Great Lives from History

The Middle Ages

477 - 1453

Great Lives from History

The Middle Ages

477 - 1453

Volume 1

Pietro d'Abano-Kōbō Daishi

Editor
Shelley Wolbrink
Drury University

Editor, First Edition
Frank N. Magill

Salem Press
Pasadena, California Hackensack, New Jersey

Editor in Chief: Dawn P. Dawson
Editorial Director: Christina J. Moose
Project Editor: Rowena Wildin
Developmental Editor: Leslie Ellen Jones
Copy Editor: Desiree Dreeuws
Assistant Editor: Andrea E. Miller
Editorial Assistant: Dana Garey
Photograph Editor: Philip Bader
Acquisitions Editor: Mark Rehn
Research Supervisor: Jeffry Jensen
Production Editor: Joyce I. Buchea
Graphics and Design: James Hutson
Layout: William Zimmerman

Cover photos: Library of Congress

∞ The paper used in these volumes conforms to the American National Standard for Permanence of Paper for Printed Library Materials, Z39.48-1992 (R1997).

Some of the essays in this work originally appeared in the following Salem Press sets: *Dictionary of World Biography* (1998-1999, edited by Frank N. Magill) and *Great Lives from History* (1987-1995, edited by Frank N. Magill).

Library of Congress Cataloging-in-Publication Data

Great lives from history. The Middle Ages, 477-1453 / editor, Shelley Wolbrink.— 1st ed.
p. cm.
Includes bibliographical references and index.
ISBN 1-58765-164-5 (set : alk. paper) — ISBN 1-58765-165-3 (v. 1 : alk. paper) — ISBN 1-58765-166-1 (v. 2 : alk. paper)
1. Biography—Middle Ages, 500-1500. 2. Middle Ages—History. I. Wolbrink, Shelley.
CT114.G74 2005
920′.009′02—dc22

2004016696

First Printing

PRINTED IN THE UNITED STATES OF AMERICA

Contents

Publisher's Note

Great Lives from History: The Middle Ages, 477-1453 is the second installment in the revised and expanded *Great Lives* series, initiated in 2004 with *Great Lives from History: The Ancient World, Prehistory-476* C.E. It will be joined by *Great Lives from History: The Renaissance & Early Modern Era, 1454-1600*, planned for 2005, and in successive years by volumes covering the *Seventeenth Century, Eighteenth Century, Nineteenth Century*, and *Twentieth Century*—each two or more volumes in length. The entire series, when complete, is expected to cover more than 2,500 lives in essays ranging from 3 to 6 pages in length.

Expanded Coverage

This ongoing series is a revision of the 10-volume *Dictionary of World Biography* (*DWB*) series (1998-1999), which in turn was a revision and reordering of Salem Press's 30-volume *Great Lives from History* series (1987-1995). The expanded *Great Lives* differs in several ways from *DWB*:

- The original essays are enhanced by the addition of new entries covering a wider geographical area and including many more women. The coverage of each set has been increased significantly. In the current two volumes on *The Middle Ages*, for example, 59 new essays have been added to the original 297 for a total of 356 essays covering 361 historical figures (5 essays address closely allied pairs).

- In an effort to align coverage with curriculum, the new series provides more logical breaks between eras. For example, *The Ancient World* now ends at 476 C.E. (the fall of Rome), and the current two volumes on *The Middle Ages* consequently begin at 477 and end at 1453 (the fall of Constantinople)—as opposed to the more arbitrary 1400 in the old *DWB*.

- 109 regnal tables and dynastic lists have been added to enhance and supplement the text throughout, and a section of 11 maps has been added to allow students to locate personages geographically and to place rulers dynastically.

- Essays from the original *DWB* on all personages falling into the new time frame are reprinted in this new series with updated and annotated bibliographies.

Scope of Coverage

The geographic and occupational scope of the individuals covered in *Great Lives from History: The Middle Ages, 477-1453* is broad. Coverage is worldwide, with individuals identified with one or more of the following areas: 9 with Africa, 52 with the British Isles, 11 with the Byzantine Empire, 3 with Central Asia, 23 with China or Mongolia, 51 with France, 25 with German states, 61 with Italy, 15 with Japan, 1 with Korea, 42 with the Middle East or Persia, 16 with Russia and Central Europe, 17 with Scandinavia and the Low Countries, 9 with South or Southeast Asia, and 20 with Spain or Portugal. Only 1 individual, Itzcóatl, represents the Americas; it must be recalled that the cutoff date for this set, 1453, precluded identifiable figures who could sustain the minimum length of the essay, 1,500 words. (Figures such as Deganawida, Doña Marina, Montezuma II, Huascar, and others from the Americas are covered in *Great Lives from History: The Renaissance & Early Modern Era, 1454-1600*, slated to appear in 2005.)

The editors have sought to provide coverage that is broad in areas of achievement as well as geography, while at the same time including the recognized shapers of history essential in any liberal arts curriculum. Major world leaders appear here—emperors, conquerors, kings, and khans—as well as the giants of religious faith who were central to the medieval world: popes, monks, and saints who left their imprint on political as well as spiritual institutions. The set also includes figures who have received little or no attention in the past—from the seventh century queen of the Berbers Damia al-Kāhina to the eleventh century Italian gynecologist Trotula. By category, the contents include more than 120 world leaders, 56 religious figures, 38 writers, 23 artists, 20 historiographers, 16 philosophers, 13 military leaders, 8 scientists, 7 medical practitioners, 6 musicians, 4 educators, 4 explorers, 4 figures identified with the law, 4 mathematicians, 3 architects, 3 geographers, 2 patrons of the arts, 2 social reformers, and 2 linguists. Among these architects of today's civilization are 53 women of the medieval world: writers, scholars, scientists, and national leaders.

Essay Length and Format

Each essay ranges from 1,500 to 4,000 words in length (roughly 3 to 6 pages), with the majority falling in the range of 2,000 to 2,500 words. The familiar standard format offers easy access to biographical information.

Ready-reference top matter identifies the person and provides vital data:

- The essay title is the name of the individual; editors have chosen the name as it is most commonly found in Western English-language sources.
- The individual's *nationality or ethnicity* and *occupation or historical role* follow on the second line, including reign dates for rulers.
- A *summary paragraph* highlighting the individual's historical importance indicates why the person is studied today.
- The *Born* and *Died* lines list the most complete dates of birth and death available, followed by the most precise locations available, as well as an indication when these are unknown, only probable, or only approximate; both medieval and modern place-names (where different) are listed.
- *Also known as* lists all known versions of the name, including full names, given names, alternative spellings, pseudonyms, and common epithets.
- *Area(s) of achievement* lists all categories of contribution, from Architecture and Art through Warfare and Women's Rights.

The body of each article is divided into six parts:

- *Early Life* provides facts about the individual's upbringing and the environment in which he or she was reared, as well as the pronunciation of his or her name, if unusual. Where little is known about the individual's rearing, historical context is provided.
- *Life's Work*, the heart of the article, consists of a straightforward, generally chronological, account of the period during which the individual's most significant achievements were accomplished.
- *Significance* is an overview of the individual's place in history.
- *Further Reading* is an annotated bibliography, a starting point for further research.
- *See also* is a list of cross-references to essays in the set covering related personages.
- *Related articles* lists essays of interest in Salem's companion publication, *Great Events from History: The Middle Ages, 477-1453* (2 vols., 2005).

SPECIAL FEATURES

Several features distinguish this series as a whole from other biographical reference works. The front matter includes the following aids:

- *Key to Pronunciation*: a key to in-text pronunciation guidelines, in both volumes.
- *Complete List of Contents*: this alphabetical list of contents appears in both volumes.
- *List of Maps and Tables*.
- *Maps*: In the front matter to each volume, a section of 11 maps displaying major regions of the world in the period 477-1453 appear grouped together for easy reference.

The back matter to Volume 2 includes several appendices and indexes:

- *Rulers and Dynasties*: a geographically arranged set of tables listing major rulers and their regnal dates, covering 37 regions of the world.
- *Chronological List of Entries*: individuals covered, arranged by birth year.
- *Category Index*: entries by area of achievement, from architecture to women's rights.
- *Geographical Index*: entries by country or region.
- *Personages Index*: an index of all persons, both those covered and those additionally discussed within the text.
- *Subject Index*: a comprehensive index including personages, concepts, terms, events, civilizations, and other topics of discussion, with full cross-references from alternative spellings and to the Category and Geographical Indexes.

USAGE NOTES

The worldwide scope of *Great Lives from History* resulted in the inclusion of many names and words that must be transliterated from languages that do not use the Roman alphabet, and in some cases, there is more than one transliterated form in use. In many cases, transliterated words in this set follow the American Library Association and Library of Congress (ALA-LC) transliteration format for that language. However, if another form of a name or word was judged to be more familiar to the general audience, it is used instead. The variants for names of essay subjects are listed in ready-reference top matter and are cross-referenced in the subject and personages indexes. The Pinyin transliteration was used for Chinese topics, with Wade-Giles variants provided for major names and dynasties. In a few cases, a common name that is not Pinyin has been used. Sanskrit and other South Asian names generally follow the ALA-LC transliteration rules, although again, the more familiar form of a word is used when deemed appropriate for the general reader.

Titles of books and other literature appear, upon first mention in the essay, with their full publication and translation data as known: an indication of the first date of publication or appearance, followed by the English title in translation and its first date of appearance in English; if no translation has been published in English, and if the context of the discussion does not make the meaning of the title obvious, a "literal translation" appears in roman type.

Throughout, readers will find a limited number of abbreviations used in both top matter and text, including "r." for "reigned," "b." for "born," "d." for "died," and "fl." for "flourished." Where a date range appears appended to a name without one of these designators, the reader may assume it signifies birth and death dates.

Finally, in the regnal tables dispersed throughout the text, the reader will find some names appearing in small capital letters. These figures are covered in their own separate essays within these two volumes.

THE EDITORS AND CONTRIBUTORS

Salem Press would like to extend its appreciation to Professor Shelley Wolbrink, Department of History, Drury University, Editor of *Great Lives from History: The Middle Ages, 477-1453*. In addition, we extend appreciation to the many academicians and scholars who prepared essays for this work. Without their expert contributions, a project of this nature would not be possible. A full list of contributors and their affiliations appears in the front matter of volume 1.

Contributors

James W. Alexander
University of Georgia

William Allison
Weber State University

Edward Allworth
Columbia University

J. Stewart Alverson
University of Tennessee at Chattanooga

Norman Araujo
Boston College

Martin Arbagi
Wright State University

Madeline Cirillo Archer
Duquesne University

Stanley Archer
Texas A & M University

Tom L. Auffenberg
Ouachita Baptist University

James R. Banker
North Carolina State University

John W. Barker
University of Wisconsin-Madison

Jeffrey G. Barlow
Lewis & Clark College

Dan Barnett
Butte College

Thomas F. Barry
Himeji Dokkyo University

Judith R. Baskin
University of Oregon

Michael E. Bauman
Hillsdale College

Martha Bayless
University of Oregon

Erving E. Beauregard
University of Dayton

Richard P. Benton
Trinity College

Beverly Berg
Linfield College

S. Carol Berg
College of St. Benedict

Robert L. Berner
University of Wisconsin-Oshkosh

David M. Bessen
Ball State University

Cynthia A. Bily
Adrian College

Quentin Bone
Indiana State University

Harold Branam
Savannah State University

John R. Broadus
University of North Carolina

Robert I. Burns
Loyola Marymount University

William H. Burnside
John Brown University

Joseph P. Byrne
Belmont University

Clare Callaghan
The Catholic University of America

Edmund J. Campion
University of Tennessee

Byron D. Cannon
University of Utah

Joan E. Carr
Washington University

M. G. Carter
New York University

James A. Casada
Winthrop College, South Carolina

Nan K. Chase
Appalachian State University

Dennis C. Chowenhill
Chabot Community College

John J. Contreni
Purdue University

Bernard A. Cook
Loyola University

Weston F. Cook, Jr.
University of North Carolina at Pembroke

Raymond J. Cormier
Wilson College

Loren W. Crabtree
Colorado State University

Kenneth E. Cutler
Indiana University-Purdue University

Ronald W. Davis
Western Michigan University

Frank Day
Clemson University

Andrea E. Donovan
Western Michigan University

Desiree Dreeuws
Independent Scholar

Thomas Drucker
University of Wisconsin-Whitewater

Ronald Joseph Duncan
Oklahoma Baptist University

David G. Egler
Western Illinois University

Robert P. Ellis
Worcester State College, Massachusetts

Clara Estow
University of Massachusetts-Harbor Campus

Gary B. Ferngren
Oregon State University

Edward Fiorelli
St. John's University

Charles J. Fleener
Saint Louis University

Michael J. Fontenot
Southern University at Baton Rouge

Robert J. Forman
St. John's University, New York

Robert J. Frail
Centenary College

Ronald K. Frank
Pace University

Shirley F. Fredricks
Regis College

Ronald H. Fritze
Lamar University

C. George Fry
University of Findlay

Gloria Fulton
Humboldt State University

Paul C. Gaige
Tulane University

John G. Gallaher
Southern Illinois University at Edwardsville

Catherine Gilbert
Independent Scholar

Paul E. Gill
Shippensburg University

K. Fred Gillum
Colby College

Nancy M. Gordon
Independent Scholar

Karen K. Gould
Independent Scholar

Daniel G. Graetzer
University of Washington Medical Center

Candace Gregory
Loyola University of New Orleans

William C. Griffin
Appalachian State University

Hassan S. Haddad
St. Xavier College

Irwin Halfond
McKendree College

Gavin R. G. Hambly
University of Texas at Dallas

Katherine Hanley
St. Bernard's School of Theology & Ministry

David V. Harrington
Independent Scholar

Sandra Hanby Harris
Tidewater Community College

Fran J. Hassencahl
Old Dominion University

Carlanna L. Hendrick
Governors School for Science & Mathematics

Mark C. Herman
Edison Community College

Michael Hernon
University of Tennessee at Martin

Elton D. Higgs
Independent Scholar

Richard L. Hillard
University of Arkansas at Pine Bluff

Michael Craig Hillmann
University of Texas at Austin

Samuel B. Hoff
Delaware State University

John R. Holmes
Franciscan University of Steubenville

John J. Hunt
St. Joseph College

E. D. Huntley
Appalachian State University

Paul Hyer
Brigham Young University

Amy J. Johnson
Berry College

Lynn Marie Johnson
Towson University

Philip Dwight Jones
Bradley University

Yoshiko Kainuma
University of California, Los Angeles

Mathew J. Kanjirathinkal
Park University

Thomas O. Kay
Wheaton College

Karen A. Kildahl
South Dakota State University

Leigh Husband Kimmel
Independent Scholar

Paul W. Knoll
University of Southern California

Z. J. Kosztolnyik
Texas A&M University

Richard J. Kubiak
Mercyhurst College

Dale E. Landon
Indiana University at Pennsylvania

Eugene S. Larson
Los Angeles Pierce College

Harry Lawton
University of California, Santa Barbara

Joseph W. Leedom
Hollins College

Thomas Tandy Lewis
Anoka Ramsey Community College

San-pao Li
California State University-Long Beach

Christopher G. Libertini
Suffolk University

James L. Livingston
Northern Michigan University

R. C. Lutz
CII

Peter F. Macaluso
Montclair State College

William McCabe
Independent Scholar

Clyde S. McConnell
University of Calgary

Rhonda L. McDaniel
Western Michigan University

Margaret McFadden
Appalachian State University

James Edward McGoldrick
Greenville Presbyterian Theological Seminary

Nancy McLoughlin
University of California, Santa Barbara

Kerrie L. MacPherson
State University of New York College at Buffalo

David K. McQuilkin
Independent Scholar

Kenneth G. Madison
Iowa State University

Bill Manikas
Gaston College

Ralph W. Mathisen
University of South Carolina

Timothy May
University of Wisconsin-Madison

David Harry Miller
University of Oklahoma

Mary Emily Miller
Independent Scholar

Randall L. Milstein
Oregon State University

Terence R. Murphy
American University

John E. Myers
Simon's Rock of Bard College

Gregory Nehler
Independent Scholar

Edwin L. Neville, Jr.
Canisius College

Frank Nickell
Southeast Missouri State University

Steven M. Oberhelman
Texas A&M University

Glenn W. Olsen
University of Utah

Kathleen K. O'Mara
State University of New York College at Oneonta

Eric W. Osborne
Texas Christian University

Lisa Paddock
Independent Scholar

Robert J. Paradowski
Rochester Institute of Technology

Michael C. Paul
University of Miami

Brian A. Pavlac
King's College

Joseph R. Peden
Baruch College, CUNY

John M. Pederson
University of Nebraska-Lincoln

Mark Stephen Pestana
Grand Valley State University

R. Craig Philips
Michigan State University

Susan L. Piepke
Bridgewater College

Ernest R. Pinson
Union University

David Pitre
The Dunham School

John Powell
Cumberland College

Joseph M. Pucci
Brown University

Charles H. Pullen
Queen's University

John D. Raymer
Independent Scholar

Dennis Reinhartz
University of Texas at Arlington

Rosemary M. Canfield Reisman
Charleston Southern University

Richard Rice
University of Tennessee at Chattanooga

Betty Richardson
Southern Illinois University at Edwardsville

St. John Robinson
Montana State University at Billings

William B. Robison
Southeastern Louisiana University

Carl Rollyson
Baruch College of the City University of New York

Joseph Rosenblum
University of North Carolina, Greensboro

Robert L. Ross
Independent Scholar

Thomas E. Rotnem
Southern Polytechnic State University

Thomas Ryba
Michigan State University

Joyce E. Salisbury
University of Wisconsin-Green Bay

Hilel B. Salomon
University of South Carolina

Jason D. Sanchez
Tulane University

Daniel C. Scavone
University of Southern Indiana

Randy P. Schiff
University of California, Santa Barbara

Bernard Schlessinger
Independent Scholar

June H. Schlessinger
University of North Texas

Steven P. Schultz
Loyola University of Chicago

Thomas C. Schunk
Independent Scholar

T. A. Shippey
St. Louis University

J. Lee Shneidman
Adelphi University

R. Baird Shuman
University of Illinois at Urbana-Champaign

Anne W. Sienkewicz
Independent Scholar

Thomas J. Sienkewicz
Monmouth College

Shumet Sishagne
Christopher Newport University

Ralph Smiley
Bloomsburg University of Pennsylvania

Clyde Curry Smith
University of Wisconsin

Ronald F. Smith
Independent Scholar

Van Mitchell Smith
University of Texas at Arlington

Katherine Snipes
Independent Scholar

Richard B. Spence
University of Idaho

Joseph L. Spradley
Wheaton College

David R. Stevenson
Kearney State College

Paul Stewart
Southern Connecticut State University

Jean T. Strandness
North Dakota State University

Fred Strickert
Wartburg College

Paul Stuewe
Green Mountain College

Bruce M. Sullivan
Arizona State University

Donald D. Sullivan
University of New Mexico

Charlene E. Suscavage
University of Southern Maine

Roy Arthur Swanson
University of Wisconsin-Milwaukee

Patricia E. Sweeney
Independent Scholar

Glenn L. Swygart
Tennessee Temple University

Hoyt Cleveland Tillman
Arizona State University

David Treviño
Donna Klein Jewish Academy

Frank H. Tucker
Colorado College

William L. Urban
Monmouth College

Larry W. Usilton
University of North Carolina at Wilmington

Fred R. van Hartesveldt
Fort Valley State College

Sem Vermeersch
Academia Koreana, Keimyung University

Anne R. Vizzier
University of Arkansas

Paul R. Waibel
Belhaven College

William T. Walker
Chestnut Hill College

John R. Wallace
University of California, Berkeley

Larry C. Watkins
University of Kansas

Delno West
Northern Arizona University

Robert I. Willman
Mississippi State University

John D. Windhausen
Saint Anselm College

Michael Witkoski
University of South Carolina

Shelley Wolbrink
Drury University

Frank Wu
Independent Scholar

Vincent Yang
Independent Scholar

Clifton K. Yearley
State University of New York at Buffalo

Kristen L. Zacharias
Albright College

William M. Zanella
Hawaii Loa College

Ronald Edward Zupko
Marquette University

Key to Pronunciation

Many of the names of personages covered in *Great Lives from History: The Middle Ages, 477-1453* may be unfamiliar to students and general readers. For these unfamiliar names, guides to pronunciation have been provided upon first mention of the names in the text. These guidelines do not purport to achieve the subtleties of the languages in question but will offer readers a rough equivalent of how English speakers may approximate the proper pronunciation.

Vowel Sounds

Symbol	**Spelled (Pronounced)**
a	answer (AN-suhr), laugh (laf), sample (SAM-puhl), that (that)
ah	father (FAH-thur), hospital (HAHS-pih-tuhl)
aw	awful (AW-fuhl), caught (kawt)
ay	blaze (blayz), fade (fayd), waiter (WAYT-ur), weigh (way)
eh	bed (behd), head (hehd), said (sehd)
ee	believe (bee-LEEV), cedar (SEE-dur), leader (LEED-ur), liter (LEE-tur)
ew	boot (bewt), lose (lewz)
i	buy (bi), height (hit), lie (li), surprise (sur-PRIZ)
ih	bitter (BIH-tur), pill (pihl)
o	cotton (KO-tuhn), hot (hot)
oh	below (bee-LOH), coat (koht), note (noht), wholesome (HOHL-suhm)
oo	good (good), look (look)
ow	couch (kowch), how (how)
oy	boy (boy), coin (koyn)
uh	about (uh-BOWT), butter (BUH-tuhr), enough (ee-NUHF), other (UH-thur)

Consonant Sounds

Symbol	**Spelled (Pronounced)**
ch	beach (beech), chimp (chihmp)
g	beg (behg), disguise (dihs-GIZ), get (geht)
j	digit (DIH-juht), edge (ehj), jet (jeht)
k	cat (kat), kitten (KIH-tuhn), hex (hehks)
s	cellar (SEHL-ur), save (sayv), scent (sehnt)
sh	champagne (sham-PAYN), issue (IH-shew), shop (shop)
ur	birth (burth), disturb (dihs-TURB), earth (urth), letter (LEH-tur)
y	useful (YEWS-fuhl), young (yuhng)
z	business (BIHZ-nehs), zest (zehst)
zh	vision (VIH-zhuhn)

Complete List of Contents

Volume I

Volume 2

List of Maps and Tables

Eastern Hemisphere c. 800 C.E.

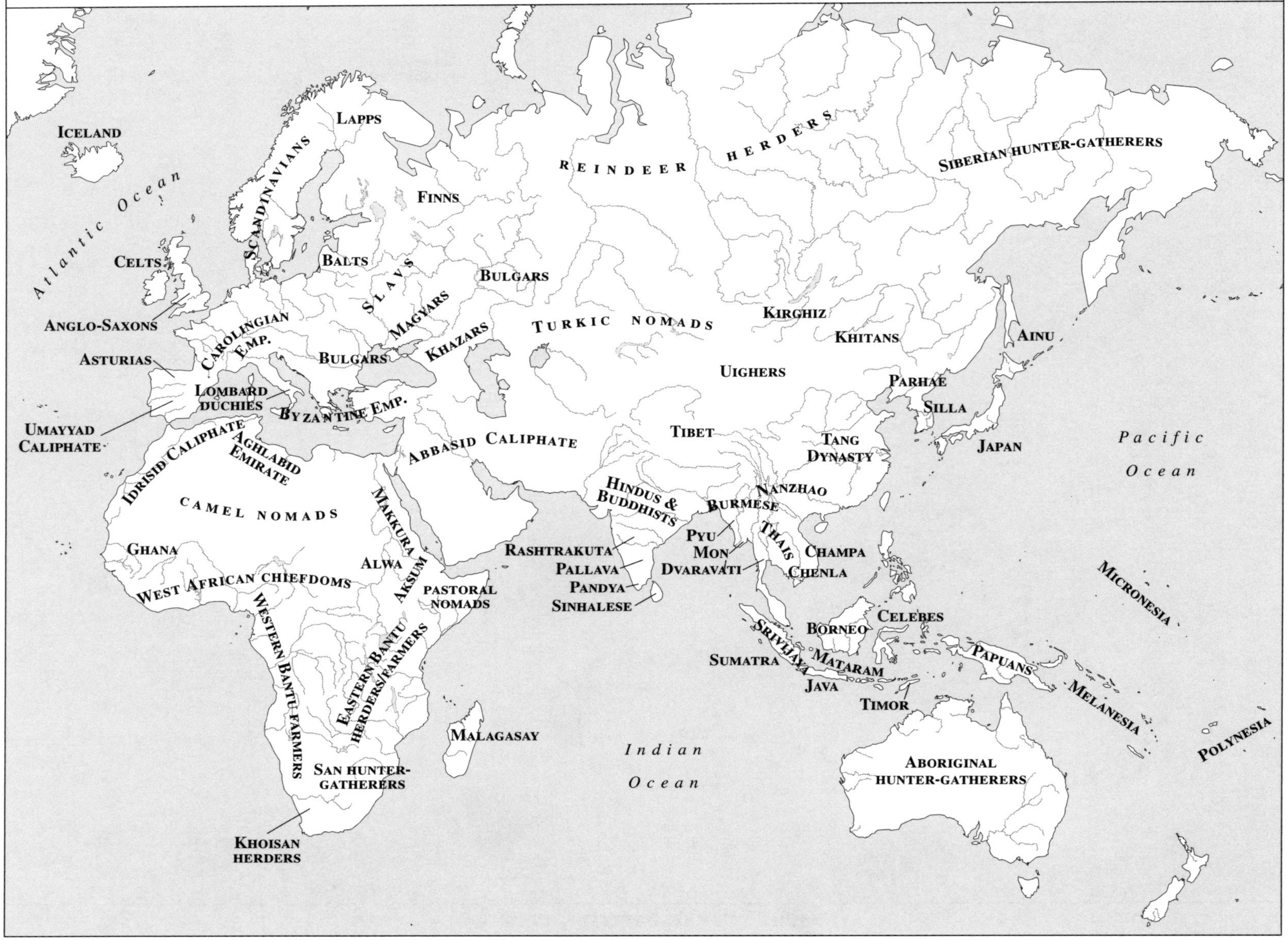
Iceland
Atlantic Ocean
Celts
Anglo-Saxons
Asturias
Umayyad Caliphate
Lombard duchies
Carolingian Emp.
Scandinavians
Lapps
Finns
Balts
Slavs
Magyars
Bulgars
Bulgars
Khazars
Byzantine Emp.
Idrisid Caliphate
Aghlabid Emirate
Camel nomads
Ghana
West African chiefdoms
Western Bantu farmers
Makkura
Alwa
Aksum
Pastoral nomads
Eastern Bantu herders/farmers
San hunter-gatherers
Khoisan herders
Malagasay
Abbasid Caliphate
Reindeer herders
Turkic nomads
Siberian hunter-gatherers
Kirghiz
Khitans
Uighers
Ainu
Parhae
Silla
Japan
Tibet
Tang Dynasty
Hindus & Buddhists
Nanzhao
Burmese
Pyu
Mon
Thais
Champa
Chenla
Dvaravati
Rashtrakuta
Pallava
Pandya
Sinhalese
Borneo
Celebes
Srivijaya
Sumatra
Mataram
Java
Timor
Papuans
Melanesia
Micronesia
Polynesia
Pacific Ocean
Indian Ocean
Aboriginal hunter-gatherers

Eastern Hemisphere c. 1000

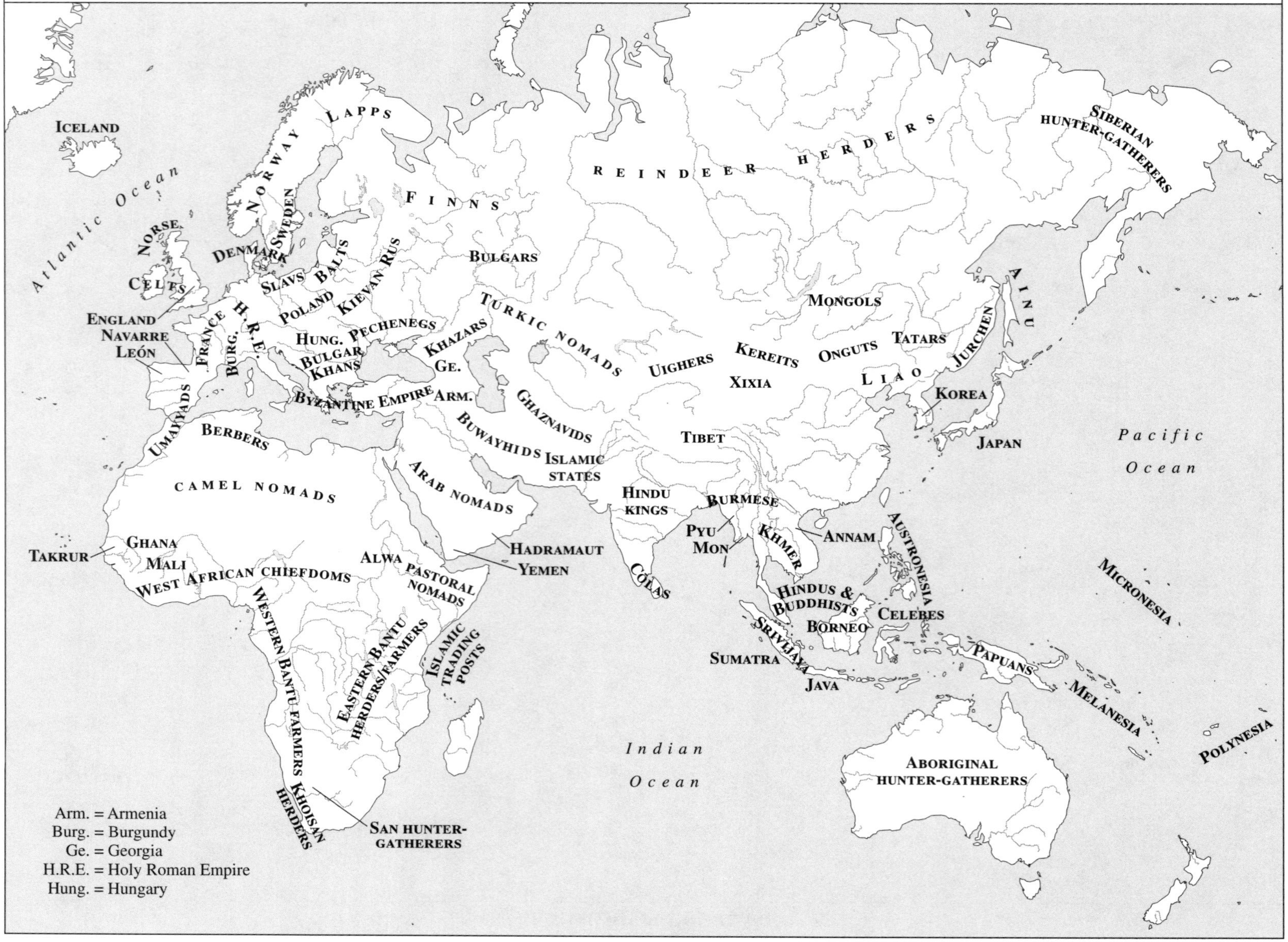
Iceland
Atlantic Ocean
Norse
Celts
England
Navarre
León
France
Burg.
H.R.E.
Denmark
Norway
Sweden
Lapps
Finns
Slavs
Balts
Poland
Kievan Rus
Hung.
Pechenegs
Bulgar Khans
Byzantine Empire
Khazars
Ge.
Arm.
Bulgars
Turkic Nomads
Reindeer Herders
Siberian Hunter-Gatherers
Ainu
Jurchen
Korea
Japan
Mongols
Tatars
Onguts
Kereits
Uighers
Xixia
Liao
Tibet
Ghaznavids
Buwayhids
Islamic States
Umayyads
Berbers
Camel Nomads
Arab Nomads
Hadramaut
Yemen
Takrur
Ghana
Mali
West African Chiefdoms
Alwa
Pastoral Nomads
Western Bantu Farmers
Eastern Bantu Herders/Farmers
Islamic Trading Posts
Khoisan Herders
San Hunter-Gatherers
Hindu Kings
Colas
Burmese
Pyu
Mon
Khmer
Annam
Austronesia
Hindus & Buddhists
Borneo
Celebes
Srivijaya
Sumatra
Java
Papuans
Melanesia
Micronesia
Polynesia
Pacific Ocean
Indian Ocean
Aboriginal Hunter-Gatherers
Arm. = Armenia
Burg. = Burgundy
Ge. = Georgia
H.R.E. = Holy Roman Empire
Hung. = Hungary

Eastern Hemisphere, 1279

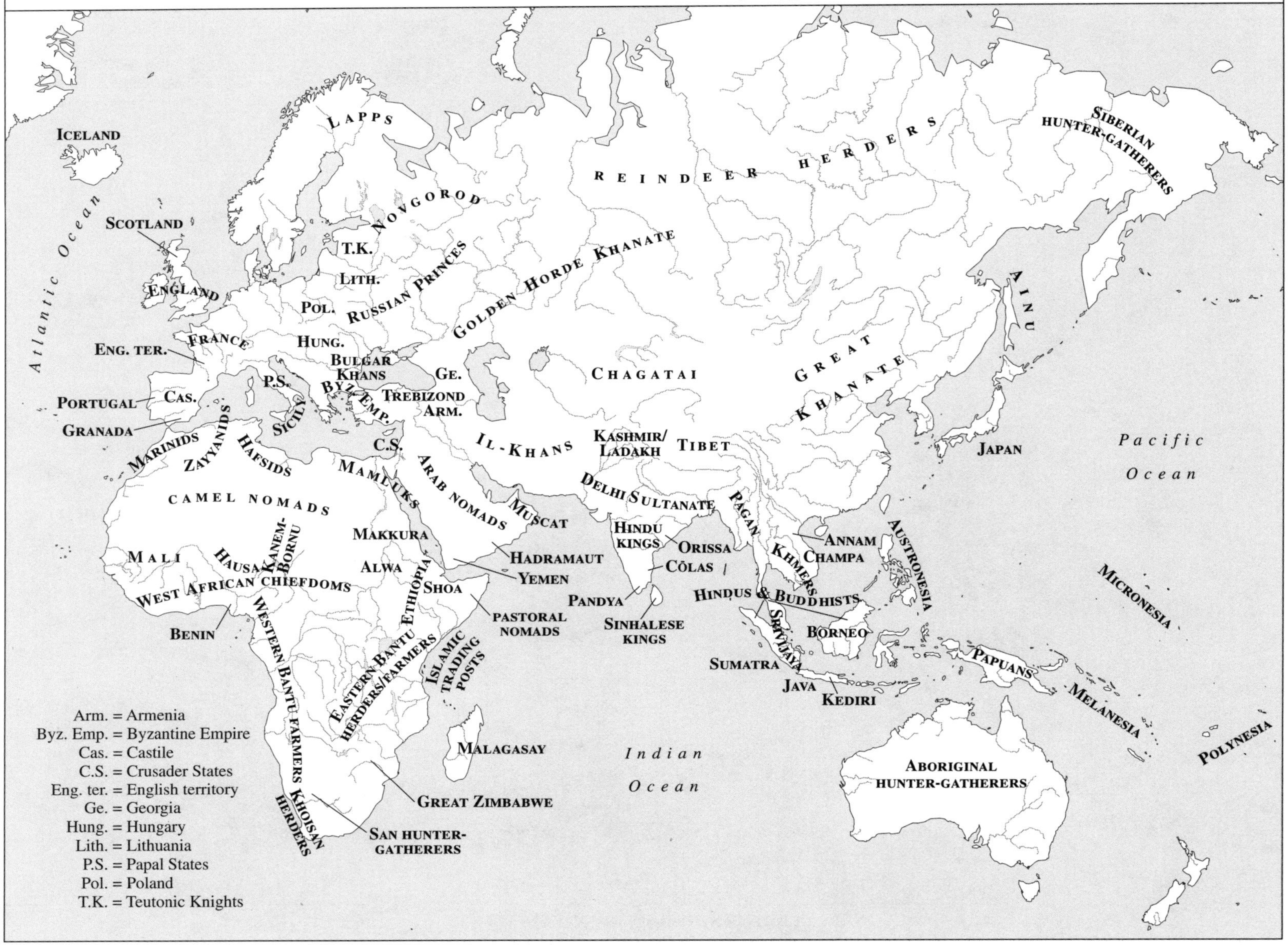

Eastern Hemisphere, 1492

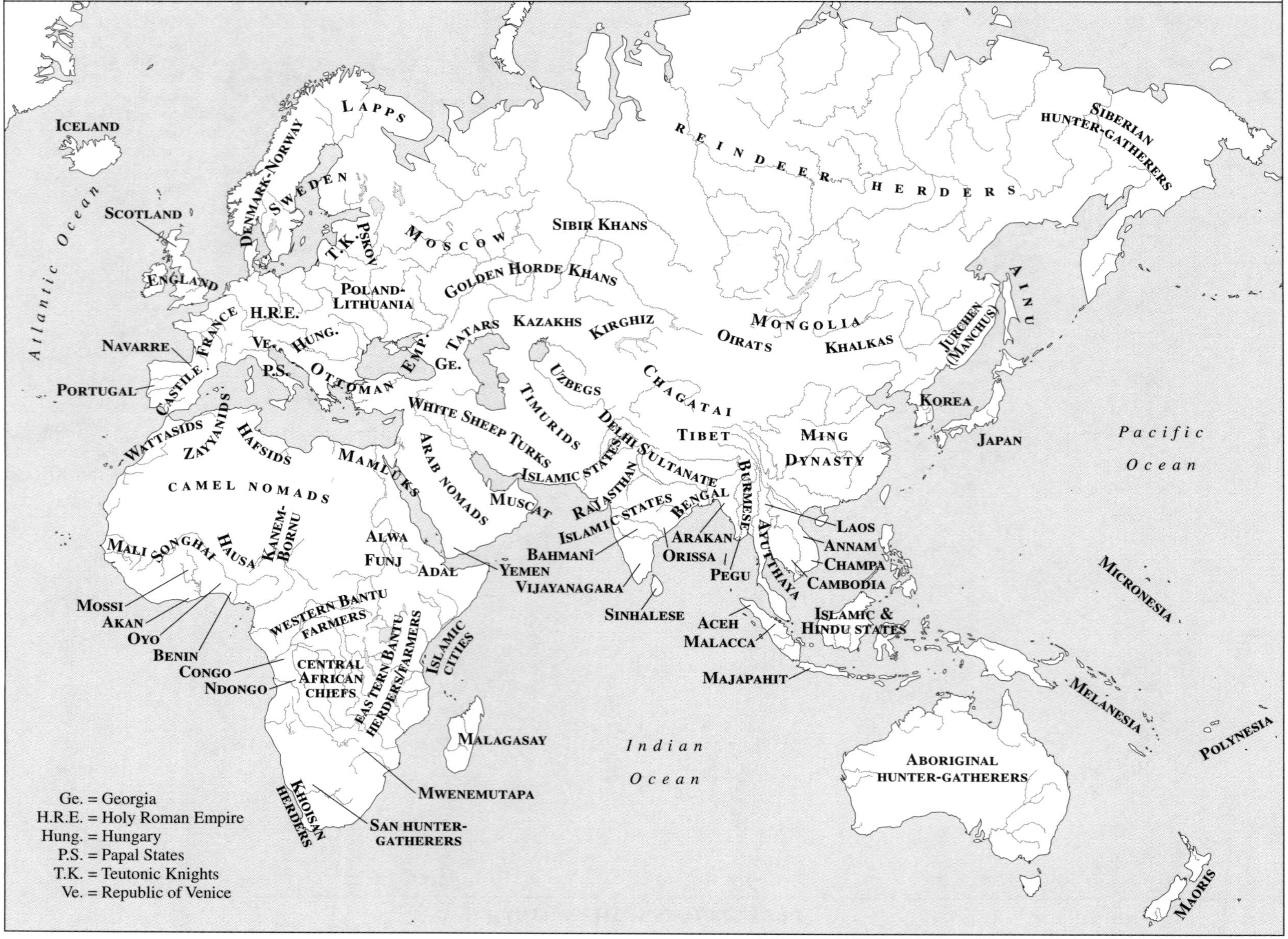

EUROPE AT CLOVIS'S DEATH, 511 C.E.

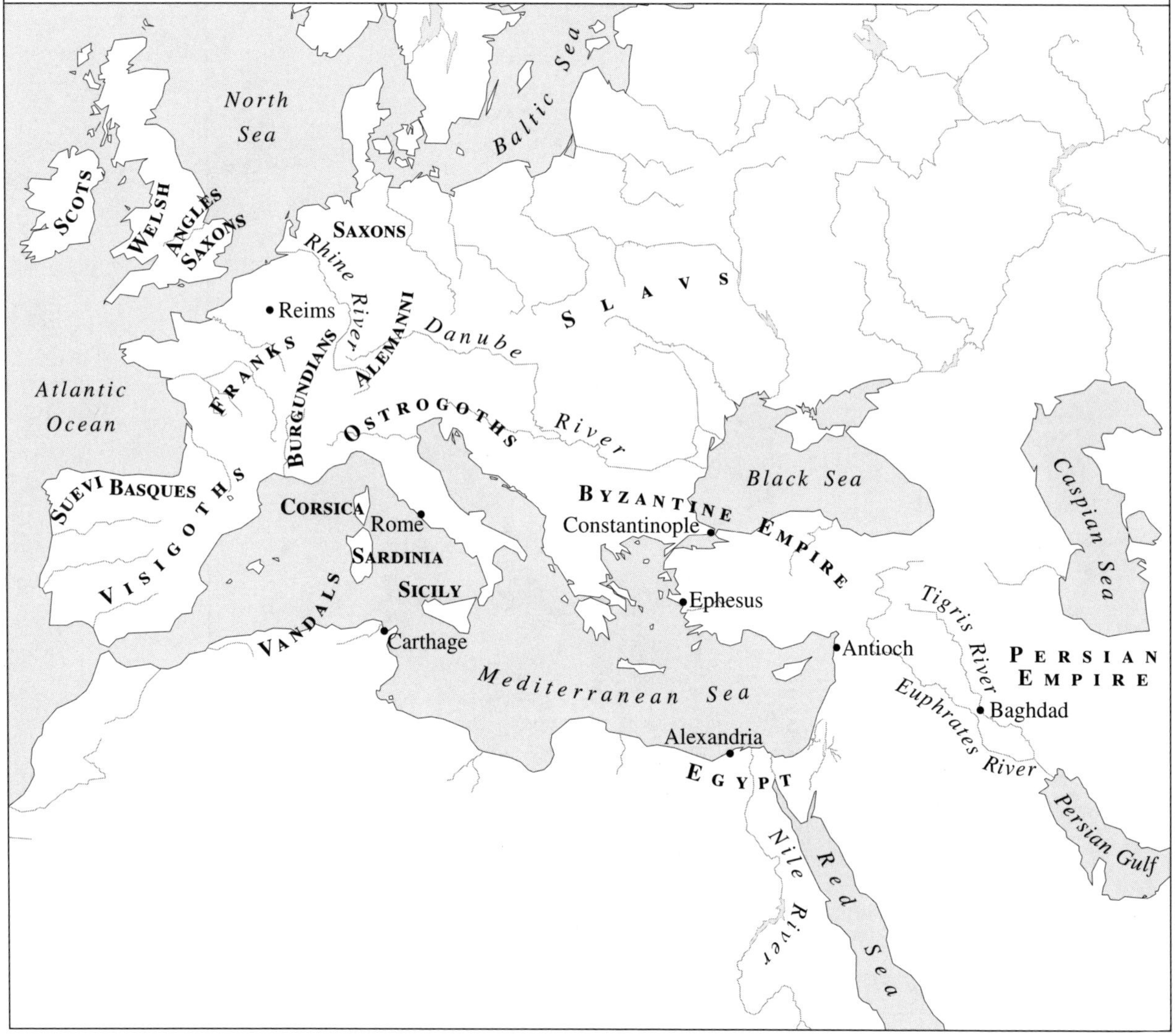
North Sea
Baltic Sea
SCOTS
WELSH
ANGLES
SAXONS
SAXONS
Rhine River
Reims
FRANKS
BURGUNDIANS
ALEMANNI
Danube River
SLAVS
Atlantic Ocean
OSTROGOTHS
SUEVI
BASQUES
VISIGOTHS
CORSICA
Rome
SARDINIA
SICILY
VANDALS
Carthage
BYZANTINE EMPIRE
Constantinople
Black Sea
Ephesus
Caspian Sea
Tigris River
PERSIAN EMPIRE
Antioch
Baghdad
Euphrates River
Mediterranean Sea
Alexandria
EGYPT
Nile River
Red Sea
Persian Gulf

Byzantine Empire at Justinian's Death, 565 C.E.

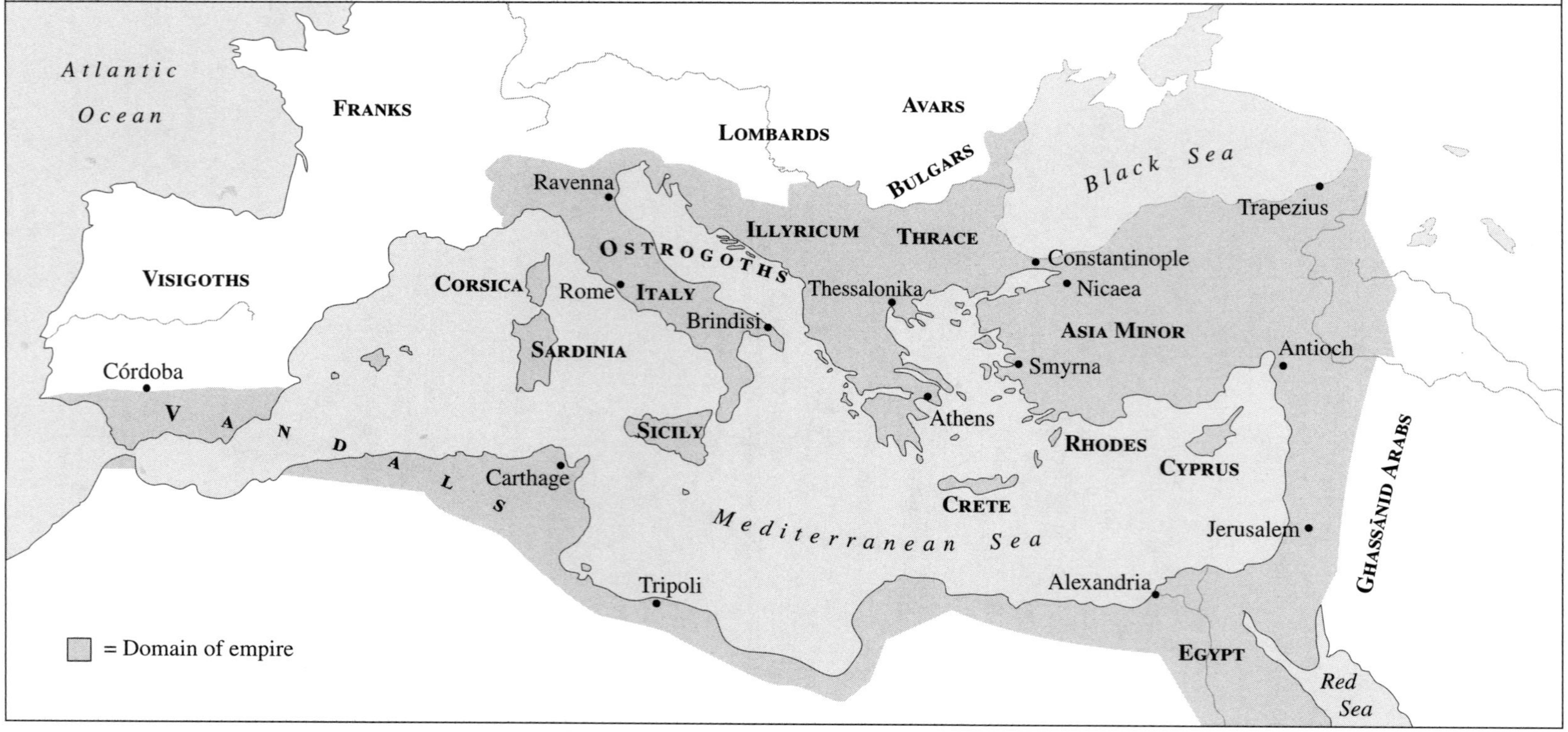

Carolingian Empire, 768-814 c.e.

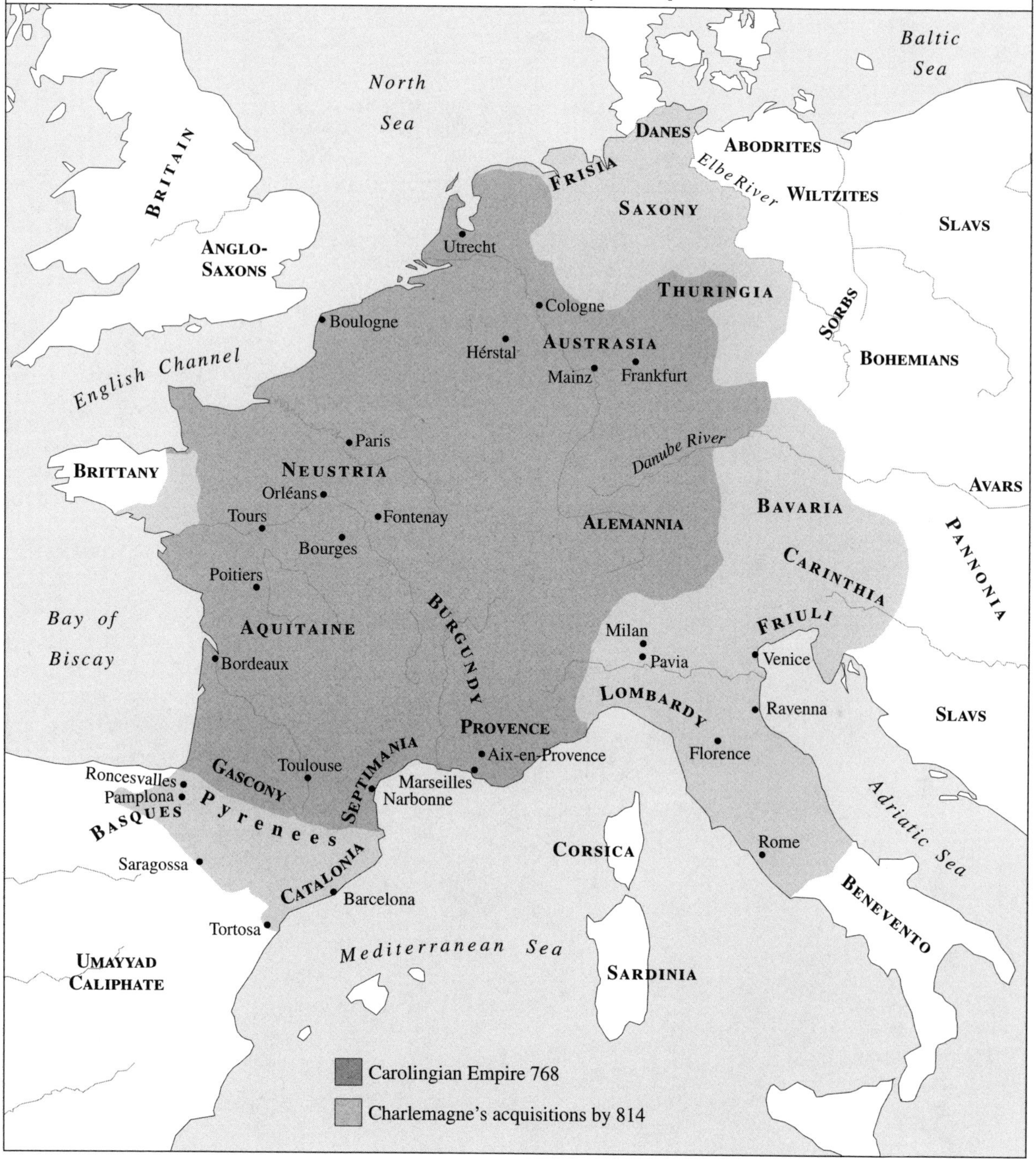

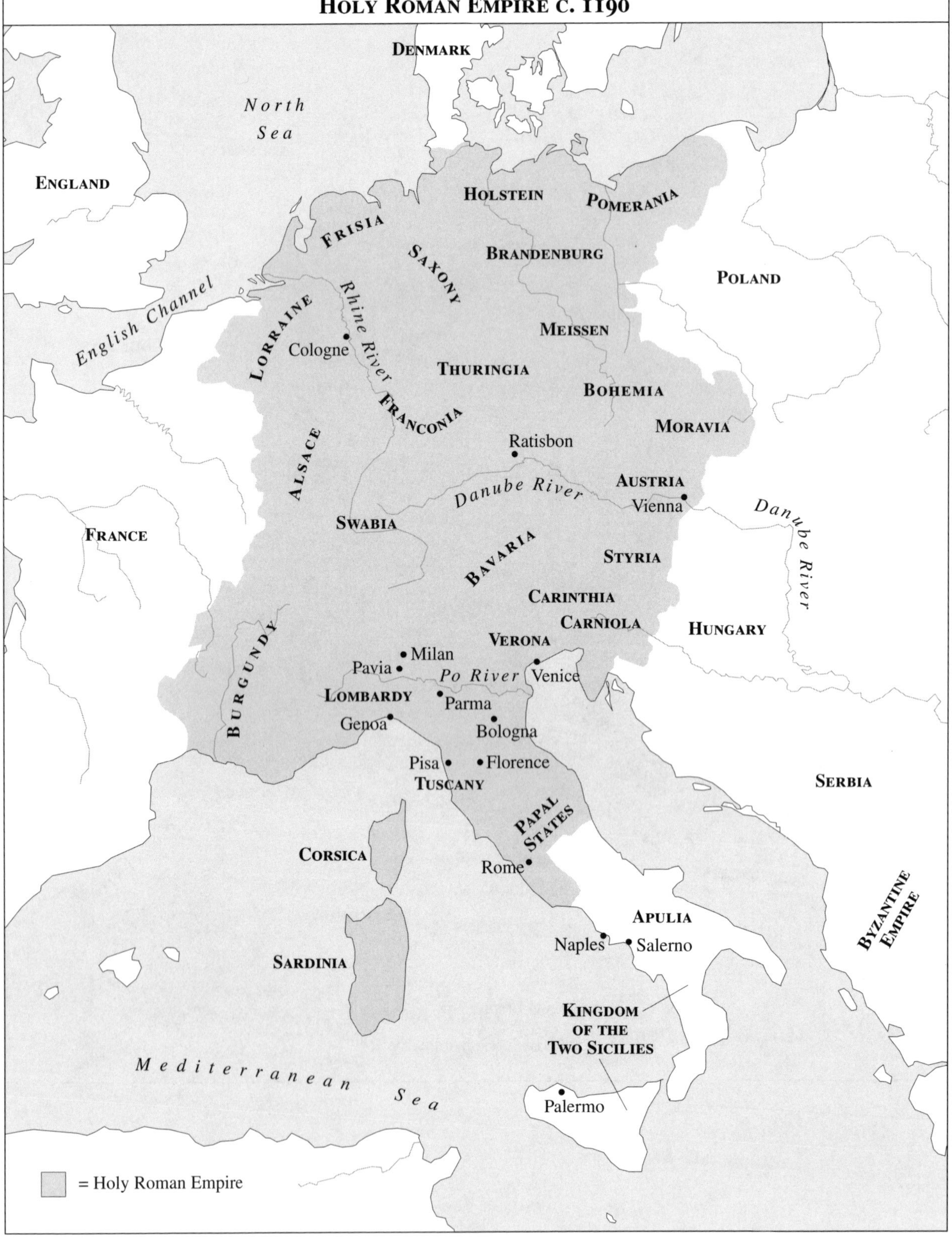
Holy Roman Empire c. 1190
Denmark
North Sea
England
Holstein
Pomerania
Frisia
Saxony
Brandenburg
Poland
English Channel
Lorraine
Rhine River
Cologne
Meissen
Thuringia
Bohemia
Franconia
Moravia
Alsace
Ratisbon
Austria
Danube River
Vienna
Danube River
Swabia
France
Bavaria
Styria
Carinthia
Carniola
Hungary
Burgundy
Verona
Milan
Pavia
Po River
Venice
Lombardy
Parma
Genoa
Bologna
Pisa
Florence
Tuscany
Serbia
Papal States
Corsica
Rome
Byzantine Empire
Apulia
Naples
Salerno
Sardinia
Kingdom of the Two Sicilies
Mediterranean Sea
Palermo
= Holy Roman Empire

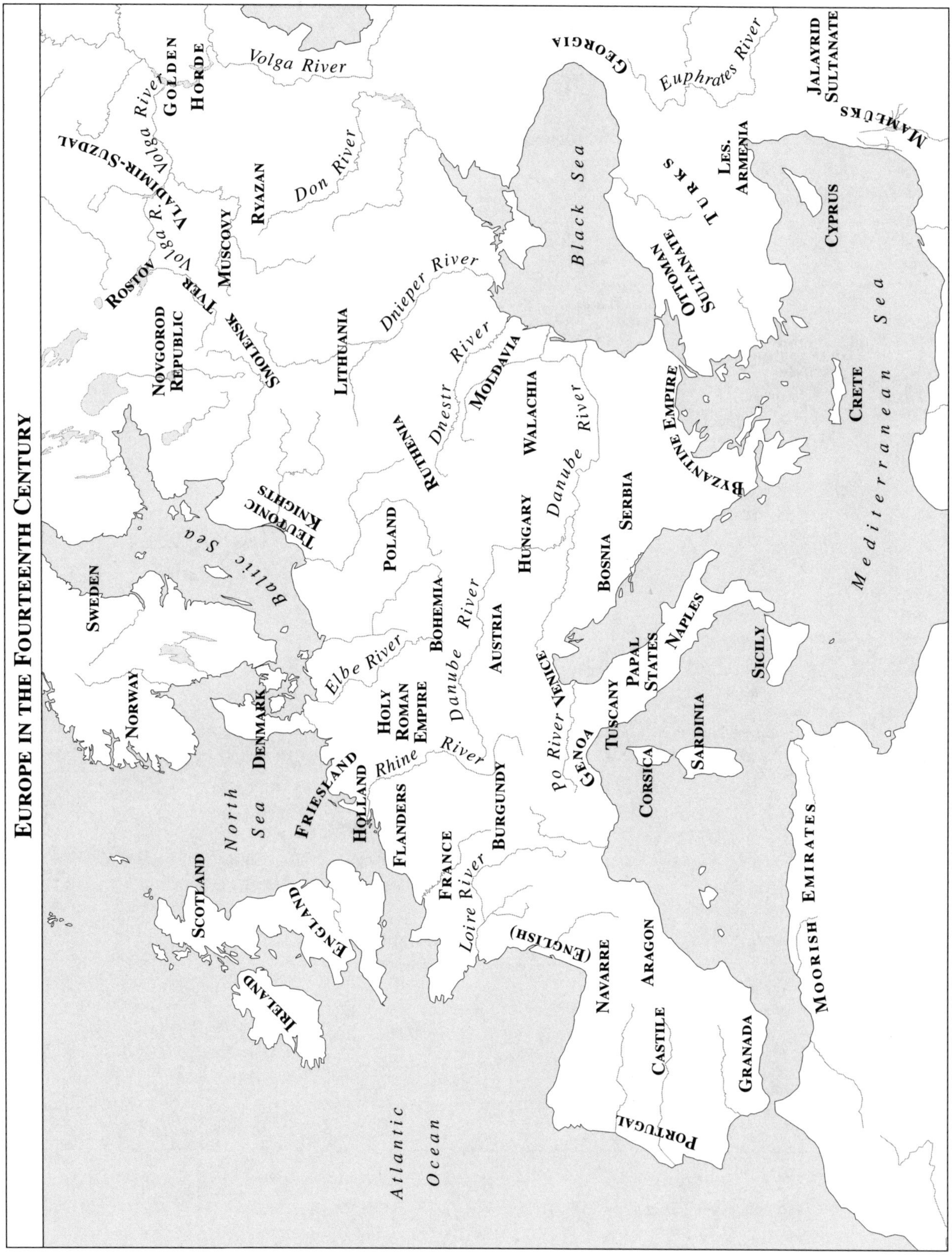
EUROPE IN THE FOURTEENTH CENTURY
Atlantic Ocean
North Sea
Baltic Sea
Black Sea
Mediterranean Sea
IRELAND
SCOTLAND
ENGLAND
NORWAY
SWEDEN
DENMARK
FRIESLAND
HOLLAND
FLANDERS
FRANCE
(ENGLISH)
PORTUGAL
CASTILE
NAVARRE
ARAGON
GRANADA
MOORISH EMIRATES
BURGUNDY
HOLY ROMAN EMPIRE
BOHEMIA
AUSTRIA
POLAND
TEUTONIC KNIGHTS
LITHUANIA
RUTHENIA
HUNGARY
WALACHIA
MOLDAVIA
BOSNIA
SERBIA
VENICE
GENOA
TUSCANY
PAPAL STATES
NAPLES
CORSICA
SARDINIA
SICILY
CRETE
CYPRUS
BYZANTINE EMPIRE
OTTOMAN SULTANATE
TURKS
LES. ARMENIA
MAMLUKS
JALAYRID SULTANATE
GEORGIA
SMOLENSK
NOVGOROD REPUBLIC
ROSTOV
TVER
MUSCOVY
RYAZAN
VLADIMIR-SUZDAL
GOLDEN HORDE
Loire River
Rhine River
Elbe River
Danube River
Po River
Dnestr River
Dnieper River
Don River
Volga River
Volga R.
Euphrates River

Africa c. 1000-1500

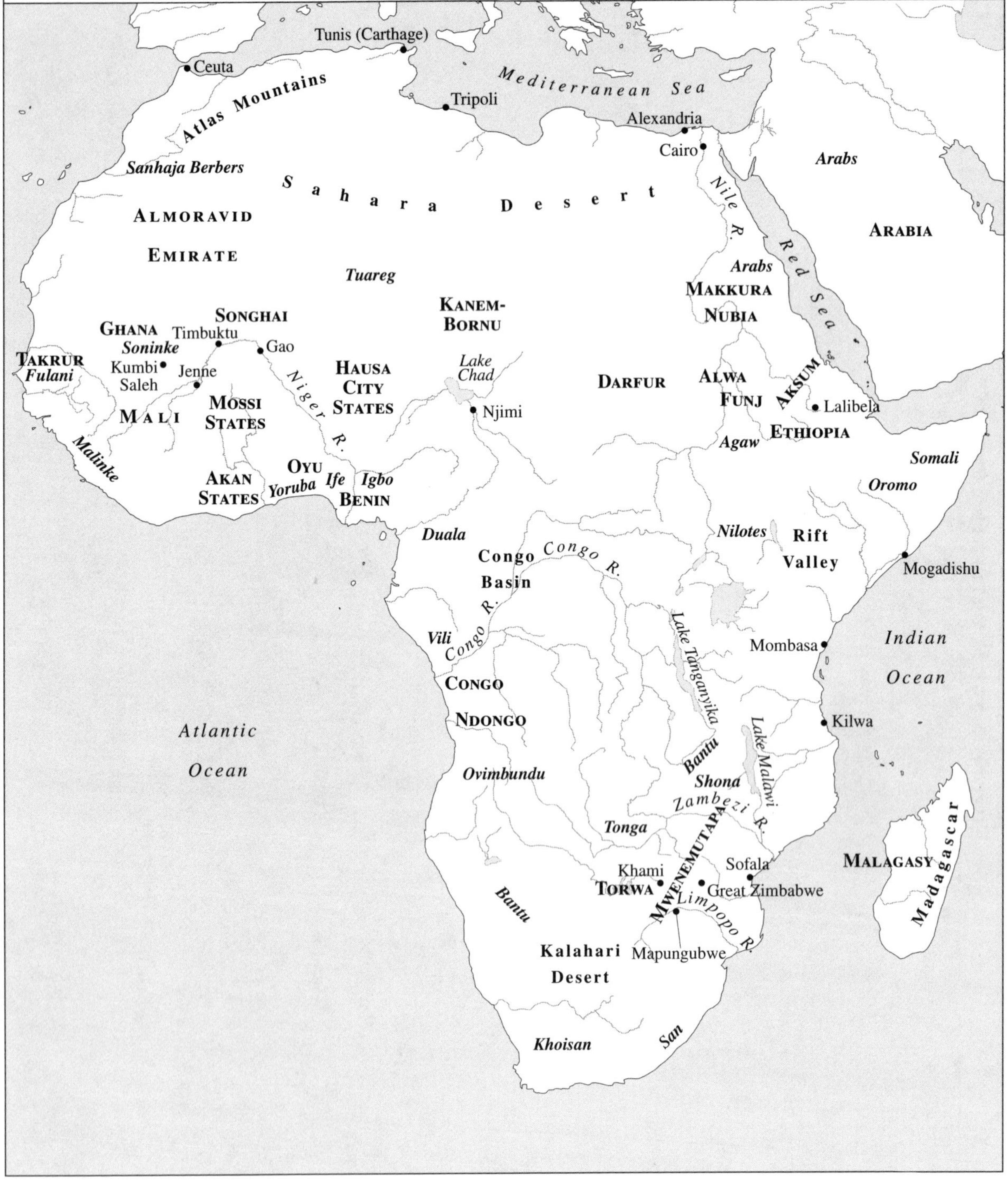

Tunis (Carthage)
Ceuta
Atlas Mountains
Tripoli
Mediterranean Sea
Alexandria
Cairo
Arabs
Sanhaja Berbers
Sahara Desert
Nile R.
Red Sea
Arabia
Almoravid Emirate
Arabs
Tuareg
Makkura Nubia
Songhai
Kanem-Bornu
Ghana
Soninke
Timbuktu
Gao
Takrur
Fulani
Kumbi Saleh
Jenne
Niger R.
Hausa City States
Lake Chad
Darfur
Alwa
Funj
Aksum
Lalibela
Mali
Mossi States
Njimi
Ethiopia
Agaw
Malinke
Akan States
Oyu
Yoruba
Ife
Igbo
Benin
Somali
Oromo
Duala
Congo Basin
Congo R.
Nilotes
Rift Valley
Mogadishu
Vili
Lake Tanganyika
Mombasa
Indian Ocean
Congo
Ndongo
Kilwa
Lake Malawi
Atlantic Ocean
Ovimbundu
Bantu
Shona
Zambezi R.
Tonga
Mwenemutapa
Sofala
Malagasy
Madagascar
Khami
Torwa
Great Zimbabwe
Limpopo R.
Bantu
Kalahari Desert
Mapungubwe
Khoisan
San

The Americas to c. 1500

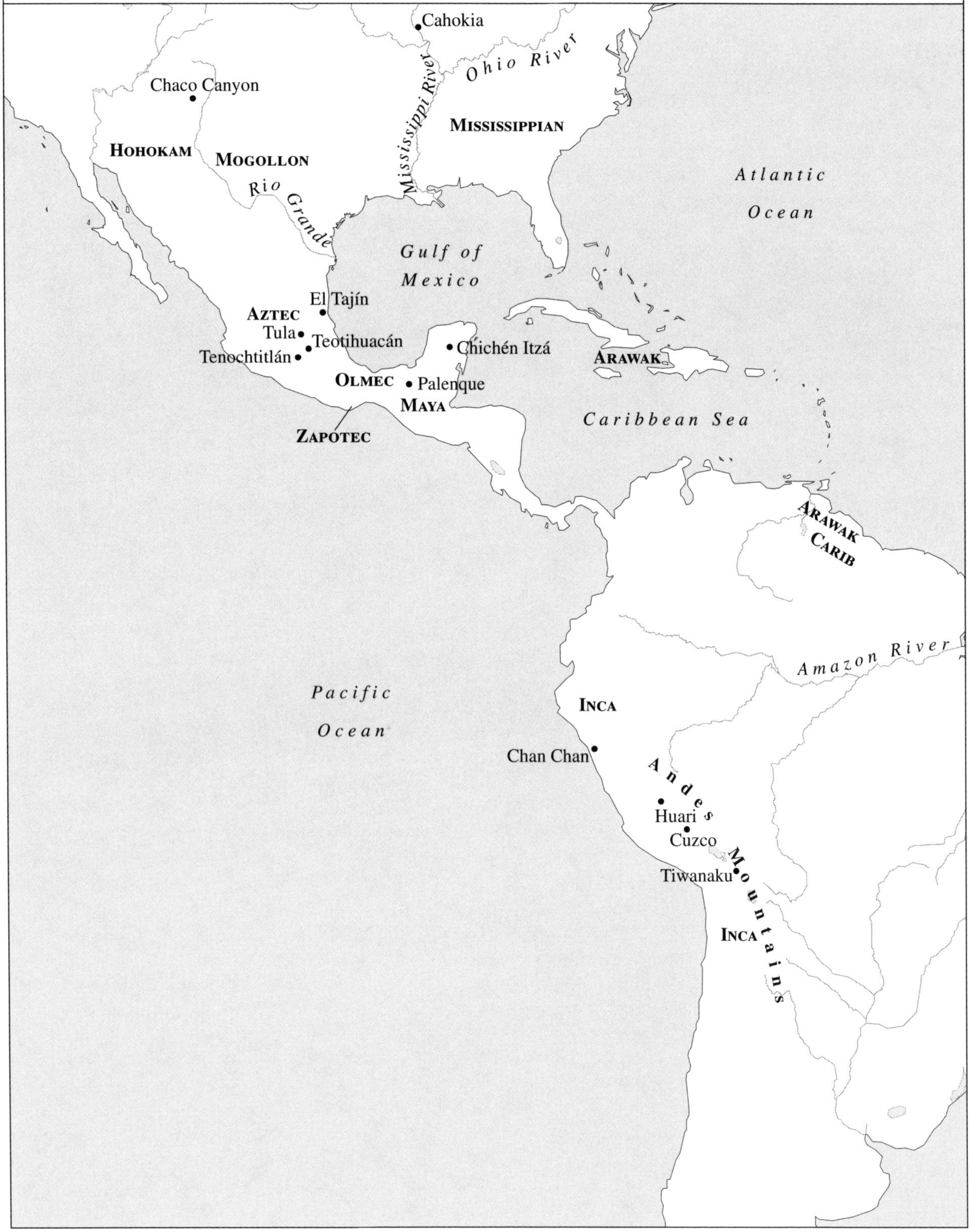
Cahokia
Ohio River
Mississippi River
Chaco Canyon
Mississippian
Hohokam
Mogollon
Rio Grande
Atlantic Ocean
Gulf of Mexico
El Tajín
Aztec
Tula
Teotihuacán
Tenochtitlán
Chichén Itzá
Arawak
Olmec
Palenque
Maya
Zapotec
Caribbean Sea
Arawak
Carib
Amazon River
Pacific Ocean
Inca
Chan Chan
Andes Mountains
Huari
Cuzco
Tiwanaku
Inca

Great Lives from History

The Middle Ages

477 - 1453

PIETRO D'ABANO

Italian scholar and scientist

Abano founded the Paduan school of medicine, introducing elements of Arabic knowledge into Italy, and worked toward a synthesis of medieval, classical, Arabic, and Jewish philosophy.

BORN: c. 1250; Abano, near Padua (now in Italy)
DIED: 1316; Padua
ALSO KNOWN AS: Peter of Abano; Petrus de Apono; Petrus Aponus; Petrus Aponensis
AREAS OF ACHIEVEMENT: Medicine, philosophy

EARLY LIFE

Pietro d'Abano (PYEH-troh duh-BAW-noh) was born in the village of Abano, now in northern Italy. Not much is known concerning his family background or early years. His father was a public notary and seems to have been reasonably well-to-do, for Pietro was able to receive an unusually good education. As a youth, he went to Greece and Constantinople, where he gained a mastery of the Greek language; among his early writings are translations of works of Aristotle into Latin. The ability to read the Greek classics in the original was quite unusual in Western Europe before the invading Ottoman Turks began to force Greek scholars to flee westward from the collapsing Byzantine Empire in the mid-fifteenth century.

On his return from Constantinople, Pietro attended the University of Paris, perhaps the best of the few institutions of higher learning that existed in late thirteenth century Europe. He studied philosophy, mathematics, and medicine for a number of years and earned a doctorate. Pietro's fame as a scholar and teacher quickly spread, and he became known as "the great Lombard."

LIFE'S WORK

In addition to his scientific and philosophical studies, Pietro was very interested in the pseudoscience of astrology. He often included astrological considerations and prayer in his medical prescriptions. Later in his life, he was responsible for the inscription of some four hundred astrological symbols on Padua's city hall. His reaching for supernatural forces was probably a reaction to the limited scientific knowledge of the fourteenth century. Pietro himself, for example, asserted firmly that it was impossible to determine the constituent parts of a compound. Thus, without outside help, the medieval scientist was so restricted as to be almost helpless. His astrological interests, however, eventually led to trouble with the Church.

Pietro was more a man of the Middle Ages than of the early Renaissance. His idea of the four elements—earth, water, air, and fire—was typical of medieval understanding of chemistry, but he went further than most medieval scholars through experimentation and critical translation of classical manuscripts. Pietro was also an eager collector of new information. He left record of an interview with the explorer Marco Polo held shortly before the latter returned to Venice in 1295. Pietro inquired about natural phenomena and drugs such as camphor, aloe, and brazil, which were imported from Asia. He made no mention of magic or other supernatural matters.

Pietro is often called a disciple of the Arabic scholar Avicenna and even more so of Averroës, whose ideas he is supposed to have introduced into Europe. Pietro's ideas about the stages of disease—onset, increase, fullness, and decline—correspond to those of Avicenna, as does his preference for simple, natural medicines. Scholar Lynn Thorndike, however, argues quite effectively that the supposed influence of Averroës has no basis in Pietro's writings. Averroës' ideas about chemistry were more sophisticated than those of medieval Europeans such as Pietro, and Thorndike finds no reason to think that Pietro's theological ideas came from the same source. Other writers, however, suggest that Pietro's adoption of a corruption of Averroës' idea of the soul was one of the principal sources of his trouble with the Church.

In addition to numerous translations from Arabic and Greek, Pietro wrote at least ten books. The most famous is the *Conciliator differentiarum philosophorum et praecipue medicorum* (1472; conciliator of the various medical philosophies and practices), in which he attempted to reconcile the teachings of Greek, Arabic, Jewish, and Latin writers in philosophy and medicine. Although done with the usual medieval resort to authority and syllogism, this work contains much original comment and makes clear Pietro's deep commitment to astrology.

Pietro's second major work, *De venenis eorumque remediis* (1473; English translation, 1924), is a description of all important known poisons with descriptions of symptoms and antidotes or treatments. Reportedly done for a pope—possibly John XXII—it too is a mixture of astrology and superstition, but the listing of poisons and symptoms is well done.

Pietro's writings other than translations are *Expositio problematum Aristotelis* (1475; exposition of Aristotelian problems), *Hippocratis de medicorum astrologia*

Pietro d'Abano. (Library of Congress)

libellus Graeco in Latinum (1476; Hippocratus's astronomical medicine translated from Greek to Latin), *Textus Mesue emendatus Petri Apponi medici in librum* (1505; the text of Mesue amended by Dr. Pietro d'Abano), *Astrolabium planum, in tabulis ascendens, continens qualibet hora atque minuto aequationes domorum coeli, significationes* (1502; clear astronomical tables, containing the heavenly signs for any hour and minute), *Joannis Mesue additio* (1505; additions to John Mesue), *Decisiones physiognomicae* (1548; judging a person's character by physical features), *Geomantia* (1549; *Magical Elements*, 1655), and *De balneis* (1553; on baths). Many of these works were considered authoritative into the sixteenth century.

Although the details are in some dispute, Pietro's return to Padua from Paris seems to have been marked by serious trouble with the Church. Either shortly before or after his arrival in Padua, Pietro was accused of heresy and necromancy. The charges were made through the Dominican order of friars and were based on reports of a physician named Petrus de Reggio. There are a number of reported accusations, including that he used magic to get all the money he spent returned to him, that he claimed that some biblical miracles had natural explanations, and that he adhered to the rationalistic philosophy of Averroës. Charged with several others, Pietro had to face the Inquisition. Thanks to the intervention of influential patrons—there is one report that Pietro went to Rome and won the support of Pope Boniface VIII—he was exonerated in 1306. In 1314, Pietro was offered the chair of medicine at the new University of Treviso, but he fell ill and died before he could move there. His death was fortuitous in one sense, for in 1315, the charges of heresy were renewed. Posthumously, he was condemned and orders were issued for the exhumation and burning of his body. Although most authorities maintain that friends spirited the body away to a new tomb and only an effigy was burned in the public square of Padua, Thomas of Strassburg, Augustinian prior general, claims to have seen the body burned. The distinction seems academic at best.

Thorndike, who has made the most thorough study of Pietro, rejects much of the story of his troubles with the Inquisition. It was, Thorndike argues, constructed of whole cloth in the fifteenth and sixteenth centuries. Pietro may have had one brush with Church authorities, but the embellishments about the body being spirited away have no basis in original sources. Thorndike is not even convinced that Pietro died on the traditionally accepted date of 1316 and suggests that he may, in fact, have taught for some years at Treviso after that date. Thorndike's arguments are well marshaled, but they have not been widely adopted by other scholars.

SIGNIFICANCE

Pietro was a medieval scientist, but he showed some of the qualities that would mark the Renaissance as well. His critical attitude and experimental approach were signs of the future. The importance he placed on astrology and prayer as elements in medical prescriptions, however, harked back to the past.

Pietro played an important role in the development of Padua and its university into a major intellectual center. Although in the thirteenth century the University of Padua was known mostly for the study of law, by 1500 it could boast of having had many of the major scientists of the Italian Renaissance as professors or students. Pietro founded the Paduan school of medical thought, introducing both classical and Arabic sources. His willingness to question established views and to seek new information rather than depending wholly on authority was important in shaping the growing scholarly tradition of Padua.

—*Fred R. van Hartesveldt*

Further Reading

Brown, Horace. "*De venenis* of Petrus Abbonus." *Annals of Medical History* 6 (1924): 25-53. A translation of Pietro's work about poisons and their symptoms and treatments, this is the only conveniently available English translation of any of Pietro's writings. It provides a good sample of the mix of superstition and science that marked his approach to medicine.

French, R. K. *Medicine Before Science: The Rational and Learned Doctor.* New York: Cambridge University Press, 2003. This examination of the role of physicians in the Middle Ages provides information on the age in which Pietro lived.

Hyde, J. K. *Padua in the Age of Dante.* New York: Barnes and Noble Books, 1966. An excellent description of late medieval Padua that provides valuable background information about the milieu in which Pietro worked.

Olschki, Leonardo. "Medical Matters in Marco Polo's Description of the World." In *Essays in the History of Medicine Presented to Professor Arturo Castiglioni on the Occasion of his Seventieth Birth Day*, edited by Henry E. Sigerist. Baltimore: Johns Hopkins University Press, 1944. Contains a discussion of Pietro's interview with Marco Polo showing the former's scientific approach to collecting new data.

Thorndike, Lynn. *A History of Magic and Experimental Science.* Vol. 2. New York: Columbia University Press, 1947. A magisterial work in eight volumes tracing the development of the techniques of modern science. Contains a thorough study of Pietro.

_______. "Peter of Abano: A Medieval Scientist." *Annual Report of the American Historical Association for the Year 1919* 1 (1923): 317-326. Contains a summary of Pietro's life but is focused on historiographical sources. Attempts to show that many common beliefs about Pietro are misconceptions based on secondary sources from the fifteenth and sixteenth centuries.

See also: Alhazen; Arnold of Villanova; Averroës; Avicenna; Boniface VIII; Guy de Chauliac; Paul of Aegina; Marco Polo; al-Rāzī; Trotula.

Related articles in *Great Events from History: The Middle Ages, 477-1453*: 1233: Papal Inquisition; 1271-1295: Travels of Marco Polo.

ʿAbd al-Malik

Islamic caliph (r. 685-705)

ʿAbd al-Malik solidified the Islamic Empire under the Marwanid Dynasty through his victory in the second fitna, or Islamic civil war. This victory ensured the continued rule of the Marwanids, a branch of the Umayyad family. He also introduced the first Arabic coinage, established Arabic as an official language, and oversaw the construction of the Dome of the Rock.

Born: c. 646; Medina, Hijaz (now Medina, Saudi Arabia)

Died: October 705; Damascus, Syria

Also known as: ʿAbd al-Malik Ibn Marwān

Areas of achievement: Government and politics, warfare and conquest, architecture

Early Life

ʿAbd al-Malik (ahb-dewl mah-LIHK) was the son of Marwān ibn al-Hakam (r. 684-685) during the reign of ʿUthmān ʿAffān (r. 644-656), the third caliph. Following the first *fitna*, the Umayyad family took control of the caliphate, and Muʾāwiyah (r. 661-680) became the caliph. The Umayyads had been a large, powerful family well before their conversion to Islam. Under Muʾāwiyah, Marwān was appointed the governor of the Hijaz, an area formerly the center of Islam, which included Mecca and Medina. ʿAbd al-Malik was born in Medina, and received the education and lifestyle that resulted from being a governor's son and member of a powerful Arab family. This education was due to the nature of Umayyad society, which consisted of "not so much a nation as a hereditary social caste which one could enter by birth" (according to Bernard Lewis in *The Arabs in History*, 1993).

Following the death of Muʾāwiya in 680, a second civil war broke out over the succession. Muʾāwiya had secured the succession of his son, Yazīd (r. 680-683). Followers of ʿAlī (r. 656-661), the fourth caliph, disputed the succession. This struggle was the second *fitna*.

In 680, Yazīd massacred ʿAlī's son, al-Ḥusayn, and some of his followers at Karbala. This inspired a revolt in Medina. While putting down this revolt in the Hijaz, Yazīd died. Following Yazīd's death in 683, Marwān and ʿAbd al-Malik moved from Medina to Damascus. The son of Yazīd, Muʾāwiyah II, became caliph but soon died, and his death fractured the entire Islamic world into competing factions. Two Arabian tribes, the Qays and the

Kalb, both supported contenders for the caliphate. Marwān was supported by the Kalb and Ibn al-Zubayr was supported by the Qays. Marwān was victorious and became caliph in 684. He then negotiated to ensure that one of his sons, either ʿAbd al-Malik or ʿAbd al-ʿAzīz, was appointed his successor. In 685, Marwān died of plague, and ʿAbd al-Malik became caliph. On his ascension, this Islamic world was divided into three main factions: ʿAbd al-Malik controlled Syria, Ibn al-Zubayr controlled the Hijaz, and al-Mukhtar controlled Iraq. ʿAbd al-Malik was forced to reunite the Islamic world.

Life's Work

For the first two years of his reign, ʿAbd al-Malik concerned himself with securing his center of power. He struggled with the Byzantine Empire for control of northern Syria and also struggled to contain Zufar, who led the Qays and was allied with Ibn al-Zubayr. Other revolts in Syria were from separate members of the Umayyad family. In 689, ʿAmr ibn Saʿid al-Ashdaq, the head of another branch of the Umayyads, led a revolt in Damascus. ʿAbd al-Malik brutally suppressed this revolt by killing ʿAmr ibn Saʿid, supposedly under a truce flag.

During ʿAbd al-Malik's struggle for control of Syria, al-Zubayr's brother Musʿab, the governor of Iraq, managed to defeat al-Mukhtar and establish control over most of Iraq in 687. Musʿab then concentrated on his struggle with the Kharijites, a rival faction that would acknowledge only the authority of a caliph they selected. In 691, while Musʿab was mainly occupied with the Kharijites, ʿAbd al Malik advanced into Iraq with his army. The caliph first offered to let Musʿab keep the governorship of Iraq, but Musʿab refused. Musʿab was killed in battle that October. ʿAbd al-Malik then established control over Iraq and continued to suppress opposition such as the Kharijites. The Kharijites were completely driven out of Iraq under ʿAbd al-Malik. ʿAbd al-Malik then sent his general, al-Ḥajjāj ibn Yūsuf, to deal with al-Zubayr. Al-Ḥajjāj, known for his brutality, advanced on Mecca, where al-Zubayr was based. The resulting seven-month siege led to the destruction of the Kaaba. Al-Ḥajjāj managed to defeat al-Zubayr in late 692, and then, in two years as governor of the region, managed to suppress all opposition. ʿAbd al-Malik had now secured control over the majority of the Islamic world. Following this unification, ʿAbd al-Malik renewed his struggle against the Byzantine Empire.

Following the solidification of the Islamic world, ʿAbd al-Malik made significant reforms in the government and administration of the empire. Under ʿAbd al-Malik, the beginnings of a standing army were created. Also, service in the army became a way to advance one's career. ʿAbd al-Malik's general and eventual governor of Iraq, al-Ḥajjāj, came from humble origins and gained his position through military skill. Also, ʿAbd al-Malik is credited with changing the official language of the administration to Arabic. Traditionally, the Arabs had assimilated the languages of the previous administrations of the areas they conquered; Greek, Coptic, and Persian were used in various parts of the region. Additionally, the provincial administrations were standardized, although they remained under the local governors' control. This governmental centralization took time; however, it was a significant break from previous Arab traditions.

ʿAbd al-Malik instituted the first Arabic coinage. As with the administrative languages, the Arabs had previously adapted existing, mainly Byzantine, coinage for commerce. According to some accounts, ʿAbd al-Malik began minting Arabic coins called dinars in Kufic script in response to changes in Byzantine coinage. These changes were made because of a reported dispute with the Byzantine emperor. However, the change in Byzantine coinage probably was more a result of changes made a few years later. The coins were originally minted in Damascus and later in the Hijaz. Because of their high concentration of precious metal, they replaced the lesser quality Byzantine coins rapidly. Additionally, ʿAbd al-Malik began a process of fiscal reforms. The economic reorganization coupled with the establishment of a centralized bureaucracy was the beginning of a transformation from a coalition of tribes to a true empire.

The Umayyad Caliphs, 661-750

Reign	*Caliph*
661-680	Muʾāwiyah I (Muʾāwiyah ibn Abī Sufyna)
680-683	Yazīd I
683	Muʾāwiyah II
684-685	Marwān I
685-705	ʿABD AL-MALIK
705-715	al-Walīd I
715-717	Sulaimān
717-720	ʿUmar II
720-724	Yazīd II
724-743	Hishām
743-744	al-Walīd II
744	Yazīd III
744	Ibrāhīm
744-750	Marwān II

The most dramatic example of this transformation during ʿAbd al-Malik's reign was the construction of the Dome of the Rock in Jerusalem, completed sometime in the 690's and built on the rocky outcropping called the Temple Mount, where the caliph ʿUmar I is believed to have entered the city during the Muslim conquest. The building was funded by seven years' worth of revenues from Egypt, ʿAbd al-Malik's richest province. There are several explanations for why ʿAbd al-Malik built the Dome of the Rock. Tradition says that it was to replace the Kaaba as the destination of the pilgrimage (*hajj*) during the struggle with al-Zubayr. This reason would allow ʿAbd al-Malik to gather revenues from the *hajj* as well as increase his legitimacy as the rightful caliph. This explanation, however, has generally been discarded.

During the second *fitna*, four opposing factions jointly made the pilgrimage to the Kaaba in Mecca, and during the siege of Mecca, ʿAbd al-Malik's army requested entry to the city for a pilgrimage. Additionally, by trying to usurp Mecca as the center of the Islamic world, ʿAbd al-Malik would have lost legitimacy, instead of gaining it. Others believe the dome was built to demonstrate the legitimacy of Islamic culture. The region around Jerusalem was predominantly Jewish and Christian, with grandiose temples and churches. The dome's shape was unique to Muslim buildings, and it more closely resembled Christian architecture. Regardless of ʿAbd al-Malik's original motives, the Dome of the Rock was a significant architectural achievement, and it demonstrated the ongoing transformation of a unified civilization between Jews, Christians, and Muslims. The Dome of the Rock also has important historical significance in regard to Islam as a religion. The inscriptions on the inside of the building are the earliest datable Qurʾānic texts, and they provide the first reference to the religion of Muḥammad as "Islam."

Significance

The reign of ʿAbd al-Malik marked a significant transitional point in Islamic history. For the previous sixty years, the Middle East had seen the rise of Islam and the subsequent conquest of most of the region. The organization of this conquest was mostly tribal, with little centralization. During ʿAbd al-Malik's reign, he managed to defeat several factions vying for control of this empire, unifying it once again. Concurrent with unification, he also began the long process of transforming a collection of tribal conquests into a centralized civilization. Instead of adapting the bureaucracy and currency of previous or neighboring empires, he instituted the Arab language as the official language of government and began minting Islamic coins. A result of this centralization was the creation of a standing army and the resulting, albeit small, amount of social mobility through martial skill. This change meant that instead of seasonal campaigns in areas near their home, armies were stationed or deployed from North Africa to Iraq and were units designed to control and expand the empire.

Finally, ʿAbd al-Malik solidified the caliphate as a dynastic monarchy. ʿAbd al-Malik had four sons who later became caliphs, and the only interruption of this was by a cousin, ʿUmar bin ʿAbd al-ʿAzīz (r. 717-720). While all Umayyad caliphs after 685 were descendants of Marwān, ʿAbd al-Malik was the true founder of the Marwanid Dynasty. The Umayyad family became the first dynasty of Islam, and through the success of ʿAbd al-Malik, the Marwanid branch dominated the empire. ʿAbd al-Malik turned the Islamic Empire into a true imperial empire.

The significance of this unification and transformation was seen by the success of the Islamic Empire during and following ʿAbd al-Malik's death. Under ʿAbd al-Malik's son and successor al-Walīd (r. 705-715), the Umayyads conquered Spain and built the Umayyad Mosque in Damascus. Initial military probes into India were also conducted. The conquest into Europe continued until the Battle of Tours in 732, which halted the Muslim advance. Finally, the Islamic Empire became a major world center of science and the arts during a time when Western Europe was still in the Dark Ages.

—*Paul C. Gaige*

Further Reading

Flood, Finbarr Barry. *The Great Mosque of Damascus: Studies on the Makings of an Umayyad Visual Culture*. Boston: Brill, 2001. Examines the visual culture, including architectural elements, of the Umayyads and the empire's far-reaching cultural influences. Illustrations, extensive bibliography, and index.

Goitein, Shelomo Dov. "The Historical Background of the Erection of the Dome of the Rock." *Journal of the American Oriental Society* 70, no. 2 (April-June 1950). This article discusses the various explanations for the construction of the Dome of the Rock as well as details the significance of the building.

Hawting, G. R. *The First Dynasty of Islam: The Umayyad Caliphate A.D. 661-750*. New York: Routledge, 2000. Provides an excellent historical narrative of the Umayyad caliphate's development into a dynasty. Includes excellent genealogical tables and a good explanation of the tribal organization and history of the Arabs. Maps, bibliography, index.

Lewis, Bernard. *The Arabs in History*. New York: Oxford University Press, 1993. Provides a general, narrative overview of the Arabs and their historical significance, with a concentration on social and economic history. Focuses mostly on the social, everyday impact of historical events.

Raby, Julian, and Jeremy Johns, eds. *Bayt-al-Maqdis: ʿAbd al-Malik's Jerusalem*. New York: Oxford University Press, for the Board of Faculty of Oriental Studies, 1992-1999. Vol. 1 in a two-volume set that explores the architecture of al-Malik and the history of religious architecture in the city of Jerusalem. Part of the Oxford Studies in Islamic Art series. Some text in French. Bibliography.

See also: al-Ḥasan al-Baṣrī; John of Damascus; Damia al-Kāhina; ʿUmar I.

Related articles in *Great Events from History: The Middle Ages, 477-1453*: c. 610-632: Muḥammad Receives Revelations; 685-691: Building of the Dome of the Rock; April or May, 711: Ṭārik Crosses into Spain; October 11, 732: Battle of Tours; 843: Treaty of Verdun.

ʿAbd al-Muʾmin

Berber founder of the Almohad Dynasty (r. 1130-1163)

Through military prowess and administrative skill, ʿAbd al-Muʾmin founded the Almohad Empire in North Africa and the Iberian Peninsula, initiating a period of thriving commerce and artistic creativity.

Born: 1094; Tagra, Kingdom of the Ḥammādids (now in Algeria)

Died: May 2, 1163; Rabat, Almohad Empire (now in Morocco)

Also known as: ʿAbd al-Muʾmin ibn-ʿAlī ibn Makhlūf ibn Yuʿla ibn Marwān (full name); Abū Muḥammad al-Kūmi; Amir al-Muʾminin

Areas of achievement: Government and politics, warfare and conquest, patronage of the arts

Early Life

Born ʿAbd al-Muʾmin ibn-ʿAlī ibn Makhlūf ibn Yuʿla ibn Marwān in Tagra in 1094, ʿAbd al-Muʾmin (ab-dool-MOO-mihn) was the son of Alī, a humble potter and member of the Koumiya, an Arabized section of the Berber Zanata tribe. Legends arose concerning marvelous happenings in his youth: Swarms of bees were said to have alighted on him without stinging, and a holy man prophesied that the boy would conquer countries at the four cardinal points.

Alā decided that his son must have an education. Thus, ʿAbd al-Muʾmin studied at the school in Tagra and then at the mosque in the important Algerian city of Tlemcen. One historian noted his intelligence: "In the time it takes a man to grasp one question, he understood ten." To further his knowledge, ʿAbd al-Muʾmin, accompanied by uncle Yaʿlu, determined to go to the East. In 1117, that plan was scrapped at Mallala, Algeria, because of ʿAbd al-Muʾmin's momentous meeting with Ibn Tūmart.

Ibn Tūmart, a Masmuda Berber of southern Morocco, founded the Almohad movement, the name being a corruption of the Arabic *al-muwaḥḥidūn*, meaning "the movement of the unitarians." Ibn Tūmart placed special stress on the oneness of God and introduced into North Africa the Shīʿite notion of an infallible *mahdī* (divinely guided one). It was as he was returning from his pilgrimage to Mecca that Ibn Tūmart met ʿAbd al-Muʾmin at Mallala. According to tradition, Ibn Tūmart had prophesied their meeting.

ʿAbd al-Muʾmin became Ibn Tūmart's first disciple, accompanying him to Morocco. In 1121, Ibn Tūmart established headquarters at his native village, Igliz, moving to Tinmel three years later. In 1125, Ibn Tūmart proclaimed himself the *mahdī*, the imam known and infallible. ʿAbd al-Muʾmin served as Ibn Tūmart's trusted lieutenant, spreading his doctrine, helping to organize Almohad society, and fighting against the Almoravid regime. In May, 1130, ʿAbd al-Muʾmin suffered wounds in the Almohad defeat by the Almoravids at the Battle of al-Buhaira. On August 13, 1130, Ibn Tūmart died, having designated ʿAbd al-Muʾmin as the Almohad leader. For three years, Ibn Tūmart's death was concealed because certain Almohads disputed ʿAbd al-Muʾmin's succession, arguing that he was an outsider. By 1133, however, his supporters had managed to establish his leadership.

Life's Work

ʿAbd al-Muʾmin determined to conquer the entire Maghreb for the Almohad cause. For several years, he prepared meticulously, gaining adherents to the Almohad message and attracting mountaineers to his army in Tinmel. Then, systematically employing guerrilla tactics against the Almoravid Dynasty, he conquered the western mountain ranges of North Africa one after another: the High Atlas, the Middle Atlas, the Rif, and the range south of Tlemcen. Emboldened, ʿAbd al-Muʾmin moved from the mountains. In 1144, he defeated the Almoravid ally Reverter and his Christian militia. A year later, ʿAbd al-Muʾmin crushed the Almoravid monarch Tashfin ibn Alī ibn Yusuf and took Oran and Tétouan. Next, after a nine-month siege, ʿAbd al-Muʾmin captured Fez, and, in 1147, following an eleven-month siege, Marrakech, where he executed the last Almoravid ruler. ʿAbd al-Muʾmin made Marrakech the Almohad capital and proceeded to massacre the Lemtuna Berbers.

Thereupon, ʿAbd al-Muʾmin turned his attention to the Iberian Peninsula, where the Christians had been recovering territory because of the Almoravid decline. Because of their rigid doctrine, the Almohads encountered resistance from Iberian Muslims and Christians alike. As a result, by 1148, ʿAbd al-Muʾmin's authority extended to only the southwestern part of the Andalus. Regarding the Iberian Peninsula as a diversion from the task of consolidating Almohad rule in the Maghreb, ʿAbd al-Muʾmin pushed no farther into Europe.

After conquering Morocco, ʿAbd al-Muʾmin focused attention on the central Maghreb. Here the Ḥammādid kingdom existed in decline under Yaḥyā. In 1151, by forced marches and in secrecy, ʿAbd al-Muʾmin and his army reached Algiers and then Bougie, the Ḥammādid capital, which surrendered. Next, ʿAbd al-Muʾmin's son took and sacked Qalʿa. In 1152, the Hilalians, Arab Bedouins of the region, joined the attempt to push the Almohads to the far west. ʿAbd al-Muʾmin, who had been returning to Morocco, hurried back and met the enemy at Sétif, where he triumphed after a four-day battle. In this case, however, he treated the vanquished leniently.

ʿAbd al-Muʾmin devoted the years between 1152 and 1159 to organizing his state. He had taken the title caliph of Ibn Tūmart, imitating Abū Bakr, caliph of Muḥammad. He also became Amir al-Muʾminin (prince of the faithful), the first non-Arab to be so honored. Members of his family, known as sayyids, formed the elite. In 1154, ʿAbd al-Muʾmin proclaimed his son as successor, displacing Abū Hafs ʿUmar, the first designee. ʿAbd al-Muʾmin sent his other sons to the principal provinces as governors. With each of them, ʿAbd al-Muʾmin sent a leading Almohad sheikh as counselor, thus joining the religious leaders to his family. ʿAbd al-Muʾmin used Abū Hafs ʿUmar as his first vizier and then as a personal adviser; the latter's family ranked next to the sayyids. Ibn Tūmart's Council of the Fifty, a consultative assembly that had representatives from the original tribes of the Almohad movement, was retained. These elements formed the aristocracy of the empire.

Using Ibn Tūmart's teachings, ʿAbd al-Muʾmin aimed to build a unified Muslim community in the Maghreb. The bases for legislation were the Qurʾān, the tradition of Muḥammad, and the concord of Muḥammad's companions. Practical needs of justice, however, drove ʿAbd al-Muʾmin to tacit toleration of the Malikite system of law. To maintain and enforce Ibn Tūmart's doctrine, ʿAbd al-Muʾmin devised special training for provincial administrators. He personally selected young men from the Masmuda tribes and trained them in Ibn Tūmart's writings, archery, horsemanship, and swimming. The ruler's sons received this education as well.

As an administrator, ʿAbd al-Muʾmin shone in masterminding an immense geographical survey of the Maghreb. According to a Muslim historian, one-third of this area was deducted for mountains, rivers, salt lakes, roads, and deserts, and the remainder was made subject to the land tax (*kharaj*), with a fixed amount in grain and money

ALMOHAD CALIPHS (SPAIN AND NORTH AFRICA)

Reign	*Caliph*
1130-1163	ʿABD AL-MUʾMIN
1163-1184	Abū Yaʿqūb Yūsuf
1184-1199	Abū Yūsuf Yaʿqūb al-Manṣūr
1199-1213	Muḥammad ibn Yaʿqūb
1212	Christians defeat Almohads at Las Navas de Tolosa
1213-1224	Yūsuf II Abū Yaqūb
1224	ʿAbd al-Wāḥid Abū Muḥammad
1224-1227	ʿAbd Allāh Abū Muḥammad
1227-1235	Yaḥyā Abū Zakariyyāʿ
1227-1232	Idrīs I ibn Yaʿqūb
1228-1229	Retreat from Spain
1232-1242	ʿAbdul-Wāḥid ibn Idrīs I
1242-1248	ʿAlī ibn Idrīs I
1248-1266	ʿUmar ibn Isḥāq
1266-1269	Idrīs II ibn Muḥammad
1269	End of Almohad domination in North Africa

to be paid by each tribe—a first in Barbary. ʿAbd al-Muʾmin used the survey to ascertain his fiscal resources. The treasury drew revenue from the taxes imposed by the Qurʾān and from a large part of the *kharaj*. The latter applied to "unbelievers," paying the tax as a sort of rent on their former property, its ownership having been taken by the state. The unbelievers comprised all non-Almohad Muslims and also those Almohads who were judged unzealous.

The pragmatic ʿAbd al-Muʾmin did not subject all tribes to the *kharaj*. He needed the help of nomads for manning his army in the Iberian Peninsula and for keeping order in the Maghreb. These nomads included the Hilalians, who were brought to Morocco from Tunisia, the Zanata Beni ʿAbd al-Wad in the area between Mina and the Moulouya, and another tribe camped in the Bougie district. Members of these tribes enforced the payment of the *kharaj* on settled tribes.

ʿAbd al-Muʾmin encountered internal opposition to his regime. His restricting the succession to the Almohad leadership to his own family caused a rebellion in 1155. The ringleaders were Ibn Tūmart's brothers, ʿAbd al-ʿAziz and ʿIsa. They besieged Marrakech but were defeated and executed. Along with them, ʿAbd al-Muʾmin executed numerous chiefs of the Hargha tribe who had been suspected of fomenting treason. Sensitive to opposition, ʿAbd al-Muʾmin dealt cautiously with the proud Masmuda tribes, which claimed Ibn Tūmart as their own son. ʿAbd al-Muʾmin allowed only the Masmuda to have the honor of being called Almohads; they were also the sole group permitted to discuss and elaborate Ibn Tūmart's doctrine. Furthermore, ʿAbd al-Muʾmin gave the Masmuda preferential treatment in taxation.

While organizing his government, ʿAbd al-Muʾmin gave thought also to Ifriqiya (Tunisia). Muslims there sought his help against the Norman occupation under King William I of Sicily. In two years of preparation, ʿAbd al-Muʾmin built seventy warships and an army of 200,000. In 1159, he led the army into Ifriqiya, his navy following along the coast. He sent one force to besiege Tunis, whose ruler was a Muslim Sanhaja chief under Norman protection. ʿAbd al-Muʾmin led his main army against heavily fortified Mahdia, the major Norman stronghold. On January 22, 1160, a seven-month siege ended, the Almohad navy having defeated a Norman relieving fleet from Sicily. ʿAbd al-Muʾmin and the Normans negotiated: The Normans evacuated Mahdia, and ʿAbd al-Muʾmin gave them safe passage to Sicily. Thus ended Norman rule in Africa. At this time, the Almohads captured Tunis and the interior of Ifriqiya. Now, moreover, the Muslims of Tripolitana, who had evicted the Normans in 1157, swore allegiance to ʿAbd al-Muʾmin.

ʿAbd al-Muʾmin's achievements extended to still another activity: patronage of architecture. He ordered the construction of a palace and of the impressive Kutubia mosque at Marrakech, as well as the mosque at Taza. To commemorate Ibn Tūmart, ʿAbd al-Muʾmin built a mosque at Tinmel. The design of this structure reveals influences from the surrounding area, the East, and Moorish Spain. Another of his buildings was the fortress of Ribat al-Fath.

On May 2, 1163, ʿAbd al-Muʾmin died at Rabat. He was buried near Ibn Tūmart at Tinmel.

SIGNIFICANCE

ʿAbd al-Muʾmin created a new chapter in the history of North Africa. Designated by the *mahdī*, Ibn Tūmart, as his successor in leading the Almohad movement, ʿAbd al-Muʾmin converted that spiritual body into a political regime lasting from 1130 to 1269. Throwing off his deference to Abū Hafs ʿUmar, ʿAbd al-Muʾmin built by war an empire in North Africa and southern Spain which his family, the Muʾminid, ruled. His long military activity angered some of the original Almohads, who tried unsuccessfully to assassinate him in 1160. The conspirators also hated his magnanimous policy toward the empire's Arabs.

The reigns of ʿAbd al-Muʾmin, his son Abū Yaʿqūb Yūsuf (r. 1163-1184), and his grandson Abū Yūsuf Yaʿqūb al-Manṣūr (r. 1184-1199) marked the golden age of Barbary. They brought a general revival of commerce, for the Almohads had the best fleet in the Mediterranean, and they opened the sea to Christian and Muslim traffic. Urban life continued the development begun under the previous Almoravid rule, with a new burst of creative activity stemming from Ibn Ṭufayl and Averroës.

Art flourished in Morocco and Spain under ʿAbd al-Muʾmin and his dynasty. ʿAbd al-Muʾmin was the founder of a new architectural style—the most original and impressive in North Africa. He gave to Andalusian artists a new spirit: an austere and simple style that resulted in a magnificent union of Andalusian subtlety and Moroccan strength.

Nevertheless, ʿAbd al-Muʾmin contributed to the ultimate Almohad decline and fall. The mechanical and official nature of his piety began to loosen the Muʾminid state from the passionate and radiant zeal of Ibn Tūmart, whose uncompromising stand had created the Almohad movement. Furthermore, ʿAbd al-Muʾmin settled some Arab Bedouin tribes in Morocco, where he wanted to train them to further his realm in Spain. Later, members of these tribes became unruly, causing anarchy in the heart of the Almohad Empire.

Still, ʿAbd al-Muʾmin's great achievement cannot be denied: He led the Berbers in the first unification of North Africa.

—*Erving E. Beauregard*

Further Reading

Abun-Nasr, Jamil M. *A History of the Maghrib*. 2d ed. Cambridge, England: Cambridge University Press, 1975. This compact account of ʿAbd al-Muʾmin links his creation of a unified Muslim community to Ibn Tūmart's doctrine. The relationship of the Almohad regime with previous and later dynasties is discussed. Brief bibliography; index, map.

_______. *A History of the Maghrib in the Islamic Period*. Cambridge, England: Cambridge University Press, 1987. A brief but excellent depiction of ʿAbd al-Muʾmin, more scholarly treatment than Abun-Nasr's book. Unannotated bibliography, index, map.

Falola, Toyin, ed. *Africa*. Durham, N.C.: Carolina Academic Press, 2000. A good history of the continent. Bibliographic references, index.

Hopkins, J. F. P. *Medieval Muslim Government in Barbary Until the Sixth Century of the Hijra*. London: Luzac, 1958. One section describes the Almohad hierarchy. The entire system may have existed solely on paper. Treatment of the elaborate organization may be of interest only to scholars. One map.

Julien, Charles-André. *History of North Africa: Tunisia, Algeria, Morocco*. Translated by John Petrie, edited by C. C. Stewart and Roger Le Tourneau. London: Routledge & Kegan Paul, 1970. Very good treatment of the Almohads (forty-seven pages), placing ʿAbd al-Muʾmin on center stage in his varied roles. Apt quotations from sources; one map, fine bibliography.

Ki-Zerbo, Joseph, and Djibril Tamsir Niane, eds. *Africa from the Twelfth to the Sixteenth Century*. Berkeley: University of California Press, 1997. Includes several chapters on the Maghreb, including "The Unification of the Maghrib Under the Almohads." Illustrations, maps.

Le Tourneau, Roger. *The Almohad Movement in North Africa in the Twelfth and Thirteenth Centuries*. Princeton, N.J.: Princeton University Press, 1969. Excellent in integrating ʿAbd al-Muʾmin into the Almohad movement and showing his strengths and weaknesses. Brief but good treatment of contemporary accounts and historical studies. Helpful index.

See also: Afonso I; Averroës; Ibn Khaldūn; al-Idrīsī; James I the Conqueror.

Related articles in *Great Events from History: The Middle Ages, 477-1453*: 1062-1147: Almoravids Conquer Morocco and Establish the Almoravid Empire; 1190: Moses Maimonides Writes *The Guide of the Perplexed*; 1230: Unification of Castile and León.

ʿAbd al-Raḥmān III al-Nāṣir

Spanish emir (912-929) and caliph (929-961)

ʿAbd al-Raḥmān became the first full-fledged caliph of Córdoba, on the Iberian Peninsula, inaugurating the Umayyad caliphate in Spain. His reign, characterized by sound administrative, fiscal, and religious policies, military successes, astute diplomacy, and patronage of learning, marked the apex of Islamic power in Spain.

Born: January, 891; Córdoba (now in Spain)
Died: October 15, 961; Córdoba
Areas of achievement: Government and politics, religion and theology, military, patronage of the arts

Early Life

The grandson of Emir ʿAbd Allāh and his Christian wife, great-grandson of Emir al-Mundhir and a Christian princess from Navarre, and grandnephew of the powerful Navarrese queen Toda, ʿAbd al-Raḥmān III al-Nāṣir (uhb-dool-rahk-MAHN uhl-NAH-sihr) spent his youth in the wealth and culture of his grandfather's palace in Córdoba. This ancestry illustrates the complex nature of Spanish society in the tenth century. Clearly the Christians and the Muslims were in conflict, but the conflict was rooted more in political and economic rivalries than in religious or cultural antagonisms. This background provided ʿAbd al-Raḥmān with perspective and connections that he was able to exploit effectively, as his grandfather had not. When ʿAbd al-Raḥmān inherited the emirate, his authority extended only to the area around Córdoba.

During the preceding decades, Arab aristocrats and Berber military men had amassed huge landed estates that gave them a power base from which to ignore central authority. This independence was apparent particularly in certain areas of Aragon, Toledo, and Estremadura. Religious fanatics of one kind or another were in repeated revolt. Through sporadic raids and warfare, the Christian princes in the north had regained vast tracts of land that the emirate had controlled earlier. The absence of political unity and social stability had devastated the economy of Spain. Although ʿAbd Allāh was not the strongest or wisest of emirs, he did make one outstanding decision: From among his many grandchildren, he chose ʿAbd al-Raḥmān as his heir.

LIFE'S WORK

In 912, when ʿAbd al-Raḥmān was twenty-one, he became the emir. He immediately undertook to rectify the political, economic, and social problems that he had inherited. His interests were many, but he gave primary attention to three major activities: the unification of his kingdom, the construction of the Madinat az-Zahra palace, and the promotion of an economic revolution.

The first of these tasks, the unification and centralization of his kingdom, took the first twenty years of ʿAbd al-Raḥmān's reign. He neutralized the power of the aristocracy and curbed the bellicosity of the Berber tribes by establishing a standing army, made up of slaves and foreigners from the whole of the Mediterranean world, soldiers whose first loyalty was to the caliph. This army ultimately numbered one hundred thousand and was supported by a third of the royal revenues.

ʿAbd al-Raḥmān defeated the religious rebels whose power centered on Bobastro and who had virtually declared their independence from the central government. He deliberately broke the independence of the governors of Saragossa, Toledo, and Badajoz, restoring their function as frontier marches whose purpose was to prevent Christian intrusion into the Córdoban kingdom. He campaigned repeatedly, though not always successfully, against the Christian kingdoms of León, Castile, Navarre, and Galicia. In the end, it was to the caliphate that the Christians went in search of physicians, musicians, architects, negotiators, tutors, and marriage alliances.

By the end of his reign, ʿAbd al-Raḥmān had centralized his authority over Islamic Spain. He had made the Christian kingdoms tribute states but allowed them to retain governmental autonomy. By 937, he had stopped the westward expansion of the Fāṭimids out of Tunis, extending his sovereignty over Morocco and western Algeria. In recognition of his power, rulers of all European and eastern Islamic kingdoms commissioned emissaries to his court.

CÓRDOBA'S UMAYYAD CALIPHS, 756-1031

Reign	*Ruler*
756-788	ʿAbd al-Raḥmān I (emir)
788-796	Hishām I (emir)
796-822	al-Hakam I (emir)
822-852	ʿAbd al-Raḥmān II (emir)
852-886	Muḥammad I (emir)
886-888	al-Mundhir (emir)
888-912	ʿAbd Allāh (emir)
912-961	ʿABD AL-RAḤMĀN III AL-NĀṢIR (emir 912-929, caliph 929-961)
961-976	al-Hakam II al-Mustanṣir
976-1009	Hishām II al-Muayyad
1009-1010	Muḥammad II al-Mahdī
1009-1010	Sulaimān al-Mustaʿīn
1010-1013	Hishām II (restored)
1013-1016	Sulaimān (restored)
1016-1018	Alī ben Hammud
1018	ʿAbd al-Raḥmān IV
1018-1021	al-Qasim
1021-1022	Yaḥyā
1022-1023	al-Qasim (restored)
1023-1024	ʿAbd al-Raḥmān V
1024-1025	Muḥammad III
1025-1027	Yaḥyā (restored)
1027-1031	Hishām III
1031	End of Umayyads; dissolution of Umayyad Spain into small states

Note: Islamic rulers on the Iberian Peninsula were emirs until 929.

To add to his prestige and focus his authority, in 929, ʿAbd al-Raḥmān declared himself caliph of Islamic Spain, based on his Umayyad lineage. He also took the titles "commander of the believers" and "defender of the religion of God," tacitly supporting the Malikite theological position, which was then dominant among Muslims in Spain. His assumption of these titles allowed petty chieftains in North Africa to recognize the Spanish caliph as their sovereign, rather than the schismatic and fanatical Fāṭimids. It also did much to focus the emerging patriotism and loyalty of his Spanish subjects.

In the economic sphere, ʿAbd al-Raḥmān met with equal success. Production of gold, iron, silver, lead, and rubies increased. He improved and extended the canals and irrigation systems. Despite the Qurʾānic dictates against wine drinking, the growing of grapes and the making of wine became important economic enterprises.

Agriculture was diversified and expanded. Rice, peaches, oranges, apricots, sugar, cotton, pomegranates, figs, and saffron had been introduced by the Muslims into Spain; traditional crops such as wheat, other grains, and olives also continued to be cultivated.

This diversification and increased agricultural production were key elements of the prosperity of ʿAbd al-Raḥmān's caliphate, but industry played a crucial role as well. The caliphate became known for its fine leather, superb steel, olive oil, and paper. These products were traded as far east as India for slaves, cloth, and exotic spices. ʿAbd al-Raḥmān expanded the navy in order to protect trade routes and the merchant fleet from attacks by the Normans, Byzantines, or ʿAbbāsids. In the end, ʿAbd al-Raḥmān's navy and merchant marine came to dominate the western Mediterranean.

In 936, ʿAbd al-Raḥmān embarked on the construction of his great palace, Madinat az-Zahra (which means "she of the shining face"). Az-Zahra was the caliph's favorite wife; curiously, initial funding for the palace came as a gift to the caliph from one of his concubines. The construction of the palace became a major public works project, employing ten thousand workers and three thousand animals for twenty-five years at an expense of one-third of the annual royal revenues. Materials such as ebony, gold, and ivory were imported to decorate the palace; luxurious gifts for its embellishment were received from other rulers. This sprawling palace complex, located about three miles outside Córdoba, provided a beautiful view of the city and surrounding countryside. Some have deemed it the crowning achievement of ʿAbd al-Raḥmān's reign.

Significance

ʿAbd al-Raḥmān III al-Nāṣir died at the age of seventy, leaving the caliphate to al-Hakam II, his son by his Basque Christian wife, Subh. ʿAbd al-Raḥmān had been a determined and successful ruler. His energy was boundless, his ability undisputed, his power immense and wisely controlled. He demanded respect; he extended charity. He carefully and intelligently tended to the demands of state and religion, while conscientiously expanding the culture, refinement, and economic well-being of his realm. He had established not only the most magnificent but also the most powerful kingdom in Europe—and nowhere was this better exemplified than in his capital, Córdoba.

Half a million people populated the city, whereas London had perhaps five thousand; indeed, the population of Spain as a whole had exploded during ʿAbd al-Raḥmān's reign. The streets of the city were paved and lighted. Resplendent with palaces, seven hundred mosques, and at least three hundred public baths, Córdoba contained seventy libraries, countless bookstores, and twenty-seven free schools.

The caliph founded the University of Córdoba in the Great Mosque and established chairs and scholarships there; it was an institution that attracted teachers and students from the whole Mediterranean world and western Asia. During the reign of his son, the royal library founded by ʿAbd al-Raḥmān reached 400,000 volumes, a number of which serve today as the basis of the Arabic collection in the Library of the Escorial. In addition to the university, a leading center for Jewish theological studies flourished in Córdoba. Indeed, ʿAbd al-Raḥmān's physician, Hasdai ibn Shaprut (915-970), was Jewish, a member of the Ibn Ezra family educated at the University of Córdoba. A man of tact and goodwill, he became a diplomatic, financial, and commercial adviser for the caliph. He patronized learning and gave scholarships and books to deserving students. It is said that the stature of a leader can, at least in part, be determined by the quality of those who serve him; Hasdai, then, serves as a case in point.

Córdoba became one of the three great cultural centers of the medieval world, rivaling both Constantinople and Baghdad. Its glory, however, was not only cultural. The economic power of the caliphate centered in Córdoba as well. The city processed and marketed the products of the agricultural revolution of the tenth century. Great brass, glass, pottery, paper, and leather works were located there. The city housed at least thirteen thousand silk, wool, and cotton weavers. Through Córdoba and Seville (the premier port of the caliphate) flowed Spain's exports in marble, sugar, figs, cotton, olives, olive oil, wine, and saffron. Revenues from import-export duties alone financed the caliphate.

The awe and admiration inspired by this "jewel of the world" that was Córdoba was only a reflection of the stature of the caliph himself. Never again could Islamic Spain claim such a one as ʿAbd al-Raḥmān III al-Nāṣir.

—*Shirley F. Fredricks*

Further Reading

Chapman, Charles E. *A History of Spain*. 1918. Reprint. New York: Free Press, 1965. A classic survey of Spanish history, this work remains a standard reference because of its objectivity, detail, and organization.

Christopher, John B. *The Islamic Tradition*. 1972. Reprint. Lanham, Md.: University Press of America, 1987. This is one of the best short introductions to the history, the basic religious tenets, and the great medieval cultural synthesis of Islam, including that which occurred in Spain. Indeed, it is out of this rich medieval cultural heritage that Islam faces the modern world.

Coppée, Henry. *History of the Conquest of Spain by the Arab-Moors: With a Sketch of the Civilization Which They Achieved and Imparted to Europe*. 2 vols. Piscataway, N.J.: Georgia Press, 2002. This work, originally published in 1881, explores the conquest of Spain in 711 and the resulting Arab influences on European civilization.

Durant, Will. *The Age of Faith: A History of Medieval Civilization—Christian, Islamic, and Judaic—From Constantine to Dante, A.D. 325-1300*. New York: MJF Books, 1992. This is the fourth volume of the author's *Story of Civilization* series, a massive synthesis. Good bibliography, helpful explanatory notes, and index.

Hayes, John R., and George N. Atiyeh, eds. *The Genius of Arab Civilization: Source of Renaissance*. 3d ed. New York: New York University Press, 1992. A lively collection of essays, suitable for the general reader, discussing Arab intellectual and cultural accomplishments. Includes a bibliography and index.

Hillgarth, J. N. *Spain and the Mediterranean in the Later Middle Ages: Studies in Political and Intellectual History*. Burlington, Vt.: Ashgate Variorum, 2003. A survey of the political and intellectual history of Spain from 711 through the sixteenth century. Includes bibliography and index.

Hitti, Philip K. *Capital Cities of Arab Islam*. Minneapolis: University of Minnesota Press, 1973. Describes the uniqueness of six great capitals of Islam, including Córdoba.

_______. *History of the Arabs: From the Earliest Times to the Present*. 10th ed. New York: Palgrave, Macmillan, 2002. A complete and useful study of the rise of Islam in Spain and elsewhere.

Jackson, Gabriel. *The Making of Medieval Spain*. New York: Harcourt Brace Jovanovich, 1972. A most insightful and evenhanded examination of medieval Spain. It stresses the rich results of the long intermingling of the Islamic, Christian, and Jewish cultures. Packed with information, this short text is lucid and extremely well written. Includes many excellent illustrations and a short but enlightening bibliographic essay.

Watt, W. Montgomery, and Pierre Cachia. *A History of Islamic Spain*. Edinburgh: Edinburgh University Press, 1965. This well-informed study details the influence of Islam on the cultural development of Spain—and through Spain, all Europe. Special attention is focused on the Umayyads, of whom ʿAbd al-Raḥmān was the greatest.

SEE ALSO: Alfonso X; Averroës; Avicenna; Roger Bacon; al-Bīrūnī; El Cid; Dante; Fakhr al-Dīn al-Rāzī; al-Ghazzālī; Moses Maimonides; al-Rāzī; Ṭārik ibn-Ziyād; Thomas Aquinas.

RELATED ARTICLES in *Great Events from History: The Middle Ages, 477-1453*: April or May, 711: Ṭārik Crosses into Spain; c. 950: Court of Córdoba Flourishes in Spain; 1031: Caliphate of Córdoba Falls; November 1, 1092-June 15, 1094: El Cid Conquers Valencia; c. 1150: Moors Transmit Classical Philosophy and Medicine to Europe; 1230: Unification of Castile and León.

PETER ABELARD

French philosopher

Abelard developed the theory of conceptualism to reconcile Platonic idealism with nominalism. His use of the dialectic to explore Scripture helped shape Scholasticism, and many of his religious views, condemned as heretical in his own lifetime, subsequently influenced Church doctrine.

BORN: 1079; Le Pallet, Brittany (now in France)
DIED: April 21, 1142; the Priory of Saint-Marcel, near Chalon-sur-Saône, Burgundy (now in France)
ALSO KNOWN AS: Pierre Abailard; Petrus Abaelardus (Latin name)
AREAS OF ACHIEVEMENT: Philosophy, religion and theology

EARLY LIFE

Peter Abelard's father, Berengar, was lord of the village of Le Pallet and a knight in the service of the count of Brittany; because Abelard was the oldest son, his parents expected him to succeed to these titles. Nevertheless, they did not object when he showed more interest in intellectual than physical jousting. At fifteen, Abelard left his parents, his three brothers—Raoul, Porcaire, and Dagobert—and his sister, Denise, to study under Roscelin of Compiègne. By 1100, he had moved on to Paris, where he attended the lectures of William of Champeaux, head of the cathedral school and archdeacon of Notre Dame.

At the school, Abelard demonstrated the combination of brilliance and indiscretion that was to earn for him the title *Rhinoceros indomitus*—the unconquerable rhinoceros. William, an extreme Platonist, maintained that universal concepts such as "tree" exist independent of any specific examples. Thus, there is no substantial difference between one maple tree and another, or between an oak, a maple, or an elm. Moreover, the quality of "treeness" is independent of any individual example. In public debate, Abelard forced William, regarded as the leading dialectician of the age, to abandon this position and accept Abelard's own view of conceptualism. Without denying universal categories (which nominalists rejected), Abelard argued that one knows those universals only because of individual examples; if those specimens did not exist, neither would the universal.

LIFE'S WORK

Abelard's victory won for him the respect of his fellow students and the enmity of William; both factors prompted him to leave Notre Dame and set up his own school, first at Melun (1102) and then at Corbeil, within five miles of the French capital. The rivalry with Abelard may have influenced William's decision to leave Paris as well; outside the city he established a new monastery, dedicated to Saint Victor, where he continued teaching.

William's departure left a vacancy at the cathedral school, and after Abelard recovered from an illness that had caused him to return to Brittany, he was invited to assume the chair of his former master (c. 1108). As soon as William learned of the appointment, he hastened back to Notre Dame and forced Abelard to leave. Retreating first to Melun, Abelard soon was teaching at Sainte-Geneviève, at the very gates of Paris, drawing all but a handful of the students from the cathedral.

His teaching was interrupted again in 1111 when his parents decided to take holy orders, a common practice among the elderly in the twelfth century. Abelard had to go to Brittany to settle the family estate; then, perhaps at the urging of his mother, Lucia, he went to study theology under Anselm of Laon.

Just as William had been the most noted logician, so Anselm was the most famous religious teacher of the period, and just as Abelard had shown himself a better logician than William, so he would prove himself a better teacher of theology than Anselm. Finding the lectures at Laon dull, Abelard absented himself frequently. Students loyal to the old master challenged this lack of respect, and Abelard retorted that he himself could teach more effectively. Considering the little time that he had devoted to the subject, such a boast seemed absurd; his fellow students challenged him to make good his claim.

Abelard readily agreed, promising to lecture the next day on Ezekiel, one of the most abstruse books in the Bible. Even his opponents thought that matters had now gone too far and urged him to take time to prepare. Abelard refused; thus, when he rose to speak, he saw only a few people in the audience, all eagerly waiting for the upstart to make a fool of himself. Instead, his exegesis was so brilliant that within two days virtually all Anselm's students were attending Abelard's lectures and begging him to continue the series. Anselm thereupon forbade Abelard to teach anywhere in Laon.

By now, though, William's old post was vacant once more, and in 1112 or 1113 Abelard assumed it without opposition, inaugurating his tenure by concluding his explication of Ezekiel. Handsome, of medium height, with piercing brown eyes, he was, as even his enemies conceded, "sublime in eloquence." As *magister scholarum* of the leading school in France, if not of northern Europe, he was immensely popular. In part he owed this success to his unorthodox teaching methods. Rejecting the traditional *lectio*, in which the master read a text and then the commentaries on it, Abelard championed the *disputatio*, posing problems and resolving them through logic and careful textual analysis. Recalling those years, Héloïse wrote:

> Who among kings or philosophers could equal thee in fame? What kingdom or city or village did not burn to see thee? Who, I ask, did not hasten to gaze upon thee when thou appearedst in public, nor on thy departure with straining neck and fixed eye follow thee?

Among those impressed with Abelard's teaching was a canon of Notre Dame named Fulbert, the uncle and guardian of Héloïse. She had been educated at the convent of Argenteuil, and, by the age of fourteen, she could read Latin, Greek, and Hebrew. "La très sage Héloïs," as François Villon referred to her in 1461 in "Ballade des dames du temps jadis" ("Ballad of Dead Ladies"), may have already attended some of Abelard's lectures when in 1117 Fulbert invited Abelard to live with him on the Île de la Cité in the rue des Chantres. In return, the thirty-eight-year-old Abelard would tutor the seventeen-year-old Héloïse.

Tall, thin, with thick brown hair, gray eyes, fine features, a gracious manner, and intelligence, she might have tempted a saint left alone in her company: The sequel was not surprising. As Abelard recorded,

> More words of love than of our reading passed between us, and more kissing than teaching. My hands strayed oftener to her bosom than to the pages; love drew our eyes to look on each other more than reading kept them on our texts.

Peter Abelard and Héloïse. (Library of Congress)

Finally, even Fulbert realized his mistake and evicted Abelard, but Héloïse was already pregnant. To protect her from her uncle's anger Abelard took her to Brittany, where their son, Astrolabe (or Astrolabius), was born. To reconcile themselves to Fulbert, Abelard offered to marry Héloïse, under the condition that the marriage remain secret, and Fulbert agreed.

Héloïse strongly opposed this step, recognizing it as the worst possible solution. If the purpose of the marriage was to lessen Fulbert's shame, secrecy would not satisfy him. Any marriage would also remove Abelard's prospects for advancement in the Church, and even his reputation as a philosopher would be diminished. She argued,

> What harmony can there be between pupils and nursemaids, desks and cradles, books or tablets and distaffs, pen or stylus and spindles? Who can concentrate on thoughts of Scripture or philosophy and be able to endure babies crying, nurses soothing them with lullabies, and all the noisy coming and going of men and women about the house?

Moreover, she did not regard marriage as necessary to bind her to Abelard, to whom she was linked by a love stronger than any church vows.

Whether because of his desire to redeem Héloïse's honor, concern over Fulbert's possible vengeance, or fear that Héloïse might eventually marry another, Abelard rejected her sage advice, though to keep the marriage secret they lived apart. As Héloïse had predicted, Fulbert soon was boasting of his alliance with France's leading philosopher, and when Abelard and Héloïse denied having wed, Fulbert began to abuse his niece. Abelard thereupon removed her to the convent at Argenteuil, where she would be safe from Fulbert but close enough for him to visit.

Fulbert was now convinced that Abelard intended to force Héloïse to become a nun and thereby dissolve his marriage, leaving him free for ecclesiastical advancement. The enraged canon devised a revenge that would at once block such promotion and fittingly punish Abelard's lechery. Bribing Abelard's servant to leave the door unlocked, Fulbert, accompanied by some ruffians, burst into Abelard's bedroom one night and castrated him.

Paris rallied to Abelard's support. Fulbert was stripped of his canonry and expelled from the city. The two culprits who were apprehended—one of them Abelard's feckless servant—were blinded and castrated. Seeing his suffering as divine retribution, Abelard gave up his post at Notre Dame and retired to the monastery of Saint-Denis, where he became a monk (c. 1119). He also ordered Héloïse to assume the veil, though she had no religious vocation; indeed, he insisted that she take her vows first. Was this another sign that he feared she might marry another? If so, he little understood her deep love for him.

At Saint-Denis, Abelard lost little time in making new enemies by pointing out that the monks were not adhering to the Benedictine rule. Therefore, when Abelard asked permission to resume teaching, the abbot gladly allowed him to establish a school at the priory, removed from the monastery. Students again surrounded him, and for them, he prepared *Tractatus de unitate et trinitate divina* (a treatise on the trinity; c. 1120), a work he would expand and revise several times over the next sixteen years.

Although the monks of Saint-Denis were delighted with Abelard's absence, others were not pleased with his teaching. Among the disciples of Anselm who still resented Abelard's behavior at Laon were Alberic of Rheims and Lotulph of Novara. They maintained that a monk should not teach philosophy, that Abelard lacked the training to teach theology, and that his book, which sought to use logic to demonstrate the existence and nature of the Trinity, was heretical. They organized a council at Soissons in 1121 to try the book, and they secured Abelard's condemnation. Even the presiding papal legate regarded the decision as unjust and immediately allowed Abelard to return to Saint-Denis.

At the monastery, Abelard embroiled himself in further controversy by challenging the identity of the monks' supposed patron saint. So inflamed were passions against him that he fled to Provins. The friendly Count Theobald arranged for him to establish a hermitage near Troyes, and Abelard dedicated it to the Paraclete, or Holy Spirit. Again the orthodox objected; traditionally, hermitages were dedicated to the entire Trinity or to Christ, never to the Paraclete.

Students cared nothing about the name, though. Leaving the comforts of Paris they came in the thousands to till the fields and build accommodations in order to listen again to the words of Abelard, who rewarded them with stimulating lectures and treatises. *Sic et Non* (c. 1123; yes and no) responded to criticism that authority did not need the support of logic to establish faith. Abelard assembled some 160 seemingly contradictory statements by the Church fathers and argued that only through reason could one reconcile these. *Ethica* (c. 1138; *Ethics*, 1935) postulated that sin derives from intention, not action. Performing a good deed for evil purposes is not meritorious; committing wrong unknowingly is not sinful.

These heterodox views disturbed Saint Bernard of Clairvaux and Norbert, archbishop of Magdeburg. In his

MAJOR WORKS BY PETER ABELARD

Date	*Work*
c. 1120	*Logica ingredientibus*
c. 1120	*Tractatus de unitate et trinitate divina*
c. 1120	*Dialectica*
c. 1120	*Theologia "summi boni"*
c. 1123	*Sic et Non*
c. 1125	*Theologia Christiana*
c. 1132	*Historia calamitatum* (*The Story of My Misfortunes*)
c. 1135	*Theologia Scolarium*
c. 1138	*Ethica* (*Ethical Writings*)
c. 1141	*Apologia*
1141-1142	*Dialogus inter philosophum, Judaeum et Christianum* (*Dialogue of a Philosopher with a Jew and a Christian*)
1713	*Letters of Abelard and Heloise*

treatise on baptism (1125), Bernard rejected Abelard's view on sin, and Abelard was so uneasy about this opposition that around 1125 he accepted the post of abbot at the monastery of Saint-Gildas-de-Rhuys (in Brittany), a place so remote that even his devoted students did not follow him there.

The buildings at the Paraclete were abandoned but soon found another use. The abbot of Saint-Denis claimed the convent of Argenteuil and expelled the nuns. Around 1128, Abelard offered his former hermitage to a group under Héloïse, and they accepted. Soon the convent was so successful that other nunneries placed themselves under Héloïse's jurisdiction, and daughter institutions had to be established to house all the members.

Abelard did not fare as well in Brittany. As at Saint-Denis, his efforts to reform the dissolute monks met with hostility. Twice they tried to poison him; when he learned of a plot to cut his throat, he fled.

Hiding and in despair, Abelard composed *Historia calamitatum* (c. 1132; *The Story of My Misfortunes*, 1922). After a copy reached Héloïse, she promptly wrote to Abelard the first of a brief but poignant series of love letters that reveal how truly she meant her statement in 1118 that she would prefer to be Abelard's mistress than Caesar Augustus's wife.

Though her love had not abated, Abelard's had. "If . . . you have need of my instruction and writings in matters pertaining to God, write to me what you want, so that I may answer as God permits me," he replied to her impassioned lines, urging her to forget their former life together. Ever obedient, preferring Abelard's religious treatises to silence, she requested and received sermons, psalms, biblical exegeses, a rule more suitable for convents than that devised by Benedict for monasteries. As she had inspired Abelard to compose love poetry during their short time together, so now she served as a religious muse.

Abelard's movements in the early 1130's are unclear, but by 1136 he was again teaching in Paris. This return to prominence aroused his enemies, chief among them Saint Bernard of Clairvaux, who saw in Abelard's reliance on reason a challenge to faith. Whether Bernard's extensive letter-writing campaign against Abelard would have succeeded is unclear, but in 1140 Abelard's students challenged Bernard to debate their master at an assembly at Sens. Bernard at first refused, knowing that he was no match for the *Rhinoceros indomitus*. Bernard's supporters insisted that he attend, however, and he finally agreed.

Yet he had no intention of engaging Abelard in any intellectual combat. On the day before the scheduled encounter, Bernard persuaded the gathered religious leaders to condemn Abelard unheard; when Abelard entered the church of Saint-Étienne on June 3, 1140, Bernard began reading out a list of seventeen charges of heresy. Realizing that he was facing a trial, not a debate, Abelard immediately stopped the proceedings by appealing to Rome for judgment. He then left the Church, intending to plead his case before the pope.

Bernard's letters moved faster than the aging Abelard, however, and Pope Innocent II owed his tiara to Bernard. At the abbey of Cluny, Abelard learned that Rome had confirmed Bernard's verdict, and the local abbot, Peter the Venerable, now urged Abelard to make peace with his old antagonist. Although Abelard consented, the rhinoceros remained unconquered. In *Dialogus inter philosophum, Judaeum et Christianum* (1141-1142; *Dialogue of a Philosopher with a Jew and a Christian*, 1979), he still maintained that unless theologians could use reason, they could not defend their faith.

Abelard composed this treatise at the monastery of Saint-Marcel, near Chalon-sur-Saône, in Burgundy, where he had gone for his health, and there he died on April 21, 1142. He had asked to be buried at the Paraclete, and so he was. Twenty-two years later, Héloïse was laid to rest beside him. According to a chronicler, as her body was lowered into the grave, Abelard reached up to embrace his wife. Over the centuries their bodies were moved several times, but they now lie in the famous Père-Lachaise cemetery in Paris beneath the inscription, "Abelard: Héloïse—For Ever One."

SIGNIFICANCE

In his epitaph for Abelard, Peter the Venerable called his friend "the Socrates of the Gauls, the great Plato of the West, *our* Aristotle." Yet Abelard was neither a secular philosopher nor a religious skeptic. As he wrote in his *Apologia* (c. 1141), "I do not wish to be a philosopher by dissociating myself from Paul; I do not wish to be an Aristotle by separating myself from Christ, since there is no other name under heaven by which I can be saved."

While Bernard was wrong to view Abelard as a heretic, he was right to see Abelard as a threat to the old order. Abelard's popularity as a teacher helped create the university system, which spelled the end of the power of monastic schools. His fusion of logic and theology fostered a new scholasticism that was spread by his students, who included three future popes and the greatest classicist of the twelfth century, John of Salisbury. His manuscripts contributed to the era's intellectual renaissance.

Abelard is best remembered, however, for his association with Héloïse; over the centuries writers have found in their story an inspiration for poems, plays, and novels. A strange new twist to that famous story was introduced in the 1980's, when a computer-assisted stylistic analysis of the correspondence between Abelard and Héloïse suggested that all the letters, including those attributed to Héloïse, were in fact written by Abelard himself. Thus the possibility exists that Abelard was not only a philosopher but also, in a peculiar way, a gifted writer of fiction.

—*Joseph Rosenblum*

FURTHER READING

Abelard, Peter. *Abelard and Heloise: The Story of His Misfortunes and the Personal Letters*. Translated by Betty Radice. London: Folio Society, 1977. Abelard's account of his life and his and Héloïse's letters, which provide primary information about Abelard's life from his birth until around 1132.

Clanchy, M. T. *Abelard: A Medieval Life*. Malden, Mass.: Blackwell, 1999. A biography on Abelard focusing on theology in France during the Middle Ages.

Grane, Leif. *Peter Abelard: Philosophy and Christianity in the Middle Ages*. Translated by Frederick Crowley and Christine Crowley. New York: Harcourt, Brace and World, 1970. An excellent survey of Abelard's life set against the history, religion, and philosophy of the twelfth century. Chapter 5 neatly summarizes Abelard's views on metaphysics and religion.

Lloyd, Roger Bradshaigh. *The Stricken Lute: An Account of the Life of Peter Abelard*. London: L. Dickson, 1932. A biography that touches lightly on Abelard's philosophy and stresses his modernity.

Luscombe, David Edward. *The School of Abelard: The Influence of Abelard's Thought in the Early Scholastic Period*. Cambridge, England: Cambridge University Press, 1969. Draws on a variety of sources, especially Abelard's manuscripts and the writings of his pupils. Includes a twenty-eight-page bibliography of works by and about Abelard.

Marenbon, John. *The Philosophy of Peter Abelard*. New York: Cambridge University Press, 1997. Analyzes Abelard's philosophical work, with a focus on logic, theology, perception, knowledge, ethics and society, and more.

Sikes, Jeffrey Garrett. *Peter Abelard*. Cambridge, England: Cambridge University Press, 1932. A scholarly and still authoritative biography. Much attention is given to Abelard's views on religious and philosophical matters.

Worthington, Marjorie. *The Immortal Lovers: Heloise and Abelard*. Garden City, N.Y.: Doubleday, 1960. A popular biography of the two lovers. Contains extensive quotations from *The Story of My Misfortune* and the letters as well as novelistic re-creations of various episodes. Good on twelfth century background.

SEE ALSO: Saint Anselm; Saint Bernard of Clairvaux; Christine de Pizan; Joan of Arc; Lady Alice Kyteler; Raymond Lull; Thomas Aquinas; John Wyclif.

RELATED ARTICLES in *Great Events from History: The Middle Ages, 477-1453*: c. 1010-1015: Avicenna Writes His *Canon of Medicine*; c. 1025: Scholars at Chartres Revive Interest in the Classics; 1100-1300: European Universities Emerge; c. 1150: Moors Transmit Classical Philosophy and Medicine to Europe; November 11-30, 1215: Fourth Lateran Council; 1233: Papal Inquisition; 1305-1417: Avignon Papacy and the Great Schism; c. 1310-1350: William of Ockham Attacks Thomist Ideas; 1377-1378: Condemnation of John Wyclif; 1440: Donation of Constantine Is Exposed.

ABŪ ḤANĪFAH

Muslim theologian and legal scholar

Abū Ḥanīfah, celebrated eighth century Muslim jurist and theologian, was the founder of the first of four orthodox schools of Islamic law, the Hanifite. His brilliant use of reason and his gift for systematic thought provided Muslim civilization with a coherent and applicable system of law.

BORN: c. 699; Al-Kūfa (now in Iraq)
DIED: 767; Baghdad (now in Iraq)
ALSO KNOWN AS: Abū Ḥanīfah al-Nuʿman ibn Thābit (full name)
AREAS OF ACHIEVEMENT: Law, religion and theology

EARLY LIFE

Abū Ḥanīfah (ah-bew hahn-EE-fah) was born in the city of Al-Kūfa. Though some traditions assert that he was descended from Persian royalty, the more likely genealogy is Afghan. It seems that his grandfather, Zuta, was brought as a slave from Kabul, Afghanistan, to Al-Kūfa. Zuta came into the possession of the prominent Taym-Allāh ibn Thaʾlaba family. For unknown reasons, Zuta was set free. He and his descendants, however, remained clients (*mawla*) of the Thaʾlaba family. Though born into the non-Arab or client class of Muslims in Al-Kūfa, Abū Ḥanīfah was no stranger to wealth. His father, like the Prophet Muḥammad, was a successful merchant.

Abū Ḥanīfah followed in his father's footsteps and won fame as a silk trader and cloth manufacturer. Like Muḥammad, the merchant Abū Ḥanīfah won a reputation for his honesty and generosity. Abū Ḥanīfah endowed scholarships for needy students and shared liberally with the poor.

Economic prosperity enabled Abū Ḥanīfah to turn from business to scholarship. With a sharp wit, a facile tongue, and a logical mind, Abū Ḥanīfah was well fitted for the world of letters. For a while, he pursued the study of theology. His primary interest, nurtured while he was yet a merchant, was the problem of equity, establishing norms for a network of right or just relationships between human beings. As a devout Muslim, Abū Ḥanīfah believed that ethical and legal norms were given by God through divine revelation, the Qurʾān. On the basis of the Qurʾān and the Hadith (a compendium of Islamic traditions), theologians, philosophers, and jurists developed rules for just living. Abū Ḥanīfah thus turned his energies to the sacred law (Shariʿa). Living, as he did, in one of the great intellectual centers of the medieval Arab world, he was able to study with a number of noted jurists, including ʿAṭāʾ (d. c. 732) and Jaʿfar aṣ-Ṣādiq (699/700 or 702/703-765), the founder of Shīʿite law (the minority or dissenting tradition in Islam, as opposed to the Sunni, the majority persuasion). For eighteen years, Abū Ḥanīfah worked with one of the most brilliant of all Muslim jurists, Hammad ibn ʿAlī Sulayman.

Abū Ḥanīfah's students remembered their master as a tall, stately man of very impressive appearance. His demeanor was serious. Abū Ḥanīfah had the bearing of a scholar, and an air of piety permeated his every act. He was respected as a man of firm conviction, reasoned conclusions, uncompromising integrity, and determined opinions. Because Abū Ḥanīfah had independent means, he was not in need of royal, private, or religious patronage. His wealth gave him the freedom to exercise his native virtues of fearlessness, independence, and total disregard for the opinions and rewards of the world.

LIFE'S WORK

On the death of his mentor, Hammad, in 738, Abū Ḥanīfah emerged as the leading legal thinker in Al-Kūfa and in much of the Muslim world. Because of his personal wealth, he was able to devote himself entirely to teaching and research. Under no necessity to accept either private donations or governmental appointment, Abū Ḥanīfah had complete academic freedom. This financial security and his love of independence may explain, in part, why one of Islam's most eminent jurists never sat on the bench as a *kadi* (judge). Like the Greek philosopher Plato, who established his own Academy, Abū Ḥanīfah attracted his own students. Relatively free of governmental pressures and of the burdens of a practicing attorney, Abū Ḥanīfah could concentrate on the theoretical foundations of Muslim law.

In his teaching, Abū Ḥanīfah relied heavily on dialectic, lectures, and discussions with his disciples. Like Socrates, he is said to have written little (indeed, nothing survives from his pen). His teachings, however, were copiously recorded by his students, among whom were his son Hammad and his grandson Ismāʿil (both of whom eventually became distinguished jurists); another disciple included the eminent thinker Abū Yūsuf. Abū Ḥanīfah's principal achievement as a teacher was twofold: He was the founder of the systematic study of Islamic law, and he was also the founder of a particular school of jurisprudence, one named in his honor—the Hanifite school.

As a jurist, Abū Ḥanīfah employed a variety of

sources. He was able to draw on his own rich experience as a merchant, a man of practical affairs. Reflected in his thought are his extensive travels in the Muslim world. As one familiar with the many levels of a complex and sophisticated society, Abū Ḥanīfah could discuss conditions of places as varied as the royal court, the slave market, and the business bazaar. In his formal legal work, Abū Ḥanīfah, as an orthodox Muslim, accepted two primary sources for Islamic law: the divine revelation, written in the Holy Qurʾān and given by God through the Prophet Muḥammad, and the human tradition, reported in the Hadith, the sayings passed down by the Muslim community from the time of Muḥammad. The relationship of Qurʾān and Hadith was similar to that of Torah and Talmud in Judaism, for God spoke in the Qurʾān to human conscience and in the Hadith to human intelligence. Abū Ḥanīfah, however, recognized the need for interpretation of these given authorities; for that reason, he was inclined to accept other authorities. Perhaps these were in a very real sense "secondary" to the primary sources, but since Muslim survival required interpretation and adaptation, the supplementary means became crucial in his thinking. Abū Ḥanīfah allowed personal interpretation on the part of the jurist. As the one closest to the case, the judge had to trust his own intelligence and instincts, experience and evaluation. Believing all truths to be ultimately related (a corollary of the belief that God is one), Abū Ḥanīfah also permitted argument by analogy and reasoning from the known to the unknown (by means of comparison and contrast). As a legal thinker, Abū Ḥanīfah also permitted the notion of consensus, the consideration of the majority opinion of the Muslim world. Some dispute later arose regarding how Abū Ḥanīfah intended such a consensus to be determined: Was it the majority opinion of the jurists, the educated classes, or the masses of Islam? Apparently, Abū Ḥanīfah was envisioning an implicit agreement among the intellectual elite of Islam, both past and present.

The major problem that Abū Ḥanīfah faced as a jurist was the growing complexity and confusion of Islamic law in his generation. For a century and a half, Islamic law had developed unsystematically, without clear direction or a discernment of underlying fundamental principles. Individual lawyers and judges had argued on the basis of specific situations and particular cases; the result was that conflicting verdicts were being offered in various parts of the Muslim world. Amid this cacophony of variant opinions, it was often impossible to arrive at either fundamental principles or clear lines of direction for the law in the future. Abū Ḥanīfah's great contribution—one that was revolutionary in its implications—was to approach the law not situationally but systematically. Many jurists had looked at particulars; Abū Ḥanīfah determined to find principles. Sifting through the vast legal writings of his time, Abū Ḥanīfah sought universal norms and standards that would be applicable regardless of time or place. By reviewing the problems that had previously been faced by Muslim jurists, Abū Ḥanīfah also tried to anticipate which cases might arise next and to speculate as to the proper approach to be followed.

In his work as a legal theoretician, Abū Ḥanīfah evolved several main principles. First, the law was to be studied systematically rather than situationally, rationally rather than empirically, abstractly rather than concretely. The purpose of such a study was to locate, beneath the welter of contradictory decisions and traditions, the unifying principles of Islamic justice. Second, at all times, Abū Ḥanīfah looked for the way of moderation or the via media between extreme positions; like the legal sage of ancient China, Confucius, Abū Ḥanīfah held to the philosophy of the Golden Mean.

Third, Abū Ḥanīfah permitted the use of natural law, the findings of reason based on the physical and social sciences; this approach, as ancient as the Greek philosopher Aristotle, allowed material not covered in the Qurʾān or the Hadith to be employed in court. God, Abū Ḥanīfah believed, was the author of two books: nature, as the Creator, and the Qurʾān, as the Revealer. Fourth, Abū Ḥanīfah put a balanced emphasis on various tests of truth. One was coherence, or internal logic, another was consistency with other known truths, and a final was consequence, or the implications of an action or decision.

Finally, as a rationalist, Abū Ḥanīfah trusted the role and rule of reason in all matters not resolved by the Qurʾān or the Hadith. In this respect, he was similar to the emperor Justinian I, the systematizer of Roman law, and to Aristotle, the father of Greek philosophy and science. For Abū Ḥanīfah, the law was not simply a matter of external relationships between persons but also an issue of internal integrity (within the mind of the judge).

The work of Abū Ḥanīfah within his lifetime was recognized as superior to that of his contemporaries in four respects. First, he made the law wider than had been the case in existing codes; it became not only more broadly based but also more universally applicable. Second, Abū Ḥanīfah made the law deeper, firmly grounding it in the judge's reason and experience and the Muslim intellectual community's interpretation of Scripture, tradition, and nature. Third, Abū Ḥanīfah made the law higher: No longer accidental and incidental, it had become intensely cerebral, theoretical, refined, and technical. Finally, the law had become narrower, for it now rested on universal moral principles, applied through a rigorous process of reasoning.

Because of his brilliant intellect, Abū Ḥanīfah also influenced the development of Muslim theology. As a philosophical theologian, Abū Ḥanīfah inclined toward a movement in his time that was named Murjiʾism. This tendency emphasized the universal community of Islam, upholding the unity of the fellowship (*umma*) against divisive or sectarian movements. It focused on the confessional character of Islam as opposed to moralistic definitions; Islam was envisioned as the public confession of certain cardinal doctrines (God, revelation, prophecy) rather than a society composed of ethically perfect persons. Moreover, the community was seen as inclusive: If a person professes the true faith, actions and even moral failures cannot sever a person from the Muslim nation. In these respects, Abū Ḥanīfah was an advocate of Muslim ecumenism and inclusivism.

Apparently, Abū Ḥanīfah tried to avoid political involvement. His century was a time of dynastic upheaval in the Muslim world. There was a growing difference of opinion as to whether the Muslim community should be led by a direct descendant of the Prophet Muḥammad (the opinion of the Shīʿites, or partisans of ʿAli, Muḥammad's son-in-law) or by a caliph, a successor chosen from among the majority party (the Sunnis) in Islam. Two rival caliphates came into existence, the Umayyads (after 750 exiled to Spain) and the ʿAbbāsids (established in Baghdad). It seems likely that Abū Ḥanīfah had contempt for both the Umayyads and the ʿAbbāsids. In spite of his attempted neutrality, he was arrested and imprisoned. The circumstances surrounding his death are not clear. One account insists that the ʿAbbāsid caliph al-Manṣūr (or possibly the Umayyad governor of Al-Kūfa) asked Abū Ḥanīfah to accept appointment as a judge; on his refusal, the jurist was flogged and imprisoned. Another version contends that Abū Ḥanīfah's family sympathized with the followers of ʿAlī (a tradition states that "ʿAlī blessed his father and his descendants"). In any case, it is known that Abū Ḥanīfah died in Baghdad in 767, either while still in prison or shortly after his release. His tomb, surmounted by a lovely dome erected by admirers in 1066, is still a shrine for pilgrims.

Significance

Islamic law, along with that of the Romans and the Anglo-Saxons, is one of the great systems of human jurisprudence. The Hanifite school founded by Abū Ḥanīfah was the earliest, and became the most widespread, of the four schools of orthodox (Sunni) Islamic law. An appealing system of justice, it has been influential in India, Pakistan, Turkey, China, Central Asia, and much of the Arab world. With a concern for equity as the chief goal of law, it has given judges latitude to exercise private opinion (*raʾy*) and to draw on natural law. Regarded as the most liberal or tolerant of the Islamic legal systems, it stands in opposition to the position of the Hanbalite school (the more fundamentalist persuasion, represented by the Wahhabis of Saudi Arabia, who accept only the Qurʾān and the Hadith as sources of Muslim law). It is also a more moderate system than the other two schools of Islamic law—the Malikite (prevailing in parts of North Africa) and the Shafite (influential in Egypt, Indonesia, and sections of Africa). As the pathfinder of Muslim law, Abū Ḥanīfah ranks as one of the great jurists of Arab civilization and one of the major legal philosophers of the entire human community.

—*C. George Fry*

Further Reading

Boer, T. J. de. *The History of Philosophy in Islam*. Translated by Edward R. Jones. 1903. Reprint. Richmond, Surrey, England: Curzon Press, 1994. This is a standard though older survey that is still useful for placing Abū Ḥanīfah in context. Bibliography, index.

Coulson, Noel J. *A History of Islamic Law*. Edinburgh: Edinburgh University Press, 1964. A helpful survey of Muslim legal thinking, part of Islamic studies series. Includes a bibliography.

Edge, Ian, ed. *Islamic Law and Legal Theory*. New York: New York University Press, 1996. Presents a chapter on Abū Ḥanīfah, a "champion of liberalism and tolerance in Islam." Also includes a chapter with sources on Islamic legal theory published in English. Bibliography, index.

Fyzee, Asaf A. A. *Outlines of Muḥammadan Law*. 4th ed. New York: Oxford University Press, 1999. In spite of the obsolete word "Muḥammadan" in its title, this volume is useful as a comprehensive study of Islamic jurisprudence. Bibliography, index.

Schacht, Joseph. *An Introduction to Islamic Law*. 1964. Reprint. New York: Clarendon Press, 1982. This volume provides a critical analysis of Islamic legal concepts and precepts. Because of its approach, some Muslims have found it offensive. Extensive bibliography, index.

_______. *The Origins of Muḥammadan Jurisprudence*. 1950. Reprint. Oxford, England: Clarendon Press,

1975. This is a thoughtful study by a Western scholar who has edited and translated numerous works on Islamic law. Includes a bibliography.

Watt, W. Montgomery. *Islamic Philosophy and Theology: An Extended Survey.* 2d ed. Edinburgh: Edinburgh University Press, 1995. A brilliant study by one of the most celebrated of Occidental authorities, this work places Abū Ḥanīfah within the mainstream of Muslim thought. Bibliography, index.

_______. *Islamic Political Thought: The Basic Concepts.* 1968. Reprint. Edinburgh: Edinburgh University Press, 1998. In this book, the noted British scholar introduces the fundamental principles of Muslim political thought in terms understandable to Western readers. Bibliography, index.

Wensinck, Arent Jan. *The Muslim Creed: Its Genesis and Historical Development.* Cambridge, England: Cambridge University Press, 1932. Though an older work, this text is still a useful survey of the evolution of the complex of Muslim theology-philosophy-law.

Williams, John Alden, ed. *Islam.* New York: George Braziller, 1961. This readily accessible anthology is helpful for the beginning student of Muslim thought and life. Includes a bibliography.

See also: Pietro d'Abano; Aḥmad ibn Ḥanbal; Avicenna; Ibn Gabirol; al-Ghazzālī; Justinian I; al-Ṭabarī.

Related articles in *Great Events from History: The Middle Ages, 477-1453*: 529-534: Justinian's Code Is Compiled; 637-657: Islam Expands Throughout the Middle East; 780: Beginning of the Harem System; c. 950-1100: Rise of Madrasas; 11th century: Expansion of Sunni Islam in North Africa and Iberia.

Abul Wefa

Persian mathematician and astronomer

Abul Wefa played a major role in mathematics by developing sines and cosines as they apply to the field of trigonometry and used them to correct astronomical calculations carried forward from classical into Islamic times.

Born: June 10, 940; Buzjan, Khorāsān (now in Iran)
Died: July 15, 998; Baghdad (now in Iraq)
Also known as: Abūʿ-Wafā; Muḥammad ibn Muḥammad ibn Yaḥyā ibn Ismāʿīl ibn al-ʿAbbās Abū ʿal-Wafāʾ al-Būzajānī (full name)
Areas of achievement: Mathematics, astronomy, science and technology

Early Life

Born in 940, during the reign of the ʿAbbāsid caliph al-Mutaqqī, Abul Wefa (ah-BEWL weh-FAH) lived during a period of extraordinary cultural and intellectual productivity. His own fields of accomplishment, mathematics and astronomy, were already widely recognized as essential elements of high Islamic civilization. Very little seems to be known about Abul Wefa's early life. Apparently, his early education in mathematics occurred under the tutelage of two uncles, one of whom (Abū ʿAmr al-Mughazili) had received formal training from the famous geometrician Abū Yahya al-Marwazī.

Whatever the possible source of patronage for the young man's further education may have been, his decision to move to Baghdad at the age of nineteen (in 959) greatly benefited the ʿAbbāsid court. Baghdad at this time was troubled politically, following the seizure of de facto control by a military clique headed by the Persian Buyid emirs; thereafter, the Buyids dominated the house of the caliphs until their fall from power in 1055. The Buyids were inclined to favor talented Persians who were drawn toward scholarly circles in the center of the empire. It is reported, for example, that it was Abul Wefa, himself then forty years of age and well established (c. 980), who introduced the Persian scholar and philosopher Abū Ḥayyān al-Tawḥīdī into the Baghdad entourage of the vizier Ibn Saʿdān. Abū Ḥayyān soon became famous under the vizier's patronage, composing a major work, *Al-Imtaʾ waʾl muʾanasa* (a collection of notes drawn from philosophical and literary salon meetings), under a dedication to Ibn Saʿdān.

Patronage for Abul Wefa's work in courtly circles, however, must have come from a different milieu, that of the so-called Baghdad School. This scientific assembly flourished in the ʿAbbāsid capital in the last century before its conquest by the Seljuk Turks in 1055. According to some historians, patronage for the natural sciences in particular came precisely during the period in which Abul Wefa passed into the main stages of his scholarly career. The Buyid emir ʿAdūd al-Dawlah (r. 978-983) had nurtured an interest in astronomy through his own studies. He passed this interest on to his son, Saraf al-Dawlah, who built an observatory next to his palace and called scholars from all regions of the empire to glorify the reputation of his reign by carrying out scientific experiments. Abul Wefa was among this group.

Life's Work

The environment for learning in the Baghdad School, with its circle of eminent Islamic scientists, may explain how the young Persian scholar mastered so many technical fields in such a limited period of time. Beyond mere speculation regarding Abul Wefa's early personal contacts, however, one must consider the importance of translation work in the Baghdad School. Abul Wefa himself translated the work of the Greek algebraist Diophantus (fl. c. 250), who had explored the field of indeterminate algebraic equations. Abul Wefa was also known for his studies of, and commentaries on, Euclid. There are, however, no surviving texts to indicate what use he made of the work of these two forerunners from the classical pre-Islamic period.

By contrast, Abul Wefa's attention to the work of the second century Greek astronomer Ptolemy not only contributed to the preservation and transmission to the medieval West of the classical knowledge contained in Ptolemy's *Mathēmatikē suntaxis* (c. 150; *Almagest*, 1952) but also earned for him an original and lasting reputation as an Islamic mathematician. The *Almagest* examined the field of trigonometry, which proposed mathematical relationships in terms of the angles and sides of right triangles. This called for the development of sines, or systematic relationships defined in a right triangle working from one of the acute angles, symbolically represented as *A*. Modern trigonometry expresses this relationship as $\sin A = a/c$, or $\sin A$ is equal to the ratio of the length of the side opposite that angle (a) to the length of the hypotenuse (c).

Ptolemy, in pioneering the field of spherical trigonometry, had laid down an approximate method for calculating sines (which he described as chords). Abul Wefa, however, drew on his studies of Indian precedents in the field of trigonometry that were unknown to Ptolemy, as well as models provided by Abul Wefa's predecessor al-Battānī (858-929), to perfect Ptolemy's chords. This was done by applying algebraic, instead of geometric, methods of systematizing the sines. In particular, Abul Wefa's development of the half-chord made it possible to achieve much more precise measurements that would eventually be used in surveying and navigation. The most immediate application of his tables of sines, however, was in the field of astronomy.

One of Abul Wefa's contributions that left a legacy that lasted for many centuries involved the study of evection, or irregularity, in the longitude of the Moon. Later European commentators, including Louis Pierre E. A. Sédillot in the nineteenth century, looked at the Islamic astronomer's work and concluded that he, not Tycho Brahe (1546-1601), had been the first scientist to posit the theory of the "third inequality of the moon." Although this theory was later proved to be erroneous, the debate at least drew attention to the importance of Abul Wefa's originality in the field.

Abul Wefa himself compiled, in addition to his well-known tables of sines, a book of astronomical tables entitled *Zij al-wadih* (that which is clear). Like his earlier work on sines, this text is not extant in the original. Scholars tend to agree, however, that certain anonymous manuscripts preserved in European libraries, such as the *Zij al-shamil*, are taken from Abul Wefa's work.

Works that have survived and that have been at least partially translated include a book of arithmetic entitled Kitāb *fi ma yahtaj ilayh al-kuttab wa l-ʾummal min ʿilm al-hisab* (961-976; book on what is necessary from the science of arithmetic for scribes and businessmen), the *Kitāb fi ma yahtaj ilayh al-sani ʿmin al-aʾmal al-handasiyha* (after 990; book on what is necessary from geometric construction for the artisan), and a book entitled *Kitāb al-kamil* (translated by Carra de Vaux in the *Journal Asiatique* of 1892). It is thought that Abul Wefa may have still been in Baghdad at the time of his death in 998.

Significance

Study of the Islamic cultural milieu in which Abul Wefa lived suggests a high level of syncretic interaction between ethnic subjects of the Baghdad caliphate—Arab, Persian, Greek, and other minorities. Abul Wefa's own career seems also to provide an example of a syncretic social hierarchy. Scientists and intellectual figures, it seems, had no reason to doubt that their accomplishments would be appreciated and supported by a ruling military elite whose social status was obviously determined by very different criteria. In this rather cosmopolitan period in Islamic history, there was room not only for scholars of diverse national origins at the caliph's court but also for representatives of different disciplines, secular and religious, to live side by side in a community that was truly representative of a world civilization. One can only understand the flourishing in Islam of such different disciplines (and the pure sciences in particular), however, if attention is given to the multiplicity of pre-Islamic sources that contributed both to the Baghdad caliphate itself and to the highly developed cultural institutions that it supported.

—*Byron D. Cannon*

FURTHER READING

Bell, Eric T. *The Development of Mathematics*. New York: McGraw-Hill, 1945. Begins with a historical review of the field of mathematics from the first-known texts through successive stages of discoveries, ending at midpoint in the twentieth century. The chapter of most interest to students of Islamic science is entitled "Detour Through India, Arabia, and Spain, 400-1300." This title underscores the importance of the medieval period of Oriental history for the conservation of classical Western sources that only returned to Europe via the Islamic core zone, from eastern Iran to Spain.

Cajori, Florian. *A History of Mathematics*. 1931. 5th ed. Providence, R.I.: AMS Chelsea, 2000. This classic work has several important characteristics that still merit mention. It covers not only standard non-Western mathematical traditions (Hindu and Islamic) but also traditions from little-studied areas such as Mayan Central America and Japan. Includes detailed information on individual mathematicians' original findings.

Hogendijk, Jan P., and Abdelhamid I. Sabra, eds. *The Enterprise of Science in Islam: New Perspectives*. Cambridge, Mass.: MIT Press, 2003. A collection of essays surveying the history of Islamic science, including mathematics and astronomy. Illustrations, bibliography, index.

Huff, Toby E. *The Rise of Early Modern Science: Islam, China, and the West*. 2d ed. New York: Cambridge University Press, 2003. Provides a strong cross-cultural background for the rise of science in the Muslim world. Illustrations, bibliography, index.

Kennedy, Edward S. *Astronomy and Astrology in the Medieval Islamic World*. Brookfield, Vt.: Ashgate, 1998. Discusses astronomy, astronomers, math, and mathematicians, including Abul Wefa's calculation of the distance between Baghdad and Mecca. Index.

_______, ed. *Studies in the Islamic Exact Sciences*. Beirut: American University of Beirut Press, 1983. Provides a rather technical treatment of several scientific disciplines that flourished in early Islamic times, including the development, through trigonometry, of accurate astronomical calculations. A specific elaboration of Abul Wefa's work is included.

Nasr, Seyyed Hossein. *Islamic Science: An Illustrated Survey*. London: World of Islam Festival, 1976. A carefully researched photographic record of the tools of Islamic science. Textual treatment of historical figures such as Abul Wefa is more limited than in Nasr's text below. The choice of illustrations, however, particularly from Islamic astronomy, is so rich that the field itself becomes a much more coherent entity.

_______. *Science and Civilization in Islam*. Cambridge, Mass.: Harvard University Press, 1968. Because this work deals with the subject of science in Islamic civilization only, it can take time to explore individual contributions at some length.

SEE ALSO: Pietro d'Abano; Alhazen; Roger Bacon; al-Battānī; Jean Buridan; al-Khwārizmī; Omar Khayyám.

RELATED ARTICLES in *Great Events from History: The Middle Ages, 477-1453*: 595-665: Invention of Decimals and Negative Numbers; 7th-8th centuries: Maya Build Astronomical Observatory at Palenque; 1040-1055: Expansion of the Seljuk Turks; c. 1100: Arabic Numerals Are Introduced into Europe.

ADAM DE LA HALLE
French composer and writer

One of the few medieval musicians who composed both monophonic and polyphonic music, Adam de la Halle produced musical and literary works in virtually every genre of the thirteenth century.

BORN: c. 1250; probably Arras, France
DIED: c. 1285-1288; Naples (now in Italy) or possibly England
ALSO KNOWN AS: Adam the Hunchback; Adam le Bossu; Adam le Boscu d'Arras; Adam d'Arras
AREAS OF ACHIEVEMENT: Music, literature

EARLY LIFE

With almost no documentary evidence—except a few bits of information here and there in his works—any account of the life of Adam de la Halle (ah-dahm duh lah ahl) must be based on educated guesses. More than likely, he was born in the prosperous town of Arras; his name appears variously as Adam d'Arras and Adam le Boscu d'Arras. His name appears most commonly as Adam le Bossu (meaning "Adam the Hunchback"), although in *Le Roi de Secile* (written after 1285), Adam protests that while he might be called a hunchback, he is not one at all. No records reveal the origin of the name; his family may have adopted it to distinguish itself from the other Halle families in Arras. Possibly an illustrious ancestor was a hunchback, and the family retained the appellation.

In another of Adam's works, *Le Jeu de la feuillée* (pr. c. 1275; *The Greenwood Play*, 1971), Adam de la Halle's father is named as a Maistre Henri de la Hale. In *Nécrologe de la Confrérie des jongleurs et de bourgeois d'Arras*, the death of Henri de la Hale's wife was recorded as 1282; the death of a Maistre Henri Bochu was recorded as eight years later, in 1290. Whether these are the composer's parents is unknown. *Nécrologe* also contains references to two women, either of whom could have been Adam's wife: Maroie li Hallee is mentioned in 1274; Maroie Hale in 1287. Given the possibilities for variation in an age when spelling had not been standardized, it would be difficult to choose between these two. Some scholars refer to *Jeu d'Adam* as evidence supporting Maroie Hale; in this work, Adam refers to his wife as still living.

LIFE'S WORK

About the rest of Adam's life, most of the clues exist in his work or in commentary about his work. There is circumstantial evidence that he studied in Paris: In *Jeu d'Adam*, he expresses his longing for his student days in Paris; furthermore, his contemporaries often described him as "maistre," indicating that he completed a more rigorous course of study than he might have received in a provincial town. Adam probably returned from Paris sometime around 1270, a date suggested by two facts: He wrote sixteen *jeux-partis* with Jehan Bretel of Arras, who died in 1272, and Bretel referred to him in the contemporaneous *Adan, a moi respondés* as well educated, suggesting that the younger trouvère (narrative poet) had already undertaken a major part of his training. The *jeux-partis* on which he collaborated with other trouvères of Arras—he also wrote one with Jehan de Grivilier—indicate that Adam was a member of the Arras *pui*, a fraternity or professional group of "actors" or trouvères. The trouvère was a court poet whose work celebrated the authority and responsibilities of the aristocratic lord whom he served and was a composer and performer who responded to the tastes and needs of an elite audience from a closely circumscribed world. As for Adam's marriage, it more than likely took place in the early 1270's. In several poems, Adam speaks of having given up school and friends in order to marry his young wife, to whom he was deeply devoted.

Of Adam's fifty-four monophonic (for one voice only) works, eighteen are *jeux-partis*, on the majority of which he collaborated with other trouvères. The form of the *jeu-parti* involves a "questioner" who sings the first musical phrase (and therefore composes the melody) and a "respondent." Adam is the respondent in thirteen of the sixteen *jeux-partis* on which he worked with Jehan Bretel, indicating that the melodies were composed by the older man. This early collaboration was to be an important influence on Adam's musical style. Scholars have noted the strong stylistic similarities between the melody of *Adan, a moi respondés* and the melody composed by Adam for two of his chansons (a cabaret or music-hall song), and between other *jeux-partis* and Adam's chanson *De cuer pensieu*. Adam's work shares tonality and range and phrasing with Bretel's, but Adam's melodies are more formal and sophisticated. Adam's other monophonic works, the chansons, for the most part remain close to the older courtly tradition of French monophonic song.

Adam de la Halle remained in Arras for only a few years after his return from Paris, and again the evidence is suggestive rather than conclusive. His *Jeu d'Adam* and his *Le Congé*, written at about the same time (c. 1276-1277), are both farewells in which Adam declares his intention to return to Paris to continue his studies. There is some evidence that he intended to leave his adored wife in his father's care, indicating that the absence was not to be a long one; in fact, two later lyrical pieces describe his return and the joy he feels at coming back to his own land.

Jeu d'Adam is a peculiar combination of topical humor and sheer fantasy, written to amuse Adam's friends just before his departure for Paris. Lacking a fully realized plot, the rambunctious play (*jeu* means "game") involves a meeting between certain townsfolk of Arras and a group of fairies on the eve of Pentecost when, traditionally, the shrine of Notre Dame is displayed beneath a *feuillée*, or canopy of green leaves. Much of the play is devoted to humorous allusions to real persons: gluttons, alcoholics, scolding wives, submissive husbands, a loose woman and her lovers, unethical government clerks (called "bigames") who married more than one woman for financial gain. Even Adam's own family comes in for its share of the burlesque. His father is described as a fat, stingy bigamist who loves alcohol more than anything else. Adam even pretends to be bored with his wife, thus gaining an excuse to detail her charms, which no longer excite him. Buried not too deeply in the songs and games of the play is Adam's occasionally bitter criticism of the class warfare that was destroying the social fabric of Arras.

Structurally the play consists of spoken dialogue, exchanges of songs, dances, games, jokes, and horseplay. Probably written only for the amusement of a select group of friends and acquaintances, the play may have had only one complete performance in Arras.

At some point after his second return to Arras, Adam de la Halle left his native town once more and traveled to Italy, where he entered the service of Robert II, count of Artois, who was on a diplomatic mission for his uncle, Charles of Anjou, who was to become King Charles II of Naples. Later, Adam joined the entourage of Charles, whom he served during the wars against the Sicilians until Charles died in 1285. During his service either with Robert or with Charles, Adam wrote *Le Jeu de Robin et de Marion* (pr. c. 1283; *The Play of Robin and Marion*, 1928), apparently as a part of the Christmas entertainment for the amusement of expatriate northern French soldiers who were resting between battles.

In its most basic form, the plot of *The Play of Robin et de Marion* describes how the shepherd, Marion, repulses the amorous advances of a roving knight in favor of her rustic country lover, Robin. The story of a rustic maid desired by both a courtly lover and a country swain appears in dozens of pastoral lyrics popular in Adam's day. What Adam did was to dramatize a conventional story by retaining its framework (names, specific incidents, popular songs connected with the story), adding a fully realized background, and amplifying or manipulating key elements of the narrative, particularly the *bergerie*, a lyric piece describing songs, dances, and games indulged in by shepherds and their loves. The result is a highly entertaining theatrical piece.

Adam's original audience would have recognized the major characters from the courtly pastorals, but would also have been delighted with the realistic details incorporated into the traditional story. The knight takes his rebuff lightly instead of being discomfited; Robin is an amusingly awkward peasant whose affection for Marion is genuine; Marion is a simple lass who is nevertheless resourceful in her handling of the knight's advances. The games incorporated into the action are real games, popular at the time and still played today in some parts of France. Also, the dialogue is natural, even coarse at times.

In addition to his inclusion of naturalistic elements in the familiar plot, Adam added a number of popular songs, dances, and instrumental melodies. Although some of the dances would have been accompanied by singing alone, others were probably performed to the music of bagpipes, horns, and flutes. The sixteen melodies are short and rhythmic, and probably belong to a group of popular courtly melodies called refrains.

Among Adam's polyphonic works, the rondeaux have excited the most commentary for their characteristics that point ahead to the secularization of polyphonic music in the fourteenth century. Two of these rondeaux are typical of the thirteenth century understanding of the rondeau form, which at that point in the development of music encompassed virtually all songs with periodically recurring refrains; hence, these two are not true rondeaux in the sense that later masters would have recognized. One is a virelay (a medieval French song form featuring a refrain before and after each stanza); the other, a ballade (a medieval narrative poem, either sung or recited, containing three stanzas and an envoi).

Five motets have been conclusively identified as Adam's work; six others are said to be his on the basis of characteristics shared with the genuine motets. Adam's motets are basically conservative, and many include refrains quoted from his other works. The motets whose provenance is uncertain are written in a later style.

What Adam did after Charles's death is open to conjecture, although it is reasonably safe to assume that he never returned to Arras. There are only two pieces of evidence about his movements in later years, and those two are contradictory. The earlier piece is a posthumous tribute to Adam de la Halle, written in 1288 by his nephew, known variously as Jean Madot or Jehanes Mados (who may or may not be the Mados mentioned in *Jeu d'Adam*), who says that Adam left Arras to seek entertainment and company and points out that this action was foolish, since Adam was popular at home. The date of this tribute indicates that Adam died in or before 1288. The confusion comes from an English source from 1306 in which a certain "maistre Adam le Boscu" is listed among the European minstrels who have been engaged to participate in the coronation ceremonies for Edward II in 1307. "Boscu" is an unusual name, especially in conjunction with an Adam who has earned the appellation "maistre." Clearly the possibility exists that Adam did not die in Naples, although the trouvère who was invited to England could be a younger member of the same family, even Adam's son.

Significance

Adam de la Halle's works survive in more than two dozen manuscripts, one of which is an almost complete edition of his works classified by genre. Coming as he did between traditions, Adam wrote in a variety of genres that reflected the old (the courtly lyric, the *chanson de geste*, the "songs of deeds") and the new (the decidedly bourgeois *Jeu d'Adam* and *Le Jeu de Robin et de Marion*). His position in the thirteenth century is problematic for music historians for several reasons. First, he was a master of the monophonic chanson and motet, both of which belonged even then to a dying tradition. Second, he composed a body of work that combined traditional texts with innovative settings, lyric poetry with the polyphony that was becoming a force to be reckoned with in music. Finally, his dramatic creations were so far ahead of his time that nothing like them was written until decades later. In fact, it is Adam's theatrical works that are his most distinctive contribution: The prose drama *Jeu d'Adam* is regarded by many to be the earliest comedy in French; the musical play *Le Jeu de Robin et de Marion* is commonly considered a precursor to comic opera with its combination of sung and spoken parts.

—E. D. Huntley

Further Reading

Butterfield, Ardis. *Poetry and Music in Medieval France: From Jean Renart to Guillaume de Machaut*. New York: Cambridge University Press, 2002. A discussion of medieval music and poetry that covers Adam de la Halle and his *Le Jeu de Robin et de Marion*. Bibliography and indexes.

Caldwell, John. *Medieval Music*. Bloomington: Indiana University Press, 1978. A discussion of Western music from about 950 to 1400, with considerable attention paid to notation, which is the key to medieval musical style. The text is well illustrated with relevant examples and has an excellent bibliography and listing of manuscript sources and their locations.

Cook, William R., and Ronald B. Herzman. *The Medieval World View: An Introduction*. 2d ed. New York: Oxford University Press, 2004. An examination of the Middle Ages.

Dane, Joseph A. *Res/Verba: A Study in Medieval French Drama*. Leiden: E. J. Brill, 1986. Examines Adam de la Halle's *Le Jeu de Robin et de Marion* as well as a play by Jean Bodel.

Frank, Grace. *The Medieval French Drama*. Oxford, England: Clarendon Press, 1960. A comprehensive study of both liturgical and secular plays from the medieval period. An entire chapter is devoted to the plays of Adam and their theatrical and social milieu. Includes a comprehensive bibliography.

Nichols, Stephen J., Jr. "The Medieval Lyric and Its Public." In *Medievalia et Humanistica*, edited by Paul Maurice Clogan. Cleveland, Ohio: Press of Case Western Reserve University, 1972. A careful analysis of the nature of the audience who patronized the medieval poet-musicians.

Wilhelm, James. *Seven Troubadours: The Creators of Modern Verse*. University Park: Pennsylvania State University Press, 1970. Presents seven distinct lyric voices—some of them contemporaries of Adam—of the twelfth and thirteenth centuries whose work shows the Christian-secular heritage of the High Middle Ages. Although Adam is not one of the featured seven, the book is valuable for the light it sheds on his artistic and philosophical milieu.

See also: John Dunstable; Hrosvitha; Francesco Landini; Johannes de Muris; Pérotin; Philippe de Vitry; Zeami Motokiyo.

Related article in *Great Events from History: The Middle Ages, 477-1453*: c. 1100: Rise of Courtly Love.

Adrian IV
English pope (1154-1159)

Adrian IV served as Vatican diplomat to Scandinavia and later established policies and direction that led the medieval Papacy to its thirteenth century zenith of power.

Born: c. 1110; near St. Albans, Hertfordshire, England
Died: September 1, 1159; Anagni, Papal States (now in Italy)
Also known as: Nicholas Breakspear or Brekespere (given name); Hadrian IV
Areas of achievement: Church government, diplomacy, monasticism, religion and theology

Early Life

Few details are available on the early years of Nicholas Breakspear. His father, Robert, was a younger son of a landed family with no hope of receiving an inheritance. A man of meager resources, Robert married and had two sons. Discouraged by his struggles to live, and with the consent of his wife, he entered the monastery of St. Albans to become a monk. Although this practice was by no means common, there were a number of such examples in the medieval church. Robert hoped that his son Nicholas might join him in the cloister as a student and a future cleric.

At his first request for admission to the abbey, Nicholas was refused. The abbot suggested that he be patient, continue his studies, and make himself a worthy candidate. The reasons for the early rejection are unclear, but Robert berated his son for his failure, and they became estranged. Breakspear left England shortly afterward to search for a more congenial atmosphere in France. He achieved considerable success in his studies at Paris, wandered for a period after their completion in the area of Montpellier, studied at Arles, and finally entered the Monastery of St. Rufus near Avignon, an order of canons regular.

Described by contemporaries as an elegant person, of pleasing face, greatly skilled in speech, highly disciplined, and popular with his fellows, Nicholas quickly rose within the monastery. About the year 1137, he was unanimously elected abbot. What occurred to reduce his popularity is unknown, but sharp disagreements between the monks and their superior led to virtual rebellion of the community. Although there were suggestions that the monks regretted having elevated a foreigner to the abbacy, it may be that Breakspear's devotion to discipline eroded the relationship. Charges were brought by the monks against Nicholas, and Pope Eugenius III intervened twice in the dispute.

In 1146, Breakspear went to Rome for discussions with the pope. He never returned to the monastery, but remained in Rome, either because the pope considered resolution of the monastic quarrel hopeless or because he found in Breakspear a man who might serve a different purpose. Eugenius elevated Breakspear to the bishopric of Albano, and in due course he was named cardinal. At that point in his life, he began to earn the reputation that led him to the papal office.

Life's Work

Between 1152 and 1154, Breakspear represented the pope as a diplomat or reformer in reorganizing the Church in Scandinavia. The history of this northern region in the eleventh and twelfth centuries was extremely complex. The kingdoms of Denmark, Norway, and Sweden were taking shape politically, but in terms of ecclesiastical organization, they were subject to the German archbishop of Hamburg-Bremen. At the opening of the twelfth century, the Papacy answered many petitions and transferred power of decision making in the Scandinavian area to the Danish archbishopric of Lund. Norway and Sweden, however, continued to demand their own archbishops and autonomy in church affairs. Breakspear's mission was to quiet the growing unrest, resolve increasing political difficulties, and reorganize and reform the Church.

Breakspear successfully resolved many questions and preserved the peace of the area, calling for meetings with powerful men, negotiating, reconciling, and offering his services for arbitration. The Norwegians regarded him as a hero who had quieted an era of unrest. At his return to Rome in 1154, he was honored for his work in the north and became a figure of much admiring attention.

Breakspear and his sixteen fellow cardinals were called to meet within a few months of his return in order to elect a new pope at the death of Pope Anastasius IV. Breakspear's reputation undoubtedly led to his unanimous election to the chair of Peter on December 4, 1154. Taking the name Adrian IV, he soon discovered that the position of vicar of Christ on Earth, a title he is credited with originating or popularizing, was a difficult and lonely one. Yet for the years of his pontificate, he was tireless, firm, and determined to maintain the papal prerogative in European affairs as he understood it.

Pope Adrian IV. (Library of Congress)

This was not an easy task, for at the middle of the twelfth century many changes were taking place in the society of Western Europe. A spirit of lay involvement, new dialectics in the schools in the wake of Peter Abelard's teaching, and the growth of feudal monarchy in England, France, and the Germanies seemed to threaten the traditional papal role.

The city of Rome, discontented with the temporal claims of the Papacy and incited by the radical reformer Arnold of Brescia, became openly hostile and menacing toward the new pope. Arnold, one of Abelard's students at Paris, had a long history of activism against the temporal claims of the Papacy. His oratorical powers and impassioned appeals for a return to the greatness of the Roman republic aroused the city to action. Expelled from Rome in 1155, Arnold was captured by the German emperor, who returned him to Rome for trial. Tried and convicted, Arnold was executed the same year but left a legacy of violence that created continuing difficulties for Adrian.

The pope's relationship with other political powers was no less troublesome. Frederick I Barbarossa, the ambitious German monarch, wanted control of the rich cities of northern Italy and the title Holy Roman Emperor, a title historically granted by the Papacy. Yet he wished to avoid the appearance of holding a fief from papal hands. His journey to Italy often had the aspect of an invasion and his relations with Adrian were marked by argument, misunderstanding, maneuvering, and finally uneasy compromise. The iron-willed Adrian, unwilling to surrender the important elements of papal tradition to the German emperor, was challenged by others at the same time.

The Norman state to the south posed threats to the security of the southern boundaries of the papal states as the Germans did to the northern boundaries. William, ruler of the Norman kingdom, which included the southern provinces of Italy and the island of Sicily, had succeeded to an inheritance that contained a strong party of rebellious nobles. This insurgent faction approached Adrian, asking for help against William and papal protection of their persons and property. Hoping that the rebels might become a bulwark against William's threatened encroachment on papal claims, Adrian gathered troops and marched to the south.

At this time, an embassy from Manuel I Comnenus, the Byzantine emperor at Constantinople, sought audience with Pope Adrian. The emperor offered troops and money if Adrian would grant three coastal cities in Norman Italy to him. The Byzantine government considered the Normans usurpers of land and formidable enemies. The possibility of reuniting the Western and Eastern churches, separated in the eleventh century, was offered as an additional incentive.

William, recognizing the threat of combined papal and Byzantine troops, now made overtures to Adrian, conceding on several contested issues and offering to subdue the discordant elements in Rome. Adrian was willing to negotiate but deferred to his cardinals, who believed that further concessions might be wrung from the embattled king. Against his better judgment, Adrian rejected William's offer.

William attacked the Eastern emperor's forces, now on Italian soil and, with courage born of his desperate circumstances, defeated the foreign armies. The rebellious party of Normans seemed to disappear at the remarkable victory, and Adrian found himself at a disadvantage in dealing with the Norman power. Sending most of his cardinals away, only three of the most trusted remaining, Adrian awaited the arrival of William. His diplomatic experience helped the pope salvage a bad situation. The Papacy emerged somewhat restricted in its rights in Sicily, but thanks to Adrian's skill, its power was essentially undiminished. Adrian confirmed William in his possessions. He did not forget the nobles who had asked his help against William, and their freedom and property were protected in the settlement.

Throughout the brief pontificate, all the major protagonists continued to trouble the Papacy. Adrian was vigilant, constantly moving from one part of Italy to another, finding time to solve local problems and build and repair churches. Other powers had to be watched with care. Henry II of England asked the pope's approval to conquer Ireland. It has been suggested that Adrian approved, in the papal bull *Laudabiliter.* Great controversy has grown up about this episode. There has been a lengthy debate as to the bull's authenticity and, if authentic, to its purpose. At minimum, the bull did reveal the latitude of interest and the energy to meet all challenges that made this brief pontificate noteworthy. Suddenly falling ill at Anagni, Adrian IV died on September 1, 1159.

When the old St. Peter's was demolished in 1607, Adrian's sarcophagus was opened. An archaeologist reported that the pope was small in stature and adorned in a dark silk chasuble. The tomb was closed and placed in the new St. Peter's.

SIGNIFICANCE

Adrian IV was an important representative of the Papacy in a momentous era. Not a man of theory but one of action, his efforts were directed toward concretizing the theoretical claims of the Papacy developed from the days of the Gregorian reform movement. The constant turmoil of his pontificate obscures Adrian's moral stature and its effects on his many relationships with contemporary powers. Personally blameless of many of the faults of his Curia, he showed no avarice or meanness of spirit. Despite his early history, he bore no ill will toward the monasteries of St. Albans or St. Rufus but received their abbots in friendship and granted them several requests. Spiritually oriented, he believed deeply in the church that he represented. His contemporaries, even his greatest enemies, respected him.

Adrian's policies played an important part in leading his successors to the culmination of power in the reign of Innocent III. Innocent III clearly recognized the importance of the only Englishman to wear the papal tiara. In many ways, Adrian IV was an able feudal monarch.

—Anne R. Vizzier

FURTHER READING

Bolton, Brenda, and Anne J. Duggans, eds. *Adrian IV, the English Pope, 1154-1159: Studies and Texts.* Burlington, Vt.: Ashgate, 2002. A collection of sources and documents related to Adrian's role as pope. Includes a bibliography and an index.

Boso. *Life of Alexander III.* Translated by G. M. Ellis. Totowa, N.J.: Rowman and Littlefield, 1973. Accessible translation of an original source that contains significant material on Adrian IV and his biographers.

Mann, Horace K. "Hadrian IV." In *The Lives of the Popes in the Early Middle Ages.* Vol. 9. Wilmington, N.C.: Consortium Books, 1979. Complete coverage in English. Though dated and uncritical of sources, a useful work.

Munz, Peter. *Frederick Barbarossa: A Study in Medieval Politics.* Ithaca, N.Y.: Cornell University Press, 1969. Excellent discussion of the struggle between pope and emperor.

Southern, Robert W. "Pope Adrian IV." In *Medieval Humanism.* New York: Harper and Row, 1970. First-rate interpretation of Adrian and his career set against the background of the period.

Ullmann, Walter. "The Pontificate of Adrian IV." *Cambridge Historical Journal* 11 (1955): 234-251. An excellent discussion that possibly exaggerates the importance of symbolism and ceremony.

SEE ALSO: Peter Abelard; Frederick I Barbarossa; Henry II; Innocent III.

RELATED ARTICLES in *Great Events from History: The Middle Ages, 477-1453*: 1152: Frederick Barbarossa Is Elected King of Germany; 1169-1172: Normans Invade Ireland; 1305-1417: Avignon Papacy and the Great Schism.

ÆTHELFLÆD

Queen of Mercia (r. 899-918)

Æthelflæd continued to rule Mercia and direct its armies after her husband King Ethelred's death in 911, successfully beating back Danish incursions into Anglo-Saxon territories.

BORN: c. 870; Wessex, England
DIED: June 12, 918; Tamworth, England
ALSO KNOWN AS: Ælfled; Ethelfleda
AREAS OF ACHIEVEMENT: Government and politics, warfare and conquest

EARLY LIFE

Æthelflæd (EH-thuhl-flehd) was the firstborn child of West Saxon king Alfred the Great and Ealhswith, a noblewoman of the royal family of Mercia. Although the year of Æthelflæd's birth is not certain, Asser's life of Alfred says that she married Ethelred of Mercia around 890 "as the time for matrimony approached," that is, before age twenty, placing the birth of the princess in the early 870's.

While much of Æthelflæd's success must be due to her natural gifts, some credit should go to her early education. Most women of her class in the tenth century would have received a classical education only by pursuing a religious education as a cloistered nun. Æthelflæd, however, was educated in her father's court alongside her brother Edward (d. 924), who would succeed his father Alfred as King Edward the Elder (r. 899-924). The sibling tie, together with their common education, made Æthelflæd and Edward a powerful political team, and the political effectiveness of Edward's reign largely depended on Æthelflæd's own power and influence.

The close confederacy between Wessex and Mercia was of crucial strategic importance at the beginning of the tenth century. Mercia's eastern half was under Danish control and from eastern Mercia the Danes could assault Alfred's kingdom of Wessex. Two factors cemented Wessex and Mercia at the end of Alfred's reign. First, the ruler of Mercia, Ethelred, declined the title of king, claiming only those of ealdorman (earl) and Myrcna hlaford (lord of the Mercians). Second, Alfred strengthened the fealty of Ethelred by giving him Æthelflæd in marriage.

One indication of the central role played by such political marriages as Æthelflæd's in Anglo-Saxon society is that one of the West Saxon words for "wife" was *frithuwebbe* (peace weaver). A chieftain could settle a feud with a rival nation or form a political union by marrying his daughter to a rival or confederate. In Æthelflæd, however, Lord Ethelred would find more than a typical peace weaver, which she would be in uniting Ethelred's Mercia and Alfred's Wessex. She would do more than any other political leader of her century to strengthen the defense of Mercia and win back the lands it had lost from the Danes.

Nothing is mentioned of Æthelflæd in the first decade of her marriage, aside from the birth of her daughter Ælfwynn in 898, but with the death of her father in 899 and the accession of her brother Edward, her name appears in connection with Edward's struggle to keep the throne. Æthelflæd's cousin Æthelwold contested Edward's claim to kingship in Wessex and enlisted the Northumbrian Danes to aid his cause. Edward counted on his sister's help to repel the Danes and not his brother-in-law Ethelred. The Mercian Register makes no mention of Ethelred in its accounts of Mercian military assistance to Edward, but as the tenth century began, Æthelflæd was increasingly mentioned as coordinating the Danish campaigns with her brother. An Irish chronicle known as *The Three Fragments* implies that Ethelred was too infirm after 902 to direct the campaigns, but Æthelflæd, half her husband's age and educated in her father's court, had both the strength and the military acumen to do so. One group of Irish and Danish immigrants under the Viking warrior Ingimund was given written permission to settle in Wirral in 902: The document is signed by Æthelflæd, not her husband, suggesting that she was then the de facto head of state.

Æthelflæd's kindness to Ingimund was repaid by treachery: In 905, Ingimund attacked the Mercian town of Chester. Æthelflæd's response would set the pattern for her activity in the disputed Mercian territories over the next decade. She turned Chester from a *tun* (town) to a *burh* (fortified city) by building walls and battlements around it in 907.

LIFE'S WORK

Æthelflæd's military accomplishments were primarily defensive, but she did not hesitate to direct offensive strikes early in her struggle with the Danes. In 909, she joined her brother Edward in a successful raid into East Anglia, where the pagan Danes held the body of the seventh century English king and martyr Saint Oswald, much revered by the Christian English. Returning in triumph, Æthelflæd presented the saint's remains to Saint Oswald's Priory in Gloucester.

A year later, on the feast of Saint Oswald (August 5, 910), Edward led a daring surprise attack against the biggest Danish stronghold in York, defeating the Danes in the Battle of Tettenhall. The Battle of Tettenhall was proof of the success of Edward's and Æthelflæd's strategy in the border country. Danish advances in the ninth century had been gained by lightning raids followed by retreats to Danish strongholds. The highly mobile Danish army could not sustain the prolonged siege warfare that English garrisons along the border would provide. When she saw the role that English fortifications played in the victory at Tettenhall, Æthelflæd built another *burh* at Bremesburh in 910. Each new fort made the Danish raid-and-retreat strategy more difficult.

When Ethelred died in 911, Mercia set a new precedent in English government. Rather than declaring a new lord of Mercia, the *witangemot*, or parliamentary body charged with determining royal succession, hailed Æthelflæd as Myrcna hlæfdige (lady of the Mercians). This was the feminine counterpart of the title claimed by her husband: that is, the highest-ranking official of Mercia, yet acknowledging fealty to the West Saxon king (at that point her brother Edward). It was as lady of the Mercians that Æthelflæd scored her greatest achievements, both military and political.

A first glance at Æthelflæd's earliest fortifications on the map of central England might suggest a preparation more for retreating from the Danes than for standing up to them. Her first *burhs* were at Chester and Bremesburh (on what is now the Welsh border)—both far from the Danes. Æthelflæd's strategy in strengthening these frontiers first, however, makes perfect sense. Away from Danish eyes, Mercia could perfect the techniques of fortification and move the construction projects closer to the Danish strongholds gradually. By the time the Danes saw what was happening, Mercian garrisons were too strong for the Danish blitzkrieg tactics to work.

Æthelflæd's next two fortifications, in 912, were also on the Welsh border country, along the Severn River. The first, Bridgenorth, was aptly named. The narrowest and shallowest point of the Severn for miles around, it was literally the "bridge north," the point at which the Danes liked to cross into Wales on the relatively few occasions they ventured that far. Æthelflæd's second fort was at Scergeat, whose location is unknown in modern times, though it was probably upriver north and west from Bridgenorth. At the same time Edward moved east to the already fortified town of Hertford, where a second fort was built. Thus, by the end of 912, Æthelflæd had an impenetrable line, a fall-back position in case Danish belligerence increased before the more eastern and northern borders could be secured.

Danish aggression came the following spring (913) when Danish forces at Leicester looked west to find two new English forts, one at Tamworth and another at Stafford. Thus cut off, they marched south to the English village of Banbury, joining forces with the Danes of Northampton for a coordinated attack on the hapless English town. This would be one of the last of the successful destroy-and-retreat raids of the Danes. Æthelflæd moved in immediately, fortifying the largest town south of Danish Northampton, Buckingham, in 914. At Buckingham, Æthelflæd upped the ante, building not one but two forts, one on each side of the River Ouse. The show of force worked: The Danish armies of Northampton and Bedford submitted to Æthelflæd's army at Buckingham, allowing King Edward to establish a fort at Bedford in 915, directly across the Ouse from the former Danish camp.

Æthelflæd's string of forts now formed a nearly straight southeast line from Chester to Hertford, with only two significant gaps: the midlands between Tamworth and Buckingham and the mouth of the Mersey River, just out of reach of Æthelflæd's first fort at Ches-

ANGLO-SAXON KINGS OF ENGLAND, 802-1016

Reign	*Ruler*
802-839	EGBERT
839-856	Æthelwulf
856-860	Æthelbald
860-866	Æthelbert
866-871	Ethelred (Æthelred) I
871-899	ALFRED THE GREAT
899-924	EDWARD THE ELDER (with sister ÆTHELFLÆD)
924-939	Æthelstan
939-946	Edmund the Magnificent
946-955	Eadred
955-959	Eadwig (Edwy) All-Fair
959-975	Edgar the Peaceable
975-978	Edward the Martyr
978-1016	ETHELRED (ÆTHELRED) II, THE UNREADY
1016	Edmund II Ironside
1016	Ascendancy of Canute the Great (Danish line begins)

ter. Æthelflæd closed the Mersey gap with two *burhs*, Eddisbury (914) and Runcorn (915), and fortified the midpoint between Tamworth and Buckingham at Warwick. Developments on the Danish side helped shift the momentum toward both the Mercian and the West Saxon English. A Danish Viking named Ragnald, who had seized power after the Battle of Tettenhall, solidified his power in the lands that remained to him, defeating the Scots in the First Battle of Corbridge in 914. It was largely his army against which Æthelflæd fortified Mercia. However, in defeating Scots and Irish in the north, Ragnald turned possible allies against him and sent them over to the English.

Æthelflæd took full advantage of this development, and in 917, she signed a treaty with two Scottish kings, both named Constantine, ensuring their alliance against the Danish York. The Danes, unwilling to face Æthelflæd's forces, attempted a Second Battle of Corbridge, defeating the Scots again but cutting their forces in half in the effort. This weakening of the Danish forces allowed Æthelflæd to take offensive action. In July of 917, while Edward was fighting the Danes in the east (Towcester, Bedford, Wigingamere, and Tempsford), Æthelflæd's troops marched into the major Danish center of Derby (in north-central England) and took it handily. The following year, which would be the last year of Æthelflæd's life, marked the final, crushing defeat of the Danes by the tandem of Edward and Æthelflæd.

The 918 campaign began in mid-May with Edward building a *burh* in Stamford, causing the Danes there to submit to him without a fight. To the west, Æthelflæd marched into Leicester, where the Danes surrendered, again without bloodshed. The only remaining Danish enclaves, at Nottingham and Lincoln, would fall to the West Saxons by the end of summer, but Æthelflæd would not live to see it. Falling back to Tamworth after her victory at Leicester, she died on June 12, 918. She was buried in Saint Oswald's Priory in Gloucester, where a decade earlier she had celebrated her victory over the East Anglian Danes.

SIGNIFICANCE

If part of Æthelflæd's legacy is demonstrating a woman's military and political leadership, then that legacy lived on in Mercia for a few months after her death. Again faced with choosing a leader for the former kingdom, the Mercian *witangemot* that had named Æthelflæd lady of Mercia bestowed the same title on her twenty-year-old daughter Ælfwynn. By the spring of 919, however, Ælfwynn's uncle, King Edward, had called her to his court and officially annexed Mercia. No one would claim either title, lord or lady of Mercia, again.

—*John R. Holmes*

FURTHER READING

Hadley, D. M. *The Northern Danelaw: Its Social Structure*. London: Leicester University Press, 2000. A useful resource on Æthelflæd's central England from the point of view of the English Danes.

Nelson, Janet L. "Anglo-Saxon England." In *The Oxford Illustrated History of Medieval England*, edited by Nigel Saul. New York: Oxford University Press, 1997. Offers complete background not only to Æthelflæd's reign but also to the development of West Saxon power that preceded and followed her.

Stafford, Pauline. "The King's Wife in Wessex, 800-1066." In *New Readings on Women in Old English Literature*, edited by Helen Damico and Alexandra Hennesey Olsen. Bloomington: Indiana University Press, 1990. Gives a thorough picture of the nature of queenship in Æthelflæd's time.

Wainwright, F. T. "Æthelflæd, Lady of the Mercians." In *The Anglo-Saxons*, edited by Peter Clemoes. London: Bowes and Bowes, 1959. A complete source of information on Æthelflæd. Includes a map of fortifications.

SEE ALSO: Alfred the Great; Edward the Elder.

RELATED ARTICLES in *Great Events from History: The Middle Ages, 477-1453*: 850-950: Viking Era; 878: Alfred Defeats the Danes.

Afonso I

King of Portugal (r. 1139-1185)

Through astute leadership in military victories over Muslims and Christian Iberian neighbors, Afonso created the independent monarchy of Portugal and became its first king.

Born: c. 1108; Guimarães, Portugal
Died: December 6, 1185; Coimbra, Portugal
Also known as: Afonso Henriques; Afonso the Conqueror
Areas of achievement: Government and politics, military, warfare and conquest

Early Life

In 1087, many French knights were invited by Christians of the Iberian Peninsula to help in the fight against the Muslim Almoravids. These Moroccan warriors had invaded the divided Islamic areas of Spain, and through military victories were uniting the Muslims and threatening the Christian kingdoms. One of the French nobles was Henry of Burgundy, who ingratiated himself with the emperor of León, Alfonso VI, and married his illegitimate daughter, Princess Teresa. The county of Portugal was conferred on Henry by his father-in-law. He was charged with the defense of the western frontier from the Muslims. Henry established his court at Guimarães, in northern present-day Portugal. It was close to Braga, which had been restored as a bishopric in 1070. One of Henry's successes was helping to achieve papal recognition of Braga's elevation to a metropolitanate.

Sometime around 1108, Teresa gave birth to a son, Afonso. The prince was reared at the court, where he was surrounded by Portuguese barons who had been appointed by Henry to be his chief officers. Henry's policy was to reward native aristocrats with estates, thus winning their loyalty and identifying his rule with the Portuguese.

Henry died in 1112, leaving Afonso, not yet five years of age, as his heir. Teresa became the regent of Portugal and used the title of queen. It was argued that this term was appropriate, as she was the daughter of an emperor. Teresa's rule was characterized by complicated intrigues. She took a lover, Fernando Peres, a Galician noble, and they produced a daughter. Teresa and Peres attempted to expand the Portuguese domain to the north, cutting into Galicia. Alfonso VII of León, Teresa's half brother, invaded Portugal in 1127, and she was forced to surrender the territory she had acquired in southern Galicia.

Young Afonso was maturing in a society that was in constant preparation for warfare. Theoretically, the enemies were the Muslims to the south, but in actuality, fellow Christians to the north in Galicia and to the east in León and Castile were a constant threat to the physical integrity of the county.

The Portuguese barons blamed Teresa and her Galician paramour for a decline in their fortunes. They began to range themselves behind someone they considered one of them: Afonso. On July 24, 1128, on the field of São Mamede, near Guimarães, the army of Teresa and Fernando faced Afonso's barons. The young count was victorious, capturing his mother and her lover and expelling them. Afonso, Portuguese born and bred, became the ruler of the county.

Life's Work

Afonso was in his early twenties when he gained control of Portugal. No contemporary likeness of him exists, but the chronicles describe him as a man of gigantic stature with a flowing beard and enormous strength. It is also clear that he had a calculating and shrewd mind. From the beginning, he seems to have aspired to the creation of an independent Portuguese kingdom.

In the first decade of his reign (1128-1138), he was involved with various skirmishes with his Christian neighbors, and he was compelled to make token political submission to the authority of Castile. On the ecclesiastical front, Afonso was more successful in this earlier period. A resourceful and diplomatic Cluniac priest, John Peculiar, became his disciple and ally. Afonso had him installed in the episcopal office in Oporto and then saw him elevated to the archbishopric of Braga. After long and complicated intrigues, the bishop and the count achieved the jurisdictional independence of the Portuguese church from Santiago de Compostela and Toledo.

In the political arena, a new Muslim invasion of southern Iberia offered Afonso an opportunity to extend his authority southward. According to the royal chronicles, Afonso and his Portuguese army encountered the Almohad forces at a place known as Ourique. On the night before the battle, a vision of Jesus Christ inspired Afonso, so that on the next day, July 25, 1139, the Feast of Saint James, the outnumbered Portuguese were able to route the Islamic forces. The results of this encounter were impressive. Christian strongholds were established south of Coimbra, and the important Muslim city of Santarém was forced to pay tribute.

THE PORTUGUESE MONARCHY, 1139-1640

Reign	*Ruler*
1139-1185	AFONSO I
1185-1211	Sancho I
1211-1223	Afonso II
1223-1245	Sancho II
1245-1279	Afonso III
1279-1325	Diniz (Denis)
1325-1357	Afonso IV
1357-1367	Peter I
1367-1383	Ferdinand I
1385-1433	John I of Avis
1420's-1460	Golden age of Portuguese exploration: Prince Henry "the Navigator" underwrites naval expeditions
1433-1438	Edward I
1438-1481	Afonso V
1481-1495	John II
1495-1521	Emanuel I
1521-1557	John III
1557-1578	Sebastian I
1578-1580	Cardinal Henry
1580-1598	Philip I of Portugal (Philip II of Spain)
1598-1621	Philip II of Portugal (Philip III of Spain)
1621-1640	Philip III of Portugal (Philip IV of Spain)
1640	Revolt of Portugal

Afonso's success at Ourique may have convinced him to declare the fullness of his dominion in Portugal, which he considered to be the area north of the Tagus River. Documents of the time reveal that after 1139, instead of referring to himself as simply *infans* or *princeps*, as he had in the past, he adopted the title of *Portugalensium rex*; this was a virtual declaration of independence. By placing his kingdom under papal protection and pledging loyalty to the Holy See, he took another significant step to strengthen and secure his independence. Proclaiming himself a knight of Blessed Peter and of the Roman Empire, he promised to pay an annual tribute of four ounces of gold in return for papal protection. A formal document setting forth these terms was published on December 13, 1143. Earlier that year, Alfonso VII met Afonso at Zamora and, evidently accepting the fait accompli, recognized him as king of Portugal. In the spring of 1144, Pope Lucius II wrote to Afonso graciously accepting the proffered tribute and extending protection, but the letter was addressed simply to the *Portugalensium dux*. Not until 1179, when the independence of Portugal was firmly established, did Pope Alexander II address Afonso as king.

The mid-twelfth century was the era of the early Crusades, and Afonso actually used the Crusaders who often put into Portuguese ports on their way to Palestine. In 1140, with the help of a fleet staffed by many Englishmen, he forced Muslim Lisbon to pay him tribute. By 1147, he was ready to denounce his truce with the Moors, and in that year he captured Santarém on the Tagus.

In May of the same year, a fleet of 164 ships and almost 13,000 men, with contingents from Germany, Flanders, Normandy, and England, set sail from Dartmouth, England. They arrived at Oporto, where they were greeted by the bishop, who invited them to aid the king in an attack on Lisbon. The bishop declared that this was a just war, worthy of their talents: "Act like good soldiers, for the sin is not in fighting war, but in fighting for the sake of booty." When the fleet reached Lisbon on June 28, Afonso outlined his proposals, and an alliance was concluded. He guaranteed to the Crusaders the plunder of Lisbon and the ransom of captives; those who wished to settle there would be given lands and would be assured the protection of their native customs and liberties. The king also exempted them and their descendants from the payment of tolls in any part of his realm. He promised to continue the siege until surrender unless he was forced to desist because of mortal illness or an attack on his kingdom from some other quarter.

The archbishop of Braga was sent to persuade the Muslims to surrender. He charged that they had "held our cities and lands already for 358 years," and he urged them to "return to the homeland of the Moors." When this drew a negative response, the siege commenced in earnest. Catapults and towers were constructed, and the city was blockaded on all sides. The defenders appealed in vain to their fellow Muslims for relief, but at least one of their messengers was captured by the Christians, who realized their enemies' plight. When the Muslims became aware that their chances of victory were steadily lessening, they eventually asked for a truce to negotiate the terms of surrender. After a siege of seventeen weeks, the Christians made their triumphal entrance into Lisbon on October 24, 1147. Although the Muslims were permitted to leave freely, the city was sacked and many were killed.

The conquest of Lisbon, which has been described by one Anglo-Norman priest, rivals the capture of Toledo (1085) and Saragossa (1118) in importance.

Afonso set to work to repopulate the newly conquered lands. Crusaders who were willing to settle received land grants near the Tagus. The Templars were given castles for the defense of the valley, and the Cistercians established monasteries to foster agricultural development. Throughout Afonso's long reign, raiding and counter-raiding persisted. He carried his frontiers beyond the Tagus Valley, annexing Beja in 1162 and Évora in 1165. Afonso's battling days came to an end when he was wounded in a skirmish with Christians at Badajoz. His leg was fractured, and he was no longer able to ride. Captured by his opponents, he was held for two months while his vassals raised ransom funds. As part of the agreement to gain his freedom, he renounced any claim to Galicia.

Afonso had renewed his connection with the House of Burgundy by marrying Mafalda, the daughter of a count of Savoy. He associated his son, Sancho I, with his power, knighting him at Coimbra in 1170. When Afonso died in 1185, his son inherited a stable and independent monarchy and his father's plans for driving the Moors out of the lands south of the Tagus.

SIGNIFICANCE

It could be argued that were it not for Afonso I the Iberian Peninsula would be politically united today. Through his military, ecclesiastical, and political victories, he underscored the distinctiveness of the westernmost regions of Iberia. Through his successful negotiations with the Papacy and his military prowess, he achieved the recognition of Portugal as an independent kingdom, the fifth into which the Christian-dominated part of the peninsula was divided. The other kingdoms were Castile, León, Aragon, and Navarre.

In modern republican Portugal, 1139 is accepted as the birth date of the State of Portugal, and Afonso I is considered the father of his nation. Similar sentiments were expressed by contemporaries of Afonso. The *Chronica Gothorum* expressed the era's view:

> He received the Kingdom and the Lord, through him, extended the frontiers of the Christians and expanded the bounds of the faithful people from the River Mondago, that flows by the walls of Coimbra, to the River Guadalquivir, that flows by the City of Seville, and from the Great Sea to the Mediterranean Sea.

—*Charles J. Fleener*

FURTHER READING

Dos Passos, John. *The Portugal Story: Three Centuries of Exploration and Discovery.* Garden City, N.Y.: Doubleday, 1969. The author, a fluent and engaging stylist, focuses on the emergence of the Portuguese empire, summarizing Afonso's achievements and recounting the siege of Lisbon.

Kennedy, Hugh. *Muslim Spain and Portugal: A Political History of al-Andalus.* New York: Longman, 1996. Presents a history of the Muslims in Spain and Portugal, including the time of Afonso's reign up to 1385. Also includes discussion of the Muslim Almoravids and the Almohad.

Livermore, Harold V. *A New History of Portugal.* 2d ed. New York: Cambridge University Press, 1976. Excellent chapters on the origins of Portugal. Clearly traces Portugal's history from county to kingdom and discusses Afonso as the founder of Portugal, the conqueror of Lisbon, and an agricultural hero.

Marques, A. H. de Oliveira. *The History of Portugal: From Lusitania to Empire.* 2d ed. New York: Columbia University Press, 1976. One of Portugal's outstanding contemporary historians traces Afonso's career in the chapter "The Formation of Portugal." This author stresses social history and provides the reader with convincing glimpses of life in both Christian and Muslim medieval Portugal.

O'Callaghan, Joseph F. *A History of Medieval Spain.* Ithaca, N.Y.: Cornell University Press, 1983. This massive survey of the history of the Iberian Peninsula from 415 to 1479 places the career of Afonso in the context of the surging Christian Reconquest of the twelfth century. An excellent place to begin a bibliographic search for additional aspects of this era in Portuguese history.

Payne, Stanley G. *A History of Spain and Portugal.* 2 vols. Madison: University of Wisconsin Press, 1973. The chapter in Volume 1 on the emergence of Portugal provides an excellent survey of the medieval era in that region of the Iberian Peninsula. Places the story of Afonso within an Iberian-wide context.

Power, Daniel, and Naomi Standen, eds. *Frontiers in Question: Eurasian Borderlands, 700-1700.* New York: St. Martin's Press, 1999. Chapter 2 explores the conflicts and tensions between the overlapping "borders" and "boundaries" of Muslims and Christians in the Iberian Peninsula in the time immediately preceding Afonso's birth. Includes bibliography and index.

Stephens, H. Morse. *The Story of Portugal.* 1891. Reprint. New York: AMS Press, 1971. This classic survey of Portuguese history includes an extended chapter on Portugal becoming a kingdom under the reign of Afonso. The author calls his work "an episodical history."

SEE ALSO: Alfonso X; El Cid; Innocent III; Ṭāriq ibn-Ziyād.

RELATED ARTICLES in *Great Events from History: The Middle Ages, 477-1453*: April or May, 711: Ṭārik Crosses into Spain; November 27, 1095: Pope Urban II Calls the First Crusade; March 21, 1098: Foundation of the Cistercian Order; c. 1120: Order of the Knights Templar Is Founded; 1147-1149: Second Crusade; c. 1150: Moors Transmit Classical Philosophy and Medicine to Europe; 1189-1192: Third Crusade; 1230: Unification of Castile and León; 1415-1460: Prince Henry the Navigator Promotes Portuguese Exploration.

AḤMAD IBN ḤANBAL

Muslim theologian and jurist

Ibn Ḥanbal sought to conjoin jurisprudence closely with the study of texts recording the teachings and practices of the Prophet Muḥammad. Ibn Ḥanbal's ideas and his example of steadfast resistance to political persecution inspired the formation of the fourth classical school of Islamic law—Hanbalism.

BORN: December, 780; Baghdad (now in Iraq)
DIED: July, 855; Baghdad
ALSO KNOWN AS: Aḥmad ibn Muḥammad
AREAS OF ACHIEVEMENT: Law, religion and theology

EARLY LIFE

Aḥmad ibn Muḥammad (ahk-mahd ihb-ehn KAHN-behl), who generally became known by the surname Ibn Ḥanbal, handed down from his grandfather, was descended from the Arab tribe of Banū Shayban, which had played a notable part in the conquest of Khorāsān. The parents of Aḥmad ibn Ḥanbal moved from Merv, on the northeastern frontiers of Iran, to Baghdad shortly before he was born in 780. His father, who had pursued a military career, died when Aḥmad was about three years old; a small family estate, however, provided for many of his needs during his early years. Aḥmad's education centered particularly on grammar and religious texts; he displayed a marked interest in accounts of the Prophet Muḥammad and his mission. By 795, such concerns prompted him to commence a series of travels across Arabia, Yemen, and Syria; within Iraq he also visited Al-Kūfa and Basra. Over a period of about eleven years, beginning at the age of twenty-three, he performed five pilgrimages to Mecca. During this time he became acquainted with a number of specialists on Islamic law and history; these contacts helped him to begin to define his own position.

Early legal theory, which had developed alongside the exegesis of Muslim traditions, was associated with schools that followed the teachings of major scholars. In addition to the Qur'ān, many jurists accepted precedent established by custom (*sunnah*). Sayings attributed to the Prophet had been passed along from his contemporaries to their descendants and students until eventually they were transcribed; these were also regarded as authoritative. The Hadith, or tradition, thus was also applied to the settlement of disputes at law. Some care, however, had to be taken when sources of doubtful veracity were presented. Other forms of legal reasoning were based on the process of consensus (*ijma*) that had evolved during the Prophet's time; some jurists accepted a wider consensus, recognizing the opinions of later scholars as well. Argument from analogy was used when a precedent for a given situation had not yet been established. Among some specialists, it was held permissible for judicial authorities to formulate an opinion (*ra'y*) on matters for which precedent and texts were lacking. The first school of law, the Hanifite school, founded by Abū Ḥanīfah (c. 699-767), allowed considerable latitude in forms of legal reasoning; this school had gained influence particularly in Iraq and Syria. During the course of his studies, Ibn Ḥanbal encountered proponents of Hanafi law; as his own views became more definite, he rejected such teachings.

Other legal doctrines were somewhat more narrowly concerned with the reconciliation of religious writings and teachings with the requirements of judicial decision making. Theologian Mālik ibn Anas (c. 715-795) had contended that, after the Qur'ān, traditions recorded in Medina, where the Prophet's work as a statesman had commenced, should be accorded preponderant weight; similarly, the consensus of Muslim scholars should be construed in the light of the practices sanctioned in that city. The Malikite school had become important particularly in western Arabia, where local memories and interests supported such views.

The teachings of Abū ʿAbd Allāh ash-Shāfiʿī (767-820), whom many regarded as the founder of systematic jurisprudence (*fiqh*), established criteria by which the preeminence of original revealed authority could be upheld. In making distinctions between strong and weak traditions, he attempted to resolve problems of inconsistency that had arisen when sources of varying degrees of authenticity were cited as evidence of the Prophet's position on an issue. When further opinion was needed, Shāfiʿī insisted on a consensus of the Muslim community in its entirety. His doctrines had acquired a notable following in Baghdad and Cairo, where he lived and taught. It is known that Ibn Ḥanbal met him in about 810, while both of them were in Iraq, and that Ibn Ḥanbal had access to some of Shāfiʿī's works. It has been claimed that at one time Shāfiʿī commended Ibn Ḥanbal for his piety and learning in the traditions. Although Ibn Ḥanbal's teachings in some ways resembled those of Shāfiʿī, in other ways they were more like those of ʿAbd al-Malik, particularly in his reliance on available traditions and unwillingness to accept other authority as legally binding.

Life's Work

Descriptions of Aḥmad ibn Ḥanbal characterized him as having an impressive bearing and demeanor; those around him evidently were taken with his air of great learning and dignity. One biographical chronicle describes him as a man of middle height; his hair was reddish from being tinted with henna (a common practice at that time). He was married twice and, in addition to having six children by a concubine, he was the father of one son by each of his wives; these two sons, Salih and ʿAbd Allāh, later played instrumental roles in the dissemination of their father's doctrines. In his personal habits Aḥmad ibn Ḥanbal displayed an exemplary devotion to the principles he taught. It was said that, in the absence of traditions that would authorize him to do so, he refused to eat watermelon. He was painstakingly scrupulous in his piety; he fasted often and, following a schedule that left little time for sleep, he prayed at length during the mornings and evenings and at other set times.

Ibn Ḥanbal's teachings uniformly emphasized the primacy of revealed authority, and he stalwartly opposed rationalistic innovations that would permit greater scope for interpretation in questions of law and theology. He denounced conceptions that appealed to sources of judgments beyond the established law of the Qurʾān and the traditions. In particular, his views clashed with those of the Mutazilites, members of a dogmatic school whose political and theological ideas reveal Hellenistic influence. The various thinkers associated with this school contended that free will rather than determinism should be accepted as a principle of humanity's place in the universal scheme. One of the critical questions for the Mutazilites was the problem of whether the Qurʾān had been created; they maintained that it had. On a more immediate level, they posited notions of divine origins that could be used to elevate political rulers beyond the level granted them by previous doctrines. An important political implication of Mutazili ideas was that theological and judicial issues were subject to review on the part of the state. In 827, Caliph al-Maʾmūn, anxious to shore up his government against dissension and external challenges, officially adopted tenets of the Mutazilites as a means of underscoring his authority on matters of faith.

Although the philosophical impulses that were at the source of Mutazili beliefs were of a liberal sort, in urging that reason be consulted on difficult questions of theology, the attempt to transform this position into a political creed produced an unfortunate episode known as the *mihnah* (inquisition or trial). While other thinkers bowed to the wishes of the caliph, Ibn Ḥanbal steadfastly refused to assert that the Qurʾān had been created. In 833, he and another man were taken in chains and summoned before the caliph, who was then at Tarsus in southern Anatolia. Along the way it was learned that al-Maʾmūn had died during a campaign against the Byzantine Empire. Ibn Ḥanbal was returned to Baghdad, where he was kept successively in three prisons. The new caliph, al-Muʿtaṣim (r. 833-842), was unwilling to abandon the policies of his predecessor. The caliph called Ibn Ḥanbal before him and interrogated him on the origins of the Qurʾān; after he would not yield on this question, Ibn Ḥanbal was scourged and returned to prison.

Eventually, however, he was set free. The scars that remained on his body were taken by his followers as testimony to his willingness to suffer in the cause of his convictions. After al-Wathīq became caliph in 842, Ibn Ḥanbal, after a few public lectures, remained in relative seclusion; he neither took part in nor encouraged an insurrection that broke out in 844. The inquisition continued for a time, and some prominent individuals were executed or died in prison. All along, however, public opinion had opposed the state's intervention in matters of conscience, and efforts to enforce such policies increasingly had aroused consternation and disapproval. Shortly after the accession of al-Mutawakkil (822-861), in 847, the government relented; thereafter, the *mihnah* was abandoned and the caliph reaffirmed conventional Sunnism. Ibn Ḥanbal was officially honored by invitations to assist in the education of the young prince al-Muʿtazz, but because of his age and declining health, he excused himself from such a position.

Ibn Ḥanbal composed a number of works that became the basis for the school of law that bears his name. The statement that he preferred a weak tradition to a strong analogy has often been cited in connection with his teachings. For some time his renown as a traditionist surpassed his reputation as a jurist. His most extensive effort, the *Musnad*, was a collection of traditions that, with exacting care, he had traced back to their original sources. Long after it was compiled, the first printed edition of this work appeared in six volumes, containing an estimated twenty-eight or twenty-nine thousand traditions. Other writings recorded his ideas on religious and political questions; some were cast in the form of dialogues, in which he answered questions put to him by students with expositions of law according to the traditions. In short discourses, he also expounded his positions on faith and prayer; a polemical work, which he evidently wrote while he was in prison, was meant to define and refute certain heresies. Some materials were also collected and edited by his sons and followers. By the time Ibn Ḥanbal died in Baghdad, in July of 855, he had won the admiration of many people; hundreds of thousands of people were said to have joined his funeral procession.

SIGNIFICANCE

It has commonly been maintained that Ibn Ḥanbal founded not simply the fourth and last but also the most rigid and least influential among the classical schools of Islamic law. Nevertheless, his work was extremely important—sometimes in ways that belied the usual preconceptions. As a traditionist, he provided important material for the studies of leading scholars in that field, including al-Bukhārī (810-870) and Muslim al-Ḥajjāj (c. 817-875). For centuries Hanbali doctrines were widely taught, particularly in Baghdad, but also in Damascus and to some extent in Egypt; in portions of Syria, Palestine, Iraq, and some outlying Muslim lands such ideas were received avidly. The important theorist Ibn ʿAqīl (1040-1119) demonstrated the breadth and range of inquiry possible within a highly traditionalist framework. Among leading works in jurisprudence that set forth the applications of Ibn Ḥanbal's teachings were treatises by Muwaffaq al-Dīn ibn Qudāmah (1146-1223) and Ibn Taymīyah (1263-1328). During later medieval times, the Hanbali school may have declined in importance. Later, the Ottoman Empire made use of the Hanafi interpretation of Muslim law, limiting the propagation of other doctrines in central Islamic lands. In Arabia, the Wahhabi movement of the eighteenth century depended largely on Hanbali ideas in Ibn Taymīyah's formulation for doctrinal support; later still, the kingdom of Saudi Arabia adopted this school of law in its official practice. Muslim reform movements, notably in Egypt, have been indebted to Hanbali teachings. In the twentieth century, legislation in other Arab countries on certain points has borne the imprint of Ibn Ḥanbal's juridical conceptions.

—*John R. Broadus*

FURTHER READING

Ahmed, Ziauddin. "Ahmad b. Hanbal and the Problems of *ʿIman*." *Islamic Studies* 12 (1973): 261-270. This brief consideration of Ibn Ḥanbal's conception of religious faith takes particular note of the differences that arose on this count among the various Muslim schools of law.

_______. "Some Aspects of the Political Theology of Ahmad b. Hanbal." *Islamic Studies* 12 (1973): 53-66. Ibn Ḥanbal was willing to tolerate imprisonment and suffering partly because he rejected open rebellion against established authority; this brief study examines the bearing his views about succession to the caliphate and political legitimacy had on his own life and thought.

Coulson, Noel J. *A History of Islamic Law.* Edinburgh: Edinburgh University Press, 1964. In this important survey of stages in the development of legal theory and practice, the author considers representative problems in jurisprudence to illustrate the uses of doctrine and sources among the various schools of law.

Edge, Ian, ed. *Islamic Law and Legal Theory.* New York: New York University Press, 1996. Discusses Islamic jurisprudence and legal theory. Also includes a chapter with sources on Islamic legal theory published in English. Bibliography, index.

Fyzee, Asaf A. A. *Outlines of Muḥammadan Law.* 4th ed. New York: Oxford University Press, 1999. This volume is useful as a comprehensive study of Islamic jurisprudence. Bibliography, index.

Hurvitz, Nimrod. *The Formation of Hanbalism: Piety into Power.* New York: RoutledgeCurzon, 2002. A biographical study of Ḥanbal and his foundational work during the formative years of Islam. Bibliography, index.

Khadduri, Majid. *The Islamic Conception of Justice.* Baltimore: Johns Hopkins University Press, 1984.

The theory and practice of Muslim jurisprudence are considered in the light of many facets of legal and philosophical thought that have developed since early times. This study by a leading specialist discusses the applications of methods and texts to issues surrounding major movements in Islamic law.

Makdisi, George. "The Hanbali School and Sufism." *Humaniora Islamica* 2 (1974): 61-72. Although it has commonly been maintained that the Hanbali school rejected mystical forms of thought, the author points out that several eminent jurists found means to reconcile concepts of religious inspiration with Ibn Ḥanbal's doctrines.

Patton, Walter Melville. *Ahmed ibn Hanbal and the Mihna: A Biography of the Imâm Including an Account of the Mohammedan Inquisition Called the Mihna, 218-234 A.H.* Leiden, The Netherlands: E. J. Brill, 1897. This work, based on original materials, has maintained a favorable reputation as an important and detailed study.

Schacht, Joseph. *An Introduction to Islamic Law.* 1964. Reprint. New York: Clarendon Press, 1982. This sound and thorough work, which is recognized as a standard treatment of the subject, deals first with historical developments and then considers applications of law. The positions of the classical law schools are discussed in connection with patterns of influence and doctrine.

Watt, W. Montgomery. *Islamic Philosophy and Theology: An Extended Survey.* 2d ed. Edinburgh: Edinburgh University Press, 1995. A brilliant study by one of the most celebrated of Occidental authorities, this work places Islamic theologians and philosophers within the mainstream of Muslim thought. Bibliography, index.

SEE ALSO: Pietro d'Abano; Abū Ḥanīfah; Avicenna; al-Ghazzālī; Justinian I; al-Ṭabarī.

RELATED ARTICLES in *Great Events from History: The Middle Ages, 477-1453*: c. 610-632: Muḥammad Receives Revelations; 637-657: Islam Expands Throughout the Middle East; 11th century: Expansion of Sunni Islam in North Africa and Iberia.

ʿALĀʾ-UD-DĪN MUḤAMMAD KHALJĪ

Khaljī sultan of Delhi (r. 1296-1316)

ʿAlāʾ-ud-Dīn usurped the throne of Delhi from his uncle and, after defeating several Mongol invasions, launched a series of raids into central and southern India, further extending the frontiers of Muslim expansion.

BORN: Date unknown; place unknown
DIED: 1316; place unknown
AREAS OF ACHIEVEMENT: Warfare and conquest, government and politics

EARLY LIFE

ʿAlāʾ-ud-Dīn Muḥammad Khaljī (ah-LAH-eh-DEEN muh-KHAHM-mehd khahl-JEE) belonged to the Khaljī tribe. There has been much discussion regarding the origins of the Khaljīs, although contemporary writers clearly distinguished them from Turks. The Khaljīs were associated with the area around the upper Helmand River in southwestern present-day Afghanistan. Originally, they were either Turks who had settled in the area and intermarried with the indigenous population, assimilating their characteristics, or indigenous nomads who underwent a process of Turkification during Ghaznavid and Ghūrid times (eleventh-twelfth centuries). Various historical sources mention Khaljīs among the Muslim troops invading northwestern India, and during the 1190's, a Khaljī, Muḥammad ibn Bakhtiyar, commanded an army that overran Bihar and Bengal.

When ʿAlāʾ-ud-Dīn was born, the throne of Delhi was occupied by the formidable slave-soldier (*mamlūk*) turned sultan, Ghiyās-ud-Dīn Balban (r. 1266-1287). Within three years, however, the ruling family was superseded by ʿAlāʾ-ud-Dīn's uncle, the aging Jalāl-ud-Dīn Fīrūz Khaljī (r. 1290-1296), an experienced fighter against the Mongols on Delhi's northwest frontier. ʿAlāʾ-ud-Dīn was the eldest son of Sultan Jalāl-ud-Dīn's younger brother. Not much is known of his early life. Even his date of birth is not recorded. Because his father is never mentioned in the chronicles, he must have died young, for ʿAlāʾ-ud-Dīn and his brothers were brought up by Jalāl-ud-Dīn, and they would certainly have received a military training. At the time of Jalāl-ud-Dīn's accession in 1290, ʿAlāʾ-ud-Dīn was appointed *amīr-i tuzuk* (master of ceremonies), an important position in the court hierarchy. Later, in that same year, he was appointed governor of Kara, near Allahabad (now in India).

He had been given one of Jalāl-ud-Dīn's daughters in marriage (her name is not recorded), but it proved a rancorous relationship, and there were no children. ʿAlāʾ-ud-Dīn took a second wife, Mahru, a sister of Alp Arslan, a Turk destined to become one of ʿAlāʾ-ud-Dīn's most loyal supporters. On one occasion, the sultan's daughter attacked the second wife, beating her with her sandal (in Islamic society, an ignominious insult). ʿAlāʾ-ud-Dīn intervened, a scuffle ensued, and both the sultan's daughter and her mother complained to Jalāl-ud-Dīn regarding ʿAlāʾ-ud-Dīn's behavior. Such feuds characterized harem life, where dynastic marriages and concubinage often led to violent rivalries. Mahru later became his principal wife, known as Malikat-i Jahan (queen of the world), and the mother of his eldest sons.

In Kara, if not before, ʿAlāʾ-ud-Dīn had begun to plot to usurp the throne. In 1296, crossing from the central Gangetic plain to the northwestern Deccan, ʿAlāʾ-ud-Dīn attacked the Yādava kingdom of Devagiri (Deogir, later Daulatabad, India); it was the first time that a Muslim army had penetrated south of the Narbada River. He sacked the city and forced its ruler, Rācandra (r. 1271-c. 1309), to submit and pay tribute. ʿAlāʾ-ud-Dīn immediately returned to Kara with fabled wealth, which he offered to share with his uncle if the latter would visit him in Kara. When Jalāl-ud-Dīn did, his nephew promptly had him assassinated. ʿAlāʾ-ud-Dīn then marched on Delhi, where he formally mounted the throne on October 20, 1296, eliminating the sons of Jalāl-ud-Dīn and other potential rivals.

LIFE'S WORK

ʿAlāʾ-ud-Dīn's accession was not without problems. The Khaljīs were resented by the old Turkish *mamlūk* elite, and there were conspiracies that the new sultan put down with habitual ruthlessness. The sultanate also continued to be threatened by almost annual Mongol invasions until 1306. Despite these, ʿAlāʾ-ud-Dīn embarked on a series of spectacular raids into central and southern India that carried Islam into the very heartlands of Hindu civilization. In 1299, he invaded the rich province of Gujarat, where he extracted great booty. Here, he purchased a Hindu eunuch, Kāfū, who would become his principal commander and who would finally contribute to the downfall of the dynasty. In 1300, ʿAlāʾ-ud-Dīn attacked the Rājput princes of Rajasthan, sending expeditions against Ranthanbor in July, 1301, against Chitor in 1303, and in 1308 against the more remote fortresses of Siwana and Jalor.

According to the poet-chronicler Amir Khusrau (d. 1325), after the taking of Chitor, ʿAlāʾ-ud-Dīn resolved to seize the kingdoms of the southern rajas. In 1305, therefore, his forces advanced into Malwa, displaced the Hindu Paramāra Dynasty, and took the capital, Māndu. In 1309, he subdued the Chandellas of Bundelkhand (now in Madhya Pradesh, India) and captured their capital, Mahoba. In 1306-1307, the sultan sent his favorite Kāfū, who had become *malik naib* (the sultan's deputy), against Devagiri. Then, in 1309, Malik Kāfū invaded the northwestern Deccani kingdom of Tilangana, besieging the capital of Warangal (near modern Hyderabad). In 1310-1311, he moved against the Hoysaḷa kingdom of Dōrasamudra (Dvārasamudra; modern Halebīd), overthrowing the ruler and sacking his capital. He then marched into Ma'bar (southern Coromandel). The historian Ziyāʾ-ud-Dīn Baranī (1285-after 1357), an eyewitness, described Malik Kāfū returning to Delhi with 612 elephants, 20,000 horses, 96,000 *mans* of gold (reckoned at 241 tons), and countless jewels, pearls, and slaves.

Throughout the early part of ʿAlāʾ-ud-Dīn's reign, Mongol incursions were almost annual affairs, some reaching Delhi itself. In 1305, according to Amir Khusrau, after the invaders were driven off, the heads of eight thousand Mongol prisoners were mixed into the cement of the walls of the sultan's new suburb of Siri. These raids ended only with the death of Duwa, the reigning Chaghataid khan, in 1306. Many Mongols had also migrated into India, turned Muslim, and entered the sultan's army. Their behavior had not been above suspicion, and according to Baranī, around 1313, ʿAlāʾ-ud-Dīn ordered a general massacre of twenty thousand to thirty thousand Mongol men, whose wives and children were given as slaves to their executioners.

By this time, the sultan was entering his dotage, and his last years were decidedly inglorious. There was a struggle to the death between Mahru's brother, Alp Arslan, whose daughters had married the sultan's two eldest sons, Khizr Khan and Shadi Khan, and the indefatigable Malik Kāfū, who personally assassinated Alp Arslan as he entered the royal apartments. Malik Kāfū now persuaded ʿAlāʾ-ud-Dīn to disinherit his eldest sons in favor of his youngest, six-year-old ʿUmar. Khizr Khan was sent as a prisoner to Gwalior, Shadi Khan was imprisoned in Siri, and Mahru was confined to the harem.

When ʿAlāʾ-ud-Dīn died in 1316, Malik Kāfū ordered the blinding of Khizr Khan and Shadi Khan, and the enthronement of ʿUmar as Sultan Shihāb-ud-Dīn. For thirty-five days, Malik Kāfū acted without restraint, preparing to seize the throne for himself. He sent four henchmen to blind Mubārak, another captive son of the late sultan, but Mubārak neatly turned the tables on him, bribed his would-be assassins, and sent them back with orders to kill Malik Kāfū, which they did. Mubārak now pre-

Khaljī Dynasty, 1290-1320

Reign	Ruler
1290-1296	Jalāl-ud-Dīn Fīrūz Khaljī
1296-1316	ʿAlāʾ-ud-Dīn Muḥammad Khaljī
1316	ʿUmar Shāh
1316-1320	Mubārak Shāh
1320	Khusraw Khān Barwārī

sented himself as regent for his younger brother, only to seize power, order the blinding of Shihāb-ud-Dīn, and mount the throne himself as Quṭb-ud-Dīn Mubārak Shāh (r. 1316-1320), last of the Khaljī sultans.

Opinions differ as to the style of ʿAlāʾ-ud-Dīn's government. In some respects, it was conventionally Islamic, with a censor of morals (*muhtasib*) appointed to suppress alcoholism, gambling, prostitution, and sodomy. For reasons of state, however, he restricted the authority of the Muslim jurists (*ulamā*) to matters of religious law and theology. Baranī was baffled that a sultan who subordinated religious law (*Shariʿa*) to political self-interest did not incur divine punishment. Later writers represented his campaigns against Hindu kingdoms as holy wars (*jihad*), but the motives for his expansionism were more predatory than pious.

The treachery with which ʿAlāʾ-ud-Dīn had usurped his uncle's throne and the conspiracies that occurred in the early years of his reign left him deeply suspicious of those around him, and he imposed a system of surveillance, intimidation, and expropriation to terrorize elite groups. For his own security, he organized what was in effect a standing army, maintained by state revenues. To maintain these safeguards, he enforced a ruthless system of revenue collection and imposed strict price controls, which were apparently effective, and aroused much interest on the part of the chroniclers, especially Baranī.

Although ʿAlāʾ-ud-Dīn was probably illiterate, his reign saw the flourishing of certain Indo-Islamic cultural trends begun in the previous century. Although at first suspicious of the Sufis, especially those belonging to the Chishtī order of dervishes, he developed a close relationship with the greatest Chishtī of the age, Shaykh Niẓām-ud-Dīn Awliyā (1236-1325), to whom he sent Khizr Khan and Shadi Khan as disciples. Khizr Khan is said to have commissioned the Jamāʿat Khanah mosque in the *dargāh* (shrine-complex) of the saint, the earliest example of an Indian mosque built in an Islamic style and originally intended for the saint's tomb.

Persian poetry flourished during the sultan's reign. Among the shaykh's disciples was Amir Khusrau, regarded as the greatest of Indo-Persian writers. Amir Khusrau was very close to ʿAlāʾ-ud-Dīn, and several of his poems are elaborately ornate accounts of the reign. More prosaic forms of Persian historiography also flourished, culminating in the works of Baranī and Isami. ʿAlāʾ-ud-Dīn also appeared in several legendary epics in which love and war served as mirrors for the Muslim advance into the subcontinent.

ʿAlāʾ-ud-Dīn laid out an extensive suburb known as Siri north of the core of Muslim Delhi, and to the west of it he excavated the reservoir known today as Hauz-i Alaʾi (now Hauz-i Khās). The sultan also expanded the Quwwāt al-Islām mosque-complex to accommodate the growing Muslim population. He enlarged the enclosure, building four gateways, two on the east side and one each on the north and south sides, of which only the latter survives. Known as the Alaye Darwaza, it is one of the finest surviving structures of the early sultanate period and displays Seljuk influence, perhaps because of the migration of craftspeople to Delhi from Iran. ʿAlāʾ-ud-Dīn apparently ordered repairs to the Quṭb Mīnār, as a Nagari inscription on the minaret refers to it as his victory-column (*vijaya-stambha*). Later, he planned to construct an enormous minaret to the north of Quṭb Mīnār, which, had it been built, would have been double the height of Quṭb Mīnār. To the southwest of the complex is a structure believed to have been a religious college (*madrasa*), commissioned by him to contain his tomb.

Significance

ʿAlāʾ-ud-Dīn is reckoned among the greatest of India's Muslim rulers, primarily for extending the frontiers of Muslim domination to the remote south of the peninsula. His conquests were not effectively integrated into the administrative system of the sultanate, and the ravaged lands tended to revert to their former Hindu rulers; however, following these campaigns, the Deccan and peninsular India were increasingly exposed to Muslim influence through the activities of military adventurers, merchants, missionaries, and Sufis. Of great significance for the future, the proto-Urdu spoken in the northern Indian camps was carried to the Deccan with the invading Khaljī armies, thereafter becoming the Dakani Urdu of later times.

—*Gavin R. G. Hambly*

Further Reading

Digby, Simon, and I. Habib. "Northern India Under the Sultanate." In *The Cambridge Economic History of*

India. Vol. 1. Cambridge, England: Cambridge University Press, 1982. Excellent for its description of ʿAlāʾ-ud-Dīn's economic policies.

Habib, Irfan. "The Price Regulations of ʿAlaʾʿuddin Khalji." In *Money and the Market in India, 1100-1700*, edited by S. Subrahmanyam. Delhi: Oxford University Press, 1998. An important discussion of economic policy.

Hardy, Peter. *Historians of Medieval India*. London: Luzac, 1960. Detailed discussion of the historiography of the reign.

Jackson, Peter. *The Delhi Sultanate*. Cambridge, England: Cambridge University Press, 1999. A good general history of the period.

_______. "The Problems of a Vast Military Encampment." In *Delhi Through the Ages*, edited by R. E. Frykenberg. Delhi: Oxford University Press, 1986. Discusses the growth of Delhi.

Lal, K. S. *History of the Khaljīs*. London: Asia Publishing House, 1967. A detailed account of the sultan's reign.

SEE ALSO: Genghis Khan; Kublai Khan.

RELATED ARTICLES in *Great Events from History: The Middle Ages, 477-1453*: 1204: Genghis Khan Founds Mongol Empire; 1299: ʿAlāʾ-ud-Dīn Muḥammad Khaljī Conquers Gujarat.

SAINT ALBERTUS MAGNUS

German philosopher, theologian, and scientist

Albertus expanded scientific knowledge through experimentation and observation. As an Aristotelian, he reconciled reason with revelation.

BORN: c. 1200; Lauingen, Swabia (now in Germany)
DIED: November 15, 1280; Cologne (now in Germany)
ALSO KNOWN AS: Albert, Graf von Bollstädt; Albert of Cologne; Albert the Great; Doctor Universalis
AREAS OF ACHIEVEMENT: Religion and theology, philosophy, education, science and technology, scholarship

EARLY LIFE

Albertus (al-BURH-tuhs) was born at Lauingen in Swabia, the eldest son of the count of Bollstädt. The exact date of his birth is not known; it could have been as early as 1193 or as late as 1207. Albertus matured during the most dynamic decades in medieval history, decades marked by the rule of great medieval sovereigns such as Pope Innocent III, Philip II in France, and Ferdinand III in Castile. The Albigensian and the Fourth Crusades were fought at this time, and in England, King John signed the Magna Carta. The dates, places, and content of Albertus's education are still open to speculation. Most scholars believe that he studied the liberal arts for some months in 1222 at the newly founded University of Padua.

As the University of Padua had just broken away from the University of Bologna over the issue of civil versus canon law, it would appear that Albertus's father planned for him to become a civil lawyer. That would account, too, for the strong objections of Albertus's family when, in 1223, at about the age of sixteen, he joined the Dominican order.

As a novice, Albertus studied theology, probably at Bologna, where he was immersed in the writings of theologians ranging from Saint Augustine to Robert Grosseteste. Despite the constitutions of his order, issued in 1228, which forbade the study of books written by pagans and philosophers, Albertus knew a large number of these works, which profoundly influenced him. He read the works of Averroës, Avicenna, Pliny, Plato, and especially Aristotle. He also knew Pythagorean arithmetic, though Roger Bacon would later claim that Albertus was never a mathematician.

LIFE'S WORK

In 1228, Albertus left Bologna for Cologne, where he began his career as a teacher. In 1233, his order assigned him the lectorship in Hildesheim. Subsequently, he taught at Fribourg, Ratisbon, and Strasbourg. In 1240, he went to the University of Paris, where he earned his degree as a doctor of theology. While there, he ensured his reputation as one of the great minds of his age as a result of two diverse activities.

First, he began work on his commentaries on Aristotle, which ultimately included treatises on physics, metaphysics, logic, psychology, geography, zoology, botany, mineralogy, astrology, alchemy, chiromancy, and celestial phenomena. So well conceived and detailed were these writings that Albertus was quoted as an authority even during his lifetime. With this work, Albertus contributed significantly to the creation of Christian Aristotelianism.

Second, in 1240, as a result of polemical attacks on the Talmud, Blanche of Castile and her son, Louis IX, called for a public debate of the merits of those attacks. Albertus was one of seven people chosen to discuss the issue. Because of this debate, Albertus's skills as a negotiator were in frequent demand.

Twice he settled disputes between the citizens of Cologne and Archbishop Conrad von Hochstein, typical examples of the struggle between feudal authority and the rising power of the middle-class townsmen. Albertus negotiated a trade agreement between Cologne and Utrecht. He settled a property dispute between Mecklenburg and the Knights of Saint John at the request of Pope Clement IV.

After receiving his doctor's degree, Albertus stayed in Paris, where he taught theology at the university from 1242 to 1248. This is the period when Thomas Aquinas and Siger of Brabant studied with him. In 1248, the Dominicans sent Albertus to Cologne to found and administer the first Dominican school in Germany. There he collaborated with Thomas and others in the formulation of a standard course of study for the schools of the order. Later, he was appointed for three years the provincial over all German Dominicans.

Albertus's administrative ability must have been equal to the quality of his teaching and negotiating, because the pope, over the objections of both Albertus and the general of the Dominicans, Humbert of Romans, appointed Albertus bishop of Ratisbona in 1260, a position from which he resigned in 1262. Almost immediately thereafter, Pope Urban IV sent him to preach the Eighth Crusade, an assignment that lasted two years. In 1264, he returned to teaching, first at Würzburg and then in Strasbourg, after which he finally returned to Cologne in 1272.

He left this oft-sought, much-desired seclusion only a few more times before his death in 1280; the first time was to attend the council at Lyon in 1274. The second occurred in 1277, when Albertus went to Paris to defend his former student Thomas (who had died in 1274) and Aristotelianism, under attack for heresy. As Albertus may have been past eighty at this time and was apparently not in good health, this action clearly indicates his dedication to Aristotelian thought and his support of Thomas.

In addition to boundless energy and practicality in everyday affairs, Albertus possessed an encyclopedic mind, unflagging curiosity, and an undaunted commitment to scholarly endeavors, as is illustrated by the subjects about which he wrote. A prolific writer, he produced at least thirty-eight volumes on interests ranging from alchemy to zoology. Albertus's scientific approach was rooted in experimentation and observation rather than in philosophical speculation and revelation. He had no patience with those who accepted dogmatic knowledge without investigation. Where experience disagreed with accepted dogma, he followed experience, preferably his own. While conceding that all things must ultimately be attributed to divine will, he argued that God worked through nature, which could be understood through reason.

More specifically, Albertus thought that there were two kinds of knowledge, that of theology, faith, and revelation and that of philosophy and natural reason. According to Albertus, there was no contradiction. Instead, he saw each activity as separate but not exclusive of the other; he harmonized the whole, using each kind of knowledge in its appropriate sphere of human inquiry.

Saint Albertus Magnus. (Library of Congress)

Albertus began all of his investigations with Aristotle's work and mindful of the Christian faith. Anchored in these, he allowed his empirical observations to refine, redefine, elaborate, and correct. He felt free to exercise reason on all natural phenomena.

De vegetabilibus et plantis, written around 1250, became the chief source of biological knowledge in Europe for the next three hundred years. Albertus relied almost exclusively on observation. He noted how ecological conditions, such as heat, light, and moisture, affected the way things grew. His study of plants led him close to an understanding of mutation and species modification, something he could not transfer to his investigation of animals, probably because it brought him too close to humans.

De animalibus (thirteenth century) recorded Albertus's thinking on zoology. In it, his observations about German whaling and fishing were outstanding. To the standard Aristotelian catalog, he added descriptions of animals that he had observed in northern Europe. Unfortunately, his understanding of animals, especially the reproductive process, fell prey to the standard misconceptions of his day; for example, he thought that the birth of monstrosities resulted from "defective female matter" that the male "vital heat" could not overcome. Nevertheless, he identified correctly the function of the umbilical cord and the placenta. Through observation, he disproved many of the traditional mystical origins and theological definitions of animals.

It was in his works *De mineralibus et rebus metallicis* (c. 1260; *Book of Minerals*, 1967) and *De causis proporietatum elementorum* (thirteenth century), however, that Albertus made his most original contributions. In them, he scientifically described various precious stones and minerals, although he often included descriptions of mystical properties. He also correctly explained why sea fossils could be found high on a mountainside. Finally, Albertus believed that the world was a sphere and held the near-heretical notion that people lived on the "underside" of that sphere; yet he still believed that Earth was the center of the universe, with all else revolving around it.

Albertus remains one of the greatest medieval theorists on physical science. Although many of his inquiries produced traditional answers, his methodology was a harbinger of modern science. He provided the framework for an understanding of the operations of the physical world, which he saw as a system of activity and constant change; this conception was contrary to the thinking of many of his contemporaries, who defined the world in static terms. He died in Cologne in 1280.

SIGNIFICANCE

The life of Albertus Magnus, the "Christian Aristotle," spanned most of the thirteenth century. He was part of the great outburst of philosophical speculation that characterized the medieval mind. He dealt effectively with at least twelve different popes, beginning with Innocent III, popes who often challenged his methodology and thought. Albertus became the most learned man and the greatest teacher of his day; he is still the patron saint of Catholic schools.

Because of the overwhelming quantity and quality of his work and because of his excellence as a teacher, Albertus earned the titles Magnus and Doctor Universalis (universal teacher). A man of common sense, with an insatiable and healthy curiosity, he sought truth, accepted it when he found it, and conveyed it honestly to his students. Roger Bacon, who was by no means one of Albertus's supporters, conceded that Albertus was one of the greatest scholars of their day. Nevertheless, many were the pedestrian minds who accused Albertus of magic and consorting with the Devil, thinking that such breadth of knowledge could not have been gained in any other way. At times, he was considered a pantheist, although this doctrine would never have appealed to Albertus, who was a man deeply committed to God as the creator and source of all knowledge. In his belief, to understand nature was to understand God.

Although his teaching and administrative career was primarily confined to Germany, Albertus's reputation was European. While he reflected much of the temper of his age, he also helped to create it. More than anyone else, he constructed the Scholastic world system. He awakened the scientific spirit that would dominate the intellectual life of subsequent centuries. Little wonder that his contemporaries called him Magnus.

—*Shirley F. Fredricks*

FURTHER READING

Albertus Magnus: Zum Gedenken nach 800 Jahren, neue Zugänge, Aspeckte und Perspektiven. Berlin: Akademie Verlag, 2001. A collection of academic papers. In German.

Brandt, William J. *The Shape of Medieval History: Studies in Modes of Perception*. New Haven, Conn.: Yale University Press, 1966. This is an excellent study of medieval perceptions of nature, human nature, and human action, which illustrates how those perceptions defined the world for the medieval thinker. Contains extensive explanatory notes, which offset the lack of a bibliography.

Crombie, A. C. *Medieval and Early Modern Science*. Vol. 1. Garden City, N.Y.: Doubleday, 1959. This is an excellent analysis of Albertus's contributions to the sciences and empirical methodology. Highly readable and contains an excellent bibliography.

Durant, Will. *The Story of Civilization*. Vol. 4, *The Age of Faith: A History of Medieval Civilization—Christian, Islamic, and Judaic—from Constantine to Dante, A.D. 325-1300*. New York: Simon & Schuster, 1950. An enjoyable work of popular history, providing an excellent introduction to Albertus.

Gilson, Étienne. *History of Christian Philosophy in the Middle Ages*. London: Sheed and Ward, 1955. Gilson is the leading modern follower of Saint Thomas Aquinas, who thought that truth was perennial and, like Albertus, that there need not be a contradiction between reason and faith.

Haskins, Charles Homer. *The Rise of Universities*. Ithaca, N.Y.: Cornell University Press, 1923. Haskins interpretively outlines the rise of the medieval university, commenting briefly on Albertus's role. This study sparked a generation's study of medieval education.

Heer, Friedrich. *The Intellectual History of Europe*. Translated by Jonathan Steinberg. Cleveland, Ohio: World, 1968. An excellent analysis of the development of Western thought, with Albertus seen as a pivotal figure. This is a detailed scholarly study; the sources must be culled from copious notes.

Leff, Gordon. *Medieval Thought: St. Augustine to Ockham*. Baltimore: Penguin Books, 1958. Leff gives the reader an easily understood description of the development of the medieval mind. Describes Albertus's contributions as a synthesizer, an experimenter, an Aristotelian who reconciled reason and faith; according to Leff, he foreshadowed René Descartes and John Locke in methodology. Limited bibliography.

Thorndike, Lynn. *A History of Magic and Experimental Science*. Vols. 1 and 2, *The First Thirteen Centuries of Our Era*. New York: Columbia University Press, 1923. Thorndike remains one of the great historians of science. In this work, he describes Albertus's empirical method.

Weisheipl, James A. *The Development of Physical Theory in the Middle Ages*. Ann Arbor: University of Michigan Press, 1971. Weisheipl stresses Albertus's elaboration and extension of Aristotelian science, particularly in physics. The reader is persuaded that there was much originality in medieval scientific thought. The bibliography for this short, perceptive, and interpretive essay contains the standard works on the history of science.

SEE ALSO: Blanche of Castile; Jean Buridan; Saint Dominic; Louis IX; Siger of Brabant; Thomas Aquinas; William of Moerbeke.

RELATED ARTICLES in *Great Events from History: The Middle Ages, 477-1453*: 1100-1300: European Universities Emerge; c. 1250-1300: Homosexuality Criminalized and Subject to Death Penalty; c. 1265-1273: Thomas Aquinas Compiles the *Summa Theologica*.

ALBOIN

King of the Lombards (r. c. 565-572)

Alboin was a powerful and aggressive king of the Lombards who successfully invaded northern Italy in 568, countering the Byzantines and establishing a kingdom that lasted for more than two centuries.

BORN: Sixth century; Pannonia (now in Hungary)
DIED: 572; Verona, Lombardy (now in Italy)
AREAS OF ACHIEVEMENT: Government and politics, warfare and conquest, military

EARLY LIFE

The Lombards, a northwestern Germanic tribe that may have originated in Scandinavia, flourished on the borders of the Roman Empire during the fifth century. They moved across the Danube to occupy Hungary in the 520's under the leadership of Waccho. It was there, in Pannonia, that Alboin (al-BOH-uhn) was born to the Lombard king Audoin, ruler from approximately 547 to 565, by his first wife, Rodelinda. Little is known about Alboin's early years, since much of his life remained undocumented until the Lombards moved into Italy in 568.

Alboin's childhood and young adulthood were shaped by an ongoing conflict with a neighboring tribe, the Gepids, a feud that continued into Alboin's rule. As a young adult, Alboin killed a Gepid prince, Thorismund, in a Gepid-Lombard battle that took place around 554. Alboin's success made such an impression on the other Lombard warriors that on their return to his father's court, the warriors proclaimed Alboin's power and bravery to Audoin.

Alboin is described as a young man by the historian Paulus Diaconus (Paul the Deacon) in *Historia Langobardorum* (c. 770-786). According to Diaconus, Alboin was tall, with the frame and attitude of a born warrior and leader. Alboin's appearance and demeanor, his lineage, and his triumphant encounter with the Gepids made him an obvious favorite for the Lombard throne, and on Audoin's death sometime prior to 565, Alboin became king.

On Alboin's succession to the throne, he married Chlotsuinda, daughter of Chlotochar I, king of the Franks. The two had a daughter, Albsuinda, who would be Alboin's only child; he thus would leave no suitable heir to the Lombard throne. It is probable that Alboin married Chlotsuinda primarily because of her Frankish background. This would have been a strategic maneuver for two reasons. First, the Franks were located to the west of the Lombards and were often invading periphery lands, and this union would have helped to protect the Lombards. Second, the Franks were Catholic, as were the Holy Roman and Byzantine Empires. A tie to Catholicism would have been of value to the Lombards, who practiced the Arian version of Christianity. Alboin apparently used the association with Catholicism as a political tool, and he allowed Arian religious practices to continue through his reign.

LIFE'S WORK

Although he was king of the Lombards for a relatively short period, Alboin did much to change the nationalistic map of developing Europe. His greatest accomplishment was the successful move of his people into northern Italy, where they established a Lombard kingdom. His first task, however, was to put to rest the long-running feud with the Gepids. The feud had taxed the resources of both tribes for such a long time that it had kept either side from advancing economically or growing in numbers and strength.

Engraved depiction of Alboin's entry into Pavia. (F. R. Niglutsch)

By the time Alboin became king of the Lombards, the Gepid king Thorisind, father of the slain Thorismund, had died and been succeeded by Cunimund. Therefore, the two major figures in the Gepid-Lombard war had changed, with Alboin and Cunimund now heading the feuding nations. Further, a new threat came from the northeast as the Avars, a group of Asiatics of Hunnish origin, menaced the peoples and lands of Europe. At the time of Alboin's accession, the Avars were situated to the east of the Gepid lands, with the Lombards to the west of the Gepids. To gain favor with the Avars and to remove the Gepids as a threat, Alboin suggested that the Avars and the Lombards together attack the Gepids, after which the Avars could have all the Gepid land and half the spoils of war. In addition, Alboin promised the Avars the Lombard lands of Pannonia, since he planned to invade northern Italy and move his people there after the destruction of the Gepids.

The Avars agreed to the combined invasion, and the Gepids were overthrown quickly and nearly completely. Alboin himself killed the Gepid king, Cunimund, in battle. Alboin allegedly removed Cunimund's head and had the skull made into a drinking goblet, which afterward was filled with wine and given to the king during festivals and receptions. The other "trophy" that Alboin claimed from the Gepid war was Cunimund's daughter, Rosamund. Because Alboin's first wife Chlotsuinda had died, Alboin took Rosamund as his queen. The Gepids essentially ceased to exist as a tribe, as the survivors became subjects of either the Lombards or the Avars.

Alboin then began to prepare to invade northeastern Italy. He gathered men and supplies and began the march in the early spring of 568. The Lombard troops crossed the Alps at the Predil Pass, where, according to legend, Alboin looked down and viewed Italy for the first time. The march through Venetia, including Verona, proceeded rather easily, and there is speculation that the invasion may not have been opposed. Alboin and his troops spent the winter of 568-569 in Venetia, during which time he set up a Lombard government, the duchy of Forum Julii, in a town now called Cividale. Alboin appointed his nephew Gisulf as first duke of Forum Julii.

In 569, Alboin continued west through the province of Liguria, into Milan, and to the Alps. Once he conquered Milan, Alboin began to refer to himself as the "lord of Italy," and he counted that date as the beginning of his reign in Lombard Italy. The whole invasion was met with little resistance except at Pavia, just south of Milan. Pavia held out through a siege for three years but finally succumbed to hunger and disease. Despite the barbaric tradition of the Lombards, the Italian people seem to have suffered little during the invasion; when Pavia finally surrendered under the conditions that its church be left intact and its people unharmed, Alboin did not seek vengeance on the city.

Alboin did choose Pavia as the new Lombard capital and the depository of the Lombard riches. While Pavia was under siege, Alboin also conquered the Po Valley, moved into central Italy to conquer Tuscia and Umbria, and progressed into southern Italy, laying the foundations for the Lombard duchies of Spoleto and Benevento.

Throughout these conquered regions, the Lombards held many of the major cities and much of the countryside, but the Lombard hold was not exclusive and many important areas, including Genoa, Perugia, Rome, Naples, Salerno, and much of the Riviera and the province of Bruttii, remained out of their hands. Nevertheless, in Alboin's time, much of Italy came under Lombard rule, and the stage was set for eventual Lombard domination.

Several factors assisted Alboin's conquest of Italy. First, when the Lombards entered Italy, the country had already been devastated by the long years of the Gothic Wars. Second, disease had decreased the population of Italy so severely that towns had become almost extinct; large regions of the country had become deserted. Finally, a famine that raged in 570 across northern Italy further decreased the population. With these factors in mind, there has been some speculation among historians that Alboin was invited to "invade" Italy by the Byzantines in the hope of seeing the country repopulated. Regardless, by the close of Alboin's career, the Lombard people had successfully settled northern Italy and moved well into central and southern Italy.

In 572, shortly after Alboin's greatest successes, his career was cut short by murder. In the spring of that year, Alboin attended a banquet in Verona. At the festivities, he reportedly asked for the goblet fashioned out of the Gepid king Cunimund's skull, and he forced his wife Rosamund, Cunimund's daughter, to drink from it. Rosamund, apparently seeking vengeance, entered into a deal with Alboin's adviser and foster brother, Helmechis, and chamberlain Peredeo, to kill Alboin. Together, the assassins conspired to stab Alboin during an afternoon nap.

Lombard Kings, 565-774

Reign	*Ruler*
565-572	Alboin
573-575	Celph
575-584	Unstable
584-590	Authari
590-591	Theodelinda
591-615	Agilulf
615-625	Adaloald
625-636	Arioald
636-652	Rotharis
652-661	Aribert I
661-662	Godipert
662-671	Grimoald
671-674	Garibald
674-688	Bertharit
688-700	Cunibert
700-701	Liutpert
701	Raginpert
701-712	Aribert II
712-744	Liutprand
744-749	Rachis of Friuli
749-756	Aistulf of Friuli
756-774	Desiderius
774	Frankish conquest

The Lombard people mourned their king. Although Helmechis apparently had hoped to be chosen as Alboin's successor, he, Peredeo, Rosamund, and Alboin's daughter Albsuinda fled to Ravenna. Peredeo and Albsuinda were taken to Constantinople, but nothing more is known of their fates. Helmechis and Rosamund were found poisoned in Ravenna.

Significance

As a side effect of his campaigns and conquests, Alboin helped to spread Lombard traditions of government, society, and aesthetics. The Lombards were more artistically and architecturally advanced than the then-dominant Byzantines, and the influence of Lombard law codes and economic traditions is evident in later Italian practices.

Alboin's most notable achievement, however, was the Lombard invasion of Italy. To accomplish this, Alboin had to engineer the displacement of a huge number of people, as the entire Lombard nation moved from the area of modern Hungary into northern Italy. Further, because of his maneuvering, the Gepids were eliminated from history, and the Avars ceased to ravage Europe. Moreover, the north of Italy, in Alboin's time severely underpopulated, became sufficiently populated to continue its economic and social progression. Regions not directly affected by Alboin's invasion included unconquered areas of Italy and southern France. Peoples along the south of France moved to higher and less accessible grounds to protect themselves from the Lombards, and the occupants of unconquered areas of Italy built up and fortified their towns. In all, Alboin caused a huge number of people to change the ways they lived, worked, and ultimately developed.

—*Andrea E. H. Donovan*

Further Reading

Christie, Neil. *The Lombards: The Ancient Longobards*. Cambridge, England: Blackwell, 1992. Incorporates material-culture and archaeological evidence on the Lombards, addressing issues thematically and chronologically.

Geary, Patrick J. *The Myth of Nations: The Medieval Origins of Europe*. Princeton, N.J.: Princeton University Press, 2002. Analyzes nation-building in Europe—including Italy—during the Middle Ages, and discusses nationalism in relation to immigration, ethnicity, race, and xenophobia.

Harrison, Dick. *The Early State and the Towns: Forms of Integration in Lombard Italy, A.D. 568-774*. Lund, Sweden: Lund University Press, 1993. A look at the history of the towns of Lombard Italy. Includes maps, bibliography, and index.

Hodgkin, Thomas. *Italy and Her Invaders, 553-600*. 1895. Reprint. New York: Russell and Russell, 1967. Covers the history of Italian invasions, from the expulsion of the Goths from Italy to the death of the Lombard king Liutprand.

Koenigsberger, Helmut G. *Medieval Europe, 400-1500*. Harlow, England: Longman, 1987. An insightful study of medieval Europe that discusses political events, society, and culture.

Tabacco, G. *The Struggle for Power in Medieval Italy: Structures of Political Rule*. Cambridge, England: Cambridge University Press, 1989. Deals with the many political struggles in medieval Italy, emphasizing the ways in which power is set up and rationed.

Villari, Pasquale. *The Barbarian Invasions of Italy*. 2 vols. New York: Scribner, 1902. Discusses in clear and well-documented detail the ancient and medieval invaders of Italy, from the Goths and Byzantines to the Franks.

Wolfram, Herwig. *The Roman Empire and Its Germanic Peoples*. Translated by Thomas Dunlap. Berkeley: University of California Press, 1997. Includes a chapter on the Lombards in northern Italy and how their new kingdom affected the transformation of the Roman world. Includes maps, bibliography, and index.

See also: Alcuin; Charlemagne; Charles Martel; Gregory the Great.

Related articles in *Great Events from History: The Middle Ages, 477-1453*: 568-571: Lombard Conquest of Italy; 590-604: Reforms of Pope Gregory the Great; 890's: Magyars Invade Italy, Saxony, and Bavaria.

ALCUIN

English-born scholar and teacher

Alcuin became court tutor and educational and religious adviser to Charlemagne, king of the Franks and Lombards. Reforms inspired by Alcuin made an indelible impression on the later traditions and practices of the Catholic Church.

BORN: c. 735; probably near York, Yorkshire, England
DIED: May 19, 804; Tours, France
ALSO KNOWN AS: Alhwini or Ealhwine (given name); Albinus or Alcuinus (Latin name)
AREAS OF ACHIEVEMENT: Education, literature, religion and theology

EARLY LIFE

Alcuin (AHL-kwihn) was an Anglo-Saxon. As he began to correspond and later to work with people who knew no English and used Latin as their professional language, however, his English name must have seemed difficult to spell, if not barbarous. It was accordingly latinized to Alcuinus or Albinus. The misnomer serves as a reminder that Alcuin was for much of his life an exile in a culture that, if not alien to him, was not native either.

In fact, Alcuin was a product of the first golden age of Anglo-Saxon Christianity. One hundred years before his birth, the northern area of England was still pagan; one hundred years after his death, it had once again passed under the control of pagans, this time Viking armies, a process whose beginning Alcuin lived to see. In the interval between these two heathenisms, Christian scholarship in England was developed, with Alcuin at its heart.

Alcuin was sent to the cathedral school at York Minster when only a small child. He must have been one of its first students, but it is not clear why his allegedly noble parents sent him there. It is unlikely that he was an oblate (a child literally "offered up" by his parents to the monastery), for although he ended his life as an abbot, strict monastic vows would have barred him from his life of travel and court service. Alcuin was also never ordained as a priest, signing himself always as "deacon" or as "humble deacon." Alcuin seems in fact to have functioned as a pure scholar, not aiming primarily at ecclesiastical promotion. He entered the York school in the early 740's and stayed there almost forty years. He clearly studied the seven liberal arts, which moved from grammar, rhetoric, and dialectics to arithmetic, astronomy, music, and geometry, and participated in the buildup of books at York, which he mentions with great pride in a poem written during that time, *De pontificibus et sanctis ecclesiae Eboracensis* (c. 780; *The Bishops, Kings, and Saints of York*, 1982).

Probably around 766 Alcuin became the *scholasticus*, or headmaster, of the cathedral school. On at least two occasions he went on officially sanctioned trips to the Continent. In 781, however, a new archbishop sent Alcuin to Rome to fetch the archbishop's pallium from the pope. As he returned, Alcuin met Charlemagne, king of the Franks and Lombards, at Parma (now in Italy). He was offered a post at the royal court, returned home to get permission from his king and his archbishop, and then accepted. Alcuin then traveled to France in 782 to begin the principal, if long-delayed stage of his career.

LIFE'S WORK

Many have described Alcuin as a pedant, but this characterization is unfair: He was a schoolmaster. He did with the members of the royal family—Charlemagne, his wife, and his children—what he did with the boys at York: He taught them Latin grammar above all. His treatises on grammar and spelling survive and are now universally dismissed as obvious. They were, however, at the highest level for that period, and it may have been a considerable advantage to Alcuin to be English, a native speaker of a Germanic language. The native language of much of Charlemagne's realm could be called either very early French or very late, corrupt Latin. Thus, Frankish clerics were inclined to allow their Latin to be contaminated by the popular language. To Alcuin, Latin was the language of books. He spoke it as it had been written. Accordingly, his treatises are full of elementary advice: Do not confuse *beneficus*, a doer of good, with *veneficus*, a poisoner; do not confuse *vinea*, a vine, with *venia*, permission. Just the same, the advice was certainly necessary. Alcuin acted not as a researcher but as a preserver of knowledge.

His position at the court also gave him immense influence. It seems very likely that Charlemagne, a king of great energy who was coming into a period of success against outside enemies such as the Saxons, the Lombards, and the nomadic Avars, was concerned about the poor quality and lax discipline of his own clergy. Around 787, a few years after Alcuin had joined him, he issued a capitulary giving wide-ranging instructions to senior abbots. The abbots were, he said, to keep their rules strictly and to study grammar. The letters the king had been re-

Alcuin. (Library of Congress)

ceiving from monasteries were well intentioned but uncouth in language. According to the ordinance, it was doubtful whether the writers could even understand the Bible. Charlemagne urged the abbots to select qualified schoolmasters and raise the standard of education. It is clear that Alcuin the former *scholasticus* was behind these reforms. Later instructions insist that not only would-be monks but also all male freeborn children should be educated (an extremely ambitious project for the time).

Alcuin seems, then, to have been influential in preserving good Latin. The point about understanding the Scriptures was also a concern. Several of his own commentaries on the Bible survive, but once again he was more influential on large-scale projects. He seems to have been responsible for the massive reorganization of the Frankish liturgy—that is, the instructions for what was to be said, read, and done at all services in all Frankish churches. Many of these decisions are still being followed in modern times.

In addition, Alcuin presided over a major revision and reediting of the increasingly corrupt and badly copied texts of the Latin Bible itself. It is true that no single copy of an "Alcuinian" Bible survives—not even the copy that Alcuin presented to Charlemagne as the only suitably magnificent gift on the occasion of Charlemagne's coronation as emperor of the Holy Roman Empire by Pope Leo III on Christmas Day, 800. This absence is, however, a proof of success. Like much of Alcuin's work, the revised Bibles were "read to pieces." They have not survived because they were in continual use. As with grammar and liturgy, though, in editing the Bible Alcuin may have done nothing new. What he did was to reduce error and introduce a correct standard.

Alcuin had other and more public triumphs. During the 790's, he confronted clerics of the Spanish church, who were promoting a new doctrine, Adoptionism, and rather unusually for the history of the Church, he reasoned them into retracting rather than having the king declare a crusade against them. Alcuin was also dispatched at least once to England, possibly to help smooth over dissension between Charlemagne and Offa, the powerful king of Mercia. Alcuin also enjoyed considerable literary prestige. His best-known poem is *The Bishops, Kings, and Saints of York*, which he wrote after he left York but which is filled with pride and affection. His other poems are generally believed to be correct and skillful rather than inspiring; more than was usual at the time, they stray from religious themes to imitation of pre-Christian Latin classics. Often they appear to have been written for a court coterie of writers in whom Charlemagne took great pride. Indeed, Alcuin is said to have reproved the king for wishing for more scholars than the King of Heaven himself could provide.

A further major body of work was written, however, after Alcuin had been given permission to retire in 796, taking up the vacant appointment of abbot at the abbey of Saint Martin of Tours. These are his letters, correspondence with Charlemagne and other kings, clerics, and senior political figures of England. In one letter, he grieves with the abbot of Lindisfarne after the first, horrible, unexpected assault of the Vikings on that island monastery. In another letter, Alcuin writes a famous condemnation of secular, native song, which many scholars have seen as the oldest allusion to orally transmitted poems such as the epic *Beowulf* (first transcribed c. 1000). In other letters, he writes warningly to the king of Northumbria and encouragingly to Offa. In yet another letter, written after the deaths of both Offa and his son, he makes it clear that he thought Offa's reign was stained by judicial murder. These letters are among the clearest and most useful historical documents of the time. Their value is shown by the efforts made to preserve them.

Alcuin's influence may indeed have continued beyond his retirement, for some believe that the elevation of

Charlemagne to imperial status was masterminded by his faithful adviser and deacon. Certainly, in the last decade of his life Alcuin's output remained extraordinarily high, amounting not only to hundreds of letters but also to several hagiographies and theological works. He died on May 19, 804, at Saint Martin's abbey in Tours.

SIGNIFICANCE

Alcuin represents a particularly successful example of "cross-fertilization." In his maturity, the best scholarship in Europe was to be found in the northern part of England. Alcuin exported this scholarship to a country in sore need of it and set both religious and secular study on a sounder basis. The favor was to be returned, for as the Viking attacks on England grew stronger, both Christianity and learning fell into ignominious decline. Indeed, the great library at York, of which Alcuin was so proud, was in the end destroyed so thoroughly that not a single book from it is known to have survived. Learning was reestablished in England largely by men from the Continent. If it had not been for Alcuin's reforms, there might have been no such men to come to the rescue.

Alcuin's effect in other areas is even harder to evaluate. No one sees him as a great literary figure, and his works are rarely translated. Yet it is quite probable that the entire daily practice of the Roman Catholic Church, apart from its theory or dogma, was affected by Alcuin's decisions as to which of many conflicting forms and rituals should become standard. It has even been suggested that Church Latin is an Alcuinian "invention," Latin before that being read not as it was written but as native French or Italian speakers would naturally pronounce it. Alcuin and his colleagues brought a new rigor to the Frankish church and, indeed, to the whole of Western Christianity.

—*T. A. Shippey*

FURTHER READING

Duckett, Eleanor S. *Alcuin, Friend of Charlemagne: His World and His Work.* New York: Macmillan, 1951. This volume is a complete, straightforward biography. At times hagiographical in tone and reluctant to take a critical stance on politics or literary talent, the author has, nevertheless, written a very useful book on Alcuin.

Ellard, Gerald. *Master Alcuin, Liturgist: A Partner of Our Piety.* Chicago: Loyola University Press, 1956. Written by a Jesuit, this extremely technical work attempts to determine how much of later liturgical practice can be traced back to Alcuin. It makes good use of the otherwise inaccessible Latin "Life of Alcuin."

Godman, Peter. *Poets and Emperors: Frankish Politics and Carolingian Poetry.* New York: Clarendon Press, 1987. Alcuin is treated here as part of an entire "court circle," and his works are set in the contexts of flattery, policy, and decision making. Included are valuable sections on Alcuin's contemporaries, such as Theodulf of Orleans and Paul the Deacon.

_______, ed. *The Bishops, Kings, and Saints of York.* New York: Clarendon Press, 1982. A complete edition of a major poem by Alcuin, with full commentary and introduction. Argues that the poem was written after Alcuin emigrated, although the poem is valuable chiefly as a guide to Alcuin's early intellectual life.

Houwen, L. A. J. R., and Alasdair A. MacDonald, eds. *Alcuin of York: Scholar of the Carolingian Court.* Groningen, The Netherlands: E. Forsten, 1998. Essays from the Third Germania Latina Conference covering Alcuin's cultural influence, his role in the emergence of monastic schools, his social world, and more. Includes a bibliography.

Levison, Wilhelm. *England and the Continent in the Eighth Century.* 1946. Reprint. Oxford, England: Clarendon Press, 1966. A clear account of the relations between England and Europe in Alcuin's century, including the missionary drive that Alcuin supported and the liturgical work.

Waddell, Helen, ed. and trans. *Medieval Latin Lyrics.* 1933. Reprint. Baltimore: Penguin Books, 1968. Graceful translations of several poems by Alcuin and other members of the "court circle." Particularly useful is the "Disputation Between Spring and Winter," which has been doubtfully ascribed to Alcuin yet is in a pastoral mode he employs elsewhere.

Whitelock, Dorothy, ed. and trans. *Circa 500-1042.* Vol. 1 in *English Historical Documents*, edited by David C. Douglas. 2d ed. New York: Routledge, 1996. This volume includes translations of a dozen of Alcuin's major letters and other items of correspondence to or from Charlemagne that refer to the political scene of Western Europe in Alcuin's lifetime.

SEE ALSO: Charlemagne.

RELATED ARTICLES in *Great Events from History: The Middle Ages, 477-1453*: 781: Alcuin Becomes Adviser to Charlemagne; June 7, 793: Norse Raid Lindisfarne Monastery; 850-950: Viking Era; c. 1025: Scholars at Chartres Revive Interest in the Classics.

SAINT ALEXANDER NEVSKY
Grand duke of Vladimir (r. 1252-1263)

Alexander strengthened the Republic of Novgorod by defeating Swedish, Livonian, and German invaders. By skillful diplomacy and appeasement policies, he also secured limited autonomy for the entire Grand Duchy of Vladimir-Suzdal from the Tatars of the Golden Horde.

BORN: c. 1220; Northern Pereiaslavl, Vladimir-Suzdal (now in Russia)
DIED: November 14, 1263; Gorodets, Vladimir-Suzdal
ALSO KNOWN AS: Aleksandr Nevsky; Aleksandr Yaroslavich (given name)
AREAS OF ACHIEVEMENT: Government and politics, diplomacy, warfare and conquest

EARLY LIFE

Alexander Nevsky (NYAYF-skee), nephew of Grand Prince Yuri Vsevolodovich (1189-1238), was born to Prince Yaroslav II Vsevolodovich of Northern Pereiaslavl, a principality located in Suzdal. Alexander, who had seven paternal uncles and seven brothers, spent his youth in Northern Pereiaslavl and then in Novgorod. Yaroslav was hired as a Novgorodian service prince in 1222, mainly to defend the merchant-dominated society from foreign attackers. In 1236, Yaroslav left to assume the princely throne at Kiev, compelling the Novgorodians to accept his sixteen-year-old son, Alexander, as successor in the republic. Yaroslav held Kiev but a short time before he was ousted by Michael of Chernigov. Meanwhile, young Alexander attempted to build a stronger government and a wider territorial base for Novgorod.

LIFE'S WORK

Alexander's rule in Novgorod began in 1236. Three years later he married Alexandra, princess of Polotsk, a principality between Smolensk and Lithuania. In the 1250's, Lithuania began its absorption of the old lands of Kievan Russia, including part of Polotsk, held in special regard for Nevsky because of his wife's family there. Eventually all the lands of Polotsk would become part of Lithuania. Nevertheless, Alexander was able to repel Lithuanian attempts to seize Novgorod and its tributary principality of Pskov. In response to Lithuanian raids on Smolensk and Kamno in 1239, he erected a number of defensive forts in the south along the Shelon River. Conflict erupted with Lithuania in 1245, when troops invaded areas to the north and south of Novgorod. Alexander's armies from Novgorod, Tver, Pskov, and Dmitrov stopped the invasions, causing the deaths of eight Lithuanian princes and the Russian recapture of booty and lands. Three years later another Lithuanian invasion near Smolensk was stopped, but one of Alexander's brothers was killed in the warfare.

Alexander's leadership in the defense of Novgorod and the other Russian lands from incursions of Swedes and Germans is equally well known. Some sources portray him as a hero, the savior of Orthodoxy. Twice Alexander was engaged in defense against Swedes; one of these battles took place along the Neva River on July 15, 1240, and explains the sobriquet "Nevsky." Alexander's mounted brigade surprised the encamped Swedes, while infantry attacked Swedish ships in dock to prevent arrival of reinforcements. These battles (or skirmishes, as one authority avers) were part of the continuing struggle between Russians and Scandinavians for control of the Finnish lands and not, as some early sources attest, part of a papal plan of Germans, Danes, and Swedes to absorb Novgorod at a time when it was weakened by Tatar rule.

Describing the defense against German Teutonic Knights (the Order of Swordbearers of Livonia) is more complicated because of German support both in Pskov and in Novgorod itself. The nature of such support and the reasons for it are unclear, but the prince of Pskov and the mayor allowed Germans entry to the city. The German party in Novgorod influenced Nevsky to leave the city with his family for northern Pereiaslavl after returning from the encounters with the Swedes. German invasions, however, prompted the assembly to recall Alexander on his own terms. On his return, several German partisans in the city were executed. Alexander's military forces then drove the Germans from the north of the city and retook Pskov, punishing those who had aided the knights. The stage was set for the celebrated "battle on the ice" against German and Estonian forces near Lake Peipus.

Alexander's tactic was to lure the German forces toward the shoreline by feigning a flight, enabling the cavalry detachments to descend from the flanks on the forces in disarray; it is said that five hundred Germans died in the battle. The victory on April 5, 1242, was followed by a march of fifty German and Estonian knights as prisoners through the streets of Pskov, after which the order signed a treaty ceding all of its conquered lands. Stories of Nevsky's battles assume epic, even biblical, proportions in the romantic accounts of contemporaries. The difference between the numbers killed and taken prisoner in Russian and Estonian accounts is immense, and some modern authorities are convinced that the battles involved far fewer combatants than the Russian chroniclers attest.

Family rivalries played a major part of Alexander's mature life. When Yaroslav died in 1246, Alexander's uncle Sviatoslav Vsevolodovich became grand prince and confirmed the patrimonies that Yaroslav had assigned to his sons. Within a year, Alexander's brother Andrew overthrew his uncle and seized the grand princely throne, which required the approval of the Tatars. Andrew and Alexander went to Saray to debate the issue, but Mongolian ruler Batu Khan (d. 1255) dispatched them to distant Karakorum for a final decision. Andrew, though younger than Alexander, was awarded the title, and Alexander was given the rule of Kiev and the lands of southern Russia. They returned to Russia in 1249, and Andrew remained the grand prince for three more years.

When troubles arose between Andrew and the Golden Horde, a Tatar army drove Andrew from his capital, Vladimir, on the Kliazma River. Andrew and his brother Yaroslav defended the region as best they could but in the end were forced to flee: Andrew to Sweden and Yaroslav to Pskov. Andrew and his father-in-law, Daniel of Galicia-Volhynia (1202-1264), had conspired against the Tatars, who discovered the plot. The Tatars conferred with Alexander and then attacked, before Andrew and Daniel could coordinate their plans. Thus, Alexander became grand prince. The brothers later made peace; Andrew was given Nizhni Novgorod and Suzdal in 1255, and Yaroslav was later provided with Tver.

Alexander Nevsky. (Hulton|Archive at Getty Images)

The rule of Alexander (1252-1263) as grand duke or prince of Vladimir was marked by continued accommodation to the Golden Horde, strong support for Russian Orthodoxy vis-à-vis the Roman Church, and a firm policy against opposition within his realm. His chief support came from Metropolitan Kirill, who crowned him in Vladimir, later buried him with full honors, and probably commissioned the biography of Alexander. Kirill encouraged his conciliation of the Tatars and established an Orthodox bishopric in Saray itself. Kirill gained much for the Orthodox Church from the Golden Horde: no taxation, no conscription, and no inclusion in the census. He persuaded Alexander to reject the blandishments from the Roman pope and strengthened the historical image of Alexander as the savior of the Orthodox Church from the West.

Throughout his reign, Alexander continued to defend the frontiers against incursions of Germans, Lithuanians, and Swedes. In 1253, Russian forces under Alexander's son Dmitry seized Tartu from the Teutonic Knights. When Swedes built a fortress on the Narva River in 1256, Alexander himself led a Novgorodian army that frightened them away, after which there were no more Swedish incursions for nearly twenty-five years. In 1262, the king of Lithuania switched allegiances from Rome and the Teutonic Knights to Suzdal, whereupon a combined Russian-Lithuanian-Polotskian army attacked the German post at Tartu. The murder of the Lithuanian king later that year ended the promising alliance.

Relations with the Mongol or Tatar Southeast were different. Rejecting Andrew's idea of uniting all against the Golden Horde, Alexander chose to submit for the sake of limited independence. Novgorod was the trouble spot in this pro-Tatar policy, since antagonism to the Golden Horde was keen there. When Alexander sent his twelve-year-old son Vasily (1240-1271) to rule for him, Novgorodians replaced him with his uncle Yaroslav. Alexander marched on the city, forcing his brother to flee and threatening to punish the lesser boyars, the mer-

PRINCES OF VLADIMIR, 1169-1331

Reign	Ruler
1169-1174	Andrei I Bogolyubsky
1175-1176	Michael
1176-1212	Vsevolod III
1212-1217	Yuri II
1217-1218	Constantin
1218-1238	Yuri II (restored)
1238-1246	Yaroslav II
1240	Mongol conquest
1246-1247	Svyatoslav III
1248-1249	Michael
1249-1252	Andrei II
1252-1263	SAINT ALEXANDER NEVSKY
1264-1271	Yaroslav III of Tver
1272-1276	Vasily
1276-1281	Dmitry
1281-1283	Andrei III
1283-1294	Dmitry (restored)
1294-1304	Andrei III (restored)
1304-1319	Saint Michael of Tver
1319-1326	Yuri III of Moscow
1326-1327	Alexander II of Tver
1328-1331	Alexander III

chants, and the mayor. Only the intercession of the archbishop prevented violence.

New troubles arose in 1257, when the Tatars sent census takers and tax collectors to the city. Young Vasily supported the resistance, and when the Tatars and Alexander arrived, he fled to Pskov, only to be captured and imprisoned by his father. Vasily's supporters were either executed or mutilated. The angry Tatars then summoned Alexander and his two brothers Yaroslav and Andrew to Saray. Alexander, his troops, and Tatar officials went to Novgorod in 1260 in order to enforce the census and tax. Again, the city divided between the greater boyars who supported the grand prince and other citizens who chose resistance. The grand prince's troops easily overcame the rebels, and Alexander, with Tatars by his side, rode through the streets of the city. Novgorod had submitted.

The famed rising of 1262 against Tatar rule came not in Novgorod, however, but in Rostov, Vladimir, Suzdal, and Yaroslavl, occasioned by Tatar demands for slaves and conscripts for the Persian War. The princely class did not support the rebels, and the movement took on the character of a general popular uprising. Alexander was again summoned to Saray to explain the behavior of his subjects. Did he save Russians from reprisals or simply explain his inability to control his subjects? The sources are unclear, but Mongol ruler Berke Khan (d. 1267) kept him there for the winter of 1262-1263, when he became ill. Alexander left in the spring, but instead of going to Vladimir, he went north to Gorodets, in Andrew's patrimony. There, he took monastic vows and died about six months later, on November 14, 1263. His body was taken for burial in Vladimir eleven days later.

The timing of Alexander's death has led to speculation that he was poisoned by the Golden Horde, since his father and younger brother Yaroslav also died after leaving the Tatar capital. In any case, his last mission was at least successful because the Tatars launched no punitive expedition northward and ceased the demands for conscripts.

SIGNIFICANCE

Alexander Nevsky remains an intriguing figure in Russian medieval history. Ironically regarded as a hero even by the Soviet state, he had openly submitted to the mighty Golden Horde. For somewhat similar reasons, medieval churchmen and modern statesmen magnify Nevsky's role in withstanding the challenges of the West. Yet some analysts discount the danger of a major Western invasion, noting that Alexander's defense of the borders was little more than what previous princes had done. The Orthodox Church, ever conscious of its rivalry with Rome, saw security in the conciliatory policies of Alexander, but Tatar policies were always tolerant of foreign religions. Was Alexander's delicate treatment of Saray responsible for the paucity of Tatar reprisals against Russians, or were the Tatars simply too busy with the military threats from Persia? Clearly, Alexander's defeat of his brothers signaled the end of effective Russian resistance to the Golden Horde for more than a century. Also, Andrew's policy of resistance can be seen as unrealistic when one recalls that Daniel died without the Western Crusade that he and Andrew had expected.

Alexander's accession to the grand princely throne in 1252 may mark the real beginnings of the "Tatar Yoke," since there was no further resistance to this administration for nearly 125 years. Furthermore, the accession of Alexander to the principality of Kiev a few years earlier discontinued the political links between northern and southern Russia, since the prince never went to Kiev; its lands were absorbed by the expansionist state of Lithuania.

After Alexander's death, his sons were either too weak (Vasily) or too young (Dmitry, Andrew, and Daniel) to succeed him. News of Alexander's death prompted Novgorodians to replace his son Dmitry with Yaroslav of

Tver. Berke Khan chose Yaroslav over the older Andrew to be grand prince. Although Alexander had failed to change the method of lateral succession, his son Daniel became the first permanent ruler of Moscow, founding a junior princely line that would produce the first czar, Ivan IV Vasilyevich (r. 1547-1584), also known as Ivan the Terrible, who presided over the canonization of Alexander in 1547; later, Czar Peter I (Peter the Great; r. 1696-1725) moved Alexander's body to St. Petersburg to rest in a monastery dedicated to him at the end of Nevsky Prospekt.

No paintings of Alexander have survived, but his helmet is prominently displayed in the Moscow Armory. Residing in the Leningrad Hermitage is an enormous silver tomb for Nevsky constructed by master craftsmen in 1750-1753 in Petersburg. A cathedral in Sofia, Bulgaria, was named after Alexander in honor of Russian support during the nineteenth century. Sergei Eisenstein's film about Alexander Nevsky was released in 1938, and during World War II Joseph Stalin established the Order of Alexander Nevsky to honor Red Army soldiers.

—*John D. Windhausen*

FURTHER READING

Dukes, Paul. *A History of Russia: Medieval, Modern, Contemporary, circa 882-1996*. 3d ed. Durham, N.C.: Duke University Press, 1998. Part 1 of this historical study introduces medieval Russia and the construction and then collapse of Kiev (882-1240). Extensive bibliography and an index.

Fennell, John. *The Crisis of Medieval Russia, 1200-1304*. New York: Longman, 1983. A critical account of Alexander and his betrayal of his brothers Andrew and Yaroslav. Bibliography, index.

Halperin, Charles J. *Russia and the Golden Horde: The Mongol Impact on Medieval Russian History*. Bloomington: Indiana University Press, 1985. The author is sympathetic to Alexander's policy of appeasement and its results. The text also minimizes the magnitude of Novgorod's resistance to the Tatar tax collectors. Maps, bibliography, index.

Hartog, Leo de. *Russia and the Mongol Yoke: The History of the Russian Principalities and the Golden Horde, 1221-1502*. New York: British Academic Press, 1996. Explores the Mongolian beginnings of the Russian Empire and the Golden Horde. Covers the Mongolian invasion and subsequent dominance of Russia, the rise of Moscow and Lithuania, and more. Includes a genealogy of principal persons, maps, a bibliography, and index.

Manz, Beatrice F., ed. *Central Asia in Historical Perspective*. Boulder, Colo.: Westview Press, 1994. Discusses the historical legacy of the Mongols and the Tatars in Central Asia. Bibliography, index.

Michell, Robert, and Nevill Forbes, trans. *The Chronicle of Novgorod, 1016-1471*. New York: AMS Press, 1970. An indispensable source, first published in 1914, for the study of Alexander's role in Novgorod—but written from the biased outlook of medieval churchmen. The author of the chronicle is unknown.

Paszkiewicz, Henryk. *The Rise of Moscow's Power*. Translated by P. S. Falla. Boulder, Colo.: East European Monographs, 1983. In a full account, the author argues that Alexander was poisoned by the Tatars because he had outlived his usefulness and was, in any case, too popular. Bibliography, index.

Presniakov, A. E. *The Formation of the Great Russian State: A Study of Russian History in the Thirteenth to Fourteenth Centuries*. Translated by A. E. Moorhouse. Chicago: Quadrangle Books, 1970. First published in Russian in 1918, this seminal work analyzes the disintegration of Russian political affairs. The author stresses Alexander's family relationships and the centrifugal trends, inevitable despite the presence of charismatic leadership.

Riasanovsky, Nicholas V. "Lord Novgorod the Great" and "The Mongols in Russia." In *A History of Russia*. 6th ed. New York: Oxford University Press, 2000. A historical text with two particularly relevant chapters, one on Alexander and the other on the Mongol influence in Russian history. Bibliography, index.

Vernadsky, George. *The Mongols and Russia*. New Haven, Conn.: Yale University Press, 1953. The classic account by the late dean of American scholars of medieval Russia. It should be read in conjunction with the revisionist version by Fennell.

Zenkovsky, Serge A., ed. "Tale of the Life and Courage of the Pious and Great Prince Alexander." In *Medieval Russia's Epics, Chronicles, and Tales*. Rev. ed. New York: E. P. Dutton, 1974. The basic account that depicts Alexander as the savior of the land from the West. Its omissions are as revealing as the hagiography.

SEE ALSO: Giovanni da Pian del Carpini; Genghis Khan; Saint Olga; Rurik; Tamerlane.

RELATED ARTICLES in *Great Events from History: The Middle Ages, 477-1453*: 1204: Genghis Khan Founds Mongol Empire; July 15, 1240: Alexander Nevsky Defends Novgorod from Swedish Invaders; July 15, 1410: Battle of Tannenberg.

ALEXANDER III
Italian pope (1159-1181)

Despite decades of controversy, through patience, moderation, and practicality, Alexander III established administrative and legal reforms that strengthened the papal monarchy and contributed to the development of canon law.

BORN: c. 1105; Siena, Tuscany (now in Italy)
DIED: August 30, 1181; Cività Castellana (now in Italy)
ALSO KNOWN AS: Roland Bandinelli (given name)
AREA OF ACHIEVEMENT: Religion and theology

EARLY LIFE

Little is known of the early years of Roland Bandinelli, the future Alexander III, pope from 1159 to 1181. His family, probably descended from a French émigré of the previous century, was prominent in city affairs. The earliest substantiated fact places him as professor of theology and canon law at Bologna from 1139 to 1142. Because Siena's schools were not considered distinguished and the appointment was prestigious, it is thought that Bandinelli probably attended school at Bologna as well.

In 1148, he began his career at the Curia in Rome, having been deacon and canon at Pisa and probably having taught in the schools there. A series of appointments advanced his ecclesiastical career. In 1150, Bandinelli was named cardinal deacon. In 1151, he became cardinal priest and by 1153 was appointed papal chancellor, which led to his becoming one of Pope Adrian IV's closest advisers. He was entrusted with a number of diplomatic missions that enhanced his reputation among churchmen and laity. One such embassy, however, would become significant in negative ways during his own troubled papacy.

In October, 1157, Adrian IV sent a delegation of cardinals, headed by Bandinelli, to the imperial diet of the German emperor at Besançon, Burgundy. Relations between the emperor Frederick I Barbarossa and the pope had cooled after the signing of the Concordat of Benevento in 1156. As part of the continuing struggle between spiritual and secular jurisdiction in Europe, the pope had concluded a treaty with William I, the Norman ruler of southern Italy and Sicily. The situation in Italy was stabilized, and the treaty represented a counterbalance to the emperor's pretensions in northern Italy, where his policy was to dominate the rich cities of Lombardy. Furthermore, an important churchman traveling through Frederick's dominions had been captured, and although the man was later freed, his captor had not been disciplined by the emperor. Papal letters had been ignored. Adrian IV considered it essential to ensure cooperation of the emperor in the future.

Admitted to an audience with the emperor and his imperial diet, Bandinelli read a letter from the pope voicing his concerns and pointing out that the Church had accorded honor to Frederick in his coronation at Rome. The letter suggested that full cooperation with the Papacy might lead to greater benefits. The letter, written in Latin, used the word *beneficia*, which meant "benefits" in classical Latin. Rainald of Dassel, the militant German chancellor, translated it into German as *fief*, a word used to designate a landholding granted to a vassal by a lord. Angrily, he asked if the pope meant that the emperor held his office and power as a fief from the Papacy. Tempers flared and heated discussion followed in which intemperate words were used on both sides. Frederick restrained his men but was also angered. The delegation was dismissed and sent from imperial territory. Frederick remembered the name of Roland Bandinelli.

LIFE'S WORK

When Adrian IV died on September 1, 1159, tensions between empire and Papacy were still strong. Frederick sought support from the Romans and from individual cardinals by granting them gifts and honors. When the conclave met on September 4, 1159, a small but influential group nominated Cardinal Octavian, a member of a noble Roman family supportive of the emperor.

Electoral procedures were not yet clearly defined, and much confusion clouds the extant accounts. A majority of the cardinals favored the election of Bandinelli. He was a recognized scholar and jurist with a dozen years of experience in papal administration and diplomacy. He had enjoyed the confidence of Adrian IV. Of the thirty cardinals in attendance, twenty-two supported Bandinelli and seven or eight Octavian. Both men claimed the succession, Bandinelli as Alexander III and Octavian as Victor IV. The Church of Rome found itself divided for the second time in the twelfth century.

The Council of Pavia, convened by the emperor in 1160, supported the antipope Victor IV. Within six months, the kings of England and France declared for Alexander III. Other rulers from Spain to Denmark followed their lead. The greater part of western Christian Europe supported Alexander III, which enabled him to carry out ordinary papal administration and accomplish many of his goals despite exile from Rome. Aided by the regular clergy, especially the Cistercians, Alexander III was able to maintain strong lines of communication. Skillful use of legates and his own moderate position and pursuit of negotiated settlements eventually bore fruit.

The most significant accomplishment of his exile in France was convening the successful Council of Tours. On May 19, 1163, it formally opened at the Church of Saint Maurice. The numbers of those in attendance (accepted by historians) include seventeen cardinals, 124 bishops, and 414 abbots as well as clerks and influential clergy and laity. The eight or nine canons resulting from the council furthered reform of the Church by combating both clerical abuses and "heretical" movements.

Important points included prohibitions of dividing church holdings, granting church property to laypeople, or priests hiring others to perform duties for an annual payment. Clerical usury was forbidden. No payments were to be exacted from those entering religious life. Fees were not to be levied for burial rites or assessed for anointing the faithful with chrism or oil. In short, no payment was to be demanded for any spiritual service, and all irregularities were to cease. Church property was declared immune from secular intervention. Bishops and archbishops were not to delegate their duties to priests or deacons. All those ordained to holy orders by Victor IV were declared to be invalid priests.

The canon on heresy was directed against the growing Catharist movement in southern France. The sect was condemned. No Catharist was to be granted land or refuge by any authority. No commercial dealings were to be conducted with them. When known, Catharists might be held in custody by local authority and their property confiscated. The death penalty was not mentioned at this point, but inquisitorial methods were discussed and are considered a prelude to the establishment of the later, infamous tribunal.

From 1164 to 1170, Alexander III was also troubled by the struggle between Archbishop of Canterbury Thomas Becket and Henry II of England. Initiated by Becket's condemnation of the *Constitutions of Clarendon* (1164), which stated regalian rights as opposed to ecclesiastical, the controversy became heated. Becket insisted that the document's claims were incompatible with reformed canon law. Old legal precedents encouraged Henry II to push his claims. Challenged by continuing difficulties with Frederick, Alexander III was criticized by some contemporaries for failing to support Becket strongly and consistently. Yet many of the papal letters to the king are firm and concise, if not particularly bold. Becket's actions in numerous instances were both rash and intemperate. Undoubtedly Alexander III proceeded cautiously both because of his own problems and his position of moderation. Following the brutal murder of Becket in December, 1170, a long period of shock and indignation resulted in Becket's early canonization. It took several more years for the legates to reopen the see of Canterbury and complete the penitential duties of the Crown.

In 1165, Alexander III returned to Rome. Victor IV had died in 1164, but a new antipope, Paschal III, succeeded him. Frederick's invasion of Rome in 1167, despite heroic resistance on the pope's behalf, sent Alexander III in flight to the southern part of the papal states. Again, Alexander III was able to continue his diplomatic and administrative activities, sometimes enjoying cordial relations with other states after complicated negotiations. Hungary, the Crusader states of the Levant, and other Christian communities became strong allies. Correspondence with the Byzantine emperor began a cautious exploration of possible reunion.

The long schism came to an end with a series of misfortunes suffered by Frederick. The decimation of his

Pope Alexander III. (Library of Congress)

army by plague shortly after his capture of Rome, the loss of Rainald of Dassel, the growth of power in northern Italy represented by the Lombard League, which inflicted a defeat on imperial forces at Legnano in 1176, and the guiding of his own conscience led to reconciliation with Alexander III in Venice in 1177. It would be difficult to assess the victory of either participant. Theoretical statements were avoided and individual compromises were made. Each could believe that he had not done badly in the settlement.

Although the situation in Rome continued to be tumultuous and difficult, Alexander III returned to the area, often residing outside the city itself. In 1179, he convened the Third Lateran Council, to his great satisfaction. Considered to be one of four Lateran councils best studied as a whole, Alexander presented a wide array of subjects for discussion. If he did not resolve them, he enhanced the chances for possible later solutions.

In 1181, still troubled by his problems with the fickle Romans, he died, bringing to a close one of the longest and most troubled papal reigns of the Middle Ages.

SIGNIFICANCE

The difficulty in evaluating Alexander III's role in the development of papal monarchy from Gregory VII to the pinnacle of its power in the pontificate of Innocent III lies in the complexity of the changes occurring in the twelfth century. It is necessary to understand Alexander III's place in the twelfth century world. He was a product of a great renaissance of learning and a contemporary of Gratian, the great expositor of Roman law, whose *Decretum* (c. 1140) was the basis for the flowering of canon law. Scholars have proved that Alexander III depended heavily on Gratian's work. He was a contemporary, too, of Peter Abelard, the brilliant logician, theologian, and teacher, whose new dialectics created a debate that divided the Church to the days of Saint Thomas Aquinas. That Abelard influenced Alexander III is equally clear. Abelard's insistence on the role of reason, even to illuminate revealed faith, found in Alexander III a strong advocate. This pope was a man of learning and a lawyer. If his interests were not as wide as those of his fellow scholars, they were equally deep. Not given to broad theocratic principles or statements, Alexander III worked more successfully to solve specific problems dealing with the role of the church in the affairs of the world. His work for clarity and consistency in law had great influence. He was also interested in marriage law, insisting that mutual consent was the basis for the legality of the contract.

Alexander III was also a religious man. Even the most bitter of opponents acknowledged his moral stature. He admired the austere life and believed that to judge fairly, preach fervently, and give worthwhile penances made a good pope as well as a good priest. He was committed to missionary work, particularly in Scandinavia. His interest in crusading activity in the East was strong.

If Alexander III proved contradictory in his actions or inconsistent in his support of individuals or causes, it would seem to have been dictated by the struggles of the moment. He produced much given the constant threats of exile and schism and the very real danger he frequently faced. As his funeral cortege approached Rome, an angry mob threw mud and dirt on his bier. Alexander III's problems were not solved even by his death.

—*Anne R. Vizzier*

FURTHER READING

Baldwin, Marshall. *Alexander III and the Twelfth Century.* New York: Newman Press, 1968. First-rate discussion of the role of the pope and his place in twelfth century history. Contains useful introductory material; individual chapters cover major problems of the Pontificate. Conclusion, notes, and bibliography are useful.

Barlow, Frank. *Thomas Becket.* London: Weidenfeld and Nicolson, 1986. A biography of Becket, looking at his secular and Christian work. Index and bibliography.

McBrien, Richard P. *Lives of the Popes: The Pontiffs from Saint Peter to John Paul II.* San Francisco: HarperSanFrancisco, 1997. An overview of the popes that touches on Alexander III. Bibliography and indexes.

Mann, Horace K. *The Lives of the Popes in the Early Middle Ages.* Vol. 2. Reprint. Wilmington, N.C.: Consortium Books, 1980. An old but still valuable study of the lives of the popes to 1305. A good starting point for the student. Continuing scholarship has superseded this work on numerous specific points.

Munz, Peter. *Boso's Life of Alexander III.* Translated by G. M. Ellis. Totowa, N.J.: Rowman and Littlefield, 1973. A splendid translation and edition of an original source by a contemporary and associate of Alexander. The introduction by the editor is extremely useful, incorporating the best scholarship to date. Understandably pro-Alexander.

_______, ed. *Frederick Barbarossa: A Study in Medieval Politics.* Ithaca, N.Y.: Cornell University Press, 1969. Probably essential for an understanding of imperial policy. Well written but lengthy. specially useful as a balance to the overly sympathetic accounts from the papal point of view. Excellent example of the use of biography as a means of focusing on complex historical problems.

Somerville, Robert. *Pope Alexander III and the Council of Tours: A Study of Ecclesiastical Politics and Institutions in the Twelfth Century.* Berkeley: University of California Press, 1977. Contains lists of canons, titles, and names relating to the council. Sections on preparation for convening the council and its formalities help understanding of such sessions. Demonstrates how historians use primary material.

SEE ALSO: Peter Abelard; Adrian IV; Saint Thomas Becket; Frederick I Barbarossa; Thomas Aquinas.

RELATED ARTICLES in *Great Events from History: The Middle Ages, 477-1453*: November 27, 1095: Pope Urban II Calls the First Crusade; March 21, 1098: Foundation of the Cistercian Order; 1147-1149: Second Crusade; 1152: Frederick Barbarossa Is Elected King of Germany; December 29, 1170: Murder of Thomas Becket; November 11-30, 1215: Fourth Lateran Council.

ALFONSO X

King of Castile and León (r. 1252-1284)

Alfonso's wide-ranging interests earned for him the title El Sabio, or "the Wise." In literature, law, historiography, and the arts, this king of Castile and León sponsored numerous advances of lasting consequence for Spanish culture.

BORN: November 23, 1221; probably Burgos, Castile (now in Spain)
DIED: April 4, 1284; Seville, Andalusia (now in Spain)
ALSO KNOWN AS: Alfonso the Wise
AREAS OF ACHIEVEMENT: Patronage of the arts, government and politics, literature, historiography

EARLY LIFE

Alfonso X was born the eldest of fourteen children. His father was the revered Ferdinand III, who took advantage of rapidly moving events and expanded his double kingdom of Castile and León into the rich and densely populated regions of southern Spain. Alfonso's grandfather Alfonso VIII had won a most decisive battle in the centuries-long war between Christians and Moors for control of the Iberian Peninsula. This victory by Christians at Las Navas de Tolosa in 1212 made it possible for Ferdinand III to capture the major cities of Córdoba (1236), Jaén (1246), and Seville (1248). Thus, the heart of Islamic al-Andalus (Andalusia) was incorporated into the kingdom of Castile and León.

Prince Alfonso spent his early childhood in Galicia, under the care of surrogate parents. His education was of a high order, and his military training was not neglected.

Although his first thirty years were spent in the shadow of his father, Alfonso did demonstrate military prowess in the field as well as political initiative. When barely twenty years of age, Alfonso negotiated and applied military pressure to force the Muslim kingdom of Murcia to pay tribute to Castile, thus giving the central power a window on the Mediterranean. In 1248, Alfonso was involved in the successful siege of Seville.

Alfonso was betrothed to Violante of Aragon in 1242; their family eventually numbered five sons and five daughters. Unfaithful after the fashion of powerful men of his era, Alfonso fathered at least one illegitimate child, Beatriz, who eventually became queen of Portugal.

LIFE'S WORK

From the moment Alfonso crowned himself in 1252, he entertained grandiose ambitions of becoming emperor of all Spain. His father had died while planning to invade Africa to ensure the safety of his conquests on the peninsula. These schemes to take the war to the infidels' homeland, however, were not successful. On another international front, Alfonso sought to become Holy Roman Emperor through claims that he had inherited through his German mother. After paying enormous bribes, he was indeed elected in 1257. The next fifteen years, however, were marked by obsessive but fruitless efforts to validate his title from afar. His competitor, Richard of Cornwall, was able to go to Germany and press his claim in person. After Richard died in 1272, Alfonso was finally able to travel over the Pyrenees Mountains to appeal to Pope Gregory X, who persuaded him to renounce his claim.

Throughout his reign, Alfonso was beset by revolts; in 1252, there was a Muslim uprising, and a group of Christian nobles followed suit in 1254. In 1264, Moroccan forces crossed the Mediterranean to support Granada and Murcia in a revolt against Christian Andalusia. Alfonso was able to put down this threat and annex Murcia to his kingdom. Granada was thus left as the only Muslim state

Engraving of Alfonso X patterned on a votive statue in the Toledo Cathedral. (Frederick Ungar Publishing Co.)

on the peninsula; it paid tribute to Alfonso from 1266 onward.

In 1275, North African armies again invaded Christian Spain. Alfonso's eldest son, Ferdinand (Fernando de la Cerda), was killed in the fighting, and his second son, Sancho, became a hero by defeating the invaders. This seeming success laid the foundation for Alfonso's final and greatest political debacle.

Son Sancho, the hero, proceeded to claim the position of heir apparent. According to Alfonso's recently proclaimed laws, however, the slain Ferdinand's son was next in line. The issue of succession was complicated by the fact that Ferdinand's male children were also nephews of the king of France. Alfonso vacillated; in 1281, he seemed to bend to French demands. Taking advantage of accumulated grievances against his father, Sancho then declared himself regent and led a rebellion of nobles against Alfonso. Sancho gained the backing of the Valladolid Cortes (the parliament of Castile) as well as that of Aragon, Portugal, and Islamic Granada. Alfonso was forced to flee to his beloved Seville, where he died.

It is clear, then, that Alfonso did not earn the title El Sabio on the strength of his political acumen. A review of his economic policies reveals a similarly mixed legacy. On the positive side, Alfonso promoted the establishment of town fairs to enhance trade in his domains. He ordered the incorporation of the Mesta, the guild of the sheep and wool industry, which was to become a vital element in central Castile's economy during the late Middle Ages. On the other hand, Alfonso spent prodigiously on his many political and cultural projects; his pursuit of the Holy Roman emperorship, for example, was extremely expensive. The results of this extravagance were increased taxation, the consequent alienation of his subjects, and inflation, which led to the devaluation of Castile's currency.

It is on the cultural front that Alfonso's achievements are most laudable. His patronage of—and personal involvement in—scholarship and the arts resulted in an outpouring of creative works from his court. Alfonso's name is associated with major translations, law codes, works of fiction and poetry, astronomy, advances in education, chronicles, and even games.

A year before his coronation, he oversaw the publication of *Calila e Digna* (1251; *Kalila and Dimna: Or, The Fables of Bidpai*, 1819), a translation of the Arabic tales of the *Kalila wa-Dimna*. The Alfonsine astronomical tables, with their suggested astrological impact, were published during the first decade of his reign. His compilation of Roman law, the *Espéculo* (speculum), appeared in 1260. A most original and impressive work, and the project that most clearly reveals his direct involvement, is the *Cántigas de Santa María* (c. 1279; songs to Saint Mary; English translation, 1889). This complex masterpiece, twenty-five years in the making, represented a fusion of poetry, music, and dance. The *Cántigas de Santa María* appeared in Galician, the language then considered proper for lyric poetry. Alfonso is well known, however, for his use and promotion of Castilian, which became the foundation of modern Spanish. Indeed, some have called him the father of Castilian prose.

Most scholars probably would point to Alfonso's monumental law code, *Las Siete Partidas*, as his most important single work. Based on Roman law, it contained discourses on manners and morals and developed a theory of the king and his people as a corporation. It moved beyond feudal conceptions of monarchy in representing the monarch as the agent not only of God but also of his subjects. In 1348, long after Alfonso's death, *Las Siete Partidas* was proclaimed the law of all Castile and León. It continues to influence jurisprudence in Spain and abroad. In fact, in the month of the seventh centennial of Alfonso's death, April, 1984, the U.S. Supreme Court cited *Las Siete Partidas* in a decision concerning lands in California.

Alfonso can be said to have founded Spanish historiography. He was responsible for the *Crónica general*, a history of Spain that was completed by his son Sancho, as well as for a more general history that began with an account of the Creation. Here, as in his other works, Alfonso's desire to synthesize knowledge from diverse sources—classical, Hebrew, Christian, and Islamic—is evident.

One of Alfonso's most popular works, and yet another demonstration of his wide-ranging interests and accessibility to readers throughout the ages, is his celebrated book on chess. It appeared in 1283, not long before his tragic death.

Kings of Castile, 1035-1516

Reign	*Ruler*
1035-1065	Ferdinand I
1065-1072	Sancho II
1072-1109	Alfonso VI
1086	Reconquista begins
1109-1126	Urraca I (wife of Alfonso I of Aragon)
1126-1157	Alfonso VII (king of León)
1147	Almohad incursions
1157	Castile restored as separate principality
1157-1158	Sancho III
1158-1214	Alfonso VIII
1212	Battle of Las Navas de Tolosa: Christians defeat Muslims
1214-1217	Henry I
1217-1252	Saint Ferdinand III
1236-1248	Ferdinand captures Córdoba (1236), Jaén (1246), and Seville (1248)
1252	Castile subsumes León, dominates central Spain
1252-1284	ALFONSO X (emperor)
1264	Moroccan forces cross into Spain
1284-1295	Sancho IV
1295-1312	Ferdinand IV
1312-1350	Alfonso XI
1350-1369	Peter the Cruel
1369-1379	Henry II
1379-1390	John I
1390-1406	Henry III
1406-1454	John II
1454-1474	Henry IV
1474-1504	Isabella I
1492	Fall of Granada completes the Reconquista
1504-1516	Juana the Mad (d. 1506) & Philip I of Habsburg
1516	Formation of Kingdom of Spain

Significance

After reviewing the career of Alfonso X, one might conclude that it is more appropriate to translate his sobriquet, El Sabio, as "the Learned" or "the Erudite" rather than "the Wise." The sixteenth century Jesuit historian Juan de Mariana summarized Alfonso's reign by suggesting that he turned his back on practical political life in order to pursue scholarship and that thus, "meditating on the stars, he lost the earth."

Of incalculable importance was Alfonso's decision that almost all of his publications and royal decrees should be issued in Castilian rather than medieval Europe's usual Latin. In this way Alfonso, almost single-handedly, elevated Castilian into a flexible, sophisticated vernacular tongue. Eventually, his language of choice came to dominate most of the Iberian Peninsula, and he may be considered the father of the language now called Spanish and spoken by millions around the world.

While Alfonso's end was tragic, his achievements on all levels were impressive. He was directly involved, as prince and king, in some of the most spectacular triumphs of the Spanish Reconquest. He restructured the administration of his expanded realms, promoted a legal and cultural renaissance, and supported commercial and technological breakthroughs. Additionally, Alfonso presided over a period of wide-ranging cultural exchanges among Christian, Islamic, and Jewish cultures, a cross-fertilization that affected the evolution of Western civilization on many levels. More than seven hundred years after his death, Alfonso el Sabio is considered by historically conscious Spaniards to be one of their nation's greatest monarchs.

—*Charles J. Fleener*

FURTHER READING

Alfonso X. *Las Siete Partidas*. 5 vols. Translated by Samuel Parsons Scott. Philadelphia: University of Pennsylvania Press, 2001. An excellent translation of the seminal legal code of Alfonso.

Burns, Robert I., ed. *Emperor of Culture: Alfonso X the Learned of Castile and His Thirteenth-Century Renaissance*. Philadelphia: University of Pennsylvania Press, 1990. A study of the intellectual and cultural life of Spain under Alfonso. Includes a bibliography and index.

_______. *The Worlds of Alfonso the Learned and James the Conqueror: Intellect and Force in the Middle Ages*. Princeton, N.J.: Princeton University Press, 1985. Seven scholars present papers on the theme of "intellect and force in the Middle Ages" of Spain. The editor's introduction and epilogue contain excellent summaries of the achievements of Alfonso.

Fraker, Charles F. *The Scope of History: Studies in the Historiography of Alfonso el Sabio*. Ann Arbor: University of Michigan Press, 1996. Discusses, among other topics relevant to Alfonso's historiography, the *Crónica general*.

Hillgarth, J. N. *The Spanish Kingdoms, 1250-1516*. 2 vols. New York: Oxford University Press, 1976-1978. This synthesis of the late medieval era begins with the reigns of Ferdinand III and Alfonso X. The latter, through the chronicles he sponsored, is a primary source for the historian of his age. The bibliography in this volume is a good place to start a search for Alfonso's creative works, many of which have been translated into English.

Keller, John Esten, and Annette Grant Cash. *Daily Life Depicted in the Cantigas de Santa Maria*. Lexington: University Press of Kentucky, 1998. A study of the representation of everyday life and manners and customs in Alfonso's *Cantigas*. Includes bibliography and index.

O'Callaghan, Joseph. *Alfonso X, the Cortes, and Government in Medieval Spain*. Brookfield, Vt.: Ashgate, 1998. Discusses Alfonso's parliamentary and political roles. Includes bibliography and index.

_______. *A History of Medieval Spain*. Ithaca, N.Y.: Cornell University Press, 1983. This massive survey of the history of the Iberian Peninsula from 415 to 1479 places the career of Alfonso within the context of the Reconquest and the Spanish medieval renaissance.

Payne, Stanley G. *A History of Spain and Portugal*. 2 vols. Madison: University of Wisconsin Press, 1973. The chapter on Castile-León in the era of the Reconquest provides an excellent survey of the exploits of Alfonso VIII, Ferdinand III, and Alfonso X. The author places the story of this text within an Iberian-wide context.

Reilly, Bernard F. *The Kingdom of León-Castilla Under King Alfonso VII, 1126-1157*. Philadelphia: University of Pennsylvania Press, 1998. Covers the "political organization of Christian Iberia," "Crusade, Reconquista, and Dynasty," the church and towns of Alfonso's realm, and a guide to documents of Alfonso and his reign.

Thought: A Review of Culture and Ideas 60 (December, 1985). In this special issue devoted to an examination of "the emperor of culture," eight scholars focus on the polymath's cultural achievements. The essays develop aspects of Alfonso's successes.

SEE ALSO: El Cid; Jean Froissart; Gregory of Tours; Vincent of Beauvais.

RELATED ARTICLES in *Great Events from History: The Middle Ages, 477-1453*: April or May, 711: Ṭārik Crosses into Spain; c. 950: Court of Córdoba Flourishes in Spain; c. 1150: Moors Transmit Classical Philosophy and Medicine to Europe; c. 1200: Fairs of Champagne; 1230: Unification of Castile and León.

ALFRED THE GREAT
King of England (r. 871-899)

Alfred, through courage, leadership, and practical good sense, preserved the English kingdom of Wessex from Viking armies and laid the foundation for the later reconquest and unification of all England.

BORN: 849; Wantage, Berkshire, England
DIED: October 26, 899; place unknown
ALSO KNOWN AS: Ælfred
AREAS OF ACHIEVEMENT: Warfare and conquest, military, government and politics, literature, education

EARLY LIFE

Alfred was born the fifth son and sixth child of King Ethelwulf of Wessex and his Mercian first wife, Osburh. Even these few facts reveal important implications for Alfred's future. One is that as a fifth son he could never have expected to be king; even his name is significant, for all of his elder brothers—Æthelstan, Æthelbald, Æthelbert, and Æthelred—as well as his sister Æthelswith, contained in their names the Anglo-Saxon word "ethel," meaning "noble," an element closely associated with royalty. It may have been a sign of Alfred's apparent ineligibility for any future succession to the throne that he was not so distinguished. It is also striking that Alfred was not born in Wessex but (apparently) just over the border, in the neighboring English kingdom of Mercia. Relations between Wessex and Mercia were to be among the most critical issues of Alfred's life.

When Alfred was four, his father sent him to Rome, where he met Pope Leo IV. *The Anglo-Saxon Chronicle* (compiled c. 890 to c. 1150), composed starting some forty years later when Alfred was the hero of his age, insists that the pope consecrated Alfred "as king"—which would have been highly improper and much resented by Alfred's father and brothers. It seems likely that Pope Leo in fact made the little boy an honorary consul of Rome, in gratitude for his father's presents, and that Saxons in the audience much later credited the pope with supernatural foresight.

In fact, Alfred's real youth must have been strained and insecure. His biographer Asser, who wrote an incomplete life of the king when Alfred was forty-five, insists that Alfred remained illiterate until he was twelve, or even later, and tells an amusing story of how Alfred won a book of poems from his brothers, not by learning to read it (as his mother intended) but by memorizing passages and reciting them. Asser also gives a confused but suggestive account of his subject's ill health, from which it appears that Alfred suffered badly from hemorrhoids in early youth, that he recovered from this (as a result of prayer, Asser said), but that hemorrhoids were replaced by another and unknown disease from which the king was still suffering in maturity and which first struck him on the day of his marriage, in 868, to the Mercian noblewoman Ealhswith. Many commentators believe that Alfred's illness must have been psychological, but there are no clues as to what disease it was.

Alfred had legitimate reason to fear for his life. His father and elder brothers died off with unpredictable speed, Æthelstan in the 850's, Æthelwulf in 858, Æthelbald in 860, Æthelbert in 866, Æthelred in 871. In the intervening years, Alfred's mother died, and while his father was absent in France contracting marriage to Judith, daughter of the French king, Æthelbald had rebelled. On this occasion, the Wessex royal family had managed to avoid civil war and made an arrangement between all the parties concerned. Yet the Vikings were a growing menace.

These marauders had plagued England for many years, Alfred's grandfather Egbert having made great slaughter of them, according to *The Anglo-Saxon Chronicle*, at the Battle of Aclea (851) close to Alfred's birth. As time went by, though, the Vikings became more numerous and dangerous, and they developed the ominous habit of not returning home to Scandinavia each winter but taking bases in England instead, as if they meant to stay. In 865, a particularly formidable army appeared, called by the Anglo-Saxons the Great Army or the Great Host. Within a very few years, the Vikings had destroyed the English kingdom of Northumbria and East Anglia and thoroughly intimidated the Mercians. In 870, with Alfred's one surviving brother on the throne, the Great Army turned on Wessex.

LIFE'S WORK

Alfred's main achievement was to repel this army and to place Wessex in a position of strength for dealings with its descendants. He could hardly have succeeded to the throne under worse circumstances. During the winter of 870-871, the West Saxons, under King Æthelred and his brother Alfred, fought one battle after another against the Vikings; *The Anglo-Saxon Chronicle* counts nine "general engagements," in addition to innumerable skirmishes. It seems likely that the Saxons lost nearly all of those battles. Even the Battle of Ashdown (871), which the chronicle insists the West Saxons won and which Asser said was decided by Alfred charging uphill "like a wild boar" in his brother's temporary absence, led only to a further remorseless Viking advance southward. After Easter of 871, Æthelred died, perhaps worn out by campaigning. Alfred, now king, continued fighting but with little support. Almost the first action of his reign was the dishonorable one of negotiating a peace with the Vikings, which could not have been arranged without the Saxons' paying tribute.

On the other hand, the Vikings must have believed that Wessex was at least prepared to fight. In the next few years, they attacked Mercia, driving its king overseas with humiliating ease and setting up an English puppet king in his place. Many of the Vikings settled permanently in Northumbria. It was not until 875 that they returned to Wessex, when they fought an inconclusive and little-known campaign with Alfred. Three years later, however, they caught Alfred and Wessex totally by surprise.

The Vikings struck in midwinter, just after Twelfth Night in January, 878. The West Saxon levies were no doubt all at home, completely unprepared, and there was no immediate Saxon resistance. Many of the English fled overseas or surrendered. Alfred, however, escaped, and instead of going to Rome to retire (as the king of Mercia had done), he hid in the marshlands of Athelney and waged what would now be called guerrilla warfare against the Vikings.

The fact that Alfred did not abandon them seems to have rallied the West Saxons. In the summer of 878, while still under Viking occupation, they gathered an army and for perhaps the first time clearly and indisputably defeated the Great Host in the field at the Battle of Edington. They then besieged the survivors in their camp and forced them in turn to make a humiliating peace, including the proviso that the Viking king Guthrum ("battle-snake") should accept baptism.

Alfred the Great acknowledged as the king of England. (F. R. Niglutsch)

At this moment, Alfred showed a most unexpected quality for a Dark Age war leader, namely, a magnanimity extending to statesmanship. He treated Guthrum well and set the foundation for a relatively stable peace of respect between equals. The Great Host went away, some Vikings settling permanently in East Anglia or Mercia, some trying their luck in France, leaving Alfred with fairly secure boundaries.

Between 878 and 892, Alfred's main political problem must have been English Mercia. Other English kingdoms were settled and controlled by Vikings (mostly Danes). If the Danes also took over the whole of Mercia, the center of England, Wessex would be isolated. Fortunately for Alfred, the Danes—probably overstretched—had left several Mercian counties, including the richest and most populous, more or less to themselves. Alfred must have thought that if he could control the area from Middlesex (now part of Greater London) to Stafford he would be on much more even terms. The Mercians, however, had never obeyed a West Saxon king and probably saw no reason that they should. Alfred's task was to persuade them to think of themselves as the English and not as Mercians.

Alfred once again employed magnanimity. In a brilliant stroke, he reconquered London from the Vikings and handed it over to a Mer-

Anglo-Saxon Kings of England, 802-1016

Reign	*Ruler*
802-839	Egbert
839-856	Æthelwulf
856-860	Æthelbald
860-866	Æthelbert
866-871	Ethelred (Æthelred) I
871-899	Alfred the Great
899-924	Edward the Elder (with sister Æthelflæd)
924-939	Æthelstan
939-946	Edmund the Magnificent
946-955	Eadred
955-959	Eadwig (Edwy) All-Fair
959-975	Edgar the Peaceable
975-978	Edward the Martyr
978-1016	Ethelred (Æthelred) II, the Unready
1016	Edmund II Ironside
1016	Ascendancy of Canute the Great (Danish line begins)

cian alderman named Æthelred (no relation to Alfred's brother). Shortly afterward, he arranged a marriage between Æthelred and his daughter Æthelflæd, later the queen of Mercia. The arrangement seems to have been (though it may never have been put into words) that Alfred would leave Mercia alone if Æthelred did not establish himself as king, leaving open the possibility for Wessex and English Mercia to unite. Whatever the agreement, when the Vikings returned to Wessex in 892, assisted by their former companions now settled in England, they met a united front and a new style of defense. They faced an army with a developed system of reliefs, a network of fortresses that they could not usually reduce, continuous harassment by small forces to prevent them scattering to plunder, rivers blocked to prevent them using their ships, and counterstrokes by English naval forces with ships built to the king's own design. In four years of campaigning (892-896), the Vikings were never beaten decisively. They showed no sign of winning, however, and never succeeded in extorting tribute.

Alfred had preserved his kingdom militarily. He had also—in a most surprising way for one so uneducated—conducted an equally determined campaign for the strengthening of learning and Christianity. Works that survive from his era include his own personal translations of at least four Latin books, interspersed with his own reflections on statecraft. Several other works, including *The Anglo-Saxon Chronicle*, were created at his orders or by his inspiration. His personal prestige enabled him to force through vital reforms on every level, such as compelling all West Saxon reeves and aldermen to learn to read—which, says Asser, they did "sighing greatly from the bottom of their hearts." He saw his country at peace when he died. In his relatively short life, he became one of the most successful and farsighted kings England ever had.

Significance

Arguably, if King Alfred the Great had given up in 878, as so many others did, the world's "universal" language would now be a form of Danish. Less dramatically, but of equal significance, if he had not devised his enlightened policy of nonprovocation of English Mercia, England might have remained much more permanently divided between the South and West (Wessex), and the center, North, and East (Mercia, Northumbria, and East Anglia). The consequences of this for English, European, and U.S. history are unimaginable.

Alfred did not totally rely on force. He was no doubt ruthless at times—*The Anglo-Saxon Chronicle* records his hanging of captured Vikings, and his laws offered no forgiveness to traitors. His recorded works, however, show a strange persuasiveness and a readiness not to take all that was his due. He also seems to have been a very early practitioner of lateral thinking, creating novel solutions to a variety of problems: ship design, river-blocking, and geography. He even discovered a method of telling time by using candles. Finally, his writings show a highly attractive and immediately personal blend of decisiveness and humility. He said often that he would have liked to do better.

—*T. A. Shippey*

Further Reading

Brooke, Christopher. *The Saxon and Norman Kings*. 3d ed. Malden, Mass.: Blackwell, 2001. Contains a chapter on Alfred, together with a discussion of his successors and the problems of writing early biography.

Keynes, Simon, and Michael Lapidge, eds. *Alfred the Great*. New York: Penguin Books, 1983. Contains translations of important sources, including Asser's *Life of Alfred*, coupled with an exhaustive introduction, bibliography, and notes.

Reuter, Timothy, ed. *Alfred the Great: Papers from the Eleventh-Centenary Conference*. Burlington, Vt.:

2003. A wide-ranging collection covering topics such as literature and the Alfredian canon, poetry and prose during Alfred's reign, gender and inheritance in Alfred's family history, urban policies, and more.

Shippey, T. A. "Wealth and Wisdom in King Alfred's Preface to the Old English *Pastoral Care*." *English Historical Review* 94 (1979): 346-355. Close analysis of Alfred's proposal for educational reform, focusing on the king's own words.

Stenton, F. M. *Anglo-Saxon England*. 3d ed. New York: Oxford University Press, 1989. A complete history of the period, with extensive commentary on Alfred's reign.

_______. *Preparatory to Anglo-Saxon England*. Edited by Doris Maris Stenton. New York: Clarendon Press, 1970. Contains valuable pieces on Alfred's last years.

Swanton, Michael, ed. and trans. *The Anglo-Saxon Chronicle*. Rev. ed. London: Phoenix, 2000. A full translation.

SEE ALSO: Æthelflæd; Canute the Great; Edward the Elder; Egbert.

RELATED ARTICLES in *Great Events from History: The Middle Ages, 477-1453*: 731: Bede Writes *Ecclesiastical History of the English People*; June 7, 793: Norse Raid Lindisfarne Monastery; 850-950: Viking Era; 878: Alfred Defeats the Danes.

ALHAZEN

Arab physicist, astronomer, and mathematician

Alhazen, Islam's greatest scientist, devoted his life to physics, astronomy, mathematics, and medicine. His treatise Optics, *in which he deftly used experiments and advanced mathematics to understand the action of light, exerted a profound influence on many European natural philosophers.*

BORN: 965; Basra (now in Iraq)
DIED: 1039; Cairo, Egypt
ALSO KNOWN AS: Ibn al-Haytham; Abū ʿAlī al-Ḥasan ibn al-Haytham (full name)
AREAS OF ACHIEVEMENT: Physics, astronomy, science and technology, mathematics, medicine

EARLY LIFE

Alhazen (ahl-HAH-zehn) was born in Basra. He was given a traditional Muslim education, but at an early age he became perplexed by the variety of religious beliefs and sects, because he was convinced of the unity of truth. When he was older, he concluded that truth could be attained only in doctrines whose matter was sensible and whose form was rational. He found such doctrines in the writings of Aristotle and in natural philosophy and mathematics.

By devoting himself completely to learning, Alhazen achieved fame as a scholar and was given a political post at Basra. In an attempt to obtain a better position, he claimed that he could construct a machine to regulate the flooding of the Nile. The Fāṭimid caliph al-Ḥākim (r. 996-1021?), wishing to use this sage's expertise, persuaded him to move to Cairo. Alhazen, to fulfill his boast, was trapped into heading an engineering mission to Egypt's southern border. On his way to Aswān, he began to have doubts about his plan, for he observed excellently designed and perfectly constructed buildings along the Nile, and he realized that his scheme, if it were possible, would have already been carried out by the creators of these impressive structures. His misgivings were confirmed when he discovered that the cataracts south of Aswān made flood control impossible. Convinced of the impracticability of his plan, and fearing the wrath of the eccentric and volatile caliph, Alhazen pretended to be mentally deranged; on his return to Cairo, he was confined to his house until al-Ḥākim's death around 1021.

Alhazen then took up residence in a small domed shrine near the al-Azhar Mosque. Having been given back his previously sequestered property, he resumed his activities as a writer and teacher. He may have earned his living by copying mathematical works, including Euclid's *Stoicheia* (c. fourth century B.C.E.; *Elements*, 1570) and Ptolemy's *Mathēmatikē suntaxis* (c. 150; *Almagest*, 1952), and may also have traveled and had contact with other scholars.

LIFE'S WORK

The scope of Alhazen's work is impressive. He wrote studies on mathematics, physics, astronomy, and medicine, as well as commentaries on the writings of Aristotle and Galen. He was an exact observer, a skilled experimenter, and an insightful theoretician, and he put these abilities to excellent use in the field of optics. He has been called the most important figure in optics between antiquity and the seventeenth century. Within optics itself, the range of his interests was wide: He discussed theories of light and vision, the anatomy and diseases of the eye, reflection and refraction, the rainbow, lenses, spherical and parabolic mirrors, and the pinhole camera (camera obscura).

Alhazen's most important work was *Kitāb al-Manāzir*, commonly known as *Optics*. Published first in Latin (*Opticae thesaurus Alhazeni libri vii*, 1572) and partially in English as *The Optics of Ibn al-Haytham: Books I-III, On Direct Vision* (1989), it attempted to clarify the subject by inquiring into its principles. He rejected Euclid's and Ptolemy's doctrine of visual rays (the extramission theory, which regarded vision as analogous to the sense of touch). For example, Ptolemy attributed sight to the action of visual rays issuing cortically from the observer's eye and being reflected from various objects. Alhazen also disagreed with past versions of the intromission theory, which treated the visible object as a source from which forms (simulacra) issued. The atomists, for example, held that objects shed sets of atoms as a snake sheds its skin; when a set enters the eye, vision occurs. In another version of the intromission theory, Aristotle treated the visible object as a modifier of the medium between the object and the eye.

This frontispiece to Alhazen's Opticae thesaurus *depicts various uses of optics, including Archimedes' defense of Syracuse with mirrors*. (Library of Congress)

Alhazen found the atomistic theory unconvincing because it could not explain how the image of a large mountain could enter the small pupil of the eye. He did not like the Aristotelian theory because it could not explain how the eye could distinguish individual parts of the seen world, since objects altered the entire intervening medium. Alhazen, in his version of the intromission theory, treated the visible object as a collection of small areas, each of which sends forth its own ray. He believed that vision takes place through light rays reflected from every point on an object's surface converging toward an apex in the eye.

According to Alhazen, light is an essential form in self-luminous bodies, such as the sun, and an accidental form in bodies that derive their luminosity from outside sources. Accidental light, such as the moon, is weaker than essential light, but both forms are emitted by their respective sources in exactly the same way: noninstantaneously, from every point on the source, in all directions, and along straight lines. To establish rectilinear propagation for essential, accidental, reflected, and refracted radiation, Alhazen performed many experiments with dark chambers, pinhole cameras, sighting tubes, and strings.

In the first book of *Optics*, Alhazen describes the anatomy of the eye. His description is not original, being based largely on the work of Galen, but he modifies traditional ocular geometry to suit his own explanation of vision. For example, he claims that sight occurs in the eye by means of the glacial humor (what would be called the crystalline lens), because when this humor is injured, vision is destroyed. He also uses such observations as eye pain while gazing on intense light and afterimages from strongly illuminated objects to argue against the visual-ray theory, because these observations show that light is coming to the eye from the object. With this picture of intromission established, Alhazen faces the problem of explaining how replicas as big as a mountain can pass through the tiny pupil into the eye.

He begins the solution of this problem by recognizing that every point in the eye receives a ray from every point in the visual field. The difficulty with this punctiform analysis is that, if each point on the object sends light and color in every direction to each point of the eye, then all this radiation would arrive at the eye in total confusion; for example, colors would arrive mixed. Simply put, the problem is a superfluity of rays. To explain vision, each point of the surface of the glacial humor needs to receive a ray from only one point in the visual field. In short, it is necessary to establish a one-to-one correspondence between points in the visual field and points in the eye.

To fulfill this goal, Alhazen notices that only one ray from each point in the visual field falls perpendicularly on the convex surface of the eye. He then proposes that all other rays, those falling at oblique angles to the eye's surface, are refracted and so weakened that they are incapable of affecting visual power. Alhazen even performed an experiment to show that perpendicular rays are strong and oblique rays weak: He shot a metal sphere against a dish both perpendicularly and obliquely. The perpendicular shot fractured the plate, whereas the oblique shot bounced off harmlessly. Thus, in his theory, the cone of perpendicular rays coming into the eye accounts for the perception of the visible object's shape and the laws of perspective.

Book 2 of *Optics* contains Alhazen's theory of cognition based on visual perception, and book 3 deals with binocular vision and visual errors. Catoptrics (the theory of reflected light) is the subject of book 4. Alhazen here formulates the laws of reflection: Incident and reflected rays are in the same plane, and incident and reflected angles are equal. The equality of the angles of incidence and reflection allows Alhazen to explain the formation of an image in a plane mirror. As throughout *Optics*, Alhazen here uses experiments to help establish his contentions. For example, by throwing an iron sphere against a metal mirror at an oblique angle, he found that the incident and reflected movements of the sphere were symmetrical. The reflected movement of the iron sphere, because of its heaviness, did not continue in a straight line, as the light ray does, but Alhazen did not contend that the iron sphere is an exact duplicate of the light ray.

Alhazen's investigation of reflection continues in books 5 and 6 of *Optics*. Book 5 contains the famous "Problem of Alhazen": For any two points opposite a spherical reflecting surface, either convex or concave, find the point or points on the surface at which the light from one of the two points will be reflected to the other. Today it is known that the algebraic solution of this problem leads to an equation of the fourth degree, but Alhazen solved it geometrically by the intersection of a circle and a hyperbola.

Book 7, which concludes *Optics*, is devoted to dioptrics (the theory of refraction). Although Alhazen did not discover the mathematical relationship between the angles of incidence and refraction, his treatment of the phenomenon was the most extensive and enlightening before that of René Descartes. As with reflection, Alhazen explores refraction through a mechanical analogy. Light, he says, moves with great speed in a transparent medium such as air and with slower speed in a dense body such as glass or water. The slower speed of the light ray in the denser medium is the result of the greater resistance it encounters, but this resistance is not strong enough to hinder its movement completely. Because the refracted light ray is not strong enough to maintain its original direction in the denser medium, it moves in another direction along which its passage will be easier (that is, it turns toward the normal). This idea of the easier and quicker path was the basis of Alhazen's explanation of refraction, and it is a forerunner of the principle of least time associated with the name of Pierre de Fermat.

Optics was Alhazen's most significant work and by far his best known, but he also wrote more modest treatises in which he discussed the rainbow, shadows, camera obscura, and Ptolemy's optics as well as spheroidal and paraboloidal burning mirrors. The ancient Greeks had a good understanding of plane mirrors, but Alhazen developed an exhaustive geometrical analysis of the more difficult problem of the formation of images in spheroidal and paraboloidal mirrors.

Although Alhazen's achievements in astronomy do not equal those in optics, his extant works reveal his mastery of the techniques of Ptolemaic astronomy. These works are mostly short tracts on minor problems, for example, sundials, moonlight, eclipses, parallax, and determining the *gibla* (the direction to be faced in prayer). In another treatise, he was able to explain the apparent increase in size of heavenly bodies near the horizon, and he also estimated the thickness of the atmosphere.

His best astronomical work, and the only one known to the medieval West, was *Hayʾat al-ʾalan* (tenth or eleventh century; *Ibn al-Haytham's On the Configuration of the World*, 1990). This treatise grew out of Alhazen's desire that the astronomical system should correspond to the true movements of actual heavenly bodies. He therefore attacked Ptolemy's system, in which the motions of heavenly bodies were explained in terms of imaginary points moving on imaginary circles. In his work, Alhazen tried to discover the physical reality underlying Ptolemy's abstract astronomical system. He accomplished this task by viewing the heavens as a series of concentric spherical shells whose rotations were interconnected. Alhazen's system accounted for the apparent motions of the heavenly bodies in a clear and nontechnical way, which accounts for the book's popularity in the Middle Ages.

Alhazen's fame as a mathematician has largely depended on his geometrical solutions of various optical problems, but more than twenty strictly mathematical treatises have survived. Some of these deal with geometrical problems arising from his studies of Euclid's *Elements*, whereas others deal with quadrature problems, that is, constructing squares equal in area to various plane figures. He also wrote a work on lunes (figures contained between the arcs of two circles) and on the properties of conic sections. Although he was not successful with every problem, his performance, which exhibited his masterful command of higher mathematics, has rightly won for him the admiration of later mathematicians.

SIGNIFICANCE

Alhazen was undoubtedly the greatest Muslim scientist, and *Optics* was the most important work in the field from Ptolemy's time to the time of Johannes Kepler. He extricated himself from the limitations of such earlier theories as the atomistic, Aristotelian, and Ptolemaic and integrated what he knew about medicine, physics, and mathematics into a single comprehensive theory of light and vision. Although his theory contained ideas from older theories, he combined these ideas with his new insights into a fresh creation, which became the source of a new optical tradition.

His optical theories had some influence on Islamic scientists, but their main impact was on the West. *Optics* was translated from Arabic into Latin at the end of the twelfth century. It was widely studied, and in the thirteenth century, Witelo (also known as Vitellio) made liberal use of Alhazen's text in writing his comprehensive book on optics. Roger Bacon, John Pecham, and Giambattista della Porta are only some of the many thinkers who were influenced by Alhazen's work. Indeed, it was not until Kepler, six centuries later, that work on optics progressed beyond the point to which Alhazen had brought it. Even Kepler, however, used some of Alhazen's ideas, for example, the one-to-one correspondence between points on the object and points in the eye. It would not be going too far to say that Alhazen's optical theories defined the scope and goals of the field from his day to today.

—Robert J. Paradowski

FURTHER READING

Bakar, Osman. *The History and Philosophy of Islamic Science*. Cambridge, England: Islamic Texts Society, 1999. Discusses questions of methodology, doubt, spirituality and scientific knowledge, the philosophy of Islamic medicine, and how Islamic science influenced medieval Christian views of the natural world.

Grant, Edward, ed. *A Source Book in Medieval Science*. Cambridge, Mass.: Harvard University Press, 1974. A compilation of readings from medieval natural philosophers, including several selections in English translation from the works of Alhazen. Bibliography, index.

Hayes, John R., ed. *The Genius of Arab Civilization: Source of Renaissance*. 3d ed. New York: New York University Press, 1992. In this beautifully illustrated book, several international authorities discuss the intellectual achievements of Islamic culture. Sabra's chapter on the exact sciences contains an account of Alhazen's work in the context of Islamic intellectual history. Bibliography, index.

Hogendijk, Jan P., and Abdelhamid I. Sabra, eds. *The Enterprise of Science in Islam: New Perspectives*. Cambridge, Mass.: MIT Press, 2003. A collection surveying the history of science, including mathematics, optics, and astronomy, in Islam, with a chapter on Alhazen's work. Illustrations, bibliography, index.

Huff, Toby E. *The Rise of Early Modern Science: Islam, China, and the West*. 2d ed. New York: Cambridge University Press, 2003. Provides a strong cross-cultural background for the rise of science and medicine in the Muslim world. Illustrations, bibliography, index.

Lindberg, David C. *Theories of Vision from al-Kindi to Kepler*. Chicago: University of Chicago Press, 1981. Surveys visual theory against the background of ancient accomplishments. The chapter on Alhazen's intromission theory is excellent. Bibliography, index.

________, ed. *Science in the Middle Ages*. Chicago: University of Chicago Press, 1978. Through the expertise of several historians of medieval science, this book examines in depth all major aspects of natural philosophy in the Middle Ages. The approach is not encyclopedic but interpretative. Includes a chapter on optics, in which Alhazen's work is clearly explained.

Nasr, Seyyed Hossein. *Islamic Science: An Illustrated Study*. Westerham, England: World of Islam Festival, 1976. The first illustrated study ever undertaken of the whole of Islamic science. Using traditional Islamic concepts, the author discusses various branches of science, including optics.

_______. *Science and Civilization in Islam*. Cambridge, Mass.: Harvard University Press, 1968. This book is the first one-volume work in English to deal with Islamic science from the Muslim rather than the Western viewpoint. Its approach is encyclopedic rather than analytic, but it does contain a discussion of Alhazen's work in its Muslim context.

Sabra, Abdelhamid I. *Optics, Astronomy, and Logic: Studies in Arabic Science and Philosophy*. Brookfield, Vt.: Variorum, 1994. A history of science, specifically optics and astronomy, in the Muslim world of Alhazen's time. Includes discussion of Alhazen and his work. Illustrations, index.

_______. *Theories of Light from Descartes to Newton*. New York: Cambridge University Press, 1981. Though this book is mainly centered on seventeenth century theories of light, the author discusses in detail the impact of Alhazen's ideas on the optical discoveries of such thinkers as Descartes and Christiaan Huygens. Bibliography, index.

SEE ALSO: Pietro d'Abano; Abul Wefa; Roger Bacon; al-Battānī; Jean Buridan; al-Khwārizmī; Omar Khayyám; John Pecham; al-Rāzī.

RELATED ARTICLES in *Great Events from History: The Middle Ages, 477-1453*: 972: Building of al-Azhar Mosque; c. 1150: Moors Transmit Classical Philosophy and Medicine to Europe.

ALP ARSLAN

Seljuk sultan (r. 1063-1072 or 1073)

The second sultan of the Seljuk Dynasty, Alp Arslan consolidated and extended the conquests of his predecessor, Toghrïl Beg. His reign, together with that of his son Malik-Shāh, constituted the zenith of the empire of the Great Seljuks.

BORN: c. 1030; Khorāsān, Persia (now in Iran)

DIED: November, 1072, or January, 1073; near Tirmidh, Transoxiana (now Termez, Uzbekistan)

ALSO KNOWN AS: ʿAṣud al-Dawla Abū Shujaʿ Muḥammad ibn Dāʾūd Chāghrï Beg (full name)

AREAS OF ACHIEVEMENT: Government and politics, warfare and conquest, military

EARLY LIFE

Alp Arslan (AHL-pahr-SLAHN), the second and most famous of the sultans of the Seljuk Dynasty, was born to Chaghrï Beg, brother of the Turkish warlord Toghrïl Beg. During the 1040's, Toghrïl invaded Iran with his Turkmen followers, became the protector of the ʿAbbāsid caliph in Baghdad and thereby the champion of Sunni (orthodox) Islam, and founded an empire that extended over much of the Middle East. Alp Arslan's Turkish name (his Arabic names and titles were ʿAṣud al-Dawla Abū Shujaʿ Muḥammad ibn Dāʾūd Chāghrï Beg) was a combination of the words *alp*, meaning warrior or hero, and *arslan*, meaning lion, apt sobriquets for so renowned a military leader.

His great-grandfather, Seljuk, the eponymous ancestor of the Seljuk Dynasty, had been a clan leader among the tribes that composed the confederacy of the Oğhuz Turks, who in the tenth century occupied the steppes between the Aral Sea and the Volga River. Seljuk himself had thrown off his allegiance to the *yabghu*, as the supreme ruler of the Oğhuz was known, and led his clansmen and a growing body of Turkmen followers as soldiers of fortune in the service of the rulers of Khwārizm and Transoxiana. His base of operations was in the neighborhood of Jand, on the north bank of the Syr Darya River, where eventually he was buried. One source states that he went to the aid of one of the last rulers of the Sāmānid Dynasty of Bukhara, under attack from the Qarakhanid Turks, advancing from what is now Chinese Central Asia. By then, he had become a Muslim. His sons, Arslan Isrāʾīl, Mikhail, and Musa, followed their father's example in taking advantage of the anarchy in Central Asia that accompanied the fall of the Sāmānids and the rise of the Qarakhanids. The unusual personal names of these three have led scholars to wonder whether they are indicative of Nestorian Christian or Jewish Khazar influence.

Mikhail's sons, Toghrïl Beg and Chaghrï Beg, were the founders of Seljuk rule in the Middle East. Even before their defeat of the Ghaznavid sultan (until then, ruler of much of the Iranian Plateau as well as Afghanistan) at Dendenkan, between Merv and Sarakhs, in 1040, Toghrïl Beg had entered Neyshabur, the principal city of Khorāsān, and proclaimed himself sultan. After Dendenkan, Chaghrï Beg turned east to occupy Balkh and Tukharistan in northern Afghanistan. Toghrïl Beg then proceeded with the systematic conquest of central and western Iran and of Iraq. He occupied Baghdad in 1055 and again in 1058, where he assumed the role of protector of the caliph. In 1062, in a reluctant break with past precedent, the latter agreed to Toghrïl Beg's marriage to his daughter.

While Toghrïl Beg was pursuing his triumphant course in the west, Chaghrï Beg was acting as the quasi-independent ruler of Khorāsān and part of the Amu Darʾya (Oxus) River valley, with his headquarters at Merv. His eldest son, Qavurt, had embarked on the conquest of Kerman and southeastern Iran (where his descendants were to rule until 1186), while his other sons (among them Alp Arslan) accompanied Toghrïl Beg on his campaigns in Iraq and western Iran. During his last years, Chaghrï Beg chose, perhaps as a result of poor health, to make use of Alp Arslan in the government of Khorāsān, thereby providing him with administrative experience that would stand him in good stead for the future. It was during this period, under his father's tutelage, that he came into contact with the man who would eventually become his chief minister and adviser, Niẓām al-Mulk, whom Chaghrï Beg on his deathbed urged Alp Arslan to appoint as his vizier. Undoubtedly, a significant factor in the success of Alp Arslan's reign was his appreciation of the talents of Niẓām al-Mulk as an administrator and the consequent partnership of sultan and vizier in the government of the empire. At Chaghrï Beg's death (c. 1060), Toghrïl Beg confirmed Alp Arslan as the new ruler of his father's vast appanage in the northeast.

No likeness of Alp Arslan survives, but he was said to have been a tall and imposing figure of exceptional strength, his great height enhanced by his preference for an unusually high headdress. A quaint tradition records that before he drew his bow, a servant had to tie back his immense mustache, which would otherwise have become entangled in his bowstring.

LIFE'S WORK

Like other ruling groups from Central Asia, the early Seljuks viewed sovereignty as being invested in the family as a whole, rather than in a single individual, an attitude that Toghrïl Beg had done little to discourage. At his death in 1063, therefore, there was a predictable familial struggle over the succession. Childless himself, Toghrïl Beg had designated as his successor another of Chaghrï Beg's sons, Sulaimān, the favorite candidate of the late sultan's powerful vizier, al-Kunduri. Perhaps because Sulaimān's accession would have confirmed the already dominant position enjoyed by al-Kunduri, some of Toghrïl Beg's former *mamlūk* (slave) commanders favored Alp Arslan, who had already established a formidable reputation as ruler of Khorāsān. In the contest that followed, Sulaimān was easily outmaneuvered, and al-Kunduri was executed at the instigation of Niẓām al-Mulk.

A more formidable threat was posed by Alp Arslan's kinsman Qutlumush ibn Arslan Isrāʿīl, the able and energetic son of Alp Arslan's granduncle. Qutlumush's power base lay in the northwest, in the direction of the Caucasus, and he commanded the loyalty of formidable numbers of Turkmen warriors who were dismayed at the centralizing processes that marked the transformation of Seljuk rule from predatory raiding to empire building. Qutlumush pressed his own claim to the throne with an appeal to the traditions of the steppes: "By right, the sultanate should come to me, because my father was the senior and leading member of the tribe." His forces advanced to the vicinity of Rayy (near what is now Tehran) but were defeated by troops loyal to Alp Arslan. Qutlumush himself died shortly afterward, apparently killed by a fall from his horse. His followers were not so easily dealt with, and it was largely on their account that Alp Arslan was eventually drawn into direct confrontation with the Byzantines.

There were other challenges to Alp Arslan's authority. Toghrïl Beg had married a daughter of the ruler of Khwārizm who had a son by a previous marriage, and although this son was not a Seljuk, he attracted some support among the disaffected. More serious was the revolt in Kerman of Alp Arslan's older brother, Qavurt, whose delayed resentment at the elevation of his younger sibling surfaced in 1067. Alp Arslan was forced to invade Kerman and also Fārs, which Qavurt had previously seized from a local dynasty, but the two brothers were eventually reconciled.

Alp Arslan must have been familiar with the course of Toghrïl Beg's difficult negotiations with the ʿAbbāsid caliph, and it seems that he himself was determined to avoid situations in which disputes might develop as to the respective powers and prerogatives of caliph and sultan. On his accession, he obtained formal recognition from the long-reigning caliph al-Qāʾim, with whom his uncle had dealt, but he declined to visit Baghdad in person or to become involved in the intrigues of the caliphal court. While keeping his distance, he did, however, keep a close watch on affairs in Baghdad. Alp Arslan's prime concern was to prevent any augmentation of the influence of the Fāṭimid caliphs in Cairo, Shīʿites whose secret emissaries worked assiduously for the Fāṭimid cause in a region (Iraq) where a number of the Arab emirs were themselves Shīʿites. To that extent, at least, he and the ʿAbbāsid caliph had common ground for cooperation.

SELJUK GREAT SULTANS, 1037-1157

Reign	*Sultan*
1037-1063	Toghrïl Beg
1063-1072/73	ALP ARSLAN
1073-1092	Malik Shāh I
1092-1093	Maḥmūd I
1093-1104	Berk Yaruq (Barkyaruk, Barkiyarok)
1104-1105	Malik Shāh II
1105-1117	Muḥammad Tapar
1117-1157	Aḥmad Sanjar (Sinjar)

Hence, he was careful to ensure that his military representative (*shahna*) in Iraq was personally acceptable to the caliph, while Niẓām al-Mulk endeavored to work closely with the caliph's successive viziers. The policy of avoiding Baghdad while treating the caliph with a blend of courtesy and firmness undoubtedly paid off: In 1066, when Alp Arslan designated his son, Malik Shāh, as *valiahd* (heir apparent) and had his name read in the *khutba* together with his own, he was able to secure caliphal recognition for him, and in 1071-1072, one of Alp Arslan's daughters was married to al-Qāʿim's heir, al-Muqtadi.

Although Alp Arslan's reputation as one of the greatest medieval Muslim rulers arose in part from his spectacular success against the Byzantines at Manzikert in 1071, it is unlikely that he cherished the ambition to be a *ghāzī* (frontier warrior for the faith). On the other hand, he cannot have been unhappy to see the restless Turkmens devote their energies to jihad (holy warfare) on the Byzantine marches, an undertaking that deflected their attention from the heartlands of the Seljuk Empire. The danger was that the Turkmens, who included many former followers of Qutlumush, as they pressed forward, would wholly emancipate themselves from Seljuk control and perhaps even set up an independent state. Thus, Alp Arslan was compelled early in his reign to turn his attention to the northwest. Several major dynasties based on the Iranian Plateau (for example, the Sāsānids, the Il-Khans, and the Safavids) found it necessary to seek control of the strategic region between the Black Sea and the Caspian, bounded on the north by the Caucasus and on the south by the Araks River; to this rule Alp Arslan was no exception.

In 1064, therefore, within a year of his accession and the overthrow of Qutlumush, he invaded Byzantine Armenia, capturing its administrative capital, Ani, and obtaining the submission of the great fortress of Kars. He then advanced into Georgia, where he married a niece of the Georgian king. Three years later, in 1067, he marched into Arran (the country between the Araks and Kura rivers), where he received the formal submission of its Shaddadid ruler. Shortly afterward, the ruler of Shirvan also submitted, with the result that Seljuk's suzerainty was extended along the western shores of the Caspian as far north as Darband. Then, in 1068, a further invasion of Georgia, this time led by the Shaddadid ruler of Arran, reaffirmed Alp Arslan's overlordship over that now-isolated Christian kingdom (Armenia had finally come under Muslim rule and the Byzantine frontier had contracted in a westerly direction).

Initially, the Seljuks, as they advanced into the Middle East, had appeared to have as their goal the occupation of the Iranian Plateau. That achievement, however, had inevitably led to the conquest of Iraq, partly because of the need to put down the prevailing anarchy there and partly to counter long-standing Fāṭimid ambitions in that area. Toghrïl Beg's occupation of Baghdad had forced the Seljuk sultanate and the ʿAbbāsid caliphate into a symbiotic relationship, which committed the sultan to restoring Sunni orthodoxy and combating Shīʿite heterodoxy in the Fertile Crescent. In consequence, a principal concern of Alp Arslan from the time of his accession was the question of the military frontier with the Fāṭimids in northern Syria. By 1070, the matter of relations with the Fāṭimids was coming to a head: That year, the sharif of Mecca informed Alp Arslan that the *khutba* in Mecca was no longer being said in the name of the Fāṭimid caliph in Cairo but in that of the ʿAbbāsid caliph and the Seljuk sultan, a circumstance that the sultan sought to turn to his advantage. Furthermore, a delegation of rebellious Egyptian emirs was seeking his assistance in overthrowing Fāṭimid rule. Alp Arslan therefore began to plan the invasion of Fāṭimid Syria and perhaps to contemplate a subsequent invasion of Palestine and Egypt.

Meanwhile, however, the virtually independent Turkmens were raiding deep into Byzantine Anatolia, plundering throughout the countryside and, wherever possible, breaking into the cities, including those two later centers of Seljuk rule, Konya and Kayseri. The Byzantines, predictably, reacted to protect the line of communication with their most easterly outposts: Malatya, Diyarbakir, Antioch, and Edessa. In 1070, therefore, the Byzantine emperor, Romanus IV Diogenes, sent an expedition to reinforce these cities. While much obscurity surrounds Seljuk-Byzantine relations of this period, it appears that Alp Arslan, preoccupied with his plan to attack the Fāṭimid strongholds in Syria, agreed to sign a truce with the emperor. While the two imperial powers sought to stabilize the border zones between them, however, the sultan was in no position to control the Turkmens in eastern Anatolia, and it was their ongoing predatory raids that finally provoked the emperor into mounting a major military expedition against them. Assembling a huge force at his base in Erzurum, he proceeded to lead his troops into the Armenian districts north of Lake Van.

Alp Arslan, regarding this move as a breach of the recent truce, abandoned his siege of a Fāṭimid client in Aleppo and hastened to bar the emperor's further advance. The two armies met at Manzikert (now Malazgirt) and fought the great battle of August 26, 1071, which resulted in the utter destruction of the Byzantines and the capture of the emperor himself. Alp Arslan treated his captive honorably, releasing him in exchange for a ransom, promises of tribute and a marriage alliance, and probably cession of territory, but these arrangements were voided by the emperor's deposition and blinding on his return to Constantinople that same year. Hence, the issues at stake between the two empires were left unresolved. Following Manzikert, Alp Arslan had only a year to live, but during the reign of his son Malik Shāh (1073-1092), Sulaimān ibn Qutlumush, the son of Alp Arslan's old rival, penetrated Anatolia as far west as the Aegean Sea, capturing Nicaea (now İznik) around 1077.

The Battle of Manzikert has been correctly viewed as one of history's decisive battles, for it marked the formal beginning of the process whereby the Byzantines eventually suffered the permanent loss of provinces that were major sources of revenue and recruits; the Turks became the conquerors of, and eventually the dominant ethnic group in, Anatolia; and Christian and Hellenistic Asia Minor became Muslim Turkey. Indirectly, Manzikert led to the appeal by later Byzantine emperor Alexius I Comnenus (r. 1081-1118) for military assistance from Latin Christendom and hence to Pope Urban II's famous sermon at Clermont in 1095, which unleashed two centuries of crusading zeal in the Middle East and the eastern Mediterranean. In this light, the account of Manzikert that reached the Latin West through the writings of the historian of the First Crusade, William of Tyre, who heard that the battle "was fiercely contested by almost equal forces," bears examination. William was completely mistaken as to Alp Arslan's treatment of Romanus Diogenes, but his account, the stuff of legend, conformed to Christian preconceptions of their Islamic adversaries.

> The foe, magnificent but infidel, elated by his great success and rendered still more arrogant by victory, commanded that the emperor be brought before him. Seated upon his royal throne, he ordered Romanus to be thrown beneath his feet, and, to show his contempt for the Christian name and faith, in the presence of the attendant princes, he used the emperor's body as a footstool, mounting and dismounting upon it.

Although throughout his reign Alp Arslan's main concern (like Toghrïl Beg's) seems to have centered on western Iran and the Fertile Crescent, he could not altogether ignore his eastern borders with his Ghaznavid and Qarakhanid neighbors. As far as the Ghaznavids were concerned, the treaty that had followed the 1040 Seljuk victory at Dendenkan continued in force. With the Qarakhanids, now masters of Transoxiana (Bukhara, Samarqand, and western Farghana), there remained residual tension, for they were long-standing antagonists of the Seljuks and now their possessions included territory formerly ruled by Alp Arslan's father, Chaghrï Beg. Early in Alp Arslan's reign, the sultan had campaigned in the western Qarakhanid khanate, which was then ruled by the pious and respected Tamghach khan Ibrāhīm ibn Nasʿr. As the years passed, however, the two rulers gradually had developed a kind of modus vivendi exemplified by a series of marriage alliances, including the marriage of a daughter of Alp Arslan to Ibrāhīm's successor, Shams al-Mulk Nasʿr, and the marriage of Alp Arslan's heir, Malik Shāh, to a Qarakhanid princess. War broke out between Alp Arslan and Shams al-Mulk Nasʿr, however, in 1072. One version of the story asserts that Shams al-Mulk Nasʿr had caused the death of the sultan's daughter, suspecting her of having urged the Seljuks to invade his territory; Alp Arslan thereupon led a large army across the Amu Daryʾa. Soon after the crossing, he ordered the execution of a *mamlūk* who had disobeyed him. The condemned man, enraged at what he regarded as an act of injustice, broke loose from his escort and stabbed the sultan to death.

Significance

Building on the foundations laid by Toghrïl Beg, Alp Arslan consolidated and extended his predecessor's conquests to create an empire extending almost from the Mediterranean to the Pamirs. Under the aegis of his brilliant minister, Niẓām al-Mulk, that empire acquired the character of a traditional Irano-Islamic monarchy, with the Seljuks cast in the role of renovators of a hitherto decrepit political order. Inevitably, war and administrative tasks left Alp Arslan little opportunity to establish a reputation as a great patron, and the achievements of the

Seljuks in literature, architecture, and the decorative arts belong to a later age.

At Manzikert, Alp Arslan changed the course of Middle Eastern history, for his victory foreshadowed the end of Byzantine Christian dominance in Asia Minor and its ultimate Turkification and Islamization, while also contributing to the call for a crusade in Latin Christendom. Alp Arslan figures in the Muslim historiographical tradition as a brave soldier, a pious Muslim, a champion of the faith, and a just and, for the most part, magnanimous ruler.

—*Gavin R. G. Hambly*

FURTHER READING

Barthold, W. *Turkestan Down to the Mongol Invasion.* Translated by T. Minorsky. Edited by C. E. Bosworth. 4th ed. London: Gibb Memorial Trust, 1977. This authoritative study of those areas of Central Asia ruled by the Russian czars in the nineteenth century is the work of one of the greatest of Russian Islamicists. Covering the Islamic period down to the first quarter of the thirteenth century, it is especially good on the Seljuks and their contemporaries.

Bosworth, Clifford Edmund. *The New Islamic Dynasties: A Chronological and Genealogical Manual.* 1967. Rev. ed. New York: Columbia University Press, 1996. A historical survey of the Islamic dynasties, including the Seljuks in eastern Persian lands and elsewhere. Bibliography, index.

_______. "The Political and Dynastic History of the Iranian World (A.D. 1000-1217)." In *The Cambridge History of Iran*, vol. 5, edited by J. A. Boyle. Cambridge, England: Cambridge University Press, 1968. This chapter provides a masterly and very detailed review of the Seljuk period. The reign of Alp Arslan and the vizierate of Niẓām al-Mulk are both discussed.

Cahen, Claude. "Alp Arslan." In *The Encyclopaedia of Islam.* Vol. 1. 2d ed. Leiden, The Netherlands: E. J. Brill, 1960. This is the best short account of the career of Alp Arslan from an authoritative source.

_______. *Pre-Ottoman Turkey: A General Survey of the Material and Spiritual Culture and History, c. 1071-1330.* New York: Taplinger, 1968. This definitive study of the Seljuk period of Turkish history gives a straightforward, scholarly account of the rise of the Seljuks and their involvement in Anatolia prior to 1071.

Friendly, Alfred. *The Dreadful Day: The Battle of Manzikert, 1071.* London: Hutchinson, 1981. A highly readable but also very detailed account of Manzikert and the events leading up to it. Written for the nonspecialist.

Irwin, Robert. "Muslim Responses to the Crusades." *History Today* 47, no. 4 (April, 1997). Presents a rich overview of the Muslim perspective on the Crusades, including the responses of the Seljuks before the First Crusade in the late eleventh century. Provides photographs and a short list of further readings.

Lambton, Ann K. S. "The Internal Structure of the Saljuq Empire." In *The Cambridge History of Iran.* Vol. 5. Edited by J. A. Boyle. Cambridge, England: Cambridge University Press, 1968. This is an excellent account, by a leading authority, of the political and administrative institutions of the Seljuk Empire. It can be usefully supplemented by the same author's *Continuity and Change in Medieval Persia* (Albany: State University of New York Press, 1988).

Lev, Yaacov, ed. *The Medieval Mediterranean: Peoples, Economies and Cultures, 400-1453.* Vol. 9 in *War and Society in the Eastern Mediterranean, Seventh-Fifteenth Centuries.* Leiden, The Netherlands: Brill, 1997. Explores the world of the Crusades and other military encounters in the Middle East and the greater Mediterranean area, including Egypt from the time before the Seljuks to the fall of Constantinople in 1453. Topics include armaments and supplies, regional administration, and the impact of the Crusaders on rural populations. Good for a broad overview of a thousand year history of military conflict between Christians, Muslims, Jews, and other peoples.

Luther, K. A. "Alp Arslān." In *Encyclopaedia Iranica.* Vol. 1. Edited by Ehsan Yarshater. Boston: Routledge and Kegan Paul, 1985. Particularly valuable for its listing of the sources available for the study of Alp Arslan's reign.

Müneccimbasi, Ahmet ibn Lutfullah. *A History of Sharvan and Darband in the Tenth-Eleventh Centuries.* Translated and edited by V. Minorsky. Cambridge, England: W. Heffer, 1958. This translation and abridgment of an eleventh century work dealing with the minor Islamic dynasties of the Seljuk period in the area north of the Araks River and south of the Caucasus Mountains is essential reading for understanding the circumstances that drew Alp Arslan into this region.

Rice, Tamara Talbot. *The Seljuks in Asia Minor.* New York: Praeger, 1961. A popular account of the Seljuks, their culture and arts, in the series Ancient Peoples and Places. Attractively illustrated, it is particularly useful as a guide to the better known Seljuk monuments in Turkey.

Vryonis, Speros. *The Decline of Medieval Hellenism in Asia Minor and the Process of Islamization from the Eleventh Through the Fifteenth Century.* Berkeley: University of California Press, 1971. This fine study of the complex interaction of political, social, and cultural developments as Byzantine rule gave way to that of the Turks in Anatolia sheds much light on the circumstances under which the Turkmens penetrated the Byzantine frontier both before and after the Battle of Manzikert.

See also: Maḥmūd of Ghazna; Niẓām al-Mulk; Omar Khayyám; Osman I; Urban II.

Related articles in *Great Events from History: The Middle Ages, 477-1453*: 1054: Beginning of the Rome-Constantinople Schism; August 26, 1071: Battle of Manzikert; 1077: Seljuk Dynasty Is Founded; November 27, 1095: Pope Urban II Calls the First Crusade; 1147-1149: Second Crusade; 1150: Venetian Merchants Dominate Trade with the East; 1189-1192: Third Crusade; 1204: Knights of the Fourth Crusade Capture Constantinople; 1217-1221: Fifth Crusade.

Amalasuntha

Queen of the Ostrogoths (r. 534-535)

Amalasuntha ruled the Ostrogothic realm with success. She issued legislation protecting women's marriages while still regent for her young son, after whose death she asserted her own right to the throne.

Born: c. 495; probably Ravenna, Kingdom of the Ostrogoths (now in Italy)

Died: April 30, 535; an island in Lake Bolsena, Tuscany (now in Italy)

Also known as: Amalasuentha; Amalasuintha; Amalaswintha

Areas of achievement: Government and politics, women's rights

Early Life

Amalasuntha (ah-mahl-ah-SUHN-thah) was the youngest daughter of Theodoric the Great, king of the Germanic tribe of the Ostrogoths (East Goths), who, with the approval of the East Roman (Byzantine) emperor Zeno in Constantinople, established Ostrogothic rule in Italy. In 493, Theodoric entered Ravenna, the city at the mouth of the River Po in northeastern Italy, which became his capital. Theodoric swiftly arranged a series of political marriages to strengthen his ties to the other Germanic tribes, who were likewise establishing kingdoms in the former western Roman provinces. His two daughters, the fruit of a youthful relationship, were married to the rulers of the Visigoths (West Goths) and the Burgundians, while Theodoric himself took to wife Audefleda, the sister of King Clovis of the Franks, who during those years was establishing his rule over France. Amalasuntha was the only child of this marriage.

A mosaic still to be seen on the walls of the church of Sant'Apollinare Nuovo in Ravenna depicts the city as it looked in the days when Amalasuntha was growing up. The palace of Theodoric had a vast arcaded courtyard with marble columns that undoubtedly were the spoils from some pagan temple, for the Ostrogoths had been converted to the Arian form of Christianity in the fourth century. As Arians they held that Christ was lesser in majesty than God the Father, a creed that differentiated them sharply from the Orthodox Italians over whom they had established their hegemony. Behind the palace, the mosaicist shows two round domes, belonging to the baptistries, one for the Arians, one for the Orthodox, which still stand, and a sturdy crenellated wall surrounding the town.

Amalasuntha, whom Theodoric chose to carry on his line, was given an education fit for a queen. Cassiodorus, the Italian who was to become her secretary, waxes eloquent in a letter to the Roman senators on her linguistic ability. Not only does she speak her native Gothic, he says, but also she is fluent in both Greek and Latin, conversing easily in those tongues with envoys. Her knowledge of literature, which Cassiodorus extols, would have included Greek and Latin classics, and probably some saints' lives. Italy was prosperous under the wise and just rule of Theodoric, and no discrimination was allowed against the Orthodox, Jews, or Samaritans. One of the mosaics of Sant'Apollinare, which contains the earliest extended sequence of depictions of the life of Christ, shows him at the well with the Samaritan woman, who is dressed in a colorful striped robe. The picture would have reminded Amalasuntha to practice tolerance.

Bishop Gregory of Tours tells a story, best discounted

as slanderous rumor against the Arian sect, in his *Historia Francorum* (late sixth century; *The History of the Franks*, 1927), that Amalasuntha had poisoned her own mother with the wine of communion. God, asserts Gregory, would not have permitted such crimes in an Orthodox church. The reason he gives for the quarrel of the princess with her mother may, however, have some truth in it. He says Audefleda interrupted the elopement of Amalasuntha with the low-born Traguilla, who was punished with death. Amalasuntha's family belonged to the royal clan of the Amals, from whom Gothic rulers were chosen. Her father discovered a portionless Amal named Eutharic living in Visigothic Spain and arranged for him to marry Amalasuntha in 515.

KINGS OF THE OSTROGOTHS, 474-774

Reign	*Ruler*
474-526	THEODORIC THE GREAT
526-534	Athalaric
534-536	Theodahad (with AMALASUNTHA)
536-540	Vitiges (Witiges)
540	Theodobald (Heldebadus)
541	Eraric
541-552	Totila (Baduila)
552-553	Teias
553-568	Roman domination (Byzantine emperor Justinian I)
568-774	Lombard domination
774	Frankish conquest

Eutharic was ceremonially adopted by the Byzantine emperor Justin I (uncle of Justinian I) to strengthen the rights of the couple. They had two children, a girl, Matesuntha, and a son, Athalaric, whom Theodoric hoped would someday rule his kingdom. The mosaics of Sant'-Apollinare show Christ enthroned on one side of the altar, his mother, Mary, on the other, seated on a Byzantine-style throne and robed in royal purple, her infant son on her lap. Mary's prominent position in the mosaics may reflect the showcasing of Amalasuntha and her son at the court of Theodoric, and Amalasuntha herself could well have been shown leading a procession of court ladies with gifts for the Virgin, for the train of women saints that now graces the wall is an Orthodox replacement for earlier mosaics of Theodoric's time.

LIFE'S WORK

Amalasuntha's husband Eutharic predeceased King Theodoric, who died in 526. As was customary in both Gothic and Roman tradition, Amalasuntha, as a woman, was passed over as heir in favor of her son Athalaric, a boy of about eight. Amalasuntha, then about thirty, became regent and directed the government. It was a century of powerful queen mothers, such as the Frankish Fredegunde and her rival Brunhilde.

Two independent contemporary accounts exist of the rise and fall of Amalasuntha, one by Jordanes, *Getica* (551; *The Gothic History Jordanes*, 1908, revised 1915), who was a Goth residing in Italy, and the other, more circumstantial narrative, by the Greek Procopius, *Polemon* (552; *The History of the Wars of the Emperor Justinian*, 1653). Procopius praises Amalasuntha for her intelligence and zeal for justice but disparages her personality as too masculine. A stone-portrait head of the queen shows her with a mild, round face and soulful eyes, but Procopius judges her determination to rule as unfeminine.

It is from the letter collection of her secretary Cassiodorus, *Variae* (537; *The Variae of Magnus Aurelius Cassiodorus Senator*, 1886; better known as the *Variae*), that one can best understand the policies of Amalasuntha during her son's regency and her own short period of independent rule. In his encomium addressed to the Roman senate, Cassiodorus praises not only her learning but also her military preparedness, reporting that the troops under her generals have campaigned on the Danube and stood firm against the Franks. At the same time, Cassiodorus attempts to show her modestly feminine demeanor by characterizing her as quiet, judging legal cases in a few words.

Cassiodorus's letter collection includes additions to the laws of Theodoric issued during the regency of Amalasuntha. Her edicts show that one of her concerns was to repress expropriation of land by the Goths from the Italians; all were to have their rights under her government. She wished one law to apply to both Goths and Romans, and she sought to protect the status of married women. If a man attempted to seduce the wife of another, he would be severely punished. His own marriage would be dissolved, or, if a bachelor, he would be forbidden to marry. Bigamy was outlawed, and if a married man established an extramarital relationship his concubine and her children would become the slaves of his wife.

A letter to the Roman senate insisting that teachers not have their salaries curtailed reflects Amalasuntha's concern for education. How much more important it is to reward teachers of ethics and rhetoric, the letter points out, than the actors whom the government maintains for the enjoyment of the populace. Her interest in art and the adornment of her city is shown in a letter to the Byzantine emperor Justinian I requesting that he facilitate the shipping of marble statues collected in his realm by her agents.

The cultivated education Amalasuntha was giving her son, however, met with opposition from a faction of the Goths who insisted that Athalaric be brought up in their native tradition. Amalasuntha was forced to give way and lost all influence with the young king. The hardy warrior upbringing of his ancestors was not substituted for Greek and Latin. Instead, Athalaric was encouraged to run wild with a group of slightly older Ostrogothic boys and, Procopius reports, he fell into drunkenness and promiscuity while still a young teen.

Amalasuntha realized her situation was precarious. In her world a boy was considered an adult at the age of fourteen. Athalaric was now of age but was unfit to rule and was estranged from his mother. She therefore negotiated with the emperor Justinian, who promised her a place of refuge should it become necessary. At the same time, she moved boldly to have assassinated three leading members of the Gothic opposition, whom she considered traitors to her government. In the midst of these dangers, in 534, Athalaric died at age sixteen. According to Procopius, his debaucheries killed him.

Gothic custom decreed an Amal should wear the crown, but the rule of a woman in her own right was unprecedented. Women had, indeed, ruled the Roman Empire in the previous century, but always with a male colleague. The daughter of Emperor Theodosius, Galla Placidia, had ruled the west from Ravenna in the name of her lackluster brother and then her son. Pulcheria, the granddaughter of Theodosius, had ruled the east with her brother. After his death, despite her early vow of virginity, she entered into a nominal marriage with Marcian in order to have a male associate on the throne.

For Amalasuntha, her co-ruler must be a man and an Amal. The only candidate was her cousin Theodahad, the son of Theodoric's sister. He had fallen foul of Amalasuntha's decree forbidding Goths to despoil the property of Italians and she had forced him to give up some of his vast Tuscan estates. Some historians have therefore deemed it folly for Amalasuntha to share the rule of Ostrogothic Italy with her cousin, but in fact she had no other choice. They became joint rulers, as Pulcheria had shared rule with her brother Theodosius II.

Theodahad speedily showed himself a villain. He had Amalasuntha confined to an island in Lake Bolsena in Tuscany. Soon thereafter she was murdered in the steam bath. We know the killers were relatives of the three Ostrogoths whose assassination she had earlier arranged, but it is less clear who was behind their deed. In *The History of the Wars of the Emperor Justinian*, Procopius blames Theodahad, and it is indeed unlikely that her cousin was ignorant of the conspiracy, although he protested his innocence. Procopius, however, also wrote a secret version of the history of his times, *Anecdota* (c. 550; *Secret History of the Court of the Emperor Justinian*, 1674), published after the death of Justinian. In this work, Procopius alleges that it was Justinian's envoy to Italy, Peter, who urged Theodahad to have Amalasuntha killed. The emperor was innocent of the deed, but his wife, Theodora, fearful lest the beautiful Amalasuntha be given refuge in the east and steal the heart of Justinian, engineered her death.

So writes Procopius, but his hatred of Theodora was by no means rational. There is, however, some independent confirmation of his charges. Cassiodorus continued in his post as royal secretary and preserved in his letter collection a missive from Theodahad to Theodora darkly hinting that the king had carried out the wishes of the empress. Likewise a letter from his wife Queen Gudeliva to Theodora alludes mysteriously to a favor done the empress. Whether or not Theodora ordered the death of Amalasuntha, it seems likely that Theodahad and Gudeliva knew it would not be unwelcome to her. Amalasuntha was about forty at the time of the death. Her daughter Matesuntha survived her and was married first to a Goth and then to Germanus, the nephew of Justinian I.

Significance

In a century of strong queens, such as Theodora, Brunhilde, and Fredegunde, Amalasuntha stands out as a woman of pure life and high ideals. She believed in justice for Goth and Italian alike, she advocated education for youth, and she worked to eliminate corruption. Amalasuntha courageously attempted to maintain her right to the throne as the daughter of Theodoric after her son's death. Other women could learn from Amalasuntha's career, despite her tragic end. Her people mourned their loss and swiftly spurned Theodahad. Italy, prosperous under her rule, was subjected to incessant war as the troops of Justinian invaded, proclaiming vengeance for her death. These forces were at length replaced by the Germanic Lombards, and at the end of the sixth century Italy again found a great Germanic queen in Theodelinda.

—*Beverly Berg*

FURTHER READING

Browning, Robert. *Justinian and Theodora*. New York: Praeger, 1971. Browning includes coverage of the career of Amalasuntha and photographs of her stone portrait head and the mosaics of Sant'Apollinare Nuovo. This is a good introduction to the age of Justinian.

Duckett, Eleanor Shipley. *The Gateway to the Middle Ages*. New York: Macmillan, 1938. This well-written study of the sixth century and its writers has never been bettered. There is extensive coverage of Cassiodorus, and in the process Duckett recounts much of the story of his patrons, Theodoric and Amalasuntha.

Frankforter, A. Daniel. "Amalasuntha, Procopius, and a Woman's Place." *Journal of Women's History* 8, no. 2 (Summer, 1996): 41ff. Considers Procopius's writings on Amalsuntha and the reasons for her murder.

Thiebaux, Marcelle, ed. *The Writings of Medieval Women*. 2d ed. New York: Garland, 1994. Thiebaux has a good chapter on Amalasuntha, including a translation of the four letters in Cassiodorus's collection issued in her own name rather than that of her son.

Wallace-Hadrill, J. M. *The Barbarian West, A.D. 400-1000*. New York: Harper, 1962. A compact and reliable account of early medieval times, including the Ostrogothic kingdom of Italy.

SEE ALSO: Cassiodorus; Clovis; Fredegunde; Gregory of Tours; Theodora; Theodoric the Great.

RELATED ARTICLES in *Great Events from History: The Middle Ages, 477-1453*: 496: Baptism of Clovis; 524: Imprisonment and Death of Boethius; 568-571: Lombard Conquest of Italy.

AN LUSHAN

Chinese rebel leader

An Lushan led an attempted coup d'état *against reigning Tang emperor Xuanzong, which triggered a tumultuous, decades-long civil war, leading to centuries of China's decline at the hands of its neighbors.*

BORN: 703; Sogdiana, Central Asia (now in Uzbekistan)
DIED: 757; Shaanxi Province, China
ALSO KNOWN AS: An Lu-shan (Wade-Giles)
AREAS OF ACHIEVEMENT: Military, warfare and conquest

EARLY LIFE

An Lushan (ahn loo-shahn) was the general commanding the three armies of China during the reign of Emperor Xuanzong (Hsüan-tsung, r. 712-756) during the Tang Dynasty (T'ang; 618-907). The truth of his parentage, early life, and upbringing are difficult to interpret from official Chinese accounts, as many events have clearly been fabricated to disparage An Lushan's reputation. An Lushan's rebellion (755-763) counted as one of the final chapters in the long, famous rule of Emperor Xuanzong and one of the first steps in a long decline of China's fortunes. In China, the story of the An Lushan rebellion is principally told from the point of view of the emperor Xuanzong and his beautiful concubine, Yang Guifei (Yang Kuei-fei), as a cautionary tale warning of the impermanence of worldly love and the dangers of being distracted from crucial tasks.

Virtually all the accounts of the young An Lushan variously describe him as a depraved thief, an orphan, and a vicious thug. Although it is probable that as a young man he led a seminomadic and sordid existence, the accusations against him have primarily been made by later ethnic Chinese writers to vilify a man they held responsible for the destruction of the empire.

Scholars have likewise puzzled over the truth of An Lushan's name and origin. His name suggests that he was of Sogdian descent, from the Central Asian steppes, and various other sources claim his family may have been Turkish or from Samarqand. His given name, Lushan, is a Chinese corruption of Roxana, who was the Iranian wife of Alexander the Great, bolstering the theory that An Lushan was of Sogdian or Parthian descent. He was keenly aware that his race was held against him throughout most of his life.

For all these reasons, not much is known about the early life of An Lushan until he became a member of the Chinese military border patrol, in northeastern China near the Korean border, perhaps as early as age eighteen. It is not certain how the An family arrived in northeastern China from Central Asia. An Lushan's father may have worked in the markets along the Silk Road as a trader, and many accounts mention that An Lushan was fluent in numerous languages. Other scholars point to clan warfare in Central Asia that may have dislodged the family, as An Lushan's mother came from a noble family. Regardless, by 713, An's family had fled Central Asia and settled in China. Nothing is known of his existence for the next few decades, until his name surfaces again in 733, as the lieutenant of a military general who won a major victory over the border tribes of the Xi (Hsi) and the Khitan in the northeast. As it is unlikely that he could have risen to this high rank and been given the authority to command troops in battle without long service in the military, presumably An Lushan had served for more than a decade in the army by the time he was thirty-three years old.

LIFE'S WORK

The Tang Dynasty, during which An Lushan's military career progressed, represented China at its height militarily, economically, and culturally. Its influence dominated Central and South Asia, reaching Vietnam, and East Asia, extending to Japan. Despite its strengths, however, the dynasty lurched from succession crisis to succession crisis, interrupted by long periods in which a capable ruler would consolidate the bureaucracy and resume the upward trend of the dynasty's fortunes.

A succession crisis had marked the beginning of Xuanzong's reign. Although Xuanzong is often revered as the greatest ruler of China during the imperial period, it is remarkable that he ever became emperor. The Tang Dynasty had precipitously lurched from ruler to ruler ever since the abdication of the second emperor of the dynasty, Taizong (T'ai-tsung; r. 627-649). Although many of Taizong's later years were absorbed with the succession, the emperor never found a capable heir and eventually was succeeded by Gaozong (Kao-tsung; r. 650-683), a well-meaning but inept son. Gaozong suffered a stroke in 660, and his reign was overshadowed by the domination of his wife, the later empress Wu Hou (r. 690-705). Wu Hou was the true power behind the throne in China from 660 to 690 and ruled in her own name from 690 until her death in 705. Xuanzong had barely survived as an infant during Wu Hou's reign of terror. His mother, the concubine Dou, had been executed, and most of his childhood had been spent as a virtual prisoner in the imperial palace. On becoming ruler of China, however, Xuanzong fully lived up to his honorific title of Ming Huan (brilliant emperor).

As emperor, Xuanzong's first steps included dismantling the harem and removing the courtiers and concubines who had been running the government since the 660's. He replaced those in power with impartial officials who had acquired their positions by passing the civil service examinations. The emperor strictly forbade his wife's family from interfering in politics or becoming involved in nationally sensitive industries such as iron, silk, or salt. Xuanzong retained power over the provinces by enforcing a system that regularly rotated provincial governors and forced accountancy before and after each rotation. This greatly curtailed the corruption that had run rampant through the country over the past four generations. Xuanzong's reliance on scholar-officials directly contributed to the success of the administration, but a closer look reveals a subtle politics that laid the groundwork for An Lushan's rebellion.

The court during the height of Xuanzong's reign was roughly split between two factions: the literati, who had passed the civil service examinations and placed emphasis on writing memorials to the throne, studious readings of history, and cultivating a sense of culture, art, and poetics, and the pragmatists, who prided themselves on problem solving and practical experience. The latter group had not had the privileges of education or a noble birth but instead had made their name as capable administrators.

The pragmatists were led by Li Linfu, who helped restore order to the census rolls and diversify the state's reliance on taxes on silk. Li Linfu was a minor provincial official who made his name through the provision of grain and other key products to military units on the frontier. A series of rapid promotions brought him to the highest levels of imperial power. The ascendancy of Li Linfu was to begin a subtle reshaping of the Chinese imperial court. The literati resented the new administrators, and seemingly innocent clashes involving political policy masked the direct attempts both sides were making to seize total control.

Meanwhile, Xuanzong's wife had failed to bear a male heir. The frustrated Xuangzong began to consort with Yang Guifei, a courtesan of divine beauty. Her real name was Yang Yuhuan; *guifei*, which meant "first-class prostitute," was a somewhat pejorative title. Soon after entering the emperor's court, Yang Guifei entranced Xuanzong, who soon lost his profound interest in governing and began to focus solely on her comforts and interests. Although he had prevented his wife's family from taking on court positions, Xuanzong granted major positions and powers to Yang Guifei's family, and in particular her cousin, Yang Guozhong (Yang Kuo-chung).

Such was the situation when the first major battle between East Asia and Central Asia was waged. In the Battle of Talas River (751), a Muslim Arabic army dealt a devastating blow to the Tang forces, who were commanded by general Gao Xianzhi. The humiliating defeat led to a settlement of Uighur Turks living in Hami, in modern Gansu Province, and the ultimate loss of Dunhuang, the famous Buddhist settlement on the Silk Road.

Li Linfu was able to heap blame on the literati for the disaster and install An Lushan as the new general commanding the three armies. Yang Guifei, seeing the importance of counterbalancing political and military interests, adopted An Lushan as her son.

As the intrigue grew, palace ministers were torn between backing military leaders and the family of Yang Guifei. As the emperor lost interest in all but his affair with his concubine, two sides emerged: the family of Yang Guifei, as represented by Yang Guozhong; and the military generals of An Lushan, backed by his minister Shi Suming (Shih Ssu-ming) and Li Linfu.

The proximate cause of An Lushan's rebellion was Yang Guozhong's accession as prime minister in 755, a post An Lushan himself coveted. When An Lushan marched on the capital that winter, Chang'an fell without a battle. Xuanzong escaped to Chengdu (in modern Sichuan Province) but was forced by his bodyguard to order the execution of Yang Guifei en route. Perhaps there is no more fitting description of the situation than that of the legendary Chinese poet Bo Juyi (Po Chü-yi; 772-846):

> The emperor could not save her. He could only cover his face
> And later when he looked, that place of blood and tears
> Was hidden in a yellow dust blown by cold wind . . .
> Earth endures, heaven endures; sometime both shall end,
> While this unending sorrow goes on forever.

However, neither the death of Yang Guifei nor that of An Lushan himself would end the rebellion. Xuanzong escaped to Chengdu and abdicated in favor of his son Suzong (Su-tsung; r. 756-762). An Lushan was slain in 757 by his own son, while his ally Shi Suming remained in power. The majority of Suzong's reign was taken up with fighting the civil war, which did not end until 763.

The war was an absolute disaster for China. Both sides employed scorched-earth and forced-conscription tactics, which resulted in a near total destruction of agriculture. The ensuing famines, coupled with the war, resulted in almost unimaginable numbers of deaths. China's population dropped from 53 million in 754 to 17 million in 764. Although ultimately Suzong's heir, Daizong (Tai-tsung; r. 762-779), would end the war and restore the legitimacy of the Tang, the devastation prohibited the dynasty from ever regaining its previous level of achievement. Invasion on all sides led to the loss of significant territories, and the Song Dynasty (Sung; 960-1279) would fail to achieve the restoration of the power and glory of the Tang.

SIGNIFICANCE

The impact of the An Lushan rebellion on world history cannot be overstated. Before the rebellion, China was unquestionably the most powerful nation on earth, with economic and military influence that ranged from Japan to Indonesia to the Middle East. The nearly 60 percent drop in population and retrenchment of its border military forces led to the loss of Chinese suzerainty over nearly 50 percent of its land area and hastened the fall of the Tang Dynasty. With the serious decline in military forces and population, China was forced to continually retrench and sign numerous iniquitous treaties with border kingdoms for the sake of peace. Although it recovered somewhat in the Song Dynasty, China failed to restore its former glory, making it an easy target for the Mongols, who made it their first target during the conquests of Genghis Khan.

—*Jason D. Sanchez*

FURTHER READING

Ebrey, Patricia. *Chinese Civilization: A Sourcebook*. New York: Free Press, 1993. A useful overview on Chinese history from ancient times to the present, including excellent bibliographies.

Graff, David. *Medieval Chinese Warfare, 300-900*. New York: Routledge, 2002. Covers military service on the frontier, where An Lushan served before becoming a Chinese general. Deals directly with the An Lushan uprising and gives highlights of a few of the major battles.

Li Chenyang, ed. *Sage and the Second Sex: Confucianism, Ethics, and Gender*. Chicago: Open Court, 2000. Explores, among other topics, how the Yang Guifei affair was viewed by the court and the backlash that women's rights took after the restoration of imperial sovereignty.

Pulleyblank, Edward G. *The Background of the Rebellion of An Lu-Shan*. New York: Oxford University Press, 1955. Pulleyblank's work remains the classic regarding the period and has an excellent bibliography.

SEE ALSO: Genghis Khan; Kublai Khan; Taizong; Wu Hou.

RELATED ARTICLES in *Great Events from History: The Middle Ages, 477-1453*: 618: Founding of the Tang Dynasty; 690-705: Reign of Empress Wu; 751: Battle of Talas River; 755-763: Rebellion of An Lushan; 907-960: Period of Five Dynasties and Ten Kingdoms; 960: Founding of the Song Dynasty; 960-1279: Scholar-Official Class Flourishes Under Song Dynasty.

Blessed Angela of Foligno
Italian mystic

Blessed Angela of Foligno, a Franciscan mystic, explored the ways to experience God within one's soul in her works; her desire to suffer the agony of Christ's crucifixion won widespread admiration.

Born: 1248; Foligno, Umbria (now in Italy)
Died: January 4, 1309; Foligno, Umbria
Also known as: Lella; Mistress of the Theologians
Area of achievement: Religion and theology

Early Life

Blessed Angela of Foligno (ahn-JEHL-ah uhv foh-LEEN-yoh) was born to wealthy parents in the town of Foligno. Little is known about her childhood. She was no doubt influenced by the reputation of Saint Francis of Assisi (c. 1181-1226) who experienced a public conversion in Assisi, only a few miles from Foligno. Angela spoke in the Umbrian dialect of Italian and may have learned to read and write as well. She was married with several children.

Sometime in her late thirties, Angela began her religious conversion, moving toward a life of spiritual penitence and intense religiosity. In her later writings, she related that she underwent a spiritual crisis in which she began to fear hell and claimed to have committed sins so shameful that she could not tell her confessor, even as she continued to take Communion. Although one scholar has speculated that she may have committed a grave "sin of the flesh," it remains highly probable that she was referring only to rich foods, fancy clothes, and intimate relations with her husband in an environment that cherished fasting, poverty, and chastity. Inspired by a vision of Saint Francis of Assisi, Angela eventually confessed to a Franciscan friar, thereby introducing herself to Franciscan ideals of poverty and the sacrament of penance to atone for one's sins. Scholars believe this portion of her conversion may have been complete by 1285. As a symbol of her commitment to her new life, and in imitation of Saint Francis, Angela visited the Church of Saint Francis in the Foligno square, removed her status-laden clothing, and stripped naked, pledging to remain perpetually chaste. She also began to put aside food, head coverings, and her better clothes.

Angela's account of her journey to know and experience Christ allowed her to reflect on her life as mother and wife. Modern readers are surprised by Angela's deprecating remarks concerning her familial burdens. Feeling no love and embroiled in her husband's "slanders and injustices," Angela wrote that the rapid deaths of her husband, children, and mother came as a relief to her, as she had prayed to be free from them and her mother was an obstacle to her new religious life. Soon after the death of her family and after a pilgrimage around 1291, Angela sold her properties, gave away most of what she owned to the poor, and made the decision to became a Franciscan tertiary, a layperson associated with the Franciscan order.

Life's Work

As a tertiary, Angela remained part of the lay community. Wearing a simple gray cloak, Angela lived in a Foligno house in the company of a woman, Masazuola. Her dedication to the life of Saint Francis meant imitating his compassion for the poor, lepers, and the sick.

In her early forties, Angela began to receive visions and alternately achieved bouts of ecstasy and despair. Angela's journey to an intimate relationship with Christ was recorded by a Franciscan friar, Frater A., a relative who served as her spiritual adviser and was affiliated with the Church of Saint Francis in Foligno. Scholars frequently refer to this "Frater A." as Fra Arnaldo, although no evidence establishes this link. As her confessor, Frater A. heard her elaborate visions and, although initially skeptical, began to record her words.

The collaboration between the friar and Angela produced the *Memoriale* (1296 or 1297; translated together with the *Instructionum* as *The Book of the Visions and Instructions of Blessed Angela of Foligno*, 1888; best known as *Memoriale*), a thirty-step account of Angela's path to experience Christ within her soul. In her account of her experiences until around 1296, Angela depicted the arduous road that sinners such as herself must confront. Initially consumed by extraordinary sinfulness, misery, and sorrow, Angela, after numerous public confessions, ultimately succeeded in her journey to feel divine grace, rapture, and enlightenment. After she united with the Holy Trinity, God provided her with approval of her life and hoped that her life would serve as a model for others. Jesus told her in one mystical encounter:

> God almighty has deposited much love in you, more than in any woman of this city. He takes delight in you and is fully satisfied with you and your companion. Try to see to it that your lives are a light for all those who wish to look on them. A harsh judgment awaits those who look at your lives but do not act accordingly.

The *Memoriale* served as a manual for others to achieve a mystical union with God, and for this reason, Angela related her initial lack of confidence in achieving her spiritual quest and her exposé of previously "sinful ways." Her own struggles were intended to serve as a source of inspiration for others, and indeed they did, as this work became popular in the Middle Ages.

When Angela dictated in her Umbrian dialect, the friar took down her words as she spoke them and translated her ideas into Latin, reading back the text to check for errors. Although she admitted that all that he had written was "true and without lie," she once scolded her scribe for not conveying the divine essence of the vision. The friar sometimes expressed shock and embarrassment over Angela's extreme behavior. However, he was careful to point out that Angela represented the Church's viewpoints, and even examinations by inquisitors, Franciscans, and cardinals could find no false teachings. In the medieval mindset, the text represented a collaboration of God who sent the visions to Angela, Angela who revealed the visions, and the confessor and scribe who asked questions of Angela pressuring her to respond, listened to and copied down her responses, and then translated the responses into Latin, sometimes organizing the material for clarity.

Scholars debate the degree to which the *Memoriale* represents the authentic voice of Angela. While acknowledging collaboration between the friar and Angela, many scholars argue that is possible to extract Angela's words, ideas, and meaning from the text, especially in an age in which mystics prized the oral tradition and dictation was commonplace. One scholar has noted that many of the most revered religious men and women dictated their ideas, including Jesus, Buddha, and Hildegarde of Bingen. In doing so, the sacredness and immediacy of the visionary experience is preserved.

The *Memoriale* began to be circulated around 1297, and after Angela's death, hand-written and dictated letters as well as spiritual treatises were compiled to form thirty-six chapters of *Instructionum*. Together these two works are sometimes referred to as the *Beatae Angelae de Fulginio visionum et instructionum liber* (*The Book of the Visions and Instructions of Blessed Angela of Foligno*, 1888), and it is through these texts that Angela has come to be viewed as an author, mystic, and penitential.

Angela's visionary experiences are unique for their vividness, their accessibility, and their focus on the crucified body of Christ. She was nicknamed the "mistress of the theologians," and her texts remain immensely significant for understanding the religious environment of the Middle Ages. The goal of the *Memoriale* was to establish emotional and spiritual contact with God. As Angela stated, "What I wanted was that God would make me actually feel." She did not want to hear a sermon about the Holy Trinity unless she felt the presence of the Trinity within herself. She described the process of "elevating the soul" in order to see Christ as one of reflecting on his suffering and crucifixion, even speaking aloud if necessary to achieve a mystical union with him. Her dialogue with God was intimate and emotional, frequently described as an amorous relationship.

The intensity of Angela's visions allowed her to see the physicality of Christ. In various visions, Christ appeared, revealing his throat, neck, or arms, beautiful and divine. Other times, his eyes became visible in the host, and once the Christ child appeared in the host, enthroned and about twelve years in age. The vision of a wounded, bleeding Christ allowed her to drink the blood from his wounds: "He called me and said that I should put my mouth to the wound in his side. And I was given to understand that that by this he would cleanse me." Christ embraced her, and on one visit to his tomb, she kissed his mouth, "from which, she added, a delightful fragrance emanated." So intense was Angela's passion for Christ that tears often burned her flesh, and she was forced to cool her body with water. This emotionalism and direct link to Christ through amorous dialogue allowed her to come to know that her soul was married to God.

In her search to imitate Jesus and experience Christ within herself, Angela frequently sought extreme measures. Self-defilement, the denial of food, and severe abjection were part of a greater plan to come to know Christ in her soul. After they had finished bathing the feet of lepers, Angela and her companion Masazuola drank the water, reflecting on its sweetness and comparing it to Holy Communion. Reflecting continuously on the suffering and torture of Christ's passion, Angela asked to die, to be tortured, to be made to bleed, to have a rope tightened around her neck, and to be crucified "by a very vile instrument." For Angela, this was necessary as Christ himself had been crucified because of her sinful nature.

As a spiritual mother, Angela also provided leadership within the Franciscan order, advising members of the order whom she dubbed "my sons" and "my little children." Ubertino da Casale, a member of the Spiritual Franciscans, attributed his conversion to Angela's "ardent virtue." Angela died in 1309, and her tomb may be visited today in the Church of Saint Francis in Foligno. Although never canonized officially as a saint, she was revered locally, beatified in 1701, and today the Franciscan order celebrates her feast day.

Significance

Angela remains one of the greatest mystics of the Middle Ages, exerting tremendous influence on later mystics. Like other holy women of the Middle Ages, Angela of Foligno found power and status in religion, expressed herself through the oral and written word, and came to be venerated despite her lay status. Angela's text was widely read throughout Europe, and it remains one of the earliest printed Italian texts in the vernacular. Her book was frequently read to understand the immediacy of Christ, and like other medieval mystics of the thirteenth century, her visions and accounts were seen as symbols of sanctity.

Angela is frequently included among those holy women who sought self-mortification in the extreme. Although remembered today for her desire to drink the blood of Jesus, she remains significant as an author of one of the most important texts of medieval mysticism and as a supreme example of a medieval woman admired for her religiosity and for openly living the life she desired.

—*Shelley Wolbrink*

Further Reading

Angela da Foligno. *Complete Works*. Translated by Paul Lachance. New York: Paulist Press, 1993. An English translation of Angela's works with a detailed introduction and footnotes.

Arcangeli, Tiziana. "Re-reading a Mis-known and Misread Mystic: Angela da Foligno." *Annali d'italianistica* 13 (1995): 41-78. A useful article for understanding the historiography of Angela and for detailing misconceptions.

Lavalva, Rosamaria. "The Language of Vision in Angela da Foligno's *Liber de vera fidelium experientia*." *Stanford Italian Review* 11 (1991): 103-122. Argues for the importance of the oral tradition of Angela's visions.

Mazzoni, Christina, ed. *Angela of Foligno's Memorial*. Translated by John Cirignano. Rochester, N.Y.: D. S. Brewer, 2000. Abridged text with insightful analysis.

Petroff, Elizabeth. "Writing the Body: Male and Female in the Writings of Marguerite D'Oingt, Angela of Foligno, and Umiltå of Faenza." In *Body and Soul: Essays on Medieval Women and Mysticism*. New York: Oxford University Press, 1994. An analysis of the gendered images of body employed by medieval mystics, including Angela.

Sagnella, Mary Ann. "Carnal Metaphors and Mystical Discourse in Angela da Foligno's *Liber*." *Annali d'italianistica* 13 (1995): 79-90. Discusses the rigorous asceticism of Angela's mystical union with Christ.

See also: Beatrice of Nazareth; Saint Catherine of Siena; Saint Francis of Assisi; Hildegard von Bingen; Joan of Arc; Julian of Norwich; Margery Kempe; Marguerite Porete.

Related articles in *Great Events from History: The Middle Ages, 477-1453*: 12th-14th centuries: Social and Political Impact of Leprosy; April 16, 1209: Founding of the Franciscans.

Fra Angelico

Italian artist

Fra Angelico is best known for adapting the most advanced artistic techniques of his time (perspective and brilliant use of color and line) to extraordinary evocations of purely spiritual subjects.

Born: c. 1400; Vicchio, Tuscany, Republic of Florence (now in Italy)
Died: February 18, 1455; Rome (now in Italy)
Also known as: Guido di Pietro (given name); Giovanni da Fiesole; Il Beato Fra Giovanni Angelico
Area of achievement: Art

Early Life

Not much is known about the early life of Fra Angelico (frah awn-JAY-lee-koh). His baptismal name was Guido di Pietro, but he was also named Giovanni da Fiesole. Il Beato Fra Giovanni Angelico is the name he was given after his death, even though he was never actually beatified. He was apparently an extremely devout man who, about 1425, took his vows in the Dominican order. The first painting of his that can be confidently dated is the *Madonna Linaivoli Altarpiece* (1433), which is in Saint Mark's Convent in Florence, Italy. It is thought that he began painting perhaps ten years earlier, working on small pictures and miniatures, such as *Saint Jerome Penitent*, which is in the collection of Princeton University.

As researcher Giulio Carlo Argon puts it, Fra Angelico was a man of "saintly habits, a learned and zealous friar." He seems to have turned to art not only as a way of glorifying God but also as a way of demonstrating the sacred contents of his world. This meant painting angels and holy figures in vivid color and specific detail; there is nothing abstract or stilted about Fra Angelico's human and divine figures. They are a recognizable part of the viewer's world, set off only by their brilliance and repose.

Fra Angelico may have achieved a significant place of authority among the Dominicans. One unverified account claims that the pope wished him to be archbishop of Florence. What is certain is that Fra Angelico enjoyed the respect of the Vatican and worked for many years on papal commissions. From 1449 to 1452, he was prior of the convent of San Marco. Still, his fame as a painter far exceeded his accomplishments in the Church. His paintings reveal such skill, clarity, and intensity that many critics have presumed that the artist's aim was to combine Renaissance Humanism with an exalted portrayal of Christian doctrine.

Fra Angelico. (Library of Congress)

LIFE'S WORK

Fra Angelico's main purpose was to give depth, resonance, and substance to his spiritual conception of existence. What separates his work from earlier medieval religious painting is his use of perspective, the portrayal of objects or people on a flat surface so as to give the illusion of three dimensions. In other words, Fra Angelico learned the technique of making his religious figures stand out, as though what he painted had an objective, concrete existence in the world of the senses. Perspective was a fifteenth century invention, and it is likely that Fra Angelico learned it from his contemporaries in Florence. At about 1420, the Florentine architects Filippo Brunelleschi and Leon Battista Alberti designed two panels depicting architectural views of Florence. For the first time, viewers of these panels could get a sense of the space in and around objects rather than having each object or image appear flattened out along the same plane. It was as if the viewer could look into a painting and not simply at it.

In *The Annunciation*, painted sometime in the 1430's, the Virgin Mary and the archangel Gabriel are framed by two arches that curve over them and create a coherent, concrete space that they can be seen to inhabit. This architectural detail is not merely decorative; it serves the function of creating a scene, a small drama that draws the viewer's attention to the entrance of the angel into the human realm. Gabriel is depicted leaning forward, with the tail ends of his golden wings and of his heavily ornamented pink-and-gold gown bisected by one of the pillars of an arch. Mary, on the other hand, is completely separate in her own panel, save for a small piece of her royal blue gown edged with gold that extends slightly into Gabriel's space. The Annunciation, Gabriel's announcement that Mary will bear the Son of God, is rendered in three streams of gold lines that penetrate the pillar that separates Mary's panel from Gabriel's. Visually, the two archways are linked by the representation of the Annunciation, yet their very solidity and the openness to the viewer suggests the simultaneous separation and unity of the human and divine worlds. Gabriel's index finger on his right hand points at Mary while his left hand is slightly raised, his fingers pointing upward. Mary, with her head inclining slightly toward him and her hands crossed on her breast, assumes the pose appropriate to receiving the Word of God. As Argon observes, "every line in the Virgin's figure is galvanized and taut, as she starts from her absorption in the prayer book on her knee." The delicacy with which these figures are profiled within the archways makes them intriguing, integral parts of a spiritual allegory.

In 1436, the Dominicans of Fiesole took up residence in Saint Mark's Convent in Florence. Their protector, Cosimo de' Medici (1389-1464), the first of his noble family to rule Florence, made it possible for Fra Angelico to supervise the preparation of the frescoes of the building. One of the most ambitious projects was *The Presentation in the Temple*, a work renowned for its deeply receding perspective and its portrayal of interior lighting. As many critics have pointed out, the color schemes and lighting of Fra Angelico's paintings and frescoes account for much of his success, for they reveal his intense concern with natural and artificial environments, and the contrast between nature and architecture. The presentation of the Christ child, for example, is depicted in a scene of semidarkness. In three panels—the largest of which is set off by two archways with pillars—the artist assembles three figures in the foreground that emit the most light and that are naturally set apart from the dim interior. Slightly behind Jesus, Joseph, and Mary are two votaries, a male and female, emerging from the archways and entering the center panel in prayerful and respectful poses. This arrangement of space was at the service of Fra Angelico's effort to show how God had proportioned the world, with the sight lines of the painting converging on the Christ child.

Other works, such as *Christ on the Cross Adored by Saint Dominic*, *The Crucifixion*, *Christ Scorned*, and *The Transfiguration*, all of which were completed after 1437, suggest the artist's growing concern with spiritual insight. They evince the effort of a devout man bent on creating objects of meditation. These paintings appeared in the Dominicans' cells, and they represent (much more than Fra Angelico's earlier work) an intimate concern with the relation of the individual soul to its Maker. There is, for example, Saint Dominic's contracted brows and the tightness of his jaw and pursed lips as he devoutly gazes upward at Christ, whose blood streams down the Cross. Saint Dominic is kneeling at the base of the Cross, his hands gripping it as though to steady himself or to look directly at Jesus. This is the study of a man undergoing the agony of his own faith.

In painting after painting in the last ten years of his life, Fra Angelico concentrated on Christ as the very light of human life. In *The Transfiguration*, Jesus is depicted in his threefold aspect as martyr, creator, and savior. Enclosed in an oval light, with his arms outstretched and level with his shoulders, his hands, palms open, emerge from the light in benediction of the prophets and saints encircling him with expressions of supplication, yearning, thanksgiving, and contemplation. In *The Transfiguration*, the artist invokes the whole community of faith.

SIGNIFICANCE

In 1445, Pope Eugenius IV called Fra Angelico to Rome to design the Cappella del Sacramento in the Vatican. Although he accepted other commissions in the late 1440's, his greatest work was accomplished in Rome during his final years with his rendering of episodes from the lives of Saints Stephen and Lawrence, some of which was undoubtedly completed by his pupils. In 1449, Nicholas V was finally successful in healing the breach in the Catholic Church known as the Great Schism, and that probably accounts, in part, for the themes of Fra Angelico's frescoes, which emphasized the unity of the religious community and the renewal of the faithful.

Although Fra Angelico continued to paint after his years in Rome, his return to Florence in 1449 as the prior of San Marco evidently meant that he had much less time for his art. None of the works from his very last period of creativity amplifies in any significant respect the achievement of his mature years. He never painted a subject that was not religious. All of his work was suffused with the Humanism of the Renaissance. His religious figures are vibrantly alive with his age's growing interest in the human personality. An innovator in art, Fra Angelico sought to adapt the latest advances in painting to a depiction of the greatest spiritual subjects. The faith he professed had to be palpable and demonstrable, in vivid color and in space that had a sculptural clarity of form and depth. His Christianity took the shape of an art that made a union of seeing and believing and put religion in a realm of the senses that every human being could experience.

—*Carl Rollyson and Lisa Paddock*

FURTHER READING

Douglas, Langton. *Fra Angelico*. London: G. Bell & Sons, 1902. Still informative as a general treatment of the artist's life and career. Douglas examines Fra Angelico's work, his influence on subsequent painting, and his use of architectural forms. The critic maintains a careful discussion of the differences between Fra Angelico's early and late work. Seventy-three plates, a bibliography, and an index of the artist's work, as well as a general index, make this a study worth consulting.

Gilbert, Creighton. *How Fra Angelico and Signorelli Saw the End of the World*. University Park: Pennsylvania State University Press, 2003. Gilbert examines the frescos at Capella della Madonna di San Brizio, which were begun by Fra Angelico. Index.

Hood, William. *Fra Angelico: San Marco, Florence*. New York: G. Braziller, 1995. An examination of the great fresco cycles of the Renaissance, including the work of Fra Angelico in the priory of San Marco. Illustrated.

Kanter, Laurence B., and Carl Brandon Strehike. *Rediscovering Fra Angelico: A Fragmentary History*. New Haven, Conn.: Yale University Art Gallery, 2001. An exhibition catalog of the works of Fra Angelico.

Pope-Hennessy, John. *Fra Angelico*. Ithaca, N.Y.: Cornell University Press, 1974. A systematic study of the artist's life, early works, panel painting and frescoes, period in Rome, and late works. Includes a catalog of works attributed to Fra Angelico. The index and black-and-white and color plates are presented with impeccable scholarship drawing on sources from both the artist's period and modern times.

Schottmüller, Frida. *The Work of Fra Angelico Da Fiesole*. New York: Brentanos, 1913. A biographical introduction situates the artist's life and work in the context of the Middle Ages, the Renaissance, and Western art generally. Especially valuable for a discussion of Fra Angelico's contemporaries. Contains 327 black-and-white plates.

Spike, John T. *Fra Angelico*. New York: Abbeville Press, 1996. A biography of the painter Fra Angelico. Includes discussion of the painter's innovative techniques and his Renaissance altarpieces featuring Mary, the baby Jesus, and saints. Indexes.

SEE ALSO: Filippo Brunelleschi; Cimabue; Donatello; Duccio di Buoninsegna; Jan van Eyck and Hubert van Eyck; Lorenzo Ghiberti; Giotto; Pietro Lorenzetti and Ambrogio Lorenzetti; Simone Martini; Andrea Orcagna; Jean Pucelle; Rogier van der Weyden.

RELATED ARTICLE in *Great Events from History: The Middle Ages, 477-1453*: 1305-1417: Avignon Papacy and the Great Schism.

ANNA, PRINCESS OF THE BYZANTINE EMPIRE

Byzantine princess

Anna resolved the strategic concerns of the two expanding and rival empires of Byzantium and Kievan Rus by consenting to marry Vladimir I, but only after insisting on his conversion to Christianity. The whole of Russia, too, would soon convert to Christianity.

BORN: March 13, 963; Byzantine Empire
DIED: 1011; Kiev, Kievan Rus (now in Ukraine)
ALSO KNOWN AS: Anna "Porphyrogenita" ("born of the purple," born of imperial lineage)
AREAS OF ACHIEVEMENT: Religion and theology, government and politics

EARLY LIFE

Anna was a Byzantine princess, the daughter of Empress Theophano and Emperor Romanus II (r. 959-963) and sister of the emperors Basil II (r. 976-1025) and Constantine VIII (r. 976-1028). She lived during a time of diplomatic intrigue between two rival kingdoms—Byzantium and Kievan Rus—in the late tenth century. Her marriage to Prince Vladimir I—after Anna's insistence that he convert to Christianity—significantly influenced the Christianization of the pagan Slavs after 989.

Little is known of Anna's life before she met and married Prince Vladimir in 989. It is believed that she was highly educated and took a certain interest in the way her brother, Basil II, ruled the Byzantine Empire. Byzantium in the late tenth century was a poor, rural backwater. Approximately 90 percent of its citizens were illiterate and engaged in subsistence agriculture. However, by medieval standards Byzantium was a highly developed society with a stable, diversified economy, a well-educated and efficient bureaucracy, and a capital city, Constantinople, which had no rival in all of Europe. During the ninth and tenth centuries, the Byzantine Empire enjoyed a particularly stable period—an era that brought growing prosperity, territorial expansion, and a lucrative trading relationship with Scandinavian and Baltic Sea kingdoms through Kievan Rus, a Slavic kingdom to the east.

Women in the Byzantine Empire, even before Anna's time, had more opportunities than those in other societies of that era. Indeed, several women ruled the empire, some as regents, others in their own right. Moreover, many women were educated and became nuns, abbesses, writers, and doctors. It also appears that women were believed capable of playing a part in public life.

Parallels to the quasi-empowered woman of Byzantium may also be seen in Kievan Rus, Byzantium's neighbor. In the middle of the tenth century, Princess Olga (later Saint Olga), ruled the Kievan Rus domain. Her life would later be intertwined with that of Princess Anna. As early as 945, Olga—the wife of Prince Igor (r. 912-945), who had been killed by assassins in 945—had claimed political power on behalf of her youthful son, Svyatoslav I. Ruling as regent for Svyatoslav I and the grandmother of the future Prince Vladimir, Princess Olga also became interested in the Christian religion of the Byzantines. Regent from 945 to 964, Olga made a state visit to Constantinople in 957. The first female barbarian potentate to ever see Byzantium, Olga had earlier converted to Christianity in Kiev in either 954 or 955.

However, she did not attempt to convert her people, the Eastern Slavic tribes inhabiting present-day Ukraine.

Olga did later strive to get her son, Svyatoslav I, to convert from his pagan religion to the Orthodox Christianity of the Byzantines. Her efforts were to no avail. Indeed, Svyatoslav I remained a pagan all his life and, besides mounting a continuous campaign of warfare against neighboring eastern tribes and the Bulgarian kingdom to the west, he actively sought to extend the belief in various pagan deities among his Kievan Rus people. Indeed, some sources claim that Svyatoslav I maintained a strong allegiance to paganism in order to preserve an important alliance with pagan allies to the north.

Before Svyatoslav I's death in 972, the prince entrusted various regions of his domain to each of his sons. Iaropolk and Oleg were given Kiev and Polotsk, respectively, while Vladimir, the youngest son, was sent to manage Novgorod in the north. On Svyatoslav's death, a civil war raged among the brothers. By 980, Vladimir finally arose the victor in the post-Svyatoslav struggle for control of Kievan Rus.

In his early years as ruler, Vladimir I continued the pro-pagan policies of his plucky, pugilistic predecessor, Svyatoslav. A small, secretive Christian movement had been afoot within the realm of Vladimir I since at least the early tenth century. Indeed, the peace treaty signed between Kiev's Prince Igor (Olga's husband) and the Byzantine Empire in 945 suggests that a small Christian community, with its own church, resided in Kiev. However, the majority of people within Vladimir's realm practiced paganism, following most specifically the god Perun, the god of thunder; Volos, the god of wealth; Svarog, the god of the heavens; Dazhbog, the god of fertility; and Stribog, the god of rain and wind. Polygamy was sanctioned by the pagan religion and Vladimir had taken for himself at least three, and possibly as many as seven, wives, along with dozens of concubines.

Prince Vladimir also continued efforts to extend the realm of Kiev by attacking Galicia in 981, the Yatvingians along the Baltic coast in 983, the Volga Bulgars in 985 and, finally, the Byzantine Empire in the Crimea in 987. It was the latter campaign that brought him and Anna together, a campaign that would change Russia forever.

Life's Work

Vladimir I is usually given credit for converting Russia, hence the appellation ascribed to him, Vladimir Ravnoapostolny, or, "ranking with the apostles." However, it may be that his Byzantine wife, Anna, deserves greater credit.

Vladimir I knew that surrounding nations were converting to organized religion. The Khazars to the east had converted to Judaism, the Volga Bulgars had accepted Islam, the Poles and Hungarians had become Catholic converts, and the Bulgarians to the west had accepted the Eastern Orthodox religion of the Byzantines.

In response, during the mid-980's, Vladimir sent emissaries abroad to scrutinize the diverse religious alternatives that existed. According to *The Russian Primary Chronicle* (c. 1113; English translation, 1930), the prince of Kievan Rus tried to determine which religion was most suitable for his growing realm. In the end, the envoys allegedly reported back that the ceremonies they had observed at St. Sophia Cathedral (also known as the Hagia Sophia or the Church of the Holy Wisdom) in Constantinople proved to them that

> . . . we knew not whether we were in heaven or on earth. For on earth there is no such splendor or such beauty, and we are at a loss how to describe it. We only know that God dwells there among men, and their service is fairer than the ceremonies of other nations. . . . [translation by Samuel Cross, 1953]

Though curious about neighboring religions, Vladimir did not convert to Christianity until he met and married Anna, which followed on an appeal to Vladimir for military assistance from Anna's elder brother, Basil II. Basil II, later known as Basil Bulgaroktonus—the Bulgar Slayer—reigned as imperial master of the Byzantine realm from 976 to 1025, a period of singular achievement in the Middle Byzantine period. However, in the early years of Basil's rule, he was opposed by usurpers from both within his kingdom and without. In 988, Basil asked Prince Vladimir for aid in his struggle against Bardas Phokas, a rival to the Byzantine throne, and the Bulgars to the west of Kievan Rus. Prince Vladimir duly dispatched six thousand soldiers—the dreaded Varangians—to assist Basil but not without securing from him a promise that he could wed Basil's younger sister, Anna. In the end, the army of Bardas Phokas was conquered at Abydos on April 13, 989, and Vladimir's capture of the former Byzantine city of Kherson on the Crimean peninsula occurred shortly thereafter.

At the time of her marriage to Vladimir, Anna was twenty-six years old, for that era a rather old age to first marry. Anna had at first declined Basil's attempt to marry her off to the Slavic heathen. She reportedly stated that it would be better to stay in Constantinople and die rather than be married to the eastern upstart. In the end, however, she relented, but insisted that Prince Vladimir con-

RULERS OF KIEVAN RUS, C. 862-1167

Reign	*Ruler*
c. 862-879	RURIK
879-912	Oleg
912-945	Igor
945-964	SAINT OLGA (regent)
964-972	Svyatoslav I
972-980	Yaropolk
980-1015	VLADIMIR I (with ANNA)
1015-1019	Sviatopolk I
1019-1054	Yaroslav
1054-1073	Iziaslav
1073-1076	Svyatoslav II
1076-1078	Iziaslav (restored)
1078-1093	Vsevolod
1093-1113	Sviatopolk II
1113-1125	Vladimir II Monomakh
1125-1132	Mstislav
1132-1139	Yaropolk
1139-1146	Vyacheslav
1146-1154	Iziaslav
1149-1157	Yuri I Dolgoruky
1154-1167	Rostislav

vert to Christianity before their marriage. The young empress apparently gave her assent in order to cement stronger ties between the two empires, while also reclaiming for Byzantium the city of Kherson. Moreover, Anna apparently also sought to play a part in the Christianization of the heathen Slavs. Thus, it was in Kherson in 989 that Vladimir was baptized, the two were married, and the introduction of Christianity into Russian lands began on a large scale.

Thereafter, Anna and Vladimir I set out to convert their people to Christianity, at times forcibly. Pagan statues were destroyed or thrown into rivers, while Vladimir's concubines were converted into nuns and his former wives were cast off. As well, Anna actively sought to convert Vladimir's children.

Anna also played a role in managing portions of Vladimir's realm and maintained a large entourage on her own authority as princess of Kievan Rus. In addition, Princess Anna served Vladimir as a close adviser, and most sources agree that it was on her initiative that the first Christian churches in Kiev were instituted.

Before dying in 1011 from an unknown illness, Anna bore two sons, Boris and Gleb, and one daughter, Mariya. Mariya later continued the custom of "bridal diplomacy" by marrying the Polish king, Karol the Restorer.

SIGNIFICANCE

The historical importance of Anna and her marriage to Prince Vladimir I is immeasurable. Although pagan beliefs and ceremonies continued to exist among the Russian people for several centuries thereafter, the betrothal brought the Russian people solidly into the camp of Eastern Orthodoxy. With that came the Cyrillic (Slavic) alphabet; Byzantine church law; monastic communities at Kiev, Chernigov, Belgorod, and Pereyaslav; and wider Byzantine cultural influences in art, literature, and architecture. In addition, the exceedingly important notion of the "divine right of kings" entered into the Russian political lexicon with Vladimir's conversion to Orthodoxy, an idea that would continue to provide a source of legitimacy for the Russian czars up to the early twentieth century. The Christian faith Anna brought to the Russians also served to help unite the young nation, bestowing on it a powerful unifying culture. At the same time, however, Anna's marriage to Vladimir also had some adverse ramifications for later Russian political development. The close cultural ties with Byzantium would later serve to sever Russia from the dramatic and important periods of the Reformation and the Enlightenment, historical eras that deeply altered Western Europe's political and cultural trajectory.

—*Thomas E. Rotnem*

FURTHER READING

Alan, Rupert, and Anna Marie Dahlquist. *Royal Families of Medieval Scandinavia, Flanders, and Kiev*. Kingsburg, Calif.: Kings River, 1997. This book provides the reader with colorful insight into the royal lineage of families that receive too little attention from mainstream history.

Cross, Samuel H., trans. *The Russian Primary Chronicle*. Vol. 12 in *Harvard Studies and Notes in Philology and Literature*. Cambridge, Mass.: Harvard University Press, 1953. This work is one of the more faithful translations of the early work by the Russian historical chroniclers.

Dukes, Paul. *A History of Russia: Medieval, Modern, Contemporary, Circa 882-1996*. 3d ed. Durham, N.C.: Duke University Press, 1998. Part 1 introduces medieval Russia and the rise and then collapse of Kiev (882-1240). Extensive bibliography and an index.

Fennell, John. *A History of the Russian Church: To 1448*. London: Longman, 1995. A volume on the life of the early Russian Church, it also contains considerable detail concerning the ties between Byzantium and the early Russian metropolitans.

Franklin, Simon, and Jonathan Shepard. *The Emergence of Rus: 750-1200*. New York: Longman, 1996. This book examines the medieval origins and development of the Slavic peoples of Eastern Europe, focusing on Scandinavian, Byzantine, and barbarian influences. Maps, extensive bibliography, list of genealogies, and excellent index.

Gurney, Gene. *Kingdoms of Europe*. New York: Crown, 1982. This general purpose work provides a succinct overview of many of the major dynasties of Europe, ancient and modern.

Obolensky, Dimitri. *Byzantium and the Slavs*. Crestwood, N.Y.: St. Vladimir's Seminary Press, 1994. Surveys Slavic relations with the Byzantine Empire in the Middle Ages. Includes a chapter on "Russia's Byzantine Heritage." Bibliography, map, index.

Riasanovsky, Nicholas V. *A History of Russia*. 6th ed. New York: Oxford University Press, 2000. This volume provides an excellent, in-depth overview of Russia's history, beginning with the premodern period.

Roesdahl, Else. *The Vikings*. 2d ed. Translated by Susan M. Margeson and Kirsten Williams. New York: Penguin Books, 1998. Provides a solid, meticulous survey of Viking expansion into Kiev Rus and Kiev's relations with Byzantium. Includes maps, illustrations, an extensive bibliography, and indexes.

Warnes, David. *Chronicle of the Russian Tsars*. London: Thames and Hudson, 1999. A valuable text about Russian imperial families from the medieval period to the twentieth century.

SEE ALSO: Anna Comnena; Basil the Macedonian; Saint Clotilda; Clovis; Rurik; Queen Tamara; Theophanes the Confessor; Vladimir I.

RELATED ARTICLES in *Great Events from History: The Middle Ages, 477-1453*: 496: Baptism of Clovis; 726-843: Iconoclastic Controversy; 740: Khazars Convert to Judaism; c. 850: Development of the Slavic Alphabet; 850-950: Viking Era; 976-1025: Reign of Basil II; 988: Baptism of Vladimir I; 1077: Seljuk Dynasty Is Founded.

ANNA COMNENA

Byzantine princess and historian

Anna Comnena composed the Alexiad, *a history of her father, Byzantine emperor Alexius I Comnenus, and his reign, which became a critical historical source for the early Crusades.*

BORN: December 1, 1083; Constantinople, Byzantine Empire (now Istanbul, Turkey)
DIED: After 1148; Constantinople, Byzantine Empire
ALSO KNOWN AS: Anna Komnene
AREA OF ACHIEVEMENT: Historiography

EARLY LIFE

Anna Comnena (ah-nah kahm-NEE-nuh) was the first child of Byzantine emperor Alexius I Comnenus—and a porphyrogenite, a princess "born in the purple" while her father reigned. Alexius, an energetic young aristocrat and warlord, had seized the throne in 1081 as a kind of usurper-protector after a series of court upheavals. He had won the approval of the powerful Ducas family by marrying one of its members, Irene Ducas (c. 1066-1120), and by guaranteeing the rights of the legitimate dynast, the feeble young Constantine X Ducas (1007?-1067). When Anna was born, Alexius extended that commitment by betrothing her as a baby to Constantine (then only nine years of age). Anna grew up expecting to marry him, and she seems to have been genuinely fond of him.

When, however, Alexius's first son, the future John II (r. 1118-1143), was born (1088), Alexius could at last dream of consolidating his own hold on the throne and of founding his own dynasty. With his position made more secure by his smashing victory over the menacing Pechenegs in 1091, he began to move in that direction. Constantine was deprived of his rights and pushed into the shadows. Anna's "usefulness" as a marital pawn was then shifted to securing an alliance with another powerful aristocratic family. Thus, about 1097, at age fourteen, she was married to the noble Nicephorus Bryennius (1062-1137), a soldier and an educated and cultured man. She wrote of this marriage as a happy one, and it produced four children.

Anna came of a society that did not totally deny secular education to women, especially to those who were princesses. Over the centuries, Byzantium produced several imperial women of advanced learning and literary talent, extending beyond the palace as well. Anna understandably was proud of her learning, which she pursued from an early age through her entire life. In her writing, she exhibits a comprehensive and solid command of the ancient Greek traditions of literature, philosophy, science, and medicine. She was also acquainted with the writings of her Byzantine compatriots. As a member of the reigning family, Anna observed through youthful eyes the momentous events of that epoch, including her father's struggles with a range of menacing enemies (the Normans, Pechenegs, Turks, Latins). Notable among these were the forces of the First Crusade, who passed through Constantinople just at the time of her marriage. Combined with her good memory was access to the important personalities and documents of the day. She would draw on these sources in her great literary work.

Life's Work

There are no details about much of Anna's life during her father's rule, but there seems to have been much ill will between her and her brother John. Ever cautious about his dynastic intentions, Alexius never formally proclaimed his son John as colleague or heir. Indeed, in 1111 Anna's husband was given the title of caesar, which usually made the bearer heir apparent to the throne. Anna herself seems to have believed very strongly in her rights as firstborn, a belief apparently encouraged by her mother. In Alexius's last days, intrigue flourished, and Anna and her mother applied intense pressure on the dying emperor. However, he foiled them by discreetly opening his son's path to succession. Frustrated, Anna attempted to organize a coup against her brother, urging her husband to claim the throne for himself on the basis of her rights. He refused, and Anna was obliged to sit on the sidelines as her hated brother reigned.

Anna was regarded with suspicion thereafter, though her husband was still kept in high office, and the two seemed relatively safe until Bryennius died in 1137. Thereafter, she was effectively confined to the convent of the Kecharitomene, which had been founded by her mother as her own place of retirement. There she was able to pursue her scholarly interests and her cultural patronage, surviving her brother but none too happy with her nephew, the next emperor, Manuel I. Anna did not actually become a nun, however, until just before her death, a date that is not known for certain. She clearly lived past 1148 (when, it is estimated, the *Alexiad* may have been finished), but she was apparently dead by 1154.

Anna's only surviving literary work is one of the crown jewels of Byzantine historical writing, and one of the most significant histories written during the Middle Ages, important both as a historical source and as a work of literature. Her *Alexías* (in the original Greek), or *Alexiad* (c. 1148; English translation, 1928), is a laudatory history of her father's life and reign, a prose narrative in Greek. Its title, however, consciously evokes that of the *Ilías* or *Iliad* (c. 750 B.C.E.; English translation, 1611), by her favorite poet, Homer, casting her father as a veritably epic character. It is not known when she began to write, but the bulk of the work, and certainly the latter portions, clearly date from the 1140's, some three decades after her father's death. The work reflects her resentments against her brother, Emperor John II, and the frustrations of her later years. It has been suggested that she also meant to praise her father's glories as a critique of her nephew (John's son), Emperor Manuel I (1143-1180). Indeed, as a work it belongs to the literary and cultural context of Manuel's reign, rather than to that of Manuel's grandfather, Alexius I.

One stimulus for its creation came from established traditions of Byzantine historical writing; it was conventional for a writer to pick up from the point in time about which a predecessor had stopped writing. Some time after Alexius's death, Anna's husband Nicephorus Bryennius had written a memoir of the years 1070 to 1079, describing the struggles among leading aristocratic families for the throne. Anna felt an obligation to pick up the thread of narrative from her husband. However, his possible hints of criticism of the young Alexius may have prompted her to create a glowing and nostalgic picture of her father. Recent scholarly discussion has raised the possibility that the work was essentially written by her husband and merely taken over and finished by Anna, but such an argument seems exaggerated, and her rights of full authorship still stand secure.

Anna knew the responsibilities of historical writing, writing to which she pays earnest tribute in the work's prologue. She casts her work in fifteen books, the first two of which trace her father's career up to his accession, the remainder covering his reign until his death. Anna's chronology, however, is frequently less than strict or clear, and she sometimes omits relevant information. At some points her self-pity gets the better of her. Readers should be aware of the idyllic picture she gives of her family life and relationships.

Nevertheless, Anna is remarkably thorough and conscientious. Her account of the First Crusade and its passage through Byzantium, if written at a remove of thirty or forty years (and possibly flavored by her observation of the unfortunate Second Crusade), is one of the most important histories of the Crusades, certainly in giving the Byzantine viewpoint on these encounters between Christian East and West. Consistent with her portrayal of Alexius as a great warrior-hero, she is particularly fascinated by military operations, and she gives some invaluable descriptions of weapons and tactics. This is in marked contrast to her most important predecessor in Byzantine historical writing, the philosopher-politician Michael Psellus (1018-c. 1078), whom she greatly respected but whose overwhelming concentration on court life she avoided emulating in her own work. Nevertheless, like Psellus, she had a strong feeling for personalities, and she draws some remarkably perceptive and subtle portraits of leading characters she encountered. Among these are her formidable grandmother Anna Dalassena (fl. eleventh century), the heterodox Byzantine philosopher John Italus (fl. eleventh century), the Norman leader Robert Guiscard (c. 1015-1085), and his son Bohemond I (c. 1052-1111)—for whom she apparently had ambivalent feelings of passionate hatred and reluctant admiration.

Conservative in her viewpoint, Anna displays strong biases. Though her learning tempered her own religious beliefs, she detested heresy and expresses unseemly exultation in the martyrdom of the heresiarch Basil the Great (c. 329-379). Both socially and culturally, she was certainly elitist, though she avoided the narcissistic smugness of Psellus. With characteristically Byzantine ethnic pride, she is contemptuous of all things foreign, especially regarding Western Europeans and the Roman Church. Her accounts of her father's dealings with Crusade leaders are particularly vivid, as are her horrified reactions to the Latin hordes who descended on her world so unexpectedly. She displays ostentatious disgust at foreign names, and she does her best to retain archaic nomenclature. Beyond that typical trait, her Greek style displays all the foibles of classicizing artificiality favored by Byzantium's intellectuals—which involved using a deliberately archaic written Greek, quite different from the evolving spoken language. Still, her style is by no means as inflated as that of Psellus, nor quite as intricate as that of her greatest successor, Nicetas Choniates (c. 1150-1213), who was later to report on the collapse of the Comnenian Dynasty and on the catastrophe that the Fourth Crusade visited on Byzantium in 1204.

Significance

Anna Comnena's life and writing have tempted latter-day commentators to evaluate them in terms of modern feminism. Though a strong, educated woman, she must be understood ultimately in terms of her culture and her time. To its legacy, she contributed notably. Though Anna's history is not without faults and deficiencies, many of them derive from her society and her cultural background. Anna herself stands as a writer and historian of undeniable stature, whose work still has the power to bring alive the personalities and events of a dramatic era.

—*John W. Barker*

Further Reading

Angold, Michael J. *The Byzantine Empire, 1025-1204: A Political History.* 2d ed. New York: Longman, 1997. Outstanding treatment of this transitional segment of Byzantine history that includes chapters on Alexius, John, and Manuel.

Buckler, Georgina. *Anna Comnena: A Study.* 1929. Reprint. London: Oxford University Press, 1968. Though dated, a thorough analysis of Anna and her work.

Chalandon, Ferdinand. *Essai sur le règne d'Alexis 1er Comnène (1081-1118).* Vol. 1 in *Les Comnène.* Paris: Société de l'école de Chartres, 1900. Dated, but a classic and comprehensive study in French on Alexius's reign.

Dalven, Rae. *Anna Comnena.* New York: Twayne, 1972. A brief biography and study of Anna's work. Includes a bibliography.

Diehl, Charles. "Anna Comnena." In *Byzantine Empresses.* Translated by Harold Bell and Theresa de Kerpely. New York: Knopf, 1963. Originally published in 1927, a somewhat romanticized but still appealing sketch.

Garland, Lynda. *Byzantine Empresses: Women and Power in Byzantium, A.D. 527-1204.* New York: Routledge, 1999. Explores the empresses of the Byzantine Empire, from the early reigns of Theodora and Irene to those of Alexius's time and beyond. Includes a map, bibliography, and index.

Gouma-Peterson, Thalia, ed. *Anna Komnene and Her Times.* New York: Garland, 2000. Discuss Anna's scholarship, the *Alexiad*, the issue of gender and power, women's literature in Byzantium, and more. Illustrations, bibliography, and index.

Hamilton, Janet, and Bernard Hamilton, trans. *Christian Dualist Heresies in the Byzantine World, c. 650-c. 1450: Selected Sources.* New York: Manchester University Press, 1998. Provides a chapter on Anna's account of the trial and martyrdom of Basil the Great. Maps, bibliography, and index.

Mullett, Margaret, and Dion Smythe, eds. *Alexios I Komnenos.* Belfast: Belfast Byzantine, Queen's University of Belfast, 1996. Papers from a colloquium held in 1989, offering significant new appraisals of Alexius's reign and age.

Thiébaux, Marcelle, trans. *The Writings of Medieval Women: An Anthology.* New York: Garland, 1994. A collection that includes a chapter on Anna's writings on the First Crusade. Bibliography, index.

SEE ALSO: Bohemond I; Urban II.

RELATED ARTICLES in *Great Events from History: The Middle Ages, 477-1453*: 1054: Beginning of the Rome-Constantinople Schism; November 27, 1095: Pope Urban II Calls the First Crusade; 1147-1149: Second Crusade.

SAINT ANSELM

Italian theologian and philosopher

Combining a tenacious attachment to principle with a penetrating mind, Saint Anselm maintained the independence of the English church while making major contributions to the inductive argument for the existence of God.

BORN: c. 1033; Aosta, Lombardy (now in Italy)
DIED: April 21, 1109; possibly Canterbury, Kent, England
AREAS OF ACHIEVEMENT: Religion and theology, philosophy

EARLY LIFE

Saint Anselm (AN-sehlm) was born in Aosta, an Alpine town in Lombardy, today the Piedmont section of Italy, near the St. Bernard Pass. His parents were wealthy: Gundulf, his father, was a Lombard who assumed the extensive property of his wife, Ermenberger of Aosta, who may have been related to German royalty. They had one other child, a daughter, Richera, younger than Anselm. Ermenberger's piety was the most important influence on the young Anselm. Placed under the tutelage of a strict disciplinarian, the young boy nearly lost his mind until his mother restored him to normality with kindness.

At age fifteen, Anselm decided to become a Benedictine monk, but the abbot of Aosta refused to accept the underage boy for fear of offending Gundulf. Anselm responded by pursuing worldly amusements, only to be recovered again by his pious mother. When Ermenberger died, Anselm resumed worldly pursuits and had repeated conflicts with the censorious Gundulf. At the age of twenty-three, he left home with a clerical companion. Anselm made his way to the monastery at Becin Normandy, taking up studies with the celebrated teacher, Prior Lanfranc. Anselm was determined to become a scholar and a monk and avidly pursued literary studies. When his father died, he briefly considered returning to Burgundy to administer the family estates but instead chose the religious life in 1060. Hence, at age twenty-seven, he was accepted into the monastery at Bec by Abbot Herlwin. Three years later, as a result of his scholarship and exemplary commitment to monastic duties, Anselm succeeded Lanfranc as prior when the teacher left to become abbot of Saint Stephen's Monastery in Caen. Anselm was then just thirty years old.

LIFE'S WORK

As prior, Anselm set aside time each day to render advice in person and in writing to persons even of high position (and to his own nephew, also named Anselm). At night, he corrected the books of the monastic library or wrote devotional literature. Rejecting the prevailing instructional methods for the education of young boys, which included severe constraints and physical beatings, Anselm, recalling his own unhappy experience at the hands of the tutor in Aosta, stressed a blend of kindness and punishment, freedom and discipline. While still at Bec, he wrote his *Monologion* (1076; *Monologium*, 1903, better known as *Monologion*) and the *Proslogion* (1077-1078; *Proslogium*, 1851, better known as *Proslogion*).

Fifteen years after becoming prior, Herlwin died. Anselm was elected abbot in 1078, and in the following year, he was consecrated. That year he journeyed to England to examine the English properties of the monastery and also to visit with his old teacher, Lanfranc, now the archbishop of Canterbury. At Lanfranc's request, Anselm addressed the religious at Canterbury on sundry theological and monastic topics. It was there that Anselm met his future biographer and lifelong friend, Eadmer.

When William the Conqueror lay dying from a wound at Rouen, he sent for Abbot Anselm to hear his confession. Anselm's own illness prevented his arrival, and the king died in 1087. After Lanfranc died in May, 1089, King William Rufus (William II) seized the opportunity to tax the clergy and acquire the revenues of the English churches and monasteries. No new archbishop was allowed to be appointed; the king sought to use his added revenues for a military campaign in Normandy. English nobles invited Anselm to come and intercede with the king on behalf of the oppressed churchmen. His visit with the king in September, 1092, was, however, unsuccessful. When King William became seriously ill the following year, he was frightened into naming Anselm as the new archbishop of Canterbury. Anselm demanded that all the former lands of the see be restored to church control, that additional properties long claimed by the see be recognized, and that the king take him as his personal counselor. William accepted the first demand but not the other two. With considerable reluctance, Anselm consented and was consecrated archbishop on December 4, 1093, by Thomas of Bayeux, archbishop of York. Anselm was sixty years of age. Although there may have been the customary election of the archbishop, the records do not reveal one.

As an administrator of church affairs, Anselm is best remembered for his protection of ecclesiastical independence and properties from the depredations of English royalty. Shortly after his consecration as archbishop, King William Rufus demanded a gift of one thousand pounds. Anselm refused for fear that the public would perceive such a large gift as simony. When the king refused his offer of five hundred pounds, Anselm ordered the sum given to the poor. King and primate also quarreled over the former's insistence on possessing the revenues of the abbeys.

Anselm wished to go to Rome in 1095 to receive the symbol of papal approval, the archiepiscopal pallium (a woolen shoulder vestment that was a sign of investiture) from Pope Urban II. King William refused to recognize Urban as pope and so denied Anselm's request for a safe-conduct document. The papal election was disputed between Urban and Clement III, and England had not yet decided whom to recognize. Anselm did not deny the king's right to withhold support for a pope whose election was disputed; rather, he held that his support for Urban was announced before his own acceptance of the see. Normandy had accepted Urban, but a convocation of English bishops and nobles in 1095 resulted in the craven submission of the bishops to King William. The nobles, however, supported Anselm and negotiated a truce. Anselm agreed not to go to Rome. Now William sought to deal with the pope; determining that Urban was, indeed, the rightful pontiff, he asked that the pallium be delivered to himself for bestowal on someone other than Anselm. The Roman agents refused to accept his scheme, and the pallium arrived in Canterbury for Anselm only on June 10, 1095.

During the next two years, 1095-1097, church-state disputes ceased, enabling Anselm to administer routine affairs of the Church, consecrating new bishops, erecting buildings, and other tasks. During these years he also began work on his famous book, *Cur deus homo* (1098; *Cur Deus Homo: Or, Why God Was Made Man*, 1854-1855). He even raised two hundred pounds to aid the king's temporary acquisition of Normandy when Robert, his brother, accepted Urban's appeal to go on the First Crusade. Still, William angered Anselm by refusing to consider other church reforms.

Hence, in 1097, Anselm again wished to travel to Rome; as before, William refused. The king feared the papal interference with his own prerogatives and, this time armed with the support of both bishops and nobles, informed Anselm that if he left for Rome, he could not return. After personally blessing the king, Anselm left for Italy in November, 1097, whereupon the king confiscated all of his properties. Anselm's reception in Rome was unusually warm. While resting in Apulia, he finished his work *Cur Deus Homo*. The pope did not accept

Saint Anselm of Canterbury. (Library of Congress)

his request to be relieved of his see. Anselm attended the Council of Bari in 1098, which concerned the *Filioque* doctrine that caused such division with the Church in the East. The address that Anselm delivered at the council later formed the basis of his book *De processione Spiritus Sancti* (1102; *The Theology of Saint Anselm Concerning the Procession of the Holy Spirit to Confute the Opposition of the Greeks*, 1953). This gathering specifically denounced King William of England for simony and would have excommunicated the king had it not been for Anselm's intercession. In Rome the next year, Anselm attended the Vatican Council of 1099, which declared for excommunication of laypeople who invested church offices. Stopping in Lyon on his way home, Anselm wrote *De conceptu virginali et originali peccato* (1099-1100; *Concerning Virginal Conception and Original Sin*, 1954) and *De humani generis redemptione* (1099; *Meditations Concerning the Redemption of Mankind*, 1701). A number of miracles were attributed to him during these months. Before he reached England, both Pope Urban II and King William II died, the latter by an assassin's arrow.

The new English king, Henry I, William's brother, quarreled with Anselm on the very same issues and demanded that the archbishop be reinvested and render homage for his see. Henry secured a truce in order to send agents to Rome to beg the pope to relax the recent decrees. During this respite in the quarrel, Anselm pleased the king by allowing him to marry Mathilde of Scotland, who was charged with having entered a convent as a nun. The archbishop's council decided otherwise, and Anselm blessed the royal marriage on November 11, 1100. Once again, he served the king's interest by supporting his claim to Normandy vis-à-vis that of his brother, Robert, and so helped to avert a war. When Pope Paschal's letter arrived and maintained the former decrees, however, Anselm concluded that he must obey Rome. In 1103, Anselm began his second exile, traveling to Rome to see Pope Paschal II. King and pope were deadlocked over who held the right of investiture. The archbishop had agreed to go to Rome to clarify the situation, but the pope reiterated his positions, doing so in a manner designed to soothe and compliment the English king. Anselm went to Lyon again, to study with his friend, Archbishop Hugh. After written negotiations between Anselm and Henry proved fruitless, the two parties agreed to meet in Normandy in July, 1105. There they were reconciled, and Anselm returned to Canterbury in September, 1106. The English bishops were chafing now under royal taxes and finally came to Anselm's support. Hence, at the conference at Westminster, the king promised never again to invest bishops and abbots with the ring and crosier, while Anselm agreed to render homage to the king for the temporal possessions of the archbishopric, a formula that was approved by Pope Paschal II. This agreement was the model for the Concordat of Worms in 1122, which resolved a similar dispute within the Holy Roman Empire.

Anselm wrote a work called *De concordia praescientiae et praedestinationis et gratiae dei cum libero arbitrio* (1107-1108; *The Harmony of the Foreknowledge, the Predestination, and the Grace of God with Free Choice*, 1976). The next year, he became seriously ill; he died on April 21, 1109. He was called Beatus by the new archbishop, Theobald; Saint Thomas Becket requested his canonization in 1163. Sometime before Becket's martyrdom on December 29, 1170, Anselm may have been formally canonized, but no explicit record has been discovered. Others contend that his canonization was only executed by the notorious Borgia pope, Alexander VI, in 1494. Pope Clement XI declared him a doctor of the Church in 1720.

Significance

Intellectually, Saint Anselm's contributions to philosophy and theology were pivotal in the transition from early medieval thought to the Scholasticism of the later era. Anselm always regarded belief in God as something in accordance with unaided reason, yet his approach was still Platonic rather than Aristotelian. In the *Monologion*, he sought not only to demonstrate the reasonableness of belief in God but also to explicate his attributes. In his most remembered work, the *Proslogion*, Anselm argued that the very idea of perfection implied its existence. Although Thomas Aquinas later rejected Anselm's ontological argument, it was defended by René Descartes in the seventeenth century, and it has continued to interest philosophers of religion.

Anselm's successful defense of church prerogatives in the face of royal demands was crucial to the maintenance of limited authority that marked late feudal England and that was a lasting political legacy of English history for the modern era. Indeed, the triumph of limited government in Western history can in part be attributed to the fact that the contests between church and state in the Middle Ages were between equal forces, neither of which was able to dominate the other. The compromise of Westminster between Anselm and King Henry was just such a case.

—John D. Windhausen

Further Reading

Anselm, Saint. *The Letters of Saint Anselm of Canterbury.* Translated by Walter Frölich. Kalamazoo, Mich: Cistercian Publications, 1990. Frölich's introduction provides a concise view of Anselm's life and works as well as sheds light on his letters.

Colleran, Joseph M. Introduction and notes to Anselm's *Why God Became Man*, and *The Virgin's Conception and Original Sin*. Albany, N.Y.: Magi Books, 1969.

Eadmer. *The Life of Saint Anselm, Archbishop of Canterbury.* Translated and edited with an introduction and notes by R. W. Southern. Oxford, England: Clarendon Press, 1979. The principal source for Anselm's life, this work is important not only for what it reveals about the archbishop but also for what it tells about the community of monks that shaped both author and subject.

Fortin, John R., ed. *Saint Anselm: His Origins and Influence*. Lewiston, N.Y.: E. Mellen Press, 2001. A collection of essays on Anselm, touching on topics such as *Proslogion* and Anselm's religious arguments. Bibliography.

Hartshorne, Charles. *Anselm's Discovery: A Re-examination of the Ontological Proof for God's Existence.* 1965. Reprint. La Salle, Ill.: Open Court, 1991. An examination of Anselm's argument that attempted to prove God's existence. Bibliography and indexes.

Schufreider, Gregory. *Confessions of a Rational Mystic: Anselm's Early Writings*. West Lafayette, Ind.: Purdue University Press, 1994. This work includes Anselm's *Proslogion* and a translation as well as discussion of Anselm's attempts to prove the existence of God. Bibliography and index.

Van Fleteren, Frederick, and Joseph C. Schnaubelt, eds. *Twenty-five Years (1969-1994) of Anselm Studies: Review and Critique of Recent Scholarly Views*. Lewiston, N.Y.: E. Mellen, 1996. A collection of essays regarding various theories and research produced by scholars studying Saint Anselm.

Viola, Coloman, and Frederick van Fleteren, eds. *Saint Anselm, A Thinker for Yesterday and Today: Anselm's Thought Viewed by Our Contemporaries*. Lewiston, N.Y.: E. Mellen Press, 2002. A collection of essays presented at the International Anselm Conference in Paris. Bibliography and indexes.

See also: Saint Thomas Becket; Henry I; Thomas Aquinas; Urban II; William the Conqueror.

Related articles in *Great Events from History: The Middle Ages, 477-1453*: 596-597: See of Canterbury Is Established; November 27, 1095: Pope Urban II Calls the First Crusade.

Saint Anthony of Padua

Portuguese-born preacher, teacher, and scholar

Anthony of Padua was one of the most eloquent Franciscan preachers and the first teacher of the Franciscan school of theology. He is credited with introducing the theology of Saint Augustine into the order and was named a doctor of the Church.

Born: August 15, 1195; Lisbon, Portugal

Died: June 13, 1231; Arcella, near Padua, Verona (now in Italy)

Also known as: Ferdinand (or Fernando) de Boullion (given name)

Areas of achievement: Religion and theology, education

Early Life

Anthony of Padua (PAJ-ew-wuh) received the name Fernando (Ferdinand) at baptism. It is asserted that his father was Martin de Boullion, descendant of the renowned Godfrey de Boullion, commander of the First Crusade, and that his mother, Theresa Travejra, was a descendant of Froila I, fourth king of Asturias.

After he had completed the course at the Cathedral School of Saint Mary, Ferdinand, at the age of fifteen, joined the Canons Regular of Saint Augustine in the convent of Saint Vincent outside the city walls in September, 1210. Two years later, he went to the Monastery of the Holy Cross in Coimbra, where he remained for eight years. In Coimbra, he became an expert in biblical studies. It is believed that he was ordained a priest in 1218.

In 1220, he saw the bodies of the first five martyrs of the Franciscan order (Saints Berard, Peter, Otho, Aiuto, and Accursio) being returned from Morocco, where on January 16, 1220, they had been killed for their faith. Ferdinand was so moved by the desire for martyrdom that he set his heart on becoming a friar minor. That same year, 1220, he received the Franciscan habit from the friars of the Convent of the Holy Cross at Olivares (near Coimbra), who were accustomed to beg alms from the canons. He took the name Anthony, a name that was later assumed by the convent at Olivares itself.

LIFE'S WORK

At his own request, Anthony was sent as a missionary to Morocco in December, 1220. There, however, he was stricken with a severe illness that affected him the entire winter, and he was compelled to return to Portugal the following spring. Driven off course by a violent storm, his ship landed in Sicily.

Anthony was informed by the Franciscans in Messina that a general chapter of the order was to be held at Assisi on May 30, 1221. He arrived in time to take part in the famous Chapter of the Mats, in which three thousand friars participated. It was here that he met Saint Francis of Assisi and was assigned to Bologna, in the province of Romagna.

For a time, Anthony resided in solitude and penance in the hermitage of Monte Paolo near Forlì. It was at Forlì that his talents as a preacher became known. Because of the absence of the regularly appointed preacher for the ordination of some Dominicans and Franciscans at Forlì, in 1222, Anthony was asked to preach the sermon. His eloquence and the depth of his knowledge astonished the audience.

Francis wrote to Friar Anthony in 1223 and appointed him the first professor of theology for the Franciscan order. He commanded him to teach in such a manner as to perpetuate the spirit of prayer and piety advocated in the rule. Anthony is credited with introducing the theology of Saint Augustine to the Franciscan order—a union that was to become the characteristic mark of Franciscan theology.

Anthony spent some time in Vercelli between 1222 and 1225, where he discussed mystical theology with Thomas of Saint Victor, known as Thomas Gallus (d. 1246), the founder and abbot of the monastery of Saint Andrew. They became personal friends. Thomas was well known for his translation, commentary, and synthesis of the Pseudo-Dionysian works. Thomas had a strong influence on early Franciscans such as Alexander of Hales, Saint Bonaventure, and Adam of Marisco. He was so impressed by Anthony's knowledge that he asserted that "aided by divine grace, he drew most abundantly from the mystical theology of the Sacred Scripture."

Anthony taught successively at Bologna, Toulouse, and Montpellier. In 1223, he started a school of theology for the friars, who called him Pater Scientiae and Doctor Veritatis. This school eventually developed into the school of theology of the University of Bologna. At Arles, Toulouse, and Montpellier, he taught in the order schools, not in the city universities. Toulouse had no public faculty of theology before 1229; Montpellier's was founded after 1240 and Bologna's after 1300. During this period, five Franciscan houses were founded—at Nice, Bordeaux, La Réole, Saint-Jean-d'Angély, and Le Puy-en-Velay.

Sculpture of Saint Anthony of Padua. (Library of Congress)

Because he was such an inspiring preacher, Anthony was commissioned to preach against the heretics in northern Italy (from 1222 to 1224) and against the Albigensians in southern France in 1224. Between 1227 and 1230, his preaching mission brought him back to Italy. During Lent in 1231, he preached daily in Padua.

Anthony's sermons attracted enormous crowds. People would begin to gather in the middle of the night to obtain good seats, shops would close, and Anthony had to be protected from souvenir hunters and the press of the crowd. He avoided preaching during harvest time so as not to interfere with this important farm work.

Only two series of Anthony's sermons have survived, one for saints' feast days and one for Sunday. He is the only early Franciscan preacher whose actual words have been preserved. The printed sermons are in Latin, and they are very long and argumentative. The sermons can be described as moral and penitential in tone; it is known, however, that the later ones became more dogmatic. Anthony underscored his points by frequent reference to Scripture. Though the Franciscans were not the first to introduce biblical examples into sermons, their development of this practice revolutionized the art of preaching.

After the death of Francis of Assisi on October 3, 1226, Anthony returned to Italy, where he was elected provincial of Romagna-Emilia. After his election as guardian of the convent at Le Puy-en-Velay, he became the leader of the more rigorous party in the Franciscan order, who were opposed to the modifications introduced by Elias of Cortona, general of the order.

During the year 1228, Anthony preached in the Venetian province and gave the Advent sermons in Florence; he preached a Lenten series in Florence the following year. At the end of 1229, he took up his last permanent residence at Padua, at a convent he founded in 1227. At the general chapter on May 30, 1230, he resigned his provincial office, but in June he was sent as a member of a special commission to Rome to confer with Pope Gregory IX concerning the interpretation of the rule. (Gregory was the same pope who had invited Anthony to preach in Rome in 1227.) During the winter of 1230-1231, he worked on a revision of his sermons. In 1231, he preached his last course of Lenten sermons.

Anthony's audience at times numbered as high as thirty thousand. Because church buildings could not accommodate his listeners, he was obliged to speak in the open air. He preached to the public perched in an oak tree at Camposanpiero in 1231.

Two weeks before his death, Anthony stood on the summit of a hill that overlooked Padua and blessed the city—as the dying Francis had once blessed his beloved Assisi—saying, "Blessed be thou, O Padua! Beautiful is thy site, rich thy fields, but Heaven is about to crown thee with a glory still richer and more beautiful."

Before he could return to Padua, Anthony died in Arcella on June 13, 1231, at the age of thirty-five. At the first news of his death, children ran about the streets crying out, "The saint is dead!" At his canonization on May 30, 1232, Gregory IX declared him to be a "teacher of the Church," and Pius XII, on January 16, 1946, made him a doctor of the Church with the title doctor evangelicus.

Significance

Besides being a scholar and teacher, Anthony was a preacher of great force and persuasiveness. In mystical theology, he prepared the way for Saint Bonaventure, Saint Teresa of Avila, and Saint John of the Cross. With other members of the Franciscan school, in infused contemplation he attributed the primary force to the will. He was a forerunner of John of the Cross in teaching the classical doctrines of the passive, sensitive, and intellectual activities of the soul. Anthony's mysticism was, however, not as austere as Saint John's, for he says that the devout individual may request the spiritual consolations that increase his love for God.

In 1263, when the relics of Saint Anthony were being transferred to a new chapel erected in his honor at Padua, it is said that Bonaventure found the saint's tongue preserved whole amid Anthony's ashes. Picking it up, Bonaventure said: "O blessed tongue, which always blessed the Lord and caused others to bless Him, now it is revealed how great was thy merit before God." Because of the many miracles recorded at Anthony's tomb, he is chiefly remembered as a wonder-worker, and he continues to be widely venerated in the Roman Catholic Church.

—*Peter F. Macaluso*

Further Reading

Clasen, Sophronius. *St. Anthony: Doctor of the Gospel.* Translated by Ignatius Brady. Chicago: Franciscan Herald Press, 1973. A good short biography of Anthony. This 140-page work has 32 pages of pictures and many quotations from Anthony's sermons. This work is useful because it attempts to present an authentic life of Anthony and omits unverifiable legends or tales.

Dent, Francis. *Saint Anthony of Padua and the Twentieth Century.* New York: P. J. Kennedy and Sons, 1899. This study is an old but useful examination of Anthony's life. The author's last four chapters describe how the devotion to Anthony grew and gives detailed accounts of the particular favors attributed to his intercession.

Franciscans of the U.S.A. *St. Anthony, Doctor of the Church Universal: Souvenir of the Commemorative Ceremonies.* Washington, D.C.: Catholic University of America Press, 1946. A collection of five essays dealing with Anthony as a preacher and theologian and with his relationship with the people. These essays contain analysis and interpretation not found in other works. A good summary of Anthony's contributions.

Huber, Raphael. *St. Anthony of Padua, Doctor of the Church Universal: A Critical Study of the Historical Sources of the Life, Sanctity, Learning, and Miracles of the Saint of Padua and Lisbon*. Milwaukee, Wis.: Bruce, 1948. This critical study is an indispensable and comprehensive source for the life and work of Anthony of Padua. Well-organized and well-documented chapters examine his life, his preaching and teaching career, and the authentic and the spurious writings. Included is a literary evaluation of the works on Anthony from a historical perspective, texts of three sermons, and an annotated bibliography.

Kerry, Margaret Charles, and Mary Elizabeth Tebo. *Saint Anthony of Padua: Fire and Light*. Boston: Pauline Books, 1999. A brief biography introducing Saint Anthony and his family origins, family life, and historical context, written especially for young, "intermediate" readers.

Moorman, John. *A History of the Franciscan Order: From Its Origins to the Year 1517*. Chicago: Franciscan Herald Press, 1988. A scholarly study of the Franciscan order that is filled with references and a large bibliography. It is an indispensable source for Anthony and his age, for it contains numerous references to primary materials arranged chronologically.

Nugent, Madeline Pecora. *Saint Anthony: Words of Fire, Life of Light*. Boston: Pauline Books, 1995. A fictionalized biography "narrated" by contemporaries of Anthony. Includes very helpful explanatory chapter notes

O'Brien, Isidore. *Enter Saint Anthony*. Chicago: Daughters of St. Paul, 1976. An inspiring life of Anthony that provides accurate and stimulating information on the career and work of Anthony and the temper of the age.

Stoddard, Charles Warren. *St. Anthony: The Wonder-Worker of Padua*. 2d ed. Rockford, Ill.: TAN Books, 1978. Written for the general reader, this book does justice to the life and career of Anthony. It is a well-rounded, brief account.

Zawart, A. "The History of Franciscan Preaching and of Franciscan Preachers 1209-1927."In *Franciscan Educational Conference*. Vol. 9. St. Bonaventure, N.Y.: St. Bonaventure University Press, 1927. A detailed study of the character of Franciscan preaching as a new development in medieval religious practice. A valuable analysis of the character of religious life in Anthony's time.

SEE ALSO: Saint Bonaventure; Saint Francis of Assisi; Gregory IX.

RELATED ARTICLES in *Great Events from History: The Middle Ages, 477-1453*: November 27, 1095: Pope Urban II Calls the First Crusade; c. 1175: Waldensian Excommunications Usher in Protestant Movement; April 16, 1209: Founding of the Franciscans; 1209-1229: Albigensian Crusade.

ARNOLD OF VILLANOVA

Catalan physician and scholar

The first great figure of European medicine and physician to kings and popes, Arnold joined Arabic theory to European empiricism. His more than seventy scientific works and translations made him an influential medical theorist beyond the sixteenth century, just as his radical theology and stormy life made him lastingly controversial.

BORN: c. 1239; probably Valencia, Aragon (now in Spain)

DIED: September 6, 1311; at sea, near Genoa (now in Italy)

ALSO KNOWN AS: Arnald of Villanova

AREAS OF ACHIEVEMENT: Medicine, religion and theology

EARLY LIFE

France, Italy, and Spain have claimed Arnold as a native son. The name "Villanova" (vihl-luh-NOH-vuh) may have derived from Villeneuve-les-Vence, or else Villeneuve-Loubet, in Provence, where he had relatives. By one theory, his family were Jews who, on converting to Christianity, moved to Catalonia and then Valencia. Arnold himself said that he was "born of the soil, lowly and obscure" and called himself "an unlearned country-fellow." Contemporaries called him a Catalan, which he accepted, and his early editors used that as an alternate surname. The only language in which he wrote, besides Latin, was Catalan. The kingdom of Valencia, just conquered from the Muslims by Catalonia-Aragon, always claimed Arnold for its own. The great fourteenth century

Valencian writer Francesc Eiximenis took it as common knowledge, within a lifetime of Arnold's death, that the latter was a native of Valencia. The settlers in Valencia, and even those in Murcia to its south, were called "true Catalans" by the contemporary memoirist Ramón Muntaner; famous medieval Valencians such as Vicent Ferrer and the Borgia popes, as well as the Majorcan Anselm Turmeda, were also called Catalans. Thus, Arnold was probably born in Valencia, after the fall of its capital in 1238. Arnold had properties in Valencia and, more significant, was ordained as a cleric in minor orders in the Valencian diocese; his daughter Maria became a nun at Valencia city in 1291.

In 1982, John Benton published a note from a medieval manuscript archived in Pasadena, California, indicating that Arnold was born at Villanueva de Jilóca near Huesca in Aragon and that some of his relatives still lived there in the mid-fourteenth century. Benton suggested that Arnold learned his Arabic from the conquered Muslims there and was an Aragonese by early training. There is no evidence, however, that Arnold knew any Aragonese, while he is a major figure in Catalan literature. Moreover, it is unlikely that Aragon's acculturated Muslim farming communities, with their Arabic dialect, were the source of his classical Arabic and his knowledge of its literature. Valencia was an advanced Islamic society, barely come under colonial rule, with its Muslim aristocracy, savants, and schools intact during the long decades of Arnold's education. As a Valencian, Arnold's environment would have been multiethnic, among affluent Muslim and Jewish communities in a land of international ports, lush farmlands, and dangerous revolts on the part of the Muslim majority—a far cry from the bleak and rocky uplands of Aragon.

LIFE'S WORK

Arnold of Villanova (Arnau de Vilanova in his native Catalan) was graduated around 1260 from the celebrated medical university in Montpellier, then part of the wider realms of Aragon-Catalonia. He may have done postdoctoral work at Naples under the physician Giovanni de Casamicciola. Presumably during his Montpellier sojourn, he married Agnès Blasi of that city, herself of a lineage of physicians. In the early 1280's, he studied Hebrew and the Talmud under the Arabist-Hebraist Ramón Martí at the Dominican school in Barcelona. Famous by 1281, Arnold became the main physician to King Peter III of Aragon-Catalonia, receiving the huge stipend of two thousand Barcelonan sous on condition of living in Barcelona near the court (another indication that his home was not Catalonia but Valencia). Other gifts included the castle of Ollers. Arnold continued to enjoy royal support under Peter's successors, Alfonso III (r. 1285-1291) and James II (r. 1291-1327), and he was released to reside in Valencia, which he did from 1286 to 1289.

Arnold of Villanova. (New York Academy of Medicine)

Called to teach at Montpellier for a decade, Arnold began to publish apocalyptic religious works, prophesying the coming of Antichrist in 1345 (later revised to 1368) and demanding moral reform. When James II sent the respected doctor on a diplomatic mission to Philip IV of France, Arnold spread his radical theology so passionately that the theologians of the University of Paris had him tried and condemned in 1299. Pope Boniface VIII and King Philip secured his release. Grateful for Arnold's cure of his renal affliction, the pope lent him the castle of Scorcola near Anagni as a retreat in which to study and write. Arnold returned to his post with the royal family in 1302. He soon became embroiled in a theological battle with the Dominicans of Gerona and Castellón de Ampurias, and he disputed before the archbishop at Lérida and the king at Barcelona. At Valencia, his polemics prompted the Inquisition to excommunicate him. His patient and protector Boniface VIII died in 1303, but the new pope (Benedict XI, whom Arnold treated for gallstones) shielded him. Further religious polemic got Arnold imprisoned briefly at Perugia in Italy. Under the protection of Frederick III of Sicily, however, he continued his religious writings at Messina.

In 1305, Arnold returned to Barcelona to exhort James II to crusade against Islamic Almería. Continuing to write on medical and religious topics, and by now the European leader of the visionary evangelical movement called the Spirituals, Arnold went to Narbonne and Marseilles; in 1308, he was in Messina, where he interpreted an obsessive dream for King Frederick. In 1309, he was at the court of his friend and patient Pope Clement V in Avignon; in 1310, he was back with Frederick III briefly and in the siege of Almería and then at Messina again. Journeying by sea to Avignon, he died near Genoa and was buried there in 1311.

During all these travels, he had enthusiastically propagated the astrological, alchemical, and occult themes then popular in Islam. His method of exegesis by symbolic letters, borrowed from the Jewish Cabalists, disturbed some contemporaries. Suspected of converting to Judaism, he was in reality an anti-Judaic proselytizer. In 1316, the Inquisition at Tarragona condemned a number of his religious approaches. At the same time, he was hailed internationally as a great physician.

In later medieval Mediterranean Europe (as distinguished from the inland and northern regions), a physician was a prestigious personage, expected to be a general savant, a repository of philosophical and even theological ancient knowledge, and also a man active in public affairs. He was a welcome decoration in the courts of the powerful. This model echoes the Islamic *hakim*, extending to the Jews with Arabist training who functioned at the court of the kings of Aragon-Catalonia. Training of physicians in Europe, though often still accomplished through private apprenticeship, had become a university function, so that the university title "doctor" and the renown of the universities themselves were reflecting more glory on the profession. Seen in this light, Arnold's almost comic embroilment in the Spirituals' cause makes more sense; it was then the premier public polemic in Europe. Arnold's diplomatic projects are also thus explained. He never lost sight, however, of his own priorities: He was a physician, in an era of revolutionary advances in surgery, anatomy, and the professionalization of medical work.

Arnold's medical theory has been summed up as "Galen Arabicized." He not only translated Arabic medical works into Latin, including those of the Valencian Abū Salt, but also revered the classic Muslim physicians and integrated their findings with Western medical knowledge and practice. His *Aphorismi de gradibus* (aphorisms on the degrees), completed in the late 1290's, revolutionized the study of pharmacology with its theory of compound medicines and its application of mathematics. It organized traditional knowledge into one unified field, while rejecting previous forms of classification. Arnold composed some seventy medical books and treatises in Latin, over a wide range of topics. His work on preventive medicine and hygiene, *Regimen sanitatis Salernitanum* (1307; *Regimen sanitatis Salerni: This Booke Teachyng All People to Governe Them in Health*, 1575), enjoyed great popular success; the queen of Aragon ordered a version translated into Romance for wider diffusion, and a Hebrew version appeared. In all, Arnold wrote eleven such books. He also wrote a book titled *De conservatione juventutis et retardatione senectutis* (1290; *The Conservation of Youth and Defense of Age*, 1544). Other works specialized in bleeding, fevers, poisons, sexual intercourse, conception, sterility, dreams, food for the sick, eye troubles, epilepsy, wines, waters, antidotes, leprosy and contagious diseases, the heart, meat-eating, and medical theory. He discoursed on the value of bathing, kinds of baths, and their effects. He also took up questions on surgery, an art being revolutionized by the treatise of Abulcassis (al-Zahrawi) that he had translated and by pioneering theories on disease as anatomically focused.

The historian of Spanish medieval medicine Luis García-Ballester sees Arnold as a frontier phenomenon, a fusion of Arabic, Jewish, and European medical traditions that flowered until supplanted by the Scholastic model of the Italians. Arnold was an academician, and his talent was for joining practice to theory. A catalog of his library survives, affording insights into his intellectual tastes. He was not interested, for example, in Islamic theology. He collected not only Arabic books but also works in Greek, a language he learned only late in life.

SIGNIFICANCE

Arnold was the greatest physician in the West since ancient Rome. Physician and spiritual adviser to four kings, physician to three popes, and for a decade the most celebrated teacher at Europe's greatest medical university, Montpellier, Arnold was a tireless author and translator of medical works. More than any medieval figure, he represents the juncture of Arabic with European medicine, theory with practice. At the same time, he was a major figure in public affairs, from diplomatic missions to crusade propaganda; he became the leader of the apocalyptic Spirituals movement then agitating Europe. His writings show his contribution to the evolution of the Catalan language and literature. He had close associations with the Jewish community in southern France, partly to borrow Cabalistic knowledge and partly with proselytizing intent. His incessant travel, and the explosive energies visible both in his production of books and in the disputations that made him leader of the Spirituals (and landed him in prison several times), made him one of the best-known public men of his age.

—*Robert I. Burns*

Further Reading

Amundsen, Darrel W., ed. *Medicine, Society, and Faith in the Ancient and Medieval Worlds*. Baltimore: Johns Hopkins University Press, 1996. Covers the connections between medicine and religious faith, canon law on medical practice, medical ethics, and more.

Arnold of Villanova. *Arnaldi de Villanova: Opera Medica Omnia*. Vols. 2 and 16. Edited by Michael R. McVaugh. Granada, Spain: Seminarium Historiae Medicae Granatensis, 1975. Despite the work's Latin title and edited text, the introductions to these volumes are in English, written by a major authority on Arnold. The second volume, *Aphorismi de gradibus*, has 143 pages in English on Arnold's contribution to medieval pharmacology.

Benton, John F. "The Birthplace of Arnau de Vilanova: A Case for Villanueva de Jilóca near Daroca." In *Viator: Medieval and Renaissance Studies*. Vol. 13. Berkeley: University of California Press, 1982. An exciting contribution to the study of Arnold's early years, though controversial in its interpretation. Contains additional information on his career and a bibliography in notes.

Burns, Robert I. "The Medieval Crossbow as Surgical Instrument: An Illustrated Case History." *Bulletin of the New York Academy of Medicine* 48 (September, 1972): 983-989. Reprinted as chapter 7 of Burns's *Moors and Crusaders in Mediterranean Spain* (London: Variorum, 1978). Six thirteenth century panels illustrate a surgical procedure, including the preparation of the patient beforehand by assistants and the formal dress of physicians. The case is explained from contemporary surgical manuals, with relevant bibliography.

García-Ballester, Luís. *Medicine in a Multicultural Society: Christian, Jewish, and Muslim Practitioners in the Spanish Kingdoms, 1222-1610*. Aldershot, England: Ashgate, 2001. A history of medicine, medical practice, and religion in Arnold's time. Includes an index.

Kibre, Pearl. *Studies in Medieval Science: Alchemy, Astrology, Mathematics, and Medicine*. London: Hambledon Press, 1984. Discusses treatises by medieval medical writers found in the medieval libraries of Western Europe.

Kotek, Samuel S., and Luís García-Ballester, eds. *Medicine and Medical Ethics in Medieval and Early Modern Spain: An Intercultural Approach*. Jerusalem: Magnes Press, 1996. Discusses Jewish medical practitioners in Spain and the ethics of patient-doctor relations at the time of Arnold.

McVaugh, Michael R. "Quantified Medical Theory and Practice at Fourteenth-Century Montpellier." *Bulletin of the History of Medicine* 43 (September-October, 1969): 397-413. An early presentation of themes expanded by the author in his later introduction to Arnold's works on mathematical formulas applied to compound medicines.

Siraisi, Nancy G. *Taddeo Alderotti and His Pupils: Two Generations of Italian Medical Learning*. Princeton, N.J.: Princeton University Press, 1981. An excellent introduction to the new medicine of the thirteenth century, a panoramic and profound examination of a Mediterranean region then vying with Arnold's Montpellier and Catalonia. Includes an extensive bibliography.

Ziegler, Joseph. *Medicine and Religion, Circa 1300: The Case of Arnau de Vilanova*. New York: Oxford University Press, 1998. Covers medicine in the context of religion and religious speculation, "a sermon for students of medicine," and more.

See also: Pietro d'Abano; Averroës; Avicenna; Jacqueline Félicie; Saint Fulbert of Chartres; Hildegard von Bingen; Saint Isidore of Seville; Moses Maimonides; Paul of Aegina; Philip IV the Fair; al-Rāzī; Trotula.

Related articles in *Great Events from History: The Middle Ages, 477-1453*: 809: First Islamic Public Hospital; c. 1010-1015: Avicenna Writes His *Canon of Medicine*; 1100-1300: European Universities Emerge; c. 1150: Moors Transmit Classical Philosophy and Medicine to Europe.

ARNOLFO DI CAMBIO
Italian architect and sculptor

As chief architect of Florence during the end of the thirteenth century, Arnolfo directed the construction of some of Florence's principal monuments and brought the Italian classical tradition together with elements of the French Gothic.

BORN: c. 1245; Colle di Val d'Elsa (now in Italy)
DIED: Between 1302 and 1310; Florence (now in Italy)
AREAS OF ACHIEVEMENT: Architecture, art

EARLY LIFE

Little is known of the early years of Arnolfo di Cambio (awr-NOL-foh dee KAWM-byoh). From 1266 to 1268, he worked as chief assistant to Nicola Pisano, Italy's first great sculptor; together they created the pulpit in the cathedral in Siena, Italy. Arnolfo may also have worked with Pisano at about the same time on the tomb of Saint Dominic in the Church of San Domenico in Bologna. Around 1272, Arnolfo constructed the monument to Cardinal Annibaldi in the Church of San Giovanni Laterano of Rome. This work may have been commissioned by Emperor Charles I of Anjou, who became Arnolfo's patron in 1271, when the sculptor went to Florence after leaving Pisano's shop. The monument to Annibaldi reflects the characteristics of Arnolfo's early work, with graceful yet stiff drapery and simple treatment of the facial features—expressing the restraint of classical Roman sculpture, which was Arnolfo's model.

Arnolfo continued to distinguish himself as a sculptor of funerary monuments during the first stage of his artistic career. Two of Arnolfo's notable works of this period are the monument to Cardinal Guillaume de Braye in San Domenico in Orvieto (1282) and the ciborium (an ornamental altar canopy) in San Paolo Fuori le Mura in Rome (1285). The monument to Cardinal de Braye combines the energetic Gothic figures of Saint Peter and Saint Dominic with a restrained, classical rendering of the Virgin Mary as an empress holding her son. The strong horizontal lines, maintained by the ornamentation of the pedestal and sarcophagus, temper the vertical quality of the Gothic design. Similar effects are found in the ciborium in San Paolo Fuori le Mura. The figures of the saints reflect the restrained, sober classicism of early Christian work. Moreover, the Gothic design is consistently controlled: The trilobed arches are gently rounded, conveying spaciousness rather than strong upward movement; the pediment gables and pinnacles are countered with strong horizontal lines accented by the decorative use of nearly black marble. These two characteristics of Arnolfo's sculptures—the serene, controlled spirit of sculptured portraits and the de-emphasis of vertical movement—are also trademarks of Arnolfo's architectural work.

LIFE'S WORK

Arnolfo's classicism, distinctive in his sculptures in Rome, is most evident in the Tuscan capital of Florence, where he served as the city's *capomaestro*, or chief architect, probably beginning in 1284. In many respects, Tuscany was based on classical precedent, and Florence, of all Tuscan cities, took this precedent most seriously, modeling its own republican government after the Roman Republic. Giovanni Villani, in 1338, referred to Florence as "the daughter and creature of Rome." As *capomaestro* of Florence, Arnolfo was charged with extensive city planning, culminating in the reconstruction for which Florence has been famous ever since. Pressured by the city's growth (its population had surpassed fifty thousand by the end of the thirteenth century) and strengthened by the success of the city's banking and wool industry, the guilds and prominent families of Florence were eager to have the city stabilized through comprehensive city planning. Arnolfo directed a building campaign for a new set of city walls (it would be the third set, the last having been built in 1170). These walls would draw into the city's circumference the enclaves, at opposite edges of the city, of the two powerful brotherhoods, the Dominicans and the Franciscans, as well as the neighborhoods along the banks of the south side of the Arno River. The building campaign also called for a new cathedral and a new town hall, the Palazzo Vecchio. In addition, the communal granary, also a monument to the city's guilds, was slated for renovation.

These three focal points of the new city—cathedral, town hall, and guild hall—were to be united by the widening of the straight thoroughfare, Via Calzaioli. Thus public monuments would dominate over private ones, and the republic of Florence would become a more vivid expression of classical ideals, including Aristotle's notion that city walls add strength and beauty and the Roman contention that wide, straight streets (*pulchrae, amplae, et rectae*) contribute health, convenience, and beauty to a city. Arnolfo was designer and director of all these projects, although none was completed during his lifetime. In addition to these public works, Arnolfo started restorations of the Franciscan abbey church known as the Badia and designed the Franciscan Church of Santa Croce, one of the most famous monuments of Florence. Arnolfo was probably also responsible for refacing the baptistry, situated a few yards west of the new cathedral.

By the time Arnolfo began the work of enlarging Florence and constructing its major religious and secular buildings, the city had already established an architectural tone that was consistent with Arnolfo's tastes. Italian Gothic was a combination of classical and French Gothic influences, with the classical dominating. This classical influence is most dramatically represented in the Italian Romanesque style found in the Benedictine Abbey Church of San Miniato al Monte, located on a hill across the Arno from the site of Santa Croce. San Miniato al Monte's round arches supported by columns and its triangular pediment are imitative of classical architecture. The stark contrast between the white and dark green marble used as paneling for the church's façade is pure Romanesque, having no parallel in antiquity, but the classical proportions emphasized by the façade's geometric patterns are strong echoes of classical forms, whose gentle curves and strong horizontal lines are the antithesis of the Gothic style. The Church of San Miniato al Monte was begun in 1013, but the Florentines of the thirteenth century regarded it as far older than it was, a survival from Roman antiquity. For an architect of Arnolfo's time, influenced by the attraction to classical forms that was to become a trademark of the Renaissance, this accessible "ancient" model could not be ignored.

The Church of Santa Maria Novella, begun a generation before Arnolfo became *capomaestro* of Florence, offered a precedent of compromises between these Italian classical ideals and the French Gothic tradition so popular throughout the Middle Ages. The ceiling of the church is a stone vault instead of the open timbered roof of other Tuscan churches, such as San Miniato al Monte. The usual effect of this vaulting is a feeling of vertical thrust, but in this Tuscan rendering the vertical thrust is minimized by many elements. The spacing of the interior columns along the nave of the church creates square nave bays and proportionally longer aisle bays than are found in Gothic churches. The heights of the arcade and clerestory are nearly equal, creating the illusion that the roof is shorter than it is. In addition, the vaults and arches are made from *pietra serena*, a dark gray stone of Tuscany, and stand outlined against the plaster walls. The effect of these features is an interior that feels spacious, light, and broad, unlike a narrow and vertical Gothic interior. In these respects, the Church of Santa Maria Novella is the structural predecessor to Arnolfo's two great churches, Santa Croce and Florence's cathedral, Santa Maria del Fiore.

Arnolfo designed Santa Croce closely after Romanesque models. The ceiling of Santa Croce takes after San Miniato al Monte rather than Santa Maria Novella; the church has an open-trussed, wooden roof rather than stone vaulting. The lighter weight ceiling allows for lighter supporting columns, which give the church's nave its Tuscan openness. Gothic influence, however softened, is evident not only in its pointed arches but also in its long, rather narrow aisle bays and nave bays wider than they are long.

The Cathedral of Santa Maria del Fiore is perhaps Arnolfo's chief achievement. The most striking monument of Florence, it brings together the dominant elements of Tuscan art. Santa Maria del Fiore is the architectural culmination of an age, integrating native Tuscan qualities with the Italian Romanesque and the French Gothic. To appreciate Arnolfo's design, however, one must ignore the alterations that were made by later designers who finished the cathedral complex. Giotto (c. 1266-1337), who succeeded Arnolfo as *capomaestro*, did not attempt working on the church proper but designed and began construction of the bell tower. Francesco Talenti, a subsequent *capomaestro*, altered the church's façade and enlarged the floor space, extending the nave and broadening the transepts and chancel. Although they violated the original scale of the building, Talenti's changes otherwise respected Arnolfo's design. Arnolfo's original plan survives in manuscript, and his design for the façade is depicted in a thirteenth century painting by Bernardino Poccetti.

The Tuscan tradition is evident in Santa Maria del Fiore's interior, which is similar to the interior of Santa Croce and Santa Maria Novella in its openness and classical pilasters. Like Santa Croce, it has horizontal lines coursing the interior perimeter above the aisle arches. The cathedral's Gothic vaulted ceiling, like that of Santa Maria Novella, is lightened through the use of *pietra serena* and plaster. The colored marble outlining geometric patterns on the exterior is an Italian Romanesque feature. In the interior, the octagonal opening at the crossing mirrors the octagonal form of the baptistry. It is this octagon that is the most distinguishing feature of the cathedral, giving shape to the open center of the interior. The dome above it, spanning the complete width of the nave, creates a spaciousness unmatched by other Italian churches of the period. Arnolfo, no doubt responding to pressure from Florentine patrons to outdo rivaling cathedrals in Pisa and Siena, was intent on the octagonal form, but such a design required very sophisticated engineering. This problem would not be solved until more than one hundred years later, when Filippo Brunelleschi (1377-1446) came up with a plan that enabled the dome to be built. With its completion, Arnolfo's intention was realized: The French Gothic style that was so influential in the late Middle Ages informs and gives grace to this cathedral, which nevertheless leaves as its dominant impression a light spaciousness, the quality that was native to the architecture of Arnolfo's Italian heritage.

SIGNIFICANCE

In his time, Arnolfo's talents were well recognized. The Florentines, in 1300, declared him officially exempt from tax obligations because he was the best known and most highly respected architect of church buildings. As sculptor, architect, and city planner, he can also be appreciated for his range of talents, a sort of precursor of the ideal of the Renaissance man.

Arnolfo's legacy as a sculptor is his creation of a blend of classical and contemporary Italian forms. His subdued, classical draperies and his warmly human, yet austere, portraits look forward to the human figures painted by Giotto (many of which appear as frescoes in Arnolfo's Church of Santa Croce). Arnolfo's funerary monuments, particularly the monuments to Cardinal Annibaldi in Rome and to Cardinal de Braye in Orvieto, became the principal models of Gothic funerary art.

Arnolfo's distinctive architecture, however, became his most wide-ranging contribution. The architecture of Italy's Renaissance, which had Florence as its capital, generally carries forward the synthesis of styles that Arnolfo realized. Evidence of this is seen most notably in Brunelleschi's Florentine churches, Santo Spirito and San Lorenzo. Though Brunelleschi, as a Renaissance architect, was concerned with consistent mathematic proportions in his buildings to an extent not realized in Arnolfo's age, he nevertheless maintains the same uniquely Italian balance of the Romanesque, Tuscan, and Gothic styles that Arnolfo first mastered. Even Brunelleschi's balanced proportions can be seen foreshadowed in the evenly radiating aisles of the broad central octagon at the center of Florence's cathedral.

Creator of a native art, like Dante writing in the vernacular and Giotto expressing biblical themes in classically influenced Italian portraits, Arnolfo strengthened and gave longevity to the Italian style in art.

—*Dennis C. Chowenhill*

FURTHER READING

Kostoff, Spiro. *A History of Architecture: Settings and Rituals*. New York: Oxford University Press, 1985. An extremely accurate and thorough source of information about the architectural precedents to Arnolfo and Arnolfo's achievement. Two chapters contain information on Arnolfo: "The Urbanization of Europe: 1100-1300" and "Edges of Medievalism." Useful photographs, drawings, and maps pertaining to Arnolfo's buildings in Florence. Scholarly, but readable. Contains a glossary and an index. A bibliography is included at the end of every chapter.

Mayernik, David. *Timeless Cities: An Architect's Reflections on Renaissance Italy*. Boulder, Colo.: Westview Press, 2003. Mayernik's examination of Italian Renaissance cities includes a look at Florence and Siena. Bibliography and index.

Murray, Peter. *The Architecture of the Italian Renaissance*. New York: Schocken Books, 1986. Includes an excellent, clear account of Romanesque and Gothic influences in Tuscany before and during Arnolfo's time. Discusses Arnolfo's achievement, with more accurate information than is available in older accounts. Also includes drawings and photographs of Arnolfo's architectural work, a carefully annotated bibliography, and an index.

Vasari, Giorgio. *Lives of Painters, Sculptors, and Architects*. Reprint. New York: Alfred A. Knopf, 1996. A classic biography of Italian artists by a Renaissance Italian painter, written more than two hundred years after Arnolfo's death. Though riddled with inaccuracies (Vasari indiscriminately mixed legend with history), it is still valuable as an appreciation of the genius of Arnolfo from an artist's point of view. Treats Arnolfo as Arnolfo di Lapo, a composite figure that includes Arnolfo di Cambio. If not a consistently reliable account, it nevertheless shows how Arnolfo was viewed until the twentieth century.

SEE ALSO: Filippo Brunelleschi; Lorenzo Ghiberti; Giotto; Andrea Orcagna; Andrea Pisano; Nicola Pisano and Giovanni Pisano; Claus Sluter; Suger.

RELATED ARTICLE in *Great Events from History: The Middle Ages, 477-1453*: April 16, 1209: Founding of the Franciscans.

ÁRPÁD

Magyar founder of Hungary

Árpád, the first great leader of a united Hungarian people and the founder of a dynasty, led the tribal Magyars in a conquest and settlement of the land that is now Hungary.

BORN: c. 850; southern Siberia
DIED: 907; Óbuda, Hungary (now Budapest, Hungary)
AREAS OF ACHIEVEMENT: Government and politics, warfare and conquest, military

EARLY LIFE

Details of the childhood and formative years of Árpád (AHR-pahd) are scarce. Most of the information concerning the early history of the Hungarians comes from accounts written hundreds of years later that relied on traditional lore passed through the generations by word of mouth. According to the *Chronica Hungarorum* (1488; *Chronicle of the Hungarians*, 1991), the Hungarians were originally from the western portion of southern Siberia. Their society was nomadic; they subsisted by fishing and herding and by using mounted archers to raid and loot other peoples. Seven tribes, the Nyek, Magyar, Kürtgyarmat, Tarján, Jenó, Kara, and Kaza, left Siberia during the ninth century and migrated southwest, acquiring territory to the north of the Black Sea. They named this region Lebedia after their chieftain, Lebed, who had guided them during the migration. The exact date of their settlement is unknown, but contemporaries first recorded their presence in 839 in the region around the lower Danube. Árpád was born in Lebedia around 850 and assumed a prominent role in the affairs of his tribe, the Magyars, led by his father Almos. The Hungarians portray their hero as a short, stocky man about five feet tall who as a boy was well trained in the art of war and horsemanship.

Conflict between the Hungarians and the indigenous population of Lebedia soon forced Árpád's people to look for another site for settlement. The Petchenegs, a people of Turkish origin, attacked and defeated the Hungarians in 889 and prompted them to move farther west. The Hungarians named their second settlement Etelköz, now known as the region of Bessarabia. The defeat at the hands of the Petchenegs created conditions that brought Árpád to power soon afterward.

LIFE'S WORK

The chieftains of the seven tribes met soon after the move to Etelköz to appoint a leader to rule over the whole of the Hungarian people. This was previously unheard of in times of peace, but the chieftains realized that there was much greater strength in unity than in divided leadership such as they had in the past. They first chose Lebed to be their permanent leader, but he was quite old and declined the honor. He suggested that either Almos of the Magyar tribe or his son Árpád should receive the post. Almos became leader, with the understanding that Árpád would inherit the position. The existing sources conflict on the exact date of Árpád's assumption of power, but by 896, he had become the leader of the united nation of Hungarians; according to ancient custom, when he assumed power he was raised on a shield and presented to the people. Henceforth, ethnic Hungarians became known as "Magyars" after his tribe, which was the strongest of the seven.

Árpád assumed the title of *gyula*, the military commander of the nation. Another post, the *kundu*, was held by a man named Kurszán. The *kundu* was technically the religious and political head of the nation, but the position held nominal power because the success or failure of the nation depended on events on the battlefield. Árpád wielded the majority of the power in the newly united Hungarian nation and officially assumed both positions following the death of Kurszán in 904. Subsequent leaders also combined the powers of these two posts as absolute rulers of the Hungarians.

The settlement of Etelköz, on the northern border of the Byzantine Empire, attracted the attention of the Byzantines soon after the Hungarians settled there. The Byzantines sent merchants to trade with the newly established nation who returned with a report on the new Hungarian ruler. The merchants described Árpád as a wise man who was valiant and quite capable of governing a nation. More important, these merchants also reported that Árpád was a strict disciplinarian with a well-trained army. Because of the potential security concern that the Hungarians posed to the Byzantine Empire, the Byzantine emperor, Leo VI (r. 886-912), did not take the information lightly. To the west of Etelköz lay the Bulgar Empire, which had been expanding its borders to include not only present-day Bulgaria but also most of present-day Hungary. Leo VI believed that the possibility of an alliance between the Bulgars and the Hungarians constituted a serious threat on his northern border. His solution was to entice Árpád into an alliance and to make war on the Bulgar Empire. The threat would be greatly reduced if one of the two nations were destroyed in war.

Leo was successful, and the alliance of Árpád and Leo declared war on Czar Simeon the Great (d. 927) of the Bulgars in 895. The Byzantines provided ships for Árpád's troops to sail across the Danube River to attack the Bulgars. This army, led by Árpád's son Levante, crushed the Bulgar army and devastated Simeon's kingdom. However, the destruction of the Bulgarian army proved to be a crucial turning point in Árpád's life that was initially for the worse. Leo VI had accomplished his goal with the defeat of the Bulgarians, and he consequently made a separate peace with Simeon in 895. This peace held disastrous consequences for Árpád and his people, as it deprived Árpád's army of the ships they needed to cross the Danube and return home to Etelköz. Levante and the army were thus trapped in the Bulgar Empire.

Czar Simeon took advantage of the situation by concluding an alliance with the Petchenegs, the old foes of the Hungarians. Árpád found his nation attacked on the western frontier of Etelköz by the Bulgarians and in the east by the Petchenegs. This combined attack defeated the Hungarians, who were without the aid of Levante's army. Faced with the possibility of continuing attacks that would inevitably destroy his nation, Árpád made the decision in 895 to move the Hungarian nation a third time, to a place that was more easily defendable than Etelköz.

The plan to evacuate Etelköz was a well-orchestrated operation founded on information Árpád received from a band of Hungarians who had conducted raids across the Carpathian Mountains in the region between the Danube and Tisza Rivers in 894. They reported that this area, the Pannonian Plain, had good land in which to settle and was well protected by dense forest to the east and north and high mountains to the south. The Bulgars had laid claim to the area, but Árpád realized that they could not defend the territory alone. Isolated from their Petcheneg allies by the Carpathian mountains, the Bulgars were easy prey to the superior power of the well-trained Hungarian army. Árpád heeded the advice of his subjects that the Pannonian Plain was the best place in which to resettle the Hungarian nation.

Árpád realized that an immediate evacuation of Etelköz was impossible, given the threat of attack on two fronts from the Bulgars and the Petchenegs. Following a thorough exploration of the proposed resettlement area, Árpád resolved to invade the region by numerous different routes and to withdraw from Etelköz gradually. This plan kept the Hungarians' enemies unaware of the move

Árpád, in center on horseback, presides over the union of the Magyar tribes in Hungary. (Hulton|Archive at Getty Images)

ÁRPÁD KINGS OF HUNGARY, C. 896-1301

Reign	Ruler
c. 896-907	ÁRPÁD
d. 947	Zsolt
d. 972	Taksony
997	Géza
997-1038	SAINT STEPHEN (ISTVÁN) I
1038-1041	Peter Orseleo
1041-1044	Samuel
1044-1046	Peter (second rule)
1047-1060	Andrew I
1060-1063	Béla I
1063-1074	Salamon
1074-1077	Géza I
1077-1095	SAINT LÁSZLÓ (LADISLAS) I
1095-1116	Kalman
1116-1131	Stephen II
1131-1141	Béla II
1141-1162	Géza II
1162-1163	László II
1163-1172	Stephen III
1163-1165	Stephen IV
1172-1196	Béla III
1196-1204	Imre
1204-1205	László III
1205-1235	Andrew II
1235-1270	Béla IV
1270-1272	Stephen V
1272-1290	László IV
1290-1301	Andrew III

and also allowed the migrants to gain a foothold in the new country before most of them had left for their new home. Except for the route he himself traveled, the paths that Árpád chose for his people to take are uncertain. According to the chroniclers, Árpád and his contingent traveled north, entering the Pannonian Plain via the Verecke Pass in the northeast Carpathian mountain range. The other paths were probably through the southeast Carpathians and across the lower Danube.

Árpád's plan succeeded, and by 898, the entire Hungarian nation had evacuated Etelköz, conquered the indigenous population of the Pannonian Plain, and established a firm base from which to expand. In the ensuing years, Árpád augmented his new kingdom with the conquest of much of the land to the south of the Pannonian Plain, his armies reaching as far as Bavaria, Austria, and the northern border of Italy. The final stage of Árpád's conquest was the occupation in 902 of Moravia, which was weakened by internal strife that undermined its defenses. With the fall of Moravia, Árpád established a large eastern European kingdom that would be consolidated by his descendants. He died in 907 and is believed to be buried in Óbuda, part of modern Budapest.

SIGNIFICANCE

Árpád's contribution to history is apparent despite the lack information on his reign. His leadership allowed the Hungarian nation to survive certain defeat and subjugation by the Bulgars and Petchenegs. More important, through his conquests, he became the father of modern Hungary. He had little time to consolidate his realm before his death, but the Árpád dynasty dominated Hungarian history until 1301, when the last of the line, Andrew III, died. Árpád's successors built on his work, transforming Hungarian society from a largely nomadic one to a society based on agriculture. Future leaders also established a firm hold on the territorial holdings won by Árpád, ensuring Hungary's position as one of the most powerful nations of medieval Europe.

—*Eric W. Osborne*

FURTHER READING

Bowlus, Charles R. *Franks, Moravians, and Magyars: The Struggle for the Middle Danube, 788-907*. Philadelphia: University of Pennsylvania Press, 1995. Controversial in its contention that Great Moravia was actually located in modern Serbia. This text is considered a lightning-rod for renewed debate about early Magyar history. Maps, bibliography, index.

Györffy, György. *King Saint Stephen of Hungary*. Boulder, Colo.: Social Science Monographs, 1994. Although largely devoted to the life of Árpád's successor, Stephen I, this work contains a summary of Árpád's reign and highlights the difficulties collecting concrete information on the early history of the Hungarians. Maps, bibliography, index.

Halász, Zoltán. *Hungary: Geography, History, Political and Social System, Economy, Living Standard, Culture, Sports*. 2d ed. Budapest: Corvina Press, 1963. Includes sections on history and geography that are useful examining Árpád's life and legacy. The history section contains a discussion of his conquests and the geography section illustrates the gradual expansion of the Hungarian state.

Kosztolnyik, Z. J. *Hungary Under the Early Árpáds, 890's to 1063*. Boulder, Colo.: East European Monographs, 2002. A historical survey of the House of Árpád. Discusses the early years of the Magyars, their

migrations and settlement patterns, military campaigns, and more. Genealogical tables, maps, bibliography, index.
Lázár, István. *Hungary: A Brief History*. Translated by Albert Tezla. 6th ed. Budapest: Corvina Press, 2001. Presents a brief but concise history of Hungary, from its beginnings during the days of Árpád through the present day. Maps, index.
Lukinich, Imre. *A History of Hungary in Biographical Sketches*. 1937. Reprint. Translated by Catherine Dallas. Freeport, N.Y.: Books for Libraries Press, 1968. Covers the history of Hungary through a biographical examination of each of its major figures. Contains a chapter on Árpád and the early history of the Hungarians as well as good sections on other Árpád Dynasty rulers.
Macartney, C. A. *The Magyars in the Ninth Century*. London: Cambridge University Press, 1968. Examines the existing source material on Árpád and his successors and comparatively evaluates the usefulness of each source.
Róna-Tas, András. *Hungarians and Europe in the Early Middle Ages: An Introduction to Early Hungarian History*. New York: Central European University Press, 1999. A comprehensive survey of the history of Hungary. A good introduction for general readers unfamiliar with the region. Maps, extensive bibliography, index.
Sinor, Denis. *History of Hungary*. 1959. Reprint. Westport, Conn.: Greenwood Press, 1976. A good account of Hungarian history from before Árpád's rise to power. Provides a good description of ninth century Hungarian society and how it changed following the migration from Etelköz. Maps, index.
Thuróczy, János. *Chronicle of the Hungarians*. Translated by Frank Mantello. Bloomington, Ind.: Indiana University, Research Institute for Inner Asian Studies, 1991. The best known and most widely accepted account of Árpád's reign, this fifteenth century work serves as a base for study about Árpád and the early history of the Hungarians.
Vámbéry, Ármin. *Hungary in Ancient, Mediaeval, and Modern Times*. 1886. Reprint. Freeport, N.Y.: Books for Libraries Press, 1972. Provides a good summary of Árpád's contributions and importance. The section concerning Árpád focuses on his defeat of the Moravians, which ended his conquests. Illustrations.

SEE ALSO: Boris I of Bulgaria; János Hunyadi; Saint László I; Stephen I.
RELATED ARTICLES in *Great Events from History: The Middle Ages, 477-1453*: 890's: Magyars Invade Italy, Saxony, and Bavaria; 893: Beginning of Bulgaria's Golden Age; August 10, 955: Otto I Defeats the Magyars; November, 1330: Basarab Defeats the Hungarians; June 28, 1389: Turkish Conquest of Serbia; 1442-1456: János Hunyadi Defends Hungary Against the Ottomans.

ĀRYABHAṬA THE ELDER

Indian mathematician and astronomer

Āryabhaṭa the Elder's treatise, The Aryabhatiya, *is the first work of Indian mathematics that has a definite author and date. It indicates what Indian mathematicians had accomplished by the end of the fifth century.*

BORN: c. 476; possibly Ashmaka or Kusumapura (now in India)
DIED: c. 550; place unknown
ALSO KNOWN AS: Āryabhaṭa I; Āryabhaṭṭa
AREAS OF ACHIEVEMENT: Mathematics, astronomy, science and technology

EARLY LIFE

Āryabhaṭa (ahr-yah-BAH-tuh) the Elder is a figure of whom almost nothing is known other than his work. His only surviving book, the *Aryabhatiya* (499; *The Aryabhatiya*, 1927), indicates that it was written in 499 and that he was twenty-three years old at the time, which provides the traditional date for his birth. There is a good deal of disagreement about the exact date, as well as about the place of his birth. One of his successors in the field of Indian mathematics refers to Āryabhaṭa as being from Ashmaka, a region in the northwestern part of modern India. There was a migration from that region to a more southerly part of India, and Āryabhaṭa is likely to have been born there, as it is close to the only geographic region in which he is known to have worked. He is called Āryabhaṭa the Elder to distinguish him from a later mathematician who wrote under the same name. The later Āryabhaṭa may have chosen to use that as the signature for his works as a tribute to his predecessor.

In the course of the mathematical section of *The Aryabhatiya*, the author refers to the town of Kusumapura. Most scholars believe that this refers to the town where he was doing his academic work rather than his birthplace, but others argue that this town was where the mathematician was born. Kusumapura is frequently identified as the modern-day Patna, the capital of the region of Bihar. Because his work was to prove influential in the Kerala school of astronomy, practiced at the very south tip of India, some scholars have claimed that he spent his career there, but evidence to support that claim is no easier to come by than evidence regarding any other feature of Āryabhaṭa's life.

The nature of the education that Āryabhaṭa received is unknown, but from the text of his work it is clear that he studied Greek mathematics and astronomy as well as the Indian traditions in both areas. Because Āryabhaṭa's work is the first systematic treatment of these subjects that has survived from that part of the world, it may be that he was dependent on odd scraps of knowledge from his predecessors. He would have had plenty of examples of particular sorts of calculation from which to learn. Because he wrote in Sanskrit verse, his training would have been literary as well as scientific. From the religious tone of his invocations, it seems safe to conclude that he was not a Buddhist, as he pays reverence to Brahman and the astronomical bodies.

LIFE'S WORK

From later references, it appears that Āryabhaṭa wrote a book on astronomy as well as *The Aryabhatiya*. There were periods of time when neither work was available to students, but *The Aryabhatiya* was subsequently made generally available. The work on astronomy is not known to have survived.

The Aryabhatiya is a Sanskrit poem divided into four sections: an introduction, a mathematical section, a section on time measurement, and a section on celestial spheres. The opening section is written in a different verse form than the others, as though it may have been more like an invocation. There is an invocation at the start of the section on mathematics as well. The entire mathematical section is only thirty-three verses long, which attests to the brevity of his style. As a result, there is no illustration of the techniques and ideas he describes by numerical examples.

By Āryabhaṭa's time, the use of numerals that were the ancestors of the Hindu-Arabic system was already common. Because Āryabhaṭa was writing a poem, however, that form of number was not convenient for fitting into the meter. As a result, he introduced a system of words in the first section of the poem to correspond to numbers. His numerical vocabulary therefore is not as wide as the range of numbers already in use in Indian computation but sufficed for the writing of his poem.

After the opening invocation in the section devoted to mathematics (*ganita*, in Sanskrit), Āryabhaṭa lists in the second stanza the names for classes of numbers. The third stanza is on the subject of geometry; it points out that the product of two equal numbers was called by the same name as both the square of a figure and its area. He points that the same consideration applies in three dimensions to the cube and the product of three equal quantities.

The following two stanzas (four and five) present methods for calculating the square root and the cube root of a number. From the form of the instruction, it is clear that Āryabhaṭa recognized that the square root and cube root were not generally going to terminate in a finite number of places. The geometrical points made in the previous stanzas could have come out of the Greek tradition of theoretical mathematics, but these techniques for calculation could be part of a native Indian tradition. In general, the issue of how far Āryabhaṭa was indebted to Greek sources is hard to resolve, and the discussion often revolves about political issues as well as mathematical or scholarly ones.

The next four stanzas all take up the area and volume of various two-dimensional and three-dimensional figures. The formulae for the area of a triangle and a circle are correct, as is that for the volume of a pyramid, but the formula for the volume of a sphere is incorrect. If Āryabhaṭa were drawing on the Greek geometrical tradition throughout, it is hard to see how he could have made this error, which seems to be based on an analogy with the area of a circle. In addition, he gives the area for a trapezoid and plane figures more generally. The more general formulae may be suggested by the kind of averaging involved in handling the trapezoid. It is worth remembering that all the so-called formulae are really expressed in the language of poetry rather than written out as equations.

The tenth stanza includes one of the most interesting features of *The Aryabhatiya*, an approximation for π (the ratio of the circumference of a circle and its diameter). The specific numerical values given by Āryabhaṭa lead to a decimal approximation good to four places, and there is plenty of discussion about how this compares with the best possible values that the Greeks obtained. In principle, for example, the method of exhaustion of Archimedes (c. 287-212 B.C.E.) could produce approximations to an arbitrary degree of exactness. What is clear is that Āryabhaṭa recognized that his value remained only an approximation.

The following two stanzas deal with the calculation of quantities related to the trignometric sine function. The centrality of the sine function in the mathematics of Āryabhaṭa came from its appearance in the tradition of calculating orbits of planets that goes back to Greek explanations of observations, records of which survive from Babylonian times. The mathematical astronomy of Ptolemy (c. 100-178 C.E.) was probably brought to India in the course of the centuries before Āryabhaṭa's work, as there were Greek and Egyptian traders in India and Indian traders in the centers of culture of Europe and the Mediterranean. However, there was also a native tradition of astronomy going back many centuries, although it is not clear how mathematical a form it had taken. Āryabhaṭa's interests seemed to merge those of Greek mathematics and Hindu astronomy.

Greek mathematics took issues of construction as seriously as proofs, and Āryabhaṭa includes a stanza on the construction of various figures. The next three stanzas take up matters relating to the construction of sundials, not surprising in view of the section following that on mathematics being devoted to time measurement. The seventeenth stanza then turns to the Pythagorean theorem about the relationship between the sides of a right triangle. Historians have found references to the theorem in many mathematical cultures other than the Greek, and it could easily have been part of an Indian tradition as well. Because there is no reference to a proof, it is hard to see any connection with the version given in Euclid (c. 330-c. 270 B.C.E.).

After a stanza on the lengths of chords in a circle, Āryabhaṭa explains how to calculate the sum of the terms in an arithmetic series (where the difference between successive terms is constant). He also provides the way to calculate the number of terms involved if one has the sum, and this presupposes a knowledge of the quadratic formula, the way to derive the roots of a quadratic (second-degree) equation. The quadratic formula had been used by Babylonian mathematicians much earlier, and it is hard to tell how it fit into the rest of Āryabhaṭa's algebraic knowledge. The formulae he then proceeds to give for the sum of the squares and cubes of arithmetic series also come without derivation.

A couple of stanzas are devoted to getting the values of individual terms from various ways in which they can be combined. After a stanza (number 25) on interest (in which compounding takes place), Āryabhaṭa introduces the rule of three, the standard method of dealing with proportions for algebraists for millennia. In subsequent stanzas, he provides a guide to calculating common denominators for fractions and resolving problems by using the inverse of the operations in which the problems are posed. The range of subjects continues to widen, as he gives a way of getting a sum from differences, of calculating the value of an object with an agreed monetary standard, and of calculating the distances between planets.

The height of Āryabhaṭa's mathematical originality comes in the final two stanzas, in which he presents the general techinique for solving Diophantine equations of the first degree. Diophantus (fl. c. 250 C.E.) had presented solutions of number of special cases, but Āryabhaṭa clearly developed more general forms. The additional detail given to the method (by taking an extra stanza) and its position at the end of the section suggests that Āryabhaṭa recognized the extent of what he had accomplished.

The third section of *The Aryabhatiya* looks at issues relating to time but largely through the medium of astronomy. The final section takes up the celestial sphere, and both sections had an influence on subsequent Indian astronomy as well as being brought subsequently to the West. The work as a whole ends with a couple of stanzas celebrating his own accomplishments and criticizing those who disparage the field of astronomy. It is safe to say that this was in response to critics, but it is not clear what the basis was for their objections.

After Āryabhaṭa's death, subsequent Indian mathematicians, especially Brahmagupta (c. 598-c. 660), disparaged his accomplishments for not having been presented systematically. On the other hand, his work remained the starting point for Indian mathematics and astronomy for many years. Commentaries were published on *The Aryabhatiya* for more than a thousand years, and it has also drawn the attention of modern scholars. As historians of mathematics look for sources outside the Greek tradition, Āryabhaṭa's work is both attractive for its style and worthy of investigation.

Significance

Āryabhaṭa stands at the head of the Indian tradition of mathematics. There was clearly a stream of predecessors on which he drew, but their anonymity makes their importance a trifle elusive. The work of Āryabhaṭa provided a spur for a thousand years of mathematical research. The form in which he presented his work also helped make sure that it could be taken as a classic contribution to Indian scholarship, not merely a mathematical thesis.

When India launched its first satellite in 1976, it was the 1500th anniversary of Āryabhaṭa's birth, and the satellite was named after him. At present, there is an Āryabhaṭa Forum centered in the United Kingdom working on issues in the history of mathematics. The legacy of Āryabhaṭa continues to serve as a reminder that not all mathematics can be assumed to have come through the Greek pipeline.

—*Thomas Drucker*

Further Reading

Menon, K. N. *Aryabhata: Astronomer, Mathematician.* New Delhi, India: Ministry of Information, 1977. Part of the spate of literature produced by the 1500th anniversary of Āryabhaṭa's birth, this work is typical in that it claims all sorts of achievements for Āryabhaṭa at the expense of both other mathematical cultures (like the Greek) and other Indian mathematicians.

Proceedings of the International Seminar and Colloquium on Fifteen Hundred Years of Aryabhateeyam. Kochi, India: Kerala Sastra Sahitya Parishad, 2002. This was sparked by the 1500th anniversary of Āryabhaṭa's book rather than his birth. The collection of articles covers a good deal not connected with Āryabhaṭa, but it does provide evidence for continued disagreements over some of the basic facts of his life.

Velukutty, K. K. *Heritages to and from Aryabhatta.* Elipara, India: Sahithi, 1997. Another assault on the standard accounts of the details of Āryabhaṭa's life. It follows up some other Indian mathematical traditions with attention to details of practice.

See also: Brahmagupta.

Related articles in *Great Events from History: The Middle Ages, 477-1453*: 595-665: Invention of Decimals and Negative Numbers; c. 1100: Arabic Numerals Are Introduced into Europe.

al-Ashʿarī

Muslim theologian

Al-Ashʿarī initiated a theological movement that gave human reason only a limited role in demonstrating religious truths. To al-Ashʿarī, dialectical argument was acceptable if it remained subordinate to revealed facts.

Born: 873 or 874; Basra, southern Mesopotamia (now in Iraq)

Died: 935 or 936; Baghdad (now in Iraq)

Also known as: Abū al-Ḥasan al-Ashʿarī (full name)

Areas of achievement: Religion and theology, philosophy

Early Life

Al-Ashʿarī (ahl-ash-ah-REE) was born in Basra in southern Mesopotamia. He may have been a descendant of the famous Abū Mūsā al-Ashʿarī (d. 662 or 663), a companion of the Prophet Muḥammad. Nothing is known about al-Ashʿarī's early life, though it is evident from his subsequent activities that he received the usual education of his time: studies in grammar, the Qurʾān, traditions of the Prophet Muḥammad, canon law, and Scholastic theology. It can also be assumed that he was deeply influenced by the intellectual turmoil of an age of violent ideological conflict, during which renewed interest in Greek philosophy intensified the clash between the ultrarationalist Mutazilites and the fundamentalist theologians. He became a pupil of the leading Basran Mutazilite, Abū ʿAlī Muḥammad ibn ʿAbd al-Wahhāb al-Jubbāʿī (d. 915 or 916), and flourished as an aggressive debater in law and dogmatics.

At about the age of forty, in 912 or 913, al-Ashʿarī underwent a radical conversion away from the extreme rationalism of his master al-Jubba'i, and made a declaration of repentance in the mosque, announcing his return to strictest orthodoxy and rejecting outright the subordination of religious beliefs to rational principles. About this abrupt change of direction two different stories are told, which, although they are later embellishments to al-Ashʿarī's biography, are significant because they reflect his role in the development of Islamic theology.

The first story tells of three dreams; in two of them the Prophet orders al-Ashʿarī to return to traditional orthodoxy, but in the third he commands him not to abandon dialectical theology either. In the best-known version of the second story, al-Ashʿarī silences al-Jubba'i with an unanswerable riddle of three brothers, one dying as a baby (hence too young for Paradise or Hell), one rewarded with Heaven for his virtuous life, and one sent to

Hell for his sins. The infant challenges God on his fate: Why was he not allowed to live and earn salvation? Al-Jubba'i replies that God would say that God knew that the child would grow up to be a sinner, and out of divine justice, he brought his life to an early end. On hearing this, the third brother now cries out from Hell: Why did he not kill me too, before I had a chance to sin? Al-Jubba'i, naturally, is incapable of resolving the dilemma. It was this demonstration of the incapacity of human reason that was said to have turned al-Ashʿarī away from the Mutazilite movement, one of whose central beliefs was that God could not be anything but absolutely just.

LIFE'S WORK

There are two ways to approach al-Ashʿarī: evaluating him either by his reputation or by his writings. He is credited with a large number of works (106 titles are known), but not all of the few that have survived are accepted as genuine. Furthermore, their character varies according to whether they were composed before or after his conversion.

Four works may be considered representative of al-Ashʿarī's output. His *Maqalat al-Islamiyin wa-ikhtilaf al-musallin* (*Discourses of the Muslims*, 1930) is noteworthy as one of the first treatises on the Islamic sects and was an important source for later historians of religion. It is divided into two parts, one dealing with the Muslim sects and the other with the views of the Scholastic theologians (*mutakallimun*). There may also have been a third part examining the opinions of the philosophers. *Al-Ibanah ʿan usul al-diyanah* (*The Elucidation of Islam's Foundation*, 1940) is an outline of the principles of Islam, perhaps written soon after his conversion to strict orthodoxy and therefore extremely hostile to the unbridled use of human reason in theological argument. A third work, *Risalat isthsan al-khawd fi ilm al-kalam* (best known as *al-Haththʿala al-bahth*; *Incitement to Investigation*, 1953), strongly defends the use of reason and is critical of those same orthodox thinkers whose ranks al-Ashʿarī had so dramatically rejoined. To their claim that rational speculation is heretical, al-Ashʿarī replies that to prohibit the use of reason in the absence of all Qurʾānic and extra-Qurʾānic support is itself a heresy. Finally, the *Kitāb al-luma* (*Book of Highlights*, 1953) should be mentioned. It is a late work, similar to *Incitement to Investigation* in its rigorous defense of Islam by the use of dialectic, and it was probably al-Ashʿarī's most popular treatise, to judge by the commentaries and refutations it provoked.

Far more significant than al-Ashʿarī's writings is the body of ideas attributed to him and constituting the theological system named for him. Ashʿarism's general aim was to achieve a true synthesis of purely logical argument and the transcendental elements of revealed religion. A non-Muslim is likely to be unimpressed by the apparent contradictions this method produces, but it would be a gross error to devalue the absolute importance of all the issues involved by relegating them to the status of mere Scholastic quibbles.

Al-Ashʿarī's method typically combines rational argument with an appeal to Qurʾānic authority, so that each reinforces the other. Thus, to refute the Mutazilite preference for mechanical causality (which threatened to make God subject to natural laws), al-Ashʿarī attacks on two fronts. Rationally, it is self-evident that humans are not in control of the universe and cannot create themselves; humankind's continued existence therefore must be attributable to a higher cause. Hereupon, al-Ashʿarī invokes Qurʾānic verses to confirm by revelation what he has just established by reason. God's unity is similarly demonstrated by pointing out the logical absurdity of predicating omnipotence of more than one deity, and again the case is supported by Qurʾānic quotations.

By this type of argument, Ashʿarism constructed a theology that resolved—or at least acceptably accounted for—all the major points of doctrinal dispute. The rather numerous individual topics may be conveniently subsumed under two broad categories: dogma relating to God and dogma in which humans are the main focus.

The Qurʾān and the subsequent tradition are very explicit regarding God's qualities. Logic is equally insistent that the oneness of God is incompatible with the medieval scientific principle of substance and accident, that is, that all beings are complex insofar as their attributes are additional to their substance. There are two extreme solutions to this dilemma: One is to prohibit inquiry into the question altogether, which was approximately the position of the fundamentalists, and the other is to affirm the unity of God by denying that he has any attributes at all, which was essentially the view of the Mutazilites. Either way, the theological consequences were disturbing: The fundamentalists were obliged to accept things that they could not understand (God's location, for example; the Qurʾān describes him as sitting on a throne), while the Mutazilites reduced God to a construct of the mind ruled by the laws of thought (the faithful will not see him in the afterlife, because it is inconceivable that he should be anywhere to be seen).

Al-Ashʿarī and his followers arrived at a reconciliation of this type of contradiction by combining belief in revealed truth with acceptance of logical arguments designed to show that God's attributes were of a different nature from humankind's, thus neither depriving him of attributes nor negating his oneness. It is important to stress here that al-Ashᶜarī was seeking not a compromise between the two opposing views but a total victory for fundamentalist theology, expressed in terms that would silence both sides. The weaknesses of the two extremes are clear, but the intention of al-Ashᶜarī's reasoning was to make the fundamentalist position logically unassailable.

Humankind's theological status was equally problematical, especially in the matter of free will. The fundamentalists naturally adhered to the Qurʾānic assertions of God's unqualified omnipotence, while the Mutazilites had to argue that there could be no responsibility (hence no reward for virtue or punishment for sin) without free will, thereby restricting God's powers. Al-Ashᶜarī's solution is simply brilliant. Human actions are indeed all created by God, including even the accountability for those actions that a person "acquires" as he or she performs them. This "acquisition" (*kasb*) is one of al-Ashᶜarī's most inspired theological insights: Drawing on a commercial metaphor in the Qurʾān ("every man must stand surety for what he has acquired"—that is, he will be judged accordingly), he elaborated a perfectly coherent doctrine of individual responsibility. A person "buys" his or her actions, which is to say, he or she accepts them exactly as a purchaser does under Muslim law, with eyes open and with full satisfaction (*rida*). The concept is ethically watertight: A person acts as he or she is predestined to act, but does so always knowing what God has determined to be right or wrong, and it is the acceptance (*kasb*) of that knowledge that will send the individual eventually to Heaven or Hell.

SIGNIFICANCE

A brief description of Ashᶜarism cannot give an adequate impression of the subtlety and breadth of al-Ashᶜarī's ideas, which ranged from the most abstruse questions of metaphysics to practical matters of worldly ethics. What must be stressed, however, is that his solutions were found acceptable by numerous Muslims of undoubted intellectual superiority, of whom the greatest is al-Ghazzālī (1058-1111), the single most influential Muslim thinker. Ashᶜarism clearly answered Islam's need to harmonize the intellectual's insistence on systematic coherence with the fundamentalist's refusal to question matters of revelation. Even Sufi mystics are among his followers, and the foundation of the Nizamiyya College in Baghdad in 1070 represents the elevation of Asharism to an officially sponsored state doctrine. Ironically, this reconciliation of faith and reason is exactly what al-Ashᶜarī's bitterest opponents, the Mutazilites, strove for and failed to accomplish.

Although al-Ashᶜarī's position in the history of Islamic theology is clearly defined in the Muslim tradition, there is still much uncertainty about him in Western scholarship. Disagreement among non-Muslims springs from the difficulty of accepting Islamic religious premises and an understandable inclination to regard Islamic theological speculation as sterile and abstract. Al-Ashᶜarī is thus a somewhat contradictory figure to non-Muslims; indeed, he has been called a "man with two faces" for his apparent vacillation between the extremes of blind fundamentalism and radical enlightenment. To see al-Ashᶜarī in this polarized way, however, is to deny the very synthesis he created. In theological terms, he was never anything but ultraconservative, yet he also managed to remove from Islam (or at least to make it possible through his champion al-Ghazzālī) that fear of intellectualism that had made the Mutazilites so unpopular despite their pious intentions. In fact, al-Ashᶜarī's hostility toward the unthinking kind of Muslim who believes by mere "imitation" (*taqlid*) was far stronger than his opposition to the inquisitive Mutazilites.

How much of Ashᶜarism is al-Ashᶜarī's personal achievement and how much is attributable to natural adjustments within Islam as it progressed toward doctrinal maturity may not be very important to determine. Ideological movements in Islam usually spring from the teachings of a major figure and then take on a life of their own, so that the question of originality retreats into the background. None of al-Ashᶜarī's ideas is totally without precedent; the use of reasoned theological argument (*kalam*) to analyze and defend religious doctrine, the tone of uncompromising orthodoxy, and concepts such as "acquisition" (*kasb*) can all be observed in or traced to earlier sources. In the end, therefore, al-Ashᶜarī should perhaps be judged in terms of the tradition that bears his name, which gives a full and satisfying role to the powers of a person's intellect in working with a set of revealed Islamic beliefs.

—*M. G. Carter*

FURTHER READING

Abdul Hye, M. "Ashᶜarism." In *A History of Muslim Philosophy*, edited by M. M. Sharif. Vol. 1. 1963. Reprint. Karachi, Pakistan: Royal, 1983. Chapter 9 contains a detailed and informative account of al-Ashᶜarī and his ideas from the Muslim perspective. Clearly and concisely summarizes doctrinal issues, setting al-Ashʿarī in the wider context of Islamic theology.

Ashʿarī, ʿAlī ibn Ismail al-. *Abūl-Ḥasan ʿAlī ibn Ismāīl al-Ašʿarī's Al-Ibānah an ʿuṣūl ad-diyānah (The Elucidation of Islām's Foundation).* 1940. Reprint. Edited and translated by Walter Conrad Klein. New York: Kraus, 1967. Translation of a major work, with a convenient introduction giving a brief outline of al-Ashʿarī's life and doctrines.

_______. *The Theology of al-Ashʿarī.* Translated by Richard J. McCarthy. Beirut: Imprimerie Catholique, 1953. Accurate and well-annotated translation of two of al-Ashʿarī's most important works, the *Kitāb al-luma* and the *al-Haththʿala al-bahth*, with the original Arabic text and useful biographical and bibliographical material. A reliable rendering of the key ideas and issues.

Frank, Richard M. *Al-Ghazzālī and the Asharite School.* Durham, N.C.: Duke University Press, 1994. Presents a history of the Asharite school of Islamic law and the work of al-Ghazzālī in that context. Bibliography, index.

_______. "Elements in the Development of the Teaching of al-Ashʿarī." *Muséon* 101 (1988). Thorough analysis of al-Ashʿarī's views on the rational approach to theology, the attributes of God, and the nature of the Qurʾān. Emphasizes the consistency of al-Ashʿarī's thinking in spite of his apparent changes of allegiance.

Goldziher, Ignaz. *Introduction to Islamic Theology and Law.* Translated by Andras and Ruth Hamori. Princeton, N.J.: Princeton University Press, 1981. The classic treatment of the topic, this work is widely accepted. This edition contains an updated bibliography and notes. Chapter 3, "The Growth and Development of Dogmatic Theology," discusses al-Ashʿarī.

Hourani, George F. *Reason and Tradition in Islamic Ethics.* New York: Cambridge University Press, 1985. Chapter 9, "Ashʿarī," is a short, lucid account, supplemented by many other references that help to locate al-Ashʿarī and his school in the general context of Islamic theology.

Makdisi, G. "Ashʿarī and the Ashʿarites in Islamic Religious History." *Studia Islamica* 17-18 (1962-1963): 37-80, 19-39. A radical reassessment of al-Ashʿarī that rejects the authenticity of the *Incitement to Investigation* and argues that al-Ashʿarī's real opponents were not the Mutazilites or Hanbalites but the Shāfʿī school of law.

Martin, Richard C., Mark R. Woodward, and Dwi S. Atmaja. *Defenders of Reason in Islam: Mutazilism from Medieval School to Modern Symbol.* Boston: Oneworld, 1997. Examines Mutazilism in Islam during the Middle Ages and through the twentieth century. Bibliography, index.

Watt, W. Montgomery. *The Formative Period of Islamic Thought.* Boston: Oneworld, 1998. Part 2 of this historical work includes the chapters "The Attraction of Reasoning" and "The Great Mutazilites." Extensive bibliography, index.

_______. *Free Will and Predestination in Early Islam.* London: Luzac, 1948. Chapter 6 describes al-Ashʿarī's solution to the problem of free will and offers some valuable corrections to common misconceptions regarding al-Ashʿarī's true position in the debate between fundamentalists and rationalists.

_______. *Islamic Philosophy and Theology: An Extended Survey.* 2d ed. Edinburgh: Edinburgh University Press, 1995. The best starting point: concise and readable summaries with guidance for further reading, placing al-Ashʿarī in the wider theological context.

SEE ALSO: Abū Ḥanīfah; Aḥmad ibn Ḥanbal; Fakhr al-Dīn al-Rāzī; al-Ḥallāj; al-Jāḥiẓ; al-Masʿūdī; al-Rāzī; Thomas Aquinas.

RELATED ARTICLES in *Great Events from History: The Middle Ages, 477-1453*: 637-657: Islam Expands Throughout the Middle East; c. 950-1100: Rise of Madrasas; c. 1265-1273: Thomas Aquinas Compiles the *Summa Theologica*.

ASHIKAGA TAKAUJI

Japanese shogun (1338-1358)

Through dogged military prowess and ruthless political decisiveness, Ashikaga Takauji prevented Japan from swinging back to an outdated Chinese-style imperial government and placed powerfully in the hands of rising new military clans. The Ashikaga shogunate that he founded hastened innovations in politics, culture, and economics.

BORN: 1305; Ashikaga, Japan
DIED: June 7, 1358; Kyoto, Japan
AREAS OF ACHIEVEMENT: Government and politics, military

EARLY LIFE

Ashikaga Takauji (ah-shee-kah-gah tah-kah-ew-jee) was born in 1305, the son of Ashikaga Sadauji of the Seiwa Genji branch of the Minamoto clan, which had founded the first shogunate, or military government, at Kamakura in 1185. His mother was of the Hōjō family, which had dominated the latter years of the Kamakura shogunate (1185-1333). The only portrait reputed to be of Takauji shows him mounted in a heroic pose, brandishing his curved sword in full armor. He is bullnecked with a black mustache and goatee. It is typical of the battle portraits of the day. In fact, Takauji was thoroughly typical of a time in which, paradoxically, family loyalties and spartan courage were revered but betrayal and intrigue played a major part in politics.

The Kamakura shogunate under which Takauji was reared exemplified the Japanese genius for maintaining the fiction of an emperor while allowing administration by the military powers. The charade of an emperor "appointing" a shogun to oversee the details of politics served to protect the imperial court, rendering the emperor a mere figurehead. Courtiers and warriors alike drew their incomes from agricultural estates called *shōen*, which were overseen by stewards appointed by the shogun. Provincial military governors, like the Ashikaga, were appointed by and owed their loyalties to the Kamakura shogunate.

Although the system had been stable for more than a century, unrest was growing by the beginning of the fourteenth century. Dwindling returns from the *shōen* led everyone to seek a larger share. In 1318, the emperor Go-Daigo (r. 1318-1339), heir to one of the two family lines that systematically alternated in the imperial reign, legally acceded to the throne and began a movement to take back into the emperor's hands all administrative power. In 1333, the shogunate, determined to exterminate this movement, dispatched an army under the command of Takauji.

LIFE'S WORK

There was widespread resentment in Japan against the Kamakura shogunate, which, having grown stale and overly complex at the top, was unable to distribute satisfactory rewards. Sensing this, Takauji suddenly declared for the emperor and promptly seized the shogunate's offices in Kyoto, while another army attacked and captured the shogunate's main headquarters at Kamakura. Victory over the Hōjō gave Go-Daigo his chance to assert direct personal imperial rule. Known as the Kemmu Restoration, from 1333 to 1336, it was a naïve and unrealistic program to bring the institutions of military rule under long-superseded organs of pre-1185 imperial government. Takauji, who aspired to be shogun, was bypassed in favor of Go-Daigo's son, Prince Morinaga. By 1335, Takauji had turned against Go-Daigo, whom he drove out of Kyoto, and proceeded to set up the emperor Komyō (r. 1336-1348) of the rival alternate line in his place. Go-Daigo thereupon fled to the town of Yoshino, south of Kyoto, where he and his successors maintained their claim as rightful rulers. From 1336 to 1392, therefore, two emperors contested the throne. The period, known as the Northern and Southern Courts (Nanboku-cho), is one of extensive fighting during which, until his death, Takauji strove to maintain his vision of a new order.

Takauji received the title of shogun from the emperor of the northern court at Kyoto in 1338 and thus became the first in a line of Ashikaga shoguns who ruled Japan as military dictators for the next 235 years. During most of his time as shogun, Takauji had to deal simultaneously with the civil war against the supporters of the southern court and with the infighting among his own supporters. The internal strife centered on the antagonism between Takauji's brother, Ashikaga Tadayoshi, and the vassal chieftains Ko no Moronao and his brother Ko no Moroyasu. Tadayoshi had closely supported his brother in his defeat of the Kamakura shogunate and then in his turnabout against Go-Daigo. Takauji's shogunate, in fact, divided responsibilities between Takauji, who handled military affairs, and Tadayoshi, who oversaw many of the judicial and administrative matters. An able administrator, Tadayoshi at first worked harmoniously with his brother.

Moronao, a loyal vassal with high ambitions, was charged with military recruitment among the small clans in the Kyoto area. In this capacity, he sought to dispossess court nobles of their *shōen* in order to offer further rewards to the military. Tadayoshi, fundamentally more conservative than either Moronao or Takauji, opposed this plan and plotted to have Moronao assassinated. The plot was discovered, and Tadayoshi was ordered, as punishment, to become a monk in 1349. In 1350, he offered his services to the southern court and then attacked his own brother in 1351, killing Moronao in battle. In turn, he was defeated and taken prisoner. Takauji evidently had him poisoned in 1352. Fratricide was not uncommon in medieval Japan, but the disarray it caused among Takauji's allies kept the southern court's fortunes alive longer than might have been expected. Nevertheless, by the time of his death in 1358, Takauji managed to bequeath to his son Ashikaga Yoshiakira a fairly stable regime that had at last overcome its internal strife and eliminated the offensive power of the southern court.

The atmosphere in which two imperial courts battled for legitimacy had produced more than its share of dissidents, rebels, double-crossers, and malcontents. That meant that Takauji and his successors had to be both able generals and fast-footed administrators. Takauji had to innovate for his political survival by establishing a government significantly different from that of Kamakura predecessors while still retaining whatever shreds of tradition would lend legitimacy to his rule. The basic Ashikaga code, the Kemmu Formulary of 1336, was declared to be an addendum to the Kamakura Code established in 1232. Also, Takauji appointed many Kamakura bureaucrats in a bid for legitimacy based on continuity. He also eliminated many encrusted and outdated layers of bureaucracy inhabited by imperial aristocrats and recruited new social elements, including merchants, whose talents answered the needs of a society and an economy that was changing and expanding. He and his successors, moreover, were willing to promote mercantile wealth and, eventually, to license foreign trade, which speeded diversification away from self-centered agrarianism.

Takauji chose to place his shogunate in Kyoto, the old imperial capital, partly to distance himself from the failed Kamakura shogunate but principally to take advantage of the prestige of being at the seat of the imperial government. Militarily, Kyoto was a more strategically central location. The surrounding region was the most agriculturally productive area in Japan. Because of its long association with the imperial government, it was one of the few truly urban areas of Japan at that time, with a comparatively large market. The interaction between this market and the growing production was to produce the core of a sophisticated money economy, with a large free-labor class working for wages, an advanced credit and banking system, and an active craft producing establishment.

Takauji took care not to ignore the outlying areas. The eastern provinces, which were the heartland of many in the Ashikaga camp, were particularly volatile. Takauji shifted trusted officials back and forth between Kyoto and the eastern administrative center of Kamakura. Takauji himself ruled from Kamakura during his struggle with Tadayoshi and left his son Yoshiakira there for a time. In the process, Kamakura took on the status of "deputy shogunate." In the southern island of Kyushu, where the Ashikaga had no real vassal ties, Takauji established a permanent shogunate representative.

The finances of the Kamakura shogunate had been based on fixed shares of the incomes of supervisory estate stewards and of the provincial governors, all of which were appointed by the shogun from among those with vassal ties to the shogun's family. Thus, they relied

MAJOR EMPERORS OF THE MUROMACHI PERIOD, 1336-1573

Emperors: Southern Court

Reign	*Ruler*
1318-1339	Go-Daigo
1339-1368	Go-Murakami
1368-1383	Chōkei
1383-1392	Go-Kameyama

Ashikaga Pretenders: Northern Court

Reign	*Ruler*
1336-1348	Komyō
1348-1351	Sukō
1351-1371	Go-Kogon
1371-1382	Go-En'yu

Later Emperors

Reign	*Ruler*
1382-1412	Go-Komatsu
1412-1428	Shōkō
1428-1464	Go-Hanazono
1464-1500	Go-Tsuchimikado
1500-1526	Go-Kashiwabara
1526-1557	Go-Nara
1557-1586	Ogimachi

MAJOR SHOGUNS OF THE ASHIKAGA SHOGUNATE, 1338-1573

Reign	*Shogun*
1338-1358	ASHIKAGA TAKAUJI
1359-1368	Ashikaga Yoshiakira
1368-1394	Ashikaga Yoshimitsu
1395-1423	Ashikaga Yoshimochi
1423-1425	Ashikaga Yoshikazu
1429-1441	Ashikaga Yoshinori
1449-1473	Ashikaga Yoshikatsu
1449-1473	Ashikaga Yoshimasa
1474-1489	Ashikaga Yoshihisa
1490-1493	Ashikaga Yoshitane
1495-1508	Ashikaga Yoshizumi
1508-1521	Ashikaga Yoshitane (second rule)
1522-1547	Ashikaga Yoshiharu
1547-1565	Ashikaga Yoshiteru
1568	Ashikaga Yoshihide
1568-1573	Ashikaga Yoshiaki

for their revenues on loyalties that were almost familial. Takauji presided over a much more complex and potentially unstable structure, so he sought to immunize himself from dependence on vassal ties for taxation by supporting his government directly from the Ashikaga estates, some sixty *shōen* scattered throughout the country. He continued the practice of appointing military governors to provinces, and his main authority was exerted through these governors, but his government income was personal. Takauji died in 1358.

SIGNIFICANCE

When his regime was first founded, Takauji asked his legal experts for advice on the shaping of his government. They responded, "Does one follow the path of an overturned wagon?" The meaning he evidently derived from this response was that, while precedent must not be utterly violated, one must be willing to carve new paths in a brutal and uncertain world. Takauji and his successors, in fact, introduced the bulk of Japan's major political innovations for the next three centuries. Yet the meaning of most of what he had set in motion by his victories and by his political arrangements was not apparent at the time he died.

It was his grandson, the third Ashikaga shogun Yoshimitsu (ruled 1368-1394), who reaped the economic benefits of foreign trade and enhanced mercantile activity. The later Ashikaga shoguns also witnessed the extraordinary cultural flowering of arts and religion that is the main contribution of feudal Japan to the modern nation. It was during the Ashikaga shogunate that Zen culture permeated art, philosophy, and drama. Takauji was exceptionally pious, a diligent Zen practitioner and talented poet, but it was his successors who saw Zen combine with aristocratic culture to transform the rude samurai into poets, artists, connoisseurs, and meditators.

—*David G. Egler*

FURTHER READING

Grossberg, Kenneth Alan. *Japan's Renaissance: The Politics of the Muromachi Bakufu*. Cambridge, Mass.: Harvard University Press, 1981. This volume is a highly literate and knowledgeable account of the economy, bureaucracy, and military of the Ashikaga shoguns. Focusing mainly on Takauji's successors, Grossberg argues that the Ashikaga shoguns, often dismissed in general histories as presiding over a loose and uncoordinated polity, can be compared favorably to European Renaissance rulers.

Hall, John Whitney. *Government and Local Power in Japan, 500-1700: A Study Based on Bizen Province*. Princeton, N.J.: Princeton University Press, 1966. This study grew out of field investigations conducted in the 1950's in Okayama Prefecture. Despite the title, the book frequently departs from strictly local events to fill in developments in Japan as a whole. Hall's analysis of land administration and the transformation of provincial governors into leaders of independent principalities has become the point of departure for a whole generation of American scholars.

Kitabatake, Chikafusa. *A Chronicle of Gods and Sovereigns: "Jinno shotoki" of Kitabatake Chikafusa*. Translated by H. Paul Varley. New York: Columbia University Press, 1980. A translation of the *Jinno shotoki*, written in 1339 and revised in 1343 by Kitabatake, a prominent southern court loyalist and the major combatant against Takauji. Kitabatake asserts forcefully the unbroken descent of Japanese emperors from the gods who created Japan, and his chronicle is a polemic for a return to the type of imperial rule Japan had before the shoguns, whose exercise of a monopoly of power he regarded as a perversion.

Sansom, George Bailey. *A History of Japan, 1334-1615*. Vol. 2. Stanford, Calif.: Stanford University Press, 1961. The second volume of a three-volume history of Japan that is arguably the most complete general history of premodern Japan available. This well-illustrated work, based entirely on Japanese sources, is indispensable for anyone writing on medieval Japan. Includes a wealth of detail on the political changes wrought by military defeats and victories, on changing alignments, and on matters of religion and art.

The Taiheiki: A Chronicle of Medieval Japan. Translated by Helen Craig McCullough. 1959. Reprint. Tokyo: Charles E. Tuttle, 1979. A straightforward translation of one of the most famous of Japanese war tales, ironically titled "the great peace." Largely favorable to the Ashikaga family, it was compiled sometime between the 1330's and 1370's by an unknown person and is the record of the battles and, to some extent, the intrigues of the period during which Takauji was rising to power. Contains an introduction and notes.

SEE ALSO: Fujiwara Michinaga; Minamoto Yoritomo; Taira Kiyomori.

RELATED ARTICLES in *Great Events from History: The Middle Ages, 477-1453*: 538-552: Buddhism Arrives in Japan; 792: Rise of the Samurai; 858: Rise of the Fujiwara Family; 1156-1192: Minamoto Yoritomo Becomes Shogun; 1175: Hōnen Shōnin Founds Pure Land Buddhism; 1219-1333: Hōjō Family Dominates Shoguns, Rules Japan; 1336-1392: Yoshino Civil Wars.

AVERROËS

Islamic philosopher

Jurist, physician, and philosopher Averroës, also widely known as Ibn Rushd, was one of the last of a line of medieval Muslim scholars who sought to reconcile the truths of revealed religion and dialectical reasoning. He exercised an overwhelming influence on Latin and European thought through his commentaries on Aristotle.

BORN: 1126; Córdoba (now in Spain)

DIED: 1198; Marrakech, Almohad Empire (now in Morocco)

ALSO KNOWN AS: Ibn Rushd; Abū al-Walīd Muḥammad ibn Aḥmad ibn Muḥammad ibn Rushd (given name)

AREAS OF ACHIEVEMENT: Philosophy, medicine, religion and theology

EARLY LIFE

Abū al-Walīd Muḥammad ibn Aḥmad ibn Muḥammad ibn Rushd, generally known as Ibn Rushd, and to the medieval Christian West as Averroës (a-VEHR-oh-weez), was born into a distinguished Spanish-Arab family of jurists in Córdoba, the former capital of the Umayyad Caliphate in Spain. His grandfather, who died in the year of his birth, had been a distinguished Malikite jurisconsult, who had held the office of chief *qāḍī* (Muslim judge) of the city, as well as imam (prayer leader) of its great mosque, still one of the most celebrated monuments of early Islamic architecture. Ibn Rushd's father was also a *qāḍī*, and in the course of time he too would follow the family calling.

Ibn Rushd's biographers state that he was given an excellent education in all the branches of traditional Islamic learning, including medicine, in which he was the pupil of a celebrated teacher, Abū Jaʿfar Hārūn al-Tajali (of Trujillo), who may also have initiated him into a lifelong passion for philosophy. The young scholar was also influenced by the writings of one of the most famous thinkers of the previous generation, Ibn Bājjah of Saragossa (c. 1095-1138 or 1139), known to the Latin Schoolmen as Avempace.

By 1157, Ibn Rushd, at age thirty, had made his way to Marrakech in Morocco, at that time the capital of the North African and Spanish empire of the Almohads, where he was perhaps employed as a teacher. Ibn Rushd lived during a very distinctive period in the history of Islam in Spain and the Maghreb. A century before his birth, the disintegration of the caliphate of Córdoba had led to the fragmentation of Muslim Spain among the so-called Party Kings (Arabic *muluk al-tawāʿif*), who in turn had been overthrown by the Berber tribal confederacy of the Almoravids (Arabic *al-murabitun*, those dwelling in frontier fortresses). These fanatical warriors from the western Sahara had quickly succumbed to the hedonistic environment of Spanish Islam, only to be replaced by another wave of Berber fundamentalists, the Almohads (Arabic *al-muwaḥḥidūn*, those who affirm God's unity). Under ʿAbd al-Muʾmin (r. 1130-1163), who assumed the title of caliph, the Almohads conquered all southern and central Spain as well as the North African littoral as far east as modern Libya.

Within the context of the cultural and intellectual history of the Muslim West, the Almohads played a highly ambiguous role. The spearhead of a puritanical movement sworn to the cleansing of Islam of latter-day accretions and to a return to the pristine mores of the days of the Prophet and the Rightly-Guided Caliphs (Arabic *al-Khulafā al-Rāshidūn*), they were also the heirs, through their conquests, to the intellectually precocious and culturally sophisticated traditions of Muslim Spain. The ruling elite seems to have dealt with this paradox by developing a deliberate "double standard": Within the walls of the caliph's palace and of the mansions of the great, the brilliant civilization of an earlier age continued to flourish, while outside, in street and marketplace, obedience to the Shariʿa, the law of Islam, was strictly enforced at the behest of the clerical classes, the *ʿulama* (persons learned in the Islamic sciences) and the *fuqaha* (those learned in jurisprudence). The life of Ibn Rushd himself points to a similar dichotomy. Outwardly, he was a *qāḍī* and a *faqih*, a judge and a jurisprudent; inwardly, he was a *faylasuf*, a philosopher with an insatiable urge to pursue speculative inquiry by rational argument and to delve deeply into the infidel wisdom of the ancients.

In 1163, ʿAbd al-Muʾmin was succeeded by his son, Abū Yaʿqūb Yūsuf, who throughout his reign (r. 1163-1184) was to be a generous patron and friend to Ibn Rushd. Apparently, it was a contemporary scholar, Ibn Tufayl (c. 1105-1184), known to the Latins as Abubacer, who first presented Ibn Rushd to Abū Yaʿqūb Yūsuf, probably around 1169. Tradition relates that, at their first meeting, the caliph began by asking Ibn Rushd (who may already have been working on a commentary on Aristotle's *De caelo*) about the origin and nature of the sky. While the latter hesitated, uncertain as to how to reply to questions that raised dangerous issues of orthodoxy, the caliph turned to converse with Ibn Tufayl, and in so doing revealed his own extensive learning. Reassured, Ibn Rushd embarked on a discourse that so displayed the depth and range of his scholarship that the delighted caliph thereafter became his ardent disciple. It was on this occasion, too, that Abū Yaʿqūb Yūsuf complained that the existing translations of the works of Aristotle were too obscure for comprehension and that there was need for further commentaries and exegeses. Ibn Tufayl remarked that he himself was too old to assume such an undertaking, at which Ibn Rushd agreed to assume the task that was to become his life's work.

Averroës. (Library of Congress)

LIFE'S WORK

The name of Ibn Rushd is inextricably linked with that of Aristotle, and it is for his commentaries on the works of Aristotle that, under the name of Averroës, he became so famous in the Christian West. Since the end of antiquity, no one had studied the writings of Aristotle, or what passed for his writings, so carefully as Ibn Rushd, and in his numerous commentaries, many of which are now lost or are known only through Hebrew or Latin translations, he set out to remove the exegetical accretions of earlier ages. The Great Commentator, as the Latin Schoolmen liked to call him, did not perhaps have a very original mind, but he did have a highly analytical one, capable of great critical penetration.

Ibn Rushd understood Aristotle better than his predecessors had because his powers of analysis enabled him, almost alone in the Arabo-Aristotelian philosophical tradition, to circumvent the glosses superimposed on Aristotle by a spurious tradition that had for so long concealed the real Aristotle, consisting of such works as the *Theologia Aristotelis* derived from Plotinus, the *Liber de causis* of Proclus, and the commentary on Aristotle of Alexander of Aphrodisias. This "contamination of Aristotle," as David Knowles, in *The Evolution of Medieval Thought* (1962), has described it, laid on medieval Arab and Jewish scholars alike the temptation to undertake "a synthesis in the systems of Plato and Aristotle," but this was a false trail that, for the most part, Ibn Rushd avoided following, largely on account of his intellectual acuity.

On the other hand, Ibn Rushd was a man of his times. Preoccupied as he was with political thought and its relationship to personal conduct, he nevertheless did not have access to Aristotle's *Politics*. He was therefore forced to rely on Plato's *Politeia* (388-368 B.C.E.; *Republic*, 1701) and *Nomoi* (360-347 B.C.E.; *Laws*, 1804) and Aristotle's *Ethica Nicomachea* (348-336 B.C.E.; *Nichomachean Ethics*, 1797), and was heavily dependent on his predecessor al-Fārābi. Ibn Rushd had no knowledge of Greek. Therefore, he was compelled to study both Aristotle and Aristotle's Greek commentators in Arabic translations made from Syriac or, more rarely, from the original Greek. This fact alone makes his achievement the more remarkable. It helped him that, from the outset of his career as a scholar, his unabashed admiration for Aristotle as a thinker drove him to try to uncover the authentic mind beneath the palimpsests of later generations, the mind of the man who, in his words (as quoted by Knowles),

> was created and given to us by divine providence that we might know all there is to be known. Let us praise God, who set this man apart from all others in perfection, and made him approach very near to the highest dignity humanity can attain.

Although Ibn Rushd has come to be known first and foremost as a philosopher, to his contemporaries he was probably regarded primarily as a jurist and a physician. In 1169, the year that saw the beginning of his long and fruitful intellectual friendship with Abū Yaʿqūb Yūsuf, he was appointed *qāḍī* of Seville, where, always preoccupied with his writing, he complained of being cut off from access to his library in Córdoba. He returned to Córdoba as *qāḍī* in 1171, but it seems that throughout the 1170's he traveled extensively within the caliph's dominions, perhaps undertaking roving judicial commissions for the government. In 1182, he was summoned to Marrakech to succeed Ibn Tufayl as the caliph's physician. He had already written extensively on medical subjects, for in addition to the celebrated *Kulliyāt* (general medicine, c. 1162-1169; a seven-part encyclopedia, later translated into Latin as *Colliget*), he had written several commentaries on Galen. It is not certain how long he served as Abū Yaʿqūb Yūsuf's physician, for not long afterward he was appointed chief *qāḍī* of Córdoba, the post that his grandfather had formerly held. Since Abū Yaʿqūb Yūsuf was killed in battle at Santarém (Portugal) in 1184, it is possible that the prestigious appointment was made by Abū Yaʿqūb Yūsuf's son and successor, Abū Yūsuf Yaʿqūb al-Manṣūr (r. 1184-1199). For most of his reign, Abū Yūsuf Yaʿqūb showed himself as well disposed toward Ibn Rushd as his father had been, but during 1195 the philosopher experienced a brief period of disgrace and danger.

The Christian powers of the north were now mustering their forces, and Abū Yūsuf Yaʿqūb needed to rally his subjects for the approaching struggle. For that, he needed the unqualified support of the *ʿulama* and *fuqaha*, which in turn involved his unequivocal commitment to orthodoxy. The *fuqaha* insisted that Ibn Rushd be silenced for spreading doctrines that were subversive of faith, such as the Aristotelian theory of the eternity of the world, which denied God's act of creation, and for his rejection of the divine knowledge of particulars, which called into question God's omniscience. Ibn Rushd was compelled to appear before some kind of hostile gathering in Córdoba, his books were publicly burned, and his enemies bombarded him with false accusations and scurrilous libels. His actual punishment, however, was quite mild—temporary exile to the town of Lucena, south of Córdoba—and it cannot have done much to assuage the wrath of his foes. Shortly afterward, the caliph won a great victory over the Christians at Allarcos, midway between Córdoba and Toledo (July 19, 1195), the last triumph of Muslim arms in the peninsula. In consequence, he apparently felt less dependent on the goodwill of the *fuqaha*, and on returning to his capital of Marrakech, he summoned Ibn Rushd to join him. The old man (now in his seventies) did not have long to enjoy his restoration to favor. He died in 1198 in Marrakech, where his tomb still stands, although he was subsequently reinterred in Córdoba. Abū Yūsuf Yaʿqūb died within months of the passing of his most celebrated subject.

As a thinker, Ibn Rushd was in the mainstream of Muslim Scholasticism, as well as being one of its last significant practitioners. Like his great predecessors in the Muslim East, he sought to establish an honored place for philosophy within the broader context of Muslim thought and learning. Contrary to the later and quite erroneous Christian notion of him as a champion of rationalism who denied the truths of revealed religion, Ibn Rushd was a devout Muslim who never set philosophy on a pedestal in order to challenge religious belief. Throughout his life, he stoutly denied that there was any inherent contradiction between philosophical truth, as established by the speculative thinker, and the certainties of faith embodied in the Qurʾān and the Shariʿa, the religious law that provided the social bounds within which the Muslim community and the individual Muslim lived their lives—

and which, as a *qāḍī*, it was his duty to uphold. In his celebrated *Tahāfut at-tahāfut* (c. 1174-1180; *Incoherence of the Incoherence*, 1954)—a defense of philosophy against the attacks made on it by the theologian and mystic al-Ghazzālī (1058-1111) in his *Tahāfut al-falāsifah* (1095; *Incoherence of the Philosophers*, 1958)—he takes it as axiomatic that the philosopher will subscribe to the teachings of the highest form of revealed religion of the age in which he lives (by which he meant Islam). In *Kitāb fasl al-maqāl* (c. 1174-1180; *On the Harmony of Religion and Philosophy*, 1961), he assumes the compatibility of philosophical truth and revelation: Where there appears to be a conflict, that is the result of human misunderstanding, as in the case of diverse interpretations of scripture. The Muslims, he writes,

> are unanimous in holding that it is not obligatory either to take all the expressions of Scripture in their apparent meaning or to extend them all from their apparent meaning to allegorical interpretation. . . . The reason why we have received a Scripture with both an apparent and an inner meaning lies in the diversity of people's natural capacities and the difference of their innate dispositions with regard to assent.

In other words, people can believe only what their natural abilities allow them to comprehend, and this affects, among much else, the relationship between religion and philosophy, and the philosopher's place in society.

Significance

Ibn Rushd was one of the most formidable thinkers in the entire intellectual history of Islam, but he was also, in a very real sense, the end of a line. In the Muslim East, of which he lacked direct experience, the heritage of speculative philosophy had long since withered away in the face of Ashʿarite orthodoxy and a growing preoccupation with transcendent mysticism. In the Muslim West, which was his home, the end came more rapidly and more completely. It was an accident of history that during the late twelfth century, the caliphs of the puritanical Almohads had tolerated such men as Ibn Tufayl and Ibn Rushd. Fourteen years after Ibn Rushd's death, the Almohads went down in defeat in one of history's truly decisive battles, Las Navas de Tolosa (1212), which heralded the end of Muslim rule in Spain and, with it, Arabo-Hispanic civilization. Thereafter, the Maghreb turned in on itself, and the intellectual life of the Muslim West, to which Ibn Rushd had contributed so much, slowly drew to its close. Its last representative, the Tunisian Ibn Khaldūn (1332-1406), ended his days in Cairo.

Yet Ibn Rushd, whom the Muslim world soon forgot, enjoyed a posthumous and enduring fame in lands he had never visited and in a civilization that, had he known it, he would probably have despised. A principal component of the twelfth century European renaissance was the work of the translators of Toledo (reconquered by Alfonso VI of Castile from the Muslims in 1085), who made available in Latin the riches of Arabic, Hebrew, and Greek thought. When the pace of translation intensified during the thirteenth century, attention centered on the works of Aristotle and on the Aristotelian commentaries of Ibn Rushd. Among Christian translators, Michael Scott (1180-1235) made available Ibn Rushd's commentaries on *De caelo* and *De anima*, among others; Hermann the German translated the middle commentaries on the *Nichomachean Ethics*, *Rhetoric*, and *Poetics*; and the Italian William of Lunis translated the commentaries on Aristotelian logic. No less prominent were the Jewish translators. Jacob Anatoli made available Ibn Rushd's middle commentaries on the *Categories, De interpretatione*, *Analytica priora*, and *Analytica posteriora*; Solomon ben Joseph ibn Ayyūb, the middle commentary on *De caelo*; Shem-Tob ben Isaac ibn Shaprut, the middle commentary on *De anima*; and Moses ben Samuel ibn Tibbon, a record output of commentaries. As a result of this activity, Ibn Rushd became, along with Aristotle, one of the most explosive elements in the development of medieval Christian thought.

Misread and misunderstood, Ibn Rushd became the personification of human reason, unaided by divine illumination, arrogantly pitting itself against Providence. Almost from the first appearance of Latin translations of his works, there was an odor of brimstone about him. In 1277, the bishop of Paris censured 219 errors held by Aristotle or Averroës, by which time his alleged disciples, the Latin Averroists, headed by Siger of Brabant, were drawing on themselves the magisterial denunciations of Thomas Aquinas, whose schematic endeavor to reconcile faith and reason nevertheless derived from the labors of Ibn Rushd a century earlier. Dante, encountering him in Limbo, was correct in his emphasis when he wrote, "Averroës, che'l gran comento feo" (Averroës, who made the Great Commentary), but even he could not have imagined the extent of Ibn Rushd's influence on the intellectual history of late medieval Europe.

—*Gavin R. G. Hambly*

Further Reading

Arnaldez, R. "Ibn Rushd." In *Islamic Desk Reference*. Edited by E. van Donzel. Leiden, The Netherlands:

E. J. Brill, 1994. This is a strongly recommended, succinct, detailed article on Ibn Rushd's life and thought, to which is added an excellent bibliography.

Averroës. *Averroës' Middle Commentaries on Aristotle's Categories and "De interpretatione."* Translated by Charles E. Butterworth. Princeton, N.J.: Princeton University Press, 1983. This is the first volume in a series of translations of Ibn Rushd's middle commentaries, based on the critical edition of the Arabic texts.

_______. *Averroës on Plato's "Republic."* Translated by Ralph Lerner. Ithaca, N.Y.: Cornell University Press, 1974. The translator maintains that his version is "an improvement in accuracy and intelligibility" over its predecessor, Erwin Rosenthal's *Commentary on Plato's "Republic"* (Cambridge, England: Cambridge University Press, 1956). The Arabic original is missing, and this translation is based on a Hebrew translation of the early fourteenth century by Samuel Ben Judah. This work provides an excellent example of Ibn Rushd's methods as a commentator.

_______. *On the Harmony of Religion and Philosophy.* Translated by George F. Hourani. London: Luzac, 1961. A translation of the *Kitāb fasl al-maqāl*, in which Ibn Rushd argues that the apparent contradictions between faith and reason are reconcilable.

_______. *Tahāfut al-tahāfut (Incoherence of the Incoherence).* Translated by Simon van den Bergh. London: Luzac, 1954. This is an excellent translation of Ibn Rushd's spirited rejoinder to the assault made on philosophy by al-Ghazzālī in *Incoherence of the Philosophers*.

Fakhry, Majid. *Averroës (Ibn Rushd): His Life, Works, and Influence.* Oxford, England: Oneworld, 2001. Part of the Great Islamic Thinkers series, this concise biography looks at Averroës and his realm.

Hitti, Philip K. *Makers of Arab History.* New York: St. Martin's Press, 1968. The chapter on Ibn Rushd in this collection of popular biographies provides a lively introductory account of the man and his thought, a useful starting point for further study. The book also contains biographies of al-Ghazzālī, al-Kindī, and Avicenna.

Kemal, Salim. *The Philosophical Poetics of al-Fārābi, Avicenna and Averroës: The Aristotelian Reception.* New York: Routledge Curzon, 2003. Explores Aristotle's poetics and aesthetics in the light of work by Averroës, al-Fārābi, and Avicenna. Includes a bibliography and index.

Knowles, David. *The Evolution of Medieval Thought.* 1962. 2d ed. New York: Longman, 1988. A classic in the field, by one of the twentieth century's most well respected medievalists.

Peters, F. E. *Aristotle and the Arabs: The Aristotelian Tradition in Islam.* New York: New York University Press, 1969. A scholarly as well as lively and stimulating account of the place of Aristotelian thought within the Islamic intellectual tradition. This book is essential reading for anyone seriously interested in the background to Ibn Rushd's life and work, written by one of the leading Western scholars in the field.

Rosenthal, Erwin I. J. *Political Thought in Medieval Islam: An Introductory Outline.* 1958. Reprint. Westport, Conn.: Greenwood Press, 1985. Provides an excellent discussion of Ibn Rushd's political and social thought, based on his knowledge of such Platonic and Aristotelian texts as were available to him, as well as the writings of al-Fārābi, but stressing Ibn Rushd's undoubtedly original contribution.

Watt, W. Montgomery. *Islamic Philosophy and Theology.* 2d ed. Edinburgh: Edinburgh University Press, 1995. This is one of the best and shorter general accounts of Islamic philosophy, written by a leading scholar in the field.

Whaba, Mourad, and Mona Abousenna, eds. *Averroës and the Enlightenment.* Amherst, N.Y.: Prometheus Books, 1996. This collection, based on an international philosophy conference held in Cairo, includes chapters on Averroës' influence on Enlightenment thought concerning religion, law, philosophy, and Western science. Several chapters also address his place in Islamic and African scholarship.

SEE ALSO: Pietro d'Abano; ʿAbd al-Muʾmin; Peter Abelard; Saint Albertus Magnus; Avicenna; Roger Bacon; Jean Buridan; Dante; al-Ghazzālī; Guy de Chauliac; Ibn al-ʿArabī; Ibn Khaldūn; Levi ben Gershom; Raymond Lull; Moses Maimonides; Siger of Brabant; Thomas Aquinas; William of Moerbeke.

RELATED ARTICLES in *Great Events from History: The Middle Ages, 477-1453*: c. 950: Court of Córdoba Flourishes in Spain; 1031: Caliphate of Córdoba Falls; 1062-1147: Almoravids Conquer Morocco and Establish the Almoravid Empire; c. 1150: Moors Transmit Classical Philosophy and Medicine to Europe; 1190: Moses Maimonides Writes *The Guide of the Perplexed*; c. 1265-1273: Thomas Aquinas Compiles the *Summa Theologica*; 1328-1350: Flowering of Late Medieval Physics.

Avicenna

Persian philosopher and scholar

Avicenna was the first Islamic thinker to synthesize the philosophy of Aristotle and Plato with Islamic traditions. His writings on medicine were studied in Europe as late as the seventeenth century.

Born: August or September, 980; Afshena, Transoxiana Province of Bukhara, Persian Empire (now in Uzbekistan)

Died: 1037; Hamadhan (now in Iran)

Also known as: Abū ʿAlī al-Ḥusayn ibn ʿAbd Allāh ibn Sīnā

Areas of achievement: Medicine, philosophy, law, astronomy, science and technology

Early Life

Avicenna (av-a-SEHN-a) was born to ʿAbd-Allāh of Balkh (now in Afghanistan), the well-to-do governor of an outlying province under Sāmānid ruler Nūh II ibn Manṣūr. Avicenna may have descended from a Turkish family on his father's side, but his mother, Sitara, was clearly Iranian.

After his brother, Maḥmūd, was born five years later, the family moved to Bukhara, one of the principal cities of Transoxiana and capital of the Sāmānid emirs from 819 to 1005. Exhibiting an early interest in learning, young Avicenna had read the entire Qurʾān by age ten. His father was attracted to Ismāʿīlī Shīʿite doctrines, preached locally by Egyptian missionaries, but Avicenna resisted his father's influence. There was much discussion in his home regarding geometry, philosophy, theology, and even accounting methods. Avicenna was sent to study with an Indian vegetable seller who was also a surveyor. It was from him that Avicenna became acquainted with the Indian system of calculation, making use of the zero in computations.

A well-known philosopher came to live with the family for a few years and had an extraordinary influence on the young scholar. Abū ʿAbd Allāh al-Natili stimulated Avicenna's love of theoretical disputation, and the youth's earlier readings in jurisprudence enabled him to tax al-Natili's powers of logic daily. The tutor convinced ʿAbd-Allāh that Avicenna's career should be only in learning. Avicenna was studying Aristotelian logic and Euclidean geometry when the teacher decided to move to a different home. Soon Avicenna had mastered texts in natural sciences and metaphysics, then medicine, which he did not consider very difficult. He taught physicians, even practicing medicine for a short time. At the age of sixteen, he was also engaging in disputations on Muslim law.

For the next year and a half, Avicenna returned to the study of logic and all aspects of philosophy, keeping files of syllogisms and praying daily at the mosque for guidance in his work. So obsessed did he become with philosophical problems and so anxious to know all that he hardly took time for sleep. Aristotle's *Metaphysica* (*Metaphysics*) became an intellectual stumbling block until his reading of a work by al-Fārābi clarified many ideas for him. Soon all of Aristotle became understandable, and Avicenna gave alms to the poor in gratitude.

When Sultan Nūh ibn Manṣūr of Bukhara became ill, he sent for Avicenna, on the advice of his team of physicians. Because of his help in curing the ruler, Avicenna gained access to the palace library, thus acquainting himself with many new books. When not studying, Avicenna was given to drinking wine and satisfying a large sexual appetite that he retained to the end of his life. Avicenna claimed that after the age of eighteen he learned nothing new, only gained greater wisdom. When the palace library was destroyed in a fire, critics blamed Avicenna, who, they said, wished to remove the sources of his ideas. There is no proof of that charge.

Life's Work

Avicenna's writing career began in earnest at the age of twenty-one with *al-Majmu* (1001; compilation), a comprehensive book on learning for Abū al-Ḥasan, a prosodist. Then he wrote *al-Hasil wa al-mahsul* (c. 1002; the sun and substance), a twenty-volume commentary on jurisprudence, the Qurʾān, and asceticism. There soon followed a work on ethics called *al-Birr wa al-ithm* (c. 1002; good works and evil). The sponsors made no copies of them, a matter of some concern to the author.

His father died in 1002, and Avicenna was forced to take government service. He reluctantly left Bukhara for Gurganj, the capital of Khwārezm, where he met Emir ʿAlī ibn Maʾmūn. From Gurganj, he moved to Fasa, Baward, Ṭūs, Samanqan, and then to Jajarm on the extreme end of Khorāsān. Avicenna served Emir Qābūs ibn Wushmagir until a military coup forced him to leave for Dihistan, where he became ill. After recovering, he moved to Jurjan.

In Jurjan, Avicenna met his pupil and biographer, Abū ʿUbayd al-Juzjani, who stayed with him throughout much of the remainder of his life. Al-Juzjani thought him exceptionally handsome and wrote that when Avicenna went to the mosque on Friday to pray, people would gather to observe firsthand "his perfection and beauty." While in Jurjan, Avicenna wrote *al-Mukhtasar al-awsat* (the middle summary on logic), *al-Mabdaʿ wa al-maʿād* (the origin and the return), and *al-Arsad al-kulliya* (comprehensive observations). There also Avicenna wrote the first part of *al-Qanun fi al-tibb* (1010-1015; *Canon of Medicine*, 1930), *Mukhtasar al-Majisti* (summary of the *Almagest*), and yet other treatises. One modern scholar lists one hundred books attributed to him. Another says that the list of Avicenna's works includes several hundred in Arabic and twenty-three in Persian.

From Jurjan, Avicenna next moved to al-Rayy, joining the service of al-Saiyyida and her son, Majd al-Dawlah. Civil strife forced him to flee to Qazwin; from there he moved to Hamadhan. He was called to the court of Emir Shams al-Dawlah to treat the ruler for colic, after which Avicenna was made the vizier of his emirate. Because of a mutiny in the army, however, the emir was forced to discharge him. After matters calmed down, Avicenna was called back and reinstated as vizier. During this period, public affairs occupied his daytime hours, and he spent evenings teaching and writing. When the emir died, Avicenna went into hiding, finishing work on his *Kitāb al-shifa* (book of healing; partially translated, 1927). He was arrested for corresponding with a rival ruler, but when Emir Alāʾ al-Dawlah attacked Hamadhan four months later, Avicenna was set free.

Avicenna. (Library of Congress)

Avicenna left Hamadhan for Isfahan with his brother, two slaves, and al-Juzjani to serve Emir ʿAla al-Dawlah. The emir designated every Friday evening for learned discussions with many other masters. Not present was a famous scholar and rival of Avicenna, al-Bīrūnī, with whom he carried on a rather bitter correspondence. They had been clients at many of the same courts, but never at the same time. At Isfahan, Avicenna completed many of his writings on arithmetic and music. He was made an official member of the court and accompanied the emir on a military expedition to Hamadhan.

When he was rebuked by the emir's cousin, Abū Manṣūr, for feigning expertise in philology, Avicenna was so stung by the criticism that he studied this subject frantically, compiling his discoveries in a book entitled *Lisan al-ʿArab* (the Arabic language). During these years, he also continued other experiments in medicine and astronomy. He introduced the use of medicinal herbs and devised an instrument to repair injured vertebrae. He understood that some illnesses arose from psychosomatic causes, and he wrote extensively on the pulse, preventive medicine, and the effects of climate on health. On May 24, 1032, he observed the rare phenomenon of Venus passing through the solar disk.

When he became ill in Isfahan, one of his slaves filled his meal with opium, hoping for his death and an opportunity to steal his money. Yet Avicenna managed to recover under self-treatment. Soon, however, he had a relapse; he died in 1037. Most authorities say that he died and was buried in Hamadhan.

SIGNIFICANCE

The *Canon of Medicine* remained a principal source for medical research for six centuries, perhaps second only to the Christian Bible in the number of copies produced. Between 1470 and 1500, it went through thirty editions in Latin and one in Hebrew; a celebrated edition was published on a Gutenberg press in Rome in 1593.

Avicenna's principal literary contribution was the invention of the Rubaiyat form, quatrains in iambic pentameter, later made famous by Omar Khayyám. Most important of all, Avicenna's philosophical system helped to stimulate a genuine intellectual renaissance in Islam that had enormous influence not only in his own culture but in Western Europe as well. Thomas Aquinas, Averroës, John Duns Scotus, Albertus Magnus, and Roger Bacon learned much from Avicenna, even though they disagreed on some particulars.

Most intriguing to the medieval Scholastics were Avicenna's insistence on essences in everything, the distinction between essence and existence (a notion derived from al-Fārābi), the absence of essence in God (whose existence is unique), and the immortality of the soul (which animates the body but is independent of it).

According to some scholars, Avicenna's insistence on observation and experimentation helped to turn Western thought in the direction of the modern scientific revolution. His theories on the sources of infectious diseases, his explanation of sight, his invention of longitude, and his other scientific conclusions have a truly remarkable congruence with modern explanations. The application of geometrical forms in Islamic art, his use of the astrolabe in astronomical experiments, and his disputations on the immortality of the soul demonstrate Avicenna's universal genius.

—*John D. Windhausen*

FURTHER READING

Afnan, Soheil M. *Avicenna: His Life and Works*. London: Allen and Unwin, 1958. A biography in which the author stresses the impact of Avicenna's philosophy on the thinkers of the Arabic-speaking world.

Avicenna. *The Life of Ibn Sina: A Critical Edition*. Translated by William E. Gohlman. Albany: State University of New York Press, 1974. Contains an annotated edition of Avicenna's autobiography. Part of the Studies in Islamic Philosophy and Science series. Bibliography.

Bakar, Osman. *The History and Philosophy of Islamic Science*. Cambridge, England: Islamic Texts Society, 1999. Discusses questions of methodology, doubt, spirituality and scientific knowledge, the philosophy of Islamic medicine, and how Islamic science influenced medieval Christian views of the natural world.

Brown, H. V. B. "Avicenna and the Christian Philosophers in Baghdad." In *Islamic Philosophy and the Classical Tradition*, edited by S. M. Stern, Albert Hourani, and Vivian Brown. Columbia: University of South Carolina Press, 1972. A clear presentation of Avicenna's philosophical differences with both Aristotle and the Peripatetic thinkers of the Baghdad School.

Copleston, Frederick. *A History of Philosophy*. Vol. 2. Westminster, Md.: Newman Press, 1955. Clarifies not only the contributions of Arab philosophy to European medieval thought but also the diversity within this Islamic renaissance. Particular attention is focused on Avicenna and Averroës.

Goichon, Amélie M. *The Philosophy of Avicenna and Its Influence on Medieval Europe*. Translated by M. S. Khan. Delhi: Motil al Banarsidass, 1969. A fine work on the main theses of Avicenna's philosophy, the adaptation of the Arabic language to Hellenic thought, and the influence of Avicenna's ideas on European intellectual developments in the Middle Ages. Not addressed are Avicenna's contributions to medicine and the natural sciences.

Hitti, Phillip K. *Makers of Arab History*. New York: St. Martin's Press, 1968. This eminent historian of the Arab world discusses Avicenna and twelve other outstanding figures, from Muḥammad to Ibn Khaldūn. A valuable feature of this work is its incorporation of eight historical maps.

Huff, Toby E. *The Rise of Early Modern Science: Islam, China, and the West*. 2d ed. New York: Cambridge University Press, 2003. Provides a strong cross-cultural background for the rise of science and medicine in Avicenna's time. Includes illustrations, a bibliography, and index.

Maurer, Armand A. *Medieval Philosophy*. 1962. Reprint. Toronto: Pontifical Institute of Medieval Studies, 1982. Presents a summary of Avicenna's arguments on being, necessity, and essence; on proofs for the existence of God; on the doctrine of creation; and on intuitive knowledge of the human soul.

Morain, Lloyd L. "Avicenna: Asian Humanist Forerunner." *The Humanist* 41 (March-April, 1981): 27-34. A valuable article containing numerous reproductions of artifacts and sketches of Avicenna. Features anatomical drawings used in Avicenna's writings and other depictions of his medical treatments, portraits, and a photograph of his mausoleum.

Peters, F. E. *Aristotle and the Arabs: The Aristotelian Tradition in Islam*. New York: New York University Press, 1968. This text discusses the notion of *falsafah*, the tenth century reception of classical Greek science and philosophy. Part of the Studies in Eastern Civilization series. Bibliography.

Wisnovsky, Robert, ed. *Aspects of Avicenna*. Princeton, N.J.: Markus Wiener, 2001. Chapters explore Avicenna's psychology, epistemology, natural philosophy, metaphysics, and ideas on substance and materiality and intuition and thinking. Bibliography, index.

_______. *Avicenna's Metaphysics in Context*. Ithaca, N.Y.: Cornell University Press, 2003. Chapters cover Avicenna's ideas on perfection and the soul and explore the synthesizing of his philosophy within the work of other his contemporaries. Bibliography, index.

SEE ALSO: Pietro d'Abano; Saint Albertus Magnus; Averroës; Roger Bacon; John Duns Scotus; Fakhr al-Dīn al-Rāzī; Ibn Khaldūn; Omar Khayyám; Thomas Aquinas.

RELATED ARTICLES in *Great Events from History: The Middle Ages, 477-1453*: c. 950: Court of Córdoba Flourishes in Spain; c. 1010-1015: Avicenna Writes His *Canon of Medicine*; c. 1150: Moors Transmit Classical Philosophy and Medicine to Europe.

ROGER BACON

English scientist and scholar

Bacon was a pioneer in the development of the scientific experimental method, and he advocated educational reform based on secular, scientific disciplines.

BORN: c. 1220; Ilchester, Somerset, England
DIED: c. 1292; probably Oxford, England
AREAS OF ACHIEVEMENT: Science and technology, education, philosophy, religion and theology

EARLY LIFE

Roger Bacon was born into a family of minor nobility. Although very little is known concerning his life prior to 1239, he was trained in his youth in the classics and in the *quadrivium* (arithmetic, geometry, astronomy, and music). He studied the liberal arts at Oxford University and received his baccalaureate from either Oxford University or the University of Paris around 1239. Soon thereafter, he received a master of arts degree from the University of Paris and began his teaching career there as a regent master on the arts faculty.

During Bacon's early professional years, he lectured on Aristotelian and pseudo-Aristotelian treatises—especially the *Secretum secretorum* (fourth century B.C.E.; secret of secrets), a long letter of advice on kingship and practical affairs supposedly written by Aristotle to Alexander the Great—but he exhibited no indication of his later preoccupation with science. As an eclectic thinker during this period from 1239 to 1247, Bacon blended his Aristotelian ideas with certain Neoplatonist elements derived from many different sources. Nevertheless, he was one of the first Parisian masters to lecture on the forbidden books of Aristotle soon after the Church lifted the ban. There he wrote his early scholastic works and commentaries on grammar, dialectics, physics, metaphysics, and astronomy. He also popularized the ideas of Avicenna, al-Ghazzālī, and Averroës, thus integrating Arabic thought with that of the West. Again, his eclecticism led him to criticize the Muslim savants on many issues, especially when they espoused concepts that he considered to be anti-Christian or antiscriptural.

About 1247, a major change occurred in Bacon's intellectual development. Abandoning his teaching position in Paris to return to Oxford, he devoted all of his time and large sums of money raised mainly from family members to experimental research, to acquiring certain "secret" books, to constructing scientific instruments and tables, to training assistants, and to conferring with scholars of like mind. These activities marked a definite departure from the usual routine practiced by his colleagues. Through these endeavors he became immensely impressed with the benefits that science could bestow on religion—a "universal" science that would address all the secrets of nature.

This change probably was caused by the Oxford environment and the influence exerted there by Robert Grosseteste (whom Bacon may never have met personally), a leader in introducing Greek learning to the West and an early advocate of the experimental method. Bacon was also impressed by Adam Marsh, Grosseteste's most famous associate, and by Thomas Wallensis, the bishop of St. David's.

From 1247 to 1257, Bacon devoted himself to the study of languages, optics, alchemy, astronomy, and mathematics. He campaigned against hearsay evidence; denounced rational, Platonist deductions; and extolled experimentation so relentlessly that he began to anger the more traditional scholars. Although his role as an experimenter may be exaggerated historically and his originality may not have produced significant scientific or technological breakthroughs, he did operate a laboratory for alchemical experiments and did carry out systematic observations with lenses and mirrors. Also important was his work on the nature of light (reflection, refraction, and spherical aberration) and on the rainbow. Of lesser significance were his ideas on flight, gunpowder, mechanically propelled land vehicles and seacraft, and eclipses of the sun.

LIFE'S WORK

About 1252, Bacon joined the Franciscan order (soon after Grosseteste had bequeathed his library to them), but from the beginning he appears to have been unhappy. He had difficulty acquiring scientific equipment, he abhorred his colleagues' disinterest in his work, and he resented the preference shown by his superiors to the more orthodox teachers on the faculty. Within several years, he became embittered and began to level criticisms (often unjust) at some of the best minds of his age. Yet for a time, he was permitted to engage in scientific speculation and observation without interference.

In 1257, he was transferred to the Friars Minor convent at Paris, possibly because of the aforementioned personal difficulties but certainly not for his scientific endeavors. His feverish activity, amazing credulity, sup-

Depiction of Roger Bacon patterned on a print by Flemish painter Aegidius Sadeler. (Library of Congress)

posed superstition, and vocal contempt for those who opposed him obviously irritated the established English members. He would always feel suspicion, and his increasing physical infirmities and lack of support would plague him for the remainder of his life.

From 1257 to 1266, Bacon taught mathematics, perspective, and philosophy at the Franciscan *studium*. Eventually, the order's hostility to his ideas forced him to appeal to Pope Clement IV (Guy Le Gros Foulques), whom he may have known when the latter was in the service of the Capetian kings. In correspondence of 1266, the pope referred to letters that he received from Bacon that described various aspects of the natural world, mathematics, languages, physics, and astrology. Bacon envisioned the production of an encyclopedia—a massive compendium of all verifiable knowledge—to be put to the ultimate service of theology. He stated that such a scientific work would be of great value in confirming Christian faith, in maintaining the welfare of the Church and the universities, and in sponsoring educational reform. Desiring a fuller understanding of this project, the pope ordered Bacon to send him detailed information and to proceed in total secrecy because of the Franciscan rule against unauthorized writing.

In obedience to the pope's command, Bacon set to work in 1266 and in a remarkably short period of approximately eighteen months produced the *Opus majus* (1267; great work), the *Opus minus* (1267; lesser work), and the *Opus tertium* (1267-1268; third work). The *Opus majus* contains all of his basic ideas for educational reform based on the supremacy of the sciences. The second and third works were largely synopses. The death of the pope in November of 1268 dealt a crushing blow to Bacon's chances of an official reception and extinguished his lifelong dream. The pope may not have read any of them.

Bacon divided the *Opus majus* into eight sections. The first delineated four barriers to truth: submission to untrustworthy authority, influence of custom, popular prejudice, and concealment of ignorance within philosophical jargon. The second showed the close relationship between philosophy and theology since they were both revealed by God to humanity. In section 3, Bacon stressed that all true scholars must be proficient in Hebrew, Greek, and Arabic if they desired to do meaningful research. Section 4 was a defense of the intimate correlation of the sciences with theology. Section 5 contained his theories of vision and optical science. In the sixth section—the most important—Bacon formulated his notion of experimental science. To him, experimentation certified the conclusions of deductive or mathematical reasoning, added new information to existing knowledge, and served to increase technological proficiency in both war and peace. The last two sections dealt with philosophical and political science questions that would be examined in greater depth by another Parisian master in the early years of the next century—Marsilius of Padua in his *Defensor pacis* (1324; defender of the peace).

Soon after the completion of these masterpieces, Bacon returned to England. He did little significant writing thereafter, save for some nonscientific works on grammar and philosophy. In 1272, he issued a highly polemical pamphlet directed against his opponents, and this produced more trouble for him within his order. A later source (the *Chronicle of the Twenty-four Generals* of 1370) reveals that he was imprisoned sometime between

1277 and 1279 for "suspected novelties" by the general of his order, Jerome of Ascoli (later Pope Nicholas IV). It is difficult, however, to determine what these novelties were, since his ideas did not differ greatly from those of his contemporaries except in overall emphasis. The imprisonment, if indeed it were a true incarceration, was undoubtedly for personal reasons rather than for his scientific work. In any case, he was freed shortly before his death.

SIGNIFICANCE

Roger Bacon was instrumental in laying the early foundation of modern scientific thinking. He was keenly aware of the interrelatedness of all the separate sciences and of the contributions that science makes to the understanding of reality. He explained the role of the experimental method in confirming or refuting speculative hypotheses. He insisted on the practical value of scientific speculation and believed in the importance of an ethical superstructure that would act as a system of checks and balances on the discovery of new knowledge.

During his many years of scientific research, Bacon endeavored to discover all that could be known, but it seems clear that although he did some experimental work himself, his real claim to fame rests on his achievements as a scientific thinker and synthesist of other scholars' work. He has been credited, sometimes erroneously, with the introduction of gunpowder, eyeglasses, the telescope, and other technological developments. His works certainly describe these things and he understood the principles on which they were based, but he never claimed credit for their invention. His experimental method may not be compatible with modern scientific method, but given the limitations of his time, his formulation was valid. In his conception of the immediate practical use of science, he was a harbinger of later work that led to the age of science in the early modern world. Bacon did not create modern science; he inspired it.

—*Ronald Edward Zupko*

FURTHER READING

Bacon, Roger. *Roger Bacon's Philosophy of Nature: A Critical Edition*, edited by David C. Lindberg. South Bend, Ind.: St. Augustine's Press, 1998. A collection of Bacon's philosophical perspectives on nature and the natural sciences.

Clegg, Brian. *The First Scientist: A Life of Roger Bacon*. New York: Carroll and Graf, 2003. A biographical look at Bacon and his scientific work.

Crombie, A. C. *Medieval and Early Modern Science*. 2 vols. 2d ed. Cambridge, Mass.: Harvard University Press, 1961. Extensive bibliographic coverage with detailed analyses of Bacon's contributions to calendar reform, scientific classifications, education, geography, geology, ophthalmology, optics, and physics.

_______. *Robert Grosseteste and the Origins of Experimental Science, 1100-1700*. Oxford, England: Clarendon Press, 1953. A detailed examination of experimentation in the thirteenth century and its relationship to modern scientific method.

Easton, Stewart C. *Roger Bacon and His Search for a Universal Science*. Westport, Conn.: Greenwood Press, 1970. Valuable for its emphasis on Bacon's early life, educational experiences, Paris professorship, scientific contributions, religious conflicts, and impact on science and education.

Hackett, Jeremiah, ed. *Roger Bacon and the Sciences*. New York: Brill, 1997. A look at Bacon's work in the sciences.

Leff, Gordon. *Paris and Oxford Universities in the Thirteenth and Fourteenth Centuries*. New York: John Wiley and Sons, 1968. Bacon is cast within an institutional context that emphasizes university regulations, curricular requirements, teaching privileges, and intellectual developments. Special emphasis is placed on Aristotelianism and its influence on later medieval education.

Steele, R. "Roger Bacon and the State of Science in the Thirteenth Century." In *Studies in the History and Method of Science*, edited by Charles Singer. Oxford, England: Clarendon Press, 1921. The best early attempt to show the continuity of Bacon's scientific thought.

Westacott, Evalyn. *Roger Bacon in Life and Legend*. New York: Philosophical Library, 1953. Among the more important topics covered are Bacon's principal works (in synopses, notably the *Opus majus*), his role as a medieval philosopher and scientist, and his creativity in the secular disciplines.

SEE ALSO: Saint Albertus Magnus; Alhazen; Averroës; Avicenna; al-Ghazzālī; Petrus Peregrinus de Maricourt; William of Auvergne; William of Moerbeke; William of Rubrouck.

RELATED ARTICLES in *Great Events from History: The Middle Ages, 477-1453*: c. 1150: Moors Transmit Classical Philosophy and Medicine to Europe; 1328-1350: Flowering of Late Medieval Physics.

JOHN BALL

English priest and social reformer

The rebel John Ball, who described himself as Sometime Saint Mary Priest of York and now of Colchester, was one of the leaders of the Peasants' Revolt of 1381.

BORN: 1331; probably Peldon, Essex, England
DIED: July 15, 1381; St. Albans Abbey, Hertfordshire, England
AREAS OF ACHIEVEMENT: Church reform, social reform, government and politics, religion and theology

EARLY LIFE

The outline of John Ball's life is blurred by the lack of historical records and complicated by the apparent existence of another John Ball. The John Ball of the Peasants' Revolt (also known as Wat Tyler's Revolt) was probably born in Essex in 1331 and became parochial chaplain at St. James's Church, East Hill, in Colchester, a position comparable to an appointment today as an assistant curate. The other John Ball served as rector of St. James, and his separate identity is confirmed by church records that report his death in 1394, more than a decade after the rebel John Ball was hanged, drawn, and quartered for his role in the Peasants' Revolt. An unbiased account of Ball's life is impossible to find in the chroniclers of his time, for even the most talented of them, the Frenchman Jean Froissart, was an upper-class historian who approached the Peasants' Revolt as a "pestillensse" and Ball as an evil madman.

Parochial chaplains were drawn from the peasantry and for that reason could be expected to sympathize with the distressed subjects to whom they ministered. Although Ball's preachings reveal some parallels to the doctrines of John Wyclif and the Lollards, no conclusive evidence links Lollardy to Ball's peasant movement. The best evidence of Ball's thought comes in the six widely read letters that he wrote in code to the Essex peasants. The messages are oblique and allegorical, with such moralizing as "Now the clergy for wealth work themselves woe. God give us redress, for now is the time!" These letters reveal the unmistakable influence of William Langland's long allegorical poem *The Vision of William, Concerning Piers the Plowman* (c. 1362-1393), which is interpreted by most scholars as a key to the meaning and social context of Ball's exhortations to his followers. Whether these letters were distributed by a revolutionary people's organization known as Magna Societas, or the Great Society, is not clear, as historians differ on whether such a disciplined, well-structured group existed.

Ball's success as a preacher led to his being called before the archbishop of Canterbury in 1366 to answer charges of preaching error and scandal. As a result, all people were warned to shun his sermons or face excommunication. Not long after this brush with authority, Ball was excommunicated for preaching in the diocese of Norwich and, on King Edward III's order, arrested and imprisoned in Essex. Barred from preaching his Christian communism after his release, Ball spoke against corruption in the church and the greed of the wealthy classes, finding audiences in marketplaces, churchyards, and roadside gatherings. He is commonly identified with the popular rhyme, "When Adam delved and Eve span/ Who was then the gentleman?" ("When Adam dug the earth and Eve spun the cloth, where then were class distinctions?"). Threatened by the effectiveness of Ball's eloquence and moral earnestness in arousing the people, the archbishop of Canterbury, Simon of Sudbury, had him imprisoned at Maidstone just before the revolt broke out.

LIFE'S WORK

The English economy was suffering, partly because of the cost of war in France, and taxes were already oppressive when in November, 1380, a new poll tax was imposed on everyone age fifteen or older. Mass protests ensued, and when tax collectors appeared in Kent in June, 1381, a mob assaulted the dungeons at Rochester and freed the prisoners. A former soldier, Wat Tyler, was named the rebels' leader, and in less than a week he had earned the allegiance of about twenty thousand men from Kent and rescued John Ball from Maidstone prison. After Tyler and Ball, the most important rebel leader was Jack Straw, who may have been the rector of Fobbing in Essex. Tyler's leadership genius and Ball's inspirational presence combined to attract more followers. Perhaps as many as fifty thousand people eventually joined the movement. The sudden success of the rebellion, with citizens joining from many regions, supports the argument for a well-established Great Society. Exactly when John Ball wrote his letters cannot be determined, but they probably went out soon after his release from Maidstone.

The throng marched toward London and arrived on June 12 at Blackheath, where they told messengers from the fourteen-year-old King Richard II that they would not go home until they had parleyed with the king. The next morning, Ball celebrated Mass on Blackheath Common and preached a moving sermon pleading for social equality. According to Froissart, the sermon began:

> Ah, ye good people, the matters goeth not well to pass in England, nor shall do till everything be common, and there be no villeins or gentlemen, but that we may be all united together, and that the lords be no greater masters than we be. What have we deserved, or why should we be kept thus in servage? We be all come from one father and one mother, Adam and Eve; whereby can they say or show that they be greater lords than we be, saving by that they cause us to win and labour for that they dispend?

Another source, an anonymous monk, reported that Ball urged the rebels to take revenge on their persecutors, killing the lords, the lawyers, the justices, and all others hostile to their vision of egalitarianism.

Ball's sermon was cheered enthusiastically by the throng on the common, who shouted their wish that Ball be their new archbishop and chancellor in place of Simon of Sudbury, who was in hiding with the king and his followers in the virtually impregnable Tower of London. Inspired by Ball and their success in moving unhindered, the rebels marched on London and made camp on June 12 at Mile End, just outside the northeast corner of the city. By this time, the combined forces from Essex and Kent exceeded one hundred thousand men, and they were awaited eagerly by most of London's thirty thousand inhabitants.

They were welcomed cordially the next morning by two London aldermen, who lowered the drawbridge for them to enter the city. Before crossing London Bridge, however, the militants—probably influenced by Ball's preaching on Christian marriage and morality—stopped at Southwark and burned the brothels to the ground, just as they had earlier burned down the Colchester brothels. The brothels were housed in buildings leased from the bishop of Winchester, William Wykeham, by the lord mayor of London, William Walworth, who employed Flemish girls from across the English Channel.

The first target of the insurgents in the city of London was the Savoy, the mansion of John of Gaunt, the king's uncle. The leaders in the destruction of the Savoy were probably Londoners, assisted by men from Kent and Essex. From the Savoy, the rebels went on to free the inmates in the Fleet prison and destroy the lawyers' quarters in the Temple, where many documents were housed. Other buildings sacked were the residence of Sir Robert Hales, the hated treasurer, and the priory of St. John's at Clerkenwell.

The king, meanwhile, was secure in the Tower with his mother, Hales, Archbishop Sudbury, the bishop of London, and other notables. On the advice of the earl of Salisbury, Richard agreed to meet the rebels the next morning, June 14, at Mile End. In the ensuing confrontation with the king, Ball and Tyler demanded an end to serfdom and demanded cheap land rentals, freedom to trade, and common justice, to all of which the king agreed. The other major issue of the conference—punishment of those who had been judged to be traitors—is unclear and disputed by historians. One source claims that the king gave permission only for the rebels to pursue the traitors and bring them before him for punishment, whereas another—the official city record—maintains that the king allowed the rebels to punish their captives themselves. Whatever the agreement, four hundred men hurried to the Tower, set up a block on Tower Hill, and beheaded Sudbury, Hales, John Legge, the sergeant-at-arms, Brother William Appleton, the king's physician and confessor, and three other officials. Others regarded as enemies were later executed. Numerous foreigners were assaulted before Richard issued the agreed-on charters and the force retired to Mile End.

The king took up quarters in the Great Wardrobe, near St. Paul's cathedral. After consulting anxiously with his advisers while rebellions flared up across the kingdom, he informed the rebels that he would meet them at the Smithfield cattle market, outside Aldersgate, that same day, June 15. Whether the king's intentions were peaceful is unclear; all of his party wore armor and carried weapons, however, suggesting to many historians that he was deliberately leading Ball, Tyler, and their followers into a trap. In the meeting, Tyler rode across the field with a single companion to meet the king, only to die in an altercation with Lord Mayor Walworth and another attacker.

With Tyler dead and the charters voided, the rebellion continued sporadically in the rural areas but sputtered to a halt on July 2, when the king and five hundred soldiers announced at Colchester that the serfs and villeins would continue in their low status. Ball was hiding in nearby St. Runwald's Church with several other ringleaders, and he fled to Coventry on hearing of the king's vindictive speech.

Ball's security did not last. On July 13, he was arrested and immediately arraigned before Justice Robert Tresilian in St. Albans. Ball confessed to his role in the uprising, admitted sending the inflammatory letters, and refused to ask for pardon. He was indicted for rebellion and writing seditious letters. Although he was apparently tried by jury and acquitted of all but writing the letters, Ball was sentenced by Tresilian to be hanged, drawn, and quartered. The execution took place on July 15 in the public square near St. Albans Abbey. Fifteen local businessmen were executed with him, their only crime having been to petition for charters of freedom. On July 15, 1981, a plaque to Ball's memory was erected in Colchester's Dutch Quarter.

SIGNIFICANCE

Ball was the kind of figure—obviously talented but frustratingly obscure—who easily polarizes the historians who judge him. He lived in a time when the common people of England found their lives uncommonly difficult, and with his eloquence he could incite popular feeling against their oppressors. Scholars sympathetic to Ball and Tyler minimize the rebels' actions in London, viewing them as heroes who were tricked by a corrupt king when they thought they were poised to ally themselves with him in establishing a just rule for all. More hostile historians condemn the rebellion for its offenses against law and order and see Ball, Tyler, and Jack Straw as irresponsible rabble-rousers. Despite the disparity of opinion, nothing suggests that Ball was anything but a decent man, devoted to the poor people in his pastoral care and courageous enough to work for their general good even though his actions led to his gruesome death.

—*Frank Day*

FURTHER READING

Bird, Brian. *Rebel Before His Time: The Story of John Ball and the Peasants' Revolt*. Worthing, England: Churchman, 1987. Excellent, radically sympathetic account that identifies Peldon as Ball's birthplace and includes translations of Ball's six letters.

Dobson, R. B., ed. *The Peasants' Revolt of 1381*. New York: St. Martin's Press, 1970. Indispensable collection of contemporary documents about the revolt, plus a chronology. Includes letters by Ball and accounts of him by several of his contemporaries.

Dunn, Alastair. *The Great Rising of 1381: The Peasants' Revolt and England's Failed Revolution*. Stroud, England: Tempus, 2000. An account of the revolt in the context of the English and revolutions in general. Includes a bibliography and index.

Hill, Douglas, comp. *The Peasants' Revolt: A Collection of Contemporary Documents*. Amawalk, N.Y.: Jackdaw, 1998. A study guide especially helpful as introductory material.

Hilton, R. H., and T. H. Aston, eds. *The English Rising of 1381*. New York: Cambridge University Press, 1984. Eight scholarly essays on the historical background of the Peasants' Revolt.

Lindsay, Philip, and Reg Groves. *The Peasants' Revolt of 1381*. 1950. Reprint. Westport, Conn.: Greenwood, 1974. An excellent introduction to the subject, with a good bibliography. Two chapters on John Ball, one a moving account of his death.

Morris, William. *A Dream of John Ball*. New York: Oriole Chapbooks, 1971. The British poet's evocative fictionalization of John Ball's dream of an egalitarian community.

Oman, Charles. *The Great Revolt of 1381*. New York: Haskell House, 1968. Valuable for its appendices, maps, and region-by-region account of the revolt. Reveals little sympathy for the rebels.

Zelitch, Simone. *The Confession of Jack Straw*. Seattle, Wash.: Black Heron, 1991. A lively political novel about the Peasants' Revolt featuring Jack Straw, and John Ball figures as one of the major characters.

SEE ALSO: Edward III; Jean Froissart; Richard II; Wat Tyler; John Wyclif.

RELATED ARTICLES in *Great Events from History: The Middle Ages, 477-1453*: 1373-1410: Jean Froissart Compiles His *Chronicles*; May-June, 1381: Peasants' Revolt in England.

BASIL THE MACEDONIAN

Byzantine emperor (r. 867-886)

Through his strength, intelligence, and excellent administration, Basil established the Macedonian Dynasty, which brought the Byzantine Empire to great heights. He imparted such vitality to an ancient imperial tradition that it has been emulated by modern nations.

BORN: 812 or 813; Charioupolis, Macedonia, Byzantine Empire (now in Greece)
DIED: August 29, 886; Constantinople, Byzantine Empire (now Istanbul, Turkey)
ALSO KNOWN AS: Basil I
AREAS OF ACHIEVEMENT: Government and politics, military

EARLY LIFE

Basil the Macedonian was the eldest son of a couple commonly called Constantine and Pancalo. The father of Constantine appears to have been an Armenian, Hmayeak, known sometimes by his name in Greek form, Maiactes. The mother of Constantine may have been a daughter of Leo V, the ruler of the Byzantine Empire from 813 to 820, also of Armenian descent. Scholar Cyril Toumanoff has traced Hmayeak's ancestry through the Armenian Mamikonian princes and the Arsacid rulers to the Achaemenid monarchs of Persia. The presence of the Armenians in Macedonia was not unusual, as the Byzantine Empire often moved groups of its minorities to areas it wished to strengthen and develop. Macedonia was under attack by the Bulgars during Basil's childhood, and there are unconfirmed reports that he and his family were taken captive by them for a time.

Basil did not learn to read and write until late in life, but he credited his father with being his principal instructor in the wisdom of life. A large, handsome man, he became a skilled rider and breaker of horses and developed impressive strength and athletic ability. These traits helped open his path to greatness when, as a young man, he moved to Constantinople. Also helpful were well-placed fellow Armenians, one of whom engaged Basil as his stable master. This man was a courtier with access to Emperor Michael III, who ruled from 842 to 867. When a wrestler was needed at the palace to defeat a Bulgarian challenger, Basil was taken there and won easily. On a royal hunting trip, Basil was present when the emperor's horse ran away. Vaulting into the saddle with great skill, he brought the steed back safely. The tall and personable Basil became a favorite of Michael III.

LIFE'S WORK

Basil divorced his first wife, Maria, the mother of his son Constantine, in 865 and married Eudocia, Michael III's concubine. In 866, Michael had Basil crowned as a coemperor of the Byzantine Empire, but in 867, Michael had a new favorite, so Basil, with the help of several relatives and friends, murdered Michael, becoming sole emperor of the eastern empire in 867. With Eudocia, Basil had three sons: Leo, born in 866; Alexander, born in 870; and Stephen, born in 871. The favorite son, Constantine, was crowned coemperor in 869, as was Leo in 870, these steps being taken to provide for an orderly succession to the throne.

Basil had great plans for his beloved Constantine. In 868, he tried to arrange his marriage to the daughter of Louis II, Roman emperor in the West. Because Louis had no sons, such a marriage could have reunited the two halves of the Roman Empire. Basil's extension of Byzantine control in southern Italy annoyed Louis, however, and the perennial quarrel about papal claims to authority over the Christians of the eastern empire also divided them. The marriage project failed, and the death of Constantine in 879 came as a bitter blow to the emperor. There are scholars who claim that the next heir, Leo, was actually the son of Michael III, but an analysis of the funeral oration delivered by Leo VI when Basil died shows him to be Basil's son, as does the fact that Basil could have eliminated Leo and arranged for the succession of one of his younger sons.

Under Basil I, the Byzantine navy became a dominant power in the eastern Mediterranean. When the Arab fleet attacked along the eastern shore of the Adriatic Sea, laying siege to Dubrovnik in 867, a strong Byzantine naval force compelled them to abandon the siege and retire to the southwest. Byzantine missionary efforts led to the Christianization of the Serbians and the Slavic groups on the southeastern shore of the Adriatic, and progress was made with conversions in Bulgaria and Macedonia. There and in Russia, the use of Slavic languages in Slavic letters—an alphabet devised by missionaries of Greek origin—aided the spread of the faith. The drawing of the Slavic peoples of the Balkans and Russia into the Byzantine cultural, religious, and political orbit was a major achievement. Although Syracuse in Sicily was lost to the Muslims, the Byzantine position in the mainland of southern Italy was improved, against both Muslims and the adherents of the Roman Empire in the West.

Conditions were exceptionally favorable for the Byzantine Empire at this time because of Muslim divisiveness. Egypt established its own rulers in 868, and there were civil wars among the Arabs of North Africa. In the eastern part of the Islamic world, the rising power of the Turks was causing disunity. The Byzantine forces were able to advance their frontiers into what is now southeastern Turkey. The Armenians and their neighbors were thus shielded somewhat from Muslim pressures, and Armenia's relations with the empire were generally positive.

The Byzantine occupation of Tephrice, capital of the Paulicians—a deviant Christian sect—also moved the border eastward. That victory came in 872, and in the next year Basil's army moved forward in the region of the Euphrates River, taking Zapetra and Samosata. Basil was a ruthless and cruel leader, but he knew how to select highly effective commanders for his forces on land and sea. He motivated them thoroughly, supervising and coordinating them well. The concept of the Christian Empire, which had often been weakened by the divisive influence of the iconoclasts—those who opposed the use of holy images in the Church—exercised an inspirational and unifying role. Basil began the forging of real nationalism, or "uniculturalism."

Basil was more a military leader than an intellectual, but his dynastic and family arrangements made it possible for his successors, some of whom tended to be more intellectual or even ineffectual, to blend their rulership's legitimacy with leadership from the armed forces. This was sometimes done by the marriage of legitimate heirs to successful generals or by regency and coemperorship between such partners. Basil also bequeathed an intricately organized civil service, administrative continuity, and a foundation of much-improved law codes.

Basil desired to revive and update the legal system of the empire by preparing an overarching code of Greco-Roman legislative acts. Emperor Justinian I, who ruled from 527 to 565, had codified the laws of ancient Rome, collecting and publishing all the valid imperial edicts. He

Engraving of Basil the Macedonian attacked by a stag while hunting. (Hulton|Archive at Getty Images)

had also published the collected writings of the classical Roman jurists, thus bringing the vast and frequently conflicting rulings of those jurists into one orderly system. Basil saw that the updating of such a system would provide an underlying unity for a regime that rested on an uneasy partnership of rough soldiers and cultivated bureaucrats, bridging their mutual suspicion and dislike. Not only would government and individual affairs be properly regulated but also a better framework would underlie the expanding commerce of the empire. The Byzantine Empire was the center of flourishing trade between Europe and Russia on the one hand and the commercial routes eastward into Asia on the other. The traders who moved goods through Mesopotamia and Persia, as far as India and China, contributed significantly to the economic well-being of the realm.

BYZANTINE EMPERORS: MACEDONIAN LINE, 842-1056

Reign	*Emperor*
842-867	Michael III (last of the Phrygian line)
846	Arabs sack Vatican
865	Varangian (Russian) incursions
867-886	BASIL I THE MACEDONIAN
867	Siege of Dubrovnik
886	Venice independent
886-912	Leo VI the Wise (the Philosopher)
907	More Varangian attacks
912-913	Alexander
913-919	Constantine VII Porphyrogenitus
919-944	Romanus I Lecapenus
944	Treaty with Russians
944-959	Constantine VII (restored)
959-963	Romanus II
963	Basil II Bulgaroktonos
963-969	Nicephorus II Phocas
969-976	John I Tzimisces
971	Bulgaria conquered
976-1025	Basil II (restored)
989	Russia converted to Christianity
1018	Macedonian Bulgaria annexed
1025-1028	Constantine VIII
1028-1034	Zoë and Romanus III Argyrus
1034-1041	Zoë and Michael IV the Paphlagonian
1041-1042	Zoë and Michael V Calaphates
1042	Zoë and Theodora
1042-1050	Zoë, Theodora, and Constantine IX Monomachus
1050-1055	Theodora and Constantine IX
1055-1056	Theodora

Basil wished to adapt the legal system to changed conditions, adding the many laws issued after Justinian's time. Not only was a housecleaning of the old material needed, but Basil also planned to accompany the code with explanations of the Latin words and phrases in Greek. The Greek language would be used for the code, but the old Latin references need not remain obscure.

The new compilations prepared under Basil's administration included a manual of legal science to explain the law and its penalties. Basil realized that the full code might not be issued in his time, and, as it turned out, most of the material was published in the reign of his son, Leo VI. Basil did publish *Procheiron* (English translation, 1931) and *Epanagoge* during his lifetime. The voluminous codes, in two sets of forty and sixty volumes, were drafted under Basil and published by his successor as the *Basilica* (from *basilikos*, meaning imperial). The influence of these ambitious works was felt not only during the ensuing six centuries of Byzantine history but also in Russia, where the works from Basil's reign were quoted in seventeenth century documents of the government and courts.

Especially interesting in Basil's legal material is the general theory set forth on the rights and duties of the various components of the government and the church authorities, under the emperor and the patriarch of the Church. These two supreme heads had parallel functions, the first to serve the material needs of the people, the second to see to their spiritual condition. The two were to cooperate for the benefit of all humankind.

In August of 886, Basil was mortally injured during a hunt. Taken back to Constantinople, he died nine days later, on August 29, 886. To his son, now Leo VI, he left a stable, well-organized nation, extending from southern Italy east to the Caucasus and from the banks of the Danube River on the north to Syria in the south.

SIGNIFICANCE

The firm foundation laid by Basil the Macedonian, through strong government and a homogenized culture, unified a multiracial empire that could have been dissolved by its diversity. The Armenian and Slavic minorities were two groups that took a major part in leading the empire's forces, running its government, and enriching its commerce. Basil also resolved several potential religious schisms during his reign.

Basil's dynasty spread Byzantine influence throughout Europe. His great-great-granddaughter, Theophano, married the Western Roman emperor Otto II and became a forebear of Edward I of England and most later European dynasties. Her sister Anna married Prince Vladimir I of Kiev, the Christianizer of Russia. Vladimir's granddaughter, Anna, was the wife of King Henry I of France; her son was the first of many kings in the West to be named Philip. She was mindful, in selecting the name, of her supposed descent from Philip II, king of Macedonia, the father of Alexander the Great. The uses of these two names by the much later rulers of expansionist Spain and Russia, respectively, demonstrate the vitality even into modern times of the dynamic Byzantine imperial concept.

The heirs of Basil I were well advised to emulate his governmental acumen, but with respect to aggressive empire-building, this emulation has been a tragic force in history. For centuries, Russia saw itself as the Third Rome, Constantinople having been the second. Many modern imperialists have dignified their tyrannies as continuations of the ancient empires, appropriating such symbols as the fasces, eagles, and the titles czar and kaiser, derived from the earlier term, caesar.

—*Frank H. Tucker*

Further Reading

Charanis, Peter. "The Armenians in the Byzantine Empire." *Byzantinoslavica* 22 (1961): 226-240. A detailed account of the Armenian minority of Byzantium, with special attention to the time of Basil and his dynasty.

Diehl, Charles. *Byzantine Portraits*. Translated by Harold Bell. New York: Alfred A. Knopf, 1927. A dated but still-important text that provides sketches of major figures of the empire, including Basil.

_______. *Byzantium: Greatness and Decline*. Translated by Naomi Walford. New Brunswick, N.J.: Rutgers University Press, 1957. A well-organized work in four sections: "Evolution of Byzantine History," "Elements of Power," "Elements of Weakness," and "Byzantium's Contribution to the World." Includes an extensive bibliography.

Ostrogorsky, George. *History of the Byzantine State*. Translated by Joan Hussey. Rev. ed. New Brunswick, N.J: Rutgers University Press, 1969. An excellent, thorough history. Contains an especially good explanation of the sources on the subject, such as original contemporary materials.

Sherrard, Philip. *Byzantium*. New York: Time-Life Books, 1966. Notable for being composed of many pictures drawn from very early chronicles, showing events in Byzantium. Much attention to Basil.

Tougher, Shaun. *The Reign of Leo VI (886-912): Politics and People*. New York: Brill, 1997. Surveys the reign of Basil and his son Leo VI, the establishment of the Macedonian Dynasty, Leo's wives, military affairs, and more. Includes a map, bibliography, and index.

Treadgold, Warren. "The Persistence of Byzantium." *Wilson Quarterly* 22, no. 4 (Autumn, 1998). Presents a detailed history of the Byzantine Empire and argues for its recognition as one of the greatest empires in the history of the world.

Vasiliev, A. A. *History of the Byzantine Empire, 324-1453*. 2 vols. 1928-1929. 2d ed. Madison: University of Wisconsin Press, 1964. A standard authority, but especially recommended for its chapter on the study of Byzantine history.

Vryonis, Speros. *Byzantium and Europe*. New York: Harcourt, Brace and World, 1967. Good source on a key aspect of Basil's role in forming history and ideology.

Wagner, Anthony. *Pedigree and Progress*. London: Phillimore, 1975. Contains a detailed account of the Asian antecedents of Basil, his dynasty, and its marriages and relationships with the European nations. Provides relevant, translated portions of Cyril Toumanoff's *Manuel de Généalogie et de Chronologie pour l'Histoire de la Caucasie Chrétienne* (Rome, 1976), not otherwise available in English.

See also: Anna, Princess of the Byzantine Empire; Edward I; Justinian I; Philip II; Vladimir I.

Related articles in *Great Events from History: The Middle Ages, 477-1453*: 529-534: Justinian's Code Is Compiled; 563: Silk Worms Are Smuggled to the Byzantine Empire; 726-843: Iconoclastic Controversy; c. 850: Development of the Slavic Alphabet; 864: Boris Converts to Christianity; 976-1025: Reign of Basil II; May 29, 1453: Fall of Constantinople.

AL-BATTĀNĪ

Arab astronomer and mathematician

Al-Battānī examined and corrected, through application of trigonometry, astronomical theories first put forward by the second century Alexandrian Ptolemy.

BORN: 858; near Haran, Mesopotamia (now in Turkey)
DIED: 929; Qaṣr al-Jiss, region of Sāmarrā᾽ (now in Iraq)
ALSO KNOWN AS: Abū ᶜAbd Allāh Muḥammad ibn Jābir ibn Sinān al-Battānī al-Ḥarrānī al-Ṣabi᾽ (full name); Albatenius; Albategnius; Albategni (Latin names)
AREAS OF ACHIEVEMENT: Astronomy, mathematics, science and technology

EARLY LIFE

Born near Haran, the young al-Battānī (ahl-bah-TAH-nee) moved with his and several other families to Rakka on the Euphrates River midway on the caravan route between Aleppo and the Upper Mesopotamian city of Mosul. This migration may be explained in part by the *nisba*, or nickname, retained by the future Islamic astronomer. "Al-Sabi᾽" may refer to his family's earlier adherence to the so-called Sabian sect, which was reputed to follow a mixture of Christian and Islamic principles. Whatever the family's original religious orientation, al-Battānī's later fame was won under the banner of Islam, the faith he ultimately followed. After his move to Rakka as a youth, al-Battānī spent the remainder of his life in the same geographical and cultural environment.

No specific information is available on al-Battānī's formal education. It is not known, for example, whether his original training was obtained in a fully secular "scientific" or in a religious setting. It was as a youth in Rakka, however, that al-Battānī decided to devote himself to careful study of ancient texts, especially those of Ptolemy, which provided him with the knowledge needed to carry out the series of astronomical observations that would make him famous, not only in the Islamic world but in the medieval European West as well.

LIFE'S WORK

Al-Battānī, known to the West as Albatenius, contributed greatly to advances in the field of trigonometry. To carry out key calculations, he relied on algebraic rather than geometric methods. Like his somewhat lesser known later follower Abul Wefa (940-998), al-Battānī focused much of his attention on the theories of the second century Alexandrian astronomer Ptolemy. Several Islamic scholars before him had been intrigued by Ptolemy's approach to the phenomenon of the oscillatory motion of the equinoxes. Al-Battānī's contemporary Thābit ibn Qurrah (c. 836-901) tried to account for this by supplementing Ptolemy's theory, merely adding a ninth sphere to the Greek scientist's assumption of eight spheres; al-Battānī, however, remained doubtful. He was convinced that trigonometry should be developed more effectively for the purpose of achieving greater precision in already known methods of making these and other astronomical calculations. This goal led him to explore and expand the relevance of sines. His use of the Indian sines, or half chords, enabled him to criticize Ptolemy's conclusions in several areas.

For example, Ptolemy had insisted that the solar apogee was a fully immobile phenomenon. Al-Battānī, however, was able to observe that in the seven centuries since Ptolemy's time, there had been a notable increase in the Sun's apogee. His further observations suggested that the apogee was affected by the precession of the equinoxes. To explore this theory required a substantial revision of methods of proposing equations to represent the passage of time in accurate astronomical terms; room had to be made for accommodating slow secular variations. As part of this process, al-Battānī set out to correct Ptolemy's theory of the precession of the equinoxes.

The phenomenon of eclipses was also a field incompletely pioneered by Ptolemy. Interest in this subject motivated al-Battānī to make a variety of studies that aided subsequent astronomers in their calculations to determine the time of the visibility of the new moon. His treatment of the phenomena of lunar and solar eclipses provided the basic information that would be used by European astronomers as late as the eighteenth century. Most notably, Richard Dunthorne used al-Battānī's work in his 1749 study of the apparent acceleration of the motion of the Moon. In addition, mention of solutions al-Battānī proposed for the field of spherical trigonometry appears in many earlier European works, including those of Regiomontanus (1436-1476).

In a somewhat more practical vein easily appreciated by the layperson, al-Battānī's observations allowed him to determine the length of the tropic year and, significantly, the precise duration of the four seasons of the year.

One of the most original areas of al-Battānī's work

involved the use of horizontal and vertical sundials. Through their use, he was able to denote the characteristics of a so-called "horizontal shadow" (*umbra extensa*). These he used to reveal cotangents, for which he prepared the first-known systematic tables. Similarly, his study of "vertical shadows" (*umbra versa*) provided pioneer data for calculating tangents.

Most of al-Battānī's important findings in the field of astronomy were contained in his major work, *Kitāb al-zij* (c. 900-901, book on astronomy; best known as *Zij*, *De motu stellarum*, or *De scientia stellarum*). As the Latin titles suggest, this magnum opus was first circulated widely among scholars of the early period of the European Renaissance. The work was translated originally by Robertus Retinensis in Spain in the twelfth century. In the thirteenth century, King Alfonso X of Spain had a direct Arabic-to-Spanish translation prepared. *De scientia stellarum* later gained added attention from modern scholars such as the Italian C. A. Nallino, who edited and translated the Latin text, providing essential commentaries that enhance contemporary understanding of the Islamic scholar's original contributions.

Unfortunately, modern scholars' familiarity with other important writings by al-Battānī is limited to what can be gleaned from references to them in other Islamic authors' works. A "Book of the Science of Ascensions of the Signs of the Zodiac," a commentary on Ptolemy's *Apotelesmatika tetrabiblos*, and a third work on trigonometry, for example, are all lost in their original versions.

SIGNIFICANCE

The scholarly career of al-Battānī provides an example of the diversity of pre-Islamic sources that contributed to the rise of Islamic science. It also illustrates the importance of such scientists' work in saving traces of pre-Islamic contributions to knowledge during the Dark Ages of European history, when much of the classical heritage of Western civilization was lost. To speak of al-Battānī's role as that of an interim transmitter of knowledge, however, would be to miss the essential importance of scientific endeavors in his era. It is clear, for example, that al-Battānī was dissatisfied with interpretations offered by his classical and Indian forerunners. By the time his work of reinterpretation was translated for transmission to the European world, it reflected numerous original contributions. Thus, in regard to the reemergence of Western science during the classical revival period of the Renaissance, it can be said that many of the principles on which it was based came from Islamic sources.

The fact that such advances in several fields of "pure" science were actively sponsored by the early Islamic caliphs—themselves assumed to be primary guardians of the religious interests of their realm—is of major significance. In al-Battānī's age, knowledge was still recognized as something necessarily derived from syncretic sources. Tolerance for the exploration of different secular scientific traditions did not, however, survive many successive generations. Narrowness of views in the eastern Islamic world a mere century and a half after al-Battānī's contributions would make the role of Western translators of Arabic scientific works just as vital to the conservation of cumulative knowledge in world culture as the work of Islamic translators and commentators had been after the end of the classical era. Outstanding figures such as al-Battānī, therefore, definitely span world civilizations and reflect values that are universal. These are easily recognized as such beyond the borders of their chronological time or geographic zone.

—*Byron D. Cannon*

FURTHER READING

Anawati, G. "Science." In *The Cambridge History of Islam*, edited by P. M. Holt, Ann K. S. Lambton, and Bernard Lewis. 1970. Reprint. Cambridge, England: Cambridge University Press, 1977. This chapter places the general field of science within the overall framework of Islamic civilization and explores interrelationships between religious and scientific attitudes toward knowledge and how each of the two domains was affected by developments in the other. The body of the chapter consists of a field-by-field review of the most important Islamic accomplishments, including advances in arithmetic, algebra, geometry, trigonometry, optics, mechanics, astronomy and astrology, and medicine.

Bakar, Osman. *The History and Philosophy of Islamic Science*. Cambridge, England: Islamic Texts Society, 1999. Discusses questions of methodology, doubt, spirituality and scientific knowledge, the philosophy of Islamic medicine, and how Islamic science influenced medieval Christian views of the natural world.

Bell, E. T. *The Development of Mathematics*. New York: McGraw-Hill, 1945. This comprehensive work on mathematics begins with a historical review of the field from the first-known texts through each successive stage of discovery, ending at the mid-point of the twentieth century. Includes the chapter "Detour Through India, Arabia, and Spain, A.D. 400-1300." Covers the specific contributions of Islamic scholars such as al-Battānī and examines topical subsections of the field of mathematics, including geometry, invariance, and others. Bibliographical references.

Cajori, Florian. *A History of Mathematics*. 1931. 5th ed. Providence, R.I.: AMS Chelsea, 2000. This classic work has several important characteristics that still merit mention. It covers standard non-Western mathematical traditions (Hindu and Islamic). The author gives detailed information on individual mathematicians' original findings.

Hogendijk, Jan P., and Abdelhamid I. Sabra, eds. *The Enterprise of Science in Islam: New Perspectives*. Cambridge, Mass.: MIT Press, 2003. A collection surveying the history of Islamic science, including mathematics and astronomy. Illustrations, bibliography, index.

Kennedy, Edward S. *Astronomy and Astrology in the Medieval Islamic World*. Brookfield, Vt.: Ashgate, 1998. Discusses astronomy, astronomers, math, and mathematicians during the Islamic Middle Ages. Includes an index.

Nasr, Seyyed Hossein. *Islamic Science: An Illustrated Study*. London: World of Islam Festival, 1976. Contains an attractive collection of illustrations that bring to life the world of Islamic science. These include intricate miniatures depicting cosmic charts and photographs of astronomical instruments and remains of observatories similar to the ones that would have been used in al-Battānī's time. Glossary and bibliography.

_______. *Science and Civilization in Islam*. Cambridge, Mass.: Harvard University Press, 1968. This survey text deals only with scientific endeavors in Islamic civilization, which allows it to examine individual contributions thoroughly. Extensive bibliography.

Sabra, Abdelhamid I. *Optics, Astronomy, and Logic: Studies in Arabic Science and Philosophy*. Brookfield, Vt.: Variorum, 1994. A history of science, specifically optics and astronomy, in the Muslim world of al-Battānī's time. Illustrations, index.

Stephenson, F. Richard. *Historical Eclipses and Earth's Rotation*. New York: Cambridge University Press, 1997. Explores "Solar and Lunar Eclipses Recorded in Medieval Arab Chronicles," "Observations of Eclipses by Medieval Arab Astronomers," and "Eclipse Records from Medieval Europe." Illustrations, bibliography, index.

See also: Abul Wefa; Alhazen; al-Khwārizmī; Omar Khayyám.

Related articles in *Great Events from History: The Middle Ages, 477-1453*: 595-665: Invention of Decimals and Negative Numbers; 7th-8th centuries: Maya Build Astronomical Observatory at Palenque; c. 950: Court of Córdoba Flourishes in Spain.

Baybars I

Mamlūk sultan of Egypt and Syria (r. 1260-1277)

Through military prowess, administrative skill, courage, and practical good sense, Baybars rose from slavery to become the virtual founder and most eminent representative of the Mamlūk Dynasty in medieval Egypt.

Born: c. 1223; northern shore of the Black Sea

Died: July 1, 1277; Damascus (now in Syria)

Also known as: al-Malik al-Ẓāhir Rukn al-Dīn Baybars al-Ṣāliḥī (full name)

Areas of achievement: Military, government and politics, religion and theology

Early Life

Baybars I (BAY-bahrz) was born in what is now southern Russia. A member of the tribe of Kipchak Turks living on the north shores of the Black Sea, Baybars was a victim of the Mongol invasion of his native region in the late 1230's. By the time he was fourteen, Baybars had become a prisoner of war; he was sold in the slave market in Sivas, Anatolia. Syrian merchants took Baybars deep into the Arab world, where he eventually became the property of Ṣāliḥ Najm al-Dīn Ayyūb, sultan of the Ayyubid Dynasty in Egypt.

This was a time of political fragmentation in the Arab world, following the breakup of the ʿAbbāsid Empire (750-1258) and the fall of Baghdad to the Mongols. Various local regimes, or principalities, had arisen in the void created by the collapse of the ʿAbbāsid state. The Ayyubids in Egypt, like other territorial princes, began to rely heavily on imported Turkish slave troops for their defense. It was for this purpose that Baybars was either sold or given to the sultan.

Sultan al-Salih sent Baybars off to an island in the Nile for military training. The adolescent Turk did well and, following graduation from a military academy and emancipation, was enrolled in the sultan's prestigious Bahriyya regiment. Baybars had found his place in life, and the events had been set in motion that would make him "the Napoleon of medieval Egypt."

A double danger faced the Ayyubids in Egypt in the mid-thirteenth century. One threat was from the west, the other from the east. Both perils were military in nature. By sea, across the Mediterranean, came the French Crusaders. By land, across the steppes of Asia, came the Mongols. Both intruders had to be repelled if Muslim Egypt was to develop in security. As Napoleon Bonaparte later made his reputation by defending the French Revolution, so Baybars secured his fame by protecting Egypt from these two dangers.

Baybars's initial assignment was to repel a French invasion of Egypt. Since 1096, Crusaders from Western Europe had attempted to regain control of the Holy Land. While many European nations participated in the Crusades, the French kingdom often took the leadership. This was the case with the last of the two "traditional" Crusades, the Seventh and the Eighth. Both were undertaken by Louis IX of France (r. 1226-1270), a Catholic celebrated for his piety; they were occasioned by the loss of the Crusader kingdom of Jerusalem to the Mongols in 1244. Louis was persuaded that the best way to liberate Jerusalem was not by means of a direct or frontal attack but by diversionary measures in Arab North Africa. These would distract Muslim attention from Jerusalem. Louis, as a matter of fact, would die in the second of these invasions of North Africa (at Tunis in 1270). His initial adventure in Arab Africa was almost equally fatal. Louis invaded the Ayyubid sultanate, taking Dumyat (Damietta) in the Nile Delta. At this juncture, the sultan turned to Baybars for help. The elite forces of the Ayyubid army, the Bahriyya, led by Baybars, defeated the French at Al-Manṣūrah in February, 1250. Louis was captured and was held by the Ayyubids for ransom. As a result, the reputation of Baybars was established, and the Ayyubid Dynasty was relieved of the danger of invasion.

Before Baybars could direct his attention toward the other danger, the Mongols, there was an internal crisis within the Ayyubid regime. Conscious of their own power, the *mamlūk*, or Turkish slave soldiers, with Baybars's cooperation, rose in revolt against the new Ayyubid sultan, Tūrān Shāh. Tūrān Shāh was murdered, and a period of confusion followed that was resolved when the first Mamlūk sultan, Aybak, came to power. For reasons that are not entirely clear, Baybars offended the first Mamlūk sultan and, like the Old Testament soldier David who offended his commander-king, Saul, he had to go into exile in 1254. For six years, Baybars was a "soldier of fortune" in Syria.

Baybars, however, was much too valuable a person for the Mamlūks not to employ. A new sultan, Quṭuz (d. 1260), invited him to return to Egypt in 1260. Baybars was restored to his rank in the Mamlūk army and was given a suitable income. Now he was assigned to the task of delivering Egypt from the Mongol threat. Baybars took his forces to the Holy Land, where he defeated a Mongol army at the Battle of Aīn Jalūt in 1260. Apparently, Baybars was disappointed when, following this victory, he was denied a suitable reward (it is thought that he wanted the city of Aleppo). During a quarrel that may have been occasioned by a Mongol slave girl, Baybars joined other officers in a palace coup; Quṭuz was assassinated. Thus, for the second time, Baybars had been involved in the murder of his master. The ambitious officer now became Baybars I, the fourth Mamlūk sultan. For all practical purposes, Baybars was the true founder of the Dawlat al-atrak (the dynasty of the Turks). Perhaps he had set a dangerous precedent in obtaining power by assassination. Other Turkish tribes, such as the Ottomans, however, used a similar procedure, the "law of strangulation," whereby the most powerful of the sultan's sons ascended the throne after murdering his brothers. Baybars, however, proved able to maintain himself on the throne of Egypt.

Baybars ruled effectively because of his outstanding personal qualities. Known as a strict Muslim, Baybars, like the Prophet, was a man given to victory in battle and generosity in peace. Celebrated for his athletic ability, Baybars enjoyed hunting, polo, jousting, and archery. A man of courage, he inspired enormous loyalty among his followers and was capable of commanding great sacrifice from his soldiers. Though he came to power by assassination, Baybars ruled securely and retained the respect and obedience of his subordinates. Baybars came to be celebrated in the popular imagination as a "fair and able ruler." He came to be known as the subject of a body of folk literature, the *Sirat Baybars* (thirteenth century; *Life of Baybars*, 1956). Thus, not only was Baybars a legend in his own lifetime but he also became an archetypal symbol of the just king for later generations.

Life's Work

Baybars was to be the greatest of the Mamlūk sultans. For seventeen years (1260-1277), he devoted himself to carrying out three great roles: warrior, ruler, and reformer.

Baybars's reign was dominated by war. One of the great military commanders of the Middle Ages, Baybars conducted thirty-eight campaigns in Syria, fought nine battles with the Mongols, and was involved in five major engagements with the Armenians. It is reported that Baybars took personal command of the army in fifteen battles. Because of the military requirements of his reign, Baybars was outside his capital city, Cairo, for almost half the time he was sultan. On twenty-six occasions, Baybars left Cairo, traveling more than sixty-six thousand miles.

The assignment Baybars faced as sultan was the same that he had received as a staff officer: to secure the safety of Egypt from both the Crusaders and the Mongols. He began by taking up the campaign against the Crusaders. From 1265 to 1271, Baybars conducted a war against the Crusaders in Palestine. As a result, Baybars forced the Knights Hospitallers to surrender Arsuf in 1265, and within a year Safad, which had been in the control of the Knights Templars, fell. Jaffa and Antioch were occupied by May, 1268, and within another three years the ultimate doom of the Crusaders was sealed. Their eventual expulsion from the Middle East had been assured.

Having secured his realm from French invasion, Baybars turned his attention eastward. While the Mongols were his main enemy, there were also other threats in Asia. From their bases in Iran, the Mongols had felt free to invade Syria. Baybars prevented this by refortifying Syria, attacking the Armenians (who had been allies of the Mongols), and waging unrelenting war on the Mongols. As a result, Syria was pacified, secured, and united to Egypt. Baybars also destroyed the power of a militantly anarchist Muslim sect, the Assassins of Syria, and was able to invade Anatolia, taking the city of Caesarea (now Kayseri) from the Seljuk Turks in 1276. Concurrently, campaigns were undertaken in Africa to guarantee the safety of Egypt. Expeditions southward to Nubia and westward into Libya both proved successful.

Many scholars have tried to explain the military success of Baybars. Eight factors are usually offered as reasons for his brilliance as a warrior. First, he had a very fine model: Baybars consciously chose to imitate Saladin. The founder of the Ayyubid Dynasty in Egypt, Saladin (1138-1193) is regarded by many as the greatest Muslim military hero of all time. Baybars attempted to live up to the high standards of courage, courtesy, and character embodied by this great warrior. Second, Baybars had outstanding personal qualities and mental attitudes; he was an energetic man "who dominated events with an imperturbable optimism." Third, he was committed to careful planning. Attention to detail meant that he left nothing to chance. To the extent that preparation made it possible, Baybars was in control of the situation.

Fourth, under his leadership Egypt was remilitarized and turned into an adequate base of operations. Fortifications were rebuilt; arsenals, warships, and merchant vessels were constructed. Fifth, Baybars's foresight, his sense of a world perspective, and his understanding of regional military realities enabled him to capitalize on Egypt's geographic location at the crossroads of the Middle East.

Sixth, Baybars relied on an excellent communications system. News came to him from all parts of his empire at least twice a week; more urgent matters were brought to

Mamlūk Sultans, Baḥrī Line

Reign	*Ruler*
1252-1257	Aybak al-Turkumānī
1257-1259	ʿAlī I
1259-1260	Qutuz al-Muʿizzī
1260-1277	Baybars I (defeats Mongols 1260)
1277-1279	Baraka (Berke) Khān
1279	Salāmish (Süleymish)
1279-1290	Qalāwūn al-Alfī
1290-1293	Khalīl
1291	Fall of Acre
1293	Baydarā (?)
1293-1294	Muḥammad I
1294-1296	Kitbughā
1296-1299	Lāchīn (Lājīn) al-Ashqar
1299-1309	Muḥammad I
1303	Earthquake destroys Pharos lighthouse
1309-1310	Baybars II al-Jāshnakīr (Burjī)
1310-1341	Muḥammad I
1341	Abū Bakr
1341-1342	Kūjūk (Küchük)
1342	Aḥmad I
1342-1345	Ismāʿīl
1345-1346	Shaʿbān I
1346-1347	Ḥājjī I
1347-1351	al-Ḥasan
1351-1354	Ṣāliḥ
1354-1361	al-Ḥasan
1361-1363	Muḥammad II
1363-1377	Shaʿbān II
1377-1382	ʿAlī II
1382	Ḥājjī II
1389-1390	Ḥājjī II

the sultan's attention by means of carrier pigeons. Seventh, Baybars established a brilliant espionage system so that he was able to know in advance of his enemies' moves. Eighth, perhaps the keystone in this entire arch of military brilliance was Baybars's talent as a field commander. He was able to make quick decisions, to command the unflinching loyalty of his troops, to furnish an example of personal courage and vitality, and to evoke love and respect from his supporters at home.

As a ruler, Baybars was known for achievement in several major areas. He maintained the strength of the military, for he realized that his power was based on the army. It was his decision to continue the already established pattern of recruiting Turkish slaves. An alliance with the Mongols of the Golden Horde in southern Russia made this possible.

Moreover, Baybars expanded the influence of Egypt. The annexation of Syria was one expression of this goal; the establishing of diplomatic relations with the various Mediterranean powers was another. Baybars's envoys were favorably received by Emperor Michael VIII Palaeologus in the Byzantine Empire, securing the grain trade and once more opening the Bosporus and the Black Sea to Egyptian navigation. Ambassadors were also sent to various courts, including those of Manfred of Sicily, Charles of Anjou (later king of Naples and Sicily), James I the Conqueror of Aragon, and Alfonso X of León and Castile. Such an aggressive foreign policy, coupled with Baybars's military brilliance, reestablished Egypt as the key state in the Arab world.

Baybars was clearly successful in legitimizing his regime. Here again, a comparison with Napoleon Bonaparte is helpful. As Napoleon invited the pope, the representative of a world faith, to attend his coronation, so Baybars won the endorsement of the caliphate for his government. In 1261, Baybars invited the exiled heir of the ʿAbbāsid caliphate to take up residence in Cairo. While the caliph lacked political power, he had enormous popular prestige and spiritual influence. Offering sanctuary to the spiritual leader of Islam was an act of absolute brilliance. It cost Baybars nothing, but it gained respectability for his government throughout the orthodox (Sunni) Muslim world. This prestige would endure until Egypt's defeat by the Ottoman Turks in 1515 and the concomitant removal of the caliphate from Cairo to Istanbul.

Baybars was a reformer. As a devout Muslim, he was persuaded that the very center of a society must be religious faith. Accordingly, the restoration of religion was a major aim of his regime. Among his many building projects was the great mosque complex in Cairo that was named in his honor. Baybars recognized all four schools of orthodox Islamic law—Hanifite, Hanbalite, Shafite, and Malikite—and appointed judges from each of these traditions to serve in his courts. A strict moralist, he prohibited the sale and consumption of alcohol, commanded the giving of alms, facilitated the pilgrimage to Mecca, enforced the fast, and richly endowed Muslim schools and mosques. Baybars could not reform the principles of his religion, for he regarded them as ultimate and eternal, but he could promote the ardent practice of the faith. It is in that sense that Baybars was a genuine reformer.

One can only speculate as to the further extent of his accomplishments had Baybars not died prematurely on July 1, 1277, in Damascus; a poisoned cup intended for another had come to his hand. His body was buried at the al-Zahiriyah (national library) in Damascus, but his spirit lived on in the imagination of the Arab people.

SIGNIFICANCE

In a time of fragmentation and confusion throughout the Muslim world, Baybars I was able to create a strong Arab state at the very heart of the Middle East. The real founder of the Mamlūk Dynasty, which survived not only his death but also the Turkish conquest in 1515, perishing finally with the arrival of Napoleon in Egypt in 1798, he brought stability and order to Egypt. A military genius, Baybars defended the Mideast against major adversaries from both the west and the east: the Crusaders and the Mongols. Had he not come to power, Egypt might have been carved up into Crusader kingdoms, as had been the case along the Levantine coast, or, worse still, the Mongols might have devastated not only Palestine and Syria but also the North African coast. It can be said, then, that Baybars was not simply the Napoleon of the Arab Middle Ages and the real founder of the Mamlūk Dynasty but a genuine savior of Egypt as a nation and as a culture.

—*C. George Fry*

FURTHER READING

Amitai-Preiss, Reuven. *Mongols and Mamlūks: The Mamlūk-Ilkhanid War, 1260-1281*. New York: Cambridge University Press, 1995. A detailed account and analysis of the conflict between the Mamlūk sultanate of Egypt and the Mongol state in Persia. Also explores the Battle of Aīn Jalūt and other military battles of the time. Maps, bibliography, index.

Ayalon, David. *Studies on the Mamlūks of Egypt, 1250-1517*. London: Variorum, 1977. A useful introduction to the slave dynasty in medieval Egypt. The volume is made up of addresses, essays, and lectures by the author. Bibliography, index.

Hitti, Philip K. *History of the Arabs*. 10th ed. New York: St. Martin's Press, 1974. This is still the standard text for the entire spectrum of Arab history. Includes illustrations, genealogical tables, maps, and bibliographical references.

Hodgson, Marshall G. S. *The Venture of Islam: Conscience and History in a World Civilization*. 3 vols. Chicago: University of Chicago Press, 1974. A masterful history of the Muslim world, this work skillfully combines narrative and interpretation. Hodgson's study begins with Islam's classical age and ends with modern times. Bibliography, index.

Holt, P. M. *Early Mamlūk Diplomacy, 1260-1290: Treaties of Baybars and Qalawun with Christian Rulers*. New York: E. J. Brill, 1995. Presents a historical survey through source examples of the "diplomatic" relations between Baybars and Muslim Egypt with Christian rulers of Europe. Maps, bibliography, index.

Holt, Peter Malcolm, Ann K. S. Lambton, and Bernard Lewis, eds. *The Cambridge History of Islam*. Cambridge, England: Cambridge University Press, 1977. This valuable survey of the history of Islam places the time of Baybars in context. Illustrations, maps, bibliographies.

Lane-Poole, Stanley. *A History of Egypt in the Middle Ages*. 1901. Reprint. New York: Haskell House, 1969. This classic work remains a comprehensive and valuable study. Part of the History of Egypt series. Illustrations, map, bibliography.

Lev, Yaacov, ed. *The Medieval Mediterranean: Peoples, Economies and Cultures, 400-1453*. Vol. 9 in *War and Society in the Eastern Mediterranean, Seventh-Fifteenth Centuries*. Leiden, the Netherlands: Brill, 1997. Explores the world of the Crusades and other military encounters in the Middle East and the greater Mediterranean area, including Muslim Egypt up to the fall of Constantinople in 1453. Topics include armaments and supplies, regional administration, and the impact of the Crusaders on rural populations. Good for a broad overview of a thousand-year history of military conflict between Christians, Muslims, Jews, and other peoples.

Muir, William. *The Mameluke: Or, Slave Dynasty of Egypt, 1260-1517 A.D.* New York: AMS Press, 1973. With the work of Lane-Poole above, this book remains a standard survey of the Mamlūk era. Originally published in London in 1896. Includes illustrations.

Runciman, Steven. *The Kingdom of Jerusalem and the Frankish East, 1100-1187*. Vol. 2 in *A History of the Crusades*. Cambridge, England: Cambridge University Press, 1951-1958. The definitive study of the Crusades by a respected British scholar. Illustrations, maps, and a genealogical table.

Von Grunebaum, Gustav Edmund. *Classical Islam: A History, 600-1258*. Translated by Katherine Watson. New York: Barnes and Noble Books, 1996. This excellent survey, first published in 1970, provides useful background on the Umayyad and ʿAbbāsid caliphates that set the stage for the "age of principalities," in which Baybars was crucial.

See also: Alfonso X; Genghis Khan; James I the Conqueror; Louis IX; Maḥmūd of Ghazna; Saladin.

Related articles in *Great Events from History: The Middle Ages, 477-1453*: 630-711: Islam Expands Throughout North Africa; 1040-1055: Expansion of the Seljuk Turks; 1077: Seljuk Dynasty Is Founded; November 27, 1095: Pope Urban II Calls the First Crusade; c. 1120: Order of the Knights Templar Is Founded; 1147-1149: Second Crusade; 1204: Genghis Khan Founds Mongol Empire; 1227-1230: Frederick II Leads the Sixth Crusade; 1248-1254: Failure of the Seventh Crusade; September 3, 1260: Battle of Ain Jālūt.

BEATRICE OF NAZARETH

Flemish mystic and writer

Beatrice of Nazareth's Of Seven Manners of Holy Loving *was one of the first texts of Christianity to reveal mystical visions primarily based on personal experience. Beatrice's documented revelation was in stark contrast to Church tradition, which maintained that mystical experience could only be learned through biblical study.*

BORN: 1200; Tienen, Flanders (now in Belgium)
DIED: 1268; Nazareth monastery, near Antwerp, Flanders
ALSO KNOWN AS: Beatrice; Blessed Beatrix; Beatrijs of Nazareth; Beatrijs van Tienen
AREAS OF ACHIEVEMENT: Religion and theology, monasticism

EARLY LIFE

Perhaps the most striking aspect of the early years of Beatrice (BAY-uh-trees) is the young age at which she entered monastic life, becoming an oblate, that is, a member of a religious community without taking vows, at age ten. At seventeen, Beatrice began to have visions. What is known about her early life and about her adult life as a nun, mystic, and writer is gleaned from a set of four extant manuscripts called *Vita Beatricis* (c. 1320; *The Life of Beatrice of Nazareth*, 1991), written by an anonymous male cleric beginning around 1320.

Beatrice was the youngest of six children. Her mother (name unknown) died when Beatrice was only seven. Her father, Bartholomew of Tienen, thought to be a merchant, later sent Beatrice from her family's home in Tienen (near what is now Louvain, Belgium) to live with Beguines in the nearby town of Zoutleeuw. The Beguines were a mainly thirteenth century religious community of women not under vows to the Catholic Church, living in the Frankish realm of Flanders (now in the Netherlands and Belgium). The Beguines continued with the education Beatrice first received from her mother, who had taught her the scholastic arts, an exceptional education for a young girl in medieval times, but not entirely out of the ordinary for a girl in a religious community.

A year or so had passed, and Beatrice left the Beguines in Zoutleeuw for home, possibly called back by her father but for unknown reasons. Beatrice convinced her father, even at her young age, that she wanted to live a monastic life, the life of the spirit and devotion to God. She soon set out for the Cistercian abbey at Bloemendaal, a monastery of nuns possibly managed by her father. Beatrice's basic education—likely in grammar, rhetoric, and the arts, called the trivium in medieval schooling—continued at the abbey at Bloemendaal for about six years. After she turned fifteen, she expressed a desire to become a novice so that she could be admitted to the religious community of the abbey for a probationary period as a "beginning" nun. Her superiors first refused to consider her request because of her age and her inability to pay the expense, but they soon relented and granted her wish. After a year as a novice, she formally affirmed and accepted her vows to the religious community at Bloemendaal, an act called a profession.

LIFE'S WORK

The Cistercian order, of which Beatrice was a part for most of her sixty-eight years, was founded in 1098 in France. It is a monastic order that sprang from the Benedictine tradition. The Benedictines, which included men and women, devoted themselves to theological study, scholarship, and liturgical worship. However, within a matter of years, the Cistercians separated from the Benedictines because they wished for a more simple and austere spiritual life and wanted to be part of a community that was open to institutional change when changes in monastic values were for the good. They moved to a life of more physical labor, poverty, contemplation, and social reform and less liturgy, study, ostentation, and social isolation.

Beatrice's life, Bernard McGinn has argued, was profoundly influenced by a twelfth century monasticism that began to move away from the traditional ideal of the cloister, with its life of prayer, penance, and the "personal appropriation of the mystical understanding of the Bible." Before one could truly tell others about his or her vision of God, one had to know how to convey that vision based on what the Bible says makes a mystical vision. Experience does not count. However, in some circles, the tradition began to move toward a monastic mysticism where one's experience of God, unencumbered by rules about how the Bible defines a mystical experience, came to prominence. Beatrice's work, *Van seun manieren van heiliger minnin* (after 1235; *Of Seven Manners of Holy Loving*, 1964), was just this sort of mysticism: Her work shows that personal experience can equal mystical vision. Bernard of Clairvaux, the founder of the Cistercian order, was key in the move toward this new, experience-based, mysticism. In his *Sermones super Cantica* (c. 1135; *Eighty-six Sermons on the Song of Songs*, 1957-1977), he wrote, "Today we are reading in the book of experience."

The anonymously written *The Life of Beatrice of Nazareth* tells one particular story of Beatrice's life, but her own work, *Of Seven Manners of Holy Loving*, reveals a story of living the spiritual life through the personal, soulful acts of loving God and of being loved by God, acts that can help one live a life of hope for humanity. Why love God but not fear Him? Beatrice writes in the First Manner,

> The first way is a desire that most certainly originates from love, for the good soul that wants to follow faithfully and wants to love durably is being drawn on by the craving for this desire—to be loved and to be guarded most strongly—in order to exist in purity and freedom and nobility in which she is made by her creator, after His image and to His resemblance. . . . For certain, such a way of desire of such a great purity and nobility originates from love and not out of fear. Because fear makes one suffer. . . .

Beatrice's first task after her profession at Bloemendaal was to learn the art of manuscript writing (or copying), a common job performed by Cistercian women. She was sent to the Cistercian community at La Ramée, where she would learn how to copy manuscripts—copy by hand, that is—the words of one text to another, an almost unthinkable task today. At La Ramée, Beatrice met Ida of Nivelles, another Cistercian nun three years her senior, who would impact her spiritual life and learning significantly and who would remain her lifelong friend.

Ida opened the proverbial gates of Heaven for Beatrice when she assured her that she would encounter the Lord in a vision. Beatrice had her first mystical experience at age seventeen, a vision in which, according to *The Life of Beatrice of Nazareth*, she had seen the Trinity—the Father, the Son, and the Holy Spirit—"not with bodily but with intellectual eyes, with eyes not of the flesh but of the mind." Between 1217 and about 1221, Beatrice had returned to Bloemendaal and then entered the monastery at Maagdendal, was consecrated a virgin around 1225, and stayed at Maagdendal until 1235 or 1236. In about 1236, Beatrice was elected prioress of a newly built monastery called Nazareth, the place she would spend the rest of her life and where it is believed she wrote her life's work, *Of Seven Manners of Holy Loving*, written in Middle Dutch (more accessible to lay readers) instead of the scholarly Latin.

One of the main conflicts between scholars working on Beatrice's life is centered on the primacy she affords the body and feelings versus the mind and spirit in her religious commitment. First, there exists the Bynum thesis, so called after Carolyn Walker Bynum proposed that Beatrice's work indicates a sort of somatic mysticism, whereby women's bodies are not rejected as barriers to the spiritual life but are instead elevated as the place of possibility, the means for the spiritual life and closeness to God. However, scholars such as Amy Hollywood argue precisely the reverse, that Beatrice countered her contemporaries and the religious, philosophical, and even common thought of the time, which believed that to be a woman meant to be anything but spiritual and holy. To be a woman meant to be of the body and of emotion—and, therefore, unholy. Beatrice's *Of Seven Manners of Holy Loving* evokes a spirituality that differs radically from what was thought to be the norm for women conveying their mystical experiences. Most medieval, and even modern, accounts of women's mystical visions relate experiences of the body, such as being attacked by demons or suffering panic and fever or feeling ecstasy, and not "reasonable" experiences or contemplation. Beatrice's work in actuality, the argument continues, differs remarkably from how it has been interpreted by men of the Church (in Beatrice's case by a male cleric) who were given the job of documenting the lives of women mystics and theologians. Hollywood and others argue that *The Life of Beatrice of Nazareth* is a prime example of how misinterpretation, tradition, and expectation twisted the deeply thoughtful intent of her work.

Having been educated from a young age in topics mostly taught to boys and men, Beatrice likely knew and understood the traditional ways in which monastic women related their visions. She might also have known of the storytelling and mythmaking power held by the interpreters, biographers, hagiographers, and chroniclers of these women's lives, but we cannot be certain of this. Beatrice's *Of Seven Manners of Holy Loving*, however, articulated a different spiritual path. Her writing, which uses the pronoun "she" throughout, clearly shows that a woman is speaking of her love for God.

Katrien Vander Straeten has argued that *Of Seven Manners of Holy Loving* prioritizes neither the body nor the soul in the search for God. Beatrice evokes a searching that depends on the changing reactions both of the body and of the mind in seven steps toward spiritual fulfillment, the "seven manners of holy loving."

In a remarkably rich and vivid Seventh Manner, Beatrice tells of how the soul, full of love for the spirit, is pulled to overflowing by both the desire and despair of the body and the desire and despair of the mind. Beatrice writes that, "So profound is she here sunk in love and so strong is she pulled by her desire, that her heart is moved strongly and is restless inside, so that her soul flows out and melts of love, and her mind is ardently connected to a strong desire." An everlasting and unrelenting conflict—of desire, delight, pain, and despair brought about by yearning for God—erupts from the soul, as it is yanked and prodded by a combination of feelings and thoughts. Recognizing this absolute mind-body connection is a necessary step on the path leading to spiritual perfection. In a series of what could now be called metaphors about acts such as "surrendering" and "submitting to," and of "not resisting" the powers of love, metaphors that might trouble or concern some readers today because they imply weakness, Beatrice is adamant that one must embrace the loving power of the soul: It is the soul's ability to perpetually love God, a love absolutely unattainable and timeless, to which one should surrender. Timeless love means a hope forever unfulfilled, an eternal hope, so hope for love is what maintains one's never-ending faith in God.

Beatrice's *Of Seven Manners of Holy Loving* indicates an individual being "taken" by an all-powerful love that nothing could counter, a love of give and take. More significantly, her work considered this moment not a failing of the body or the mind—a literal giving in to—but a union, in which the soul is both protected and strong in its love for God: "This superior power of love has drawn the soul and has accompanied, guarded and protected it." This union of flesh and spirit, of body and soul and mind, is a perfect state of life on Earth and of life everlasting for Beatrice: "This is freedom of conscience, sweetness of heart, well-disposedness, nobility of soul, exaltation of the spirit, and the beginning and foundation of everlasting life. This is to live the life of angels here in the flesh."

SIGNIFICANCE

Beatrice of Nazareth spent a lifetime trying to show that hope cannot be maintained simply through personal salvation and individual spiritual growth, despite what *Of Seven Manners of Holy Loving* might imply with its focus on personal, bodily, and mindful experience. Beatrice and other medieval women monastics and mystics, especially the Cistercians and the Beguines, showed through example a spiritual life in service both to God and Church and to everyday people outside the religious community. They maintained an ascetic life of hard physical work and self-reliance. Beatrice preached that loving God and humanity meant also a life of "work" and "drudgery"; the heart "never rests" nor "does it subside from searching, demanding and learning." This unrest of the loving, forever-yearning heart translated, for Beatrice and like-minded medieval mystics, into a three-part spirituality of commitment: to oneself, to one's community, and to God.

Paul Rorem argues that Beatrice and many other medieval female mystics and religious writers, including Hildegard von Bingen, Saint Clare of Assisi, Marguerite Porete, Julian of Norwich, Hadewijch, Hilda of Whitby, Dhuoda, Mechtild von Magdeburg, Christina of Markyate, Catherine of Siena, Saint Brigit, and Margery Kempe, "directed their writings outward, for the sake of others, intending change or reform." They lived a life of contemplation coupled with community service. The Cistercian life demanded such a multitiered commitment, and Beatrice demanded such a commitment from herself, as her life's work has shown.

—Desiree Dreeuws

FURTHER READING

Beatrice of Nazareth. "There Are Seven Manners of Loving." Translated by Eric Colledge. In *Medieval Women's Visionary Literature*, edited by Elizabeth Alvilda Petroff. New York: Oxford University Press, 1986. The first translation in English, with a different title, of Beatrice's work. Bibliography, index.

Bowie, Fiona, ed. *Beguine Spirituality: Mystical Writings of Mechtild of Magdeburg, Beatrice of Nazareth, and Hadewijch of Brabant*. Translated by Oliver Davies. New York: Crossroad, 1990. Focuses on the female mystics and Beguines of Germany, the Netherlands, and Belgium. Map and bibliography.

Bynum, Carolyn Walker. *Fragmentation and Redemption: Essays on Gender and the Human Body in Medieval Religion*. New York: Zone Books, 1992. This detailed, scholarly study discusses the experiential literary voices of medieval women mystics and emphasizes the physical, bodily nature of women's mystical experiences.

De Ganck, Roger, trans. *The Life of Beatrice of Nazareth*. Cistercian Fathers Series 50. Kalamazoo, Mich.: Cistercian, 1991. Considered the best translation of the *Vita Beatricis*, by a scholar known for his work on Beatrice.

Hollywood, Amy. "Inside Out: Beatrice of Nazareth and Her Hagiographer." In *Gendered Voices: Medieval Saints and Their Interpreters*, edited by Catherine M. Mooney. Philadelphia: University of Pennsylvania Press, 1999. Argues that Beatrice's intent, in *Of Seven Manners of Holy Loving*, was to express an inner and not an outer, or bodily, mysticism, as *The Life of Beatrice of Nazareth* indicates. Bibliography, index.

McGinn, Bernard. *The Flowering of Mysticism: Men and Women in the New Mysticism, 1200-1350*. New York: Crossroad, 1998. An important, exhaustive study of medieval mysticism, and especially the emergence of women as mystics, during and after Beatrice's time. Extensive bibliography, index.

Pedersen, Else Marie Wiberg. "Can God Speak in the Vernacular? On Beatrice of Nazareth's Flemish Exposition of the Love for God." In *The Vernacular Spirit: Essays on Medieval Religious Literature*, edited by R. Blumenfeld-Kosinski, D. Robertson, and N. Bradley Warren. New York: Palgrave, 2002. This essay compares the Latin version of *Of Seven Manners of Holy Loving* found in the *Vita Beatricis* with Beatrice's *Of Seven Manners of Holy Loving* written in the vernacular Middle Dutch. Also discusses the contemporary resistance to writing in the vernacular instead of the expected scholarly Latin. Bibliography, index.

_______. "The In-carnation of Beatrice of Nazareth's Theology." In *New Trends in Feminine Spirituality: The Holy Women of Liège and Their Impact*, edited by Juliette Dor, Lesley Johnson, and Jocelyn Wogan-Browne. Turnhout, Belgium: Brepols, 1999. Discusses *Of Seven Manners of Holy Loving* as a text misinterpreted and misrepresented as one relating a physical experience of mystic love instead of a spiritual experience.

Rorem, Paul. "The Company of Medieval Women Theologians." *Theology Today* 60 (2003): 82-93. Argues that mystics such as Beatrice practiced a life of contemplative action, taking their messages into the social realm through community action or through writing in the vernacular, or both. Bibliographical footnotes.

SEE ALSO: Saint Brigit; Saint Catherine of Siena; Christina of Markyate; Saint Clare of Assisi; Dhuoda; Saint Hilda of Whitby; Hildegard von Bingen; Julian of Norwich; Margery Kempe; Mechthild von Magdeburg; Marguerite Porete.

RELATED ARTICLES in *Great Events from History: The Middle Ages, 477-1453*: March 21, 1098: Foundation of the Cistercian Order; 1136: Hildegard von Bingen Becomes Abbess; April 16, 1209: Founding of the Franciscans; November 11-30, 1215: Fourth Lateran Council.

SAINT THOMAS BECKET

English statesman and archbishop of Canterbury (1162-1170)

Becket accepted martyrdom in defending the rights of the Church as developed under the Gregorian reforms against the encroachment of the secular power of the state.

BORN: December 21, 1118; London, England
DIED: December 29, 1170; Canterbury, Kent, England
ALSO KNOWN AS: Thomas à Becket; Thomas of London
AREAS OF ACHIEVEMENT: Religion and theology, government and politics, church government

EARLY LIFE

Though born in London, Saint Thomas Becket (BEHK-uht) was not of native Saxon lineage, as had long been assumed. His parents came from the province of Normandy. His father, a merchant, was a man of substance and of considerable standing in the city. When ten years old, Thomas was sent to a priory school in a nearby county, where he learned Latin grammar. After four years he entered one of the London schools, and at the age of eighteen he went to Paris to continue his studies for another four years. Following a short term of employment by a kinsman, Thomas entered the household of Theobald, the archbishop of Canterbury. Wishing to groom his young protégé for the post of archdeacon, Theobald sent him to study civil and canon law first in Bologna (now in Italy) and then in Auxerre (now in northeast-central France), where there was also a famous school of law. Probably on Theobald's recommendation, Becket was appointed the royal chancellor by Henry II three months after the young king's accession to the throne.

Affable, witty, and adept at repartee, Becket soon became the boon companion of his youthful master despite his fifteen years' seniority. Becket was fond of the hunt, especially of the royal art of falconry, which he had learned at an early age. The king's loyal and obedient servant, he lived in almost regal splendor, dining sumptuously on the choicest foods and wearing the finest fabrics. Fastidious in his personal grooming, he insisted that his living quarters be kept in impeccable order. About the time Henry appointed him, he was still youthful in appearance, described as slender, unusually tall, pale of complexion, with dark hair, a long nose, and well-formed facial features.

LIFE'S WORK

During the eight years of his chancellorship, Becket served his king obediently and adroitly. Much to Archbishop Theobald's disappointment, he forced submission of the bishops to Henry's demands. On two occasions he crossed the Channel to assist Henry in defending his French fiefs. He successfully carried through the embassy to arrange a marriage contract between the son of his king and the infant daughter of the French king, Louis VII. He was such an official as Henry could not afford to lose.

On Theobald's death in 1162, Henry took it as a matter of course that Becket would serve him as archbishop of Canterbury with the same fidelity that had marked his conduct as chancellor. Soon after being appointed, Becket resigned the office of chancellor. This about-face was considered an unfriendly act by Henry, but Becket was nothing if not thoroughgoing. As archbishop, he served a new master, realizing that his championship of the Church would lead to conflict with Henry.

A sore point on which the imperious king expected Becket's compliance concerned jurisdiction over the clergy. That category had been extended in practice far beyond those who exercised a spiritual office to include students and practically anyone who could speak a few lines of Latin. "Criminous clerks" tried in the much more lenient Church courts escaped due punishment for serious crimes. Henry II wanted them to be turned over to the royal courts for sentencing if found guilty of charges in the Church courts. Becket refused to concede to Henry's wish and only reluctantly did so on the insistence of Pope Alexander III.

Even so, King Henry, possessed of the violent temper characteristic of his family, was enraged by Becket's obstinacy. He resolved to set down the terms of relationship between royal power and Church authority in writing. He commanded Becket to appear at the meeting of the royal council at Clarendon, where the *Constitutions of Clarendon* (1164) were presented. The *Constitutions of Clarendon* prescribed the procedure in punishment of criminous clerks, forbade appeals to Rome without royal permission, and prohibited the excommunication by the pope of any of the king's vassals or officials unless the king consented. Rather surprisingly, Becket, who could be adamant in opposition, accepted the *Constitutions of Clarendon*. Becket, however, reversed his position on learning that the pope had condemned the document.

Outraged by Becket's renunciation, the vindictive king summoned Becket to a council at Northampton to stand trial for having wrongfully taken land from one of the royal officials and to recover debts that Becket had failed to pay when he was chancellor. Becket accepted the judgment of the court in the first case but protested that he had received quittance of his debts as chancellor when he was raised to the archbishopric. At one point in the proceedings, Becket broke in on the court and heatedly asserted that the laymen who were sitting there had no legal right to try an archbishop. As he left the room, some of the barons grabbed rushes from the floor to hurl at him, and cries of "traitor" were heard as he walked through the door. Unwilling to submit to the sentence that was certain to ensue and fearful for his life, Becket that same evening secretly stole away from Northampton in a heavy rainstorm and by stages managed to make his way to exile in the French kingdom.

Becket was to remain in exile from November, 1164, until December, 1170. At first, the pope temporized in trying to deal with the quarrel between Henry and Becket, but on January 19, 1170, he decreed the terms under which a settlement would be reached, including the restitution of Canterbury to Becket and Becket's submission to Henry except for the articles of the *Constitutions of Clarendon*. Becket and Henry met at Fréteval in France and conversed amiably, though nothing was said about the restoration of property or the *Constitutions of Clarendon*. All of the specifics were to be settled later. Inwardly, however, Henry was not reconciled. He feared the interdict and excommunication that might easily result if he did not show some compliance to the pope's terms. Wishing to have his son Henry crowned king before his own death, he had the ceremony of coronation performed by the archbishop of York and six other bishops before Becket could return to England, knowing that the archbishop of Canterbury had the exclusive right to preside at coronations. Because of this breach in Church law, the pope gave Becket permission to excommunicate all bishops who had overstepped their authority whenever the time might be opportune.

Becket returned to England amid the tumultuous acclaim of the populace on December 2, 1170. Shortly afterward, he executed the power of excommunication against the offending bishops as had been authorized by the pope. On hearing of Becket's retribution, the king, who remained in his fief of Normandy across the Channel, flew into a rage. "What a set of idle cowards I keep in my kingdom," he allegedly said, "who allow me to be mocked so shamefully by a low-born clerk." Four members of his household secretly crossed the Channel to avenge their king. They were not mere knights, but barons of substance, great men of the realm. They confronted Becket in the north transept of Canterbury Cathedral as he was going to Vespers, and after some altercation, hacked off the top of his skull.

For some time that evening, Becket's corpse lay unattended where it had fallen, the monks having been scattered by the armed assassins. When later the monks came to prepare the body for burial in a crypt of the cathedral, they discovered beneath the monastic habit that Becket wore a hair shirt (worn for penance) tightly sewn around his body. Not even Becket's clerks had been aware of this mortification: He had wholly committed himself to the religious and ascetic life after becoming primate of England.

Western Christendom was aghast over the horrendous crime. A church was supposed to be a place of asylum even for the most heinous criminals. Two years later, Thomas Becket was canonized, and a cult developed around the martyrdom of the saint. Canterbury became one of the great shrines of Europe, as attested in Geoffrey Chaucer's *The Canterbury Tales* (1387-1400).

For Henry II the murder was a disaster. All who were involved in the crime were excommunicated by the pope. Henry feared that an interdict might be imposed on England and that he might himself be excommunicated. After evading the heat of censure for a time by going to Ireland, where a revolt threatened, he ultimately had to renounce the *Constitutions of Clarendon* and to admit full jurisdiction of Church courts over criminous clerks. He also was forced to undergo public scourging at the hands of the cathedral monks on the very spot where Becket had been struck down, as a gesture of penance for the responsibility he bore in the murder.

SIGNIFICANCE

The whole episode of the dispute between King Henry and Thomas Becket was a dramatic story. It has been presented with varying interpretations by playwrights such as T. S. Eliot and Jean Anouilh. Until the later nineteenth

Saint Thomas Becket felled by assassins on the steps of the church altar in Canterbury. (Library of Congress)

century, writers usually presented the narrative as the struggle of a heroic and devout clergyman defending the liberties of the Church against a tyrannous and overbearing monarch. Since the research and writings of the magisterial constitutional historian William Maitland, another view has modified the former opinion. Maitland revealed the legal and administrative reforms that were promoted by Henry II, so that a more secular age sees a real point in the king's argument against the archbishop. The epic reduces itself into a contest between two poles, the spiritual and the secular.

—*Quentin Bone*

FURTHER READING

Becket, Thomas. *The Correspondence of Thomas Becket: Archbishop of Canterbury, 1162-1170*, edited by Anne J. Duggan. New York: Oxford University Press, 2000. A collection of Becket's letters while he served as archbishop. Includes a bibliography and index.

Jones, Thomas M., ed. *The Becket Controversy*. New York: John Wiley and Sons, 1970. Contains selections from a few of the chronicles of the twelfth century, some of the letters written by Becket and others, and selections from works on Becket published in the eighteenth, nineteenth, and twentieth centuries.

Knowles, David. *Thomas Becket*. Stanford, Calif.: Stanford University Press, 1971. A thoroughly researched work on Becket by a premier scholar on the subject and an exposition of Church history and canon law. Includes an informative bibliographical essay.

Maitland, Frederic William. *The Collected Papers of Frederic William Maitland*. 3 vols. Edited by H. A. L. Fisher. 1911. Reprint. Holmes Beach, Fla.: Gaunt, 1999. Presents the papers of the influential scholar of British constitutional history.

Smalley, Beryl. *The Becket Conflict and the Schools: A Study of Intellectuals in Politics*. Totowa, N.J.: Rowman and Littlefield, 1973. Presents the arguments of twelfth century scholars on the dispute between Archbishop Becket and Henry II. The fundamental issue was that of the legal relationship between *sacerdotium* (priestly authority) and regnum (kingdom).

Staunton, Michael, trans. *The Lives of Thomas Becket*. New York: Palgrave, 2001. A biographical look at Becket. Part of the Manchester Medieval Sources series. Includes a bibliography and an index.

Winston, Richard. *Thomas Becket*. New York: Alfred A. Knopf, 1967. Based on documentary evidence, including the published archives at Canterbury relevant to the life of Becket. A resource for the general reader unacquainted with medieval institutions.

SEE ALSO: Alexander III; Saint Anselm; Geoffrey Chaucer; Eleanor of Aquitaine; Henry II.

RELATED ARTICLES in *Great Events from History: The Middle Ages, 477-1453*: 1169-1172: Normans Invade Ireland; December 29, 1170: Murder of Thomas Becket; 1387-1400: Chaucer Writes *The Canterbury Tales*.

SAINT BEDE THE VENERABLE

English scholar, historian, and theologian

Bede, who wrote the Ecclesiastical History of the English People, *was considered the father of English history. He also set an example of piety and devotion by his saintly life and his dedication as a teacher.*

BORN: 672 or 673; Wearmouth, Northumbria (now Sunderland, Tyne and Wear, England)

DIED: May 25, 735; Jarrow, Durham (now in England)

ALSO KNOWN AS: Beda; Bæda; Venerable Bede

AREAS OF ACHIEVEMENT: Historiography, literature, monasticism, religion and theology

EARLY LIFE

Bede (beed) was born of Saxon parents, south of the Tyne River on land that in 674 was incorporated into the monastery of St. Peter founded at Wearmouth by Benedict Biscop. At the age of seven, Bede was placed by his parents in the care of Abbot Benedict to receive an education. A year later, in 681 or 682, he was transferred to the newly founded, and associated, nearby monastery of St. Paul at Jarrow, under the authority of Abbot Ceolfrith. In 686, a plague so ravaged the monastery that, according to Ceolfrith's anonymous biographer, only the abbot himself and one boy were well enough to sing the antiphons in the choir. This boy probably was Bede, who even at this young age was able to fulfill the duties of a choir monk.

Bede was reared in a scholarly environment. His first abbot, Benedict Biscop, had been trained at the famous monastery of Lerins on the French Riviera. Benedict had visited Rome several times and was a Greek and Latin scholar and expert in art, astronomy, music, and theology. Bede derived great benefit from the monastic library, assembled by Benedict and subsequently doubled in size by Ceolfrith. In spite of his relative isolation, he had much of contemporary European scholarship ready at hand; what was not available often could be borrowed from another monastery. Most of the books available to Bede would have been the writings of the church fathers, such as Ambrose of Milan, Jerome, Augustine, and Gregory the Great, on whom Bede based most of his theological study. He was much less familiar with—or at least had less access to—the writings of the classical Latin authors, many of which were not rediscovered until the Renaissance.

Bede eventually became a master of both Latin and Greek, and he even knew some Hebrew. While still in his teens, Bede was recognized for his learning and scholarship. At the age of nineteen, in 692 or 693, he was made a deacon by Bishop John of Hexham, even though the canonical age for such an office was twenty-five. At thirty he was made a priest by the same bishop. Both promotions were made on the recommendation of his abbot, still Ceolfrith.

Saint Bede the Venerable. (Library of Congress)

LIFE'S WORK

Bede rarely traveled far from home, although he did visit the monastery at Lindisfarne before 721, and his friend Egbert, archbishop of York, in 733. He also may have visited the learned king Ceolwulf of Northumbria, who eventually abdicated and himself became a monk.

Bede is known primarily for his literary activities, to which he gave devoted and incessant effort. He said of himself,

> I have spent all . . . of my life in this monastery and devoted myself entirely to the study of the Scriptures. And while I have observed the regular discipline and sung the choir offices daily in church, my chief delight has always been in study, teaching, and writing.

His occupation with such activities also would have enabled him to escape much of the drudgery endured by the other, less intellectually oriented, monks.

A great number of Bede's works still survive, although many of the shorter works still have not been edited adequately. Much of this writing consists of commentaries, mostly allegorical in nature, on the Scriptures. Bede said of them,

> from the time of my receiving the priesthood until my fifty-ninth year, I have worked, both for my own benefit and that of my brethren, to compile short extracts from the works of the venerable Fathers on Holy Scripture and to comment on their meaning and interpretation.

Indeed, Bede wrote voluminously on both the Old Testament and the New Testament, as well as several works of ecclesiastical history and biography. Of the former, the best known is his *Historia ecclesiastica gentis Anglorum* (731; *Ecclesiastical History of the English People*, 1723). He also wrote *Vita sanctorum abbatum monasterii in Wiramutha et Girvam, Benedicti, Ceolfridi, Easteruini, Sigfridi, atque Huaetbereti* (c. 725; *Lives of the First Abbots of Wearmouth and Jarrow: Benedict, Ceolfrid, Eosterwine, Sigfrid, and Huetbert*, 1818), about the abbots of his own monastery, and a life in verse and prose of the monk and bishop Cuthbert. He translated the lives of Saint Felix and Saint Anastasius, and he compiled a martyrology, or list of the feast days of various saints.

Another group of works can be classified as scientific, primarily on chronology: the six ages of the world, the resting places of Israel, the words of Isaiah 24.22, the bisextile year, and Anatolius's explanation of the equinox. He also wrote linguistic and literary works: a book on orthography, a book on the art of poetry, a book on tropes and figures, a book of hymns, a book of epigrams—the list goes on. Bede was not only prolific but also wide-ranging in the matters he took up for consideration, even in a time when the distinctions between the various "fields" of scholarship were not as clearly delineated as they are today.

Bede's most famous work, *Ecclesiastical History of the English People*, completed near the end of his life, is simple and straightforward. In its earlier sections, it is little more than a compilation. Unlike many writers, Bede nearly always named his sources. He also often quoted his source documents verbatim and at great length. Those of his sources that survive indicate that he attained a high level of accuracy in his quotations. He paid particular attention to chronology, attempting to make it as exact as he could. He introduced the idea that the *adventus Saxonum* (arrival of the Saxons) marked the beginning of a new period in British history, even though he wrongly saw it as a single, distinct event of the mid-fifth century rather than as a continuing process begun earlier.

Although Bede diligently studied and used his source material, he was not always sufficiently critical in his use of it. He sometimes fell victim to the errors in his sources, especially for the more distant past. His dependence on oral traditions and the obscure sixth century writer Nennius for the fourth through the sixth centuries, for example, led him to repeat Nennius's errors and misconceptions. Much of his chronology for this period has had to be corrected on the basis of the extant Easter tables and Gallic Chronicles, which discuss some of the same events. The closer Bede came to his own times and his own experiences, however, the more vivid his history became.

Bede's history also is limited, from a modern point of view, by its concentration on ecclesiastical matters. He considered secular matters only when they had some impact on the affairs of the Church. Even these mentions, however, demonstrate the contemporary lack of political unity in Britain. Bede also discussed in detail the role played by the English kings in the spread of Christianity in Britain and in the functioning of the Church. The history and his *Lives of the First Abbots* contain much useful information about the ecclesiastical life and practices of the day, such as miracle stories, missionary activities, and the operations of the English monasteries. His character sketches of individuals from all levels of society are especially realistic. Bede also discussed some of the ecclesiastical controversies, such as that over the date of Easter. In this, he had some bias against Celtic church practices, as when he said in *Ecclesiastical History of the English People*, "The Britons . . . have a national hatred for the English, and uphold their own bad customs against the true Easter of the Catholic Church."

Bede died after a short illness at the age of sixty-three, still in the midst of an unfinished translation of the Gospel of Saint John. In the eleventh century, his remains were stolen and placed in the coffin of Saint Cuthbert at Durham, and in 1104, they were moved yet again and placed in a gold and silver casket in Durham Cathedral. In 1541, the casket was looted and the bones were lost. Bede seems to have acquired the cognomen (surname) Venerable as early as the ninth century. Such an appellation, however, was commonly given to ecclesiastics of the time. In 1899, he was recognized as a saint and doctor of the Church.

SIGNIFICANCE

Bede was one of the three greatest English scholars of his time, the other two being Aldhelm, abbot of Malmesbury and bishop of Sherborne, and Alcuin, who ultimately served at the court of Charlemagne. More than anything, Bede was a teacher. He had little desire to be original or innovative; rather, he was content to pass his knowledge on to his students. His writings became accepted reference works even while he was still alive.

Bede's voluminous and detailed *Ecclesiastical History of the English People* immediately became the standard account of early post-Roman Britain. It was soon translated into Old English by King Alfred the Great. It gave the first coherent British account of the troubled times of the fifth and sixth centuries, during which the native Romano-British population was gradually overwhelmed by the newly arriving Anglo-Saxons. It also provided a detailed account of how the insular practices of the "Celtic" church in Britain, in which the abbot usually held supreme authority, gave way in the seventh century to Continental, "Roman," usages, in which the bishop was supreme. During this period, Britain once again was incorporated into the mainstream of Continental culture.

Bede's own life reflects the extent to which the monastic life had taken hold of England. Yet, even though he was totally committed to the monastic way of life himself, he concluded his history with a cautionary note: "As such peace and prosperity prevail in these days, many . . . have laid aside their weapons, preferring to receive the tonsure and take monastic vows rather than study the arts of war. What the result of this will be the future will show." Bede's words foretell the troubles that were soon to follow, as the Danes began to ravage the English shores.

—*Ralph W. Mathisen*

Further Reading

Alcock, Leslie. *Arthur's Britain: History and Archaeology, A.D. 367-634*. New York: Penguin Books, 2001. A detailed discussion of the use of Bede's historical work as a source for fifth and sixth century Britain.

Bede. *Bede: A History of the English Church and People*. Translated by Leo Sherley-Price. New York: Penguin Books, 1985. A translation of Bede's most significant work, with a map and twenty-four-page introduction.

_______. *The Ecclesiastical History of the English People, the Greater Chronicle: Bede's Letter to Egbert*. Edited by Judith McClure and Roger Collins. New York: Oxford University Press, 1999. A translation of Bede's major work. Part of the Oxford World's Classics series. Includes bibliography and index.

_______. *Historical Works*. Translated by J. E. King. 2 vols. Reprint. Cambridge, Mass.: Harvard University Press, 1994-1996. A Latin text with English translation on facing pages of Bede's historical works, with an introduction.

Owen, Gale R. *Rites and Religions of the Anglo-Saxons*. New York: Dorset Press, 1985. A discussion of the religious background of the age of Bede, with special concentration on the transition from Anglo-Saxon pagan rites to Christianity.

Rey, Roger. *Bede, Rhetoric, and the Creation of Christian Latin Culture*. Jarrow, England: St. Paul's Church, 1997. Publication of the Jarrow Lecture, a lecture series concerned with biblical criticism and interpretation.

Stenton, F. M. *Anglo-Saxon England*. New York: Oxford University Press, 1989. A standard history of the period during which Bede lived and the subsequent period of the Danish raids.

See also: Alcuin; Alfred the Great; Cædmon; Priscian; Saint Sergius I.

Related articles in *Great Events from History: The Middle Ages, 477-1453*: 596-597: See of Canterbury Is Established; 635-800: Founding of Lindisfarne and Creation of the *Book of Kells*; 731: Bede Writes *Ecclesiastical History of the English People*; 781: Alcuin Becomes Adviser to Charlemagne.

Saint Benedict of Nursia

Italian monk

During fifty years of his life, Saint Benedict took the Greek pattern for the monastic life and adapted it for systematic use in the Latin church; the resulting Benedictine Rule became the model for all subsequent monastic movements.

Born: c. 480; Nursia, Umbria, kingdom of the Lombards (now in Italy)

Died: c. 547; Monte Cassino, Campania (now in Italy)

Areas of achievement: Religion and theology, monasticism

Early Life

Although the dates of his life are in doubt, it appears that Saint Benedict of Nursia (NUR-shee-uh) was born while Simplicius was bishop of Rome and Odoacer was king of Italy. Benedict's parents, according to ancient tradition, were Euproprius and Abundantia, people of rather high social standing. It is possible that Benedict's father was a town councilman or a magistrate.

The only primary source for the study of Benedict's life is the *Dialogi* (sixth century; *The Dialogues of Saint Gregory, Surnamed the Great*, 1608) by Gregory the Great, pope from 590 to 604. This source relates practically nothing about Benedict's parents, but it does contain something about his sister Scholastica and his nurse. Tradition says that Benedict and his sister were twins. Gregory reported that the two loved each other dearly and that both, from an early age, wanted to serve God. The nurse's name may have been Cyrilla, for that is what early biographers of Benedict called her. There is, unfortunately, no reliable information about the home life of these two future saints, but Gregory indicates that Benedict and Scholastica had no interest in worldly pursuits.

Benedict received what Gregory called a liberal education in Rome. This indicates that he attended a Latin grammar school, where he was offended by the evil conduct of other students. He finally decided to discontinue his education and to adopt an ascetic life as the way to

God. At about age seventeen, he forsook family, school, and possessions to become a monk. The exact circumstances surrounding this decision are not known, but he left Rome in search of a way to practice piety.

Life's Work

By renouncing worldly pleasures, Benedict committed himself to a monastic life that was to last about fifty years. He joined monks at Enfide, east of Rome, but he remained there for only a short time. For the next three years, he lived secluded in a cave near Subiaco, about 40 miles (65 kilometers) from Rome, a barren place where Emperor Nero had once maintained a villa.

Life in the hermitage was difficult—just as Benedict wished, for he sought to win God's favor by rigorous self-denial. He suffered severe temptations at times, despite the isolation of his residence, and at one point, he became so inflamed with lust that he almost abandoned asceticism. The monk, however, defeated the temptation by leaping into a thicket of thorn bushes, from which he emerged bruised, cut, and bleeding—but rid of his lust. He later reported that this experience had given him final victory over sexual desires.

When Benedict arrived at Subiaco, Romanus, a monk from the nearby house at Vicovaro, met him and led him to the cave that became his home for three years. Romanus and his associates eventually asked Benedict to become their abbot, and after much hesitation, he agreed. Although he disliked leaving his solitude, he saw an opportunity to lead a community of ascetics that was greatly in need of reform. Benedict sought to eliminate laxity and to restore faithful adherence to the principle of self-denial. His efforts aroused animosity from some monks, and they conspired to remove him. After some dissidents tried to poison him, the abbot left the community and resumed the life of a hermit.

His solitude did not, however, last long. Benedict was concerned for the souls who came to him for counsel, and he eventually organized them into twelve houses, which were united under his authority in an association of monasteries—the first Benedictine institutions in history. The monks' reputation for piety soon attracted adherents from Rome, who joined a movement that corresponded closely to the monastic pattern common in the Church of the East.

Benedict might have remained at Subiaco for the rest of his life had not a vicious plot destroyed his tranquillity. The saint's enemy was Florentius, a local priest of ungodly character who was embarrassed by the devout lives of Benedict and his monks. The cleric feigned friendship by sending the abbot a gift of food, which he had poisoned. When that effort failed, Florentius employed seven women to dance in the monastery garden to entice the monks. Benedict believed that the priest's hatred for him was the motive behind his machinations, so the abbot determined to leave Subiaco to protect his disciples from further attacks on their virtue. He explained to his brethren that God, by a direct revelation, had commanded him to depart, so his decision was irrevocable. Florentius did not, however, enjoy his triumph very long. As the hate-filled priest stood

Saint Benedict of Nursia. (Hulton|Archive at Getty Images)

on a balcony watching Benedict leave Subiaco, the porch collapsed under him, and he was killed, which Gregory concluded was divine retribution.

With a small band of disciples, Benedict terminated his thirty-year ministry at Subiaco and traveled to Monte Cassino, about 80 miles (130 kilometers) south of Rome. This area had once been the site of altars and sacred groves for the worship of Apollo and other pagan gods. Some of the local peasants were still members of pagan cults when the monks arrived. Benedict demolished at least one altar in current use and cut down a sacred grove. He replaced the implements of paganism with chapels in honor of Saint Martin of Tours and Saint John the Baptist.

Although Benedict went to Monte Cassino to found a monastery for the practice of the ascetic life, he soon accepted an obligation to seek the conversion of pagans in the neighborhood, an endeavor that succeeded well. The most enduring feature of Benedict's work at Monte Cassino is, however, the monastic rule that ever since has borne his name. This is the only writing from the saint's own hand to survive.

The Benedictine Rule gradually became the standard for monastic practice throughout the Western church. It was not, however, entirely original with Saint Benedict. Later research has shown that it was preceded by the *Regula magistri*, an anonymous document from which Benedict borrowed heavily. The Benedictine Rule quotes from the Bible and the church fathers, especially Augustine, Jerome, Cyprian, and Leo. It reveals the author's familiarity with Eastern fathers such as Pachomius and Basil, who wrote rules for monks of Greek Christendom. Benedict's reliance on the *Regula magistri* and other sources shows that he did not consider himself an innovator or the founder of a new religious movement. He instead accepted the concepts of his predecessors and adapted them to his own needs and those of his disciples. The synthetic character of the Benedictine Rule was actually part of its strength, which may account for the broad acceptance it achieved.

It is rather interesting that, in composing his rule, Benedict drew extensively from the writings of two earlier monastic leaders who held contradictory doctrines of salvation. Saint Augustine (354-430) had produced a rule for monks of his diocese in North Africa, and Cassian (360-435) had done the same for those in southern Gaul. Augustine was the champion of salvation by grace alone, while Cassian contended that grace enabled people to perform works of righteousness that, if sufficiently meritorious, God would reward with salvation. Cassian's view, commonly called Semi-Pelagianism, became very popular in southern Gaul, but the Catholic Church condemned it as heresy at the Synod of Orange in 529. Condemnation did not, however, lead to the demise of Semi-Pelagianism, as the Benedictine Rule shows clearly. In the prologue to his rule, the abbot wrote:

> Let us encompass ourselves with faith and . . . good works, and guided by the Gospel, tread the path He [Christ] has cleared for us. Thus may we deserve to see Him who has called us into His Kingdom. . . . If we wish to be sheltered in this Kingdom, it can be reached only through our good conduct.

Although Benedict affirmed that divine grace enables individuals to perform good works, it is evident that he regarded such works as meritorious toward salvation. In fact, Cassian and those who espoused his teaching saw clearly that the Augustinian belief that salvation is a free gift of grace undermines the entire philosophy of monasticism, something that the great bishop of Hippo had failed to perceive.

The Benedictine Rule prescribes a style of life intended to win salvation by self-denial. Benedict ordered that monks subscribe to vows of poverty, chastity, and obedience. He wanted his disciples to forsake individualism and to perform spiritual and physical good works in the community. He wanted monasteries to be self-sufficient so that monks would "not need to wander about outside, for this is not good for their souls." He made the abbot master of the community, to whom the monks owed unqualified obedience. The rule is not all-inclusive but allows the abbot considerable latitude. It is more a compendium of principles than a code of precise precepts. The Frankish emperor Charlemagne (r. 768-814) promoted ecclesiastical reforms that featured observance of the Benedictine Rule, and the emperor's son Louis the Pious (r. 814-840) made it the standard for monastic houses in Germany and France. Although Benedict did not presume that his rule would gain universal acceptance in the Catholic Church, all later monastic characters have been chiefly modifications of his original work.

Benedict died at Monte Cassino, forty-six days after his sister Scholastica. Although he had shown no signs of illness, six days before he died, he told his followers to open his grave so that he could see the remains of Scholastica, with whom he was to be buried.

Pope Gregory believed that Benedict worked miracles and that he possessed the gift of prophecy. In *The Dialogues of Saint Gregory, Surnamed the Great*, therefore, miracle tales abound. Among them are wonders that correspond to events in the Bible, such as bringing water out of rocks, causing an iron blade to rise from the bottom of a lake, and enabling a disciple to walk on water. There is one account of the abbot restoring a dead person to life.

Significance

The significance of Benedict for the development of Latin Christendom can scarcely be exaggerated, even if one discounts the miracles that Gregory the Great attributed to him. Benedict's monks soon established a daughter house at Terracina, the first of many extensions—eventually thirty-seven thousand others dotted the landscape of Christendom. Although he did not produce syllabi for scholarly activities, his order became famous for the learned writings of medieval authors such as Saint Bede the Venerable and Alcuin. When, by the tenth century, monasticism in general had declined, the Cluniacs and Cistercians arose to restore adherence to the Benedictine Rule.

In 1964, Pope Paul VI made Benedict patron saint of Europe. Although he was not the first Latin monk, he was surely the most influential, and the prevalence of the Semi-Pelagian doctrine of salvation in modern Catholicism bears witness to the pervasiveness of the ascetic world-and-life view that monks have, since his time, promoted. Benedict's motto was *Ora—Labora*, Praise and Work.

—James Edward McGoldrick

Further Reading

Benedict, Saint. *The Rule of Saint Benedict in English.* Edited by Timothy Fry and Imogen Baker. New York: Vintage Books, 1998. Critically prepared text with very helpful biographical sketch of author.

Clark, Francis. *The "Gregorian" Dialogues and the Origins of Benedictine Monasticism.* Boston: Brill, 2003. An analysis of the writings of Gregory the Great on Saint Benedict and an investigation into the beginnings of Benedictine monasticism. Index.

Dreuille, Mayeul de. *The Rule of Saint Benedict: A Commentary in Light of World Ascetic Traditions.* New York: Newman Press, 2002. Dreuille examines the monastic rule developed by Saint Benedict and compares it with other ascetic practices. Bibliography and index.

Dudden, F. Homes. *Gregory the Great, His Place in History and Thought.* 2 vols. New York: Russell and Russell, 1967. Despite its age, this is still the major work on the subject; valuable for Gregory's view of Benedict.

Gregory the Great. *Life and Miracles of Saint Benedict: Book Two of the Dialogues.* Translated by Odo J. Zimmerman and Benedict R. Avery. Reprint. 1949. Westport, Conn.: Greenwood Press, 1980. The only surviving primary source on Benedict, in a readable translation.

Kardong, Terrence. *Benedict's Rule: A Translation and Commentary.* Collegeville, Minn.: Liturgical Press, 1996. A translation of Saint Benedict's work, with notes on the man and his writings. Bibliography and index.

See also: Alcuin; Saint Bede the Venerable; Charlemagne; Gregory the Great.

Related articles in *Great Events from History: The Middle Ages, 477-1453*: 590-604: Reforms of Pope Gregory the Great; 731: Bede Writes *Ecclesiastical History of the English People*; 781: Alcuin Becomes Adviser to Charlemagne; 963: Foundation of the Mount Athos Monasteries.

BENJAMIN OF TUDELA

Spanish rabbi and traveler

Benjamin's account of his travels presents the best record available of the number, the leaders, and the social, religious, and economic conditions of the Jews in southern Europe and the Middle East during the twelfth century. At the same time, he provided the best documentation of trade and commerce in these areas in the period between the Second and Third Crusades.

BORN: Twelfth century; Tudela, Navarre (now in Spain)
DIED: 1173; Castile (now in Spain)
ALSO KNOWN AS: Rabbi Benjamin ben Jonah of Tudela (full name)
AREAS OF ACHIEVEMENT: Geography, exploration, historiography, religion and theology

EARLY LIFE

All that can be learned of the life of Rabbi Benjamin ben Jonah of Tudela (tew-DAY-lah) is found in his only surviving literary work, *Massaʿot* (c. 1173; *Itinerary of Benjamin of Tudela*, 1840), and its Hebrew preface, written by a contemporary of Benjamin. This preface refers to Benjamin as "a wise and understanding man, learned in the Law and the Halacha [Book of Practices]," and observes further that "wherever we have tested his statements we have found them accurate, true to fact and consistent; for he is a trustworthy man." Unfortunately, Benjamin stood outside his narrative, revealing little about himself as he chronicled what he had seen and heard during his travels.

The Hebrew preface speaks of Benjamin as a rabbi, and in his observations Benjamin demonstrated a familiarity with the rabbinical literature of his time as well as a thorough knowledge of the Hebrew Bible. He wrote in a formal medieval Hebrew sometimes called Rabbinic Hebrew. He seems to have known Arabic, for his account is filled with phrases from that language. In fact, in that his native city, Tudela, was located in al-Andalus, or Muslim Spain, Arabic may well have been his mother tongue. Benjamin no doubt grew to maturity in two cultural worlds: one of Arabic science and culture and another of Jewish culture based on the Bible and the classical works of the rabbis such as the Talmud. His careful description of commercial activities indicates that he was probably a merchant by profession.

Benjamin did not explain his reasons for making his journey. He may have gone as a pilgrim to worship before the relics of the Hebrew past, many of which he described in the course of his travels, or his object may have been trade and mercantile operations, since he spent so much time describing those that he saw among the people he visited. He may also have been motivated by a concern for his fellow Jews. The period of the Crusades had already witnessed the extermination by Christian Crusaders of whole communities of Jews in Germany and along the routes to Palestine, and even in Benjamin's Spain his Jewish brethren were caught between the Christian soldiers of the Reconquista (Reconquest) and the occupying Muslims of al-Andalus. Perhaps he hoped to find places of asylum for his fellow Jews in the lands he visited. This would account for his careful descriptions of independent communities of Jews that had rulers of their own and owed no allegiance to outsiders. Indeed, Benjamin may have been motivated by all these considerations.

LIFE'S WORK

The only claim to importance of Benjamin of Tudela is *The Itinerary of Benjamin of Tudela*, his record of a journey he took from his birthplace in northern Spain to Baghdad and perhaps beyond, and his return by way of Egypt and Sicily. He left Tudela in 1159 or 1160 and was back in Spain by 1173, the year in which he died.

Most scholars make a distinction between what Benjamin saw and what he heard. His descriptions of communities in Spain, southern France, Italy, the Byzantine Empire, Palestine, and Iran are detailed and accurate, so that there is little doubt that he visited them. Of areas to the east of Baghdad, however, his descriptions are brief, sketchy, and filled with fabulous stories, so that most who have studied Benjamin's work agree that his accounts of places beyond the Persian Gulf are based on what he heard from merchants and other travelers whom he met in Baghdad, where he spent considerable time. On his return route, Benjamin visited Aden, Yemen, Egypt, and Sicily. He makes reference to Germany, Bohemia, Russia, and northern France at the end of his account, but there is little reason to believe that he actually visited them. Of the nearly three hundred locations mentioned by Benjamin, those communities given the most coverage are Rome, Constantinople, Nablus, Jerusalem, Damascus, Baghdad, Cairo, and Alexandria.

The importance of *The Itinerary of Benjamin of Tudela* is that it is the earliest, the best, and, in some cases, the only source of information for many facets of the history of the regions through which he traveled at the time of the Crusades. Without question, Benjamin's account is the fullest and most accurate record of the condition and numbers of the Jews in the twelfth century. For most of the Jewish communities that Benjamin actually visited, he provides the reader with the names of the leaders and the sizes of the congregations; in many cases, he lists the occupations of the people—silk and purple cloth makers in Thebes, dyers in Jerusalem, silk cloth makers and merchants in Constantinople, glass makers in Tyre. Indeed, until the discovery in the nineteenth century of merchant letters stored in the attic of the synagogue in Cairo, Benjamin's account was the sole source of information for the vast and diverse trade on the Mediterranean Sea and the Indian Ocean during the period in which he wrote. While the letters augment Benjamin's account, they do not challenge its basic accuracy.

On numerous other matters, Benjamin was the first European commentator. He was the first from the West to describe with accuracy the sect of the Assassins in Syria and Iran, the first to point to the island of Kish (or Kis) in the Persian Gulf as the chief emporium in the Middle East for the goods of India, and the first to refer to China by its modern name.

Benjamin's account is also valuable for showing the diversity of religious beliefs and practices among the people he met or of whom he heard, whether they were Jews, Christians, Muslims, or pagans. He described strange worship patterns, burial customs, diets, and other deviations from what he considered to be normal practice. For example, he described the Jews of Nablus, whose alphabet lacked three letters. While they knew the law of Moses, their alphabetical deficiency, according to Benjamin, deprived them of dignity, kindness, and humility. Benjamin was also aware of the issues that separated the Roman Christians from those of the Byzantine Empire, as well as the struggle between the Protector of the Faithful in Cairo and the Protector of the Faithful in Baghdad, which disrupted the unity of the Muslim community.

Two of the most extensive and useful descriptions in Benjamin's account are those of the cities of Constantinople and Baghdad, two cities that in his estimation had no peer. Constantinople was visited by merchants from every country, and its storehouses of silk, purple, and gold were without equal. He estimated that the city received twenty thousand gold pieces every year as tribute from merchants who entered by sea and land, and from the rents of shops and markets. According to Benjamin, the Greek inhabitants were very rich: "They go clothed in garments of silk with gold embroidery, and they ride horses, and look like princes." To protect themselves, the Greeks hired mercenaries, for they were "not warlike, but . . . as women who have no strength to fight." No Jews were permitted in the city, except one who was the emperor's physician, and through him the oppression of the Jews who lived outside the city was somewhat alleviated.

Baghdad is clearly the city that made the greatest impression on Benjamin. He noted that there were twenty-eight synagogues, ten rabbinical academies, and forty thousand Jews there, all dwelling "in security, prosperity and honour under the great Caliph." While devoting much space to the wonders of the city and the character of the caliph—a ruler who supported himself by the work of his own hands and gave generously to the poor but kept members of his family bound by iron chains and under perpetual guard for fear of rebellion—Benjamin was most eloquent when he described the exalted role held by the exilarch, whom the Jews called Our Lord, the Head of the Captivity of All Israel. This man, according to Benjamin, had been given authority by the caliph over all the Jews in the Muslim Empire. Every subject of the caliph, Jew and Muslim alike, was required to rise up before the exilarch and salute him. Each Thursday a triumphal parade through the streets of Baghdad preceded the exilarch's meeting with the caliph at the royal palace. The exilarch, possessed of great property, bestowed charity and benevolence on his people.

Aside from the more serious aspects of his account, readers may find much of interest in Benjamin's retellings of fanciful stories that he heard. He tells, for example, of the pillar of salt into which Lot's wife was turned, observing that "the sheep lick it continually, but afterwards it regains its original shape." Stranger still is his fable of the sun-worshipers of Khulam (Quilon), who embalmed their dead with spices and then placed them in their homes "so that every man can recognize his parents, and the members of his family for many years."

SIGNIFICANCE

Although Benjamin's account undoubtedly reflects his interests as a pilgrim, a merchant, and a Jew who may have been seeking places of asylum for his coreligionists, it is the good fortune of his readers that his other interests were diverse. Though he was at his best in describing the conditions of the Jews in the communities he visited, as well as the economic endeavors in which they and other peoples engaged, Benjamin was also skillful in discussing architectural wonders, religious relics, social customs, religious beliefs and practices, and forms of government. His analysis of the power of the caliph of Baghdad and the exilarch has been noted; he also offers useful discussions of the power exercised by the Old Man of the Assassins, the leaders of the Turkish tribes, and the priests of Ceylon, who controlled their people through trickery and witchcraft.

The ultimate significance of Benjamin's narrative can be judged by the numerous editions and translations through which it has passed. Cited by various writers in the Middle Ages, when it circulated in manuscript, it was first printed in 1543. Since then it has gone through many printings, both in the original Hebrew and in modern languages. No scholarly work on the Middle East in the twelfth century can be complete without drawing directly or indirectly on this work. While recent research has cast additional light on many of the topics covered by Benjamin's work, regarding those things he claims to have seen himself few significant errors have been exposed. In large part, *The Itinerary of Benjamin of Tudela* has stood the test of time.

—*Paul E. Gill*

Further Reading

Ahituv, Shmuel, ed. *A Historical Atlas of the Jewish People: From the Time of the Patriarchs to the Present.* New York: Continuum, 2003. A finely detailed and well-illustrated presentation about the global history of the Jews—including migrations to the Middle East in medieval times—with maps, photographs, drawings, chronologies, and extensive commentaries. Also provides a bibliography and an index.

Baron, Salo W. *A Social and Religious History of the Jews.* 8 vols. New York: Columbia University Press, 1952. Vols. 3-7 contain numerous citations of Benjamin, in which his data are compared and contrasted with information from other sources for the same period.

Beazley, C. Raymond. *The Dawn of Modern Geography: A History of Exploration and Geographical Science.* 2 vols. 1897-1906. Reprint. New York: Peter Smith, 1949. Vol. 2 of this work focuses on the period from 900 to 1260, including a fifty-page analysis of Benjamin's writings. Where errors in Benjamin's account are noted, the appropriate corrections are made.

Benjamin of Tudela. *The Itinerary of Benjamin of Tudela.* Translated with an introduction and notes by Marcus Nathan Adler. London: H. Frowde, 1907. Contains an improved translation of the text, a useful introductory essay, notes, an English index to the text, and a map showing the route taken by Benjamin.

_______. *The Itinerary of Rabbi Benjamin of Tudela.* Translated with an introduction and notes by A. Asher. 2 vols. London: A. Asher, 1840. Vol. 1 contains the earliest English translation of the text, an informative introductory essay, and a bibliography. Vol. 2 contains extensive notes on the text and two expository essays.

Murray, Alexander Calander, ed. *After Rome's Fall: Narrators and Sources of Early Medieval History.* Buffalo, N.Y.: University of Toronto Press, 1998. A study of the major chronicles of medieval history, including Benjamin's and his contemporaries' work on "Jews, pilgrimage, and the Christian cult of saints." Also includes a bibliography.

Signer, Michael A. Introduction to *The Itinerary of Benjamin of Tudela.* New York: Joseph Simon, 1983. This volume includes a reprint of the Adler translation along with Adler's and Asher's introductory essays. The excellent introduction gives fresh insights into Benjamin's motives for making the journey and writing his account. Maps included.

Signer, Michael A., and John van Engen, eds. *Jews and Christians in Twelfth-century Europe.* Notre Dame, Ind.: University of Notre Dame Press, 2001. An extensive collection of articles surveying the history of Christians and Jews in the Europe of Benjamin's time. Includes a chapter on Jewish-Christian conflict in the context of the First and Second Crusades.

See also: Jean Froissart.

Related articles in *Great Events from History: The Middle Ages, 477-1453*: 1147-1149: Second Crusade; 1189-1192: Third Crusade; 1290-1306: Jews Are Expelled from England, France, and Southern Italy; 1373-1410: Jean Froissart Compiles His *Chronicles*.

SAINT BERNARD OF CLAIRVAUX
French monk and religious leader

Bernard epitomized the monastic ideal and served as adviser and critic to kings, popes, bishops, abbots, and other leading figures in Western Europe.

BORN: 1090; Fontaines-les-Dijon, Burgundy (now in France)
DIED: August 20, 1153; Clairvaux, Champagne (now in France)
AREAS OF ACHIEVEMENT: Religion and theology, church reform, monasticism

EARLY LIFE

Bernard of Clairvaux (klehr-voh) was born the son of Tescelin le Sor, a rich and valiant Burgundian knight. Aleth, his mother, was a dutiful wife; her saintly behavior had a considerable impact on Bernard. At an early age, Bernard was enrolled in a church school at Châtillon-sur-Seine, where he impressed everyone with his love of learning. He mastered the *trivium* and became somewhat familiar with the *quadrivium*. After his mother's death, he was left with the difficult choice of a vocation in the secular world, perhaps that of a knight like his father, or in the Church, which had been his mother's preference. Bernard was tall and attractive with a noble countenance, but he was too delicate and sensitive to become a warrior. Thus, he was destined from before birth, according to one account, to become a monk.

There followed a period of preparation. In a short time, Bernard's charismatic personality influenced many others to eschew the secular world. Around 1113, Bernard and about thirty companions were admitted to the Cistercian monastery of Cîteaux, which was renowned for its austerities. Not only was this an important step in Bernard's life, but it was also a significant event in the history of the fledgling Cistercian order.

LIFE'S WORK

During his novitiate, Bernard earned the admiration and wonder of all with his ascetic behavior. In the meantime, Cîteaux had grown so rapidly that it became necessary to found new colonies. In 1115, although only twenty-four years old, Bernard was selected to lead one of these expeditions. He and twelve companions took up residence in the Valley of Wormwood and began construction of the monastery known as Clairvaux. Cîteaux's newest daughter prospered under Bernard's guidance, but the rigors of office, coupled with an inclination toward extreme asceticism, ruined his health and brought him close to death. At the behest of Guillaume de Champeaux, bishop of Châlons-sur-Marne, Bernard was relieved of his abbatial duties for a year to regain his strength.

At the end of the year, Bernard returned to his monastic office, but he never fully recovered. At times he had such difficulty digesting his food that he had to vomit into a pit dug for the purpose near his seat in choir. Pale and emaciated, his appearance was at once forbidding and ethereal. Bernard's happiest moments were spent in his cell praying, fasting, studying, and writing. During infrequent intervals of leisure, Bernard wrote a prodigious number of sermons and letters. The sermons were written on spiritual subjects such as humility, pride, the love of God, the Virgin Mary, and church reform, while the letters were addressed to kings, popes, bishops, monks, and others on a multitude of subjects.

Bernard became the most famous monk of his day, preaching a doctrine that called on ecclesiastics and laypeople alike to repent of their sins, embrace Christ, and live a monastic life. Many were won to monasticism, the Cistercian order in particular. Even the famous, such as the brother of the French king, sought the peace of the cloister. So eloquent was Bernard that mothers hid their children lest they be led away by the monastic Pied Piper. As the order grew in numbers, new houses were founded in France, Germany, Italy, Spain, England, and Scandinavia. In 1135, Clairvaux found it necessary to relocate closer to the Aube River to permit additional growth.

Bernard would have been quite happy to restrict himself to the management of Clairvaux and its daughter houses, yet the great abbot lived in close proximity to a violent and chaotic world whose repercussions sometimes reached Clairvaux. Never a shrinking violet, Bernard became involved in nearly all the important political and ecclesiastical issues of Western Europe during a period of thirty years. Sometimes he advised kings. On other occasions, he took issue with their policies, especially those that threatened the freedom of the Church. Louis VI of France was reproved for intervening in the affairs of the bishop of Paris and for appointing a prelate as seneschal, while his son, Louis VII, was censured many times for inappropriate behavior.

Nor was the Church spared Bernard's whip. Among other issues, Bernard was determined to carry forward the ecclesiastical reform movement begun in the eleventh century by Pope Gregory the Great.

Convinced that Cistercian monasticism was superior to all other forms, Bernard never ceased to castigate others, especially the Cluniacs, who, he believed, had lost their religious zeal and become spiritually decadent. In 1137, he prevented a Cluniac from becoming bishop of Langres, gaining the office for one of his own Cistercian monks. In such matters, Bernard was often intransigent and self-righteous, but he was also capable of great warmth. Although Bernard and Peter the Venerable, the abbot of Cluny, had their differences, they became good friends.

Bernard was also concerned about those who had become enamored of the world and its pleasures. Suger, the abbot of Saint-Denis and adviser to both Louis VI and Louis VII, was scolded for his great wealth and earthly concerns. Bernard found the secular clergy and even the peasantry guilty of similar offenses. Even the pope did not escape Bernard. In *De consideratione* (*Treatise on Consideration*, 1641), composed late in his life and addressed to Eugenius III, a former disciple, Bernard reminded the pontiff of his Christian responsibilities and exhorted him to reform a corrupt Curia.

When he was not lecturing popes and kings, Bernard lashed out at those who threatened the orthodoxy and unity of the Church. One particularly difficult issue that occupied much of his time was the schism of 1130. In that year, on the death of Honorius II, two popes were elected by disputing factions within the College of Cardinals. Innocent II was eventually compelled to flee Italy when his adversary, Anacletus II, became violent. At the Council of Étampes, convened by Louis VII, Bernard threw his support to Innocent, who, he believed, had been properly elected and was the more worthy of the two. Over the next seven years, Bernard worked to win recognition of Innocent, traveling throughout Europe, crossing the Alps three times in one winter, meeting and corresponding with the most important political and ecclesiastical figures in Europe. With the death of Anacletus in 1137, Bernard's choice was finally enthroned, and the schism was ended.

Nevertheless, there was little rest for the weary monk. In 1139, Bernard's close friend, William of Saint-Thierry, informed him that Peter Abelard, one of the most brilliant intellectuals of the age, was teaching a dangerous theology that substituted reason for revelation. Abelard also espoused heretical ideas about the Trinity; among other things, he said that the Holy Spirit was not coequal with the Father and the Son. It was with great reluctance and possibly some trepidation that Bernard left Clairvaux to confront Abelard at the Council of Sens in 1140.

Saint Bernard of Clairvaux exhorts his listeners to participate in the Second Crusade. (Gihon)

Bernard refused to debate the issues, preferring instead a stratagem that condemned Abelard's entire approach. Humiliated, Abelard withdrew from the encounter, fell ill, and died several years later at Cluny. Bernard won, but he has been severely criticized through the ages for his narrow-minded approach to the debate.

Although Bernard successfully quashed Abelard's heresy, there was much work to be done. In 1145, Europe received the shocking news that Edessa had fallen to the Muslims. The event was of special interest to Bernard. In his youth, the First Crusade had captured Jerusalem. Later, in 1128, at the Council of Troyes, Bernard drew up a charter for the Knights Templar, a military-monastic group whose chief concern was the defense of Palestine. Thus Bernard emerged from the cloister to prepare for what would be his last major battle. In 1146, he preached the Second Crusade at Vézeley and then spent considerable time and energy promoting the venture in France and Germany. As a result, both Louis VII of France and Conrad III of the Holy Roman Empire took up the cross. The Crusade eventually failed, and Bernard's popularity suffered greatly. Nevertheless, in spite of failing health, Bernard remained very active in his last years, and he even dreamed of leading another expedition to liberate the Holy Land. He died at Clairvaux on August 20, 1153.

SIGNIFICANCE

For more than thirty years, Bernard of Clairvaux was the spokesperson for Western Christendom. Although his first love was the contemplative life of the monastery, he was frequently summoned by the outside world. He was a friend and adviser to kings, popes, bishops, and abbots. Nothing that might impact adversely on the Church escaped his notice. Many times he left his monastery to reprove those who threatened the Church—truculent feudal magnates, wealthy prelates, heretics, and the infidels who threatened Palestine.

His impact on the Cistercian order, monasticism, the Church, indeed, Western Europe, is inestimable. When he and his monks settled at Clairvaux, there were only five Cistercian houses. By the time of his death in 1153, there were 343 abbeys, 68 of which had been founded directly from Clairvaux. Without a doubt, Bernard's charismatic personality was the single most important factor in the rapid growth of the order. Moreover, his humility, ascetic lifestyle, and devotion to God earned for him the admiration of both ecclesiastics and laypersons. He was, in many ways, a miracle worker, and in 1174, less than twenty-five years after his death, he was canonized.

—*Larry W. Usilton*

FURTHER READING

Balzani, Count Ugo. "Italy, 1125-1152." In *The Cambridge Medieval History.* Vol. 5. Cambridge, England: Cambridge University Press, 1948. In a chapter from one of the most comprehensive multivolume surveys of the Middle Ages, the author discusses Bernard's role in the schism of 1130 and the Second Crusade.

Butler, Edward Cuthbert. *Western Mysticism: The Teaching of Saint Augustine and Saint Bernard on Contemplation and the Contemplative Life.* Vol. 3. Rev. ed. London: Kegan Paul, 1999. Essays on and a selection of classic writings of Saint Bernard and other mystics, discussing contemplation, the concept of mysticism, mystical theology, spiritual practice, and more.

Daniel-Rops, Henri. *Bernard of Clairvaux.* New York: Hawthorn Books, 1964. Examines Bernard's life and the history of the Cistercian order from his death to the present. An excellent introductory work.

Evans, G. R. *The Mind of St. Bernard of Clairvaux.* Oxford, England: Clarendon Press, 1983. An advanced study and chronology of Bernard's intellectual life and life in general. Focuses primarily on his education, preaching, sermons, and theology.

Hoyt, Robert S., and Stanley Chodorow. *Europe in the Middle Ages.* 3d ed. New York: Harcourt Brace Jovanovich, 1976. A good general history of the Middle Ages. Included is a brief sketch of Bernard's life that considers his influence on literature, art, and ideas.

Hufgard, M. Kilian. *Bernard of Clairvaux's Broad Impact on Medieval Culture.* Lewiston, N.Y.: E. Mellen Press, 2001. Art-historical analysis of Bernard's views on art, beauty, and goodness, appreciations for which he was accused of lacking.

Knowles, David. *Christian Monasticism.* Reprint. New York: McGraw-Hill, 1977. An excellent introduction to monasticism, ranging from the earliest Christian monks to the modern world. Bernard's impact on the Cistercian movement is discussed briefly in a chapter on monastic expansion.

Lawrence, C. H. *Medieval Monasticism: Forms of Religious Life in Western Europe in the Middle Ages.* New York: Longman, 1984. A brief history of the monastic movement from the desert hermits to the friars, including a valuable chapter on Bernard and the Cistercian order.

Painter, Sidney, and Brian Tierney. *Western Europe in the Middle Ages, 300-1475.* 4th ed. New York: Alfred A. Knopf, 1983. An excellent general history of Western Europe, with scattered references to Bernard. Includes

a brief overview of his career with reference to his impact on the Cistercian order.
Strayer, Joseph R. *Western Europe in the Middle Ages*. 2d ed. Englewood Cliffs, N.J.: Prentice Hall, 1974. A brief survey of medieval civilization with a number of references to Bernard, including a short biography.
Tamburello, Dennis E. *Bernard of Clairvaux: Essential Writings*. New York: Crossroad, 2000. Covers the historical context of the time and includes Bernard's writings on "divine grace and human freedom," "conversion," "the love of God," "union with God," and "spirituality and leadership," and ends with a discussion of Bernard's legacy.

See also: Peter Abelard; Saint Benedict of Nursia; Blanche of Castile; Saint Fulbert of Chartres; Gregory the Great; Hildegard von Bingen; Joachim of Fiore; Melisende; Suger; William of Saint-Thierry.

Related articles in *Great Events from History: The Middle Ages, 477-1453*: 590-604: Reforms of Pope Gregory the Great; 963: Foundation of the Mount Athos Monasteries; November 27, 1095: Pope Urban II Calls the First Crusade; March 21, 1098: Foundation of the Cistercian Order; c. 1120: Order of the Knights Templar Is Founded; 1147-1149: Second Crusade; c. 1200: Scientific Cattle Breeding Developed.

al-Bīrūnī

Arab scholar and scientist

One of the greatest scholars of medieval Islam, al-Bīrūnī was both a singular compiler of the knowledge and scientific traditions of ancient cultures and a leading innovator in Islamic science.

Born: September, 973; Khiva, Khwārizm, Khorāsān (now in Turkmenistan)
Died: December 13, 1048; Ghazna, Ghaznavid, Afghanistan
Also known as: Abū al-Rayḥān Muḥammad ibn Aḥmad al-Bīrūnī (full name)
Areas of achievement: Historiography, science and technology

Early Life

Al-Bīrūnī (al-bee-REW-nee) was of Iranian descent and spent most of his childhood and young adult years in his homeland of Khwārizm, south of the Aral Sea. His sobriquet derives from *bīrūn*—"suburb"—in reference to his birth in an outlying neighborhood of Khiva. Little is known of al-Bīrūnī's childhood except for the important matter of his education, which was directed by the best local mathematicians and other scholars; his exceptional intellectual powers must have become apparent very early. Al-Bīrūnī's religious background was Shīʿite, although in later years he professed agnostic leanings. A precocious youth, while still a student in Khwārizm, al-Bīrūnī entered into correspondence with Avicenna (Ibn Sīna), one of the leading lights of Islamic medicine. Some of Avicenna's replies are preserved in the British Museum.

Although he published some material as a young student, the scope of al-Bīrūnī's intellectual powers became apparent only when he left Khwārizm to travel and learn further. In al-Bīrūnī's age, the key to scholarly success lay in attaching oneself to a powerful and influential court society and obtaining noble patronage. He found the first of many such benefactors in the Sāmānid sultan Manṣūr II, after whose demise he took up residence in the important intellectual center of Jurjan, southeast of the Caspian Sea. From here, al-Bīrūnī was able to travel throughout northeastern Iran.

Life's Work

While at Jurjan, al-Bīrūnī produced his first major work, *al-Āthār al-bāqīyah ʿan al-qurūn al-khāliyah* (tenth century; *The Chronology of Ancient Nations*, 1879). This work is an imposing compilation of calendars and eras from many cultures; it also deals with numerous issues in mathematics, astronomy, geography, and meteorology. The work is in Arabic—the major scientific and cultural language of the time—as are nearly all al-Bīrūnī's later writings, although he was a native speaker of an Iranian dialect. As would have been common among Muslim scholars of his time, al-Bīrūnī also was fluent in Hebrew and Syriac, the major cultural and administrative languages in the Semitic world before the Arab conquest.

Around 1008, al-Bīrūnī returned to his homeland of Khwārizm at the invitation of the local shah, who subsequently entrusted him with several important diplomatic missions. In 1017, however, his tranquil life as a scholar-diplomat took a rude turn. The shah lost his life in a military uprising, and shortly thereafter, forces of the power-

al-Bīrūnī. (Library of Congress)

ful Ghaznavid Dynasty of neighboring Afghanistan invaded Khwārizm. Together with many other scholars—as part of the booty of war—al-Bīrūnī found himself led away to Ghazna, which was to become his home base for the remainder of his life.

Ironically, this deportation afforded al-Bīrūnī his greatest intellectual opportunity. The Ghaznavids appreciated scholarly talent, and the sultan, Maḥmūd of Ghazna (r. 997-1030), attached al-Bīrūnī to his court as official astronomer/astrologer. Maḥmūd was in the process of expanding his frontiers in every direction. The most coveted lands were in India, and during the sultan's campaigns there, al-Bīrūnī was able to steep himself in the world of Hindu learning. In India, he taught eager scholars his store of Greek, Persian, and Islamic knowledge. In return, he acquired fluency in Sanskrit, the doorway to what was, for al-Bīrūnī, essentially a whole new intellectual universe.

In 1030, al-Bīrūnī completed his marvelous *Tār'īkh al-Hind* (translated by Edward Sachau as *Al-Beruni's India*, 1888). This masterpiece remains, in the eyes of many scholars, the most important treatise on Indian history and culture produced by anyone before the twentieth century. The degree of scholarly detachment and objectivity displayed in *Al-Beruni's India* is almost without parallel for the time, and the work consequently is still of enormous value to contemporary scholars.

Almost at the same time, al-Bīrūnī produced another work dedicated to the sultan Masʿūd ibn Maḥmūd (r. 1031-1041), heir to the Ghaznavid throne. *Kitāb al-qanūn al-Masʿūdī* (c. 1030; *Canon Masudicus*, 1954-1956) is the largest and most important of al-Bīrūnī's mathematical and geographical studies.

During his long and productive life, al-Bīrūnī authored many other treatises of varying length—he himself claimed to have produced more than one hundred—in addition to those mentioned above. They include essays on arithmetic, geometry, astronomy, and astrology, a pioneering effort in mineralogical classification, and, toward the end of his career, material on the medical sciences. His compendia of Indian and Chinese minerals, drugs, potions, and other concoctions, still not systematically studied, may be of immense value to pharmacology. Some of these works have been lost; they are known only through references by other scholars. Many survive but await translation into European languages.

SIGNIFICANCE

In the golden age of medieval Islam, a small number of incredibly versatile and creative intellects stood at the interface of Semitic, Hellenistic, Persian, and Hindu culture and learning. Their syntheses and insights often brought about quantum leaps in scientific and historical thought in Islam—so vast, in fact, that in some cases their achievements were fully appreciated only by later ages better prepared to comprehend them. Al-Bīrūnī was one of these intellects, to some historians the most important of all. *The Chronology of Ancient Nations*, for example, constitutes an unprecedented attempt to periodize the history of the known world by comparing and cross-referencing large numbers of chronologies and calendrical systems. His work provides a basis for chronological studies that has yet to be fully exploited.

Al-Bīrūnī's immense store of astronomical and geographical knowledge led him to the verge of modern scientific ideas about the earth and the universe. He was familiar with the concept that Earth rotates on its axis to produce the apparent movement of celestial bodies, rather than those bodies revolving around Earth (although he did not necessarily endorse the idea). His insights with respect to geography were profound. On the basis of reports of various flotsam found in the seas, al-Bīrūnī reasoned that the continent of Africa must be surrounded by water, thus taking exception to the Ptolemaic cosmography popular in Christendom, which held that Africa extended indefinitely to the south. On examining the Indus Valley in what is now Pakistan, al-Bīrūnī correctly guessed that it had once been a shallow sea filled in through the centuries by alluvial deposits from the river. Al-Bīrūnī also explained the operation of artesian springs and wells essentially in terms of modern hydrostatic principles. He devised a system of geographical coordinates that is still a marvel to cartographers.

In medieval Islam, the significance of scholarship may often be determined by how frequently a scholar's materials were copied by later generations of researchers (a practice for which modern scholars are grateful, as much otherwise would now be lost). The thirteenth century geographer Yaqut, for example, cited al-Bīrūnī extensively in his own work. Yaqut's material on oceanography and general cosmography is drawn almost verbatim from his illustrious predecessor.

Like many scholars in Islam's golden age, al-Bīrūnī was a polymath, a Renaissance man before there was a Renaissance. Some modern scholars have criticized him for writing extensively on astrology, usually at the behest of his noble patrons. Astrology, however, was in a certain sense a means of popularizing the science of the time, and al-Bīrūnī most likely used it to reach a lay audience, just as contemporary popular science writers often simplify and make use of analogy. He seems to have regarded astrology as a gesture to simple people who wanted immediate, practical results from science.

Al-Bīrūnī's astounding versatility has prompted some to place him in a league with Leonardo da Vinci as one of the greatest geniuses of all time. The most appropriate description, however, comes from his students, patrons, and other contemporaries. To them, al-Bīrūnī was simply the "Master."

—*Ronald W. Davis*

Further Reading

Acts of the International Symposium on Ibn Turk, Khwārezmī, Fārābī, Beyrūnī, and Ibn Sīnā. Ankara, Turkey: Atatürk Culture Center, 1990. A collection of essays from an international symposium on al-Bīrūnī and other scholars. Bibliography.

Chelkowski, Peter J., ed. *The Scholar and the Saint: Studies in Commemoration of Abu'l-Rayhan al-Biruni and Jalal al-Din al-Rumi.* New York: New York University Press, 1975. These essays from a 1974 conference cover such topics as al-Bīrūnī's concepts of India, his use of Hindu historical material, Sanskrit astronomical texts, Muslim times of prayer and their relation to seasonal changes in daylight, and other topics.

Kazmi, Hasan Askari. *The Makers of Medieval Muslim Geography: Alberuni.* Delhi, India: Renaissance, 1995. Kazmi looks at al-Bīrūnī's contributions to the study of the geography of Central Asia.

Kennedy, E. S., ed. and trans. *The Exhaustive Treatise on Shadows.* Vol. 2. Aleppo, Syria: Institute for the History of Arabic Science, University of Aleppo, 1976. This volume presents a commentary on al-Bīrūnī's treatise on shadows; a consideration of his overall influence on the history of science is also included.

Khan, M. A. Saleem. *Al-Biruni's Discovery of India: An Interpretive Study.* New Delhi, India: South Asian Publishers, 2001. An examination of al-Bīrūnī's trip to India. Bibliography and index.

Nasr, Seyyed Hossein. *An Introduction to Islamic Cosmological Doctrines: Conceptions of Nature and Methods Used for Its Study by the Ikhwān al Ṣafā', al-Bīrūnī, and Ibn Sīnā.* Rev. ed. Albany: State University of New York Press, 1993. Part 2 of this work concentrates on al-Bīrūnī and his theories regarding the creation of the world and astrology.

Said, Hakim Mohammad. *Al-Bīrūnī Commemorative Volume.* Karachi: Hamdard National Foundation, Pakistan, 1979. Proceedings of the international congress in Pakistan on the millenary of al-Bīrūnī. Examines al-Bīrūnī and science in the Islamic Empire.

Said, Hakim Mohammad, and Ansar Zahid Khan. *Al-Bīrūnī: His Times, Life, and Works.* Karachi, India: Hamdard Academy, 1981. A biography of al-Bīrūnī. Covers his life and works and pays special attention to his astronomy. Bibliography and index.

See also: Avicenna; Maḥmūd of Ghazna.

Related articles in *Great Events from History: The Middle Ages, 477-1453*: 637-657: Islam Expands Throughout the Middle East; c. 1010-1015: Avicenna Writes His *Canon of Medicine*; 1225-1231: Jalāl al-Dīn Expands the Khwārizmian Empire.

BLANCHE OF CASTILE

Spanish-born queen of France (r. 1223-1252)

Blanche of Castile helped to consolidate French royal authority and power in the thirteenth century in the face of baronial revolt and English royal claims to territory in France.

BORN: March 4, 1188; Palencia, Castile (now in Spain)
DIED: November 26 or 27, 1252; Paris, France
ALSO KNOWN AS: Blanche de Castille; Banca de Castilla
AREA OF ACHIEVEMENT: Government and politics

EARLY LIFE

Blanche of Castile (ka-STEEL) was born to King Alfonso VIII and Queen Eleanor. Blanche was their third daughter and, through her mother, the granddaughter of Henry II of England and Eleanor of Aquitaine. She spent her childhood at her parents' court, which was reputed to be both cultivated and entertaining. It was also consumed by the threat posed by the Muslim forces in the Iberian Peninsula, and Blanche's father was active in the military struggle against them.

LIFE'S WORK

It was through the agency of her grandmother, Eleanor of Aquitaine, queen of England, that Blanche was engaged to marry the heir to the French throne, Louis, son of Philip II. Blanche was twelve years old when her grandmother took her to France to marry Louis. The ceremony took place soon thereafter, on May 23, 1200.

Blanche was to remain in France for the rest of her long life. This marital strategy placed Blanche—a descendant of the Plantagenets—in line to share the French throne with the Capetian heir Louis and provided some grounds for the Capetians to claim the English throne as Blanche's inheritance should Eleanor of Aquitaine's own royal English sons fail in issue. Thus would Plantagenet blood have a role in the future.

Whatever designs may have prompted her grandmother to arrange the marriage, after the event Blanche assumed the goals and ambitions of the Capetians as her own. Safeguarding her new family's interests preoccupied her for the rest of her life. As the historian Robert Fawtier argued, "To all intents and purposes," Blanche "may be counted among the kings of France." From the death of her husband, Louis VIII, in 1226 until her own death in 1252, Blanche had ample opportunity to prove her mettle as a ruler. In 1226, her son, Louis IX, was a minor. Louis VIII, knowing he was dying, designated Blanche to serve as ruler during their son's minority. Blanche had worked tirelessly to gather French baronial support for her husband's excursion to England, proving not only her dedication to French royal interests but also her ability to deal confidently with the great barons in urging them to fulfill their responsibilities to the Crown. Louis IX relied heavily on his mother's judgment not only during his minority but also after he assumed power. She accompanied him in council meetings and met officially with foreign ambassadors. She guided him in matters of policy, piety, and justice. When he left on the Seventh Crusade in 1248, Louis IX officially put the reins of power in Blanche's hands; he returned to France only when he heard of her death. The two kings' confidence in Blanche was not misplaced.

During the twelfth and thirteenth centuries, the French monarchy faced a major challenge to its power and authority from the great nobility. The latter wished to increase their own power in their territories and assert their independence of the Crown. Shifting alliances and coalitions of the hostile French nobility against the Capetians were a constant threat. The kings of England also claimed territory in France: Normandy, Anjou, and Gascony. At times, they also put forth claims to the French throne. The French barons and the English monarchs often joined forces against the French crown in pursuit of their respective ends. In meeting these challenges, the French monarchs consolidated the power of the Crown. Blanche had witnessed the glorious successes of Philip II and her husband against the English and their allies, culminating in the Battle of Bouvines in 1214. In addition, Louis VIII, acting on behalf of the Papacy against the Cathar (Albigensian) heretics, brought the unruly southern region of Languedoc under control just before his death. By the time of Louis VIII's death in 1226, the Crown had acquired a dominant position over the nobility, territories, and resources of France.

During Blanche's rule, however, the Crown's hard-won gains were tested. The same lords who had been subdued or their descendants, including those of the English kings, would attempt to revive their previous power and independence in France. Historians agree that the combination of forces arrayed against the French crown at this time was one of the fiercest challenges faced by any French ruler. Blanche, however, proved equal to the situation. She demonstrated determination, courage, a formidable intelligence, and the ability to take decisive action to safeguard her family and the Crown. She used every means at her disposal: outright conquest of territory that could then be added to the Crown lands, military action against coalitions, strategic marriages, gifts, favors, and alliances with the communes, which had their own reasons for preferring royal over baronial control. She demonstrated her grasp of policy especially in the use of marriages and other favors. She appeased some disgruntled noblemen by arranging their marriages, or those of their successors, to heiresses with the promise of secure riches and territory. She also arranged several marriages between the heiresses of French fiefs and her own kinsmen. Thus did she secure the loyalty of those regions.

Blanche's mercy toward former enemies also gained her adherents. Flanders was notoriously problematic for the French crown in this period. Blanche used the occasion of Louis IX's coronation to release its count, Ferrand of Portugal, from prison, a move that gained his support for the Crown. As these examples demonstrate, Blanche did not attempt to destroy the nobles or their ability to govern in their own territories. Instead, she wanted to secure their loyalty to the Crown, their recognition of their military responsibilities to support the Crown and the whole realm of France, and their recognition of the Crown's ultimate suzerainty over the realm. Thus, Blanche sought the feudal solution to the problem of royal government: to create a feudal monarchy over the whole realm. In this, she continued the policies of her father-in-law and husband. When she died at the age of sixty-four, she left her son an orderly state. She had not merely maintained the gains of the previous rulers of France, but had improved on them.

Blanche was also known for her piety. Perhaps the greatest legacy of that quality she left to France was her son Louis IX, who was later canonized. His celebrated character, so deeply informed by a sense of piety, developed in an environment congenial to religious sensibility. Blanche was responsible for that environment as she consciously surrounded herself and her growing children with individuals she regarded as properly religious. In Blanche's mind, piety and politics should be practiced together. Although she was untiring in her efforts to consolidate royal rule, she was consistent in attempting to make that rule a principled one. One of the most famous remarks attributed to Blanche is found in Jean de Joinville's chronicle of the reign of Louis IX (*Livre des saintes paroles et des bons faiz nostre roy saint Looys*, 1309; *The Life of Saint Louis*, 1955). There she is reported to have said that she preferred to see her son dead than in mortal sin.

She also set an example of substantial and sustained royal patronage to certain religious houses. It appears that some of the religious donations often assumed to derive from Louis's hand should be attributed to Blanche instead. She favored the Cistercians and founded and built the abbey of Royaumont around 1228. Several members of the royal family were subsequently buried there. Blanche's own burial place was in Maubuisson, one of the two Cistercian convents she founded. In the light of the Cistercian hostility to women who took religious vows, even those belonging to its own order, Blanche's decision to found these convents suggests that she wished to use her patronage to criticize those who would deny women an active role outside the family and home. After she became ill in 1252, Blanche expressed a wish to take vows and enter the convent of Maubuisson. Her death came too soon for that.

Blanche's piety did not, however, prevent her from upholding the rights of the Crown to judge in matters that concerned the Church. The papal reform movement had attempted to further papal and clerical jurisdiction over

Blanche of Castile. (Hulton|Archive at Getty Images)

THE CAPETIANS

Reign	*Ruler*
987-996	Hugh Capet
996-1031	Robert II the Pious
1031-1060	Henry I
1060-1108	Philip I the Fair
1108-1137	Louis VI the Fat
1137-1179	LOUIS VII THE YOUNGER (with ELEANOR OF AQUITAINE, r. 1137-1180)
1179-1223	PHILIP II AUGUSTUS
1223-1226	Louis VIII the Lion
1223-1252	BLANCHE OF CASTILE (both queen and regent)
1226-1270	LOUIS IX (Saint Louis)
1271-1285	Philip III the Bold
1285-1314	PHILIP IV THE FAIR
1314-1316	Louis X the Stubborn
1316	Philip, brother of Louis X (regent before birth of John I and during his short life)
1316	John I the Posthumous
1316-1322	Philip V the Tall
1322-1328	Charles IV the Fair

ecclesiastical lands and personnel throughout Europe. Ecclesiastical claims often brought Church officials into conflict with temporal rulers. However, Blanche—as did many other rulers—countered these claims with a growing sense that all cases in the realm involving justice concerned the Crown and that royal jurisdiction overrode ecclesiastical jurisdiction. She and her son successfully assumed the right to settle a dispute between the townspeople of the episcopal city of Beauvais and the city's ecclesiastical governors. Just before her death, during her son's absence, Blanche tried to prevent the chapter of Notre-Dame de Paris from exacting heavy fees from its serfs. She tried to force the case into the royal courts but, in this case, was unsuccessful. After her death it was ruled that the Crown's jurisdiction did not extend to cover the chapter's treatment of its serfs.

Blanche's personal and emotional life seems, by all accounts, to have been as fulfilling and remarkable as her public role. Her childhood was blessed by the close and exemplary marriage of her parents. Her own marriage to Louis VIII was observed to be close, devoted, and companionable on both sides. She was devoted to her children, especially to the royal heir, Louis IX. Some resented her influence over Louis IX and her demands on his attention. Famously, Joinville portrayed Blanche as bitterly jealous of Louis's wife, Queen Margaret, and any time he spent with her. Such feelings on Blanche's part are not unimaginable. However, she never swerved from her political goals because of them. Her popular reputation at the time of her death was high, and her death was met by a public outpouring of grief. Throughout her life, she directed her considerable energy, spirit, and intelligence to great personal and public deeds. She faced extraordinary challenges—both personal and political—and rose to each occasion.

SIGNIFICANCE

Blanche's historical significance is important in both French and European contexts. She preserved the French crown and the Capetian Dynasty at a critical time. She understood and carried on the goals of royal government as previous Capetian rulers had defined them. In doing so, she was engaged in the same process as many other European rulers, that of asserting royal domination over the great territorial barons. Thus, she participated in one of the great turning points of European medieval history and must be seen as one of the architects of the European state at its early stages.

—*Lynn Marie Johnson*

FURTHER READING

Fawtier, Robert. *The Capetian Kings of France: Monarchy and Nation, 987-1328.* Translated by Lionel Butler and R. J. Adam. London: Macmillan, 1960. Looks at the entire period of Capetian rule in France, devoting a section to the period of Blanche's activity. The author is emphatic about Blanche's historical significance.

Hallam, Elizabeth M., and Judith Everard. *Capetian France, 987-1328.* 2d ed. New York: Longman, 2001. This excellent scholarly book is firmly grounded on the most basic and practical aspects of the Capetian era. The author agrees with Fawtier on Blanche's significance, but the coverage of Blanche in this text is more extensive. Includes maps, genealogical tables, and a bibliography.

McCash, June Hall, ed. *The Cultural Patronage of Medieval Women.* Athens: University of Georgia Press, 1996. A historical overview of medieval women who were cultural benefactors. Includes a chapter on Blanche. Also offers an extensive bibliography and an index.

Pernoud, Régine. *Blanche of Castile.* Translated by Henry Noel. London: Collins, 1975. A full-length study of

Blanche based on a wide range of primary documents. Also provides substantial contextual material on Blanche's historical significance. Includes family charts, illustrations, and a bibliography.

Poulet, Andre. "Capetian Women and the Regency: The Genesis of a Vocation." In *Medieval Queenship*, edited by J. C. Parsons. New York: St. Martin's Press, 1993. Provides material for comparing and contrasting women rulers of the Capetian Dynasty.

SEE ALSO: Saint Albertus Magnus; Eleanor of Aquitaine; Henry II; Louis IX; Philip II.

RELATED ARTICLES in *Great Events from History: The Middle Ages, 477-1453*: 987: Hugh Capet Is Elected to the French Throne; March 21, 1098: Foundation of the Cistercian Order; 1209-1229: Albigensian Crusade; July 27, 1214: Battle of Bouvines; 1227-1230: Frederick II Leads the Sixth Crusade; 1248-1254: Failure of the Seventh Crusade.

GIOVANNI BOCCACCIO

Italian writer and scholar

Boccaccio was the father of Italian and European narrative. He was also a pioneer of Latin and Greek scholarship in the late Middle Ages and, along with Petrarch, a precursor to the Renaissance Humanists.

BORN: June or July, 1313; Florence or Certaldo (now in Italy)
DIED: December 21, 1375; Certaldo (now in Italy)
AREA OF ACHIEVEMENT: Literature

EARLY LIFE

Giovanni Boccaccio (jyoh-VAHN-nee boh-KAHT-choh) was the illegitimate son of a merchant of Certaldo, identified as Boccaccio di Chellino. Some scholars believe that Boccaccio was the product of a relationship between his father and an unknown Parisienne. That, however, is unlikely. Although his father did travel to Paris for extensive periods and the identity of his mother is not known, Boccaccio was absolutely Tuscan in blood and spirit. His father legitimized him about 1320 and gave him a decent education, sending him to the school of a famous educator, Mazzuoli da Strada, whose son, Zanobi, later to achieve some fame as a poet, remained a lifelong friend and correspondent of Boccaccio.

In 1327, Boccaccio's father was sent to Naples to head the branch of the Bardi banking company there. He took his son with him, having clearly planned for him a life in commerce. The king of Naples, Robert of Anjou, was eager to establish lines of credit with the major Florentine banking houses. Under the Angevins, Naples was a commercial hub, and because King Robert had a taste for culture, it was a major center of learning. Boccaccio's formative years were spent in this vibrant southern capital. While in theory he was learning the business of banking (for which he had little inclination), his attention was drawn to the dynamic life of the port and the tales of merchants who arrived from all corners of the Mediterranean. Through the royal court and library, he came into contact with some of the most distinguished intellectuals of his day. Among them was Cino da Pistoia, a contemporary of Dante and surviving member of the *dolce stil nuovo* (sweet new style) school of poets, who introduced Boccaccio to vernacular love poetry in the Tuscan tradition. Paolo da Perugia, the royal librarian, probably inspired Boccaccio's later, encyclopedic works; the scholar Dionigi da Borgo san Sepolcro introduced him to the genius of Petrarch; and an encounter with Barlaam da Calabria began Boccaccio's lifelong fascination with the Greeks.

Naples was also a city of beautiful women, who both stimulated the young man's senses and inspired his first literary efforts: romances in prose and verse that were close to the tradition of French love poetry (the height of fashion in Angevin Naples). Like Dante's Beatrice and Petrarch's Laura, Boccaccio's Fiammetta served as a Muse, inspiring the works of the first half of his career. She has frequently been identified as Maria of Aquino, the illegitimate daughter of King Robert. Yet, like the notion of Boccaccio's Parisian mother, this idea must be dismissed as myth, in part encouraged by Boccaccio himself, who sought to romanticize his life into a story that overshadowed the cloud of illegitimacy.

An important friend of Boccaccio during this period was the Florentine Niccolò Acciaiuoli, who was to exercise considerable influence over the life of the writer. Acciaiuoli had embarked on a political career that was to make him a major figure in the history of the Angevin Dynasty, both before and after the death of King Robert in 1343; yet he was also to prove an unreliable friend to the scholarly Boccaccio, who tended to be dazzled by his countryman's charisma.

Engraving of Giovanni Boccaccio patterned on a print by Cornelius Van Dalen. (Library of Congress)

Before leaving Naples, Boccaccio had composed *La caccia di Diana* (c. 1334; Diana's hunt), a bucolic narrative in *terza rima* (a verse form first used by Dante), and the lengthy *Il filostrato* (c. 1335; *The Filostrato*, 1873), a version of the tale of Troilus and Cressida in octave form. He had completed the prose romance *Il filocolo* (c. 1336; *Labor of Love*, 1566) and had certainly begun the *Teseida* (1340-1341; *The Book of Theseus*, 1974), the story of Palamon and Arcite. *The Filostrato* and *The Book of Theseus* are of particular interest because they are, respectively, the sources of Geoffrey Chaucer's *Troilus and Criseyde* (1382) and "The Knight's Tale" from *The Canterbury Tales* (1387-1400).

Life's Work

When Boccaccio returned to Florence at the end of 1340, he found a city in crisis. His father had preceded him in 1338, following the closing of the Bardi office in Naples. An upheaval in the banking world had brought many major Florentine companies close to bankruptcy. Boccaccio's father, having weathered severe financial setbacks, had been married again, to a woman for whom the son expressed little sympathy. Naples must have seemed far away, and Florence a dreary alternative.

During the next decade, however, Boccaccio established himself as the leading storyteller of his generation. *Il ninfale d'Ameto*, also known as *Commedia delle ninfe* (1341-1342; comedy of the nymphs), is modeled after Dante's *La vita nuova* (c. 1292; *Vita Nuova*, 1861, better known as *The New Life*, 1867). *L'amorosa visione* (1342-1343; English translation, 1986) is a lengthy disquisition on love in *terza rima* and is a direct predecessor of Petrarch's *Trionfi* (1470; *Tryumphs*, 1565, also known as *Triumphs*, 1962). The *Elegia di Madonna Fiammetta* (1343-1344; *Amorous Fiammetta*, 1587, better known as *The Elegy of Lady Fiammetta*) is a psychological novel, entirely in prose, which tells of Fiammetta lamenting the departure from Naples of a young Florentine merchant. All the previously mentioned works show Boccaccio closely bound to the medieval tradition of moral reflection on, and allegorization of, love. In particular, Boccaccio was faithful to the *dolce stil nuovo*, which derived from contemporaries of Dante who celebrated the themes of sacred and profane love.

Although the Black Death of 1348 was profoundly disastrous, it actually furthered Boccaccio's career by providing the starting point for his masterpiece, *Decameron: O, Prencipe Galeotto* (1349-1351; *The Decameron*, 1620). This collection of one hundred stories, carefully grouped around three central themes (fortune, love, and wit), established Boccaccio as one of the founders of European narrative and served as a sourcebook for future storytellers (including Chaucer and William Shakespeare). It is a wonderful literary synthesis, weaving the idealized loves of the medieval tradition into the lives of merchants and adventurers. Set against the backgrounds of cities such as Florence, Naples, and Milan, the stories emphasize intelligence and individual initiative. They move beyond the Middle Ages, pointing the way toward the Renaissance. The plague killed Boccaccio's father and stepmother, making him the head of the family and the arbiter of its affairs. The fact that the book grew out of this period of despair indicates the author's desire for the restoration of order out of chaos and his respect for human law in the midst of social dislocation.

Crucial to Boccaccio's spiritual and artistic development in these years was his friendship with Petrarch, whom he had admired from a distance but finally met in Florence in September, 1350. The devotee of Laura was en route to Rome when he was entertained at Boccaccio's house and introduced to a distinguished circle of admirers. In the spring of 1351, Boccaccio led a delegation to Padua, where Petrarch was residing, bringing with him the official restoration of citizenship to the poet

(Petrarch's father having been exiled, along with Dante, in the political crisis of 1300). Boccaccio also offered Petrarch a professorship at the newly established University of Florence—which he declined. In a garden in the shadow of the city cathedral, these two masters of Italian letters spent weeks in intimate conversations (faithfully transcribed by Boccaccio, who always regarded himself as the "disciple") on questions of literature, such as the nobility of Latin authors, the strengths of the vernacular, and the moral function of poetry. They also discussed political matters, expressing their devotion to the ideals of freedom in the Florentine republic and the hatred of tyranny as embodied by the Visconti of Milan.

Two years later (July, 1353), Boccaccio was offended to learn that his noble friend had accepted a stipend from that same dynasty he had condemned in writing and conversation and had settled in the despised Milan. There was in Petrarch's character both a conservatism and a cultivation of self-interest that set him apart from his more consistent and idealistic admirer. Boccaccio—a true Florentine—could not contain himself and gave vent to his indignation in an angry epistle to which Petrarch did not reply. In time, however, the two friends were reconciled, and their correspondence on literary and moral matters continued unabated until Petrarch's death in 1374. There would be further encounters: one in the hated Milan (1359), a visit marked by the planting of an olive tree in Petrarch's garden, and another (March, 1363) in Venice, which afforded Boccaccio great consolation, since it followed a most dispiriting visit to Naples in search of preferment from his old acquaintance and nemesis, Acciaiuoli, who appears to have treated the author of *The Decameron* with cavalier indifference. Furthermore, when Boccaccio experienced a religious crisis in 1362, Petrarch persuaded his dear friend not to abandon the vocation of literature and not to burn (for whatever symbolic reasons) the manuscript of *The Decameron*.

In all these years, Boccaccio was also at the service of the republic when required and actively engaged in diplomatic activities. He twice led delegations to the papal court in Avignon (in 1354 and 1365). The intention was to assure the pope of Florence's devotion to the Papacy, as well as to encourage Urban V to restore the pontificate to Rome. In spite of his age and growing corpulence, as well as the dangers from bandits, both journeys were diplomatically successful and rich in pleasant memory, including visits to Petrarch's old estate in idyllic Vaucluse.

By early 1361, Boccaccio had retired to Certaldo, following a reported conspiracy against the current Guelph faction then governing Florence in which several of the writer's most influential friends were said to be implicated. It seemed a politic moment to remove himself to the country. Certaldo thereafter remained his home and refuge. In this final chapter of his life, three themes persisted: fidelity to relatives and friends (notably Petrarch), prompt service to the republic, and tireless devotion to literature.

SIGNIFICANCE

Clearly reflecting the influence of Petrarch, Boccaccio's work reveals a man with scholastic and classical interests and a wish for partial withdrawal from the world. *De casibus virorum illustrium* dates from the period between 1355 and 1374 (*The Fall of Princes*, 1431-1438), and *De mulieribus claris* (c. 1361-1375; *Concerning Famous Women*, 1943) was clearly written as its companion volume. The most ambitious of these scholarly works, the *Genealogia deorum gentilium* (c. 1350-1375; genealogies of the Gentile gods), was written and revised dur-

MAJOR WORKS BY GIOVANNI BOCCACCIO

Date	*Work*
c. 1330-1340	*Rime*
c. 1335	*Il filostrato*
c. 1336	*Il filocolo* (*Labor of Love*)
1340-1341	*Teseida* (*The Book of Theseus*)
1341-1342	*Il ninfale d'Ameto* (or *Commedia delle ninfe*)
1342-1343	*L'amorosa visione*
1343-1344	*Elegia di Madonna Fiammetta* (*The Elegy of Lady Fiammetta*)
1344-1346	*Il ninfale fiesolano* (*The Nymph of Fiesole*)
1349-1351	*Decameron: O, Prencipe Galeotto*
c. 1351-1366	*Buccolicum carmen* (*Boccaccio's Olympia*)
1351, 1360, 1373	*Trattatello in laude di Dante* (*Life of Dante*)
c. 1355	*Corbaccio*
1355-1374	*De casibus virorum illustrium* (*The Fall of Princes*)
c. 1360	*Genealogia deorum gentilium*
c. 1361-1375	*De mulieribus claris* (*Concerning Famous Women*)
1373-1374	*Esposizioni sopra la Commedia di Dante*

ing the last twenty years of his life, but a first draft was complete by about 1360. To these major compilations, one must add Boccaccio's devotion to Greek studies and his invitation to the great Greek scholar Leontius Pilatus to live with him in Florence in 1360. Boccaccio not only worked with Pilatus on a translation of Homer but also had him appointed professor of Greek at the university in Florence.

These Latin works emphasize his contribution to the burgeoning climate of Humanism (meaning, on one level, a devotion to classical learning), which was the central feature of intellectual life in the Renaissance. Boccaccio's works in Latin are quite different from those of Petrarch in that they are compendia and intended as reference works for future scholars. Largely forgotten by modern scholars, they earned for Boccaccio enduring fame throughout the Renaissance and into the nineteenth century. For later storytellers, they offer a rich source of material for fiction and fable.

Boccaccio's religious crisis of 1362 helps to explain the strong thread of moral reflection on the vagaries of human fortune in these works, which all told illustrate a conscious redirection of energies toward religious contemplation. Connected with these themes are the fourteenth and fifteenth books of the *Genealogia deorum gentilium*, which amount to a defense of poetry as a force for moral improvement and religious regeneration. A similar impulse lies behind Boccaccio's *Trattatello in laude di Dante* (1351, 1360, 1373; *Life of Dante*, 1898) and the public lectures he gave on Dante (from 1373 to 1374). *Life of Dante* was begun in the 1350's and continued to be revised into the last years of his life. It represents Boccaccio's modest devotion to the poet who, although ill-treated by his countrymen, was still upheld as one of the great glories of the republic. Those public lectures on Dante and the news of the death of Petrarch in July, 1374, link the three founders of Italian literature, who established the standards of achievement in the epic, the lyric poem, and the short story for succeeding generations.

—*Harry Lawton*

FURTHER READING

Boccaccio, Giovanni. *The Decameron*. Translated by G. H. McWilliam. Harmondsworth, England: Penguin Books, 1972. An excellent modern English translation of Boccaccio's masterpiece. Includes a lively introduction, along with some interesting observations on the history of the various English translations.

Branca, Vittore. *Boccaccio: The Man and His Works*. Translated by Richard Monges. New York: New York University Press, 1976. This work is the indispensable biography of Boccaccio, on which all students of the writer depend. It is a careful reconstruction of the major events in the life, with reference to the literary works, correspondence, and contemporary documents. A comprehensive portrait of the author emerges, while popular myths (too long in circulation) are demolished. Includes the English translation of *Profilo biografico*, a biography by Branca.

Koff, Leonard Michael, and Brenda Deen Schildgen, eds. *"The Decameron" and the "Canterbury Tales": New Essays on an Old Question*. Cranbury, N.J.: Associated University Presses, 2000. A collection of essays on the relationship between the two works. Bibliography and index.

Serafini-Sauli, Judith Powers. *Giovanni Boccaccio*. Boston: Twayne, 1982. A very useful introduction to Boccaccio's works. Introductory chapters deal with the writer's background and the early years in Naples. Each section is preceded by biographical information as a preface to the commentary. Contains a good bibliography, with details of the works in Italian, Latin, and English translations.

SEE ALSO: Dante; Petrarch.

RELATED ARTICLES in *Great Events from History: The Middle Ages, 477-1453*: c. 1306-1320: Dante Writes *The Divine Comedy*; c. 1320: Origins of the Bubonic Plague; 1347-1352: Invasion of the Black Death in Europe; c. 1350-1400: Petrarch and Boccaccio Recover Classical Texts; 1387-1400: Chaucer Writes *The Canterbury Tales*.

Boethius

Roman philosopher

Adding knowledge of Greek thought to his Christian Roman background, Boethius became one of the most important mediators between the ancient and medieval worlds.

Born: c. 480; Rome (now in Italy)
Died: 524; Pavia (now in Italy)
Also known as: Anicius Manlius Severinus Boethius (full name)
Areas of achievement: Philosophy, religion and theology, literature

Early Life

Anicius Manlius Severinus, better known as Boethius (boh-EE-thee-uhs), was born into the patrician Roman family of the Anicii, whose members figure prominently in Roman history as far back as the Third Macedonian War in the second century B.C.E. The Manlius and Severinus families also could boast of eminent forebears. Boethius's own father held several important offices under Odoacer, the first Germanic ruler of the Italian peninsula. In 480, the supposed year of Boethius's birth, the old Roman families were adjusting and contributing to the reign of a "barbarian" king. When Boethius's father died, perhaps in the early 490's, another distinguished Roman, Quintus Aurelius Memmius Symmachus, became the boy's guardian.

An old tradition that Boethius was sent to Athens to study Greek has no basis in fact; he might as well have been sent to Alexandria, which by the late fifth century had replaced Athens as a center of Greek studies. Wherever he studied, it is clear that Boethius mastered Greek at a time when it was becoming a lost skill in Rome, and in the process, he developed a strong interest in the great Greek philosophers on whom Roman thinkers had depended heavily for centuries. It is likely that Plato's *Politeia* (388-368 B.C.E.; *Republic*, 1701) convinced him of the advisability of philosophers entering public life, and he combined an ambitious program of study and writing with public service. As a young man, he married Rusticiana, his guardian's daughter, with whom he had two sons. Boethius may have met the Ostrogothic king Theodoric the Great, who had displaced Odoacer, in 500 when the ruler, who maintained his headquarters at Ravenna, visited Rome. At any rate, many of the traditional Roman offices persisted, and Boethius rose to the consulship in 510, when he was about thirty.

Life's Work

Boethius's earlier writings cannot be dated with any confidence. Of his five theological tractates, *De trinitate* (on the Trinity), dedicated to his father-in-law, Symmachus, shows his determination to use reason in support of a doctrine that he recognized as standing firmly on a foundation of Christian faith. His interest in harmonizing revealed religion with the discoveries of pre-Christian thinkers foreshadows the work of the medieval Scholastic philosophers many centuries later. *De trinitate* represents his attempt to reconcile for intellectual Christians the seemingly contradictory doctrines that God was one but consisted of three persons.

In addition to the tractates, Boethius wrote on all four subjects of the ancient *quadrivium*—arithmetic, music, geometry, and astronomy—although his works on the last two subjects have not survived. His most voluminous extant works, however, deal with one of the subjects of the *trivium*: logic. He translated treatises by Aristotle and Porphyry, wrote commentaries on these works as well as on Cicero's *Topica* (45-44 B.C.E.; *Topics*, 1848), and produced original monographs on such subjects as categorical syllogisms and systems of logical classification. His overriding ambition, to harmonize the philosophies of Plato and Aristotle, probably bogged down amid the pressures of his public career.

After serving as consul, he became a Roman senator according to ancient tradition, and in 520 or 522 he obtained an important post with authority over most other government positions, the *magister officiorum*, or master of offices. This appointment would have involved moving to Theodoric's court at Ravenna and leaving behind the library at Rome that had sustained his scholarly endeavors. Also in 522, his sons were both appointed as consuls, although Boethius himself at this time could not have been much more than forty years of age.

With family prestige at this high point, Boethius was drawn into the struggle between Italy's Ostrogothic king and the Roman senate. Theodoric, who had been educated in Constantinople and who owed his kingship to the Eastern Roman emperor Zeno, brought with him a substantial retinue of his Germanic brethren, many of them subscribers to the Arian heresy, which held that Jesus was not coeternal with God the Father. Despite the potential for ethnic and religious conflict, Theodoric established a reputation for tolerance, impartiality, and devotion to the goals of peace and prosperity. Yet it was

Theodoric who imprisoned, tortured, and eventually executed the renowned scholar and previously trusted official, Boethius.

Like philosophically minded civil servants before and after his time, Boethius found much to distress him in government, including rampant corruption. "Private pillage and public tributes," as he put it, depleted the treasury, and when he interceded to protect principled officials from the clutches of greedy courtiers, he made influential enemies. His troubles mounted when he rose to the defense of a fellow former consul and senator named Albinus, who was suspected of treason. It appears that Boethius was motivated primarily by a desire to defend the reputation of the senate as a whole from suspicions of complicity in the alleged treachery. Boethius apparently admitted to the suppression of evidence that he considered damaging to the integrity of the senate, a course of action inevitably leading to charges against him. Accused of plotting against Theodoric in favor of Justin I, the reigning Eastern emperor, Boethius was conveyed to Pavia in 522 and imprisoned there. Under the strain of a conviction he considered entirely unjustified, he produced his masterpiece, *De consolatione philosophiae* (523; *The Consolation of Philosophy*, late ninth century). If his previous writings and his government service had made him a notable man, this work commanded the attention of the West for more than a thousand years thereafter.

Boethius. (Library of Congress)

Although conceived as a tribute to philosophy and exhibiting features of his plan to synthesize the best in Greek philosophy, *The Consolation of Philosophy* endures as a human record of doubt, discouragement, and suffering transformed by a rethinking of basic philosophical tenets into a triumph of the spirit. Even more than his Christian faith, philosophy sustained Boethius in his two years of confinement. This work consists of five main divisions or "books," each formed of alternating verse and prose sections. The prose parts develop the situation and introduce the thoughts that it generates; the verses concentrate lyric bursts of emotion and meditations on his plight.

To dramatize the conflicts within him, Boethius resolves his mental and emotional state into two components represented by the discouraged prisoner and an awesome visitor to his cell, Lady Philosophy. She listens to his complaints and gradually brings him around to the reaffirmation and fuller understanding of conviction, which his ordeal has undermined. In some poems is heard the prisoner's voice, in some the sage counselor's. In this way, Boethius externalizes and gives artistic shape to the inner dialogue that he must have conducted in his cell to forestall despair. First, Philosophy must convince him that Fortune, while not a source of happiness, is not truly the prisoner's enemy either. Her presumed benefits—worldly prosperity, honors, and other pleasures that the historical Boethius had enjoyed—have no intrinsic value. The source of all goodness is God, who permits evil and an apparently random distribution of adversity and prosperity. Boethius's questions lead Philosophy to the relationships of fate, chance, God's omniscience, Providence, and free will. With the prisoner now able to view the mind as free to surmount all human confinement, book 5 plumbs the deeper problem of human freedom in general. Philosophy upholds the paradoxical freedom of the will in the sight of an omniscient and providential God. At length, she convinces Boethius that no human or divine necessity stands in the way of the most valid exercise of the will: the pursuit of virtue.

Though presumably reconciled to his unjust sentence, Boethius reached no reconciliation with his accusers, and he died in prison in 524, either from the effects of torture or by explicit order. Almost immediately, his friends and admirers began to regard him as a martyr for his faith; his local followers in Pavia acclaimed him as a saint. The existing evidence suggests that he suffered and died not for specifically religious convictions but for moral and political ones. Even after his other works ceased to be generally read, *The Consolation of Philosophy* continued to attract readers and translators. He would have been pleased to know that two of England's greatest monarchs, Alfred the Great in the ninth century and Queen Elizabeth I seven centuries later, became philosopher-kings enough to make their own translations. Like his beloved Plato, Boethius had found a form for his philosophy that earned for it the status of a literary classic.

Significance

Although Boethius possessed both literary ability and the discipline of a professional writer, it took imprisonment to make him a philosophical poet. His earliest admirers valued not only his thought but also the integrity and courage that shine through both metrical and prose sections of *The Consolation of Philosophy.* These readers, members of an increasingly Latinate culture, could hardly have appreciated fully his efforts to keep the West in touch with Greek antiquity. At the same time, the rise of vernacular tongues and the Church's adaptation of Latin to its own purposes meant that the classical Latin verse forms that Boethius could still practice proficiently became a lost art. In this sense, he can be considered the last of the classical Latin poets as well as one of the last representatives of Greco-Roman culture generally.

Boethius also became that quintessentially medieval scholar, the Catholic theologian, and although little of the theologian shows through in his last work, there is not the slightest reason to believe that he ever abjured Christianity. On the contrary, he was believed to have been put to death for trying to protect the Church from persecution by heretics. None of his medieval enthusiasts saw anything remarkable in his exclusion of specifically Christian doctrine from *The Consolation of Philosophy.* He was simply operating as a philosopher and thus keeping theology and philosophy distinct.

In time, Boethius's versatility was bound to recommend him to scholars, among them the recoverers of the Greek heritage that had slipped almost completely from sight in the centuries between the breakup of the Roman Empire and its comeback through Arabic sources beginning in the eleventh century. Successive waves of intellectuals, from the Scholastics of the twelfth and thirteenth centuries to the scientists of the sixteenth and seventeenth centuries, were in a better position than were early medieval people to understand the import of Boethius's pursuit of Greek learning. By modern times, Boethius could be seen as a pivot between the ancient and medieval worlds generally, between classical and Christian Latinity, and between pre-Christian Hellenism and Renaissance Humanism.

Had he lived longer and found more extensive opportunities to translate Greek texts and synthesize Greek thought, Boethius might well have forestalled the loss of the Greek intellectual heritage, but his work was sufficient to demonstrate that "pagan" philosophy could animate the life of a practicing Christian and even provide spiritual sustenance in adversity. It is hardly surprising, then, that *The Consolation of Philosophy* held its grip on posterity for so long. Revered by the two greatest Catholic medieval poets—Dante and Geoffrey Chaucer—translated by Renaissance Protestants such as Queen Elizabeth I and Henry Vaughan, and admired by later skeptical historians such as Edward Gibbon and Arnold Toynbee, Boethius achieved a universal appeal. Because there are greater and more representative philosophers, theologians, and poets in his tradition, Boethius is far less generally known than Plato or Saint Thomas Aquinas or Dante, but it is difficult to think of another figure of Western civilization who combined so competently all these activities. This competence is particularly astonishing given the nature of the early sixth century, the beginning of the period long designated the "Dark Ages."

—*Robert P. Ellis*

Further Reading

Astell, Ann W. *Job, Boethius, and Epic Truth.* Ithaca, N.Y.: Cornell University Press, 1994. The book argues for the continuous existence of a theory of heroic epic from antiquity through the Middle Ages to the Renaissance. Astell sees *The Consolation of Philosophy* as transmitting the classical epic to the Middle Ages.

Barrett, Helen M. *Boethius: Some Aspects of His Times and Work.* Cambridge, England: Cambridge University Press, 1940. Reprint. New York: Russell and Russell, 1965. One of the older books on Boethius, it remains a good introduction. It provides an introductory historical survey, sets Boethius firmly in this context, and interprets the scanty details of his life in a balanced and sensible way. Subsequent scholarship has supplemented but rarely contradicted the picture of Boethius given here.

Chadwick, Henry. *Boethius: The Consolations of Music, Logic, Theology, and Philosophy.* Oxford, England: Clarendon Press, 1981. Unlike other writers, who have tended to concentrate on the Christian, the poet, the philosopher, or the educational theorist, Chadwick aims to show Boethius's career as a unified whole. He has succeeded in writing the most comprehensive book about his life and work.

Hoenen, Maarten J. F. M., and Lodi Nauta, eds. *Boethius in the Middle Ages: Latin and Vernacular Traditions of the "Consolatio philosophiae."* New York: Brill, 1997. Translations and analysis of *The Consolation of Philosophy*. Bibliography and indexes.

Marenbon, John. *Boethius*. New York: Oxford University Press, 2003. A biography of Boethius in the Great Medieval Thinkers series. Bibliography and index.

Reiss, Edmund. *Boethius*. Boston: Twayne, 1982. Reiss argues the case against accepting too literally the autobiographical details in what he regards as a highly polished work of fictional art. He tends to reject the assumption that the quotations and other specific knowledge demonstrated in *The Consolation of Philosophy* constitute a feat of memory by a prisoner without access to a library.

Scott, Jamie S. *Christians and Tyrants: The Prison Testimonies of Boethius, Thomas More, and Dietrich Bonhoeffer.* New York: P. Lang, 1995. An analysis and comparison of three Christians who were imprisoned.

SEE ALSO: Geoffrey Chaucer; Dante; Odoacer; Theodoric the Great.

RELATED ARTICLE in *Great Events from History: The Middle Ages, 477-1453*: 524: Imprisonment and Death of Boethius.

BOHEMOND I

Prince of Antioch

Bohemond was one of the leaders of Europe's most successful Crusade to the Holy Land and the founder and first prince of Antioch.

BORN: c. 1052; somewhere in what is now southern Italy

DIED: March 7, 1111; Caossa, Apulia (now Canosa di Puglia, Italy)

ALSO KNOWN AS: Marc (given name); Bohemond of Otranto; Bohemund I of Antioch

AREAS OF ACHIEVEMENT: Warfare and conquest, government and politics

EARLY LIFE

Bohemond I (BOH-uh-muhnd) was the firstborn son of Robert Guiscard, the most successful of that small band of eleventh century Norman adventurers who reclaimed southern Italy and Sicily from Byzantine, Italian, and Muslim forces. By the time of his death in 1085, Guiscard had become duke of Apulia and Calabria, overlord of Sicily (then being subdued by his younger brother Roger), and vassal, ally, and protector of the pope.

Guiscard's first wife, a Norman woman named Alberada, gave birth to their son Bohemond in the early 1050's, perhaps 1052. While Bohemond was still a small boy, Guiscard had his marriage to Alberada annulled so that he could make a more advantageous union with Sigelgaita, sister of the prince of Salerno. Little else is known about Bohemond's early years, except that he probably learned to read and write Latin and that he certainly learned the art of war as his father's apprentice. Bohemond grew to be a very tall, broad-shouldered, muscular man with a slightly stooped carriage. He had fair skin, yellow hair, and blue-gray eyes.

In 1081, Guiscard and Bohemond attempted the conquest of the Byzantine Empire, which then dominated the southern Balkans and Greece. On the eve of the invasion, Bohemond's stepmother deprived him of his inheritance as firstborn by persuading Guiscard to name the eldest of their three sons, Bohemond's half brother Roger, heir to the duchy. Had the conquest of the Byzantine Empire succeeded, Bohemond's inheritance probably would have come out of the spoils.

The invasion began well. Bohemond, who was then about twenty and already skilled enough to be second in command, secured a beachhead by conquering Avlona, participated in the successful sieges of Corfu and Durazzo, and defeated Byzantine armies in the field. Meanwhile, the Byzantine emperor Alexius I Comnenus encouraged his German allies to invade Italy and Guiscard's ever-restive barons in southern Italy to rebel. Because the Normans had insufficient monies and troops to handle all the conflicts simultaneously, they withdrew to Italy in late 1083.

In October, 1084, the Normans invaded again. Their initial successes were followed by an outbreak of disease in their camp. Bohemond became ill and returned to Italy to recuperate. Before he could return to the war in the summer of 1085, his father died, and his half brother

Roger, the new duke, called off the invasion and brought the troops home.

Bohemond declared war on Duke Roger in order to win from him a share of the patrimony from which he had been excluded. By 1090, Bohemond had seized most of Apulia (the heel of Italy), including important towns such as Taranto and Bari. What chiefly prevented him from conquering more was intervention by his uncle, Count Roger of Sicily, whose own advantage lay in keeping southern Italy divided between his nephews.

Thwarted by his uncle and half brother, Bohemond found an outlet for his acquisitiveness and bellicose energy when Pope Urban II preached the Crusade in 1095. Then vast new opportunities opened for him.

Life's Work

With protestations of goodwill toward his former enemy Alexius, Bohemond led a large contingent of Norman warriors and kinsmen to Constantinople late in 1096 to take part in the Crusade to liberate the Holy Land from Turkish Muslims. By the following spring, a number of small armies led by other European warlords had also arrived at Constantinople. Those forces constituted the First Crusade.

Bohemond I leads his soldiers at Dorylaeum during the First Crusade. (F. R. Niglutsch)

The Crusaders were united in their overall objective but in little else. The greed, pride, and jealousy of their leaders resulted in a lack of unified command and in dangerous rivalries among them, especially between Bohemond and Count Raymond IV of Toulouse. The Crusaders also disagreed about the extent of obligation and alliance to their host, Alexius. Bohemond became his vassal, a status that later caused trouble, as it gave Alexius a claim to what Bohemond acquired.

A joint Crusader-Byzantine army invaded Asia Minor in the spring of 1097 but cooperated only long enough to besiege and liberate the city of Nicaea. Thereafter, while Alexius stayed behind to secure western Asia Minor, the Crusaders struck out toward the Holy Land. Near Dorylaeum on July 1, Turkish cavalry attacked. In the battle that ensued, Bohemond commanded one of the Crusader contingents. The Turks were defeated so decisively that the Princes' Crusade could pass through the remainder of Asia Minor without incident.

The Crusade emerged onto the plains of northern Syria in the autumn of 1097 and there began what proved the most difficult, and for Bohemond the most important, operation of the campaign—the siege of ancient, rich, and well-fortified Antioch. Bohemond and Raymond both coveted the city as spoil. For Bohemond, the challenge was to work with Raymond to capture Antioch at the same time he worked against him to secure it as his own.

The siege of Antioch took eight months (from October, 1097, to June, 1098). Famine, disease, desertions, and occasional attacks by Turkish relief columns slowed progress. A breakthrough finally came when a disgruntled defender of one of Antioch's towers offered secretly to betray the city to Bohemond. Bohemond negotiated the price of this treachery and then approached his fellow captains with the proposal that whoever first breached the defenses would be named governor. Raymond would not agree, but once the other captains did, Bohemond led his troops to the tower commanded by the traitor and began the predictably successful final assault. Antioch fell on June 3. Raymond's forces seized the Bridge Gate Tower and the former governor's palace to prevent Bohemond's control of the city, but before Bohemond could combat them, a greater threat appeared outside the walls.

A Turkish army under Kerboga of Mosul appeared at Antioch a few days after the Crusaders captured the city and began a siege. The Crusaders then had to defend the city, which was low on provisions as a result of their own recent siege. The miraculous discovery of what was alleged to be the Holy Lance that pierced the side of Jesus boosted the morale of the Crusaders, but it was Bohemond who finally saved them. He persuaded them that the best defense was to attack, and then, on June 28, 1098, he led the attack that defeated and drove off Kerboga's army. Antioch was secure, yet its ownership was not determined until the following spring, when, in the absence of his colleagues who had gone to liberate Jerusalem, Bohemond forcefully ejected Raymond's garrisons from their positions in the city.

Bohemond's tenure as prince of Antioch lasted five years (from 1099 to 1104). Most of that time, he spent at war or in prison. He fought to defend his principality from Alexius, who demanded that Antioch be surrendered to him; he fought to defend it from Raymond, who still wanted it; and he fought to enlarge it at the expense of his Muslim neighbors. While fighting Muslims in the summer of 1100, Bohemond was captured. He spent the following three years in a Turkish prison, until ransomed for 100,000 gold pieces. Meanwhile, his nephew Tancred had served as regent in Antioch. Bohemond resumed control of the principality briefly on his release in 1103. The following year, however, he reinstalled Tancred as regent so that he could return to Europe, ostensibly to raise money for the debts incurred by his wars and his ransom but actually to raise an army with which to relieve pressure on Antioch by attacking Alexius's empire from the west.

Bohemond's reputation as a great warrior guaranteed for him a favorable reception by the pope and the great men of Italy and France, whom he visited during the years from 1105 to 1107. He regaled his hosts with tales of the Crusade and of Byzantine treachery and extorted from them financial and military backing for a crusade against Alexius. Philip of France also gave him the hand in marriage of his daughter Constance.

In October, 1107, approximately thirty-four thousand Italian and French Crusaders under Bohemond invaded the Byzantine Empire, using the same strategy that Bohemond and Guiscard had used in the 1080's. They took Avlona but were resisted while besieging Durazzo. The defenders thwarted all their efforts to breach, to mine, and to surmount Durazzo's walls, while Alexius's land and naval forces denied them access to the interior and easy communications with Italy. Those obstacles, plus disease, hunger, and desertion, sapped the strength of the invaders and forced Bohemond to negotiate withdrawal to Italy. By September, 1108, the Crusade was over. Bohemond returned to Apulia in disgrace.

The humiliation of the failed Crusade wore off in time. By the spring of 1111, Bohemond was again collecting an army, probably to take to Antioch. Before completing his preparations, he became ill and died. He was then approximately fifty-nine years of age.

Bohemond and Constance had had two sons during their five-year marriage; the first died in infancy, and the second, named Bohemond, succeeded his father in Apulia and eventually also in Antioch.

SIGNIFICANCE

Bohemond I was a conspicuously successful example of the bellicose, acquisitive warlord of medieval Europe. From landless warrior in 1085, he rose to become, by 1106, the leader of Apulia and Antioch and the son-in-law of the king of France. Self-interest seems to have motivated him more than high principle; he participated in the Crusade for what he might win more than for the pious intent of the enterprise. Indeed, he visited Jerusalem only once, briefly, after it had been liberated.

What was his goal? Were his accomplishments part of a larger unrealized plan? Here scholars are left to speculate, for Bohemond kept his own counsel. It could be that his acquisition of Antioch was simply successful opportunism. It could also be that taking Antioch was part of a larger plan to link in profitable commerce the ports of Apulia with a major Levantine trading center. More ambitious still, it could be that Antioch was part of a plan to conquer the Byzantine Empire—his father's unrequited ambition. There was contemporary precedent for such grandiose schemes in William, duke of Normandy's conquest of England. If Bohemond made such plans, it was lack of resources more than lack of skill that prevented their realization.

Indeed, in military skills, Bohemond was among the most adept of that age, the failed Crusade of 1107-1108 notwithstanding. At Dorylaeum and at Antioch, he displayed his competence in the major facets of contemporary war: pitched battle and siege craft. Had it not been for his skills, the First Crusade might have failed at Antioch, and the two hundred years of crusades that helped broaden European horizons during the Middle Ages might not have followed.

Bohemond's administrative skills might also have been considerable. Antioch proved to be one of the most durable of the Crusader states, but how much of Antioch's government was designed by Bohemond during his brief tenure as its prince remains uncertain. Contemporary accounts by both his friends and enemies concentrate mostly on his career as a warrior.

—*Kenneth E. Cutler*

FURTHER READING

Asbridge, Thomas S. *The Creation of the Principality of Antioch, 1098-1130*. Rochester, N.Y.: Boydell Press, 2000. An examination of the formation of the principality of Antioch which touches on Bohemond, its first prince.

Foss, Michael. *People of the First Crusade*. Boston: Little, Brown, 1997. This work on the First Crusade focuses on the people involved. Bibliography and index.

France, John. *Victory in the East: A Military History of the First Crusade*. New York: Cambridge University Press, 1994. France studies the First Crusade in detail, primarily as a military campaign. Bohemond's role in it is amply discussed.

Hill, Rosalind, ed. *The Deeds of the Franks and the Other Pilgrims to Jerusalem*. New York: T. Nelson and Sons, 1962. The anonymous author of this work was one of Bohemond's vassals. His account covers the Crusade to 1099 and was published almost immediately thereafter. Bohemond took this work with him to Europe in 1005 and disseminated it. Virtually every other twelfth century account of the First Crusade was borrowed from this one.

Nicholson, Robert L. *Tancred: A Study of His Career and Work in Their Relation to the First Crusade and the Establishment of the Latin States in Syria and Palestine*. 1940. Reprint. New York: AMS Press, 1978. Illuminates not only the military exploits of Tancred but also his complex and largely cooperative relationship with Bohemond.

Riley-Smith, Jonathan. *The First Crusaders, 1095-1131*. New York: Cambridge University Press, 1997. The story of the First Crusade, including recruitment, preparation, preaching, the holy war, and the return. One appendix lists the Crusaders. Illustrations, maps, and index.

Yewdale, Ralph B. *Bohemond I, Prince of Antioch*. 1924. Reprint. New York: AMS Press, 1980. An uncompleted Princeton dissertation published after Yewdale's death by a teacher who thought it a significant contribution to the field. Yewdale is sympathetic to Bohemond but not uncritical. Excellent bibliography of primary sources and lengthy, if now dated, list of secondary sources.

SEE ALSO: Tancred; Urban II.

RELATED ARTICLES in *Great Events from History: The Middle Ages, 477-1453*: November 27, 1095: Pope Urban II Calls the First Crusade; 1127-1130: Creation of the Kingdom of Sicily; 1147-1149: Second Crusade; 1189-1192: Third Crusade.

SAINT BONAVENTURE

Italian philosopher

Saint Bonaventure combined an early commitment to the ideals of Saint Francis of Assisi with great preaching and teaching abilities. Noted for his ability to reconcile differing groups and individuals, he proved to be a defender of both human and divine truth and an outstanding witness for mystic and Christian wisdom.

BORN: 1217 or 1221; Bagnoregio, Papal States (now in Italy)

DIED: July 15, 1274; Lyon (now in France)

ALSO KNOWN AS: Bonaventura; Giovanni di Fidanza (given name); John of Fidanza; Seraphic Doctor

AREA OF ACHIEVEMENT: Religion and theology, monasticism

EARLY LIFE

Not much is known of the family of Saint Bonaventure (bahn-uh-VEHN-chur). His father was a medical doctor, Giovanni di Fidanza. (Fidanza was not a family name, but the name of a grandfather.) His mother was called Maria di Ritello, or simply Ritella. He was very ill as a boy and was said to have been saved from death by the intercession of Saint Francis of Assisi. Bonaventure recorded his cure in his life of Saint Francis. It is recorded that the young Bonaventure received his early schooling at the Franciscan friary in Bagnoregio. He showed scholastic ability and was sent to be a student at the University of Paris in 1235 or 1236.

It was in Paris that Bonaventure met many of the Franciscan friars and entered the Franciscan order (in either 1238 or 1243). Called Giovanni since birth, he received the name Bonaventure soon after entering the order. In accordance with the Franciscan regulations of the time, he was considered a member of the Roman province of his birth. After receiving a master of arts degree from the University of Paris in 1243, he studied theology at the Franciscan school in Paris for the next five years, under Alexander of Hales and John of La Rochelle, until their deaths in 1245. He probably continued with the masters Eudes Rigauld and William of Meliton; later, he was influenced by the Dominican Guerric of Saint-Quentin and the secular master Guiard of León.

During these years, Bonaventure began teaching the brothers in the local Franciscan friary. In 1248, he became a teacher of Scripture, lecturing on the Gospel of Luke and other portions of the Bible. From 1250/1251 to 1253, he lectured on the *Sententiarum libri IV* (1148-1151; *The Books of Opinions of Peter Lombard*, 1970; better known as *Sentences*) at the University of Paris. This work was a medieval theology textbook written by Peter Lombard, a twelfth century Italian theologian. Bonaventure's commentaries on Scripture and *Sentences* enabled him to receive the licentiate and doctorate from the chancellor of the University of Paris. The chancellor acted in the name of the Church; therefore, this licentiate allowed Bonaventure to teach anywhere in the Christian world at the end of the 1252-1253 academic year. He was placed in charge of the Franciscan school in Paris, where he taught until 1257.

Paris at that time was a hotbed for theological study. Thomas Aquinas had arrived to study in 1252; he and Bonaventure became good friends. Yet the secular masters opposed the Mendicants (Franciscans and Dominicans), and although Bonaventure presented at least three series of disputed questions in Paris between 1253 and 1257, some authors claim that he was not accepted into the guild, or corporation, of the masters of the university until October 23, 1257.

LIFE'S WORK

The years between 1248 and 1257 proved to be a productive time for Bonaventure. He produced many works: not only commentaries on the Bible (not all of which have survived) and on *Sentences* but also the *Breviloquium* (1257; English translation, 1946), which provided a summary of his theology, showing his deep understanding of Scripture, early church fathers (especially Saint Augustine), and philosophers (particularly Aristotle). He adapted the older Scholastic traditions, perfecting and organizing a fresh synthesis. Bonaventure urged that the theologian be allowed to draw on logic and all the profane sciences. He thought of truth as the way to the love of God. In 1256, he and the Dominican Thomas Aquinas defended the Mendicants from an attack by William of Saint-Amour, a university teacher who accused the Mendicants of defaming the Gospel by their practice of poverty and wished to prevent them from attaining any teaching positions.

The Franciscan order itself was experiencing an internal struggle, between those who wanted a more rigorous poverty and those who wanted to relax the strict views of poverty established by Saint Francis. Pope Alexander IV commanded the minister general of the Franciscans, John of Parma, to resign his office. A chapter gathering was called at Rome late in January, 1257. Because of his defense of the Franciscans and the fact that he was an exemplary person patterning himself after Saint Francis, Bonaventure was elected minister general on February 2, 1257. He was to hold that post for seventeen years.

By placating the Spirituals (who opted for a more rigorous poverty) and reproving the Relaxati, Bonaventure reformed the order in the spirit of Saint Francis. The restoration of peace and reconciliation of opponents, a special talent of Bonaventure, was accomplished through extensive visits to all the provinces of the order and through his own practice of the Franciscan way of life. It was during these travels, despite health problems, that his reputation as a preacher was earned. His election to office had ended his teaching career, but it created preaching opportunities. Throughout Europe, his eloquence, knowledge, and simplicity caught the attention of high dignitaries and the laity. He also administered the order, presiding over the general chapters and guiding the continued growth of the Franciscans.

Bonaventure's new tasks did not prevent him from continuing his writing. In his visits to the provinces in October, 1259, he stopped at La Verna. There he wrote *Itinerarium mentis in Deum* (1259; *The Journey of the Soul to God*, 1937; also known as *The Journey of the Mind to God*, 1993). At this time, without ceasing to be a Scholastic, Bonaventure became a mystic, aligning himself more clearly with the inner life of Saint Francis. He merged Augustine's intellectual contemplation of truth with the Dionysian notion of truth as the ecstatic knowledge of God. He used as his model Saint Francis, whose vision of the seraphim at La Verna had shown how the heights of contemplation could be reached. Bonaventure also had the example of Brother Giles of Assisi, although to a lesser degree than Saint Francis. He wrote other works in this period, including *De triplici via* (1260; *The Enkindling of Love, Also Called the Triple Way*, 1956) and *De perfectione vitae ad sorores* (1260; *Holiness of Life*, 1923).

In 1260, Bonaventure was in France preparing for the Pentecost Chapter at Narbonne, which was to codify the Franciscan ordinances into a new set of constitutions. It was this chapter that charged him with writing a new biography of Saint Francis. To gather material, Bonaventure visited all the places that had been significant to Francis and interviewed those of the early friars who were still alive. While working on this project, he presented himself to the new pope, Urban IV, elected in August, 1261. Late in that year or in the following year, Bonaventure was forced to submit the previous minister general, John of Parma, to a trial because of John's continued adherence to Joachism. On April 8, 1263, Bonaventure was in Padua for the transferral of the relics of Saint Anthony, and on May 20 he was in Pisa for a general chapter in which some forty liturgical statutes and rubrics were introduced, ending about fifty years of work in the Franciscan order. Bonaventure gave each of the thirty-four provincials present a copy of his new *Legenda maior* (1263; *The Life of Saint Francis of Assisi*, 1868). That year he also wrote *De sex alis seraphim* (1263; *The Virtues of a Religious Superior: Instructions by the Seraphic Doctor*, 1920).

In 1264, he spent some time at the papal court, and in the spring he gave a sermon on the Body of Christ at a consistory of Urban IV. In March, 1265, he was at

Saint Bonaventure, from a fresco by John of Florence in the Chapel of Nicholas V in the Vatican. (Frederick Ungar Publishing Co.)

Perugia to present himself to the new pope, Clement IV. In November, the new pope nominated Bonaventure to be archbishop of York, but he refused the post. At the general chapter at Paris, May 16, 1266, Bonaventure continued to correct abuses in the order, especially those regarding matters of poverty. The chapter also ordered that all other biographies of Francis be destroyed because Bonaventure had provided a new one.

Until as late as mid-1268, Bonaventure lived at a small friary in Mantessur-Seine, France, where he continued his ascetical writings and preached at the university. His Lenten conferences of 1267 (on the Ten Commandments) and 1268 (on the gifts of the Holy Spirit) attacked current trends. On July 8, 1268, he was in Rome receiving the Archconfraternity of the Gonfalonieri into spiritual communion with the Franciscans, staying in Italy through the chapter of Assisi in May. When he returned to Paris, he found that Gerard of Abbeville, a teacher of theology, had renewed the charge of William of Saint-Amour against the Mendicants. Bonaventure responded by upholding the Christian faith while denouncing unorthodox views in a work that was not only a refutation of heretical opinions but also the presentation of a positive theology of religious life in imitation of Christ. It showed that Bonaventure was less interested in external regulations than building up an inner spirit of prayer and devotion and creating right attitudes using the examples of Christ and Francis. Here one can see Bonaventure's doctrine of illumination, discussed in *The Journey of the Mind to God*, in operation: the cooperation given the soul when it acts as the image of God.

In June, 1272, Bonaventure was in Lyon for the Pentecostal General Chapter. The following spring, 1273, he was in Paris for the last time; there, he began work on *Collationes in Hexaemeron* (1273; *Collations on the Six Days*; 1970), his theological testament to refute those who exaggerated the rationalism of Aristotle in opposition to the inspiration of the Scriptures. In this same year, Pope Gregory X named him the cardinal bishop of Albano, Italy. He was consecrated as bishop November 11 or 12, 1273, and proceeded with the pope to Lyon for the Second Council of Lyon. In the capacity of legate, Bonaventure helped the pope prepare for the Council of Lyon, which opened on May 7, 1274. To continue his work at the council, he resigned as minister general of the Franciscans. Bonaventure continued to lead in the reform of the church, reconciling the secular (parish) clergy with the Mendicants. He preached at least twice at the council and effected a brief reunion of the Greek church with Rome.

Bonaventure died unexpectedly on the night of July 15, 1274, leaving his last work unfinished. He was buried in the Franciscan church in Lyon, with the pope attending. At the fifth session of the council, July 16, all priests of the world were ordered to celebrate a mass for his soul.

The impression Bonaventure made on contemporaries is summarized in the notes of the Council of Lyon, which indicate sorrow at his death. He was canonized on April 14, 1482, by Pope Sixtus IV, who also enrolled him with the mass and office of a confessor bishop. On March 14, 1588, another Franciscan pope, Sixtus V, gave Bonaventure the designation doctor of the Church. In 1434, his body was transferred to the church dedicated to Saint Francis in Lyon, with an arm taken to his native Bagnoregio. During the Huguenot uprising in France, his body, except the head, was destroyed by fire. His head was destroyed by fire during the French Revolution.

Significance

Saint Bonaventure is properly considered the second father of the Franciscans and a prince of mystics. He personified the ideals of Saint Francis of Assisi in teaching, in preaching, in writing, and in living his life. He had an immediate and a lasting influence on the Scholastics of the thirteenth century. He was an influential guide and teacher of spiritual life, particularly in Germany and the Netherlands. His influence has been maintained through the Roman College of Saint Bonaventure, founded by Pope Sixtus V in 1587. He was depicted in medieval art, and modern scholars consider him one of the foremost men of his age, a true contemporary of Thomas Aquinas.

—*Mary-Emily Miller*

Further Reading

Analecta Franciscans, sive chronica aliaque varia documents ad historium fratrum minorum spectantia. 10 vols. Florence: Quaracchi, 1885-1941. An excellent source for original documents on the Franciscans. For Bonaventure, see especially volume 3, pages 323-355, which contain a review of his early life and more details on the years 1257 to 1274. A knowledge of Latin is necessary, particularly where there are corrections of some errors in Luke Wadding's scholarship.

Bonaventure, Saint. *The Life of Saint Francis*. Translated by E. Gurney Salter. London: J. M. Dent and Co., 1904. There are other translations of this work in numerous languages. It was this work that became the official biography in 1266. Not only does this work aid in an understanding of Francis, but it also contributes to a deeper understanding of Bonaventure.

Delio, Ilia. *Simply Bonaventure: An Introduction to His Life, Thought, and Writings*. Hyde Park, N.Y.: New City Press, 2001. A biography of the saint that covers his life, works, and theology. Index.

Hellmann, J. A. Wayne. *Divine and Created Order in Bonaventure's Theology.* New York: Franciscan Institute, 2001. An examination of Saint Bonaventure's theology. Bibliography and indexes.

Wadding, Luke, ed. *Annales Minorum seu Trium Ordinum.* 25 vols. Rome: St. Francisco Institutorum, 1731-1886. An indispensable reference for the history of the Franciscans, though later scholarship has pointed to some errors in Wadding, mostly concerning dates. A knowledge of Latin is necessary for an understanding of the annotations and general comments.

See also: Saint Francis of Assisi; Thomas Aquinas; William of Saint-Amour.

Related articles in *Great Events from History: The Middle Ages, 477-1453*: April 16, 1209: Founding of the Franciscans; 1233: Papal Inquisition; c. 1265-1273: Thomas Aquinas Compiles the *Summa Theologica.*

Saint Boniface

English missionary and archbishop (732-754)

Boniface left England to assist in the conversion of pagan Germany. He brought Christianity to many areas and, in others, set the Church on a new and sounder basis, earning the title Apostle of Germany.

Born: c. 675; Crediton, Devonshire, England

Died: June 5, 754; Dokkum, Frisia (now in the Netherlands)

Also known as: Wynfrith or Wynfrid (given name); Bonifatius (Latin name); Apostle of Germany

Areas of achievement: Literature, religion and theology, church government

Early Life

As a young child, Boniface (BAHN-uh-fas) was sent to the monastery at Exeter to be reared as a monk. In later years, he would claim to be of humble birth, but it seems likely that this claim was only a conventional profession of humility. Several of his relatives appear to have had noble rank. There is a tradition that he was born at Crediton, and though it cannot be traced further back than the fourteenth century, Crediton is near enough to Exeter for the story to be plausible.

Exeter does not seem to have satisfied Wynfrith (his given name), and perhaps in the 690's he transferred to the monastery at Nursling, near Southampton, also a Benedictine house and also in the kingdom of Wessex, but possibly with better scholarly endowments. Wynfrith gained a reputation for his learning and piety (though in the unchristianized England of that time there may have been few competitors). He compiled England's first Latin grammar; it is interesting to note, though, that according to *Vita sancti Bonifati* (*The Life of Saint Boniface*, 1916), written by the priest Willibald, when Wynfrith was first introduced to Pope Gregory II in 719, he begged to make his profession of faith in writing, as his spoken Latin did not meet Vatican standards.

Wynfrith's English colleagues thought well of him. In 712, a synod of Wessex priests and bishops chose him as their emissary to the archbishop of Canterbury. After he had made a first, brief visit to the Christian mission in Frisia (now in the Netherlands) in 716, the monastery of Nursling tried to hold this valuable man by making him abbot. They were, however, too late. Wynfrith had decided to leave England and work with the already established Christian missions in Germany. In 718, he left England, never to return.

Life's Work

The problems facing Wynfrith were complex. From the time of their own conversion, the Anglo-Saxons had felt a strong urge, even a responsibility, to spread the Gospel to their Germanic cousins who had remained on the Continent. The kinship, it seems, was recognized on both sides. Later, in a letter of 738 asking for the prayers of the English, Boniface says that even the pagans declare, "We are of one and the same blood and bone." Yet, however welcome a friendly mission from the Anglo-Saxons might be, the next neighbor of many of the Germanic tribes, especially of the Saxons and the Frisians, was the aggressive Christian kingdom—later empire—of the Franks. The pagans, as a result, were very likely to see behind the missionary the Frankish imperialist and to react in very hostile fashion. In addition, relations between the English missionaries and the Frankish church were

Saint Boniface. (Hulton|Archive at Getty Images)

rarely good. The English thought the Franks corrupt, immoral, and self-interested; the Franks thought the English were moving in on their territory.

Wynfrith, accordingly, did not plunge straight into missionary work but went to Rome. In 719, he introduced himself to Pope Gregory II, and on May 15, he received a mandate from him, letters of support and introduction, and, in recognition of his new status, the new name of Bonifatius, or Boniface. Boniface in this way received protection from Frankish interference. Gregory and his successors, in turn, would have new provinces added to the Church, whose example in the end affected even the disorganized and unreliable Franks.

Boniface returned to the mission in Frisia established by his famous countryman Saint Willibrord (658-739) and worked there for three years. Like the monks of Nursling, Willibrord tried to retain him by offering him a bishopric, but Boniface refused. It was not that there was no work to do, for the Frisians (though situated handily close to England on the North Sea coast running up from the what is now the Netherlands through Germany to Denmark) remained among the most obdurate pagans of all. Boniface may have believed that there were less stubborn souls to win elsewhere, or he may have preferred independence. In any event, he returned to Rome, was consecrated a bishop there on November 30, 722, gave a personal oath of loyalty to the pope, and returned not to Frisia but to central Germany. He took with him a letter of recommendation from the pope to Charles Martel, the powerful ruler of the Franks. Boniface's success would depend in no small part on this combination of papal support and government protection.

Boniface worked in Germany for some sixteen years, mostly in the provinces of Hesse and Thuringia. The most famous story about him comes from Willibald's account, written by an otherwise unknown English monk not long after Boniface's death, though it seems that Willibald had not known Boniface personally. He relates that Boniface had decided to challenge the pagans by felling the sacred oak at Geismar in Hesse, which was dedicated to Donar, the god of thunder (the German equivalent of the Norse god Thor). In the presence of many angry pagans, Boniface lifted his ax to it. At the first strike, the oak fell into four parts, as if blown down from Heaven. If the story has any truth, it may show that Boniface believed in a policy of confrontation—which was, in the end, to cause his death.

Assisted by many Anglo-Saxon volunteers, Boniface established churches and monasteries, converting and baptizing large numbers. He was made an archbishop in 732 by Pope Gregory II but had no bishops under him for several years. Possibly as a result of this odd status, Boniface made a third trip to Rome in 738 to confer with the pope, then turned to a new phase of large-scale organization.

Moving to the relatively Christianized south of Germany, he set up a new Bavarian "province" of the Church, with four bishoprics in it. He also established bishoprics in Hesse, Thuringia, and Franconia, ending with eight bishops subordinate to him. This looks rather like an exercise in empire-building, but Boniface seems to have succeeded in it, first because the new bishops were often Boniface's Anglo-Saxon assistants, who had no doubt volunteered to join him because of his own personal prestige, and second because he was careful always to clear himself with successive popes. The exercise was in any case necessary and had many good effects. With eight bishops, and the support of Carloman and Pépin III the Short, the heirs of Charles Martel, Boniface was able to call a series of synods between 740 and 747 to reform the Frankish church. The Frankish church was shamed into reluctant imitation and cooperation. One final problem was solved when Boniface—until then an archbishop without a seat—was given Cologne for his base. His base was later changed to Mainz, as a result of Frankish objections.

With these successes behind him, Boniface, by this time in his late seventies, decided to return to the scene of his first mission in Frisia, in 753. There, however, resistance to the Franks and the Christians was still strong, exacerbated by decades of war. When Boniface tried to hold a mass baptism on June 5, 754, near the town of Dokkum, armed pagans attacked him. Boniface forbade resistance and was killed, by tradition holding up a Gospel book. Many of his followers were killed with him. Willibald's *The Life of Saint Boniface* rather gloatingly reports that the Christian Frisians, unencumbered by Boniface's scruples about nonviolence, armed themselves and successfully counterattacked the pagans. Even if this story is true, it made no difference to the overall situation in Frisia. Boniface's body was recovered and taken for burial to the abbey at Fulda in Hesse, which he had founded.

A considerable part of Saint Boniface's correspondence has survived. It makes, for the most part, rather uninspiring reading. With the exception of the general "Letter to the English" of 738, which makes a straightforward appeal to love and piety, Boniface's letters are those of a busy administrator. He worries about recurring problems, often related to being short of assistants: What is he to do about priests unworthy of their cloth? Can he still use them, or must they be discarded? Is the pope supporting him, or are people going behind his back to reverse his decisions? More technical queries include the degrees of kinship prohibiting marriage; pagan and Christian definitions of incest often differed. Can food offered to idols be used after it has been blessed in Christian fashion? What are the rules about re-baptism? It would appear to a modern reader that Boniface often fusses needlessly over details—for example, ordering re-baptism in cases in which a priest, through ignorance, has made a mistake in his Latin. The deed and intent were not enough for him; the words also had to be right.

On the other side, those writing to Boniface must often (one senses) have driven him close to despair. The bishop of Winchester, who had probably never met a hostile pagan, sent Boniface advice on how to convert people. One of the several popes Boniface served so loyally asked him to be sure that bishops' sees were established in proper cities, not mere townships. Where Boniface was to find these cities, in the forests of central Germany, the pope did not say. Meanwhile, though the king of Mercia appears not to have replied to the strong letter of reproof that Boniface sent to him in 746/747 regarding his sins, the king of Kent did write in the most cheerful fashion, in or near 750, saying how delighted he was that Boniface was praying for him. He also asked Boniface to send him a pair of good German falcons, preferably big enough to attack crows. Letters such as these both attest Boniface's international prestige and offer insight into the unexpectedly mundane problems of missionary life.

Significance

Boniface's main achievement, perhaps, was to live so long and remain so undiscouraged. Sparks of Christianity often fell on the pagan North. Usually they were snuffed out after a few years. Boniface was one of the few who survived hostility from the pagans, jealousy or indifference from the Christians, and the discouragement and death of his supporters. He built missionary fervor into a structure that, perhaps most important, would no longer need fervor to sustain it. When he died, the Church in Germany was too strongly rooted to need great individuals for survival. Boniface made scattered missions into an organized Church, and, by his example to the Franks, brought the whole of northwest Europe into a better relationship with Rome. Later kings, popes, and emperors were to build on this stable foundation.

—*T. A. Shippey*

Further Reading

Albertson, Clinton, ed. and trans. *Anglo-Saxon Saints and Heroes*. Bronx, N.Y.: Fordham University Press, 1967. Contains seven lives of Anglo-Saxon saints, the last being Willibald's *The Life of Saint Boniface*. Provides annotations.

Duckett, Eleanor S. *Anglo-Saxon Saints and Scholars*. Hamden, Conn.: Archon Books, 1967. Provides a major chapter on the life of Boniface. While written in a novelistic style, it is backed by solid research. Includes often revealing anecdotes about the period.

Emerton, Ephraim, ed. and trans. *The Letters of Saint Boniface*. New York: Columbia University Press, 2000. One of the best complete English versions of the more than one hundred letters. While the letters are sometimes frustratingly bureaucratic, they offer a picture of an eighth century personality almost unrivaled in detail.

Levison, Wilhelm. *England and the Continent in the*

Eighth Century. Reprint. New York: Clarendon Press, 1966. The work is especially valuable in setting Boniface in the context of earlier missions and of general European politics. An appendix gives a full account of the manuscripts of the letters.

Stenton, F. M. *Anglo-Saxon England*. 3d ed. Reprint. New York: Oxford University Press, 1989. Though Boniface is not treated extensively in this general history, the author's account includes a useful map and valuable observations on the letters, on political realism, and on events after Boniface's death.

Talbot, C. H., ed. and trans. *The Anglo-Saxon Missionaries in Germany*. New York: Sheed and Ward, 1954. A well-chosen selection from Boniface's correspondence, together with a translation of Willibald's biography and lives of four other early missionaries. Includes a short introduction and a good bibliography (largely of foreign-language material).

Whitelock, Dorothy, ed. and trans. *Circa 500-1042*. Vol. 1 in *English Historical Documents*, edited by David C. Douglas. 2d ed. New York: Routledge, 1996. In addition to fourteen letters to, from, or about Boniface and two extracts from Willibald, this volume contains large selections of similar letters and lives, as well as of chronicles and narrative sources, which help to put Boniface in the context of his times.

SEE ALSO: Saint Bede the Venerable; Charlemagne; Charles Martel; Widukind.

RELATED ARTICLE in *Great Events from History: The Middle Ages, 477-1453*: 735: Christianity Is Introduced into Germany.

BONIFACE VIII

Italian pope (1294-1303)

Though pope for only nine years, Boniface VIII represents both the zenith and nadir of papal power. In his clash with the secular rulers of Western Europe, Boniface insisted on the ultimate earthly authority of the Papacy.

BORN: c. 1235; probably Anagni, Papal States (now in Italy)

DIED: October 11, 1303; Rome, Papal States (now in Italy)

ALSO KNOWN AS: Benedict Caetani (given name)

AREAS OF ACHIEVEMENT: Religion and theology, church government

EARLY LIFE

Boniface VIII (BAHN-uh-fas), christened Benedict Caetani, was one of the younger sons of Roffred Caetani and his wife, Emilia, the niece of Pope Alexander IV. His family seems to have been moderately wealthy, owning some land, and well-connected to the Church. Very little is known of Benedict's life before 1275. In the 1250's and 1260's, however, he apparently joined his uncle Peter, who had been made bishop of Todi in 1252, and studied civil law there with Master Bartolus, traveling on occasion to Spoleto to study with other masters. In 1263 or 1264, he probably studied law for a short time at the great law school in Bologna. At about the same time, Benedict embarked on his career in the Church, first working as a secretary of Cardinal Simon of Brie and, from 1265 to 1268, accompanying Cardinal Ottoboni Fieschi on a diplomatic mission to England. When Ottoboni became Pope Adrian V in 1276, Benedict was appointed to supervise the collection of certain papal taxes in France. Achieving this post marks the beginning of Benedict's rapid ascent through the ranks of the growing papal bureaucracy. From tax supervisor to papal notary to inquisitor's assistant, Benedict learned not only the complex workings of the Church's government but also the intricacies of canon law. When his old master Simon of Brie became Pope Martin IV in 1281, the new pope rewarded his former secretary by making him a cardinal—the cardinal-deacon of Saint Nicholas in Carcere Tulliano.

A cardinal in the late thirteenth century could wield much power within the Church's bureaucracy, especially by managing the incomes of numerous benefices and overseeing delicate diplomatic negotiations. Medieval popes perceived themselves to be the peacemakers of Christendom, individuals who could nurture truces or settle disputes between warring secular powers or churchmen. They relied on their industrious cardinals or legates to aid in the maintenance of peace. To support the great business of the cardinals, the pope granted numerous benefices—churches, canonries, and deaconries, each producing an annual income—to his trusted officers. In addition, cardinals, such as Benedict, often received gifts and gold from kings, princes, bishops, and noblemen who sought the cardinals' favors or political support.

Throughout the 1280's and the early 1290's, Cardinal Benedict served as a legate for Popes Martin IV, Honorius IV, and Nicholas IV, traveling to France and throughout Italy to aid in keeping the peace between often quarrelsome monarchs. Having gained much experience in the service of the Papacy, Benedict achieved even greater prominence in 1285 when Honorius IV appointed him chief examiner of bishops, an office that offered much prestige and permitted Benedict to establish political liaisons with many of the bishops appointed to dioceses across Europe.

Pope Boniface VIII. (Library of Congress)

LIFE'S WORK

When Pope Nicholas IV died in 1292, political rivalries between two great Italian families kept the papal election process from a speedy conclusion. After wrangling for twenty-seven months, the cardinals, including Cardinal Benedict Caetani, selected a hermit, Peter of Morrone, to be the new pope, Celestine V. The politically convenient solution of choosing a nonentity to be pope proved disastrous. Although the cardinals who had supported the rival factions in the college thought that a hermit pope would permit them to continue to jockey for power, Celestine turned out to be semiliterate, untrained in religious and doctrinal matters, and partial to rustic rather than courtly life. During the nearly four months that Celestine ruled, it became painfully obvious that he did not wish to be pope and that his performance of papal duties was unsatisfactory and irregular. On December 13, 1294, Celestine took the unprecedented step of announcing his abdication. Ten days later, the College of Cardinals reassembled to choose a successor and, on Christmas Eve, 1294, Benedict Caetani was elected pope, adopting the name Boniface VIII. In later years, suspicion was cast on this election because Cardinal Benedict had been one of the legal experts who provided advice on Celestine's resignation. Some were to argue that this advice had been self-serving.

Boniface's nine-year reign was one of the most controversial pontificates of the Middle Ages. As pope, he not only directly confronted the royal power of the English and French monarchs but also raised questions about his own faith (he believed in the power of amulets and magic) and the propriety of his defense of the Church.

Boniface's relationship with the secular monarchs of Europe focused on the question of precisely what powers a monarch could exercise over clergymen who lived within his or her kingdom. In the final years of the thirteenth century, the kingdoms of England and France once again found themselves engaged in conflict, and the monarchs of both kingdoms desperately needed funds to support their costly war efforts. The monarchs claimed the power to collect taxes not only from their lay subjects but also from their clerical ones, since all subjects, regardless of their status, received the benefits of royal protection within the kingdom. Boniface opposed the clerical payment of royal taxes, primarily because he himself desired to collect taxes from clergymen to finance his own struggles against the Colonna family in Italy and the Ghibellines, who advocated a strong, antipapal, imperial presence in papally dominated Italy. Furthermore, Boniface felt that by allowing monarchs to tax clergymen, the Church would be compromising its hard-won supremacy, fought for and defended for two centuries. In response to the taxation measures of Edward I of England and Philip IV the Fair of France, Boniface issued the bull *Clericis laicos* in 1296, in which he declared that, according to canon law, the clergy was composed of individuals who had special personal and property privileges not accorded to others. Because of this special quality, clergymen could be taxed only after the pope had given his authorization. Failure to obtain this authorization could result in the excommunication of anyone who collected tax revenues from the clergy.

Neither Philip nor Edward was intimidated by Boniface's declaration. Philip ordered an end to the export of money from France—effectively ending the collection of taxes by the Papacy in France—and Edward declared all clergymen who refused to pay taxes to be outlaws, thereby removing them from royal protection and subjecting them to banditry. In the face of this opposition, Boniface backed down in 1297, saying that in times of emergencies—determined by the secular rulers—clergymen could make voluntary "gifts" to monarchs, in lieu of tax payments. The pope's retreat, however, was not to last long.

Four years later, Philip arrested and tried Bernard Saisset, bishop of Pamiers, for crimes of treason, heresy, simony, and the uttering of offensive statements. Saisset was found guilty and imprisoned by his archbishop. The royal court asked Boniface to remove Saisset from his bishopric. Boniface refused the royal request, despite the facts of the case against Saisset, and demanded that the king have Saisset immediately released. More drastically, Boniface revoked all the privileges previously granted to the king for limited influence in church affairs. Boniface acted from his firm belief that the Church and the Papacy must be completely independent of secular control or interference. This uncompromising position was, perhaps, bolstered by the fact that as an Italian, deeply involved in interclan rivalries within Italy, Boniface seems to have harbored an anti-French bias.

Philip's response to Boniface's demand and revocation of privileges was powerful and unwavering. Beginning in 1302, his administration flooded France with antipapal propaganda, and royal officers drew up a list of twenty-nine accusations against the pope, charging him with blasphemy, simony, heresy, fornication, and the murder of the recently deceased Celestine V, whom Boniface allegedly had to kill in order to prevent Celestine from testifying to the French charge that Boniface had induced him to abdicate in 1294. Philip's government insisted that a council of cardinals, archbishops, and bishops from across Europe be held to determine the propriety of Boniface's actions and his suitability for the papal throne.

Boniface convoked a council in November of 1302, and the outnumbered French clergymen who attended were unable to prevent the council from approving of Boniface's actions. At the end of the meetings, Boniface issued a papal decree—the boldest and most confident statement ever made in the history of the Church about the powers of the pope. The decree, *Unam sanctam*, contains a series of legal arguments dredged up from the archives of the Church and the writings of several twelfth century canon lawyers. Basically, the document describes Boniface's perception of Christian society: Christendom was a society in which there were two "swords," the sword of secular monarchs and the sword of the pope. The secular monarchs used their swords to protect the Church physically, while the pope used his for spiritual defense. Boniface also argued that "every human creature must be subject to the Roman pontiff" if that individual wished to gain salvation. In the pope's mind, every human committed sins, and the Church, which the pope controlled, was the institution to which humans were required to turn to seek forgiveness of their sins. Thus, *Unam sanctam* declared that the pope was the single most powerful ruler of Christian society because he controlled all human ability to gain salvation.

King Philip fired the last shot in this ongoing conflict between the pope and a secular monarch. In June, 1303, the king assembled representatives of the clergy, nobility, and towns of France and, after much careful staging and intimidation, convinced them to pass a resolution demanding that Boniface VIII be tried by a church council on the twenty-nine accusations the French had made against him. With the delicately orchestrated show of popular resentment against Boniface, the French king felt obliged to respond to his people's demand. When Philip learned that Boniface intended to have him excommunicated, Philip sent a small band of French soldiers to the papal palace at Anagni, where Boniface VIII was captured on the night of September 7. Though the inhabitants of Anagni won the release of the pope two days later, Philip's message was clear: The pope could produce legal arguments that described and defended his supreme position in Christian Europe, but forceful military action ultimately determined who held real power in Christendom. Five weeks later, on October 11, Boniface VIII died at the palace in Rome, a broken man and a conquered pope.

SIGNIFICANCE

Boniface VIII's pontificate marked the end of a 225-year phase of papal history, a period characterized by the Papacy's struggle to maintain itself as the premier political force in Christendom on the basis of complex legal and doctrinal arguments. Boniface, having received legal training and having worked his way through the ranks of the Church's bureaucracy, not only understood the functions and intricacies of the Church as an institution but also appreciated the political value of the claim to papal supremacy. His stubborn insistence on the complete independence of the Church from secular interference reveals his devotion to an old tradition within the Church, as well as a certain unawareness of the changing realities of early fourteenth century politics. While Europeans still piously believed in the importance of the Church in the gaining of salvation, their political support and devotion were gradually being courted and won by national monarchs who had their own ideas about power and the needs of Christian society.

—*David M. Bessen*

FURTHER READING

Barraclough, Geoffrey. *The Medieval Papacy*. 1968. Reprint. New York: W. W. Norton, 1979. A handsomely illustrated, readable history of the Papacy as an evolving institution in Europe.

Boase, T. S. R. *Boniface VIII*. 1933. Reprint. Wilmington, Del.: International Academic Publishers, 1979. Though somewhat dated, this is still the most useful English-language biography of Boniface VIII. Boase traces Boniface's life throughout his career, focusing especially on the factional problems of the Papacy and the various clashes with Philip IV.

Denton, Jeffrey Howard. *Philip the Fair and the Ecclesiastical Assemblies of 1294-1295*. Philadelphia: American Philosophical Society, 1991. An account of the interactions between Philip IV the Fair and Boniface VIII. Indexes.

Ullmann, Walter. *A Short History of the Papacy in the Middle Ages*. 1972. Reprint. New York: Routledge, 2003. A careful survey of papal history from its development in the late Roman imperial period to the Protestant Reformation.

Wood, Charles T., ed. *Philip the Fair and Boniface VIII: State vs. Papacy*. 1967. Reprint. New York: Holt, Rinehart, and Winston, 1971. Wood has collected several primary documents and historical interpretations of the struggle between Boniface and Philip, providing the reader with an overview of the papal and French perspectives of the crucial events of Boniface's pontificate.

SEE ALSO: Edward I; Philip IV the Fair.

RELATED ARTICLE in *Great Events from History: The Middle Ages, 477-1453*: November 18, 1302: Boniface VIII Issues the Bull *Unam Sanctam*.

BORIS I OF BULGARIA

Czar of Bulgaria (r. 852-889)

Boris brought Bulgaria into the framework of Christian Europe while preserving its political independence and cultural identity. His efforts made Bulgaria a center of Slavonic Christian culture and laid the foundation for the first Bulgarian Empire.

BORN: 830; probably Pliska, Bulgaria
DIED: May 15, 907; Preslav (now Veliki Preslav), Bulgaria
ALSO KNOWN AS: Mikhail; Michael
AREAS OF ACHIEVEMENT: Government and politics, religion and theology

EARLY LIFE

Boris's father was Svinitse, the second of three sons of Khan Omortag, who ruled between 814 and 831. The pagan Bulgars were polygamous, and the identity of Boris's mother is unknown. She was probably the daughter of a prominent noble, or boyar, family. Few reliable reports about the details of Boris's physical appearance are available. In numerous frescoes and mosaics, almost all of them posthumous, he is portrayed as a bearded, dark-haired warrior-saint dressed in Byzantine-style robes.

The pre-Christian Bulgarian society that Boris came to rule was a rather complex affair, and understanding something of its nature is essential to appreciating Boris's subsequent policies. The original Bulgars were an Asiatic, nomadic people closely related to the Huns. In 679, a large number of them crossed the Danube River and established themselves in what is now northern Bulgaria. This region was already inhabited by numerous Slavic tribes, whom the Bulgars proceeded to subjugate. The Slavs subsequently provided most of the manpower of the Bulgarian state, while the Asiatic Bulgars constituted the military aristocracy—a relationship somewhat similar to the one later established between Normans and Saxons in England. By Boris's day, there had already been considerable blending of the two groups, but the Asiatic element was still distinct and dominant. One of

Boris's major accomplishments was to promote the general Slavicization of his realm's language and culture.

Boris followed his uncle Malamir to the throne in 852. Malamir had apparently been a weak ruler, and his reign remains as a hazy episode in Bulgarian history. His wars with the Byzantines and Serbs were largely unsuccessful, and he left no son to succeed him. Young Boris was initially determined to reestablish his nation's military prestige and expand the conquests of his forebears. The campaign he proceeded to launch against the Byzantine Empire, however, achieved little, and he was diplomatically outmaneuvered by the empress Irene. In 853, he invaded the Carolingian part of Croatia, again without notable success; in 860, he initiated an effort to conquer the Serbs on his northwestern frontier, but this campaign ended in disastrous defeat. Boris did, however, consolidate Bulgarian control over most of Macedonia, a region that would later become the cultural watershed of the Bulgarian Empire.

LIFE'S WORK

His lack of success as a conqueror soured Boris on military adventures and influenced him to take a closer look at the internal and diplomatic state of his realm. In both areas, the matter of religion was a paramount cause for concern. Boris turned his attention to this issue and there achieved his most important and lasting impact.

The traditional faith of the Bulgars was a brand of shamanism, revolving around the worship of the Sun and the Moon. Animal and human sacrifice was widely practiced. The Slavs also had numerous pagan cults, the most important of which was that of the god Perun. The shamans and priests of these cults were closely linked to the boyar nobles, who provided the state with most of its military leaders and administrators. Like their counterparts in Western Europe, the boyars were generally opposed to expansion or consolidation of the monarch's power.

Christianity had already made inroads into Bulgar society. Its most active agents were the Byzantines, who exported their faith as a kind of diplomatic weapon. The Byzantine, or Orthodox, Church adhered to the doctrine of caesaropapism, under which their emperor served as head of both state and church. Thus, a Bulgar who accepted the Orthodox faith was technically obligated to accept the Byzantine ruler as the rightful sovereign, a position that made his conversion tantamount to treason. As a result, the Bulgar khans had generally opposed the spread of Christianity among their subjects.

The alternative to the Orthodox Church was the Roman church, headed by the pope. Although the final split between the Eastern and Western churches was still some two centuries away (1054), these two branches of Christianity were already locked in a bitter struggle for dominance, a conflict that Boris exploited to his advantage.

Boris accepted the Orthodox faith in 864 or early 865. His conversion has been variously attributed to his contemplation of a vivid painting of the Last Judgment, the influence of a Greek Christian slave, and a threat of invasion from Byzantine emperor Michael III (r. 842-867). The first version is almost certainly fanciful, but both of the others probably contain some core of truth. Still, his conversion was undoubtedly a deliberate and practical decision. Boris had tolerated numerous Christians, including his sister, in his court. He could also see that the pagan cults had lost their spiritual vitality as well as the allegiance of much of the population. Furthermore, by breaking the power of the cults, he could reduce the influence of the boyars. Finally, he recognized that as long as Bulgaria remained pagan it would never be accepted by the Christian powers as a legitimate state; thus, it would remain isolated from the material and cultural benefits of Christian civilization.

Boris's challenge was to bring his country into the Christian fold without surrendering its independence to either the emperor or the pope. At his baptism, Boris accepted Michael III as his godfather and even adopted Michael as his Christian name. Boris proceeded to demand that all of his subjects follow his example, and where there was resistance he was not averse to using force. In 866, diehard pagans, led by dissident boyars, rebelled, but they were quickly and ruthlessly crushed. Fifty-two leading boyars were slaughtered along with their entire families; the noble opposition was thus left without leadership.

Boris hoped that the Byzantines would accept an autonomous archbishop at the head of the Bulgarian church, thus guaranteeing it some measure of independence from imperial control. Instead, the country was flooded with Greek priests who regarded Bulgaria as a Byzantine province.

In retaliation, Boris turned to Rome, and in 866, he recognized the supremacy of the pope. The opportunity to establish his authority directly on the Byzantines' doorstep was tempting to Pope Nicholas the Great (822-867). He offered Boris guidance in both religious and governmental policies and sent a mission from Rome to take over the stewardship of the Bulgarian church. The Greek priests were replaced by Latin-speaking clerics whose language and manners were completely alien to the Bulgars. Moreover, the pope refused to grant any measure of autonomy to the Bulgarian Christians.

CZARS OF BULGARIA, 852-1018

Reign	*Czar*
852-889	BORIS I
865	Boris converts to Christianity
889-893	Vladimir
893-927	Simeon I the Great
927-969	Peter I
969-972	Boris II
971	Bulgaria conquered by John I Tzimisces
1018	Basil II annexes Bulgaria to Macedonia

As a result, Boris initiated a rapprochement with the Byzantines, a move abetted by the coincidental deaths of Pope Nicholas and Emperor Michael in late 867. Two years later, the Orthodox patriarch Ignatius consecrated an autonomous archbishop for Bulgaria, the candidate handpicked by Boris.

Bulgaria's adoption of the Orthodox rite, if not a foregone conclusion, was always the most likely outcome. Physical proximity alone assured the Byzantines a predominant influence. Boris was also attracted to the caesaropapist doctrine of state over church, whereas Rome insisted on submission to the pope in all affairs.

Boris, however, had no intention of turning his domain into a cultural satellite of Byzantium. In 881, he briefly played host to Saint Methodius (c. 825-884), one of the original Orthodox apostles to the Slavs. Four years later, Boris gave permanent refuge to Methodius's followers, who had been driven from Moravia by Latin persecution. These men brought with them the Slavic Cyrillic alphabet, which freed the Bulgars from their dependence on Greek as a written and liturgical language. As a result, Bulgaria soon became the center of a flourishing Slavonic Christian culture. Boris had succeeded in using Christianization and Slavicization as means to unify his realm. His six children (by his Christian wife) were all given Slavic or biblical names. Boris himself largely abandoned the title khan in favor of the Slavic *kniaz* (prince) or Greek *arkhon* (sovereign).

Nearly sixty years old and in declining health, Boris surrendered the throne in 889 and retired to the monastery of St. Panteleimon at Preslav. He was succeeded by his eldest son Vladimir, who showed no intention of following in his father's footsteps. Vladimir attempted to revive the pagan cults and actively courted the support of the old boyar hierarchy. The situation grew so chaotic that in 893 the aged Boris was forced to intervene against his son; Vladimir was quickly overthrown and blinded. Boris, however, did not resume the throne, but elevated his remaining son Simeon, a monk. Boris returned to the monastery, but until his death in 907, he remained Simeon's closest adviser. Soon after his death, Boris was canonized by the Bulgarian church.

SIGNIFICANCE

Boris I inherited an embattled pagan kingdom, ruled by tribal custom and devoid of a unified or literate culture. During his reign of almost forty years, he transformed his domain into a powerful and respected Christian state under a strong central monarchy and made it the center of a vital Slavic culture.

Like many other successful ruler-reformers, Boris was both a visionary and an opportunist. His conversion to Christianity, for example, was an act of both sincere piety and practical political necessity. He openly embraced much of the style and organization of the Byzantine Empire, yet carefully avoided becoming a mere imitator or puppet. Boris was patient and, when necessary ruthless in the pursuit of his goals. His effort to establish an autonomous Bulgarian church took almost twenty years, and his goal was finally achieved without alienating or unduly provoking the powerful Byzantine Empire.

Boris's changes laid the foundation for the first Bulgarian Empire, which would endure for another hundred years. More important, however, Boris created the foundations of a unique Bulgarian culture and nation that would later survive centuries of foreign domination and reemerge as an independent state in the late nineteenth century.

—*Richard B. Spence*

FURTHER READING

Anastasoff, Christ. *The Bulgarians, from Their Arrival in the Balkans to Modern Times: Thirteen Centuries of History.* Hicksville, N.Y.: Exposition Press, 1977. A useful general survey of Bulgarian history with a good chapter on the early medieval period. Particularly useful for putting Boris's reign into perspective with later Bulgarian history.

Crampton, R. J. *A Concise History of Bulgaria.* New York: Cambridge University Press, 1997. Contains a brief but useful treatment of Boris in the chapter on medieval Bulgaria, as well as an extensive bibliography.

Fine, John V. A., Jr. *The Early Medieval Balkans: A Critical Survey from the Sixth to the Late Twelfth Century.* Ann Arbor: University of Michigan Press, 1983. Contains a concise but informative discussion of Boris's reign. Overall, a good description of the character and conditions of the Balkans in this formative period.

Hussey, J. M., ed. *The Cambridge Medieval History.* Vol. 4. London: Cambridge University Press, 1966-1967. Vol. 4 of this standard reference work concentrates on the Byzantine Empire, but it does contain an excellent chapter on the early Bulgarian state and Boris's reign.

Lang, David Marshall. *The Bulgarians: From Pagan Times to the Ottoman Conquest.* Boulder, Colo.: Westview Press, 1976. This readable survey of medieval Bulgarian history offers a generous treatment of Boris and his time. Contains numerous illustrations, plates, maps, and an excellent bibliography.

Obolensky, Dmitri. *The Byzantine Commonwealth: Eastern Europe, 500-1453.* London: Weidenfeld and Nicolson, 1971. Chapters 2 and 3 contain an objective and informative discussion of Boris, the early Bulgarian state, and Bulgar-Byzantine relations.

Runciman, Steven. *A History of the First Bulgarian Empire.* London: G. Bell and Sons, 1930. Still probably the best work on Boris and early medieval Bulgaria. Its style and its bibliography are dated, but the critical analysis of contemporary and modern sources is excellent. Also contains several useful appendices.

Tzvetkov, Plamen S. *A History of the Balkans: A Regional Overview from a Bulgarian Perspective.* 2 vols. Lewiston, N.Y.: E. Mellen Press, 1993. One of the most comprehensive histories of Bulgaria available in English, this set includes significant treatment of medieval Bulgaria and Boris's rule.

SEE ALSO: Árpád; Saint Cyril and Saint Methodius; Saint Irene; Saint Ludmilla; Nicholas the Great.

RELATED ARTICLES in *Great Events from History: The Middle Ages, 477-1453*: c. 850: Development of the Slavic Alphabet; 864: Boris Converts to Christianity; 893: Beginning of Bulgaria's Golden Age; 1054: Beginning of the Rome-Constantinople Schism.

HENRY DE BRACTON

English jurist and legal scholar

Bracton was the author of a comprehensive account of the common law of England as it had developed to the middle of the thirteenth century. His book was extremely influential throughout the medieval period and was consulted by legal authorities through the sixteenth and seventeenth centuries.

BORN: Early thirteenth century; Devon or Somerset, England

DIED: 1268; probably Exeter, Devon, England

ALSO KNOWN AS: Henry de Bratton; Henry de Bretton

AREAS OF ACHIEVEMENT: Historiography, law, literature

EARLY LIFE

Nothing is known of the early years of Henry de Bracton. He probably was born during the reign of King John (r. 1199-1216), and on circumstantial grounds, his birth and upbringing have been linked with the village of Bratton Clovelly, with Bratton Fleming in Devon, or with Bratton Court in Somerset. Tradition has long associated him with Oxford University, although like a number of English men of learning of the thirteenth century, he may also have studied at Paris or Bologna, the latter already celebrated as a center for the study of Roman law, with which, as is clear from his writings, Bracton was well acquainted.

At Oxford, Bracton would have taken courses to qualify first for the baccalaureate and then for a master of arts degree, and although his subsequent career was to be that of a judge, his formal education and his social status were those of a cleric. Furthermore, his employment by the Crown was paid for with income derived from clerical patronage. He was, for example, a canon of Wells cathedral from 1247 or 1249 until his death in 1268. Toward the end of his life, he enjoyed quite lucrative ecclesiastical preferment. He held a prebendary stall at Exeter (that is, he was in receipt of a stipend as a canon of the cathedral there) and another at Bosham (now West Sussex), both in the gift of the bishop of Exeter. In 1263, Bracton was named archdeacon of Barnstable in Devon, resigning after a few months in order to assume, in 1264, the chancellorship of Exeter cathedral. Because his successor in that position was inducted in September, 1268, it is likely that Bracton died some time before that event. His connection with Exeter and the patronage provided by its bishop indirectly confirms the tradition that his family roots were in the West Country.

LIFE'S WORK

Bracton's adult life was spent in the service of Henry III, primarily as a judge. Typical of the bureaucratic character of Angevin government during the thirteenth century, Bracton's career was that of a royal "clerk," well educated in the ecclesiastical learning of the age, who was recruited to the king's service to be employed thereafter in affairs of state and, in particular, in the increasingly busy world of the royal courts of justice. This was important and exacting work, and it could be well rewarded, offering opportunities for substantial advancement for able men, including persons of relatively obscure social background.

Little is known of the details of Bracton's career. He apparently joined the royal service in 1239, and he may have owed his early advancement, at least in part, to the patronage of the king's brother, Richard, earl of Cornwall, later king of the Romans, from whom, in 1242-1243, he held a knight's fee (land held on condition of homage and service) in Alverdiscott in Devon. At the outset of his career, Bracton's earliest judicial patron was William Raleigh, an eminent judge who in 1239 became bishop of Norwich and in 1242 bishop of Winchester. The seventeenth century antiquary Sir William Dugdale stated that in 1245 Bracton acted as an itinerant justice of assize for Nottinghamshire and Derbyshire. For 1246, he served as a member of a judicial commission sent to Northumberland, Westmoreland, Cumberland, and Lancaster. He is also named in the records of Waltham Abbey for that same year, together with two other justices known to belong to the curia (the king's court), strongly implying that Bracton also belonged. There are further references to him as an itinerant justice for the western counties between 1260 and 1267. It may be assumed, therefore, that during at least the middle decades of the thirteenth century, he was fully occupied on judicial business, either in court at Westminster or as a traveling justice of assize. There is a late tradition that he became chief justice of the realm, but no mention of this appears in the contemporary records. Presumably, his posthumous reputation as a great authority on the law accounts for this supposition.

Bracton's fame and his unique place in the history of the common law are almost exclusively attributable to his authorship of the treatise *De legibus et consuetudinibus Angliae* (c. 1235; *Bracton on the Laws and Customs of England*, 1968). Much discussion has centered on when he completed this enormous undertaking, but the widely accepted date is 1259. Bracton's was certainly not the first attempt to contain within a single work the ever-expanding corpus of royal enactments and judge-made case law. Bracton's book had a famous predecessor, *Tractatus de legibus et consuetudinibus regni Angliae* (c. 1188; treatise on the laws and customs of the kingdom of England), attributed to Henry II's justiciar, Ranulf de Glanville.

Glanville's work, however, was inevitably superseded by Bracton's larger and more comprehensive compendium, which was both a practical handbook for judges and also an attempt to provide a coherent, systematic account of the way in which the common law had taken shape. This most formidable undertaking required of its author not only very extensive practical experience of the day-to-day workings of the courts, which he undoubtedly possessed, but also a lucidity of mind and an intellectual breadth of understanding capable of reducing to a meaningful synthesis what had hitherto been an inchoate mass of custom (*ius*), law that existed since time immemorial, and law (*lex*), meaning royal enactments (the statutes and ordinances of later times) and the decisions of the king's justices.

In undertaking this task, Bracton can be seen as typical of the thirteenth century, an age of encyclopedic scholarship, of which the most characteristic monuments of intellectual endeavor are the theological summae of Thomas Aquinas, Saint Albertus Magnus, and John Duns Scotus. Bracton's achievement gains in perspective if placed beside the *Sachsenspiegel* (c. 1220; the mirror of Saxon law) of Eike von Repgow, the *Liber Augustalis* of the emperor Frederick II, Philippe de Beaumanoir's *Coutumes de Beauvaisis* (c. 1280-1283; *The Coutumes de Beauvaisis of Phillipe de Beaumanoir*, 1992), and other thirteenth century legal compilations. Since Gratian's *Concordia discordantium canonum* (c. 1140; harmony of contradictory laws; also known as *Decretum Gratiani*, Gratian's decree), the Decretalists had been shaping the canon law into an elaborate and sophisticated code to meet the growing needs of the Church. Parallel with this development, there had been a vigorous revival of Roman law, emanating from Bologna, where it had been studied since the time of Irnerius, and it had come into its own during the late twelfth century under the patronage of the German Hohenstaufen emperors. It was natural, therefore, that a very learned judge of a philosophical turn of mind at the English king's court would wish to go beyond the immediate demands of utility in order to provide the common law, which had grown up insulated from both the Roman and canon law traditions, with a firm intellectual framework.

The nineteenth century legal historian Sir Henry Maine argued that Bracton had attempted to force the common law into the conceptual framework of Roman law. Denying this, scholar F. W. Maitland maintained that Bracton simply sought to apply to it Roman law concepts in order to provide coherence. At the same time, Maitland felt that Bracton had drawn on analogies from Roman law without properly comprehending the latter system. Modern-day scholar Hermann Kantorowicz has put the case that Bracton's writings reveal that he possessed a genuinely broad legal culture. *Bracton on the Laws and Customs of England* shows that Bracton was thoroughly familiar with the code, the institutes and the digest of Justinian's jurists, with Gratian, and with leading contemporary works such as the two summae on the code and the *Institutes* of Azo of Bologna (1150-1230), the *Glossa Ordinaria* (the great gloss) on the digest of Fransiscus Accursius (1220-1250), and probably the writings of the Dominican canonist Raymond of Peñafort. He was also widely read in the nonlegal literary learning of the age.

It has frequently been remarked that Bracton's comments on English kingship are ambiguous and contradictory. Bracton was no political theorist, but he was emphatic that no authority existed on earth superior to that of the English king. At the same time, he held that the king was answerable not only to God but also to the law, a position that has provoked considerable discussion on the part of his commentators. Scholar Charles H. McIlwain, however, paid Bracton the ultimate compliment when he wrote that as regards "the true character of the general principles underlying the medieval English constitution there is no indication so clear as the book on the laws and customs of England by Henry of Bratton, or Bracton—the greatest of medieval books on English law and constitutionalism, if not on the law of any European nation."

SIGNIFICANCE

Bracton codified the common law so well that virtually every subsequent attempt to give coherence to the apparent formlessness of English law has turned back to him as a first point of reference, at least until the close of the seventeenth century. Thus, within a half century of his death, the anonymous authors of the two legal treatises known as "Fleta" and "Britton" were based on his book, as was the compendium produced by Gilbert Thornton (chief justice of King's Bench, 1290-1295). It is significant that forty manuscripts of his bulky work have survived from before the invention of printing. None of these is complete, but the publication of the first printed version, which was complete, by Richard Tottell in 1569 ensured the availability of Bracton's work for later generations of legal scholars in the age of Sir Edward Coke, John Selden, and Sir Matthew Hale. More than Glanville, more than Henry II even, Bracton was the true father of the common law of England.

—*Gavin R. G. Hambly*

FURTHER READING

Bracton, Henry de. *Bracton on the Laws and Customs of England.* Translated by Samuel E. Thorne. 4 vols. Cambridge, Mass.: Harvard University Press, 1968. The definitive English translation.

Kantorowicz, Hermann. *Bractonian Problems.* Glasgow: Jackson and Son, 1941. Provides an important scholarly discussion and reevaluation of earlier research.

McIlwain, Charles Howard. *Constitutionalism: Ancient and Modern.* 2d ed. Ithaca, N.Y.: Cornell University Press, 1947. Contains a brilliant review of Bracton's contribution to the development of constitutional thought.

Maitland, F. W., ed. *Bracton's Note Book: A Collection of Cases Decided in the King's Court During the Reign of Henry the Third.* 3 vols. 1887. Reprint. Buffalo, N.Y.: W. S. Hein, 1999. An important source for the study of Bracton.

________. *Select Passages from the Works of Bracton and Azo.* London: B. Quaritch, 1895. Useful for a comparative approach.

Plucknett, T. F. T. *Early English Legal Literature.* New York: Cambridge University Press, 1958. Bracton in the setting of his times by a distinguished historian of medieval legal history.

Richardson, H. G. *Bracton: The Problem of His Text.* London: Selden Society, 1965. An illuminating overview of the subject by a leading constitutional historian.

Schulz, Fritz. "Bracton on Kingship." *English Historical Review* 60 (1945): 136-176. In this and a number of other articles, the author has made a major contribution to Bractonian studies.

Thorne, S. E. "Henry de Bracton, 1268-1968" and "The Text of Bracton's *De Legibus Angliae.*" In *Essays in English Legal History.* Ronceverte, W.Va.: Hambledon Press, 1985. Explores Bracton's life and work.

Turner, Ralph V. *The English Judiciary in the Age of Glanvill and Bracton, c. 1176-1230.* Holmes Beach, Fla.: Gaunt, 2001. Looks at the history of the English judiciary system in Bracton's time.

SEE ALSO: Saint Albertus Magnus; John Duns Scotus; Frederick II; Henry III; Raymond of Peñafort; Thomas Aquinas.

RELATED ARTICLE in *Great Events from History: The Middle Ages, 477-1453*: c. 1200: Common-Law Tradition Emerges in England.

BRAHMAGUPTA
Indian mathematician

Brahmagupta wrote Brahmasphuṭasiddhānta, *a book in verse expounding a complex system of astronomy and containing two chapters on arithmetic, algebra, and geometry. His work on indeterminate equations and the introduction of negative numbers greatly influenced the development of science in both India and Arabia.*

BORN: c. 598; Bhillamala, Rajputana (now Bhinmal, India)
DIED: c. 660; possibly Ujjain, Kingdom of Magadha (now in India)
AREAS OF ACHIEVEMENT: Mathematics, astronomy, science and technology

EARLY LIFE

The Hindu astronomer and mathematician Brahmagupta (brah-mah-GEWP-tah) was born to a man named Jishnugupta from the town of Bhillamala. The suffix *-gupta* may indicate that the family belonged to the Vaiśya caste (composed mostly of farmers and merchants).

In contrast to his predecessor, Āryabhaṭa the Elder (c. 476-c. 550), who lived in relative obscurity at Kusumapura (modern-day Patna, Bihar), Brahmagupta had the opportunity to live, study, and teach in Ujjain, a town in the state of Gwalior, Central India. Ujjain was then the center of Hindu mathematics and astronomy and had the best observatory in India. At Ujjain, Brahmagupta also had access to the writings of many great scientists who came before him, including Hero of Alexandria (fl. 62-late first century C.E.), Ptolemy (c. 100-178 C.E.), Diophantus (fl. c. 250 C.E.), and Āryabhaṭa the Elder. Brahmagupta later drew heavily on these sources in his own writings, often correcting their errors. For example, he corrected Āryabhaṭa's mistake regarding the formulas for the surface areas and volumes of the pyramid and cone. Brahmagupta even borrowed mathematical problems, including one calling for the calculation of the position of a break in a bamboo pole. This problem had first appeared in the Chinese text *Jiuzhang shuanshu* (c. 50 B.C.E.-100 C.E.; arithmetic in nine sections), the authorship and date of which are uncertain.

Another influence of Ujjain was on Brahmagupta's style of writing. Like other Hindu scientists, including Āryabhaṭa, he wrote his mathematical texts as poetry. The Indian practice was to clothe all arithmetical problems, especially those in schoolbooks, in poetic garb, fashioning them into puzzles that served as a popular amusement. Brahmagupta wrote that his mathematical problems were undertaken only for pleasure and that a wise man could invent a thousand more or solve those presented by others, thereby eclipsing their brilliance, just as the sun eclipses the other stars in the sky.

At Ujjain, the thirty-year-old Brahmagupta completed his masterwork, the *Brahmasphuṭasiddhānta* (c. 628; the improved astronomical system of Brahma). The date of this work has been determined by consulting both commentary from later Hindu scholars and, appropriately, astronomical data.

LIFE'S WORK

The first ten chapters of Brahmagupta's *Brahmasphuṭasiddhānta* deal with various astronomical issues, including the mean and true longitudes of the planets, diurnal motion, lunar and solar eclipses, heliacal risings and settings, the lunar crescent and "shadow," conjunctions of the planets, and their conjunctions with the stars. The following thirteen chapters take up an examination of previous work on astronomy (including Āryabhaṭa's), additions and problems (and their solutions) supplementing six of the earlier chapters, mathematics, the gnomon, meters, the sphere, instruments, and measurements. The work's twenty-fourth and final chapter summarizes the principles of Brahmagupta's astronomical system in a compendious treatise on astronomical spheres. (Some manuscripts include an additional chapter containing tables.) All but two of the chapters deal with astronomy, but scholars have chosen those two chapters, 12 and 18, which deal with algebra and mathematics, to study most intensely.

Although Brahmagupta studied mathematics only for its applicability to astronomy and considered knowledge of the rules of arithmetic a prerequisite to be a *ganaca* (a student of astronomy), most scholars in the ages since he lived have studied his mathematics more closely than his astronomy. Of particular interest is his work on indeterminate equations, building on the work of both Diophantus and Āryabhaṭa. Brahmagupta's work, along with that of Bhāskara II (1114-c. 1185), solved the so-called Pell equation, $y^2 = ax^2 + 1$, where a is a nonsquare integer. Brahmagupta showed that from one solution where x, y, and xy do not equal zero, a general formula indicating an infinite number of solutions could be derived. Brahmagupta also stated that the equation $y^2 = ax^2 - 1$ could not be solved with integral values of x and y unless a was equal to the sum of the squares of any two integers. Brahmagupta's work on these equations, with additions by Bhāskara, is highly regarded because it was not for several centuries that another mathematician, namely Joseph-Louis Lagrange (1736-1813), could completely work out the Pell equation.

Brahmagupta also studied indeterminate equations of the first order, such as this one: Two ascetics live on top of a hill of h units of height, whose base is mh units away from a nearby town. One ascetic descends the hill and walks directly to the town. The other, being a wizard, flies straight up a certain distance, x, then proceeds in a straight line toward the town. If the distance traveled by each ascetic is the same, and h is 12 and mh is 48, find x. The solution comes from the formula $x = mh/(m + 2)$, or in this case, $x = 8$.

Brahmagupta's work on the geometry of quadrilaterals, which was probably inspired by his studies of Ptolemy and Hero, is also a landmark in the history of Hindu mathematics. Brahmagupta found the formulas, for the first time, for the diagonals (defined as m and n) of a quadrilateral having sides of length a, b, c, and d and opposite angles of A and B, and C and D. He calculated the diagonals thus:

$$m^2 = (ab + cd)(ac + bd)/(ad + bc) \text{ and}$$
$$n^2 = (ac + bd)(ad + bc)/(ab + cd).$$

These formulas were later studied by Bhāskara, who, failing to understand that they applied only to quadrilaterals inscribed in a circle, incorrectly pronounced them unsound. Brahmagupta also figured that, if a, b, c, A, B, and C are positive integers such that $a^2 + b^2 = c^2$ and $A^2 + B^2 = C^2$, then the cyclic quadrilateral having consecutive sides aC, cB, bC, and cA (which came to be called a Brahmagupta trapezium) has rational area and diagonals, and the diagonals are perpendicular to each other. These formulas are most remarkable; nothing like them had previously appeared in Hindu geometry.

Brahmagupta borrowed from Hero of Alexandria the formula for the triangular area, but he brilliantly extended Hero's formula to work with quadrilaterals that can be inscribed within circles. This idea was later built on by the ninth century Hindu mathematician Mahāvīra and was much admired by later commentators. Brahmagupta's other advances in mathematics included proving the Pythagorean theory of the right triangle, deriving formulas for the areas of a square and a triangle inscribed in a circle, and showing that a rectangle whose sides were the radius and semiperimeter of a circle had the same area as that circle.

Although he is now remembered mostly for his advances in mathematics and his influence on the mathematical work of later Hindus such as Mahāvīra and Bhāskara, Brahmagupta considered himself primarily an astronomer. Almost every Hindu commentator on astronomy discusses his work. Indeed, some of his work in astronomy is quite admirable. He provided fairly accurate figures for the circumference of Earth and the length of the calendar year. Brahmagupta gives a figure different from Āryabhaṭa's for the circumference of Earth: 5,000 *yojanas*. Assuming that Brahmagupta's *yojana* was a short league of about 4.5 miles, that would convert his figure to 22,500 miles, which is not too far off the mark. He also tried to correct Āryabhaṭa's computation for the length of the year, which was 365 days, 15 *ghati*, 31 *pala*, and 15 *vipala*, or 365 days, 6 hours, 12 minutes, and 30 seconds. His own figure was slightly more accurate: 365 days, 15 *ghati*, 30 *pala*, 22 *vipala*, and 30 *pratipala* (365 days, 6 hours, 12 minutes, and 9.0 seconds).

Much of his astronomy, however, is quite erroneous. Like many Hindu scientists of the time, Brahmagupta was vehemently opposed to Āryabhaṭa's ideas that Earth revolved around the Sun and spun on its axis. Why then, Brahmagupta asked, do not the lofty bodies fall down to Earth? He also questioned Āryabhaṭa's theory of an aerial fluid that causes Earth to rotate.

SIGNIFICANCE

Although Brahmagupta greatly extended the work of many preceding mathematicians and presented numerous valid theories of his own, it must be acknowledged that he did make some serious scientific errors. In addition to denying Āryabhaṭa's theories of the place of Earth in the solar system, he gave a faulty formula for the area of an equilateral triangle. In his studies on the circle, he alternately used 3 and the square root of 10 as values for π.

Yet Brahmagupta's importance as a scientist must have been recognized during his lifetime, because he was accused of propagating scientific falsehoods to please the priests and the ignorant commonfolk. The priests were particularly opposed to the ideas that Earth was round and that it rotated around the Sun. Perhaps Brahmagupta had lied to avoid the fate of Socrates (c. 470-399 B.C.E.).

Despite these accusations, at least two of Brahmagupta's algebraic formulations, although originally devised for use in astronomy, became widely used by Hindu traders. Of particular practical use was his rule of three, in which the Argument, the Fruit, and the Requisition are the names of the terms. The first and last terms have to be similar. The Requisition multiplied by the Fruit and divided by the Argument yielded the Produce.

Brahmagupta also introduced the use of negative numbers, which he used to unify three of Diophantus's quadratic equations under a general equation. These negative numbers were especially useful to merchants in representing debts, along with positive numbers, which represented assets. Another advance in mathematics that the merchants must have found helpful was Brahmagupta's work on interest rates.

By 700, Hindu merchants had introduced Brahmagupta's mathematics to the Arabs, with whom they carried on a high volume of trade. In 772, a table of sines from Brahmagupta—which, incidentally, was probably based on work by Āryabhaṭa—reached the ʿAbbāsid caliph al-Manṣūr, and it was ordered to be translated into Arabic. The entirety of the *Brahmasphuṭasiddhānta* was translated into Arabic by 775, around the time works by other Greek and Hindu mathematicians were being translated by Arab scholars. Together, these works would greatly influence the nascent Arabic mathematics, with Brahmagupta's greatest contributions coming in the study of negative numbers and indeterminate equations.

—*Frank Wu*

FURTHER READING

Ball, W. W. Rouse. *A Short Account of the History of Mathematics*. 4th ed. London: Macmillan, 1908. A thorough overview of the history of mathematics, with a section on Brahmagupta and his work on quadratic equations, right triangles, and algebra, plus scattered information on his later influence on Hindu and Arab mathematicians.

Cajori, Florian. *A History of Mathematics*. 5th ed. Providence, R.I.: AMS Chelsea, 2000. Gives the solution to Brahmagupta's broken bamboo problem, plus formulas for Brahmagupta's work on triangles and quadrilaterals.

Eves, Howard. *An Introduction to the History of Mathematics*. 6th ed. Philadelphia: Saunders College, 1990. Includes information on Brahmagupta's studies on indeterminate equations, the Pell equation, cyclic quadrilaterals, and the rule of three, along with a discussion of his place in the history of mathematics. Some problems (with solutions) based on his formula for the cyclic quadrilateral are included.

Joseph, George Gheverghese. *The Crest of the Peacock: The Non-European Roots of Mathematics*. Rev. ed. Princeton, N.J.: Princeton Unversity Press, 2000. Joseph examines the history of mathematics in cultures throughout the world, including India. Its wide coverage places India within the greater scope of mathematical development. Bibliography and indexes.

Lakshmikantham, V., and S. Leela. *The Origin of Mathematics*. Lanham, Md.: University Press of America, 2000. Lakshmikantham argues that the importance of the early Indian mathematicians has been underestimated. Bibliography and index.

Prakash, Satya. *A Critical Study of Brahmagupta and His Works*. New Delhi, India: Indian Institute of Astronomical and Sanskrit Research, 1968. A comprehensive study of Brahmagupta, his works, his sources, and the influence of his work on later writers. Contains an extensive bibliography.

Puttaswamy, T. K. "The Mathematical Accomplishment of Ancient Indian Mathematicians." In *Mathematics Across Cultures: The History of Non-Western Mathematics*, edited by Helaine Selin. Boston: Kluwer Academic, 2000. Examines the early Indian mathematicians and their importance.

SEE ALSO: Āryabhaṭa the Elder.

RELATED ARTICLES in *Great Events from History: The Middle Ages, 477-1453*: 595-665: Invention of Decimals and Negative Numbers; c. 1100: Arabic Numerals Are Introduced into Europe.

SAINT BRIGIT

Irish abbess

Brigit founded the first Christian religious community of women in Ireland at Kildare—which became the most important religious center in Ireland—and was a leader in the Irish church.

BORN: c. 450; Faughart, near Dundalk, County Louth, Ireland
DIED: February 1, 525; Kildare, Ireland
ALSO KNOWN AS: Brigid; Bridget; Bride
AREAS OF ACHIEVEMENT: Religion and theology, monasticism, literature

EARLY LIFE

Brigit was named after the chief Celtic goddess Brid (or Brig), the goddess of fire and wisdom, who was also the patron of song and poetry, the flames of knowledge. Unlike the biographies of some other saints, the biographical data on her life is inferior. What is known comes from the tradition found in hymns and poetry. Saint Ultán's hymn from the seventh century devoted to Brigit is perhaps the oldest hymn in the Irish language. The oldest life of Brigit was composed in Irish and in meter by Saint Broccan, who died in 650. A Latin verse version was composed between 650 and 690 by a Kildare monk and Brigit's biographer, Cogitosus (*Vita prima sanctae Brigitae*; *On the Life of St. Brigit*, 1878). This is the earliest extant life of any Irish saint and possibly the first written, but it consists principally of a collection of pre-Christian folktales dealing with the marvels of the goddess Brid retold in a Christian context. Subsequent lives of Brigit are attributed to Saint Ultán, Saint Aileran, and the monk Coelan.

Most of the history of Brigit's life must be drawn from these miracle stories, many of which mirror the miracles of Jesus, albeit with an Irish touch. She is said to have healed lepers, restored sight to the blind, and helped to speak those who previously could not. The religious kernel of the stories, however, is Brigit's faith and trust in God and her tremendous compassion for and care of the needy. The miracle stories also are replete with accounts of wonder-working associated both with animal and human fertility. These legends could have been incorporated to embellish the life of Brigit or to transform Brigit into a Christian replacement for Brid. In *Cormac's Glossary* (ninth century; *Sanas Chormaic*; 1868), Brigit is transformed into a pre-Christian Celtic goddess. She is identified as the daughter of Dagda, the "good god," and referred to as the goddess of poetry. Also, according to *Cormac's Glossary*, Brigit's sisters were the goddesses of smithing and healing, two activities ascribed to the patronage of Saint Brigit by the Christian tradition. The imagery of sun and fire in early Brigitine sources leads some to assert a connection with traditions of a goddess of sun or fire. However, sun and fire have an important role in Christian symbolism.

Though the stories of Brigit are partly made of Irish legend, she certainly existed as a person. The church at Kildare was for centuries an important episcopal center under female governance, under her leadership and, later, her influence.

Even though there are discrepancies in the early accounts of Brigit's life, several seventh century sources claim that her mother, Brocca, was a Christian slave in the court of her father, Dubthach, a chieftain of Leinster. A late eighth or early ninth century life of Brigit in both Irish and Latin, which Oliver Davies called "The Irish Life of Brigit," asserts that Brigit was raised in the house of a Druid and through her piety and miracles not only freed her mother from slavery but also affected the conversion of the Druid. Brigit, according to "The Irish Life of Brigit" and in accord with aspects of the saga tradition of pre-Christian Ireland, was brought by her father to Dúnlang in Leinster to be sold as a slave to the king because Brigit had angered her stepmother by giving too much to the poor. While her father was meeting with the king, Brigit gave his prized sword to a leper. When her father took her to task for giving away the sword, Brigit responded, "Even if I had the power to give the whole of Leinster, I would give it to God." When the enslaved Brigit was miraculously restored to her father, the king of Leinster affirmed "Truly, Dubthach, this girl can neither be sold nor bought." After returning to her father's house, Brigit, according to "The Irish Life of Brigit," rejected a suitor but told him where to find a suitable replacement and bestowed on him the gift of blarney to enable him to win her heart. When Brigit's brothers, anxious to obtain a dowry, insisted that she marry, she defaced herself. Her father then relented and consented to her taking the veil as a consecrated virgin and dedicating her life to the Lord.

LIFE'S WORK

Brigit took the veil from Saint Mac Caille, a disciple of Saint Mel of Armagh, either at Uisnech, a place with mythological associations as the "navel of Ireland," or at

Croghan (now in County Offaly). She lived with seven other virgins at the foot of Croghan Hill. She took her vows before Saint Mel. Also, "The Irish Life of Brigit" claimed that Mel, "intoxicated by the grace of God," did not realize that he was reading the wrong rite and instead of consecrating Brigit as a virgin "consecrated Brigit with the orders of a bishop." Mel then affirmed, "Only this virgin in the whole of Ireland will hold Episcopal ordination." Cogitosus described Brigit journeying across the plain of Mag Breg "in the manner of a bishop." Nevertheless, when a pagan, who had offered Brigit and her companions hospitality, agreed to be baptized, Brigit said "there is no man in orders with me." It is said that she sent a messenger to Saint Patrick so that a bishop or priest might baptize him. Patrick then told Brigit not to go about without a priest serving as her driver. (This story is meant most likely as an assertion of patriarchy. Patrick, who died in 461, would have been unable to give Brigit this directive.)

Around 468 Brigit and Mel's pupil Mac Caille went with Mel to Teffia in Meath. About two years later she moved to Druin Criadh, in the plains of Magh Liffe, where under a large oak tree, the site of a Druid sanctuary, she built her convent of Cill Dara (church of the oak), now in County Kildare. She extinguished the ritual fire of Brid and kindled a Christian replacement dedicated to Christ, Light of the World. This replacement was faithfully tended until it was extinguished by agents of Henry VIII. Brigit, who had been given the authority of abbess by Mel, founded two monasteries, one for females and another for males. Under the leadership of Brigit, Cill Dara became a religious center and eventually a cathedral city. Cogitosus wrote that the church founded by Brigit was "the head of almost all the churches of Ireland."

Brigit undoubtedly played a unique role in the Irish church. She selected Saint Conleth, a hermit, and called him from his solitary life to serve as bishop of Kildare. Some have asserted that it was she who gave him canonical jurisdiction. Cogitosus unambiguously stated that Brigit selected Conleth "to govern the Church along with herself." He wrote that they "established their chief church in felicitous and mutual cooperation." Her actions and authority established the precedent for the church in Kildare to be led jointly by the abbot-bishop and abbess. Because of Brigit's prestige among the Irish, the abbess of Kildare was regarded as the superior of all religious houses for females in Ireland. The abbess of Kildare also exercised jurisdiction over the monasteries in the southwest of Ireland until the suppression of the monasteries by the English after the Reformation.

Brigit made Kildare a center of scholarship and a school of art that produced both ironwork and remarkable illuminated manuscripts. The most famous of these was the *Book of Kildare* (sixth century; English translation, 1911). In the twelfth century Giraldus Cambrensis praised the book as incomparable. Unfortunately, the book disappeared following the Reformation.

Brigit died at Kildare on February 1, 525. Saint Ninnidh gave her the last sacraments and was thereafter known as Ninnidh of the Clean Hand, because he reputedly had his right hand encased in metal after he had used it to anoint the dying Brigit. Brigit was buried on the right side of the high altar of the cathedral in Kildare, and her tomb became a popular pilgrimage site. Around 878, because of Viking raids, Brigit's remains were moved to Downpatrick in County Down in the north of Ireland, where they were placed, as legend tells it, with the remains of Saint Patrick and Saint Columcille. In 1185, the relics of Brigit, Patrick, and Columcille were solemnly entombed in Downpatrick cathedral.

SIGNIFICANCE

Through the school she founded at Kildare, Brigit contributed to the preservation of literate culture in Europe following the collapse of the Roman Empire. Because of Brigit's powerful personality and the role she played in the founding of Kildare, her successors as abbesses at Kildare continued to play a significant role in the church in Ireland. Brigit, whose recognition for sanctity preceded her death, was venerated from her death as a saint and became with Saint Patrick and Saint Columcille one of the three most important saints of Ireland. The ninth century *Book of Armagh* (*Liber Ardmachanus*; 1913) considered Brigit and Patrick "the columns of Ireland." The veneration of Saint Brigit became an integral part of the social and cultural life of Ireland. Her feast day, February 1, occurs at the time of the ancient Irish festival *imbolc*, a fertility festival, fertility being intimately connected with her veneration. Many rituals and articles of folk art, such as the *brideog*, a figurine of Brigit, are associated with the arrival of spring in the Irish countryside.

—*Bernard A. Cook*

FURTHER READING

Catháin, Séamas Ó. *The Festival of Brigit: Celtic Goddess and Holy Woman*. Dublin: DBA, 1995. Discusses Saint Brigit's Day and Brigit as a Celtic deity.

Curtayne, Alice. *St. Brigid of Ireland*. New York: Sheed and Ward, 1954. A traditional saint's life that does a very good job of placing Brigit in the context of the Ireland of her day.

Davis, Oliver, trans. *Celtic Spirituality.* New York: Paulist Press, 1999. A very useful sourcebook with a good historical introduction. Includes chapters on the tradition of Brigit and the power of women within Celtic spirituality.

De Paor, Liam. *Saint Patrick's World: The Christian Culture of Ireland's Apostolic Age.* Notre Dame, Ind.: University of Notre Dame Press, 1993. Contains a translation of Cogitosus's *On the Life of St. Brigit* and an informative chapter, "Women Founders of Churches."

Sharpe, Richard. *Medieval Irish Saints' Lives: An Introduction to Vitae Sanctorum Hiberniae.* New York: Oxford University Press, 1991. Connects Brigit's life to traditions of earlier pre-Christian Irish mythology.

Staunton, Michael. *The Story of Christian Ireland: From St. Patrick to the Peace Process.* Dublin: Emerald Press, 2001. Discusses Ireland before Christianity and the lives of Brigit and other saints.

SEE ALSO: Christina of Markyate; Hildegard von Bingen; Joan of Arc; Julian of Norwich; Mechthild von Magdeburg; Saint Patrick.

RELATED ARTICLES in *Great Events from History: The Middle Ages, 477-1453*: 1136: Hildegard von Bingen Becomes Abbess; c. 1380: Compilation of the Wise Sayings of Lal Ded.

ROBERT BRUCE

King of Scotland (r. 1306-1329)

Bruce led Scotland to victory in the struggle for independence from English control. He consolidated Scottish political autonomy and secured English recognition of Scotland as an independent nation in the Treaty of Northampton, signed by King Edward III in 1328.

BORN: July 11, 1274; Turnberry Castle, Carrick, Ayrshire, Scotland

DIED: June 7, 1329; Cardross, Dumbartonshire, Scotland

ALSO KNOWN AS: Robert the Bruce; Robert I; Robert VIII de Bruce

AREAS OF ACHIEVEMENT: Diplomacy, government and politics, military

EARLY LIFE

Robert Bruce's roots lay six generations deep in the western lowlands of Scotland, but the Brus (or Bruys) originated among the Norsemen, who settled in Normandy and went to England with William the Conqueror in 1066. They moved to Yorkshire in the north of England, where the first of the Bruces acquired great estates and was an important royal agent under King Henry I. His son, also Robert Bruce, was a close friend of David I, king of Scotland, who made him lord of Annandale, where the Bruces remained permanently. Annan was the main western gateway into Scotland through the wild, boggy country of the western lowlands. The Bruces built two castles, Annan and Lochmaben, to guard the way.

To understand the Scotland of Robert Bruce (later known as King Robert I), one must have some knowledge of the feudal system that formed the basis for the legal system and for political relationships in the Middle Ages. In the later Middle Ages, nationalism was just beginning to come into conflict with feudalism as an important historical force. The tension between these two concepts is seen in the life of Bruce.

Feudal lords were like provincial kings who controlled and administered their hereditary lands under a system of mutual obligation. They held their land grant, or fief, under the authority of their king and owed to him military service, counsel, and political loyalty. The lords governed their manors and administered their fiefs in the name of their king, who was dependent on the services and payments of feudal dues by their vassals. Thus a system of mutual obligation developed. An extension of the system was the manorial system, whereby serfs were allowed to work the land and graze their livestock on the lords' fiefs in exchange for payment in kind and civil obedience. In Scotland, where the system merged with the ancient clan tradition, military service as foot soldiers was also required of the peasants or cotters.

This political, economic, and legal system often crossed national lines. For example, at one time the English king held half of France in fief. The British Isles were particularly interrelated, and many Scots lords married the daughters and heiresses of English barons and earls. Family and feudal relationships prompted a stronger sense of loyalty than did ties of nationalism. There was a certain competition as well as cooperation among the nobility, many of whom had ties to royal families. Robert Bruce, for example, was a direct descendant of King David I.

Bruce was born in 1274 at Turnberry Castle, heir to the earldom of Carrick and to the lordship of Annandale. Little is known of his childhood, but it may be surmised that his education and upbringing were typical for children of his social standing and position in medieval Scotland. He had to be trained in courtly manners and in the complexities and diplomacy of the feudal system. He was exposed to the arts, literature, and law, and he learned basic theological beliefs and the subtleties of the relationship of the Church to the political system and social structure. Like other sons of noble birth, Robert grew up bilingual in French and Gaelic. If he spoke fourteenth century English, it was as an acquired language, as was his Latin. He also had to manage his estates and needed training in administration and business management, but for his life's work he particularly needed military training. Bruce was physically strong and was a formidable foe in hand-to-hand knightly combat, as later battles demonstrated. He learned the details of medieval combat and developed into a brilliant strategist and tactician. He was a born leader and inspired courage and discipline in his men. He was exceptionally persistent and had that sense of perspective that great leaders possess.

Robert Bruce. (Library of Congress)

LIFE'S WORK

On March 18, 1286, Alexander III, king of Scotland, left from Edinburgh Castle to return to his new young wife at his royal manor across the Firth of Forth. It was midnight. The distance was twenty miles over bad roads and a two-mile ferry crossing over choppy waters. It had been snowing and was bitterly cold. Escorted by only three men, the king slipped in the winter storm and was found dead on the shore the next morning. Only forty-four years of age at his death, Alexander had outlived his first wife, Margaret of England, their two sons, and his daughter, the queen of Norway (also known as "the maid of Norway"). His three-year-old granddaughter was now legitimately Margaret, queen of Scots.

The king's council appointed a commission of regency with three guardians for the north of Scotland and three for the south. The great-uncle of the child queen was Edward I, king of England, who sought to arrange a marriage between Queen Margaret and his own son, Prince Edward. The kingdoms of England and Scotland would then be united by marriage. Margaret, however, died at the age of seven, and Scotland was left without a ruler.

The two principal claimants to the throne were John de Baliol, lord of Galloway, and Robert Bruce (grandfather of the future king). To avoid civil war between the two factions, Edward I was called in as a neutral arbitrator to help decide which had the superior claim. He was the brother-in-law of Alexander III and the great-uncle of Queen Margaret. England and Scotland had close relations, and many of both Scottish and English nobility held fiefs in both nations. King Edward was the logical choice to help solve the dispute, but the Scots had not counted on Edward's ambition to annex Scotland as part of his empire: The king had signed the Treaty of Birgham (1290) recognizing the integrity of Scotland as a separate kingdom.

Despite the fact that Bruce had a stronger claim to the throne (including a declaration to that effect by Alexander II), Edward declared in favor of Baliol, presumably because he would be more compliant than the Bruces. At the same time, Edward took many steps to exert his alleged feudal superiority over Scotland. On November 19, 1292, the kingdom of Scotland was formally conveyed to the new King John as a vassal of Edward. The Bruces, in order to avoid civil war, decided not to contest.

In 1295, Edward prepared for war against France and ordered John de Baliol, king of Scots, to join him in London with his Scottish forces to invade France. John refused and joined in an alliance with France instead. Edward responded by seizing all English estates held by Scots nobles who remained in Scotland. John reciprocated, and both kingdoms prepared for war.

Superior English forces defeated the Scots at Dunbar in 1296, and Edward declared himself lord of Scotland and appointed the earl of Surrey as guardian of his kingdom there. The Scottish nobility rallied around William Wallace, one of the guardians of Scotland, who defeated the English at Stirling Bridge in 1297 and parried several English invasions from 1297 to 1304. Finally, in 1305, the English captured and executed Wallace.

At that critical stage of Scottish history Bruce, grandson of the original claimant to the throne, decided to take the leadership in the Scottish War for Independence. In doing so, he took a historically decisive step away from feudalism in favor of nationalism. Through incredible adversity, Bruce clung tenaciously to the goal of freedom for his country, and his perseverance ultimately triumphed. He had the immediate and loyal support of his subjects on his estates, reflecting his generosity as a feudal lord as well as Scots patriotism. The Scottish nobility took sides, some on the side of English suzerainty, others with King Robert I, for so was Bruce crowned in 1306. Indeed, the king was not free to fight the English until he had defeated his Scottish opposition, including the rival Comyn family, one of whom he killed in a violent personal confrontation.

It was of great significance that the battle for Scottish independence from England was fought and won in the ecclesiastical and theological sphere before it was won on the battlefield. The common folk sided with their king largely because their patriotic Scottish bishops did and were persuasive in their justification for so doing. Bishop Wishart of Glasgow provided the robes for the king to wear at his coronation and brought out of hiding the forbidden flag of the lion with the scarlet lilies of the king of Scots. Imprisonment by the English did not dissuade the clergy. King Edward retaliated by appointing Englishmen to the higher posts in the Scots church. In 1310, Scottish bishops issued this manifesto:

> By the providence of the Supreme King under whose government kings rule and princes bear sway, we have with divine sanction agreed on the said Lord Robert, and with the concurrence and consent of the people he was chosen to be king; and with him the faithful people of the kingdom will live and die as with one who is worthy of the name of king and the honour of the kingdom, since, by the grace of the Saviour, he has by the sword restored the realm thus deformed and ruined.

Manifestos, though, do not win wars. Though the Scots had the advantage of fighting in their home country with shorter logistical lines, the greatest advantages by far were with the English, who outnumbered the Scots five to one. Their military leadership was outstanding, including that of the king himself. Moreover, their weapons, especially the longbow, were superior. English cavalry was formidable, heavier, and much more numerous. Funding for military campaigns was much easier for the English.

When Bruce was crowned king in 1306, Scotland was, in effect, a conquered country. His position was desperate and dangerous. Yet in an incredible eight years Scotland was to regain its freedom under Bruce's leadership. Bruce was joined by most of the church leaders, 135 landed gentry with their armed men, and many patriotic volunteers.

King Edward ordered that all those taken with military arms and all who sheltered Scottish fighting men were to be hanged or beheaded. He petitioned the exiled pope in Avignon, France, Clement V, to excommunicate Bruce, which he did. The archbishop of Canterbury followed the pope's directive, but the Scots clergy were not much impressed.

The English surprised and defeated the Scots, many of whom were executed or imprisoned. King Robert and his small band hid out in the Grampian mountains. Their wives were outlawed with them by Edward, and they, too, took to the field. In a sharp skirmish, three Scottish brothers attacked the mounted king alone, but Bruce managed to kill all three of them. Seeking a stronghold for his wife and child, Bruce parted from them and did not see them again for eight years, years of fighting during which Bruce struggled to keep the independence movement alive. The English won many small victories, but the Scots often retaliated in force, not to win territory but to demonstrate that the guerrilla movement was still alive. Meanwhile, Bruce's force was increasing.

On June 7, 1307, King Edward I died on the English border. He had fought to conquer Scotland for eleven years, yet the resistance was very much alive. His death proved to be a turning point in Scottish history, for his son was not nearly the aggressive commander in chief that his father had been. Sporadic uprisings against Edward II occurred in many parts of his realm. Internal dissension in England made the Scottish war all the more difficult for him. He decided to return to England for a while and went as far south as York.

The English king was no sooner out of the country than the Scottish king launched a counteroffensive against northern England, partly for booty and partly to demoralize the English. They burned and looted towns and monasteries and captured prominent citizens to hold them for ransom, which was readily paid. Northern English shires agreed to pay indemnities to King Robert to persuade him to return to Scotland, which he did, some twenty thousand pounds richer.

The Scots captured English garrisons in southern Scotland and held national parliament at Ayr, demonstrating their independent status. The only stronghold north of the Firth of Forth still in English hands was Perth, some 50 miles (80 kilometers) north of Edinburgh on the Firth of Tay. For six weeks, the Scots laid siege to the walled town, with its deep moat and huge stores of provisions. Without artillery, it could not be taken by assault. The king himself went scouting during the long, dark nights around Christmas to find a weakness in the defenses. In the freezing weather, he personally took soundings of the moat until he found a place scarcely 5 feet (1.5 meters) deep.

At the beginning of the New Year 1313, Bruce ordered the siege raised and the garrison watched from the walls as the besiegers packed their gear and prepared to leave. However, they did not leave. Unseen by the English, the Scots made scaling ladders and, choosing a dark night, crept silently to the moat where the king had located the shallowest spot. Bruce was first across, with a ladder in one hand and his lance in the other sounding his way. Scores of Scots scaled the walls and attacked the garrison. Few people on either side were killed, and there was no unnecessary slaughter when the commander surrendered. The Scots razed the walls of Perth and filled the moat with debris.

One Scottish success followed another, including the conquests of Edinburgh Castle and of Dumfries. Edward II prepared for a showdown battle. The place was Bannockburn, and the time was June 23 and 24, 1314. The English amassed a force of more than twenty thousand soldiers with twenty-five hundred heavy cavalry against seven thousand Scots and five hundred light cavalry. Despite the enormous disparity in numbers, the Scots had two vital advantages: First, they had a volunteer force dedicated to their cause, well drilled and well disciplined (in spite of the traditional individualism of Scottish culture); second, Bruce had the opportunity and the intelligence to choose a superb position for the type of fighting that had to be conducted. Bannockburn flowed through an S-shaped gorge that was 18 meters (60 feet) high, and both cavalry and infantry could cross only in a narrow formation. With the battle actually under way the English could not use their superior numbers and force but were confined to fighting an equal number of Scots at any single time.

The English, too, were overconfident. The Scots had spent the night in prayer before the battle. Early the next morning, when Edward, in his shining armor and jeweled weaponry, saw them across the way, he commented, "They kneel." "Aye, Sir King," answered one of his aides, "but to God. Not to us."

The courage and leadership of Robert Bruce had always been significant throughout the war. No better example was that demonstrated at Bannockburn. In the reconnaissance and maneuvering before the battle, a brave English knight,

KINGS OF SCOTLAND, C. 858-1371

Reign	*Ruler*
c. 858	Kenneth I breaks with England
1005-1034	Malcolm II: Lothian added
1034-1040	Duncan I: Strathclyde added
1040-1057	Macbeth
1057-1058	Lulach
1058-1093	Malcolm III Canmore
1093-1094	Donaldbane
1094	Duncan II
1094-1097	Donaldbane (second rule)
1097-1107	Edgar
1107-1124	Alexander I
1124-1153	DAVID I
1153-1165	Malcolm IV
1165-1214	William I the Lion
1214-1249	Alexander II
1249-1286	Alexander III
1286-1290	Margaret
1290-1292	Interregnum
1292-1296	John Baliol
1296-1306	Interregnum
1306-1329	ROBERT I THE BRUCE
1314	Robert the Bruce defeats England
1329-1371	DAVID II
1371	Ascendancy of Robert II, House of Stuart

Henry de Bohun, and his men came on King Robert and his small staff observing and positioning their men. For the moment the king had ridden forward to watch the English movements and was alone. The knight saw an opportunity to rid the English of their nemesis in one bold stroke. He unslung his lance and charged. The king had no lance, but only a light ax, and he was mounted only on a small, gray, sure-footed pony. Coolly he held his ground and watched the huge horse and knight in full armor bear down on him at full speed. Just short of the impact, Bruce quickly moved his pony to sidestep the charging steed and with perfect timing stood in his stirrups as De Bohun thundered past and split his helmet and skull in one awful blow, breaking the ax shaft.

The Scots went on to win that most famous of battles by immobilizing the English within their own lines so that effective use could not be made of either archers or cavalry. English losses were great, Scottish casualties few. The English retreated back into England, and prisoner exchanges freed most Scots still held by the English.

The war was won, but not over. It dragged on listlessly for another fourteen years. In order to persuade the English crown to denounce its alleged suzerainty over any part of Scotland, King Robert spasmodically raided and blackmailed northern England. He even began to grant lands to his supporters in Northumbria. This pressure finally had its desired effect, and in 1328 the Treaty of Northampton was concluded in Scotland in formal recognition of Scottish sovereignty and ratified by Edward III at the parliament of Northampton.

That same year, the king's son, David Bruce, age four (who became King David II in 1329), and Edward's sister, Joanna, age six, were married to cement the friendship of the two kingdoms. It was only one year later that Bruce died, just short of his fifty-fifth year, content to see the accomplishment of his life's work, the independence of Scotland.

SIGNIFICANCE

As important to Scotland as that independence was, Robert Bruce's influence continues much beyond that time and place. In a remarkable document sent to Pope John, known as the Declaration of Arboath (1320), the king, with the help of the lords of the realm, sketched the history of the constitutional struggle in Scotland and explained the basis in political philosophy of their determination to be free and independent. The Second and Third Estates acknowledged in an accompanying letter their support of the Declaration. Referring to Bruce, the Declaration states:

> The Providence of God, the right of succession by the laws and customs of the kingdom (which we will defend till death), and the due and lawful consent and assent of all the people, made him our king and prince. . . . But after all, if this prince shall leave these principles he hath so nobly pursued, and consent that we or our kingdom be subjected to the king or people of England, we will immediately endeavour to expel him as our enemy, and as the subverter both of his own and our rights, and will make another king who will defend our liberties. For so long as only a hundred of us stand, we will never yield to the dominion of England. We fight not for glory nor for wealth nor honour, but for that freedom which no good man surrenders but with his life.

Surely this document needs to share the honored place of the Magna Carta, the English bill of rights, and the U.S. and Dutch declarations of independence. "Liberty of conscience" is not an empty phrase when one is called on to defend that principle with one's life. Freedom in the world today is based on the concept of limited government guaranteed by a constitution giving both the powers and limitations of each part of the government. In fourteenth century Scotland, that meant that the king must rule by consent, first of the leaders of society, then followed by the consent of the common person. In Scotland the term "community of the realm" described the consent of the governed, and all subjects were considered to participate in the national debate over public policy.

In spite of political turmoils and wars, Scotland maintained its free and independent status until after the death of Queen Elizabeth in 1603, when King James VI of Scotland became also King James I of England and began the Stuart Dynasty in English history. It is ironic how many rulers of England have been of Scottish descent. The Scots participated in the English civil war of the 1640's and the Glorious Revolution of 1688. Under Queen Anne, the Act of Union (1707) took effect, voluntarily merging the two kingdoms into one Great Britain. Tension between north and south still exists, and Scottish national identity and liberty of conscience are very strong even today.

—*William H. Burnside*

FURTHER READING

Barrow, G. W. S. *Kingship and Unity: Scotland, 1000-1306*. Toronto: University of Toronto Press, 1981. A valuable discussion of life under the feudal system at the time of Bruce, and an explanation of the concept of the "communities of the realm."

_______. *Robert Bruce and the Community of the Realm*

of Scotland. Berkeley: University of California Press, 1965. Discusses the community of the realm concept from Bruce's perspective and looks at the Scottish struggle for independence.

Duffy, Seán, ed. *Robert the Bruce's Irish Wars: The Invasions of Ireland, 1306-1329*. Charleston, S.C.: Tempus, 2002. A historical overview of the military invasions of Ireland during Bruce's reign. Includes maps.

Fry, Michael. *The Scottish Empire*. East Lothian, Scotland: Tuckwell Press, 2001. A history of Scottish imperialism, including its struggles for independence.

Grant, Alexander. *Independence and Nationhood: Scotland, 1306-1469*. London: Edward Arnold, 1984. A clear, concise interpretation of the relationships between Bruce and Edward I of England and John de Baliol of Scotland. Places Bruce in the sociopolitical context of his time.

MacKay, James A. *Robert Bruce: King of Scots*. London: Robert Hale, 1974. Excellent account of the political and diplomatic situation in Scotland at the time of Bruce. Analyzes Bruce's motivations, personality, and character, and the events leading to his leadership in securing Scottish independence.

Mackenzie, Agnes Mure. *Robert Bruce King of Scots*. 1934. Reprint. Freeport, N.Y.: Books for Libraries Press, 1970. A detailed account of the Scottish war for independence, including analysis of the site of the Battle of Bannockburn. Recognizes the underlying importance of political philosophy in the life of Bruce.

Mitchison, Rosalind. *A History of Scotland*. London: Methuen, 1982. A brief survey of and a good introduction to Scottish history. Places the Scottish independence movement in the broader context of several centuries of Scottish history.

Roberts, John L. *Lost Kingdoms: Celtic Scotland and the Middle Ages*. Edinburgh, Scotland: Edinburgh University Press, 1997. A history of Scotland from the eleventh to the seventeenth century, including a chapter on Bruce and Scottish independence.

Stephens, Peter John. *Outlaw King: The Story of Robert the Bruce*. New York: Atheneum, 1964. Lively, intriguing account written especially for the young reader. Clearly explains complicated political and diplomatic events.

SEE ALSO: David I; David II; Edward I; Edward II; Philippa of Hainaut; William Wallace.

RELATED ARTICLE in *Great Events from History: The Middle Ages, 477-1453*: June 23-24, 1314: Battle of Bannockburn.

FILIPPO BRUNELLESCHI

Italian sculptor and architect

Brunelleschi's architectural accomplishments, as well as his dedication to the principles of perspective, established a vigorous new classical Renaissance style that influenced building design for centuries.

BORN: 1377; Florence (now in Italy)
DIED: April 15, 1446; Florence
ALSO KNOWN AS: Filippo Brunellesco
AREAS OF ACHIEVEMENT: Architecture, art, engineering, science and technology

EARLY LIFE

Filippo Brunelleschi (fuh-LEE-poh brew-nayl-LAYS-kee) was born the second of three sons of Ser Brunellesco di Lippi and Giuliana degli Spini, the daughter of an established Florentine banking family. His father was a notary and middle-level public official frequently employed in various capacities by the republican government. Young Filippo thus grew up in a household heavily involved in the complex politics of Tuscany's leading city. His elder brother, Tommaso, became a goldsmith and died in 1431, and his younger brother, Giovanni, entered the priesthood and died in 1422.

As a child, Brunelleschi received the traditional education of boys of his class. Although his father may have wished him to follow him in a notary career, young Filippo early exhibited a penchant for art and mechanics. The elder Brunelleschi consequently apprenticed his second son to the Silk Guild for training as a goldsmith. His training there included a study of literature and the abacus as well as rigorous mathematical instruction. In 1398, Brunelleschi applied for registration as a goldsmith with the Silk Guild and was admitted as a full master six years later.

Even before this last event, the young artist had established a reputation for himself as one of the most promising figures in the Florentine artistic community. In the early 1400's, he made several silver figures for the altar of the cathedral in Pistoia. Two busts of prophets and two full-length figures of saints survive from this endeavor.

One of the turning points in Brunelleschi's early career concerned his participation in the 1401 competition sponsored by the Signory and Guild of Merchants for the commission to do a series of relief sculptures for the north doors of the Florence cathedral baptistery. Brunelleschi was one of the two finalists, but in 1402, the judges selected a panel submitted by his fellow goldsmith Lorenzo Ghiberti as the winner. Brunelleschi's competition panels on the theme of the sacrifice of Isaac have been preserved in the National Museum of Florence. Brunelleschi's defeat in the competition had important consequences for his future. Virtually the rest of Ghiberti's long career was consumed by the task of the north doors and a subsequent set for the eastern entry. Brunelleschi found himself free for other endeavors, and he increasingly became more interested in architecture in preference to sculpture.

LIFE'S WORK

Although he was active in many artistic and engineering projects, Brunelleschi's main contribution during the last four decades of his life was in the field of architectural inventiveness. He most probably left Florence shortly after his 1402 defeat and spent several years in Rome with his fellow Florentine, the sculptor Donatello. In Rome, he studied ancient buildings in minute detail, making careful drawings of classic arches, vaulting, and other architectural features.

The Florence to which he returned in the early 1400's provided a fertile field of opportunities for the energetic and talented young Brunelleschi. The city's wealthy elite had an increasing thirst to commission city palaces, country villas, and burial chapels. Even more important, the civic Humanists dominating the Florentine government were eager to employ painters, sculptors, and architects to make Florence the premier city in Italy. The most important project to the city fathers was the completion of the great cathedral of Santa Maria del Fiore, an undertaking that gave Brunelleschi his most challenging and famous commission.

Begun in 1296 and designed in the traditional Tuscan Gothic style, the cathedral essentially stood finished by the late fourteenth century except for the dilemma of constructing a dome to cover the 140-foot (43-meter) octagonal space created by the crossing at the east end. No previous architect had found a solution to the technical problems and expense entailed in this problem. It remained for Brunelleschi, who had been involved with various facets of the cathedral's construction as early as 1404, to provide the answer.

Marble bust of Filippo Brunelleschi. (Library of Congress)

In 1418, the cathedral's officials announced a competition for a workable design for the dome. Based on his studies of ancient Roman and Byzantine vaulting, Brunelleschi proposed an innovative solution that entailed constructing the cupola without the traditional costly wooden centering or exterior scaffolding. After two years of feasibility studies, the commission finally jointly awarded the prize to Brunelleschi and his rival Ghiberti, but the latter soon largely retired from the project.

Brunelleschi personally invented much of the machinery necessary to erect his revolutionary dome. His eventual plan used a skeleton of twenty-four ribs (eight of them visible from the exterior) that enabled the cupola to be self-supporting as it rose from its base 180 feet (55 meters) from the ground. The ribs soared some 100 feet (30 meters) and converged in an oculus meant to be topped by a lantern tower. To keep the weight of the structure to a minimum, Brunelleschi designed the first double shell in architectural history and placed the brickwork in herringbone patterns on the framework of the stone beams. When completed in 1436, his masterpiece was by no means a mere copy of classical patterns, but a unique and daring creation notable for its visual impressiveness from the outside, unlike such Roman structures as the Pantheon. It became the single most identifiable architectural landmark in the city. In 1436, Brunelleschi won yet another competition, this one for the design of the lantern that anchored the top of his cupola. This lantern was not completed until 1461, fifteen years after his death. He also designed the lateral tribunes that graced the structure.

Despite its overwhelming importance, Brunelleschi's work on the Florentine cathedral was not representative of the main thrust of his architectural style. Much more typical were his plans for the Ospedale degli Innocenti (foundling hospital), a building commissioned by the Silk Guild in 1419. His most important contribution to the project was a graceful portico of rounded arches that extended across the facade. The entire exterior reflected Brunelleschi's dedication to proper geometrical proportions, symmetry, and classical detail.

Classical elements also dominate the two basilican churches that Brunelleschi designed in his native city, San Lorenzo and Santo Spirito. Although neither was completed before his death and each was somewhat modified from his original plans, both reflected his dedication to mathematical proportion and logical design to provide visual and intellectual harmony. Their interiors of Roman rounded arches and pillars became hallmarks of the Renaissance style.

One of the Florentine master's greatest undertakings in church architecture was the Pazzi Chapel, a chapter house for the monks of the cloister of Santa Croce. Although his commission came in 1429, actual work did not begin until 1442 and continued into the 1460's. In this chapel, Brunelleschi again produced an edifice noted for harmonious proportions and clarity of expression, breaking with Gothic mystery and grandeur in favor of restraint and geometrical harmony. The interior, dominated by a dome-covered central space, became a highly influential model for future architects. Brunelleschi employed darkly colored pilasters against lightly colored walls to create a harmonious and peaceful atmosphere notable for its simplicity and classical beauty.

Churches were by no means Brunelleschi's sole architectural preoccupation. Despite the proliferation of palace building in Florence during this time, only one such structure—the Palazzo di Parte Guelfa—was definitely designed by him. His model for a palace for Cosimo de' Medici was rejected as too ostentatious and imposing. Florence and other cities throughout Tuscany frequently employed him as a consultant to design fortifications and bridges and to supervise other public works projects. In 1430, for example, he became involved in an unsuccessful scheme to divert the Arno River in order to turn the city of Lucca into an island.

Brunelleschi did not completely abandon sculpture after his loss in the competition of 1401. His polychrome wood statue of the Virgin for the Church of Santo Spirito perished in a 1471 fire, but several other works have been attributed to him, including the terra-cotta evangelists in the Pazzi Chapel.

A lifelong bachelor, in 1417, Brunelleschi adopted five-year-old Andrea di Lazzaro Cavalcanti, more commonly known as Il Buggiano, as his heir. This foster son became his apprentice in 1419 and eventually collaborated with his mentor on many projects. Brunelleschi continued working actively on his numerous projects until his death on April 15, 1446. In 1447, city officials authorized the interment of his remains in the same cathedral that had played such an important part in his long and productive career.

SIGNIFICANCE

At the time of his death, only a few of Brunelleschi's designs had been completed. Most, such as the great basilicas of San Lorenzo and Santo Spirito and the lantern for his great dome, were finished many years after his death. Nevertheless, during his active career of nearly half a century, Brunelleschi established himself as the premier architect in Florence and the first architect of the new Renaissance style. Unlike his younger contemporary Leon Battista Alberti, he never produced a book about his architectural theory, but his landmark buildings served as textbooks for numerous future architects such as Michelangelo.

With his profound respect for classical values, Brunelleschi personified the self-confident optimism of the early Renaissance Humanists. Much like Leonardo da Vinci later in the century, he was interested in a wide variety of subjects, including hydraulics, watchmaking, and practical mechanics. Sometime between 1410 and 1415, he drew two panels, now lost, which effectively rediscovered the principles of linear perspective. This had a profound impact on painters of the era, such as Brunelleschi's young acquaintance Masaccio. Linear perspective helped revolutionize the style of fifteenth century Italian painting.

It is through his architectural accomplishments, however, that Brunelleschi made his major contribution. He was undoubtedly the pivotal figure in assuring Florentine supremacy in the field throughout the fifteenth century. Works such as his great cathedral dome and the Pazzi Chapel revived admiration for classical styles without resorting to slavish imitation of Greco-Roman forms. Brunelleschi thus created a vibrant, self-confident classical Renaissance style that profoundly influenced architecture for centuries.

—*Tom L. Auffenberg*

FURTHER READING

Battisti, Eugenio. *Filippo Brunelleschi*. London: Phaidon, 2002. A translation and revision from an earlier Italian version, this scholarly study thoroughly examines Brunelleschi's life and career, including such aspects as his military engineering, theatrical machinery, and verse. Illustrated. Contains an index.

Funari, Michele. *Formal Design in Renaissance Architecture: From Brunelleschi to Palladio*. New York: Rizzoli, 1995. This study of Renaissance architecture examines the works of Brunelleschi, among others. Illustrations, map, and indexes.

King, Ross. *Brunelleschi's Dome: How a Renaissance Genius Reinvented Architecture*. New York: Walker, 2000. King focuses on Brunelleschi's construction of the dome of the cathedral of Santa Maria del Fiore. Illustrations and index.

Klotz, Heinrich. *Filippo Brunelleschi: The Early Works and the Medieval Tradition*. London: Academy Editions, 1990. Klotz examines Brunelleschi's early architectural works, determining how they fit in with the Renaissance and Medieval traditions. Illustrations and index.

Saalman, Howard. *Filippo Brunelleschi: The Buildings*. London: Zwemmer, 1993. This work, part of the Studies in Architecture series, examines the architectural works of Brunelleschi. Illustrations, bibliography, and index.

Walker, Paul Robert. *The Feud That Sparked the Renaissance: How Brunelleschi and Ghiberti Changed the Art World*. New York: William Morrow, 2002. Walker examines the interactions of Brunelleschi and Ghiberti, including their competitions. Illustrated with eight pages of plates. Bibliography and index.

SEE ALSO: Arnolfo di Cambio; Donatello; Lorenzo Ghiberti; Giotto; Masaccio; Andrea Orcagna; Andrea Pisano; Nicola Pisano and Giovanni Pisano.

RELATED ARTICLE in *Great Events from History: The Middle Ages, 477-1453*: c. 1410-1440: Florentine School of Art Emerges.

LEONARDO BRUNI

Italian scholar and writer

Bruni was a leading Italian Renaissance figure, a Humanist scholar whose work was important in the development of historiography.

BORN: c. 1370; Arezzo, Republic of Florence (now in Italy)
DIED: March 9, 1444; Florence
ALSO KNOWN AS: Leonardo Bruno; Leonardo Aretino
AREAS OF ACHIEVEMENT: Historiography, literature, government and politics

EARLY LIFE

Leonardo Bruni (BREW-nee) was the son of Cecco Bruni, a small grain dealer in Arezzo. As a result of civil war, Bruni and his father were imprisoned in 1384, with the young Bruni held apart from his father in a castle room on the wall of which was a portrait of Petrarch. Bruni would later write that his daily viewing of the painting of this famous Italian poet and Humanist inspired him with an eagerness for Humanist studies. The years following the war and his imprisonment were difficult for Bruni. His father died in 1386, his mother in 1388; family resources declined sharply.

In spite of the family hardship, Bruni moved to Florence, perhaps to live with relatives, and began his studies. From 1393 to 1397, he studied law in Florence and came to the attention of the medieval scholar Lino Coluccio Salutati. In 1396, another scholar, Manuel Chrysoloras, moved to Florence and did much to broaden Bruni's career and education. In 1397, Bruni shifted to the study of Greek, in which Chrysoloras educated and then inspired him to complete a series of translations of several classical literary items from ancient times, many of which had been overlooked for centuries. These included works by Xenophon, Saint Basil, Procopius, Polybius, Demosthenes, Plutarch, Thucydides, and Aristotle. Before he was thirty-five, Bruni's achievement in this work led to his stature among contemporaries as the leading authority on the subject of ancient literature.

Life's Work

As a result of his recognition as a literary figure and because of his proficiency in Latin and Greek, Bruni received an appointment in 1405 as a secretary to Pope Innocent VII. Except for a brief period in 1410 and 1411, he would spend ten years with the papal court in Rome. In 1411, when he was forty-one years of age, he married. Although little is known about his wife or her family, it is known that she brought to the marriage a dowry that reflects a family of wealth and status. Bruni also became a close acquaintance of Baldassarre Cossa, who became Pope John XXIII during the schism of the Papacy until the famous deposition in 1415 at the Council of Constance (1414-1418). As a result of the loss of power by his patron, Bruni returned to Florence, where he settled into an active life in historical study and writing, Florentine politics, and personal investments.

It was as a historian that Leonardo Bruni became a great Renaissance scholar. Through translations, dialogues, biographies, commentaries, and his monumental *Historiae Florentini populi* (*History of the Florentine People*, 2001), Bruni changed historical writing and thought so significantly that he was referred to as the "father of history" for at least two centuries after his death. Numerous Italian historians were influenced by his methods and style, and his impact extended into other disciplines. Although there is no complete chronology of Bruni's historical works, the list is impressive. It begins with his *Laudatio Florentinae urbis* (in praise of the city of Florence) and the *Dialoghi ad Petrum Paulum historum* (dialogues dedicated to Pier Paolo Vergerio), both produced between 1401 and 1405.

Laudatio Florentinae urbis is an attempt to present a thorough view of the Florence city-state in its geographic and historical perspectives, a total view of the city. The work is based, in part, on the model of Aristides' eulogy of Athens in ancient Greece. Bruni sought to explain how Florentine institutions and politics evolved from the Italian past, in itself a new historical method. It was also in this work that Bruni's civic Humanism emerged. He expressed the view that the health of the state must ever be based on the educated and ethical sense of the citizenry, factors that, in his view, had contributed much to the glory and fame of Florence. *Dialoghi ad Petrum Paulum historum* was a combination of two dialogues that served as reproductions of conversations between scholars from two Florentine generations. Here Florence is presented as the preserver of the best features of Republican Rome and classical Greece. Together the two works are credited with marking the beginning of a new Humanism, a new civic sentiment, and a new view of the past.

Bruni's greatest work was his *History of the Florentine People*, the first and, as some would argue, the greatest achievement of Renaissance historical writing. Bruni intended this work to be a complete history of Florence to 1404 in order to explain the greatness of this Italian city-state. He concluded that the civic virtue of its citizens and the republican form of its government were key explanations for its greatness. In his view, Florence was the shining example of what people living in political freedom could accomplish. The setting for much of his history was the conflict between Florence and Milan. Although some scholars have criticized Bruni's continued use of the rhetorical methods of Greek and Roman historians and his heavy emphasis on the symbols of the classical age, the work served as a model for historians for many years. Bruni's research was in response to clearly articulated questions and in pursuit of relevant causal relationships. He became more than a chronicler and instructed those who followed him that history must be true, utilitarian, documented, instructive, readable, thematic, respectful of the past, viewed in epochs or eras, and focused on those matters that human beings can control, specifically politics. Finally, *History of the Florentine People* is important for the significant narrative techniques it introduced.

There are other writings for which Bruni received recognition. These include his *De militia* (1421; on knighthood), in which he advanced the establishment of the idea of a citizen-army for Florence; his 1427 funeral oration for a Florentine general, Nanni degli Strozzi, who had fought successfully against Milan, thus serving to promote the interests of freedom and humanity; and his *De studiis et litteris* (1421-1424; *Concerning the Study of Literature*, 1897), one of the first treatises to advance a program of education based on the humanities that offers a demonstrated concern for women as well as men. In his later years, he published his memoirs, *Rerum suo tempore gestarum commentarius* (1440-1441; commentary on the history of his own times), a perspective on contemporary history that substantially departed from the work of previous chroniclers.

The success of his literary career led Bruni into a prominent political role in Florence by the middle of the 1420's. He became a member of a number of prominent trade and professional guilds, served as an ambassador to Pope Martin V in 1426, and in 1427 became the chancellor of Florence. In the latter position, he would play a major role in the political and military affairs of the state, an influence he would continue until his death in 1444. Tax records indicate that by 1427, he was one of the wealthiest persons in Florence, possessing a series of farms, houses, and investments. In 1431, his son Donato married into a prominent family and would himself occupy a visible place in the affairs of Florence for many years. Clearly Bruni spent a considerable amount of time promoting his personal political power and personal wealth.

The important role of Bruni in the affairs of Florence is borne out by the elaborate public funeral given on his death in 1444. This proved to be an event of major importance, attended by figures of prominence from a wide area. His funeral oration was given by a leading statesman, and one of the most gifted sculptors of Florence prepared a marble tomb for him. Niccolò Machiavelli, the famous author and statesman of the Italian Renaissance, was buried beside Bruni on his death in 1527.

SIGNIFICANCE

Bruni was one of the outstanding figures of the Italian Renaissance. In the first half of the fifteenth century, he was the leading figure in the development of Humanism, history, and political thought. His translations of ancient Greek texts from Aristotle and Plato made a major contribution to European scholars for centuries. He was clearly the greatest authority on ancient literature for his time. His own biographies, dialogues, histories, and commentaries created a virtual revolution in historical writing and thought. He divided the past in new ways, placed a new emphasis on sources, developed new narrative forms, and established Humanism as a political necessity in the struggles among the Italian city-states. He is the most important example of civic Humanism in the early Renaissance.

—*Frank Nickell*

FURTHER READING

Bruni, Leonardo. *The Humanism of Leonardo Bruni: Selected Texts*. Translated and introduced by Gordon Griffiths, James Hankins, and David Thompson. Binghamton, N.Y.: Medieval and Renaissance Texts and Studies in conjunction with the Renaissance Society of America, 1987. Commentaries on the translations provide valuable information about the author.

Cochrane, Eric. *Historians and Historiography in the Italian Renaissance*. Chicago: University of Chicago Press, 1981. A superb study of the emergence, growth, and decline of Renaissance historiography. Places Bruni in historical perspective. References are made to several hundred historical writings of the period. An outstanding work on an important period in the development of historical writing.

Griffiths, Gordon. *The Justification of Florentine Foreign Policy: Offered by Leonardo Bruni in His Public Letters, 1428-1444*. Rome: Istituto Storico Italiano per il Medio Evo, 1999. Griffiths presents an analysis of Bruni's attitude toward Florentine foreign policy, based on documents from the Florentine and Venetian archives. Bibliography.

Hankins, James. *Repertorium Brunianum: A Critical Guide to the Writings of Leonardo Bruni*. Vol. 1. Rome: Istitute Storico Italiano per il Medio Evo, 1997. In this volume, the first of three, Hankins provides a list of manuscripts by Bruni.

Ianziti, Gary. "Bruni on Writing History." *Renaissance Quarterly* 51 (Summer, 1998): 367. The author examines the evolution of Bruni's writings during the period between 1404 and 1443, in particular the *Cicero novus*, *Commentarii de primo bello punico*, and the *De bello italico*.

Kallendorf, Craig W., ed. *Humanist Educational Treatises*. Cambridge, Mass.: Harvard University Press, 2002. Kallendorf provides a translation and analysis of Bruni's *The Study of Literature*, along with other essays on education by Humanists of the same period. Bibliography and index.

Witt, Ronald G. *In the Footsteps of the Ancients: The Origins of Humanism from Lovato to Bruni*. Boston: Brill, 2000. Contains a chapter on Bruni and his contributions to Humanism. Bibliography and indexes.

SEE ALSO: Petrarch.

RELATED ARTICLES in *Great Events from History: The Middle Ages, 477-1453*: May 20, 1347-October 8, 1354: Cola di Rienzo Leads Popular Uprising in Rome; July 15, 1410: Battle of Tannenberg.

Hubert de Burgh
English justiciar

De Burgh served as justiciar throughout the reign of Henry III and strengthened the power and prestige of the monarchy in the face of baronial faction and opposition.

Born: Late twelfth century; Burgh, Norfolk, England
Died: May 12, 1243; Banstead, Surrey, England
Area of achievement: Government and politics

Early Life

Virtually nothing is known of the early life of Hubert de Burgh (HYEW-burt duh BURG). It is probable that he joined the king's service as a knight of the household during the last years of the reign of King Henry II, thereafter serving both King Richard I and King John. In 1200, de Burgh was a member of an embassy sent to Portugal, and in 1201, he became one of the royal chamberlains. After Arthur of Brittany (King John's nephew) was taken captive by the king in August, 1202, de Burgh, according to one chronicler, was his jailer in the castle of Falaise, a source for some of the most dramatic scenes in William Shakespeare's *King John* (pr. c. 1596-1597). From this time onward, John seems to have regarded de Burgh as one of his most trustworthy servants. During the campaigns that saw the loss of most of John's continental possessions to the French king Philip II, de Burgh was castellan of the great fortress of Chinon on the Loire. From the spring of 1203 until early in 1205, he vigorously resisted the besieging French forces, abandoning his charge only after a final, tremendous onslaught. Even then he continued to fight outside the walls, suffering wounds and then taken prisoner.

During the following decade, de Burgh served John well, and he was well rewarded for his services, receiving grants of several sheriffdoms. By 1214, he had risen to be seneschal (king's steward) of Poitou. During the last stages of the revolt that led to the granting of the Magna Carta in June, 1215, he was constantly with the king. He appears in the preamble to the Great Charter as seneschal of Poitou, and he is said to have been one of the twenty-five barons elected to uphold it. In that same month of June, 1215, de Burgh was appointed justiciar, making him the king's deputy. This office was the highest in the kingdom. The justiciar held court in the king's name, and he issued administrative writs in his own name and on his own initiative, confirming them with his own seal. In his person were combined the supreme administrative, judicial, and financial functions of government beneath the throne.

De Burgh assumed the justiciarship at a time of extreme crisis. Many barons continued in revolt even after the signing of the Great Charter, and in May, 1216, the heir to the French throne, the future Louis VIII, landed in England with an army to support the rebels. John ordered his justiciar to hold Dover Castle, regarded as the gateway to England. There, de Burgh withstood a determined siege from July 22 to October 14, 1216, by which time the tide had begun to turn against the French. John, who was hated by many of his subjects, died on October 18, and on October 28, his nine-year-old son, Henry III, was crowned in Gloucester Abbey. Although lengthy royal minorities usually boded ill for the welfare of a kingdom, the transition of authority in the autumn of 1216 was remarkably smooth. A regency council was established, with William Marshal, earl of Pembroke, at its head, supported by the papal legate, Cardinal Guala, and the archbishop of Canterbury, Stephen Langton. De Burgh was retained as justiciar.

Yet Louis and his French troops were still in the field, and when it was learned that a French fleet was about to bring reinforcements and supplies to the invaders, de Burgh sailed out of Dover to intercept it as it headed north for the mouth of the Thames. Although contemporary accounts of the engagement differ in detail, it appears that de Burgh won a decisive victory and disembarked to a hero's welcome. The defeat of the French fleet left Louis in an impossible situation, and shortly thereafter, the Treaty of Lambeth (September 11, 1217) enabled him to withdraw without loss of face. Two years later, in 1219, William Marshal died, and while the regency council was now dominated by a triumvirate consisting of the justiciar, the new papal legate, Cardinal Pandulf, and the bishop of Winchester, Peter des Roches, for all practical purposes, de Burgh was in control.

Life's Work

At the outset of Henry's reign, the English system of government was perhaps the most elaborate and efficient to be found north of the Alps. Yet the rebellion during the last years of John's reign, the French invasion, and the disorders that inevitably surfaced during a minority together threatened to bring about a collapse in effective control by the center. It was de Burgh's task to restore the authority of the Crown, repair the financial damage, enforce the king's peace, and ensure that when Henry eventually came of age, he would find his patrimony intact.

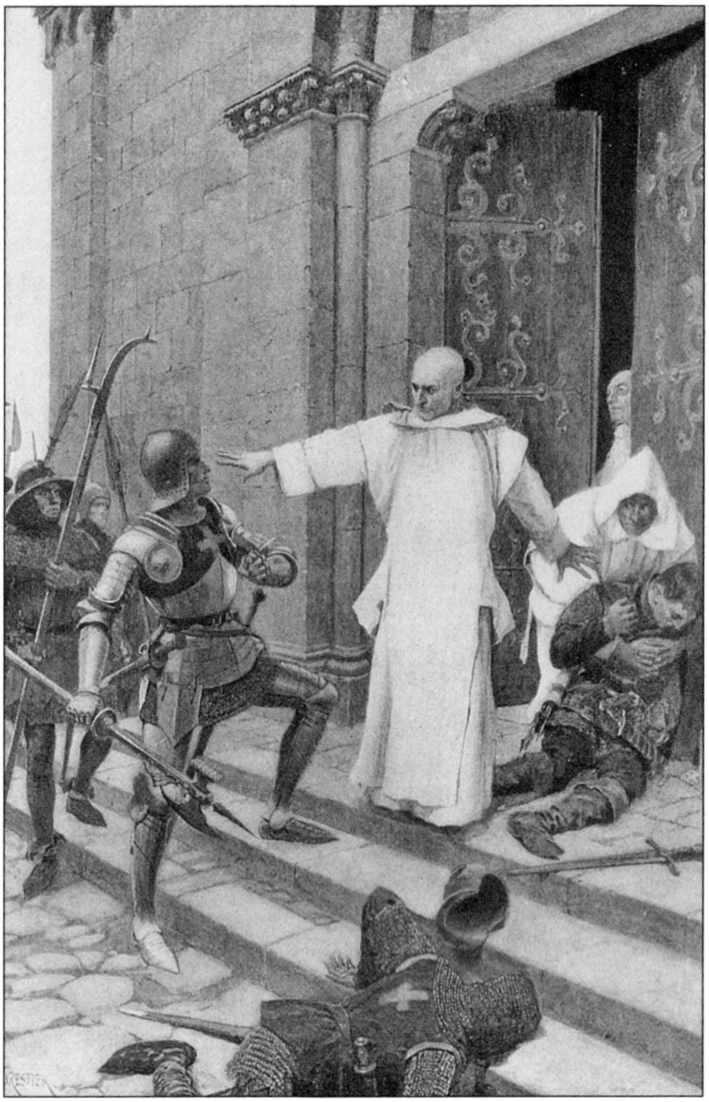

Hubert de Burgh seeks sanctuary to evade an arrest order issued by Henry III. (F. R. Niglutsch)

His immediate problem was the prevailing insubordination of the baronage and their retainers, an inherent characteristic of a rapacious, undisciplined feudal aristocracy no longer subject to the watchful scrutiny of the late king. The problem was exacerbated by long-standing familial and regional rivalries. For the justiciar, a particular bugbear was the presence of John's erstwhile foreign favorites, who had acquired a substantial share of the estates. Those foreigners were bitterly disliked, and de Burgh seems to have deliberately represented himself as the spokesperson for "English" interests. Among the targets of popular resentment, none was more hated than John's old companion at arms, Fawkes de Breauté, although among the aliens, de Burgh's personal enemy was Peter des Roches, a Poitevin, the holder of one of the richest bishoprics in the country, the former confidant of John and now the young king's mentor.

De Burgh's position was an unenviable one. To govern firmly meant repossessing illegally seized Crown lands and disturbing newly acquired interests. In consequence, the justiciar made many enemies. He was sustained by the affection of Henry and the backing of Archbishop Langton, a positive force in the kingdom. On the other hand, de Burgh himself conducted the government harshly and high-handedly and was seen to be greedy and self-serving.

In 1221, de Burgh determined to take over in the king's name those castles and estates that had been illegally acquired by John's former favorites and others during the years of civil war and anarchy. Few were prepared to surrender without a fight. In the council itself, he faced a vociferous and ongoing opposition on behalf of kinsmen and clients, and it was probably to deflect this opposition that he sought and obtained from Pope Honorius III in 1223 permission to proclaim the king, who was a papal ward, competent to govern. Thus the king was able to set the seal of royal authority on the government's resumptions.

Reinforced by Henry's support, de Burgh ruled the country for the next three years as firmly as ever. Despite a display of arrogance that provoked further resentment, he well knew how to ride out the feuds and factional fighting around him and was skilled in demonstrating his ability to assist friends and punish foes. What he failed to apprehend was that the greatest danger to his position lay in the personality of his royal master, capricious and unpredictable by nature yet increasingly eager to exercise authority.

In January, 1227, Henry, now turned twenty, declared himself to be of age. This move was bound to affect the justiciar. It would prove difficult for someone who had been virtual dictator of England for the past decade to relinquish gracefully the substance of power, while the young king was straining at the leash to prove himself. As the king came into his own, the justiciar's enemies found themselves better placed to drive a wedge between the two.

De Burgh had long been not only the most powerful man in England but also one of the richest, arousing envy and bitterness. He had profited enormously from his service to the Crown and had also contrived to benefit from a series of advantageous marriages to conveniently short-lived heiresses. His first wife had been the daughter of the earl of Devon; his second, Beatrice de Warenne, the daughter of William de Warenne; and his third, Isabella, daughter and heiress of the earl of Gloucester, repudiated first wife of King John and widow of the fifth earl of Essex. In 1221, he married his fourth wife, Margaret of Scotland, daughter of William the Lion and sister of Alexander II. He also vigorously pursued the aggrandizement of his kinsmen. His brother, Geoffrey, became bishop of Ely. A nephew became bishop of Norwich. For another nephew, he procured the widow of the sixth earl of Essex, while for another, he sought to win the widow of the earl of Salisbury, supposedly lost at sea, only to be later denounced to the king by the returning earl, who proved to be very much alive. When the latter died in 1226, as with the death of the justiciar's old enemy, Fawkes de Breauté, rumors of poisoning circulated.

In 1228, de Burgh was made earl of Kent. Otherwise, it was a difficult year. His longtime ally Langton died, and de Burgh became embroiled in a dispute between the king and his brother, Richard, earl of Cornwall, the future king of the Romans, thereby earning the latter's enmity. Also, he led an expedition into Wales, which proved a dismal failure. Meanwhile, Henry's French vassals were urging the king to mount an expedition on the Continent to ward off the encroachments of Louis IX's officials. De Burgh cautioned against it, for the treasury was virtually empty, but the king was enthusiastic and resented the justiciar's negative attitude. Eventually, an expeditionary force was assembled at Portsmouth in the autumn of 1229, but the arrangements proved unsatisfactory, and only half the anticipated number of ships were available. The king exploded with rage, blamed de Burgh for the fiasco, and publicly abused him. After a while, the famous Plantagenet rage abated, de Burgh was restored to the king's favor, and in 1230, both went off to Gascony and Poitou, a wasteful and ineffective excursion, as was the raid into Wales that the justiciar led on his return from France.

De Burgh now became embroiled with the Church, allegedly giving support to a violent protest movement against local clerics by lay landowners who felt that advowson (the right to present a nominee to a vacant ecclesiastical benefice in their "possession") was being eroded by the growing papal practice of providing candidates. Furthermore, in 1231, he became involved in a suit with the archbishop of Canterbury, Richard Grant, over the custody of Tonbridge Castle, which was eventually transferred to Rome, where the archbishop had much to say about de Burgh's high-handed administration. The king, always well-disposed toward the Papacy and with the vindictive bishop of Winchester now his favorite counselor, resolved to break with his justiciar. Characteristically, he moved deviously, presumably intending to remove any prior suspicions de Burgh might have, for in June, 1232, the latter was appointed justiciar of Ireland for life. Then, on July 29, 1232, the blow fell. De Burgh was stripped of all his offices, his property was seized, an audit was ordered with regard to all of his financial dealings, going back to his early years in the royal service, and a series of extreme and quite implausible charges were laid against him. Twice he took sanctuary, once at Merton Priory and once at Brentwood, but he was retaken and imprisoned in the Tower of London and, subsequently, in Devizes castle, perhaps escaping judicial murder only through his friends spiriting him away to Chepstow, beyond the Wye.

When the saintly Edmund Rich (canonized in 1248) became archbishop of Canterbury in 1234, he procured the dismissal of Henry's evil counselors on threat of excommunication and brought about a reconciliation with de Burgh, whose outlawry was now reversed, "one of the most impressive vindications of the rule of law in our history," according to the historian T. F. T. Plucknett. De Burgh's properties were restored, and he again took his place in the king's council. In 1239, however, Henry revived many of the charges against his old servant, and although de Burgh was once more acquitted, he was compelled to surrender four of his castles as surety for his future good behavior. These were later restored, following yet another reconciliation with the king.

He died on May 12, 1243, and was buried in the London Church of the Black Friars, to whom he bequeathed his town house beside the Thames adjacent to Westminster. This property was eventually purchased by the archbishop of York and was to become the archiepiscopal residence known as York Place, which on the fall of Thomas Wolsey passed to Henry VIII and became the palace of Whitehall. It is a curious irony that this site should link the careers of de Burgh and Wolsey. Perhaps no two commoners in English history wielded greater power or profited more materially in the service of their respective masters, yet both were ignominiously disgraced and abandoned to the vengeance of their enemies.

SIGNIFICANCE

Hubert de Burgh's remarkable career exemplified the way in which a man of middling rank and no great inherited wealth could, by applying himself in the king's service, acquire the remunerative appointments, the grants of land, and the marriage settlements that would enable him to rise into the highest ranks of feudal society. Yet de Burgh's intense ambition and personal acquisitiveness should not be allowed to obscure the fact that he dedicated his active professional life to upholding and enlarging royal authority, consciously implementing policies that, in retrospect, can be seen to have assisted the emergence of a genuinely national English monarchy. Surviving sources reveal a detailed picture of how that monarchy functioned under de Burgh's direction. The mainsprings of its political life—in particular, the obsessive and seemingly incomprehensible victimization of the fallen statesman by his ungrateful master—are more difficult to understand. Like many medieval figures, de Burgh himself remains unknowable.

—*Gavin R. G. Hambly*

FURTHER READING

Carpenter, David. *The Minority of Henry III.* Berkeley: University of California Press, 1990. An account of Henry's early years as king. Includes bibliography and index.

Duby, Georges. *William Marshal: The Flower of Chivalry.* Translated by Richard Howard. New York: Pantheon Books, 1986. A penetrating study of de Burgh's older contemporary, providing valuable insights into the knightly ethos, both chivalrous and mercenary, of which de Burgh was a part.

Ellis, Clarence. *Hubert de Burgh: A Study in Constancy.* London: Phoenix House, 1952. A biography of the great justiciar.

Plucknett, T. F. T. *Early English Legal Literature.* New York: Cambridge University Press, 1958. English legal history by a distinguished historian of medieval legal history.

Powicke, F. M. *King Henry III and the Lord Edward.* Oxford, England: Clarendon Press, 1966. A detailed study of the Plantagenet king and his son.

_______. *The Thirteenth Century, 1216-1307.* 2d ed. Oxford, England: Clarendon Press, 1962. Provides an excellent scholarly account of the political setting in which de Burgh operated.

Tout, T. F. *Chapters in the Administrative History of Mediaeval England.* 6 vols. 1920. Reprint. New York: Barnes and Noble Books, 1967. Volume 1 provides a good account of the administrative system during the minority of Henry III, as supervised by de Burgh.

Wilkinson, B. *The Constitutional History of Medieval England, 1216-1399.* 3 vols. London: Longmans, 1963. Volume 1 contains an excellent summary of English constitutional history, supported by contemporary documentation.

SEE ALSO: Henry II; Henry III; King John; Louis IX; Richard I.

RELATED ARTICLE in *Great Events from History: The Middle Ages, 477-1453*: June 15, 1215: Signing of the Magna Carta.

JEAN BURIDAN
French philosopher

A distinguished natural philosopher, Buridan wrote critical commentaries on the works of Aristotle, laid the foundations of the modern science of mechanics, and defined objectives and a methodology that separate science from philosophy and theology, making him a major figure in the development of modern science.

BORN: c. 1295; Béthune, France
DIED: c. 1358; Paris, France
ALSO KNOWN AS: Joannes Buridanus (Latin name)
AREAS OF ACHIEVEMENT: Philosophy, physics, science and technology

EARLY LIFE

Jean Buridan (zhahn bew-ree-dahn) received his early education at church schools in the diocese of Arras. His great intellectual gifts were soon manifested, and as a young cleric he studied at the University of Paris. He studied philosophy and was profoundly influenced by Ockhamism. William of Ockham, an English Franciscan, espoused nominalism, a doctrine holding that individuals are the primary reality and that universal concepts have no objective referents but are only mental descriptions for similar features among individuals. Buridan's later writings often reflect Ockham's ideas and methods.

After receiving his master of arts degree around 1320, Buridan became a lecturer in natural, metaphysical, and moral philosophy at the University of Paris. He quickly achieved recognition as a gifted philosopher, but he remained a secular cleric rather than becoming a member of a religious order, and he never sought a degree in theology. Nevertheless, he was willing to introduce theology into physical questions; for example, he argued that God could create a vacuum even though Aristotle posited the vacuum's impossibility. As a teacher and writer, Buridan was not a narrow specialist and he felt free to discuss problems as wide-ranging as the dogmas of the Christian faith and the formation of mountains.

The first documentary mention of Buridan is dated February 2, 1328, and the occasion was his appointment as university rector. The document shows that he was held in high esteem by his colleagues, and records in the Vatican indicate that benefices and honors were conferred on him several times during his successful career as a lecturer and administrator. Around 1330, he traveled south to visit the papal court at Avignon, and en route he climbed Mount Ventoux to make some meteorological observations.

In 1340, he again became rector of the University of Paris, and in that capacity he signed, on December 29, 1340, a statute strongly condemning certain members of the faculty of arts for applying strict logical analysis to scriptural texts without sufficiently considering the holy authors' intentions. Many scholars think that this decree was directed against Nicholas of Autrecourt, a rival Scholastic philosopher whose skeptical views have since garnered for him the name "the medieval Hume." The mild temperament discernible in many of Buridan's writings was set aside when he attacked Nicholas's errors. These condemnations, however, were not anti-Ockhamist, since Ockham's philosophy was firmly based on the principle of natural causation, which is what was impugned by Nicholas. Throughout Buridan's career, he used Ockham's doctrines to defend both natural knowledge and real secondary causes.

LIFE'S WORK

Aristotle's fourth century B.C.E. writings profoundly influenced Europeans in the thirteenth and fourteenth centuries, and Buridan's extant writings consist almost entirely of detailed commentaries on Aristotelian treatises. These writings clearly derived from his lectures at the University of Paris, whose curriculum was largely based on the study of Aristotle's works. For example, Buridan wrote commentaries on *Physica* (335-323 B.C.E.; *Physics*, 1812), *Metaphysica* (335-323 B.C.E.; *Metaphysics*, 1801), *De anima* (335-323 B.C.E.; *On the Soul*, 1812), *Politica* (335-323 B.C.E.; *Politics*, 1598), and *Ethica Nicomachea* (335-323 B.C.E.; *Nichomachean Ethics*, 1797).

Although much of his work evolved from his study of Aristotle, Buridan was not merely an explicator of Aristotelian ideas. On the contrary, he leveled some devastating attacks against this great philosopher, and he used these criticisms to develop his own ideas, which were themselves important advances in scientific and philosophical thought. This approach can be seen in Buridan's works on logic, in which, while commenting on Aristotle, he developed a method now known as logical analysis. He used this method to formulate philosophical problems as questions about the meaning and reference of terms and the truth condition of sentences. In his primer on logic, *Summula de dialectica* (1487; English translation, 2001), as in his other logical works (*Sophismata*, 1488; English translation, 1966; and *Consequentie*, 1493; English translation, 1985), Buridan showed himself to be a follower of *logica moderna* (the new logic), in which Aristotle's logic was reconstructed on new foundations. Buridan achieved this reconstruction through the theory of the supposition of terms. Medieval logicians used the word "term" to designate descriptive signs occupying the subject or predicate positions in propositions. Ockham defined supposition as the "standing for something else" of a term in a proposition. In his opinion, as in Buridan's, what primarily determined the supposition, or referential use, of a subject or predicate term in a proposition was the verb.

Buridan went beyond Ockham by applying the new logic to many problems never before treated. One such problem was the analysis of statements in indirect discourse. Since the terms occurring in the subordinate clauses of sentences in indirect discourse purport to designate what actually is said to be known, the question of what such terms denote boils down to the question of what kinds of entities constitute the object of knowledge. Do these terms stand for really existing individual things or Platonic essences or simply the words themselves?

Buridan's most extensive treatment of this problem is found in *Sophismata*, a work devoted to the analysis of paradoxical statements that appear to be both true and false. The famous "liar" paradox is an example: Is the statement "What I am now saying is false" true or false? According to Aristotelian logic, this statement is true if it is false and false if it is true. Buridan thought that the person who makes that statement and says nothing else really is saying something false, because this sentence has to be considered together with the circumstances of its utterance, and one of these circumstances is that sentences cannot be both true and false. Thus, in this case the sentence and its circumstances make the statement false.

In philosophy, Buridan was a moderate nominalist; he supported the condemnation of both the radical Ockhamism of Nicholas and the extreme Aristotelianism of the followers of Averroës. Among his philosophical discussions, Buridan is best known for his theory of the relationship of will and reason. He proposed that a person must will what is revealed to reason as the greater good but stated that the will is free to delay choice until the reason has more extensively inquired into the values and motives involved. The classic illustration of this analysis is the parable of "Buridan's ass," a story not found in the extant writings. An ass is situated between two equidistant and equivalent bundles of hay. Because the ass has no reason to choose one bale over the other, he would remain in perpetual indecision and starve to death. Later philosophers attacked Buridan's theory of the will. In their view, when reason can find no preference, the will is still capable of decision when it is clear that delay is pointless, stupid, or even dangerous.

Despite his perceptive logical and philosophical analyses, Buridan made his most important contributions in science. Aristotle had defined science as the knowledge of universal and necessary conclusions made by demonstration from necessary though indemonstrable premises. Buridan, on the other hand, sharply distinguished between premises determined logically, through definitions of the terms, and those determined empirically, through inductive generalization from conditional evidence. He therefore rejected the thesis, common among many Scholastic philosophers, that the principles of physics are necessary in the sense that their contradictories are logically impossible. Buridan did not require the same logical rigor from the scientist as from the mathematician. According to him, if scientific truths could be imposed under pain of contradiction, then physical science would be destroyed. Through this analysis he was able to concede the possibility of God's interference with the natural order while still excluding supernatural events as irrelevant to the scientific enterprise.

In his treatment of physics and cosmology, Buridan accepted Aristotle's ideas as a basic framework for natural philosophy, but he also entertained alternative ideas as both logically possible and empirically preferable to explain certain phenomena. His most incisive criticism was directed against Aristotle's account of motion. An obvious weakness of Aristotle's theory was its inability to explain projectile motion satisfactorily. For Aristotle, a thrown object required an external moving cause continuously in contact with it. He theorized that the air, disturbed by the violent motion of throwing the projectile, kept pushing the object forward for a time. Buridan first refuted Aristotle's theory by several empirical arguments; for example, he showed that disturbing the air was not sufficient to move the projectile. He then proposed his theory of impetus as a solution.

Impetus, to Buridan, was a motive force impressed by the thrower on the projectile. He regarded this impressed force as permanent and believed that were it not for air resistance and gravity, impetus would maintain the projectile at a uniform speed. Buridan also quantified impetus as the product of the amount of matter and the speed, the same quantities defining momentum in Sir Isaac Newton's physics, although Newton's momentum is a measure of the effect of a body's motion whereas Buridan's impetus is a cause of motion. Also significant for later physics is Buridan's statement that impetus is an "enduring reality," for it suggests Newton's law of inertia: An object, once set in motion, tends to remain in motion at a uniform speed. An important difference between Newton's inertia and Buridan's impetus is that impetus would persist indefinitely for an object moving both in a circle and in a straight line, whereas Newton's momentum would persist only in a straight line and would need a force to bend it into a circle.

Buridan used impetus to explain many phenomena: the acceleration of an object falling to earth, the vibration of plucked strings, the bouncing of balls, and the everlasting rotations of heavenly bodies. This last application is the most important one, and Pierre Duhem, the great French physicist, dated the beginning of modern science to Buridan's rejection of Intelligences as movers of the heavenly bodies. Buridan believed that the heavenly bodies, having been put in motion by God, continued to move because of the impetus God impressed on them; they consequently required no everlastingly active angels to keep them moving. Buridan explained rotational motion by a rotational impetus analogous to the rectilinear impetus for projectile motion. Galileo Galilei held similar views; it was not until Newton that the movements of heavenly and earthly bodies were correctly explained.

In the light of the great changes that Nicolaus Copernicus would cause in astronomy two centuries later, it is interesting that Buridan himself investigated the question of whether Earth is at rest. He believed that the daily motion of the stellar sphere and the planets could be explained by assuming either a stationary heaven and rotating Earth or the reverse. In other words, he recognized that the problem was one of relative motion. To support the theory of a rotating Earth, Buridan stressed, in typical Ockhamist manner, the desirability of explaining the phenomena by the simplest means possible. Since it was simpler to move the smaller Earth than the much larger stellar sphere, it seemed reasonable to attribute rotation to Earth while leaving the stellar sphere at rest. Despite this and other arguments favorable to a daily terrestrial motion, Buridan finally opted for a nonrotating Earth because, in his judgment, a rotating Earth could not explain why an arrow shot vertically into the air fell back to its origin rather than far to the west.

Although Buridan believed that Earth did not rotate, he nevertheless did not believe it was perfectly stationary. Indeed, he thought that Earth experienced incessant, though slight, motions that arose from continual shifts of Earth's center of gravity, caused by the redistribution of matter on its surface. Buridan explained that streams and rivers carried material from the mountains to the sea, and in this way the elevated regions of Earth became lighter and the watery regions heavier. His explanation is similar to the modern theory of isostasy, which plays a major role in physical geology.

It is not known which work written by Buridan was his last. The final documentary mention of him is dated July 12, 1358, in a statute in which his name appears as a witness to an agreement between the Picard and English students and teachers of the University of Paris. Buridan, who came from this region of northern France, represented the Picards. It is possible, though there is no real evidence to support it, that he fell victim to the Black Death, which in the late 1350's took the lives of many of those who had survived its first outbreak in 1348-1349.

SIGNIFICANCE

To many historians of science, Buridan is the key figure in the development of medieval dynamics and an important precursor of modern mechanics. He successfully challenged Aristotle's theory of motion and proposed an alternative dynamics that had potentially revolutionary implications. Unfortunately, he did not generalize impetus into a theory of universal inertial mechanics. Although he used impetus to explain both terrestrial and celestial motion, he never tried to formulate a single mechanics for the whole universe because he accepted the Aristotelian dichotomy between terrestrial and celestial bodies. Buridan's ideas on terrestrial and celestial movements were developed by Albert of Saxony and Nicole d'Oresme, and his theory of impetus came to have wide acceptance in fifteenth and sixteenth century France, England, Germany, and Italy.

Other scholars see Buridan's importance more in the questions he raised than in the answers he proposed. Even when his specific contributions to physics were forgotten, the influence of his conception of scientific evidence and method lived on. In particular, he helped eliminate explanations in terms of final causes from physics. His work marks a shift from a metaphysical to an empirical attitude toward scientific problems. He vindicated natural philosophy as a field of study in its own right, and he defined the objectives and methodology of science in a way that guaranteed its autonomy with regard to theology and philosophy. In this sense, Duhem is correct in saying that Buridan's work marks the start of modern science.

—*Robert J. Paradowski*

FURTHER READING

Clagett, Marshall. *The Science of Mechanics in the Middle Ages*. Madison: University of Wisconsin Press, 1959. Presents documentary material on which to base studies of medieval science, and contains excerpts and helpful discussions of several works by Buridan on mechanics and cosmology.

Dijksterhuis, E. J. *The Mechanization of the World Picture: Pythagoras to Newton*. Translated by C. Dikshoorn. Reprint. Princeton, N.J.: Princeton University Press, 1986. This classic work is a detailed account of the origins and development of the physical sciences.

Duhem, Pierre. *Medieval Cosmology: Theories of Infinity, Place, Time, Void, and the Plurality of Worlds*. Translated and edited by Roger Ariew. Chicago: University of Chicago Press, 1985. Presents excerpts from a discussion of Buridan and others that demonstrates the sophistication of medieval physics and cosmology.

Grant, Edward. *A Source Book in Medieval Science*. Cambridge, Mass.: Harvard University Press, 1974. Part of a series in classical papers that have shaped the history of various sciences. Several selections have been translated into English from Buridan's works on natural philosophy and are presented with commentary and annotations.

Lindberg, David C., ed. *Science in the Middle Ages*. Chicago: University of Chicago Press, 1978. Analysis of major aspects of the medieval scientific enterprise in some detail and a discussion of Buridan's work in chapters on medieval philosophy, mechanics, and cosmology.

Moody, Ernest A. *Studies in Medieval Philosophy, Science, and Logic: Collected Papers, 1933-1969*. Berkeley: University of California Press, 1975. A collection of several of the author's influential papers on Buridan, among them "John Buridan on the Habitability of the Earth" and "Buridan and a Dilemma of Nominalism."

Thijssen, J. M. M. H., and Jack Zupko, eds. *The Metaphysics and Natural Philosophy of John Buridan*. Boston: Brill, 2001. An analysis of Buridan's metaphysics, physics, and natural philosophy. Includes an extensive bibliography and an index.

Zupko, Jack. *John Buridan: Portrait of a Fourteenth-Century Arts Master.* Notre Dame, Ind.: University of Notre Dame Press, 2003. A survey of Buridan's science of logic; of his views on the question of bodies and souls, knowledge, freedom, and natural science; and of his legacy in the history of philosophy and science.

SEE ALSO: Alhazen; Averröes; Nicholas of Autrecourt; William of Ockham; Thomas Aquinas; William of Auxerre.

RELATED ARTICLES in *Great Events from History: The Middle Ages, 477-1453*: 595-665: Invention of Decimals and Negative Numbers; c. 1025: Scholars at Chartres Revive Interest in the Classics; 1100-1300: European Universities Emerge; c. 1150: Moors Transmit Classical Philosophy and Medicine to Europe; c. 1265-1273: Thomas Aquinas Compiles the *Summa Theologica*; 1328-1350: Flowering of Late Medieval Physics; 1347-1352: Invasion of the Black Death in Europe.

CÆDMON

English poet

Cædmon, an unlettered monk of the seventh century, is recognized as the first English poet identified by name, from whom a work has survived.

BORN: Early seventh century; Northumbria (now in England)
DIED: c. 680; Whitby Abbey, Northumbria
AREA OF ACHIEVEMENT: Literature

EARLY LIFE

Cædmon (KAD-muhn) had two significant contemporaries. The first, Aldhelm (c. 639-709), perhaps preceded him, but Aldhelm's English verses have not survived. Cædmon's second significant contemporary, Cynewulf (fl. ninth century), signed four religious poems with runic letters indicating his authorship, but he probably lived slightly later than Cædmon. The sole source of information on Cædmon's life is the *Historia ecclesiastica gentis Anglorum* (731; *Ecclesiastical History of the English People*, 1723) by Saint Bede the Venerable (672 or 673-735). Bede, a monk who lived in the monastery at Jarrow, sought to account for the development of Christianity in England from Roman times to his own day. He was particularly concerned with tracing the divisions that existed within the two main branches of English Christendom. All that he wrote—though much was historically correct—had an overriding religious intent.

The story of Cædmon is presented as the origin of religious poetry in the English vernacular. According to Bede, Cædmon was a simple, unlettered herdsman, probably employed on a monastic landed estate. During celebrations or feasts, it was the custom to pass the harp around the table so that each celebrant might sing in turn. Lacking the ability to sing or accompany himself, Cædmon often felt inadequate and habitually left the table before the harp reached him. One evening, he was assigned to watch over the domestic animals while the others celebrated, and on this occasion he fell asleep at the cattle pens. In a dream, a stranger appeared to him and said, "Cædmon, sing me something." At first, Cædmon protested that he was unable, but he was told that he had to sing. When he inquired what he should sing, the stranger replied, "Sing about the Creation."

Cædmon then began to recite verses, producing a nine-line hymn in Anglo-Saxon alliterative verse. Translated literally, it reads as follows:

> Now we must praise the Keeper of Heaven's Kingdom,
> The Maker's might and His mind-thoughts,
> Work of the Glory-Father, as He each of wonders,
> Eternal Lord, established in the beginning.
> He first shaped for bairns of men
> Heaven as a roof, holy Creator;
> Then the middle-yard Guardian of mankind,
> Eternal Lord afterward made—
> Earth for men, Lord almighty.

After Cædmon recited his poem to his superior, he was taken to the abbess Saint Hilda, who was in charge of a combined convent and monastery at Whitby. After hearing his poem, she concluded that Cædmon was truly inspired, and she urged him to become a monk, even though he was beyond the normal age for entry into the monastic life. He entered the monastery at Whitby and devoted the remainder of his life to poetry and monastic discipline.

As a monk, Cædmon produced divine poems based on biblical texts. According to Bede, he listened to others reading biblical passages aloud and then formed the lines into Old English verses. Apart from Cædmon's work as a poet, Bede narrated little about his life, but Bede included a detailed account of Cædmon's death in a passage designed to inculcate piety. Bede reported that Cædmon had a premonition of his death at a time when his companions thought he was in good health. Bede recorded that, to the surprise of his fellows, Cædmon in a mood of mirth asked for the sacraments to be administered to him; after receiving the Eucharist, he ended his life by falling asleep peacefully.

LIFE'S WORK

A just assessment of Cædmon's contribution to English literature is difficult to achieve owing to the lack of sources. Bede wrote that Cædmon limited his entire poetic output to sacred themes, avoiding secular subjects altogether. He translated large portions of the biblical books into Old English alliterative verse, including "all the history of Genesis; . . . the Exodus of Israel out of Egypt and entrance into the promised land; and many other stories of sacred scripture, about the Lord's incarnation, and his passion, resurrection and ascension into heaven; about the advent of the Holy Spirit and the teachings of the apostles." In addition, he wrote about the horrible punishments of hell, the heavenly kingdom, and divine love and justice.

This passage led scholars to conclude that the poems found in the Old English Junius Manuscript, located in

Oxford University's Bodleian Library, were by Cædmon. The four poems, totaling about five thousand lines, are *Genesis*, *Exodus*, *Daniel*, and *Christ and Satan*. Those that purport to be biblical translations are in reality loose paraphrases of the biblical books, with many omissions and interpolations. None represents a complete version of the book on which it is based. Although *Christ and Satan* deals with biblical themes, it represents an independent treatment of New Testament material. All four titles adapt sacred themes to Anglo-Saxon civilization, mores, and culture with a freedom that in later translations would be inadmissible.

Subsequent scholarship has established that these works are by various hands, and most scholars now agree that their style and probable dates of composition make it unlikely that Cædmon contributed anything to their composition. Though the works have been characterized as belonging to the "School of Cædmon," this claim seems inadequately founded. All that relates them to Cædmon is the reference in Bede to their subject matter and a few tenuous formulaic similarities to the *Hymn*.

This leaves the nine-verse *Hymn* as Cædmon's surviving contribution to English literature, yet the poem itself poses serious textual problems. The earliest surviving version is in Bede's Latin text, recorded not later than 731. The word order and tone of Bede's text strongly suggest a previously extant Anglo-Saxon text that was known to Bede. Cædmon's monastery was located not far from Bede's, some fifty miles, and his life may well have overlapped Bede's. Thus, arguably, Cædmon's work and reputation could have been known in Jarrow while the poet was still alive. In addition, Bede informs the reader that his Latin translation, like all poetic translations, fails to capture the beauty of the original. This wording suggests that he had either seen or heard an earlier version in English. The scholarly consensus appears to be that the *Hymn* is rightly attributable to Cædmon and that Bede somehow knew an earlier version.

In addition to Bede's Latin text, at least seventeen Old English versions of the poem, or a portion of its verses, exist in early manuscripts. The majority represent translations into the West Saxon dialect dated from the late tenth through the eleventh centuries. These were produced as a result of the translation of Bede's entire *Ecclesiastical History of the English People* into Old English during the revival of learning inspired by King Alfred the Great (849-899, r. 871-899). To the translators, Bede's Latin lines were easily rendered into the standard poetic dialect of Old English.

Four of the seventeen versions, however, are in the Northumbrian dialect, derived from the Angles who settled that area of England. Of these, two date from the early eighth century. While Northumbrian would have been Cædmon's vernacular dialect, these versions were recorded long after Cædmon's death and were related to Bede's text. It appears that monastic copiers of Bede's Latin added the Old English version of the poem in the margins. Scholars have put forth the plausible argument that the Old English text was known to the translators independently of Bede's Latin. In addition to differences attributable to dialect, the early holographs include some minor variations of diction, and these have been the subject of careful scrutiny by scholars of the period.

Like much Old English poetry, Cædmon's work was heavily indebted to the oral tradition. According to Bede, he composed by hearing the biblical texts read and then turning the passages into Anglo-Saxon poetry. There is no indication that Cædmon ever learned to read and write. How, then, did he learn to compose poems? Bede would have his readers believe that Cædmon received divine inspiration from a miraculous dream vision. A more skeptical, less exalted view suggests that he learned to create verses through hearing the oral performances of his fellow herdsmen and agricultural workers. Bede's account suggests that their oral secular verses, though never recorded, preceded those of Cædmon. Further, such a view is consistent with the known customs of celebration among the Anglo-Saxons and the Teutonic tribes from which they came.

Significance

Although Cædmon's surviving poetic output is small, he holds an important place in literary history as the founder of English vernacular poetry. His *Hymn* embodies the vigorous expression, style, and conventions of later Anglo-Saxon poems, with their strong metaphors, alliterative verses as an aid to memory, unrhymed verses, half-line construction, and memorable epithets.

Aldhelm recited Anglo-Saxon verse to his parishioners in order to motivate them to attend church, but none of his verses has survived. Cynewulf left four early Anglo-Saxon religious poems, but nothing is known about his life. Among the named seventh century English poets, only Cædmon is known as a poet and a person.

—*Stanley Archer*

Further Reading

Bede. *Bede: A History of the English Church and People*. Translated by Leo Sherley-Price. New York: Penguin Books, 1985. A translation of Bede's most significant work, with a twenty-four-page introduction and a map.

Bessinger, Jess B., Jr., and Stanley J. Kahrl, eds. *Essential Articles for the Study of Old English Poetry.* Hamden, Conn.: Archon Books, 1968. A collection of twenty-six articles on Old English poetry. Offers general studies of stylistics, themes, oral influences, and metrics as well as studies of individual poets and works. The *Hymn* is mentioned numerous times.

Curran, S. Terrie. *English from Cædmon to Chaucer: The Literary Development of English.* Prospect Heights, Ill.: Waveland Press, 2002. A look at the development of English literature, including the work of Cædmon.

Farmer, David Hugh. *The Oxford Dictionary of Saints.* New York: Oxford University Press, 2003. A reputable source that looks at the lives of saints in Great Britain.

O'Keeffe, Katherine O'Brien. *Visible Song: Transitional Literacy in Old English Verse.* New York: Cambridge University Press, 1990. Analyzes the composition of most extant versions of the *Hymn*, relates Cædmon's *Hymn* to the rich tradition of oral poetry, and explores scribal awareness of the distinctions between Old English transcription and classical Latin verse.

Smith, A. H., ed. *Three Northumbrian Poems.* New York: Appleton-Century-Crofts, 1968. Provides texts of and extensive commentary on three Old English poems: Bede's *Death Song*, Cædmon's *Hymn*, and *The Leiden Riddle.*

Stevens, Martin, and Jerome Mandell, eds. *Old English Literature: Twenty-two Analytical Essays.* 2d ed. Lincoln: University of Nebraska Press, 1980. Contains several essays that discuss Cædmon and his work.

Wrenn, C. L. *A Study of Old English Literature.* New York: W. W. Norton, 1967. A chronologically arranged study of Old English that offers a highly informed overview of Anglo-Saxon literature.

SEE ALSO: Adam de la Halle; Alcuin; Alfred the Great; Saint Bede the Venerable; Giovanni Boccaccio; Boethius; Charles d'Orléans; Alain Chartier; Geoffrey Chaucer; Dante; Firdusi; Saint Hilda of Whitby; Marie de France; Petrarch; Jalāl al-Dīn Rūmi; Walther von der Vogelweide; Wang Wei.

RELATED ARTICLES in *Great Events from History: The Middle Ages, 477-1453*: 731: Bede Writes *Ecclesiastical History of the English People*; c. 1306-1320: Dante Writes *The Divine Comedy.*

CANUTE THE GREAT

Danish king of England, Denmark, and Norway (r. 1016-1035)

Canute's conquest and strong kingship gave England a period of peace and prosperity that began to repair damage, destruction, and demoralization wrought by centuries of Viking attacks. A fierce young Viking himself, Canute matured into a ruler who appeared to be the ideal Christian king, lawgiver, and protector of his people. However, Canute's very success not only foreshadowed but also helped to bring about the Norman Conquest of 1066.

BORN: c. 995; Jelling?, Denmark

DIED: November 12, 1035; Shaftesbury, Dorset (now in England)

ALSO KNOWN AS: Knut; Knud; Canute I; Canute Sveinson

AREAS OF ACHIEVEMENT: Government and politics, military

EARLY LIFE

Canute (kuh-NYEWT) Sveinson was born probably in the Danish royal residence of Jelling in Jutland. His was a Danish royal name, and the standard spelling "Canute" is an Anglicization of the Latin form Cnuto of the Viking name Cnut, Knut, Knutir, or still other variant spellings. Canute seldom used his Christian name, Lambert, which he took when he was finally baptized, probably during the 1010's. The obscurity surrounding Canute's birth and childhood derives both from the fact that he was a younger son, having an elder brother Harold, and from the cultural isolation and political turbulence of Denmark around the year 1000.

Canute's father was Sweyn Forkbeard, who was king of Denmark from 987 to 1014. Sweyn's father, whom Sweyn's army slew in battle, was Harold II Bluetooth, king of Denmark (r. c. 950-987). Sweyn had been baptized as a child but apostatized, rose to power on a tide of Viking heathenism, and persecuted Christianity. Sweyn was a wild Viking sea rover who had dreams of becoming king of a dual monarchy of Denmark and England.

Canute's mother was a Polish princess who took the Danish name Gunnhild. She was the daughter of

Mieszko I, duke and first ruler of Poland. Gunnhild's brother Bolesław I the Brave, duke of Poland from 992 to 1025, would become in 1025 the first king of Poland. Canute's mother belonged to the Polish ducal and royal house of Piast, which embraced Christianity in self-defense because the Germans employed conversion of the Slavs as the pretext for conquest. Neither Sweyn nor Gunnhild were devout Christians, and their son Canute was reared a heathen Viking.

Many Northmen during the Viking Age took Christianity very lightly. King Olaf II, who is revered in Scandinavia as Saint Olaf of Norway, was Canute's contemporary and rival, and another fierce Viking mercenary warrior. Saint Olaf fought for the English and Norwegians against both Sweyn and Canute until Canute's soldiers finally slew him in Norway in 1030. Saint Olaf left his mark on England when in 1013, fighting for Ethelred II, the Unready (r. 978-1013 and 1014-1016), against Sweyn, he had his Viking war party pull down London Bridge, perhaps originating the old nursery rhyme.

Christianity and heathenism were practiced together by many Vikings, who might wear amulets combining the Cross of Christ and the Hammer of Thor or sculpt Viking stones such as those at Gosforth Church in Cumberland combining the Crucifixion, Thor's heroic feats, and the heathen apocalypse Ragnarok. Sagas tell of baptized Vikings who prayed to Christ when seas were calm but in rough seas and storms prayed to Thor.

Canute the Great. (Library of Congress)

Young Canute was sent to be fostered with Thorkell the Tall, a redoubtable Viking mercenary, at Jomsborg on the Baltic Sea at the mouth of the Oder River. Jomsborg was fabled in saga as a Viking military community that was organized like a heathen monastery for mercenary soldiers and pirates. What religious instruction Thorkell gave his foster son was probably heathen, because as late as 1020 in England, Thorkell was implicated in cases of witchcraft and murder in his own family that had heathen overtones. There were powerful tensions in Viking society and within individual Vikings between Christianity and heathenism.

The names of the Viking age are emblematic of its rough and violent culture and politics: Ivar the Boneless, Erik the Priest-hater, Eric Bloodaxe, Thorkell the Skull-splitter, John the Wode or Berserk, Ragnar Hairy-breeches, the poet Eyvind the Plagiarist, and the musician Einar Jingle-scale. One favorite Viking art form was called "cutting the blood-eagle," in which the Viking would mutilate the corpse of an enemy by splitting the chest and artistically pulling back the ribs. One Viking earned the contemptuous surname "the Children's Man" because he refused to play one of the merriest Viking games, "Impaling the Baby on a Spear." There is little wonder that Christian priests in Western Europe added to the Mass the new petition, "From the fury of the Northmen, O Lord, deliver us."

The degeneracy of the English during the reign of Ethelred II, the Unready, had become so flagrant that Wulfstan, archbishop of York, in his great *Sermo Lupi ad Anglos* (English translation, 1939) in 1014 could thunder that the English had become indistinguishable from Vikings. There were a few exceptional Englishmen such as the holy and learned Ælfric, but more typical was the sinister, treacherous, and violent Eadric Steona, earl of Mercia. The first Viking raid had occurred at Lindisfarne in 793, the latest in 1016, and there had been vast spiritual as well as material destruction. Two episodes in the early eleventh century illustrate this degeneracy: the Saint Brice's Day Massacre of 1002, when Ethelred ordered the English to slaughter all Danish residents in England, and the martyrdom of Ælfheah, archbishop of Canterbury, in 1013, when at a Viking feast drunken warriors pelted the saintly Ælfheah to death with table refuse. Ethelred ordered another massacre of Danes in 1014, but it was evidently less notorious and more localized than the massacre of 1002. Cruel treachery had become the norm.

Canute first made his mark as a warrior when he accompanied his father in the Danish invasion of England in 1013-1014. Even among these fierce Danes and Jomsvikings, young Canute stood out for his cruelty and ruthlessness. On the sudden death of Sweyn early in 1014, the Vikings elected Canute their leader in England. Canute thereupon committed the atrocity of mutilating Anglo-Saxons whom Sweyn had held hostage and landing them ashore at Sandwich to terrify the English. Canute also deserted his allies, the Danes of Lindsay, against whom the English retaliated brutally. In 1014, Canute sailed back to Denmark, where his elder brother Harold had succeeded their father Sweyn as king. Civil war raged on in England for the next few years, the English led by Ethelred II, the Unready, and briefly after his death in 1016 by his son Edmund Ironside. Canute decisively defeated Edmund Ironside at Ashington in 1016.

Between his victory at Ashington and his journey to Denmark in 1019-1020, Canute behaved like a Viking conqueror and ruled England oppressively. He murdered real and alleged opponents and rival claimants, divided England into four great earldoms or military districts on the Danish model, and levied an enormous Danegeld. He paid off most of his Viking mercenaries but kept enough to guard himself and garrison England. Both the Danelaw and the Anglo-Saxon parts of the realm were exhausted, bereft of English leadership, and sullen in their acquiescence to Canute's rule. During those same years, however, Canute married the widow of Ethelred, Emma of Normandy (d. 1052), in 1017; took part in two English coronation ceremonies at Bath and Westminster, also in 1017; and summoned in 1018 a national assembly of both Danes and Anglo-Saxons who swore to uphold the good laws of King Edgar the Peaceable.

In 1018, Canute's brother Harold, king of Denmark, died, leaving Canute as his only heir, but the Danish Vikings were restless and menacing because Canute's kingship now placed England out of bounds for Viking pillaging and piracy. In 1019-1020, Canute went to Denmark to secure his inheritance, control the Viking sea rovers, and establish his father's plan of dual monarchy of Denmark and England. Canute's own vision went beyond Sweyn's, as Canute appears to have had the dream of a Northern Sea empire or thalassocracy over the British Isles, Scandinavia, and the coasts and islands of the Baltic and North Seas and possibly of the north Atlantic Ocean.

LIFE'S WORK

By the early eleventh century in England, Danes and Anglo-Saxons regarded each other with hatred, vengeance, and distrust. Canute, who had lost an aunt, an uncle, a foster uncle, and friends in the Saint Brice's Day Massacre of 1002 and lost his father (or so the Vikings believed) to the magic of the East Anglian royal martyr Saint Edmund of Bury (841-869), had fought against the Anglo-Saxons from 1013 to 1016 and committed many horrible atrocities. Canute seemed to promise not peace and reconciliation but bloodbath and religious persecution. Canute in 1017 was still a young Jomsviking who had been elected leader of the Danish forces in England in 1014, after the death of Sweyn. Canute may have been baptized, but baptism had meant little for Sweyn. He was known by the heathen name Canute, not by his Christian name, Lambert. Burning, pillaging, and slaughtering, Canute had shown no Christian virtues.

The great transformation of Canute came after his journey to Denmark to secure his inheritance after the death of his brother Harold in 1018. Canute was in Denmark in 1019 and returned to England in 1020. Canute set out at once to reform the English laws through the work of his adviser Wulfstan, archbishop of York. Canute's laws covered secular and religious affairs, Englishmen and Danes, and presented themselves as a return to the laws of King Edgar the Peaceable. In his legislation, Canute stood squarely in the Anglo-Saxon tradition of royal dooms and law codes, and indeed Canute's code was so comprehensive that long after the Norman Conquest in 1066 Canute's time was remembered as a legal golden age. Thus, Canute appeared as a great lawgiver.

Also beginning in 1020, Canute tried to seem the ideal Christian king: He made spectacular public gestures of piety; lavishly endowed shrines, monasteries, and churches; and suppressed the vestiges of heathenism. His benefactions placed literate churchmen in his debt and gained him respectability, good public relations, and a great historical reputation, since churchmen wrote the history chronicles. The assumption that Canute was cynically building a public image is borne out by the fact that his pious deeds were done very conspicuously with monastic chroniclers in attendance. For example, on one of his journeys to the north of England, Canute departed from his itinerary to walk barefoot 6 miles (10 kilometers) to Durham, where he visited the shrine of Saint Cuthbert. Another motive might have been Canute's superstitious wish to propitiate the saints and win them to his side. His other benefactions, including lavish almsgiving, served similar public relations purposes. The most spectacular pious gesture was the magnificent translation of the relics of Saint Alphege from London to Canterbury in 1023. Canute, Emma, Harthcanute, Thorkell the Tall, and other Vikings participated. Thorkell's role was especially symbolic because he had been present at Aelfheah's martyrdom in 1013.

King Canute journeyed forth several times from his realm of England. He went to Denmark in 1019-1020, 1022-1023, and 1025-1027, to Rome and Scotland in 1027, and to Norway and Denmark in 1028-1029, but he spent seasons of all these years in England and never was an absentee king. Canute ruled England well. Except for his pilgrimage to Rome in 1027, which also had diplomatic significance, those trips from England were military expeditions or brief supervisory visits to his other kingdoms, which he ruled through regents. For most of his reign, Canute resided in England—at his capital, Winchester, in London, or on progress around the country.

Canute's visibility succeeded in immortalizing him in English folklore as "Good King Canute," the hero of many edifying folktales such as "King Canute Commands the Tides to Halt" and "King Canute Subjects Himself to His Own Harsh Laws" and even his own nursery rhyme.

> Merrily sang the monks of Ely,
> As King Canute came rowing by,
> "Row to the shore, knights," said the king,
> "And let us hear these churchmen sing."

This rhyme survives in an old Anglo-Saxon version that is supposed to have been extemporized by Canute himself. The reputation of Good King Canute in English folklore is well deserved because he did heal the wounds of the Viking invasions, bring Anglo-Saxons and Danes together in England, and act like the ideal Christian king.

King Canute was regal in appearance, tall, athletic in build, fair of hair and complexion, and handsome, with piercing blue eyes and a prominent, slightly aquiline, nose and a blond forked beard like his father's. For his personality, his two-faced seal may supply a clue. Canute played his part as a civilized Viking and Christian king and lawgiver very ably indeed. His coinage, portraits such as the lovely miniature of Canute and Emma in the *Liber Vitæ* of Winchester, skaldic praise poetry, and other contemporary descriptions of him agree that he looked the part of a great civilized Viking and ideal Christian king. Primary sources also agree that he had a bad temper, which he usually kept in check. His subjects regarded Canute with affectionate awe in which there was no small measure of terror. The Viking savage who had mutilated English hostages in 1014 did occasionally reappear in King Canute, as when he had Earl Ulf stabbed to death in sanctuary in a cathedral in Denmark in 1026. Canute died when he was barely forty and before he could realize his ambitions of a sea empire to rival the Western Roman Empire on the Continent. His empire was crumbling in 1035, but he had been set back before in 1014 and 1026 and had recovered strongly, regained power, and gained greater power.

DANISH KINGS OF ENGLAND, 1016-1066

Reign	*Monarch*
1016-1035	CANUTE THE GREAT
1035-1040	Harold I Harefoot
1040-1042	Harthacnut
1043-1066	EDWARD THE CONFESSOR
1066	HAROLD II

Note: Both Edward and Harold II were of mixed Danish and Saxon ancestry.

Canute had two sons who succeeded him and ruled briefly as kings of England. By his Anglo-Danish concubine, Ælfgifu of Northampton, he had Harold Harefoot, who ruled as regent for his younger legitimate half brother from 1035 to 1037 and then took the kingship himself and ruled from 1037 to 1040. By his lawful Christian wife, Emma of Normandy, Canute had Harthacnut, who ruled England from 1040 to 1042. Canute had another illegitimate son named Sweyn, who died in 1036, and a legitimate daughter named Gunnhild, who, before she died in 1038, was briefly married to Henry, the son of the Western Roman emperor Conrad II. All of Canute's offspring died young, and in 1042, there succeeded the son of his old enemy Ethelred II and Emma of Normandy, Edward the Confessor, who ruled England from 1043 to 1066. Dynastically, Canute's usurpation proved only a brief Danish interruption of the English succession and historically only a breathing space. He did not make drastic changes in government, law, or administration but was content to salvage the Anglo-Saxon institutions.

SIGNIFICANCE

Canute the Great was the first Viking ruler who was admitted to fellowship with pope and emperor and the Christian kings in Christendom. He envisioned a great northern thalassocracy that would rival the Holy Roman

Empire or surpass it. He achieved but part of his vision, and even that crumbled before his death. Still, he gave England nearly twenty years of peace, prosperity, and good government. Less happily, Canute's earldoms, housecarls (members of body guard), intricate dynasticism, and very success as an alien usurper set precedents for the Norman Conquest of 1066. As king of the English, Canute deserves the epithet "the Great" for saving the monarchy, which Alfred the Great had begun and Ethelred II, the Unready, nearly demolished.

—*Terence R. Murphy*

FURTHER READING

Barlow, Frank. *The English Church, 1000-1066: A Constitutional History.* London: Longmans, Green, 1963. Learned monograph that is somewhat critical of Canute and skeptical about his religious sincerity, but it contains fascinating details about Canute that are otherwise inaccessible.

Brondsted, Johannes. *The Vikings*. Translated by Kalle Skov. Baltimore: Penguin Books, 1965. Still indispensable for background on the Vikings.

Campbell, Alistair, ed. *Encomium Emmae Reginae*. London: Royal Historical Society, 1949. Reprint. New York: Cambridge University Press, 1998. A primary source, published with the editor's critical apparatus and commentary. Very important for the study of Canute.

Davidson, H. R. Ellis. *Gods and Myths of Northern Europe*. Harmondsworth, Middlesex, England: Penguin Books, 1977. Indispensable for understanding Viking heathenism. Includes a bibliography and index.

Fisher, D. J. V. *The Anglo-Saxon Age, c. 400-1042*. London: Longman, 1973. A full narrative nicely incorporating research and interpretation.

Fletcher, Richard. *Bloodfeud: Murder and Revenge in Anglo-Saxon England*. New York: Allen Lane/Penguin Press, 2002. Addresses the often brutal history of Anglo-Saxon times, including the roles of Canute and Ethelred II in that history. Includes a bibliography and an index.

Larson, Laurence Marcellus. *Canute the Great, 995 (circ.)-1035, and the Rise of Danish Imperialism During the Viking Age*. Reprint. New York: AMS Press, 1970. The standard biography, although outdated on many details and general interpretation. It has stood the test of time far better than most works of history because of its reliance on primary sources.

Loyn, H. R. *The Vikings in Britain*. Rev. ed. Cambridge, Mass.: Blackwell, 1995. The author devotes three chapters to the early raids and subsequent large-scale invasions of England by Scandinavians. A highly regarded history of the Viking Age and a useful overview with some insights on Canute.

Marsden, John. *The Fury of the Northmen: Saints, Shrines and Sea-Raiders in the Viking Age A.D. 793-878*. New York: St. Martin's Press, 1995. Details Viking depredations on monasteries, particularly Lindisfarne, quoting medieval sources extensively. Views the Vikings as barbarian pirates and the monasteries as repositories of civilization.

Rumble, Alexander R., ed. *The Reign of Cnut: King of England, Denmark and Norway.* Rutherford, N.J.: Fairleigh Dickinson University Press, 1994. Explores Canute's reign, with an introduction placing him in historical context and chapters on his Scandinavian empire, military exploits and achievements, possible influence on urban policy and place-names in England, coinage, and more. Includes several appendices, a bibliography, and an index.

Stenton, F. M. *Anglo-Saxon England*. 3d ed. New York: Oxford University Press, 1989. A classic history of the period and the standard source for reference purposes.

Whitelock, Dorothy, David C. Douglas, and Susie I. Tucker, eds. *The Anglo-Saxon Chronicle*. 2d ed. New Brunswick, N.J.: Rutgers University Press, 1989. The basic primary source, contains very brief entries, by year, for Canute's reign. Editorial footnotes are judicious but abbreviated.

SEE ALSO: Alfred the Great; Edward the Confessor; Ethelred II, the Unready; Harold II; Saint Olaf; William the Conqueror.

RELATED ARTICLES in *Great Events from History: The Middle Ages, 477-1453*: June 7, 793: Norse Raid Lindisfarne Monastery; 850-950: Viking Era; 878: Alfred Defeats the Danes; 1016: Canute Conquers England; c. 1025: Scholars at Chartres Revive Interest in the Classics; October 14, 1066: Battle of Hastings.

GIOVANNI DA PIAN DEL CARPINI

Italian religious leader

Carpini extended the work of the Franciscans to Saxony, Germany, northern Europe, Spain, and North Africa. After returning from the first formal Christian mission to the Mongols, he wrote an important work on the history of the peoples of Central Asia.

BORN: c. 1180; Pian del Carpini, Umbria (now Piano della Magione, Italy)

DIED: August 1, 1252; possibly Perugia (now in Italy)

ALSO KNOWN AS: John of Plano Carpini

AREAS OF ACHIEVEMENT: Religion and theology, historiography, exploration

EARLY LIFE

Giovanni da Pian del Carpini (jyoh-VAHN-nee dah pyahn dehl kawr-PEE-nee) was born in Pian del Carpini (now Piano della Magione), northwest of the Umbrian city of Perugia, which was on the route to Cortona, Italy. In the Umbrian countryside, fields and low hills were often covered in a light haze; the blue sky was reflected in nearby Lake Trasimene. The area was dominated by the ancient city of Perugia, proud and warlike, near the Tiber River. Here passed the famous and the not-so-famous, from emperors to Provençal minstrels, on their way to Rome. Across the Tiber River lay the city of Assisi, an ancient enemy.

The rising middle class in Assisi had ended the domination of the feudal nobility and sent many aristocratic families into exile in 1198. The refuge that Perugia gave these exiles resulted in a battle fought near the Tiber River in November, 1202, in which Assisi was defeated. The contentious spirit of the times was also reflected in disputes among church officials, noblemen, and city officials over property rights and sources of income.

In this unsettled, economically depressed time, young Carpini grew up. It is possible that he took part in the battle against Assisi, or he may have been studying at Bologna. In any case, he would soon have been aware of young Francis of Assisi at Portiuncula. A band of youthful followers had gathered around Francis, attracted by his spirit of simplicity, penance, and prayer. By spring, 1209, the group, now numbering twelve, went to Rome. Pope Innocent III gave his approval to the rule establishing the Order of Friars Minor to preach penance to the people.

Amid the political turbulence of the early thirteenth century, the number of Francis's disciples grew rapidly. One, Brother Giles, was assigned to the small hermitage of San Paola di Favarone outside Perugia between 1215 and 1219. Here he developed a life combining contemplation, meditation, and action. He attended the great spring, 1217, general chapter (conference) at Portiuncula, where great crowds gathered to hear Francis and the Franciscan missions were organized.

Carpini may have become a follower of Francis at this gathering or at the one in the spring of 1219 during which, according to the chronicler Giordino di Giano, ten new members were added to Francis's order. The first extant mention of Carpini notes his 1221 appointment, because of his eloquence and proficiency in Latin, to be part of a mission to Germany under Caesar of Speyer. Carpini was about forty years of age.

LIFE'S WORK

The mission to Germany was no easy assignment, for the missionaries sent out in 1219 had been badly treated and those who had gone to Morocco had been martyred. After a rocky start, however, the 1221 mission to Germany fared better. The Franciscans' first center was established in Trent. In October, the brothers met at Augsburg. Carpini and a German friar, Barnaby, were sent as missionaries to Würzburg.

In September, 1223, when Germany was divided into four administrative units, Carpini was placed in charge of Saxony as *custos* (warden). According to the chronicle of the mission, his preaching was very effective. As warden of Saxony, Carpini preached Franciscan ideals in towns along the Elbe River, at the frontier of European Christianity.

At the chapter gathering on August 12, 1224, at Würzburg, he was assigned to be the provincial's envoy at Cologne. In this post, Carpini was responsible for directing Franciscan activities in Germany. It was he who reported Francis of Assisi's death at Portiuncula in 1226 to the brothers.

At the Pentecostal Chapter at Cologne in 1228, the same year that Francis was canonized by Gregory IX, Carpini was designated provincial (minister) of Germany. The chronicles describe Carpini as being very fat, so fat that he had to ride about on a donkey. This man of courage and talent defended the faith before bishops and princes with a sweet nature and carried out his leadership role in a manner that his contemporaries compared to the way a mother deals with her children or a hen her chicks.

He was diligent in extending the Franciscan mission, sending brothers into areas of eastern and northern Europe and establishing a convent at Metz and others in Lorraine.

In 1230, Carpini was appointed minister of Franciscans in Spain. In 1232, at the general chapter in Rome, he was named minister of Saxony. In mid-May, 1235, Pope Gregory IX sent a letter to the king of Tunis designating "Giovanni" as the papal ambassador and Franciscan provincial in Barbary. The reference may have been to Carpini. The appointments to Spain and possibly Barbary enabled him to develop some knowledge of Islam and the Arab world. He returned to Germany, was removed on May 15, 1239, by a general chapter, and returned again in 1241, overseeing the province of Cologne during the Mongol invasions of Eastern Europe.

After the Western losses at the Battle of Liegnitz in Silesia near the Oder River on April 9, 1241, Pope Gregory IX preached a crusade to save Poland and end the attacks of the Mongols. Although the struggle between the pope and rulers of the Holy Roman Empire prevented any such action, fear of the Mongols continued. Further, while the death of the Great Khan Ogatai in December, 1241, together with rivalry among Mongol princes, had the effect of reducing the pressure on Western Europe, Christian Russia became a province of the Mongols. Various plans were made in the West for defense and for establishing contact with the Mongols. In 1245, the new pope, Innocent IV, chose Carpini to lead a mission to the Mongols. At this time, Carpini was about sixty-five years old and had been serving as penitentiary at the Papal Court.

Carpini left Lyon on Easter Day, April 16, 1245, with Stephen of Bohemia. In their journey across Germany and Eastern Europe, they were aided by church officials and various princes. At Breslau, Benedict the Pole joined the mission. By stages, they made their way to Cracow, where they were provided with beaver skins to present as gifts to the Mongols. At Volhynia, the Russian prince provided them with envoys to conduct them across Lithuanian territory to Kiev, then under Mongol control. The friars were unable, however, to obtain from the Russian rulers promises regarding escorts for their return trip.

Battling illness, Carpini's band continued on their mission, arriving at Kiev, where they exchanged their horses for Mongol ponies. Leaving early in February, 1246, they traveled south on the Dnieper River, reaching the first Mongol outpost on February 23. Here they left the ill Stephen of Bohemia and their servants. Using the Mongol post system and Mongol escorts, they continued down the Dnieper on the ice, then headed east to the Sea of Azov and the Don River, reaching Batu's center at Sarai on the Volga River on April 4. Batu received them, read the pope's letters (translated by a Russian in the entourage of Prince Alexander Nevsky), and arranged for them to go on to the great council in central Asia for the election and enthroning of the next supreme khan.

The Franciscans left on Easter Monday, April 8, full of uncertainty. Their legs were wrapped in puttees to protect against the friction of riding. Having fasted during Lent, they were weak and had had nothing to drink but snow melted in a kettle. They arrived at the Mongols' imperial summer station, Sira Ordu, on July 22. Since leaving Sarai, Carpini and his band had covered nearly three thousand miles (nearly five thousand kilometers) in 106 days. The fact that they had survived such a journey was a marvel in itself.

At the great council, there were three thousand envoys from all the Mongol subject peoples of Russia and China. The friars had little status among the host. By the time they were finally admitted to see the Great Khan Güyük, they had no gifts left to offer and were shunted off to the outskirts of the camp. Only the help of Cosmos, a Russian who was Güyük's favorite goldsmith, prevented them from starving. Not until November would the khan receive the friars. This delay, however, gave them the time to talk to other envoys and make the observations of the Mongols that would later be so important to the West. The khan prepared a rather belligerent answer to the pope's letter, indicating that if the West wanted peace, the pope, emperors, kings, and all the important men would have to come to him to learn his will.

The friars received the khan's letter on November 13 and were sent on their way four days later. They traveled all winter, often sleeping in the snow, not reaching Sarai until May 9, 1247. Batu gave them safe conduct to Mochi's camp, where they found Stephen of Bohemia and their servants safe. They reached Kiev in late spring and were received with great joy. The Russian princes Daniel and Basil received them at Vladimir and charged them with letters to the pope acknowledging the supremacy of the pope and the Roman church. The mission then returned to Western Europe, reaching Cologne late in September. From there they traveled to Liège and Champagne, reporting to the pope at Lyon on November 18, 1247.

As they traveled through Western Europe, Carpini gave lectures on their experiences based on an incomplete written version of their travels, of which five early manuscripts have survived. These lectures were attended by many who were eager to hear a firsthand account of the feared Mongols. Benedict the Pole also wrote an account of the trip while they were at Cologne.

The pope was quite pleased with the results of Carpini's mission and kept him at Lyon for about three months. Here Carpini wrote a fuller account, *Historia Mongalorum quos nos Tartaros appellamus*. This version exists in two manuscripts, one at Corpus Christi College, University of Cambridge, and the other at Leyden University Library. Carpini's accounts were the first of the Mongols available to the West.

Early in 1248, the pope sent Carpini to Louis IX in Paris. The French king was preparing for the Seventh Crusade (1248-1254); the pope hoped to delay the king's departure, but this mission was unsuccessful. It was probably at this time that the chronicler Vincent of Beauvais, who was frequently at the court of Louis IX, acquired Carpini's manuscript and, with abridgments, included it in the last section of his work. This ensured the survival and distribution of Carpini's work. It was also in France in the spring of 1248 that the historian Salimbene heard a reading of Carpini's work at Sens.

After the mission to France, the pope appointed Carpini as bishop of Antivari (Bar) in Dalmatia. His jurisdiction was disputed, however, by the archbishop of Ragusa. After Carpini was ousted, he traveled to Italy to appeal to the Roman Curia and to Innocent IV, who had gone to Perugia. It was here apparently that he died on August 1, 1252, around the age of seventy-two.

SIGNIFICANCE

Carpini's history was the most widely known of the early Western accounts of the Mongols. His information was vital to the West. The short version was published by Richard Hakluyt in his 1598 compilation of travel writings, but the complete version was not published until 1839 by M. A. P. d'Avezac for the Société de Géographie of Paris. Although others such as William of Rubrouck and Marco Polo traveled to the East later in the thirteenth century, Carpini was the first to offer a new understanding of the size of Asia and accurate information on the Mongols. His journey was undertaken after he had spent twenty-five years helping to establish the Franciscan order in Spain and northern and eastern Europe. The chroniclers refer to him as a fine preacher and a learned man, yet one of great humility. Carpini was a true practitioner of the original ideals of Saint Francis of Assisi.

—*Mary-Emily Miller*

FURTHER READING

Beazley, C. Raymond, ed. *The Texts and Versions of John de Plano Carpini and William de Rubruquis, as Printed for the First Time by Hakluyt in 1598 Together with Some Shorter Pieces*. London: Hakluyt Society, 1903. The introduction includes comments on the five existing Carpini manuscripts of the shorter version of his account of the Mongols. His work appears here in both Latin and English. A brief account of the main events in Carpini's life is included in the notes. Index.

Dawson, Christopher, ed. *The Mongol Mission: Narratives and Letters of the Franciscan Missionaries in Mongolia and China in the Thirteenth and Fourteenth Centuries*. New York: Sheed and Ward, 1955. This work, part of the Makers of Christendom series, presents a brief account of the conditions of the thirteenth century and of Western Europeans' interest in the Mongols, followed by accounts of the key Franciscan travels. Helpful bibliography and genealogy tables. Includes translations of the writings of Carpini, several papal bulls, and other letters. Index and map.

Morgan, David. *The Mongols*. 1986. Reprint. Cambridge, Mass.: Blackwell, 1990. An overview of the history of the Mongols. Illustrated.

Reid, Robert W. *A Brief Political and Military Chronology of the Mediaeval Mongols, from the Birth of Chinggis Qan to the Death of Qubilai Qaghan*. Bloomington, Ind.: Mongolia Society, 2002. Reid's account shows what the Mongols would soon become after the missions.

Rockhill, William Woodville, ed. and trans. *The Journey of William of Rubruck to the Eastern Parts of the World, 1253-55, with Two Accounts of the Earlier Journey of John of Pian de Carpine*. London: Hakluyt Society, 1900. Reprint. Nedeln, Liechtenstein: Kraus Reprint Limited, 1967. An introduction summarizes the history of the early thirteenth century. There is an extensive bibliography to 1900, a good index, and an excellent route map showing Carpini's and Rubrouck's travels. The translations include explanatory footnotes.

Skelton, R. A., Thomas E. Marston, and George D. Painter. *The Vinland Map and the "Tartar Relation."* New Haven, Conn.: Yale University Press, 1965. This work represents the most complete version and discussion printed to date of Carpini's travels among the Mongols. The *Tartar Relation* manuscript, another account of the history and culture of the Mongols, was apparently finished by a Franciscan friar, C. de Bridia, in 1247, around the same time that Carpini was recording his observations. This volume contains valuable maps, analyses, notes, an extensive bibliography, and indexes.

SEE ALSO: Saint Francis of Assisi; Gregory IX; Innocent IV; Louis IX; Marco Polo; Vincent of Beauvais; William of Rubrouck.

RELATED ARTICLES in *Great Events from History: The Middle Ages, 477-1453*: 1204: Genghis Khan Founds Mongol Empire; April 16, 1209: Founding of the Franciscans; 1233: Papal Inquisition; 1248-1254: Failure of the Seventh Crusade; 1271-1295: Travels of Marco Polo.

CASIMIR THE GREAT

King of Poland (r. 1333-1370)

Casimir inherited a reunited Poland and shaped it into a major Central European power that was subsequently nurtured through a brilliant golden age lasting three centuries.

BORN: April 30, 1310; Kujavia, Poland
DIED: November 5, 1370; Kraków, Poland
ALSO KNOWN AS: Casimir III; Kazimierz Wielki
AREAS OF ACHIEVEMENT: Government and politics, law, military

EARLY LIFE

Casimir (KAHZ-ih-mihr) was born the third son, sixth and youngest child, of Queen Jadwiga and King Władysław I. Stephan, the oldest, had died in 1306, and Władysław, the second oldest, died in 1312, leaving Casimir heir to the throne almost from birth. He was destined to become the most notable, but unfortunately the last, monarch of the ancient Polish royal dynasty—the Piasts.

As a prince, Casimir received a limited education. His tutors, Archdeacon Jarosław Bogoria (later archbishop of Kraków) and Spytko of Melsztyn, the castellan of Kraków, instilled in him an appreciation of diplomacy and of the written law. From his father he learned the military craft, sharing the responsibilities of leadership with the king on numerous campaigns.

The prince's experiential education was further deepened in 1329, when he was sent on a diplomatic mission to the Hungarian court in search of military aid for his father's future campaigns. Sometime later, Casimir was made administrator of Great Poland, plus the districts of Sieradz and Kujawia, ruling through his father's royal authority. The objective here was to strengthen the frontiers against German encroachment. It is clear that Władysław was grooming his only surviving son for the kingship.

This practical learning took deep root, and Casimir developed into a thoughtful long-range planner and very able ruler. Yet at the same time, the future king was a person who believed in enjoying life to the fullest. His personality is best described as jovial, energetic, and highly passionate. One might imagine that this latter characteristic greatly concerned his mother, a restrained, pious woman who once a year ate and slept in a nearby convent dedicated to Saint Clare.

Władysław, hoping to sober the prince's spirits by marriage, arranged his son's betrothal to Jutta, daughter of John of Luxembourg, king of Bohemia (r. 1310-1346), in 1322. Such a union might have reconciled the houses of Piast and Luxembourg as well as providing Poland with an ally against the Teutonic Order. Unfortunately for diplomacy, but happily for love, the negotiations collapsed.

Casimir's romantic interests were to be realized in Aldona, a daughter of Gediminas, grand duke of Lithuania. A Polish-Lithuanian alliance was signed in the fall of 1325 and was sealed with the engagement of Casimir to Aldona. She was to bring as her dowry not gold or silver but Polish prisoners held in Lithuanian captivity. The future bride was also required to be baptized. (She took the Christian name Anna.) The couple married on October 16 of that year.

Casimir's new wife loved games and dances and was accompanied by handmaidens, drummers, and flutists wherever she went. She enlivened a very restrained court but was not well liked by her contemporaries. In fact, the queen mother tried to prevent Aldona's being crowned alongside Casimir. Failing in the attempt, Jadwiga eventually entered her beloved convent of Saint Clare, where she spent the rest of her life. Yet clearly Aldona had pleased her husband very much, for at her death in 1339, he went into deep mourning and despair.

The coronation took place on the Feast of Saint Mark (April 23, 1333) and was a grand affair. Casimir was royally garbed by the nation's bishops in the palace on Wawel Hill. The nearby cathedral was the scene of his consecration and coronation, along with the installation of his wife as queen of Poland. Celebrations in the form of dances, tournaments, and general merriment continued unabated for days. At the same time, the young king was provided with an able adviser, his former tutor Spytko of Melsztyn, who served the last Piast well.

Engraved sigillum, or seal, containing the likeness of Casimir the Great. (Library of Congress)

LIFE'S WORK

Casimir was a more versatile political talent than his father. The coronation set in motion a brilliant reign that prepared the way for the Jagiellons and initiated Poland's golden age. The twentieth century scholar Oskar Halecki suggests three major divisions of Casimir's reign. The first decade was devoted to resolving problems inherited from his father, which necessitated finding at least temporary solutions for the protection of Polish interests. Second, the significance of Casimir's eastward expansion, undertaken to compensate for territorial concessions in the West, was critical, for it set the state's direction for the next five centuries. The final phase of Casimir's reign dealt with economic, constitutional, social, and cultural considerations.

Throughout all of these was the issue of the succession, the importance of which increased as the king entered his later years and the possibility of an heir decreased.

Pressure from the Germans of Bohemia and Brandenburg and the Teutonic Knights (or Teutonic Order) was Poland's major problem in the fourteenth century. The order, then at the height of its power, sought outright annexation of Polish territory. John of Luxembourg put forth a claim to the Polish throne and continually referred to Casimir as "king of Kraków." The remaining states supported the Bohemians and the Teutonic Knights in promoting German interests to Poland's detriment.

War had been Władysław's answer to German pressure, especially that of the Teutonic Order, but this had proved costly and of limited effect. Casimir, recognizing this, sought to normalize relations with the order. Extensions of an earlier truce gave the Poles a respite in 1334 and again in 1335.

Also in 1335, John of Luxembourg was induced to renounce his claims to Poland in exchange for 400,000 silver groats and Casimir's recognition of John's suzerainty over most of Silesia. John also agreed to act as arbitrator along with the Hungarian king in territorial disputes between Poland and the Teutonic Knights. The price was high, but improved relations with Bohemia were worth the cost.

Meanwhile, Poland and the Teutonic Order were trying to reach some understanding concerning the disputed territories. In 1320, an ecclesiastical court convened to hear the claims of the parties, but the ruling, though in Poland's favor, was not enforced. In 1339, Pope Benedict XII (1334-1342) appointed two French clerics along with his nuncio to review the issues once again. The court heard testimony in Warsaw from February 4 to September 15. The Teutonic Knights chose not to defend themselves against the charges but to object to the legality of the proceedings, as they had some twenty years earlier. Most of the time the order kept no representation at the hearings, while Polish representatives flooded the transcript with testimony.

More than one hundred witnesses, representing a cross section of Polish society (clergy, nobles, knights, burghers, and commons), presented testimony in response to the judges' questions. Views were expressed on Poland's right to the disputed areas, on the nature of the kingdom's frontiers, and on the destructiveness of the order's repeated invasions. The judges noted whether the witness was literate, his or her age, and other circumstances that might have influenced the person's statements. A remarkable picture of Polish national feeling emerges from these documents. The judges again found in favor of the Crown. All territory was to be returned to Poland, and the Teutonic Knights were ordered to pay a huge indemnity to compensate for their destruction of property. They were also to pay the costs incurred by the Church for the hearing.

Despite the fact that the pope himself believed that the indemnity was too harsh (about twice the annual income of the Polish state) and even though no international enforcement was available, the decision helped move the order to an agreement with Casimir. Public opinion as a result of the 1321 and 1339 decisions could have restricted the flow of western funds and manpower to the Teutonic Knights, while Poland's interests would be best served by relief from western pressure and the cost of war. The Treaty of Kalisz in 1343 was the result. The order kept Chełmno, Michalów, and Pomorze (the bulk of the disputed area), while Casimir received Kujawia and Dobrzyń and a payment of ten thousand florins as an indemnity. The needed peace was finally achieved.

These concessions to German expansion in the west, especially the loss of Pomorze and Silesia, were met with much national resistance. The king was accused by both clergy and nobles of having gone too far; the latter underscored their point with raids into the order's possessions. It was against this background that Casimir began Poland's eastward movement.

Various reasons for this initiative have been offered over the centuries. Jan Długosz, the fifteenth century historian, suggested that wars with the Lithuanians and Ruthenians convinced the king to secure his western frontiers and then to expand the state to the southeast as compensation. In other words, Ruthenia drew him away from Pomorze. Others have since argued that Casimir sought to acquire Ruthenia in order to strengthen his kingdom, planning with the added power to retake these western concessions later.

The opportunity for this eastward move came when the king's cousin, the childless Bolesław, was poisoned to death by his boyars. Bolesław was a Piast prince who through family ties inherited Ruthenia and, in turn, designated Casimir as his heir. Some of this area had been historically Polish but was now peopled by Ruthenians and contested by Lithuanians and Tatars. Casimir sought to gain popular support in this region by respecting local customs and guaranteeing the rights of the Orthodox Church. A number of boyars resisted his overtures—even favoring the Tatars over the Poles—while Lubart of Lithuania sought the area for himself and occupied Volhynia. The only Polish ally in these eastern campaigns was King Louis the Great of Hungary and Poland (r. 1342-1382 and 1370-1382), Casimir's nephew and the son of the deceased Hungarian king, Charles I (Charles Robert of Anjou; r. 1308-1342). After years of seesaw contests with various opponents in the region, Casimir succeeded in controlling twenty-six thousand square miles of Ruthenian territory, thus irrevocably setting Poland's pattern of expansion eastward.

Internal issues occupied the king throughout his reign. One of the most important of these was his intent to create a uniform legal code for the entire country; he managed, however, only to produce separate statutes for Little Poland and Great Poland. In 1347, diets were called to develop a code for each region.

POLAND'S PIAST DYNASTY, 962-1370

Reign	*Ruler*
962-992	Mieszko I
992-1025	Bolesław I the Brave
1025-1034	Mieszko II
1034-1037	Instability
1037-1058	Casimir I the Restorer
	Instability
1058-1079	Bolesław II
1079-1102	Władysław (Vladislav or Ladislas) I
1102-1106	Zbigniev (rival to brother Bolesław III)
1102-1138	Bolesław III
1138-1146	Instability following Bolesław III's division of Poland into five principalities
1146-1173	Bolesław IV
1173-1177	Mieszko III
1177-1194	Casimir II
1194-1227	Leszek I
1227-1279	Bolesław V
1228-1288	Instability: arrival of Teutonic Knights followed by Mongol incursions
1288-1290	Henry Probus
1290-1296	Przemyslav II (crowned 1295)
1297-1300	Instability
1300-1305	Wenceslaus (Vacław) I
1306-1333	Władysław I (Vladislav IV, Lokietek)
1333-1370	CASIMIR III THE GREAT
1370	End of the Piast Dynasty

Traditional customary law served as the basis for these efforts but was significantly augmented from Bohemian, Hungarian, and Italian sources. (Naturally, Italy was the home of Roman law and medieval legal studies.) The Church also contributed the influence of canon law. The codification was inspired by a desire to protect all levels of Polish society. This code provided the basis for the evolution of Polish law.

Along with the code, Casimir promoted the studies of young Poles abroad. Yet difficulties in traveling the great distances to Italian schools, plus a desire to establish higher education in his country, prompted the king to request a Polish university charter from Pope Urban V (1362-1370). Conditions conducive to establishing such a center in Poland were now present. Political stability and economic prosperity had been achieved, many contacts with the West had been established, and the country had built a number of lesser schools, which provided the necessary intellectual climate. The Papacy saw this foundation as a base from which Catholicism might spread eastward in the wake of Polish expansion.

May 12, 1364, is the traditional date associated with the University of Kraków's foundation. The charter provided for the establishment of one chair in liberal arts, two in medicine, three in canon law, and five in Roman law. Clearly, the king's intent was the development of legal studies as paramount, probably to train civil servants for his growing administrative needs. Funds for maintaining the institution came from the royal salt monopoly at nearby Wieliczka. Control of the school was given to the crown chancellor, rather than to the local bishop as was customary in many foundations. The city of Kraków granted privileges to the university's staff and their families on the same day. Unfortunately, many matters regarding the school's early years are not known. Scholars do not know its first location and know little about its faculty, its student body, and, most frustrating of all, why it apparently collapsed and had to be resurrected by the first Jagiellon ruler of Poland in 1400.

On September 9, 1370, during a hunt for stags, Casimir's horse fell, and the king suffered abrasions to his left shin. Soon he was beset with a fever, which appeared intermittently for varying periods of time. By October 30, the king appeared to be in the terminal phase of his illness. He died, probably of pneumonia, about sunrise on November 5, 1370. So ended Poland's medieval dynasty.

SIGNIFICANCE

Poland in this period was embarking on a three-century-long odyssey, a golden age. Scholarship, art, culture, and military and economic power were all components of this creative explosion that began with the reign of Casimir the Great.

One has only to travel the modern highways and byways of Casimir's medieval kingdom to appreciate the grand scale of his construction efforts. Impregnable castles and fortified towns protected the kingdom from the Teutonic Knights in Pomorze. This line then continued along the Polish-Silesian frontier, providing the same strength to Kraków. To the southeast, three other defensive systems aimed at preventing incursions from Ruthenia and helped to anchor Polish power there. To this day, it would be unusual to pass through a community of any size in this area that does not boast a church, monastery, or municipal edifice funded by the king.

Along with encouraging the economic growth and physical expansion of the towns, Casimir involved burghers and the lower gentry in national life. His promotion of members of these social classes to important administrative posts won for him their devotion. In a successful effort to weaken regionalism, he sent gentry administrators from Great Poland to Little Poland and vice versa, thus creating new ties within various provinces.

Casimir has often been referred to as "king of the peasants." He defended them from abuses and famine, establishing state granaries for the latter purpose. He was rewarded with their devotion. Often, country folk and the poor would clog the roadway to Wawel Hill before dawn to bring the king simple gifts, tokens of their affection. He was also viewed as a protector of the Jews who fled to Poland, especially from Germany, in large numbers during his reign. Casimir twice reconfirmed the Charter of Privileges granted Jews by Bolesław the Chaste in 1264. The Eastern Orthodox in Ruthenia were also protected, and the king sought the establishment of the first metropolitan in their major city of Halicz.

Casimir's greatest failure lay in not providing for an heir to continue the Piast Dynasty. He had several daughters and three sons from various unions, but none of the latter had legal claim to paternity. As a result, the succession to the Polish throne passed to Louis of Hungary. The choice reflected the close relationship that existed between Poles and Hungarians in this period as well as the friendship and affection of Casimir for Charles I, Louis's father. Formal agreements between the two states assured the outcome. (The last agreement was signed at Buda in 1355.) On this basis, the crown of the Piasts passed to the Hungarian royal house when Casimir died.

Casimir is the only Polish monarch to have been granted the title "the Great" by his country folk. His calls for peace over war, diplomacy over confrontation, and stability over uncertainty justify the appellation. He was a soother of the national spirit and a builder of the national wealth. He husbanded the country's resources and nurtured the Polish intellect. Most important, he protected his people.

—*Richard J. Kubiak*

FURTHER READING

Davies, Norman. *The Origins to 1795*. Vol. 1 in *God's Playground: A History of Poland*. New York: Columbia University Press, 1982. Contains an excellent chapter dealing with the significance of Władysław I and Casimir in the context of Polish history through the eighteenth century.

Halecki, Oskar. *A History of Poland*. New York: Roy, 1943. This historical survey of Poland includes a comprehensive chapter on Casimir's statecraft.

Jasienica, Pawel. *Piast Poland*. Translated by Alexander Jordan. New York: Hippocrene Books, 1985. A history of Poland under the Piasts, covering the dynasty from its beginnings through Casimir's reign.

Knoll, Paul W. "Casimir the Great and the University of Cracow." *Jahr-bücher für Geschichte Osteuropas*, n.s. 16 (June, 1968): 232-249. Discusses the foundation of the University of Kraków and Casimir's involvement.

_______. *The Rise of the Polish Monarchy: Piast Poland in East Central Europe, 1320-1370*. Chicago: University of Chicago Press, 1972. A detailed study of the development of Poland from reunification to major power under the last Piasts.

Lukowski, Jerzy, and Hubert Zawadski. *A Concise History of Poland*. New York: Cambridge University Press, 2001. A general introduction to Polish history. The chapter on the Piast Dynasty places Casimir in the context of his forebears and followers.

Reddaway, W. F., et al., eds. *The Cambridge History of Poland*. Vol. 1, *From the Origins to Sobieski (to 1696)*. New York: Octagon Books, 1971. Contains a chapter which deals with Casimir's wide-ranging achievements.

Vetulani, Adam. "The Jews in Medieval Poland." *Jewish Journal of Sociology* 4 (1962): 274-294. A discussion of the Jewish medieval experience in Poland, including the period of Casimir's reign. Written by one of Poland's premier legal historians.

SEE ALSO: Władysław II Jagiełło and Jadwiga.

RELATED ARTICLES in *Great Events from History: The Middle Ages, 477-1453*: c. 960: Jews Settle in Bohemia; 1228-1231: Teutonic Knights Bring Baltic Region Under Catholic Control; July 15, 1410: Battle of Tannenberg.

CASSIODORUS

Italian statesman and writer

Cassiodorus aided in the cultural synthesis of Germanic, Greco-Roman, and Christian cultures in the transition period between the late Roman Empire and the early Middle Ages and was a key conservator of ancient manuscripts for later generations.

BORN: c. 490; Scyllacium, Calabria, Kingdom of the Ostrogoths (now Squillace, Italy)

DIED: c. 585; Vivarium, Calabria (now in Italy)

ALSO KNOWN AS: Flavius Magnus Aurelius Cassiodorus (full name)

AREAS OF ACHIEVEMENT: Government and politics, historiography, monasticism

EARLY LIFE

When the Roman Empire collapsed and fell to invading Goths, Ostrogoths, and Vandals, the Germanic tribes dealt with the Romans in contrasting ways. Vandals in North Africa treated Romans as conquered subjects and sought to destroy their culture. The Ostrogoths in Rome were quite different: They valued the existing Greco-Roman culture and attempted to build on it and assimilate what they considered worthwhile. Many had already accepted Arian Christianity and were drawn to the education and the arts of the classical world. To that end, they hired cultured, well-educated Romans to serve in their courts and to preserve the culture of the Roman world. One of the officials who were used in that capacity by Theodoric the Great, king of the Ostrogoths, was Flavius Magnus Aurelius Cassiodorus, usually known as Cassiodorus (kash-ee-uh-DOHR-uhs).

Cassiodorus was born on a luxurious estate on the south coast of the Ionian Sea, near the modern Gulf of Squillace. The temperate climate produced grapes, grains, and olives. Cassiodorus's grandfather was a Roman general and his father was a wealthy, aristocratic diplomat, esteemed by the king, who was in charge of the imperial lands and, later, of the royal treasury. He was also the governor of Sicily and of Calabria. His family was noted for its honesty and integrity in public service.

Cassiodorus benefited from an excellent classical education and entered public office in the service of the Ostrogothic rulers. He was schooled in Latin and Greek literature and, typical for aristocratic students, in rhetoric. This educational foundation helped to develop Cassiodorus's literary gifts; he became one of the most distinguished writers of the period.

Cassiodorus was reared a good Catholic, and he remained orthodox all of his life. It is most interesting that he and Theodoric were able to produce a cultural synthesis of Roman, Greek, and Gothic elements. Indeed, one of Cassiodorus's principal works was *History of the Goths* (519), which is no longer extant. Theodoric's Arianism did not cause undue tension with Cassiodorus's orthodox Catholic faith. Each man respected the other, and both wished to see a coexistence between clashing cultures. Theodoric achieved a working relationship between Romans and Goths. He emulated much of the Roman political system, retaining the offices and titles of imperial Rome. The architecture and furnishings of his palace resembled Constantinople. The army was made up of Goths, and the civil government was largely composed of Romans. Cassiodorus was a key government administrator.

LIFE'S WORK

Cassiodorus served as his father's *consiliarius*, a legal assistant, and Theodoric appointed him, at the age of twenty, a quaestor, the king's private secretary and legal adviser in the preparation of administrative law. Later, Theodoric made him a consul and in 527 a magister-officiorum, giving him responsibility for polishing the writings and speeches of the quaestors. Cassiodorus's literary ability was obvious: He worded many public documents and was a confidant of the king. King Athalaric, Theodoric's grandson, appointed Cassiodorus praetorian prefect for Italy, in effect making him prime minister of the Ostrogothic civil government from 533 to 538. Cassiodorus supervised the collection of taxes and the administration of justice. Vicars, provincial governors, proconsuls and all were subordinate to him.

He ended his public career when the Byzantine emperor Justinian I defeated the Goths in 551 and expanded westward into Italy. After fifteen years in Constantinople, Cassiodorus returned to his family's estates overlooking the Ionian Sea; in retirement, he began a second career almost as long and productive as his civil service.

Cassiodorus was sixty-five years old when he established two monasteries on his estates at Vivarium (meaning "fish pond," named after his landscaped gardens). He was primarily interested in an intellectual, peaceful monastic life, but he also sought to refresh travelers and provide for the poor from his irrigated gardens. He channeled the river Pellena into his fish ponds and used the power of the river to turn the monasteries' mills. Fresh water was abundant in this earthly paradise within sight and sound of the Mediterranean Sea.

For nearly thirty years, Cassiodorus collected a large library, supervising the preservation and copying of invaluable ancient manuscripts. His monks copied and studied the Bible, works of the church fathers, and ancient Greek and Latin classics. Cassiodorus also prepared a guide for monastic education, which was used for many generations, sought refined learning under the authority of Scripture and church tradition, and prepared a bibliography of studies on all the sections of the Bible. In his detailed instructions for accurate transcription of texts in the scriptorium, he allowed slight stylistic emendation of texts, with the exception of the text of Scripture, where particular care was made to compare the ancient copies. Cassiodorus continued writing and working into his ninety-third year; he died, at the age of ninety-five, on the peaceful estate where he had dedicated many years to preserving ancient manuscripts and to studying and teaching theology.

SIGNIFICANCE

Cassiodorus inspired scholarly pursuits in other monasteries as well as his own. His example helped enormously in the preservation of ancient manuscripts and in creating copies of works from the classical world and from the early Christian centuries. His own writings, too, greatly enhanced historical knowledge of his own era. For example, *Variae* (537; *The Variae of Magnus Aurelius Cassiodorus Senator*, 1886; better known as the *Variae*), a work in twelve volumes collected during his years in public office, contains voluminous letters, proclamations, official appointments, edicts, records of judicial decisions, and administrative orders of the Ostrogothic kingdoms. It is an invaluable source of information concerning all aspects of life in that period of history: economic, cultural, political, and diplomatic. *History of the Goths* is adulatory and one-sided, but it, too, provides detailed information concerning the Goths and their perspective of their struggle and coexistence with the Romans.

Modern knowledge of church history would be much sparser without his twelve-volume *Historia ecclesiastica tripartita* (c. 540-559), which became the principal source used in the Middle Ages for the history it covered, while *De orthographia* (c. 583) was designed to systematize the rules for copying manuscripts. The care with which the monks of the Middle Ages copied and preserved ancient manuscripts has been an indispensable link for modern knowledge of the ancient and medieval worlds.

In addition to these historical efforts, Cassiodorus designed a complete book of instruction for the Western monasteries, *Institutiones divinarum et humanarum lectionum* (562; *An Introduction to Divine and Human Readings*, 1946, better known as *Institutiones*), which includes a catalog of the books contained in the library at Vivarium. His division of scholarship into categories was followed throughout the Middle Ages: grammar, rhetoric, dialectic, arithmetic, music, geometry, and astronomy. Finally, Cassiodorus's *Expositio Psalmorum* (c. 540-548; *Cassiodorus: Explanation of the Psalms*, 1990-1991) was one of his most famous expositions of Scripture and devotional works, of which he wrote many.

Cassiodorus is only a small part of the larger story in which he was a participant, but he was particularly significant historically. He played a key role in the transition from the Roman Empire to the early Middle Ages and helped to synthesize the Gothic-Greco-Roman-Christian culture that was emerging. He was a good steward for the Gothic kings but was faithful to his culture, his church, and his God also. He helped perpetuate his love of learning and organized the European monastic educational system. He organized, sorted, and classified scholarly materials that became essential tools of medieval Scholasticism. Above all, he was an essential conservator of the literary treasures of antiquity and the early Church for future generations.

—*William H. Burnside*

FURTHER READING

Burns, Thomas S. *A History of the Ostrogoths*. Bloomington: Indiana University Press, 1984. To understand the historical importance of Cassiodorus, one needs to have a knowledge of the Ostrogoths he served. This book portrays their culture and values as well as their history. It describes the synthesis of two cultures: Germanic and Roman.

Cassiodorus. *Cassiodorus: An Explanation of the Psalms*. Translated and annotated by P. G. Walsh. 3 vols. New York: Paulist Press, 1990-1991. The commentary that accompanies this translation sheds light on the psalms and on their author.

_______. *An Introduction to Divine and Human Readings*. Translated by Lewlis Webber Jones. 1946. Reprint. New York: Octagon Books, 1966. This translation of *Institutiones* provides an understanding of the writer and statesman as well as of the work itself.

_______. *The "Variae" of Magnus Aurelius Cassiodorus Senator*. Translated with notes and introduction by S. J. B. Barnish. Liverpool: Liverpool University Press, 1992. This translation and notes provide valuable information on Cassiodorus.

O'Donnell, James J. *Cassiodorus*. Berkeley: University of California Press, 1979. An important study of Cassiodorus, it analyzes the books he wrote, his career in the service of the Ostrogoths, and his establishment of and life in the monasteries of Vivarium. An unusual feature of this book is the author's explanation of his sources and the procedures used in their critical analysis.

Previté-Orton, C. W. *The Shorter Cambridge Medieval History*. 2 vols. 1962. Reprint. New York: Cambridge University Press, 1971. The first volume focuses on the period from the later Roman Empire to the twelfth century. Illustrations, maps, and index.

SEE ALSO: Justinian I; Theodoric the Great.

RELATED ARTICLES in *Great Events from History: The Middle Ages, 477-1453*: 529-534: Justinian's Code Is Compiled; 568-571: Lombard Conquest of Italy.

SAINT CATHERINE OF SIENA

Italian nun and mystic

This patron saint of Italy and doctor of the Church helped to persuade the Avignon Papacy to return to Rome. She is also known for her mystic writings, which advocate a combination of personal ecstatic experience with active service in the world.

BORN: March 25, 1347; Siena, Tuscany (now in Italy)
DIED: April 29, 1380; Rome (now in Italy)
ALSO KNOWN AS: Caterina Benincasa (given name)
AREAS OF ACHIEVEMENT: Religion and theology, church government

EARLY LIFE

Caterina Benincasa was born in Siena (see-EHN-uh), Italy, the twenty-third child of Giacomo Benincasa, a cloth dyer, and his wife, Lapa Piacenti. Lapa was more than forty years old when Catherine and her twin sister, Giovanna, were born and did not believe that she could nurse both infants. She sent Giovanna to a wet nurse and nurtured Catherine herself. In her old age, Lapa remembered Catherine as a specially favored child, nursed by her mother for a full year and brought to robust health, while her less fortunate twin died. Catherine remained attached to her family throughout her life, and images of nurturing pervade her writings.

The young Catherine was also influenced by Sienese life in the mid-fourteenth century. When she was a year old, the Black Death (bubonic plague) swept through the city, beginning a series of epidemics that brought death and panic. The Benincasa family was not prosperous enough to leave the city; Catherine lost a number of siblings and spent her early years surrounded by the fear of death and of God's punishment.

Catherine also heard of momentous happenings in the larger Christian world. The Dominican monks who preached in Siena told of the popes who lived in Avignon, France, instead of in Rome. She also heard of the Christian hope for a crusade that would once and for all free the Holy Land from the Muslims who held it. These events and expectations influenced the causes that she championed later in her life.

Catherine was drawn early to the religious life. At the age of six or seven, she had her first vision of Christ smiling at her. Between the ages of seven and twelve, she continued to grow spiritually, secretly making a vow of chastity and attempting to recapture the sweet vision that had so moved her.

When Catherine reached adolescence, her family wanted to find for her a good husband. For a while, Catherine accepted this role, but when she was fifteen, her favorite older sister died in childbirth. From that time on, Catherine actively rejected the world and began the strict self-denial that marked her life. She slept little, bound an iron chain tightly about her hips, and whipped herself daily. She consumed only bread, water, and raw vegetables, and a few years later she gave up the bread and ate almost nothing at all. She wanted to conquer all fleshly desires and leave room only for the spiritual life.

By the time she was sixteen, all these activities had persuaded her family that she was serious about her calling, and she joined the Dominican order in the congregation of the Sisters of Penance. This order of nuns did not stay in a convent, so Catherine continued to live at home with her family. From 1364 to 1367, she lived in isolation, praying and having ecstatic religious experiences in which she felt that Christ was one with her in a form of spiritual marriage. These experiences would continue throughout her life. In 1370, Catherine received the command to go into the world to do God's work.

LIFE'S WORK

Catherine began her work of serving God in Siena. She cared for the poor, giving away all of her possessions and many of her family's goods. She also patiently cared for the sick. During this time of activity, she continued to abuse her body to overcome the flesh, and these austerities took their toll on her health. She was strikingly thin and often had to take to her bed, exhausted by her fasting and the ecstatic experiences that made her seem to be in a trance.

In these early years of activity, Catherine began to acquire a following. She became the spiritual mother of a group of disciples that surrounded her until her death. At this time, she also acquired critics, who did not believe that she did not eat or that her religious trances were real. She became well-known, and her influence began to extend from caretaking to political action.

The Christian world was experiencing exciting political developments in 1370. In that year, Pope Urban V abandoned the city of Rome, to which he had returned briefly, to take the Papacy back to southern France. In the following year, the new pope, Gregory XI, called a Crusade. Throughout 1372, Catherine was an eager supporter of that crusade. She urged people to give money and other support to the venture. The Crusade never materialized, but Catherine increased her reputation as advocate of the Church's causes.

In 1374, Catherine was summoned to Florence to testify before the Dominican order. Church officials wanted to see if this young woman who was acquiring such a reputation for sanctity was in fact a servant of God. After questioning her, the officials agreed that she was indeed holy, but to be sure that she would remain so, they assigned Raymond of Capua to be her companion and confessor. Raymond stayed with Catherine throughout her life and wrote her biography. The Dominican officials were as concerned about the correctness of Catherine's perpetual fast as some of her neighbors had been, and they ordered her to eat. To demonstrate her obedience to church authority, she obeyed the order to eat but suffered severely from the food in her stomach until she forced herself to vomit. By her obedience in trying to eat, Catherine earned permission to continue her fasting.

In 1374, Catherine's political activity began to increase. Although she had never learned to read and write, she dictated letters to Italy's political figures, urging them not to take part in Florence's war on the Papacy that had been declared in 1375. She traveled to Pisa to try to dissuade other Italian cities from joining the antipapal league. She even wrote to the famous mercenary soldier John Hawkwood to urge him to Christian behavior. She believed that many of these internal Italian wars were increased by the pope's continued absence in France, and she took up the cause of persuading him to return to Rome.

These political activities did not interfere with her spiritual growth. She continued her religious trances, and in 1375, she received the stigmata, the piercing of her hands and feet as Christ had been pierced. This mark of union with Christ was a high honor, but Catherine was so modest that she asked God to keep the marks invisible. (Most who received the stigmata bled from their hands and feet.) Needless to say, there was controversy for centuries about whether Catherine had received the marks because there was no visible evidence for it. (In 1630, Pope Urban VIII pronounced her stigmata authentic, and since then, it has been accepted by the Church as fact.)

In 1376, Catherine traveled to Avignon to talk to the pope. She urged him to reform the Church, and as a critical part of that reform, she wanted him to return to Rome. In September, 1376, Catherine's dream was fulfilled and Pope Gregory XI left Avignon to return to Rome, where he would be plagued by political problems until his death in March, 1378. Catherine's part in influencing the pope's return is remembered as her major political accomplishment, although historians have since downplayed her role in the papal move, emphasizing the unrest and violence in France at the time as a more prominent reason for the pope's decision.

Catherine returned to Italy, where between 1377 and 1378 she composed her great mystical work, which she simply called "Book," but which has come to be known as *Libro della divina dottrina* (*The Dialogue of the Seraphic Virgin, Catherine of Siena*, 1896; better known as *The Dialogue*). In this work, she articulated more fully the mystical theology of love and service that was evident in her many letters. Catherine must have believed that her major life's work was accomplished; she had written her mystic vision and she had brought the pope back to his rightful home in Rome. However, political events were once more to draw her into the secular world.

After Gregory XI's death in 1378, the Papacy underwent a crisis even more serious than the pope's residence in France. Urban VI was elected to be Gregory's successor, but in September of 1378, thirteen disaffected cardinals returned to Avignon and elected Clement VII to be

Saint Catherine of Siena. (Library of Congress)

pope. The Church was now split into two factions. The Great Schism would last until 1415, when the Council of Constance (1414-1418) was able again to reunite the Catholic world under one head. Catherine rallied to the support of Urban VI, whom she considered to be the rightful pope. She dictated letters to cardinals and kings, rebuking them for their betrayal of the unity and reform she had advocated. She moved to Rome to support Urban VI with her advice and prayers. Political events, however, had gone beyond that which she could change. In January, 1380, she turned to the only thing that she could control—her body. She increased her fast by refusing to drink even water. She would be a final sacrifice to save the Church. Her last months were plagued by pain and visions of demons, and on April 29, 1380, Catherine died with a final vision of the weight of the ship of the Church (that she had worked so hard to save) descending onto her shoulders.

Significance

In 1395, Catherine's confessor, Raymond of Capua, completed his *Legenda major* (*The Life of Catherine of Siena*, 1960). He wrote the long biography based on interviews with Catherine's mother and other followers. This biography was widely read and copied. In 1477, an Italian translation was made of Raymond's Latin text, and this became one of the first printed books. Catherine's life was a model for others who wanted to serve the Church through a life of self-sacrifice and mystic longing. Her influence also extended beyond the example of her life. In 1461, she was declared a saint by Pope Pius II, and she is considered, with Saint Francis of Assisi, as a patron saint of Italy.

Catherine's influence has been recognized into the twentieth century. In 1970, Pope Paul VI declared Catherine to be a doctor of the Church. She and Saint Teresa of Ávila are the only women who have been granted this status. By bestowing the title of doctor on Catherine, the pope declared that Catherine's writings are worthy to be studied by all Catholics.

There were several reasons that the pope found Catherine's writings worthwhile. The first was that her mysticism, her religious ecstasies, did not cause her to retire from the world. On the contrary, Catherine believed that her mystic connection with Christ required that she work actively to help her neighbors, her church, and her world.

A second important theme in her works was that there could be no Christian life outside the hierarchic structure of the Catholic Church. She believed that the blood of Christ flowed through the Church, so no one should be separate from that structure even if they had, like she, been joined mystically to Christ. This made her work actively to support the Church and the Papacy. This effort was particularly important during the late fourteenth century, when the hierarchic church was troubled by so many tensions and political problems. Hers was a voice that reminded the Church that its task was a spiritual one and reminded believers of their intimate relationship to that church.

Finally, Pope Paul VI declared her spirit of self-sacrifice to be worthy of awe. It is perhaps for this spirit that Catherine remains best known. The pious child who starved herself and abused her body to rebel against her parents' desire that she marry and to rebel against her own desires for physical comfort later continued those sacrifices to join spiritually with Christ and to serve the Church. At the end, she starved herself in a final sacrifice, attempting to save the Church she had worked all of her short life to reform.

—*Joyce E. Salisbury*

Further Reading

Catherine of Siena, Saint. *Catherine of Siena: Passion for the Truth, Compassion for Humanity.* Edited, annotated, and introduced by Mary O'Driscoll. New Rochelle, N.Y.: New City Press, 1993. A translation of selected writings of the saint, with introductory notes that provide valuable information on her life and theology. Bibliography.

_______. *The Dialogue: Catherine of Siena.* Translated by Suzanne Noffke. New York: Paulist Press, 1980. The introduction gives a short summary of the saint's life and thought and describes the structure of *The Dialogue.* Indispensable for those who seek a full understanding of Catherine's theology. Contains a complete bibliography and index.

_______. *The Letters of Catherine of Siena.* Translated by Suzanne Noffke. Tempe, Ariz.: Arizona Center for Medieval and Renaissance Studies, 2000. The first volume in the new English edition of Catherine of Siena's letters. Bibliography and indexes.

Cavallini, Giuliana. *Catherine of Siena.* New York: G. Chapman, 1998. A biography of Catherine that deals with her life, her writings, and her theological beliefs as well as her political interactions with the Church. Bibliography and index.

Hilkert, Mary Catherine. *Speaking with Authority: Catherine of Siena and the Voices of Women Today.* New York: Paulist Press, 2001. Hilkert discusses Catherine of Siena and her role in the Church. Bibliography.

Noffke, Suzanne. *Catherine of Siena: Vision Through a Distant Eye*. Collegeville, Minn.: Liturgical Press, 1996. Written by a leading authority on Catherine of Siena, this series of essays is divided into two parts: The first examines aspects of Catherine's vision in her theology and spirituality; the second offers resources for further exploration of Catherine's person and thought, of her world, and of what others have written of her in English. There is a very helpful annotated bibliography.

Raymond of Capua. *The Life of Catherine of Siena*. Translated by Conleth Kearns. Wilmington, Del.: Michael Glazier, 1980. Provides a translation of the *Legenda major*, which was completed in 1395 by her friend and confessor and forms the basis for all subsequent biographies. The introduction gives a good background of the life of Raymond and serves to complement the life of Catherine presented in this accessible translation.

See also: Saint Brigit; Saint Clare of Assisi; Saint Elizabeth of Hungary; Hildegard von Bingen; Saint Irene; Saint Isidore of Seville; Joan of Arc; Saint Ludmilla; Saint Olga.

Related articles in *Great Events from History: The Middle Ages, 477-1453*: 1248-1254: Failure of the Seventh Crusade; 1305-1417: Avignon Papacy and the Great Schism; c. 1320: Origins of the Bubonic Plague; 1347-1352: Invasion of the Black Death in Europe.

Guido Cavalcanti

Italian poet

Through his unique treatment of the theme of love, Cavalcanti became one of the major poets of the so-called dolce stil nuovo *school. He exerted a major influence on Dante and the love poets of the early Renaissance.*

Born: c. 1259; Florence (now in Italy)
Died: August 27 or 28, 1300; Florence
Area of achievement: Literature

Early Life

The importance of Guido Cavalcanti (kah-vahl-KAHN-tee) as one of the early masters of European love poetry becomes all the more remarkable in view of the paucity of information about his life. He was born in the middle of the thirteenth century, the period in which the vernacular Italian literature first arose. His family was aristocratic, proud of its status as one of the most powerful families of the Guelphs, a political faction that allied itself, generally, with the pope, as opposed to the so-called Ghibellines, who favored the cause of the emperor. Throughout the thirteenth century, factious rivalries between Guelph and Ghibelline parties often resulted in bloody feuding as well as in political chaos.

Cavalcanti himself seems to have been a proud, contentious man who was disdainful of the lower classes and often upheld his honor with his fists. Yet by contemporary accounts, he was also highly educated, introspective, scholarly, and philosophical. Giovanni Boccaccio (1313-1375), in his famous *Decameron: O, Prencipe Galeotto* (1349-1351; *The Decameron*, 1620), related a popular story about Cavalcanti, illustrative of his character and wit. A group of idle young gentlemen are riding one morning and spot Cavalcanti in a pensive mood, walking among the tombs in a graveyard. They begin teasing him about his reputation as an unbeliever, as a man of little faith who sought to prove that God did not exist. Cavalcanti looks up at them and calmly answers that they can say of him anything they wish, because men should be allowed to speak freely in their own houses. The cryptic nature of Guido's retort, by which the taunters were themselves impugned as being among the dead, their intellects entombed, as it were, by their own ignorance, is indicative of the subtlety of his thought and, ultimately, of his poetry. Cavalcanti did not deny his atheism, but by turning the tables on the young gentlemen, he did not confirm it either.

Certainly the image of entombment was associated with the Cavalcanti family in a scene in Dante's *Inferno*, part of *La divina commedia* (c. 1320; *The Divine Comedy*, 1802). In this circle of Hell, the heretics are encased in their sepulchers. Among these heretics and Epicureans—those philosophers who believed, among other things, that the soul perished with the body—is Cavalcanti's father. The father cries out, looking for his son, who, he implies, will also be damned for his philosophical pride.

Life's Work

Yet if Dante condemned Cavalcanti for his heretical views, part of which formed the basis of Cavalcanti's theory of love as mortality, he also respected the man as a poet. The two, in fact, were close friends. Dedicating his *La vita nuova* (c. 1292; *Vita Nuova*, 1861; better known as *The New Life*) to Cavalcanti, whom he called his "first friend," Dante relates that he once wrote a sonnet expressing in symbolic terms his vision of love and that Cavalcanti admired the poem and replied to it with a sonnet of his own. Thus from about the early 1280's, Cavalcanti and Dante were admirers of each other's work, and Dante's early poetry shows the unmistakable influence of the older man.

Yet the factiousness of Florentine politics, together with Cavalcanti's own disputatious personality, resulted in a split between the two friends. As a leader of the White Guelphs, rivals of the powerful Blacks, Cavalcanti was involved in the bloody feuds near the close of the century, and there were rumors that several attempts had been made on his life. Early in 1300, Dante, then a magistrate of Florence, found himself forced to banish Cavalcanti in the interest of peace. Guido went to Saranza, but while there, he contracted malaria. He was allowed to return to his native city, and it was there that he died in August, 1300, the same year in which the narrative of *The Divine Comedy* begins.

Cavalcanti's reputation rests on a handful of poems, his total output numbering about fifty sonnets, ballades, and *canzone*. Though his most characteristic poems are fraught with delicate complexity and rigorous analysis—as if he were, in effect, a philosopher or scientist parsing a rational solution to a central enigma in humankind's experience—his most appealing works are those sonnets that he addressed to his love, whom he named Primavera (springtime). These are marked by a humanity, a simple honesty that enhances their lyric beauty:

> Who is she who comes, on whom all gaze,
> Who starts the air to tremble, flooded with light?

Such poems as these placed Cavalcanti at the head of a school of poets whose work Dante later characterized as the *dolce stil nuovo*, the sweet new style. The subject matter of these poems might not have been new. (Indeed, the Provençal poets and troubadours of an earlier time had sung of love and its joys.) However, the treatment of love was new. Love, to these new poets, was an ennobling experience, sanctified, as it were, by the object of that love, a woman. She was not necessarily beautiful of face; it was her gentle heart, a sort of spiritual incandescence, that was crucial in the lover's apprehension of his love. The woman's gentle heart as both the source and repository of love was an idea that took on an almost mystical significance. The loved one became an ideal of Beauty, a representation of the Divine, and, therefore, a means of salvation.

One of the earliest Italian poets to treat love in this idealized manner was Guido Guinizelli, who died about 1275. Guinizelli first identified the noble heart, *cor gentil*, as the residence of love, and Cavalcanti seems to have adopted from this older poet the idea of love as ennobling. Greater than those of Guinizelli, Cavalcanti's poems are individualistic, personal responses to the experience of love. Like the generation of English Metaphysical poets of the early seventeenth century, Cavalcanti projects a voice, a personality of lyric subtlety and power. There is an intensity in the voice, an earnestness that evokes brilliantly the force and strength of love, as in the sonnet "Glimiei folli occhi," translated as "My Foolish, Reckless Eyes." Here the poet compares his state to that of a prisoner being hauled to court, sentenced, and punished with no hope of appeal.

A characteristic of Cavalcanti's work—that quality that sets it apart from the work of his contemporaries—is this intensity by which the best of his poems maintain a tension between the experience of love as ultimate joy and as physical torture relieved only by death. His poem "Della forza d'amore" ("On the Power of Love") clearly allies joy with despair, life with death, and concludes with the poet's cursing the hour when he first fell in love.

Cavalcanti's poems treat love not so much as an emotional but as a psychological experience, a tangle of contrary forces that, tragically, kill the very subject it seeks to redeem. In many of the poems, death and grief are central to the lover's condition; love, in Ezra Pound's phrase from one of Cavalcanti's sonnets, keeps "death-watch upon the heart." For Cavalcanti, death is a metaphor emblematic not so much of the physical destruction of the body as of the psychological disintegration of the mind. A later age would use the image of the lovesick courtier, pale and wan and pining away for his beloved, but Cavalcanti's lover is not of this kind. He is not the subject of parody, but of tragedy—a personality to whom love is not spiritually invigorating but psychically ruinous. Love alienates the soul from the rational principles on which it functions.

A rational explanation of love, in fact, is found in what is often regarded as Cavalcanti's most famous poem. Obscure, scientifically analytic, the *canzone* "Donna me prega" ("A Lady Asks Me") was the subject of many commentaries for more than two centuries. In it, Cavalcanti dissects the subject of love: He tells where it resides, who begets it, and what its nature, power, essence, and action are. This method of analysis is more characteristic of a Scholastic philosopher, well versed in Aristotle, than of a poet. Because of its abstruseness, the poem is not among his most popular, but it is important for an understanding of Cavalcanti's theory of love.

In declaring love to have its seat in the memory, that part of the soul that was then considered material, Cavalcanti suggests that love is purely physical and thus subject to death; merely material, love is an illusion of the mind, a distraction, a madness. The poem thus uses reason to indict the irrational quality of love and is a good example of Cavalcanti's contradictory aspect—a poet who sings sweetly of love though conscious of love's destructive force.

Significance

Cavalcanti's contribution to the *dolce stil nuovo* was his treatment of love as a conflict between pleasure and pain, a salvific force that should redeem and purify but which in reality more often destroys. Behind the images that have become commonplace in love poetry—the beauty of the lady's eyes, her loveliness of form, her angelic face—lies a darker meaning. Love is akin to tragedy, a contradiction that men must endure to become better creatures, though it brings but bitter consolation and an agony of spirit. There is, however, little cynicism even in the darkest of Cavalcanti's poems, for love is a sweetness, a genuine ecstasy that defies explanation. As he writes in his famous *canzone:* "No one can imagine love who has never been in love."

—*Edward Fiorelli*

Further Reading

Ardizzone, Maria Luisa. *Guido Cavalcanti: The Other Middle Ages*. Buffalo, N.Y.: University of Toronto Press, 2002. Ardizzone provides criticism and interpretation of the works of Cavalcanti, along with biographical information.

Cavalcanti, Guido. *The Complete Poems*. Translated and with an introduction by Marc A. Cirigliano. New York: Italica Press, 1992. Features parallel texts in English and Italian of Cavalcanti's poems. Introduction and notes contain discussions of his poetic works and life. Bibliography and index.

_______. *Thirty-three Sonnets of Guido Cavalcanti*. Translated by Ezra Pound. San Francisco: Arion Press, 1991. The introductory essays by Hugh Kenner and Lowry Nelson, Jr., provide useful information on Cavalcanti's works and life.

Pound, Ezra. *Make It New*. New Haven, Conn.: Yale University Press, 1935. One of the earliest modern studies of Cavalcanti is found in an appreciative essay in this book, together with Pound's translation of the *canzone*.

Rebay, Luciano, ed. *Italian Poetry: A Selection from Saint Francis of Assisi to Salvatore Quasimodo*. New York: Dover Books, 1969. Besides containing several fresh translations of the poems, the book is a good brief source of background material, particularly on the *dolce stil nuovo*.

See also: Cædmon; Charles d'Orléans; Alain Chartier; Geoffrey Chaucer; Christine de Pizan; Dante; Guillaume de Machaut; Marie de France; Petrarch.

Related articles in *Great Events from History: The Middle Ages, 477-1453*: c. 1100: Rise of Courtly Love; c. 1306-1320: Dante Writes *The Divine Comedy*; c. 1350-1400: Petrarch and Boccaccio Recover Classical Texts.

Charlemagne
Holy Roman Emperor (r. 800-814)

By 800, when he was crowned emperor by Pope Leo III, Charlemagne had revived the Roman idea of universal empire, had preserved through the Carolingian Renaissance much of the written legacy of the ancient world, and had established the foundation for a European civilization distinct from that of ancient Rome and from the contemporary Byzantine and Islamic Empires.

Born: April 2, 742; probably Aachen (also known as Aix-la-Chapelle), Austrasia (now in Germany)
Died: January 28, 814; Aachen
Also known as: Charles (birth name); Charles I; Charles the Great; Karl der Grosse; Carolus Magnus
Areas of achievement: Government and politics, warfare and conquest, religion and theology

Early Life

Charlemagne (shahr-luh-mahn-yuh or SHAHR-luh-mayn) was born in the kingdom of the Merovingian Franks, founded on the ruins of Roman Gaul by Clovis I, whose people's nominal conversion to Roman Christianity made them the allies of the Papacy against the Arian heresy. Under Clovis's factious and often inept successors, whose cruelty was anything but Christian, the kingdom was at times split into as many as four parts. Though it was reunited by the end of the seventh century, real power by then had passed from the Merovingians to Charlemagne's ancestors, who became hereditary holders of the office of mayor of the palace. Charlemagne's grandfather, Charles Martel, ruled over an increasingly powerful Frankish state from 714 to 741, during much of which time there was no Merovingian on the throne. On his death, power passed to his sons, Pépin III the Short and Carloman, though the latter entered a monastery in 747, leaving his elder brother as mayor to Childeric III. Charlemagne was the eldest child of Pépin III and Bertrada, his Friedelehe—more than a concubine, but not canonically a wife, so that their son was arguably illegitimate. He was called Charles—the name Charlemagne, which means "Charles the Great," is an anachronism, though its usage is so common that to avoid it is pointless.

Charles Martel and especially Pépin III and Carloman brought the still nearly pagan Franks more firmly within the Christian fold through cooperation with pro-papal Anglo-Saxon missionaries, the most important of whom was Saint Boniface of Wessex. This helped facilitate good relations with Pope Zacharias, whose approval allowed Pépin in 751 to depose Childeric I and take for himself the title king of the Franks without fear of the stigma of usurpation. At Pépin's coronation, Pope Stephen II, who had journeyed from Rome to Saint-Denis, personally placed the crown on the new king's head. At that time, the pope recognized as Pépin's joint heirs Charlemagne and his younger brother, Carloman, who was born in 751 and was unquestionably legitimate, since by then his father and Bertrada were legally married. Charlemagne accompanied Pépin on his campaigns against the Lombards in northern Italy, undertaken at the behest of the pope. On Pépin's death in 768, however, the seventeen-year-old Carloman—perhaps because of the circumstances of his birth—received by his father's will the central portion of the kingdom, while the twenty-six-year-old Charlemagne was left with an unwieldy strip of land running along the Atlantic coast and turning inland beyond the Rhine River. Relations between the brothers were thereafter bitter, and in 769, Carloman refused to aid Charlemagne in putting down a rebellion in Aquitaine. Carloman died in 771, however, and his vassals paid homage to Charlemagne, thus reuniting the kingdom of the Franks.

Einhard, Charlemagne's biographer and a resident at his court for twenty-three years, provided a detailed description of the ruler in his *Vita Karoli magni imperatoris* (c. 829-836; *Life of Charlemagne*, 1880), though this work—modeled on the Roman historian Suetonius's rather eulogistic lives of the Caesars—must be read critically. While admitting that Charlemagne was paunchy and had a short, thick neck and a high-pitched voice, Einhard stressed his favorable features and huge physique—the opening of his tomb in 1861 revealed that he was nearly 6 feet, 4 inches (193 centimeters) tall, so that at a time when malnutrition stunted the growth of many, he was truly a giant among men. The king was cheerful, generous, and fond of the hunt, boon companions, and especially his daughters; he was also capable of fearsome anger. Einhard, the monk Alcuin of York, and others attributed to Charlemagne virtues both Christian and Stoic—wisdom, devotion to the Church, love of learning, clemency, self-control, and temperance in eating and drinking (temperance being a relative term).

By his first marriage to the Frankish Himiltrude, probably a Friedelehe, Charlemagne produced a son, Pépin the Hunchback (who was later barred from the succession, revolted, and was forced into a monastery). In 770, the king's mother, Bertrada, persuaded him to put aside his first wife and marry the daughter of Desiderius, king of the Lombards, though a year later, Charlemagne repudiated her as well. He then married a Swabian noblewoman, Hildegarde, who bore him four sons—Charles, Pépin, Lothair, and Louis the Pious—and three daughters—Rotrude, Bertha, and Gisela. Later he married Fastrada (the mother of Theoderada and Himiltrude), who was followed by Lintgard and a series of concubines.

Life's Work

Charlemagne was above all else a warrior, carrying out some sixty campaigns, about half of which he led personally. His only failure came in 778, when he crossed the Pyrenees to do battle with the Christian Basques in Spain, was unsuccessful in an attempt to capture Saragossa, and had to settle for establishing a Spanish march (buffer state) in Barcelona. Ironically, this is his most famous campaign, for the defeat of his rear guard at Roncevaux during the return home became the basis for the *Chanson de Roland* (twelfth century; *Song of Roland*, 1880), the greatest of the medieval French *chansons de geste* (songs of deeds), in which Charlemagne and his soldiers appear as idealized heroes. Elsewhere the king was victorious. In 773, he invaded the Lombard kingdom of Desiderius, whose daughter Charlemagne had recently repudiated and who was harboring Gerberga, his brother Carloman's widow, and her sons, potentially rivals to the Frankish throne. After successfully besieging Pavia and seizing the Lombard crown in 774, Charlemagne visited Pope Hadrian I in Rome, strengthening his ties with the Papacy by reconfirming the Donation of Pépin, in which his father had granted to the popes the lands in central Italy known as the Papal States.

By 772, Charlemagne had begun a long series of hard-fought wars against the Saxons to the north of Frankland, which were not complete until 804. Over and over Charlemagne's forces invaded Saxony and forced the inhabitants to accept Frankish rule and the Christian faith, only to have them renounce Christ and rebel at the first opportunity. Though Charlemagne, at the beginning of these wars, destroyed the Irminsul, a wooden pillar considered sacred in Saxony, the Saxons clung fiercely to paganism, which the Frankish king found particularly offensive. Though he broke the back of Saxon resistance in 779 with the defeat of the chieftain Widukind and began sending in Christian missionaries, the Saxons revolted again in 782, so provoking Charlemagne that he had more than forty-five hundred Saxons massacred. In the last decades of the struggle, there were further massacres, massive deportations, and virtual colonization by the Franks. Thereafter Christianity took firmer root, and by a curious twist of fate it was a Saxon ruler, Otto I (Otto the Great), who in the mid-tenth century revived in Germany the claim to universal empire earlier resurrected by Charlemagne, for by 800, the latter ruler had laid the foundation for a Carolingian Empire, harking back to the days of Roman domination in the West.

Charlemagne. (Library of Congress)

Meanwhile Charlemagne put down rebellions in 776 in Lombardy and in 788 in Bavaria, where Duke Tassilo III had been causing trouble for Frankish rulers intermittently since the reign of Pépin III the Short. The addition of Bavaria to Charlemagne's ever-expanding territories brought him into contact with the Avars (or Huns as they were sometimes called), who occupied Hungary and Austria and had wreaked havoc on the Byzantine Empire since the days of Emperor Justinian. In 791, Charlemagne drove the Avars back into the valley of the Danube River, and by 795 his son Pépin (the son of Hildegarde) had pushed them out of Carinthia in southern Austria, capturing in the process an immense Avar treasure accumulated in part from tribute paid by the Byzantine Empire. This treasure was so great that, according to Einhard, it required fifteen wagons pulled by four oxen apiece to carry it. In any case, it was sufficient to finance Charlemagne's patronage of scholarship, support of the Church, and building of a suitably "imperial" capital at Aix-la-Chapelle. Though there were additional, for the most part punitive, campaigns against Slavic peoples to the east, the victories against the Avars and the Saxons marked the extent of Charlemagne's conquests; these were essentially complete by 804, even if he later faced rebellion from Brittany and in 810 marched against the Danish king Guthrodr (or Godefrid), who was assassinated before a battle could take place.

By the turn of the century, then, Charlemagne controlled all of Western and Central Europe except for southern Italy (still controlled by the Byzantine Empire), the Iberian Peninsula (most of which was held by Muslims), the British Isles (in the hands of various groups of Anglo-Saxons and Celts), and Scandinavia (from which groups of Danish, Norwegian, and Swedish Vikings were already beginning to issue). He spread his influence still further through diplomatic contacts with other rulers. Between 771 and 777, he and the Byzantine empress, and later saint, Irene carried on eventually unsuccessful negotiations for the marriage of his daughter Rotrude and the young Constantine VI. After Irene deposed and blinded Constantine, Charlemagne apparently proposed marriage to her, in spite of her advanced age, but she too was deposed in 802. (These proposals have led some to flights of fancy about the union of the eastern and western claimants to the Roman imperial mantle, but in practice, the difficulties associated with such a project would have been insurmountable.) Charlemagne also corresponded between 789 and 796 with the most powerful of the contemporary Anglo-Saxon kings, Offa of Mercia; exchanged envoys with the mighty Islamic caliph of Baghdad, Hārūn al-Rashīd; and established contacts with various other rulers. Finally, by threatening Byzantine possessions in Italy, he compelled Emperor Michael I to recognize his claim to the title of emperor in the West in 813, thirteen years after his coronation by Pope Leo III on Christmas Day, 800.

Charlemagne's coronation, during his fourth visit to Rome (the earlier visits occurred in 774, 781, and 787), is perhaps the most controversial feature of his reign. The king had gone to Rome to restore Leo to power after an antipapal rebellion in 799 drove him across the Alps to seek assistance. Scholars are uncertain whether it was Charlemagne's advisers or those of the pope who first proposed the imperial coronation. The *Annales regni Francorum* (c. 788-829; *Frankish Royal Annals*, 1970) indicate that it was the Franks, but according to the attributed author of the *Annales*, Einhard, the king was surprised and infuriated when the pope placed the crown on his head just as he was about to rise from prayer. If the latter is true, Charlemagne eventually accepted the coronation, as is indicated by his insistence on Byzantine recognition. The coronation was also part of later debates about the relationship of secular and ecclesiastical authority, but there is no doubt that Charlemagne exercised enormous influence over the Church inside the Carolingian Empire, even if it did not quite approach the caesaropapism of the emperors in Constantinople. Charlemagne generally cooperated with the Papacy but yielded little power—in his cartularies (or book of charters and title deeds of an estate) he frequently made law for the Church himself.

Charlemagne's support was crucial to the success of Roman Christianity in the West, where he lent it moral, political, and financial support and spread the faith into newly conquered territories, though often by the harsh means of baptism at the point of a sword. He also built churches, like that in his capital at Aix-la-Chapelle, and it was faith that led to his patronage of that revival of learning known as the Carolingian Renaissance. From all of Europe, Charlemagne brought scholars—men such as Theodulf of Orléans, Paul the Deacon, and Einhard—to work under the leadership of Alcuin of York to preserve the written legacy, both pagan and Christian, of the ancient Roman world. It is true that these clerics were no innovators and that their work made little impression on contemporary society at large, but through their preservation of knowledge, they exerted an immeasurable influence on an emerging European civilization that outlived both Charlemagne and the Carolingian Empire.

The Carolingian Kings

Reign	Ruler
687-714	Pépin II of Heristal (mayor of Austrasia/Neustria)
714-719	Plectrude (regent for Theudoald)
719-741	Charles Martel (the Hammer; mayor of Austrasia/Neustria)
747-768	Pépin III the Short (mayor of Neustria 741, king of all Franks 747)
768-814	Charlemagne (king of Franks 768, emperor 800)
814-840	Louis the Pious (king of Aquitaine, emperor)
840-855	Lothair I (emperor)
843	Treaty of Verdun divides Carolingian Empire into East Franks (Germany), West Franks (essentially France), and a southern and middle kingdom roughly corresponding to Provence, Burgundy, and Lorraine)
843-876	Louis II the German (king of Germany)
843-877	Charles II the Bald (king of Neustria 843, emperor 875)
855-875	Louis II (emperor)
877-879	Louis II (king of France)
879-882	Louis III (king of France)
879-884	Carloman (king of France)
884-887	Charles III the Fat (king of France)
887-898	Odo (Eudes; king of France)
887-899	Arnulf (king of Germany 887, emperor 896)
891-894	Guy of Spoleto (Wido, Guido; emperor)
892-898	Lambert of Spoleto (emperor)
893-923	Charles III the Simple (king of France)
915-923	Berengar I of Friuli (emperor)
923-929?	Robert I (king of France)
929-936	Rudolf (king of France)
936-954	Louis IV (king of France; Hugh the Great in power)
954-986	Lothair (king of France; Hugh Capet in power 956)
986-987	Louis V (king of France)

Note: The Carolingians ruled different parts of the Frankish kingdom, which accounts for overlapping regnal dates in this table. The term "emperor" refers to rule over what eventually came to be known as the Holy Roman Empire.

Significance

When Charlemagne died in 814, he was by far the most powerful man in Western Europe and ruled over an empire that rivaled in size that of his Roman predecessors. Yet the Carolingian Empire barely outlived him by a generation. Indeed, the seeds of its destruction were already present at his death, for even if Charlemagne had taken—or had been given—the title of emperor, with all of its historic connotations, his realm lacked the administrative machinery that had kept the Roman Empire going for centuries, even under weak, criminal, or lunatic rulers. Charlemagne owed his success to his own personality and ability, to the dynamics of an expanding empire, and to being in the right place at the right time. All these things were transient.

In administering his far-flung empire, Charlemagne was dependent on the aid of semiautonomous counts ruling over vast tracts of land. By giving them enough authority to be effective, he also made them powerful enough to be potentially dangerous rebels. He supervised these unpaid, noble officials by grouping together counties outside the old Frankish kingdom under provincial governors known as dukes, margraves, or prefects, and by annually sending out officers called *missi dominici* to inquire into local administration. Yet such supervision was at best less than stringent, communication was poor, and ultimately the entire system rested on officials' loyalty to the king's person, their fear of his wrath, and his ability to offer them the prospect of further rewards as the empire continued to grow. Moreover, rebellion was a problem in even the most dynamic period of growth; by 804, the empire had ceased to expand; and a decade later, its architect and the focus of fifty years' allegiance was gone. By 843, in the Treaty of Verdun, the sons of Charlemagne's heir Louis the Pious—Lothair, Charles the Bald, and Louis the German—had split the Carolingian Empire into three parts. Over the next century, these too would disintegrate.

Yet the legacy of Charlemagne lived on. The idea of universal empire was revived by the Holy Roman Emperors and continued into the modern era to influence both Napoleon Bonaparte and Adolf Hitler. More important, it was in the age of Charlemagne that barriers among the various peoples of Western Europe were broken down and that there first came into existence a new European civilization, sharing elements with, but different from, ancient Rome, Byzantium, and Islam—a civilization that, despite the political fragmentation of the ninth and tenth centuries, would survive, with a shared heritage, a common culture, and a single faith.

—*William B. Robison*

FURTHER READING

Becher, Matthias. *Charlemagne*. Translated by David S. Bachrach. New Haven, Conn.: Yale University Press, 2003. A brief biography of Charlemagne that also discusses the history of the Holy Roman Empire and the history of France to the year 987. Includes a bibliography and index.

Chamberlin, Russell. *The Emperor: Charlemagne*. New York: Franklin Watts, 1987. This popular biography with a very useful introduction is based on essential primary and secondary sources and is rich in detail.

Einhard and Notker the Stammerer. *Two Lives of Charlemagne*. Translated by Lewis Thorpe. Baltimore: Penguin Books, 1972. An English translation of Einhard's biography written between 829 and 836, the *Vita Karoli magni imperatoris*, and of Notker's *Gesta Karoli magni*, as published in 1867.

Fichtenau, Heinrich. *The Carolingian Empire: The Age of Charlemagne*. Translated by Peter Munz. Toronto: University of Toronto Press, 1991. This excellent study stresses the role of religion in the emperor's career and examines Charlemagne as an individual, the question of the imperial title, the Carolingian Renaissance, the role of the nobility and officials, the circumstances of the poor, and the decline in the emperor's final decade.

Ganshof, F. L. *The Carolingians and the Frankish Monarchy: Studies in Carolingian History*. Translated by Janet Sondheimer. Ithaca, N.Y.: Cornell University Press, 1971. This work contains articles on Einhard, Alcuin, government and institutions, Charlemagne's use of the oath and the written word, Frankish diplomacy, Charlemagne's "failure," and the decline of the Carolingian Empire.

Halphen, Louis. *Charlemagne and the Carolingian Empire*, edited by Richard Vaughan. Vol. 3 in *Europe in the Middle Ages: Selected Studies*. Translated by Giselle de Nie. New York: North-Holland, 1977. A very highly regarded study, this work covers Charlemagne's predecessors and the establishment of the Carolingian Empire, the empire under Louis the Pious, and its disintegration following the Treaty of Verdun. It is a more thorough study than most. Contains a number of plates and several very useful maps.

Havighurst, Alfred F., ed. *The Pirenne Thesis: Analysis, Criticism, and Revision*. 4th ed. Lexington, Mass.: D. C. Heath, 1976. This collection contains a series of articles by a distinguished group of medievalists examining the famous thesis of Henri Pirenne, who argued that rather than a sharp break between the ancient world and the Middle Ages, there was a gradual change, and that a new European civilization emerged only in the eighth century (a view now widely accepted), with Islam rather than Charlemagne as the principal agent of change (a view generally disregarded here).

Loyn, H. R., and John Percival, eds. *The Reign of Charlemagne: Documents on Carolingian Government and Administration*. New York: St. Martin's Press, 1976. This work contains selections from several biographies of Charlemagne, Louis the Pious, and the latter's sons; from a number of Charlemagne's capitularies; from letters of Charlemagne, Alcuin, and Pope Adrian I; and from various charters and other documents. Useful primary material, also of interest to the nonspecialist desiring to get something of the flavor of the age.

Morrissey, Robert. *Charlemagne and France: A Thousand Years of Mythology*. Translated by Catherine Tihanyi. Notre Dame, Ind.: University of Notre Dame Press, 2003. Detailed coverage of Charlemagne and his influences, his legendary place in history, his life and literature, and more. Includes a bibliography and index.

Scholz, Bernhard W., and Barbara Rogers, trans. *Carolingian Chronicles: Frankish Royal Annals and Nithard's Histories*. Ann Arbor: University of Michigan Press, 1970. An English translation of the royal annals. This is one of the essential primary sources for Charlemagne's life and reign.

SEE ALSO: Alcuin; Saint Boniface; Charles Martel; Charles the Bald; Clovis; Dhuoda; Egbert; Hārūn al-Rashīd; Saint Irene; Louis the German; Otto I; Rabanus Maurus; Rollo; Rurik; Widukind.

RELATED ARTICLES in *Great Events from History: The Middle Ages, 477-1453*: 726-843: Iconoclastic Controversy; 735: Christianity Is Introduced into Germany; 754: Coronation of Pépin the Short; 781: Alcuin Becomes Adviser to Charlemagne; 786-809: Reign of Hārūn al-Rashīd; June 7, 793: Norse Raid Lindisfarne Monastery; 843: Treaty of Verdun; 850-950: Viking Era; c. 850: Development of the Slavic Alphabet; 890's: Magyars Invade Italy, Saxony, and Bavaria; August 10, 955: Otto I Defeats the Magyars; 987: Hugh Capet Is Elected to the French Throne; 1054: Beginning of the Rome-Constantinople Schism; 1154-1204: Angevin Empire Is Established; September 17, 1156: Austria Emerges as a National Entity; January 10, 1356, and December 25, 1356: Golden Bull.

CHARLES D'ORLÉANS

French poet, military leader, and duke of Orléans

Defeated and taken prisoner while leading French troops at Agincourt, Charles spent twenty-five years in captivity in England writing lyric poetry in French and English. After being released, he contributed to peace negotiations and maintained a poetry salon.

BORN: November 24, 1394; Paris, France
DIED: January 4, 1465; Amboise, France
AREAS OF ACHIEVEMENT: Literature, government and politics

EARLY LIFE

The parents of Charles d'Orléans (sharl dohr-lay-ahn) were Louis, duke of Orléans and brother of King Charles VI, and Valentina, daughter of the duke of Milan. Louis was powerfully influential in French politics but was a man of dissolute habits; Valentina was a gentle, cultured woman. On June 29, 1406, at age fourteen, Charles married Isabelle, daughter of Charles VI and child-widow of England's Richard II, and who was five years older than he. Isabelle died September 13, 1409, after giving birth to a daughter.

In 1407, two years before Charles lost his wife, his father was murdered by hired assassins of John the Fearless, duke of Burgundy, whose interest was in destroying rivals for control over Charles VI, who was often mentally unstable. Charles's mother, apparently exhausted by the combination of sorrow, appeals for justice, and burdens in administering the estate, died a year later.

With support from friends of his father, Charles assumed the title duke of Orléans himself and in 1410 married Bonne, the daughter of Bernard d'Armagnac. With this alliance, Charles tried for years to avenge Burgundy's crime, coming closest in 1415 by gaining support from the king and receiving consolation in memorial masses clearing his father's name and condemning the murder; he could not, however, punish Burgundy.

Later that same year, Charles was the most important of many French nobles captured in the astonishing defeat of the massive French army at Agincourt by the much smaller English forces led by King Henry V. He was kept prisoner in England for twenty-five years, from 1415 to 1440.

LIFE'S WORK

The English considered the duke of Orléans their most important political prisoner because of his high rank and the antagonism between England and France in these last decades of the Hundred Years' War. Henry V insisted on strong security to prevent escape and never asked ransom for Charles's deliverance. In later years, the brother of Henry V, Humphrey, duke of Gloucester, continued this strong opposition to Charles's release. Charles probably never was actually in what most people would consider a jail; he was, however, moved every few years from such castles as Windsor to Pontefract in 1417, Fotheringhay in 1421, Bolingbroke in 1422, London in 1425, Canterbury in 1427, Peterborough in 1428, Amthill in 1430, Dover and London in 1433, Wingfield in 1434, Calais in 1435, and London in 1437 until 1440. These frequent movements may have been to prevent him from ingratiating himself with his primary guardians.

During most of this time, he was permitted to keep servants and to receive money and household goods, including wine from France. Charles was able to send messengers to oversee affairs on his estates in France and to make political appointments. He was clearly on friendly terms with at least one of his guardians, William de la Pole, earl of Suffolk, a minor poet in English himself.

Charles d'Orléans. (Hulton|Archive at Getty Images)

In fact, when Suffolk was later accused of treason and then assassinated in 1450, one of the charges against him was that he supported release of the duke of Orléans for ransom.

For posterity, Charles's most important activity while in captivity was writing poetry, principally love lyrics. His most characteristic verse form in these years was the ballade (sometimes called ballad), an intricate verse form requiring at least three stanzas of equal length and a refrain at the end of each stanza. Charles used twenty-one stanzaic patterns and wrote in both eight-syllable and ten-syllable lines, preferring the eight-syllable line.

During his lifetime, Charles was respected for his poetry in French. Some of his correspondence included an occasional lyric, often with a request for a poem in response, especially in letters to the later duke of Burgundy, Philip the Good. While in captivity, however, he seems also to have written in English. A large collection of ballades, rondels, and occasional verses (6,531 lines) survives in the manuscript Harley 682. The speaker of these poems identifies himself as Charles, duke of Orléans; some of them are approximate translations of his French poems, others are unique. All the poems correspond in theme and verse forms to his French poems, but like Middle English verse generally, his English poems lack the grace and precision of the French lyrics.

Both in French and English, the poems written during these years in England make much use of personification and allegory, a manner of expression derived from *Le Roman de la rose* (c. 1230; the romance of the rose), a lengthy narrative started by Guillaume de Lorris but completed by Jean de Meung more than a century before Charles's work. Charles employed such personifications as Hope, Despair, Disdain, and Sadness to represent his inner experience in these shorter lyrics, particularly in ballades. The speaker in these poems is a man restricted in his activities, frequently feeling ignored or rejected and rarely gaining satisfaction. He often calls himself a prisoner of love.

Some commentators quarrel over whether these love lyrics have historical references or are merely conventional exercises in an outmoded tradition. Attempts to identify the lady or ladies alluded to in these poems include speculation that the Peerless Lady might be Charles's first wife, Isabelle (who died six years before his capture at Agincourt); his second wife, Bonne; and various English ladies. More than one scholar has pointed to the earl of Arundel's second wife, Maud Lovell.

An intriguing candidate for the replacement in the poet's heart following the death of the Peerless Lady is Anne Moleyns, a woman related by marriage to the earl of Suffolk. The first letters of one of Charles's English poems spell out ANNE MOLINS, but no other evidence besides this acrostic points to such a relationship. This beloved mistress has even been identified as a personification of France itself, indicating a reappearance of Charles's patriotism for that country after years of captivity deadened any emotional ties. Most recent scholars give up on identifying the ladies and urge the beautiful expression of complex feeling in Charles's poetry as valuable for any sensitive reader.

When released from English captivity for ransom in 1440, the duke of Orléans sincerely attempted peace negotiations between the two great powers, but not with much success. The French themselves were less interested in peace at this time because their own military power was ascending and the might of the English was in decline. Also in 1440, Charles married Marie de Clèves, niece of Philip the Good, duke of Burgundy. Among the children was a son, Louis, born in 1462, who later became King Louis XII. Charles tried unsuccessfully to reclaim property in Asti, Italy, that he had inherited from his mother. Again, however, the more important activity in this later phase of his life was writing poetry. Though he continued to write ballades as before, his preference now was for the rondel (some commentators call these same poems rondeaux). Charles's rondels are primarily composed of thirteen or fifteen eight-syllable lines divided in three stanzas using only two rhyme sounds. Most characteristically he communicates with irony or even bawdy humor in this later poetry, often with expression of indifference to the desires or pains of love.

In his last years, while living in Blois, Charles maintained a poetry salon in his home and invited noble guests, members of his household, and other poets, such as François Villon, to participate in poetic entertainments. The duke of Orléans died on January 4, 1465, while on a trip to Amboise.

SIGNIFICANCE

The status of Charles d'Orléans as a major French medieval poet seems secure and even improving; he ranks alongside François Villon and above Guillaume de Machaut and Eustache Deschamps when measured by comparable representation in selective anthologies. He does not refer to historic events or draw extensively from classical or European literature for allusions. Thus, in his poetry, he is not scholarly or intellectual by Renaissance and later standards. No one can deny, however, the elegance and concision of his best poems, especially the rondels.

The question of evaluating his English poetry remains open partly as a result of uncertainty about his authorship but also as a result of insufficient attention by Middle English specialists to fifteenth century lyrics. Charles's English poetry may in fact surpass that of any English poet of his era while still falling short of his own standard in French.

In review of his achievements as a government leader, one must credit him with good intentions, as he battled for many worthwhile causes, but he is most famous for defeat. He never truly avenged his father's murder, though John the Fearless was assassinated early in Charles's captivity; the Battle of Agincourt stands as one of the most astonishing defeats in history; his attempts to gain release from captivity meant many years of frustration; and he failed to regain his property in Italy. Nevertheless, he always earned respect from his captors and loyal followers; Joan of Arc even spoke of freeing the duke of Orléans as one of her objectives. His enforced leisure as prisoner probably led to his finding consolation in writing poetry. He was a man who achieved much in the midst of great adversity.

—David V. Harrington

FURTHER READING

Arn, Mary-Joe, ed. *Charles d'Orléans in England, 1415-1440*. Rochester, N.Y.: D. S. Brewer, 2000. A biographical account of Charles's poetry, its reception by his contemporaries, his writing in two languages, and more.

_______. "The Structure of the English Poems of Charles of Orléans." *Fifteenth Century Studies* 4 (1981): 17-23. Argues that Charles's English poems constitute a single work representing love as an incurable disease.

Champion, Pierre, ed. *Charles d'Orléans: Poésies*. 2 vols. Reprint. Paris: Librairie Honore Champion, 1966. The standard edition of the French poems, including the eleven English poems in two predominantly French manuscripts.

Coldiron, A. E. B. "Toward a Comparative New Historicism: Land Tenures and Some Fifteenth-Century Poems." *Comparative Literature* 53, no. 2 (2001): 97-116. The author, while presenting a historical account of Charles, his work, and the milieu in which he wrote, argues for a multilingual approach to the study of literature in order to get a more accurate account of events.

Fein, David A. *Charles d'Orléans*. Boston: Twayne, 1983. Contains a brief biography and careful analysis of the major French poems (with English translations) but omits coverage of the English poems. The author describes the early ballades as inwardly centered with personified emotions for exploring thoughts and feelings.

Fox, John H. *The Lyric Poetry of Charles d'Orléans*. Oxford, England: Clarendon Press, 1969. A study of the French poems (with English translations) reviewing literary background, style, and Charles's distinctive poetic personality.

Goodrich, Norma Lorre. *Charles Duke of Orléans: A Literary Biography*. New York: Macmillan, 1963. Written much like a historical novel. The author embellishes historical facts about Charles with descriptions of places, analogous anecdotes, and brief biographies of major contemporaries.

_______. *Charles of Orléans: A Study of Themes in His French and in His English Poetry*. Geneva: Librairie Droz, 1967. Compares French and English poems to prove single authorship, based on themes such as self-analysis, hope, disdain, war, peace, and craftsmanship.

Jacob, E. F. *The Fifteenth Century: 1399-1485*. Oxford, England: Clarendon Press, 1961. An admirable, authoritative study of Lancastrian England. The author's attention to political and economic concerns and the personalities of Henry V and Henry VI gives background for Charles's imprisonment and his difficulty with peace negotiations.

McLeod, Enid. *Charles of Orléans: Prince and Poet.* London: Chatto and Windus, 1969. An engaging biographical study with bold interpretations of persons and events alluded to in his poetry.

Newman, Karen. "The Mind's Castle: Containment in the Poetry of Charles d'Orléans." *Romance Philology* 33 (1979): 317-328. Takes the image of containment in Charles's verses as implying intellectual-spiritual levels of meaning in addition to imprisonment by enemies or by love.

Spearing, A. C. "Prison, Writing, Absence: Representing the Subject in the English Poems of Charles d'Orléans." *Modern Language Quarterly* 53, no. 1 (March, 1992). Considers some understudied poems of Charles, particularly from manuscript Harley 682, written while he was imprisoned.

Steele, Robert, and Mabel Day, eds. *The English Poems of Charles of Orléans.* Reprint. London: Oxford University Press, 1970. A scholarly edition with a description of manuscripts, an argument in favor of Charles's authorship, and notes and a glossary.

See also: Boethius; Cædmon; Geoffrey Chaucer; Dante; Firdusi; Henry V; Joan of Arc; Guillaume de Machaut; Marie de France; Petrarch; Philip the Good; Walther von der Vogelweide.

Related articles in *Great Events from History: The Middle Ages, 477-1453*: c. 1100: Rise of Courtly Love; 1337-1453: Hundred Years' War; August 26, 1346: Battle of Crécy; May 4-8, 1429: Joan of Arc's Relief of Orléans.

Charles Martel

Frankish mayor of the palace (719-741)

Through skill, good fortune, and ruthless ambition, Charles Martel rose to dominate the kingdom of the Franks and its weak Merovingian kings, laying the groundwork for his son Pépin III the Short to be recognized as the first Carolingian king of the Franks and for his grandson Charlemagne to emerge as the first Holy Roman Emperor. Charles also led Frankish forces to check the Muslim advance into southern France.

Born: c. 688; Herstal, near Liège (now in Belgium)
Died: October 22, 741; Quierzy-sur-Oise, Aisne (now in France)
Also known as: Carolus Martellus (Latin name); Charles the Hammer
Areas of achievement: Government and politics, military

Early Life

In 687, two years before Charles Martel (shahrl mahr-tehl) was born, his father, Pépin II of Herstal, became sole "mayor of the palace" after defeating his Neustrian rival near Aachen. This position gave Pépin, an Austrasian, dominant power in the Frankish kingdom. A weak series of kings of the Merovingian family held mainly symbolic power during the seventh century under strong mayors (a term that meant "first man of the house") who controlled land appointments and government policies. Charles's mother, Apaida, was part of a large landholding family in the lower valley of the Muese. The land bordered the area under the direct control of Pépin's family.

Although a marriage contract was drawn between Pépin and Apaida, Pépin was already married to Plectrude, who had borne him three sons. Although polygamy was still common among higher noble families in the early Middle Ages, Charles's "illegitimacy" made him an unlikely candidate to succeed his father as mayor. Charles spent most of his life at Pépin's court learning the intricacies of the mayor's power. Loyal followers were bought with land grants, and Pépin had already begun the process of taking land from the church to increase his power base. Meanwhile, Pépin's oldest son, Drago, died in 708. His second son became bishop of Rouen in 720, taking him out of the line of succession. The youngest son, Grimoald, was murdered in 714 while praying at the shrine of Saint Lambert at Liège. Coincidentally, the shrine was in territory controlled by the family of Charles's mother. Charles thus became a logical candidate for the mayor of the palace position.

Pépin II died on December 16, 714, leaving Charles with no inheritance. Power and the treasury were transferred to Pépin's wife Plectrude, to rule in the name of her young grandson Theudoald, who was the son of the recently murdered Grimoald. Fearing revolt, Plectrude immediately had Charles imprisoned. However, he soon escaped and fled to his mother's family in the lower Muese. Plectrude would face not only forces raised by an enraged Charles but also Neustrian armies eager to retake the mayor's position from any of Pépin's heirs. By 716, the mayor's position was taken by the Neustrian leader Ragenfred, who immediately began purging from church and governmental office all appointees of Pépin II.

LIFE'S WORK

With a tenuous claim on the inherited mayorship, and faced by so many adversaries, Charles might well have engaged in a venture less risky than trying to gain a position as powerful as that held by his father Pépin. Charles, though, gathered around him a band of followers who would be richly rewarded with land and church possessions in the event of his succession. Charles attacked Neustrian forces at Amblève (716) and won a decisive victory. A further triumph at Vincy (717) caused the Neustrians to flee to Paris. Charles chose not to follow the entrenched Neustrian forces. Instead, he turned his attention back to affairs in Austrasia. To consolidate his powers, Charles defeated Plectrude's forces and forced Plectrude to turn over to him the remainder of Pépin II's treasury. After declaring himself Austrasian mayor of the palace, Charles had a member of the Merovingian family crowned as King Choltar IV. In the meantime, the crippled Neustrians gained aid from the duke of Aquitaine. Charles, however, was able to defeat the forces of his combined enemies at Soissons (719), fragmenting their power. By 721, he was able to appoint his own candidate to the Merovingian throne, Theodoric IV, and to gain recognition as sole Frankish mayor of the palace.

To ensure his continued domination of Neustria, Charles took every opportunity to appoint relatives and loyal supporters to every possible position, both lay and ecclesiastic. Every excuse was used to secularize ecclesiastic lands and goods. While working out feasible consolidation strategies, Charles was also interested in expansion deep into neighboring German territories. He launched a dual land-and-sea attack, a rarity in early medieval warfare, against the Frisians, and he succeeded in killing the Frisian king Bubo and sacking pagan temples. Campaigns against the Saxons, Alamanni, and Bavarians were also successful. Yet in order to expand his control in a meaningful way, Charles supported, using Frankish armies, the work of such noted Anglo-Saxon missionaries as Willibrord's followers in Frisia and Boniface's disciples in Thuringia and Hesse.

Charles Martel. (B. F. Waitt)

While trying to introduce into the continent the Roman variety of Christianity, Charles was also able to use religion as a vehicle to introduce his own interpretation of political rule in Germany. Paradoxically, while standing as the major secular force in the spread of Roman Catholicism, Charles used every opportunity to appoint his supporters, even lay people, to head abbeys and bishoprics. Ultimately, Charles was able to annex both Frisia and Alamannia, drive the Saxons across the Rhine River, and extend Frankish domination over Bavaria. His relationship with Bavaria was sealed when, after the death of his wife Chorotrude, Charles married Sunnichild, a relative of the duke of Bavaria.

The rapid increase of the number of Charles's followers related to his liberal awarding of estates for life to those warriors who took an oath of loyalty to him, fought for him, and continued to serve him after becoming vassals. During the early Middle Ages, land served as a substitute for money payments and was the major source of power, privilege, and status. Yet oaths alone were not enough to explain Charles's success. He had also pioneered the use of calvary with the newly introduced stirrup, which enabled heavily armored Frankish calvary to remain stable in the saddle while swinging swords or leveling lances at their adversaries. Stirrups, though, had to be purchased with "hard" money, and Charles's most readily available assets were in the form of church property.

Frankish stability faced a danger of another sort. Arabic invaders had entered Spain in 711. With their superior cavalry, they extended Islamic rule throughout most of Visigothic Spain. In 732, Islamic expeditionary forces under ʿAbd al-Raḥmān al-Ghāfiqī, the Moorish governor of Spain, crossed the Pyrenees and rode through southern France. In response, Charles gathered together an army and won a victory near Poitiers; the engagement became known as the Battle of Tours. ʿAbd al-Raḥmān al-Ghāfiqī was killed in the battle. For his victory, Charles was given the surname Martel, the Hammer, and gained renown as the savior of Christian France. Charles, though, failed to take advantage of his victory, allowing the defeated enemy to fade away overnight. Islamic forces continued to seize southern towns, including Arles and Avignon, and to destroy cities in Provence. Eventually, Charles would stop the remaining Islamic forces at Narbon, causing them to return to Spain.

The Islamic invasion not only raised Charles's stature throughout Europe but also provided him with a golden opportunity to extend his own control throughout southern France. He took Bordeaux in 735, ousted the current bishop, and replaced him with his own appointee. Whenever he faced opposition, Charles followed a scorched-earth policy, thus making prolonged resistance uneconomical for the local nobility. Consequently, Charles emerged from southern France in control of a large empire.

When the Merovingian "puppet king," Theodoric IV, died in 737, Charles did not even bother to replace him. Instead, he made decisions in the dead king's name. The

THE CAROLINGIAN KINGS

Reign	*Ruler*
687-714	Pépin II of Heristal (mayor of Austrasia/Neustria)
714-719	Plectrude (regent for Theudoald)
719-741	CHARLES MARTEL (the Hammer; mayor of Austrasia/Neustria)
747-768	Pépin III the Short (mayor of Neustria 741, king of all Franks 747)
768-814	CHARLEMAGNE (king of Franks 768, emperor 800)
814-840	Louis the Pious (king of Aquitaine, emperor)
840-855	Lothair I (emperor)
843	Treaty of Verdun divides Carolingian Empire into East Franks (Germany), West Franks (essentially France), and a southern and middle kingdom roughly corresponding to Provence, Burgundy, Lorraine)
843-876	LOUIS II THE GERMAN (king of Germany)
843-877	CHARLES II THE BALD (king of Neustria 843, emperor 875)
855-875	Louis II (emperor)
877-879	Louis II (king of France)
879-882	Louis III (king of France)
879-884	Carloman (king of France)
884-887	Charles III the Fat (king of France)
887-898	Odo (Eudes; king of France)
887-899	Arnulf (king of Germany 887, emperor 896)
891-894	Guy of Spoleto (Wido, Guido; emperor)
892-898	Lambert of Spoleto (emperor)
893-923	Charles III the Simple (king of France)
915-924	Berengar I of Friuli (emperor)
923-929?	Robert I (king of France)
929-936	Rudolf (king of France)
936-954	Louis IV (king of France; Hugh the Great in power)
954-986	Lothair (king of France; Hugh Capet in power 956)
986-987	Louis V (king of France)

Note: The Carolingians ruled different parts of the Frankish kingdom, which accounts for overlapping regnal dates in this table. The term "emperor" refers to rule over what eventually came to be known as the Holy Roman Empire.

Franks could have no clearer message about who was in charge of the kingdom. To establish administrative control in this large kingdom, Charles set up an annual assembly of nobles known as the *campus martius*.

In 739, as Pope Gregory III was battling against his northern neighbors, the Lombards, he offered Charles the ancient Roman position of consul, or chief executive, if Charles would come to his aid. The pope was grateful for Charles's support of Anglo-Saxon missionaries in Germanic territories, such as the work of Boniface and his disciples in Thuringia and Hesse and the work of Willibrord in Frisia. However, in this and all of his ventures, Charles followed his own interests. He used missionaries to extend his control in German territories and used bishoprics and abbeys to install his own relatives and close supporters. One of his nephews, Hugo, received the archbishopric of Rouen, the bishoprics of Paris and Bayeux, and two rich abbeys. Clearly, the church was an institution to control for patronage and political power. Hence, Charles found it easy to reject the pope's request for aid, since Charles wanted good relations with the Lombards' king Liutprand, whose support he might need if Islamic forces returned to France.

By 740, Charles became increasingly ill, and his thoughts turned to the matter of succession. He had produced many sons, both legitimate and illegitimate. Charles decided to make Carloman, his eldest son, mayor of Austrasia, Alamannia, and Thuringia. His younger son, Pépin III the Short, who had been educated by the clergy at Saint-Denis, would receive control of Neustria, Burgundy, and Provence. When he died on October 22, 741, in his palace at Quierzy, Charles Martel's remains were taken to Saint-Denis to be buried alongside the Merovingian kings. Ten years later, Pépin III, now sole mayor of the Franks, would use his close ties with the pope to depose the Merovingian Dynasty, establishing Charles's Carolingian family as hereditary heirs to the Frankish throne.

Significance

Against unbelievable odds and a wide variety of enemies, Charles was able not only to fight his way into the mayor's position formerly held by his father but also to expand the Frankish kingdom deep into Germany and southern France. In so doing, he was able to dominate both the weak Merovingian king and the church. His masterful use of political patronage in awarding feudal fiefs, bishoprics, and abbeys introduced feudalism throughout the kingdom along with secular control of the Frankish church. His support of missionary work helped to spread Roman Catholicism in Germany along with his own political control.

By employing mounted knights, which would become the dominant military force of the Middle Ages, Charles was able to check the advance of Islam in southern France and to earn a somewhat undeserved status as "savior" of Christian Europe. He also gained the opportunity to incorporate southern France into his kingdom and to pass this area as an inheritance to his son Pépin III the Short. The powers Charles amassed enabled Pépin to depose the puppet Merovingian king and establish the Carolingian Dynasty on the Frankish throne, an act that was legitimized by the pope. Following in his grandfather's footsteps, Charlemagne, who reigned from 800 to 814, extended Carolingian control over a vast empire by waging almost continual warfare.

—*Irwin Halfond*

Further Reading

Bledsoe, Helen Wieman. "Destined to be Great." *Calliope* 9, no. 7 (March, 1999). Discusses the lives of Charles and his son Pépin the Short and grandson Charlemagne.

Fouracre, Paul. *The Age of Charles Martel*. New York: Longman, 2000. Provides historical background on the Merovingian Dynasty and Charles's connections with Burgundy, Aquitaine, Provence, Southern Germany, and other areas. Also discusses Charles's military, his family, and his relations with the Church.

Geary, Patrick J. *Before France and Germany: The Creation and Transformation of the Merovingian World*. New York: Oxford University Press, 1988. Provides an interesting regional breakdown of Merovingian feudal politics. Chapters 5 and 6 contain a comprehensive analysis of how Charles contributed to Merovingian obsolescence.

Gerberding, Richard. *The Rise of the Carolingians and the Liber "Historiae Francorum."* Oxford, England: Oxford University Press, 1987. Chapter 7 provides in-depth analysis of the career of Charles using primary source documents.

James, Edward. *The Origins of France: From Clovis to the Capetians, 500-1000*. New York: St. Martin's Press, 1982. A study of the sociopolitical institutions that helped form early France. Chapter 6 provides a solid study of the mayor of the palace position, and chapter 7 provides keen insights about the Carolingian experiment.

McGill, Sara Ann. "The World of Knights and Lords: The Feudal System." *Events and People of the Middle*

Ages (2000). This journal article discusses the development of the feudal system during the time of Charles and its further development under Charlemagne. A short but detailed text. No journal issue number.

Riché, Pierre. *The Carolingians: A Family Who Forged Europe*. Translated by Michael Allen. Philadelphia: University of Pennsylvania Press, 1993. Provides excellent background material and a good account (chapter 4) of the reign of Charles.

Wallace-Hadrill, J. M. *Early Medieval History.* New York: Barnes and Noble Books, 1976. An excellent source for the major themes and background information related to the age of Charles, along with details of his career.

Wood, Ian. *The Merovingian Kingdoms, 450-751*. New York: Longman, 1994. Chapters 15 and 16 provide a detailed look at Charles's role in Merovingian politics, based on an analysis of documentary materials.

SEE ALSO: Saint Boniface; Charlemagne.

RELATED ARTICLES in *Great Events from History: The Middle Ages, 477-1453*: April or May, 711: Ṭāriq Crosses into Spain; October 11, 732: Battle of Tours; 735: Christianity Is Introduced into Germany; 754: Coronation of Pépin the Short.

CHARLES THE BALD

King of France (r. 840-877) and Holy Roman Emperor (r. 875-877)

Reigning during one of the most turbulent periods in European history, Charles managed to survive and pass the crown of the West Frankish kingdom to his posterity.

BORN: June 13, 823; Frankfurt am Main (now in Germany)

DIED: October 6, 877; Avrieux or Brides-les-Bain (now in France)

ALSO KNOWN AS: Charles le Chauve; Charles II (Holy Roman Emperor)

AREA OF ACHIEVEMENT: Government and politics

EARLY LIFE

Charles the Bald was the grandson of Charlemagne and the son of the Frankish emperor Louis the Pious and his second wife, Judith. At the time of Charles's birth, the emperor already had three sons: Lothair, the eldest; Louis the German; and Pépin. Indeed, in 817 Louis had published a decree establishing the method by which the empire would be divided among the three at his death. Lothair was to succeed as emperor and Louis the German and Pépin were to hold kingdoms under his rule. Louis the German and Pépin had already been invested with the kingdoms they were to hold.

This situation was further complicated by the fact that the new empress, Judith, was of the Welf family, a noble family prominent in that section of the empire known as Alamannia (modern Alsace). This portion of the realm had been very difficult for the Carolingian Frankish rulers to control, and Louis the Pious, in marrying a daughter of this aristocratic family, believed that he could establish closer and friendlier ties. When Judith and Louis had a son, the future of Alamannia seemed secure. The elder brothers of the new prince, however, had no intention of allowing their portions of the territory to diminish. Because Judith did not want the young heir's interests to be ignored, the situation intensified. The result was civil war when, in 829, Charles was given a portion of land taken from the portions already allotted his brothers. The warring continued intermittently until Louis the Pious died in 840.

LIFE'S WORK

Charles's half brother Pépin was already dead when their father, Louis the Pious, died. Although Pépin had a son of his own, Pépin II, Charles received title to the land previously allotted to Pépin I, reserving the rights of Pépin II in Aquitaine, which Pépin II was to hold as a subkingdom under Charles's suzerainty.

In the division of the empire among the brothers, Charles received the western portions of the empire, which conformed, loosely, to what is now the nation of France, while Louis the German received the eastern portion of the empire, conforming loosely to what is now Germany. Lothair, the eldest brother and the new emperor, obtained a long, narrow strip of territory situated between what are modern France and Germany and including the modern territories of the Low Countries, Luxembourg, Alsace, Switzerland, and Italy.

Louis the German and Charles the Bald almost immediately attacked Lothair with the intention of adding to their portions bits of land detached from his. When Lothair died in 855, he was succeeded by his sons Lothair II in Lorraine, Charles in Provence, and Louis in Italy. Lothair II died in 869, after which Charles the Bald and Louis the German partitioned his realm.

Within his own kingdom, Charles the Bald had considerable difficulties. During the whole of his reign, the kingdom of France was subjected to repeated attacks by the Vikings. The Meuse, Seine, and Loire Rivers were navigable by the Viking longboats for considerable distances upstream, which meant that no region, even in the interior, was safe from their raids. The speed of the Viking attacks was such that it was not possible for Charles to organize an efficient defense; as a result, he usually had to bribe the Vikings to go away.

In addition, Charles had continuing difficulties with the subkingdom of Aquitaine, ruled by his nephew Pépin II; Pépin tended to ignore his overlord and uncle, and Charles wished to dispossess Pépin. The Aquitanian nobles generally supported Pépin but kept the controversy alive as a means to prevent any stable central government from limiting their influence. Charles tried to imprison Pépin II in 855 but had to release him when Louis the German sent his sons Louis the Younger and Charles the Fat to take advantage of the situation and seize Aquitaine for themselves. Charles the Bald did not take control of Aquitaine until 864, when he imprisoned Pépin a second time, after which Pépin disappeared. In the end, Charles was never able to rule Aquitaine.

As if these problems were not enough, Charles had great difficulty keeping his nobles loyal. The partitioning of the realm had taken place amid constant conflicts among members of the imperial family. This climate of general disorder was exacerbated by the inability of the Crown to deal adequately with the Vikings.

Despite all these problems, Charles the Bald managed to create at his court an atmosphere of cultivation and scholarship. Several of the most distinguished scholars of the Western world—including John Scotus Erigena, Lupus of Ferrières, Walafrid Strabo, and Hincmar of Reims—were active in the affairs of Charles's realm.

At the end of his life, Charles became emperor. His nephew Louis of Italy had succeeded to the imperial title in 869 when Lothair had died. Conditions in Italy were disturbed as a result of the invasion of the peninsula by Muslim armies from North Africa. When Louis died in 875, Pope John VIII called on Charles for assistance. Charles made an expedition to Italy in 875 and was crowned emperor on December 25 of that year, the seventy-fifth anniversary of the imperial coronation of his grandfather, Charlemagne. Yet Charles was unable to stem the Muslim threat to Rome and the Papacy and, discouraged, retired from Italy in 877. It was while he was on the way home from Italy, with his own kingdom under attack by the Germans, that Charles died

Engraved depiction of Charles the Bald's wedding celebration, interrupted by an embassy from his brother Louis the German. (F. R. Niglutsch)

on October 6. He was succeeded by his son Louis the Stammerer.

SIGNIFICANCE

During his fifty-four years, Charles the Bald witnessed the destruction of the great European empire created by his grandfather and the Frankish armies. Ultimately, the empire disintegrated, because it was too unwieldy and too ethnically diverse to be integrated into a cohesive whole. The chronic wars among the descendants of Charlemagne, to which Charles the Bald was a party, were merely symptomatic of larger problems that the political and social structures of the period simply could not solve.

Nevertheless, Charles the Bald was, in certain ways, a successful ruler. He managed to preserve and support the cultural activities of the Carolingian renaissance. He was also a dutiful son of the Church, cooperating fully with his bishops and promoting the continuing Christianization of the western Frankish lands. Moreover, the seeming chaos of his reign should not obscure the fact that in surviving and keeping the Crown amid myriad difficulties he achieved as much as was humanly possible.

—*David Harry Miller*

FURTHER READING

Barraclough, Geoffrey. *The Crucible of Europe: The Ninth and Tenth Centuries in European History.* Berkeley: University of California Press, 1976. A useful guide to the general context of late Carolingian affairs.

Duckett, Eleanor Shipley. *Carolingian Portraits: A Study of the Ninth Century.* Ann Arbor: University of Michigan Press, 1962. Contains studies of Lupus of Ferrières, Hincmar of Reims, and Walafrid Strabo—influential scholars of the time of Charles the Bald.

Dunbabin, Jean. *France in the Making, 843-1180.* Oxford, England: Oxford University Press, 1985. Chapter 1 deals with Charles the Bald.

Engreen, F. E. "Pope John VIII and the Arabs." *Speculum* 20 (1945): 318-330. One of the very few studies addressing the Arab problem in Italy during the time of Charles the Bald.

Halphen, Louis. *Charlemagne and the Carolingian Empire.* Translated by G. de Nie. Amsterdam: North Holland, 1977. Part 3 of this volume discusses the affairs of Charles the Bald and his brothers.

Hen, Yitzhak. *The Royal Patronage of Liturgy in Frankish Gaul to the Death of Charles the Bald.* Woodbridge: Boydell Press for the Henry Bradshaw Society, 2001. Hen, a lecturer in history at the Ben-Gurion University of the Negev, Israel, shows that royal patronage of liturgy characterized early medieval Francia and became an important means of political power. Bibliography, indexes.

Jeep, John M., et al., eds. *Medieval Germany: An Encyclopedia.* New York: Garland, 2001. An A-Z encyclopedia that addresses all aspects of the German- and Dutch-speaking medieval world from 500 to 1500. Entries include individuals, events, and broad topics such as feudalism and pregnancy. Bibliographical references, index.

McKitterick, Rosamond. *The Frankish Kingdoms Under the Carolingians.* New York: Longmans, Green, 1983. A useful synthesis, although it does not supersede Halphen's study. The latter portion discusses the period of Charles the Bald's life.

Moore, Robert Ian. *The First European Revolution, c. 970-1215.* Malden, Mass.: Blackwell, 2000. According to the publisher, "a radical reassessment of Europe from the late tenth to the early thirteenth centuries [arguing that] the period witnessed the first true 'revolution' in European society," supported by transformation of the economy, family life, political power structures, and the rise of the non-Mediterranean cities. Bibliography, index.

Nelson, Janet L. *Charles the Bald.* New York: Longman, 1992. A biography that discusses political and historical features of Charles's reign. Bibliography, index.

Poupardin, René. "The Carolingian Kingdoms, 840-877." In *Germany and the Western Empire.* Vol. 3 in *Cambridge Medieval History.* New York: Macmillan, 1922. A detailed and invaluable account of the period of Charles the Bald's life and the complicated affairs of the divided empire.

Wallace-Hadrill, John Michael. *A Carolingian Renaissance Prince: The Emperor Charles the Bald.* London: British Academy, 1980. An analysis of Charles from the proceedings of the British Academy. Bibliography.

SEE ALSO: Charlemagne; Dhuoda; Louis the German; Ratramnus.

RELATED ARTICLES in *Great Events from History: The Middle Ages, 477-1453*: June 7, 793: Norse Raid Lindisfarne Monastery; 843: Treaty of Verdun; 850-950: Viking Era.

CHARLES IV
Holy Roman Emperor (r. 1355-1378)

The greatest ruler of medieval Bohemia and the last important medieval Holy Roman Emperor, Charles was an efficient and effective administrator. He stabilized German political affairs, strengthened the power of his family in Bohemia and in Europe, and influenced the culture of his time.

BORN: May 14, 1316; Prague, Bohemia (now in the Czech Republic)
DIED: November 29, 1378; Prague, Bohemia
ALSO KNOWN AS: Charles of Luxembourg; Charles I (king of Bohemia)
AREA OF ACHIEVEMENT: Government and politics

EARLY LIFE

Charles was the oldest son of John of Luxembourg and the grandson of Holy Roman Emperor Henry VII, who died in 1313. In the confused years following the death without direct heir of Wenceslaus (Václav) III, the last Přemyslid king of Bohemia, Henry had arranged for John to succeed to the Bohemian throne in 1310 and to marry Elizabeth, Wenceslaus's sister. This political marriage strengthened the Luxembourg position in Bohemia, and when Charles was born in 1316 the future of the new dynasty seemed assured.

Charles's early education was unsystematic. His mother schooled him in the traditions of government and foreign policy established by the last Přemyslids and instilled in him a love of the Bohemian land. His father, whose political and cultural tastes were oriented more toward France than toward Germany, involved him in many of his European ventures. John never felt particularly comfortable or welcome in Bohemia, and the time he spent there was chiefly for obtaining the financial resources to support his activities elsewhere. It was perhaps not surprising that he and Elizabeth should quarrel, and in 1323, he took Charles from Prague to Paris to be brought up at the court of King Charles IV of France. Periodically, John included his son on his numerous knightly campaigns. As a result, Charles rapidly learned the skills of survival in the world of political intrigue.

Charles's education was not, however, wholly practical and pragmatic. While in Paris, he made contact with the eloquent and learned abbot of Fécamp, Pierre Roger, whom he asked to become his tutor. Their friendship endured and was an important factor later, when Pierre became Pope Clement VI.

The next stage in Charles's education was in the arena of practical politics. In 1331, John took him on an expedition to Italy in support of Louis IV Wittelsbach of Bavaria, who had been Holy Roman Emperor since 1314. Charles was placed in a position of authority as imperial vicar in the region of Lombardy, and for two years he gained experience with the politically unstable world of the northern Italian communes. In October, 1333, he returned with his father to Bohemia, and the next year he was named margrave of Moravia. This position gave him royal power in the absence of the king, occasions that were frequent because of John's restless knight-errantry. For most of the period between 1334 and 1346, Charles was the de facto ruler of the kingdom of Bohemia. He governed wisely and well, restoring administrative efficiency and recovering many royal prerogatives and properties.

LIFE'S WORK

Events in 1346 changed Charles's status. Opposition to the rule of Louis IV had been growing in Germany, much of it fueled by hostility from the Papacy. When Pierre Roger became pope in 1342, he had embarked on a program to depose Louis and replace him with Charles. On July 11, 1346, a majority of electors in Germany withdrew support from Louis and elected Charles in his place. Although the electoral decision in 1346 was challenged, Charles's position was confirmed the following year when Louis died of a stroke. While some observers, both then and in later times, charged that Charles was a mere ecclesiastical puppet (they applied to him the derogatory term *Pfaffenkönig*, or papal king), the fact was that the Luxembourg family had an independent imperial tradition and Charles was a practiced and adroit politician who had broad support in Germany. His relations with the Papacy were to be close, but he was always an autonomous and powerful figure. Indeed, after Clement VI's death in 1352, Charles was really the dominant figure in continental Europe.

Immediately after his election, Charles left to join his father in a military campaign with the French against the English as a part of the Hundred Years' War. At Crécy on August 26, John was led into battle by his retainers—he had been blind for a number of years—and in the subsequent French disaster, he was killed. Charles then withdrew from the conflict so that, as a contemporary observed, Bohemia would not lose two rulers in a single day. Now both emperor and king, Charles returned to

Prague and began a thirty-two-year reign of great consequence for both Germany and Bohemia.

Charles's primary concern as ruler was the dynastic aggrandizement of his family. He increased the Crown lands in Bohemia and Moravia, added areas in Silesia to the family holdings, obtained the district of Eger (Cheb) on the border between Bohemia and the German lands, purchased the region of Lower Lusatia in 1367, and gained control of Brandenburg in 1373 in complicated negotiations with the Wittelsbach family and the Estates of Brandenburg. As a result, the Luxembourg family achieved a prominent position in Europe, one that may be compared with the later eminence of the Habsburg and Hohenzollern families.

Subordinate, but related, to Charles's dynastic interests was his royal policy in Bohemia. He tried to strengthen kingly power against the high Bohemian nobility. He prepared a written law code, known as the Majestas Carolina, which was submitted to the Bohemian Estates at the diet in 1355. They recognized the degree to which it would limit their traditional role as a law-interpreting body, and they refused to accept it. In other respects, and by other means, however, Charles was able to enhance royal authority. His support of urban development and commercial activity ushered in an era of prosperity for Bohemian cities. Charles used his position as emperor to ensure that Venetian trade routes with Bruges and London were shifted eastward in order to benefit the towns and merchants of his kingdom. Nowhere is Charles's impact more clearly seen than in Prague itself, for it was transformed into an imperial capital. Charles had already arranged in 1343 with his former tutor, now Pope Clement VI, to have Prague raised to an archdiocese. Now, as king, he undertook an extensive building program and founded a new commercial and settlement district.

In the lands of the Holy Roman Empire, Charles pursued a policy that was realistic and moderate. He recognized that the centuries-long imperial tradition of trying to rule northern Italy as well as the German lands was an anachronism. He went to Italy to be crowned emperor in 1355, but he made no attempt to enforce imperial claims over the unstable and contentious communes of northern Italy. Elsewhere, he arranged to be crowned king of the old Burgundian royal domain of Arles in 1365. Nevertheless, Charles had no illusions that this kingdom could effectively be ruled as imperial territory. He eventually bestowed an imperial vicarate on the French dauphin for the whole kingdom except for the region of Savoy.

Charles's realism was best revealed in his issuance of the Golden Bull of 1356. This imperial constitution (named for the golden seal—*bulla*) defined an orderly procedure for electing subsequent rulers; it identified the electors (four secular rulers and three ecclesiastical dignitaries), from whom a majority vote was necessary; it established the city of Frankfurt-am-Main as the meeting place for an election; and it prescribed the ceremonial procedural to be followed. While these details codified a process that had been evolving for a century, the bull nevertheless represented a statesmanlike resolution of problems that had plagued the empire for generations. Of particular note is the fact that the Wittelsbachs of Bavaria and the Habsburgs of Austria were excluded from the electorship. Moreover, there was no mention of papal prerogatives of assent to, or participation in, the election. Of equal importance for the future of German affairs was that the bull declared the electoral territories of the secular rulers to be indivisible and strengthened these electors in their own principalities to such a degree that they became practically sovereign rulers. Because the king of Bohemia was identified as one of the electors, Charles himself was confirmed in his territorial prerogatives. This accomplished what had earlier been frustrated in the Majestas Carolina.

Engraved sigillum, or seal, containing the likeness of Charles IV. (Library of Congress)

House of Luxembourg: Holy Roman Emperors

Reign	*Ruler*
1308-1313	Henry VII (crowned 1311)
1346-1378	Charles IV (crowned 1355)
1378-1400	Wenceslaus (deposed)
1410-1437	Sigismund (crowned 1433)

Charles's activities were not limited to family affairs or internal politics. Within central Europe he was clearly the leading figure in relations with Poland, Hungary, and Austria. He tended to support France against England in the Hundred Years' War. In his dealings with the Papacy, Charles promoted the popes' return to Italy from Avignon, where they had been resident since the early fourteenth century. He was a supporter of ecclesiastical reform, both in Germany and especially in Bohemia. With the outbreak of the Great Schism (or Western Schism) in 1378, though he supported the Roman pope Urban VI, Charles tried to intervene to heal the division between the two claimants to the pontifical throne. His health failed him, however, and he died in Prague late in November, 1378.

Significance

From Charles's third marriage, to the niece of the Hungarian king, there came his son Wenceslaus (also spelled Wenzel or Václav), who was born in 1361 and who succeeded Charles without incident in 1378. This easy transition revealed the degree to which Charles had been successful in stabilizing and regulating German affairs. His statesmanship had given focus and direction to a process that had proceeded haphazardly in earlier generations. The effect of the Golden Bull of 1356 was not limited to the electors alone; in all the empire's principalities and city-states the same development toward territorial control may be observed. Charles recognized that the emperor had little power without a firm territorial base. His reign established the principality as the focus of German politics for the next several centuries.

Charles was also an influential religious and cultural patron. He was involved in the planning and building of the Gothic-style Saint Vitus's Cathedral in Prague, he endowed many religious establishments throughout the kingdom and the empire, and he himself wrote a biography of the patron saint of Bohemia, Saint Wenceslaus (c. 907-929). He also wrote a revealing autobiography, one of the few to come from a layperson in the medieval period. At his court, Charles entertained learned intellectuals and figures involved with the early Italian Renaissance. Charles was also patriotic about his Czech heritage. He referred to Bohemia as "the sweet soil of my native land," he prided himself that he could speak the language "like any other Czech," and he encouraged and patronized historians of Bohemia.

In 1347, Charles founded a university in Prague. It was the first north of the Alps and east of the Rhine. The University of Prague, which was allowed by the Papacy to have a theological faculty, quickly established its reputation under Charles's patronage as an important center of learning. By the end of the fourteenth century, it would become the European center of religious and theological controversy.

Charles's greatness lay not in wars waged or in conquests won but rather in his statesmanship, vision, and political realism. He was regarded by later Czech generations as "the father of his country."

—Paul W. Knoll

Further Reading

Charles IV. *Autobiography of Emperor Charles IV; and, His Legend of St. Wenceslas*. Edited by Balázs Nagy and Frank Schaer, with an introduction by Ferdinand Seibt. New York: Central European University Press, 2001. Charles IV in his own words, available in English for the first time. Genealogical tables, maps, bibliographical references, indexes.

Du Boulay, F. R. *Germany in the Later Middle Ages*. New York: St. Martin's Press, 1984. Although the scope of this volume goes far beyond the figure and rule of Charles, it is a useful book for understanding the larger context of Charles's reign as well as some specific aspects of his rule in Germany. It was abreast of the most recent scholarship at the time of its publication. The treatment of towns, the Church, and the structures of society and governance is especially good. The section devoted specifically to Charles (pages 36-42) draws effectively on the important German biography by Ferdinand Seibt.

Jarrett, Bede. *The Emperor Charles IV*. London: Eyre and Spottiswoode, 1935. This biography is largely uncritical and is based on secondary materials, with little reference to the sources. The one exception is that the author provides a partial translation of Charles's autobiography. The translation is a loose one and misses many important nuances of this effort by Charles to present some of his imperial ideals, but it does communicate some of the directness of Charles's literary style.

Krofta, Kamil. "Bohemia in the Fourteenth Century." In *Decline of Empire and Papacy.* Vol. 7 in *The Cambridge Medieval History.* 1932. Reprint. New York: Cambridge University Press, 1958. Though it deals with more than the reign of Charles, the primary focus of this chapter is on the years from 1333 to 1378. The political narrative is detailed and reliable, and the judgment on Charles is generally favorable. A good treatment of Charles in the context of Czech history.

Stoob, Heinz. *Kaiser Karl IV. und seine Zeit.* Graz, Austria: Styria, 1990. A rare biography, in German. Illustrations, maps on lining papers, bibliographical references, indexes.

Thomson, S. Harrison. "Learning at the Court of Charles IV." *Speculum* 25 (1950): 1-20. A full and scholarly treatment of the cultural aspects of Charles's reign. The author not only analyzes the formal literary and educational activities connected directly with Charles but also gives attention to the general cultural milieu, including the development of the Czech vernacular and the restructuring of the German language in the royal chancery.

Walsh, Gerald Groveland. *The Emperor Charles IV, 1316-1378: A Study in Holy Empire Imperialism.* Oxford, England: Basil Blackwell, 1924. Provides a short sketch of Charles's imperial ideals but treats these in a rather old-fashioned way, reflecting many of the categories of nineteenth century German scholarship. There is very little discussion of Charles's Bohemian policy and none of his leadership in the cultural sphere, except as it might be related to his political theory.

Waugh, W. T. "Germany: Charles IV." In *Decline of Empire and Papacy.*Vol. 7 in *The Cambridge Medieval History.* 1932. Reprint. New York: Cambridge University Press, 1958. Treats the political details of Charles's German policy in depth and with accuracy. The emphasis is on the way Charles maneuvered among the other political leaders in Europe and on his family policy. The evaluation of his accomplishments is generally negative. This is especially true with regard to what the author considers Charles's surrender of imperial prerogatives.

SEE ALSO: Jan Hus; William of Ockham; Petrarch; Cola di Rienzo; Philippe de Vitry; Wenceslaus.

RELATED ARTICLES in *Great Events from History: The Middle Ages, 477-1453*: August 1, 1323-August 23, 1328: Peasants' Revolt in Flanders; 1337-1453: Hundred Years' War; August 26, 1346: Battle of Crécy; May 20, 1347-October 8, 1354: Cola di Rienzo Leads Popular Uprising in Rome; January 10, 1356, and December 25, 1356: Golden Bull.

ALAIN CHARTIER

French poet and scholar

Chartier's skillful use of the French language and his imaginative, elegant literary style significantly influenced the development of French poetry in the fifteenth century. As royal secretary to Charles VII of Valois, Chartier played an active role in the complex political world during the Hundred Years' War, a world that he accurately recorded in prose works of extraordinary literary and historical importance.

BORN: c. 1385; Bayeux, Normandy, France
DIED: c. 1430; Avignon, France
AREAS OF ACHIEVEMENT: Literature, government and politics

EARLY LIFE

Alain Chartier (ah-lan shahr-tyay), the most famous poet of early fifteenth century France, the canon of the Notre-Dame de Paris, a chronicler of his time, and the creator of the literary school known as the Grands Rhétoriqueurs, was the eldest of three sons of a prominent Norman family. One of his younger brothers, Guillaume, became bishop of Paris, and another, Thomas, like Alain, held a post as royal secretary and notary. Such distinguished service to the kings of France by the three Chartier brothers suggests that the family enjoyed a certain social and economic prominence. The young Alain attended the University of Paris and may even have been a *maître* (lecturer-teacher) at the University of Paris for a short while.

LIFE'S WORK

Although little is known of his youthful activities, by 1417, Chartier was well established both in his profession as royal secretary and as a poet. The office of "notary and secretary of the king" was a very desirable position. In addition to guaranteeing the holder a secure place within the court, it provided a rather substantial salary. A small number of notaries were also "secretaries"; that is, as the name implies, they were empowered to sign secret letters. In his position as secretary, Chartier had almost daily contact with the king while at court and, when serving as ambassador abroad, he would have been entrusted with the most sensitive matters of state politics.

For a writer and scholar such as Chartier, the secretarial post provided intellectual benefits far beyond financial security. During untroubled times, he had time to compose his lyric poetry, he had easy access to the works of earlier poets through the king's magnificent library at Paris and through the renowned papal library at Avignon, and he enjoyed the companionship, inspiration, and encouragement of other poets who resided at court.

Miniature from Alain Chartier's Book of Hope, *in which the author, reclining in bed, is comforted by Hope.* (Frederick Ungar Publishing Co.)

Life at court, however, was not without difficulties for Chartier. On several occasions, he vehemently criticized the self-serving interests at court. In *De vita curiali* (1489; *The Curial*, 1888), he wrote:

> The court is an assembly of people who under the pretence of acting for the good of all, come together to diddle each other. . . . The abuses of the court and the habits of courtiers are such that no one lasts there without being corrupted and no one succeeds there without being corruptible.

From 1410 to 1425, Chartier moved regularly with members of the king's household as they fled before the invading English armies led by Henry V. During most of Chartier's career at court, France was ravaged by constant attacks from the English as part of the Hundred Years' War, and by a virulent civil war. Chartier was deeply immersed in the political machinations of this most complex period in French history, yet he proved to be both an able ambassador and a talented and thorough chronicler. For example, his *Epistola de Puella* (letter concerning the maid, Joan of Arc), written in 1429, describes in accurate and lengthy detail Joan of Arc's exploits and victories, including the breaking of the siege at Orléans and the crowning of Charles VII at Reims.

The last four years of his life, Chartier served as royal ambassador on a number of important missions abroad, including one to the Holy Roman Emperor Sigismund of Luxembourg in 1425 and another to the court of James I of Scotland in 1428. These were troubled times to be serving as royal ambassador; the office called for men of great talent and even greater courage. As a direct result of the prolonged and bitter fighting between the French and English, royal ambassadors faced the constant danger of assassination or being taken hostage. Chartier often mentioned in his correspondence concern for his personal safety.

In 1428, while visiting the court of James I of Scotland, Chartier negotiated an alliance that would result in military support for France. Charles also authorized Chartier to arrange for the marriage of James's daughter, Margaret Stuart, to Charles's son, Louis XI. Chartier's association with Margaret's marriage contract led to one of the most famous, yet clearly apocryphal, anecdotes of the fifteenth century. According to this often-repeated story, the beautiful young dauphin secretly kissed the sleeping Chartier on the lips and offered these words in defense of her action: "I kissed not the man, but rather the precious mouth from which so much beautiful poetry and so many virtuous words have issued."

The charming story of the youthful lady embracing the aging poet quickly seduced the court of Charles VII, for Chartier's ugliness, like his lyric poetry, had become proverbial. While still in his early forties, the poet's physical appearance already betrayed the effects of the rigorous and taxing life he had led as servant to the king. According to his own writings, his body had withered, his face had wrinkled, and he had become thin and pale. Nevertheless, Margaret did not appear at the French court until 1436, six or seven years after Chartier's death, and at that time she was only twelve years old—hardly mature enough to have been overwhelmed by the poetic power of Chartier's lyrical works.

The connection between Chartier's professional life and his literary production is readily apparent. His poetry reflects the traditional medieval interest in allegory and the lofty concerns of love; it was written for a court audience that anticipated the use of conventional forms and commonplace subject matter. His prose, more measured, more engaged, was informed by his royal service and reflects many of the political and social concerns of the age. His literary production was relatively small, and his reputation rests largely on one poem, "La Belle Dame sans merci" (1424; "The Beautiful, Pitiless Lady"), and one long prose piece, *Le Quadrilogue invectif* (1489; *The Invective Quadrilogue*, late fifteenth century).

In "La Belle Dame sans merci" (the French title is still most often used in English, probably because of the influence of John Keats's poem of the same name), a young lover engages in a debate with his pitiless lady. The young man professes a love that, if unrequited, will lead to his death. Repeatedly, the young lover's advances are repulsed by the uncompromising arguments of the lady as she defends her freedom and steadfastly resists submitting her liberty to the mastery of a man. Finally, she loses patience and summarily dismisses the lover. Devastated, he ultimately dies of a broken heart.

Reaction to Chartier's poem was swift and venomous. The professional male suitors of the court took umbrage at the disparaging portrait of the merciless lady and her lachrymose lover. They demanded a quick trial and severe punishment for the poet from the Court of Love, an actual institution that had been founded by a group of scholars and poets at the court of Charles VI on Saint Valentine's Day, 1401. The charter of the Court of Love clearly stated its purpose to "honor and praise . . . all women." According to his critics, Chartier's poem had maligned the good name of all women; as punishment, he was to be banished immediately from the court. Chartier was sufficiently troubled by the harsh reaction of the court that he penned "L'Excusation" ("The Excuse"), in which he maintained that he had simply recorded a dialogue that he had innocently witnessed while attending a party. Unappeased, the court continued to pursue the poet, adamantly calling for a public retraction and even hiring lawyers. The ultimate outcome of the matter has not been clearly determined; yet both the reaction of the court and of the poet reveal the exceptional popularity of the poem. For two centuries it was attacked, praised, imitated, and repudiated.

Despite his profound influence on the development of French poetry, many critics maintain that Chartier's greatest contribution to French letters is his prose work, *The Invective Quadrilogue*. The word "quadrilogue" refers to the fact that four allegorical figures (France and the three "estates," or orders of French society: the knights, the clergy, and the peasantry) are involved in a heated debate (*invectif*) concerning the defeat of France at the hands of the English. Written shortly after the signing of the humiliating Treaty of Troyes (1420), the work provides an astonishingly honest and reasoned critique of the social and political problems facing France in 1422. The plundering of the provinces by Henry V, the devastating civil conflict, the widespread starvation as a result of the war, and the dearth of leadership, which collectively had drained France of all of its former glory, set the political context for the work.

Chartier wondered whether France's ills were not the result of internal weaknesses more than foreign invasions. In the midst of his reverie, he fell asleep and had a vision of a beautiful lady, the personification of France, standing beside a dilapidated palace, its former richness now only barely evident. Kneeling before her were three troubled men, representing the knights, the clergy, and the peasantry. The lady admonished the men for their laziness and cowardice and forthrightly blamed their indolent behavior for the destruction of France. Responding to the lady's bitter attacks, the knight and the peasant accused each other of causing France's defeat. As the dialogue became more quarrelsome, the clergy intervened and demanded an end to the destructive bickering, because, he observed, it is just such petty behavior that is at the very root of France's problems. For France to regain her rightful place among nations, all three estates must work together. In the end, the lady underscored the wisdom of the clergy as she reminded her people that a love of the common good will overshadow individual needs and lead France to glory. If all will work together, she counseled, then the fortunes they seek individually will accrue to them all collectively. *The Invective Quadri-*

logue affected its readers powerfully in 1422 (when it was written) and through the centuries has been cited as one of the finest statements of patriotic "prose propaganda."

After November, 1428, no records or official documents bear the name of Alain Chartier. Most likely, he was promoted to member of the royal council as the reward for long and faithful service to the king; thereafter, he would have had his own secretary. He died at Avignon and was buried there in the Church of Saint-Antoine.

His life was one of devotion to public service and to his art. First and foremost, he was a patriot, willingly serving his country as artist and ambassador. His work revealed his love of France and its people, as well as his fervent desire to find ways to reconcile the combative elements within French society.

SIGNIFICANCE

Chartier's prose style, always controlled, often elegant, set the standard for French writers for more than two hundred years. A prominent modern critic, Gustave Lanson, calls Chartier a fifteenth century Balzac, referring to his ability to control and elevate the French language. Generations of poets have looked back on Chartier as the father of French eloquence. Although modern readers may find Chartier's didactic works tiresome, his lyric works frivolous, and his use of medieval rhetorical devices pedantic, it was not so in his own time. His humanism and his erudition were greatly admired by his contemporaries, who referred to him respectfully as Master Alain.

—*William C. Griffin*

FURTHER READING

Brown, Cynthia J. "Allegorical Design and Image-Making in Fifteenth-Century France: Alain Chartier's Joan of Arc." *French Studies* 53, no. 4 (October, 1999): 385-404. Argues that allegory served as a means to understand and overcome moments of crisis, leading to the making of the figure and image of Joan of Arc.

Cayley, Emma J. "Collaborative Communities: The Manuscript Context of Alain Chartier's Belle Dame Sans Mercy." *Medium Aevum* 71, no. 2 (2002): 226-240. A scholarly discussion of the what the author calls the "play" of competition and dialogue between the text of the poem and the poet Chartier.

Hale, J. R., J. R. L. Highfield, and B. Smalley, eds. *Europe in the Late Middle Ages*. Evanston, Ill.: Northwestern University Press, 1965. This collection of essays provides valuable background information on life in fourteenth and fifteenth century Europe. Lewis's essay supplies helpful information on political and social life at court and makes direct reference to Chartier's work.

Hoffman, Edward J. *Alain Chartier: His Life and Reputation*. New York: Wittes Press, 1942. One of the earliest and most complete treatments of Chartier's life and works. This volume includes a full account of Chartier's life and analyses of his major works. Portions of major works are cited in their original version, and the author assesses Chartier's influence on French letters.

Laidlaw, J. C., ed. *The Poetical Works of Alain Chartier.* London: Cambridge University Press, 1974. Provides brief but helpful introductions to all the poems and detailed study of the 113 manuscripts that contain Chartier's poetical works. A thorough treatment.

Patterson, Warner Forrest. *Three Centuries of French Poetic Theory: A Critical History of the Chief Arts of Poetry in France, 1328-1630*. 2 vols. New York: Russell and Russell, 1966. Volume 1 contains an informative introduction to the historical and intellectual context in which Chartier and his contemporaries wrote. Volume 2 contains examples of Chartier's work in the original French.

Tilley, Arthur, ed. *Medieval France*. New York: Hafner Press, 1964. A standard text that provides an account of the history, literature, art, and architecture of medieval France. Offers a concise introduction to the principal writers of the early fifteenth century and places Chartier in this context.

SEE ALSO: Geoffrey Chaucer; Chrétien de Troyes; Christine de Pizan; Eleanor of Aquitaine; Gottfried von Strassburg; Hartmann von Aue; Henry V; Joan of Arc; Marie de France; Marguerite Porete; Walther von der Vogelweide; Wolfram von Eschenbach.

RELATED ARTICLES in *Great Events from History: The Middle Ages, 477-1453*: c. 1100: Rise of Courtly Love; 1337-1453: Hundred Years' War; c. 1350-1400: Petrarch and Boccaccio Recover Classical Texts; May 4-8, 1429: Joan of Arc's Relief of Orléans.

GEOFFREY CHAUCER

English poet and diplomat

Chaucer was a great innovator and a great master of English poetry who used his descriptive and narrative skill to express a comic vision of humanity undimmed by the passage of six centuries.

BORN: c. 1343; London?, England
DIED: October 25?, 1400; London, England
AREAS OF ACHIEVEMENT: Literature, government and politics

EARLY LIFE

John and Agnes Chaucer, the parents of Geoffrey Chaucer (JEFF-ree CHAW-suhr), were London property owners; John and other members of the family were vintners, wine wholesalers, and holders of offices in the customs service. Records such as deeds, wills, and inventories suggest that fourteenth century residents of Vintry Ward near the Thames River in London lived prosperously and comfortably. Although no record of Chaucer's schooling has been found, he would most likely have been educated, like other merchants' sons, at a school such as the one attached to St. Paul's Cathedral, which had in its library—and doubtless in its curriculum—works of Latin grammar and classical poetry of Vergil, Ovid, and other favorites of the mature Chaucer.

In 1357, Chaucer served in the household of Elizabeth de Burgh, countess of Ulster, perhaps as a page. The English nobility traveled often, and the young Chaucer likely experienced trips to the country estates of other aristocrats; certainly he often expressed his fondness for the country and the beauties of nature. In 1359, the young man took part in one of the military operations of the Hundred Years' War between England and France. Captured by the enemy near Reims, Chaucer may have seen Reims Cathedral and nearby Chartres. He was ransomed in March of 1360; later that year there is a record of his having carried documents from Calais to England for Prince Lionel, the countess of Ulster's husband. Undoubtedly the expedition marked his first direct contact with a culture that influenced his poetry heavily from the start.

Nothing is known for certain of Chaucer's activities between 1360 and 1366. In the latter year, his father died. Also, Chaucer was granted a safe-conduct to Navarre, perhaps as part of a diplomatic mission, perhaps for a pilgrimage (Navarre being on the direct route to the shrine of Saint James of Compostela in Spain). A final event of that year was his marriage to Philippa, probably the daughter of Sir Gilles de Roet, another of whose daughters, Katherine, would marry John of Gaunt, a later patron of the poet. In 1367, Chaucer was in the household of King Edward III and may also have been studying law at the Inner Temple. Chaucer's poetry shows familiarity with the Inns of Court, and though evidence connecting him with the Inner Temple is hearsay, the kinds of skills it taught prospective lawyers would have been useful at court and in his later official positions. Possibly Chaucer began to write poetry at this time, for anyone who could imitate the popular French courtly verse would find encouragement. The poet depicts himself as sedentary and bookish; his portrait, which was executed some years after his death, shows a grave man with wide-set eyes, a long, straight nose, and a mustache and forked beard. He looks like a man who might be trusted with a diplomatic mission, not necessarily like the possessor of the priceless sense of humor that his literary works reveal him to have been.

LIFE'S WORK

The earliest Chaucerian poem that can be dated even approximately is *The Book of the Duchess* (c. 1370), written after the death of Blanche of Lancaster in 1368 and offering consolation, though in a whimsical way, to her widower, John of Gaunt. This 1,334-line poem exemplifies Chaucer's characteristic interest in love as a subject and in the rhymed couplets popular in French poetry of the time. He continued to serve King Edward, and his 1372 diplomatic journey to Genoa and Florence may well have contributed significantly to his development as a poet, for the three greatest Italian writers of the century, all of great interest to Chaucer, had Florentine connections. Dante had died some fifty years earlier, but both Petrarch and Giovanni Boccaccio were living. If Chaucer, remaining in Italy several months, did not meet them, he could hardly have avoided extending his knowledge of their work. Returning early in 1373, Chaucer was again sent to Genoa later that year.

In 1374, the mayor and aldermen of London leased to Chaucer a dwelling over Aldersgate rent-free, and the king appointed him as controller of the export taxes levied on wool, sheepskin, and leather in the nearby customhouse, a post that made him responsible for receipts averaging nearly twenty-five thousand pounds per year. A line in Chaucer's poem *The House of Fame* (1372-1380) that refers to his "reckonings" suggests that the work dates from this period, though whether in the early, middle, or late 1370's cannot be determined. Although it is in the form of a dream vision, as had been *The Book of the Duchess*, *The House of Fame* displays greater technical mastery. The narrator falls asleep and dreams of being in a temple of the goddess Venus, on the walls of which he sees representations of famous legendary events, particularly those dealing with love, such as Aeneas's encounter with Dido in Vergil's *Aeneid* (c. 29-19 B.C.E.). Emerging from the temple, the narrator meets an eagle with golden feathers that seizes him in its claws and soars high into the air. The eagle proves to be friendly, however, and very talkative, promising to take his prisoner to the House of Fame, where he can learn more about love than he has ever learned from his books. On arrival, he discovers the House of Fame to be a large, chaotic, puzzling place. He is about to meet a "man of great authority" who will presumably interpret the confusion; then the poem breaks off, after 2,158 lines.

In the later 1370's, Chaucer made several trips to the European continent, including another to Italy in 1378, after which he seems not to have gone abroad until after his customs duties ended in 1386. During the interim he almost surely wrote several other major works. *The Parlement of Foules* (1380), another dream vision, in honor of Valentine's Day, has been thought to refer to the negotiations involving Anne of Bohemia and her suitors, one of whom, Richard II, had succeeded Edward III on the latter's death in 1377. Regardless of whether a political meaning is intended in Chaucer's poem, wherein three male eagles argue their cases for marriage to a young female before a court of birds presided over by Dame Nature, it remains a charming poem. Another major endeavor was *Boece* (c. 1380), a prose translation of one of the most widely influential of all medieval philosophical works, Boethius's *De consolatione philosophiae* (523; *The Consolation of Philosophy*, late ninth century). Chaucer's knowledge of Boethius's work also permeates *Troilus and Criseyde* (1382), which some critics consider his masterpiece. Based on a story of two lovers frequently told in the Middle Ages, Chaucer's poem owes most to Giovanni Boccaccio's *Il filostrato* (c. 1335; *The Filostrato*, 1873), but the English poet exhibits great originality in his depictions of its three main characters: a Trojan prince, the widowed daughter of a Trojan priest, and the latter's uncle, Pandarus. The narrative, told in five books comprising 8,239 lines, or 1,177 rime royal stanzas, has elements of romance, comedy, tragedy, and what the modern world would call the psychological novel.

Chaucer's last important poem before *The Canterbury Tales* is called *The Legend of Good Women*, and it probably dates from between 1380 and 1386, by which time he had moved to Kent and was in fact representing the shire in Parliament as that body was beginning to assert itself against the young King Richard II. *The Legend of Good Women* purports to have been written at the request of "Queen Alceste" (possibly a representation of Richard's Queen Anne) to atone for Chaucer's negative portrayal of Criseyde by recounting the stories of "good women." (Whether that was Chaucer's true intention, however, is called into question by the work's satirical overtones.) Chaucer left the work unfinished, but the prologue, which exists in two versions, contains a much-admired description of Chaucer's favorite season, spring.

Indications are that Chaucer wrote the "General Prologue" to *The Canterbury Tales* in the late 1380's, a period of change in his life: He was replaced at the customhouse, he made his last trip to the Continent (to Calais in 1387), and his wife, Philippa, died, presumably also in 1387. Twice in 1388, he was sued for debt. In the midst of these troubles, however, he was planning and beginning to carry out his most ambitious poem, the fruit of a life-

Engraving of Geoffrey Chaucer. (Library of Congress)

MAJOR WORKS BY GEOFFREY CHAUCER

Date	Work
c. 1370	*The Book of the Duchess*
c. 1370	*Romaunt of the Rose*
1372-1380	*The House of Fame*
1372-1380	*The Legend of St. Cecilia*
1372-1380	*Tragedies of Fortune*
c. 1380	*Anelida and Arcite*
c. 1380	*Boece*
1380	*The Parlement of Foules*
1380-1386	*Palamon and Ersyte*
1380-1386	*The Legend of Good Women*
1382	*Troilus and Criseyde*
1387-1392	*A Treatise on the Astrolabe*
1387-1400	*The Canterbury Tales*

time of shrewd observation of human nature and a carefully honed narrative gift. In 1389, King Richard II appointed him to another responsible position. As clerk of the king's works, Chaucer oversaw the construction and maintenance of royal residences, hunting lodges and preserves, and such facilities as the Tower of London, which was not only a residence but also a fortress, armory, prison, mint, and storehouse for records. Although he had assistants, his duties were now more extensive than they had been in the customhouse. Two years later, he relinquished this task for another as deputy forester of the royal forest in Somerset, which may have allowed him more time to work on *The Canterbury Tales*.

Chaucer's last years were marked by a power struggle at court, with Henry IV triumphing over Richard and forcing his abdication in 1399. Sometime after Henry IV's coronation in October of 1399, Chaucer addressed to the new king a short poem, "The Complaint of Chaucer to His Purse," the last work known to have come from his pen. Chaucer is often ironic, and it is difficult to determine how seriously to take his lack of funds, but clearly he depended on the royal goodwill for his livelihood throughout his career. He may well have continued to work on *The Canterbury Tales*, which he left incomplete at his death, but what he left stands as one of the most substantial and brilliant literary works in English.

Late in 1399, Chaucer took a long-term lease on a house near Westminster Abbey, but on or about October 25, 1400, he died, and as a tenant and parishioner of the abbey was permitted burial there. Although no one realized it at the time, his entombment marked the beginning of Poets' Corner at the Abbey.

Not because of his poetry but because of the commercial prominence and social connections of the Chaucer family, Geoffrey Chaucer is the first English poet for whom something like a full biography can be pieced together. Because he wrote in the dialect of London, eventually the standard dialect of English, Renaissance critics could, with some difficulty, read his poetry and recognize his genius, whereas excellent poets such as William Langland (c. 1332-c. 1400) and the anonymous author of the Arthurian poem *Sir Gawain and the Green Knight* (second half of the fourteenth century), whose dialects proved more troublesome, fell into neglect. Although literary historians now recognize the excellence of these contemporaries of Chaucer, he continues to be the great favorite, indeed the only English poet to be read and enjoyed continuously for six hundred years.

SIGNIFICANCE

Chaucer's practice established accentual syllabic meter as the norm of English verse for five centuries thereafter. Beginning with the four-stress lines of *The Book of the Duchess* and *The House of Fame*, which imitated the French poets of his time, Chaucer developed the five-stress line that became the backbone of the major poetry of William Shakespeare, John Milton, Alexander Pope, William Wordsworth, and many others. He appears to be the deviser of the rhymed pentameter couplet and of the seven-line stanza, which became known as rime royal. He filled those verse forms with a wide variety of narrative types from the rough-and-tumble of the fabliau in "The Miller's Tale" to the serious romance as exemplified by "The Knight's Tale." His descriptions of the assembled Canterbury pilgrims bring alive a variety of late medieval types, from gentlefolk to artisans. Many modern readers readily identify Chaucer's fourteenth century men and women with their modern counterparts. Everyone has known someone like the hearty and assertive but parsimonious proprietor of the Tabard Inn, Harry Bailey; or like that brazen confidence man, the Pardoner; or like the fastidious, self-indulgent Prioress. In the Wife of Bath, Chaucer created one of the great comic characters in literature, larger than life, an imperious feminist, outrageous, but fiercely and somehow admirably resolute.

From his earliest work, Chaucer radiated good humor, boundless love of nature, and keen interest in people, but he worked away from the dream visions favored by poets of his time to the sharp daylight world of the Canterbury pilgrimage. Incorporating social criticism into his work, Chaucer nevertheless accepted society with all of its defects; as a dutiful Christian who saw this life as a pilgrimage to a greater and eternal life, he still cherished this world and its denizens, including its moral wanderers. John Dryden's reaction in 1700 still applies: "Here is God's plenty."

—*Robert P. Ellis*

FURTHER READING

Brewer, Derek. *Chaucer.* 3d ed. London: Longmans, 1977. This relatively short biography for the general reader by a respected Chaucerian scholar judiciously interprets the somewhat sparse and sometimes puzzling facts of the poet's life.

_______. *The World of Chaucer.* Rochester, N.Y.: D. S. Brewer, 2000. An illustrated look at Chaucer's work and the intellectual life of his time. Includes bibliography and index.

Chute, Marchette Gaylord. *Geoffrey Chaucer of England.* Rev. ed. New York: E. P. Dutton, 1962. This general reader's life of Chaucer, first issued in 1946, remains the best of its type. The style is clear and unpretentious, and the facts are set forth in the context of needed background information. The author discusses the poet's literary achievement but is more successful at conveying the flow of his life.

Coghill, Nevill. *The Poet Chaucer.* 1949. 2d ed. New York: Oxford University Press, 1967. Interweaves three biographical chapters with discussions of Chaucer's poetry, emphasizing matters that influenced his writing and omitting details of his official life.

Crow, Martin M., and Virginia E. Leland. "Chaucer's Life." In *The Riverside Chaucer,* edited by Larry D. Benson. 3d ed. Boston: Houghton Mifflin, 1987. This biographical essay briefly but authoritatively presents the principal known facts of Chaucer's life.

Crow, Martin M., and Clair C. Olson, eds. *Chaucer Life-Records.* Austin: University of Texas Press, 1966. A compilation of known records pertaining directly to the poet.

Hirsh, John C. *Chaucer and the Canterbury Tales: A Short Introduction.* Malden, Mass.: Blackwell, 2003. An introduction to *The Canterbury Tales* for the general reader.

Horobin, Simon. *The Language of the Chaucer Tradition.* Rochester, N.Y.: D. S. Brewer, 2003. A discussion of the development of Middle English during Chaucer's time.

SEE ALSO: Thomas Becket; Giovanni Boccaccio; Boethius; Edward III; Henry IV (of England); Richard II.

RELATED ARTICLE in *Great Events from History: The Middle Ages, 477-1453*: 1387-1400: Chaucer Writes *The Canterbury Tales.*

CHRÉTIEN DE TROYES

French poet and writer

Chrétien de Troyes is one of the great names in early French literature and is known as the principal articulator of many significant medieval Arthurian legends.

BORN: c. 1150; France
DIED: c. 1190; France?
AREA OF ACHIEVEMENT: Literature

EARLY LIFE

Information about Chrétien de Troyes (kray-tyan duh trwah) comes almost solely from indirect evidence in his works, and scholarly speculation has led to much controversy on this subject. A dedication in *Lancelot: Ou, Le Chevalier à la charrette* (c. 1168; *Lancelot: Or, The Knight of the Cart,* 1913) to Marie de Champagne and another in *Perceval: Ou, Le Conte du Graal* (c. 1180; *Perceval: Or, The Story of the Grail,* 1844) to Philip of Flanders suggest that the poet was connected with the courts of Champagne in Troyes and in Flanders. Like most courtly clerks in this period, Chrétien was doubtless well educated in the Latin tradition of the seven liberal arts. Under the influence of the mid-twelfth century romances and tales of antiquity and working in the vernacular with a style forged by contemporary rhetoric, he describes himself in the prologue to his second romance, *Cligés: Ou, La Fausse Morte* (c. 1164; *Cligés: A Romance,* 1912), as having already completed certain works in Old French: *Erec et Enide* (c. 1164; *Erec and Enide,* 1913), adaptations of several Ovidian poems, and a version of the Tristan legend (a story that nearly became his shirt of Nessus). It also appears likely, based on several precise topographical references in *Cligés,* that Chrétien visited England at some point in his career.

LIFE'S WORK

Most scholars agree that Chrétien's canon embraces five romances. These include *Erec and Enide, Cligés, Yvain:*

Ou, Le Chevalier au lion (c. 1170; *Yvain: Or, The Knight with the Lion*, c. 1300), and *Lancelot*; the latter two seem to have been composed simultaneously. Chrétien's last work, *Perceval*, dates from about 1180 (when his patron, Philip of Flanders, died). Besides these, there are two poems in the Provençal troubadour style and an attributed romance, *Guillaume d'Angleterre* (c. 1170; *King William the Wanderer: An Old British Saga from Old French Versions*, 1904), that draws on the Saint Eustace legend, a non-Arthurian story with obvious hagiographic themes.

The texts of Chrétien's main works are preserved in a fairly large number of manuscripts, the oldest of which dates from the early thirteenth century. He composed the romances in octosyllabic rhyming couplets—averaging seven thousand lines in length—in a language that philologists consider to be standard Old French, although some Champenois or Picard dialectal traits persist, possibly because of his scribes or copyists.

Under Chrétien's powerful influence, courtly literature took on new meaning in the midst of the twelfth century renaissance. The reciprocity of love and friendship, the stress on the values of psychological metamorphosis and self-discovery, and the humanistic rejection of the enthralling obsession and selfish adultery of the Tristan legend all make the romances enduring monuments to his innovative artistry, purity of style, and rich imagination. His ethos embraces a personal freedom actively pursued by his characters (especially the heroines) and an insistence, particularly for his heroes, on a superhuman quest for happiness purified by knightly trials of valor. He presents all of this as an intellectual pastime for a polite, courtly society; it is accomplished with humorous detachment as well.

Chrétien saw himself and is seen still as a synthesizer of several traditions: the Greco-Roman heritage (Vergil, Ovid, Statius), the rich storehouse of Celtic folklore, and occasional scriptural allusions. Chrétien's skillful combination of separate adventures into a unified, well-knit story led Dante to praise him for having made France a leader in narrative poetry. The complicated question of the Welsh traditional tales that form doublets with several of his romances raises the kind of critical issues scholars continue to debate.

Chrétien's first major work is also considered the first Arthurian romance on the Continent. (This general observation must exclude the early Welsh traditional tale *Culhwch ac Olwen*, c. 1100; "how Culhwch won Olwen.") *Erec and Enide*, a brilliant bipartite study in human psychology, poses a timely dilemma: In what manner, after marriage, must a knight maintain that prowess and glory with which he won his beloved in the first place? Can honor and arms and love all be served at the same time? Numbed by marital bliss with his young, submissive bride, Erec neglects his own fame until reminded by Enide that she has heard malicious gossip about him. The hero brusquely undertakes a series of extraordinary adventures, in the company of his bride, and both are put to the test. Enide in fact proves her love by disobeying Erec's commands. Their paired quest leads ultimately to a glorious conclusion.

Arms versus love is a question to which Chrétien adverts again in *Yvain*. It is with his second major work, *Cligés*, however, that he departs from the Arthurian mold by basing his story on popular Greco-Byzantine materials. With great literary virtuosity, dazzling metaphors, and dramatic analyses, he exalts the reciprocal love of Fenice and Cligés. His heroine is a victim of a forced marriage. Many interpretations of the text stress its ironic and mirrored echoing of Iseult's adulterous passion for Tristan. The evidence for profound intertextuality of this romance with classical, especially Ovidian, sources has yet to be fully appreciated.

Interrelationship between texts is quite obvious when discussing *Yvain* and *Lancelot*. Chrétien's third and fourth romances were most likely composed more or less simultaneously, as certain events dealing with the location of the characters suggest. The incomplete *Lancelot* recounts another famous story of adultery, that of the hero with his overlord's wife, Guinevere (Arthur's queen). The theme—apparently representing a "case" for debate—was possibly suggested by Marie de Champagne, a confusing but necessary conclusion because of the striking contrast with Chrétien's otherwise frequent praise for fidelity in marriage. That may explain the text's excessive irony and humor, often noted by critics. Lancelot, the servile lover of the imperious Guinevere, is treated with ridicule. With both *Yvain* and *Lancelot*, however, what becomes truly significant for the author is less the vindicated couple predestined to rule than the individual hero's destiny and place in society.

Yvain is considered by many Chrétien's consummate masterpiece, a sophisticated, witty, and finally wise extravaganza in which the romantic situation of *Erec and Enide* is reversed. Yet the conflicting obligations of marriage and chivalry are treated again. Chrétien's trademark—a deep understanding of human nature and the creation of extraordinary adventures—is clearly embedded in this seductive, persuasive, and humorous treatment of the widow's too hasty marriage to her husband's slayer. Yvain decides, in order to avenge his cousin's honor, to take action before the other knights of the Round Table do so. The failed adventure leads the hero to try to compensate for it. He voyages to the magical storm-provoking fountain in Brocéliande Forest and, as his cousin had done before him, pours water on the stone—which provokes an immediate challenge and attack by the lord of the castle, Esclados, whom Yvain defeats and mortally wounds. In fact, Yvain chases Esclados back to his nearby castle. Lunete, the wily servant of Esclados's widow, Laudine, proceeds to hide Yvain; the knight is smitten with the grieving widow, marries her, and thereby becomes the fountain's new champion.

At the fountain, Yvain must now challenge the visiting retainers of King Arthur, whom he bests, but Gawain, Arthur's nephew and the model of chivalry, encourages the knightly hero to depart from this land and his marriage and go a-journeying. Laudine grants the wish, with the condition that he must return within one year. Absorbed by his feats of arms, Yvain forgets to return, is denounced by Laudine, and falls from grace: In shame and grief, he goes stark mad. Magically cured, he rescues a lion, who expresses his gratitude by becoming Yvain's companion. Penitent and valorous after a complex series of liberating adventures, Yvain wins Laudine's pardon, and their happiness in the end restores favor and fulfillment.

Chrétien's last and most curious romance was, like *Lancelot*, left unfinished. Interpreted as a story of initiation, *Perceval* does relate the psychological and spiritual development of the story's protagonist. Arms, love, and religion all figure in the narrative—viewed by some as allegorical. Perceval's naïveté leads to amusing social blunders, but the humiliating intrigue of the whole episode at the Grail Castle, including the mysterious procession, leaves both the young hero and the reader unsatisfied. After numerous fantastic adventures, all becomes clear on a certain Good Friday: Perceval is touched by grace, and true charity is revealed to him. He learns that his lack of charity in hastening toward his own self-fulfillment—instead of rushing to his mother's side as she fell in a swoon from grief—prevented him from asking his host (in fact, his uncle) the crucial questions about the Grail and the Bleeding Lance. The quest for the latter, a restorative-destructive instrument, is undertaken by Gawain in a mysterious series of interrelated yet self-indulgent adventures.

MAJOR WORKS BY CHRÉTIEN DE TROYES

Date	*Work*
c. 1164	*Erec et Enide*
c. 1164	*Cligés: Ou, La Fausse Morte* (*Cligés: A Romance*)
c. 1168	*Lancelot: Ou, Le Chevalier à la charrette* (*Lancelot: Or, The Knight of the Cart*)
c. 1170	*Yvain: Ou, Le Chevalier au lion* (*Yvain: Or, the Knight with the Lion*)
c. 1180	*Perceval: Ou, Le Conte du Graal* (*Perceval: Or, The Story of the Grail*)

SIGNIFICANCE

Chrétien's lasting influence extends well beyond twelfth century France. An obvious debt is owed to him by the many compilers of later prose romances, beginning with the Vulgate cycle. Middle High German writers, such as Hartmann von Aue and Wolfram von Eschenbach, and others who composed Dutch, Scandinavian, and Provençal works, adapted his romances freely for their special audiences. From "The Franklin's Tale" in Geoffrey Chaucer's *The Canterbury Tales* (1387-1400) to the heroic and fairy-tale-like elements in Edmund Spenser's *The Faerie Queene* (1590, 1596), the French-derived Arthurian legends even found their way into the Wakefield and York mystery-play cycles and, more important, into Sir Thomas Malory's *Le Morte d'Arthur* (1485), which itself has inspired modern adaptations, from Alfred, Lord Tennyson's *Idylls of the King* (1859-1885) to John Boorman's adventure-fantasy film *Excalibur* (1981).

Chrétien's genius conferred on the matter of Britain (as the Arthurian legends also were known) new prestige; his talent exploited the resources of a fledgling vernacular so that aesthetic awareness, logic, and harmony began to emerge in this period. Purity in vocabulary and clarity in syntax are also part of his legacy to the French language, as is the supple rhyme of his narrative poetry. Medieval romance took a giant step with Chrétien, a leap into fantasy, legend, adventure, self-discovery, and especially self-actualization, through a tradition of values—marital, erotic, poetic, and literary.

—*Raymond J. Cormier*

FURTHER READING

Cazelles, Brigitte. *The Unholy Grail: A Social Reading of Chrétien de Troyes's "Conte du Graal."* Stanford, Calif.: Stanford University Press, 1996. Argues that *Perceval* is a masked account of historical crisis, in

this case the tradition of chivalry, in feudal society.
Chrétien de Troyes. *Chrétien de Troyes: The Knight with the Lion: Or, Yvain.* Edited and translated by William W. Kibler. New York: Garland, 1986. This fine edition, which complements Kibler's translation of *Lancelot* (1981), provides an excellent introduction, a modern English translation facing the Old French text, and a detailed bibliography.
Frappier, Jean. *Chrétien de Troyes: The Man and His Work.* Translated by Raymond J. Cormier. Athens: Ohio University Press, 1982. This illustrated critical work includes extensive notes and an index and is written for the general reader.
Kelly, Douglas. *Chrétien de Troyes: An Analytic Bibliography.* Rochester, N.Y.: Tamesis, 2002. This volume is an indispensable reference tool. Includes index.
Loomis, Roger Sherman, ed. *Arthurian Literature in the Middle Ages.* 2d ed. Oxford, England: Clarendon Press, 1961. A comprehensive, illustrated collection of articles on a wide array of Arthurian topics.
Topsfield, L. T. *Chrétien de Troyes: A Study of the Arthurian Romances.* Cambridge, England: Cambridge University Press, 1981. A useful survey by a specialist in troubadour poetics.
Uitti, Karl D., and Michelle A. Freeman. *Chrétien de Troyes Revisited.* New York: Twayne, 1995. An overview of Chrétien's work, including an analysis of *Perceval* as continuing themes introduced in Chrétien's earlier romances.

SEE ALSO: Geoffrey Chaucer; Edward III; Jean Froissart; Geoffrey of Monmouth; Hartmann von Aue; Marie de France; Wolfram von Eschenbach.
RELATED ARTICLES in *Great Events from History: The Middle Ages, 477-1453*: c. 1100: Rise of Courtly Love; c. 1180: Chrétien de Troyes Writes *Perceval.*

CHRISTINA OF MARKYATE
English ascetic

Christina of Markyate became an ascetic over the objections of her parents and others and attained the highest possible rank for a woman in the Catholic Church of that time, mother superior of a convent.

BORN: c. 1096; Huntingdon, England
DIED: 1160; Markyate, England
ALSO KNOWN AS: Kristina of Markyate; Christina of Markgate; Theodora (given name)
AREA OF ACHIEVEMENT: Religion and theology

EARLY LIFE

Christina of Markyate (MAHRK-yeht), named Theodora at birth, was the daughter of Autti and Beatrix of Huntington, England. Her family members were part of the gentry, possessing not titles of nobility but land and social standing. The exact date of Christina's birth was unrecorded, but most scholars place the date around 1096, almost two generations after the Norman Conquest of 1066. During this period, tensions remained strong between the Anglo-Saxon common folk and the Norman nobility. Because Christina's parents bear Anglo-Saxon rather than Norman-French names, it is likely that they were members of the old Anglo-Saxon nobility co-opted into the Norman system of governance.

The *Life of Christina of Markyate* (twelfth century; English translation, 1959), a contemporary hagiography (biography of a saint, with an emphasis on showing the person's holiness as an example for the reader's spiritual edification) originally written by one of Christina's chaplains, claimed that Christina was selected by God before birth for a life as a holy person. According to this account, Christina's mother was visited by a miraculous apparition of a white dove, which in Christian symbolism has long been regarded as a symbol of the Holy Spirit.

When Christina was a young girl, her family visited the Abbey of St. Albans. After seeing the devotion of the monks, Christina was filled with religious fervor and swore a private vow of perpetual virginity. As a sign of her determination, she scratched the sign of the cross into the door of the abbey with her fingernails. On her return to her home, her vow was confirmed by the local priest, Sueno, canon of Huntingdon. Such private vows, unlike the formal vows sworn by a person entering a monastery or convent, were considered to be binding on the conscience of the individual, but they conferred no formal ecclesiastical status. As a result, the person making such a vow could easily come into conflict with the social demands that might impose a role contrary to the terms of the vow.

LIFE'S WORK

Only a few years after her vow, Christina experienced just such a conflict. At the age of sixteen, she repulsed the immoral advances of Ranulf Flambard, bishop of Durham and former chancellor of England. By underhanded means, he contrived to have the young maiden brought to his bedchamber, and while they were alone, he immorally propositioned her. She kept her wits about her and tricked him into letting her escape through a carelessly worded promise to bolt the door. He failed to require that she bolt it on the inside, and she promptly slipped through and bolted it on the outside, trapping him within. He was so infuriated by this humiliating rejection that he arranged for Christina to be betrothed to his crony Burhtred.

Determined to fulfil her religious vow, Christina refused to be wed. Her parents saw her response as mere childish self-will rather than religious fervor and used every effort available to them to force her will. They denied her all contact with religious people and prevented her from attending any form of church services, and they surrounded her by all manner of worldly people who flattered her and undermined her determination. Her mother resorted to verbal abuse and also hired wisewomen to give her various concoctions to force her to fall in love with her betrothed. Her father hired men to rape her, but she outwitted every one of them. When she was forced to meet Burhtred, she sought to convince him to follow the example of several saints who, although married, lived in perpetual chastity and ultimately took monastic vows. Several visions are ascribed to her during this period, including one of the Virgin Mary.

Christina's parents also called on Fredebert, the Augustinian prior of Huntington, to attempt to change her mind, explaining that perpetual virginity was not the only road to salvation and that virtuous married women could also be saved. She remained steadfast in her determination to fulfill her vow, arguing that if she turned back on it, even to obey her parents, she would be guilty of having abandoned a greater good for a lesser one. She appealed to Bishop Robert Bloet of Lincoln, who at first agreed that she should be permitted to fulfill her religious vocation. However, after a substantial bribe was offered by her father's wealthy associates, he reversed his decision.

Having heard of the level of persecution Christina had faced both from her parents and from the ecclesiastical authorities, Ralph d'Escures, archbishop of Canterbury, encouraged Christina to flee. She accomplished this with the aid of Eadwine (also known as Edwin), an anchorite—or religious hermit—whom she approached, claiming to need spiritual guidance. He took her to the hermitage of Alfwen, an anchoress (female hermit) at Flamstead. There she set aside the fine garments that had been her custom as a daughter of the gentry and clothed herself in rough wool. Because she had to hide from her parents' agents, she could not participate in the manual labor that was commonly undertaken by monks and nuns. Instead, she remained within a hidden chamber in Alfwen's hermitage, continually praying and meditating on the psalter.

After two years with Alfwen, Christina had to leave that refuge. Her contemporary biographer gave no details of the reasons, but some scholars have surmised that there were differences between the two women, based on the absence of any further mention of Alfwen in the account. Christina departed to take refuge in Caddington with Roger, a monk of St. Albans who lived apart in a hermitage while maintaining obedience to the abbot.

Because of ongoing unfavorable interest in Christina, Roger concealed her in a tiny cell in the back of his hermitage. There she silently suffered the agonies of daily deprivation for four years. The cell was so tiny that she could not even wear warm clothes in the winter, and in the summer the cell became a sweatbox. Because Roger barred the door with a rock too large for Christina to move, she could not attend to her bodily needs except in the evening when darkness would conceal her presence and movements. During this period of extreme privation, Christina is said to have experienced numerous visions of the Virgin Mary as well as spectacular attacks by the devil, apparitions that would have driven others insane. In one of the vivid temptations recorded by her biographer, her tiny refuge was overrun by hideous toads (toads symbolize Satan), but she remained steadfast in her prayer and eventually they vanished.

When Roger died, the sympathetic Archbishop Thurstan of York arranged for other accommodations for Christina. She stayed briefly with an associate of his until Robert Bloet, the bishop of Lincoln who had betrayed her, died. At this point Christina settled in Markyate as a recluse. She soon developed a strong reputation in the surrounding countryside as a holy woman and worker of wonders. A number of miraculous healings are associated with her, including that of a woman from Canterbury who had contracted the falling sickness (which may have been epilepsy or could have been psychosomatic in nature, particularly in the light of the extreme regularity of its occurrence). During this period, Christina herself suffered from a bout of paralysis, which may have been of psychological origin. After all efforts to treat her had failed and she seemed to be in immediate danger of death, she was suddenly cured by the attention of a mysterious woman. This woman was regarded by Christina's biographer to have been a manifestation of the Virgin Mary.

As a result of Christina's growing renown as a holy

woman, a number of religious leaders urged her to lead religious communities in their areas. Thurston of York invited her to become the mother superior of a convent there, but she declined. She remained in her hermitage until Abbot Geoffrey of St. Albans created a convent associated with the monastery and invited her to become its mother superior. Although she accepted, such was the intensity of her religious fervor that she wondered whether she could truly testify to her virginity after all the trials and temptations she had endured. She is then said to have experienced a miraculous apparition in which angels crowned her with an elaborate headdress and hailed her as a virgin, approved by Christ himself.

Subsequently, Christina is said to have endured many visions and apparitions from both good and evil spirits. She also became the acquaintance of many wealthy and powerful individuals who approached her for blessings and spiritual advice. Her piety is said to have exerted a strong beneficent influence on Abbot Geoffrey and the other monks of St. Albans.

In 1139, Christina's life intersected the politics of the age when Abbot Geoffrey was called on to travel to Rome and meet with Pope Innocent II. This meeting related to English king Stephen's battles with two English bishops whom he regarded as excessively involved in worldly affairs and as having too much power. The Church objected to his desire to punish them himself because the discipline of clergy was an affair of the Church rather than secular authorities. While Geoffrey was struggling with this difficult journey, Christina is said to have received visions of his troubles and to have interceded with God to protect the abbot. As a result of her piety, Geoffrey's superiors finally recalled him to England and spared him the journey.

Although the account of Christina's life stops somewhat short of her death, she is known to have been alive and active in the religious community as late as 1155. King Henry II made a grant to her, and she is known to have given three miters and a pair of sandals to Pope Adrian IV, via Abbot Robert, Geoffrey's successor at St. Albans. Her death is unrecorded but is believed to have occurred in 1160. She was subsequently canonized as a saint of the Church, and her feast day is December 26 (Boxing Day).

SIGNIFICANCE

By swearing a vow of perpetual virginity, Christina was not merely rejecting sensuality. In a time when pregnancy and childbirth were life-threatening events, she was making a choice that would place her on a completely different life path. In addition, becoming a member of a religious order was one of the few ways in which a woman with intellectual interests could escape the narrow role strictures women of that time faced in the secular world.

—*Leigh Husband Kimmel*

FURTHER READING

Farmer, Sharon, and Barbara H. Rosenwein, eds. *Monks and Nuns, Saints and Outcasts: Religion in Medieval Society*. Ithaca, N.Y.: Cornell University Press, 2000. A history that includes discussion of the often marginalized nuns and other spiritual outcasts of Europe during the Middle Ages.

Furlong, Monica, ed. *Visions and Longings: Medieval Women Mystics*. Boston: Random House, 1996. Lives of Christina and several of her female contemporaries, comparing and contrasting their experiences and relationships with their respective societies.

Goetz, Hans-Werner. *Life in the Middle Ages: From the Seventh to the Thirteenth Century*. Translated by Albert Wimmer. Notre Dame, Ind.: University of Notre Dame Press, 1993. An overview of life during the Middle Ages, including a section on the role of the Church, monasteries, and religious recluses in medieval society.

Grégoire, Réginald. *The Monastic Realm*. New York: Rizzoli, 1985. A general account of monastic life during the medieval period and of its relationship to the secular world.

Schmitt, Miriam, and Linda Kulzer, eds. *Medieval Women Monastics: Wisdom's Wellsprings*. Collegeville, Minn.: Liturgical Press, 1996. Surveys the lives of several contemporary female saints and monastics in Christina's time.

Stanton, Robert. "Marriage, Socialization, and Domestic Violence in the *Life of Christina of Markyate*." In *Domestic Violence in Medieval Texts*, edited by Eve Salisbury, Georgiana Donavin, and Merrall Llewelyn Price. Gainesville: University Press of Florida, 2002. Argues that the original author of the *Life of Christina of Markyate* was critical of the cultural burdens placed on the nobility and the violence against Christina by her parents and fiancé, and that the author highlighted Christina's influence on the concept of consent by both partners regarding whether or not to marry.

Talbot, C. H., ed. and trans. *The Life of Christina of Markyate: A Twelfth Century Recluse*. Toronto: University of Toronto Press, 1998. This volume contains the original Latin text with facing-page translations as well as an extensive introduction giving cultural and historical context.

Venarde, Bruce L. *Women's Monasticism and Medieval Society: Nunneries in France and England, 890-1215.* Ithaca, N.Y.: Cornell University Press, 1997. Discusses the expansion of female monasticism in the Middle Ages, including the social and economic contexts in which women lived a life of piety and devotion.

SEE ALSO: Adrian IV; Hildegard von Bingen; Joan of Arc; Julian of Norwich; Margery Kempe; Mechthild von Magdeburg; King Stephen.

RELATED ARTICLES in *Great Events from History: The Middle Ages, 477-1453*: 1136: Hildegard von Bingen Becomes Abbess; c. 1380: Compilation of the Wise Sayings of Lal Ded.

CHRISTINE DE PIZAN

French poet and writer

The first woman of letters in France and the first woman in Europe known to have earned her living by writing, Christine was a prolific, versatile, and acclaimed lyric poet, didactic writer, and Humanist scholar; she was a precursor to the femmes savantes *of the Renaissance and to nineteenth and twentieth century feminists.*

BORN: c. 1365; Venice (now in Italy)
DIED: c. 1430; probably at the Convent of Poissy, near Versailles, France
ALSO KNOWN AS: Christine de Pisan
AREA OF ACHIEVEMENT: Literature

EARLY LIFE

Shortly after Christine de Pizan (krees-teen duh pee-zah) was born, her father, Tommaso di Benvenuto da Pizzano, who held a chair in astrology at the University of Bologna (where he had also studied medicine and astrology), was offered two attractive invitations—to go to Hungary to the court of Louis I or to Paris to the court of Charles V. Although he was reluctant to leave his family (the invitations were for him alone), Tommaso found the offer to go to the city of the celebrated University of Paris particularly attractive, and he agreed to go to the French court for one year. The king, pleased with the counsels of Thomas de Pizan (as his name was gallicized) in medical, scientific, and political matters, persuaded him to stay as the royal astrologer, alchemist, and physician; in 1368, Thomas sent for his wife and young daughter.

Thus Christine was reared in the stimulating environment of the court of Charles V, known as "the Wise," an intellectual and progressive monarch. Under his patronage, Thomas prospered and acquired property—the feudal estate of Orsonville—and Christine was reared in a literate and cultured home frequented by leading intellectuals. She studied the liberal arts under the tutelage of her father, whose intelligence and knowledge she admired—despite the fact that her mother disapproved of academic learning for girls. Later, Christine would complain that her education had been restricted on account of her gender, but she was able to learn to read and write, opportunities usually reserved for very high-ranking women.

At about the age of fifteen, Christine married Étienne du Castel, a twenty-four-year-old graduate scholar born of a noble, though not wealthy, family in Picardy, who became a court notary and secretary. Christine had known Étienne since infancy, and he was well regarded by her father. Étienne promised that they would be "true friends" when they married, and he seems to have kept his promise: The period of her marriage was a very happy one. The two had three children: a daughter, born in 1381, who later became a nun at the Poissy convent; a son who died in infancy; and a second son, Jean, born in 1385, who as a youth was reared in England by Christine's patron, the earl of Salisbury, and later joined the household of the dukes of Burgundy.

After 1380, when Charles V died, Christine's father began to lose his prestige and was eventually dismissed from his court appointment. Within a few years, he became ill and died, disillusioned and poor. A greater sorrow followed: In 1389, while accompanying Charles VI to Beauvais on matters of state, Étienne fell victim to the plague and died, at the age of thirty-four. Within two years, Christine had lost both father and husband, the two people to whom she was closest and who had also been her mentors.

LIFE'S WORK

Her husband's unexpected and premature death precipitated an abrupt turning point in Christine's life, which she later referred to as her "mutacion de fortune" in a book of that name. At twenty-five, she was forced into

Christine de Pizan, reclining on a bed, is urged by the Three Virtues to write a book of instruction for women in this fifteenth century miniature from an unpublished manuscript. (Frederick Ungar Publishing Co.)

"the role of a man," responsible for providing for her children and herself. She had no income or means of support and, in order to recover a small inheritance from her husband, had to engage in protracted and frustrating legal proceedings for the next ten years. Yet she determined to support herself rather than remarry; in a famous ballade, written shortly after her husband's death, she declared, "Seulete suy et seulete vueil estre" (I am alone and I want to be alone).

Christine's initial lyrics, considered to be some of her finest work, focus on her love for her husband and her grief over his death. Nevertheless, she soon turned to themes of chivalry and courtly love, more suited to the nobles who became her patrons. Immediately successful, she wrote prolifically on these topics for the next decade in lyric poems, short narratives, and didactic works. There is some evidence to suggest that she worked also as a manuscript copyist during these years to supplement her income from writing.

In 1398, Christine embarked on a rigorous, interdisciplinary program of study (including history, science, religion, philosophy, and literature, both classical and contemporary) and soon began to write her first mature works, *Le Livre de la mutacion de fortune* (1400-1403; the book of changes in fortune) and *Le Livre du chemin de long éstude* (1402-1403; the book of the road of long study). By this point, she had stopped writing about chivalry and courtly love, whose antimarriage and pro-infidelity themes she in fact rejected, suggesting in subsequent writings that the courtly love ethic was devised by men for men and had no redeeming value for women. In *Le Livre de la mutacion de fortune*, a scholarly, allegorical, seven-part poem, she initially recounts her own encounter with the Roman goddess of fortune, whose capriciousness Christine blames for the death of her husband and for transforming her into a man—though at the same time she acknowledges that without the necessity of having to support herself, she would never have become a scholar and writer. The remainder of the encyclopedic, philosophical work presents an account of fortune's influence in specific moments in world history. (The wheel of fortune was a common motif in medieval culture and was used to explain apparently arbitrary vicissitudes of human experience.)

Le Livre du chemin de long éstude, an allegorical voyage analogous to Dante's *La divina commedia* (c. 1320; *The Divine Comedy*, 1802), concerns the evils of the world and how to remedy them; Christine dedicated the work to the young Charles VI. On the basis of the renown she achieved from these two works, Christine was commissioned to write a biography of the late Charles V, *Le Livre des fais et bonnes mœurs du sage roi Charles V* (1404; the book of the deeds and virtues of the wise King Charles V), a monarch whose reign she considered exemplary.

During the years Christine was writing *Le Livre de la mutacion de fortune*, *Le Livre du chemin de long éstude*, and *Le Livre des fais et bonnes mœurs du sage roi Charles V*, she concurrently became an important spokesperson in *la querelle des femmes* (the women's quarrel), a debate among intellectuals in response to Guillaume de Lorris and Jean de Meung's *Le Roman de la rose* (thirteenth century; *The Romance of the Rose*, 1900). Proponents of *The Romance of the Rose*'s broad social satire saw its authors, especially Meung, as advocates of progress; its opponents censured the work for subverting public morality. Christine, whose reputation as a scholar was being established, was moved to attack the cynical satire against women in *The Romance of the Rose* and also the tradition of misogynist literature. She presented her arguments in four works: *L'Épistre au dieu d'Amours* (1399; *The Letter of Cupid*, 1721), her first feminist work, in which Cupid, who has received complaints from women about deceitful and disloyal men, issues a decree ousting slanderers of women from his court; *Le Dit de la Rose* (1402; the tale of the rose), a poem in which the goddess Loyalty founds an Order of the Rose, inducting chivalrous knights who promise to uphold the honor of women and speak no ill of them; *Les Épistres sur "Le Roman de la Rose"* (1401-1402; epistles on *The Romance of the Rose*), the collected correspondence that came out of the debate; and *Le Livre de la cité des dames* (1405; *The Book of the City of Ladies*, 1521), her most famous feminist work.

As *The Book of the City of Ladies* begins, Christine, in her study, ponders the work of Matheolus, a malicious thirteenth century misogynist. Her reading leads her to wonder why, historically, so many philosophers, clerics, poets, and rhetoricians have slandered women: Misogyny has a long and authoritative tradition. Although her own experiences with women cause her to conclude that these authorities are wrong, she nevertheless becomes discouraged and begins to doubt her own judgment. Then, in a dream vision, three crowned ladies, Reason, Righteousness, and Justice, appear to help Christine in her philosophical quest. Lady Reason carries a mirror that shows everything in its true proportions and qualities; she asserts the superiority of experience over authority. The three crowned ladies then announce to Christine that she has been given the prerogative among women to establish and build a city of ladies.

Before Christine's work, written between December, 1404, and April, 1405, the only literary work treating famous women was Giovanni Boccaccio's quasi-satirical *De mulieribus claris* (c. 1361-1375; *Concerning Famous Women*, 1943). Boccaccio wrote about famous women, both illustrious and notorious, regardless of their moral stature. He excluded Christian women, except Eve, saying that in following religious precepts, the actions of Christian women are in fact contrary to human nature—thus, they do not really qualify as exempla of woman. In addition, he wrote about only the women mentioned by the Latin *auctores*, thereby excluding contemporary women, saying that illustrious contemporary women were too few to mention.

Christine used Boccaccio's work as a major source for *The Book of the City of Ladies*; literary critics who compared the two works as recently as 1974 (such as Gianni Mombello) cited Christine's work as derivative and lacking in originality, saying that she was primarily a compiler of received ideas. Since then, literary critics (for example, Marina Warner) have noted that *The Book of the City of Ladies* is a universal history of women, much broader in scope than Boccaccio's work, because it includes both pagan and Christian women up to the time of Christine. Furthermore, in reorganizing and reconstructing the material of her sources, Christine develops original perspectives and new ideas. In *The Book of the City of Ladies*, Lady Reason suggests that "historical tradition" has in fact been shaped by the motives and biases of its writers and that Christine's interpretation of historical reality has equal epistemological validity with any other. Thus Christine takes it on herself to rewrite history, restoring the lives of virtuous women neglected by history and vindicating the reputations of women maligned.

Throughout the work Christine intersperses observations on her own society's attitudes toward women. Controlled indignation underlies a courteous manner as she discusses such topics as the disappointment women feel at the birth of a daughter; the double standard by which men rape women, then blame women for allowing them to do so; and the lack of access women have to education despite their natural affinity for learning.

Nevertheless, while Christine spent her entire career defending women's causes, her position as a feminist always remained moderate. Coming from a medieval, orthodox Catholic vantage, her concerns were with improving the conditions of women within the existing social order. She sought more equitable treatment for women but never expected total equality with men. A humanist committed to the common good, she encouraged women to seek fulfillment within the few roles open to them—marriage, family, and service to the community; she also urged society to acknowledge women's labor and to recognize their contributions.

Yet while basically accepting the hierarchical gender status quo based on the Christian tradition of the Fall, Christine also invokes Christian tradition in support of her arguments for educational and social advances for women. Referring to Genesis 1:27, she argues that woman, like man, was made in God's image and consequently was endowed by the Creator with the same moral, intellectual, and spiritual aptitude; hence, men and women are equally educable. Suggesting that Christian marriage is based on the model of Christ's caring for his church, the Bride of Christ, Christine argues that Christian marriage calls for the highest degree of moral commitment between a man and woman, and she does not condone or permit institutionalized domination. Finally, although Christine accepts medieval class/gender hierarchy, she argues that every woman has the potential for true nobility; according to Christine, the term "lady" refers to nobility of the soul rather than nobility of blood. "City of ladies" is a direct allusion to Saint Augustine's *De civitate Dei* (413-427; *The City of God*, 1610), suggesting that Christine saw her vision as part of the Christian tradition of political philosophy.

Christine's second major feminist work, *Le Livre des trois vertus* (1405; *The Book of the Three Virtues*, 1985), a companion volume to *The Book of the City of Ladies*, is a didactic work providing guidelines for women aspiring to achieve the "nobility" of the city; it is one of the first didactic works in European literature written by a woman for women. Dedicated to Marguerite of Burgundy on the occasion of her marriage to the French dauphin, Louis of Guienne, the work is nevertheless intended for women of all ages, circumstances, and social classes. The reader encounters Reason, Righteousness, and Justice again, together with Wisdom; the four provide women with instruction in moral precepts as well as in practical matters—with specific counsels according to their social class, marital status, and role in life. The work

MAJOR WORKS BY CHRISTINE DE PIZAN

Date	*Work*
1399	*L'Épistre au dieu d'Amours* (*The Letter of Cupid*)
1400	*L'Épistre d'Othéa à Hector* (*The Epistle of Othea to Hector: Or, The Boke of Knyghthode*)
1400	*Le Livre du dit de Poissy*
1400-1403	*Le Livre de la mutacion de fortune*
1401-1402	*Les Épistres sur "Le Roman de la Rose"*
1402	*Le Dit de la Rose*
1402-1403	*Le Livre du chemin de long éstude*
1404	*Le Livre des fais et bonnes mœurs du sage roi Charles V*
1405	*Le Livre de la cité des dames* (*The Book of the City of Ladies*)
1405	*L'Avision-Christíne* (*Christine's Vision*)
1405	*Le Livre des trois vertus* (*The Book of the Three Virtues*)
1406-1407	*Le Livre du corps de policie* (*The Body of Polycye*)
c. 1410	*Cent Ballades d'amant et de dame*
1410	*La Lamentation sur les maux de la guerre civile* (*Lament on the Evils of the Civil War*)
1410	*Le Livre des fais d'armes et de chevalerie* (*The Book of Fayttes of Arms and of Chivalry*)
1412-1413	*Le Livre de la paix*
1416-1418	*L'Épistre de la prison de la vie humaine*
1429	*Le Ditié de Jeanne d'Arc* (*The Tale of Joan of Arc*)

provides an interesting view of a cross section of fifteenth century medieval society—the royalty, nobility, bourgeoisie, and poor.

Christine's interests in women's issues never diminished, but in the later years of her writing career, in such works as *L'Avision-Christíne* (1405; *Christine's Vision*, 1993), *Épistre à Isabeau de Bavière* (1405; epistle to Isabelle of Bavaria), *Le Livre du corps de policie* (1406-1407; *The Body of Polyce*, 1521), *La Lamentation sur les maux de la guerre civile* (1410; *Lament on the Evils of the Civil War*, 1984), and *Le Livre de la paix* (1412-1413; the book of peace), she focused her attention on political problems in France—in the tradition made popular by the Italian Humanists. In her lifetime, Christine saw France suffer humiliating defeats in the Hundred Years' War with England, three popular uprisings culminating in the Cabochien revolt in 1413, the Great Schism within the Church, and the bitter Burgundian-Orléanist (later Armagnac) rivalry over the domination of the French regency. The latter began after the death of Charles V in 1380 and led to the murder of Louis d'Orléans in 1407; civil war followed, culminating in the slaying of Jean sans Peur, duke of Burgundy, in 1419. Meanwhile, widespread anarchy in France (and superior military tactics) permitted Henry V of England to defeat the French at Agincourt in 1415. In 1418, the Burgundians massacred a number of Parisians, and many, including Christine, fled the city and went into exile.

Christine, an ardent French patriot who believed in a divine-right, hereditary monarchy, wrote passionately about the necessity of restoring peace and stability in the kingdom. She appealed to rulers, political leaders, and the common people to stop the violence of civil war. As early as 1405, she accurately predicted the events at Agincourt when she warned about the dangers of foreign invaders attacking a weakened country. Undoubtedly Christine was able through her writings to impress influential figures, yet it is not clear that as an individual author she was able to influence in any immediate way the seemingly unstoppable course of events to which she was a witness.

Christine's last known work, *Le Ditié de Jeanne d'Arc* (1429; *The Tale of Joan of Arc*, 1977), a patriotic, narrative account of Joan of Arc, celebrates Joan of Arc's role in liberating Orléans and in leading the dauphin, Charles VII, to his coronation at Reims. News of the occasion reached Christine at the Poissy convent (where her daughter was a nun), to which she had retreated a decade earlier to escape the bloody civil war in Paris. In *The Tale of Joan of Arc*, she rejoices both at the event itself, the reinstatement of the legitimate monarchy, and at the fact that it had been brought about by a woman. It seemed as if, in these related events, the wheel of fortune were turning favorably, as the principal political and social themes of Christine's writings were realized. While the exact date of her death is not known, it is believed that Christine died soon afterward, in 1430 at about age sixty-five, at the Convent of Poissy.

SIGNIFICANCE

Gifted, intelligent, and strong-willed, Christine overcame personal loss and social prejudice to become the first known woman in Europe to earn her living as a professional writer. She gained the esteem of the aristocracy, many of whom became her patrons, and of the intellectuals of her day, with whom she engaged in philosophical debate. She was recognized as an accomplished lyric poet, and she became a highly respected and widely influential advocate of women's rights and of political theory.

At the time of her death, after a thirty-five-year career, Christine was well known in France; her fame had also spread to Portugal, Spain, Italy, Flanders, and England, where, with the advent of printing, some of her works were translated and published. Her renown continued into the fifteenth and sixteenth centuries, as evidenced by the number of authors who cite her—Matthieu Thomassin, Jean Marot, Clément Marot, Jean Bouchet, and Pierre de Lesnauderie—or are influenced by her—Alain Chartier, Charles d'Orléans, Olivier de La Marche, Jean Molinet, Jean Meschinot, François Habert, Georges Chastellain, Pierre Gringore, and Christoval Acosta.

As a literary figure, Christine did not receive notice again until the nineteenth and twentieth centuries. Critical response to her works has been divided: Her detractors argue that she is derivative, pedantic, and arduous to read; her admirers counter that she is versatile and original, intelligent and learned, and stylistically sophisticated. As more and more of her works are coming to print, Christine continues to be reevaluated. She is an important interpreter of her times, and her comments on many issues—good and bad rulers, human vice and frailty, women's status in society, and the battle of the sexes—seem as relevant in the twenty-first century as they were in the fifteenth.

—*Jean T. Strandness*

FURTHER READING

Altmann, Barbara K., and Deborah L. McGrady, eds. *Christine de Pizan: A Casebook*. New York: Routledge, 2003. A collection of essays on various aspects of Christine de Pizan, including her role as defender of women, and analyses of various works.

Campbell, John, and Nadia Margolis, eds. *Christine de Pizan 2000: Studies on Christine de Pizan in Honour of Angus J. Kennedy*. Atlanta: Rodopi, 2000. A collection of papers on Christine de Pizan, focusing on her poetry and her poetic techniques.

Christine de Pizan. *Christine de Pisan: Autobiography of a Medieval Woman (1363-1430)*. Translated and annotated by Anil De Silva-Vigler. London: Minerva, 1996. A biographical treatment of Christine de Pizan translated into English, with annotations. Illustrations.

Forhan, Kate Langdon. *The Political Theory of Christine de Pizan*. Burlington, Vt.: Ashgate, 2002. An analysis of the political and social views of Christine de Pizan. Bibliography and index.

Kennedy, Angus J., et al., eds. *Contexts and Continuities: Proceedings of the Fourth International Colloquium on Christine de Pizan, Published in Honour of Liliane Dulac*. Glasgow: University of Glasgow Press, 2002. A collection of papers from a conference held in Glasgow in July, 2000, on Christine de Pizan. Bibliography.

Smith, Sydney. *The Opposing Voice: Christine de Pisan's Criticism of Courtly Love*. Stanford, Calif.: Humanities Honors Program, Stanford University, 1990. Smith examines the political and social views of Christine de Pizan, in particular her opposition to the idea of courtly love. Bibliography.

Willard, Charity Cannon. *Christine de Pizan: Her Life and Works*. New York: Persea Books, 1984. This is a thorough and scholarly biography, with in-depth analysis of Christine's works and an extensive bibliography.

SEE ALSO: Charles d'Orléans; Henry V; Joan of Arc; Marie de France.

RELATED ARTICLES in *Great Events from History: The Middle Ages, 477-1453*: 1305-1417: Avignon Papacy and the Great Schism; c. 1306-1320: Dante Writes *The Divine Comedy*; 1337-1453: Hundred Years' War; c. 1350-1400: Petrarch and Boccaccio Recover Classical Texts.

EL CID

Spanish military leader

El Cid, through military skill and leadership, halted the Almoravid advance on the Iberian Peninsula, and by exemplifying ideals of courage, loyalty, and force of will, he became a national hero of his people.

BORN: c. 1043; Vivar, near Burgos, Castile (now in Spain)

DIED: July 10, 1099; Valencia (now in Spain)

ALSO KNOWN AS: Rodrigo Díaz de Vivar (birth name); Ruy Díaz

AREAS OF ACHIEVEMENT: Military, warfare and conquest

EARLY LIFE

Rodrigo Díaz de Vivar, known to the ages as El Cid (ehl SEED), was born in a small village to the north of Burgos in old Castile. Although not of the higher nobility, his family had long held a respected position in the history of the province and at the Castilian-Leónese court. Rodrigo himself was educated in the household of Prince Sancho, heir to the throne. In spite of the many legends and ballads dealing with his early life, little can be proven historically.

Eleventh century Spain was a swirling of shifting frontiers, an armed camp, divided into numerous Moorish and Christian kingdoms whose allegiances were constantly changing. Castile, because of its pivotal geographical position, had long been in a state of warfare. Its final independence from Navarre had been achieved only five years before Rodrigo's birth, but its King Ferdinand I quickly proceeded to unite all northwestern Spain under his rule. He then turned his attention to the Muslim principalities, the *taifas*, conquering several and subjecting many others to the payment of tribute.

Rodrigo, in such an atmosphere, quickly rose to prominence by his military prowess and strategic skills. His first military action was probably at Graus, where in 1063 the Castilians with Moorish help defeated the Aragonese. After this, Rodrigo's life seems to have been one long continuous battle. At the death of Ferdinand in 1065 and Sancho's accession to the throne, Rodrigo became commander in chief of the Castilian forces. Single combat was still the principal method of settling border disputes between rival states, and the obligation to defend Castile's honor was Rodrigo's. His victories in these duels and in battle made him famous throughout Christian Spain, earning for him the title Campeador (great warrior).

In 1072, however, Rodrigo's friend and patron Sancho was assassinated before the walls of Zamora, the last act in the bloody civil wars that had erupted immediately after the death of Ferdinand. Ignoring the lessons of his own struggle for power, Ferdinand had divided his kingdom among his five children, Sancho receiving Castile, Alfonso receiving León, García receiving Galicia, and Urraca and Elvira inheriting the livings of various monasteries. After a brief alliance with Alfonso in order to depose García, Sancho turned on the others. Legend states that it was at the incitement of Urraca, perhaps abetted by Alfonso, that Vellído Dolfos traitorously stabbed and killed Sancho at the siege of Zamora, Urraca's last stronghold. Rodrigo had grown up with the royal family, and, in spite of his position as the military leader of Sancho's forces, he had tried to mediate between the warring parties. At Sancho's death, however, Rodrigo became the spokesperson for the Castilian cause. Without a viable candidate for the throne, the Castilian nobles agreed to accept Alfonso as king if he would swear under oath three times in public assembly that he had played no part in his brother's death. This famous oath was administered by Rodrigo in the Church of Santa Gadea in Burgos. Satisfied (at least officially) of Alfonso's innocence, Rodrigo, as a loyal vassal, kissed Alfonso's ring after the oath. His king, in return, angered at this insult to his dignity and jealous of Rodrigo's reputation as the outstanding Christian military figure, stripped Rodrigo of all the offices and honors he had enjoyed under the patronage of Ferdinand and Sancho. In fact, the Castilian was never again to hold a central place at the court, which was now dominated by the powerful Leónese Vani-Gómez family, the counts of Carrión, whose hostility toward the "Castilian upstart" was to become famous in history and legend. During these years of obscurity, after Sancho's death, the only favor granted to Rodrigo was his arranged marriage in 1074 to Jimena, a niece of the king, daughter of the count of Oviedo and granddaughter of Alfonso V of León.

El Cid. (R. S. Peale and J. A. Hill)

Life's Work

Paradoxically, the essence of Rodrigo Díaz de Vivar's greatness lies not in the concrete details or consequences of what he did, but the manner in which he achieved it, in the journey he took to become El Cid. It is a journey started at the lowest ebb of his fortunes. In 1079, sent to collect the tribute due from the Moorish king of Seville, al-Muʿtamid, his forces were attacked by those of Granada assisted by García Ordóñez, the favorite of King Alfonso. Ordóñez was defeated and taken prisoner. After his release, humiliated, he spread the rumor that Rodrigo had kept part of the Sevillian tribute for himself. Gladly taking advantage of this and other pretexts, the king gave Rodrigo nine days to leave the kingdom. Shorn of all his property and rents, accompanied by vassals, relatives, and servants, but without his wife and young children, Rodrigo embarked on a life of exile. This bitter abandonment by his king is vividly portrayed in the opening of the famous epic poem *El Cantar de mío Cid* (c. 1140; also known as *Poema de mío Cid; The Poem of the Cid*, 1879).

Forbidden to give him aid, the citizens of Burgos hid behind closed doors and shuttered windows as their hero departed, never to return.

His efforts to obtain the patronage of Christian princes proving unsuccessful, Rodrigo became the commander of the Moorish army at Saragossa. There was nothing unusual in this. Although supposedly sworn religious enemies, Christians and Moors often formed alliances according to the political necessities of the moment. Saragossa at that time was one of the most brilliant courts on the Iberian Peninsula, for its leaders, al-Muqtadir and (later) al-Muʿtamin, had surrounded themselves with Jewish and Arabic scholars. They were happy to accept not only the Castilian's military services but also his renowned skill as a diplomat and legal expert. It was perhaps in Saragossa, where he remained from 1082 to 1089, that Rodrigo acquired the title Mio Cid or El Cid, which comes from the Arabic sayyid (lord or sir) and was a common title of respect throughout the Muslim world. During his own lifetime, however, the title came to be specific to Rodrigo, superseding his given name.

Although El Cid led his forces against many Christian armies and had ample reason to defy Alfonso, he never abandoned his loyalty to the man he considered to be his sovereign lord, and he refused to do anything detrimental to Castile's interests. In fact, El Cid's only son, Diego, was to die tragically at Consuegra in 1097, fighting at Alfonso's side in the terrible defeat. Relations between Alfonso and El Cid were always uneasy, but, faced with the greatest threat to the peninsula since the first Moorish invasion in 711, El Cid and the king met in Toledo in December, 1086, or January, 1087, to discuss the growing Almoravid problem. Headed by Yūsuf ibn Tāshufīn and centered in Morocco, the Almoravids were religious zealots who by 1086 ruled a vast empire. The established *taifas* of Moorish Spain considered the Almoravids little better than barbarians. Alfonso, needing a buffer between his kingdom and the fanatical newcomers, pardoned El Cid and granted him possession of all the lands he might gain by force of arms in the Levant.

The great prize was Valencia, the rich Moorish city coveted by everyone. Al-Qadir, its weak leader, was under Alfonso's protection. Therefore, when threatened by an internal revolt, he appealed to El Cid and his ally al-Mustaʿin for aid. Once in command of Valencia, however, al-Mustaʿin himself decided to claim the city, and El Cid was forced to fight against his former employer. Meanwhile, threatened Moorish emirs in other cities had persuaded Yūsuf to intervene personally. Yūsuf complied but soon left in disgust at the infighting between the Moorish factions. He returned in 1090 determined not only to humble the Christians but to scourge the *taifas* themselves of their decadence and godlessness. The Spanish Moors then realized too late that their only hope lay in cooperation and partnership with the Christian states. One by one the *taifas* fell; in Valencia, Almoravid rebels, encouraged by the news of the advancing army, murdered al-Qadir and took control of the city. After months of fruitless negotiations, El Cid placed his army between Yūsuf's and the city walls and opened up the irrigation canals to flood the fields. The Almoravids, afraid to fight their formidable opponent under these conditions, retreated. Weakened by twenty months of siege, Valencia finally surrendered, and on June 15, 1094, El Cid took possession of the city. El Cid tried to govern the Moorish inhabitants fairly but immediately set about the task of converting Valencia into a Christian outpost, even inviting the Cluniac bishop Jerome to establish a Catholic see. Installed in his fortified city, El Cid finally felt secure enough to send for his wife and children.

This newfound sense of security was brief: Yūsuf attacked again. El Cid, seeing his forces badly outnumbered, decided to take the enemy by surprise. On October 25, 1094, he led his men out of the city in darkness; attacking at dawn, El Cid became the first military leader, Christian or Moor, to defeat the Almoravid army in the field. Though he had achieved a stunning victory, during the last years of his life challenges continued to arise. His most incredible victory may have been the battle at Játiva in 1097. Trapped between towering cliffs and the Moorish army on one side and the sea and the Moorish fleet on another, with part of his army fleeing in panic, El Cid managed to rally the rest by the sheer force of his will and routed the enemy. The coast was awash with the Moorish dead who had drowned trying to reach the safety of their ships.

In 1099, Rodrigo died unexpectedly. A French chronicle comments, "His death caused the most profound sorrow in Christendom and great joy among the pagan enemies." He died in the knowledge that by his own strength and skill he had risen from obscurity to power. Shortly before his death, he had seen his daughters, María and Cristina, married into the royal families of Navarre and Catalonia.

Without El Cid, Valencia could not hold out for long. In 1102, the Almoravids laid siege to the city for seven months. Alfonso, in response to Jimena's cry for help, lifted the siege, but, realizing that it would be impossible to defend the city, ordered its destruction and abandonment. The Christians returned to Castile, bringing El Cid's body to be buried in the Monastery of San Pedro de Cardeña. It would take them 130 years to regain Valencia.

SIGNIFICANCE

El Cid, even during his lifetime, personified the hopes and aspirations of his people. Neither a powerful Moorish army nor an unjust Christian king could stop him in his path to glory. Personifying the ideal of the lone individual who conquers by force of will and persistence, his life became a symbol, the fit subject for an epic poem. Unlike the typical legendary hero, however, he was a man of flesh and blood, and even *The Poem of the Cid* never treats him as other than that. The poem celebrates the virtues and qualities of a very human man.

El Cid's life was a harsh one. He had to earn his bread by luck and the strength of his sword. His faults are well documented. He was ambitious and could be cruel and ruthless, but he was also capable of great loyalty. In concrete military terms, he saved the peninsula from being overrun by the Almoravids and gave the Christian forces time to regroup. He also seems to have been one of the few who, rising above the multitudinous petty dissensions and political divisions, saw Spain, both Muslim and Christian, as a single entity worthy to defend. He used all of his skill as diplomat and legal expert to further that end. This rare concept of national unity and loyalty can be seen in his unwavering allegiance to Alfonso.

The aptest compliment paid to him may be found in the words of an enemy. Ibn Bassām, an Arab chronicler, rejoiced at the news of El Cid's death and cited examples of his cruelty and ambition, yet added, "Although this man was the scourge of his times, yet he must also be accounted, by virtue of his restless and clear-sighted energy, his manly strength of character, and his heroic courage, one of God's great miracles."

—*Charlene E. Suscavage*

FURTHER READING

Barton, Simon, and Richard Fletcher, trans. *The World of El Cid: Chronicles of the Spanish Reconquest*. New York: St. Martin's Press, 2000. Translations—with annotations—of four historical works by El Cid's contemporaries, documenting the Reconquest. Includes a bibliography and index.

Crow, John A. *Spain, the Root and the Flower: An Interpretation of Spain and the Spanish People*. 3d ed. Berkeley: University of California Press, 1985. An impressionistic history of Spain that contains a discussion of the values underlying El Cid's elevation to national hero.

Fregosi, Paul. *Jihad in the West: Muslim Conquests from the Seventh to the Twenty-first Centuries*. Amherst, N.Y.: Prometheus Books, 1998. A history of Muslim conquests, including of Valencia during El Cid's time. Provides the chapter "Mio Cid: Valencia, 1080-1108." Bibliography and index.

MacKay, Angus. *Spain in the Middle Ages: From Frontier to Empire, 1000-1500*. New York: St. Martin's Press, 1977. Contains good background information on the civil wars that preceded El Cid's exile.

Madden, Thomas F., ed. *The Crusades: The Essential Readings*. Malden, Mass.: Blackwell, 2002. An exploration of the Crusades, including the chapter "Reconquest and Crusade in Spain, c. 1050-1150." Also provides a bibliography and an index.

O'Callaghan, Joseph F. *A History of Medieval Spain*. Ithaca, N.Y.: Cornell University Press, 1975. An interesting text that uses contemporary chronicles, not only peninsular, as source material.

_______. *Reconquest and Crusade in Medieval Spain*. Philadelphia: University of Pennsylvania Press, 2002. The author argues that the Papacy in the twelfth and thirteenth centuries regarded the conflict in Spain between Muslims and Christians, which continued after El Cid's death, to be a Crusade, and they afforded the same benefits to Crusaders in Spain as to those in the Holy Land. Includes chapters on battles, financing the conflicts, and Crusade warfare in general.

Read, Jan. *The Moors in Spain and Portugal*. Totowa, N.J: Rowman and Littlefield, 1975. Told from the Moorish point of view, this history makes use of many Arabic sources and includes a fine chapter on El Cid.

Smith, Colin. Introduction and notes in *Poema de mio Cid*. Oxford, England: Clarendon Press, 1972. Contains perhaps the definitive edition of the epic poem as well as an exhaustive introduction, a bibliography, and historical footnotes.

SEE ALSO: Afonso I; Saint Isidore of Seville; James I the Conqueror; Raymond of Peñafort; Ṭārik ibn-Ziyād.

RELATED ARTICLES in *Great Events from History: The Middle Ages, 477-1453*: April or May, 711: Ṭārik Crosses into Spain; c. 950: Court of Córdoba Flourishes in Spain; November, 1092-June 15, 1094: El Cid Conquers Valencia; c. 1150: Moors Transmit Classical Philosophy and Medicine to Europe; 1230: Unification of Castile and León.

CIMABUE
Italian painter

Cimabue introduced a more naturalistic depiction of the human body into medieval painting and is commonly regarded as a transition figure between the relatively stiff Byzantine mode of painting and the freer style that evolved in Italy during the fourteenth century.

BORN: c. 1240; Florence (now in Italy)
DIED: c. 1302; Florence
ALSO KNOWN AS: Bencivieni di Pepo (given name); Benvenuto di Giuseppe
AREA OF ACHIEVEMENT: Art

EARLY LIFE

Almost nothing is known of the early life of Cimabue (chee-MAHB-way), whose real name was apparently Bencivieni di Pepo. Cimabue, or "Oxhead," is a nickname of unknown significance. The meager facts of Cimabue's life and career are recorded in various documents and narratives, mostly in Italian, dating back as far as the painter's lifetime. Ernst Benkard's *Das literarische Porträt des Giovanni Cimabue* (1917; the literary portrait of Giovanni Cimabue) and the research of Karl Frey form the basis for examination of Cimabue's life.

A few years after Cimabue's death, the poet Dante wrote:

> In painting Cimabue thought to hold
> The field; now hath Giotto all the cry,
> So that the other's fame is less extolled.

Several later commentators also mention Cimabue in connection with Giotto. Lorenzo Ghiberti's *Commentarii* (c. 1447; *The Commentaries of Lorenzo Ghiberti*, 1948) tells of how Cimabue came on the youthful shepherd boy Giotto as he was drawing sheep on a rock and invited Giotto to become his student. Sixteenth century writers, especially Antonio Billi, continued to associate Cimabue with Giotto. Giovanni Battista Gelli referred to Cimabue's "Greek" style and called him Italy's first indigenous painter.

Although later scholars have rejected many of Giorgio Vasari's attributions of paintings to Cimabue, his famous study, *Le vite de' più eccellenti architetti, pittori, et scultori italiani* (1549-1550; *Lives of the Most Eminent Painters, Sculptors, and Architects*, 1850-1907), gives the fullest account of Cimabue's accomplishments. Vasari relates that the young Cimabue was sent to the convent of Santa Maria Novella in Florence to study literature, but the boy spent all of his time sketching men, horses, and houses. The city fathers at that time had hired numerous Greek painters to renew the art of painting, and as they worked on the chapel near Santa Maria Novella, Cimabue would escape from school and watch the painting. His passion for painting—and obvious aptitude—led his father to withdraw him from school and put him in the service of the Greek painters. Vasari's comment sums up the basis for Cimabue's enduring reputation in art history:

> From this time he labored incessantly, and was so far aided by his natural powers, that he soon greatly surpassed his teachers both in design and coloring. For these masters, caring little for the progress of art, had executed their works as we now see them, not in the excellent manner of the ancient Greeks, but in the rude modern style of their own day. Wherefore, though Cimabue imitated his Greek instructors, he very much improved the art, relieving it greatly from their uncouth manner, and doing honour to his country by the name he acquired, and by the works that he performed.

LIFE'S WORK

According to Vasari's account, Cimabue's career began with several much-appreciated paintings in Florence, including the altar of Santa Cecilia, a Virgin Mary on one of the pilasters at Santa Croce, a panel depicting Saint Francis surrounded by twenty small pictures on a gold background, and a large Madonna with angels for the abbey of Santa Trinita. For the front of the hospital of the Porcellana, he did a fresco with life-size figures of the Virgin, Jesus Christ, and Luke. Vasari praises the innovative realism of this fresco and Cimabue's imaginative advance beyond the rules of the Greek painters.

Vasari then cites a colossal crucifix painted by Cimabue for the church of Santa Croce, an execution so praised that Cimabue was requested to complete some works in Pisa. His Pisan works brought him such renown that he was invited to Assisi to paint the roof and walls of the Church of Saint Francis. Vasari lauds the work at Assisi as "truly great and rich, and most admirably executed," adding that private affairs called Cimabue back to Florence before the work was finished and that Giotto completed it many years later.

After his return to Florence, Cimabue worked on the cloister of Santo Spirito and then is said to have painted a picture of the Virgin for the Church of Santa Maria Novella, a work known as the Rucellai *Madonna* because it was suspended next to the Rucellai family chapel. Modern scholars, however, attribute this work to the Sienese painter Duccio di Buoninsegna, not Cimabue. Yet, according to Vasari, "it was carried in solemn procession, with the sound of trumpets and other festal demonstrations, from the house of Cimabue to the church, he himself being highly rewarded and honoured for it."

As a result of the fame he had acquired, Cimabue was appointed, along with the artist Arnolfo Lapi, to direct the construction of Santa Maria del Fiore in Florence. Without further narration, Vasari relates that "at length" Cimabue died in Florence, leaving behind many disciples, most notably Giotto.

SIGNIFICANCE

The life recounted by Vasari is brief, and, in addition to the Rucellai *Madonna*, many other works he ascribes to Cimabue have been attributed to others by modern scholars. Of the very few works attributed with confidence to Cimabue, the *Madonna Enthroned* that he painted for the Church of San Francesco in Pisa is judged one of his greatest. Napoleon Bonaparte appropriated it from Pisa as a prize of war, and it is now at the Louvre in Paris. It was painted at about the same time as the similar Rucellai *Madonna*, c. 1285, and its merits and its relationship to the Rucellai *Madonna* are still debated by scholars.

Scholar Alfred Nicholson provides an authoritative summation of Cimabue's genius and influence:

> He developed his peculiar idiom to its logical conclusion, and few could have approached the height of his argument. Moreover, the time was ripe for a closer observation and portrayal of man's common inheritance—the earthly and obvious. Thus the change for which the Romanized Giotto was so greatly responsible was both fortunate and inevitable. And though this by no means adequately explains the aesthetic greatness of Giotto's art, it does much to explain its immediate popularity. But it was the overwhelmingly stimulating influence of Cimabue's accomplishment that must have incited his late contemporaries, especially Giotto, to excel in other ways.

—Frank Day

FURTHER READING

Battisti, Eugenio. *Cimabue*. University Park: Pennsylvania State University Press, 1967. Translated from the Italian, this work provides an overview of Cimabue's life and work.

Bellosi, Luciano. *Cimabue*. New York: Abbeville Press, 1998. Bellosi discusses Cimabue's beginnings, his painting style, and Florence, where the painter worked. Bibliography and index.

Chiellini, Monica. *Cimabue*. Florence: Scala Books, 1988. A biography of Cimabue that discusses his works and Italian art. Index.

Lavin, Marilyn Aronberg, and Irving Lavin. *The Liturgy of Love: Images from the Song of Songs in the Art of Cimabue, Michelangelo, and Rembrandt*. Lawrence, Kans.: Spencer Museum of Art, University of Kansas, 2001. Criticism and interpretation of the works of Cimabue, Michelangelo, and Rembrandt, particularly in regard to their depictions of the Song of Songs. Bibliography and index.

Nicholson, Alfred. *Cimabue: A Critical Study*. Princeton, N.J.: Princeton University Press, 1932. Reprint. New York: Kennikat Press, 1972. An excellent, thorough study, replete with illustrations.

Van Marle, Raimond. *The Development of the Italian Schools of Painting*. 19 vols. The Hague: Martinus Nijhoff, 1923-1938. A scholarly and reliable history.

Vasari, Giorgio. *Lives of the Most Eminent Painters, Sculptors, and Architects*. Translated by Mrs. Jonathan Foster. Reprint. New York: Alfred A. Knopf, 1996. The famous history was originally published in the mid-sixteenth century.

SEE ALSO: Fra Angelico; Dante; Donatello; Duccio di Buoninsegna; Lorenzo Ghiberti; Giotto; Pietro Lorenzetti and Ambrogio Lorenzetti; Simone Martini; Masaccio; Andrea Orcagna.

RELATED ARTICLE in *Great Events from History: The Middle Ages, 477-1453*: c. 1306-1320: Dante Writes *The Divine Comedy*.

SAINT CLARE OF ASSISI

Italian abbess

Saint Clare, the first abbess of San Damiano, founded the Poor Ladies of Assisi, better known as the Poor Clares, and wrote the order's directives. The Poor Clares was the first women's religious order to be based on the Franciscan, not Benedictine, rule.

BORN: July 16, 1194; Assisi, duchy of Spoleto (now in Italy)

DIED: August 11, 1253; Assisi, duchy of Spoleto (now in Italy)

ALSO KNOWN AS: Santa Chiara di Assisi

AREA OF ACHIEVEMENT: Religion and theology

EARLY LIFE

Clare of Assisi (klauhr uhv uh-SIHS-ee) was the eldest child of Ortolana and Favarone Offreducio di Bernardino, wealthy members of the nobility in Assisi. Her father was a younger son in a well-established family. Her mother was well known for her charity and piety; she even made pilgrimages, including one to the Holy Land. Clare was educated as befitting her status as the daughter of a local aristocratic household. Evidence given by long-standing family friends at her canonization hearings indicates that Clare was both beautiful and virtuous as a girl.

Clare demonstrated her piety and charity from a young age. For example, even as a girl, she gave whatever she could to the poor of Assisi. Her good works earned her a reputation as a virtuous and generous person and probably also brought her to the attention of Saint Francis of Assisi, who was in the early stages of preaching and living his doctrine of radical poverty. Because Francis was from a merchant family and several years older than Clare, it is unlikely that they would have met earlier in their lives. However, Francis's public renunciation of his father occurred in the public square near Clare's house, so Clare most likely had heard of him before she began listening to his preaching. In her later teen years, she sought out this radical preacher, and for about two years, she was secretly instructed by him.

During the night of Palm Sunday, 1212, when she was about eighteen years old, Clare secretly left her father's house and went to Porziuncula, a small chapel near Assisi, where Saint Francis and his followers were centered. There, Clare renounced worldly goods, and Francis formally accepted her as a follower of Christ. To signify this, Clare was given simple robes and her hair was cut by Francis. The tonsure, the shorn hair, is the mark of a person newly accepted into a religious lifestyle. Clare's receiving the tonsure from Francis himself signified her deep-rooted belief in Francis's principles. Clare quickly entered her new life of poverty, selling her entire inheritance and distributing all the proceeds among the poor.

LIFE'S WORK

As the first female disciple of Francis, Clare did not immediately have a place to live. Briefly she was part of two different monasteries in the area, and then Francis advised her to settle into the monastery of San Damiano. The monastery became the gathering place for the women who would eventually come to be known as the Poor Ladies of Assisi. Clare's sister Catherine, renamed Agnes, was the first to join.

The Bernardino family was infuriated by Clare's actions. Clare was not expected to carry her charity and piety into a religious life; rather, she was expected to do as her mother had and carry those practices into her future household. Clare, however, had balked at a marriage arranged for her, then ran off to be part of the radical, poverty-focused Franciscan movement. Several times, the family, using both promises and force, had attempted to persuade Clare to return. When her sister Agnes ran away, the men of the family pursued her, and when they caught her, they attempted to carry her back home. By her prayers, Clare made Agnes weigh so heavily on them that the men were unable to carry her any farther; this is considered one of Clare's earliest miracles. Defeated, the men put Agnes down and retreated to the city. Just as he had for Clare, Francis himself gave Agnes the tonsure.

In giving Clare and Agnes the tonsure, Francis demonstrated the relationship between the women at San Damiano and the Franciscans, and in particular between Clare and Francis himself. Generally, the Poor Ladies of Assisi followed the principles of Francis's nearby Friars Minor: complete poverty and charitable works of manual labor carried out by the members themselves as well as the contemplation typical of most religious orders of the time. Many other orders not only focused on prayer and contemplation but also had accrued significant wealth, as permitted under the Benedictine Rule for religious orders.

This combination of being both wealthy and focused on prayer usually meant that the orders were insulated from the immediate problems of the poor. Frequently, the members who performed charitable actions were considered to be lesser members of the order. Although Francis also encouraged contemplation, he both preached and practiced that the members of the order should work with the poor and that they should be as poor as the people they helped. These two ideas are fundamental to the Franciscan way of life. Francis believed the religious person who practiced these ideas most truly approximated Christ in his treatment of the needy and in his poverty.

The personal relationship between Francis and Clare is reflected in Clare's description of herself as "a little plant of our holy Father Francis." She saw herself as sharing his approach to how the Gospels should be lived, and she saw herself nurtured, protected by, and growing in his example. For example, the Church of San Damiano, where Francis settled Clare and her companions, was the place where Francis believed he was given a unique mission by God. Francis ordered Clare to eat two ounces of bread a day, contradicting her wish to fast completely, and she obeyed. Francis appointed Clare the abbess of the cloister, despite her objections to being given any authority over others. Francis wrote the original principle by which the women of San Damiano were organized, and he regularly preached there.

Sculpture of Saint Clare of Assisi, left, with Saint Bernardin. (Hulton|Archive at Getty Images)

The community at San Damiano grew, although its members had to accept radical poverty and a strict work ethic. Ortolana, the mother of Clare and Agnes, joined after she became a widow. As the community expanded, it retained its focus on poverty and charitable service. For example, to demonstrate how much she valued the work of the members who aided the needy, Clare waited on them after they returned to the cloister, helping them wash their feet and serving them their meal. The members of the community who remained in the cloister were active in charity as well. For example, they worked wool given them into altar cloths that they then donated.

Clare's spiritual influence grew as Assisi accepted the vibrant San Damiano community and as similarly minded women around Europe sought Clare's counsel. Assisi's acceptance is best demonstrated by its turning to the women of San Damiano on two different occasions when the city was being invaded. Both times, Clare's prayers are credited with repelling the invaders and thus saving the city. The city came to look at the monastery as its special protector. Sisters from San Damiano established convents elsewhere in Italy as well as in Spain, France, and Bohemia. Meanwhile, women who had already begun developing communities similar in spirit to San Damiano wrote to Clare for encouragement and guidance. Clare's correspondence reveals her support of their efforts to persevere in poverty.

The Catholic Church, however, did not support these efforts, by Clare or anyone else. Cardinal Ugolino, later Pope Gregory IX, wrote a rule in 1219 for Clare and her followers, formalizing all their principles except that of poverty. Ugolino did not permit Clare to reject all possessions because he felt that cloistered women could not beg enough for their support. Ugolino had good intentions; he wanted to channel this surge of people, particularly women, interested in radical spirituality into the existing structure of religious orders, but his efforts undermined the uniqueness of their interests. As Francis resisted

Church efforts to shift his Friars Minor more toward the existing orders, Clare resisted Ugolino's rule for her community, explaining that poverty was fundamental.

For years, Ugolino, now Pope Gregory IX, pressured Clare to accept possessions in common for her cloister. When in Assisi for the canonization of Francis in 1228, Gregory even offered to absolve her from her vow of poverty. To this, Clare responded, "I crave absolution for my sins, but I desire not to be absolved from the obligation of following Jesus." The pope replied in turn by granting Clare and her women the *privilegium paupertatis*, or the formal privilege of poverty, the only such privilege ever sought or granted. This privilege, granted in 1228, modified the rule of 1219 by permitting the women of San Damiano to continue in their poverty.

After Gregory IX's death, the next pope, Innocent IV, took his turn drafting a rule for the women. In 1247, he prepared a rule based on Franciscan, not Benedictine, principles, but that still emphasized the importance of having community possessions. This emphasis, like its earlier counterpart in Ugolino's first rule, threatened the central tenet of San Damiano. This time, though, Clare responded openly, by writing her own rule.

Clare drafted her rule between 1247 and 1251; bedridden since 1226, she wrote it while her illness was worsening. Her rule blended Franciscan principles, such as the importance of the order members who serve the poor, with principles from the earlier rules, such as having a porter at the gate of the community. Francis gave the community at San Damiano their initial guidance in a brief letter. Clare's rule provided a guide for perpetuating this community centered around poverty.

Clare wrote her rule primarily to secure poverty as an integral part of women's religious life rather than as a privilege subject to revocation. She submitted it for papal consideration in 1251. In 1252, Cardinal Rainaldo, who was responsible for overseeing the order as Ugolino had been, notified her that he, as protector of the order, accepted Clare's rule. However, the pope still had concerns. Another year passed, and Clare's health radically declined. In the last days of her life, Pope Innocent IV visited her while en route from Lyon to Rome. Innocent wrote the papal bull approving her rule on August 9. It was delivered to her on August 10, and, on August 11, 1253, Clare died. She was canonized in 1255.

SIGNIFICANCE

Clare was the first Franciscan sister, both because she was Saint Francis's first female spiritual companion and because she was the first woman to follow his principles. She also became the first abbess of her community at San Damiano. She wrote the rule for the Poor Ladies of Assisi, the first religious rule written for women by a woman.

—*Clare Callaghan*

FURTHER READING

Bartoli, Marco. *Clare of Assisi*. Translated by Sister Frances Teresa. Quincy, Ill.: Franciscan Press, 1993. This scholarly biography places Clare in the larger context of later medieval Italy. In particular, her accomplishments are set against the cultural currents.

Bornstein, Daniel, and Roberto Rusconi, eds. *Women and Religion in Medieval and Renaissance Italy*. Translated by Margery J. Schneider. Chicago: University of Chicago Press, 1996. This collection examines varied aspects of the role of religious women in Italy. An essay on the early days of San Damiano is included.

Francis and Clare: The Complete Works. Translated by Regis J. Armstrong and Ignatius C. Brady. New York: Paulist Press, 1982. This edition of the writings of both Assisi saints contains comprehensive introductions to the life of each and clarifies the audience for and purpose of the different writings.

The Legend and Writings of Saint Clare of Assisi. St. Bonaventure, N.Y.: Franciscan Institute, 1953. Although an older work, this book contains the text of the "Life of Saint Clare" written by Thomas of Celano, the biographer appointed by the pope for the canonization of Saint Clare. Celano's work is the earliest known biography of Saint Clare.

Peterson, Ingrid J. *Clare of Assisi: A Biographical Study*. Quincy, Ill.: Franciscan Press, 1993. Scholarship has begun to uncover the history of women of the Middle Ages. For Clare, much of this work has been done in conjunction with the 800th anniversary of her birth.

Thomson, John A. F. *The Western Church in the Middle Ages*. New York: Arnold, 1998. This general survey of medieval Christianity places the Franciscan movement, of which Clare was an important early member, in the larger frame of contemporaneous religious development.

SEE ALSO: Blessed Angela of Foligno; Saint Benedict of Nursia; Saint Brigit; Saint Catherine of Siena; Christina of Markyate; Saint Elizabeth of Hungary; Saint Francis of Assisi; Gregory IX; Innocent IV; Saint Irene.

RELATED ARTICLE in *Great Events from History: The Middle Ages, 477-1453*: April 16, 1209: Founding of the Franciscans.

SAINT CLOTILDA
Queen consort of France (r. 493-511)

Clotilda played an instrumental role in the conversion of the Franks to orthodox Catholicism and thereby positioning France as a leading state in post-Roman Europe. Her life also foreshadows the type of role played by powerful women in medieval Europe, which was just beginning to take root during her own lifetime.

BORN: c. 474; Lyon (now in France)
DIED: June 3, 545; Tours, kingdom of the Franks (now in France)
ALSO KNOWN AS: Clotilde; Clothilde; Chlothilde; Chrotechildis; Chrodigild; Chrodechilde; Chlotilde
AREAS OF ACHIEVEMENT: Government and politics, religion and theology

EARLY LIFE

The final period of the classical ancient world witnessed the establishment of various successor states headed by Germanic tribal leaders in territory that had been at one time within the traditional boundaries of the Roman Empire. In particular, the old Roman province of Gaul (now France) was partitioned into several petty kingdoms by Germanic tribes arriving in the area during the fifth century. The region of Burgundy came to be ruled by King Gundioc (also known as Gundovic), whose granddaughter was Clotilda (cluh-TIHL-duh). On the king's death in 474, his kingdom of Burgundy was subdivided as an inheritance among his four sons Gundobad (Gundebad), Godegesil, Chilperic, and Gundomar (Gundemar).

This practice of dividing the father's estate among all his male heirs represented an ancient Germanic custom but proved to be a highly ineffective system when applied to royal households, in which the father's estate was in essence an entire kingdom. The problem with this practice was that it threatened to shatter any hope for a stable and effective central government, as the state became ever more fragmented in subsequent generations of bequeathals. The desire to prevent this type of governmental dissolution and to reestablish some type of political unity within such a subdivided kingdom quickly touched off numerous civil wars during this early period of French history and produced a chaotic, unstable society. Eventually, Clotilda's father, Chilperic, and her mother, who gave birth to Clotilda at Lyon, France, in about 474, fell victim to this civil strife when they were murdered by Chilperic's brother Gundobad.

Like other ambitious leaders of this era, Gundobad was bent on reconstituting all of Burgundy under his control and was not afraid to use whatever methods were necessary to achieve his ends, even if it meant committing fratricide. Clotilda and her sister, however, managed to escape their parents' fate and found a safe haven from Gundobad's wrath by taking up residence with their uncle Godegesil in Geneva. At this time the Burgundians in Geneva and the Salian Franks had established diplomatic relations. Clovis I, the tribal leader of the Salians, purportedly was stricken by Clotilda's beauty, grace, and intelligence, for she had received some semblance of a classical education while growing up in her parents' court located at Lyon. She had also gained insights into the Christian way of life from her mother, who had been a pious and devoted believer. Yet, it was not only out of romantic impulse that Clovis sought Clotilda's hand in marriage. The marriage also had a political undertone to it, as it was intended to solidify the growing alliance between the Burgundians and Salians, for Clovis was an ambitious leader who desired to further his conquests in the former Roman province of Gaul at the expense of rival warlords. However, to succeed in this drive for greater power he needed allies. Such politically arranged marriages among the powerful upper classes became a hallmark of the political dynamics of Europe for much of the remaining medieval period as a way to build alliances between powerful families or even states.

LIFE'S WORK

Having been raised as a devout Catholic, Clotilda immediately committed herself to trying to convert her new husband away from his pagan religion and to Christianity. In Clovis, however, she found a man of great stubbornness and passion, and so her every effort met with unflinching resistance. When their first child, Ingomer, was born, Clotilda sought to have their son baptized into the Christian faith, but Clovis opposed the idea. Not to be denied in her desire to raise her children as Christians, Clotilda had the baby baptized anyway. Soon after, however, the boy became ill and died. Clovis blamed the boy's premature death as a punishment from his pagan gods for allowing his son to be initiated into a "false" religion and so used this tragic event as proof for the illegitimacy of the Christian faith. When their second son, Chlodomer, was born, he too became deathly ill after Clotilda went ahead with having him baptized, once again over Clovis's objection. Although this time the boy recovered, Clovis still saw the event as further proof that Christianity was not a true faith.

Clotilda, however, never wavered in her persistence to bring about the conversion of her husband, and her peaceful, determined efforts finally were rewarded in 496 in a rather unlikely way. At this time the Franks under the leadership of Clovis were engaged in a bitter struggle against a rival Germanic tribe, the Alamanni, a conflict that was part of the larger chaos that surrounded the recent collapse and dissolution of the Roman Empire. Like numerous Germanic peoples before them, the Alamanni sought to expand west from their stronghold on the eastern side of the Rhine River. This attempted expansion, however, put them on a collision course with the Franks who had already established themselves in this part of Gaul.

When the armies of the two sides met at Tolbiacum, a ferocious battle ensued, in the course of which the Frankish side began to collapse. As Clovis fought at the head of his army, he sensed the coming doom, but then in this heat of battle he purportedly remembered Clotilda's unyielding appeals for him to adopt the Christian faith. Desperate to avert annihilation and convinced that his own pagan gods were powerless or unwilling to intervene on his behalf, Clovis apparently turned to Clotilda's God for assistance. According to tradition, the tide of battle then changed, and the Franks rallied to inflict a crushing defeat on the Alamanni. Attributing his unlikely victory to the intervention of Clotilda's God, Clovis finally agreed to be converted and baptized into the Christian faith. Although there is some controversy that his baptism occurred later in 506 after a second campaign against the Alamanni, tradition holds that Clovis received baptism on December 25, 496, in the city of Reims by Bishop Rémi. This event was a watershed moment in European history as it made Clovis the first major Germanic leader to accept orthodox Christianity, thereby ensuring the survival of this form of Christianity. Before, the other great Germanic leaders had accepted a heretical form of Chrisitianity—Arianism—or remained in their pagan beliefs. Following the Germanic traditions of their ancestors to follow in the footsteps of their warrior leader, many of Clovis's soldiers accepted baptism as well, thereby ensuring that orthodox Christianity would continue to flourish in the Frankish region of Gaul. From this bastion, orthodox Christianity would soon spread through much of Europe, converting its peoples away from Arianism and paganism to this orthodox system of belief.

Saint Clotilda receives the ring of Clovis, her future husband, whom she converted to Christianity. (F. R. Niglutsch)

After Clovis's death in 511, Clotilda devoted the remaining thirty-four years of her life to her family, politics, and the practice of religious devotion. Her five surviving children as adults were caught up in the chaotic struggles of this period, and Clotilda remained active in the political arena in an effort to ensure their safety during the ensuing wars and conflicts. Her attempts, however, had only marginal success as she witnessed the death of several cousins back in Burgundy at the hands of her own sons. Fratricide committed in the course of these blood feuds would eventually claim the lives of two of her sons and several of her grandchildren. Her youngest child, Chlodovald, however, somehow survived the raging climate of violent ambition and unremorseful vengeance that dominated Merovingian society at this time. Following his mother's lead concerning the practice of religion, Chlodovald became a hermit at a location near Paris and soon developed a reputation for holiness. Clotilda in her own right was renowned for her piety and sanctity, and in her later years, she lived almost the life of a female religious figure as she took up residence at Tours near a monastic house. On her death on June 3, 545, Clotilda was laid to rest in the cathedral at Tours next to her husband, Clovis.

SIGNIFICANCE

Clotilda proved to be a decisive figure in the early life of France. Her successful persistence in getting her husband to settle down and adopt the orthodox Christian faith proved to be a watershed moment in the formative and fragile years of European society, which had been trying to survive the collapse of the Roman Empire. Because of the bond in traditional Germanic culture that existed between a war leader and his warrior band during an expedition, the conversion of Clovis almost guaranteed that the rest of the nation would follow his lead. France soon became a staunchly orthodox Christian state, and because of this unique disposition it developed into a powerful ally to the Papacy in Rome. Without such a strong and faithful ally, it is hard to imagine how the Papacy and orthodox Christianity could have survived the chaotic world of the Merovingian period.

Clotilda is also a significant figure because of the social dimensions of her life. Her politically arranged marriage to Clovis, her subsequent role in politics expressed through her actions with Clovis and her sons, and her final years as a widow spent in the practice of religious devotion and piety all prefigured the life that many powerful women would lead throughout the Middle Ages. The life of Clotilda thus provides an enchanting view of how powerful women acted and worked during the medieval era.

—Christopher G. Libertini

FURTHER READING

Blumenfeld-Kosinski, Renate. "Saintly Scenarios in Christine de Pizan's *Livre des trois vertus*." *Mediaeval Studies* 62 (2000): 255-292. The author discusses Christine de Pizan's argument that particular saints, including Clotilda, lived their lives balancing spirituality, charitability, and politics.

Geary, Patrick. *Before France and Germany: The Creation and Transformation of the Merovingian World.* New York: Oxford University Press, 1988. Provides an excellent introduction and overview of the general age in which Clotilda lived and of the particular challenges faced by a society trying to establish a new order following the demise of the Roman Empire.

Gregory of Tours. *The History of the Franks*. Translated by Lewis Thorpe. New York: Penguin Books, 1974. One of early medieval Europe's greatest historians, Gregory provides a near-eyewitness account of the early Merovingian age and provides in the course of his writing some of the key details about the life of Clotilda.

James, Edward. *The Franks*. New York: Basil Blackwell, 1988. Provides an account of the Merovingian period of French history and some brief but useful details of Clotilda's place in that history.

_______. *The Origins of France: From Clovis to the Capetians, 500-1000.* London: Macmillan Press, 1982. A sound description of the society and times in which Clotilda lived, and of the succeeding period of French history that occurred under the Carolingian kings. Also includes useful genealogical tables for reference regarding the royal households of this period.

Kurth, Godefroi. *Saint Clotilda*. Translated by V. M. Crawford. New York: Benziger Bros., 1898. Although dated and written in a somewhat archaic tone, this work is still one of the most detailed accounts of the life of Clotilda.

Wood, Ian. *The Merovingian Kingdoms 450-751*. New York: Longman, 1994. A thorough review of Merovingian society during Clotilda's time.

SEE ALSO: Clovis; Fredegunde; Gregory of Tours.
RELATED ARTICLE in *Great Events from History: The Middle Ages, 477-1453*: 496: Baptism of Clovis.

CLOVIS
King of the Franks (r. 481-511)

In the early sixth century, Clovis extended his Frankish domain by conquest to form the nucleus of France and, in the process, united his interests with those of the Orthodox Church in the West, which he saved from the threat of the Arian heresy.

BORN: c. 466; probably Tournai (now in Belgium)
DIED: November 27, 511; Paris (now in France)
ALSO KNOWN AS: Chlodovech; Chlodowig; Chlodovic; Chlodovicus; Chlodowech
AREAS OF ACHIEVEMENT: Government and politics, warfare and conquest, religion and theology

EARLY LIFE

Clovis (KLOH-vuhs), or Chlodovech (meaning "noble warrior"), was born probably near the Frankish stronghold of Tournai, near the present-day Franco-Belgian border; he was the son of the Frankish chieftain Childeric I. The family was descended from a West German barbarian tribe, the Salian (dwellers by the sea) Franks, which had settled two centuries earlier near the North Sea, on the outskirts of Roman Gaul. From there, they had gradually spread in small groups perhaps as far south as the Loire River. Another branch of the Franks, the Ripuarian (dwellers by the riverbank), had settled along the west bank of the Rhine River near the city of Cologne.

Clovis was the grandson of Merovech, "the sea-fighter," who had conquered Tournai in 446 and installed the Merovingian Dynasty, which was to dominate Frankish political history for three centuries. By the time of Merovech, the Franks, unlike other generally migratory German tribes, appear to have become permanently settled in this region. They had begun to gain the acceptance of native Gallo-Romans, whom they supported against Attila and the Huns in a battle at Châlons (Mauriac Plain, 451), near Troyes. Indeed, a significant determinant of the Franks' success in creating a powerful and long-lasting kingdom in Gaul was that they expanded gradually from a homeland—a settled base of strength in which they gained the allegiance of the native population as Roman imperial control disintegrated in the West.

The acceptance of the Franks by the Gallo-Roman natives is reflected in the work of Gregory of Tours. Gregory, who lived in the second half of the sixth century, was himself a Gallo-Roman aristocrat who succeeded to the bishopric of Tours, an ecclesiastical seat long held by his family. He became a prominent political and religious leader in western Gaul, but his greatest contribution was as a historian. Gregory was the author of the *Historia Francorum* (late sixth century; *The History of the Franks*, 1927), one of the great narratives of the early Middle Ages and the one that provides the only near-contemporary account of Clovis and the early Merovingians. To Gregory, the Franks, and Clovis in particular, were the divinely ordained saviors of the Church from the heresy of Arianism, to which other German tribes had been converted. Indeed, the Clovis of history is Gregory's Clovis, and all subsequent accounts of Clovis's career, with minor modifications of later scholarship, reflect their indebtedness to the Gallo-Roman cleric.

Nothing is known of Clovis's early life, and no contemporary artistic representation of his appearance has survived. The only clues regarding his early life are found in the contents of his father's burial chamber, discovered in Tournai in 1653. Childeric's tomb contained ornaments, weapons, and hoards of coins, demonstrating that he had established important contacts with the Roman Empire as well as with the barbarians. He was, without question, a very rich man. Clovis, therefore, appears to have been groomed to succeed his father as chieftain.

LIFE'S WORK

Clovis was only fifteen years of age when he succeeded his father, in 481, as leader of the Frankish tribes that recognized the supremacy of Tournai. The use of the title "king" at this point seems premature, although it has become traditional. It would appear that Clovis was regarded by his people as nothing more than a chieftain and that the magical element associated with kingship did not come until later, after his identification of himself and his dynasty with Christianity.

Clovis spent most of his reign fulfilling the obligations of a Frankish chieftain: by cunning—and when necessary cruelty and brutality—securing booty and additional land with which to reward himself and his retainers. In the process, he created a kingdom encompassing much of what later became France and West Germany. He first contracted alliances with two relatives, Ragnachair and Chararic, who were Salian Frankish chieftains at Cambrai and Saint-Quentin. Within five years, with their aid, he moved against Syagrius, the last independent Roman ruler in Gaul, who ruled over most of the area around Soissons. Ruthlessly, Clovis put to death Syagrius, his former allies Ragnachair and Chararic, and their brother, Rigomer, who had ruled the region of Le Mans. Having conquered their territories, Clovis was recognized as Syagrius's successor in northern Gaul by certain Gallo-Roman bishops, especially Bishop Rémi of Reims. This recognition by the regional clerical hierarchy of a fait accompli was of great significance to Clovis, since he was still a pagan and not yet acknowledged by the emperor in Byzantium.

The fateful bond between the Franks and Catholicism was then strengthened by another event: During the early 490's, the most obscure period of his reign, Clovis married a Burgundian princess, Clotilda, who is credited with converting him to Christianity. Soon after, Clovis succeeded in expanding his Frankish state by bringing the Ripuarian Franks under his protection. Their allegiance to him was necessitated by their fear of the fiercest of the West German tribes, the Alamanni, who, well-armed and on horseback, were moving from Alsace in a northwesterly direction toward the Ripuarian settlements along the banks of the Rhine River. At the famous Battle of Tolbiacum (now Zülpich) in 496, on the borders of Alsace and Lorraine, the combined Frankish forces under Clovis defeated the Alamanni and extended their control as far south as Basel.

Clovis's victory at Tolbiacum was, according to Gregory of Tours, the central event of his reign and indeed of Frankish history, for it is from this battle that Gregory dates Clovis's conversion to Catholicism. All Clovis's subsequent military engagements are portrayed by Gregory as purposeful crusades for the advancement of Christianity. Although it is now generally believed that Clovis's conversion came some seven years later, the precise date of his conversion is irrelevant to its significance. According to Gregory, Clovis invoked the aid of Jesus during the course of the battle and, in the tradition of the emperor Constantine, promised his belief and baptism in return for victory. Following the victory, Queen Clotilda asked Bishop Rémi to instruct her husband in the Christian religion. There soon followed the baptism of Clovis and three thousand of his soldiers at Reims. The doubtful tradition of Clovis's baptism was important in the history of the French monarchy, for it established the feature of canonical investiture, adding a mystical religious element to the earlier military component. The site of the baptism, Reims, was also to become traditional for the coronation of French monarchs.

Of greatest contemporary significance was that Clovis and the Franks converted to orthodox Christianity and acknowledged the authority of the pope. The Franks, alone among the German tribes that moved into the western Roman Empire, never subscribed to the heresy of Arianism. This anti-Trinitarian belief had

THE MEROVINGIAN KINGS

Reign	*Ruler*
447-458	Merovech
458-481	Childeric I
481-511	CLOVIS I (with CLOTILDA, r. 493-511)
511	Kingdom split among Clovis's sons
511-524	Chlodomer (Orléans)
511-534	Theodoric I (Metz)
511-558	Childebert I (Paris)
511-561	Lothair I (Soissons 511-561; all Franks 558-561)
534-548	Theudebert I (Metz)
548-555	Theudebald (Metz)
561	Kingdom split among Lothair's sons
561-567	Charibert I (Paris)
561-575	Sigebert I (Austrasia)
561-584	Chilperic I (Soissons)
561-592	Guntram (Burgundy)
575-595	Childebert II (Austrasia 575-595, Burgundy 593-595)
584-629	Lothair II (Neustria 584, all Franks 613-629)
595-612	Theudebert II (Austrasia)
595-613	Theodoric II (Burgundy 595-612, Austrasia 612-613)
613	Sigebert II (Austrasia, Burgundy)
623-639	Dagobert I (Austrasia 623-628, all Franks 629-639)
629-632	Charibert II (Aquitaine)
632-656	Sigebert III (Austrasia)
639-657	Clovis II (Neustria and Burgundy)
656-673	Lothair III (Neustria 657-673, all Franks 656-660)
662-675	Childeric (Austrasia 662-675, all Franks 673-675)
673-698	Theodoric III (Neustria 673-698, all Franks 678-691)
674-678	Dagobert II (Austrasia)
691-695	Clovis III (all Franks)
695-711	Childebert III (all Franks)
711-716	Dagobert III (all Franks)
715-721	Chilperic II (Neustria 715-721, all Franks 719-720)
717-719	Lothair IV (Austrasia)
721-737	Theodoric IV (all Franks)
743-751	Childeric III (all Franks)

The baptism of Clovis, king of France. (F. R. Niglutsch)

been first propounded by an early fourth century priest from Alexandria, Arius, who held that Christ, the Son, was not the coequal of God the Father. Arius contended that God was self-existent throughout eternity and immutable. Christ, however, had become existent and incarnate; he had been created by God and, in human form, was subject to growth and change. Christ was different from God the Father and, being his creation, by inference, inferior. He did not fully share in divinity. Arius and his teachings had been condemned on the basis of the arguments of Athanasius, the future bishop of Alexandria, at the Council of Nicaea, called by the Emperor Constantine in 325. The Athanasian position, which the Church established as orthodox, held that the Son is "of one substance with the Father," that he had existed throughout eternity, that he was begotten, not created, and that he is God's coequal and completely divine. Christ's total divinity and his coequality with God were central to the legitimacy of the Church and its clergy, to whom Christ had entrusted the dispensation of the Sacraments and the task of mediating between Christ and the believers. As the authority of the Roman Empire declined in the West during the fourth and fifth centuries, the Church, through its clergy, assumed many former imperial functions and sought to solidify its position by enforcing religious orthodoxy. The native Gallo-Roman population submitted to orthodoxy; the German barbarian tribes, however, had converted to Arianism before they entered Western Europe. As a result, they were unacceptable to the Church there and found their beliefs to be an impediment to popular acceptance and assimilation. Clovis's conversion to orthodoxy, eliciting not only the Church's acceptance of the Franks but also its support of Clovis's campaign to conquer Arian German tribes, significantly aided in the establishment of a permanent Frankish successor state in Roman Gaul.

The chronology of the events of Clovis's reign is disputed, probably as a result of the naïve confusion of Gregory, who, obsessed with the consequences of Clovis's conversion, preferred to view additional military campaigns as religious crusades against the Arian Germans. According to tradition, after his conversion, Clovis turned his attention to the Burgundians and the Visigoths, Arian Germans located respectively in southeastern and southwestern Gaul. Having recently allied himself with the Burgundian ruler of Geneva, an orthodox Christian, Clovis defeated the army of Gundobad, the Arian Burgundian chieftain of Lyon, in battle near Dijon. Gundobad was forced to flee to Avignon, which was besieged until he agreed to pay tribute. Clovis's final campaign was against the Visigoths. At Vouillé, near Poitiers, the Visigothic leader, Alaric II, was killed. Visigothic power north of the Pyrenees collapsed to Clovis, who pillaged Alaric's treasury at Toulouse before returning to give thanks at the shrine of the Merovingian patron, Saint Martin, at Tours.

During his sojourn at Tours, Clovis received a legate from the Emperor Anastasius in Constantinople. The imperial representative brought with him letters bestowing on Clovis the title of consul. Clovis now had received imperial recognition of his legitimacy and preferment to add to his earlier recognition from the Church. Only Provence in southern France remained free of Frankish control in Gaul. Theodoric, the powerful Ostrogothic ruler of Italy, in alliance with the Burgundians permanently blocked Clovis's advance toward the Mediterranean.

After leaving Tours, Clovis returned to previously conquered Paris, which became the seat of his kingdom for the remainder of his reign. There he constructed his royal palace and, with Clotilda, oversaw the construction of the Church of Saints Peter and Paul (later known as the Church of Sainte-Geneviève), where he was subsequently entombed. In his last years, Clovis became a lawgiver and statesman rather than conqueror. On his orders, the Lex Salica (Salian law), a code of criminal law applied by Clovis to the Franks, was drawn up. Shortly before his death, he convened the first national church council held in Gaul, at Orléans. He died in November 27, 511, at forty-five years of age.

SIGNIFICANCE

Clovis's kingdom in France did not long survive him; according to Frankish tradition, it was divided among his four surviving sons. Nevertheless, Clovis left an indelible imprint on the history of early medieval Europe. He brought together all the areas, except for Provence, that would make up the nucleus of the nation of France, which, as the native and Frankish populations were assimilated, began to develop its unique identity. He also, perhaps more by necessity than conviction, saved Christian orthodoxy from the encroachments of Arianism and in so doing played a major role in subverting the Unitarian heresy in the West. In turn, having recognized his military and administrative talents, the clerical leadership in Gaul adopted Clovis and the Franks as the logical successors to secular Roman imperial authority in Gaul. Together, Clovis and the Church restored order, religious orthodoxy, and political legitimacy to a region that had long endured the chaotic political vacuum left by the decline of Roman imperial authority.

—*J. Stewart Alverson*

FURTHER READING

Cantor, Norman F. *Medieval History: The Life and Death of a Civilization*. New York: Macmillan, 1963. Although the scope of this work is broad, it is still helpful, given the dearth of material available in English on Clovis. Cantor discusses Clovis at some length and credits him with his proper significance.

Castries, Due de. *The Lives of the Kings and Queens of France*. Translated by Anne Dobell. New York: Alfred A. Knopf, 1979. Although the treatment of Clovis, whom the author portrays as the creator of France and its first king, is brief, it is balanced and contains a surprisingly large amount of information about Clovis's conversion and conquests.

Fletcher, R. A. *The Barbarian Conversion: From Paganism to Christianity*. Berkeley: University of California Press, 1999. Looks at the history of the development of Christianity in pagan Europe during the time of Clovis.

Gregory of Tours. *The History of the Franks*. Translated and edited by O. M. Dalton. 2 vols. Oxford, England: Oxford University Press, 1971. This translation of an account of the early Merovingians should be consulted by students of Clovis, for Gregory provided the portrayal of the Frankish chieftain on which all later historians have been required to base their evaluations of his significance, especially as the savior of Christian orthodoxy.

MacMullen, Ramsay. *Christianity and Paganism in the Fourth to Eighth Centuries*. New Haven, Conn.: Yale University Press, 1997. Surveys the relationship between paganism and the Christian world in the time of Clovis.

Wallace-Hadrill, J. M. *The Barbarian West, A.D. 400-1000: The Early Middle Ages*. New York: Harper and Row, 1962. Although the scope of this book is broad, the foremost modern historian of the Franks devotes considerable attention to the Franks and to Clovis. Contains a comprehensive treatment of the Franks and their significance in European history.

_______. *The Long-Haired Kings and Other Studies in Frankish History.* London: Methuen, 1962. This and the above volume are two indispensable works in English on Clovis and the Franks.

SEE ALSO: Amalasuntha; Charlemagne; Saint Clotilda; Fredegunde; Gregory of Tours.

RELATED ARTICLES in *Great Events from History: The Middle Ages, 477-1453*: 496: Baptism of Clovis; February 2, 506: Alaric II Drafts the *Breviarum Alarici*; 635-800: Founding of Lindisfarne and Creation of the *Book of Kells*.

SAINT CYRIL AND SAINT METHODIUS

Macedonian religious leaders

Through their spiritual commitment, Cyril and Methodius expanded Christianity in central and eastern Europe and established the foundations of Slavic culture and literature with the development of the Glagolitic alphabet.

SAINT CYRIL

BORN: c. 827; Thessalonica, Macedonia (now Salonika, Greece)
DIED: February 14, 869; Rome (now in Italy)
ALSO KNOWN AS: Constantine (given name)

SAINT METHODIUS

BORN: c. 825; Thessalonica, Macedonia (now Salonika, Greece)
DIED: April 6, 884; probably near Velehrad, Great Moravia (now in the Czech Republic)
AREAS OF ACHIEVEMENT: Religion and theology, linguistics

EARLY LIVES

The brothers Constantine (Cyril was a religious name taken just before his death) and Methodius (mih-THOH-dee-uhs) were born in the Macedonian city of Thessalonica, which was the second most important city of the Byzantine Empire and the provincial capital of the region to the west of Constantinople. Their father, Lev (Leo), was a high-ranking military officer in the province and a man of some importance; he was known at the imperial court in Constantinople. The younger of the two brothers, Constantine, was the more gifted intellectually and socially and certainly was better known. Methodius, by contrast, functioned in Constantine's shadow until after the latter's death in 869, despite his own considerable talents and intelligence. This lesser position is suggested by the facts that much more has been written about the early life of Constantine than has been about that of Methodius and that whenever their activities are discussed, Constantine is always cited first.

Following the death of his father in 841, Constantine was sent to Constantinople, where he became the protégé of Theoctistus, the legothete, or imperial chancellor, to the Byzantine empress Theodora. Impressed with Constantine's intellectual and linguistic capabilities, Theoctistus arranged for him to study at the imperial court academy. There Constantine studied philosophy and theology under the tutelage of Photius, the most important Byzantine philosopher and theologian of his time and a future patriarch of Constantinople. By 849, Constantine had acquired not only a reputation as an outstanding scholar of philosophical and theological matters but also the exalted title of philosopher.

Cognizant of Constantine's extraordinary skills, Theoctistus sought to use those talents for the empire by offering the scholar a place at the imperial court and marriage to his adopted daughter. Constantine, however, spurned these worldly opportunities and opted instead for a life of spiritual piety. Undaunted, Theoctistus proposed to ordain Constantine as a deacon in the Church and to appoint him to the office of chartophylax (librarian) or secretary to Ignatius, the last of the Byzantine iconoclastic patriarchs. Although initially accepting this offer, because of his disagreement with Ignatius's iconoclast policies, Constantine mysteriously disappeared. Finally, in 850, he was named professor of philosophy at the imperial academy where he had previously studied. He was only twenty-three years old. Constantine remained at the academy until 855, when he retired to join Methodius in a monastery on Mount Olympus, near the Sea of Marmora in northwestern Turkey, which was the center of monastic life in the ninth century.

As to Methodius, very little is known of his early life. There are only brief references to his activities before

863; nothing exists to illuminate his formative years or his education. It is recorded, however, that he did serve as a provincial governor in the region where he was born. Despite this eminent position, however, Methodius tired of the vicissitudes of worldly life. He became a monk and entered a monastery on Mount Olympus, where he would be joined by Constantine.

Life's Work

The main achievement of Constantine and Methodius centers on their activities among the Great Moravians of central Europe between 863 and 885. The focus of this effort was primarily religious and linguistic in that they sought to develop a Slavonic liturgy and to train an ecclesiastical hierarchy to support the emerging Christian church in Moravia. From the outset, their work was enmeshed in the religious and political rivalries involving the Byzantines, the German Franks, and the Papacy during the ninth century. Despite these difficulties, the brothers achieved their goals; their success gave rise to the later appellation "Apostles to the Slavs."

In 862, Rostislav, the king of Great Moravia, appealed to the Byzantine emperor Michael III for a group of missionaries to develop a liturgy and to train an ecclesiastical hierarchy for Moravia. In making this petition, Rostislav specifically requested the inclusion of Constantine and Methodius because their reputations as scholars and linguists had spread well beyond Byzantium. Although Rostislav couched his plea to Michael in religious terms, he was motivated by his own political interests. At issue was his desire to reduce or even eliminate the influence of the Bavarian Franks in his kingdom because their presence threatened Moravian independence. To achieve this goal, however, Rostislav needed to reduce Moravian dependence on the Franks' ecclesiastical leadership. For their part, the Byzantines were not oblivious to the political and religious advantages of Rostislav's overture. It offered the prospect for expansion of the Byzantine rite into central Europe, where Rome and Constantinople were rivals for religious authority. At the same time, it presented an opportunity to forge an alliance with Moravia against Bulgaria, whose activities threatened Byzantium. Such were the circumstances confronting Constantine and Methodius as they began their Moravian mission.

On arriving in Moravia in 863, the apostles were warmly received by Rostislav. Before they could begin their work, however, it was necessary to overcome the absence of a written Moravian language. To resolve this difficulty, Constantine turned his attention to the development of a Slavonic alphabet that would correspond to the spoken Slavonic language used by the Moravians. Constantine was well suited for this task; he was fluent in Slavonic because the language was common to Thessalonica.

To derive a Slavonic alphabet, Constantine used the letters of the Greek alphabet as a foundation. Spoken Slavonic, however, had numerous inflected sounds and diphthongs for which there were no Greek equivalents. Therefore Constantine was forced to create additional letters to represent the unique Slavonic sounds. The result was the Glagolitic alphabet, which became the basis for Old Slavonic or Church Slavonic and the precursor to the later Cyrillic alphabet. Constantine's accomplishment meant that the Moravians now possessed the means to acquire their own liturgy and to educate an independent ecclesiastical hierarchy. The next four years saw the brothers translating critical elements of the Byzantine liturgy into the new Glagolitic script for this purpose. By the autumn of 867, their mission seemingly completed,

Saint Cyril. (Library of Congress)

the apostles departed from Moravia, returning to Constantinople with the new liturgy and a group of disciples who were candidates for ordination. Once ordained, these disciples were to return to Moravia and continue the work begun by Constantine and Methodius.

Unfortunately, the apostles never completed their journey to Constantinople; fate intervened in the form of an invitation from Pope Nicholas I to visit Rome. Turning toward Rome, the brothers intended to remain there briefly and then continue their journey to Constantinople. Instead, the Roman sojourn lasted more than two years and had a major impact on their work in Moravia. As in 863, the primary cause of this situation was the continuing rivalries in central Europe. Although Constantine and Methodius attempted to remain above these conflicts and intrigues, they could not escape the impact of events.

By the time the apostles arrived in Rome in late December, 867, or early January, 868, Nicholas was dead and Adrian II was the new pope. The brothers had accepted Nicholas's invitation in part because they wished an opportunity to ordain the Moravian disciples. By doing that in Rome, the new clerics could return to Moravia and begin their work much sooner than had they proceeded to Constantinople. These hopes were quickly realized because Adrian approved not only the ordination but also Constantine's Slavonic liturgy. Certainly the reputation of Constantine and Methodius contributed to Adrian's decision. It is also possible, however, that Adrian sensed an additional political advantage for Rome. Granting a Slavonic liturgy and an ecclesiastical hierarchy for Moravia would neutralize Frankish influence there. Moreover, it afforded an opening for the extension of Roman ecclesiastical authority into the region by reversing the earlier rejection of Moravian requests for a religious mission from Rome, a rejection that had originally prompted the Byzantine mission.

Adrian's actions marked the high point of the brothers' stay in Rome as summer, 868, brought distressing news from Constantinople. Reports told of the overthrow and assassination of Michael III by his coruler, Basil the Macedonian, in the previous September. No less disturbing was the deposing of Patriarch Photius and his replacement by the iconoclast Ignatius. The cause of these events was the conflict between Constantinople and the Papacy over Roman religious penetration of Bulgaria, a circumstance both Photius and Michael adamantly opposed. By removing the two men, the new leadership in Constantinople hoped to improve relations with Rome and to eliminate Roman influence in Bulgaria. The effect of the developments was to leave Constantine and Methodius in limbo. They were uncertain of their status in Constantinople and of the future of their work. Meanwhile, Constantine, already ill, continued to decline. He died in Rome on February 14, 869. Before he died, however, he became a monk and received the name Cyril in recognition of his new spiritual standing.

The burden of their work fell to Methodius. By now it was certain that he could not return to Constantinople, but he did not wish to see the work in Moravia disrupted. It was important, he believed, for the Slavs to have their own liturgy and ecclesiastical leadership. With this in mind, he accepted the appointment by Adrian to return to Moravia as papal legate. Methodius remained there until his death on April 6, 884. It was this final demonstration of spiritual concern that ensured the preservation of the Slavonic liturgy among the Slavic peoples.

Significance

In retrospect, the significance of the work of Cyril and Methodius was not confined to their activities in central Europe. Although their mission was a major factor in the development and expansion of Christianity among the Moravians and the other Slavic peoples that inhabited the region, the broader impact of the brothers was to the east in Bulgaria and Russia. The reason for this observation can be found in the historical events that transpired after the ninth century. First, Rome was able to assert its religious and ecclesiastical influence in central Europe. The effect was the latinization of these peoples culturally, linguistically, and liturgically. Byzantine influence, never really strong there, declined. Second, the disciples of Methodius, driven eastward in the late ninth and early tenth centuries, found refuge in Bulgaria, where their Glagolitic alphabet and Slavonic liturgy took root and flourished. During the next two centuries, these elements gave rise to a distinctive Slavic culture. For the first time in their history, the Slavs had a written language. In turn, this language led to the evolution of a national literature in the form of hagiography and historical chronicles. The result was the emergence in Bulgaria of a Slavic unity where none had previously existed. In the twelfth century, the expansion of the Slavonic language and culture fostered a similar cultural and linguistic unity in Kievan Russia. Subsequently, this Slavic unity was transmitted to medieval Russia though the Russian Orthodox church and became one of the significant unifying forces of early Muscovite development. Thus, Cyril and Methodius richly deserve the appellation "Apostles to the Slavs."

—*David K. McQuilkin*

FURTHER READING

Duichev, Ivan, ed. *Kiril and Methodius, Founders of Slavic Writing: A Collection of Sources and Critical Studies*. Translated by Spass Nikolev. New York: Columbia University Press, 1985. Contains a tenth century hagiography on the life and acts of Cyril by a probable disciple of Methodius. Also includes an encomium or eulogy by the same author on the death of Methodius.

Farrugia, Edward G., Robert F. Taft, and Gino K. Piovesana, eds. *Christianity Among the Slavs: The Heritage of Saint Cyril and Methodius*. Rome: Pontifical Oriental Institute, 1988. A collection of addresses and papers presented at the international congress held on the eleventh centenary of the death of Saint Methodius. Examines the work and lives of Methodius and his brother. Bibliography and index.

Obolensky, Dimitri. *Byzantium and Slavic Christianity: Influence of Dialogue?* Berkeley, Calif.: Patriarch Athenagoras Orthodox Institute, 1998. This work, published as part of a lecture series, looks at the lives and works of Saints Cyril and Methodius, focusing on their influence on the Slavs.

_______. *Byzantium and the Slavs*. Crestwood, N.Y.: St. Vladimir's Seminary Press, 1994. Three chapters in this work on Byzantium deal with Saints Cyril and Methodius, including one on their influence in Russia. Bibliography and index.

Tachiaos, Anthony-Emil N. *Cyril and Methodius of Thessalonica: The Acculturation of the Slavs*. Crestwood, N.Y.: St. Vladimir's Seminary Press, 2001. A biography of the two saints that touches on their influence on the Slavs. Bibliography.

_______, ed. *The Legacy of Saints Cyril and Methodius to Kiev and Moscow: Proceedings of the International Congress on the Millennium of the Conversion of Russia to Christianity.* Thessalonika, Greece: Hellenic Association for Slavic Studies, 1992. A set of papers on Saints Cyril and Methodius from a conference in 1988.

Vodopivec, Janez. *The Holy Brothers Cyril and Methodius, Co-patrons of Europe: Cultural Link Between the East and the West*. Rome: Pontificia Universitas Urbaniana, 1985. An examination of the two saints and their influence on the Slavs. Contains Pope John Paul II's *Encyclical epistle Slavorum Apostoli*, in which the pope writes of the saints and their work as apostles.

SEE ALSO: Basil the Macedonian; Nicholas the Great.

RELATED ARTICLES in *Great Events from History: The Middle Ages, 477-1453*: c. 850: Development of the Slavic Alphabet; 890's: Magyars Invade Italy, Saxony, and Bavaria; 893: Beginning of Bulgaria's Golden Age.

ENRICO DANDOLO

Doge of Venice (r. 1193-1205)

As doge of Venice from 1193 to 1205, Enrico Dandolo presided over the Republic of Venice and founded its commercial, colonial, and maritime empire in the eastern Mediterranean Sea. He was the outstanding leader of the Fourth Crusade and played the key role in its diversion from the Holy Land to Constantinople.

BORN: 1108?; Venice (now in Italy)
DIED: 1205; Constantinople (now Istanbul, Turkey)
AREA OF ACHIEVEMENT: Government and politics

EARLY LIFE

Enrico Dandolo (DAHN-doh-loh) was born about 1108 into the Venetian merchant aristocracy. This birth date, which the best and earliest sources provide, has been called into question by some modern historians, who doubt that a nonagenarian who was blind and a businessman to boot could have led chivalric Crusaders into battle. The primary sources from the Fourth Crusade (1202-1204) agree that Dandolo was blind and very aged, and modern doubts would seem to involve latent prejudices about old age and physical handicaps rather than any real evidence. The birth date in 1108 would have Dandolo eighty-five years old in 1193 when he was elected doge (or duke) of Venice, which agrees well with the earliest sources.

During the early twelfth century, Dandolo made no special mark, so his early life has left little record. It may be presumed that he had the characteristic career of scions of the Venetian merchant aristocracy and served in the navy and marines; on a succession of government boards, assemblies, and councils; and in diplomatic posts overseas. In Venetian diplomatic service, Dandolo rose to the top by 1170 to become ambassador of Venice to the Byzantine Empire at Constantinople. He also worked in his family's business, married, and had children, including a son who acted as his deputy in Venice when Dandolo was overseas on crusade.

During the twelfth century, Venice, Genoa, and Pisa were commercial rivals in the Mediterranean, but Venice was almost a satellite of the Byzantine Empire, culturally in its shadow, politically often under its thumb, and economically beholden to it for trade concessions and favors. Venice's territorial ambitions along the Adriatic Balkan coast and in the islands of the Ionian and Aegean seas brought the republic into collision with the Byzantine Empire and the rising Balkan power of Hungary, which became a vassal kingdom of the Papacy. At the head of the Adriatic Sea, Venice was also placed in an exposed position between the Papacy and its allies and the Holy Roman Empire. Venice's geographic and economic situation required inspired diplomacy to maintain the republic's freedom and to increase its power.

LIFE'S WORK

While Dandolo was the Venetian ambassador at Constantinople in 1170, his life suddenly and terribly changed. In the anti-Latin rioting that year in Constantinople, the Byzantines arrested and blinded Dandolo. There survive several accounts of his blinding, the most credible being the obscure *Novgorodskaia letopis* (1016-1471; *The Chronicle of Novgorod, 1016-1471*, 1914), which is also the one most consistent with the other evidence.

Byzantine agents had identified Dandolo as the ablest of the Latins and a statesman very likely to rise to power in the Republic of Venice. The Byzantine emperor therefore ordered him seized and blinded by a fiendish apparatus of glass that used concentrated reflected sunlight to destroy his retinas without changing the appearance of his eyes or leaving any apparent injury. The intent was to disable Dandolo, demoralize and depress him, disqualify him from future leadership positions, and, in a devious manner, discredit him should he try to explain his blindness.

The disability would have crushed most men, but Dandolo persevered in his quest for the dogeship. He was not only undeterred by his disability but also strengthened in his resolve and purpose of liberating Venice from Byzantine influences. The blind Dandolo saw more perceptively than his contemporaries and even later historians the strategic geopolitical realities around 1200, when the traditional Crusade aimed at Jerusalem had become obsolescent, peripheral, and largely irrelevant.

Dandolo's notion of crusading combined diplomacy, mastery of the seas, and a plan to attack directly at centers of power in Egypt and Asia Minor, not at symbols such as Jerusalem. In this, he anticipated the later development of crusading. More controversially, Dandolo regarded the Byzantine Empire not as a necessary buffer state between Western Christendom and Islam but as a degenerate, wicked, and treacherous ally that really was an obstacle to the attainment of the goals of crusading. Dandolo's familiarity with the East and his cosmopolitan sophistication were very different from the naïve chivalry and piety of the French Crusaders, for whom crusading meant armed pilgrimage to Jerusalem, not mastery of complex power politics.

To achieve his ends, Dandolo capitalized on a series of opportunities that chance provided. First, in 1201, he negotiated the Treaty of Venice with the French Crusaders contracting for transportation across the sea to Egypt. By 1202, however, too few Crusaders had assembled at Venice to pay their part of the contract. Venice faced financial catastrophe because the republic had overextended itself on shipbuilding and provisioning the Fourth Crusade on Crusader credit.

Dandolo renegotiated the treaty and drove a hard bargain. It was argued that the Fourth Crusade would not proceed directly to Egypt but instead divert to besiege Zadar, a Christian port on the Adriatic Sea that had rebelled against the Venetian empire. Late in 1202, Christian Zadar fell to the Fourth Crusade, much to the shock of Christendom.

At Zadar, Dandolo and the Crusaders renegotiated their agreement, and taking advantage of dynastic turmoil in the Byzantine Empire and the private ambitions of some great Western noblemen, Dandolo secured another diversion of the Fourth Crusade. The Crusaders were to move from Zadar in 1203 to Constantinople, the capital of the Byzantine Empire, ostensibly to place an exiled pretender on the throne where he would further the Crusade.

In July of 1203, the Fourth Crusade stormed the fortifications of Constantinople. The Venetians breached the seaward walls, led by Dandolo in front with the Venetian banner, setting the example of bravery. He was at this time about ninety-five years old and blind. After this first conquest of the capital, new dynastic turmoil soon led to the expulsion of the Crusaders. In April of 1204, the Crusaders took Constantinople a second time and sacked the city, plundering it for three days.

The Fourth Crusade ended here and never reached the Holy Land. The Crusaders chose Baldwin of Flanders as the new emperor of what would prove to be the ill-fated Latin Empire of Constantinople (1204-1261) and divided the city and Byzantine territories. Venice received three-eighths of the city; trade concessions; the lion's share of the booty in religious relics, works of art, and precious commodities; and a network of island and peninsular territories in the Aegean and Ionian seas, the foundations of Venice's vast maritime empire. His work done, Dandolo died in Constantinople in 1205.

SIGNIFICANCE

The long life span of Dandolo saw the transformation of the crusading ideal from the religious fervor and idealism that had marked the First Crusade to the political realism and secularism that marked the Fourth Crusade. Dandolo had been trained in the hard school of power politics and could capitalize on this transformation in the interest of the Republic of Venice, which he probably regarded as in line with the interest of all Christendom. Some romantic

Engraved depiction of Byzantine emperor Alexius IV defying the conquering forces of Enrico Dandolo on the shores of Constantinople. (F. R. Niglutsch)

medievalists may criticize this crusty old bourgeois businessman for lacking the visionary idealism of a naïve French knight, but in the new age Dandolo's commercial bourgeois values certainly were more realistic and successful. Perhaps more important, Dandolo overcame serious physical disabilities and achieved resounding victory for his Republic of Venice. This blind nonagenarian businessman of unexampled bravery, vigor, and imperial vision was medieval Venice's greatest doge, diplomat, naval commander, and statesman.

—*Terence R. Murphy*

FURTHER READING

Bartlett, W. B. *An Ungodly War: The Sack of Constantinople and the Fourth Crusade*. Thrupp, Stroud, Gloucestershire: Sutton, 2000. An overview of the Fourth Crusade, focusing on the sack of Constantinople.

Brand, Charles M. *Byzantium Confronts the West, 1180-1204*. 1968. Reprint. Aldershot, Hampshire: Gregg Revivals, 1992. The Fourth Crusade and its background from the perspective of its Byzantine victim. Predictably hostile to Dandolo and skeptical about his blindness and old age, though grudgingly appreciative of his great abilities.

Clari, Robert de. *The Conquest of Constantinople*. Translated and edited by Edgar Holmes McNeal. 1936. Reprint. Toronto: University of Toronto Press and the Medieval Academy of America, 1996. Primary account of the Fourth Crusade by a French knight from the Crusader rank and file. Robert de Clari certainly admired Dandolo, though it was difficult for the knight to appreciate the doge's bourgeois values.

Madden, Thomas F. *Enrico Dandolo and the Rise of Venice*. Baltimore: Johns Hopkins University Press, 2003. A biography of Dandolo that focuses on his role in governing Venice. Bibliography and index.

Queller, Donald E., and Thomas F. Madden. *The Fourth Crusade: The Conquest of Constantinople*. 2d ed. Philadelphia: University of Pennsylvania Press, 1997. A scholarly and detailed study, sympathetic to the Venetians and an excellent secondary source on the Crusade.

SEE ALSO: Afonso I; Bohemond I; Edward I; Frederick I Barbarossa; Henry the Lion; Innocent III; James I the Conqueror; Louis IX; Richard I; Saladin; Tancred; Theoleptus of Philadelphia; Urban II; Geoffroi de Villehardouin.

RELATED ARTICLES in *Great Events from History: The Middle Ages, 477-1453*: 1054: Beginning of the Rome-Constantinople Schism; 1147-1149: Second Crusade; 1189-1192: Third Crusade; 1204: Knights of the Fourth Crusade Capture Constantinople; 1209-1229: Albigensian Crusade; 1212: Children's Crusade; 1217-1221: Fifth Crusade; 1227-1230: Frederick II Leads the Sixth Crusade.

DANTE

Italian poet

Dante's The Divine Comedy, *written in vernacular Italian terza rima, synthesizes classical and medieval thought in a confessional format that is at once universal and intensely personal.*

BORN: May or June, 1265; Florence (now in Italy)
DIED: September 13 or 14, 1321; Ravenna (now in Italy)
ALSO KNOWN AS: Dante Alighieri (full name); Durante Alagherius (variant of full name)
AREA OF ACHIEVEMENT: Literature

EARLY LIFE

A welter of legend surrounds the life of Dante (DAHN-tay), author of the tripartite masterpiece *La divina commedia* (c. 1320; *The Divine Comedy*, 1802). Still, certain facts are clear. His neighbor Giovanni Villani wrote a brief sketch, and Giovanni Boccaccio wrote a eulogy that appeared sometime after Dante's death. These accounts agree on a birth date in May of 1265. His family had noble origins at least several generations before Dante's birth, and their surname was originally Alagherius or Alaghieri. Dante's own name is a shortened form of Durante. His mother died during his childhood, and his father, who remarried, died in 1283. Dante had two sisters (one a half sister named Tana from his father's second marriage) and a half brother named Francesco. Although his family was nominally ennobled, it was neither rich nor especially prominent.

By all accounts, Dante's early life was a happy one. His family recognized the value of education and sent him to an elementary school run by the Dominicans and subsequently to the school of Santa Croce. He read both

Provençal and Italian poets during these early years and acquired a knowledge of metrics entirely on his own. His readings gave him vivid impressions of country as well as city life; he also enjoyed art and practiced drawing.

Florence was the center of the literary and artistic world in the late Middle Ages, and the city continued to flourish during the Renaissance. It was during these transitional years that the young Dante and those with whom he associated lived there. The poet Guido Cavalcanti, although Dante's senior, became "the first among [his] friends," as Dante records in *La vita nuova* (c. 1292; *Vita nuova*, 1861; better known as *The New Life*), and his literary adviser. In the *Inferno*'s circle of Epicureans, Guido's father Cavalcante de' Cavalcanti learns of his son's death in one of the canticle's most poignant scenes. Guido was a man of his times in every sense; he disliked classical verse in general and Vergil's poetry in particular, primarily because of its imperialism and religious piety.

Dante. (Library of Congress)

Brunetto Latini, a scholar and author of a French prose encyclopedia called *Li Livres dou tresor* (1266; the books of treasure), was another important influence on Dante. Much conjecture surrounds Dante's placing his mentor among the Sodomites of the *Inferno*. The best explanation, cogently argued by John Freccero, is that Dante came to recognize the pridefulness a comprehensive encyclopedia of knowledge implies and realized, as had Saint Augustine, that one could be seduced by glib language.

Practically nothing is known about the musician Mario Casella aside from Dante's affection for him—and that he serenades the Pilgrim Dante and the penitents in the *Purgatorio* and shaped Dante's love of music. Casella died sometime before 1300, the year in which *The Divine Comedy* is set. Not much more can be said of Dante's contemporaries the poets Lapo Gianni and Cino da Pistoia, except that they saw themselves as the vanguard of new poets who would change the character of Italian verse.

LIFE'S WORK

The literary ferment of Dante's time was matched and exceeded by political instability and violence, and Dante found himself thrust into this atmosphere. Florence was an essentially independent municipality controlled by its trade unions and intense partisan interests. In 1289, Dante, a young poet married for several years to Gemma Donati, participated in the Battle of Campaldino, fighting against the rival town of Arezzo. His wife was a fourth cousin of Corso and Forese Donati, perhaps of the same family as the Buoso degli Abati of the *Inferno*; certainly, however, Corso Donati was an infamous leader of the Florentine political faction known as the Blacks. Dante and his wife had at least three, possibly four, children during the period they lived together: two sons, named Pietro and Jacopo, and one or two daughters, Antonia and, less certainly, Beatrice. Dante's was an arranged marriage (with the dowry set in 1277), but it was not necessarily an unhappy one, as some contend. His wife did not follow Dante into exile in 1302, probably because her family ties to Florence were so strong.

The political conflict between Blacks and Whites had its origins in a continued class struggle between Guelphs and Ghibellines. The emerging middle class (essentially

MAJOR WORKS BY DANTE

Date	Work
c. 1292	*La vita nuova* (*The New Life*)
c. 1300-1321	*Epistolae*
c. 1306	*De vulgari eloquentia*
c. 1307	*Il convivio* (*The Banquet*)
c. 1313	*De monarchia* (*On World Government*)
c. 1316	*Epistola X*
1319	*Eclogae*
c. 1320	*La divina commedia* (*The Divine Comedy*)

Guelphs) was despised by the old military aristocracy (primarily Ghibellines), which built fortifications throughout and surrounding Florence. Although a battle fought at Benevento in 1266 brought a seemingly decisive defeat of the Ghibellines, two factions of the Guelphs reorganized around the Donati family and the Cerchi family. To assert aristocratic prerogative, the Blacks enlisted the aid of Pope Boniface VIII, who hoped to make Tuscany part of the Papal States. In 1302, Boniface sent an army into Tuscany under Charles de Valois (supposedly to establish order); the Whites, Dante among them, were driven from Florence. Dante would never return to his beloved city; he would also never forgive Boniface for what he saw as a perversion of papal authority. He alludes to Boniface with relentless bitterness in the *Inferno*.

Dante's having held municipal office in the years following 1295 had made him a conspicuous figure embarrassing to his Guelph in-laws. His publication of *The New Life* had, by this time, attracted the attention of literary Florence as well. The work was noticed first as an anthology of sonnets in Italian rather than Latin. The influence of the young Cavalcanti is clear in Dante's decision to break with tradition here. Curiosity surrounded (and continues to surround) the identity of Beatrice, a woman the poet had loved since their childhood. *The New Life* records Beatrice's death, and, although Dante does not divulge her surname, she is generally considered to have been Beatrice dei Portinari, daughter of the prominent Florentine Folco dei Portinari and wife of the banker Simone dei Bardi. Her tragic early death and innocence make her a recurring figure of saintliness in Dante's verse, and it is Beatrice who leads the Pilgrim Dante through Heaven in the *Paradiso*, the last canticle of *The Divine Comedy*.

By 1302, then, Dante was considered a brash young poet and a political troublemaker. He was separated from his wife and family, dispossessed of his property, and (cruelest of all for him) banished formally from his city under the threat of death by fire. The charges against him are vague, obliquely involving misappropriation of municipal funds left in his charge. The real reason for his expulsion involves his Guelph sympathies. He could have purchased a pardon in 1315, but he refused to do so.

For several years after the sentence of exile was imposed, Dante wandered from town to town, first consorting with exiles who appeared to have like political sympathies but ultimately, disgusted with their grandiose plans and incipient violence, going his own way and depending on his writing for his living. These were essentially rootless and wandering years. Around 1307, he wrote *Il convivio* (*The Banquet*, 1903), a popular exposition of philosophy that contains a commentary of fourteen of his own poems. Dante sought peace in its writing and probably adapted that volume from sets of lectures given in various university cities, Bologna and Paris possibly among them. He completed only four of the work's projected fifteen treatises. Also incomplete and written during these years is a formal treatise in Latin, *De vulgari eloquentia* (c. 1306; English translation, 1890).

One can only guess how Dante lived during this period. The Scala family of Verona housed and supported him for a time, generously as it appears, until the death of his patron Bartolommeo (Alboino) della Scala in 1304. In 1306, Dante acted for the Malaspina family of Lunigiana in negotiating a peace with the bishop of Luni. By 1310, he was actively involved in supporting the Holy Roman Emperor Henry VII of Luxembourg, in an attempt to reunite church and state in Northern Italy. The emperor's invasion attempt was foiled from the beginning and faced the united opposition of nearly all Tuscany. Dante's outspoken encouragement of Henry VII in the form of three letters, probably written at Pisa from 1310 to 1311, did little to endear him to his fellow Florentines, and Henry VII's inglorious death at Siena in 1313 ended Dante's hope for return to his native city.

Fortunately, Dante was able to turn again to the Scala family of Verona, and Can Grande della Scala became his new champion. By the time of his return to Verona, in 1314 or 1315, Dante had completed the *Inferno* and probably a large part of the *Purgatorio*. It was relatively soon after this, possibly as early as 1316, that Guido da Polenta, a nephew of Francesca da Rimini whom Dante had immortalized in the *Inferno*, offered Dante permanent sanctuary at Ravenna. Dante accepted the offer, probably in part because two of his children, Pietro and Antonia (who had become a nun and taken "Beatrice" as her religious name) resided there.

It appears that these final years at Ravenna were happy. Dante found respect and peace there and took some sort of diplomatic mission to Venice during this period. He continued to enjoy the friendship and patronage of Can Grande and to work on the *Paradiso*, which would ultimately be published as the final canticle of *The Divine Comedy*. He died peacefully at Ravenna, never again seeing his beloved Florence, on September 13 or 14, 1321.

Contemporary engravings of Dante, almost always idealized, portray him as a professorial-looking man of about fifty, his face unlined and seemingly untroubled by the political and personal turmoil of what would have been essentially homeless years of exile. He, like the Pilgrim Dante of *Purgatorio* and *Paradiso*, has eyes upraised toward a more sublime existence, found in some measure in the friendship of his Verona and Ravenna patrons.

SIGNIFICANCE

Perhaps Dante always knew that his real contribution would be to pioneer the *dolce stil nuovo* (sweet new style) of vernacular Italian verse. Indeed, each canto of *The Divine Comedy* presents a technical challenge to the poet that matches the physical obstacles facing the Pilgrim. It is no accident, therefore, that Dante's predecessor in poetry, Vergil, whom he calls *Maestro* (master), is left behind once the Pilgrim enters Paradiso. Vergil cannot guide the Pilgrim through Heaven because no poet has ever sought to describe the infinite nature of God in finite human language. Dante, who brought allegory from its classical associations with a sacred text to a secular poem paradoxically filled with the universal and individual search for a Divine Unity, clearly saw the struggles of his life against the difficulties of writing this sublime poem.

That is not to imply that Dante was so idealistic as to believe the wretchedness of Tuscan politics could be altered by a philosophy of poetry. Change needed an agent, and Dante looked hopefully to one earthly savior after the next. One always senses, however, despite his letters of encouragement to Henry VII, despite his prophecy of a Hound (Can Grande?) in the *Inferno* who will subdue the rapacious Wolf, that Dante knew the wait would be a long one.

—Robert J. Forman

FURTHER READING

Bloom, Harold. *Dante Alighieri*. Philadelphia: Chelsea House, 2003. A biography of Dante that also examines his works. Bibliography and index.

Boccaccio, Giovanni. *Life of Dante*. London: Hesperus, 2002. Boccaccio's biography of Dante. An important early source.

Cachey, Theodore J., Jr. *Dante Now: Current Trends in Dante Studies*. Notre Dame: University of Notre Dame Press, 1995. A collection of papers presented at a conference at the University of Notre Dame in 1993. Mostly criticism and interpretation.

Freccero, John. *Dante: The Poetics of Confession*. Cambridge, Mass.: Harvard University Press, 1986. This is a collection of Freccero's major articles on Dante, a poet he sees as heir to the Augustinian tradition of confessional literature. Freccero concentrates on Dante's ability to make his poem move beyond finite language at the same time as it reveals Dante as both Pilgrim and Poet.

Gallagher, Joseph. *A Modern Reader's Guide to Dante's "The Divine Comedy."* Liguori, Mo.: Liguori/Triumph, 1999. Criticism and analysis of Dante's major work. Bibliography and index.

Iannucci, Amileare A., ed. *Dante: Contemporary Perspectives*. Buffalo, N.Y.: University of Toronto Press, 1998. The essays in this volume contain everything from a scrutiny of Dante's attitude toward poetic authority and language to examinations of his political thought and his views on gender.

Jacoff, Rachel, ed. *The Cambridge Companion to Dante*. New York: Cambridge University Press, 1993. A collection of essays on Dante, touching on his life, his relationship to Florence, his theology, and his connection to the classic poets a well as providing an introduction to the *Inferno*, *Purgatorio*, and *Paradiso*. Index.

Lansing, Richard, ed. *The Dante Encyclopedia*. New York: Garland, 2000. An encyclopedia devoted to Dante. Covers his life and works and contains numerous appendices. Index.

_______. *Dante: The Critical Complex*. 8 vols. New York: Routledge, 2003. A collection of criticism and analysis, with volumes looking at Dante's relation to Beatrice, philosophy, theology, history, critical theory, and interpretation.

Lewis, R. W. B. *Dante*. New York: Lipper/Viking, 2001. A biography of Dante in the Penguin lives series. Bibliography.

Quinones, Ricardo J. *Dante Alighieri*. New York: Twayne,

1998. Part of the Twayne world author series, this biography of Dante looks at his life and works.

Singleton, Charles S., ed. and trans. *Dante: The Divine Comedy.* 6 vols. Princeton, N.J.: Princeton University Press, 1973-1975. This work is the classic translation and commentary on Dante's magnum opus. It contains full Italian text and apparatus for the scholar and a readable translation on facing pages. The separate commentary volumes allow for easy reference, and the commentary itself, though scholarly, is never esoteric.

SEE ALSO: Giovanni Boccaccio; Boniface VIII; Guido Cavalcanti; Chrétien de Troyes; Cimabue; Giotto; Mechthild von Magdeburg; Petrarch.

RELATED ARTICLES in *Great Events from History: The Middle Ages, 477-1453*: c. 1100: Rise of Courtly Love; c. 1306-1320: Dante Writes *The Divine Comedy*; c. 1350-1400: Petrarch and Boccaccio Recover Classical Texts; 1387-1400: Chaucer Writes *The Canterbury Tales*.

DAVID I

King of Scotland (r. 1124-1153)

David granted feudal tenures to Anglo-Normans, extended the diocesan system, encouraged monastic growth, defeated various Scottish opponents, remodeled his government along patterns found in England and France, and protected his interests along the Anglo-Scottish border, creating a more united kingdom built on the thriving European institutions of his day.

BORN: Between 1080 and 1085; Scotland
DIED: May 24, 1153; Carlisle, Cumberland, England
AREAS OF ACHIEVEMENT: Government and politics, military

EARLY LIFE

David I was the sixth son of King Malcolm III Canmore (1058-1093) and his second wife, Saint Margaret of Scotland, the daughter of Edward the Atheling and sister of Edgar the Atheling, the last male representative of the royal house of Wessex. David's earliest years were spent in an environment that had strong ties, through Saint Margaret and her intimates, with the Anglo-Saxon past and the ecclesiastical currents of the day. This peaceful childhood came to an abrupt end in the autumn of 1093. Malcolm, while on his fifth raid into northern England, and Edward, his second son but Saint Margaret's eldest son, were killed in early November. On receiving news of their deaths, Saint Margaret reportedly died of grief while attending a mass. The Scots chose the dead king's brother, Donald III, as their new king. Donald expelled the English, who had been a part of Malcolm's court. Probably about this time David and his siblings fled to the court of William II of England.

In May, 1094, Duncan, Malcolm's eldest son, with the aid of William II, invaded Scotland and expelled Donald. Duncan II, in turn, was murdered during a rebellion led by Donald and Edmund, the eldest of Saint Margaret's sons, in November, 1094.

In the autumn of 1097, with support from William II, Edgar, with his three younger brothers, invaded Scotland. In a battle, Edgar defeated Donald, who was slain by David. While the new king awarded his brothers Ethelred and Alexander with earldoms, he seems to have left David to seek his fortune at the English court.

LIFE'S WORK

In 1100, Henry I of England (1100-1135) married Matilda, David's sister. For the next few years, David, who in contemporary chronicles is repeatedly referred to as "the brother to the queen," served as a retainer to his brother-in-law, King Henry. David's position was that of a younger son of the Anglo-Norman aristocracy. Given that he had three brothers senior to him, there was only an extremely small chance that he would ever become a king. Nevertheless, his courteous and pious demeanor, coupled with his position as the brother of King Edgar of Scotland and Queen Matilda of England, made David a useful agent in Anglo-Scottish relations. For centuries, the border between the two kingdoms had been in dispute, with each kingdom claiming areas in the territory of the other. Edgar, at the time of his death, apparently granted Lothian to David. Yet Edgar's successor, Alexander I, refused to honor his predecessor's bequest until David, with the backing of Henry I, threatened to invade Scotland with a large force of Norman knights. Sometime between 1107 and 1113, David received Teviotdale, Strathclyde, including Cambria, and southern Lothian from Alexander. David's position as an important lord in southern Scotland evolved into one of the major marcher lords along the Anglo-Scottish border.

In 1113, David's presence on the border was enhanced by his marriage to Matilda, the widow of Simon de Senlis, earl of Northampton and Huntingdon, and granddaughter of Earl Waltheof of Northumberland and Adelaide, sister of William I of England. Conceived by Henry I, this marriage provided the vehicle through which Normanization of the border finally occurred. With Henry's support, David led the way for Norman colonization in the border area. Using Norman knights, he defeated the Galwegians, revived the diocese of Glasgow, began the foundation of a series of religious houses beginning with one at Selkirk in 1113, and feudalized southern Scotland with the introduction of a number of Anglo-Norman knights as landholders in his Scottish lordships. These knightly colonists were descendants of feudal families that either held estates in the earldom of Northampton and Huntingdon or originated in Brittany and western Normandy in northwest France. A second aspect of David's marriage was the possibility of a claim to the earldom of Northumberland, about which he apparently said nothing until after Henry's death in 1135.

On April 23, 1124, Earl David became King David I. Despite Alexander I having married Henry's illegitimate daughter, Sybil, he had had no children by her, thus leaving Scotland to David, who had outlived all of his brothers. At about the age of forty, David found himself a king.

Within Scotland, the new king continued his reliance on Anglo-Normans by settling numbers of them in its southern areas. In addition to these colonists, David introduced Anglo-Norman institutions as well. Several sheriffdoms modeled on English counties were created. In each, a sheriff acted as the Crown's chief local officer. At the highest level, David borrowed the concept of the "justiciar," who acted as the king's senior administrator and justice. To maintain control of the countryside, David and his Normans built a number of motte and bailey castles, whose exemplars dotted every English county. With the Norman knights and their castles came feudalism to help the king secure his hold over the lowlands and extend his influence into the highlands. To assist the development of commerce and the payment of taxes other than in kind, David began the issuance of coinage, based on English pennies, in the late 1130's.

On the death of Henry I in 1135, England found itself divided over the succession to the throne. In 1127, David I had led the Anglo-Norman feudal lords in swearing an oath to recognize Matilda, Henry's only surviving legitimate offspring, as the king's successor. Yet, on hearing of Henry's death, Stephen of Blois, the second son of William I's daughter, Adela, seized the English crown for himself, becoming King Stephen. A protracted but intermittent civil war between Matilda and Stephen followed, during which David attempted to solidify his control over Cambria and Northumbria. While honoring his oath to Matilda, David asserted claims to southern Cambria and the earldom of Northumbria. In response to Stephen's coronation, David invaded northern England. Stephen hurried to Durham, where David met him in February, 1136. They agreed that David would keep Cambria, return Northumberland to Stephen, decline to become Stephen's vassal, and permit Henry, his son, to do homage to Stephen for the earldom of Huntingdon. In answer to calls for help by Matilda, David once again crossed into England and ravaged Northumbria in the spring and summer of 1138.

Although a raid by Stephen into Lothian did not reduce King David's pressure on the north of England, an

A textual illumination of the likenesses of David I, left, with grandson and successor Malcolm IV, from the Charter of Kelso Abbey. (Hulton|Archive at Getty Images)

KINGS OF SCOTLAND, C. 858-1371

Reign	*Ruler*
c. 858	Kenneth I breaks with England
1005-1034	Malcolm II: Lothian added
1034-1040	Duncan I: Strathclyde added
1040-1057	Macbeth
1057-1058	Lulach
1058-1093	Malcolm III Canmore
1093-1094	Donaldbane
1094	Duncan II
1094-1097	Donaldbane (second rule)
1097-1107	Edgar
1107-1124	Alexander I
1124-1153	DAVID I
1153-1165	Malcolm IV
1165-1214	William I the Lion
1214-1249	Alexander II
1249-1286	Alexander III
1286-1290	Margaret
1290-1292	Interregnum
1292-1296	John Baliol
1296-1306	Interregnum
1306-1329	ROBERT I THE BRUCE
1314	Robert the Bruce defeats England
1329-1371	DAVID II
1371	Ascendancy of Robert II, House of Stuart

army of Yorkshiremen destroyed the Scottish army in August, 1138, at the Battle of the Standard. David escaped back to the border. At Durham, in April, 1139, Stephen, attempting to stabilize his northern frontier, continued to accept the arrangements made in 1136, except that David's son Earl Henry now became the earl of Northumbria, which included the counties of Northumberland, Durham, Cumberland, Westmorland, and Lancashire. When Matilda captured Stephen early in 1141, David journeyed southward to assist her. While besieging some of Stephen's supporters at Winchester, Matilda and David were attacked by a relieving force. She escaped, and David found himself captured three different times, after each of which he bought his freedom and finally returned to Scotland. Stephen regained his freedom and deprived David and Henry of their English estates. Although they lost control over Huntingdon, they retained Northumbria, which Stephen was unable to wrest from them.

In 1149, Henry of Anjou, duke of Normandy and Matilda's heir, journeyed to Carlisle seeking David's assistance. For his promise to recognize Scottish rule of Cumbria and Northumbria, Duke Henry was knighted by David. When their joint movement southward from Carlisle met a quick response from Stephen, David returned to Scotland and Henry to Normandy. Not until November, 1153, would Duke Henry come to the agreement with Stephen, which would make him king of England in 1154, Henry II.

David intended to pass Scotland to his son, Earl Henry. From the mid-1130's David had associated Henry with himself in the governance of Scotland and their English earldoms. By 1144, Henry was being referred to as *rex designatus*, king-designate. David's plan, however, came to naught: Henry died on June 12, 1152. Being about seventy, David quickly had Earl Henry's sons Malcolm and William proclaimed heir to the kingdom of Scotland and earl of Northumbria, respectively. Then, on May 24, 1153, while at Carlisle, David I died and was succeeded by twelve-year-old Malcolm IV.

SIGNIFICANCE

In the half century following David I's death, several English monastic writers described the king's achievements both as a ruler and a man. They report that he maintained a balance between his actions as a king and his behavior as a devout Christian. In him, while the roles of king and Christian affected each other, neither completely dominated the other. The English monk William of Newburgh described David as

> a man religious and pious; a man of much prudence, and of the greatest moderation in the administration of temporal things, and none the less of great devotion toward God; a man by no means on account of affairs of the kingdom more careless of divine offices: nor on account of the divine offices with which he occupied himself less capable in the affairs of the kingdom.

Scots from his day onward saw David's reign as a high point in their history. David had reasserted Scottish independence from England, had begun the revival of the Christian church, and had initiated an enduring governmental structure. His accomplishments would continue to influence the development of Scottish government, culture, and society well into the thirteenth century.

—*Kenneth G. Madison*

FURTHER READING

Anderson, Alan Orr. *Early Sources of Scottish History, A.D. 500 to 1286*. 2 vols. Edinburgh: Oliver and Boyd, 1922. Contains passages from chronicles written by non-English and non-Scottish writers as well as mate-

rial drawn from charters and other documents in English translation.
Barrow, G. W. S. *The Anglo-Norman Era in Scottish History.* New York: Clarendon Press, 1980. A fairly technical discussion of the Normanization of Scotland, for which David I was mainly responsible, by a premier scholar of medieval Scottish history.
_______. *Kingship and Unity: Scotland, 1000-1306.* 2d ed. Edinburgh: Edinburgh University Press, 2003. An exploration of David I's life and accomplishments.
Duncan, Archibald A. M. *Scotland: The Making of the Kingdom.* New York: Barnes and Noble Books, 1975. The standard historical treatment of early medieval Scotland.
Kapelle, William E. *The Norman Conquest of the North: The Region and Its Transformation, 1000-1135.* Chapel Hill: University of North Carolina Press, 1979. Provides an excellent analysis of Norman settlement along the Anglo-Scottish border until 1135.
Le Patourel, John. *The Norman Empire.* New York: Clarendon Press, 1976. Presents the wider picture of Norman expansion in England and northern France from the early 900's to the mid-1150's and discusses the background against which David I acted.
Ritchie, R. L. G. *The Normans in Scotland.* Edinburgh: Edinburgh University Press, 1954. Indispensable text on the Normanization of Scotland.
Webster, Bruce. *Medieval Scotland: The Making of an Identity.* New York: St. Martin's Press, 1997. Discusses Scottish identity in the context of place, order, faith, and struggles for independence.

SEE ALSO: Henry I; Henry II; King Stephen; William the Conqueror.
RELATED ARTICLE in *Great Events from History: The Middle Ages, 477-1453*: October 14, 1066: Battle of Hastings.

DAVID II

King of Scotland (r. 1329-1371)

David, king of Scotland during many years of its struggle for independence from the English, spent much time in exile or captivity before his return to the kingdom and a period of peace, leaving room for debate over his accomplishments as king.

BORN: March 5, 1324; Dunfermline, Scotland
DIED: February 22, 1371; Edinburgh, Scotland
ALSO KNOWN AS: David Bruce
AREAS OF ACHIEVEMENT: Government and politics, military

EARLY LIFE

David Bruce was the son of Robert Bruce, the famous Scottish warrior and then king of Scotland who had led the nation in successful revolt against English control. King Robert, a strong and energetic ruler, sought to consolidate his family's and nation's position through a marriage between his son David and Joanna, the sister of Edward III of England. This marriage was celebrated on July 12, 1328. Less than a year later, on June 7, 1329, King Robert died. David II was then crowned and anointed king and Scotland faced the uncertain prospect of a long period with a child monarch on its throne, uncertainty among its nobles, and a powerful English presence on its border.

The symbolism of the ceremony crowning David deliberately underscored Scotland's position as an independent kingdom. This independence had been threatened earlier by the weakness of John de Baliol, who had accepted the English monarch as his feudal lord; Baliol had later been thrust aside by King Robert, who had claimed the crown and driven the English from the land.

A number of Scots lords had sided with Baliol and the English during the struggle, and during the early years of David's reign, they and Edward III pressed for the return of their forfeited estates. In August, 1323, Edward de Baliol (son of John, who was by this time long deceased) and many of these nobles, known as the Disinherited, landed on the coast of Fife. They were secretly supported by Edward III, who desired at least a friendly ruler in Scotland and who eventually claimed the crown for himself. On August 11, at Dupplin Moor, the rebels defeated a Scots army led by the earl of Mar, guardian for the young king. The guardian and many of the nobility were slain, and Baliol advanced rapidly through the kingdom. In September, he was crowned at Scone.

Civil war now resumed in Scotland. The new guardian, Sir Andrew Moray, was captured by Baliol, but under his successor, Sir Archibald Douglas, supporters of David forced Baliol to evacuate Scotland. In turn, this brought Edward III into the conflict to support his ally, and on July 19, 1333, the English inflicted a serious defeat on the Scots at the Battle of Halidon Hill. Douglas, the new guardian, fell in battle, along with more of the Scots lords. Although Baliol established himself at Perth as king, his deference to Edward III was complete: All southern Scotland was surrendered to the English, and there were clear indications that Edward III contemplated possession of the entire nation.

In this uncertain situation, David and Joanna sailed for the safety of Scotland's traditional ally, France; they landed in Boulogne on May 14, 1334. The royal exiles, well-treated abroad and supported by funds from home, would remain in France for seven years.

Back in Scotland, the struggle against the English continued. The fortunes of war varied greatly, generally favoring Edward III when he campaigned in person. Edward's lieutenants were less capable, and the Scots waged a remorseless guerrilla war against them. The decision of Edward in 1337 to concentrate his strength in a French campaign was a turning point in the war, because it reduced the level of English power in Scotland.

Sir Andrew de Moray, who had been reappointed as guardian, was able to take advantage of the favorable situation and drive the English from their strongholds. After de Moray's death in the spring of 1338, the struggle was continued by the next guardian, Robert the Steward. Robert, although he was eight years older than David II, was his nephew, heir, and eventual successor. Under Robert, the Scots took Edinburgh from the English in April, 1341.

LIFE'S WORK

On May 4, 1341, David returned to Scotland. Thanks to leaders such as Robert and Moray, northern Scotland had been liberated. In a council held at Aberdeen in February, 1342, David assumed command as king. He set out with Moray on a raid on the English border to underscore his commitment to the struggle and traveled about his kingdom to be seen by his subjects. The attack on the English was ineffectual, however, and the kingdom deeply troubled.

Open warfare still raged between the supporters of Baliol and the English and those of David; personal feuds, murders, and assaults were common. The administration of justice and government was uncertain. Contemporary chronicles noted a fast-spreading disease that attacked the fowls of the kingdom; it was a forerunner of the Black Death, which would soon ravage Europe.

By 1346, Edward III was deeply involved in the siege of Calais, on the French coast. To assist his French allies while the English were weakened, David gathered his forces and moved south with twelve thousand men-at-arms and thirteen thousand other troops. William Zouche, the archbishop of York, mustered the English and, on October 17, 1346, smashed the Scots at the Battle of Neville's Cross, killing many of their leaders and capturing David himself. The king would spend the next eleven years as captive of Edward. The English were unable to exploit fully this victory because of their campaigns in France.

Robert was appointed guardian of the realm once more, and ransom negotiations began for the release of David. The negotiations were long and difficult because the English demands were considerable. A total of 90,000 marks (60,000 pounds) was set, which could be raised only with great difficulty in poor, war-ravaged Scotland. Worse, from the Scots' view, was Edward's insistence that, should David die without an heir, the kingdom go to Edward III or one of his sons.

In January, 1356, Baliol, as scholar Ranald Nicholson describes it, "took the crown from his head, lifted a handful of earth and stones from Scottish soil, and handed them to Edward III." Now that Baliol, the pretender he had supported, had renounced his claim, the English monarch openly sought the throne for himself. Later that year he led an army through southern Scotland in the "burnt Candlemas" campaign, spreading additional devastation throughout the countryside.

Edward III's position was strengthened by his success in France: In September, 1356, the Battle of Poitiers left the French routed and their monarch, King John II, a captive of the English. Realizing that their traditional ally was unable to assist them, the Scots concluded the ransom treaty with Edward, agreeing to pay 100,000 marks (66,666 pounds) over a ten-year period. Although the amount was enormous, the treaty placed no other conditions on the Scots, including matters touching the succession. On October 7, 1357, David II finally returned to Scotland as a free man.

David's return to Scotland may have restored the monarchy, but it failed to bring an immediate end to the nation's troubles. There was turmoil among the Scottish nobles, who continued to struggle among themselves and who defied his attempts to gain control of the kingdom. Their opposition was decisively countered by David, who asserted his power over his subjects through various methods, including the revocation of titles, imprisonment, and the use of armed force. Royal control over the Church was strengthened. The administration of the government was greatly improved, especially in fiscal matters, and commentary of the time remarked on the even dispensation of justice under David.

As the king established himself more firmly throughout the land, Scotland began to emerge from the trials of war. The burgesses, that class below the nobility and above the commons, assumed new and more important positions in the realm. One reason for their growing importance was the vital role they took in raising the ransom for the king; this service was their entry into political decisions affecting Scotland. A second source of their new strength was their essential participation in the rebirth of Scotland's trade. Restoration of peace permitted renewed commerce with England and with the Continent. Once again, the burgesses engaged and profited in this enterprise.

It was in the area of foreign affairs, specifically relating to England, that David proved less satisfactory to his subjects. The treaty for his release had set a large ransom but had left Scotland independent. In November of 1363, further talks were held between English and Scottish representatives, regarding nonpayment of the ransom and possible solutions; the old issue of the succession was raised once more. The English were willing to forgo the unpaid portion of the ransom if the Scots would agree that their kingdom would go to Edward III should David die without an heir.

It seems that David, while in London, personally agreed to this proposal. He apparently had a genuine respect and admiration for Edward, who was generally regarded as an outstanding example of kingly chivalry, a point of particular importance to David. The Scottish king also must have been impressed by the weakness of the French and the growing strength of England. These considerations, combined with the great difficulty in raising the annual payments, seem to have inclined him toward settling the kingdom on the English king as the best solution for his own and the kingdom's dilemma. The Scots, on the other hand, scorned the suggestion, and in March of 1364, their parliament rejected the proposed treaty. Although the Scots were in arrears on their payment of the ransom and had rejected his proposal, Edward was unable to act against them because of his continued deep involvement in France. Despite the force of Edward and the complaisance of David, Scotland remained independent.

There remained the vexatious problem of the succession. David's wife, Joanna, had joined him in London during his captivity and had died there on August 14, 1362, without ever having returned to Scotland. The next year, David married Margaret, widow of Sir John Logie. His contemporaries believed that he had been overcome by love; certainly, the alliance brought no political or dynastic advantage to the king, nor did it produce children. In 1369, a divorce was granted by the Scottish bishops.

A new marriage was contemplated, this one with Agnes Dunbar. As he was only forty-seven years old, David was still capable of siring children. As plans for the wedding were being prepared, however, David II died, on February 22, 1371, at Edinburgh Castle. His kinsman, Robert the Steward, succeeded him to the throne.

SIGNIFICANCE

The reign of David II presents an enigma to historians, particularly in regard to his policy toward England and its effect on the independence of Scotland. Assessments of David vary, according to how his actions are interpreted. Some see David as having come under the increasing domination of King Edward III, ready to cede the realm of Scotland to the more powerful monarch. According to this view, David, discouraged with the prospects of continued struggle and particularly disenchanted with his French allies, believed English victory to be inevitable and sought to make the best possible and practical arrangement for his country. Others stress, in addition, the love of chivalric pageantry and tradition that was so strong a part of David's character; this led him to an inevitable admiration for Edward III, Europe's prime example of chivalry. It would have been natural for David to accept Edward as his feudal lord, and the submission of Scotland to the English king would not have seemed shameful to him.

In some of the documents surviving from the 1363 ransom and treaty discussions, there is mention of Scotland's position should Edward inherit the throne. Promises somewhat vaguely assure the Scots that they can retain their traditional laws and customs and their internal government and administration. Perhaps David thought that, for all practical purposes, Scotland would remain independent under Edward III and that only a common ruler would link the two countries. Whether this was practical and whether this is what Edward intended is unknown. The fate of Wales under the English monarch would suggest otherwise.

Some writers see in David a more nationalistic and independent monarch, whose relationship with England and Edward was based on a realistic appraisal of his country's power and position. Whatever changes might have been discussed, none was actually implemented.

Was that what David intended, or what the Scottish lords demanded? It is certain that those lords and their followers were the ones who preserved Scottish independence during the long years of David's exile and captivity, and it is logical to conclude that after David's return they helped maintain that independence despite the inclinations of their royal master.

—*Michael Witkoski*

FURTHER READING

Bower, Walter. *Scotichronicon.* Edited by D. E. R. Watt. Edinburgh: Mercat Press, 1987-1997. A nine-volume classic on the history of Scotland, originally written in the 1440's. Volume 7 includes a survey of the years 1320 to 1390, a time period that includes the reign of David II.

Dickinson, W. Croft. *Scotland from the Earliest Times to 1603.* 3d rev. ed. Edited by Archibald M. Duncan. Oxford, England: Clarendon Press, 1977. A well-written, well-researched account of Scotland, and the section on David II is easily accessible to the general reader.

Donaldson, Gordon, and Robert Morpeth. *Who's Who in Scottish History.* New York: Barnes and Noble Books, 1973. Brief but informative entries on prominent figures in Scotland's past. The section on David II presents him in a slightly better light than most of his other biographies.

Nicholson, Ranald. *Scotland: The Later Middle Ages.* New York: Barnes and Noble Books, 1974. A thorough, narrative account of the kingdom.

Northen, Stephanie. "A Ruler Made to Be Broken." *Times Educational Supplement* (June 14, 2002). Discusses David as the first anointed king and the ruler whose death marked the end of the Bruce clan's reign in Scotland.

Packe, Michael. *King Edward III.* Edited by L. C. B. Seaman. Boston: ARK, 1985. Provides an interesting perspective on the relationship between Edward III and David, David's actions, and Scottish aspirations.

Roberts, John L. *Lost Kingdoms: Celtic Scotland and the Middle Ages.* Edinburgh: Edinburgh University Press, 1997. A history of Scotland from the eleventh to the seventeenth century, including a chapter on Scottish independence.

SEE ALSO: Robert Bruce; Edward I; Edward III; Philippa of Hainaut; William Wallace.

RELATED ARTICLES in *Great Events from History: The Middle Ages, 477-1453*: June 23-24, 1314: Battle of Bannockburn; 1347-1352: Invasion of the Black Death in Europe; 1366: Statute of Kilkenny.

DHUODA

Carolingian writer

Dhuoda's Liber Manualis *is the only work written by a woman that survives from the Carolingian period. It offers vivid insights into ninth century Western European life.*

BORN: c. 805; place unknown
DIED: c. 843; Uzès (now in France)
ALSO KNOWN AS: Dodana; Duodana; Dhuodana
AREA OF ACHIEVEMENT: Literature

EARLY LIFE

Conjecture attends all aspects of the early life of Dhuoda (dew-OH-duh). That she was married in 824—a fact she records in the *Liber Manualis* (c. 841; *Handbook for William*, 1991)—allows one to posit a birth year of about 805, while the scant evidence bearing on her birthplace and lineage points to an origin in what is now northern Germany (though France cannot be ruled out). She hailed from a distinguished family that doubtless was consanguine to Charlemagne, a heredity confirmed by her marriage to Bernard of Septimania, a close confidant and second cousin of the emperor Louis the Pious, whose own father, Charlemagne, had stood as Bernard's godfather. Louis himself attended the couple's wedding, which was held in Aachen, the imperial capital, in the emperor's own private chapel.

Dhuoda brought much to her marriage and would in time become a shrewd and talented proxy for her husband in southern France. Bernard, in turn, made an early name for himself by defending the Spanish March. Consequently, in 831, he was appointed chamberlain, which wedded his fortunes closer to those of Louis the Pious. Dhuoda gave birth in 826 to a son named William, and at some point later she and William were sent to live in Uzès in southern France.

As chamberlain, Bernard was intimately involved in the struggles of Louis the Pious against his scheming sons, who were constantly at odds with, and eventually waged war on, their father and each other. Even before Louis's death, in 840, civil war was endemic. Louis had not even been dead a year when one of his sons, Charles the Bald, began fighting in earnest for control of the empire, a mere seventeen-year-old whose youth ensured his endurance but also fueled an arrogant zealousness.

Charles the Bald's hostility toward Bernard was patent and had already manifested itself toward Bernard's cloistered sister, Gerberga, who was accused of sorcery, sealed in a wine cask, and thrown into a river to drown. To this was added the widely circulated rumor that Bernard had carried on an affair with Charles's mother, the empress Judith. In this highly charged setting, Bernard returned to Uzès in 840, reunited with Dhuoda long enough for her to get pregnant a second time, and then traveled north to pay homage to the king. Moreover, as an earnest of his good will toward the mercurial young king, Bernard delivered William to Charles's safekeeping, in effect making his son a hostage to the king's caprice. When Dhuoda's second son was born, in 841, Bernard holed the child up in Aquitaine, at a stronghold surrounded by bishops and nobles loyal to him, presumably as a safeguard to the family's future fortunes.

LIFE'S WORK

Amid the bereavement of losing her two sons in a matter of months, one of whom was a mere infant, Dhuoda struck on the idea of working through her grief by composing a book in which she would record for William those things she deemed necessary for him to survive. This book, the *Handbook for William*, belongs generically to a kind of writing known as a princely mirror, which extols the ideals of correct princely living. Dhuoda's work, however, is more than the usual mirror for a prince, for in standing for comparison with other such compositions, it is clear that Dhuoda has composed a more personal and, therefore, more original work. It is very much a mother's book.

The power of her unique view is felt at once in the book's opening lines, in which Dhuoda offers to William in exchange for her presence a book that he must use as if it were actually her, punning on the Latin word for "body"—*corpus*—which also means "book." However, what she hopes to achieve through this exchange is another matter, for, as she goes on to say, she has hidden, obscure things to tell her son.

> Many things are patent to many people that are hidden from me, and there are those like me with a hidden sense, lacking intellect, [wherein] if I say less, I am more. . . . Although I have a fragile sense and live unworthily among worthy women, still I am your mother, William, my son, and I am sending you now the discourse of my manual . . . so that . . . you might frequently read this little book directed to you by me . . . just as if you were looking in a mirror or playing a board game.

Dhuoda characterizes her own mental abilities as a species of hiddenness, suggesting a unique maternal (feminine) quality to her knowledge, which includes deeper truths hidden in the mysteries of etymology, wordplay, and numerology. Dhuoda is at her best in this regard.

> God [Deus] contains two syllables and four letters . . . and our "D," with which the name of God begins, among the Greeks is delta; and this is expressed according to their system of counting by the number 4, perfection; D in our Roman numerals, however, is 500, also suggesting a sacred mystery.

The hard work required of knowing, and the hidden bounties that are revealed to those who search for them, are suggested here in layers of meaning patiently set forth and explained—and many pages of the *Handbook for William* fit this mold, setting forth principles of correct living from beneath the veil of Dhuoda's own, rarified sources of knowing.

Many pages of the *Handbook for William* are, of course, straightforward charges to William about all manner of life's activities—praying, moral conduct, social awareness, and the like. Always, however, the priority of affect over reason looms large in Dhuoda's estimations of authentic action. Her treatment of prayer is a case in point, for Dhuoda admits that *oratio* stresses reason in its derivation from *oris ratio*, meaning "reason of the mouth." Yet in composing a prayer for William to recite, Dhuoda produces a specimen that stresses the inability of reason to ascertain the fullness and complexity of divinity—claims her own broader notion of knowing has already affirmed.

The contrast of feminine, maternal affect and masculine, hierarchical, reason is used to good effect as Dhuoda more formally considers right behavior, the correction of moral imperfection, and the balancing of human needs with spiritual progress, themes that take up a considerable portion of the *Handbook for William*. Consistently the world of power and intrigue—the masculine world of Bernard and Charles the Bald—is held up against the purer, more ephemeral world, to which Dhuoda has better access. When she instructs William in the proper attitudes he must hold toward his peers and lords, for example, Dhuoda avers that such figures and their families are owed respect, because, in the larger social structure in which she and her son exist, it is important to remain "truthful" toward such figures as these.

When Dhuoda goes on to enjoin William to be kind to great and small, however, the vocabulary and imagery of hierarchy, of masculine political power—lord to knight, son to father, vassal to lord—gives way to a parable based on Psalm 41, which begins with the image of a deer longing for the running waters. The deer points up a useful image in longing for the water, Dhuoda says, for when it needs to ford a river, the herd gather together and form a line in which each deer supports and helps the deer in front and behind. Slowly the lead deer drops back to rest and a new leader takes its place, so that the line remains refreshed and the river is more easily spanned.

This is brotherly love and compassion, Dhuoda says, but it is also an attitude that argues against respecting one's peers and their families simply in token of their status. Such respect as this, based on rank, power, and hierarchy, is contrasted here to the smooth, well-moving line of deer, who are exemplary precisely because they do not operate hierarchically, because they refuse to step on each other's backs or to submerge each other's heads. In this sense, then, Dhuoda affirms her own notion of moral fairness and right action apart from the world of male hierarchy, opting instead for a purer world framed by feeling, compassion, and the words of the psalmist, whose full sentiment, with its emotional productions, is not at a far remove from those lines of her own *Handbook for William*. In the text, speaking to God, Dhuoda declares, "my soul longs for you God, as the deer longs for the running waters."

The poetry of the psalms returns in several original poems that mark the end of Dhuoda's *Handbook for William*. One such piece highlights the singularity of Dhuoda's position as a woman and a mother, for she longs now to see how her son has physically matured, remembering how he grew from infancy to boyhood. At the same time, she laments her ill health and bad luck, which leads her to compose her own epitaph, before commending her soul to her readers by repeating those qualities of her own intellect that she holds in best esteem: her maternity and femininity; her access to deeper, rarified truths; and her knowledge of feeling and affect.

Affect looms largest perhaps in the final poem of the *Handbook for William*, in which Dhuoda speaks of her own discernment as a means to frame her desire to see William in the flesh. The idea of Dhuoda's special kind of discernment highlights her own commitment to the feelings that bind in an excellent and fair way, that commit humans most pervasively and most completely to each other. Longing never leaves her words. She writes,

> You are now 16 years old and you are yourself a lord of sorts; I long to see again how you look . . . but I'm tired, so very tired. . . . I hope you know, William, that you'll never have anyone like me—like me—because, though I am unworthy, I am your very mother.

One hopes that these words and others like them helped William in the time leading up to his father's murder in 844, and his own execution in 847, in that world his mother had warned him against so carefully. Presumably they did, precisely because they are so very much like their author.

SIGNIFICANCE

Dhuoda's *Handbook for William* is one of a kind, both in its length—eleven books of Latin prose and poetry—and in its overarching claim that feeling trumps reason in making authentic sense of the world. In terms of generic protocols, too, the *Handbook for William* strikes in fresh directions, making the princely mirror into a venue for personal expression in both prose and poetry. Dhuoda's Latin strikes for attention, in its earthy Germanicisms, its simplicity, and the ways it suggests the further development of later into Medieval Latin. Finally, the *Handbook for William* opens a window onto the social, political, and spiritual habits of the ninth century that otherwise would be permanently closed to view.

—Joseph M. Pucci

FURTHER READING

Dronke, Peter. *Woman Writers of the Middle Ages: A Critical Study of Texts from Perpetua (203) to Marguerite Porete (1310)*. New York: Cambridge University Press, 1988. A sensitive and subtle treatment of Dhuoda's *Handbook for William*.

Marchand, James. "The Frankish Mother Dhuoda." In *Medieval Women Writers*, edited by Katharina M. Wilson. Athens: University of Georgia Press, 1984. A partial translation and concise treatment of the *Handbook for William*.

Mayeski, Marie Anne. *Dhuoda: Ninth Century Mother and Theologian*. Scranton, Pa.: University of Scranton Press, 1995. Chapters discuss Dhuoda in histori-

cal and theological context, the "moral life of the Christian," and "biblical wisdom."
Neel, Carol, ed. *Handbook for William: A Carolingian Woman's Counsel for Her Son*. Lincoln: University of Nebraska Press, 1991. A translation of the *Liber Manualis* that includes an excellent introduction and bibliographical guide.
Thiébaux, Marcelle, trans. *Dhuoda: Handbook for Her Warrior Son*. New York: Cambridge University Press, 1998. A translation of the *Liber Manualis* with useful introduction and bibliography.
_______. *The Writings of Medieval Women*. New York: Garland, 1994. A partial translation and discussion.

SEE ALSO: Boethius; Cædmon; Geoffrey Chaucer; Chrétien de Troyes; Christine de Pizan; Dante; Eleanor of Aquitaine; Firdusi; Hrosvitha; Guillaume de Machaut; Marie de France.
RELATED ARTICLE in *Great Events from History: The Middle Ages, 477-1453*: 781: Alcuin Becomes Adviser to Charlemagne.

DIONYSIUS EXIGUUS
Scythian monk and scholar

Dionysius Exiguus provided a more accurate means to ascertain the date of Easter and initiated the convention of the Christian era by basing the calendar on the year of the birth of Christ.

BORN: Second half of the fifth century; Scythia
DIED: First half of the sixth century; Rome (now in Italy)
ALSO KNOWN AS: Denis the Little
AREA OF ACHIEVEMENT: Religion and theology

EARLY LIFE

Very little is known about the life of Dionysius Exiguus (di-uh-NISH-ee-uhs eh-ZIGH-yuh-wuhs). The only contemporary account of his life is a paragraph in the *Institutiones divinarum et humanarum lectionum* (562; *An Introduction to Divine and Human Readings*, 1946, better known as *Institutiones*) of Cassiodorus, who gives few details. Dionysius Exiguus was born in Scythia in central Asia, became a monk, and was summoned to Rome, where he died. By analyzing his writings, modern scholars have attempted to fix various events in his life, but no consensus exists. Because it is likely that Dionysius was a mature adult when he arrived in Rome, probably around 500, it is also likely that he died before 550, although it seems that he disappeared around 527. Dionysius assumed the appellation *Exiguus*, which translates as "short," "small," "lowly," or "less," probably not to describe his physical stature but rather to suggest his unimportance in relation to God.

Dionysius knew Latin and, because of his Eastern origin, Greek. His proficiency in translating material from one of these languages into the other attracted the attention of Pope Saint Gelasius I, who summoned him to Rome to organize the papal archives. Dionysius arrived in Rome after the pope died in 496.

Above all, Dionysius Exiguus was known as a translator. He translated several biographies of saints, a philosophical work on the creation of the human being, and texts on the heresies, including various writings on this topic by officials of the Eastern, or Greek, church.

In terms of church history, Dionysius Exiguus is best known as a canonist. His translating and compiling abilities produced the first collection of canon, or church, law. His collections included the canons of the apostles; the decrees of the councils of Nicaea, Ancyra, Neocaesarea, Gangra, Antioch, Laodicea, Constantinople, Chalcedon and Sardica, and Carthage; dedicatory epistles; and the decretals of the popes from Saint Siricius (384-399) to Anastasius II (496-498).

LIFE'S WORK

As a translator, Dionysius developed an interest in computation, or the determination of the calendar. The churches of Rome and Asia Minor had engaged in a dispute concerning the date of Easter since the second century. Based on the account of the Crucifixion of Christ in the Gospel of Saint John, the church in Asia Minor celebrated Easter on the day of the sacrifice of the lamb in the Jewish Passover, regardless of the day of the week. Passover occurred on the fourteenth day of Nisan, the first month of the Jewish year. The Roman church followed the Gospels of Matthew, Mark, and Luke, which identified the Last Supper with the Passover meal and placed the Crucifixion on the day after Passover. In the Western church, Easter became a memorial of the Resurrection and was celebrated on the Sunday following the first full moon after the spring equinox.

At the end of the second century, Victor, the bishop of Rome, threatened excommunication for anyone not observing Easter from the first Friday to Sunday after the fourteenth day of Nisan. As they adhered to a more ancient tradition, the churches in Asia Minor refused to submit. The controversy blew over, though the dispute continued. In the Western church in particular, a growing number of believers came to hold the opinion that Easter should be independent of Passover, and several means to determine Easter appeared during the third century.

The Nicene Council in 325 produced a unanimous decision that the Western and Eastern churches should hold Easter on the same day and that the date should have nothing in common with the Jewish tradition. However, no method of calculation was established at the Nicene Council; the Western church continued to use an old eighty-four-year cycle, while the Eastern churches used the more accurate nineteen-year (or Metonic lunar) cycle, known since antiquity.

The disputes and discrepancies continued. In the middle of the fifth century, Victorius of Aquitaine was charged with the recalculation of the dates of Easter, but he believed that his task was only to show the differences resulting from the employment of two sets of criteria, the pope having the final authority. Victorius did computations according to the Eastern nineteen-year cycles, but he made at least three mistakes, which caused repeated inaccuracies in the calculation of the Easter date. In some years, the Western and Eastern dates for Easter were separated by a week or even a month. For example, in 501, the Roman church held Easter on March 25, and the Eastern church celebrated it on April 22. The difference resulted from the Eastern church's practice of dating the spring equinox on March 21, while the Roman church placed the equinox on March 18.

At the request of a Bishop Petronius in 525, Dionysius Exiguus took up the Easter question in *Liber de Paschate* (*Paschal Tables*), which includes *Epistola prima scripta anno Christi 525* ("first letter written in the year of Christ 525"). In the letter, Dionysius committed a "pious" lie: He claimed that the Nicene fathers directed Christendom to accept the fourteenth day of the Paschal moon as the basis of the Easter calculation. These directives do not appear in the actual council decisions, which decreed only the universal celebration of Easter on the same day. Preserving the Nicene Council's goal of a single Easter date, Dionysius accepted the calculations of Athanas (c. 297-373), archbishop of Alexandria, and his successors, Theophil (fl. early fifth century) and Cyril (d. 444), which placed Easter on the fourteenth day of the Paschal lunation occurring during the first Hebrew month, Nisan. Based on God's commands to Moses concerning the celebration of Passover and on the *Historia ecclesiastica* (c. 300, 324 C.E.; *Ancient Ecclesiastical Histories*, 1576-1577; better known as Eusebius's *Church History*) of Eusebius of Caesarea, Dionysius noted that Nisan commenced on the day a new crescent moon appeared on or between March 8 and April 5. It was further stipulated that Easter must occur after the spring equinox.

The Alexandrians had preserved the nineteen-year cycle, in which the Easter date repeats every nineteen years, and Cyril designed a ninety-five-year cycle composed of five nineteen-year cycles. Dionysius included a Latin translation of the Easter cycle of Cyril. With his understanding of the Alexandrian method of calculation, and noting that in 525, six years of the ninety-five-year cycle remained, Dionysius provided Easter dates for the years 532 to 627, the next ninety-five-year cycle. Certain deviations from modern calculations are explained by the fact that Dionysius considered the day to begin at sunrise and not at midnight, the modern convention. Thus, while Dionysius did not invent the method of the determination of Easter, he is responsible for its introduction into use in Western Christendom.

History also credits Dionysius with the introduction of the idea of the Christian era. Actually, others before him had conceived of a calendar based on the date of Christ's birth, though at the time of Dionysius, there were several competing ways to number the years. In his calculation of the Easter date, Dionysius chose "to designate time from the Incarnation of our Lord Jesus Christ," and not from the 153d year after the Diocletian era, as Cyril did.

Dionysius took the year in which he wrote his Paschal tables to be 1278 A.U.C. (*ab urbe condita*, from the founding of the city of Rome), 783 A.U.C. to be the year of Christ's Crucifixion, and thirty to be the age at which Christ died. Thus he arrived at 525 for the year in which he was writing. History judges that he made a mistake in his calculations, for most scholars agree that Jesus was born not in 1 C.E. but rather, perhaps, in 4 or 7 B.C.E. The revised figure is based on a calculation from the year of Christ's birth, which can be more accurately determined than the year of his death.

One final issue concerning Dionysius's introduction of the Christian era deserves note. He began the Christian era not with the year 0 but rather with the year 1. This omission cannot really be considered an error; at the time, the concept of the zero did not exist in the West. Although the ancient Egyptians did have such a conception, they did not employ it regularly. The idea of the number zero appeared in Arab and Hindu thought toward the end of the eighth or the beginning of the ninth century and was introduced into Europe somewhat later.

Significance

Although Dionysius invented neither the manner of the calculation of the Easter date nor the conception of the Christian era, his works popularized both. Petronius circulated the tables Dionysius had prepared. Pope John I (523-526) learned of Dionysius's calculations and was interested in adopting them. He died in 526, however, and the next two popes were not impressed by the tables. Moreover, there is some evidence that Dionysius fell out of favor with them. During this period, Victorius's tables sufficed, but over time, the errors inherent in them became troubling.

Knowledge of the Dionysiac tables, however, spread. By 562, Cassiodorus was using them in his school. They were received and accepted as canonical in Spain before 627. The Dionysiac tables circulated widely throughout Europe in the seventh century. The majority of English churches accepted the tables in 729. Under the leadership of Charlemagne, the nineteen-year cycle was universally accepted in the Christian church.

All Dionysius's works, including his translations and his computation and canonical tables, had a single aim: to reconcile the Western and Eastern churches. Although the universal acceptance of his Easter tables provided unity on one point, there were many other political, cultural, and doctrinal differences between the Western and Eastern churches, and by the 800's, a schism between the two had begun. In 1054, Christianity divided permanently into two churches, the Roman Catholic and the Eastern Orthodox. When the Roman Catholic Church replaced the old, inaccurate Julian calendar with the Gregorian calendar in 1582, the agreement over the Easter date vanished. As a consequence, the Eastern Orthodox Easter and the Roman Catholic Easter are now sometimes celebrated on different days.

—*Kristen L. Zacharias*

Further Reading

Borst, Arno. *The Order of Time from the Ancient Computus to the Modern Computer.* Translated by Andrew Winnard. Chicago: University of Chicago Press, 1993. A 168-page history of the calendar from ancient Greece to the twentieth century. Contains a chapter on the Easter cycle and includes other references to Dionysius Exiguus.

Declercq, Georges. *Anno Domini: The Origins of the Christian Era.* Turnhout, Belgium: Brepols, 2000. An examination of Dionysius's role in establishing the Christian era. Bibliography.

Frend, W. H. C. *The Rise of Christianity.* Philadelphia: Fortress Press, 1984. A 1,022-page history of the early Christian church. Useful for an understanding of the development of the Eastern (Greek) and Western (Latin) Christian churches and their differences, including short sections on Easter dating.

Gould, Stephen J. *Questioning the Millennium: A Rationalist's Guide to a Precisely Arbitrary Countdown.* New York: Harmony Books, 1997. A 190-page book with a short discussion of Dionysius in the context of the dispute over when the third millennium begins. Places calendar issues within a social context.

Harvey, O. L. *Time Shaper, Day Counter: Dionysius and Scaliger.* Silver Spring, Md.: Harvey, 1976. An examination of the history of the calendar that looks at the part played by Dionysius.

Percival, Henry R., ed. *The Seven Ecumenical Councils of the Undivided Church.* New York: Edwin S. Gorham, 1901. Contains documents from the Council of Nicaea relating to the determination of Easter and comments concerning the following history and later role of Dionysius.

See also: Cassiodorus.

Related article in *Great Events from History: The Middle Ages, 477-1453*: 595-665: Invention of Decimals and Negative Numbers.

SAINT DOMINIC

Spanish monk and religious leader

Through faith, courage, and practicality, Dominic established the Dominican order in 1215, which revolutionized the monastic movement of the Middle Ages and filled a vital need for apostolic preaching in the Church.

BORN: c. 1170; Calaruega, Castile (now in Spain)
DIED: August 6, 1221; Bologna, Romagna (now in Italy)
ALSO KNOWN AS: Domingo de Guzmán (given name)
AREAS OF ACHIEVEMENT: Religion and theology, monasticism

EARLY LIFE

Dominic was born the third son of Jane of Aza and Felix de Guzmán, both of noble blood. Little is known about his father, and it appears that he died when Dominic was young. Dominic inherited his exceptional sensitivity to the suffering of others from his mother. When he was six or seven years old, old enough to learn how to read, Dominic was handed over to an uncle, an archpriest, to begin his education. At fourteen, Dominic went to Palencia, where he received a thorough grounding in theology and the Scriptures. As a student, Dominic was something of a loner with a reputation for being mature beyond his years. He did not, however, isolate himself from current events.

In the mid-1190's, Spain was in great misery. War had broken out against the Muslims, and with war came famine. In the course of a terrible famine that occurred while Dominic was at Palencia, few of the rich or the authorities did anything to help the starving masses. Repulsed by their indifference and inspired by Scripture (Luke 18: 18-26), Dominic sold all that he had, including his books with his personal glosses, saying that he would not study on dead skins while people were dying of hunger.

LIFE'S WORK

In 1196, Dominic became a canon and then a priest of the cathedral chapter of Osma. There he met Diego of Acebo, bishop of Osma, a man of intense zeal who would change the course of Dominic's life. Diego returned the chapter to the apostolic life as described in the Acts of the Apostles 4:32-33. He also had a gift for evangelism, and Diego quickly recognized Dominic as a gifted, deeply spiritual priest. The two became inseparable.

In 1203, Diego was sent to Rome with Dominic by King Alfonso VIII to secure a marriage contract for the king's son. Their route took them through Languedoc in southern France, and they discovered that what had been rumored in Spain was true: Languedoc was infested by the rapidly growing Waldensian and Catharist (Albigensian) heresies. The primary reason for the success of these heresies was the state of the clergy. Most of the parish priests were illiterate and lived lives hardly different from the poor people of their flock. Ignorant and worldly, they were unable to command respect and, more significant, they were unable to teach and defend the faith. The ostentation and worldly lifestyle of many, though certainly not all, of the higher clergy stood in stark contrast to the moral and humble lives of the majority of the heretics.

The contrast with the Church's position in Spain must have shocked both men. In Spain, the Church, under constant pressure from its enemy, Islam, was united and strong. In southern France, with its rich, productive land, numerous towns, and more sophisticated economy, the Church had become complacent, corrupt, and unable to inspire and win souls. This was the decisive moment in Dominic's life. The recognition of the Church's need burdened his soul and charted his life's work. Unknowingly, Diego and Dominic spent their first night in Languedoc in the home of a Catharist. They would not have known their host was a heretic by outward statement or appearance. Possibly he made some spiritual comment about the Church or expressed anticlerical feelings. In any event, Dominic passed the night in conversation with his host. After a night of honest debate, in which Dominic first tried to understand his host's position and then countered with his own beliefs, the heretic was converted back to the faith.

Their experience in southern France convinced Diego and Dominic to become missionaries. When they reached Rome, Diego asked Pope Innocent III to permit him to resign as bishop of Osma so that he, with Dominic, could be a full-time missionary. It is a measure of Diego's reputation as a bishop that Innocent III refused Diego's request, and both men returned to Languedoc.

Dominic began to perfect his approach to the heretics. Since the night he converted his host, Dominic had been convinced that genuine discussion was the only effective way to confront heresy. He went to great lengths to comprehend fully the heretics' arguments before contradicting them. He debated them without scorn or condescension, and he was not afraid to appoint a heretic to officiate at a debate and to determine the victor. Dominic saw the heretics in a humane light. He knew that they were in error, but he also realized that they had some justifiable positions and that many of them lived virtuous lives. For example, on close examination, the Waldensians were seen as Christians who took the Bible seriously and who had been pushed into heresy by not being allowed to preach. In fact, Dominic adopted some of the Waldensians' orthodox views into his own movement. It is an indication of his greatness that, in trying to understand the Waldensians, Dominic was able to take what was good and incorporate it into the Church. If priests and churchmen lived simple and virtuous lives, the great anticlerical impetus for heresy would be stopped. This approach was something new; the accepted response to heresy then in vogue was force and oppression. It is interesting to speculate how Church history would have changed had Dominic been able to elaborate his plan. Two events, however, prevented this from happening: the death of Diego and the Albigensian crusade (1209-1229).

On December 30, 1207, Diego, bishop of Osma, died. Dominic's sense of loss must have been enormous. For ten years, they had shared everything together, complementing each other perfectly. Diego had played an important part in developing Dominic's innovative approach to heresy. Dominic now faced the daunting apostolic task of evangelizing southern France alone. In the coming months, the situation would only continue to deteriorate. In January, 1208, Peter of Castelnau, Cistercian legate to Languedoc, was assassinated by a member of the household of Raymond, count of Toulouse, who if not a Catharist himself, resisted any firm actions against that sect. This set in motion a chain of events that culminated in the savage Albigensian crusade (1209-1229), which soon deteriorated into a war of conquest by the northern French nobility. Any plan to combat heresy via religious debate was quickly halted; the ravages of warfare made calm discussion impossible.

With the situation in southern France so poisoned by the Albigensian war, Dominic retreated into his religious house at Prouille. The bloodshed and savagery of the war repelled him. Dominic understood that force never truly converted anyone, and he wanted nothing to do with the violence. Dominic had attracted a small band of preachers around him and now realized that a new religious order was necessary to carry out effectively the missionary work. The members of this order would be priests who would not withdraw from the world. Rather, their designated duty would be to preach the word of God to regain for the Church those who had lost their way. They were to persuade others to Christ, and this would require that they be educated men themselves. Therefore, study was to be as important as prayer. Dominic, however, would also demand that these men live a life worthy of the Gospels, and so poverty was mandatory. Dominic's insistence on poverty, unlike that of Saint Francis of Assisi, was totally practical. It would allow the members of the order to concentrate on preaching without being distracted by material goods and would also add moral force to their mission.

An important element of Dominic's vision was the inclusion of women. His followers at Prouille included a number of female converts, apparently of noble birth. From the outset of his development of the new order, he established what was called a double monastery, with a convent for the nuns and a priory for the friars. The nuns were trained to teach the local children and to instruct converts to the faith. Dominic considered their example an essential part of the work of the order.

Placed in the context of the thirteenth century, this was a revolutionary monastic movement. In October of

Saint Dominic. (Library of Congress)

1215, after having been granted a religious house by Bishop Fulk of Toulouse in that city, Dominic requested that Innocent III formally confirm his new order. Innocent III refused. The Church was deeply concerned about the development and control of new religious orders and movements and had forbidden the creation of new orders. Innocent III understood the worsening condition of the Church and the clear need for effective preaching, but Dominic's proposed order broke too much with the past and seemed to have unreachable goals. Innocent III did concede that if Dominic would incorporate his order into an established monastic rule, it would be approved. Dominic agreed and chose the Augustinian rule, with which he had been familiar as a canon of Osma.

Dominic viewed the pope's approval of the order in 1216 only as a beginning, and he moved rapidly to expand. By 1217, he had friars in Toulouse, Paris, Bologna, Madrid, and Rome. By the time the order had its first general chapter (essentially a congress of the whole order), at Bologna on May 17, 1220, six houses had been established in Lombardy, four in Provence, four in France, three in Tuscany and Rome, and two in Spain, and groups of preachers had traveled to England, Germany, Hungary, and Scandinavia.

Dominic not only organized the order and traveled extensively but also devoted himself personally to the grueling ministry of preaching. In 1220-1221, Dominic started on an enormous mission of evangelizing in northern Italy, but the effort proved to be too much. All the deprivation and exertions of the past caught up with him, and he fell ill at Bologna.

Dominic called together his closest brothers in the order to give them his final instructions. Throughout his career, Dominic the man was hard to discern. He was a person of true humility who chose to remain in the background of events and avoided self-promotion. In his last words, some of the man is seen. Dominic told his brethren never to accept any kind of property and then confessed that, while he had remained a virgin all of his life, he had taken more pleasure in conversation with young women than with old. As his friars prayed, Dominic died, on August 6, 1221.

Significance

Dominic's emphasis on education and intellectual excellence quickly placed the order into the heart of the medieval universities. By 1245, general houses of the order had been opened at Paris, Oxford, Cologne, Montpellier, and Bologna—all centers of important universities. The order produced some of the greatest scholars of the period, such as Saint Albertus Magnus and his pupil, Saint Thomas Aquinas. Thomas would lead a successful defense of Christian doctrine against the skeptical philosophy of Averroës, and Thomas's *Summa theologiae* (c. 1265-1273; *Summa Theologica*, 1911-1921), which, in essence, reconciled faith and reason, would be the apex of medieval scholarship. Thomistic philosophy would become a foundation of Church doctrine.

The Dominicans were also leaders in the expansion and defense of the faith. Bartolomé de las Casas, author of *Historia de las Indias* (wr. 1520-1561; *History of the Indies*, partial translation, 1971), protested the horrible exploitation of the Indians by the Spaniards. By 1600, Dominicans had gone into the Philippines, China, Taiwan, and Japan.

Dominicans were in the forefront in the struggle against Protestantism; 130 Dominican bishops and theologians were present at the Council of Trent (1545-1563), and their Thomistic positions had a major influence on the council's decrees. Indeed, before the inception of the Jesuit order, the Dominicans were the chief champions of the Church. They were also the order most involved with the Inquisition. Dominic deserves no blame for this identification. The Inquisition operated in complete opposition to his beliefs, and there is no doubt that Dominic would have condemned the Inquisition in the strongest possible terms.

Possibly the Dominicans' greatest impact was on the everyday operations of the Church. In the period from 1221 to the twentieth century, there were two Dominican popes, Saint Pius V (1566-1572) and Benedict XIII (1724-1730), forty-one cardinals, and more than one thousand archbishops and bishops.

—*Ronald F. Smith*

Further Reading

Emond, James R., ed. *Dominican Bibliography and Book of Reference, 1216-1992: A List of Works in English By and About Members of the Order of Friars Preachers, Founded by St. Domini*. New York: P. Lang, 2000. A revised edition of the bibliography compiled beginning in 1216 and through 1992. This collection is made up of more than twelve hundred pages, and it includes an index.

Finley, Mitch. *The Seeker's Guide to the Christian Story*. Chicago: Loyola Press, 1998. A book oriented toward seekers of the Christian faith, with a chapter on Dominic in relation to the Crusades, the Inquisition, and Saint Francis of Assisi.

Hinnebusch, William A. *The Intellectual and Cultural*

Life to 1500. Vol. 2 in *The History of the Dominican Order*. Staten Island, N.Y.: Alba House, 1973. Discusses such topics as the importance of study to the order, the order's impact on doctrine, the development of libraries, and the writings of various Dominican authors in biblical, pastoral, and spiritual theology and history. An excellent, scholarly work best appreciated if one has a basic understanding of the order's history.

Jarrett, Bede. *Life of Saint Dominic (1170-1221)*. 2d ed. London: Burns, Oates, and Washburn, 1934. This is a standard biography of Dominic that, while not as detailed as Vicaire's, is still considered one of the better works on the life of the saint. Includes an index.

Ladurie, Emmanuel Le Roy. *Montaillou: The Promised Land of Error*. Translated by Barbara Bray. New York: G. Braziller, 1978. Based on a Dominican inquisition, this exceptional book re-creates time in the small village of Montaillou and most of its inhabitants from 1294 to 1324. While it does not discuss Dominic, this book covers the history, social life and customs, and religious life of a town that was deeply affected by the Catharist heresy. This account reveals what Dominic probably confronted on a daily basis. Includes maps, index, and bibliography.

Lehner, Francis C., ed. *Saint Dominic: Biographical Documents*. Washington, D.C.: Thomist Press, 1964. An excellent source for English translations of the principal primary sources on the life of Dominic.

Nigg, Walter. *Warriors of God: The Great Religious Orders and Their Founders*. Edited and translated by Mary Ilford. New York: Knopf, 1959. Includes a succinct account of Dominic's life and work. There is little material on his early life, but the description of his work in Languedoc, the evolution of the order, and its impact on the development of the Church is excellent.

Vicaire, M.-H. *Saint Dominic and His Times*. Translated by Kathleen Pond. New York: McGraw-Hill, 1964. Considered by many historians to be a definitive study of Dominic. The first section covers his early childhood, education, spiritual growth, encounters with heretics, and events surrounding the establishment of the order in 1215. Part 2 details Dominic's life in Rome and his successful efforts to organize and expand the order.

See also: Saint Albertus Magnus; Averroës; Saint Francis of Assisi; Innocent III; Simon de Montfort; Thomas Aquinas.

Related articles in *Great Events from History: The Middle Ages, 477-1453*: 1100-1300: European Universities Emerge; c. 1175: Waldensian Excommunications Usher in Protestant Movement; 1209-1229: Albigensian Crusade; November 11-30, 1215: Fourth Lateran Council; 1233: Papal Inquisition; c. 1265-1273: Thomas Aquinas Compiles the *Summa Theologica*; 1305-1417: Avignon Papacy and the Great Schism; c. 1310-1350: William of Ockham Attacks Thomist Ideas.

Donatello

Italian sculptor

One of the first great European artists to articulate fully the principles of perspective, Donatello has had an incalculable influence on his successors, who have derived their inspiration from his highly naturalistic and intense dramatizations of the human form.

Born: c. 1386; Florence (now in Italy)
Died: December 13, 1466; Florence
Also known as: Donato di Niccolò di Betto Bardi (full name)
Area of achievement: Art

Early Life

Donato di Niccolò di Betto Bardi, better known as Donatello (doh-nah-TEHL-loh), was the son of a wool carder. Very little is known about his life, except what can be surmised from contemporary records (such as payments to him for commissioned work) and from a biographical sketch in *Le vite de' più eccellenti architetti, pittori, et scultori italiani* (1549-1550; *Lives of the Most Eminent Painters, Sculptors, and Architects*, 1850-1907) by Giorgio Vasari, an Italian architect, writer, and painter. Vasari, however, is not entirely reliable on the subject of his predecessors. It is known that Donatello lost his father while still a young boy and that he lived with his mother until his middle forties, when she died. He never married. According to Vasari, the artist was a poor but generous man.

Donatello's native city of Florence had been an Etruscan city, founded before Rome. Florence had a long tradition as a center of commerce and pleasure, where a

Sculpture of Donatello. (Library of Congress)

young man such as Donatello could learn art and the practical skills of business. He was trained in the Stonemasons' Guild and was the master of many crafts, including goldsmithing, the making of inlays, engraving, carving, and the application of stucco ornaments to furniture.

The first record of Donatello as an artist (May, 1403) puts him in the shop of Lorenzo Ghiberti, a pioneer in the use of perspective, a technique that gives depth and three-dimensional quality to paintings and relief sculpture. By 1406, Donatello was at work on small marble figures of prophets for the Porta della Mandorla of the Duomo of Florence. On February 20, 1408, he received his first major commission, for a marble figure of David.

LIFE'S WORK

Donatello's first major work, the *David* in the Palazzo Vecchio, is a marble figure measuring 6 feet, 3.5 inches (192 centimeters). The massive head of Goliath rests at David's feet. Standing with his legs parted, David is a lithe, almost delicate figure, draped in a close-fitting cloak that emphasizes the youthful muscularity of his figure. His long right arm accentuates the power of the slingshot throw that brought Goliath to earth. The fingers of the right hand are bent in a grasping pose and were probably meant to hold a sling that has been lost. There is great vitality and strength in the sculpture, even though David is not depicted in action, because of the economy and the expressive precision of the details Donatello dramatizes, such as the way the index and middle fingers of his left hand press against his torso. Although David is a religious figure and embodies a myth, he is presented as an individual, a remarkable personality worthy of close inspection.

With the marble figure of *Saint John the Evangelist*, now in the southern aisle of the Duomo of Florence, Donatello made a larger-than-life statue that surpasses the *David* in the dynamic rendering of personality. Working with a somewhat shallow block of marble, the artist shaped the upper half of the body in high relief, thus leaving enough marble for the seated figure's thighs. By giving the figure no back, he foregrounded those aspects of Saint John's person he wished to highlight. It is the saint's human qualities, his piercing eyes and grave demeanor, that rivet the viewer. With book in hand, held meditatively, he appears as the very embodiment of the prayerful man.

Saint George and the Dragon, a marble relief on the outside of the Or San Michele in Florence, is noteworthy for Donatello's use of mountain and forest landscapes. As in his previous work, there is a beautiful rendering of naturalistic elements, a grounding in the reality of human emotions and settings. The representation of such scenes in the Middle Ages was more formulaic, more centered on a static composition of all the elements of the myth. In Donatello, rearing horse, rider, and dragon collide, so that the meaning of the myth arises primarily out of the sense of movement. Donatello's sculpture is not so much allegory (a pictorial evocation of myth) as it is an action in itself, a story evolving out of the artist's powerful dramatic technique.

The Feast of Herod (also known as the *Dance of Salome*), when compared to Pietro Lorenzetti's earlier painting of the same name, confirms Donatello's deft handling of realistic human figures in dramatic settings. In Lorenzetti's work, each of the seven figures is carefully spaced and distinctly visible in the foreground and background. The scene is frozen, made static, so that the picture is complete, the story intact. In Donatello's bronze relief for the Siena Cathedral font, five figures in the foreground of the right side of the relief draw back in horror at the presented head of John the Baptist. One man partially covers his face with his hand, as though the full sight of the head is more than he can bear. The other four figures are drawn back, but a woman in profile—perhaps the dancing Salome—stares fixedly at the head. These five figures are bunched together, obscuring a full view of their faces. Indeed, one face cannot be seen at all—only a headdress is visible. The realism, drama, and human complexity of the reactions to this atrocity demonstrate how intensely Donatello wished to convey the very life of events and personalities and not merely their symbolism. His use of composition to render the psychology of his subjects is evident in the left side of the bronze relief, where five distinctly positioned figures complete the foregrounding of the work and relieve the congestion of the right side. There is an exquisite balance achieved in the framing of the scene, quite different from Lorenzetti's proportioning of space.

Between 1411 and 1427, Donatello received commissions to work on figures of *Saint John the Evangelist* and *Saint George and the Dragon*, the *Sacrifice of Isaac*, the tomb of Baldassare Cossa (Pope John XXIII), the *Head of a Prophet*, the *Head of a Sibyl*, and others for the Or San Michele, the Opera del Duomo, and the cathedral of Orvieto—all in Florence. In 1430, he went to Rome for three years and carved several tombs. By 1433, he had returned to Florence to design several stained-glass windows, marble tombs, and bronze heads.

One of Donatello's most notable works from this period and said to have been his favorite is the so-called *Zuccone* (pumpkinhead, or baldhead). Again, it is the strong personality of the figure that is so commendable to modern taste. The long angular face, accentuated by the tilt of the head downward, the long loosely flexed right arm, with the right hand casually thrust inside a belt, are all aspects of a highly individualized figure. This is a person with his own peculiar outlook on the world, not simply a study of human form, and a figure with a posture that bends with life.

The bronze *David*, the *Equestrian Monument of General Gattamelata*, and *Mary Magdalen* are representative examples of the power and variety of Donatello's final period of creativity. It seemed to the artist's contemporaries that *David* was cast from life, so natural and playful does this slight figure appear. There is a joy and a lightness in this work that is entirely different from the earlier *David* in marble. The bronze statue of General Gattamelata, which stands in front of the Church Sant' Antonio in Padua, where the artist lived for nearly ten years, is a ruggedly determined depiction of the commander in chief of the Venetian military forces who died at Padua on January 16, 1443. The tough, chiseled quality of the face and the tight and slight grimness in the lips bespeak a man girding himself for battle with the poised calm of a great leader. As Ludwig Goldscheider notes, the wood carving of Mary Magdalen is an especially vivid example of Donatello's final naturalistic phase. The roughly hewn wood exaggerates the worn, beaten-looking, bony face, with its broken-toothed, grotesque mouth, while the strong hands, with fingers not quite touching one another in the sign of prayer, suggest the spirituality that inheres in this crude body.

SIGNIFICANCE

Donatello is regarded as one of the great innovators of Renaissance art. The bronze *David*, for example, is one of the first nude freestanding Renaissance statues. His great contributions were recognized in his time, especially at Padua, where he was the head of an enormous workshop. In his last years, he created an extraordinary set of reliefs for the pulpits of San Lorenzo. Most of his work remains in Florence, although an unfinished *David* is exhibited at the National Gallery of Art in Washington and a *Madonna* is in the Boston Museum.

The portrayal of human bodies is certainly one of Donatello's greatest achievements. The personality seems to express itself from within his dynamic figures, and there is never the sense that the faces he gives his figures are simply imposed on them. In the perfect disposition of each physical feature, of every detail of clothing and setting, the artist perfects both the objective and psychological points of view. His figures are real people in a real world, observed with sharp accuracy.

Donatello can rightly be regarded as one of the precursors of modern art because his sculpture is autonomous, a thing in itself that is never simply illustrative of the subjects he carved and casted. Like his contemporary Fra Angelico, Donatello excels in the dramatization of whole scenes, relying not only on his deft manipulation of human figures but also on his profound understanding of architecture and of the spaces his figures and objects occupy. Where he differs from Fra Angelico is in the heroic quality of so many of his human figures. It is, in the last analysis, his ability to portray depth powerfully—in his human subjects and in his settings—that continues to make his work worthy of the most serious study.

—Carl Rollyson and Lisa Paddock

FURTHER READING

Avery, Charles. *Donatello: An Introduction*. New York: Icon Editions, 1994. A concise, illustrated survey of the life and work of Donatello, this book provides balanced coverage of Donatello's sculpture in different media and in different cities of Italy, and discusses his importance and indifference. An ideal introduction for general readers, tourists, or students, Avery's book shows how Donatello's influence helped to create a new humanism that was a hallmark of the Renaissance.

Donatello. *Donatello*. Florence: Giunti, 1999. A catalog of Donatello's sculpture. Contains 44 leaves of plates, mostly color.

Gaeta Bertelà, Giovanna. *Donatello*. New York: Riverside, 1991. An analysis and examination of Donatello's works, with information on his life. Bibliography and index.

Jolly, Anna. *Madonnas by Donatello and His Circle*. New York: Peter Lang, 1998. An examination of artistic treatments of the Virgin Mary by Donatello and his contemporaries. Bibliography.

Poeschke, Joachim. *Donatello and His World: Sculptures of the Italian Renaissance*. New York: H. N. Abrams, 1993. An examination of Donatello's sculptures and other sculptures created at this time. Illustrated. Bibliography and index.

Pope-Hennessy, John. *Donatello, Sculptor*. New York: Abbeville Press, 1993. An analysis of Donatello's sculpture, including those for the Or San Michele and the Campanile and the Madonnas. Also looks at Donatello's partnership with Michelozzo. Illustrated. Bibliography and index.

SEE ALSO: Arnolfo di Cambio; Filippo Brunelleschi; Lorenzo Ghiberti; Jacopo della Quercia; Pietro Lorenzetti and Ambrogio Lorenzetti; Nicola Pisano and Giovanni Pisano; Claus Sluter.

RELATED ARTICLE in *Great Events from History: The Middle Ages, 477-1453*: c. 1410-1440: Florentine School of Art Emerges.

DU FU

Chinese poet

Du Fu is considered the greatest of the Chinese poets as well as one of the giant figures of world literature.

BORN: 712; Gongxian County, Henan Province, China
DIED: 770; Tanzhou (now Changsha), Hunan Province, China
ALSO KNOWN AS: Tu Fu (Wade-Giles)
AREA OF ACHIEVEMENT: Literature

EARLY LIFE

Du Fu (doo foo) descended from the nobility, and his family tradition was both scholarly and military. He was the thirteenth-generation descendant of Du You (Tu Yu), a marquess and an army general who was married to a princess of the imperial family. Du Fu's great-grandfather was Du Yiyi (Tu I-i), a mid-level government official. His grandfather was Du Shenyan (Tu Shen-yen), a *jinshi* (a high-level scholar) who served in minor official positions and was a respected poet. Du Fu's father, Du Xian (Tu Hsien), served in minor government posts. His mother, a woman of imperial blood, apparently died giving birth to Du Fu.

Little is known about Du Fu's childhood or teenage years and the education he received. He studied the Confucian classics to prepare himself to take the examination for the *jinshi* degree, the gateway to officialdom for most men. Evidence also suggests that he attended private schools. Apart from his acquaintance with the Four Books and the Five Classics (*Wujing*), he probably also studied Sunzi's military classic, the *Sunzi Bingfa* (c. 5th-3d century B.C.E.; *The Art of War*, 1910).

What is known about Du Fu's early life comes largely from his poems, many of which are autobiographical. In a poem written in 762, known as "Brave Adventures," he refers to himself at the age of seven when he writes, "My thoughts already concerned heroic deeds;/ My first song was on the phoenix, the harbinger of a sagacious reign." In the same poem, he refers to himself at the age of nine, when he began to practice calligraphy by writing "big characters" (that is, foot-square characters), which accumulated until there "were enough to fill a bag." He also remarks that his nature was "spirited," that he was already "fond of wine," that he "hated evil" unremittingly, and that he abandoned children his own age to associate exclusively with adults. At age fourteen or fifteen, Du Fu had entered into literary competition, and the local literati declared him a prodigy. In another poem written about the same time (c. 760), entitled "A Hundred Anxieties," Du Fu reveals that despite his seriousness about learning and writing at this age, he was still very much a boy: At fifteen, his "heart was still childish," he was as "strong as a brown calf," and in one day he "could climb the trees a thousand times."

At age nineteen, Du Fu began to see the world. He set forth in a southwesterly direction toward the lands of "Wu and Yüeh" (modern Jiangsu and Zhejiang). His journey was to last four years (731-735). He described his visit to Suzhou, a city noted for its scenic wonders and rich past. In viewing the city's ancient ruins, Du Fu recalled certain historical personages and the events associated with them. His journey completed, he returned northward by boat, eventually reaching his home in Jingzhao.

In the following year (736), Du Fu, now in the prime of life at age twenty-four, was invited by his prefecture to Chang'an to sit for the examination for the *jinshi* degree. However, for reasons unknown, he failed the examination.

Life's Work

Du Fu's failure in the examination practically put an end to his chances to have an official career. Although embittered, he never actually gave up this ambition and continually sought an official appointment by other means. In the meantime, he paid his respects to the prefect of Jingzhao and then left for his parents' residence at Yanzhou, where he would have to face their disappointment.

Soon, however, Du Fu set out on another journey. This time he went to Qi and Zhao (modern Shandong and southern Hebei). This trip would occupy him for another four years (736-740). His activities during these travels are also described in "Brave Adventures." He employed himself mainly by honing his skills in falconry, horsemanship, archery, and hunting. He recalled this period of his life in another poem, written in 766, entitled "Song of the White-Headed." In this poem, he regrets that his present age no longer permits him to perform the exciting and adventurous feats of his youth:

> Suddenly I think of youthful days,
> When frosty dew froze on the steps and door.
> On a Tatar horse I clasped an ornamented bow;
> My humming string was not loosed in vain.
> My long shaft sped after the cunning hare;
> Its swift feathers fitted to the bow's full moon.
> Mournful, the Song of the White-headed;
> Deserted now, the haunts of the gallants.

Du Fu's second journey was brought to a close by the death of his father in 740. He had to make the funeral arrangements, tend to his father's affairs, and find a place for the family to live. Du Fu chose Yanshi, northeast of

Ink drawing of Chinese poet Du Fu. (K. Kurnizki)

Luoyang, the eastern capital. There he built a house, which the family occupied in 741.

Soon Du Fu took up residence in Luoyang. There he met the older poet Li Bo (Li Po), who had just been dismissed from the court in Chang'an. With Li Bo and another distinguished poet, Gao Shi (Kao Shih), Du Fu made excursions to various historic sites in Henan. Du Fu and Li Bo met again—for the last time—the following year (745). At this time Du Fu wrote two poems concerning their friendship. (Later, about 758, not having heard from Li Bo since their parting, Du Fu wrote his two famous poems entitled "Dreaming of Li Bo—Two Poems.") Sometime between 742 and 745, Du Fu had married and fathered a child. In 746, he and his family moved to Chang'an. There, he once again sought an official appointment.

The years from about 730 to 745 may be taken as the formative stage, or First Period, of Du Fu's poetic development. Yet only four of his poems written during this period are extant. Du Fu's violation of conventional literary techniques can be seen in one of these poems, "A Poetry Contest After Dinner at the Zuo Villa." Here he departs from the traditional decorum of subgenres and their themes, since his poem is both about meeting and about departing. He draws an extensive contrast in comparing the "firmament" to a "thatched roof . . . studded with stars." He also tries to balance the demands of "the book and the sword" (*shu jian*) in the statement "We consult books. . . . We re-examine the sword."

In addition, Du Fu affirms that his victory in the poetry contest (described in the poem) was, in effect, a conquest of Wu. (He wrote that the poem was chanted in the Wu dialect.) It was an action equal to the political and military feats of the heroes of China's antiquity. Du Fu refers to the small boat of Fan Li (fifth century B.C.E.), the minister of Ku Jian, king of Wu. It is said that Fan Li, having enabled his king to gain a military victory, declined a reward for his service and sailed away in a small boat. From this poem, therefore, it is clear—as in "Brave Adventures" and "Song of the White-Headed"—that in the Tang Dynasty (T'ang; 618-907), there was no separation between the scholar and the man of action. Du Fu was a *shi* in the older sense of the Chinese "scholar-knight."

Du Fu spent the years from 746 to 759 in or near Chang'an. For ten years, he indulged in a frustrating effort to get a government post. The reigning emperor, Xuanzong (Hsüan-tsung, r. 712-756), was old and neglectful of public affairs. He left his rule entirely in the hands of a despotic minister, Li Linfu, who had many enemies—especially the heir apparent and his entourage. When Du Fu arrived in the capital, he obtained the patronage of the prince of Ruyang (Ju-yang). Although this connection was politically harmless, Du Fu also had ties with the heir apparent. Li Linfu eventually dispelled members of the heir apparent's entourage. Du Fu had family ties with the despotic minister that saved him from also being banished. Nevertheless, his connection with the heir apparent blocked Du Fu's chances for government service for some time to come.

In 747, Xuanzong held a special examination to discover new talent. Du Fu was again hopeful. Yet, fearful of the success of those taking the exams, Li Linfu arranged that all be failed. During the next three years, Du Fu tried to appeal to the emperor directly. He presented him with works of the *fu* genre that were accompanied by pleas for favor. Finally, he got the emperor's attention with his three *fu* on major rites. In 753, a special examination was prepared for him, and this time he passed. During the next five years, a turbulent period when the heir apparent finally assumed power, Du Fu was given various ceremonial posts. In 758, however, he was ousted when one of his friends fell into disfavor with the emperor.

The years from 746 to 759 constituted the maturing stage, or Second Period, of Du Fu's work as a poet. Generally, in this period he developed a new kind of "realism." His earlier tendency to combine, reconcile, and balance opposing elements—seen earlier in his merging of poetic subgenres and themes and in his balancing of the demands of "the book and the sword"—was expanded and developed in other directions. He mixed prose (*fu*) and verse (*shi*); introduced new "unpoetic'" subjects in combination with old "poetic" ones; merged private circumstances and concerns with public and national ones that embraced political, military, and economic factors; and transposed general descriptive judgments into specific ethical judgments that placed blame directly on specific persons.

Among Du Fu's most outstanding poems of this period are "The Ballad of the War Chariots," "Frontier Duties: Nine Poems," and "Five Hundred Words to Express My Feelings When I Went from the Capital to Fengxian." These first two poems were written toward the end of 750, and the third was written near the end of 755, before Du Fu knew of the outbreak of the rebellion that resulted in the heir apparent's rise to power. When Du Fu was banished from court in 758, he was sent to Huazhou, 60 miles (96 kilometers) east of the capital, to become commissioner of education.

In the early part of 759, Du Fu was sent on a mission to Luoyang. On his way home, he wrote two notable poems on recruiting officers at Xinan and Shihao. Yet not long after his return to Huazhou, he resigned his position, probably because at this time he believed that his official services were futile. Then he and his family set out on a long journey, with pauses of some duration at Tsinchow (modern Tianshui) and Tunggu (modern Zhengzhou). His journey finally ended by wintertime in Chengdu, where the following year he was to occupy his famous thatched hut. Du Fu was forty-eight years old, and he was not in good health. (He had had lung trouble since 754.) Although by this time he had written many distinguished poems, some of Du Fu's greatest poems were yet to come.

During the years from 759 to 770, the Third Period, Du Fu produced an abundance of mature poetry. Although he never actually gave up his ambition to perform public service, it seemed that age and bad health made him more content to devote himself almost entirely to his writings. He was much taken by his thatched hut, located on the outskirts of Chengdu, which he regarded as an ideal hermitage. At least two poems were inspired by the hut's location and completion: "Choice of a Domicile" and "The Hut Completed." "My Thatched Roof Whirled Away by an Autumn Gale" is one of his greatest poems, combining dismay, love, pathos, and the tragedy of aging.

Du Fu's old friend and patron Yan Wu soon was appointed military commissioner of Chengdu. He, in turn, appointed Du Fu to his military staff. Du Fu served Yan as military adviser from 764 to 765, resigning probably because of age and poor health. His ambivalent attitude toward his position can be detected in his poems "Overnight at the General Headquarters" and "Twenty Rhymes to Dispel Gloom: Presented to His Excellency Yan."

Yan Wu died suddenly in 765. It appears that Du Fu had left Chengdu just before his friend's death and at the time was sailing with his family down the Min River on his way to Rongzhou (modern Yibin), in Sichuan. His health failing, Du Fu continued to travel, eventually arriving in Kuizhou (modern Fengjie), Sichuan, to which he refers in his poetry as "the White Emperor's city." He found a generous patron there and stayed for two years. During this time, he wrote a number of distinguished poems: his *lüshi* series "Generals: Five Poems," "Thoughts on Historical Sites: Five Poems," and the series generally regarded as the finest of his masterpieces, "Autumn Thoughts: Eight Poems." He also wrote eight "in memoriam" poems, including a beautiful tribute to his deceased friend Yan Wu.

Old and sick, Du Fu died in Hunan, in the winter of 770. In Du Fu's Third Period, the ill and relatively isolated poet created works that displayed greater technical prowess and a higher level of perfection. The playful representation of the early poems gave way to the rich symbolism of the later ones, syntax became more complex and ambiguous, and realism was transformed into surrealism. The great works of this period are characterized by classical precision in versification and idiosyncratic freedom of diction and syntax.

SIGNIFICANCE

Du Fu's preeminence as a poet is unquestionable. He not only is the most celebrated poet in Chinese literature but also bears comparison to the chief figures of the various national literatures of the West. His literary accomplishment is a major contribution in the formation of literary values generally. Although no coterie formed around him during his time and the impact of his genius was not felt for decades after his death, once his preeminence was apparent, no later Chinese poet could afford to ignore his work.

Du Fu is perhaps the most learned poet of China and its most complicated stylist. His poetry is characterized by recondite allusions; a feeling for the historicity of language; rapid stylistic and thematic shifts; social, political, military, and economic analysis; ethics, cosmology, aesthetics; and a decided interest in historical context. Indeed, this last interest gave him the designation of the *shishi*, or the "poet historian." In his view of old age and of art as timeless and distinct from the changes of life, he resembles William Butler Yeats. In his appreciation of nature, rusticity, and the common man (who, to Du Fu, may be good or evil, as an aristocrat may also be), he resembles William Wordsworth. In his treatment of society and his mockery, bitterness, and humor, he resembles François Villon. In his interest in history, government, and economics, he resembles Ezra Pound.

—*Richard P. Benton*

FURTHER READING

Chou, Eva Shan. *Reconsidering Tu Fu: Literary Greatness and Cultural Context.* New York: Cambridge University Press, 1995. Chou examines the styles and techniques of Du Fu's poetry as well as his literary legacy. Contains some translations of poems. Bibliography and index.

Cooper, Arthur, comp. and trans. *Li Po and Tu Fu: Poems Selected and Translated with an Introduction and Notes.* Harmondsworth, England: Penguin Books, 1973. The translations are generally excellent, and the extensive background material on the history of Chinese poetry and literature is helpful. Discusses Du Fu's connection with Li Po.

Du Fu. *The Selected Poems of Du Fu.* Translated by Burton Watson. New York: Columbia University Press, 2002. A collection of Du Fu's poems, translated into English by a noted specialist on China.

_______. *The Selected Poems of Tu Fu.* Translated by David Hinton. New York: New Directions, 1989. A collection of Du Fu's poetic works, translated into English.

McCraw, David R. *Du Fu's Laments from the South.* Honolulu: University of Hawaii Press, 1992. An examination of Du Fu's travels in Sichuan and his poetic output. Bibliography and indexes.

Pine, Red, trans. *Poems of the Masters: China's Classic Anthology of T'ang and Sung Dynasty Verse.* Port Townsend, Wash.: Copper Canyon Press, 2003. A collection of poetry from the Tang and Song Dynasties that includes the work of Du Fu. Indexes.

Seaton, J. P., and James Cryer, trans. *Bright Moon, Perching Bird: Poems by Li Po and Tu Fu.* Scranton, Pa.: Harper & Row, 1987. This work, part of the Wesleyan Poetry in Translation series, features the works of Li Bo and Du Fu, two Tang poets. Provides some information on Tang Dynasty poetry.

Seth, Vikram, trans. *Three Chinese Poets: Translations of Poems by Wang Wei, Li Bai, and Du Fu*. Boston: Faber and Faber, 1992. A collection of poems by Du Fu, Li Bo, and Wang Wei. Commentary provides useful information.

SEE ALSO: Li Bo; Li Qingzhao; Ouyang Xiu; Sima Guang; Su Dongpo; Wang Wei.

RELATED ARTICLES in *Great Events from History: The Middle Ages, 477-1453*: 618: Founding of the Tang Dynasty; 907-960: Period of Five Dynasties and Ten Kingdoms; 960: Founding of the Song Dynasty; 960-1279: Scholar-Official Class Flourishes Under Song Dynasty.

DUCCIO DI BUONINSEGNA

Italian painter

By blending techniques borrowed from French Gothic, Florentine, and Byzantine art, Duccio created a distinct Sienese style of painting. His attempts at three-dimensionality and his inventive use of architectural structures in his painting influenced future generations of Italian and French artists.

BORN: c. 1255; possibly Siena (now in Italy)
DIED: August 3, 1319; Siena
AREA OF ACHIEVEMENT: Art

EARLY LIFE

The importance of the work of Duccio di Buoninsegna (DEWT-choh dee bwah-neen-SAYN-yah) is often overshadowed in art criticism by the exuberant praise of the work of his contemporary, Giotto, even though many of the works attributed to the latter may not have actually been done by him. Another handicap in the assessment of Duccio's work stems from the fact that he was born in Siena and not Florence, the center of Italian art in the late thirteenth and early fourteenth centuries. According to the art historian John White:

> It is hard to think of any major painter who, when it comes to generalizations about his art, is less appreciated for himself, and on his own terms, and who is more consistently considered in a framework of relative and qualitative comparisons than Duccio.

Of his personal life, little of substance is known. He was married to a woman named Taviana, with whom he had six sons and one daughter. Three of his sons later became painters themselves, yet nothing is known of their lives or work. Duccio's everyday life was apparently filled with numerous confrontations with the rigid stratification of Sienese society. A large number of recorded fines against the young artist have suggested a bohemian lifestyle to some; yet most of the infractions were petty in nature, such as breaking of curfew, failing to attend a public meeting to which he was summoned, and refusing to swear allegiance to a superior. Perhaps Duccio was as independently oriented toward his civic duties as he was toward his art.

Between 1295 and 1302, the artist undertook a series of trips, first to Paris and then to Rome. In Paris, he worked as a miniaturist, or manuscript illuminator. On seeing Chartres Cathedral, located a short distance from the capital city, Duccio succumbed to the spell of French Gothic art. His visit to Chartres profoundly affected his later work, particularly the Rucellai *Madonna*, the only true Gothic painting of the thirteenth century in Italy, which borrows directly from the famous cathedral window "La Belle Verrière." Most experts agree that the artist also traveled to Constantinople about this same time, for few can believe that the Byzantine influences so visible in Duccio's major work could have been acquired at second hand.

By the beginning of the fourteenth century, Duccio had become the head of his own large workshop, which may have included as many as twelve assistants. Although his later life would be spent in constant and profitable work that ultimately permitted him to purchase a small vineyard, not far from Siena, his children renounced his will, for it contained nothing but debts.

LIFE'S WORK

Perhaps as many as nine or ten of Duccio's paintings survive; nevertheless, his reputation hinges on three principal works: the Crevole *Madonna* (1280), the Rucellai *Madonna* (1285), and his masterwork, the climax of his career, the *Maestà* (1308-1311), a representation of the lives of the Madonna and Christ child, created for the Duomo of Siena.

The Crevole *Madonna* clearly shows its Byzantine origins, most notably, in the subtle color alterations of the Madonna's drapery, which range from a gentle pink to dark vermilion, the flowing golden hemline, the soft cream-white tunic of the Christ child, and the crystal blues of the cloaked angels in the corners. The figures themselves reflect the artist's concern for a new humanization of the Holy Mother and Child. The babe is gently extending his right hand to touch the headdress of the Madonna, yet he does not actually touch her face, suggesting both closeness and separation, reminding the viewer of both Christ's Passion and the Holy Mother's intuition of its nature. Despite the charming proportions of Christ's figure, to the modern eye, the infant resembles more a miniature of the adult Christ than an infant.

Even though the work lacks a true three-dimensional character, the chubby, cherublike representation of the child represents one of the earliest attempts at three-dimensionality in painting. Many of the innovations that characterize Duccio's mature work and set him apart from his contemporaries are in evidence here: the close attention to detail, the transparency of the draperies that distinctly reveal the figure of the child, and the precision of the facial tones and lines.

Duccio's second extant masterpiece is the Rucellai *Madonna*, commissioned in Florence on April 15, 1285, for the Chapel of the Laudesi. Signed "Duccio di Buoninsegna, the painter, of Siena," it is a majestic work, measuring 15 feet (4.6 meters) high by 10 feet (3 meters) wide. For several centuries, the work was attributed to the Florentine painter Cimabue, but most twentieth century critics agree that it was done entirely by the hand of Duccio. The work presents the immaculate Virgin Mary and the Christ child surrounded by six angels. An exquisitely feminine Mary, seated on a massive, ornately carved throne done in Byzantine fashion, cradles the child on her left arm. Of particular interest, both historical and aesthetic, is the complex pose of the child, his right arm extending across and away from the Madonna, his legs slightly crooked to convey a comfortable, childlike position of safety on his mother's knees. Of further importance is the absence of eye contact between mother and child, a symbolic foreshadowing of the tragic separation of Christ from the world after the Passion.

Duccio's Gothic heritage is again much apparent in this work. The soft, undulating folds of the Madonna's drapery model the angle of the legs beneath, so that, despite the relative absence of three-dimensional perspective, the position of the limbs beneath the garments is clearly indicated. A gilded hem serpentines across the front of her garment, accentuating the Gothic curves and cascades of material. The six angels, three on either side of the principal figures, seem to be floating in golden air, accentuating their celestial mission; Mary is obviously enthroned in Heaven, not on Earth.

The depiction of the heavenly throne on which Mary is seated reveals the innovation that Duccio was attempting. With consummate finesse, Duccio emphasizes the structural supports of the throne to create a feeling of its massive weight and stability. On observing the celestial throne, one critic noted that Duccio's technique lay "far outside the imaginative range or the executive ability of any of his contemporaries."

Despite the genius of these two early works, it is the *Maestà*, created for the high altar of the chapel of the Duomo of Siena, which has assured Duccio his place among the ranks of such masters as Giotto and Cimabue. The work has an interesting history. On the day that it was carried to the cathedral, June 9, 1311, there was a spectacular procession, as reported by one anonymous chronicler of the time:

> On the day on which it was carried to the Duomo, the shops were locked up and the Bishop ordered a great and devout company of priests and brothers with a solemn procession accompanied by the Signori of the Nine and all the officials of the Commune, and all the populace, and all the most worthy were in order next to the said panel with lights lit in their hands; and then behind were the women and children with much devotion; and they accompanied it right to the Duomo.

The work had taken two years and eight months to complete. The prestigious nature of this commission for Duccio is revealed by the fact that the *Maestà* was to replace a revered Sienese icon.

In 1771, the *Maestà* was sawed into seven pieces and disassembled to make room for a new altarpiece. Although much of the work was returned to the cathedral in 1776, many of the panels have since been scattered to various museums. In the late nineteenth century the major parts of the work were moved from the cathedral to the Museo dell'Opera del Duomo in Siena, where they have remained since.

In its original state, the *Maestà* consisted of one large, two-sided altarpiece. Duccio himself painted only the front panels; the back panels were executed by the numerous apprentices in his workshop. Forty-six panels from the original fifty-four or fifty-eight are extant. Majestic and complex, the work originally stood on a base with seven scenes from the early life of Christ, beginning with the "Annunciation" and ending with the "Teaching in the Temple." The main frontal panel, an expansive paean to the Virgin, centers on the scene of "Virgin Enthroned with Angels and Saints." Above the principal panels are half portraits of those ten apostles not represented in the central panels. Two central panels are missing from the original but were probably the "Assumption" and the "Coronation of the Virgin." These *predella*, independent yet thematically related panels arranged in chronological order, are the earliest extant examples of this technique in Italian art.

On the back are twenty-six scenes from the Passion. The series follows an imaginative order unique to Duccio's work, beginning from the bottom left with the "Entry into Jerusalem" and ending at the top right with the "Apparition on the Road to Emmaus." Six panels at the top complete the sequence. The central panels of the work represent the "Agony in the Garden," "The Betrayal," and "The Crucifixion." Two panels from the main central column are missing but were probably "The Ascension" and "Christ in Majesty."

A masterpiece of painting, architectural construction, and engineering, the *Maestà* required a precision of measurement and awareness of perspective generally unheard of at the time. The overall compositional effectiveness of the work eschews monumentality in favor of an elegant grandeur and scrupulously sustains the symbolic relationships of the various parts to the whole. The entire effect dramatically testifies to the genius of the artist.

Duccio's attention to iconographic and realistic detail, his flawless sense of harmony and unity within complexity, and his surety of line and color combine in the *Maestà* to produce a work of incomparable proportion and beauty. The narrative character of the work is typical of the period in which Duccio was working, yet here again he left his particular imprint. Rather than having the panels relate the story of Christ's life in the traditional, linear fashion, Duccio selected a sort of zigzag pattern to suggest the simultaneity of actions and events in time, as they might actually have occurred.

SIGNIFICANCE

Duccio's recognizable Tuscan style emerged out of subtle blending of the Byzantine mosaic style with French Gothic, Roman, and Florentine influences. In addition to his experimentations with proportion and perspective, and with color, shadings, and line, Duccio introduced several startling compositional innovations into his work. In one of the most famous panels of the *Maestà*, "The Healing of the Man Born Blind," Duccio produced the first surviving example of a cityscape that actually encloses the figures in the foreground. The buildings on the right side of the work, encircling the blind man, seem to lunge forward to frame the work. Although by modern standards these structures still appear flat and disproportionate, and the figures still appear to be pasted over the background, a sense of an enclosed space is dramatically present.

Duccio's attempts to represent coherently the perspective of background structures can also be seen in the panel "Annunciation of the Death of the Virgin," in which the two figures are completely enclosed by an architectural space. Never before had an artist so clearly suggested the three-dimensionality of space on a flat canvas. Always in the past, architectural space had appeared behind the figures. Such experimental techniques greatly hastened the movement of Italian art toward the new kind of realism of the Renaissance.

Although Duccio's direct influence on later generations of Italian artists pales in comparison to that of Giotto, his influence on artists outside Italy, and particularly in France, was significant. In the work of Jean Pucelle, for example, whose Parisian illumination workshop was the most famous in Europe between 1320 and 1350, Duccio's influence is explicitly present. In a well-known Book of Hours, a sort of private prayer book, for Jeanne, queen of France, the "Annunciation" illumination borrows both its composition and its general conception of interior space from the panel of the same name in the *Maestà*. Among the later Italian artists who continued to model on Duccio's work, only one disciple, Simone Martini, achieved any distinction. Although he abandoned Duccio's lyrical style, Martini continued to develop many of the master's techniques.

—*William C. Griffin*

FURTHER READING

Bellosi, Luciano. *Duccio, the Maestà*. New York: Thames and Hudson, 1999. Covers the art of Duccio, in particular the *Maestà*. Bellosi examines the parts of the work, including the Virgin and Child on the main front panel, scenes from the Passion of Christ on the main back panel, scenes from Christ's infancy and his ministry, and apparitions of Christ after the Resurrection. Bibliography and index.

Janella, Cecilia. *Duccio di Buoninsegna*. New York: Riverside, 1991. A biography of the painter Duccio that examines his life and works. Contains color illustrations and bibliography.

Satkowski, Jane. *Duccio di Buoninsegna: The Documents and Early Sources*. Athens, Ga.: Georgia Museum of

Art, 2000. An examination of the early writings on Duccio and of his times. Illustrated. Bibliography and index.

Stubblebine, James H. *Duccio di Buoninsegna and His School*. 2 vols. Princeton, N.J.: Princeton University Press, 1979. Provides a complete and reasoned analysis of Duccio's work, major and minor, and a detailed study of the author's life. Stubblebine meticulously documents the location, size, attribution, condition, and provenance of each of the artist's works, providing a critical evaluation of each. In all cases, the author presents a balanced view of the problems of influences on Duccio's work and on the debates concerning attribution.

Weber, Andrea. *Duccio di Buoninsegna: About 1255-1319*. Koln, Germany: Könemann, 1997. Part of the Masters of Italian Art series, this work examines the life and paintings of Duccio. Contains color illustrations and a bibliography.

See also: Fra Angelico; Cimabue; Donatello; Lorenzo Ghiberti; Giotto; Pietro Lorenzetti and Ambrogio Lorenzetti; Simone Martini; Masaccio; Andrea Orcagna; Jean Pucelle.

Related article in *Great Events from History: The Middle Ages, 477-1453*: 1305-1417: Avignon Papacy and the Great Schism.

John Duns Scotus

Scottish philosopher and theologian

Duns Scotus, with his closely woven synthesis of Scholastic philosophical and theological thought, created the school of Scotism. His rigorous and subtle critical method and fresh theoretical formulations have influenced important thinkers.

Born: c. March, 1266; Duns, Berwick, Scotland
Died: November 8, 1308; Cologne (now in Germany)
Also known as: Doctor Subtilis; Subtle Doctor; Joannes Scotus
Areas of achievement: Philosophy, religion and theology

Early Life

Little is known for certain about the life, early or late, of John Duns Scotus (duhnz SKOHT-uhs), both because of the period in which he was born and because his life was not one of action but of thought; he was a thinker rather than a doer. He was nicknamed by his contemporaries Doctor Subtilis (the Subtle Doctor), a tribute to the keenness of his reasoning as well as to his ability to make fine distinctions of meaning.

Duns Scotus evidently was the son of a well-to-do landowner known as Ninian Duns of Littledean. The Duns family was noted as a longtime benefactor of the Friars Minor, or Franciscans, the religious order founded in 1210 by Saint Francis of Assisi. Since the young Duns Scotus displayed a brilliant intellect as well as pious religious devotion, his uncle, a Franciscan vicar general who was stationed at the friary of Dumfries, arranged for the twelve-year-old student to come to the friary to prepare himself for a religious vocation.

Because Duns Scotus was not yet fifteen, however, he had to wait until 1280 before he could be accepted as a novice friar. In 1282, he became a candidate for the bachelor's degree, which required four years of philosophical training, and had entered Oxford for this purpose, although no extant documentation sustains this assumption. Before his studies were completed, he was ordained into the priesthood at St. Andrew's Church in Northampton on March 17, 1291. Duns Scotus apparently received his bachelor's degree from Oxford in the following year.

In 1293, Duns Scotus was sent to the University of Paris to obtain his master's degree. For some reason, however, he returned in 1296 to Oxford without having completed his master's requirements. At Oxford, he lectured from 1297 to 1301. In 1302, he returned to Paris and resumed his studies. In 1303, however, he was forced to leave the university and return to England because he supported Pope Boniface VIII in the pope's controversy with the French king, Philip IV the Fair. Duns Scotus's presence at Oxford from 1300 to 1301 is documented: His name is listed among the twenty-two Oxford Franciscans who were presented to Bishop Dalderby on July 26, 1300, and a disputation of a master of theology, Philip of Bridington, names Duns Scotus as the bachelor respondent. Following a brief exile, Duns Scotus returned to the University of Paris, where he received his master's degree in 1305.

Duns Scotus was evidently a devout monk, a zealous teacher, and an ambitious writer, but the essence of his personality must be extrapolated from his writing style, which, in general, is impersonal in line with his intention to attain absolute objectivity. Utilizing the dialectical approach to the discussion of a topic, Duns Scotus deliberately suppresses the identities of those with whom he enters into dialogue. Yet despite his meticulous analysis and his effort to be precise, his style is difficult and often obscure. Nevertheless, despite his efforts to be impersonal, his style is not fully dehumanized, however lacking it is in emotion and a sense of humor. Never seeking to portray himself in any favorable light, he sometimes falls from grace and displays pettiness, narrow-mindedness, prejudice, and even fanaticism. In his love of God he was undoubtedly sincere, but a love without a tangible object, whether it be God, the Virgin Mary, or simply everybody, can sometimes, as it appears with Duns Scotus, efface the love of the individual.

His reception of the master's degree from the University of Paris in 1305 stimulated Duns Scotus to ambitious literary activity. Having started on his *Commentaria Oxoniensia ad IV libros magistri Sententiarum* (after 1300; *Proof for the Unicity of God*, 1950; better known as *Ordinatio: Philosophical Writings*, 1962) at Oxford in 1300, he set about to complete this notable work by drawing not only on his original Oxford lecture notes but also on those made at Cambridge (exactly when he taught at Cambridge is not known, but possibly this occurred during his exile) and at Paris. This remarkable commentary, which is also known by the title *Opus Oxoniense*, on Peter Lombard's *Sententiarum libri IV* (c. 1160; *The Books of Opinions of Peter Lombard*, 1970; better known as *Sentences*), has proven to be the most important of his works, although it remained unfinished at his death.

John Duns Scotus. (Library of Congress)

LIFE'S WORK

In 1305, Duns Scotus was appointed regent master in the Franciscan chair at the University of Paris, and he lectured and disputed there in this capacity until 1307. During this period, Duns Scotus conducted several disputations worthy of note. In one, he locked horns with the Dominican master Guillaume Pierre Godin, regarding the principle of individuation, or what makes one thing different from another of the same species. Godin held that matter was the principle of individuation. Duns Scotus denied that that was so, believing instead that it was neither matter nor form nor quantity. Rather, he contended, the principle of individuation was a property in itself that was added to the others. Scotists later referred to this property as the *haecceitas*, that is, the "thisness" of a thing, which individualized it. At the same time, Duns Scotus recognized that individualized created natures must have some common denominator if scientific knowledge were to be gained of them.

Duns Scotus also conducted an important quodlibetal disputation. This was a disputation in which the master accepted questions of any kind on any topic (*de quodlibet*) and from any bachelor or master present (*a quodlibet*). Duns Scotus accepted twenty-one such questions to be disputed that concerned God and creatures. Later, he revised, enlarged, and organized them into a work called *Quaestiones Quodlibetales* (1306; *The Quodlibetal Questions*, 1975). As with his *Ordinatio*, however, he left this work unfinished at his death. Nevertheless, the *The Quodlibetal Questions* proved scarcely less important than the *Ordinatio*. Indeed, the former represented his most advanced thinking. Altogether, his fame depends chiefly on these two works.

Another important disputation in which Duns Scotus engaged at this time was his defense of his theory of the Immaculate Conception. During the Middle Ages, many doctors of the Church were disturbed by the very idea of the Immaculate Conception. Was not Mary a product of human propagation? Was she therefore not a child of Adam and Eve, one who had inherited the original sin of her primordial parents? If so, did she not need Christ as her Redeemer? Therefore, how could Mary, virgin birth notwithstanding, have been free of original sin at her conception of Christ? Although Duns Scotus agreed with the skeptics that Mary would necessarily have needed Christ as her Redeemer, he proposed that mother and Son had been united in the Incarnation and Redemption by virtue of divine predestination and hence were joined together in their life, mission, and privileges. Therefore, he concluded, Mary had been preserved from both original and actual sin by Christ's Redemption. This theory, however, was not received well by Duns Scotus's secular and Dominican colleagues and was heatedly debated. Indeed, the idea of the Immaculate Conception continued to be controversial for five centuries before it became approved Catholic dogma.

Although Duns Scotus worked out of the Augustinian-Franciscan tradition, he was influenced by a variety of predecessors. He belongs to no particular school except the one he founded. Among the ancient Greeks, he drew mostly on Aristotle; among the Apostles, he favored Saint Paul; among the Evangelists, he preferred Saint John the Divine; among the later Peripatetics, he was stimulated by Porphyry (a disciple of Plotinus); among the Latin fathers, he drew heavily on Saint Augustine of Hippo, Africa; among the Arabians of the East, he was mostly indebted to Avicenna; among the Franciscan school, he was attracted to Saint Bonaventura; among the Dominican school, he paid particular attention to Saint Thomas Aquinas; and among the Neo-Augustinians, he followed closely the doctrine of the secular Henry of Ghent.

Near the end of 1307, Duns Scotus was suddenly called away from Paris, having been unexpectedly appointed to a professorship at Cologne, Germany. According to some scholars, the reason for this abrupt departure is that his teacher and loyal friend, Master Gonsalvus of Balboa, had transferred him to Germany because he feared for his protégé's life, given the heated resistance to his defense of the Immaculate Conception. Duns Scotus's theory at this time seemed to many to conflict with the Church's doctrine of Christ's universal redemption, and he had been hotly challenged by his secular and Dominican colleagues. Indeed, at one quodlibetal disputation the secular master Jean de Pouilly had denounced the thesis as heretical and hinted that Duns Scotus deserved severe punishment. Under these circumstances, Duns Scotus's life was surely in danger if a charge of heresy could have been proved against him.

In any case, Duns Scotus had not long to live. He lectured at Cologne until near the end of 1308, when he died November 8 at the age of forty-two. His body was buried in the Franciscan church at Cologne, where it still lies. Although canonical proceedings for his beatification have been initiated twice since his death, he has never been canonized by the Church. In the Franciscan order he is known as "Blessed" Duns Scotus, and his name is included in the Franciscan martyrology. He is also thus venerated in the German dioceses of Cologne and Nola.

The basis of Duns Scotus's metaphysics is "being" (*ens*). For him, being is the primary object of human intellect. He distinguishes, however, between spiritual and material being. God, the Divine Spirit, is the Supreme Being, that is, God is "pure" being, self-generated and uncreated. Although angels are in like manner immaterial, their spirit is less pure than that of the Divine Spirit; having been created, they are distanced from God. The human soul is also immaterial; breathed into the body by God to give it life, it lodges temporarily in its prison house, further distanced from "pure" being until it is released by death.

For Duns Scotus, all created substances are composed of matter (*materia*) and form (*forma*). He calls the common substrate of all created beings *materia prima*. Passive and receptive to corporeal forms, it is the subject of substantial and accidental change without the mediation of any substantial form. In other words, it is a *terminus creationis*. Duns Scotus insists on the unity and homogeneity of matter in all created beings. Everything that is created partakes univocally of this *materia prima*, which is indeterminate, matter without form, and only just removed from "nothing."

Duns Scotus distinguishes between "essence" (what makes a thing what it is) and "existence" (actual being). Between the two, he holds, is a *distinctio formalis a parte rei*, a formal property that is partly logical and partly real. Because an imaginary being has essence without having existence, however, substance (*substancia*) is an essence that has existence. In attempting to solve the questions of what gives existence to an essence and what constitutes the individual thing, Duns Scotus proposes that every created thing is composed of two realities: the "universal" and the "particular." The universal essence is the *natura* (what is common to all concrete realities of the same species). It is "form" that confers *natura* on matter. Form and matter constitute concrete substance in the "real" world, or what is taken to be reality. Matter in itself is indeterminate, but form is determining. It is form that communicates being to matter by determining "genus" and "species." Compounded, form and matter make a "unity." It is *haecceitas*, however—the principle of individuation—that confers singularity and uniqueness on a thing. Thus haecceity, like matter and form, has its own unity. According to Duns Scotus, between the *natura* and the *haecceitas* is a difference that is partly conceptional but is also partly an objective ground in reality itself and independent of the mind. The unity of this composite is less than the numerical unity of the individual as such. What actually constitutes the individual as a concrete object is neither matter nor form nor *compositum* as such, for all three of these factors can be conceived of logically as universals. Hence the singular and unique thing is a composite of this matter, this form, and this *compositum*. Duns Scotus's view that the universal has an objective ground in reality is termed in philosophy "moderate realism."

The concepts described above are among the most important speculations in Duns Scotus's philosophy. Others of similar importance include his theory of the "plurality of forms," which he applies only to organic creation. His conception is that the essence of the whole contains the essences of all the parts and includes a plurality of partial forms. All beings that possess life share in this plurality. Another significant theory is Duns Scotus's idea of the "hierarchy of forms." He arranges the forms in their order of perfection. The perfection of a form depends on its distance or separation from matter, that is, the range from corporeal matter to the matter or stuff of which spirits are composed. The further a form is separated from corporeal matter, the more potent is its activity. Duns Scotus's theory of the plurality of forms must be distinguished from his theory of formalities and his concept of *distinctio formalis*. In this theory, he distinguishes the forms of the intellect (*distinctio rationis tantum*) from those that are "real" (*distinctio realis*) and their merely physical counterparts, or *res*. Although the idea of the plurality of forms is a metaphysical concept, that of the formalities and of *distinctio formalis* is a logical one.

Although in modern times, Duns Scotus has been admired principally for his philosophy, by profession he was a theologian. Although he considered philosophy to be the foundation of theology, at the same time he viewed the former as inferior to the latter. Only theology, he held, can solve the mysteries of religion, but it must be aided by divine revelation if certainty is to be attained, for human reason alone cannot prove the omnipotence of God or the immortality of the human soul. In philosophy, he is an empiricist in affirming that all knowledge comes through the senses and that knowledge of the particulars of sense is the foundation of higher cognition, and hence of the natural sciences and scientific knowing. In his division of the speculative sciences, his placing of logic midway between grammar and metaphysics shows his awareness of their close connection. In this way he acknowledges the importance of language in philosophical discussion.

SIGNIFICANCE

Duns Scotus, an heir to the Augustinian-Franciscan tradition, founded the Scholastic school of Scotism. Franciscan teachers tended to follow his lead. In the fourteenth century, the principle Scotists were Francis of Mayron and Antonio Andrea. During the fourteenth and the fifteenth centuries appeared the following Scotists: John of Basoles, John Dumbleton, Walter Burleigh, Alexander of Alessandria, Lychetus of Brescia, and Nicholas De Orbellis. Among the Scotists of the period that marks the transition from Scholasticism to modern philosophy were John the Englishman, Johannes Magistri, Antonius Trombetta, and Maurice the Irishman. Because Duns Scotus rejected the principle that all bodies are moved by other bodies as a physical proof of God's existence and viewed corporeal substance more dynamically, some scholars have declared that the tendency of his physics prefigured that of the German philosopher and mathematician Gottfried Wilhelm Leibniz. Duns Scotus has also been called the Immanuel Kant of Scholastic philosophy because he resembles Kant in his refusal to accept without criticism any theory, regardless of its popularity or how strongly it was supported by the authority of great names. Here the resemblance stops, perhaps, because for Kant the supreme tribunal was moral consciousness, whereas for Duns Scotus it was divine revelation.

The high quality of Duns Scotus's thought is further attested by his influence on modern philosophers and literary figures of the nineteenth and twentieth centuries. His voluntarism (which he owes to Henry of Ghent) prefigured that of Arthur Schopenhauer, Eduard von Hartmann, and Friedrich Nietzsche, although whether they were familiar with his work is uncertain. He has, however, exerted a direct influence on such thinkers as Charles Sanders Peirce, Martin Heidegger, Pierre Teilhard de Chardin, Gerard Manley Hopkins, and Thomas Merton.

Duns Scotus is not, therefore, simply another medieval Scholastic. His philosophy contains much that is original, even unique. Emphasizing criticism, his thinking displayed rigor as well as subtlety and depth as well as brilliance. It is true that he composed no single work in which the whole of his philosophy is clearly set forth as a system; nevertheless, a fairly well-rounded system can be extracted from his two major works, *Ordinatio* and *The Quodlibetal Questions*. Duns Scotus had the courage of his convictions and mercilessly attacked those masters whom he considered either inconclusive or erroneous in their thinking. He cared not that their schools might be distinguished or that their names were authoritative and prestigious.

—*Richard P. Benton*

FURTHER READING

Bettoni, Efrem. *Duns Scotus: The Basic Principles of His Philosophy*. Edited by Bernardine Bonansea. Washington, D.C.: Catholic University of America Press, 1961. Simple, relatively nontechnical, and clear exposition of Duns Scotus's ontology, epistemology, theology, and ethics.

Campbell, Bertrand James. *The Problem of One or Plural Substantial Forms in Man as Found in the Works of St. Thomas Aquinas and John Duns Scotus*. Paterson, N.J.: St. Anthony Guild Press, 1940. Compares and contrasts the Thomistic theory of the unity of form with the Scotist theory of the plurality of forms and their bearing on their respective cosmologies, especially in the concepts of space and time.

Frank, William A., and Allan B. Wolter. *Duns Scotus, Metaphysician*. West Lafayette, Ind.: Purdue University Press, 1995. Part of the History of Philosophy series, includes chapters on Duns Scotus's metaphysics, his ideas on the existence of God, and his epistemology.

Ryan, J. K., and B. W. Bonansea, eds. *John Scotus, 1265-1965*. Washington, D.C.: Catholic University of America Press, 1965. Fifteen essays by distinguished Scotist scholars covering a wide range of philosophical and theological topics.

Williams, Thomas, ed. *The Cambridge Companion to Duns Scotus*. New York: Cambridge University Press, 2003. Essays cover Duns Scotus's ideas about space and time, universals and individuation, philosophy of language and mind, cognition, natural law, and more.

SEE ALSO: Avicenna; Henry de Bracton; Saint Francis of Assisi; Philip IV the Fair.

RELATED ARTICLE in *Great Events from History: The Middle Ages, 477-1453*: 1328-1350: Flowering of Late Medieval Physics.

JOHN DUNSTABLE

English composer

Dunstable was the first great English composer and one of the most influential composers of the fifteenth century. His strategic use of dissonance and harmonic structure laid the foundation for music in the Renaissance.

BORN: c. 1390; probably Dunstable, Bedfordshire, England
DIED: December 24, 1453; probably London, England
ALSO KNOWN AS: John Dunstaple
AREA OF ACHIEVEMENT: Music

EARLY LIFE

Though he is unquestionably the first great English composer in the history of music and an important link between the medieval and Renaissance styles, little is known about the life and career of John Dunstable (DUHN-stuh-buhl). This uncertainty is not surprising when one considers the status of musicians and composers in the medieval period—a status on a level with those anonymous craftsmen and artisans who designed and built the great cathedrals of the era or who worked diligently for their masters or in the service of the Church, the great stabilizing institution of the period.

Still, there is much circumstantial evidence that teases the imagination. A Latin inscription on the cover of an astronomy book states that the volume belonged to a John Dunstable, musician in the service of the duke of Bedford. The duke was the brother of Henry V, king of England from 1413 to 1422, and served as regent to the king's nephew, Henry VI, in "occupied" France from 1422 until his own death in 1435. If, as seems likely, Dunstable, as court musician, accompanied Bedford to France, this period would be the earliest record of Dunstable's career, however speculative. It was during this period, interestingly, that Joan of Arc was captured by the English forces under Bedford and burned at the stake in 1431.

What Dunstable's formative years were and what

training he received are unknown, but his connection with astronomy suggests that he was a learned man, probably versed in the other medieval academic disciplines of mathematics, arithmetic, and certainly music. The breadth of his learning is supported by one of several epitaphs written in Latin that commemorates Dunstable as "an astrologian, a mathematician, a musician and what not."

Just when he began to compose is also problematic, but scholars have compared his work with some of the most important sources of the period, particularly the Old Hall manuscript, containing pieces by English composers, and the evidence is strong that his first work began to appear about 1415.

Ironically, the only fact about Dunstable's life that is certain is the date of his death. Once again, an epitaph provides the information. Taken from the church in which Dunstable was buried, the Latin inscription declares him to be the glory of music, who passed among the constellation of the stars, "on the day before Christ's birthday," 1453.

Life's Work

The extent of Dunstable's influence on the development of Western music may be gauged by, among other things, the famous assessment of Johannes Tinctoris, a Renaissance musicologist who wrote *De inventione et usu musicae* (c. 1487; on the discovery and practice of music) and was the editor of one of the first musical dictionaries. He affirmed Dunstable to be the founder of "the English style" of music, which spread to the Continent and which became the standard of artistic achievement. Tinctoris had even let his enthusiasm for Dunstable's work lead him to declare that nothing in music was worth hearing before Dunstable's time. As overripe as Tinctoris's esteem might appear, however, the existence of manuscripts of Dunstable's works on the Continent, particularly in Italy, attests his influence and importance as a transmitter of this new style.

Both the variety and the number of his compositions are impressive. His works total about seventy-five pieces. All of them are for voices alone (*a cappella*), mostly for two or three parts, and the majority are religious works intended for church use, though not necessarily for any specific liturgical event. As with most music before 1500 or so, the human voice was the primary medium of expression, and though there was a significant production in secular music as early as the fourteenth century, vocal music centering on the church service was the primary focus of most serious composers.

The Latin church music of Dunstable shows a mastery of the polyphonic vocal technique then reaching its flowering. Originating sometime around the eleventh century, polyphony is the simultaneous singing of two or more independent melodies. By the fourteenth century, the texture of much polyphonic writing had become rigid, complex, and technically dense. Working within his English musical traditions, Dunstable produced compositions that were freer, less obtuse, and structurally clearer than much of the work of other composers. The key to this clarity was his control of dissonance.

To the modern ear, much medieval music sounds somehow unresolved. In that period before a major and minor tonal system (a development of the Baroque period, beginning about 1600), the melodic progression of a musical composition often depended on the main melody, called the *cantus firmus*, which was supported by a second, third, or fourth voice. These voices, or parts, often embroidered the *cantus firmus* so heavily that the work resulted in a rhythmic density, technically brilliant but hard to follow. Such a density is typical, for example, of the French polyphonic tradition of the fourteenth century, called *ars nova*.

Dunstable freed polyphonic writing from this density. By taking control of the dissonance inherent in such embroidery, he simplified the melodic progression and created work of unmatched sonority. His hymn *Ave maris stella* is an excellent example of controlled dissonance, an innovation that looked ahead to the harmonic principles of a later generation.

Several types of compositions distinguish the work of Dunstable. The largest group can be classified as ballades, freestyle compositions whose origins are in the secular music of the previous century. Dunstable's ballades are characterized by a clear melody carried by one or more voices and are largely songs in praise of the Virgin. Such works as *Sancta Maria, non est*, *Salve Mater*, and *Salve Regina* are obvious examples of Dunstable's skillful adaptation of secular models for sacred purposes. Like his other works in general, these are marked at once by their seeming spontaneity, their sonority, and their melodic charm.

Dunstable's most complex works are motets. One of the most important medieval and Renaissance forms, the motet is a polyphonic composition using a biblical text. Sometimes a different, though complementary, text was assigned to each voice. Dunstable wrote more than a dozen motets in what is called isorhythmic structures, a precisely mathematical form in which the main melody is repeated several times, along with the rhythmic pattern, though the time values of the notes are proportionately reduced as the music progresses, the voices now coming together, now separating. Highly sophisticated, such works as *Veni Sancte Spiritus* (1431?) established Dunstable as one of the century's leading composers. The arithmetical precision of these motets strengthens the validity of those epitaphs that praise him as a mathematician.

For all the complexity of such isorhythmic motets, Dunstable also produced, probably between 1420 and 1435, a number of declamatory motets that scholars praise as his most original contribution to the form. His most famous of this type is *Quam pulcra es*. In this motet, the rhythm is allowed to take the pattern demanded by the text, following the natural inflections and accents of the voice. Melody is thus subordinated to the sense and rhythm of the words, and the result is an expressiveness unmatched in the period. There is a quality of improvisation in these works, an easy freedom that anticipates much of the music of the Renaissance.

Finally, Dunstable seems to have been among the earliest composers to attempt a musical unification of the Mass. Previous to him, the sung parts of the Mass—such as the Kyrie, the Gloria, and the Credo—were conceived as independent, unrelated musical structures. Though the French composer Guillaume de Machaut (c. 1300-1377) is generally credited with producing the first polyphonic setting of the complete Mass in 1364, the thematic unity of the work is questioned by some scholars, and the piece is, in any case, virtually unique amid the composer's vast body of secular compositions. Dunstable's work, however, shows a clear attempt at thematic unification of the various parts of the Mass. His *Rex seculorum* Mass unites the five sections—Kyrie, Gloria, Credo, Sanctus, and Agnus Dei—through the use of a single common melody. The music is clear, expressive, and remarkably sonorous.

Little evidence suggests that Dunstable composed after the death of Bedford in 1435. Some scholars speculate that he "retired" to London to pursue his astronomical studies, especially in the light of a book of astronomical treatises to which he contributed about 1440. Certainly he was well known on the Continent by that date and was already being praised as a musical genius. By the time of his death, in 1453, the Renaissance was in full flower.

SIGNIFICANCE

Dunstable was the acknowledged leader of a group of English composers at the end of the Middle Ages who were writing polyphonic compositions indigenous to their own musical tradition. In style and technique, the music was basically conservative, but there was an emphasis on the use of certain chords and harmonic structures that came closer to modern musical techniques than to any other music produced at that time.

The particular distinction of this English school was its development of what is called a "pan-consonant" style—music characterized by a freer melodic line, a more impromptu and spontaneous use of rhythm, a greater flexibility in the arrangement and grouping of the voices, and, especially in the case of Dunstable, a control of dissonance—what to a modern ear are those harsh and unresolved notes that do not seem to harmonize with the basic melody.

Like Johann Sebastian Bach, composing some three hundred years after him, Dunstable was less an innovator than a great synthesizer. He built his music on an older tradition, fusing it with newer elements from the French and Italian schools, and produced something fresh and original, works of unusual sweetness and euphony.

Dunstable's musical strategy was toward clarity and simplicity. If much of the polyphonic music of the era can be compared to massive cathedrals of sound, aesthetically analogous to those stone-hewn monuments of prayer that are the glories of medieval architecture, then Dunstable's music can be viewed as a magnificent church, lighter, less stupefying, but more personal, more intimate, and still wonderfully crafted.

Coming at the end of the Middle Ages, Dunstable's music is a summation of much that went before and an affirmation of what was to come: a perfect transition between the medieval and Renaissance styles. Ironically, after his own time, little of his music was known until the end of the nineteenth century, and the complete edition of Dunstable's works was not published until 1953, some four hundred years after his death.

—*Edward Fiorelli*

FURTHER READING

Bent, Margaret. *Dunstaple*. New York: Oxford University Press, 1981. A brief, close study of the technical aspects of Dunstable's work, intended largely for the student of music rather than the general reader.

Carlerius, Egidius, Johannes Tinctoris, and Carlo Valguilo. *"That Liberal and Virtuous Art": Three Humanist Treatises on Music*. Edited and translated by J. Donald Cullington. Newtonabbey, Ireland: University of Ulster, 2001. A translation of three fifteenth century treatises on church music by important musicologists of the time.

Davey, Henry. *History of English Music*. 1895. Reprint. New York: Da Capo Press, 1969. An enthusiastic account of the composer and his music.

Grout, Donald J., and Claude V. Palisca. *A History of Western Music*. 6th ed. New York: W. W. Norton, 2001. Text includes an entry discussing Dunstable and his contributions to the history of Western music.

Harrison, Frank L. *Music in Medieval Britain*. New York: Praeger, 1959. A pioneering and exhaustive look at English choral and vocal music from the Norman Conquest to about 1550.

Reese, Gustave. *Music in the Middle Ages*. New York: W. W. Norton, 1940. An excellent, thorough study of the range of Western music up to the Renaissance. The final chapters deal with polyphony in England and the death of Dunstable and suggest a creative cross-pollination between Continental and English composers.

Walker, Ernest. *A History of Music in England*. 3d ed. London: Oxford University Press, 1952. Contains an early chapter on Dunstable and the period.

SEE ALSO: Adam de la Halle; Henry V; Henry VI; Francesco Landini; Guillaume de Machaut; Johannes de Muris; Pérotin; Philippe de Vitry.

RELATED ARTICLE in *Great Events from History: The Middle Ages, 477-1453*: c. 1350-1400: Petrarch and Boccaccio Recover Classical Texts.

EDWARD THE CONFESSOR
King of England (r. 1043-1066)

Edward served as the focus of a series of events that culminated in one of the most significant episodes in English history, the Norman Conquest of England.

BORN: c. 1005; Islip, Oxfordshire, England
DIED: January 5, 1066; London, England
ALSO KNOWN AS: Eadward
AREA OF ACHIEVEMENT: Government and politics

EARLY LIFE

Edward's succession to the English throne involved an interesting intertwining of persons and politics. Edward was the son of Ethelred II, the Unready, king of Anglo-Saxon England from 979 to 1016, and his second wife, Emma, descended from the Norman aristocracy. Ethelred, beset by personal, political, and military difficulties, lost England to invading Danes. The Anglo-Saxon throne fell into the hands of Canute the Great, who attempted to forestall the claims of Ethelred's son to the throne by marrying the late king's widow; the marriage produced a son, Harthacnut, who preceded Edward to the throne and ruled England from 1040 to 1042. Emma, queen to two kings and queen mother to another, had personally and politically gravitated toward the northern Scandinavian political orbit. She had favored Edward's younger half brother over her firstborn son. Even after Edward had become king, she intrigued with another Scandinavian king (Magnus of Norway) to invade England.

Emma's political machinations, however, were thwarted by the Anglo-Danish aristocracy that had been developing in England since the time of Canute's ascendancy to the throne. It favored the ancient native dynasty. That aristocracy used the Anglo-Saxon national assembly, the Witan, which formally chose the king, to bring Edward to the English throne, bypassing both Edmund the Exile, the grandson of Ethelred from his first marriage who was living in Hungary, and any of the possible Scandinavian claimants or intriguers to the throne.

Edward had lived in exile in Normandy from 1013 until 1041. In 1041, King Harthacnut invited his half brother to England and adopted him as a member of the royal household. Edward had probably been forwarded as Harthacnut's heir. The Witan elected Edward king by popular acclaim on Harthacnut's death and even before his burial. Edward was crowned on Easter, 1043, at Winchester.

Edward's character is probably best described as enigmatic. The modern interpretations vary from a king who was a half-witted ascetic to a king who showed some ability early in his reign but in the later years was dominated by a tendency to allow things to slide. A contemporary of Edward noted that he was terrible in anger and compared him in that state to a lion. On several occasions, he did strike hard at his enemies. The consensus is that he was basically a weak personality, normally lazy, with only flashes of assertive, strong character.

LIFE'S WORK

Having lived for approximately twenty-eight years in Normandy, Edward became king of a country that was foreign to him. It was made even more foreign by the changes that had occurred during his exile. The government of Canute had produced the growth of a strong Anglo-Danish aristocracy that was politically dominated by powerful earls, now the nation's chief warriors and statesmen. The earls had no real affection for or historical attachment to Edward's dynasty. Throughout his reign, Edward had to deal with this group of families firmly established in their regional spheres of influence.

Most influential and most powerful among those families was the house of Godwin, earl of Wessex. By 1018, Godwin, an Anglo-Saxon who had little ancestral claim to political influence, had become a trusted counselor of King Canute and a chief adviser in the last years of his reign. Following Canute's death, Godwin allied with Emma to support the claim of Harthacnut, her son by Canute, to the throne. Godwin, however, switched to Harthacnut's rival Harold, the son of Canute and Ælfgifu of Northampton, once Harold's faction had gained political control. Godwin's activities in support of Harold included the arrest and surrender to Harold's control of the atheling (prince) Alfred, the younger son of Ethelred and Emma, the younger brother of Edward, and the half brother of Harthacnut. Alfred was killed at Harold's instigation. Godwin was subsequently prosecuted by Harthacnut once he became king. The earl's complicity in the murder of Edward's brother certainly had a disturbing effect on the relations between Godwin and Edward. There is no indication that Godwin resisted the popular enthusiasm that brought Edward to the throne. Godwin, moreover, was one of the leading men who accompanied Edward in 1043 when he confiscated his mother's property and lands, an act that probably was prompted by Emma's support of Magnus of Norway's claim to the throne.

Godwin's strength continued to grow in the early years of Edward's reign. In 1043, Sweyn, his eldest son, was raised to an earldom and his younger son Harold became earl of Essex, East Anglia, Cambridgeshire, and Huntingdonshire. In 1045, his daughter Edith married the king. By the end of 1050, Godwin had become the king's most prominent subject. His family had extensive lands, his own earldom extended across the south of England from Kent to Cornwall, and he had even managed to secure the recall of his disreputable eldest son Sweyn. Sweyn had seduced an abbess before abandoning his earldom and, after living in exile, had returned to England only to murder his cousin Earl Beorn and be declared a "nithing" for his atrocious treachery; he therefore again had to flee. Sweyn, twice banished, on recall was given an earldom that included the shires of Somerset, Berkshire, Hereford, Gloucester, and Oxford.

With powerful aristocrats such as the Godwin family and others such as Leofric of Mercia and Siward of Northumbria, who were strong enough at times to neutralize the Godwin power, Edward had to face serious challenges to his political control. He was a king in an unfamiliar country surrounded by trying political conditions. His search for things familiar only brought more problems.

Engraved sigillum, or seal, containing the likeness of Edward the Confessor. (Library of Congress)

In an unfamiliar country, surrounded by aristocrats with their own agendas and probably uncomfortable with manners strange to him, Edward was partial to Normans and things Norman. Yet because Germans, Lotharingians, Flemings, French, and Bretons were also among those welcomed by the king, it was important not to give special prominence to the Norman contingent. Still, Edward did choose to have Normans around him in his household, and he did at times reward them. Three Norman churchmen were apparently most influential: Ulf, bishop of Dorchester; William, bishop of London; and most notably, Robert of Jumieges, archbishop of Canterbury, because of his ecclesiastical position and his acknowledged leadership in the king's attack on Godwin.

Edward's apparent fondness for the Normans eventually produced a native resurgence. After breaking the strength of Godwin's power, forcing Godwin's family to flee into exile and dispatching his queen (Godwin's daughter) to a nunnery, the king offended native sensitivities by his increased patronage of individual Normans. His appointment of Normans as sheriffs became especially offensive when they failed in their attempts to administer a strange system of laws in a strange land. A more serious affront to native pride was the king's initiation of an attempt at devolving the English crown to the duke of Normandy. Unfortunately, the king's moments of real control of the kingdom and the problem of political succession coincided in the events of 1051 and 1052.

The developing problem of succession perhaps also owed its beginnings to Edward's long exile in Normandy. An unmarried man approaching his forties when he was crowned king, Edward may not have taken a vow of chastity as a youth (there were tales that he had been placed in a monastery at an early age), but there is no evidence that he had been much interested in women. His eventual marriage to Edith had produced no children by 1051. He was approaching his fifties, and it was perhaps most obvious to Edward himself that steps must be taken to provide for a successor. In 1052, the awkward problem of the succession to the throne was addressed. His search for a successor led him to look to Normandy and its duke.

By 1052, Edward effectively appointed William, duke of Normandy, heir to the throne. If one can believe William of Normandy's court biographer William of Poitier, Edward chose William because of kinship, past favors, and the

DANISH KINGS OF ENGLAND, 1016-1066

Reign	*Monarch*
1016-1035	CANUTE THE GREAT
1035-1040	Harold I Harefoot
1040-1042	Harthacnut
1043-1066	EDWARD THE CONFESSOR
1066	HAROLD II

Note: Both Edward and Harold II were of mixed Danish and Saxon ancestry.

duke's suitability. William of Normandy was Edward's first cousin once removed (his grandfather Richard II of Normandy, and Edward's mother, Emma of Normandy, were brother and sister). Edward had been given refuge in Normandy, and he may have received Norman aid for the expedition that he led to England in 1035. In addition, Norman assistance could have been offered to Edward to address his diplomatic difficulties in the late 1040's. The childless king might have used the promise of succession as a diplomatic asset. Most important, the powerful Godwin had been removed from the political scene.

Meanwhile, Godwin was able to use the growing native sentiment to regain his position in the kingdom's politics, but he died shortly after being restored to prominence. Godwin's son Harold, extremely competent in things political, administrative, and military, was able to assume the leadership of this powerful Godwin family and eventually position himself to secure election to the throne. The inevitability of eventual confrontation between Harold and William of Normandy for the English throne was becoming evident. Edith was returned from her sentence in the nunnery to take her place again as queen. The Normans were removed from their positions. Edward's influence in government and politics was in decline; no longer would he attempt to control, and his reliance on the Godwin family increased. In Normandy, William, with the beginnings of a claim to the English throne, would develop his political strength, and, helped by diplomatic luck, he would launch the Norman Conquest of England in 1066.

In the last years of his reign, Edward appears to have focused primarily on his plans to rebuild the poverty-stricken abbey at Westminster. His abbey, constructed in the Norman Romanesque style with round arches and built solidly of stone, was completed in 1065 and consecrated on December 28. Unfortunately, the king was too ill to attend the event. Edward died on January 5, 1066, and was buried in Westminster Abbey. Thus he was able to be surrounded by something familiarly Norman (at least until it was restructured by Henry III).

SIGNIFICANCE

Edward the Confessor's reign was significant for providing the setting for one of the great transitional events in English history. Although the personal influence of Edward was minute, he was the ingredient that brought important historical forces into a developing process culminating with the conquest of England by William of Normandy.

Edward the Confessor has enjoyed a good reputation, if an exaggerated one, in English history. His memory has benefited from the praise of monastic writers, especially the monastic writers of Normandy. His rapid elevation to sainthood (he was canonized in 1161) only served to heighten his reputation. In his last years, Edward grew increasingly religious, mystical, and removed from his world. His appearance, particularly his long white hair and beard (he has been described as a truc albino), produced a superstitious aura. He revealed his dreams and proclaimed his visions: He dreamed that the Seven Sleepers of Ephesus had all turned on their left side; on his death bed, he was said to have foretold England's future as dark and troubled. During his lifetime, people had flocked to be touched by the king so that they could be cured of scrofula; they continued to flock to his tomb after his death, and miracles were said to take place there. His tomb at Westminster became an altar-tomb confessionary, which accounts for the epithet by which he became known to later generations.

—Dale E. Landon

FURTHER READING

Ælred of Rievaulx, Saint. *The Life of Edward, King and Confessor.* Translated by Jerome Bertram. Southampton, England: Saint Austin Press, 1997. A biographical look at Edward's life and reign by his near contemporary, the abbot of Rievaulx.

Barlow, Frank. *Edward the Confessor.* Berkeley: University of California Press, 1970. A careful, scholarly, and credible study of Edward that contains many discussions of source problems.

Douglas, D. "Edward the Confessor, Duke William of Normandy, and the English Succession." *English Historical Review* 68 (1953): 526-545. A leading scholar of the Normans presents the case for the story of the succession promise as presented by the Norman chronicler William of Jumieges.

O'Brien, Bruce R. *God's Peace and King's Peace: The Laws of Edward the Confessor.* Philadelphia: University of Pennsylvania Press, 1999. Includes a translation of *Leges Edwardi Confessoris* (laws of Edward the Confessor) and chapters on connections between God's peace (religion) and king's peace in England during Edward's time.

Scholz, B. W. "The Canonization of Edward the Confessor." *Speculum* 26 (1961): 38-60. Investigates the purpose of Edward's canonization.

Stenton, Frank M. *Anglo-Saxon England.* 3d ed. New York: Oxford University Press, 1989. The classic study of Anglo-Saxon England, essential for understanding the forces in Edward's lifetime.

Walker, David. *The Normans in Britain.* Cambridge, Mass.: Blackwell, 1995. An overview of the Anglo-Norman period in England, Scotland, Ireland, and Wales, beginning with the Battle of Hastings.

SEE ALSO: Canute the Great; Ethelred II, the Unready; Harold II; Henry I; William the Conqueror.

RELATED ARTICLES in *Great Events from History: The Middle Ages, 477-1453*: 1016: Canute Conquers England; October 14, 1066: Battle of Hastings.

EDWARD THE ELDER

King of England (r. 899-924)

Building on the success of his father, Alfred the Great, and working in close collaboration with his sister Queen Æthelflæd, Edward defeated all Viking kingdoms and coalitions in England and moved toward the political unification of the country.

BORN: 870?; place unknown
DIED: July 17, 924; Farndon-on-Dee, Chester, England
ALSO KNOWN AS: Eadward; Eadweard
AREAS OF ACHIEVEMENT: Government and politics, military

EARLY LIFE

What little is known of King Edward's early life suggests a multitude of threats and pressures. He was the son of Alfred the Great, king of Wessex, and Ealhswith, the Mercian noblewoman whom Alfred had married in 868. Because Edward was in command of an army in 893, he must have been born fairly soon after the marriage. In these years, though, his father and family were under constant threat from Viking invaders. In 878, when Edward must have been no more than a young boy, Alfred and his kingdom were caught completely unawares by a Viking invasion in midwinter. If Edward stayed with his father—and there can have been no safer place for him—he must have spent some months hiding in the marshes of Athelney while his father conducted guerrilla warfare against the Vikings. At this point, the Vikings can have wanted nothing more than to find and kill Alfred, the last English leader opposing them. It is unlikely that they would have left Edward, or any other member of the royal family, alive to act as a focus for resistance. Although Alfred's policy of continuous warfare was brilliantly successful, it must have entailed extreme risks for his family. Possibly this accounts for the grinding determination to eliminate all enemies that later characterized Edward's politics.

A further threat to the young atheling (the Old English term for "prince") came from his relatives. His father, though undisputed king of Wessex (when Alfred came to the throne in 871, only an experienced warrior could have been considered), had no less than four elder brothers. Though all of them had died before Alfred became king, at least one, King Ethelred, had left descendants, his sons Ethelwold and Ethelhelm. By the later laws of England, one of those sons should rightfully have been king. Even under Anglo-Saxon law, or convention, both of them would have had the same claim to the throne as Edward. The question of who would succeed Alfred was therefore open and a matter of concern.

In practice, Alfred may well have "engineered" the succession for his own son by giving Edward early power and responsibility while keeping his nephews back. There is some indication, though, that Edward may have simultaneously been kept well in his father's shadow to eliminate any prospect of son rebelling against father (as one of Alfred's brothers had done against their father, in 855-856). *The Anglo-Saxon Chronicle* (compiled c. 890 to c. 1150) notably ignores that affair; the rebellion is known only from other sources. In exactly the same way, *The Anglo-Saxon Chronicle*, describing the Viking invasion of 892-896, records a spectacular victory by the English at Farnham in 893, a victory that ended with the Vikings penned on an island, yet it fails to identify the English leader (though it clearly was not King Alfred) and complains loudly because the Vikings were allowed to slip away before the king arrived. *The Chronicle of Ethelweard* (973) identifies the English commander as Prince Edward, who seems accordingly to have won a major victory before he was twenty-five. At least one contemporary commentator was reluctant to allow him proper credit, clearly wishing to give Alfred no rival.

King Alfred died in late 899. Edward immediately succeeded to the kingdom, and almost as immediately his cousin Ethelwold rebelled. He seized a manor, defied the king, but then slipped away—to the Vikings of Northumbria, who must have welcomed him gladly as a valuable pawn in their power struggle against Wessex, the only kingdom to defy them. For some years, Edward's anxiety must have remained; *The Anglo-Saxon Chronicle* grimly records Ethelwold's movements. Then, in 902, part of an English raiding force into the Viking kingdom of East Anglia was caught and cut off (through disobeying Edward's orders, the chronicler says). Though the English were defeated, they inflicted many casualties, and among the dead was Ethelwold.

LIFE'S WORK

Edward was still left with a very difficult political problem. Following the almost incessant warfare of 865-896, what is now England had become a bewildering patchwork of small states, in weak or shifting coalitions. On one side was Wessex, Edward's kingdom, which by this time had thoroughly assimilated Kent, Surrey, Sussex, and perhaps Cornwall. Also English, anti-Viking, and Christian was the area of south and west Mercia (roughly speaking, the southwest English midlands), which had never been occupied by the Danes. Mercia was controlled by alderman Ethelred and his wife, Queen Æthelflæd, Edward's sister. Edward knew that it would be enormously advantageous for the West Saxon kings to have this rich and populous area on their side, but Wessex and Mercia had long been in open warfare, and even King Alfred had never tried to assume direct rule there.

On the other side of England was a string of states controlled by Vikings (usually Danes). Some were kingdoms; others described themselves as the "army" of Cambridge, or of Northampton, or of the "Five Boroughs" of the Midlands. All these areas still had large numbers of English-speaking and presumably Christian inhabitants, whose loyalties must have been very uncertain. In the far north lurked English "splinter states," owing allegiance to no one, while in the northwest the position was about to be upset by an influx of Norwegian Vikings from Ireland, from whom the Danish armies would in the end be glad to be rescued. Edward seems to have decided to reduce this confused situation by what would in chess terms be described as a strong pawn push.

The center of Edward's strategy was to build fortresses and garrison them, so as to tie his mobile enemies down. His father had begun this policy, and it is hard to say which of the two was responsible for which fortress, but a document from Edward's reign known as the "Burghal Hidage" lists thirty-one fortresses demanding garrisons totaling some twenty-seven thousand men. To

Edward the Elder raised on a shield by his soldiers. (F. R. Niglutsch)

ANGLO-SAXON KINGS OF ENGLAND, 802-1016

Reign	*Ruler*
802-839	Egbert
839-856	Æthelwulf
856-860	Æthelbald
860-866	Æthelbert
866-871	Ethelred (Æthelred) I
871-899	ALFRED THE GREAT
899-924	EDWARD THE ELDER (with sister ÆTHELFLÆD)
924-939	Æthelstan
939-946	Edmund the Magnificent
946-955	Eadred
955-959	Eadwig (Edwy) All-Fair
959-975	Edgar the Peaceable
975-978	Edward the Martyr
978-1016	ETHELRED (ÆTHELRED) II, THE UNREADY
1016	Edmund II Ironside
1016	Ascendancy of Canute the Great (Danish line begins)

these Edward added more, moving from a defensive to an offensive position. He built fortresses at Hertford to threaten the armies of Bedford and Cambridge; he built others at Buckingham to threaten Bedford and Northampton. His position was eased by the events of 909-910, when Edward launched a combined West Saxon and Mercian host against Northumbria, drew a reprisal raid the following year (Vikings were not accustomed to being raided as opposed to raiding), and destroyed it so utterly at the Battle of Tettenhall in 910 that the Northumbrian Danes never quite recovered. The mixture of destruction and the threat of destruction forced army after army to come to terms.

Æthelflæd played an extremely important role in these disputes. She, too, was a potential rival: After her husband Ethelred died in 911, she seems to have run the counties of English Mercia on her own and could (following Ethelwold's example) have provided a rival focus for English loyalties. In fact, she seems to have coordinated her policies with her brother's, building fortresses on a lavish scale, conquering Derby and Leicester, fighting the Welsh, and extorting submission even from York. In response (following family tradition), Edward suppressed mention of her. West Saxon copies of *The Anglo-Saxon Chronicle* barely acknowledge her existence, although the *Mercian Register* (902-924), used by other chronicles, lists her achievements and refers proudly to her, not as "queen" or even "alderwoman" but as lady of the Mercians.

Æthelflæd died at Tamworth on June 12, 918, leaving no son, perhaps fortunately. Her daughter Ælfwynn, a possible focus for Mercian independence, was soon carried off to Wessex, and Edward became in practice king of English Mercia—a position firmly ratified by his son Æthelstan, deliberately brought up in Mercia by his aunt. Edward's power and influence reached their peak in the year before he died, when according to *The Anglo-Saxon Chronicle* he not only was master of the South and Midlands, both English and Danish, but also was accepted as "father and lord" by the king of Scots, by all the Northumbrians including "splinter states" and Norwegian Vikings, by the "Welsh" of Strathclyde, and, a year or two before, by the kings of Wales. Few of these groups, however, remained loyal: Edward was to die in Cheshire only a few days after suppressing a joint rising by the Welsh and the English Mercians of Chester. Yet even the fiercest or remotest rulers of England had to recognize and fear his authority. It must have seemed a long step from the fearful months of his childhood at Thelney, when his father's kingdom ran no farther than the cover of the marshes.

SIGNIFICANCE

King Edward the Elder is remembered almost entirely as a military leader, and his leadership contains few of the brilliant strokes of his father or his son. Nor did he show any of the magnanimous and unexpected statesmanship displayed by Alfred, though he did on one occasion ransom a Welsh bishop from the Vikings, either out of altruism or to gain support in Wales. Nevertheless, Edward converted a successful defensive position into a successful offensive one. He worked single-mindedly, and he demonstrated with Æthelflæd the ability of his family to stick together in spite of rivalry. His quarter century of rule consisted of one long campaign, which has been described as the most remorselessly efficient ever recorded in any country during the Middle Ages. In other respects, too, Edward may have left his mark on the map. He seems to have fostered a policy of quiet infiltration, by which Englishmen simply bought their way back into Danish-controlled areas; he reorganized the bishoprics of Wessex; and the familiar shires of central England, Gloucestershire, Worcestershire, Oxfordshire, and others appear to have been created during his reign as standardized military and administrative units to oppose the

Danish boroughs and armies. All these moves bear the mark of Edward's unspectacular, organizing mind. His European credibility is shown by the marriages of four of his daughters to the kings (or dukes) of France, Germany, and Burgundy.

—*T. A. Shippey*

FURTHER READING

Higham, N. J., and D. H. Hills, eds. *Edward the Elder, 899-924*. New York: Routledge, 2001. A biography of Edward from the perspective of the history of kings and rulers of Anglo-Saxon Britain.

Hill, David. *An Atlas of Anglo-Saxon England*. Toronto: University of Toronto Press, 1981. Invaluable for its maps of the complicated campaigns and interconnections of the Reconquest.

The Laws of the Earliest English Kings. Edited and translated by F. L. Attenborough. Cambridge, England: Cambridge University Press, 1922. Includes the laws of Edward as well as those of his father and his successors.

Stenton, F. M. *Anglo-Saxon England*. 3d ed. New York: Oxford University Press, 1989. An excellent account of the period, gathering together material from many fields.

_______. *Preparatory to Anglo-Saxon England*. Edited by Doris Maris Stenton. New York: Clarendon Press, 1970. Includes valuable pieces on the Battle of Farnham and *The Chronicle of Ethelweard*.

Wainwright, F. T. *Scandinavian England: Collected Papers*. Edited by H. P. R. Finberg. Chichester, England: Phillimore, 1975. Contains the chapters "Æthelflæd, Lady of the Mercians" and "The Submission to Edward the Elder."

Whitelock, Dorothy, David C. Douglas, and Susie I. Tucker, eds. *The Anglo-Saxon Chronicle: A Revised Translation*. 2d ed. New Brunswick, N.J.: Rutgers University Press, 1989. Translation of all forms of *The Anglo-Saxon Chronicle*. The major primary source for a history of the period.

SEE ALSO: Æthelflæd; Alfred the Great; Ethelred II, the Unready.

RELATED ARTICLES in *Great Events from History: The Middle Ages, 477-1453*: 850-950: Viking Era; 878: Alfred Defeats the Danes.

EDWARD I

King of England (r. 1272-1307)

Edward was highly regarded in his own time as a Crusader, conqueror of Wales, and "hammer" of the Scots, and modern historians admire him principally as lawmaker and lawgiver, the monarch who brought Parliament into partnership in the governance of England.

BORN: June 17, 1239; Westminster Palace, London, England

DIED: July 7, 1307; Burgh-on-the-Sands, near Carlisle, Cumberland, England

ALSO KNOWN AS: Longshanks; Hammer of the Scots; Law-Giver

AREAS OF ACHIEVEMENT: Government and politics, law, military

EARLY LIFE

Edward I succeeded his father, Henry III, as king of England while on crusade in the Holy Land, following a tempestuous youthful career in the conflicts between Henry and his rebellious barons, the latter led by Simon de Montfort. Edward, one of the greatest English kings, was tall, athletic, handsome, and a courageous man who gloried in battle and in tournaments and who commanded the intricacies of the law and of the art of government. Edward combined, in his complex personality, order and efficiency, the capacity not only for cool judgment but also for unreasoning fury, a religious devotion at least conventional, and a cultured mien. Capable of open honesty and of devious behavior, efficient yet a proto-Romantic, he presaged his grandson's revival of what was perceived as Arthurian chivalry. Edward I succeeded to a still-restive realm.

As was customary in the experience of kings succeeding weak or insouciant monarchs, he spent the earliest—and most fruitful—years of his reign regaining what he and his advisers considered royal rights temporarily lost. In so doing, this king created what was in fact a new form of monarchy, one based on the cooperation rather than on the domination of the politically significant elements of his realm. Edward was a great king because he was a successful politician.

Life's Work

Edward's reign was far more fruitful in government policy and in parliamentary statutes during his first twenty-five years than during the last ten; in part, this was a result of the growing distractions and expenses of the wars with Wales, Scotland, and France. Military conflict always takes precedence over domestic issues, although the former may make the latter unquiet, as it did during 1297-1307. Edward's people wearied of their sovereign's wars and, more important, of the resources in men, money, and commitment needed to support them. Before the foreign policies of Edward I interrupted his domestic program, however, this king's relations with his parliament led to the great statutes that characterize his reign and give it historical significance.

The first historically important piece of legislation issuing from the king's parliament was the Statute of Gloucester, enacted in 1278, which investigated the sources of franchise holders' claims to their jurisdictions and questioned by what right (quo warranto) a person was entitled to exercise his claimed legal authority over others. In theory, unless the claimant could exhibit written evidence of a royal grant to hold his liberties, or prescriptive tenure, the lord's right to hold his putative authority was challenged. These inquests bear an obvious relationship to growing ideas of inalienability of royal sovereignty. Although the effects of the statute were far less wide-ranging than once was thought, the resulting inquests did nevertheless abolish long use as a future justification for jurisdictional claims and prevented the growth of new franchises without royal grant. The statute *De viris religiosis* (1270) limited the alienation of lands to the Church without a royal license; six years later, *Circumspecte agatis* limited and defined the rights of church courts over secular cases at law.

The year 1285 saw two more statutes of deep significance: Westminster II, which controlled entailed estates, and *Nisi prius*, which enhanced the authority of the court of common pleas. In the same year, the Statute of Winchester marked a step in the evolution of military service from the feudal practice of basing service on landholding (the knight's fee) to one based on the monetary value of land; the apparent reason for this legislation was to make more Englishmen liable for scutage (the payment of money to the king in lieu of personal service). Edward I's last great statute—*Quia emptores* (Westminster III, 1290)—effectively halted the growth of subinfeudation (the practice whereby landholders alienated part of their holdings to others) by making the subtenant hold his landed rights from the ultimate, rather than from the immediate, possessor of the granted lands. These statutes, which in the long run undermined the feudal structure of society, were not intended to do so; they represented an attempt to modernize, rather than to destroy, feudalism.

As the legislation of Edward I in part brought non-noble elements of English society into a share in the governance of the realm, so more obviously did the growth of Parliament. By the late thirteenth century, kings had a perceived need to consult with elements of the polity beyond the nobility. Yet one must not assume that the growth of Parliament should be equated with the growth of representative government; popular representation occurred in only about 10 percent of the parliaments of the reign, and even then popular meant only politically influ-

Sculpture of Edward I. (Library of Congress)

PLANTAGENET KINGS OF ENGLAND, 1154-1399	
Reign	*Monarch*
1154-1189	HENRY II (with ELEANOR OF AQUITAINE, r. 1154-1189)
1189-1199	RICHARD I THE LION-HEARTED
1199-1216	JOHN I LACKLAND
1216-1272	HENRY III
1272-1307	EDWARD I LONGSHANKS
1307-1327	EDWARD II (with ISABELLA OF FRANCE, r. 1308-1330)
1327-1377	EDWARD III (with PHILIPPA OF HAINAUT, r. 1327-1369)
1377-1399	RICHARD II

ential nonecclesiastical and nonnoble classes, not representatives of the common people, who waited until modern times for their voice to be heard in Parliament. Parliament in the reign of Edward I was almost always controlled by the king, who used it to extend, not to restrict, his powers; Edward wanted support, not meaningful opposition.

However, despite the absence of representatives of the common people, Parliament did exhibit a broadening of consultation beyond the nobles and higher clergy, a further step away from governance by the king consulting only with the political and ecclesiastical feudality. Parliament's principal functions were not legislative; it was primarily the high court of England, and its other miscellaneous functions were distinctively secondary to its judicial role. The English Parliament differed in fundamental ways from its cognates on the Continent: Its members' actions bound all Englishmen, the members were not limited in their deliberations, they had national (rather than regional, as in France) control over taxation, and the English nobility had a sense of wider fiscal and political responsibility even to classes other than their own. The English Parliament institutionalized political restraint over the king, thus making him, unlike his contemporary in France (Philip IV the Fair), a constitutional king, a king whose actions had to be taken with the possibility of opposition in mind. Yet one must not exaggerate the often-alleged parliamentary limitations on the king; after all, even in the crises of 1297-1300, the king did achieve his aims with very little sacrifice of effective power.

Edward's relations with the borderlands of Wales and Scotland brought him grudging success in the first instance, frustration in the second. English penetration of Wales had a long history, going back to the reign of William the Conqueror. Throughout the twelfth and thirteenth centuries, Welsh princes and lords played important roles in English politics, trying to expand their powers when the English polity was weakly governed and to defend them when the English and the lords of the Welsh marches were strong; the fortunes of the two countries were becoming increasingly intertwined. Thus, when Edward I took advantage of a quarrel between Llewelyn ap Gruffydd (ruler of Snowdonia) and his brother Dafydd to intervene in Welsh politics, there was no novelty in Anglo-Welsh relations but rather a continuation of old mutual policies of pursuing targets of opportunity. In this case, Edward suspected the coalescing of Welsh loyalties around Llewelyn. The Welsh lost the war that began in 1276, yet they retained elements of peculiarity (language, culture) that persist in somewhat attenuated form today. Unlike the nascent romantic nationalism of the modern Scots, that of the Welsh had long roots. Llewelyn's power was confined to north Wales, while the denizens of the rest of the region cooperated with the English. Yet this situation proved to be ephemeral; all of Wales rose against the English in 1282; Edward and the marcher lords responded with efficiency and speed, conquering the Welsh, killing Llewelyn and subjecting his brother Dafydd to the disagreeable fate of being hanged, drawn, and quartered. The constitutional result was the Statute of Wales (1284). This statute, which should be compared with the Act of Union (with Scotland) of 1707, incorporated Wales into the royal domain, divided north Wales into shires, and subjected the area to English law and governmental procedures (although it recognized the continuance of Welsh law and custom). In 1301, the principality of Wales was created as a special entity under the eldest son of the monarch (in this case, Edward II of Caernarvon, the future Edward II). The Welsh did not go gentle into that good night; sporadic revolts occurred throughout the fourteenth and fifteenth centuries (the most famous was that of Owain ab Gruffydd, better known in the lore of William Shakespeare as Owen Glendower, during the reign of Henry IV), but in general the Welsh proved loyal, if somewhat burry, subjects of the Crown.

This could not be said of the Scots, in part because the northern Celts took advantage of English troubles with Wales and forged the Auld Alliance with France that persisted into modern times. The history of Anglo-Scottish relations paralleled that of the English and Welsh, but the Scottish kings and nobility were much more interrelated by blood and by interests with those of England. The precipitating incident that led to the Anglo-Scottish conflicts of the reign of Edward I was the death of Alexander III of Scotland in 1286; his heir was his granddaughter Margaret, the "maid of Norway." She died as Queen Margaret in 1290, leaving the Scottish crown prey to the ambitious claims of three candidates: John de Baliol, Robert Bruce, and John Hastings. Edward I intervened in the matter in his recognized capacity as overlord of Scotland.

Edward I, after examining law and tradition, recognized Baliol as king (1292). Unfortunately both for the histories of England and Scotland, Baliol was viewed by the Scottish nobles as too subservient to the wishes of Edward I. In 1295, the Scottish alliance with France was sealed; late in this year, Edward I prepared for the war that he began with the invasion of Scotland in the following March. Edward seemed easily to triumph, and the disgraced Baliol, yielding his kingdom, departed from Scotland never to return. The fabled Stone of Scone at this time was taken to England, where it remains embedded in the English coronation throne at Westminster. The Scots rose in rebellion against Edward in 1297, led by William Wallace, Andrew of Moray, Robert Bruce (later King Robert of Scotland), and the aged Robert of Wishart, bishop of Glasgow. Most of the leaders abandoned the fight against superior English power, but Wallace continued to resist, leading not magnates but men of lower social position.

The resistance took the form of what now could be called guerrilla warfare. The first large-scale battle turned into disaster for the English at Stirling Bridge (1297). Wallace was not again to win a major battle with the English, and he was delivered to the English and hanged in 1305. English attempts to treat the Scots as generously as they had the Welsh failed: The Scots had not been conquered, and they maintained a stubborn resistance against an English people tiring of war and of fiscal levies. In early 1306, another major revolt began, led by King Robert, grandson of the royal claimant of 1291. It is this revolt that brought Edward north to Burgh-on-the-Sands, where he died in 1307.

Edward's policy with regard to France was much less important than that toward his Celtic fringe, more a distraction than a dominating concern. Its chief interest lies in the ways in which the issues at contest between the kings of England and of France foretold issues important in the etiology of the Hundred Years' War, which began in 1337. Could the English monarchs maintain their lordship of Gascony in the face of growing French expansionism? Could marriage alliances between the two dynasties solve the political problems? Could naval hostilities in the Channel be confined so as to avoid aggravating a coming wider war? During and after the reign of Edward I, the answer to all these questions was no.

Significance

The reign of Edward I was as important as any in the Middle Ages in laying the foundations of national, as opposed to feudal, monarchy. He expanded the base of military service, enlarged the taxation of commerce, and was the father of the Parliament that was so central to English government in his reign and thereafter, that body that brought the community of the realm into partnership with the king in the governance of England. Nor was Edward unsuccessful in his dealings with the Church: He continued to control the Church in England (although with less notoriety than his cousin Philip IV the Fair, suppressor of the Templars and conqueror of the Papacy). Hammer of the Scots he may well have been, but they were an indestructible anvil. His addition of Wales to the realm reflects a pattern to be seen in his policies toward France as well—the expansion of the realm beyond an ethnically well-defined base.

—*James W. Alexander*

Further Reading

Chancellor, John. *The Life and Times of Edward I.* London: Weidenfeld and Nicolson, 1981. Illustrated, clearly written biography intended for the general reader with no previous knowledge of Edward I or his realm.

Morris, John E. *The Welsh Wars of Edward I.* Phoenix Mill, England: Alan Sutton, 1996. An excellent discussion of Edward and wars with the Welsh.

Plucknett, T. F. T. *Legislation of Edward I.* Oxford, England: Clarendon Press, 1962. Comprehensive introduction to Edward for those with some knowledge of the social and legal history of the reign.

Powicke, F. M. *The Thirteenth Century, 1216-1307.* 2d ed. Oxford, England: Clarendon Press, 1962. An excellent source on the life and reign of Edward and the times he dominated and personified.

Prestwich, Michael. *Edward I.* New Haven, Conn.: Yale University Press, 1997. Part of the Yale English Monarchs series, a look at Edward and his reign.

_______. *The Three Edwards: War and State in England, 1272-1377.* New York: Routledge, 2003. Focuses on the concepts and realities of war and the state, although the scope is not limited to these areas.

Raban, Sandra. *England Under Edward I and Edward II, 1259-1327.* Malden, Mass.: Blackwell, 2000. Looks at the reigns of Edward I and Edward II and their place in British history. Includes bibliography and index.

Sayles, G. O. *The King's Parliament of England.* New York: W. W. Norton, 1974. An excellent introduction to parliamentary history for the nonspecialist.

Stones, E. L. G., and Grant G. Simpson. *Edward I and the Throne of Scotland, 1290-1296.* 2 vols. New York: Oxford University Press, 1978. The indispensable collection of documents concerning the earlier phase of the struggle for the rule of Scotland.

Watson, Fiona J. *Under the Hammer: Edward I and Scotland, 1286-1307.* East Lothian, Scotland: Tuckwell Press, 1998. Focuses on Scotland's struggle for independence.

SEE ALSO: Boniface VIII; Robert Bruce; Edward II; Henry III; Isabella of France; Simon de Montfort; John Pecham; Philip IV the Fair; William Wallace.

RELATED ARTICLES in *Great Events from History: The Middle Ages, 477-1453*: 1285: Statute of Winchester; 1290-1306: Jews Are Expelled from England, France, and Southern Italy; 1295: Model Parliament; June 23-24, 1314: Battle of Bannockburn; 1337-1453: Hundred Years' War; 1366: Statute of Kilkenny.

EDWARD II

King of England (r. 1307-1327)

Edward's ineffectual leadership and weakness of character furthered the decline of the monarchy and furthered the growth of representative government in England.

BORN: April 25, 1284; Caernarvon Castle, Caernarvonshire, Wales
DIED: September 21, 1327; Berkeley Castle, Gloucestershire, England
ALSO KNOWN AS: Edward II of Caernarvon
AREA OF ACHIEVEMENT: Government and politics

EARLY LIFE

Edward II was born the fourth son of Edward I by his first wife, Eleanor of Castile. He was only a few months old when the last of his brothers died in August and he became his father's heir to the throne. His father did not neglect Edward's royal education. He was given a palatial residence of his own at an early age, and efforts were made to find a queen for him. In 1301, he became the first prince of Wales as a concession to a conquered people, and in 1302 he attended his first parliament.

As he approached twenty years of age, Edward physically resembled his father—tall, handsome, and very strong. On the other hand, there were significant differences between the two. Although the younger Edward regularly accompanied his father into battle against the Scots, he was not a warrior. In years to come, he would go out of his way to avoid battle. Instead, to the old king's great disappointment, Edward had already begun to exhibit certain irresponsible traits. He frequently lost large sums of money gambling and preferred pedestrian amusements such as amateur theatricals, rowing, digging, and thatching houses. His greatest fault, however, the one that would prove his undoing, was his blind dependence on nefarious advisers such as the Gascon knight Piers Gaveston. The king so greatly resented Gaveston's debilitating influence that he drove him into exile.

LIFE'S WORK

At first, observers could hope that the prince's faults were the natural by-products of adolescence. Unfortunately, age did not improve Edward's character. When his father died on July 7, 1307, Edward's first act was to recall his friend Gaveston. Gaveston's influence became so great that he served as regent when Edward went to France to marry Isabella, daughter of Philip IV the Fair, on January 25, 1328. Most of the barons did not share the king's high opinion of Gaveston. In 1311, these barons, led by the king's cousin Thomas, earl of Lancaster, insisted that Gaveston be banished again and that the king submit to a number of restrictions. The king could not prevent a baronial committee of twenty-one lords—appointed by the king as framers of ordinances for regulating his household—from taking control of the government. The effect was to enhance the powers of the Great Council while diminishing those of the monarchy. The new ordinances, however, could not be enforced, and Gaveston returned before the end of the year. This touched off a rebellion led by Lancaster's faction. Gaveston was captured and executed, and additional restrictions were imposed on the Crown. For the next few years, Lancaster was the real power behind the throne.

In the meantime, Edward's problems with the Scots had grown worse. Robert Bruce had taken a number of

Edward II. (Library of Congress)

fortresses and had laid siege to Stirling. Even the lethargic Edward recognized the danger of this situation. In June, 1314, the king led an army into Scotland but was decisively defeated in the Battle of Bannockburn, which effectively undid all that his father had accomplished in the north. The Scots had, for all practical purposes, achieved their independence, and it was not until 1323 that Edward was able to work out an acceptable peace treaty. Edward's humiliating defeat at Bannockburn would make him more dependent than ever on the barons.

The king, however, was not the only one with problems. Although Lancaster was wealthy and powerful, he could not gain the confidence of most of the barons. In 1318, a more moderate group of barons came to power headed by Aymer of Valence, earl of Pembroke. Ostensibly, the purpose of this group was to free the king from Lancaster's influence. Yet the king disliked Pembroke as much as Lancaster, and so he turned for advice to Hugh le Despenser, another great baronial leader. Despenser's son, Hugh le Despenser the Younger, quickly won a place in the king's heart similar to that which Gaveston had occupied in earlier years. The Despensers, however, proved even more objectionable than the king's earlier favorites, and the barons deeply resented the many favors bestowed on them. The Despensers had many enemies, such as Thomas of Lancaster and the Mortimers, a family of Welsh lords from whom they had taken much territory. In 1321, the barons attempted to banish the Despensers, but Edward, displaying unusual vigor, gathered an army and routed the rebels in the decisive Battle of Boroughbridge. Lancaster was captured and executed.

For the next five years, the Despensers would rule the kingdom. One of the most significant events of this period occurred in 1322, when a parliament was held at York and revoked the ordinances of 1311 that had been implemented by the barons alone. From this point forward, no statute was considered valid unless it was ratified by the House of Commons. This was a major step in the direction of a more representative government.

In the meantime, the Despensers' growing arrogance and greed brought them new problems. Lord Roger Mortimer, imprisoned after the Battle of Boroughbridge, had not forgotten their depredations in the Welsh Marches. In 1323, he escaped from the Tower of London and took refuge in France. Two years later, he was joined by the queen, Isabella of France, who had gone to the French court with her son on business. While there, she became Mortimer's mistress and refused to return to England while the Despensers controlled the government. In September, 1326, Isabella, accompanied by Mortimer and the young Edward, invaded England and captured and imprisoned the king. Both Despensers were captured, tried, and beheaded for their many crimes. A few months later, in January, 1327, a parliament deposed the king, whereupon he was succeeded by his fourteen-year-old son, Edward III. That, however, was not enough for Edward's enemies. He was forced to abdicate and placed in prison, where he was tortured and eventually murdered.

Edward II was probably the weakest English king since the Norman Conquest. His father had achieved fame as a warrior, Crusader, and administrator. Because there was some physical resemblance between father and son, there was some hope for a strong monarchy. Unfortunately, Edward II was not emotionally capable of duplicating or even maintaining his father's achievements. He was humiliated on the battlefield, where King Robert and the Scots won their independence in one decisive battle, and at home, he was dominated within the government by friends and enemies alike. Even his queen,

Isabella, betrayed him and later took up arms against him. He lost his family, his throne, and eventually his life.

Edward should not be blamed, however, for all of England's woes at this time. In fact, many of the problems had carried over from his father's reign. It was during Edward I's day that Parliament first became a truly representative body. The barons had come to expect at least a voice, and could hope for a personal hand, in governing the kingdom. This was a gain that they would not easily surrender. When it became obvious that the first prince of Wales was much weaker than his father, the barons set about the business of increasing their power. During his coronation, Edward II was forced to agree to abide by the laws set forth by the community of the realm. Edward found this difficult to do, and the result was two decades of strife, hatred, and intermittent civil war. Nor could Edward ever hope to solve the Scottish problem. Even a great soldier such as Edward I had found it virtually impossible to hold the Scots in check, and storm clouds were gathering again when the old king died in 1307.

SIGNIFICANCE

What was Edward II's legacy? It is easy to speak of his failures and much more difficult to find positive accomplishments. In fact, the most significant accomplishment of his reign came about as a result of the king's weakness—the continued growth of representative government. His willingness to trust friends and his interest in nonregal activities also contributed to the narrowing gap between Crown and community.

—*Larry W. Usilton*

FURTHER READING

Davies, James. *The Baronial Opposition to Edward II.* Cambridge, England: Cambridge University Press, 1918. Emphasizes the barons' attack against the royal system of administration.

Fryde, Natalie. *The Tyranny and Fall of Edward II, 1321-1326.* Cambridge, England: Cambridge University Press, 1979. A very critical study of an incompetent king and his evil ministers, the Despensers.

Haines, Roy Martin. *King Edward II: Edward of Cærnarfon, His Life, His Reign, and Its Aftermath, 1284-1330.* Montreal: McGill-Queen's University Press, 2003. An extensive biographical survey of Edward's life before taking the throne, during his reign, and the years following.

McKisack, May. *The Fourteenth Century, 1307-1399.* Oxford, England: Oxford University Press, 1959. One of the most comprehensive studies of the period that details the political events of Edward II's reign.

Myers, A. R. *England in the Late Middle Ages, 1307-1536.* 8th ed. Baltimore: Penguin Books, 1971. Edward II figures prominently in the first two chapters of this text, which discusses the waning power of the monarchy and the growing influence of the community of the realm.

Prestwich, Michael. *The Three Edwards: War and State in England, 1272-1377.* New York: St. Martin's Press, 1980. Provides a good, short biography of Edward II for the general reader.

Raban, Sandra. *England Under Edward I and Edward II, 1259-1327.* Malden, Mass.: Blackwell, 2000. Looks at the reigns of Edward I and Edward II and their place in British history. Includes bibliography and index.

SEE ALSO: Robert Bruce; Edward I; Edward III; Isabella of France; Philippa of Hainaut; Richard II.

RELATED ARTICLES in *Great Events from History: The Middle Ages, 477-1453*: June 23-24, 1314: Battle of Bannockburn; 1366: Statute of Kilkenny.

EDWARD III

King of England (r. 1327-1377)

Under Edward's reign, England witnessed an increase in the governing power of Parliament and especially that of the House of Commons, owing to the necessity for the king to seek parliamentary authority for the money to finance his wars with Scotland and with France.

BORN: November 13, 1312; Windsor Castle, Berkshire, England
DIED: June 21, 1377; Sheen, Surrey, England
ALSO KNOWN AS: Edward Plantagenet; Edward III of Windsor
AREAS OF ACHIEVEMENT: Government and politics, military

EARLY LIFE

Edward III was the son of Edward II and Queen Isabella of France. Nothing is known of his childhood. At the time of his accession to the throne in 1327, Edward was fourteen years of age. The first three years of his reign found the young king overshadowed by the rule of his adulterous mother, Isabella, and her paramour, Roger Mortimer. Their governance, however, was doomed; Isabella had no clearly conceived plans for her regency, and Mortimer was interested primarily in carving out for himself a great lordship in the west of England. Both their domestic and their foreign policies were failures, insofar indeed as they could be said to have had policies at all. In the fall of 1330, the young king, nearly eighteen years old, led a conspiracy of young lords that successfully overthrew Mortimer and Isabella, arranged for Mortimer's hanging, and packed the queen off to a convent of Poor Clares, where she lived on until 1358. Edward had come through his first crisis with skill and with bold decisiveness.

LIFE'S WORK

Edward III was one of the most interesting of medieval English kings. To his contemporaries he was the ideal monarch. The embodiment of chivalric values and virtues, Edward also loved war, the hunt, and pageantry. He was a most intelligent man who was conventional in his cultural interests, brilliant in his patronage of the uniquely English perpendicular Gothic, and respectful of learning (which he himself exhibited). This handsome, athletic leader of fighting men was also to become more of a statesman than the following of the great historical scholar Bishop William Stubbs, in the late nineteenth century, was prepared to acknowledge.

The 1330's encompassed the foundation of the king's policy toward his great barons, that class without whose cooperation he could not have ruled effectively. Edward was an astute politician in his use of royal patronage; his barons were rewarded for their support by titles and honors. In 1337, the king elevated four barons to earldoms, and as his sons achieved adulthood, they were married to wealthy, noble heiresses. From these marriages, however, descended the men who fought to secure the Crown in the Wars of the Roses. Another tie that bound selected nobles to the king was his foundation of the Order of the Garter in 1348, which united the king and his chosen intimates in a chivalric and almost mystical bond of common interests and dreams, reviving an Arthurian mystique that had never in fact existed, ornamented by round tables, tournaments, and festive pageantry.

The domestic history of the reign is chiefly important for the rise in influence of the House of Commons in Parliament. In the Middle Ages, "commons" did not mean the common people; the term meant the well-born of less than aristocratic rank who held extensive land in the countryside, as well as wealthy burgesses of the towns and cities of England. The easy cooperation of king and community so characteristic of the 1330's was threatened by a small crisis that arose in 1341. The king's problem with Parliament arose from the initial failures of the Hundred Years' War, which had commenced in 1337. Like all wars, the war was also expensive, and the king's requests for money gave the Parliament opportunity to seek royal concessions as the price of grants of money. Moreover, there was conflict between the administration in England and the officials who had accompanied the king to the Continent. At issue, too, was the question of the king's right to choose his own ministers. These uncertainties and conflicts enlarged the possibilities for Parliament to increase its role in the governance of England. The Parliament of 1341 produced a compromise by which the king reconfirmed the Magna Carta and the Charter of the Forest, both issued originally in 1216. Although these documents were anachronistic in detail by 1341, they had assumed a symbolic status in that they recognized that the king was bound by his own law. Owing to the Parliament's attempts to control the king's appointment of his officials, the compromise broke down in the Parliament of 1343, which affirmed the king's right to appoint his own counselors, as was traditional in medieval England.

Other domestic developments of the reign of Edward III were less dramatic but no less important. While domestic politics were largely eclipsed by the French war, important constitutional developments characterized the period after the early 1340's. The aristocracy cooperated with the king because they had a common interest in the pursuit of the Hundred Years' War—for sporting fun and for profit—and because of their common allegiance to England and to her king. The Statute of Treasons was promulgated by Parliament in 1352; theretofore, treason had been defined as an act against the king, a definition open to all-too-obvious political abuse. The statute defined treason as an act against the state rather than against the monarch as a person. The arrival of the Black Death in England around 1347 seems to have had little effect on royal policy, despite its devastating horror among the common people, 40 percent of whom probably were destroyed by this dread pandemic.

Edward's declining years, when he was apparently afflicted by premature senility and unduly influenced by his mistress, Alice Perrers, gave opportunity for the assertion of parliamentary authority. Edward was not altogether competent to rule, the Black Prince (Edward of Woodstock, the king's eldest son) was moribund, and the king's other sons lacked the necessary leadership qualities to lead England effectively. John of Gaunt, Edward III's second son, while not without ability, did not inspire general confidence. The Parliament of 1376 (the Good Parliament) gathered to consider the state of the kingdom and again focused on the responsibility of royal officials to the representative body. A new threat to the royal prerogative to appoint advisers emerged in impeachment, a form of trial in Parliament that saw lords acting as judges (which was not without precedent) and the Commons as the body presenting the indictment. Commons held the lever here: They could refuse taxation unless the king acquiesced in the trial of his ministers. The process was ahead of its time, however, and failed in the same year.

The Hundred Years' War, begun by Edward III, was complex in its origins. Edward III regarded the French war as an effort understood in chivalric terms rather than in the frame of reference of modern nationalism. Probably the root cause of the war was the festering English resentment at the loss of the northern French lands that had been held by the Norman and Angevin kings; these areas had been lost under Richard I and John, and Henry III's attempts to recover the territories were unsuccessful. As well, the growth in landed power of the king of France threatened the remaining holdings in France subject to the king of England, and the French government supported the Scots in their resistance to English interference in their internal affairs. In 1337, when it was apparent that war was imminent, Edward III advanced his claims to the French throne; he was the grandson of Philip IV the Fair through his mother, Isabella. The first phase of the war, ending with the Peace of Brétigny in 1360, was crowned with the success of English arms. The most notable victories of the English were at Sluys (a naval battle fought off that Flemish city in 1340), Crécy (1346), and Poitiers (1356). The English victories at the last two battles were assured by superior leadership, by strategy and tactics, and by the longbow, the master of the field both in firepower and in range. The Peace of Brétigny was favorable to the English, but it was never effectuated, and the last years of Edward's reign saw the war largely characterized by skirmishes and plundering, with no large set-piece battles involving the English. His death, on June 21, 1377, may have resulted from the complications of premature senility.

SIGNIFICANCE

Edward III assumed the monarchy at the time of its degradation; at the end of his reign, England was preeminent among European powers. His policies succeeded because of harmonious symbiosis between the king and

Engraving of Edward III, patterned on a painting in Windsor Castle. (Library of Congress)

other elements of the polity. This successful cooperation was both the cause and the result of some compromise of royal authority and prerogative. Edward's success was also fortified by the pomp and pageantry of his chivalric court and by military success. Clashes with Parliament were few, and the twin highlights of the history of this representative body were the growth in the power of Commons and the practical end of the king's right to tax without consultation. Edward was revered by his people, easily the most popular fourteenth century ruler of his island realm, an astute politician and a military hero.

—*James W. Alexander*

FURTHER READING

Barnie, John. *War in Medieval English Society: Social Values and the Hundred Years' War, 1337-99*. Ithaca, N.Y.: Cornell University Press, 1974. A pioneering study of the impact of war on the English people, examined in terms of the political and social elites, the clergy, the educated, and the laity.

Bothwell, J. S. *The Age of Edward III*. Rochester, N.Y.: York Medieval Press, 2001. Discusses Edward's redistribution of estates, politics and propaganda, peace negotiations, legal history, and more.

Fowler, Kenneth. *The Age of Plantagenet and Valois: The Struggle for Supremacy, 1328-1498*. New York: Putnam, 1967. A lavishly illustrated, clearly written overview of the Hundred Years' War and of its times.

Hewitt, H. J. *The Organization of War Under Edward III, 1338-62*. New York: Barnes and Noble Books, 1966. An original study of the home front, especially the role of civilians in supplying and supporting the war effort.

McKisack, May. *The Fourteenth Century, 1307-1399*. Oxford, England: Clarendon Press, 1959. The standard narrative history of Great Britain in the reign of Edward III.

Nicholson, Ranald. *Edward III and the Scots: The Formative Years of a Military Career, 1327-1335*. London: Oxford University Press, 1965. Reveals the complexities of relations among the English, the French, and the Scots.

Perroy, Édouard. *The Hundred Years' War*. New York: Capricorn Books, 1965. A very good general history of the war.

Prestwich, Michael. *The Three Edwards: War and State in England, 1272-1377*. New York: St. Martin's Press, 1980. A sophisticated interpretation of the reign of Edward III.

Rogers, Clifford J. *The Wars of Edward III: Sources and Interpretations*. Rochester, N.Y.: Boydell Press, 1999. Covers the Hundred Years' War and its beginnings, war strategy and organization, English armies, and the relationship between Parliament and war.

Vale, Juliet. *Edward III and Chivalry: Chivalric Society and Its Context, 1270-1350*. Woodbridge, England: Boydell Press, 1982. A brilliant book, argues with conviction that the impact of chivalry at the court of Edward III was essential to his reign, and to later generations' understanding of it.

SEE ALSO: Edward II; Henry III; Isabella of France; King John; Philip IV the Fair; Richard I.

RELATED ARTICLES in *Great Events from History: The Middle Ages, 477-1453*: c. 1200: Common-Law Tradition Emerges in England; June 15, 1215: Signing of the Magna Carta; 1295: Model Parliament; 1337-1453: Hundred Years' War; August 26, 1346: Battle of Crécy; 1347-1352: Invasion of the Black Death in Europe.

EGBERT

King of England (r. 802-839)

Egbert restored the fortunes of Wessex and established the political foundation of the future English state that, under Alfred the Great, would successfully resist Scandinavian dominance in the ninth century.

BORN: c. 770; Wessex (now in England)
DIED: 839; Wessex
ALSO KNOWN AS: Ecgbert; Ecgberht; Ecgbryht
AREAS OF ACHIEVEMENT: Government and politics, military

EARLY LIFE

Egbert was born into the royal family of the southern British kingdom of Wessex at a time when it had for more than half a century been under the overlordship of the midland kingdom of Mercia. His father, Ealhmund, may have been a descendant of both Hengist of Kent and Cerdic of Wessex, fifth century founders of their respective states. The royal line of Wessex, however, had passed to another branch of the family by the eighth century. Ealhmund therefore served under Mercian dominance as a subking of Kent (784-786). When both Ealhmund and Cynegils, the West Saxon king, died around 786, the Mercian king, Offa, feared that Egbert would unite the kingdoms of Kent and Wessex in opposition to Mercia. In alliance with a new Wessex king, Beorhtric, Offa exiled Egbert. The date and duration of Egbert's exile are uncertain, though he may have been banished as early as 789, when Beorhtric married Offa's daughter. Most sources suggest a three-year exile, though some historians contend that he was away from Britain for thirteen years.

Egbert found refuge and tutelage in Frankfurt at the court of Charlemagne, who, as the greatest European ruler of the time, may have assisted in securing Mercian acceptance of Egbert's return to England. With Beorhtric's death, Egbert ascended the throne of Wessex in 802. For the next twenty-three years, the only evidence of his reign is *The Anglo-Saxon Chronicle* (compiled c. 890 to c. 1150) report of the 815 subjugation of Cornwall. During this gap in the historical record, Egbert probably was preparing Wessex and its army for the campaigns of 825 to 830, which would make him famous.

LIFE'S WORK

In 825, Egbert launched a series of military campaigns that within five years brought most of England under his indirect control. Egbert first crushed a rebellion in western Wales (modern Cornwall). He then wheeled northward to meet the forces of Mercia, which had taken advantage of the Welsh revolt to invade Wessex. In 825 in the Ellendun region, near modern Swindon, Egbert slaughtered a force led by the Mercian king, Beornwulf, a battle commemorated in popular verse by reference to its "river of blood." Immediately after the battle, he dispatched Ethelwulf, his son; Ealhstan, the bishop of Sherborne; Wulfheard, his aldermen; and a large army to regain the kingdom of Kent, which his father had previously ruled. There the Mercian under-king, Baldred, was driven north across the Thames River, forcing Kent into submission.

After the fall of Kent, the states of Sussex, Surrey, and Essex also submitted to Egbert. Finally, Egbert led his warriors in defense of the East Angles, who accepted Egbert's overlordship in return for protection from Mercia. In a single year, Egbert had enlarged Wessex, dramatically weakened Mercia, and become overlord of Corn-

Egbert. (Library of Congress)

ANGLO-SAXON KINGS OF ENGLAND, 802-1016	
Reign	*Ruler*
802-839	EGBERT
839-856	Æthelwulf
856-860	Æthelbald
860-866	Æthelbert
866-871	Ethelred (Æthelred) I
871-899	ALFRED THE GREAT
899-924	EDWARD THE ELDER (with sister ÆTHELFLÆD)
924-939	Æthelstan
939-946	Edmund the Magnificent
946-955	Eadred
955-959	Eadwig (Edwy) All-Fair
959-975	Edgar the Peaceable
975-978	Edward the Martyr
978-1016	ETHELRED (ÆTHELRED) II, THE UNREADY
1016	Edmund II Ironside
1016	Ascendancy of Canute the Great (Danish line begins)

wall, Essex, and East Anglia, positioning himself to challenge the larger kingdoms of Mercia and Northumbria.

By 829, after regrouping and utilizing the resources of his new territories, Egbert again repelled a Mercian attack led by the Mercian king Wiglaf on the East Angles; he then invaded Mercia itself, conquering all Britain south of the Humber River. In his honor, Egbert had coins stamped proclaiming him *Rex Merciorum*, king of the Mercians. He then led his army toward Northumbria. At Dore (near modern Sheffield), the Northumbrians submitted to the overlordship of Egbert. In 830, Egbert led an army against the north Welsh (in the area of present-day Wales), and in one of his last major campaigns gained their submission, consolidating his dominance of Britain south of Scotland.

This did not mean that Egbert was the king of England in the modern sense. His direct rule extended only to Wessex and a few adjacent regions. As was common at the time, Egbert ruled through subkings who acknowledged the overlordship of Wessex. He even restored Wiglaf to the throne of Mercia under such conditions in 830, probably in order to forestall further Welsh rebellions.

The kingdom of Kent also was maintained separately because of its unique position. It had been ruled by his father and might therefore have been brought within the strict boundaries of Wessex, but it was also the seat of ecclesiastical government in England and was the area of England closest to the European continent. As a result, Egbert made his son, Ethelwulf, king of Kent, probably in 828. Whereas the Mercians had tried to suppress the authority of the Church and of the archbishop of Canterbury, Egbert supported them, thus gaining an important political and social ally. At the Council of Kingston in 838, Egbert and Ethelwulf agreed to a perpetual alliance with the Church, guaranteeing election rights and providing assurances of peace and protection.

Little is known of Egbert's domestic policy. There is some evidence to suggest that he strengthened ties between the bishops and the shires and that he organized local military forces, enabling the West Saxons to offer effective resistance to Scandinavian invaders. His final years were spent in trying to consolidate the extensive gains made during the 820's. Scandinavian raiders plundered coastal territories in both 834 and 835. These setbacks led the West Welsh to join an invasion of Wessex by the Scandinavians, but in 837, Egbert routed them at Hingston Down (Hengestdune). Two years later, he died and was succeeded by his son, Ethelwulf.

SIGNIFICANCE

The Anglo-Saxon Chronicle refers to Egbert as the eighth bretwalda, an informal title denoting a ruler of Britain and suggesting a measure of authority that he did not truly possess. Nevertheless, over a period of five years, Egbert did establish for the first time a single political framework for most of what is modern-day England. Although Wessex would later temporarily lose control of some the territories Egbert conquered, his work of consolidation was never wholly undone, and it proved to be a turning point in the process of English political unification. Three previously independent states, Kent, Surrey, and Sussex, would never be separated from the Saxon monarchy. More important was Egbert's temporary overlordship of Northumbria, which previously had been far removed from "southern" concerns. Egbert's thrust northward foreshadowed the eventual unity of the country against the Danes and prepared England for future military and political success as the idea of the modern nation-state developed.

The true accomplishment of Egbert may best be seen in the success of his successors. Ethelwulf, who had inherited a strong Wessex state, was succeeded by his fifth son, Alfred (later Alfred the Great), in 871. Alfred the

Great stood on the political and social foundations laid during Egbert's thirty-seven-year rule as he defended England from the relentless pressure of the Danes. Had the Anglo-Saxons been less prepared, and the Danes successful in their conquest, the development of the English state would have been profoundly altered.

—*John Powell*

Further Reading

Brooke, Christopher. *The Saxon and Norman Kings*. 3d ed. Malden, Mass.: Blackwell, 2001. Useful for its demonstration of the limits of modern knowledge of early Saxon kings, including Egbert.

Campbell, James, Eric John, and Patrick Wormald, eds. *The Anglo-Saxons*. New York: Penguin Books, 1991. A good if sometimes difficult narrative. Readers will benefit from its profuse illustrations and useful bibliography.

Dutton, Leonard. *The Anglo-Saxon Kingdoms: The Power Struggle from Hengist to Ecgberht*. Hanley Swan, England: SPA, 1993. Discusses the political struggles between the various kingdoms during the Anglo-Saxon period.

Helm, P. J. *Alfred the Great*. New York: Crowell, 1965. Provides a simple introduction to Egbert's lineage and its importance to the future accomplishments of Alfred the Great.

Hodgkin, R. H. *A History of the Anglo-Saxons*. 2 vols. 3d ed. London: Oxford University Press, 1959. A comprehensive evaluation of Egbert's influences, career, and accomplishments. Includes a good map illustrating Egbert's supremacy.

Jones, Gwyn. *A History of the Vikings*. Rev. ed. New York: Oxford University Press, 1984. A very good introduction to Viking culture in Scandinavia and its expansion into Britain, providing valuable insights into the political realities of Egbert's age.

Loyn, H. R. *The Governance of Anglo-Saxon England, 500-1087*. Stanford, Calif.: Stanford University Press, 1984. Treats the development and nature of royal government in the period. Extremely useful for separating early medieval concepts of kingship and rule from later conceptions.

Stenton, F. M. *Anglo-Saxon England*. 3d ed. New York: Oxford University Press, 1989. Provides an explanation of the events preceding Egbert's reign and a detailed account of his military campaigns.

Whitelock, Dorothy, David C. Douglas, and Susie I. Tucker, eds. *The Anglo-Saxon Chronicle*. 2d ed. New Brunswick, N.J.: Rutgers University Press, 1989. Includes translations of all versions of *The Anglo-Saxon Chronicle*. An important primary source relating to Egbert's reign.

See also: Alfred the Great; Charlemagne.

Related articles in *Great Events from History: The Middle Ages, 477-1453*: 850-950: Viking Era; 878: Alfred Defeats the Danes.

Eleanor of Aquitaine

Queen of France (r. 1137-1180) and queen of England (r. 1154-1189)

As queen of France, queen of England, and mother of two English kings, Eleanor of Aquitaine was probably the most powerful woman of her time. In addition, she promoted the literary and social style of courtly love and of the troubadours.

Born: c. 1122; either at Bordeaux or at the nearby castle of Belin, southern France

Died: April 1, 1204; the Abbey of Fontevrault, Anjou, France

Areas of achievement: Literature, government and politics

Early Life

The first important influence on the childhood of Elanor of Aquitaine (EHL-eh-nohr uhv Ar-kwih-tehn) was William IX, her grandfather. He was the earliest troubadour known by name and ruled Aquitaine and Poitou from 1086 to 1127. Though he was known for a scandalous private life and his defiance of the Church, he maintained control over his quarrelsome vassals and passed down to William X and ultimately to Eleanor a considerable inheritance. William X, Eleanor's father, was also a cultured man and a patron of poets and troubadours, though enormously quarrelsome and disrespectful of the Church.

Eleanor's mother, Aénor, who died when Eleanor was eight, was the daughter of the notorious Dangerosa, the wife to the viscount of Chatellerault, and the mistress to Eleanor's grandfather. William X was fond of Eleanor, his eldest child, and took her with him wherever he went. Medieval rulers could not reside quietly at some central castle. To maintain control over their vassals and administer justice throughout the land, they were almost always on the move from one residence to another.

Eleanor's education was not confined to women's arts such as needlework. She learned to read and write Latin, unusual accomplishments for a layperson, and probably to speak it as well. She also learned to read and write Provençal, the language of the lyric poetry of the troubadours. Eleanor herself became the inspiration of much troubadour poetry.

When Duke William X died in 1137, his daughter, under feudal law, automatically became the ward of the French king Louis VI. She did inherit her father's fief and the homage of his vassals, but she was vulnerable to seizure by any powerful suitor who could forcibly marry her and enjoy her inheritance. Louis VI hastened to betroth her, therefore, to his only surviving son. Even before they were actually married, the monarch made his son, then sixteen years old, claim Poitiers and Aquitaine and receive the homage of Eleanor's vassals. At age fifteen, Eleanor became the bride of the young man destined to be Louis VII. The bridegroom had a much less worldly upbringing than Eleanor, having been destined from earliest childhood to be a monk. Only the accidental death of his older brother, the crown prince, brought the "child monk" out of the monastery of Saint-Denis.

Drawing of Eleanor of Aquitaine from 1901. (Library of Congress)

Chroniclers agree that the young prince was appropriately smitten with adoration for this tall, beautiful girl who already carried herself like a queen. Even writers who did not always approve of her worldly tastes agreed that she was strikingly beautiful, with a superb figure, fine features, and lustrous eyes. On July 25, 1137, Louis and Eleanor were married in the cathedral of Saint André at Bordeaux in the presence of many lords and church dignitaries. A few days later, on August 8, they were consecrated duke and duchess of Aquitaine in the cathedral at Poitiers. During the banquet that followed, the abbot Suger, who was a trusted counselor to both King Louis VI and his son, brought the news that the king had died. Young Eleanor was crowned queen of France on Christmas Day, 1137.

LIFE'S WORK

Eleanor apparently enjoyed the next few years of married life, making her court the most splendid in Western Christendom. She filled it with troubadours from southern France and trouvères (court poets), their northern counterparts, who wrote not only love songs but also the epic *chansons de geste* (songs of deeds). In spite of his savage temper, Louis VII became known for his honesty and generosity and extended royal authority in France by issuing charters to the towns.

In 1147, Eleanor accompanied her husband on the Second Crusade. Edessa had fallen to the Saracens in 1144 and Christendom feared that the Holy Land might be lost, after having been won from the infidels at such great cost only a generation before. After attempting an overland trip through Bavaria, Hungary, and the Balkans, Eleanor and Louis were royally entertained in Constantinople by Emperor Manuel I Comnenus. The refinements of ancient Greece and Rome were still in evidence in Constantinople, as well as the luxuries of the East: Asian silks, Russian furs, and Persian carpets. This experience, combined with the royal reception later in the Latin principality of Antioch, where her uncle Raymond of Poitiers was their host, confirmed Eleanor's taste for Byzantine splendor.

The actual contact with the Saracens, however, and some of the dreadful effects of weather were not so pleasant. Emperor Manuel had reported that the German emperor Conrad III, whose Crusaders had preceded Louis, had already successfully engaged the Turks. Louis, wishing to share in such a triumph, moved hurriedly into dangerous territory. There he found that Conrad had actually suffered a disastrous defeat.

Louis and his band met with little better luck. On Christmas Day, heavy rains and floods destroyed their tents and baggage, and many horses and men were drowned. Soon after, the Saracens began to attack, shooting arrows from the saddle, then racing in with sabers. At Attalis, Louis abandoned the infantry and the pilgrims to proceed as best they could, while he and his horsemen and Eleanor took to ships. They made a stormy crossing to Saint Symeon, where Eleanor became fast friends with her uncle Raymond, the prince of Antioch.

Here Louis and Eleanor had a serious quarrel that was never to be entirely healed. Eleanor passionately supported Raymond in a plan to use the French troops to attack the Saracen strongholds and win back Edessa. Louis resented this proposal and asserted that he was leaving for Jerusalem and that his wife had to come with him. Eleanor refused, saying that she wanted their marriage annulled on grounds of consanguinity—that is, that they were too closely related. This was the favorite way of getting out of marriages among royalty in medieval times, as it avoided the stigma and complication of divorce. Louis left in the middle of the night and had his men abduct Eleanor from her quarters to accompany him.

Louis and Eleanor did reach Jerusalem, where they were royally welcomed by King Baldwin III. Louis joined an unwise expedition against Damascus, which had been a friendly Saracen city. This move ended in disaster and retreat. After Easter, 1149, Louis and Eleanor left for home by sea on separate ships. Eleanor's ship was captured once by Greeks but was liberated again by King Roger of Sicily.

Back in Paris at last, Louis and Eleanor quarreled, in spite of the efforts of both Pope Eugene III and Abbot Suger to reconcile them. On March 21, 1152, the marriage was pronounced null and void on the grounds of their being third cousins. The fact that Eleanor had borne only daughters (Marie and Alice) may have been the final motivation for Louis at last to take this step. Eleanor was again a desirable heiress, but she was also again in danger of seizure and forced marriage by ambitious suitors. She hastened to forestall this possibility by promoting a speedy alliance with Henry II. They were married on May 18, 1152, only eight weeks after her annulment.

Plantagenet Kings of England, 1154-1399

Reign	*Monarch*
1154-1189	Henry II (with Eleanor of Aquitaine, r. 1154-1189)
1189-1199	Richard I the Lion-Hearted
1199-1216	John I Lackland
1216-1272	Henry III
1272-1307	Edward I Longshanks
1307-1327	Edward II (with Isabella of France, r. 1308-1330)
1327-1377	Edward III (with Philippa of Hainaut, r. 1327-1369)
1377-1399	Richard II

Since his father had died, Henry was master of Normandy, Maine, Anjou, and Touraine already and might acquire England as well. He was a man of enormous energy, both physical and mental, a tireless horseman, unusually well educated, a master of languages, a good lover—altogether a more aggressive and formidable husband than Louis had ever been.

Henry soon went to England, while Eleanor held court in Angers, the capital of Anjou. She gave birth there to her first son, William. She also became a patron of Bernart de Ventadour, one of the most famous of the medieval troubadours. Meanwhile, Henry in England had forced King Stephen to name him as heir.

When Stephen died, the archbishop of Canterbury crowned Henry and Eleanor king and queen of England, on December 19, 1154. Henry was a vigorous monarch, restoring order in a land long dominated by robber barons who hired mercenaries to terrorize the countryside. Within three months, practically all mercenaries had left England and a thousand robber fortresses had been destroyed. He created new institutions, issued new silver coinage, reformed the law, and generally brought order out of social chaos. Henry also named as his chancellor a brilliant young man named Thomas Becket.

There was one thing Henry did not do as well as Louis: He did not share his executive functions with Eleanor. For some time, Eleanor was busy bearing his children. The first child, William, died when he was three years old, but Eleanor had four more sons—Henry, Richard, Geoffrey, and John—and three daughters—Matilda, Eleanor, and Joanne. After the birth of John, her last child, in 1167, Eleanor regained her strength and her energy to pursue some kind of political power of her own.

The king, who was having a long affair with Rosamund Clifford, was anxious to keep Eleanor out of England and decided that she would be useful in Aquitaine, which was restless and rebellious. Eleanor regained some degree of freedom to manage her own court, installing herself in Poitiers. Again, she reigned over a glittering court of poets and troubadours, including her old admirer Bernart de Ventadour, as well as Bertran de Born. Eleanor herself and sometimes her eldest daughter (by Louis), Marie of Champagne, presided over romantic song contests. The stylized games of courtly love attained their fullest expression there.

Henry's prestige and reputation in Christendom suffered a severe blow when four of Henry's knights murdered Thomas Becket, then archbishop of Canterbury, before his altar. The revolt of 1173 against Henry was a combined plot involving Eleanor and three of her sons, aided by Louis of France. Many other men throughout the king's territories were tired of his heavy-handed rule. Especially in Aquitaine, he was considered a tyrant. The plot to depose him might have been successful had not the young Henry lost his nerve and fled to King Louis VII.

Thus alerted, Henry reestablished his power with a series of swift and lucky strokes, repelling a French force that was invading Normandy, destroying Breton rebels before they could cross into England, capturing the king of the Scots who harassed the northern border, and even seizing the fifty-year-old Eleanor, disguised as a nobleman riding toward Paris. Eleanor was imprisoned thereafter in one of her husband's castles until Henry's death fifteen years later.

Henry II had been generous in making peace with his sons. When young Henry, the crown prince, died of dysentery, Henry made Richard his heir. Nevertheless, quarreling continued between Richard and John and their father. When Henry did not concede to Richard's demands, Richard made an alliance with Philip II, by then king of France. Henry, deathly ill of blood poisoning, capitulated to the combined forces of Richard and Philip II and died a bitter man.

In her old age, Eleanor showed herself to be an executive and diplomat of rare power. When Jerusalem had again fallen into infidel hands in 1187, King Richard I hastened to launch another crusade. While he was gone, Eleanor was kept busy protecting the realm from the ambitions of her son John in England and Philip II, who was trying to invade Normandy. When Richard was shipwrecked and held for ransom by King Henry VI of Hohenstaufen, Eleanor herself raised the 100,000 marks and went to Germany to ransom her son.

When her beloved Richard died in 1199, more dreary work remained for Eleanor, a losing battle to exercise some control over her least favored son John, now king. She died on April 1, 1204, at the Abbey of Fontevrault. The Angevin Empire died with her, for King John could not hold the vast inheritance from his father.

Significance

Eleanor of Aquitaine lived and participated actively in that age of artistic and intellectual awakening sometimes called the twelfth century renaissance. The literary aspects of that renaissance began in the Poitou-Aquitaine region of southern France early in the century. The intellectual ferment that was to result in new theological thought, new economic and political theories, and innovations in architecture, art, music, and poetry centered later at the University of Paris and the royal courts of France and England. New knowledge brought back by Crusaders, including the adventurous Eleanor herself, also encouraged new attitudes.

Eleanor successfully defied the conventional expectations about women in that era. Whatever enemies she made in her long career as a queen and the mother of kings, she retained the loyalty of Aquitaine through the political turmoil of a lifetime.

—*Katherine Snipes*

Further Reading

Andreas, Capellanus. *The Art of Courtly Love.* Translated by John Jay Parry. 1941. Reprint. New York: Columbia University Press, 1990. Andreas, known as the chaplain, set down a code of manners for court life. This text is a curious reversal of Ovid's instructions on how to seduce women. Here, however, woman is the mistress, man her pupil in homage, her vassal in service.

Burns, Jane E. "Courtly Love: Who Needs It? Recent Feminist Work in the Medieval French Tradition." *Signs: Journal of Women in Culture in Society* 27, no. 1 (Autumn, 2001): 23-57. Surveys feminist and other writings on the role of female protagonists in "reshaping" and "remapping" the courtly love tradition, the conditions of love itself, gender expression, and sexuality.

Kelly, Amy. *Eleanor of Aquitaine and the Four Kings.* Cambridge, Mass.: Harvard University Press, 1978. A detailed and well-written biography.

Kibler, William W., ed. *Eleanor of Aquitaine: Patron and Politician.* Austin: University of Texas Press, 1976. A collection of papers from distinguished medieval scholars on the significance of Eleanor within her own and subsequent centuries.

Lewis, C. S. *The Allegory of Love*. New York: Oxford University Press, 1976. Although this classic work, originally published in 1936, contains no specific information about Eleanor, it provides a detailed discussion of the tradition of courtly love and its significant impact on later literature and popular thought.

_______. *Eleanor of Aquitaine*. Translated by Peter Wiles. New York: Coward-McCann, 1968. An authoritative and admirable biography of Eleanor. In the original French, this work won the Pris Historia in 1966.

Rorem, Paul. "The Company of Medieval Women Theologians." *Theology Today* 60, no. 1 (April, 2003): 82-93. Argues that the tradition of women theologians during the Middle Ages included a vast "company" of religious practitioners and activists and not a company made up of those who were merely contemplating. The author notes the final years of Eleanor's life, when she was in residence at the abbey at Fontevrault.

Rougemont, Denis de. *Love in the Western World*. 1956. Reprint. Translated by Montgomery Belgion. New York: Schocken Books, 1990. This is a classic work on the meaning of love in Western civilization, including the radical change that started among the troubadours of southern France in the time of Eleanor.

Warner, Marina. *Alone of All Her Sex: The Myth and the Cult of the Virgin Mary*. New York: Vintage Books, 1983. Good for background information about the view of women in the Middle Ages, though courtly love, as practiced in Eleanor's famous courts of love, had only a very remote connection to the cult of the Virgin.

Wheeler, Bonnie, and John Carmi Parsons, eds. *Eleanor of Aquitaine: Lord and Lady*. New York: Palgrave Macmillan, 2003. A study of more than five hundred pages (with a sixty page bibliography), discussing topics such as Eleanor's positions in the government of her reigning sons, a comparison of Eleanor with other noblewomen of the time, and divorce and canon law.

See also: Adam de la Halle; Saint Thomas Becket; Blanche of Castile; Geoffrey Chaucer; Chrétien de Troyes; Edward III; Jean Froissart; Geoffrey of Monmouth; Gottfried von Strassburg; Hartmann von Aue; Henry II; Hildegard von Bingen; King John; Marie de France; Philip II; Richard I; King Stephen; Suger; Wolfram von Eschenbach.

Related articles in *Great Events from History: The Middle Ages, 477-1453*: c. 1100: Rise of Courtly Love; 1147-1149: Second Crusade; 1154-1204: Angevin Empire Is Established; December 29, 1170: Murder of Thomas Becket; c. 1180: Chrétien de Troyes Writes *Perceval*.

Saint Elizabeth of Hungary

Hungarian social reformer

Elizabeth, seeking to live according to the Christian ideal, established the first orphanage for homeless children in Central Europe and actively cared for the poor and the unemployed.

Born: 1207; Sárospatak, Hungary

Died: November 17, 1231; Marburg, Hesse (now Maribor, Slovenia)

Also known as: Elizabeth of Thuringia; Elisabeth of Thuringia

Areas of achievement: Religion and theology, social reform

Early Life

Elizabeth of Hungary was born in Sárospatak to King Andrew II of Hungary (r. 1205-1235) and Gertrud of Andechs-Meran. Her mother met a tragic death in 1213, when Hungarian conspirators had her murdered. Elizabeth's two maternal uncles, Berthold, titular patriarch of Aquileia, and Bishop Eckbert of Bamberg, who had played a role in the assassination of the king of Germany and emperor Philip of Swabia (r. 1198-1208), and sought refuge at the Hungarian court, were high ecclesiastics. In 1211, Hermann I (c. 1156-1217), landgrave of Thuringia, sent a delegation led by the knight Walter of Vargila to Pozsony to request the hand of Elizabeth in marriage for his son, Hermann.

The landgrave probably wanted to restore his weakened social and financial resources through this marriage with the Hungarian royal family. He may also have hoped to rely on the support of the Eastern monarch in the deadly struggle between Emperor Otto IV of Brunswick (1174?-1215) and emperor Frederick II (r. 1220-1250), the new papal protégé for the German throne (r. 1212-1250). Bishop Eckbert may have suggested the plan,

Engraving of Saint Elizabeth of Hungary, from a painting by Fra Angelico in the Academy of Fine Arts at Perugia. (Frederick Ungar Publishing Co.)

though it is possible that King Otakar I of Bohemia (r. 1198-1230) may have also tried to establish a triple alliance by including the king of Hungary. From another point of view, family ties between one of the leading noble families in the empire and the Hungarian court might have enhanced the diplomatic position of Andrew II against some German princes, who still looked on Hungary as a country to be invaded and plundered.

Knight Vargila successfully concluded a marriage agreement, and the four-year-old bride, richly endowed, was dispatched to the Thuringian court at the castle of the Wartburg, near Eisenach. A bathtub of pure silver and a thousand pieces of gold formed only a portion of her dowry. It is known from her second husband, Louis, that the Thuringian court had never before seen such riches. They also expressed surprise at Elizabeth's large personal entourage of servants and nurses.

Hermann I maintained an elaborate court and provided for poets and artists of the age. It may be that Walther von der Vogelweide or Wolfram von Eschenbach (while working on his *Parzival*, c. 1200-1210; English translation, 1894) spent some time at the castle at Wartburg. Hermann I and his wife, Sophia, met the young Elizabeth at Eisenach, and the official engagement celebration was held soon after at Wartburg. Elizabeth was educated at the Thuringian court; the curriculum included the study of contemporary poetry and writers, the history of leading families in the empire, art appreciation, Latin, and religion. As a child, Elizabeth liked to play, ride horses, and participate in games as well as pray in the chapel. Even as a child she displayed empathy and compassion toward the poor. Concerned with Elizabeth's appearance as a lady of society, however, her mother-in-law cautioned her about being too loud and exuberant.

In 1213, when her mother was murdered, the six-year-old Elizabeth saw her bloody, mutilated body in a dream. After that, she spent more time in prayer before the crucifix and began to dress more simply. She began to pray for the murderers of her mother. Elizabeth was nine when she lost her fiancé, Hermann, and one year later her father-in-law died. It was at this time that Louis, her fiancé's younger brother, became Elizabeth's protector and good friend. After discussing Elizabeth's uncertain future, Louis decided that she would be his wife. They were married in 1221 in the presence of the nobles of Thuringia and of other German regions. Knight Vargila led Elizabeth to the altar, and her father sent additional gifts. At the end of September, 1222, the young couple visited King Andrew at Pozsony. Traveling by horse, they were horrified at the destruction and decline of the country. It was the year of the Hungarian Golden Bull, by which the Hungarian nobles, discouraged by the nearly total disintegration of law and order in the realm, had forced the king to share his government with them.

LIFE'S WORK

Under the guidance of her confessor, Father Rodinger, a Franciscan friar, Elizabeth began to lead a deeper spiritual life, carried out charity work, and established an orphanage (the first in Central Europe). She cared for lepers, of whom she was not afraid, and constructed a twenty-eight-bed hospital for them. She then came under the spiritual directorship of Konrad von Marburg (c. 1180-1233, the noted mystic, Franciscan preacher, and chief papal inquisitor in Germany.

In 1225, Louis embarked on a military campaign summoned by the emperor, and in his absence, Elizabeth governed Thuringia. She healed the wounds caused by natural disasters and was concerned about social discrimination among the disadvantaged; she fed nine hundred poor people daily, provided tools and obtained work for the able-bodied unemployed men, and taught the women to spin. At the same time, she represented her husband in high society, received distinguished guests at the court, and participated in hunting parties.

In 1227, Louis was again summoned by the emperor and joined a Crusade; Elizabeth was expecting their third child. By the time Gertrud was born, Louis was already dead, having fallen ill at Otranto. Elizabeth's brothers-in-law, uneasy about her spending habits, forbade her to handle her own fiscal affairs, prompting her to leave Wartburg in October, 1227, with her three small children. Nobody in Eisenach, however, would accommodate them. After placing the children in foster homes, Elizabeth, accompanied by two of her royal servants, Guda and Isentrud, finally found shelter in an innkeeper's stable. She spun cloth for a living until Mechtild, abbess of Kitzingen, provided for her in the abbey. Her uncle, the bishop of Bamberg, placed his castle at Pottstein at her disposal. The bishop tried to persuade her to marry Emperor Frederick II, but Elizabeth firmly declined the proposal. Only the future of her children concerned her; for herself, she desired to live in poverty. She had her husband's remains buried in the monastery he had founded at Reinhardsbrunn. After the burial, and with Knight Vargila's support, she regained her right to manage the estates she had inherited as a widow. Making a vow in the Franciscan church in Eisenach to renounce all earthly love and free will, she retained her property for the sake of her children, Hermann, Sophia, and Gertrud, and for making provision for the poor. She did not live in the castle at Wartburg but in nearby Wehrda, in a primitive house built of blocks of dirt. She spun cloth to earn her living and assisted in the hospital she had founded.

To deepen Elizabeth's humility, Konrad used crude methods such as flagellation and beatings, the dismissal of her two servants, forbidding her to distribute large sums of money to the poor, and allowing her to give only one slice of bread each to the hungry. Elizabeth used her own bed to care for a young boy sick with dysentery; when he died, she put a girl with leprosy in her bed. Augmenting the abuse and humiliation suffered at the hand of Konrad, gossip now began to undermine Elizabeth's reputation. She was ridiculed for her loud laughter, her refusal to dress in black, and the apparent ease with which she forgot her deceased husband. There were even rumors that she was happily engaged in an affair with the friar, about which she was confronted by Knight Vargila. In response, Elizabeth showed the marks of the flagellations and beatings received from Konrad.

Knowing that she was weak and would die soon, Elizabeth stayed in bed for the last two weeks of her life, finalizing the arrangements for the distribution of her wealth and her children's future. Three days before she died, she sent everyone away from her except Konrad, who remained at her bedside. She died in the early hours of November 17, 1231. Her body lay in state for four days in the Franciscan church at Eisenach, dressed in clothing of the poor. During this time, the inhabitants of Thuringia came to her coffin not to pray for her but to ask for her intercession on their behalf. It is reported that during the following days and weeks, numerous miracles occurred at her grave.

Konrad informed Pope Gregory IX of the death of Elizabeth, and the pontiff authorized the friar to make preparations for her canonization. When Konrad was murdered in July, 1233, the bishop of Hildesheim carried on with the canonization process. It was then that the *Libellus de dictis IV ancillarum* (depositions of Saint Elizabeth's four handmaidens—Isentrud, Guda, Irmingard, and Elisabeth) was recorded in writing, followed by a strict ecclesiastical investigation. On May 26, 1235, in Perugia on the Feast of Pentecost, Pope Gregory IX entered Elizabeth's name in the canon of saints (papal bull *Gloriosus in maiestate*). The first church erected in her honor was built by her brother-in-law Konrad, who was grand master of the German Order, at Marburg. On May 1, 1236, her coffin was elevated on the altar in the presence of her children, brothers-in-law, four archbishops, eight bishops, and a multitude of German, Hungarian, Czech, and French pilgrims.

SIGNIFICANCE

Saint Elizabeth of Hungary lived according to the Christian ideal, fusing it with the pastoral concept of the mendicant orders in teaching and practicing humility and social equality. She did not believe that social stabilization could occur by suddenly elevating the lower strata; rather, she believed that the upper classes should willingly descend to the aid of the poor. In addition to building a hospital and establishing an asylum for homeless children, Elizabeth demonstrated an attitude toward the poor that was realistic as well as humane. Thus, although she developed a plan for feeding the poor, she abhorred idleness, quoting from Saint Paul that one who did not work would not eat.

—Z. J. Kosztolnyik

FURTHER READING

Bihl, Michael. "Elizabeth of Hungary." *Catholic Encyclopaedia* 5 (1909): 389-391. A thorough report on Saint Elizabeth and her time in accordance with early biographies and sermons. The work colorfully depicts the Hungarian royal court, life in Thuringia, and the background of the Crusades in the early thirteenth century.

Hawkins, Henry. *The History of St. Elizabeth, 1632*. Ilkley, Yorkshire, England: Scolar Press, 1974. Originally written in the early seventeenth century, this text is a still-useful historical study of Elizabeth's life.

Obbard, Elizabeth Ruth. *Poverty, My Riches: A Study of St. Elizabeth of Hungary, 1207-1231*. Southampton, England: Saint Austin Press, 1997. A brief look at Elizabeth's life as an ascetic and her devotion to helping the poor and needy. Bibliography, appendix.

Thurston, Herbert, and Donald Attwater, eds. *Butler's Lives of the Saints, Complete Edition*. 1956. Reprint. Vol. 3. Westminster, Md.: Christian Classics, 1990. A readable and informative account that includes quotations from the depositions of Elizabeth's loyal servants. Reveals the remarkable depth of Elizabeth and Louis' relationship, and treats Konrad's spiritual directorship dispassionately. Bibliography.

SEE ALSO: Saint Clare of Assisi; Frederick II; Gregory IX; Stephen I; Walther von der Vogelweide; Wolfram von Eschenbach.

RELATED ARTICLES in *Great Events from History: The Middle Ages, 477-1453*: 890's: Magyars Invade Italy, Saxony, and Bavaria; 12th-14th centuries: Social and Political Impact of Leprosy; April 16, 1209: Founding of the Franciscans; 1227-1230: Frederick II Leads the Sixth Crusade.

ETHELRED II, THE UNREADY

King of England (r. 978-1013 and 1014-1016)

Ethelred was the son of a powerful king and a member of one of the most successful and prestigious dynasties of the Middle Ages but was unable to cope with repeated Viking assaults. His name became associated with military and political ineptitude.

BORN: 968?; place unknown
DIED: April 23, 1016; London, England
ALSO KNOWN AS: Æthelred II, the Unready
AREA OF ACHIEVEMENT: Government and politics

EARLY LIFE

Ethelred (EHTH-ehl-rehd) II was consecrated as king at Kingston on May 4, 979. In some respects he had immense advantages. He was the son of King Edgar, who had reigned virtually unchallenged from 959 to 975. Among his immediate relatives and ancestors were Alfred the Great, Edward the Elder, and his great-uncle Athelstan, known even to his Viking enemies as "the victorious." His kingdom was rich and well organized, and he had no immediate rivals.

Against these advantages, however, were a string of disadvantages that may go some way toward explaining the failure of his reign. To begin with, what he was king of was not absolutely clear. By birth and long ancestry he was king of Wessex, in practice all of southern England. His ancestors, furthermore, had gained effective control over those shires of middle England that had not been settled by Viking invaders; by a combination of war and diplomacy, they had also subjected the Danish midlands, the Viking-settled North of England, and areas of Wales and Scotland. Yet none of these regions was absolutely secure. Much depended on the personality of the king.

Ethelred, furthermore, cannot have been more than thirteen when he came to the throne; his father, Edgar, did not marry his mother, Alfthryth, until 964, and they had one son before Ethelred, but he died young. Even more significant, Alfthryth had not been Edgar's first wife, but his second or even third; by one of the former wives, probably Æthelflæd, Edgar had had a son Edward, who immediately succeeded his father as king in 975. Ethelred would not have come to the throne at all if his half brother Edward had not been murdered at Corfe Gate in Dorset in 978 or 979. Ethelred himself cannot have been responsible for this act—he was too young. Blame was, however, variously ascribed to overzealous servants of Ethelred, and to Ethelred's mother, Alfthryth. Modern historians are not entirely convinced by these accusations. Some have pointed out that stepmothers always make popular scapegoats, and others noted the signs that Edward had already made himself unpopular. Nevertheless, the murder of a king was regarded as a peculiarly horrible deed, and there is no doubt that, by popular reaction, Edward was soon elevated to the status of sainthood.

Ethelred accordingly came to the throne under a cloud, perhaps not being held personally liable for his half brother's murder but having benefited from it and having done nothing subsequently about it. William of Malmesbury, the author of *Gesta Regum Anglorum* (1125; *The Deeds of the Kings of the English*, 1847), recorded that Alfthryth beat her son so fiercely with candles for crying over Edward's death that he developed a phobia for candles. This may represent an early half-contemptuous view of him, no good foundation for success.

For perhaps fifteen years subsequently, Ethelred appears to have been dominated by various groups of advisers: to begin with, his mother, and then the established aldermen and bishops of England. It is striking, though, that Alfthryth ceases to figure as a witness to royal land grants from 985, though she was not dead, reappearing in this role some ten years later. In surviving documents, Ethelred appears to show traces of remorse over his behavior toward the Church during this period; he is known to have expropriated land from several religious foundations and to have ordered a harrying of his own town of Rochester in Kent to punish some disobedience or resistance. A plausible explanation is that King Ethelred escaped from the control of his mother's "faction" after the death of the powerful bishop of Winchester, Ethelwold, on August 1, 984, and for some time was dominated by secular favorites such as Alfgar, son of Alfric, alderman of Hampshire. Ethelred, however, had Alfgar blinded in 993 and appears to have made up matters with his mother, the Church authorities, and the more established dignitaries of the kingdom.

The image of Ethelred II, the Unready, patterned on a likeness from an old coin. (Hulton|Archive at Getty Images)

Life's Work

The reason may well have been increasing pressure by a new wave of Viking invaders from Scandinavia. A first wave of attempts to rule over England had been decisively defeated a century before by Ethelred's ancestors, though at the price of leaving large areas controlled and settled by Danes or Norwegians. From about 991, Viking pressure once more grew steadily stronger. In that year, a raiding force was met and challenged by Byrhtnoth, alderman of Essex, on the river Blackwater near Maldon. Byrhtnoth himself was one of the great figures of Ethelred's early reign, by tradition and indeed by archaeology (for his headless body has been measured of immense size and combative disposition). His courage was his undoing, however, for he accepted a Viking "dare" to level combat and was killed with many of his men. Ethelred then paid ten thousand pounds in tribute to persuade the Viking army to go away: In so doing he set up an almost inevitable contrast between his own policy of appeasement and his ancestors' rigorously maintained one of immediate resistance.

At this point Ethelred's career falls under the spell of the one long account of his reign, written by an anonymous compiler of *The Anglo-Saxon Chronicle* (compiled c. 890 to c. 1150), working perhaps in London. This account is so powerful, so consistent, and so incisively phrased that it has determined—or ruined—Ethelred's reputation ever since. What the chronicler had to say is in essence that the Vikings continued their assaults on England from 991 to 1016, when Ethelred died, to be succeeded very soon by Canute the Great, king of Denmark. During this period, the English paid Danegeld no less than six times, the amounts rising remorselessly from the ten thousand pounds of 991 to the thirty-seven thousand of 1007 (and the eighty-three thousand of 1018). Yet not only did the wretched people of England have to contribute all this silver in taxes; they also had to suffer the consequences of continual ravaging (for the Danegeld was usually paid after the Vikings had done their looting, not before). In addition, they had to pay enormous amounts toward the upkeep of English armies and navies, though

ANGLO-SAXON KINGS OF ENGLAND, 802-1016

Reign	*Ruler*
802-839	EGBERT
839-856	Æthelwulf
856-860	Æthelbald
860-866	Æthelbert
866-871	Ethelred (Æthelred) I
871-899	ALFRED THE GREAT
899-924	EDWARD THE ELDER (with sister ÆTHELFLÆD)
924-939	Æthelstan
939-946	Edmund the Magnificent
946-955	Eadred
955-959	Eadwig (Edwy) All-Fair
959-975	Edgar the Peaceable
975-978	Edward the Martyr
978-1016	ETHELRED (ÆTHELRED) II, THE UNREADY
1016	Edmund II Ironside
1016	Ascendancy of Canute the Great (Danish line begins)

these latter rarely fought. They had in fact the worst of all worlds, paying "protection money" to both sides and getting no benefit from either. Any one of the above policies—fight, surrender, or simply do nothing—would have been better than all three of them, or so the chronicler implied. His contempt for his own government reached a peak in 1006, when he described the English army as the "innhere," the "in-harriers," and the Danish as the "uthere," the "out-harriers."

The chronicler, furthermore, said repeatedly that there was no lack of readiness to fight on the part of the English people. The levies were, however, continually betrayed by treacherous and cowardly leaders, such as Alfric in 992 and 1003 and alderman Eadric, "the grabber," in 1009 and 1015, or by internal division and ineptitude, as shown by Eadric's brother Birhtric in 1009 again. Over all of this Ethelred seems only to have presided. The chronicler's account of low morale and confusion is largely confirmed by such documents as the "Sermon of the Wolf to the English" given by Archbishop Wulfstan of York around 1014.

Nevertheless, one has to note that the chronicler wrote from hindsight, from a time when the Danes had in fact conquered England, and also that his view was a "worm's-eye view," not based (unlike earlier parts of *The Anglo-Saxon Chronicle*) on official sources and good information. If one looks again, and skeptically, at his account, one can discern some signs of royal good intentions at least. Ethelred tried to counterattack in 1000 by leading a naval force against the north of England. In 1002, he made a diplomatic marriage to Emma, sister of the powerful duke of Normandy, and in the same year tried to eliminate the Danes in loyal areas of England by the Saint Brice's Day Massacre. In 1008-1009 especially, his government not only organized a massive navy to fight the Danes but also imposed on the country a gigantic three-day penitential fast. It is true that none of these measures worked, the massacre in particular being counterproductive and the navy of 1009 expending all its energies in civil war. Still, Ethelred's government showed no sign of running out of ideas; while in a peculiar way the sporadic outbursts of English defiance, like the resistance of London in 1013, were on the whole encouraged by the presence of the king.

The English did, however, weary in the end of defeat and taxation, perhaps especially after the failures of 1009, the martyrdom of Ælfheah, archbishop of Canterbury, in 1012 (pelted to death with ox bones by drunken Vikings), and the arrival of King Sweyn of Denmark in 1013. Northern areas made a separate peace. Southern England remained loyal, but only with conditions. In 1015, Ethelred's own son Edmund Ironside defied his father to pursue the traditional Wessex policy of giving battle. In confused circumstances, with even prominent Vikings such as Thorkell "the tall" changing sides, Ethelred finally died in London on Saint George's Day, 1016. His son Edmund succeeded, and fought Sweyn's son, the formidable Canute the Great, to a draw; on Edmund's death later that year, however, English resistance came to an end, and the country for the first time acknowledged a Dane as king in all areas.

SIGNIFICANCE

Ethelred's nickname still seems apt. It is based on an Anglo-Saxon pun, which notices that Ethelred means literally "noble counsel" and adds to it the Anglo-Saxon compound noun "unraed," which means "no-counsel" or perhaps "bad-counsel." This could mean that Ethelred did not accept advice; more likely, however, it means that he himself had no plans. He merely reacted to circumstances. For all that can be said for his government's ability to make laws, mint coins, and collect taxes, this remains a fair judgment. Ethelred started badly, was initially surrounded by men older and stronger than himself, and never managed either to prevent factional fighting or to impose his own leadership. This was explicable and even excusable, but never praiseworthy. "Unraed" is a good short description of him, and was probably coined (though not recorded) in his own lifetime.

—*T. A. Shippey*

FURTHER READING

Ashdown, Margaret, trans. and ed. *English and Norse Documents Relating to the Reign of Ethelred the Unready.* Cambridge, England: Cambridge University Press, 1930. Useful edition and translation of documents from both sides of the Viking invasions.

Campbell, Alistair, ed. *Encomium Emmae Reginae.* London: Royal Historical Society, 1949. Discusses the life of Ethelred's widow Emma, a woman who remained influential long after her first husband's death.

Hill, David. *An Atlas of Anglo-Saxon England, 700-1066.* Oxford, England: Basil Blackwell, 1981. Invaluable maps of the confused political boundaries, campaigns, and countermarchings of Ethelred's reign.

Howard, Ian. *Swein Forkbeard's Invasions and the Danish Conquest of England, 991-1017.* Rochester, N.Y.: Boydell and Brewer, 2003. Discusses propaganda and legend in the context of King Sweyn's invasions, as well as possible explanations.

Jones, Gwyn. *A History of the Vikings.* Rev. ed. New York: Oxford University Press, 1984. A very good introduction to Viking culture in Scandinavia and its expansion into Britain.

Keynes, Simon. *The Diplomas of King Æthelred "the Unready," 978-1016.* New York: Cambridge University Press, 1980. Though highly specialized, this study attempts to get behind the familiar accounts of Ethelred's reign to the reality of its internal politics.

Lavelle, Ryan. *Æthelred II: King of the English, 978-1016.* Charleston, S.C.: Tempus, 2002. A biography covering Ethelred's reign.

Stenton, F. M. *Anglo-Saxon England.* 3d ed. New York: Oxford University Press, 1989. Still the best overall account of the king and of the period, given in great detail.

Whitelock, Dorothy, David C. Douglas, and Susie I. Tucker, eds. *The Anglo-Saxon Chronicle.* 2d ed. New Brunswick, N.J.: Rutgers University Press, 1989. Translation of the major early account of the life and work of Ethelred.

SEE ALSO: Alfred the Great; Canute the Great; Edward the Confessor; Edward the Elder; Harold II; Saint Olaf; Olaf I.

RELATED ARTICLES in *Great Events from History: The Middle Ages, 477-1453*: 850-950: Viking Era; 1016: Canute Conquers England.

JAN VAN EYCK AND HUBERT VAN EYCK

Flemish painters

In paintings of unprecedented accuracy of observation and coherence of form, the van Eycks achieved a fusion of Christian religious content with a passionate devotion to visual fact.

JAN VAN EYCK

BORN: c. 1390; possibly Maaseik, Bishopric of Liège, Holy Roman Empire (now in Belgium)

DIED: July 9, 1441; Bruges, Flanders (now in Belgium)

HUBERT VAN EYCK

BORN: Before 1390; possibly Maaseik, Bishopric of Liège, Holy Roman Empire

DIED: Probably September 18, 1426; Ghent, Flanders (now in Belgium)

AREAS OF ACHIEVEMENT: Art, religion and theology

EARLY LIVES

The commonplace facts of the lives of Jan (yahn) and Hubert van Eyck (HYEW-burt van ik) are almost entirely absent from the historical record. Jan's estimated year of birth, 1390, seems reasonable in view of the established details of his early career, as well as his date of death, 1441. Of Hubert, whose very existence has occasionally been called into question by scholars, evidence suggests that he was an elder brother; a taxation document from 1426 establishes that he died at about that time.

Both Hubert and Jan may have worked in The Hague (now in the Netherlands) from about 1415 to 1417, and it is certain that Jan was employed in that city from 1422 to 1424 by John of Bavaria, who as count of Holland maintained his court there. A document indicates that Jan was accompanied in his work there by at least two assistants. In early 1425, civil war broke out in Holland, and Jan sought refuge in Flanders, where Hubert had already gone. On May 19, Jan van Eyck entered the service of Philip III, duke of Burgundy. Philip the Good, as he was known, had a high regard both for Jan's artistic abilities and for his skills as a negotiator, since over the next several years Jan was engaged in various missions on Philip's behalf, including a journey in 1428 to negotiate Philip's marriage to Isabella, daughter of King John I of Portugal. Jan's role, at minimum, was to paint portraits of Isabella to help Philip come to a decision about the match. For the sake of security, two pictures were returned to Bruges, one by sea and the other by land.

Of the circumstances of Hubert's death, and of its effect on the work in which he and Jan may have been jointly engaged, there is no documentation; their artistic and professional relationship can only be inferred from the paintings that have been attributed to them. A third brother, Lambert, who survived Jan, seems not to have been an artist.

Around 1432, Jan van Eyck bought a house in Bruges. By 1434 he had married, and in that year, his son was born; a daughter was born several years later. Only the first name of Jan's wife, Margaretha, is known; of her social origins there is no record, but it may be assumed that a renowned artist of van Eyck's stature would seek a favorable marriage. Jan's portrait of her when she was thirty-three, painted in 1439, shows a woman of great intelligence, if not beauty. If Jan's painting of 1433, known as *The Man with the Red Turban*, is, as seems likely, a self-portrait, the modern viewer has a visual document of a prosperous fifteenth century husband and wife.

Jan van Eyck. (Hulton|Archive at Getty Images)

LIFE'S WORK

The dominant form of painting in northern Europe during the youth of Jan and Hubert van Eyck was manuscript illumination, a form that dominated the art of the Middle Ages and that was a particularly vital element of what came to be known as Gothic art. The small scale of manuscript illumination required extremely precise technique; that, and the need to include decorative elements and writing within the page, tended to favor qualities of abstract form and color rather than observation of nature. Around 1400, however, a trend toward naturalism in manuscript painting gained momentum in many northern European centers, including the region of Limbourg, near the van Eycks' birthplace. The origins of this new attention to natural appearances are varied, but the influence of Giotto of Florence and his successors is certain. These fourteenth century Italian masters irreversibly influenced the depiction of the human figure, presenting it as a three-dimensional mass in an illusionistic space. The representation of natural light and the convincing portrayal of action and emotion were other progressive elements of Italian art that spread to major centers of artistic production in fifteenth century Europe.

In the earlier parts of their careers, the van Eycks were almost certainly occupied with manuscript painting. Probably the earliest works attributable to Jan or Hubert are the *Heures de Turin* (the Turin hours), several paintings that were once part of a book of miniatures, *Très Belles Heures de Notre Dame*. This volume was the effort of many artists working over an extended period of time whose identities are elusive, but in the case of the *Heures de Turin*, the modernity of the use of space in landscape and the subtle modulation of tones suggest the involvement of artists of very progressive tendencies. No more likely candidates than the van Eycks have been proposed, but opinion has always been divided about which particular characteristics in the works can be attributed to Hubert and which to Jan, or in fact whether the works represent a collaborative effort at all. All that can be said with assurance is that the *Heures de Turin* represent the vital trends that reach fulfillment in later works of the van Eycks.

Generally accepted as a work of Hubert is *The Three Marys at the Sepulcher*, a painting on a wooden panel that is substantially larger than a typical manuscript illumination. Although undated, it is considered a work of Hubert's mature years and exhibits many qualities thought to be uniquely his own, such as a sharply inclined ground plane, awkward perspective, and slender, small-headed figures. There is an intensity of narrative interest in the figures thought to be atypical of the work of Jan. Its great significance, however, is that, in it, the vigor and monumentality of the style of the *Heures de Turin* are rendered on a larger scale.

The scholarly problem of distinguishing between the work of Jan and Hubert recurs in connection with the great polyptych, *The Ghent Altarpiece*, but here a consensus has emerged from decades of study. An inscription on the painting, placed there by order of the patron who commissioned it, states "Hubert van Eyck, the greatest painter who ever lived, began the work, which his brother Jan, the second in art, finished at the instigation of Jodocus Vijdt. With this verse, on 6 May [1432] he invites you to look at this work." Given such a documentary starting point, if the altarpiece were less complex, attribution of its design and execution would not be problematic. The altarpiece is, however, composed of twenty panels of differing shapes, dimensions, and representational scales. When closed, the work's eight exterior panels comprise an area 218 centimeters (86 inches) wide and 314 centimeters (124 inches) high; opened, its twelve panels together measure 455 centimeters (179 inches) in width. Within this impressive format, a multitude of figures is presented in an upper and lower register; centrally placed in the upper register is the seated figure of God, representing the Trinity. This figure, larger than life-size, is clothed in resplendent garments painted with an almost miraculous precision and vibrancy of color. To the left is the Virgin, and to the right is Saint John the Baptist. On either side of this central group are panels depicting angel musicians, and at the sides of this upper portion are the figures of Adam on the left and Eve on the right.

The lower register consists of five panels that together form a continuous landscape. The large central panel, which is the width of the four flanking panels combined, is a scene of the Adoration of the Lamb representing Revelation 7:2-10: "After this I beheld, and, lo, a great multitude, which no man could number, of all nations, and kindreds, and people, and tongues, stood before the throne, and before the Lamb, clothed with white robes, and palms in their hands." The outer panels show the Just Judges, the Warriors of Christ, the Holy Hermits, and the Holy Pilgrims. In its entirety, the Adoration panels may be considered as the evocation of either an Earthly Paradise or the New Jerusalem. There is everywhere a profusion of grass, flowers, trees, and fruit, enveloped by a radiant, unifying light.

The consensus of scholars, which seems unlikely to be changed by further study, is that Hubert was largely responsible for the design of the altarpiece and for much of its execution, while Jan was the designer and painter of the figures of Adam and Eve and of parts of the rest, including the orange trees, palms, and cypresses of the Adoration of the Lamb. The question has been raised whether *The Ghent Altarpiece* was actually envisioned from the start in its present form by either Hubert or Jan, calling into question the unity of the overall structure. Yet few believe that the difference in scale, for example, of the figures in the upper and lower parts is anything but intentional; the contrast in scale seems visually and emotionally effective, and it is theologically sound.

With *The Ghent Altarpiece*, the technique of painting reached a degree of perfection that was the envy of painters in succeeding generations. The impression was given by the Italian artist Giorgio Vasari, writing in 1550, that Jan van Eyck had invented the technique of painting with oil. Oil had been used in the Low Countries as a medium before the van Eycks, but it is clear that the reputation for brilliance and subtlety gained by their works was in some measure the result of new methods in the preparation of paint, probably involving the use of a superior oil and more painstaking grinding of the pigment. The effects of their improvements were both aesthetic—a gain in the ease and flexibility with which paint could be applied—and physical, in that the paintings proved remarkably durable.

While working on *The Ghent Altarpiece*, Jan van Eyck accepted other commissions, but his next major works appeared after its completion in 1432. *The Arnolfini Wedding*, perhaps his best-known painting, was finished in 1434. It represents the wedding of Giovanni Arnolfini and Giovanna Cenami, natives of Lucca who resided in Bruges. It has been shown that each detail of the work has symbolic meaning and that the painting is in a sense almost a legal documentation of a wedding, with the two witnesses (the painter himself, and his wife—a priest was not strictly necessary) shown reflected in a convex mirror at the back of a small room in which the ceremony takes place.

The years that remained to Jan van Eyck were as productive as those preceding *The Arnolfini Wedding*. In addition to portraits of Arnolfini, Margaretha van Eyck, and others, he completed several panels in which the donor is represented appearing before the infant Christ and the Madonna in a contemporary setting. Of these, the finest is perhaps *Madonna with Chancellor Rolin*, which places the subjects in a beautifully rendered Romanesque palace, with a view of a city on a river receding to a distant mountain landscape.

SIGNIFICANCE

Jan and Hubert van Eyck began their careers in a milieu in which artistic endeavor tended to be anonymous and guilds controlled the standards and methods of production in the arts. Jan's career—there is no direct evidence of a "career" for Hubert, in this respect—demonstrated that an artist could achieve individual distinction and be recognized not merely by fellow artists but by citizens generally. Artists began to gain status beyond that of mere specialized craftspeople. Jan van Eyck's missions on behalf of his patron Philip the Good show that he was a trusted representative in political and personal matters, and one can infer that he was a man of substantial intellect.

Regardless of the credit due individually to Hubert or Jan in their works, each possessed a receptiveness to new ways of seeing the world, with the skill and sense of organization to complete projects of major physical and spiritual scope. On the slender evidence of Hubert's attributed works, one might say that he was the more passionate and Jan the more analytical personality. Both, however, presented the world as suffused with a unifying light and color that incarnate spiritual unity. The diversity of the natural world is seen with a fresh eye, but not as purely optical phenomena.

The paintings of the van Eycks belong to the first flowering of the Renaissance in the art of northern Europe. Their conquest of natural appearances, even though it was pursued in the realm of religious art, contributed to a process of secularization that affected all facets of life.

—*Clyde S. McConnell*

FURTHER READING

Baldass, Ludwig. *Jan van Eyck*. London: Phaidon Press, 1952. This major monograph is exceptionally detailed both in text and illustrations, and it gives a good account of the historical context of the van Eycks' work and has thorough appendices. The quality black-and-white reproductions are more sympathetic to the works than those in most later publications.

Borchert, Till-Holger. *Age of Van Eyck: The Mediterranean World and Early Netherlandish Painting, 1430-1530*. New York: Thames and Hudson, 2002. Published concurrently with an exhibit held in Bruges in 2002, this collection explores painting in Southern Europe influenced by the van Eycks. One chapter looks at "Van Eyck and the Invention of Oil Painting." Includes color illustrations, a bibliography, and index.

De Hamel, Christopher. *The British Library Guide to Manuscript Illumination: History and Techniques*. Toronto: University of Toronto Press, 2001. Presents in a very brief format, with some illustrations, the ins and outs of manuscript illumination, including a history of the fine, detailed art.

De Vos, Dirk. *The Flemish Primitives: The Masterpieces*. Princeton, N.J.: Princeton University Press, 2002. A historical look at several Flemish master painters, including Jan van Eyck. Includes mostly color illustrations, a map, and a bibliography.

Faggin, Giorgio T. *The Complete Paintings of the Van Eycks*. New York: Penguin Books, 1986. Presents all the known paintings of the van Eycks. Major works are reproduced in color, many of them accompanied by enlarged details. The remainder of the reproductions are found in a separate section at the back of the book, which also contains extensive notes ranging from anecdotes to scholarly information. Includes a selection of comments on the van Eycks by writers through the centuries, a chronology, and appendices.

Foister, Susan, Sue Jones, and Delphine Cool, eds. *Investigating Jan van Eyck*. Turnhout, Belgium: Brepols, 2000. A collection of papers, most read at a symposium on Jan van Eyck in 1998, which cover topics such as Jan's painting style and technique, handwriting, and underdrawing, and the use of dress and silk textiles in his work. Includes color illustrations, a bibliography, and index.

Panofsky, Erwin. "Jan van Eyck's Arnolfini Portrait." In *Renaissance Art*, edited by Gilbert Creighton. New York: Harper and Row, 1970. This classic essay was first published in *Burlington Magazine* in 1934, introducing the theory of "disguised symbolism," which became a standard tool of art history. The author was one of the great scholars of art history, and he remains one of the most readable.

Van Puyvelde, Leo. *Flemish Painting from the Van Eycks to Metsys*. New York: McGraw-Hill, 1970. This text devotes about one-fifth of its pages to the van Eycks. Reproductions vary in quality from good to very good.

SEE ALSO: Fra Angelico; Arnolfo di Cambio; Cimabue; Donatello; Duccio di Buoninsegna; Giotto; Pietro Lorenzetti and Ambrogio Lorenzetti; Simone Martini; Masaccio; Andrea Orcagna; Philip the Good; Nicola Pisano and Giovanni Pisano; Jean Pucelle; Claus Sluter; Rogier van der Weyden.

RELATED ARTICLE in *Great Events from History: The Middle Ages, 477-1453*: c. 1410-1440: Florentine School of Art Emerges.

Fakhr al-Dīn al-Rāzī
Muslim theologian and scholar

Fakhr al-Dīn al-Rāzī was among the last representatives of Islamic theology to espouse the systematic orthodox school founded by al-Ash'arī. An itinerant scholar, al-Rāzī's personal contributions as a teacher left an indelible mark on the intellectual life of the eastern provinces of the late twelfth and early thirteenth century Islamic caliphate.

Born: 1148 or 1149; Rayy, Persia (now in Iran)
Died: 1210; Herāt, Khorāsān Province (now in Iran)
Also known as: Abū ʿAbd Allāh Muḥammad ibn ʿUmar ibn al-Ḥusayn ibn Fakhr al-Dīn al-Rāzī (full name)
Areas of achievement: Religion and theology, philosophy

Early Life

Fakhr al-Dīn al-Rāzī (FAHK-rahl-deen-ahl-uhr-rah-zee) was the son of Shaykh Diya al-Dīn ʿUmar, *khatib* (preacher) of Rayy, a key city in the north-central area of Iran. The family claimed both a long tribal ancestry (associated with the Taimi tribe) and descent from the family of Abū Bakr, the first caliph. Al-Yafii, whose biographical sketch of al-Rāzī survives in manuscript form only, cites a long pedigree of family teachers (originally named by al-Rāzī himself, in his *Tahsil al-haqq*), going back to al-Ashʿarī (873 or 874-935 or 936), the famed figure of classical Islamic orthodox scholarship. This line of scholars led in a chain to the generation and person of al-Rāzī's father, who was his first teacher in the fields that would make his fame. Some traditional Islamic biographers claim that the young student was also interested, in the early stages of his education, in alchemy and astrology. Such interests are reflected only very little within his known works as a mature scholar.

Following his father's death, al-Rāzī received specialized training not only in *fikh* (Islamic law) but in *ilm al-kalam* (Islamic theology) and philosophy as well. His teacher in the latter field, Majd al-Dīn al-Jīlī (from Jilan Province), had clearly been involved in controversial subjects, since at least one of his other students, Shihab al-Dīn al-Suhrawardī, faced a death sentence for expounding beliefs that bordered on heresy. Al-Rāzī's exposure to al-Jīlī, however, did not result in such controversy. What was most significant for this early stage of al-Rāzī's adult life, perhaps, was the opportunity he received to accompany al-Jīlī to the region of Maragheh, where the latter was engaged as a preacher. This experience, which brought a widening of both intellectual and geographical horizons for the youth, left a mark of cosmopolitanism that became characteristic of al-Rāzī's entire career.

Life's Work

At some point after passing his thirtieth year (thus in the 1180's), al-Rāzī began to travel very widely, not to the central Iraqi and Syrian provinces but to the eastern reaches of the Islamic caliphs' domains. He first left his mark as a philosophical itinerant in Khwārizm (the Amu Darya basin, north of Khorāsān Province in eastern Iran). There, representatives of the Mutazilites (best-known for their contention that the Qur'ān was created scripture, not the timeless word of God) engaged him in debates that, because of their controversial tenor, led to his expulsion by the authorities. Next came a brief sojourn (between 1184 and 1186, when al-Rāzī would have been thirty-six to thirty-eight years old) in the Iranian/Turkish frontier zone of Transoxiana.

Some traditionalists maintain that the brevity of al-Rāzī's stay in Transoxiana was connected with his involvement in the philosophical and theological debates that formed the corpus of his edited work *Munāẓarāt jarat fi bilād mā warā ʿa al-nahr* (*Transoxianian Controversies*, 1966). It is also possible that not only intellectual but also material considerations pushed the itinerant scholar from place to place. It is known that the next stage of his career was played out in the palace at Ghor, part of the Islamic domain of Ghazna (south of Kabul in modern Afghanistan). There, al-Rāzī obtained formal patronage, with material compensation, from the Ghūrid ruler Mu ʿizz al-Dīn Muḥammad. This privileged status proved to be tenuous, however, when al-Rāzī's combination of orthodox and philosophical approaches to Islamic doctrine was opposed by representatives of the extremist Karramiyah doctrine, which was championed locally.

A better climate for profitable patronage for al-Rāzī's modes of philosophical and theological analysis appeared in the eastern Iranian province of Khorāsān. There, the ruler ʿAlāʾ al-Dīn Tukush appointed al-Rāzī tutor to the crown prince, Muḥammad. Service to the eventual successor brought its rewards: first, in the form of high appointed office with privileged material status, and second, through marriage links to the Tukush court (al-Rāzī's daughter was married to the vizier, or chief minister, ʿAlāʾ al-Mulk).

Whether it was in Khorāsān or in another position of patronage (the standard accounts vary on this point), it appears that al-Rāzī's reputation as a teacher earned for him the honor of having a special *madrasah*, or Islamic seminary, built in his name and for his use. Although it is not known how long al-Rāzī retained such privileged status, by 1203, when he was in his fifties, he was able to move to Herāt, in southeastern Khorāsān, where he settled, investing some of his acquired wealth in propertied estates. The seven years he spent in Herāt before his death (in 1210) did not shield him from bitterness at having had to defend himself from critics of his thought wherever he went. Some of the scholar's resentment of the unending controversy over his ideas is reflected in his last testament. As recorded in Ibn Abī Uṣaibiʿah's biographical collection, *ʿUyun al-anba fi tabaqat al-atibba*, the testament that al-Rāzī dictated to his student Ibn ʿAlī al-Iṣfahīnī read,

> Know I was a lover of knowledge, and . . . wrote about every question that I might know its quantity and quality, irrespective of whether it was true or false. . . . I have examined the methods of theology and philosophy, but I did not find in them the profit I found in the Koran, for the Koran ascribes glory and majesty to God, and forbids preoccupations with obscurities and contradictions. These only teach us that the human intellect disintegrates in these deep narrows and hidden ways.

What was the nature of al-Rāzī's interpretations of Islamic philosophy and theology that aroused so much controversy? First, one should remember that al-Rāzī did not distinguish himself only as an author of works that were easily acceptable as reflecting Sunni (orthodox) views. In fact, in stages, and after having been tempted by rationalistic Greek thought, he became associated with the well-established Ashʿarī school, which sought to find a synthesis between orthodox religious principles (such as the uncreated nature of the Qurʾān and the absolute power and grace of God) and human efforts to use reason. Among al-Rāzī's major works that reflected such principles, the famous *Kitāb muḥaṣṣal afkār al-mutaqaddimīn wa-al-mutaʾakhkhirīn* (compendium of the ideas of scholars and theologians; best known as *Muḥaṣṣal*) is worthy of note. The *Muḥaṣṣal* discusses (among a wide variety of subjects) the general characteristics of being, cause and effect, and prophecy and eschatology. A second landmark work is his *Kitāb al-tafsir al-kabir* (great commentary on the Qurʾān). Although both of these works became Islamic classics, modern commentators on al-Rāzī, including Louis Gardet, make it clear that al-Rāzī's theology is marked by philosophical and even some scientific references to Greek sources. Gardet provides a key to understanding why those of al-Rāzī's contemporaries who were bound to strict religious tenets might have opposed the originality of his interpretations. Referring to al-Rāzī's Qurʾānic commentary, Gardet cites G. C. Anawati, who says, "It . . . is both philosophical and *biʿl-raʿy*, i.e., it does not rely on tradition alone, but on the considered judgment and reflection of the commentator."

SIGNIFICANCE

The career of al-Rāzī is a striking example of the survival, into the thirteenth century, of eclectic intellectual currents that had roots in the classical age of Greece and Rome as well as that of Persia, currents that contributed to the great tradition of Islamic scholarship. Anawati's suggestion that much of al-Rāzī's analysis of legal and theological questions reflects the use of personal opinion (*biʿl-raʿy*) is significant, especially in the light of what would follow. To be certain, Islamic religious orthodoxy had never been at ease with certain philosophers' tendency to introduce secular rational approaches into religious debates. Nor was mysticism—an element present in Islam from the earliest years following Muḥammad's death—fully or openly accepted. It was the task of great thinkers such as al-Ashʿarī and al-Ghazzālī (1058-1111) to attempt to forge *kalam*, or theology, into a set of systematic principles that could resist the criticism of full rationalists, on one hand, and satisfy the need that mystics felt for personal religion, on the other.

During this process, which was at its peak in Islam during the eleventh and twelfth centuries, the movement for orthodox systematization, of which al-Rāzī was a part, still left the *bab al-ijtihad* (door of independent reasoning) open wide enough to allow, not deviation, but at least diversification, in modes of analysis. That al-Rāzī used diverse approaches to arrive at systematic conclusions is illustrated in several scholars' appraisals of his famous commentary on the Qurʾān as containing elements of Greek thought and even Greek physical science.

The two or three centuries that followed the generation of al-Rāzī witnessed what would be called the "closing of the door of *ijtihad*." The effects of this narrowing of acceptable principles for individual scholarly analysis of theological and legal questions would be to underline further the uniqueness of al-Rāzī's latter-day contributions to Asharism. Such originality would not be seen again until currents of intellectual rationalization challenged orthodox Islamic values near the end of the nineteenth century. When that happened, there was a call for a "reopening of the door of *ijtihad*," and classical but very individualistic commentaries such as that of al-Rāzī resurfaced after centuries of near oblivion.

—*Byron D. Cannon*

FURTHER READING

Abrahamov, Binyamin. *Islamic Theology: Traditionalism and Rationalism.* Edinburgh: Edinburgh University Press, 1998. Explores the foundations of traditionalist and rationalist thought in classical Islamic theology from the third to the sixteenth century, including the criticisms between the two perspectives and the attempted reconciliations.

Gardet, Louis. "Religion and Culture." In *The Cambridge History of Islam*, edited by P. M. Holt, Ann K. S. Lambton, and Bernard Lewis. Cambridge, England: Cambridge University Press, 1977. This chapter is particularly useful for placing the life and work of al-Rāzī in the wider context of Islamic history, including the various schools of thought to which he reacted. Offers chapters titled "The Geographical Setting" and "Literature," both of which are helpful discussions of the intellectual milieu within which al-Rāzī lived.

Inglis, John, ed. *Medieval Philosophy and the Classical Tradition in Islam, Judaism and Christianity.* Richmond, Surrey, England: Curzon, 2002. Places medieval Islamic philosophy in the context of classic philosophy. Bibliography, index.

Iskenderoglu, Muammer. *Fakhr al-Dīn al-Rāzī and Thomas Aquinas on the Question of the Eternity of the World.* Boston: Brill, 2002. Explores al-Rāzī's and Aquinas's work in the Muslim and Christian contexts and the ways each thinker broke with his respective religious tradition in favor of a philosophical perspective on the question of the eternity of the world. Bibliography, index.

Kholeif, Fathalla. *A Study on Fakhr al-Dīn al-Rāzī and His Controversies in Transoxiana.* Beirut: Dar el-Machreq Press, 1966. This may be the only monographic study of al-Rāzī in English. It includes a substantial section on his life and works in general, but focuses on the text of the famous *Transoxiana Controversies*. The work is organized around sixteen questions, some of which deal with philosophy and theology and others with Islamic law.

Kraus, Paul. "The Controversies of Fakhr al-Dīn al-Rāzī." *Islamic Culture* 12, no. 2 (1938): 131-150. Argues that because al-Rāzī's *Transoxiana Controversies* is a synthesis of a number of different subjects, it can provide a better idea of the evolution of his thought than that afforded by his major works of theology and Qur'ānic commentary.

Nasr, Seyyed Hossein. *The Islamic Intellectual Tradition in Persia.* Edited by Mehdi Amin Razavi. Richmond, Surrey, England: Curzon Press, 1996. Presents a chapter on al-Rāzī's philosophy, with a look also at his predecessor, Avicenna. Bibliography, index.

Powers, David S. *Studies in Qur'ān and Hadith: The Formation of the Islamic Law of Inheritance.* Berkeley: University of California Press, 1986. This work is primarily concerned with technical questions of Islamic law. It shows how representatives of the Ashʿarī school organized their arguments around specific legal issues that were of particular interest to Qur'ānic commentators.

Rahman, Fazlur. *Islam.* London: Weidenfeld and Nicolson, 1966. A detailed and extensive study on the institutions of Islam. The discussion of schools of thought, both within and outside orthodox tradition, includes analysis of the two currents that influenced al-Rāzī most: Mutazilism and Asharism.

SEE ALSO: Al-Ashʿarī; Avicenna; al-Ghazzālī; Thomas Aquinas.

RELATED ARTICLES in *Great Events from History: The Middle Ages, 477-1453:* c. 950: Court of Córdoba Flourishes in Spain; c. 1150: Moors Transmit Classical Philosophy and Medicine to Europe.

JACQUELINE FÉLICIE

Parisian medical practitioner

Félicie challenged the legal restriction of medical practice to graduates of the University of Paris, which did not admit women as students, and successfully treated the patients that other physicians could not or would not help.

BORN: c. 1280; possibly Paris, France
DIED: After 1322; place unknown
ALSO KNOWN AS: Jacoba Felice; Jacqueline Félicie de Almania (full name)
AREA OF ACHIEVEMENT: Medicine

EARLY LIFE

Jacqueline Félicie (fehl-ih-zee) practiced medicine in Paris and its suburbs at the beginning of the fourteenth century. All of the extant information about Félicie's life and work is contained in the record of a trial conducted against her and several other Parisians accused of practicing medicine illegally.

Félicie was accused in ecclesiastical court on August 11, 1322, of wrongfully assuming the function of a physician. The accusation carried the penalties of excommunication and a fine of sixty Parisian sous. Additionally, she was forbidden to practice medicine in Paris or its environs. Although she did not deny practicing medicine, she did appeal the economic and spiritual penalties imposed on her. Félicie insisted that her medical practice was legitimate, legal, and in the interest of the public good. Her appeal continued until November 2, 1322, when she was formally excommunicated. The records of her appeal provide a window into her life and medical practice.

Félicie's trial testimony suggests that she was born in Paris around 1280. One of her patient-witnesses reported that her house was small. Because no husband or relatives are mentioned in the trial documents, it seems that Félicie lived by herself. Her patients knew her by her reputation, which seems to have spread to many different regions of the city and its suburbs.

It would be helpful at this point to discuss the professional and social atmosphere in which Félicie and other medical practitioners of Paris in the Middle Ages worked. Paris, during Félicie's lifetime, was the largest city in Western Europe and an important political and intellectual center. It also contained a large number of medical practitioners. These practitioners fell into five rough categories: physicians, surgeons, barbers, empirics, and apothecaries.

Physicians, who were university trained and licensed, treated internal diseases by administering alterative drugs or plasters. In 1271, the physicians in Paris attempted to gain control over the practice of medicine within the city. In addition to revising the qualifications for the medical license granted by the university, they attempted to restrict the practice of surgeons, barbers, and apothecaries and to eliminate the practice of empirics.

The statute that the physicians passed in 1271 limited both surgeons and barbers, who could not attend the university, to manually operating on individuals who suffered from external or local conditions. Conditions that fell under their expertise included fractured bones, mangled limbs, open wounds, hernias, cataracts, urinary-tract stones, dental extractions, and gum surgery. They also performed bloodletting.

Physicians were prohibited from performing manual operations on these conditions because such treatments would identify surgeons and barbers as manual laborers of artisan status. Similarly, surgeons and barbers could not prescribe or administer potions, laxatives, or plasters because such activities would identify physicians as elite men of medical learning.

According to the statute of 1271, apothecaries mixed drugs at the physicians' request but were not allowed to administer them. Like surgeons and barbers, however, apothecaries did not always abide by the university's restrictions. All three groups continued to be caught administering potions, treating internal conditions, and usurping the role of a physician, throughout the fourteenth and fifteenth centuries.

The practitioners who presented the greatest challenge to the university-trained physicians' aspirations regarding the control of medical practice in Paris were the empirics. Physicians defined an "empiric" as any practitioner who acted independently of a guild, lacked a license, and was self-taught. The university vigorously prosecuted the empirics whom they accused of being unlearned, of making up remedies in their heads, and of endangering the lives of their patients.

The physicians' portrayal of empirics as a danger to the public health allowed them to gain the support of popes and French kings in their appeals for more stringent regulation of medical practice in Paris. Their efforts, however, were largely unsuccessful in spite of royal and papal support. The university's struggles to regulate and discredit empirics continued at least until the beginning of the seventeenth century.

In some instances the activities of empirics failed to

catch the university's attention. Many of those who were called empirics served a population that was too humble and poor to be of interest to the university-trained physicians. In other cases, the university-trained physicians and those they considered empirics competed for the same wealthy and even royal patients. Félicie represents an instance of competition between licensed university-trained physicians and unlicensed practitioners.

Life's Work

Félicie was an ambitious and accomplished medical practitioner. Although she lacked a university education, she was able to compete with university-trained physicians to the extent that patient-witnesses at her trial supported her right to practice medicine regardless of her qualifications. Félicie also practiced the highest form of medicine, internal medicine, in spite of prejudices and legal restrictions against women in such a practice. Women could be surgeons and barbers because neither practice required a university degree. Because the university denied women admission, however, they could not legally practice as physicians. Finally, Félicie defended her right to continue practicing on the basis of her own competence.

All aspects of Félicie's trial point to the fact that university-trained physicians saw her as a threat to their monopoly over medical practice in the city. Although some of Félicie's patient witnesses were apparently of such low social status that she refused to accept payment from them for her services, she did collect forty Parisian sous from one shopkeeper after she had treated him successfully. Moreover, one patient witness reported that Félicie had treated the chancellor to the king for gout and the chancellor's nephew for impotence.

These reports suggest that Félicie was competing with university-trained physicians for the same royal and bourgeois clientele. In fact, of the seven patient witnesses who were present at Félicie's appeal, five had sought the care of licensed physicians before turning to Félicie. Moreover, in three of these cases the physicians in question were known members of the faculty of medicine at the university.

Félicie's success as a physician is further confirmed by the accusations made against her. The physicians were particularly interested in establishing that she examined the urine and pulse of her patients and also administered potions and plasters. These accusations were confirmed by witness testimony. Four of the seven patient witnesses reported that Félicie took their pulse and examined their urine. All seven were offered potions or plasters. Such practices would have readily identified Félicie as a physician because they were the standard methods for discerning the nature of and treating internal illnesses. Moreover, the cases that Félicie treated concerned the types of conditions that physicians were known to treat, such as fevers, kidney problems, rheumatism, and doubling pain. Her performance apparently convinced her patients who, when asked whether or not they were aware that Félicie was lacking in education, answered that they had not inquired about her qualifications.

Having established that Félicie "posed" as a physician, the physicians attempted to characterize her as a dangerous fraud who practiced medicine haphazardly and at great risk to her patients. Witness testimony from Félicie's trial, however, suggests that she enjoyed substantial success as a practitioner of medicine even without university medical training. This witness group included five individuals whom university-trained physicians were unable to help. Moreover, of the seven patient witnesses at her trial, all but one reported that they would not have recovered without the help of Félicie, that her potions healed them immediately, and that they had contacted her because of her reputation as a successful healer. The abstaining witness could not evaluate Félicie's healing abilities because she had refused treatment.

Unable to prosecute Félicie for dangerous incompetence, the physicians challenged Félicie on the basis of her gender. Citing a law that prohibited women from practicing law, they argued that it was much worse for a woman to endanger a person's life through her medical ignorance than it was for her to endanger the outcome of his legal case. Félicie countered this assertion with the claim that it was more proper for women patients to be treated by women than by men and that many women suffered needlessly because they were too ashamed to consult male doctors.

In short, the physicians could find no practical reason to prevent Félicie from practicing medicine. At the conclusion of her trial they dismissed all of her arguments as irrelevant on the basis that as an unlicensed practitioner of medicine she had violated the law. In other words, they disregarded all the particulars of her case for the purpose of defending their own privilege.

Félicie also challenged the law restricting medical practice to licensed practitioners. She suggested that her competence exempted her from the law that was intended to prevent those ignorant of the art of medicine from harming their patients. Because she had successfully healed patients whom other physicians could not help, she suggested that it was not in the public interest for her to stop practicing medicine. Finally, she challenged the university physicians' authority to regulate medical practice for the city of Paris without consulting all other groups in the city who were affected by such regulation. All these appeals failed and Félicie was formally excommunicated on November 2, 1322.

Because Félicie's trial is the only record of her life and accomplishments available, what happened to her after her excommunication is not clear. Medieval European Christians were expected to seek absolution from excommunications through repentance and penance. In France, all those who failed to seek absolution within a year of being excommunicated were deemed heretics and punished by secular law. Thus, Félicie's trial probably marked the end of her medical career. At the time, she was approximately forty-two years old.

SIGNIFICANCE

Although Félicie did not succeed in defending her right to practice medicine, her trial marks a significant episode in the history of the professionalization of medical practice. Félicie, as a medical practitioner who was not solely a midwife, confirms the existence of medieval women practitioners who treated men and women and a wide variety of illnesses successfully. Her competence and good practice contradict the rhetoric that developed coincident with the professionalization of medicine that characterized female practitioners as superstitious, ignorant, and dangerous. Also, her remarks challenging the university's right to regulate medical practice, as well as the fondness with which her patient witnesses described her, reveal that not all members of medieval society felt that the university's regulation of medicine was in their best interest.

Félicie's case demonstrates the complexity of issues surrounding the professionalization of medical practice in medieval Paris, particularly as it applied to practitioners who were women. Although she did not deny that ignorant practitioners should be prevented from continuing their practice, she did challenge the idea that the university-trained physicians were the best medical practitioners, and she challenged the belief that these trained physicians were in the best position to judge for the citizens of the city who was ignorant and who was not.

—*Nancy McLoughlin*

FURTHER READING

Biller, Peter, and Joseph Ziegler. *Religion and Medicine in the Middle Ages*. Suffolk, England: York Medieval Press, 2001. Addresses many of the questions regarding the relationship between heresy, theology, magic, and medicine that traditional histories of medicine often neglect.

Furst, Lilian R., ed. *Women Healers and Physicians: Climbing a Long Hill*. Lexington: University Press of Kentucky, 1997. Addresses women healers and physicians from medieval Europe to twentieth century Europe and the United States. The chapters on medieval times, in particular, address the development of negative images of women healers.

Green, Monica. *Women's Healthcare in the Medieval West: Texts and Contexts*. Aldershot, England: Ashgate, 2000. This collection of articles addresses the methodological questions inherent in the study of women's healthcare and medical practice and synthesizes recent social and cultural histories on the subject.

Kibre, Pearl. *Studies in Medieval Science: Alchemy, Astrology, Mathematics and Medicine*. London: Hambledon Press, 1984. The author is a critical figure in the study of the medieval university and medieval science. This collection includes a detailed discussion of the University of Paris's attempt to restrict medical practice to licensed physicians.

Minkowski, William L. "Physician Motives in Banning Medieval Traditional Healers." *Women and Health* 21, no. 1 (1994). Discusses Félicie's case against the Parisian faculty and the Church as well as the history of women healers and the regulation of medieval medical practice.

O'Boyle, Cornelius. *The Art of Medicine: Medical Teaching at the University of Paris, 1250-1400*. Boston: Brill, 1998. Discusses the history of the study and practice of medicine as art at the time of Félicie. Includes an extensive bibliography and index.

Siraisi, Nancy. *Medieval and Early Renaissance Medicine: An Introduction to Knowledge and Practice*. Chicago: University of Chicago Press, 1990. Synthesizes developments in medical learning and practice from the twelfth to sixteenth centuries. The author's comprehensive account recognizes different types of healers, including those who relied on spiritual remedies.

SEE ALSO: Pietro d'Abano; Arnold of Villanova; Averroës; Avicenna; Saint Fulbert of Chartres; Hildegard von Bingen; Saint Isidore of Seville; Moses Maimonides; Paul of Aegina; al-Rāzī; Trotula.

RELATED ARTICLES in *Great Events from History: The Middle Ages, 477-1453*: 809: First Islamic Public Hospital; c. 1010-1015: Avicenna Writes His *Canon of Medicine*; 1100-1300: European Universities Emerge; c. 1150: Moors Transmit Classical Philosophy and Medicine to Europe.

FIRDUSI

Iranian poet

Firdusi's Shahnamah *is the supreme example of the epic in the Persian language. Through centuries of foreign invasion and conquest, it has served as a major means of preserving Iran's cultural identity.*

BORN: Between 932 and 941; Ṭūs, Khorāsān Province (now in Iran)
DIED: Between 1020 and 1025; Tabaran, near Ṭūs, Iran
ALSO KNOWN AS: Firdawsī; Ferdowsī; Firdousi; Abū ol-Qāsem Manṣūr (given name)
AREAS OF ACHIEVEMENT: Literature, historiography

EARLY LIFE

Firdusi (fihr-DEW-see), the national poet of Iran, flourished during the tenth and early eleventh centuries. What Homer was to the ancient Greeks and Vergil was to the Romans, Firdusi has been for centuries to all speakers of Persian. He was born in the vicinity of Ṭūs, near what is now called Mashhad, in the northeastern Iranian province of Khorāsān, but nothing is known regarding his parentage or his formative years. Even his personal name is unknown. "Firdusi" is a pen name, meaning paradise (*firdaus*). What is reasonably certain is that he belonged to the ancient class of hereditary landowners known as *dihqans* and that during the earlier part of his long life he enjoyed a modest financial independence, presumably an income derived from property inherited from his father.

Apart from a visit to Baghdad, Firdusi seems to have spent his entire life in Khorāsān or in the adjoining regions of Afghanistan and Mawarannahr (now Uzbekistan). Either in Tūs or in the course of his later wanderings, he would have imbibed the cultural traditions and the pride in the values of the pre-Islamic Iranian past that were cultivated among the *dihqan* class and at the courts of local Iranian dynasts such as the Sāmānids of Bukhara, the Buyids of western Iran, and the Ziyarids of Tabaristān. Among both rulers and landowners there lingered a nostalgic attachment to the memory of the imperial Sāsānid Dynasty, which had ruled over the Iranian plateau and the surrounding regions from the early third to the mid-seventh century.

In such a milieu, Firdusi began to compose and organize his great epic, the *Shahnamah* (c. 1010; the book of kings), a paean to the glories of ancient Iran and its famous rulers. The actual completion of this enormous undertaking (*Shahnamah* manuscripts can range from forty-eight thousand to more than fifty-five thousand distichs, or two-line units) is said to have taken at least thirty-five years, with perhaps sometime around 975 as its starting point and 1010 as its terminal date. Although the twelfth century belletrist Neẓāmī-ye ʿArūẓī states that Firdusi's reason for writing the *Shahnamah* was to earn a reward sufficient to provide a proper dowry for his daughter and sole surviving child, it is difficult not to imagine its composition as a labor of love, a self-appointed mission. Nevertheless, it does appear that at some time in middle life, Firdusi's financial resources became depleted, for whatever reason, and that consequently, he was compelled to go in search of patrons.

LIFE'S WORK

The late tenth century was an inauspicious time to find a patron for a poet who sang of ancient Iranian greatness. The openhanded Iranian rulers of Firdusi's youth had all but disappeared, and the age of the Turkish warlord was dawning. In the north, beyond the Amu Darʾya (Oxus) River, the noble Sāmānids of Bukhara had been swept away by the seminomadic Qarakhanids. On the Iranian plateau itself, the celebrated Turkish conqueror Sultan Maḥmūd of Ghazna (r. 997-1030) held sway from his capital in eastern Afghanistan. To him, perhaps as a last resort, Firdusi made his way. Almost everything that is known of the dealings of Maḥmūd with Firdusi originated a century or more after the death of both men and therefore partakes more of literary legend than of historical fact. Supposedly, Maḥmūd initially encouraged Firdusi to complete his epic and to dedicate it to him (Maḥmūd was a great "collector" of poets, mainly panegyrists, and men of letters, some of whom he forcibly recruited). On receiving it, however, he declined to pay Firdusi the princely sum originally promised, dismissing him with a payment the poet regarded as insulting. It is not clear whether Maḥmūd acted thus out of stinginess or because, as some scholars have suggested, Firdusi's subject matter, the splendors of ancient Iran, offended the ruler's self-esteem as a Turk and the son of a slave. More likely than either explanation is that Firdusi's enemies at court whispered in the ear of the Sunni Muslim sultan that the poet was a secret Shīʿite.

According to Neẓāmī, Firdusi, bitterly disappointed at his paltry reward, went to a bathhouse in Ghazna, where he bathed and ordered a cup of sherbet. He then took the sultan's gift and divided it between the bathhouse keeper and the sherbet seller. To offer so public an insult to a ruler was rash in the extreme, and Firdusi promptly fled from Ghazna to Herāt, and thence to Tūs and Tabaristān. His pursuers never caught up with him. Perhaps they lost the trail or—more probably—Maḥmūd called off the hunt, unwilling to go down in history as the persecutor of the greatest poet of the age. Finally, if Neẓāmī is to be believed, Maḥmūd relented and belatedly made amends by sending to Firdusi a valuable consignment of indigo loaded on the sultan's own camels. As the caravan entered one of the gates of Tabaran, a town in the Tūs district where Firdusi had been living, however, the corpse of the poet was being carried out the opposite gate. Firdusi's daughter, a woman "of very lofty spirit," proudly spurned the sultan's gift.

The Iranians have always ranked Firdusi among their greatest poets, along with Jalāl al-Dīn Rūmī (c. 1207-1273), Saʿdi (c. 1200-c. 1291), Hafiz (c. 1320-1389 or 1390), and Jīmī (1414-1492). Unlike these other poets, however, Firdusi displays virtually no interest in contemporary religious issues or values and no trace whatsoever of a mystical calling. Still, his writing is rooted in a strong tradition of personal ethics, tempered by a strain of unmistakable pessimism, both of which are integral to his thematic concerns. The subject matter of the *Shahnamah*, which is composed in metrical rhymed couplets of ten syllables, is the entire history of Iran down to the Arab-Islamic conquests of the mid-seventh century. For the Sāsānid period (third to seventh centuries), the epoch preceding the Arab invasions, Firdusi provides detailed narratives, partly legendary and partly historical, derived from both chronicles and oral traditions. Of the long-lived Parthian regime that the Sāsānids overthrew, he has almost nothing to say; the same is true with regard to the prior Seleucids and Achaemenids, except for a fantastic episode in which King Dārāb (Darius II) marries a daughter of King Philip of Rum (in this instance, Greece) but then sends her back to her father in disgrace. He does not know, however, that she is already pregnant by him and soon to give birth to a child "splendid as the sun," Iskandar (Alexander). Meanwhile, Darab takes a new wife, who provides him with an heir, Dara, who eventually succeeds him. In this way, the stage is set for the great duel between Persia and Greece, the Achaemenids and the Macedonians, and also for the inclusion of much colorful material derived from *Iskandar nama* (an Alexander romance often referred to as the *Pseudo-Callisthenes*).

It serves no purpose to look to Firdusi for the early history of Iran, for he does not provide it. Instead, he offers an epic spanning the life histories of two wholly legendary dynasties, the Pishdadian and the Kayanian, redolent with the splendors of mighty monarchs and the heroic deeds of peerless warriors. Here is a gallery of memorable figures: wise, rash, and foolish kings, and their paladins, among whom the most famous is the Iranian Hercules or Roland, the giant Rustam (also spelled Rostam). Action centers on the ceaseless conflict between the warriors of Iran and Turan, the latter subjects of the malevolent but ultimately tragic King Afrāsiyāb. Nor is there any lack of romance, such as in the love story of Zāl and Rūdābah and that of Bijan (Bīzhan) and Manija (Manīzhah). The obsession of the impetuous Sudaba (Sudabah) for her stepson, Siyavush (Siyāvūsh), is resonant of the Qurʾānic version of the story of Joseph and Potiphar's wife, as well as of the myth of Phaedra. Finally, in the mortal conflict of Rostam (Rustam) and Sohrab (Suhrāb), father and son, there is tragic denouement of a high order (as the Victorian Matthew Arnold was quick to perceive and adapt in his 1853 poem "Sohrab and Rustum"). It is these legendary scenes in the *Shahnamah* that have so endeared it to generations of Iranian readers and audiences.

It is scarcely possible to overestimate the influence of the *Shahnamah*. Rulers and members of the elite vied among themselves to acquire sumptuous manuscripts, finely bound and illustrated. Familiarity with Firdusi's masterpiece, however, was not restricted to the literate. The epic was conceived as much for recitation as for reading, and there eventually emerged a class of professional reciters of the *Shahnamah* (known as *Shahnamah-*Khvand), who were perhaps heirs to a minstrel tradition of Sāsānid or even Parthian times. Bards who memorized the entire epic were particularly revered, and a few such have been heard of even today. Recitations took place on festive occasions such as weddings or at the time of the Nuruz (the pre-Islamic New Year celebrations), but reciters also entertained humbler audiences more informally in village teahouses or in caravansaries, where travelers sheltered for the night. Thus, the *Shahnamah* became better known among the general population than any other book (the Qurʾān excepted), influencing ordinary speech and molding popular attitudes and values, as well as contributing to a literary tradition of many imitations.

The *Shahnamah* was no less influential in the development of Persian painting. Islam prohibited representational art, especially religious subject matter, an injunction that only the Shīʿites at times disregarded. The *Shahnamah*, however, contained no material that could in any sense be viewed as Islamic, and it was brimful of graphic and picturesque episodes (battles, hunting scenes, durbars, and banquets) that were natural subjects for illustration. Consequently, both in Iran and in those lands influenced by the Persian iconographic tradition, scenes from the *Shahnamah* became favorite subjects for book illustration and miniature painting. Were an inventory to be taken of all surviving Persian miniatures down to the nineteenth century, it is probable that the great majority would consist of scenes from the *Shahnamah*.

SIGNIFICANCE

The *Shahnamah* has always held a special place in Iranian hearts. In the twentieth century, nationalists and modernizers seized on Firdusi's glorification of the remote Iranian past to belabor the "Islamic centuries" between the seventh century Arab conquests and their own day as the source of the obscurantism and backwardness of Iranian society. For such as these, Firdusi provided the model of a distant Golden Age. During the rule of the Pahlavi Dynasty (1925-1979), Firdusi's praise for the monarchical tradition of ancient Iran, associated with the concept of *farr* (in Old Persian, the divine favor reserved for kings) and of *hvarna* (the charisma of kingship), provided the government with readymade propaganda. Thus, Reza Shah Pahlavi (1878-1944), the shah of Iran, ordered the construction of a conspicuous monument on the alleged site of Firdusi's grave, proclaimed in 1934 the 1000th anniversary of the poet's birth, and issued commemorative postage stamps. Under his son Moḥammad Reza Pahlavi (1919-1980), dramatic scenes from the *Shahnamah*, especially those emphasizing loyalty or gratitude to the monarch, were regularly performed on state-run television. With the advent of the Islamic Revolution, however, Firdusi, the least Islamic among Persian poets, fell from official favor.

Western students of Persian literature have been almost unanimous in praise of Firdusi's genius, the one obvious exception being the English scholar Edward Granville Browne (1862-1926), who found the *Shahnamah* monotonous and repetitive. More typical was the Czech Iranologist Jan Rypka (1886-1968). The *Shahnamah*, he wrote,

> has become the common property of all Iranians and has contributed in no small measure to the strengthening and consolidation of the national consciousness. For the rest this was the ultimate aim of the poet himself. . . . In depicting the illustrious past the poet appeals for a rebuilding of erstwhile greatness. . . . This call to action lent strength to the nation whenever it had to raise itself up again after disintegration and subjugation.

—*Gavin R. G. Hambly*

FURTHER READING

Browne, Edward G. *A Literary History of Persia*. 4 vols. 1902-1924. Reprint. Cambridge, England: Cambridge University Press, 1964-1969. This is still the standard account of classical Persian literature, usefully woven into a historical narrative that places authors' lives and works in their contemporary setting. Vol. 2 contains valuable information relating to Firdusi. Bibliography provided in Vol. 1.

Davis, Dick. "The Problem of Ferdowsi's Sources." *Journal of the American Oriental Society* 116, no. 1 (January-March, 1996). Argues that Firdusi used mainly versified oral sources rather than written sources for his epic, and any written sources used likely were in verse form that came from an oral tradition. Bibliographic footnotes.

Firdusi. *The Epic of the Kings: Shāh-nāma, the National Epic of Persia, by Ferdowsi*. Translated by Reuben Levy. Chicago: University of Chicago Press, 1967. Few translators have dared to tackle the *Shahnamah*, most of them in the nineteenth century. This volume contains the free-flowing prose translation of some of its most famous episodes. Part of UNESCO's Persian Heritage series. (An abridged 1996 translation with a new introduction is also available from Mazda Publishers, Costa Mesa, Calif.)

_______. *The Tragedy of Sohráb and Rostám: From the Persian National Epic, the Shahname of Abol-Qasem Ferdowsi*. Translated by Jerome W. Clinton. Rev. ed. Seattle: University of Washington Press, 1996. A verse translation accompanied on facing pages by a recent edition by Russian scholars of the Persian text. The preface is helpful for putting the work into the context of its time. Illustrations, bibliography.

Huart, Claude, and Henri Massé. "Firdawsī." In *The Encyclopaedia of Islam*. Vol. 2. 2d ed. Leiden, The Netherlands: Brill, 1965. This is still the best short account of Firdusi and his work. The encyclopedia contains many other entries of interest regarding Islamic writers and their sociopolitical contexts. Includes bibliographies.

Meisami, Julie Scott. *Persian Historiography to the End of the Twelfth Century*. Edinburgh: Edinburgh University Press, 1999. Explores the writing of Persian-Iranian history during the time of the Sāmānid, Ghaznavid, and Seljuk dynasties, and discusses Firdusi's *Shahnamah* as historical prose. Maps, bibliography, index.

Nizāmī Arūzī Samarqandi. *The Chahár Maqála (The Four Discourses) of Nizāmī Arūzī Samarqandi*. Translated by Edward G. Browne. 1921. Reprint. London:

Luzac, 1978. These anecdotal accounts of poets, astrologers, and others by a twelfth century belletrist include the earliest surviving biographical information about Firdusi. Bibliography, index.

Robinson, B. W. *The Persian Book of Kings: An Epitome of the Shahnama of Firdawsi*. London: RoutledgeCurzon, 2002. Illustrations, bibliography, index. A concise introduction to and summary of Firdusi's epic work. Illustrations include early Persian paintings depicting events and actions. Includes a table listing kings in the book, a bibliography, and an index.

Rypka, Jan, with Otakar Klíma. *History of Iranian Literature*. Edited by Karl Jahn. Dordrecht, The Netherlands: D. Reidel, 1968. Pages 151-166 offer an exceptionally interesting account of Firdusi within the context of the tradition of epic poetry in Iran. Map, extensive bibliography.

Von Grunebaum, Gustave E. "Firdausi's Concept of History." In *Islam: Essays in the Nature and Growth of a Cultural Tradition*. 1955. Reprint. Westport, Conn.: Greenwood Press, 1981. This is a stimulating essay by a distinguished Islamicist on Firdusi's vision of the past. Bibliography, index.

Yarshater, Ehsan, ed. *Persian Literature*. Albany: State University of New York Press, 1988. Essays of particular interest in this volume cover such topics as early Persian court poetry, the development of epic Persian verse, and Firdusi and the tragic epic. Bibliography, index.

SEE ALSO: Jean Froissart; Hafiz; al-Jāḥiẓ; Maḥmūd of Ghazna; Omar Khayyám; Jalāl al-Dīn Rūmī; Saʿdi.

RELATED ARTICLES in *Great Events from History: The Middle Ages, 477-1453*: August 15-20, 636: Battle of Yarmūk; 637-657: Islam Expands Throughout the Middle East; 834: Gypsies Expelled from Persia; 997-1030: Reign of Maḥmūd of Ghazna; 1010: Firdusi Composes the *Shahnamah*.

SAINT FRANCIS OF ASSISI

Italian monk

Through the rejection of material values and the establishment of the Franciscan orders, Saint Francis of Assisi contributed to the reform movement of the medieval Church during the early thirteenth century.

BORN: c. 1181; Assisi, Umbria, duchy of Spoleto (now in Italy)

DIED: October 3, 1226; Assisi, Umbria, duchy of Spoleto (now in Italy)

ALSO KNOWN AS: Francesco di Pietro di Bernardone (full name)

AREAS OF ACHIEVEMENT: Religion and theology, monasticism

EARLY LIFE

Francesco di Pietro di Bernardone, better known as Francis of Assisi (uh-SIHS-ee), was the son of Pietro and Pica di Bernardone. His father was a prosperous merchant, and Francis grew up in a comfortable environment and developed an appreciation of life's pleasures. Francis was provided a Latinist education at the school associated with the Church of Saint Giorgio in Assisi. Based on his later demonstrations of knowledge of contemporary French literature and art, and the works of the famous French troubadours in particular, it has been assumed that he received instruction in French language and literature sometime during his formative period. His family's prosperity and his extroverted personality resulted in Francis being recognized as a promising young leader not only in Assisi but throughout Umbria; he was expected to assume a prominent position in the political and economic life of his society.

In about 1202, Francis participated in a war between Perugia and Assisi and was captured and imprisoned. Released by the Perugians in 1203, he returned to Assisi in poor health. After a prolonged period of recuperation, he attempted to renew his military career by involving himself in the war (1205-1206) between several northern Italian states and cities against the Holy Roman Empire. At the Appenine town of Spoleto, however, Francis had a mystical experience in which he was bidden to return to Assisi to await news of what he should undertake as his life's work. This experience redirected Francis from secular interests centered on worldly values to a life of poverty and spirituality.

LIFE'S WORK

Based on his own later writings and documented conversations, Francis of Assisi continued to have spiritual experiences that directed him toward a new life. At one time, Christ appeared to him, and on another occasion, a voice emanated from the crucifix in the dilapidated

Church of Saint Damiano and directed Francis to undertake the reformation and rebuilding of Christ's church. According to Francis, he then returned to his father's shop and took a quantity of cloth, which he sold in a nearby town. Returning to the Church of Saint Damiano, he tried to give the money to the priest, to be used in renovating the building. Pietro di Bernardone reprimanded his son for this action, and hearings before civil and religious leaders occurred. In the end, Francis repudiated his father's values and his connection with his family; he left for the outskirts of Assisi.

Francis began to renovate churches in need of repair and led a life of poverty. While attending Mass at the Chapel of Saint Mary of the Angels in February, 1208, Francis was moved by a reading from the Gospel of Matthew enjoining the active repudiation of worldliness and the need to lead a spiritually based life. Francis began to preach and to gain disciples. In the following year, a reluctant Pope Innocent III approved of his band's simple rule of life and the establishment of the Franciscan order. Francis and his followers set out to duplicate the selfless lifestyle of Christ; at the cornerstone of the Franciscan rule were faith and simplicity. Francis's sermons were free of complicated disputations. He maintained that the Franciscan friars should assist others by working in the world rather than being confined to a monastery, that they should care for the sick and the dying, that they should preach the Gospel, and that they should lead lives of poverty and chastity in order to move closer to a Christlike state.

Miniature from a thirteenth century psalter depicting Saint Francis of Assisi preaching to the birds. (Frederick Ungar Publishing Co.)

Francis of Assisi extended his new values to a theology of nature, arguing that all aspects of God's creation were interconnected and that human beings should exist in a state of respect and harmony with all other manifestations of nature. His work "Il cantico delle creature" ("Canticle of Creatures," which has been also been called "The Canticle of the Sun" and "Laudes creaturatum") was an expression of the comprehensive Franciscan worldview in which the natural elements and inanimate physical objects are recognized as integral parts of God's cosmic design.

The Franciscan order grew rapidly, extending throughout Italy and beyond. By 1215, there were more than five thousand men in the Franciscan order. In 1212, Francis had established an order for women, named the Poor Ladies of Assisi and known as the Poor Clares after its first member, Saint Clare of Assisi. In 1221, Francis set up the third order of Franciscan Brothers and Sisters of Penance. From 1212 to the early 1220's, the Franciscan order grew so rapidly that it required additional structuring to manage its affairs effectively. The position of vicar of the order was established; Peter Catanii was the first vicar, but he died shortly after his appointment. Elias of Cortona, who replaced Catanii, did much of the organizational work and managed the day-to-day operations of the order through the 1220's. A new rule, which provided for a period of orientation, training, and review, was developed; it was approved by Pope Honorius III in 1223.

Francis of Assisi dreamed of visiting the Holy Land and evangelizing the Muslims in Spain, but accidents and poor health prohibited these journeys. In 1219, however, he did go to Egypt during a crusade and had an opportunity to preach to a Muslim sultan. According to some accounts, the sultan was so impressed with Francis that he granted him and his companions the right to visit the Holy Land; there is no documentation to substantiate this tale, and it is known that Francis never did visit the Holy Land.

The last years of Francis's life were spent in Assisi and its environs. He had another mystical experience in 1224 during a prolonged fast. In a vision, an angel appeared to Francis and filled him with the experiences of the crucified Christ; the consequence was the appearance of the stigmata on his body. Francis's health declined steadily after 1224. Encroaching blindness was aggravated by a more serious but unspecified medical problem; apparently, the last two years of his life were painful, and medical remedies were applied to no avail. Francis of Assisi died on October 3, 1226, in Assisi. In 1230, his remains were moved from their temporary depository in the Church of Saint Giorgio to the new basilica that had been constructed under the supervision of Elias of Cortona. On July 16, 1228, Francis of Assisi was canonized a saint by Pope Gregory IX.

SIGNIFICANCE

Francis's life and work were representative of the conflicting forces of his age. Born to wealth and influence and seemingly destined to exercise power, Francis repudiated this inheritance and emerged as the most earnest and visible advocate of reformed values within and outside the Church during the early thirteenth century. Though an unordained layperson, Francis of Assisi became the most prominent spokesperson for change in the Church. As a leader, he established religious orders that were committed to simplicity in striving to realize the Christian ideal, to be Christlike. The religious orders that Francis founded were not in the monastic tradition, for they did not seek to isolate their members from the world but rather were committed to a mission of evangelism and charity that demanded active public involvement.

Within the medieval Church, the Franciscans emerged as a new alternative for a new age. The popularity of the orders was demonstrated by their rapid growth and expansion and by the papal recognition that was extended to them. The Franciscan orders have survived and multiplied through the centuries, becoming one of the largest and most influential religious communities in the world. The basilica at Assisi has been maintained and serves as a popular shrine for Catholics as well as others from throughout the world.

One of the most enduring legacies of Francis of Assisi was his exemplary life of simplicity and piety. His emphasis on active life within society and his views on the interdependence of all created beings have inspired subsequent generations to this day.

—*William T. Walker*

FURTHER READING

Armstrong, Regis J., J. A. Wayne Hellman, and William J. Short, eds. *Francis of Assisi: Early Documents*. New York: New City Press, 1999-2001. 3 vols. The three books of this set, *The Saint*, *The Founder*, and *The Prophet*, contain translated biographies, hagiographies, and other early writings concerning Saint Francis and the Franciscans. An excellent collection of early sources that contains explanatory notes. Maps and bibliography.

Cowan, James. *Francis: A Saint's Way*. Ligouri, Mo.: Liguori/Triumph, 2001. A devotional biography of Saint Francis of Assisi that focuses on his inner life, including questions of asceticism and poverty. Contains bibliography.

Frugoni, Chiara. *Francis of Assisi: A Life*. New York: Continuum, 1998. A biography of Saint Francis of Assisi. Bibliography and index.

House, Adrian. *Francis of Assisi*. New York: Hidden-Spring, 2001. A treatment of the life of Francis of Assisi that attempts to deal with the miracles and other legends in a way so that non-Christians can appreciate the saint's life.

Jobe, Sara Lee. *Footsteps in Assisi*. New York: Paulist Press, 1996. A look at Assisi that examines the homes and haunts of Saints Francis and Clare and deals with the spiritual life in the Middle Ages.

Robson, Michael. *Saint Francis of Assisi: The Legend and the Life*. London: Geoffre Chapman, 1999. A biography of Saint Francis that describes both the legends and his life. Bibliography and index.

Sabatier, Paul. *The Road to Assisi: The Essential Biography of Saint Francis*. Brewster, Mass.: Paraclete Press, 2003. A new edition of a classic biography of Saint Francis of Assisi by a French Protestant.

Spoto, Donald. *Reluctant Saint: The Life of Francis of Assisi*. New York: Viking Compass, 2002. In this biography of the saint, Spoto tries to distinguish between legend and fact, citing reasons for his beliefs, and describes the political scene at the time.

Wolf, Kenneth Baxter. *The Poverty of Riches: Saint Francis of Assisi Reconsidered*. New York: Oxford University Press, 2003. Wolf takes a critical look at the poverty pursued by Saint Francis of Assisi and what it meant for those impoverished people in Assisi. He examines the saint's contact with the leper and his wearing of a tunic.

SEE ALSO: Blessed Angela of Foligno; Saint Anthony of Padua; Saint Bonaventure; Giovanni da Pian del Carpini; Saint Catherine of Siena; Saint Clare of Assisi; Saint Dominic; Innocent IV; William of Ockham; Salimbene; Thomas Aquinas.

RELATED ARTICLES in *Great Events from History: The Middle Ages, 477-1453*: April 16, 1209: Founding of the Franciscans; November 11-30, 1215: Fourth Lateran Council.

FREDEGUNDE

Queen of Neustria (r. 567-597)

A powerful and active queen, Fredegunde used every means available both to dispose of challengers to her husband's throne and to destroy her archenemy, Brunhild, Frankish queen of Austrasia.

BORN: c. 550; possibly Paris, Neustria (now in France)
DIED: 597; Neustria
ALSO KNOWN AS: Fredegund; Fredegond; Fredigundis
AREA OF ACHIEVEMENT: Government and politics

EARLY LIFE

Most of the information about Fredegunde's (FREH-duh-guhnd-eh) life comes from the *Historia Francorum* (late sixth century; *The History of the Franks*, 1927) by Bishop Gregory of Tours. Although Gregory provided much detailed information about Fredegunde once she became queen, little is known specifically about her early life. Born sometime around 550, she was a child during the reign of Chlotar I (r. 511-561), fifth king of the Merovingian Dynasty (early fifth century to 751) in Gaul (now in France).

As the western portions of the late Roman Empire collapsed under the influx of migrating Germanic tribes, the warlords of a tribe known as the Franks established themselves in the former Roman province of Gaul. One of these warlords, Clodio (r. early fifth century), also known as Chlogio, reputedly set himself up as ruler, followed by Merovech (r. early fifth century), for whom the Merovingian Dynasty was named, and who was in turn followed by his son, Childeric (r. 456-481). Both of these early kings expanded the territory under Merovingian control, but it was the most famous of the Merovingian kings, Clovis (r. 481-511), who defeated the Roman general Syagrius in 486 and united most of Gaul under his own rule.

Clovis married a Christian princess named Clotilda, who converted him to Catholic Christianity in 496. Up to this point, the Germanic tribes that settled in the former Roman territories had been either pagans or Arian Christians (who believed that Christ was the highest of created beings, not equal to God the Father, in contrast to Catholic Christianity, which claimed that God the Father and Christ the Son were equal in all things). Because the Romans were Catholic Christians who believed the Arian doctrines to be heresy, the difference in religious beliefs led to considerable tension and conflict between the subjected Romans and their new Germanic overlords. This climate of tension made Clovis's conversion to Catholic Christianity a significant event, for his nobles followed his lead, and soon other Germanic kings began to do the same.

After Clovis's death in 511, his kingdom was divided among his four sons, Theuderic (r. 511-534), Chlodomer (r. 511-524), Childebert I (r. 511-558) and Chlotar I (r. 511-561), who quarreled endlessly with each other. Chlotar I became the sole ruler of a reunited kingdom after Childebert's death in 558. On his own death, Chlotar's kingdom was again divided among his own sons, Charibert (r. 561-567), Guntram (r. 561-593), Sigibert (r. 561-575), and Chilperic I (r. 561-584). The four brothers did not peacefully coexist but rather fought with each other as each attempted to gain control over the whole area of Chlotar I's kingdom. Charibert died first, and the land over which he ruled was divided among the remaining brothers, but they continued to fight with each other over the divisions of their father's kingdom.

In this climate of political unrest, Fredegunde, a serving-woman, won the notice of Chilperic I and became one of his wives. Chilperic "put away" his first wife, Audovera, Fredegunde, and his other wives in order to marry Galswinth, the sister of Sigibert's wife, Brunhild. Allegedly at Fredegunde's instigation, Chilperic had Galswinth garroted to death in 567, after which he took Fredegunde back as his wife.

LIFE'S WORK

After the murder of her sister, Galswinth, Brunhild became Fredegunde's implacable enemy. Fredegunde, however, was more than equal to her opposition. In 575, she suborned the murder of Brunhild's husband and Chilperic's brother, Sigibert, who had besieged Chilperic and threatened to kill him. By arranging for Sigibert's murder, Fredegunde preserved her husband and sons from death and struck a serious blow against Brunhild. The kingdom passed on to Sigibert and Brunhild's son, Childebert II.

Also in 575, Fredegunde bore a son to Chilperic, named Samson, who soon died. Chilperic's oldest son, Theudebert (whose mother was Audovera, Chilperic's first wife), died in battle. He was survived by two other sons of Audovera and Chilperic, Merovech and Clovis, who stood in line to inherit Chilperic's kingdom before any of Fredegunde's sons.

Merovech scandalized many by marrying Fredegunde's enemy, Brunhild, after the death of Sigibert. Such a move further threatened any chance that Fredegunde's own sons might have to inherit their father's throne. Accordingly, in 577, Fredegunde plotted with one of Sigibert's former military leaders to ambush Merovech. This ambush failed and Merovech escaped, only to be taken in a second ambush in 578. Surrounded by his stepmother's men, Merovech is reported to have ordered his servant to kill him rather than be taken alive. The servant did as he was ordered, but died a cruel death himself as the punishment for slaying his master. After Merovech's death, only Clovis remained between Fredegunde's sons and the throne.

During this same time, Fredegunde bore two more sons to Chilperic, Chlodobert and Dagobert. In 580, the plague swept through Chilperic's kingdom and both Fredegunde and her two sons fell ill. Fredegunde told Chilperic that the plague was God's judgment against them for their heavy taxation of their people. She burned the tax registers of her cities and urged Chilperic to do the same in hopes that God would relent and spare the lives of Fredegunde and their sons. No relief came, however, and both boys died, although Fredegunde recovered.

At this time, Fredegunde also turned Chilperic against Clovis, his only remaining son by his former wife, Audovera. Acting on the queen's suggestion, the king sent Clovis into an area in which the plague still raged, hoping that his son would become one of the victims of the disease. This plan did not work, for Clovis remained healthy and began to boast that he would inherit his father's kingdom in its entirety. On hearing of these boasts, Fredegunde listened to slanderous accusations against Clovis, tortured his lover and the lover's mother, and demanded that Chilperic avenge her against Clovis. The young prince was imprisoned, then stabbed to death.

Still in the eventful year of 580, a nobleman named Leudast falsely accused Fredegunde of adultery with a bishop named Bertram. Fredegunde was cleared of the charges, but became a bitter enemy of Leudast. Leudast sought refuge in a church, but was driven from the sanctuary by Fredegunde's order after he accosted several women. After being driven from his refuge, Leudast fled from the area.

A couple of years later, in 582, Fredegunde bore Chilperic another son, named Theuderic. Once again, the royal couple had an heir to Chilperic's kingdom. In the following year, Leudast returned to seek Chilperic's forgiveness for the calumnies he had spread about Fredegunde. Chilperic deferred to Fredegunde, and Leudast

Fredegunde. (W. Roberts)

threw himself at her feet to beg her forgiveness. Fredegunde, however, did not forgive him. She ordered her men to seize the hapless Leudast, whereupon he was imprisoned and beaten. Fredegunde's accuser finally met his death by being laid out on his back with a block of wood behind his neck, and then being beaten on the throat with another piece of wood until his windpipe was crushed and he died.

In 584, Fredegunde and Chilperic's son, Theuderic, died. Fredegunde heard that some of the women of Paris had engaged in witchcraft in order to bring about her son's death, and so she had many women rounded up, tortured into confessions, and then killed by various means. In addition, she had all of Theuderic's clothes and belongings burned so that she would have nothing to remind her of the death of her son. Later in that same year, she gave birth to Chlotar II.

Also in this year, Chilperic fell victim to an assassin's knife after returning from hunting. Chilperic's nephew, Childebert, son of Sigibert and Brunhild, accused Fredegunde of arranging for Chilperic's murder, along with the murders of Galswinth, Sigibert, Merovech, and Clovis. Fredegunde, however, sought the protection of Chilperic's only remaining brother, Guntram, who refused to hand her and her son over to Childebert.

During this same time, Fredegunde and Chilperic's daughter, Rigunth, departed for Iberia (modern Spain) to marry the Visigothic prince, Recared. Fredegunde loaded Rigunth with a gift of great wealth, apparently from her own resources. On the way, however, her retinue was looted, and Rigunth was held in Toulouse and never made it to her destination in Iberia. Fredegunde sent one of her men to bring Rigunth back from Toulouse. At the same time, she sent an assassin to kill Brunhild, but Brunhild found out about the man's intentions and had him returned to Fredegunde with his hands and feet cut off.

The next year, 585, Fredegunde again plotted with the king of the Visigoths to assassinate Childebert II and Brunhild. Childebert discovered the plan, but Fredegunde continued with the attempt and it failed. Fredegunde is also suspected of arranging the murder of Praetextatus, bishop of Rouen. As he lay dying, Fredegunde visited him, and he cursed her before breathing his last breaths. One of the leaders of the city confronted Fredegunde with the crime, and she poisoned him.

During the years of Chlotar II's minority, Fredegunde ruled as regent over his kingdom, under the protection of Chilperic's brother, Guntram. When Chlotar became deathly ill in 590, Fredegunde donated a large amount of money to the church of Saint Martin and ordered certain war prisoners to be freed in the hope that such deeds would earn divine mercy for her son. Chlotar became so ill that a rumor spread that he had died, but he made a full recovery. In this same year, Fredegunde again plotted the assassination of Childebert II. She sent twelve different men to kill the rival king, but Childebert's men captured one of the assassins and forced him through torture to reveal the identities and locations of the other eleven.

Fredegunde managed her son's kingdom until he reached his majority in 597. Her forces battled the army of Childebert II in 595, killing him and leaving the kingdom in the hands of Brunhild, who ruled as regent for Childebert's two infant sons. Fredegunde's forces won another decisive battle against Brunhild's army in 597, but she did not have much opportunity to relish her victory. Fredegunde died peacefully in her sleep in 597.

SIGNIFICANCE

Fredegunde's life illustrates in colorful detail both the wealth and political power that could be wielded by a capable woman in the early Merovingian times. It also depicts the politics of survival by which the kings and sometimes the queens of the Merovingian Dynasty sought to ensure their continued familial power and influence. Fredegunde's most powerful political moves and her most heinous crimes centered on preserving the lives and the power of her husband and sons—and therefore of herself. Despite her humble beginnings, this queen proved herself to be a capable manager of money and of people, retaining the loyalty of the counts in her son's kingdom while regent, directing their military actions in order to further secure her son's inheritance, and ruthlessly removing anyone who might challenge her offspring's right to Chilperic's crown.

—*Rhonda L. McDaniel*

FURTHER READING

Fletcher, R. A. *The Barbarian Conversion: From Paganism to Christianity.* Berkeley: University of California Press, 1999. Looks at the history of the development of Christianity in pagan Europe during the time of Fredegunde.

Gregory of Tours. *The History of the Franks.* Translated by Lewis Thorpe. New York: Penguin Books, 1974. The most complete source of information about Fredegunde, written by one who knew her personally. The translation reads smoothly, and the text provides an introduction with a historical overview, map, and par-

tial genealogical table of the early Merovingian kings.
MacMullen, Ramsay. *Christianity and Paganism in the Fourth to Eighth Centuries*. New Haven, Conn.: Yale University Press, 1997. Surveys the relationship between paganism and the Christian world in the time of Fredegunde.
Thierry, Augustin. *Tales of the Early Franks: Episodes from Merovingian History*. Translated by M. F. O. Jenkins. Tuscaloosa: University of Alabama Press, 1977. Provides a narrative collection of tales about Merovingian kings and queens and major events in early Frankish history.
Wallace-Hadrill, J. M. *The Long-Haired Kings and Other Studies in Frankish History*. 1962. Reprint. Toronto: University of Toronto Press, 1982. An oft-cited, classic scholarly work on the Frankish kingdoms.
Wood, Ian. *The Merovingian Kingdoms 450-751*. London: Longman, 1994. The author, one of the foremost scholars on the Merovingian kingdoms, provides a wealth of information on the history of the Merovingians and includes a chapter devoted to Fredegunde, Brunhild, and Radegund.

See also: Amalasuntha; Saint Clotilda; Clovis; Gregory of Tours; Joan of Arc.
Related articles in *Great Events from History: The Middle Ages, 477-1453*: 496: Baptism of Clovis; July 2, 1324: Lady Alice Kyteler Is Found Guilty of Witchcraft.

Frederick I Barbarossa

Holy Roman Emperor (r. 1152-1190)

For thirty-eight years Frederick ruled over the chaotic area of the Holy Roman Empire. Although he failed to unite effectively his German territories with the city-states of northern Italy, he nevertheless imposed his personality and power on a strong German feudal state.

Born: c. 1123; Waiblingen, Swabia (now in Germany)
Died: June 10, 1190; Saleph River, near Seleucia, Kingdom of Armenia (now Göksu River, Near Silifke, Turkey)
Also known as: Frederick I Hohenstaufen
Area of achievement: Government and politics

Early Life

Germany in the twelfth century was undergoing enormous social transformation. An increase in the population, unmatched by a corresponding economic revolution, put great pressure on a political structure based largely on personal loyalties. Simultaneously there was a growing division between the secular power of the Holy Roman Emperor and the ecclesiastical power of the Papacy. The Investiture Controversy (the quarrel over whether the pope or the emperor would invest the bishops with their symbol of authority) led Emperor Henry IV to subordinate himself to the pope and ultimately resulted in a compromise at the Concordat of Worms in 1107. Still, a bishop had a dual function as secular and spiritual prince, and his strength diminished the potential power of the emperor.

In these tumultuous times, Frederick Barbarossa (a name derived from his red beard) was chosen king of Germany in 1152; he was elected by the princes and bishops of Germany to succeed his uncle Conrad III. The unanimous election of so young a man—he was not yet thirty years old—reflected not only his personal strength and intellect but also, more important, the fact that he was related by blood to the two major families in Germany whose past quarrels had shaken the security of the empire. The powerful Welf and Staufen families had long dominated German politics, and Frederick's election proved an effective solution to their power struggle. During his long reign, he endeavored to centralize government and authority in Germany but, in the end, reestablished in a new and more orderly form the feudalism that caused Germany to lag behind the monarchical development of France and England.

Contemporary busts of Frederick (there are no portraits) show a smiling face with the tight, stylized curls of hair and beard reminiscent of Roman portraiture. Frederick's uncle, the historian Otto of Freising, described the monarch as well proportioned:

> He is shorter than very tall men, but taller and more noble than men of medium height. His hair is golden, curling a little above his forehead. . . . His eyes are sharp and piercing, his nose well formed, his beard reddish. . . .

In June of 1149, Frederick married Adela von Vohburg, a slightly older woman whose marriage to him reconciled old family quarrels. She was never crowned as queen, apparently because there was little closeness between them. When Frederick discovered that she had committed adultery, it gave him the excuse to dissolve a marriage that meant nothing to him personally and whose political value was of minor significance after he was elected king. Accordingly, he petitioned the pope to have the marriage annulled; the pope, eager to please the emperor, agreed.

When Frederick chose to remarry in 1156, he selected Beatrix, the daughter of Count Rainald, although she was apparently only ten years old at the time. Her appeal was enhanced by lands in Burgundy that she could claim and whose possession was important to Frederick as part of his grand design for the empire. Their alliance was both politically useful and personally fulfilling. The first of their four sons was born in 1164.

LIFE'S WORK

After his election as king of Germany in 1152, Frederick traveled through his kingdom, showing himself to the people (an act of symbolic importance in medieval Germany). He retained the major advisers of Conrad III so that there was, both in appearance and in fact, a continuity of rule. Frederick was then crowned at Aix-la-Chapelle by the archbishop of Cologne. His next move was to be crowned Holy Roman Emperor by the pope. Meanwhile, Frederick traveled through his kingdom as an arbitrator of conflicting interests, fulfilling one of his expected roles: maintainer of justice. His fame grew as he was successful in settling a variety of disputes.

The pope, Eugenius III, was eager for Frederick to come to Rome, where one of the traditional functions of the emperor was to protect the pope from social upheaval—in this case, a rebellious urban populace in Rome that wanted to establish a republic. Led by Arnold of Brescia, the common people protested the growing wealth of the Church. Frederick's defense of the pope would mean, as well, open war with King Roger II of Sicily (as a result of earlier commitments made by Conrad III). In 1153, Frederick and the pope signed the Treaty of Constance, which promised mutual assistance. It was after the signing of this treaty that the pope annulled Frederick's first marriage, leaving the way open for a more politically advantageous union.

The deaths of Pope Eugenius III in 1153 and King Roger of Sicily in 1154 did not deter Frederick from his purpose, and in 1154, he set out on his journey to Rome. He traveled through the tumultuous city-states of northern Italy and at last reached Rome, where he was met by

Engraving of Frederick I Barbarossa. (Library of Congress)

Pope Adrian IV (the only Englishman ever to be pope), whose reputation among the citizens of Rome had worsened. In spite of the unrest, Adrian crowned Frederick Holy Roman Emperor. The new emperor planned his promised war against Sicily, only to discover that his German princes had done all they intended to in Italy and were eager to return to Germany. The following year Frederick was back in Augsburg, ready to organize new plans for his empire.

In the early years of his rule, Frederick followed closely the traditional policies laid down by Conrad III (alliance with Greece against Sicily and support and defense of the pope). By 1156, however, Frederick was prepared to change directions. He was assisted by one of the major advisers of his reign, Rainald of Dassel, who served as chancellor for eleven years. (It was Rainald who brought the bones of the Three Wise Men from a rebellious Milan and placed them in his own bishopric in Cologne.) A change of political direction was also made easier by a treaty of reconciliation between the pope and the new king of Sicily, William I, thus eliminating the need for a war against Sicily.

Frederick sought to claim for himself a more active role in Germany. Traditionally, the emperor was little more than a protector of justice, maintaining old customs but without real authority to enact new laws. Frederick hoped to strengthen and enlarge his political power from a geographical base made up of the areas of Swabia and Alsace (where his family estates were centered), Burgundy (which he could claim through Beatrix, his wife), and Lombardy (the northern Italian area traditionally part of the Holy Roman Empire).

In moving to consolidate his empire, Frederick dealt first with troubles in Bavaria between two of his relatives: Henry the Lion (a Welf) and Henry Jasomirgott (a Babenberg). His division of the duchy established a new constitutional concept of a territorial state with its own ruler, who received more real authority and rights than the traditional rulers had held. Frederick actually began to move away from Germany as a power base and centered his new realm on his family lands. He began a program of constructing new castles and improving roads to connect the cities, many of which were founded under his rule. Frederick also encouraged the rise of an administrative class (*ministeriales*) to act as his agents in the governing of his enlarging territories.

Frederick's major problem in consolidating his empire was the territory of Lombardy, where economic development was different from that in his German states. He raised a large army to cross over into Lombardy, and there he came into conflict with the city of Milan. At first Milan became an imperial city, and Frederick participated in a crown-wearing festival that symbolized his embodiment of divine power as emperor. He issued a series of decrees listing the royal rights that belonged to him and declared that the judges and magistrates held their power from him. Opposition to Frederick, however, developed, eventually leading to riots and attempts on his life. In 1160, he took military action against Milan, and after two years the city succumbed to the emperor's rule.

With the death of Pope Adrian in 1159, the empire became even more unstable. Dissensions within the Church led to the election of two popes: Alexander III and Victor IV (the latter had the support of Frederick and much of the European aristocracy). Both popes were forced to leave Rome, where the citizens were divided in their support. Meanwhile, Alexander excommunicated Victor and his electors. Both popes were consecrated, however, and both continued to claim the spiritual and temporal power of the Papacy. Frederick endeavored to call a council to resolve the dispute, but Alexander refused to participate, claiming that the pope could not be judged by an emperor.

The council was convened without Alexander III and was attended by the kings of England and France, as well as the major nobles of Europe. In Alexander's absence, the council selected Victor as the legitimate pope, and Victor responded by legitimately excommunicating Alexander and his supporters. Alexander responded by excommunicating Frederick and, in a barrage of propaganda, claimed that Frederick wanted to establish power over the other lords in Europe. Victor, who found it very difficult to appear independent of Frederick, seemed to give credence to these claims.

The organizational problems of the Church became the governmental problems of Frederick because Milan had been supportive of Alexander. After the fall of Milan to Frederick's forces, Alexander fled to France. Frederick then began negotiations with Louis IV of France for the return of Alexander to Frederick's control. Frederick and Louis met at yet another council that, stacked in Victor's favor, resulted in Victor's being declared pope. Louis, however, changed his mind and refused to accept this settlement. The death of Victor in 1164 was followed by the election of Paschal III, but the highly political nature of his election led even Frederick to oppose him as a legitimate pope.

Frederick returned to Germany from the troubled area of Lombardy. Meanwhile, Alexander, reconciled with the citizens, planned to reenter Rome. Paschal rushed to reach Rome first but failed to beat Alexander to the Holy City. Frederick raised an army to enter Rome and capture Alexander but arrived too late to seize him. Frederick enthroned Paschal, but the triumph was short-lived. An epidemic struck the city and wiped out much of Frederick's army. The remaining forces returned to Germany, only to find revolt in Lombardy among the hostile cities there (long supporters of Alexander). The disaster in Rome, the death of Rainald from the plague there, and the revolt in Lombardy forced Frederick to reevaluate the plan for centralized territorial control he had devised in 1156. That grand design was abandoned, and Frederick sought a new direction for his rule.

In 1168, Paschal died in Rome and was succeeded by Calixtus III. Frederick initially recognized him as pope and promised support but, by 1169, Frederick was prepared to make overtures to Alexander. His first effort broke down over the problems in Lombardy, where revolt against the emperor continued. In 1175, Frederick cut his losses in Lombardy, and, with the Treaty of Anagni the following year, Germany at last ended the war with Lombardy and also the schism in the Papacy. Frederick and Alexander met in Venice in 1177 for a great festival of reconciliation.

Politically, Frederick now embarked on another pro-

HOHENSTAUFEN KINGS OF GERMANY, 1138-1254

Reign	*Ruler*
1138-1152	Conrad III
1152-1190	FREDERICK I BARBAROSSA
1190-1197	Henry VI
1198-1208	Philip of Swabia
1208-1215	Otto IV (married into Hohenstaufens)
1215-1250	FREDERICK II
1250-1254	Conrad IV
1254-1273	Great Interregnum

gram, this one centering on Germany, where he took advantage of the rising tide of feudalism to support the monarchy. Frederick planned to become a feudal king by extending power over as wide an area as possible. With Germany falling nicely into feudal order, Frederick turned again to his Italian territory. New agreements with the cities of Lombardy left Frederick as imperial lord, but with few actual powers, and the cities were left reasonably free to pursue their own goals. Both Alexander and his successor, Lucius III (who became pope in 1181), relied on the military support of Frederick for their positions. Lucius helped to arrange a marriage between Frederick's son Henry and Constance, aunt of the king of Sicily, which was a major diplomatic triumph and a union of once-hostile forces. Lucius died in 1185 and was succeeded by Urban III (from Milan, thus an enemy of Frederick) and later by Gregory VIII, who once again endeavored to incite the Christian kings of Europe to war against the infidel ruler Saladin, who had conquered Jerusalem in 1187.

Frederick decided that conditions at home were calm enough to enable him to join the Third Crusade as the crowning act of his long reign. Because the chief purpose of the emperor was to protect the Church, and the home of the Church was threatened, it seemed logical that he should go to its defense. At this point, also, the eschatological view of history, dominant in the twelfth century, encouraged the Crusade. Apocalyptic prophecy indicated that the last emperor would go to Jerusalem and lay down his crown and scepter at the Mount of Olives, which would signal the rule of the Antichrist and the Second Coming. Thus, at Pentecost, 1188, Frederick took the cross and departed on the Third Crusade, where he was joined by Philip II of France and Richard I the Lion-Hearted of England.

After careful preparation, Frederick and a disciplined army of knights set forth. The politics of the Byzantine land through which he passed often led to clashes, but Frederick continued. In Armenia, near the city of Seleucia, Frederick stopped to drink at the Saleph River, and there he drowned in 1190. His body was taken to Antioch and buried in the cathedral there. Bereft of its strong central ruler, Germany declined into feudal states, and Pope Innocent III emerged as the strongman within the empire.

SIGNIFICANCE

The facts of Frederick's tragic death were soon overshadowed by legends that had a powerful influence in Germany history, even during the Nazi era of the twentieth century. According to one legend, Frederick I Barbarossa never really died but was asleep atop the Kyffhäuser Mountain, and one day he would awaken and restore the glory of the German Empire. The legend was popular within a hundred years of Frederick's death and, though initially attached to Frederick III, in its final form centered on Frederick I Barbarossa. The cult of Frederick was very important, as the fragmented German states sought to reestablish a German Empire in the late nineteenth century.

Frederick Barbarossa was the first emperor to have a modern vision of monarchy, and his efforts to build a strong monarchy anticipated the stirring of German nationalism in the nineteenth century. Frederick was a man whose ideas were ahead of his time, and, had he been able to unify his territorial states (Swabia, Burgundy, and Lombardy), the history of Western Europe would have taken a different path. He failed because of the divided Papacy, the economic turmoil (which made Lombardy particularly difficult to subdue), and the independence of the German nobles.

In his later years, Frederick accepted the limits of his time and, capitalizing on local conditions in Germany, built a strong feudal state. Unquestionably one of the strongest figures of the twelfth century, Frederick cannot be overlooked in either the history of the Holy Roman Empire or the history of Germany.

—*Carlanna L. Hendrick*

FURTHER READING

Barraclough, Geoffrey. *Medieval Germany, 911-1250.* Oxford: Basil Blackwell, 1967. Useful, especially for constitutional issues raised during the reign of Frederick that had an impact on the development of modern Germany.

_______. *The Origins of Modern Germany.* Oxford: Basil Blackwell, 1966. One of the major scholars of the Middle Ages in general (and Germany in particular) examines the rule of Frederick. There is also an excellent discussion of Frederick's effort to establish his government in the state of northern Italy. One of the best short summaries of the life and impact of Frederick.

Carson, Thomas, ed. and trans. *Barbarossa in Italy.* New York: Italica Press, 1994. An epic about the events that led to Frederick's destruction of Milan in 1162, by a contemporary but anonymous poet known as the Bergamo Master. Bibliography.

Heer, Frederick. *The Holy Roman Empire.* Translated by Janet Sondheimer. New York: Praeger, 1968. One of many surveys of the Holy Roman Empire that, necessarily, focus on the rule of Frederick. This particular study emphasizes the romantic nature of Frederick's rule, especially as viewed in hindsight by later, nationalist Germans charmed with the legends of their medieval past.

Jeep, John M., et al., eds. *Medieval Germany: An Encyclopedia.* New York: Garland, 2001. An A-Z encyclopedia that addresses all aspects of the German- and Dutch-speaking medieval world from 500 to 1500. Entries include individuals, events, and broad topics such as feudalism and pregnancy. Bibliographical references, index.

Moore, Robert Ian. *The First European Revolution, c. 970-1215.* Malden, Mass.: Blackwell, 2000. According to the publisher, "a radical reassessment of Europe from the late tenth to the early thirteenth centuries [arguing that] the period witnessed the first true 'revolution' in European society," supported by transformation of the economy, family life, political power structures, and the rise of the non-Mediterranean cities. Bibliography, index.

Munz, Peter. *Frederick Barbarossa: A Study in Medieval Politics.* Ithaca, N.Y.: Cornell University Press, 1969. The definitive work on Frederick, this study covers in detail Frederick's reign and his different plans for development of the empire. A splendid analysis of the legends surrounding Frederick and their origins and impact on German history. It includes an extensive bibliography and genealogical table and an index useful for sorting out the persons who influenced Frederick's reign. Extensive footnotes also assist the reader in finding his way through the twelfth century.

Otto of Freising. *The Deeds of Frederick Barbarossa.* Translated by Charles Christopher Mierow. 1953. Reprint. Toronto: University of Toronto Press, in association with the Medieval Academy of America, 1994. The major source for information on the life of Frederick. Written during his lifetime by his uncle, it is politically slanted in favor of Frederick. It includes letters from and to the major figures of the day and provides not only useful information but also a wonderful flavor of the language and thought of the twelfth century.

Stubbs, William. *Germany in the Early Middle Ages, 476-1250.* New York: Howard Fertig, 1969. Includes a solid chapter on the reign of Frederick. Emphasis is on his rule, its chronology, and the other major figures who ruled contemporaneously with Frederick.

SEE ALSO: Adrian IV; Alexander III; Henry the Lion; Hildegard von Bingen; Innocent III; Philip II; Richard I; Rudolf I; Walther von der Vogelweide.

RELATED ARTICLES in *Great Events from History: The Middle Ages, 477-1453*: 1054: Beginning of the Rome-Constantinople Schism; c. 1150-1200: Rise of the Hansa Merchant Union; 1152: Frederick Barbarossa Is Elected King of Germany; September 17, 1156: Austria Emerges as a National Entity; 1189-1192: Third Crusade; 1204: Knights of the Fourth Crusade Capture Constantinople.

Frederick II

King of Sicily (r. 1198-1250) and Holy Roman Emperor (r. 1220-1250)

An able administrator, Frederick II reorganized the government of Sicily to create a centralized monarchy. He failed, however, in his attempts to gain power relative to the Church and over northern Italy.

Born: December 26, 1194; Iesi, near Ancona, Papal States (now in Italy)
Died: December 13, 1250; Castle Fiorentino, Apulia, Kingdom of Sicily (now in Italy)
Also known as: Frederick II of Hohenstaufen; Frederick von Staufen/Hohenstaufen; Stupor Mundi (Wonder of the World)
Area of achievement: Government and politics

Early Life

Frederick II of Hohenstaufen (HOH-uhn-shtaoo-fuhn) was born to Emperor Henry VI and Constance of Sicily, the daughter of Roger II, king of Sicily. When Frederick was two years old, his father had him elected king of Germany to ensure an uncontested succession. When Henry died in 1197, his wife assumed the regency, and the following year at Palermo, she had her son crowned king of Sicily. The boy king was reared and educated in Sicily, and at fourteen, he was declared to be of age. The following year, he married Constance, the daughter of Alfonso II of Aragon and widow of Emerich, king of Hungary.

During Frederick's youth, Germany was in a state of anarchy, with Philip of Swabia and Otto IV struggling for control. The maturing of Frederick and the death of Philip (1208) caused only a minor shift in the civil war north of the Alps. John of England continued to support Otto, and Philip II of France shifted his support to Frederick. The decisive military encounter was the French victory over Otto at Bouvines in July, 1214.

The following year, Frederick was again crowned the German king, this time at Aachen. Frederick had already begun to make concessions to the Church in Germany, and in 1215, in order to win the full support of Pope Innocent III, he vowed to go on a crusade. Five years later, he had the German nobles elect his young son Henry as German king and then went south to Rome, where Pope Honorius III, Innocent's successor, crowned him Holy Roman Emperor on November 22, 1220. To win the favor of the new pope, Frederick had again made lavish promises. He renewed his commitment to take the Cross, promised to aid the faltering Fifth Crusade, and said that he would fight against heresy. He also renounced the union of Germany and Sicily, a lingering fear of successive popes. Despite all of his promises, Frederick remained in Sicily for the next several years.

Life's Work

Frederick's prolonged absence from Sicily had been marked by rebellion and strife. Frederick first restored his authority and then reorganized the administration of the kingdom. He even founded a university at Naples in 1224. Still, the new pope, Gregory IX, was not impressed. He insisted that the emperor make good his promise to lead a crusade to reinstate Christian control over the Holy Land. To encourage him, the pope arranged, in 1225, for the widowed Frederick to marry Isabella, the daughter of John of Brienne, king of Jerusalem, with the understanding that he would have his father-in-law's title once he had conquered the Holy City. Yet the emperor, who was in no hurry, continued to postpone his departure. When at last, in 1227, Frederick did sail from Brindisi, sickness broke out aboard the ships, and the expedition was halted and again postponed.

Engraving of Frederick II. (Library of Congress)

Gregory was enraged, and he excommunicated the emperor.

The pope's ban was not lifted the following year when Frederick again set sail. Reaching Palestine, he was able to achieve his objectives through negotiating rather than fighting. Jerusalem and the surrounding lands, including Bethlehem and Nazareth, were acquired by the treaty signed on February 18, 1229, and he entered the Holy City and was crowned king of Jerusalem on March 18. Having no desire to remain in Palestine, Frederick returned to Italy in June of the same year to deal with a papal army that had invaded his territories in southern Italy and insurrections that had been inspired by Gregory. These affairs were handled with success, and the ban of excommunication was lifted.

THE HOHENSTAUFEN EMPERORS AND RIVALS, 1138-1254

Reign	*Ruler*
1138-1152	Conrad III (Hohenstaufen)
1152/55-1190	FREDERICK I BARBAROSSA (Hohenstaufen)
1190/91-1197	Henry VI (Hohenstaufen)
1198-1208	Philip of Swabia (Hohenstaufen)
1208/09-1215	Otto IV (married into Hohenstaufens)
1215/20-1250	FREDERICK II (Hohenstaufen): Last emperor crowned at Rome.
1246-1247	Henry Raspe
1247-1256	William of Holland
1250-1254	Conrad IV (end of the Hohenstaufen line)
1254-1273	Great Interregnum

For the next few years, Frederick devoted himself to the political and economic reform of his southern Italian kingdom. He strengthened the central administration at the expense of the old Norman feudal system to create a forerunner of the absolute monarchy. In this, he was several centuries before his time. He also brought about reform in the economic structure of the state. He encouraged trade and agriculture, improved roads and built bridges, held annual fairs, and even minted gold coins, which had all but disappeared in most parts of Europe. As a result of his economic policies, the Kingdom of Sicily prospered. Still, Frederick's ever-increasing needs, brought on by his continuous efforts to control northern Italy, led to increased taxation. Meanwhile, the German princes were establishing their near independence from imperial control. He had made major concessions to them over the years to gain their loyalty and material support for his crusade and wars in Italy. In addition, his oldest son Henry had also made concessions to the German princes that the emperor felt obliged to accept.

Indeed, young Henry was a problem for his father in the 1230's. As king of Germany, he favored the privileges of the towns over those of the princes. When the latter accompanied the emperor on his Crusade, Henry took advantage of their absence to strengthen his own position. On their return, however, he was forced to recognize their virtual independence and to submit to the authority of his father, whom he had defied. The prodigal son went to Italy in 1232 and was forgiven after he had sworn allegiance and obedience. Once back in Germany, however, he again rebelled against the emperor, with limited support of the German nobility. This time, he went one step further: He allied himself with his father's most persistent and bitter enemy, the Lombard League. Frederick, with the temporary support of Gregory IX, was able to stabilize his position in Italy by 1235, and with only a token force arriving in Germany. The German princes, who had never been strong supporters of King Henry, flocked to the standard of the emperor. With little fighting, the wayward son was forced to submit once again to his father. The situation this time was very much different from what it had been four years earlier. Not only was this the second time that Henry had rebelled against his father, but he had also committed the unforgivable offense of allying himself with the Lombards. In July, 1235, at the diet held in Worms, Henry was removed from his throne and imprisoned at Apulia, where he remained until his death in 1242.

In August of 1235, Frederick, whose second wife, Isabella, had died in 1228 giving birth to their son Conrad, married Isabella, the daughter of King John of England. In 1237, after a successful campaign against Frederick II, duke of Austria, which led not only to the subjugation of Austria but also to that of Styria and Carenthia, Frederick secured the election of his second son, Conrad, as German king to replace the deposed Henry. The emperor's bastard son Enzo (whom he had with his Cremonese mistress) was also provided with a kingdom. He was married to Adelasia, the heiress of Sardinia and named king of that island.

The emperor was now at the height of his reign and was determined to use all of his power and resources to bring northern Italy under imperial authority. Yet Gregory, who recognized the strong influence of the Church, threw his support to the Lombard League. The struggle continued during the last fifteen years of Frederick's reign, with the fortunes of war and diplomacy swaying back and forth. In September, 1237, the emperor defeated the army of the Cortenuova League, and it appeared as if victory was within his grasp. The failure of the Siege of Brescia the following year, however, renewed the spirits of Frederick's enemies, and in 1239, Gregory again excommunicated him. The Siege of Rome in 1240 was also a failure, and despite the death of Gregory (August, 1241) and the election of Innocent IV in 1243 (Celestine IV had died within months of his election in 1241), the struggle continued.

The new pope proved to be an even more capable adversary than Gregory. He withdrew from Italy and went to Lyon, on the French border, and held a General Council in June, 1245, at which Frederick was deposed and an antiemperor, Henry Raspe, Landgrave of Thuringia, was elected. The secular German princes, in particular Duke Otto of Bavaria, the father of King Conrad IV's wife, tended to side with the emperor; it was in Italy that he faced the greatest defections. Even in southern Italy, there were rebellions and defections.

In 1246 and 1247, the imperial forces, strengthened by the support of the very capable Enzo, held their own. Frederick and his son even laid siege to the vital city of Parma in 1247. Then, while the emperor was convalescing from an illness, an army sallied forth from the besieged city and destroyed the imperial army (February, 1248). This defeat was followed in May, 1249, by the defeat and capture of Enzo at La Fossalta by a Bolognese army. With this catastrophe, the hope of victory over the Lombard League came to an end. Frederick, who had never fully regained his health, retired to southern Italy, where he died at the Castle Fiorentino, in Apulia, on December 13, 1250. He was buried in the cathedral of Palermo.

KINGS OF SICILY AND NAPLES, 1042-1285

Reign	*Ruler (Line)*
1042-1046	William Iron Arm (Norman)
1046-1051	Drogo (Norman)
1051-1057	Humphrey (Norman)
1057-1085	Robert Guiscard (Norman)
1085-1103	Roger Borsa (Duke of Apulia)
1103-1154	Roger II of Sicily (Norman)
1154-1166	William I (Norman)
1166-1189	William II the Good (Norman)
1190-1194	Tancred of Lecce (Norman)
1194	William III (Norman)
1194-1197	Henry VI (Hohenstaufen)
1197-1250	FREDERICK II (Hohenstaufen)
1250-1254	Conrad IV (Hohenstaufen)
1250-1266	Manfred (Hohenstaufen)
1267-1268	Conradin (Hohenstaufen)
1268-1285	Charles I of Anjou (Angevin)

SIGNIFICANCE

The reign of Frederick II must be considered a failure. Of his many accomplishments, few survived even his own life span. The Holy Roman Empire would exist primarily on paper and in the minds of those who claimed its title. The German princes had gained virtual independence from the German king and emperor. Northern Italy continued in a state of anarchy for the next three hundred years, with neither kings nor emperors nor popes able to exercise domination except for the briefest periods of time. The Kingdom of Sicily, where Frederick had been the most successful in creating a centralized monarchy with an enviable economy, went into decline following the emperor's death. It had been the site of Frederick's finest achievements and the best example of his administrative abilities.

The power and influence of the Church had not been strengthened during Frederick's reign, but neither had they been noticeably weakened. The pontificate of Innocent III is frequently noted as the high point of the medieval Papacy, but Frederick, despite his near-perpetual struggle with successive popes, did not triumph over the Church. In fact, the positions of both the emperor and the Papacy declined in the first half of the twelfth century. It was the secular princes and the cities of Germany that emerged stronger north of the Alps, while in northern Italy, the independent city-states were taking shape. Finally, it should be noted that the death of Frederick II heralded the demise of the house of Hohenstaufen.

—*John G. Gallaher*

FURTHER READING

Abulafia, David. *Frederick II: A Medieval Emperor.* 1988. Reprint. London: Pimlico, 1992. A biography of Frederick II. Contains illustrations, maps, bibliography, and index.

Andrewes, Patience. *Frederick II of Hohenstaufen.* London: Oxford University Press, 1970. Part of the Clarendon Biographies series, this biography covers the life and times of Holy Roman Emperor Frederick II. Illustrations and map.

Kantorowicz, Ernst. *Frederick the Second, 1194-1250.* Translated by E. O. Lorimer. 1931. New York: Unger, 1967. Translated from the original German, this 680-page study of Frederick II is a very detailed and thorough account available in the English language. It contains an excellent index and a summary of sources, which takes the form of a brief bibliographical essay.

Powell, James M. *Anatomy of a Crusade, 1213-1221.* Philadelphia: University of Pennsylvania Press, 1986. An examination of the Fifth Crusade and Frederick II's role in it. Contains maps, illustrations, a bibliography, and an index.

Tronzo, William, ed. *Intellectual Life at the Court of Frederick II Hohenstaufen.* Hanover, N.H.: Distributed by the University Press of New England, 1994. A collection of papers from a symposium sponsored by the Center for Advanced Study in the Visual Arts in 1990. Focuses on the emperor's palaces and the arts in his court, including literature and philosophy. Also treats economy and society in the Kingdom of Sicily.

SEE ALSO: Saint Elizabeth of Hungary; Gregory IX; Innocent III; Innocent IV; Leonardo of Pisa; Louis IX; Petrus Peregrinus de Maricourt; Rudolf I; Salimbene; Valdemar II; William of Auvergne.

RELATED ARTICLES in *Great Events from History: The Middle Ages, 477-1453*: 1127-1130: Creation of the Kingdom of Sicily; 1152: Frederick Barbarossa Is Elected King of Germany; July 27, 1214: Battle of Bouvines; November 11-30, 1215: Fourth Lateran Council; 1227-1230: Frederick II Leads the Sixth Crusade; 1228-1231: Teutonic Knights Bring Baltic Region Under Catholic Control; 1233: Papal Inquisition; 1248-1254: Failure of the Seventh Crusade; 1258: Provisions of Oxford Are Established; 1290-1306: Jews Are Expelled from England, France, and Southern Italy.

JEAN FROISSART

French historian and poet

Froissart was a seminal figure in fourteenth century European historiography. In his Chronicles, *he offered a vivid panorama of an age in transition that relied for its inspiration on waning codes of chivalry and a growing spirit of Humanism.*

BORN: 1337?; Valenciennes, Hainaut, France
DIED: c. 1404; Chimay, Belgium
AREAS OF ACHIEVEMENT: Historiography, literature

EARLY LIFE

Jean Froissart (zhahn frwah-sahr), the son of a painter of arms, received a clerical education and entered the service of Margaret of Hainaut sometime between 1350 and her death in 1356. This was the first of many court appointments that enabled him to establish a network of contacts in aristocratic circles, primarily in France and the Low Countries. In 1362, he went to England in order to serve as secretary to Queen Philippa of Hainaut, wife of Edward III. He remained in her entourage as court poet until 1369, during which time he traveled to Scotland with King David II, to France and Spain with Edward, the Black Prince, and to Italy in the bridal party of Lionel, duke of Clarence, who married Yolanda Visconti of Milan in April, 1368. It was on this trip through Italy, as he visited Ferrara, Bologna, and Rome, that Froissart apparently made the acquaintance of Geoffrey Chaucer, Giovanni Boccaccio, and Petrarch.

On his arrival in England, Froissart presented to the court a verse chronicle of the Battle of Poitiers (1356) that had been warmly praised by Robert of Namur, lord of Beaufort and nephew to Queen Philippa. Froissart's early poetry was popular at the court, and two works in particular, *Éspinette amoureuse* (c. 1369) and *Joli Buisson de Jonece* (1373), contain allusions to his childhood. In addition to long narrative poetry, he produced short poems with fixed rhyme patterns in the tradition of Guillaume de Machaut, as well as lais, rondeaux, and ballades, before concentrating on what became his principal literary achievement—the four books entitled *Chroniques de France, d'Engleterre, d'Éscose, de Bretaigne, d'Espaigne, d'Italie, de Flandres et d'Alemaigne* (1373-1410; *The Chronycles of Englande, Fraunce, Spayne . . . ,* 1523-1525, better known as *Chronicles*).

Froissart learned the art of chronicle writing from Jean le Bel, canon of Liège, whose example he followed in relying not only on original documents but also on eyewitness accounts and interviews. Froissart was essentially interested in passing the traditions of chivalry to succeeding generations. Once his reputation was established, members of the aristocracy sought to provide him with the financial resources and protection necessary to gather research material. As a result, his writing reflects his patrons' system of values. He was ordained sometime after leaving England and, under the patronage of Wenceslas of Luxembourg, duke of Brabant, he obtained a sinecure as rector of Les Estinnes-au-Mont, where he remained for approximately ten years.

LIFE'S WORK

Froissart's *Chronicles* was widely reproduced throughout the fifteenth century, and numerous manuscripts have been preserved. Two of them include paintings made by Froissart himself that show him presenting a copy of the work to aristocratic patrons. Even though he was a priest, Froissart was completely at ease in sophisticated society, and his writing accurately depicts the mannerisms and idiosyncrasies in speech and dress that characterize the period.

In writing *Chronicles*, Froissart was carrying on a French tradition of secular historiography that began with the Crusades and continued into the fifteenth century in the works of Georges Chastellain and Philippe de Commynes. The primary concern of these scholars was to preserve the memorable events of the Hundred Years' War. Froissart classified himself as a historian, not merely a chronicler. The distinction he makes between chronicle and history is based on the amount of information supplied. Chronicles, particularly those following the thirteenth century annalist school established at the monastery of Saint-Denis, present a fairly simplified narrative account, whereas history demands depth and detailed description. (Chroniclers are also called annalists.)

Froissart's *Chronicles* covers significant events in European history from 1326 until 1400. The first volume, completed before 1371, begins with the coronation of Edward III and the accession of Philip of Valois to the crown of France, thus setting the stage for the Hundred Years' War. Book 1 was later revised considerably and its scope was extended to include events up to 1379. Because Froissart annotated book 1 throughout his life, it serves as a valuable indicator of his development as a historian and provides detailed information about his methods of composition.

Book 2, written between 1385 and 1388, recapitulates the events of the last three years of the preceding volume, adding new information, and concludes with the Treaty of Tournai (December, 1385) between Ghent and Philip the Bold, duke of Burgundy. After the death of Wenceslas in 1384, Froissart became chaplain to Guy de Châtillon, count of Blois, in whose honor he wrote numerous pastoral poems. In 1388, Froissart visited the court of Gaston Phoebus, count of Foix, near the Spanish border in Béarn, in order to obtain information concerning wars in Spain and Portugal. This journey, in particular, testifies to the vigorous health that Froissart enjoyed; he had to endure numerous hardships while traveling for several months over difficult terrain. Froissart's curiosity was relentless, and he worked late into the night recording from memory conversations with knights and dignitaries.

Jean Froissart. (Hulton|Archive at Getty Images)

Book 3, finished in 1392, relates events that had occurred since 1382, but it gives a fuller account of them. This work ends in 1389 with a three-year truce concluded between France and England, and it anticipates the entry into Paris of Isabella of Bavaria as queen of France. In his study of the political events in Portugal between 1383 and 1385 that led to the invasion by John of Gaunt, duke of Lancaster, Froissart made considerable use of Portuguese narrative sources and anecdotal information provided by Gascon knights at Orthez who had served under Edmund Cambridge, duke of York.

The first fifty chapters of book 4 follow closely on the material of book 3 as Froissart reexamined the political machinery of France under Charles VI. In 1392, a series of truces between France and England was announced and Froissart took advantage of this opportunity to visit England for three months, under the patronage of William, count of Ostrevant, cousin to Richard II. Froissart was well received by the English king, but he felt uncomfortable in what he sensed was a highly unstable environment. Book 4 recounts the confusion in England leading to the deposition of Richard, who—despite his tragic ineffectiveness—had maintained an uneasy peace between England and France. *Chronicles* concludes with the death of Richard and the succession of Henry IV, the first of the Lancastrian Dynasty, to the English throne. Internal evidence suggests that Froissart composed the account of his journey to England in the months before his death in 1404, while serving as treasurer and canon of the church at Chimay.

MAJOR WORKS BY JEAN FROISSART

Date	*Work*
c. 1369	*Éspinette amoureuse*
1372-1373	*Prison amoureuse* (*The Prison of Love*)
1373	*Joli Buisson de Jonece*
1373-1410	*Chroniques de France, d'Engleterre, d'Éscose, de Bretaigne, d'Espaigne, d'Italie, de Flandres et d'Alemaigne* (*Chronicles*)
1388	*Méliador*

Even though Froissart was a historian of chivalry, his *Chronicles* does not constitute a formal history of the aristocracy. In his attempt to demonstrate the relative superiority of the nobility, he used a process of selection; in this way, he was able to isolate significant aspects of gallantry and heroism. Hence he overlooked issues that attracted the attention of other chroniclers: administration of estates, enactment of laws, and tax collection. Nevertheless, Froissart commented openly on French policy during the reign of Charles V, on the relationship between the French monarchy and the vassals of Brittany and Flanders, and on the acute political intrigue found in all governments.

Chronicles was not written as a personal memoir—a form popular with other compilers. Nevertheless, Froissart did include numerous authorial injunctions in his narration. In these usually brief personal entries, he often shared his judgment of the events under discussion, thus creating a bond between chronicler and reader rarely achieved in medieval French prose. In addition, these interventions reveal the techniques of composition that resulted in the independent redactions found in the variant manuscripts of the first two volumes. The mobility evident in these texts is most likely the result of his collaboration with scribes, who may have played a major role in the elaboration of certain episodes. The *Chronicles'* form is derivative of the Arthurian romances, which also include superimposed accounts.

Froissart was an insightful observer of military warfare. One of his intentions was to give a faithful account of the ways in which castles and towns were attacked. He commanded a wide military vocabulary, and his description of siege warfare and pitched battles is graphically detailed in the light of the fact that fourteenth century combat was undergoing a significant change. The religious zeal of the early Crusades and the tradition of feudal loyalty had lost their vitality. Warriors were primarily motivated by personal honor or monetary gain through ransom. One-to-one encounters on horseback no longer had the advantage over the use of well-disciplined soldiers equipped with crossbows, longbows, and knives. Froissart's saga of military exploits naturally stresses individual action, yet his accounts make it clear that in large engagements the victor was usually the side that managed some degree of coordinated tactics. Froissart's astute analysis of tactical warfare and individual heroics lends extraordinary depth to the narrations of the most famous battles of the fourteenth century: Poitiers, Crécy-en-Ponthieu, and Nicopolis.

SIGNIFICANCE

Froissart's *Chronicles* benefited greatly from the advent of the printing press. From 1495 to 1520, the work went through at least ten editions. The appearance of Johannes Sleidanus's Latin abridgment in 1537—which was, in turn, translated into English, French, and Dutch—made the work available to Humanist scholars and aristocratic readers across Europe, who considered it prestigious to own a copy. By the middle of the sixteenth century, Froissart's *Chronicles* dominated all narratives of the first half of the Hundred Years' War. The vogue for Froissart reached its peak in 1850, when a statue in his honor was erected in Valenciennes.

Froissart's writing adumbrated the decline of chivalry as the concept of courtesy degenerated into greed and meaningless pageantry. His description of the tournament held at Smithfield in 1390 under the aegis of Richard II implies that courtesy had become a code of etiquette observed by members of the upper class in dealing with one another; it was no longer associated with the protection of the weak by the strong.

Froissart continually reminded his audience that his purpose in compiling the chronicles was to illustrate "les grans merveilles et les beaux faits d'armes" (heroic exploits and military prowess). He accomplished this aim with astonishing regularity despite errors in topology (regional history) and inconsistencies in dating. Causality is not a significant feature except insofar as the causes of events are personalized. *Chronicles* does not attempt to suggest the operation of historical principles that guide the course of events. Moreover, a certain cohesion is gained from this restriction. This emphasis on human factors, along with Froissart's objectivity, political acumen, variety, and poetic effects, gives *Chronicles* a cosmopolitan flavor that makes the full-blown phenomenon seem less austere and more circumscribed than that produced by clerical chroniclers.

Froissart rarely took sides in the conflicts of knights, although in the evolution of *Chronicles* there are signs of a shift in sympathy from the English to the French and, in book 4, to the Burgundian. He consistently chose to accentuate moderation as an ideal, exemplified by the conduct of Philip the Bold. Even though Edward, the Black Prince, was the hero of the Battle of Poitiers, Froissart criticized the brutality of his treatment of the burghers of Calais and the massacre of civilians at Limoges. In general, Froissart was concerned with deeds and actions, not with biography. Because of his accomplished literary talent, the portraits of the protagonists of *Chronicles* are imbued with a legendary quality.

Froissart often invoked Providence to justify the outcome of events. His philosophical observations reveal a conception of social order based on the controls exerted by a just prince who watches over the commonweal. His accounts of the Jacquerie movement (a peasant's revolt) in France (1358) and the English Peasants' Revolt of 1381 clearly indicate that, in his opinion, urban disintegration was a threat to national stability. Nevertheless, his portrayal of John Ball, the vagrant priest who incited the Peasants' Revolt, conveys a well-balanced appraisal of lower-class misery.

This objectivity is also noted in Froissart's attitude toward the Papal schism, which he treated as a political issue—the failure of diplomacy on the part of Charles V, who sided with the French cardinals. Froissart's ability to synthesize epic conflicts, like the struggle for hegemony in Western Europe between the Plantagenet and Valois Dynasties, gives *Chronicles* its distinctive pedigree. The comparison of the last Crusade, which ended in the defeat of the French at Nicopolis, to the twelfth century French epic *Chanson de Roland* (*Song of Roland*, 1880) implies that Froissart understood that the history of Europe was irrevocably determined. The scope and dynamism of Froissart's observations and his effort to recreate a mental and social tableau of fourteenth century life have contributed to the endurance of his reputation as a narrative historian.

—*Robert J. Frail*

FURTHER READING

Ainsworth, Peter F. *Jean Froissart and the Fabric of History: Truth, Myth, and Fiction in the "Chroniques."* New York: Oxford University Press, 1991. An impressive, comprehensive account of Froissart's ability to weave an intricate narrative out of diverse strands of information.

Archambault, Paul. *Seven French Chroniclers: Witnesses to History.* Syracuse, N.Y.: Syracuse University Press, 1974. This work contains an instructive essay on Froissart that places him within the context of the French annalist tradition and delineates the trajectory of French chronicle writing from 1200 to 1500, demonstrating that Froissart's emergence coincided with a transitional phase in secular historiography.

Coulton, George Gordon. *The Chroniclers of European Chivalry.* Reprint. Philadelphia: Richard West, 1978. A compelling analysis of Froissart's keen interest in the history of the Low Countries.

Dahmus, Joseph. *Seven Medieval Historians.* Chicago: Nelson-Hall, 1982. A well-researched, fairly comprehensive study of the way in which Froissart conceived of history as a conflict of interests among individuals of prominent rank and prestige. The chapter on Froissart includes generous extracts from *Chronicles.*

De Looze, Laurence. *Pseudo-autobiography in the Fourteenth Century: Juan Ruiz, Guillaume de Machaut, Jean Froissart, and Geoffrey Chaucer.* Gainesville: University Press of Florida, 1997. Looks at Froissart's work in the context of other autobiographical writings of the Middle Ages.

Figg, Kristen M., trans. and ed. *Jean Froissart: An Anthology of Narrative and Lyric Poetry.* New York: Routledge, 2001. Translated selections of Froissart's poetry and prose writings.

Fowler, Kenneth. *The Age of Plantagenet and Valois: The Struggle for Supremacy, 1328-1498.* New York:

Putnam, 1967. An attempt to explain the numerous complexities of war neurosis during the fourteenth and fifteenth centuries. Also includes an informative discussion of the social and artistic life of France, England, and Burgundy.

Huot, Sylvia. "Reading Across Genres: Froissart's *Joli Buisson de Jonece* and Machaut's motets." *French Studies* 57, no. 1 (January, 2003). A scholarly study of parallels between Froissart's poem and three of Machaut's motets.

Shears, Frederick S. *Froissart: Chronicler and Poet*. Folcroft, Pa.: Folcroft Library Editions, 1930. A definitive biography and a sympathetic defense of Froissart's proficiency as a historian. Explores the connection between Froissart's fourteen-thousand-line poetic masterpiece of 1370, *Méliador*, and the literary style of the *Chronicles*.

SEE ALSO: John Ball; Giovanni Boccaccio; David II; Edward III; Henry IV (of England); Isabella of France; Guillaume de Machaut; Petrarch; Philippa of Hainaut; Wat Tyler.

RELATED ARTICLES in *Great Events from History: The Middle Ages, 477-1453*: October 11, 732: Battle of Tours; c. 1100: Rise of Courtly Love; 1233: Papal Inquisition; 1305-1417: Avignon Papacy and the Great Schism; 1337-1453: Hundred Years' War; August 26, 1346: Battle of Crécy; 1373-1410: Jean Froissart Compiles His *Chronicles*; May-June, 1381: Peasants' Revolt in England.

FUJIWARA MICHINAGA

Japanese regent (1016-1017)

The greatest statesman of the Heian period, Fujiwara Michinaga maintained absolute control of the throne and court for thirty years and brought the Fujiwara family to the height of its power. He epitomizes Japanese leadership during the formative period of Japanese cultural development.

BORN: 966; Kyoto, Japan
DIED: January 3, 1028; Kyoto, Japan
AREA OF ACHIEVEMENT: Government and politics

EARLY LIFE

Fujiwara Michinaga (few-jee-wah-rah mee-chee-nah-gah) was born into the powerful Fujiwara family, the fifth son of Fujiwara Kaneie, who served as great minister of the right from 978 to 986 and as regent from 986 until his death in 990. The Fujiwara family had provided the principal support system for the imperial family since 645 and, by the end of the eighth century, had succeeded to the highest posts and greatest power in the imperial court. Beginning with Kaneie, who consolidated the family's power, a Fujiwara would occupy the regency for generations. The regency was important, for it preserved the imperial house and protected the throne. Although their power might have been overwhelming, the Fujiwara leaders were sensible enough to recognize that the prestige of their clan derived not only from their own talents but also from their blood connection with the reigning house. Both factors tended to perpetuate the monarchy, despite its impotence.

Although few details are known about Michinaga's early life, it is not surprising that at the age of fourteen, in 980, Michinaga received the office of lesser commander of the imperial guards of the left. This office carried with it junior fifth rank, lower grade, which was a relatively high distinction for a man of Michinaga's age. It was natural for him to rise rapidly in rank, and at the age of twenty-one, in 987, he became acting middle counselor and minister of the left. Then, in 992, he was named master of the empress's household, with junior second rank. It is clear that nothing was left to chance in his education and training, for he excelled, standing head and shoulders above others at court, particularly in Chinese studies, calligraphy, poetry, archery, and horsemanship.

Michinaga had two older brothers, Fujiwara Michitaka and Fujiwara Michikane, in line ahead of him for higher positions, and other relatives also competed with him for higher posts at court; thus, Michinaga was not expected to rise much further in the hierarchy of the court administration.

Michinaga was a handsome man, distinctive in his words and actions. People of his time commented on his vigor, boldness, and resourcefulness. According to tradition, he stalked his rival, Fujiwara Korechika, beating him in an archery contest and embarrassing him when he was dawdling by the carriage of the retired empress Akiko (Michinaga's sister). Reportedly, Michinaga had his horsemen whip his horses into some tents that Korechika had erected during a court festival.

When Kaneie died in 990, Michitaka succeeded him as regent. He became seriously ill in 995 and, before dying, handed over the regency to his brother, Michikane, who died seven days later. Michinaga then became head of the Fujiwara family and was appointed both minister of the right and examiner of imperial documents, an honorary title of great prestige. By 996, Michinaga enjoyed uncontested political dominance.

Life's Work

Michinaga seems to have given Japan a strict and able administration, exercising the powers of regent without assuming the post that his father and brothers held. He felt no need to take the highest rank, although any office in the land would have been his for the asking. He helped to establish a precedent in this regard, for the most powerful rulers in later Japanese history not only allowed sovereignty to remain with the emperor but also were themselves content to occupy relatively modest posts in the hierarchy. Before becoming a monk, Michinaga finally served as regent for two years, from 1016 to 1017, when his grandson became emperor. Entry into the religious life, however, did not mean the end of his political career. By giving up his official posts and having his son, Yorimichi, appointed regent (1017-1068), Michinaga was, in fact, able to devote even more of his energy to the exercise of power during the last ten years of his life.

Although Michinaga was the leading statesman of the Heian period (794-1185), not much more is known about the man than the emperors he was supposed to serve. There is no extant portrait of Michinaga, and the personal touches in contemporary records are not sufficient to produce any well-rounded picture. This is not because he had a self-effacing nature. Indeed, modesty was not one of his virtues. Michinaga had won the endemic struggle for power within the Fujiwara family—a contest between individuals, not a clash about issues. What concerned a member of the ruling aristocracy was the acquisition of a supreme office for himself and his immediate kin. Having acquired such an office and its many delightful trappings, one tended to hold it against all comers. What determined appointments was the support given to the leader who eventually won the power struggle, not administrative ability. Because none of the Fujiwara leaders can be identified with any concrete policy or constructive public service, these statesmen do not emerge as distinct individuals. (This is true even of those who were most prominent during the period, such as Michinaga.) They are usually differentiated in terms of their relative strength of ambition and skill at political intrigue.

Michinaga, however, was a man of remarkable and exceptional gifts who thought and acted with a thoroughness on a generous scale and a focus on the reality of power. Control of three major power groups formed the basis of the political stability that Michinaga maintained to the end of his life. He continued his family's policy of extensive intermarriage with the imperial house. He was generous toward his allies and his rivals, a policy that gained for him widespread support among court officials. He allied himself with the Seiwa Genji branch of the Minamoto family to maintain law and order in the capital region and expand the landholdings and wealth of the Fujiwara throughout the country.

In establishing his position, Michinaga was greatly helped by having among his fourteen children several outstandingly intelligent and attractive daughters, and he used them to forge the strongest possible link with the imperial family. Four of his daughters were married to emperors. His daughter Akiko, at the age of eleven, in 999, was married to the reigning emperor, Ichijō (r. 986-1011). She soon became the emperor's favorite, and together they had two sons. Although Emperor Sanjō (r. 1011-1016), who was the son of Emperor Reizei (r. 967-969), succeeded Ichijō when he died in 1011, Akiko's two children followed him as the emperors Go-Ichijō (r. 1016-1036) and Go-Suzaku (r. 1036-1045).

Such was the pressure on the emperors to marry Fujiwara women selected for them by Michinaga that Sanjō married Michinaga's second daughter, Go-Ichijō married the third (who was his aunt), and Go-Suzaku married the fourth (also his aunt). Michinaga's last daughter was given to a son of Sanjō, the heir presumptive (who was already married), to cover all possible situations. Clearly, Michinaga was unscrupulous in working for the interests of his own family.

Having a deep understanding of human nature, Michinaga knew how to use friends and win over enemies, and that gave him clout with court officials, who recognized that he had a firm hold on his own temper. Michinaga liked to do things on a large scale and lavished untold sums on building shrines and chapels and on Buddhist services in which thousands of monks took part. The building and dedication of the Hōjōji, a Pure Land (Jōdo) sect temple, was a brilliant display of Michinaga's wealth and power. The Heian aristocracy was much addicted to color and pageantry and benefited from Michinaga's efforts to infuse the yearly round of ceremonies with the beauty and elegance that were so important in al-

MAJOR FUJIWARA REGENTS, 866-1184

Reign	*Regent (position)*
866-872	Fujiwara Yoshifusa (sessho)
872-884	Fujiwara Mototsune (sessho)
884-891	Fujiwara Mototsune (kampaku)
930-941	Fujiwara Tadahira (sessho)
941-949	Fujiwara Tadahira (kampaku)
967-969	Fujiwara Saneyori (kampaku)
969-970	Fujiwara Saneyori (sessho)
970-972	Fujiwara Koretada (sessho)
973-977	Fujiwara Kamemichi (kampaku)
977-986	Fujiwara Yoritada (kampaku)
986-990	Fujiwara Kaneie (sessho)
990	Fujiwara Kaneie (kampaku)
990-993	Fujiwara Michitaka (sessho)
993-995	Fujiwara Michitaka (kampaku)
995	Fujiwara Michikane (kampaku)
996-1017	FUJIWARA MICHINAGA (kampaku)
1016-1017	FUJIWARA MICHINAGA (sessho)
1017-1020	Fujiwara Yorimichi (sessho)
1020-1068	Fujiwara Yorimichi (kampaku)
1068-1075	Fujiwara Norimichi (kampaku)
1075-1087	Fujiwara Morozane (kampaku)
1087-1091	Fujiwara Morozane (sessho)
1091-1094	Fujiwara Morozane (kampaku)
1094-1099	Fujiwara Moromichi (kampaku)
1106-1107	Fujiwara Tadazane (kampaku)
1107-1114	Fujiwara Tadazane (sessho)
1114-1121	Fujiwara Tadazane (kampaku)
1121-1123	Fujiwara Tadamichi (kampaku)
1123-1129	Fujiwara Tadamichi (sessho)
1129-1142	Fujiwara Tadamichi (kampaku)
1142-1151	Fujiwara Tadamichi (sessho)
1151-1158	Fujiwara Tadamichi (kampaku)
1158-1165	Fujiwara Motozane (kampaku)
1165-1166	Fujiwara Motozane (sessho)
1166-1173	Fujiwara Motofusa (sessho)
1173-1179	Fujiwara Motofusa (kampaku)
1184	Fujiwara Moroie (sessho)

Note: Some Fujiwara were regents more than once or for more than one emperor. The position of *sessho* indicates regency for an underage emperor, that of *kampaku*, regency for an adult emperor.

most every part of their lives. He also accumulated great wealth by acquiring manorial rights over land commended to him for protection and substantially rewarding those courtiers who were involved in the process.

At the same time, Michinaga could see that Fujiwara private interests were not consistent with a just administration of the affairs of the countryside and that the provincial gentry were growing more conscious of their own strength. Being aware of changes taking place in the country, he foresaw the rise of the military families. Early in his career, he made up his mind to cultivate some of the leading warriors, whom he could then trust to support him in case of need. He chose certain members of the Minamoto clan whose talents impressed him. It was their presence in the background that enabled him to defeat or intimidate his rivals. Moreover, since the metropolitan police force was incapable of preserving peace, these warriors could be relied on by Michinaga when he needed them to bring order and security to the capital. For their part, the warriors, working with Michinaga, were able to expand their own tax-free estates while at the same time aiding Michinaga in increasing Fujiwara landholdings throughout the country.

Meanwhile, in the capital, where the Fujiwara were dictators of taste and fashion, there flourished a society dedicated to elegant pursuits and happily insulated from the shocks of common life. It was a society devoted to the pursuit of beauty to a degree rarely paralleled in the history of civilization. Michinaga was a patron of architecture, painting, sculpture, music, and literature, and his influence on the development of Japanese culture has been marked.

SIGNIFICANCE

The formula for greatness gleaned from Michinaga's life might be summarized thus: Be born to a powerful family and have a handsome and personable appearance, a flair for spectacular actions, talents highly regarded by the society of the day, a certain ruthlessness, and a liberal sprinkling of good fortune. As priest, administrator, poet, and connoisseur of the good life, Michinaga carried the Fujiwara family to its highest point. A patron of arts and letters, Michinaga encouraged the preservation of history, literature, and the Japanese spirit from the distant past to the present. More has been written on him, both fact and fiction, than on any other figure in Japanese history. In an age when provincial warlords' influence was rapidly growing and the Fujiwara power base began to wane, Michinaga was able not only to hold subversive forces in check but also to carry the Fujiwaras to heights of power and glory by sheer political virtuosity.

—*Edwin L. Neville, Jr.*

FURTHER READING

Morris, Ivan. *The World of the Shining Prince: Court Life in Ancient Japan.* 1964. Reprint. New York: Kodansha International, 1994. Indispensable for under-

standing the life of the Heian period. Contains much information on the Fujiwara family and Michinaga in particular.
Okagami, the Great Mirror: Fujiwara Michinaga and His Times. Translated by Helen Craig McCullough. Princeton, N.J.: Princeton University Press, 1980. A translation of the eleventh century classic by an unknown author, which covers Japanese history from 850 to 1025 and contains biographical information on Fujiwara.
Omori, Annie S., and Koichi Doi. *Diaries of Court Ladies of Old Japan*. Boston: Houghton Mifflin, 1920. Contains three diaries of this period, one of which, Murasaki Shikibu's diary (*Murasaki Shikibu nikki*), provides insight into the character of Michinaga.
Sansom, George. *A History of Japan to 1334*. Vol. 1. Stanford, Calif.: Stanford University Press, 1958. This highly respected source contains a section on the Fujiwara, and Michinaga in particular.
A Tale of Flowering Fortunes: Annals of Japanese Aristocratic Life in the Heian Period. 2 vols. Translated by William McCullough and Helen Craig McCullough. Stanford, Calif.: Stanford University Press, 1980. Marvelous translation of the *Eiga monogatari* (c. 1092; known by other scholars as *Tales of Glory*). Two-thirds of the work written by a lady-in-waiting to the Empress Akiko is a glorification of Fujiwara Michinaga and has constantly been referred to by all scholars working in the field.
Yamagiwa, Joseph K., trans. *The Okagami: A Japanese Historical Tale*. Rutland, Vt.: Charles E. Tuttle, 1966. Written in the eleventh century, the work of an unknown hand, it covers Japanese history from 850 to 1025. Appendix 1 is a constructed biography of Michinaga, pieced together from various sections throughout the text. Contains an excellent genealogical chart of the Fujiwara and imperial families.

SEE ALSO: Ashikaga Takauji; Jōchō; Minamoto Yoritomo; Taira Kiyomori.
RELATED ARTICLES in *Great Events from History: The Middle Ages, 477-1453*: 792: Rise of the Samurai; 794-1185: Heian Period; 858: Rise of the Fujiwara Family.

SAINT FULBERT OF CHARTRES
French religious leader and teacher

Fulbert founded the cathedral school at Chartres, where the curriculum was based on the seven liberal arts. This educational and church reform helped create the twelfth century renaissance and Christian Humanism.

BORN: c. 960; Rome (now in Italy)
DIED: April 10, 1028; Chartres, France
AREAS OF ACHIEVEMENT: Church reform, education

EARLY LIFE

The eleventh century must be characterized as a time of religious zeal and reform. The much-needed reform arose from the era of the "pornographic Papacy," as historians have sometimes referred to the tenth century Church. The reform spirit created, in the minds of many, a strong commitment to support traditional theology, monastic conservatism, and the founding of such reforming movements as the Cluniac and later the Cistercian. At the same time, new knowledge from the Arabic world, particularly Spain, and the secular demands of both political and urban revival recommended the use of reason to treat the realities of the world. This viewpoint created a dynamic tension in the eleventh century and introduced several problems that would occupy intellectual life for the next two centuries. No school was more deeply involved in this debate than the one at Chartres, founded by Fulbert of Chartres (FEWL-behr uhv shahrt).

The eleventh century thus marks the awakening of the medieval mind. The first person in the history of this awakening was Gerbert of Aurillac, who taught at the cathedral school at Reims around 972; he reigned as Pope Sylvester II until his death in 1003. In his acceptance of the dialectical method, his interest in mathematics, and his familiarity with Arabic sources acquired during his stay in Catalonia, Gerbert heralded the new era of intellectual curiosity and dynamic expansion that characterized the High Middle Ages (1000-1300). Equally significant in this creation of the medieval mind was Fulbert of Chartres, one of Gerbert's outstanding students at Reims.

Although it is known that Fulbert was born in Rome about 960, not much information is available about his youth, his family, or his education. It is known, however, that Fulbert studied under Gerbert at Reims sometime between 972 and 990. After his stay at Reims and before going to Chartres, Fulbert spent time as a physician. He was practical rather than theoretical in his approach, and his treatment was characterized by his concern for the overall health of the patient rather than a specific ailment. Later, Fulbert would teach medicine, specifically the treatment of diseases, surgery, and pharmacology, all of which he is believed to have learned from Gerbert, who had first learned the practice in Catalonia.

Life's Work

In 990, when he was about twenty-seven, Fulbert appeared in Chartres, where he founded and was the first master of the cathedral school. From this school would emerge many of the great thinkers of the eleventh century. Here too was the birthplace of the twelfth century renaissance and Christian Humanism. Although many schools were founded during the eleventh century, none could claim the preeminence of Chartres. After his outstandingly successful career as a teacher, the Church appointed Fulbert to serve as the bishop of Chartres (1006-1028), a particularly prestigious position, for Chartres was a shrine to the Virgin and a popular pilgrimage center to which many miracles were attributed. Fulbert's temperament suited the assignment, as he was deeply devout and a man of saintly patience. He remained in this office until his death in 1028.

Fulbert's life work clearly began and ended with his teaching in Chartres. It was at Chartres that the Humanist movement developed to full flower, epitomized in the thought and writings of another great bishop of Chartres, John of Salisbury, a man as deeply committed to the liberal arts as Fulbert. Elegance returned to Latin as all available classics were studied, including Arabic translations of Aristotle, the Neoplatonists, and some minor works of Plato. Philosophically, Fulbert was a Humanist and a Platonist. He was also a man who maintained order and was practical; he was in tune with the needs of his society and was knowledgeable about the world around him. Fulbert's awareness of contemporary affairs was astute; in particular, he understood the operations of the socioeconomic structure, including the intricacies of feudalism.

In Fulbert's day, the cathedral schools were new institutions, his being one of the first. These schools were therefore not bound by custom and tradition, leaving them free to follow new lines of thought and inquiry developed in the new methodologies. Fulbert instigated the teaching traditions that would be continued by subsequent generations of Chartres teachers. Significant among these traditions was Fulbert's insistence that the proper role of a teacher was to encourage the development of the student's best qualities. He also set the tradition of great loyalty and an affectionate relationship between teacher and student, which gave to medieval education its particular uniqueness, strength, and vitality. R. W. Southern, the renowned Oxford medieval scholar, has called Chartres the greatest of all the cathedral schools. He attributes its excellence to the wise foundation instituted by Fulbert; the curriculum established at Chartres became the model for that century.

The academic program reflected Fulbert's own interests and training: science, medicine, theology, the Scriptures, and especially classical literature. Despite the literary and philosophical emphasis in the curriculum, study still focused on the mysteries of the faith, with the Scriptures and the writings of the church fathers accepted as supreme authority. Remaining faithful to his religious beliefs, Fulbert insisted that when the power of human reason failed to comprehend the divine creation and order of things, it should surrender and cease to look for a reasonable definition. Fulbert's curriculum, however, opened the door to a new confidence in the efficacy of human reason to master all things. Here was the first stirring of modern rationalism. Along with the emphasis on reason, skepticism and pessimism also returned to the Western mind.

The disputed issues focused on whether boundaries must exist between reason and faith and on how much reason could legitimately be applied to Christian thought. No one was more committed to resolving these questions than Fulbert's student Berengar of Tours, who insisted on submitting religious mysteries to the activity of reason, thereby denying traditional authority. His justification for challenging authority was that in reason humans most resembled God. Lanfranc of Bec, one of the great conservative minds of the day, rose to refute this position. The turmoil that accompanied the various and controversial medieval interpretations of Aristotle made Chartres the leading school of the twelfth century renaissance. It produced the Thomistic synthesis of reason and faith during the thirteenth century, a synthesis that would ultimately crumble under the weight of its own complexity.

Significance

Above all, Fulbert should be remembered as one of the most influential teachers of the eleventh century, the patriarch of the great masters produced by Chartres. Although he was never officially canonized, Fulbert is recognized as a saint. His feast day is April 10. By all accounts, he was a man of dignity, tolerance, gentle wisdom, and humanity. Though he never wrote anything particularly outstanding, he was notable among the great medieval correspondents. Fortunately, many of his letters have been preserved. They reflect his clear, concise, if not eloquent, style. He wrote in understandable Latin, something refreshing when compared to the laborious, antiquated language of most of his contemporaries.

A gifted teacher, Fulbert spoke to people in a language that they understood. Although he was intrigued by the relationship between words and reality, he started no new school of philosophy. Indeed, Fulbert contributed nothing new to learning but made what he discussed both understandable and familiar to his listeners.

Fulbert's reputation, never tarnished or diminished, was built on the success of his students and their loyalty to him. In his day it was said that Fulbert was the spring from which all the rivers of the medieval mind flowed. This influence lasted for a century after his death, drawing students from all over Europe to his school. In spite of the distinguished reputation of Fulbert and Chartres, however, the school never became a university. Instead, the focus shifted in the twelfth century to Paris, some fifty miles away.

Although Chartres is remembered today more for the beauty of its Gothic cathedral and rose windows, which were made famous by Henry Adams's book *Mont-Saint-Michel and Chartres* (1904), in the Middle Ages, it was clearly the school and its remarkable teacher and founder, Fulbert, that made it famous.

—*Shirley F. Fredricks*

FURTHER READING

Favier, Jean. *The World of Chartres*. New York: H. N. Abrams, 1990. A general work on Chartres that looks at the visionaries and craftsmen of Chartres, its buildings, and its place in society.

Fulbert, Saint. *The Letters and Poems of Fulbert of Chartres*. Translated by Frederick Behrends. Oxford, England: Clarendon Press, 1976. The introduction to the translation of the correspondence of Saint Fulbert provides valuable information on the man and his works. Indexes.

Lloyd, Roger B. *The Golden Middle Age*. Freeport, N.Y.: Books for Libraries Press, 1969. A look at education in the Middle Ages, focusing on John of Salisbury, a later bishop of Chartres.

MacKenney, Loren Carey. *Bishop Fulbert and Education at the School of Chartres*. Notre Dame, Ind.: Mediaeval Institute, University of Notre Dame, 1957. A discussion of education in the Middle Ages, in particular at the School of Chartres.

Querido, René M. *The Golden Age of Chartres: The Teachings of a Mystery School and the Eternal Feminine*. New York: Anthroposophic Press, 1987. An analysis of the intellectual life and school at Chartres. Bibliography and index.

SEE ALSO: Sylvester II.

RELATED ARTICLE in *Great Events from History: The Middle Ages, 477-1453*: c. 1025: Scholars at Chartres Revive Interest in the Classics.

GENGHIS KHAN

Mongol ruler, r. 1206-1227

A military genius, Genghis Khan united the clans and tribes of peoples later collectively known as the Mongols, leading them on conquests to the east, south, and west and organizing the Mongol Empire—which under his grandson, Kublai, came to dominate most of Eurasia.

BORN: Between 1155 and 1162; Delyun Boldog, near the Gobi Desert (now in Mongolia)
DIED: August 18, 1227; Ordos area in northern China
ALSO KNOWN AS: Temüjin (given name); Temuchin; Chinggis Khan; Jenghiz Khan; Jinghis Khan
AREAS OF ACHIEVEMENT: Warfare and conquest, government and politics, law

EARLY LIFE

Temüjin, as Genghis Khan (GEHN-ghihs kahn) was first named, was born in the village of Delyun Boldog on the Odon River in the northeastern borderlands between Mongolia and China on the fringes of the Gobi Desert between 1155 and 1162. It is said that there were great "signs" at the time of Temüjin's birth. Stars fell from the sky (possibly a meteor shower), and he was born clutching a blood clot in the shape of a human knuckle. The great-grandson of Khabul Khan, Temüjin was born into the elite Borjigin clan, the son of a Mongol lord, Yesügei, and his captive Merkit wife, Oyelun. According to Mongol custom, at the age of nine, Temüjin was betrothed to his first wife, Börte. After the treacherous poisoning death of Yesügei at a banquet hosted by a rival, Temüjin and his family fell on hard times and were periodically held captive by the Merkits. Temüjin often had to survive by hunting, fishing, and even scrounging for rodents in the desert.

Gradually, he rallied around him a group of followers from various clans and tribes, and, using his natural military ability, Temüjin emerged as a bandit-mercenary leader under the protection of Toghrïl Khan, the Nestorian Christian leader of the Kereits, sometimes linked in the West to the legendary Prester John. As an ally of Toghrïl and the Chinese in 1194, Temüjin and his band helped to defeat the Tatars. In this campaign, he clearly demonstrated his ability as a military strategist, especially in the use of the cavalry tactics for which his Mongols became so famous and so feared.

LIFE'S WORK

After the death of Toghrïl, Temüjin soon turned on his Kereit allies and subjugated them and then also the Naimans and Merkits. In 1206, he organized these diverse nomadic groups—whose principal occupations had been herding horses and sheep, banditry, mercenary soldiering, and warring with one another—into a militaristic Mongol confederacy based on kinship and personal loyalty. He assumed the title of Genghis Khan and emerged as this new state's divine ruler. He governed with skill, strength, and wisdom, but also relied heavily on popular fear of his awesome power. Quickly, Genghis Khan added to his Central Asian domains in the years 1206 to 1209 by conquering the neighboring Oyrats, Kirghiz, and Uighurs.

At the center of this state was the superior Mongol army under the brilliant command of Genghis Khan himself. Eventually, he perfected traditional Mongol cavalry and archery tactics and skillfully combined them with the use of gunpowder and siege technology adopted from the Chinese and Muslims. To keep this army in its numerous campaigns well supplied, a modern, logistic system of support was created. Effective communication between the various military groups and parts of the growing empire was maintained by a Pony Express-like postal system. Intelligence was gathered from itinerant merchants, wandering the empire, who came under the personal protection of Genghis Khan. By Börte and other wives, he had four sons: Jochi, Chagatai, Ogatai, and Tolui. They and other relatives became the leading generals and administrators of the increasingly feudal empire.

Genghis Khan established the first Mongol (Uighur-based) written language to unify his people further and promulgated the first Mongol law, a prescriptive law code that was eventually employed from China to Poland. In return for absolute obedience to Genghis Khan and his successors, the law allowed for local political autonomy and religious toleration. Under this code, a system of governance developed in the Mongol Empire similar to the satrapies employed by the ancient Persian Empire of Cyrus the Great. The law also became a basis for the law codes of many of the successor states to the Mongol Empire.

The Mongol Empire rose out of Central Asia under its dynamic leader to fill a power vacuum created by the decline of China in the east almost simultaneously with that of the Muslim states to the south and the Byzantine Empire and Kiev Rus in the west. Beginning with Xi Xia, from 1209 to 1215, Genghis Khan conquered northern China, finally entering Beijing after severely devastating it in 1215. In China, as elsewhere, Genghis Khan readily adapted aspects of the civilization and its human talent to strengthen his position and the Mongol Empire. He conversed extensively with the renowned Daoist monk Zhang Zhun but remained a shamanist. Genghis Khan also made the Chinese Yeliu Zhu his chief astrologer and a principal civil administrator. (Later, in the thirteenth century, Kublai Khan employed the Venetian Marco Polo and Polo's father and uncle as ambassadors and administrators.)

Although some historians believe that China was always the prime objective of Genghis Khan's expansionism, southern China, ruled by the declining Song Dynasty, seems to have held little appeal for Genghis Khan; after taking Beijing, he turned his attention to the West. From 1218 to 1225, he conquered the Persian Khwarizm Empire and thereby gained control of the critical trade routes between China and the Middle East. The caravans that traveled these and the other trade routes of the Mongol Empire were absolutely essential to its economic life and well-being. Eventually, Mongol-Turkish domination of these trade routes forced European navigators such as Vasco da Gama and Christopher Columbus to seek alternative ocean routes to the spices, silks, and other riches of Asia.

These southern conquests also for the first time incorporated large numbers of Muslim subjects into the Mongol Empire. In the following decades and centuries, most of the Mongols from Transoxiana and westward into Russia were converted to Islam and naturally allied themselves with the emerging Ottoman Empire. In 1223, Genghis Khan sent his brother-in-law and greatest general, Subatai, to attack the Cumans, Byzantines, and Russians and therewith begin the invasion of Europe. (In 1240, the Mongols of the Golden Horde under Batu Khan would take the Russian capital city of Kiev and eventually help to found a new Russian state under the leadership of Moscow.)

However, while Genghis Khan was in the West, his Chinese domains went into revolt. He returned east and ruthlessly resubjugated northern China from 1225 to 1227. On his return journey to the Mongol heartland, one month after the death of his son Jochi, Genghis Khan died in the Ordos region in 1227.

Genghis Khan receives advance warning about his father-in-law's plot to assassinate him. (F. R. Niglutsch)

MAJOR RULERS OF THE MONGOL EMPIRE, 1206-1294

Reign	Ruler
1206-1227	GENGHIS KHAN
1227-1229	Tolui (son of Genghis Khan), regent
1229-1241	Ogatai Khan
1241-1246	Toregene (wife of Ogatai), regent
1246-1248	Güyük
1248-1251	Oghul Qaimish (wife of Güyük), regent
1251-1259	Mongu
1259-1260	Arigböge (brother of Mongu and Kublai), regent
1260-1294	KUBLAI KHAN

SIGNIFICANCE

Genghis Khan was succeeded by his son Ogatai, who died in 1241. Under Ogatai Khan and his successors, Mongol power and influence swept into Russia, Poland, India, southern China, Indochina, and Korea, culminating in Kublai Khan's failed invasions of Japan from 1274 to 1281. Kublai Khan established the Yuan Dynasty (1279-1368) in China, and Mongol dynasties came to power in Persia, India, and elsewhere.

The Mongol Empire created by Genghis Khan was never really overthrown. The Mongols generally were culturally inferior to the peoples they conquered and gradually were absorbed by them; they became Chinese, Indian, Muslim, or Russian. Thus, with the weakening of the power and attraction of the Mongol capital, Karakorum, and the heartland and declining leadership, the once-great Mongol Empire of Genghis Khan and Kublai Khan first fragmented into numerous autonomous khanates (for example, Khanate of the Golden Horde) and finally, after several centuries, disappeared. Yet its legacy, and that of Genghis Khan, lives on in its successor states and those descended from them.

Genghis Khan remains one of the most controversial figures in the human past. He was a brutal man in a brutal time and environment. He also was one of the most brilliant military and political leaders in history. The victims of his relentless drive for personal power number in the hundreds of thousands and maybe into the millions, causing many also to judge him as one of the greatest monsters in history. He took a shattered and disparate, primitive people and unified them to form the core of the Mongol Empire, which was, in effect, the personification of his own intellect, ability, and drive. This Eurasian state he created in two short generations became one of the mightiest empires the world has yet known.

Most significant, the Mongol Empire facilitated cultural, political, economic, and technological transfer across Eurasia and thereby helped to revitalize civilization in China, India, the Middle East, and Europe. Genghis Khan once again restated civilization's debt to the barbarians. From horsemanship, the use of gunpowder, communications, military tactics and organization, and government and law to the broadening of the human biological pool, the Mongol input into human history, instigated by Genghis Khan, is long and profound.

—*Dennis Reinhartz*

FURTHER READING

Chambers, James. *Genghis Khan*. Phoenix Mill, England: Sutton, 1999. A concise biography of the Mongol ruler. Bibliography.

Hoang, Michael. *Genghis Khan*. Translated by Ingrid Cranfield. New York: New Amsterdam, 1990. A biography for the general reader, without footnotes, but which quotes extensively from the primary sources.

Juvaynī, Alā al-Dīn Atā Malik. *Genghis Khan: The History of the World Conqueror.* Paris: UNESCO, 1997. An annotated translation of a thirteenth century Arabic source on Genghis.

Komaroff, Linda, and Stefano Carboni, eds. *The Legacy of Genghis Khan: Courtly Art and Culture in Western Asia, 1256-1353*. New Haven, Conn.: Yale University Press, 2002. A catalog of an exhibition held at the Metropolitan Museum of Art in New York in 2002-2003. Illustrations, maps, and index.

Lister, R. P. *Genghis Khan*. 1969. Reprint. Lanham, Md.: Cooper Square Press, 2000. A biography of the Mongol ruler. Contains genealogical tables, bibliography, and index.

Marshall, Robert. *Storm from the East: Genghis Khan to Khubilai Khan*. Berkeley: University of California Press, 1993. A popular history of the Mongol Empire, from its beginning to the invasion of Europe and later China, to its ultimate fall. Contains dynastic tables, illustrations, maps, bibliography, and index.

Nicolle, David. *The Mongol Warlords: Genghis Khan, Kublai Khan, Hülegü, Tamerlane*. Poole, England: Firebird, 1990. An examination of the major Mongol rulers. Bibliographies and index.

Onon, Urgunge, trans. *The Secret History of the Mongols: The Life and Times of Chinggis Khan*. Rev. ed.

Richmond, England: Curzon, 2001. A literal and annotated translation of a work written only a generation after Genghis Khan's death.
Ratchnevsky, Paul. *Genghis Khan: His Life and Legacy.* Translated and edited by Thomas Nivison Haining. Cambridge, Mass.: Blackwell, 1991. A scholarly monograph on Genghis Khan. Contains a chronological survey of the conqueror's life, and the last two chapters concentrate on his personalty and on the political and administrative structure of his empire.
Roux, Jean-Paul. *Genghis Khan and the Mongol Empire.* New York: Harry N. Abrams, 2003. An examination of Genghis Khan and the empire that he created.
Togan, Isenbike. *Flexibility and Limitation in Steppe Formations: The Kerait Khanate and Chinggis Khan.* New York: Brill, 1998. A study of the Mongol tribes living in the area, particularly the Kereits, and their interactions with Genghis Khan.

See also: Kublai Khan.
Related articles in *Great Events from History: The Middle Ages, 477-1453*: 936: Khitans Settle Near Beijing; 1115: Foundation of the Jin Dynasty; 1130: Karakitai Empire Established; 1153: Jin Move Their Capital to Beijing; 1204: Genghis Khan Founds Mongol Empire; 1271-1295: Travels of Marco Polo; c. 1320: Origins of the Bubonic Plague; 1368: Tibet Gains Independence from Mongols.

Geoffrey of Monmouth

British writer and bishop

Geoffrey wrote the Historia regum Britanniae, *the work that introduced the legend of King Arthur to the European world.*

Born: c. 1100; Monmouth, Wales?
Died: 1154; Llandaff, Wales?
Also known as: Galfridus or Gaufridas Monemutensis; Galfridus or Gaufridas Arturas
Area of achievement: Literature

Early Life

Not much is known about the early life of Geoffrey, who called himself Monemutensis, "of Monmouth" (MAWN-muhth) at least three times in his work, which suggests that he was born or brought up in Monmouth, Wales. It is known that he described himself as Brito ("a Briton"), but the term could mean that he was Breton, Welsh, or Cornish. Beginning in 1075, the town of Monmouth was under the control of a Breton lord, Wihenoc. Geoffrey's family may have emigrated from Brittany to Wales during that period.

Geoffrey was in Oxford from 1129 to 1151, most likely as an Augustinian canon of the college of St. George, where he appeared as witness to a number of charters. There he signed himself Galfridus Arturus ("Geoffrey Arthur"). Some scholars have taken this to mean that Geoffrey was the son of a man named Arthur, but in such a case the word "Arturus" would most likely appear in a different form. It is more probable that the name "Arthur" was given to him, or adopted by him, in recognition of his role in disseminating the story of Arthur to the European world. It is also possible that Arturus was a given name and that he became interested in the story of Arthur because of his name, rather than vice versa.

Life's Work

Geoffrey of Monmouth wrote three major surviving works, all in Latin and all concerning the history of the pre-Norman Britons and their prominent figures. The first of these works are presented as translations of ancient prophecies made by the legendary sage and magician Merlin. The prophecies, which concerned political developments of the past, present, and future, are titled *Prophetiae Merlini* (before 1135; *The Prophecies of Merlin*, 1966). They are allegorical and deliberately vague in nature, with lines such as "A man shall wrestle with a drunken Lion, and the gleam of gold will blind the eyes of the onlookers."

The prophecies were subsequently incorporated into Geoffrey's most influential work, the mostly fictional and the phenomenally successful *Historia regum Britanniae* (c. 1136; *History of the Kings of Britain*, 1718), but they were written earlier and also circulated separately from the *History of the Kings of Britain*, fueling a zeal for political prophecy that gathered force in the later Middle Ages. The *History of the Kings of Britain* traces the history of British kings and princes from the fall of Troy (the Trojan Brutus being regarded as Britain's founding king, after whom Britain is named) to the final conquest of Britain by the Saxons. The Britons are represented as a proud and illustrious people finally brought low by internal strife and foolish choices.

MAJOR WORKS BY GEOFFREY OF MONMOUTH

Date	*Work*
Before 1135	*Prophetiae Merlini*
c. 1136	*Historia regum Britanniae* (*History of the Kings of Britain*)
After 1140	*Vita Merlini* (*Life of Merlin*)

Geoffrey's audience was most likely Norman; the Normans, having recently conquered Britain, had a natural interest in the history of their new territory. Here Geoffrey had to tread a fine line, presenting the Britons as valorous enough to serve as worthy precursors to the Normans, but not so valorous as to suggest that subsequent conquests of Britain were unjust. The narrative combines the political with the wondrous, and the history of Britain is shown to be full of magic and marvels. The most prominent purveyor of such wonders was Merlin, the son of a virgin's liaison with an incubus, who wielded extraordinary powers even as a boy. It was Merlin who was able to transform the appearance of the king, Uther Pendragon, into that of the husband of a noblewoman with whom the king was smitten. In the guise of her husband, Uther slept with the woman, bringing about the birth of Arthur. Thereafter, Merlin disappears from the story, so that in Geoffrey's account the two figures do not actually overlap. Geoffrey took the figure of Merlin from Celtic legend, which features a similar figure named Myrddin, but the shape of the story, and Merlin's connection with Arthur, are Geoffrey's invention.

The most celebrated and influential chapters of the *History of the Kings of Britain* describe the reign of Arthur, presented as a glorious king who triumphs over the Saxons and Romans, but whose kingdom is finally brought down by perfidy. Although Arthur had been a figure in Celtic legend for many years before the *History of the Kings of Britain*, it was Geoffrey who brought the king to the attention of larger Europe and who set him in a particularly political context. The story as Geoffrey told it has many of the details that were to be repeated in Arthurian literature of later centuries: his magical conception; his wife, Guinevere; his retainers, including Gawain, Bedevere, and Kay; and his betrayal by his nephew Mordred, who is finally slain at the Battle of Camlann (537). Many of these details were ultimately derived from Welsh tradition, but made their way into the pan-European literature by way of Geoffrey. The figure of Lancelot and his betrayal of Arthur with Guinevere came from French literature in later centuries and does not appear in the *History of the Kings of Britain*. Geoffrey's final summation of Arthur's career also left the door open for legends that Arthur would return. The text never describes Arthur's actual death, but said ambiguously, "Arthur himself, our renowned King, was mortally wounded and was carried off to the Isle of Avalon, so that his wounds might be attended to."

The story of Arthur takes up a disproportionate section of the *History of the Kings of Britain*, but Geoffrey also told the stories of a host of other rulers, and in so doing gave rise to legends that also became important later in history, such as the story of King Lear and his three daughters. Geoffrey claimed that the *History of the Kings of Britain* was a translation of "a certain very ancient book written in the British language," which Walter, archdeacon of Oxford, brought "ex Britannia." The phrase "ex Britannia" is ambiguous; it might mean either "from Britanny" or "from Wales." Walter was an actual person, and a friend of Geoffrey, but most scholars have cast doubt on Geoffrey's story about a single "very ancient book." Attributing a book to unverifiable older sources was a common ploy among medieval writers, used to convey an air of unimpeachable authority. Instead, it seems clear that Geoffrey confected his account from a variety of sources: texts, legends, chronicles, and his own imagination.

Geoffrey's final work, the *Vita Merlini* (after 1140; *Life of Merlin*, 1973), is an equally complex and multifaceted work. Composed in Latin hexameter verse, it tells the story of Merlin, who, in Geoffrey's account, is a Welsh king who goes mad on seeing noble young princes destroyed in battle. He flees to the woods, where he demonstrates a bleak affinity with nature, returning to human habitations only with reluctance or malice. His magical powers and ability to prophesy accurately are proven in a series of episodes. A second magical figure is also introduced: Taliesin the poet (fl. sixth century), a genuine historical poet credited with magical powers later in history, who describes the mysteries of nature and of the universe. The narrative is interrupted by lists of bodies of water with marvelous properties and other wonders of natural history and cosmology. For the *Vita Merlini*, Geoffrey drew on stories of the legendary Celtic prophet and wild man Myrddin, as well as the legend of Taliesin. Although the story is episodic and often disjointed, the poem as a whole is rich with wonders and imaginative power.

With the *History of the Kings of Britain*, Geoffrey said he intended to translate a book about the flight of the

British clergy to Brittany after a catastrophe, but there is no evidence that he actually wrote this or any work other than the three known. He must have lost his position when the Oxford college of St. George was dissolved in 1149, but in 1151 he was elected bishop of St. Asaph in Wales and served until 1154.

The Welsh countryside was in political turmoil. Many bishops never saw their bishoprics, so it is unlikely that Geoffrey ever visited his diocese. A Welsh chronicle reports that he died in 1154.

SIGNIFICANCE

Geoffrey's works, in particular the *History of the Kings of Britain*, changed the face of European literature. Before the *History of the Kings of Britain*, Arthur was a leader celebrated only in the small Celtic enclaves of western Europe; when Geoffrey brought his story to a wider audience, writers and poets across Europe made the Arthurian legends one of the enduring staples of world literature. In Geoffrey's own day, the *History of the Kings of Britain* was copied and read widely. More than 220 manuscripts—an enormous quantity—survive from the Middle Ages. A variant version, most likely revised by a different author, was quickly compiled, possibly within Geoffrey's own lifetime, and influenced writers such as Wace, who based his *Roman de Brut* (1155) on the *History of the Kings of Britain*. Works derived from the *History of the Kings of Britain* soon began to appear in the vernacular languages. Chroniclers and historians also began to incorporate "facts" from the *History of the Kings of Britain* into their own historical works, testimony to the high regard with which they regarded Geoffrey's powers as a historian.

It is in imaginative literature, however, that Geoffrey's influence was most significant, appearing in the works of many of the major writers of medieval Europe. In France, the "matter of Britain," as the Arthurian legends were known, appeared in the lays of Marie de France and the verse romances of Chrétien de Troyes, among others. In Germany, Wolfram von Eschenbach and Hartmann von Aue recast the legends of the knights of Arthur's court. England saw the creation of the important anonymous poem "Sir Gawain and the Green Knight" (c. late fourteenth century) as well as the influential prose tales of Thomas Malory's *Le Morte d'Arthur* (1485). Even the Welsh brought the European Arthur back into their own vernacular stories. Later centuries saw little abatement of Geoffrey's influence. William Shakespeare's *Cymbeline* (pr. c. 1609-1610) and *King Lear* (pr. c. 1605-1606) were both based on stories in the *History of the Kings of Britain*. John Milton considered writing an Arthurian epic before he decided on more theological material in *Paradise Lost* (1667), and John Dryden, William Wordsworth, and Alfred Tennyson wrote poems founded on Arthurian material. The twentieth century saw an explosion of literature about Arthur, from the highly literary novels of Peter Vansittart to more popular retellings such as Marion Zimmer Bradley's *The Mists of Avalon* (1983). The story of Arthur also has appeared in numerous film versions. Once Geoffrey's depiction of Arthur caught fire, it lit a passion for Arthur yet to be extinguished.

—*Martha Bayless*

FURTHER READING

Bromwich, Rachel, A. O. H. Jarman, and Brynley F. Roberts, eds. *The Arthur of the Welsh: The Arthurian Legend in Medieval Welsh Literature*. Cardiff: University of Wales Press, 1991. A collection of essays exploring the Welsh foundations of the Arthurian legend and setting Geoffrey's Arthur in context. Topics include the Welsh tradition of prophecy literature, the early character of Arthur, and Geoffrey.

Clarke, Basil, ed. and trans. *The Life of Merlin. Vita Merlini*. Cardiff: University of Wales Press, 1974. The introduction to this edition of Geoffrey's *Life of Merlin* provides a full analysis of Geoffrey's sources and of the meaning of this complex text.

Curley, Michael J. *Geoffrey of Monmouth*. New York: Twayne, 1994. A popular introduction to Geoffrey's life and work.

Echard, Siân. *Arthurian Narrative in the Latin Tradition*. New York: Cambridge University Press, 1998. Discusses Geoffrey's *Historia* and *Vita Merlini*, as well as Latin Arthurian literature in the context of medieval literature.

Gentrup, William F., ed. *Reinventing the Middle Ages and the Renaissance: Constructions of the Medieval and Early Modern Periods*. Turnhout, Belgium: Brepols, 1998. Looks at how medieval literature, including Geoffrey's work, reinterprets and re-presents historical events.

Geoffrey of Monmouth. *The History of the Kings of Britain*. Translated by Lewis Thorpe. New York: Penguin Books, 1984. The introduction to Geoffrey's classic work provides a good compact overview of Geoffrey's life, achievements, and influence.

Heng, Geraldine. *Empire of Magic: Medieval Romance and the Politics of Cultural Fantasy*. New York: Columbia University Press, 2003. Includes a chapter on Geoffrey's *History of the Kings of Britain*, its place in

romance literature, and the role of magic in the work.
Loomis, Roger Sherman. *Arthurian Literature in the Middle Ages: A Collaborative History.* New York: Clarendon Press, 1967. A clear and accessible survey of Arthurian literature throughout the Middle Ages, establishing a context for Geoffrey's achievements.
Wright, Neil, ed. *The Historia Regum Britanniae of Geoffrey of Monmouth.* Rochester, N.Y.: D. S. Brewer, 1985. A comprehensive summary of modern scholarly views about Geoffrey's life and aims.

SEE ALSO: Chrétien de Troyes; Gottfried von Strassburg; Hartmann von Aue; Marie de France; Saxo Grammaticus; Wolfram von Eschenbach.

RELATED ARTICLES in *Great Events from History: The Middle Ages, 477-1453*: 1152: Frederick Barbarossa Is Elected King of Germany; c. 1180: Chrétien de Troyes Writes *Perceval*; 1373-1410: Jean Froissart Compiles His *Chronicles*.

GERSHOM BEN JUDAH

French-German rabbi

Gershom ben Judah, a legal expert and influential teacher, played a major role in establishing the scholarly autonomy of Franco-German Jewry and in instituting structures of communal governance for the Jews of France and Germany. Among the legal innovations credited to him was a ban on polygamy for Jews living in Christian lands.

BORN: c. 960; probably Metz, Lorraine (now in France)
DIED: c. 1028; Mainz, Franconia (now in Germany)
ALSO KNOWN AS: Gershom Meʿor ha-Golah, Rabbenu (Our Rabbi Gershom); Light of the Exile
AREAS OF ACHIEVEMENT: Religion and theology, scholarship, law, literature, women's rights

EARLY LIFE

During the tenth century, the great rabbinic academies centered in Baghdad (known to Jews as Babylon)—which had maintained legal jurisdiction over the Jewish world since the redaction in the sixth century C.E. of the Babylonian Talmud (the predominant source of Jewish law, ritual observance, and custom)—were losing their domination over Jewish communities beyond the Middle East. As Talmudic studies became well established in such Jewish centers as Italy, Spain, and North Africa, local scholars emerged as legal experts who issued definitive rulings that grew out of the needs and circumstances of their own communities. Similarly, in Ashkenaz—the Hebrew designation that Jews applied to their areas of settlement in France and Germany—the Rhineland city of Mayence (Mainz), Germany, became the center of Jewish learning and judicial authority, relieving Ashkenazic Jewry of its dependence on the Babylonian academies. There several illustrious scholarly families with antecedents in Italy had settled, bringing with them the highly developed scholarship of southern Italian Jewish communities. It was in Mainz that Gershom ben Judah (guhr-shuhm behn JEW-dah) received his rabbinic education.

Very little is known about the early life of Gershom ben Judah. Although he spent most of his life in Mainz, he is generally believed to have been born in Metz, now part of France. His most influential teacher was Judah ben Meir ha-Kohen, also known as Rabbi Leontin or Sir Leon; in a *responsum* (a legal opinion in response to a query), Gershom attributes the greater part of his Talmudic learning to this teacher, whose erudition, knowledge, and reliability in legal matters he praises highly. It is known that Gershom ben Judah married a woman named Bona in 1013, following the death of his first wife, and that he had a son who was forcibly converted to Christianity in 1012 during a period of persecution of the Jews of Mainz under Emperor Henry II (the Saint, 973-1024). This son died before he could return to Jewish practice, but his father nevertheless fulfilled the laws of mourning for him according to Jewish tradition.

LIFE'S WORK

Gershom ben Judah was one of a number of outstanding Talmudists in tenth and eleventh century Mainz and the Rhineland area. His preeminence among the scholars of his time and place stems in part from his profound impact on the many students he trained in his yeshiva (academy), who went on to establish important and creative centers of Jewish biblical and rabbinic scholarship in newly expanding Jewish communities throughout France and Germany. Gershom was known as an unusually dynamic teacher who encouraged his students to debate the intricacies of the Talmud in an unconstrained and informal atmosphere of freedom and openness. Among his best-known students were Eliezer the Great, Jacob ben Jakar, and Isaac ben Judah. The foremost biblical and Talmudic commentator of medieval Ashkenaz, Rashi (1040-1105; also known as Shlomo Yitzḥaqi or Solomon ben Isaac), himself a student of Jacob ben Jakar and Isaac ben Judah, wrote in a *responsum* that Gershom ben Judah enlightened the Jews of northern Europe and that all the scholars of his own generation were the students of Gershom's students.

While later generations regarded Gershom ben Judah as the originator and source of the rich rabbinic scholarship of northern Europe, he was, in fact, the exponent of a highly developed tradition of commentary on the Babylonian Talmud, originating in Italy, that had long been transmitted orally and had expanded from generation to generation. This accrued and formalized body of traditional teachings ultimately became the foundation for a number of written Talmud commentaries that were composed in the eleventh and twelfth centuries. Gershom contributed significantly to this corpus and played a prominent role in passing it down to a large number of students, but he was not the originator or the sole creator of this large body of textual annotation. Scholars believe that the several extant commentaries on various tractates of the Babylonian Talmud attributed by tradition to Gershom ben Judah were actually expanded versions of his lectures written by his students.

Gershom ben Judah was also a pioneering textual critic who was concerned with resolving the many differences of opinion on rabbinic law and custom that resulted from different versions of the Talmud text. To resolve these inconsistencies and establish standardized readings, Gershom made a painstaking study of the texts available to him and transcribed what he believed to be a definitive exemplar of the Babylonian Talmud. He also prepared a corrected reading of the Masoretic textual traditions that accompanied and informed Jewish readings of the Hebrew Bible (Old Testament).

Gershom played a crucial role for the Jews of Ashkenaz through his willingness to formulate legal rulings to meet new situations and in his vision of structures of governance that transcended local circumstances. The rapid expansion of Jewish communities in France and Germany during the tenth and early eleventh centuries raised many challenges connected with the prerogatives of communal leadership, the limits of legal authority, and relationships among neighboring Jewish settlements. Jews also faced dilemmas related to their minority status in an often intolerant Roman Catholic culture and their involvement in international merchant activities. In this context of transition and change, a number of problems in Jewish communal life emerged that were not easily soluble according to existing Talmudic norms.

To address many of these concerns, Gershom appears to have taken a leading role in convening synods of rabbinic scholars and community leaders from across Ashkenaz to develop and ratify innovative ordinances that would apply to all Jewish communities and their members. Thus, his name is connected with a number of *taqqanot* (ordinances), and the sanctions intended to enforce them, that had an enormous and long-lasting impact on European Jewish life. Moreover, the synods he convened became a model for Jewish supercommunal government throughout the Middle Ages. While modern scholarship believes that some of the ordinances linked with Gershom ben Judah actually evolved either before or after his time, the fact that later generations attributed these distinctive features of Ashkenazic Jewish life to his authority reflects the preeminent role his leadership played in the spiritual memory of the Jews of France and Germany.

Some of the ordinances that appear to be specifically associated with Gershom ben Judah deal with the regulation of marriage and divorce and with issues of personal status. The most important of these *taqqanot* include the ban on polygyny and the prohibition of divorce without the consent of the wife. The ordinance forbidding polygyny became the most generally accepted *taqqanah* of Ashkenazi Jewry; it was accepted neither by Jews living in Muslim lands nor totally by the Jews of Spain. Both this ruling, and that requiring a wife's consent to divorce, were part of a larger legislative trend to protect and enlarge women's rights far beyond Talmudic norms. These innovations in Jewish law were strongly influenced by the insistence on monogamy in the Christian environment in which Jews lived, but they also reflect the relatively high economic and social status of women in medieval Ashkenazic society. Some contemporary scholars have also suggested that the ban on polygyny may have been intended to prevent international merchants, who traveled far afield for long periods of time, from establishing second families in their foreign ports of call.

Many other ordinances have been attributed to Gershom ben Judah as well. One reliable example, since it is quoted in his name by the commentator Rashi, forbids reminding a Jewish convert to Christianity (whether converted by force or voluntarily) of his apostasy if he has repented and returned to Judaism. Other authorities connect Gershom with the prohibition against emending Talmudic texts and with the *herem ha-yishuv*, the ban on settlement that Jewish communities could invoke against newcomers when they believed their community could not support additional members. The prohibition on the reading of a letter sent to someone else without the intended recipient's permission, often attributed to Gershom, is believed to have originated significantly later.

A number of particular questions on Jewish law and ritual were also addressed to Gershom ben Judah, and through his *responsa* (legal question-and-answer literature) he became the appellate judge for many communities of Germany and France. More than seventy of his *responsa* survive, many of which shed light on specific aspects of the social, economic, political, and religious life of the Jews of pre-Crusade Europe. These decisions were preserved because they were considered authoritative by French and German scholars of subsequent generations.

Gershom ben Judah was the first Ashkenazic scholar to compose liturgical poetry. His *selihot* (penitential hymns) and other religious verse, all written in Hebrew, reflect his exceptional poetic gifts as well as a deep knowledge of the various styles and language of Hebrew liturgical poetry. Considered noteworthy for their emotional resonance and naturalness of expression, the penitential laments may reflect Gershom's personal grief at the fate of his son, as well as his general concerns about the future destiny of the Jewish community of Ashkenaz in an era when Jewish security seemed increasingly threatened.

SIGNIFICANCE

Gershom ben Judah was an outstanding teacher who developed an effective and enduring mode of legal study for Ashkenazic Jewry based on intense dialogue between master and pupils. He transmitted to his students a large body of oral interpretation of the Babylonian Talmud that had been preserved and enhanced by the scholars of Mainz, setting the stage for the written commentaries of his successors. These commentaries, in turn, transformed the difficult text of the Talmud into an accessible reference source that could serve as the basis for ongoing legislation and communal guidance in the centuries to come.

Gershom was also an exceptional leader, convening councils of scholars and community notables that promulgated innovative legal ordinances (*taqqanot*) to address the needs of Ashkenazic Jewry. The best known of these is the ban forbidding a man from having more than one wife at the same time. Gershom ben Judah's insistence that rabbinic rulings were authoritative for all the Jews of France and Germany, overruling local practices where necessary, was also crucial in maintaining the unity of the northern European community in a time when the Jewish world was becoming increasingly fragmented.

—*Judith R. Baskin*

FURTHER READING

Agus, Irving. *The Heroic Age of Franco-German Jewry*. New York: Yeshiva University Press, 1969. A study of the economic, social, and intellectual history of the Jewish communities of Northern Europe prior to the First Crusade (1096) based on *responsa* and other literary sources connected to Gershom ben Judah and his contemporaries and successors.

Finkelstein, Louis. *Jewish Self-Government in the Middle Ages*. 1924. Reprint. New York: Jewish Theological Seminary of America, 1972. A valuable study of the development of self-governance processes in medieval Ashkenaz, including a detailed analysis of the central role of Gershom ben Judah; with Hebrew versions and annotated English translations of the ordinances attributed to him.

Grossman, Avraham. "Ashkenazim to 1300." In *Introduction to the History and Sources of Jewish Law*, edited by N. S. Hecht et al. New York: Oxford University Press, 1996. A comprehensive summary by an important contemporary scholar of the major figures (including Gershom ben Judah), literary and legal sources, and social and economic features of the medieval Franco-German Jewish community, with a particular emphasis on the assertion of legal authority by religious figures through communal enactments.

Roth, Cecil, ed. *The Dark Ages: The Jews in Christian Europe, 711-1096*. Vol. 2 in *The World History of the Jewish People: Medieval Period*. New Brunswick, N.J.: Rutgers University Press, 1966. A number of the essays in this useful work, particularly those by Irving Agus, A. M. Habermann, and Simon Schwarfuchs, discuss Gershom ben Judah's significance and contributions, including in the area of liturgical poetry.

SEE ALSO: Benjamin of Tudela; Henry II the Saint; Ibn Gabirol; Judah ha-Levi; Levi ben Gershom; Moses Maimonides; Moses de León; Naḥmanides.

RELATED ARTICLES in *Great Events from History: The Middle Ages, 477-1453*: 740: Khazars Convert to Judaism; c. 960: Jews Settle in Bohemia; 1190: Moses Maimonides Writes *The Guide of the Perplexed*; c. 1275: The *Zohar* Is Transcribed; 1290-1306: Jews Are Expelled from England, France, and Southern Italy.

Maḥmūd Ghāzān

Mongol il-khan of Iran (r. 1295-1304)

The greatest of the Mongol il-khans of Iran, Maḥmūd Ghāzān was responsible for the conversion of the il-khanate to Islam and presided over the remarkable flowering of syncretistic Central Asian and Iranian culture.

Born: November 5, 1271; Abaskun, Persia, Il-Khanid Dynasty (now in Iran)

Died: May 11, 1304; near Qazvin, Persia, Il-Khanid Dynasty

Areas of achievement: Government and politics, warfare and conquest, law, patronage of the arts, architecture

Early Life

Maḥmūd Ghāzān (MAKH-mood GAHZ-ahn) ranks as one of the most important of the medieval rulers of his country. A descendant of Genghis Khan through the latter's grandson Hülegü, he was the seventh in the line of the il-khans. These were the Mongol rulers of a khanate embracing what is today Iran, Iraq, part of Syria, eastern and central Turkey, the region of the former Soviet Union south of the Caucasus Mountains, and the greater part of Afghanistan. The word "il-khan" meant a subordinate khan, one who acknowledged the overlordship of the supreme khan, or khaqan, in distant Mongolia and China. Ghāzān seems, however, to have rejected this overlordship: Unlike his predecessors, he abandoned the practice of including the khaqan's name and title on his coinage, which consequently came to resemble that of other Middle Eastern rulers. After his conversion to Islam (which was publicly proclaimed on June 19, 1295), his adopted Muslim name of Maḥmūd was added to his Mongol name on the coinage, and as Maḥmūd Ghāzān his name was thereafter read in the *khutba*, the invocation on behalf of the ruler included in Friday prayers in the principal mosques.

Only the first two il-khans, Hülegü (r. 1256-1265) and Abaqa (r. 1265-1281), had been outstanding rulers. Hülegü, following the sack of Baghdad and the extinction of the ʿAbbāsid caliphate in 1258, had founded the il-khanate. It was Abaqa who consolidated his father's achievement. Abaqa's son and Ghāzān's father, Arghūn (r. 1284-1291), had been a ruler of fairly modest ability. Like Abaqa, he had sought the cooperation of the hard-pressed crusading states of the Holy Land and of various European rulers in the course of the Mongols' life-and-death struggle with the Mamlūk rulers of Egypt, who were also bitter foes of the Crusaders. Although rulers of Christian Europe had hoped that Arghūn would become a convert to Christianity, he was by upbringing and inclination a Buddhist, and his eldest son, Ghāzān, was also brought up in the Buddhist faith. As governor of Khorāsān during the reigns of his father and his uncle, Gaykhatu, Ghāzān is known to have ordered the construction of Buddhist places of worship in Quchan and elsewhere.

During Arghūn's reign, fighting among the Mongol nobles (*noyons*) and military commanders (emirs) seriously weakened the authority of the il-khan. At Arghūn's death, his brother, Gaykhatu, was recognized as his successor; he was formally enthroned on July 23, 1291, at Akhlat, near Lake Van in eastern Turkey. Ghāzān was confirmed in the government of Khorāsān. The new il-khan's extravagance and licentiousness, however, soon provoked resentment, and he was eventually murdered (March 26, 1295). His cousin Baydu, another grandson of Hülegü, was then enthroned as il-khan in April, 1295. Baydu's reign proved exceptionally brief (from April to October, 1295), since Ghāzān immediately challenged his accession with the support of a would-be kingmaker, Nawrūz. This great Mongol emir had been commander-in-chief in Khorāsān at the time when Ghāzān was governor there. Nawrūz had once led a revolt against Ghāzān, but he now threw his formidable weight behind Ghāzān's bid for the throne. A longtime Muslim, Nawrūz pressed on Ghāzān the political advantages of conversion to Islam, and no doubt the latter readily acknowledged the value of sharing the faith of the majority of his subjects. He may have been sincere in his conversion, but it seems more likely that, to paraphrase the famous quip attributed to Henry IV of France, Tabrīz was worth a *namaz* (formal Muslim prayer).

By the autumn of 1295, Ghāzān had gained the upper hand over his rival, who fled toward the north but was easily captured. On October 4, 1295, when Ghāzān made his triumphant entry into Tabrīz, henceforth the official capital of the il-khanate, Baydu was executed. On the same day, it was proclaimed throughout Tabrīz that Islam was now the official religion of the khanate and that Buddhist temples, Jewish synagogues, and Christian churches were to be destroyed. Court patronage of the minority faiths, hitherto normative, was now withdrawn—in theory, if not always in practice. Yet it is a measure of the shallowness of Ghāzān's conversion to Islam that, on departing from Tabrīz to winter across the Aras River, he married a woman who had formerly been a wife of his father and also of his uncle, an act utterly abhorrent to his Muslim subjects and forbidden by the Qur'ān, although customary among the shamanistic Mongol rulers.

Ghāzān was ruthless toward all who opposed him. It was not long after his accession that he began to resent the arrogance and ambition of his erstwhile ally Nawrūz. A man in Nawrūz's position had no lack of enemies, and some past double-dealing with the Mamlūk government in Cairo provided grounds for his being denounced to the il-khan, who now had a pretext to break with him. Although three of his brothers and his son were executed, Nawrūz himself escaped into Khorāsān and sought refuge with the ruler of Herāt, who owed him both his life and his position. Betrayed by his faithless host, however, Nawrūz was handed over in 1297 to a rival emir, who ordered him to be cut in half and his head sent to Baghdad, where it long adorned one of the city gates. Instrumental in the fall of Nawrūz and his family had been the principal prime minister of the il-khan, Sadr al-Dīn Zanjānī. Hitherto, this man had shown remarkable powers of survival, for he had been minister to Gaykhatu before coming over to Ghāzān. Nevertheless, in 1298 he too was denounced and executed. In their accounts of the inquiries that preceded his downfall, the sources mention for the first time the name of one of his subordinates, the historian Rashīd al-Dīn (1247-1318), a Jewish convert from Hamadān. Sadr al-Dīn soon became Ghāzān's prime minister and trusted adviser, a position he would continue to occupy under Ghāzān's successor, Öljeitü (r. 1304-1316). Meanwhile, the process of Islamicization had been gaining momentum. In November, 1297, il-khan and emirs together had formally exchanged their broad-brimmed Mongol hats, unsuitable for performing the Muslim prayers, for the traditional Middle Eastern turban.

Life's Work

During the early part of his reign, Ghāzān's prime concerns had been internal security and testing the reliability of his *noyons* and emirs. From 1299 onward, external relations and campaigning across the frontiers of the il-khanate became a major focus. The il-khanate was a formidable military power, but it was ringed by foes. To the northeast, there was the rival Chagatai khanate, ruled by descendants of Genghis Khan's second son, Chagatai (d. 1241). The Amu Dar'ya (Oxus) River served as the de facto frontier between these two aggressive neighbors, but raids into each other's territories were frequent. In the northwest, the il-khans disputed hegemony of the southern Caucasus region with the khanate of Kipchak (which the Russians called the Golden Horde), ruled by descendants of Genghis Khan's grandson Batu Khan (d. 1255). The khans of Kipchak had adopted Islam earlier than any of the other Mongol dynasties; they made common cause with the Egyptian Mamlūks, with whom they maintained important commercial and cultural contacts, against the il-khans of Iran. To the southwest, the region that later became northwestern Iraq and eastern Syria was a zone of perpetual conflict between the il-khans and the Egyptian Mamlūks, who since the time when the Mongols had first appeared in the Middle East in the 1250's had strenuously repulsed the invaders along a broad north-south front extending from Diyarbakir through Aleppo, Hama, and Homs to Damascus.

Ghāzān now had to turn his attention to the danger of encirclement, made more immediate by a 1299 coup in Cairo that brought back as sultan Nāsir al-Dīn Muḥammad, a young man who had reigned briefly in the mid-1290's and was to reign again from 1299 to 1340 (with a short break in 1309). In midsummer, 1299, a Mamlūk army crossed the Euphrates and penetrated as far as Mardin (now in southeastern Turkey), carrying off vast numbers of captives and leaving a path of devastation behind it. Ghāzān retaliated by invading Syria and, bypassing Aleppo and Hama, brought the Mamlūks to bay in the vicinity of Homs, where he won a crushing victory over them on December 22, 1299. He then captured Homs and Damascus (although in the case of the latter city, the Mamlūks held out in the citadel). In February, 1300, however, Ghāzān abruptly withdrew from Damascus, perhaps as a result of rumors of unrest in Iran or of incursions across the Amu Dar'ya frontier, and the Mamlūks soon reoccupied all that they had previously forfeited.

In the autumn of 1300, Ghāzān embarked on a second invasion of Syria, again advancing well beyond Aleppo. This time, however, there was to be no direct confrontation between Mongols and Mamlūks; excessive rain, flooding, and extremes of cold seem to have kept the two armies apart. In February, 1301, Ghāzān recrossed the Euphrates, and later in the year there were diplomatic exchanges between the two governments, although neither side was sincere in its protestations of friendship. A desultory correspondence was also carried on with Pope Boniface VIII, attempting to organize a joint Mongol-Frankish attack on Syria. Ghāzān's letter of April 12, 1302, to the pope still survives in the Vatican archives.

In the autumn of 1302, a third campaign was mounted against the Mamlūks. Ghāzān advanced into northwestern Iraq, sending an advance force under two trusted commanders, Qutlugh-Shāh and Amir Choban, to besiege Aleppo. Although the il-khan followed with the main army, he decided to relinquish the conduct of the campaign to his commanders, and he returned over the Euphrates in early April, 1303. Again, there may have been rumors of danger in the east, where his brother Öljeitü was governor of Khorāsān: Civil war was said to be raging in the Mongolian heartlands. Meanwhile, Qutlugh-Shāh had moved from Aleppo to the vicinity of Damascus, where Mamlūks and Mongols clashed in a bloody two-day battle in which the Mongols were overwhelmingly defeated (April 19-20, 1303). Qutlugh-Shāh himself was the first to inform the il-khan of the disaster, while Amir Choban brought up the rear with the wounded. An Egyptian source relates that Ghāzān was outraged at the news and that following a court of inquiry, Qutlugh-Shāh was punished and disgraced. Losses on this scale could not be made good at short notice, but the prestige of the il-khanate was at stake. Consequently, preparations began almost immediately for a fourth Syrian campaign. The plan was for the il-khan to winter in Baghdad and then advance to the front in the spring of 1304, but by now Ghāzān was a sick man, only able to travel by litter and for short distances at a time. He left Tabrīz for Baghdad in September, 1303, but early winter snow on the Zagros Mountains barred his way southward, and he passed the winter somewhere in western Iran. Perhaps sensing that his end was near, when spring came he ordered his entourage to head for Khorāsān. He died near Qazvin on May 11, 1304, having designated his brother Öljeitü as his successor, since he had no sons of his own. His body was then taken to Tabrīz for burial in the magnificent mausoleum he had built there as his final resting place.

SIGNIFICANCE

Maḥmūd Ghāzān contributed decisively to the assimilation of the infidel Mongols into the traditional Islamic culture of the Middle East, although at the time of his death the process was still far from complete. He enjoyed a formidable reputation as a military leader, but his place in Iranian history rests more on his abilities as an administrator in carrying out far-reaching reforms in taxation and the system of landholding. These aimed at alleviating the suffering of the agricultural population while maximizing the yield of revenue to the government. He also issued stern edicts to protect merchants and encourage trade, enforcing a rough-and-ready justice on bandits and those villagers tempted to plunder passing caravans. Bridges were repaired and roads were kept in good order, weights and measures were standardized, the currency was improved, and customs posts were erected at the frontiers. That these measures were actually enforced is confirmed by the survival of a number of official letters and administrative directives written by his prime minister, Rashīd al-Dīn.

Even before the accession of Ghāzān, Tabrīz had become a major international emporium on which converged trade routes from the Mediterranean, the Russian steppes, China, and India. It is a measure of its commercial importance that both the Venetians and the Genoese maintained consular representatives at the il-khan's capital. As part of his official policy of supporting Islam, Ghāzān was a munificent builder of mosques, theological colleges, and mausoleums for holy men, but it was his capital that received most of his attention. Adjacent to the west side of Tabrīz he laid out a vast suburb, known as Shenb or Ghazaniya, where his own mausoleum was located, and he enclosed both the suburb and the old city within massive new walls. Nothing now remains of these ambitious buildings. Only the shell of the mosque built by Öljeitü's prime minister, Tāj al-Dīn ʿAlīShāh, at Tabrīz and Öljeitü's magnificent mausoleum at Sulṭāniyya indicate the scale of later Il-Khanid architecture.

Aside from architecture, the il-khans were great patrons of historical writing; under them, Persian historiography experienced a veritable golden age. This was especially true of the reigns of Ghāzān and Öljeitü, during which the great histories of Rashīd al-Dīn, Vaṣṣṣāf, and Mustawfī were written. There is no reason to doubt that this flowering of historical literature owed much to the direct patronage of Ghāzān himself, whom contemporaries regarded as an authority on the history and traditions of the Mongols. Although as capable as any of his ancestors of ruthlessness and inhumanity, Ghāzān seems to have been, by Mongol standards, a man of some culture. He is said to have known several languages and to have possessed insatiable curiosity concerning a wide range of subjects. There can be no doubt that he had a more benign vision of the responsibility of the ruler toward his subjects than had any of his predecessors.

—*Gavin R. G. Hambly*

FURTHER READING

Amitai-Preiss, Reuven. *Mongols and Mamlūks: The Mamlūk-Ilkhanid War, 1260-1281*. New York: Cambridge University Press, 1995. A detailed account and analysis of the conflict between the Mamlūk sultanate of Egypt and the Mongols. Also explores the Battle of Aīn Jalūt and other military battles of the time. Maps, bibliography, index.

Amitai-Preiss, Reuven, and David O. Morgan, eds. *The Mongol Empire and Its Legacy.* Boston: Brill, 1999. A wide-ranging examination of the Mongol Empire and its historical significance. Includes chapters on the making of the Mongol states during the early years of Maḥmūd Ghāzān, before his reign; Mongol nomadism; imperial ideology; and the letters of Rashīd al-Dīn. Genealogical tables, maps, bibliography, index.

Bartold, W., and J. A. Boyle. "Ghāzān." In *The Encyclopaedia of Islam*, edited by B. Lewis, C. Pellat, and J. Schacht. Vol. 2. 2d ed. Leiden, the Netherlands: E. J. Brill, 1965. A good, short account of the career of Maḥmūd Ghāzān. Other entries give helpful information regarding numerous aspects of Islamic theology, history, and culture. Illustrations and bibliographies.

Boyle, J. A. "Dynastic and Political History of the Īl-Khāns." In *The Cambridge History of Iran*, vol. 5, edited by J. A. Boyle. Cambridge, England: Cambridge University Press, 1968. This chapter provides the reader with the most complete account available in English of the Il-Khanid period, including the reign of Ghāzān. Illustrations, maps, and bibliographies.

Lambton, Ann K. S. *Continuity and Change in Medieval Persia.* Albany: State University of New York Press, 1986. This magisterial study of the political and social structure of the Il-Khanid (as well as the Seljuk) period is an excellent account of conditions in Iran during the lifetime of Maḥmūd Ghāzān. Maps, genealogical tables, bibliography, index.

_______. *Landlord and Peasant in Persia: A Study of Land Tenure and Land Revenue Administration.* 1953. Reprint. New York: St. Martin's Press, 1991. Chapter 4 of this classical study of agrarian relations in Iran provides excellent background reading regarding Maḥmūd Ghāzān's administrative reforms. Map, extensive bibliography, index.

Morgan, David. *The Mongols.* New York: Basil Blackwell, 1987. A nonspecialist account of the Mongol Empire, this book is strongly recommended as introductory reading on the period. Maps, tables, bibliography, index.

Petrushevsky, I. P. "The Socio-economic Condition of Iran Under the Īl-Khāns." In *The Cambridge History of Iran*, vol. 5, edited by J. A. Boyle. Cambridge, England: Cambridge University Press, 1968. This chapter discusses at length prevailing social conditions as well as the government's economic policies under the Il-Khanid regime.

Roux, Jean-Paul. *Genghis Khan and the Mongol Empire.* New York: Harry N. Abrams, 2003. Although focused mainly on Genghis Khan, this work also explores the Mongolian rulers who followed him, including Maḥmūd Ghāzān. Discusses the empire's founding, its endurance, and its decline. Bibliography, index.

Wilber, Donald Newton. *The Architecture of Islamic Iran: The Il Khānid Period.* New York: Greenwood Press, 1969. Originally published in 1955, this is still the definitive study of the monuments of the Il-Khanid period (with a useful inventory to which only a few recently identified structures need to be added). This book illuminates Maḥmūd Ghāzān's role as a patron and builder. Maps, plans, bibliography.

SEE ALSO: Baybars I; Boniface VIII; Genghis Khan; Kublai Khan.

RELATED ARTICLES in *Great Events from History: The Middle Ages, 477-1453*: 637-657: Islam Expands Throughout the Middle East; 956: Oğhuz Turks Migrate to Transoxiana; 1077: Seljuk Dynasty Is Founded; 1204: Genghis Khan Founds Mongol Empire; September 3, 1260: Battle of Ain Jālūt.

AL-GHAZZĀLĪ
Muslim theologian

Al-Ghazzālī is widely regarded as the greatest theologian of Islam. His thought and writing bridged the gap between the Scholastic and the mystical interpretations of religion and formed an enduring ethical and moral structure.

BORN: 1058; Ṭūs, Khorāsān (now in Iran)
DIED: December 18, 1111; Ṭūs
ALSO KNOWN AS: Abū Hāmid Muḥammad ibn Muḥammad al-Ṭūsi al-Ghazzālī (full name); al-Ghazali
AREAS OF ACHIEVEMENT: Religion and theology, philosophy, law

EARLY LIFE

Al-Ghazzālī (ahl-guh-ZAH-lee) was one of a number of children born to a prominent family of the Ghazala, specialists distinguished for their knowledge of Muslim canon law (Shariʿa). Although little is known of his childhood, his pattern of education strongly suggests that his family intended for him to follow its professional traditions. Much of his education and religious training was at home in Ṭūs, with some time also spent at the important intellectual center of Jurjan. His advanced education was undertaken at the major university city of Nishapur. In 1085, al-Ghazzālī visited the influential Niẓām al-Mulk, the most important vizier of the early Seljuk period and a major figure himself in the propagation of education and scholarship. In 1091, Niẓām appointed al-Ghazzālī to a professorship at the university he had established in Baghdad in 1065.

For several years, al-Ghazzālī remained in Baghdad as a popular and successful lecturer, whose classes drew students by the hundreds. Beneath it all, however, al-Ghazzālī was a deeply troubled man. His views became increasingly skeptical with respect to theology and deeply critical of the corruption often associated with administration of canon law. He took up a writing campaign against the Ismāʿīlī cult of the Assassins, a political-religious terrorist group of the time whose members, holed up in the mountains of Iran, had been responsible for numerous assassinations of administrative authorities and intellectuals who took issue with the Assassins' eccentric views. Niẓām al-Mulk himself was among those who died at their hands.

Around 1095, according to some sources, al-Ghazzālī suffered a debilitating nervous illness that forced him to interrupt his career as a scholar and teacher. The illness was only a symptom of the intellectual and spiritual crisis his life had reached. Al-Ghazzālī experienced the sort of self-confrontation that inevitably reminds one of the youth of Martin Luther. He had arrived at a crossroads, and his decision was to change direction.

Al-Ghazzālī now abandoned his comfortable professorship in Baghdad (taking care to secure it for his younger brother) and embarked on years of wandering, during most of which he lived a life of poverty and celibacy as a Sufi, a Muslim mystic. After a short stay in Damascus, he went on to Palestine and thence to Mecca, participating in the pilgrimage at the end of 1096. By some accounts, he visited Egypt briefly and even contemplated a journey to the Almoravid court in faraway Morocco.

LIFE'S WORK

For more than a decade, al-Ghazzālī lived in solitude, meditating and performing mystical rituals. Near the end of this period, he produced his greatest work, *Iḥyāʾ ʿulūm al-dīn* (c. 1103; *The Revival of Religious Sciences*, 1964). Around 1106, yielding to the entreaties of the new Seljuk vizier to return to academic life, he took up a professorship in Nishapur. Shortly before his death in 1111, however, he retired once more to a life of meditation at a retreat near Ṭūs, where he gathered a small band of ascetic disciples.

Evaluation of al-Ghazzālī's thought and religious doctrine is made difficult by the uncertain authorship of many works attributed to him over the centuries. His influence was such that historians of later generations have tended to identify almost any significant theological treatise of the time with him. Shortly before the end of his life, al-Ghazzālī composed a kind of testament of his religious opinions containing much material since inferred to be biographical. The evolution of his thought must be traced using only works indisputably his own.

Al-Ghazzālī's earliest writing, late in his Baghdad professorship, sought to expose contradictions between the beliefs of Sunni Islam and the philosophy of Arabic Neoplatonism espoused by the likes of al-Fārābi and Avicenna. He first wrote a dispassionate exposition of their beliefs that, ironically, became a welcome guide in lands around the Mediterranean, where Neoplatonism remained popular among Christian and Jewish communities. Al-Ghazzālī then produced a severely critical work titled *Tahāfut al-falāsifah* (1095; *Incoherence of the Philosophers*, 1958), which went so far as to brand certain aspects of Neoplatonism as anti-Muslim.

Al-Ghazzālī's most significant work was in the application of logic to Muslim theology, in preference to the intuitive and metaphysical components of Neoplatonic thought. In particular, he made use of the Aristotelian syllogism as a frame of reference and tool for argument. To make elements of logic and philosophical argument more available to Muslim clerics and judges, he produced several handbooks.

Throughout his writing, al-Ghazzālī calls for careful evaluation and awareness of the sources of religious knowledge. His stand on behalf of logic and his warnings about the seductiveness of emotional and occult movements to those insufficiently grounded in theology partly reflect the atmosphere in northeastern Iran during his life, exemplified by the Assassins, befuddled by hashish and wandering through the countryside in search of victims.

Al-Ghazzālī's largest and most important work is *The Revival of Religious Sciences*. For the devout Muslim, it offers a complete guide to spirituality and the pious life. It provides complex prescriptions for life according to the Shariʿa and explains how such a life, virtuous and devoid of sin, contributes to human salvation. About half of the work is concerned with what al-Ghazzālī regarded as the foundational concepts necessary to devote the mind to the Muslim way.

In the contemporary West, there is a popular tendency to regard al-Ghazzālī as a mystic, or at least as sentimentally disposed to mysticism. (It is with respect to this that scholars have raised the most doubts about the authenticity of works attributed to him.) His spiritual torment may have derived in part from mystical experiences. In fact, al-Ghazzālī's ideas made it possible for Scholastic Islam and its clerics to coexist with mysticism; here lies his crucial contribution. He argued that the revelations of saintly persons supplement those of the Prophet and give individuals some spiritual independence from the authority and worldliness of the clerics. Al-Ghazzālī always insisted, however, that Muḥammad and his way must be the final authority in this world. Obedience to the Shariʿa was the pathway to piety and salvation.

Whether al-Ghazzālī's ideas constitute a reconciliation between Sunni orthodoxy and mysticism is debatable; the great complexity of his writings makes possible many interpretations. On one hand, he is concerned to defend orthodoxy against the doctrine of Ismāʿīlī Shiism, which produced the Assassins and other splinter movements in Islam. On the other, al-Ghazzālī criticizes the pedantry and corruption of the clerics in administering the Shariʿa, as well as their preference for metaphysical explanations rather than careful, logical argument in Muslim apologetics.

The writings of this singular theologian were also essential to the development of later Islamic ideas of ethical government. Al-Ghazzālī held the conservative position that a righteous king is one who enforces the Shariʿa; one who neglects the Shariʿa fails as a ruler. Although he warned that Muslims must obey unjust rulers (without condoning their injustices), his implicit judgment of secular authorities on grounds of their lack of adherence to the Shariʿa opened the way for criticism of rulers and thus potential confrontation between religious and secular leadership.

SIGNIFICANCE

In the Sunni world and beyond, al-Ghazzālī is widely regarded as the greatest and most significant Muslim after Muḥammad himself. The title Hujjat al-Islam (roof of Islam) is often applied to him. His work introduced a Greek philosophical strain into Islam that has persisted to the present. His impact on Islamic theology has been compared to that of Thomas Aquinas on Christian thought, in that he constructed an essentially Scholastic framework of explanation heavily dependent on Aristotelian reason. Indeed, his writings were so exceptionally popular that some had been translated into Latin by the middle of the twelfth century and so were known to Aquinas. Many other Christian and Jewish Scholastic theologians were influenced by al-Ghazzālī.

Some of al-Ghazzālī's critics suggest that the durability of Scholasticism in Islam, in contrast to the disintegration of this mode of thought in much of Christendom at the hands of Protestant theologians, has inhibited the adaptability of Islam to new ideas and conditions. Yet al-Ghazzālī gave legitimacy to mystical experience and promoted the devout life based on the Shariʿa, both of which strengthened Islam as a personal faith and helped to articulate standards of social and political justice. The interaction between these apparent dichotomies continues to make the writings of al-Ghazzālī of vital interest to Muslims and Christians alike.

—*Ronald W. Davis*

FURTHER READING

Abrahamov, Binyamin. *Divine Love in Islamic Mysticism: The Teachings of al-Ghazālī and al-Dabbāgh.* New York: RoutledgeCurzon, 2003. A study of the ideas of divine love in Sufism and in al-Ghazzālī's mysticism. Extensive bibliography and an index.

Binder, Leonard. "Al-Ghazali's Theory of Islamic Government." *Muslim World* 45 (1955): 229-241. Explains that al-Ghazzālī argued for a balance of powers and clerical independence for the state. Al-Ghazzālī expressed nostalgia for caliphal power in Islam, which had waned seriously by his time.

Hourani, George F. "The Chronology of Gazali's Writings." *Journal of the American Oriental Society* 79 (1959): 225-233. Provides a framework to study al-Ghazzālī's intellectual development by precise dating and sequence of works, supplemented by careful textual study of particular works.

Inglis, John, ed. *Medieval Philosophy and the Classical Tradition in Islam, Judaism and Christianity.* Richmond, Surrey, England: Curzon, 2002. Provides several chapters on al-Ghazzālī's influence on the work of contemporaries such as Averroës. Places medieval Islamic philosophy in the context of classic philosophy. Bibliography, index.

Mitha, Farouk. *Al-Ghazali and the Ismailis: A Debate on Reason and Authority in Medieval Islam.* New York: I. B. Tauris, 2001. Explores al-Ghazzālī's attempts to discredit Islamic movements such as those of the Ismāʿīlīs. Bibliography, index.

Najm, Sami M. "The Place and Function of Doubt in the Philosophies of Descartes and Al-Ghazali." *Philosophy East and West* 16 (1966): 133-141. Shows parallels between the two philosophers with respect to origin of doubt and the use of doubt to discover true knowledge.

Padwick, Constance E. "Al-Ghazali and the Arabic Versions of the Gospels." *Muslim World* 29 (1939): 130-140. An example of how Christian apologists have used al-Ghazzālī. Argues that he accepted the divine revelation of the Gospels and rejected the idea that they had been tampered with.

Sharma, Arvind. "The Spiritual Biography of Al-Ghazali." *Studies in Islam* 9 (1972): 65-85. This biographical study of al-Ghazzālī is important because it shows how he engaged in a personal rather than a merely theological quest for God and incorporated into his philosophy many tenets of the main intellectual and religious movements of his time.

Stepaniants, Marietta. *Introduction to Eastern Thought.* Translated by Rommela Kohanovskaya and edited by James Behuniak. Walnut Creek, Calif.: AltaMira Press, 2002. An introductory survey of Eastern religious and philosophical thought, including the work of al-Ghazzālī and his contemporaries, Sufism, and the Islamic tradition in general. Bibliography, index.

Watt, W. Montgomery. *The Faith and Practice of al-Ghazali.* London: Allen and Unwin, 1953. Contains a translation of al-Ghazzālī's spiritual testament, written shortly before his death.

_______. *Muslim Intellectual: A Study of al-Ghazali.* Edinburgh: Edinburgh University Press, 1963. In this study concerned with influences on al-Ghazzālī's development, the author suggests that he turned to mysticism because of the unsatisfactory state of theology and jurisprudence at the time. The author is critical of al-Ghazzālī for placing immediate experience above knowledge derived by rational means.

SEE ALSO: Pietro d'Abano; Saint Albertus Magnus; Saint Anselm; Averroës; Avicenna; Roger Bacon; Jean Buridan; Fakhr al-Dīn al-Rāzī; Judah ha-Levi; Raymond Lull; William of Ockham; Rābiʿah al-ʿAdawiyah; Thomas Aquinas; Vincent of Beauvais; William of Auxerre; William of Saint-Thierry.

RELATED ARTICLES in *Great Events from History: The Middle Ages, 477-1453*: c. 950: Court of Córdoba Flourishes in Spain; c. 950-1100: Rise of Madrasas; 1031: Caliphate of Córdoba Falls; 1062-1147: Almoravids Conquer Morocco and Establish the Almoravid Empire; 1077: Seljuk Dynasty Is Founded; c. 1150: Moors Transmit Classical Philosophy and Medicine to Europe.

LORENZO GHIBERTI

Italian sculptor

Ghiberti, one of the most famous Italian sculptors, created a sculpture for the baptistery in Florence that is often considered the first example of Renaissance art in Italy.

BORN: c. 1378; Pelago, near Florence (now in Italy)
DIED: December 1, 1455; Florence
AREA OF ACHIEVEMENT: Art

EARLY LIFE

Lorenzo Ghiberti (gee-BEHR-tee) was born in Pelago, near Florence, into a family connected to the arts. His father was a goldsmith, and Ghiberti was educated in that craft, which went beyond the obvious training in mechanical skill to an understanding of the problems of design and a general theoretical knowledge of art. Ghiberti began his career as a fresco painter, and he painted a very good fresco in the palace of Sigismondo Malatesta, the ruler of Rimini. He had probably gone there first to avoid the plague that had infested Florence, but in 1401 he was urged to return to Florence in order to enter a competition for a commission to produce a set of doors for the baptistery there, a building of considerable age and reputation to which the Pisan sculptor Andrea Pisano had added a much-admired set of decorated bronze doors in the 1330's.

The competition for this major project was formidable and included Filippo Brunelleschi, who had a considerable reputation. Ghiberti was still relatively unknown, and his credentials rested on his skills not as a sculptor but as a goldsmith and fresco painter. According to one report of the contest, the list of candidates was eventually reduced to Brunelleschi and Ghiberti, and the suggestion was made that the two men collaborate. Brunelleschi may have withdrawn because of a reluctance to work in tandem or because of friendship with Ghiberti. Whatever the case, Ghiberti was awarded the commission, and the rest of his artistic life was spent, in the main, on his work on the doors, since the first set (begun in 1403) led his sponsors to order a second set in 1425.

LIFE'S WORK

The baptistery of the cathedral at Florence is separated from the main building, standing a street's width to the west of the entrance to the church. It is a very old building, built on the site of a Roman ruin, and may have been begun as early as the fifth century. Dressed in green-and-white marble, it is a work of art in its own right. In the early 1300's, however, the Guild of Cloth Importers, which had assumed the responsibility for decorating the building, had Pisano, a Pisan sculptor, add a double-leaf door to the south side of the building. It was the first major use of bronze in Florence and proved a great artistic success, clearly indicating in its fundamentally Gothic elements the influence of classical design. This development was a precursor to the change in artistic sensibility that led to the beginnings of Renaissance sculpture.

If Pisano's door suggested that the Gothic world was passing, it has been said that Ghiberti's execution of the second set of doors marks the beginning of the Renaissance in Florence—and the beginning of the grandest period in the use of bronze sculpture in the city. It would be unfair to patronize Pisano and his work on the baptistery; Ghiberti, while generally thought to be the finer artist, had the advantage of Pisano's example, both technically and artistically. Bronze sculpture was a lost art in the Middle Ages, and Pisano had been obliged to bring a bell maker in from Venice to cast his doors. Ghiberti spent years training his crew in the art of bronze casting, and in the process he added to the sophistication and subtlety of the very difficult technique of that art. More important, perhaps, was the way in which Ghiberti took the design of the doors forward into the wider, freer, more dramatic world of Renaissance art.

The simplest, crudest definition of the birth of the Renaissance is that sensibility (social, religious, aesthetic—indeed, psychological) of Italy turned from Heaven to the world, from God to humankind, to an appreciation of the fact that life need not simply be a preparation for the afterlife but was an exciting, potentially wide-ranging celebration of existence, however fragile that existence might be. In Greek and Roman sculptures, the artists found their models for such expressions of exultation and confidence in human beings at their best. The body became the outward, aesthetic sign not only of the beautiful soul (in Neoplatonic terms) but also of the beautiful life, the boundless possibilities for the individual and for the state. That beautiful body shows up stunningly in Ghiberti's work on the doors. Indeed, Ghiberti's competition piece, which was set for all the competitors, probably shows this shift most clearly—how the Gothic inclination toward flatness and rejection of realism and drama had (with Pisano's help) been overcome. Isaac, on his knees, his glowingly muscled torso turned in *contrapposto*, his head skewed to expose his neck to Abraham's knife, is a gorgeous young man, sculpted tenderly, with an appreciation for the human body.

The Ghiberti doors did not, however, stop at graceful celebrations of human comeliness. Ghiberti's subjects were quite properly religious, and in his accommodation of the human figure to the stories from the Bible, he also added a realistic sense of place and a sense of psychological moment. The north door was his first commission; it took twenty-one years (from 1403 to 1424) to complete it. (Donatello, who was to become a far greater sculptor than his master, was a member of Ghiberti's young crew.) The subjects of the twenty-eight panels included figures from the New Testament, Evangelists, and the Fathers of the Church.

Yet such seemingly austere subjects did not deter Ghiberti from putting into play a much more dramatically exciting conception of how the panels could be used. There is something flatly stagy about the Pisano work; it is splendidly worked technically, but it is somewhat stiff. Ghiberti, however, takes to the contours of the Gothic borders of the panels (a holdover from the Pisano design) with ease and makes use of the space much more gracefully. Pisano's work is clearly rectangular, set tightly inside the flow of the margins; Ghiberti worked his design into the concave spaces, achieving a sense of space, of depth into the panels. He also possessed a deeper understanding of how to make the figures tell a story that would appeal to the emotions.

Ghiberti's determination to make his art real, to give it depth, was his greatest gift. His second set of doors, which took up the last half of his career, were begun in the mid-1420's and not completed until 1452. They are considered his masterpiece, and they allowed him to extend himself in ways that were severely limited in the earlier work. He was able to break away from the small panels into ten larger, rectangular spaces, which gave him not only more room but also a shape he really understood. As John Pope-Hennessy, one of his best critics, said, it is important to remember that he was a painter and that he knew how to put more than one thing into a seemingly flat, extended area.

With the second set, Ghiberti continued his biblical tales, often working a series of incidents into the bronze in ways that led to the culminating moment with considerable dramatic skill. He knew how to tell a story, and he knew how to divide his space horizontally, vertically, or diagonally in order to make the divisions support the narrative sequence of the various scenes. Also, he was much better at creating a sense of internal space within the panels.

Although Ghiberti's international reputation rested heavily on his work on the doors, he was not confined to working on them exclusively. He was equally adept at two-dimensional design, and his windows for the cathedral, if less well known, are also masterpieces. His window depicting the Assumption of the Virgin is strongly realistic not only in its portrayal of the Virgin's clothing but also in its depiction of her as a poignant young human being. Enthroned in a triumphant circle of swirling angels, she is proportionally sized to give a sense of depth.

There are also a handful of freestanding statues by Ghiberti in Florence. The first of these, a figure of Saint John the Baptist (1412-1416), is important for being bronze (Florentine sculptors normally worked in marble), but it is also significant because it strongly reveals an aspect of his work that can sometimes be missed in the

Detail of Lorenzo Ghiberti from a fresco at the Palazzo Vecchio in Florence, Italy. (Hulton|Archive at Getty Images)

enthusiasm for the revolutionary aspects of his bronze sculpture. This piece is clearly of an earlier time, an example of what is called the International Gothic style, and underlines the point that Ghiberti never entirely broke free from late Gothic tendencies, which can be seen closely entwined with the classical elements in all of his work, particularly in the graceful, sweeping postures that his figures often affect.

As is often the case at the beginning of a change in the artistic sensibility, Ghiberti was soon overshadowed by younger men, such as Donatello and Nanni di Banco, who were less encumbered by the last vestiges of the Gothic and whose work is less stylized, less elegantly mannered, and just slightly further down the line toward the new Humanism in their more realistic vivacity. Still, Ghiberti's work on the baptistery, particularly in the later door, called the "Porta del Paradiso," shows that he broke with tradition more as he grew older. At the National Gallery in Washington, D.C., there is a terra-cotta sculpture of the Madonna and Child—intimate, natural, and lyrically serious—which is attributed to Ghiberti; if it was indeed executed by him, it is clear that there were moments when Ghiberti was as much a Renaissance artist as Donatello.

In his later years, he kept a journal of his ideas as a practicing artist, *Commentarii* (c. 1447; *The Commentaries of Lorenzo Ghiberti*, 1948), in which he discussed not only the technical aspects of his craft but also the relation of art to society, morals, and religion. That modest pride can be seen again on the Paradise door; in one of the ornamental roundels that decorate the frame, Ghiberti's bald, round head, his arched eyebrows, and his slightly pawky look suggest that he was a man well satisfied with what he had wrought.

Significance

If Pisano was the man responsible for bringing bronze to Florence, then Ghiberti was the artist who established its use as a medium for expressing the glorious aspirations of the Renaissance. Taking the example left by Pisano almost seventy years previous, he brought it into the mainstream of intellectual and aesthetic expression. Clearly a lesser artist than Donatello, Ghiberti was no less a major contributor to the aesthetic perfection of Florence, and his doors on the baptistery in Florence well deserve the attention they have always received. Indeed, a walk around the outside of the baptistery is a journey not only through time but also through the process whereby a civilization moves forward, in this case from modest intimations of things to come in the Pisano door through the surprising leap forward in Ghiberti's first door to the aesthetic triumph of the second door.

—*Charles Pullen*

Further Reading

Borsook, Eve. *The Companion Guide to Florence*. 6th ed. Rochester, N.Y.: Companion Guides, 1997. A guidebook to the city, this volume will help place Florence's artists in context.

Krautheimer, Richard, in collaboration with Trude Krautheimer-Hess. *Lorenzo Ghiberti*. Princeton, N. J.: Princeton University Press, 1982. A biography of Ghiberti that examines his works.

Paolucci, Antonio. *The Origins of Renaissance Art: The Bapistery Doors, Florence*. Translated by Françoise Pouncey Chiarini. New York: Braziller, 1996. Discussion of Renaissance sculpture. Criticism and interpretation of works by Ghiberti, Andrea Pisano, and Batistero di San Giovanni.

Pope-Hennessy, John. *The Study and Criticism of Italian Sculpture*. Princeton, N.J.: Princeton University Press, 1980. Includes a detailed essay on Ghiberti by an expert on the subject. Excellent illustrations.

Sanders, Mary Lois. "Contest for the Doors of the Baptistery." *Calliope* 4 (May/June, 1994): 10. Sanders looks back at the contest held by the city of Florence, Italy, in 1402, in which Ghiberti and Filippo Brunelleschi competed for the honor of producing the decorations on the bronze doors of the baptistery. The influence of the competition on the development of Renaissance art and architecture are explored.

Walker, Paul Robert. *The Feud that Sparked the Renaissance: How Brunelleschi and Ghiberti Changed the Art World*. New York: William Morrow, 2002. A close look at the competition between Ghiberti and Brunelleschi and how both artists' work affected later artists. Bibliography and index.

See also: Filippo Brunelleschi; Donatello; Giotto; Jacopo della Quercia; Andrea Orcagna; Andrea Pisano; Nicola Pisano and Giovanni Pisano.

Related article in *Great Events from History: The Middle Ages, 477-1453*: c. 1410-1440: Florentine School of Art Emerges.

GIOTTO
Italian painter

Giotto, the first major figure in European painting, was among the first to concentrate on the individual, an interest later shared by Renaissance artists; his paintings are remarkable for their revelations of human complexity.

BORN: c. 1266; Vespignano, near Florence (now in Italy)
DIED: January 8, 1337; Florence
ALSO KNOWN AS: Giotto di Bondone (full name)
AREAS OF ACHIEVEMENT: Art, architecture

EARLY LIFE

Giotto (JAHT-toh), which is perhaps the shortened form of the name Ambrogiotto, was the son of Bondone, a farmer of some distinction. Although not much can be authenticated in various legends of Giotto's childhood, there is some warrant for believing that he was a precocious talent picked out at an early age by Cimabue, an important Florentine painter who died sometime around 1302. Evidently, Giotto began to sketch animals as a child without any formal training; he quickly flourished under the apprenticeship of Cimabue. By 1280, Florence was a thriving city of forty-five thousand people, renowned for its bankers, traders, artists, and craftspeople. It is thought that the artist profited from his observations of this earthy and pragmatic city and that his painting reflected a very broad and tolerant sensibility.

Giotto's painting marked such a departure from his predecessors that anecdotes of his self-confidence and originality usually are given some credit. According to one of these stories, he once painted a fly on the nose of a face on which Cimabue was working. The fly was so lifelike that the master tried to brush it off his painting several times before he grasped his student's jest. Giotto was also bold and outspoken: On one occasion he is recorded as having attacked the Franciscans for the fetish they made of their vows of poverty. It is likely that Giotto perfected his technique by traveling with Cimabue and helping him to complete many of his commissioned works.

LIFE'S WORK

Many of Giotto's paintings have disappeared, and there is still considerable debate about others that have been attributed to him. Some scholars, for example, identify the decorations in the Upper Church of the Basilica of Saint Francis as Giotto's first major work, but others question whether the painting style is congruent with other, less controversial Giotto frescoes. Perhaps his earliest surviving work is a 19-foot (6-meter) Crucifixion. It has won the admiration of some critics because Christ is depicted somewhat naturalistically, with his flesh sagging, rather than as the tense and trim figure of traditional art. At either end of the cross, the Virgin and Saint John sadly gaze at Christ—another departure from many medieval paintings, which include several allegorical scenes and various kinds of decoration. The emotion that is pictured is graphic yet austerely presented. Although some critics have not been impressed with the work's originality, doubting that it is Giotto's, Ricuccio Pucci, a parishioner of Santa Maria Novella in Florence, left funds in his will to keep a lamp perpetually burning before the crucifix "by the illustrious painter, Giotto."

In about 1304, Giotto began work on a series of thirty-eight frescoes in the Scrovegni Arena Chapel in Padua, painted a cycle of religious scenes that are considered to be some of the greatest works of Italian art, and created a three-part narrative in the Arena Chapel by arranging three horizontal strips of pictures around the walls. The top strip (scenes 1-12) portrays the early life of the Virgin. The second strip (scenes 17-27) depicts the early life of Christ. The final strip reenacts the passion of Christ—those events stemming from Judas's treachery to Pentecost, fifty days after the Resurrection, when the Holy Ghost descended on the disciples in tongues of fire and in the rushing of wind that gave them the power to speak to people of different languages.

The task the artist set for himself was enormous; it was nothing less than a retelling of the entire Christian legend. Not only did he confront the challenge of designing so many different scenes, he also had to find ways of inconspicuously indicating the narrative line and framing scenes so that they had the continuity of a story. The problem was to avoid the static, spectacle-like quality of individual panels, which might easily tire the eye. Somehow the artist had to generate movement between scenes while making them seem complete in themselves. Giotto met this technical challenge the way twentieth century filmmakers would, ensuring that each scene matched the others to form a flawless sequence. He also made sure that each scene flowed from left to right—as a page is read. The central action is in the center of the panel—as in scene 23, *The Baptism of Christ*—but the flanking figures on the left look at and past Christ, whereas the figures on the right look directly at him.

Giotto's deft management of movement in these

Giotto. (Library of Congress)

scenes is complemented by his precise and sensitive handling of the smaller details and individual figures. As one critic points out, the artist never simply paints a symbol; every object bears the mark of careful observation and drawing—as in the tree with its barren branches and the weeping angels that convey the cosmic tragedy of the Crucifixion. The angels in flight who clasp their hands, grip their faces, bow their heads, or raise their faces, evoke the many different postures of suffering, whereas the tree stands alone, to the side, a mute sign of the emptiness that accompanies grief.

The conclusion to Giotto's monumental Christian narrative in the Arena Chapel was *The Last Judgment*, a gigantic fresco on the entrance wall of the chapel. Christ sits, ringed in an oval, surrounded by the Apostles, judging the saved and the damned. Above Christ, angels roll back the heavens to reveal the gates of Paradise. Below him are the horrors of Hell, full of writhing, bent over, wretched creatures. The fresco abounds with numbers of figures strategically placed to reveal the hierarchy of Creation. The population density and the compositional dynamic are so great that the viewer is overwhelmed with the magnificence of the divine economy. On this one wall, every viewer was expected to find his or her own place in the universe. Perhaps this is one reason that Giotto put himself, as well as Enrico Scrovegni, the donor of the chapel, near the bottom of the fresco among a group of the blessed. Scrovegni is pictured presenting a model of the chapel itself, as though Giotto wanted to emphasize what human hands had wrought. The Arena Chapel is a startling work of religious art, for it invites viewers to admire an artist's conception of the Last Judgment. In a rather modern way, this conceit of the model draws attention to the work of art itself and to the artist.

Giotto went on to create beautiful frescoes in the Peruzzi Chapel and the Bardi Chapel. Among his greatest works are *Saint John the Baptist* and the *Life of Saint Francis*. As in his earlier work, the artist created cycles of scenes that told powerful stories. Nevertheless, he extended his technique by setting his monumental figures against equally monumental buildings, thus creating a deep sense of space absent from his earlier paintings. Although these works are not informed by the principles of perspective that give objects the illusion of three dimensions and measure space in mathematical proportions, the clarity and intricacy of Giotto's compositions come close to achieving the effects of the sophisticated methods perfected shortly after his death. Even when Giotto's paintings are, so to speak, out of perspective—as in the case of *The Raising of Drusiana*, where Saint John the Evangelist's fingers are much too long—the dramatic impact of exaggerating certain parts of the fresco reveal the soundness of Giotto's art. It is the simple, rugged, spiritual power of Saint John's gesturing fingers, not their size, which is important. The saint's sheer physicality makes the story of the raising of Drusiana a palpable experience.

SIGNIFICANCE

Late in his career, Giotto turned to architecture, a natural development in an artist given to creating massive frescoes peopled with so many different examples of humanity and architectural forms. Sometime after 1330, he was named chief architect of the cathedral in Florence. He lived as an artist of great influence with many pupils and admirers and was esteemed by such great literary figures as Dante, Petrarch, and Giovanni Boccaccio. Giovanni Villani, a contemporary historian, wrote that Giotto was entombed in the Florentine cathedral "with great honors and at the expense of the commune." This last observation suggests something important about his art: It was communal in the largest sense. A civilization believed that he painted for them and represented to them an encompassing vision of existence with greater imagination than any of his predecessors. The scale on which Giotto worked has never been surpassed. The epic grandeur of his frescoes, the human interest of his smaller scenes, capture the many levels on which life and art can be appreciated.

—*Carl Rollyson and Lisa Paddock*

FURTHER READING

Basile, Giuseppe, ed. *Giotto, the Arena Chapel Frescoes.* New York: Thames and Hudson. An examination of Giotto's frescoes in the Arena Chapel. Contains color illustrations and index.

_______. *Giotto: The Frescoes of the Scrovegni Chapel in Padua.* New York: Rizzolli, 2002. Focuses on Giotto's frescoes in the Scrovegni Chapel and briefly discusses his life. Color illustrations and bibliography.

Derbes, Anne, and Mark Sandona, eds. *The Cambridge Companion to Giotto.* New York: Cambridge University Press, 2004. A critical analysis of Giotto's works. Bibliography and index.

Flores d'Arcais, Francesca. *Giotto.* New York: Abbeville Press, 1995. A study of Giotto's life and works that examines the Franciscan Cycle in Assisi, his work for the Florentine bankers, and his work as an architect. Bibliography and indexes.

Haegen, Anne Mueller von der. *Giotto di Bondone, about 1267-1337.* Koln: Könemann Verlagsgesellschaft, 1998. Part of the Masters of Italian Art series, this work examines the life and works of Giotto. Contains color illustrations and a bibliography.

Ladis, Andrew, ed. *The Arena Chapel and the Genius of Giotto: Padua.* New York: Garland, 1998. A collection of essays on Giotto and his art, focusing on the Arena Chapel and Padua. Illustrated.

_______. *Franciscanism, the Papacy, and Art in the Age of Giotto.* New York: Garland, 1998. A collection of essays on Giotto and Franciscanism and other religious influences. Illustrated.

_______. *Giotto and the World of Early Italian Art: An Anthology of Literature.* New York: Garland, 1998. A collection of works on Giotto and early Italian art, looking at Giotto in Padua, Florence, Assisi, and Rome.

_______. *Giotto as a Historical and Literary Figure.* New York: Garland, 1998. A collection of essays focusing on the artist's role in history. Contains essays dealing with how artist Pietro d'Abano and biographer Giorgio Vasari viewed Giotto.

Lunghi, Elvio. *The Basilica of Saint Francis at Assisi: The Frescoes by Giotto, His Precursors, and Followers.* London: Thames and Hudson, 1996. A study of Giotto's work at the Basilica of Saint Francis at Assisi. Contains color illustrations and a bibliography.

SEE ALSO: Giovanni Boccaccio; Cimabue; Dante; Petrarch; Giovanni Villani.

RELATED ARTICLE in *Great Events from History: The Middle Ages, 477-1453*: c. 1410-1440: Florentine School of Art Emerges.

GOTTFRIED VON STRASSBURG

German poet

Gottfried was one of the great writers of the German courtly epic during the High Middle Ages.

FLOURISHED: c. 1210; possibly Alsace, Holy Roman Empire (now in France)

ALSO KNOWN AS: Godfrey of Strasbourg

AREA OF ACHIEVEMENT: Literature

EARLY LIFE

Little is known of the life of Gottfried von Strassburg (GAWT-freed fuhn STRAHS-buhrg). It is presumed that he was of middle-class origins, and since he was well educated perhaps he was also a member of the clergy. He may have been born in the Alsace region. He lived around 1200, the zenith of the European Middle Ages and the high point of German courtly culture. It was the era of feudalism, with society composed of the knightly class, the serfs, and the clergy. As the custodians of religious and secular heritage, the priests and monks were the most educated and literate of the three classes.

During this time, the court of the king and his knight-vassals was the center of worldly culture. It was the age of the courtly love lyric, a well-defined canon of poetry in which the knight proclaimed his love for his lady and pledged to do great deeds in her honor. Through such devotion, the knight was to be lifted to a higher spiritual existence. The great stories of love and adventure, the romances—from the Provençal *romans*—also had their origin in this period of European culture.

LIFE'S WORK

As one of the three greatest writers of the courtly epic in Germany (the other two being Wolfram von Eschenbach and Hartmann von Aue), Gottfried was a master of the genre and told his tales with a perfected sense of verse forms and a brilliant command of imagery. He is best known for the epic *Tristan und Isolde* (c. 1210; *Tristan and Isolde*, 1899), one of the great romances of the period. Eleven manuscript copies of his text have survived, most of them written in Alsatian dialect. His tale was never completed, and two later writers, Ulrich von Türheim and Heinrich von Freiberg, completed other versions of the Gottfried text. The love story is legendary, a fictionalized account of a historical event the details of which have long been forgotten. The primary source for Gottfried's version was that of the Anglo-Norman poet Thomas von Britanje. There had been an earlier German rendering by Eilhart von Oberge, composed around 1180, which certainly had some influence on Gottfried's tale. The themes of Gottfried's *Tristan and Isolde* are the demoniac and transcendent, or healing, powers of love.

Told in thirty chapters, Gottfried's epic relates the tragic tale of the fated lovers, Tristan and Isolde. Tristan was the child of the model English knight Rivalin and his love, Blancheflor. Their story foreshadows to a degree the later fate of their son. A knight at the court of King Mark of Cornwall, the young, inexperienced, and somewhat rash Rivalin meets the beautiful and equally youthful Blancheflor. In the typical manner of the courtly romance, they keep their love secret from the world. Their budding relationship is interrupted by the call to battle, and the brash Rivalin suffers a mortal wound. Disguised as a doctor, Blancheflor visits him on the battlefield, and they consummate their love. He is revived from his wounds by her kisses, yet after the two elope, he perishes in a battle. Blancheflor, unaware of her lover's fate, brings a child into the world but dies of grief in the course of premature childbirth when she learns of Rivalin's death. That child is Tristan—whose name, from the French *triste*, suggests sadness. He was conceived in that moment of passion that had revived his father from the brink of death and that would later lead to the loss of his mother. Thus, the story of Tristan's parents ironically establishes the association of love and tragic death that will be the theme of the son's story.

Tristan is reared by Rual and Floraete. He develops into a model student and is skilled in the manly virtues of knighthood. Like his father, he eventually goes to the court of King Mark and impresses all with his skill and learning. King Mark further undertakes Tristan's upbringing and becomes his most trusted friend. On one of his heroic adventures, Tristan visits Ireland and King Morold, who has been demanding large tributes from Mark. He engages in battle with King Morold and kills him. Wounded by the king's poisoned sword, Tristan can be healed only by Morold's sister. Disguised as a minstrel, he visits her and is healed. He then instructs her beautiful daughter, Isolde, in music and the social graces. When he returns to England, Tristan tells King Mark of Isolde's great beauty and the king decides that he must wed her. He sends Tristan back to Ireland to claim Isolde. Tristan is recognized as the one who killed King Morold and is hated by Isolde for murdering her uncle, but after slaying a dragon that has plagued the kingdom Tristan is allowed to take Isolde back as King Mark's bride.

Isolde's mother has brewed a love potion for her daughter and King Mark. On the journey to Cornwall, Isolde's servant, Brangane, confuses the potion with a drink of water she has given to Tristan and Isolde. The two fall madly in love. Tristan breaks his pledge of loyalty to Mark when he consummates his spiritual union with Isolde. The two lovers decide to deceive the king. Yet, discovered by Mark, they are banished from the court. Tristan and Isolde then seek shelter in a secluded grotto that is an enchanted domain of love. They are eventually discovered. Isolde must return to the king, and Tristan voluntarily leaves her so that she will remain safe. He goes to Normandy, where he serves as a knight and eventually marries another, Isolde Weisshand.

Gottfried's version remains incomplete at this point; the conclusion was written by his followers. Tristan is severely wounded in battle and sends for Isolde so that she might heal him with her magic arts. A white sail on the ship is the signal that she is on her way. Tristan's jealous wife, Isolde Weisshand, forces a messenger to lie and report the sighting of a black sail. Tristan dies in despair, and Isolde also perishes from grief on her arrival. In the end, King Mark has them buried side by side.

Gottfried's epic epitomizes many of the virtues of German knighthood: Tristan's prowess and courage in battle, his proper bearing at court, and his skill and learning all suggest a vision of the ideal knight. Ultimately, he is even loyal to King Mark and fights on his behalf for Isolde. It is a magic love potion that robs him of his will and causes his betrayal of his king. The breaking of the oath of fealty to one's liege lord was a serious offense within the culture of knighthood, but Tristan is clearly at the mercy of powers beyond his control. Gottfried's theme is thus very much about the irrational as it is manifested in human love. Although Gottfried lived during the great era of the courtly love lyric, a highly stylized genre that dealt with the ennobling aspects of a knight's idealized devotion for his chosen lady, his work concentrates on the more secular dimensions of love. Passion (and the irrational) is a kind of demoniac power that disrupts the normal course of society; it causes the individual to ignore its rules and prohibitions. Tristan and Isolde are therefore fated for a tragic end; those who live outside society must finally pay the price.

Yet the theme of passion is not to be interpreted solely in this negative fashion. Tristan and Isolde's love is also a transcendent power; it raises them above the everyday world into what is clearly an exalted realm of harmony and unity, into the oneness and bliss of the love experience (as in the famous episode in the grotto). Thus, love is also a spiritually healing power that abolishes the loneliness and suffering of the individual. It "cures" the ultimate sense of separateness that plagues all human beings. Isolde's healing of Tristan's wounds, for example, suggests this in a symbolic fashion. Gottfried's story of the fated lovers revolves around universal contradictions of the human experience.

Significance

As one of the great authors of the courtly epic during the Middle Ages, Gottfried von Strassburg will surely retain his place not only within German literature but also within world literature. Along with the writings of Wolfram von Eschenbach, which Gottfried abhorred, his work represents the zenith of the courtly epic genre within the German tradition. A master storyteller, his narrative style is flowing, and his verse forms are musical and well constructed. The epic foreshadowing of Tristan and Isolde's fate in the story of Tristan's parents, Rivalin and Blancheflor, suggests a writer who is in full command of the skills of his trade.

In contrast to Wolfram, whose major epic, *Parzival* (c. 1200-1210; English translation, 1894), deals with the spiritual issues of absolute truth and man's proper relationship to God, Gottfried's text treats the earthly and secular themes of beauty, passion, and love. If the Wolfram text revolves around the theme of divine love, then Gottfried's focuses on profane passion. Even when his narrative deals with aspects of physical love, it does so with circumspection and stylistic distance. He depicts these thematic concerns with a degree of elegance and grace that raises his work far above the works of his contemporaries.

Gottfried's *Tristan and Isolde* certainly remains one of the greatest love stories ever told. The intensity of the characters' passion and their tragic fate captures the mysteries and sufferings inherent in the human capacity to love. The power of his story has exerted its influence on subsequent centuries. The nineteenth century German writer Karl Immermann composed a version in 1841 that remained uncompleted, the great composer Richard Wagner wrote an opera based on the legend in 1859, and in 1903 Thomas Mann wrote a novella, *Tristan* (English translation, 1925), which incorporates themes from both Gottfried's and Wagner's versions.

—*Thomas F. Barry*

Further Reading

Batts, Michael S. *Gottfried von Strassburg*. New York: Twayne, 1971. An excellent introduction to Gottfried's life and times with an interpretive focus on his *Tristan and Isolde* and on the legend in general. Contains a bibliography.

Bekker, Hugo. *Gottfried von Strassburg's "Tristan": Journey Through the Realm of Eros*. Columbia, S.C.: Camden House, 1987. An analysis of the the medieval concept of love in Gottfried's *Tristan and Isolde*.

Chinca, Mark. *Gottfried von Strassburg: "Tristan."* Chinca, a professor of medieval literature, has published several books and essays on Gottfried. This concise introduction for students compares Gottfried's approach to literary tradition with that of previous writers and examines the reception of *Tristan and Isolde* by contemporaries and later writers.

_______. *History, Fiction, Verisimilitude: Studies in the Poetics of Gottfried's "Tristan."* London: University of London, 1993. Close readings of *Tristan and Isolde*.

Hall, Clifton D. *A Complete Concordance to Gottfried von Strassburg's "Tristan."* Lewiston, N.Y.: Edwin Mellen Press, 1992. Includes bibliographical references and an index.

Jackson, W. T. H. "The Role of Brangaene in Gottfried's *Tristan*." *The Germanic Review* 27 (1953): 290-296. A brief essay on the pivotal position of Isolde's servant. Contains notes with bibliographical information.

_______. "Tristan the Artist in Gottfried's Poem." *PMLA* 77 (1962): 364-372. This scholarly essay examines the title character and the talents he exhibits at court. Contains notes with bibliographical information.

Jaeger, Stephen. *Medieval Humanism in Gottfried von Strassburg's "Tristan and Isolde."* Heidelberg, Germany: Winter, 1977. Jaeger, a professor of comparative and Germanic literature and social/intellectual history, considers *Tristan and Isolde* in the light of the humanist tradition in Europe.

Loomis, Roger, ed. *Arthurian Literature in the Middle Ages*. Oxford: Clarendon Press, 1959. An important collection of essays on medieval literature with several on Gottfried's epic. Contains a bibliography.

Schultz, James A. "Teaching Gottfried and Wolfram." In *Approaches to Teaching the Arthurian Tradition*, edited by Maureen Fries and Jeanie Watson. New York: Modern Language Association of America, 1992. A brief but useful article for teachers.

Stevens, Adrian, and Roy Wisbey, eds. *Gottfried von Strassburg and the Medieval Tristan Legend*. Rochester, N.Y.: Boydell & Brewer, 1990. Papers from a symposium held at the Institute of Germanic Studies, London, March 24-26, 1986. Includes bibliographical references and an index.

Sullivan, Robert G. *Justice and the Social Context of Early Middle High German Literature*. New York: Routledge, 2001. A history of the Holy Roman Empire hinging on an examination of High German literature and its authors' focus on social, political, and spiritual issues during a time of transformation. Bibliographical references, index.

Thomas, Neil E. *Tristan in the Underworld: A Study of Gottfried von Strassburg's "Tristan" Together with the "Tristran" of Thomas*. Lewiston, N.Y.: Edwin Mellen Press, 1991. An analysis of the legend from its Celtic roots to its proliferation by European poets. Gottfried's source for the Tristan legend is the rendition of the French poet Thomas, to which Gottfried's work is compared. Concludes that Gottfried's work defends rather than condemns feudal order.

Willson, H. B. "Vicissitudes in Gottfried's *Tristan*." *The Modern Language Review* 52 (1957): 203-213. This essay discusses the narrative structure of Gottfried's text. Contains notes with bibliographical information.

SEE ALSO: Hartmann von Aue; Walther von der Vogelweide; Wolfram von Eschenbach.

RELATED ARTICLES in *Great Events from History: The Middle Ages, 477-1453*: After 1000: Development of Miracle and Mystery Plays; c. 1025: Scholars at Chartres Revive Interest in the Classics; c. 1100: Rise of Courtly Love; 1100-1300: European Universities Emerge; 1136: Hildegard von Bingen Becomes Abbess; c. 1180: Chrétien de Troyes Writes *Perceval*; c. 1306-1320: Dante Writes *The Divine Comedy*; c. 1350-1400: Petrarch and Boccaccio Recover Classical Texts.

GREGORY OF TOURS

French bishop and historian

Gregory provided historians with their prime source of information on Merovingian Gaul from 575 to 591. He also contributed to the Christian tradition an example of living in accord with the best principles of the Church.

BORN: November 30, 539; Clermont, Auvergne (now in France)

DIED: November 17, 594; Tours, Neustria (now in France)

ALSO KNOWN AS: Georgius Florentius (given name)

AREAS OF ACHIEVEMENT: Historiography, religion and theology

EARLY LIFE

Georgius Florentius, who would become Gregory, bishop of Tours (tewr), was born in the capital city of Auvergne. In his *De virtutibus sancti Martini* (c. 593; *The Miracles of Saint Martin*, 1949), he wrote that he was born on Saint Andrew's Day, thirty-four years before his installation in 573 as the nineteenth bishop of Tours. He was given the name of his father (Georgius) and of his father's father (Florentius), each of whom was of senatorial rank. His mother, Armentaria, was a granddaughter of Saint Tetricus, bishop of Langres (539-572) and a great-granddaughter of Saint Gregorius, who preceded his son as bishop of Langres (507-539). Gregory's lineage was clearly that of a noble family consistently influential in the Church.

His father apparently died when Gregory was a child, so he was reared by his uncle, Gallus, bishop of Clermont-Ferrand (525-551), and, after 551, he resided with the archdeacon Avitus, who became bishop of Clermont-Ferrand in the year 573. Gregory had a granduncle who was bishop of Lyon and a cousin, Eufronius, whom Gregory himself succeeded as bishop of Tours on August 20, 573.

At the age of twenty-five, he suffered a debilitating illness. He attributed his recovery to Saint Martin; it was at this time also that he was ordained a deacon. He obtained his bishopric nine years later. In the following year, 574, he suffered a deep personal loss: His brother Peter, a deacon, was murdered. Peter had been accused of murdering Silvester, bishop of Langres, who was one of their relatives. The case had been heard by Nicetius, bishop of Lyon and a maternal uncle of the accused, and Peter's oath that he was innocent had been accepted by both clergy and diocesan laymen. Within two years, however, Silvester's son attacked Peter in the street, running him through with a spear. Gregory relates the story movingly but objectively in *Historia Francorum* (late sixth century; *The History of the Franks*, 1927).

Gregory of Tours. (Library of Congress)

LIFE'S WORK

Gregory remained bishop of Tours from the date of his consecration until his death at age fifty-five. His ability during this time to maintain the tenets and principles of the Church while being privy to the political activities and ambitions of the Merovingian rulers marks him as a person of considerable shrewdness. Considerable too was his industry as a man of letters.

It is best to begin a survey of Gregory's achievements by noting his masterwork, *The History of the Franks*, as it is conventionally called; its full title is *Historia Francorum libri decem* (ten books of histories). In many of the events set down in this history, Gregory was himself a participant. The massive work in ten books opens with the author's profession of his faith and begins its record, as many medieval works of history do, with the Creation and Adam. From the Creation to the year 594, according to Gregory, 6,063 years elapsed (the number of the tally appearing in the manuscript is 5,792, probably a scribal error: Gregory's figures add up to 6,063, as noted). The first book summarizes the Old and New Testaments and moves from the death of Christ through some four centuries to the death of Martin, the patron saint of Tours and Gregory's inspiration. The second book brings the history up through the death in 511 of Clovis, the founder of the dynasty that took its name from Merovech, an early king who died in 456. Clovis had brought most of Gaul into a cohesive monarchy. Books 3 and 4 chronicle the events centering on the sons of Clovis, particularly Chlotar I, who continued to unify Gaul under Frankish sovereignty and whose sons, after his death in 561, sustained the wars, conspiracies, and assassinations that determined much of the character of Merovingian history.

There appears at the end of book 3 a report on the harsh winter of 548; book 9 also concludes with a weather report. Books 5, 6, 8, 9, and 10 all include sections on signs and portents, many having to do with the weather. Books 7 and 8 include sections on the miracles of Martin. These and similar preoccupations constitute a rather substantial part of the text.

Books 4 through 10 of *The History of the Franks* deal with events in Gregory's own time, from 549 through 593, and the last five books in particular chronicle events coinciding with Gregory's bishopric. These entail the bewildering rivalries and conspiracies of the sons of Chlotar I—particularly Kings Charibert, Sigibert, Chilperic, and Guntram—and the ambitions and schemes of Sigibert's wife, Brunhild, and Chilperic's third wife, Fredegunde. Plots, violence, bloodshed, murders, and assassinations are recounted matter-of-factly by Gregory and make for very interesting if occasionally disturbing reading.

Characteristic of his history are its amusing sidelights; Gregory has a sense of humor and tosses off many tongue-in-cheek comments. On a larger scale, there is, in the interstices of the narrative, the tale of the Falstaffian duke Guntram Boso, a thieving, conniving, but irresistible rogue for whom Gregory obviously has unwavering affection. He condemns Boso's excesses but never Boso himself and offers him the protection of sanctuary, which not even royalty can persuade him to lift, and as much help and advice as his ecclesiastical position permits. His description of the killing of Guntram Boso, pierced by so many spears that his body, propped up by them, could not fall to the ground, is an example of the memorable detail of his prose.

Gregory's Latin is anything but classical; nevertheless, it is not as bad as much other medieval Latin. He apologizes for its lack of polish in book 5 and in his preface but insists that his subject is too important to go unrecorded, however imperfect the language of record may be. History has vindicated him.

Gregory's other works were composed more or less concurrently with *The History of the Franks*. *The Miracles of Saint Martin*, mentioned above, consists of four books on the acts of his favorite saint, with periodic entries of devotion, the last datable to July 4, 593. The Latin word *virtus* (manliness, courage, excellence, goodness) is Gregory's word for "miracle." For him, a miracle is evidence of the power of goodness, a power conferred on those who are worthy of it. *Liber vitae patrum* (late sixth century; *Life of the Fathers*, 1949) considers individually twenty-two abbots, bishops, or solitaries worthy of the adjective *sanctus*—or *sancta* in the case of the nun Monegundis, the subject of section 19. *Sanctus* or *sancta* means "blessed" and refers to a person who has in some way produced a miracle. Gregory's writing antedates the formulation of official canonization procedures by about five centuries. Six of his twenty-two subjects were not subsequently canonized officially; to Gregory, however, they were all blessed. The miracles that qualified them as such may be exemplified by those attributed to Gallus. According to his biographer, Gallus put out a fire by walking toward it with a work of Scripture open in his hands, and his bed cured the fever of a man who had napped in it; at his tomb, sufferers were cured of their ailments.

The Miracles of Saint Martin (four books) and *Life of the Fathers* (one book) constitute five of what Gregory called his eight books of miracles. The others are each single volumes—*Liber in gloria martyrum* (book of the glories of the martyrs), *Liber de passione et virtutibus sancti Juliani martyris* (passion and miracles of Saint Julian, martyr), and *Liber in gloria confessorum* (*Glory of the Confessors*, 1988), all written between c. 575 and c. 593.

Gregory is as strong in his ridicule of Greek and Roman myths as he is firm in his belief in Christian miracles. One may dismiss him as naïve on this score, but it would be inadvisable to dismiss him as an unreliable observer because of his acceptance of miracles. This manifestation of his faith marks him as a practical churchman in his own time and in no way intrudes on the realism with which he describes the actual people, occurrences, and political movements of sixth century France.

Gregory also completed a short work on the miracles of the apostle Andrew, a translation into Latin of the story of the Seven Sleepers of Ephesus, and a book on astronomy that mentions a comet that preceded (or portended) the assassination of King Sigibert in 575. Two other short works, a commentary on the book of Psalms and a book on Sidonius Apollinaris's masses, are not extant.

These, then, were the three directions taken by the life's work of Gregory of Tours: his effective episcopate, his political dealings with the ruling and feuding principals of Merovingian France, and his historiography and hagiography. There was also a triad in Gregory's personal life. The first important event was his recovery from serious illness—a healing wrought, as he insists, by the intercession of Martin, to whose memory Gregory remained devoted for the last thirty years of his life. The second was his consecration as bishop. The third was the ascension to the papal throne in 590 of the deacon who was to become Gregory the Great. The historian's deep satisfaction in the election of Gregory I is reflected in his beginning the tenth book of *The History of the Franks* with a laudatory biography of the new pope and a transcription of his inaugural address. Gregory of Tours saw his namesake's elevation as a merited natural consequence of belonging to a great family of senatorial rank and ecclesiastical ambience; he had seen his own appointment to a bishopric in the same light. If pride was inherent in this attitude, so was a sense of profound responsibility.

Gregory's installation as bishop of Tours was heralded in poetry by his contemporary churchman, Venantius Fortunatus (530-609), an illustrious poet, priest, hagiographer, devotee of Saint Martin, and, after Gregory's death, bishop of Poitiers. The admiration of Fortunatus for Gregory is evidence of the esteem enjoyed by the nineteenth bishop of Tours in his lifetime. In all, two dozen poems by Fortunatus, author of the famous sixth century works *Vexilla regis prodeunt* (the royal banners forward go) and *Pange lingua gloriosi praelium certaminis* (sing my tongue the glorious battle) are directed to Gregory. Fortunatus was also a historian, but his contribution to historiography has proved to be insignificant in comparison with Gregory's. His versified life of

Martin is superior in its Latinity, but not in its devotion, to Gregory's prose account of the saint's miracles. Fortunatus's poetry, however, displays an artistry that lay well beyond the talents of Gregory. The juxtaposition of Fortunatus and Gregory supplies a reliable perspective from which to view and assess Gregory's importance. He was not a literary master, but he was duly celebrated by one who was patently not as good a historian.

SIGNIFICANCE

Gregory's *The History of the Franks* stands well above all such efforts by his contemporaries. In literary quality, it may be inferior to the history written by the next century's Saint Bede the Venerable, while it is decidedly superior in many respects to the universal history by the preceding century's Paulus Orosius—which Alfred the Great chose to translate into English. For its own century, *The History of the Franks* is without peer. Gregory's diversions on weather, plant life, and bird migrations may not, despite their compelling accuracy, appeal to most students of history; his inside record of the Merovingian royalty and his objective observations of the political machinations, disasters, and triumphs of the sixth century in Frankish Gaul, however, are not likely ever to lose their value.

—*Roy Arthur Swanson*

FURTHER READING

Auerbach, Erich. *Mimesis: The Representation of Reality in Western Literature.* Translated by Willard R. Trask. Princeton, N.J.: Princeton University Press, 2003. A classic study, first published in English in 1953, of reality, realism, and mimesis in literature. One chapter, "Sicharius and Chramnesindus," presents a segment of *The History* and analyzes its language and style. The scholar Edward W. Said provides an introduction to this anniversary edition.

Gregory of Tours. *The History of the Franks.* Translated by O. M. Dalton. 2 vols. Reprint. Oxford, England: Oxford University Press, 1971. The first volume is an extensive introduction; the second is a translation of the work. An indispensable adjunct to the study of the life and writings of Gregory of Tours.

_______. *The History of the Franks.* Translated by Lewis Thorpe. Baltimore: Penguin Books, 1974. An unpretentious translation of Gregory's history, with an excellent introduction to his life and works.

_______. *Life of the Fathers.* 2d ed. Translated and edited by Edward James. Liverpool, England: Liverpool University Press, 1991. A scholarly translation of an important hagiographical work by Gregory, with an informative introduction and helpful annotative materials.

Heinzelmann, Martin. *Gregory of Tours: History and Society in the Sixth Century.* Translated by Christopher Carroll. New York: Cambridge University Press, 2001. A shorter study of the history of Gregory as a saint and the history of Merovingian society. Includes a bibliography and index.

Lasko, Peter. *The Kingdom of the Franks: North-West Europe Before Charlemagne.* Edited by David Talbot Rice. New York: McGraw-Hill, 1971. Part of the Library of Medieval Civilization series, this study is a concise summary of Frankish art, religion, and regal power. Includes 121 illustrations, many in color. An excellent companion to *The History.*

Mitchell, Kathleen, and Ian Wood, eds. *The World of Gregory of Tours.* Boston: Brill, 2002. A collection exploring facets of Gregory's life and work, as well as his place in the historical and social context of his time. Includes bibliography and index.

Pfister, Christian. "Gaul Under the Merovingian Franks." In *The Rise of the Saracens and the Foundation of the Western Empire.* Vol. 2 in *The Cambridge Medieval History.* Cambridge, England: Cambridge University Press, 1913. An excellent standard work, which, with the introduction by Dalton to *The History of the Franks*, gives a proper introduction to a detailed study of Gregory.

Wallace-Hadrill, J. M. *The Barbarian West: 400-1000.* Rev. ed. London: Hutchinson University Library, 1957. Chapters 4 and 5 concentrate on the Franks. This is a reliable, short introduction to Gregory's milieu and to those who preceded and followed it. Helpful bibliography.

Wormald, P., ed. *Ideal and Reality in Frankish and Anglo-Saxon Society.* New York: Oxford University Press, 1983. This collection of articles includes Wood's "The Ecclesiastical Politics of Merovingian Clermont," an informative overview of that confluence of the religious and secular environments in which Gregory functioned.

SEE ALSO: Amalasuntha; Saint Bede the Venerable; Clovis; Fredegunde; Gregory the Great; Saxo Grammaticus.

RELATED ARTICLES in *Great Events from History: The Middle Ages, 477-1453*: 496: Baptism of Clovis; 590-604: Reforms of Pope Gregory the Great; 731: Bede Writes *Ecclesiastical History of the English People.*

Gregory the Great

Italian pope (590-604)

By example and direction, Gregory set the basic patterns for the medieval Church of Central and Western Europe in the areas of pastoral administration, interpretation of the Bible, and liturgical usage. He was directly responsible for sending missionaries to England and the consequent organization of the medieval English church.

BORN: c. 540; Rome (now in Italy)
DIED: March 12, 604; Rome
ALSO KNOWN AS: Saint Gregory I
AREAS OF ACHIEVEMENT: Religion and theology, church government, monasticism

Early Life

Gregory was born near the city of Rome, which once had been the center of the political and cultural world of Western civilization. About two centuries before the birth of Gregory, the capital city of the Roman Empire had been moved eastward to Constantinople. Although Rome at first remained an important city, its role continued to diminish as the years went by. During this time, invaders and migrating peoples made their way into Italy and other sections of the old Roman Empire, cutting the western half away from Constantinople and the eastern portions of the Mediterranean world. As a result, it was difficult for many people—merchants, political leaders, churchmen, and others—to maintain contact and communications with the East. Because the invaders were pagan or Arian Christians (a heretical sect of Christianity), there were unusual tensions in the Church in Gregory's homeland. These factors tended to separate further the leaders of the eastern and western churches, the pope at Rome and the patriarch at Constantinople. This problem was to become a major concern of Gregory later in his life.

The parents of Gregory were old Roman aristocrats. Hence, the young Gregory received the best education available at that time, especially in the traditional areas of grammar and rhetoric. He later studied law, a discipline that prepared him for his later career in civil and ecclesiastical administration. Gregory also was well founded in the teachings of Christianity: Some of his ancestors had served the Church, and his parents and his mother's sisters were well-known for their Christian lives and acts of piety.

Just before Gregory's birth, Rome had been restored to rule under Constantinople. In 565, however, the emperor Justinian I, who had inspired the reconquest, died. Many of his recently conquered territories, including Rome, would soon fall away to new waves of foreign conquerors. Rome was captured by the Lombards, a Germanic tribe that had entered Italy in the north. They were heretical Christians, violent and, by Roman standards, uncultured. It is at this juncture that Gregory first appeared on the scene.

Life's Work

Gregory, still a layman, was appointed prefect of the city of Rome shortly after 570. This responsibility was somewhat like that of mayor or city manager of a modern city: He presided over the senate, which was mainly a city council. He also saw to the finances, the public order, defense, and food supplies for Rome.

About 575, his father died. Gregory, believing that he had been called to renounce the cares of the secular world for the monastic life, took his inheritance and founded six monasteries in Sicily and one at the site of the family palace in Rome. To this last one he gave the name Saint Andrews, and there he spent his time in study and contemplation. His primary attention was given to the reading and study of the Latin fathers of the church and to the Bible.

In 578, because of his experience and growing reputation, Gregory was named a deacon in the Roman diocese. In the city of Rome, this was an office of honor and responsibility. From 579 to 586, Gregory served as the papal ambassador to Constantinople, where his primary task was to develop and maintain good relations with both emperor and patriarch. This was not a particularly easy job because there were rivalries and distrust between leaders at Rome and those at Constantinople. Gregory, however, won the respect of many in Constantinople. A group of Eastern monks asked him to present a series of lectures on the Book of Job. These discussions served as the basis for Gregory's most important theological writing, *Moralia in Job* (595; *Morals on the Book of Job*, 1844-1850; commonly called *Moralia*), a commentary on ethics based on Job.

In 586, Gregory returned to the monastery, serving now as abbot. The position called on his administrative expertise, as he successfully maintained strict standards of discipline and study for the monks. He continued as an informal adviser to the pope and maintained an awareness of current events. It was during this time that Gregory noticed the English youths on the slave block in the Roman marketplace and vowed to send missionaries to their land to provide the opportunity for their salvation.

During his years at the monastery, Gregory became aware of two other matters that were of great concern to him. The first was the presence in Italy, and the world in general, of heretical expressions of Christianity. To him, Arianism was the most insidious, in that it closely resembled orthodoxy and consequently drew a large following. Other heretical groups, such as Donatists and Pelagians, also concerned Gregory. He pledged to fight for orthodoxy. Second, Gregory saw his homeland suffering under natural disasters, including floods and plague, which he believed constituted God's punishment of a wayward and dissolute people. Gregory and his monks provided physical, emotional, and spiritual relief to the people of Rome.

In 590, the people of Rome turned to Gregory (for there were no cardinals in the Church at this time to carry out papal elections) and asked him to become their bishop. As the bishop of Rome, Gregory would also be pope. Gregory at first refused, believing that he was not equal to the task. When he finally accepted the call, however, he did so with an extraordinary sense of pastoral responsibility, calling for spiritual renewal and recommitment from the top down.

Gregory's first priority was to defend the city against the attacking Lombards. Deserted by his imperial benefactor in Constantinople, Gregory took matters into his own hands, leading his own army against the Lombards, negotiating with them, even offering his personal resources as tribute in an effort to buy peace. Although there was to be no end to the conflict until after 598, Gregory's method of dealing with the Lombards established a precedent for popes in the years to come.

Because of unsettled political and military conditions, there were many problems with displaced persons in Gregory's Rome. Food supplies were short and medical attention was frequently needed; adequate housing and living conditions were not always available. Gregory responded by calling on the resources of the Church: Too often, he claimed, the Church had sought to serve its own best interests and had not paid adequate attention to people who were in need. In the same spirit, Gregory was to call on each member of the clergy to ask himself whether he were fulfilling his duty. According to Gregory, in his influential work *Liber regulae pastoralis* (591; *Pastoral Care*, 1950), the clergy, like shepherds, must lead the people in God's ways. Gregory called on the pastor to demonstrate dependence on God and to be tactful, committed to others, compassionate, pure, meek, sensitive, active, disciplined, merciful, and just. Many generations of clergy have used this model for their own guidance.

Gregory sent Augustine of Canterbury to England in 597, which resulted in the conversion of the Anglo-Saxons to Christianity. Gregory also effectively opposed the spread of heresy, by means of missions to Spain. He was a strong proponent of a united Church and successfully asserted his primacy throughout the Western Church, regarding the Papacy as superior to the patriarchy at Constantinople.

Throughout his papacy, Gregory found himself embroiled in politics: with the kings of the Germanic tribes, Visigoths, Franks, and Lombards. Although Gregory's vision and goals were firmly fixed, he frequently had to

Gregory the Great. (Library of Congress)

negotiate, and this usually involved compromise. Gregory stands out as a man of principle and courage throughout his time as pope. In 602, he allowed himself to be misled into supporting the wily tyrant Phocas, emperor of Byzantium, who had come by his office through the murder of the previous emperor and his family. Phocas, as a result, propagated increasing acts of terror, although he eventually secured peace with the Lombards and thus safety for Italy. Such a peace, coming about despite Gregory's lack of foresight and at the hands of one of the most despised tyrants in history, constitutes the single outstanding flaw in Gregory's otherwise unimpeachable career.

During his years as pope, Gregory found time to write. In addition to the two books already mentioned, he wrote a book of sermons meant to prepare believers for the final judgment; a series of homilies on Ezekiel (593), which explain the text of that book of the Bible in terms that the practicing Christian could apply to his own life; fourteen books of letters, interesting for the light they throw on Gregory's papacy; and four books of "dialogues," in which Gregory explained the teachings of Saint Augustine.

Gregory also had a deep interest in the liturgy of the Church. He supported the extension of the Roman rite and the search for a uniform style of worship in the Western Church. Many of the liturgical changes that he supported came to be incorporated as a part of the medieval liturgical tradition. These changes had to do with liturgical texts, the use of the Alleluia and the Lord's Prayer, and the music of the service. Although Gregory did not actually compose music of the type known as the Gregorian chant, he did express sentiments that led to that form. Gregory did contribute some of the hymns of the Church; two of them are "Father, We Praise You" and "O Christ, Our King, Creator, Lord." Martin Luther considered the latter to be the best of the hymns.

Gregory stepped down from the papacy early in 604. Within a few weeks, in his mid-sixties, he died.

Significance

Soon after his death, Gregory's contemporaries were calling for his canonization. His writings became well known and widespread within a short time, and some of them—including *Pastoral Care*, which was translated by King Alfred into Anglo-Saxon—were published in vernacular languages and made available to a relatively large audience. The fact that Gregory's name was early and traditionally associated with the liturgical reforms gave authenticity and authority to them. Although never regarded as a scholar or eminent theologian, Gregory was highly regarded by all the great scholars of the Middle Ages, and he was the most quoted of the Latin fathers. Thomas Aquinas, perhaps the greatest of medieval theologians, cited Gregory more than any other authority; Pope Boniface VIII listed Gregory with the great "doctors" of the Church, placing him in the same category with the best scholars of Western Christendom. As the link between the ancient, classical world and the European Middle Ages, Gregory recast the ideas and teachings of the early church fathers in a new mold, one that shaped not only the medieval Church but European culture and civilization as well.

—*Thomas O. Kay*

Further Reading

Anonymous [monk of Whitby]. *The Earliest Life of Gregory the Great*. Edited by Bertram Colgrave. 1968. Reprint. New York: Cambridge University Press, 1985. Contains a bilingual text with ample notes for understanding a very early biography of Gregory.

Bremmer, Rolf H., Jr., Kees Dekker, and David F. Johnson, eds. *Rome and the North: The Early Reception of Gregory the Great in Germanic Europe*. Sterling, Va.: Peeters, 2001. A look at how Gregory the Great was perceived in early Germanic literature. Bibliography and indexes.

Cavadini, John D. *Gregory the Great*. Notre Dame, Ind.: University of Notre Dame Press, 1996. A biography of Gregory the Great that also examines early church history. Bibliography and index.

_______, ed. *Gregory the Great: A Symposium*. Notre Dame, Ind.: University of Notre Dame Press, 1995. A collection of essays on Gregory the Great and the early Church. Topics include the pope's holiness, his knowledge of Greek, and his influence on astronomy and early Middle Age doctrines on the artistic image.

Evans, G. R. *The Thought of Gregory the Great*. New York: Cambridge University Press, 1986. Evans focuses on the philosophy and thought of Gregory the Great. Includes analysis of the pope's writings. Bibliography and index.

Markus, R. A. *Gregory the Great and His World*. New York: Cambridge University Press, 1997. A discussion of Gregory the Great that focuses on his theology and his relations with religious and secular leaders as well as discusses the environment in which he functioned.

Straw, Carole E. *Gregory the Great*. Aldershot, Hampshire and Brookfield, Vt.: Variorum, 1996. A concise introduction to Gregory's life and work. Bibliography.

_______. *Gregory the Great: Perfection in Imperfection.* Berkeley: University of California Press, 1988. This is not a biography in the ordinary sense but rather a discussion of Gregory's personality and of the major topics of his thought. A well-annotated and informative study.

SEE ALSO: Saint Benedict of Nursia; Boniface VIII; Gregory of Tours; Justinian I.

RELATED ARTICLES in *Great Events from History: The Middle Ages, 477-1453*: 590-604: Reforms of Pope Gregory the Great; 596-597: See of Canterbury Is Established; 731: Bede Writes *Ecclesiastical History of the English People*; 12th-14th centuries: Social and Political Impact of Leprosy.

GREGORY VII

Italian pope (1073-1085)

As the dominant figure in the medieval Papacy, Gregory VII launched a wave of reform that brought about much of the structure of the modern Roman Catholic Church. His clash with Henry IV was merely the first in a series of struggles between the spiritual and temporal lords that characterized the Middle Ages.

BORN: c. 1020; Sanoa, Tuscany, Papal States (now in Italy)

DIED: May 25, 1085; Salerno, Principality of Salerno (now in Italy)

ALSO KNOWN AS: Hildebrand (given name)

AREAS OF ACHIEVEMENT: Religion and theology, church government

EARLY LIFE

Little is known of the early life of the man named Hildebrand who became Pope Gregory VII. He was born to a family of moderate means. Early biographers, seeking to create or emphasize parallels with the life of Christ, wrote of his early years playing among the wood chips at the feet of his father, a carpenter. Such a picture was greatly exaggerated. Though Hildebrand's father, Bonizo, a Roman citizen, was apparently of humble birth, his mother, Bertha, was well connected. Her brother was abbot of the monastery of Saint Mary, on the Aventine Hill in Rome.

Hildebrand was sent to his uncle and educated at Saint Mary's. He studied Latin rhetoric, mathematics, music, dialectics, and the teachings of the church fathers. He studied also at the Lateran Palace. Not surprisingly, after such an education, he decided to become a monk. He was appalled by the corruption of the Church and turned instead to the ascetic severities of monastic life. He entered the Benedictine order and traveled in both France and Germany.

Hildebrand returned to Rome as chaplain to Gregory VI, one of three rival claimants to the throne of Saint Peter. When all three were deposed by Emperor Henry III in favor of a German pope, Hildebrand left in exile with Gregory VI. He returned permanently to Rome with Bruno (Pope Leo IX) in 1049. According to tradition, the two traveled to Rome as pilgrims; Bruno refused the papacy until it was offered by the people and clergy of Rome. Hildebrand's subsequent term of service with Pope Leo IX began the long period of his influence in Rome and in the papal administration of the eleventh century.

Hildebrand was small and slightly built, with a swarthy complexion that was set off by his bright and piercing eyes. Though small in stature, Hildebrand played a giant's role for twenty-five years, during the reigns of Leo IX, Stephen IX, Benedict X, Nicholas II, and Alexander II. Hildebrand traveled to France to promote reform and represented the Papacy in Germany at the court of the queen regent during the minority of King Henry IV. On the death of Alexander II in 1073, Hildebrand called for three days of mourning. In the midst of the funeral service, however, the crowd shouted out their desire for Hildebrand to become pope. The cardinals led him to the throne of Saint Peter and there invested him as Pope Gregory VII.

LIFE'S WORK

Gregory VII is the dominant figure in eleventh century European religious history. He took a fragmented and corrupt Church and altered it irrevocably, establishing the norm of clerical celibacy and laying the foundation for the doctrine of papal infallibility. (Although the dogma of papal infallibility was not officially adopted by the Roman Catholic church until 1870, many popes before that time had claimed for themselves this supreme apostolic power.) His efforts to enlarge the domain of the

Pope Gregory VII. (Library of Congress)

Papacy led inevitably toward a prolonged clash with secular powers. Gregory set himself the task of establishing norms in three major areas: clerical celibacy, simony, and lay investiture.

During much of its history, the Catholic church had allowed its priests to marry. From the lowest local priests through the highest bishops, married clergy (or unmarried clergy with recognized concubines) were common in the eleventh century. Only in monasteries was celibacy required. Inspired by the reforms of the Cluny monastic movement in France, Gregory led an attack on married clergy, demanded celibacy, and endeavored (with varying degrees of success) to bar married clergy from the administration of the sacraments. Gregory believed that a married cleric would be not only diverted from single-minded devotion to God but also tempted to lay claim to the office as an inheritance for his children.

The second major reform issue was simony—the purchasing of church office. Because many church positions carried with them considerable territorial possessions and temporal power, they were often in great demand and were awarded on the basis of money paid. Gregory refused to tolerate this practice, condemning those who acquired office in this manner and refusing to allow them to officiate in religious services.

In addition to these two reforms, which concerned practices largely within the church, Gregory attacked the practice of lay investiture—and brought the Church into confrontation with the empire. Traditionally, kings had invested bishops and abbots with their emblems of office (the ring and staff), and the clergy thus invested served in a feudal relationship to the king as well as being responsible to their ecclesiastical superiors. In 1075, Gregory outlawed the practice of lay investiture. This action was truly revolutionary; predictably, it was ignored by the German emperor, Henry IV, who saw investiture as his royal prerogative (a position in which he was supported by the German clergy and nobility). It was also traditional for the king to consent to the election of the pope (though not actually to invest the pope with his official symbols).

In a document called *Dictatus papae*, Gregory listed the basic tenets of his philosophy—for it was more philosophy and politics than theology. Gregory claimed for the Papacy the right to correct abuses and laid down the foundation of papal supremacy by declaring that the clergy were dependent on the pope and that both laity and clergy were subject to the pope in all matters.

Gregory VII was also active in the secular world, seeking to extend the territorial holdings of the Papacy and to extend his authority in the German and Italian monarchies surrounding him. Inevitably, Gregory came into conflict with Henry IV, despite the fact that Henry had assented to Gregory's elevation to the papacy and the two had initially worked together. When Gregory declared that to disobey the pope was to disobey God's will, Henry became enraged. At the imperial synod at Worms in 1076, Henry deposed Gregory, who responded by excommunicating the emperor and suspending him from governing. It soon became clear to Henry that he had overreacted; he was told by his bishops and princes to seek reconciliation with the pope lest he lose his crown.

Henry determined to go to the pope and seek absolution. Crossing the Alps in midwinter, Henry met the pope at Canossa, where, barefoot and dressed in penitential sackcloth, the emperor received absolution. Although frequently viewed as a triumph of the Church over secular power (indeed, the phrase "go to Canossa" has come to mean "beg forgiveness"), it was in fact a royal victory. It suited Henry's political purposes to seek absolution from the pope, and Henry's presence in Italy created problems for Gregory.

The peace between these two strong men did not last long. Henry soon violated his agreements with the pope, and rebellious German nobles elected Rudolf of Swabia as king. In 1080, Gregory again excommunicated and deposed Henry, offering papal support to Rudolf. Meanwhile, Henry, in full control of the German clergy, declared Gregory deposed and supported the election of Guibert of Ravenna (Clement III) as antipope. Henry conquered Rome, installing Clement III in Saint Peter's; Henry was, in turn, crowned emperor by Clement in 1084. Gregory escaped Rome and fled to Salerno, where he died in 1085. According to one biographer, Gregory's last words were eloquent: "I have loved justice and hated iniquity, therefore I die in exile."

SIGNIFICANCE

Gregory VII played a major role in the development of the modern Roman Catholic Church. His pontificate was the turning point in the medieval Papacy. His insistence on clerical celibacy turned all the clergy into one great monastic order in an attempt to separate it forever from the conflicting claims of the secular world. His attack on simony and lay investiture similarly strengthened the Church, setting up barriers to the competitive claims of lay politics. Gregory's overriding achievement was to strengthen the Papacy and extend its influence. He was the first to claim for the pope universal authority. Calling the authority of the pope the authority of Christ, Gregory assumed the power to depose both bishops and emperors: As Christ had given to Saint Peter the power to bind or loose on earth, so the pope could claim such authority in Christ's name. Gregory endeavored to extend papal power over broad areas of Western Europe, seeking to establish papal authority in England, Spain, Corsica, Sardinia, Hungary, Serbia, and Kiev.

For the grandeur of his vision, his efforts to extend power, his zeal for an active life, and even his small stature, Gregory has often been compared to Napoleon. Although Gregory died in exile, deemed a failure by the world, he was triumphant in his effort to move the Church forward, reformed within and extending its power without. He fell as a result of his challenge to the power of the state in the person of Henry IV. It had not been his intention to seek conflict, but his zeal for reform and for expanded papal authority led him into the confrontation.

Gregory possessed a fiery and forceful personality, passionate beliefs, and an inflexible and uncompromising will. Such a man sowing the wind of reform—and in so doing asserting papal authority—could not fail to reap the whirlwind of opposition to his demands on the part of secular rulers. Like Luther in a later era, he could "do no other." In recognition of his formidable character and far-reaching accomplishments, Gregory VII was canonized by Pope Paul V in 1606. His papacy remains one of the rocks on which the Roman Catholic Church is built.

—*Carlanna L. Hendrick*

FURTHER READING

Cowdrey, H. E. J. *Pope Gregory VII*. New York: Oxford University Press, 1998. A comprehensive biography of Gregory VII that begins with background and examines his early years, his conflicts with Henry IV, the events at Canossa and their significance, the further conflicts between Gregory VII and Henry IV as well as with the German church, the issues in his final years, and his church reforms, including those regarding monasticism. Bibliography and index.

_______. *Popes and Church Reform in the Eleventh Century*. Burlington, Vt.: Ashgate/Variorum, 2000. A study on the topic of church reform in the eleventh century, dealing with Gregory VII's role as reformer.

Cushing, Kathleen G. *Papacy and Law in the Gregorian Revolution: The Canonistic Work of Anselm of Lucca*. New York: Oxford University Press, 1998. Primarily a work on Saint Anselm II's canonistic work, this volume also deals with Gregory VII and his influence on canon law.

Gregory VII. *The Correspondence of Pope Gregory VII: Selected Letters from the Registrum*. Translated by Ephraim Emerton. 1932. Reprint. New York: Columbia University Press, 1990. The introduction to this translation of some of Gregory VII's letters provides valuable information about his life and works. Bibliography and index.

_______. *The Register of Pope Gregory VIII, 1073-1085: An English Translation*. New York: Oxford University Press, 2002. This modern translation of Pope Gregory VII's register, along with the commentary, provides an invaluable look at the pope's life and thoughts. Bibliography and index.

SEE ALSO: Henry IV (of Germany); Leo IX; Matilda of Canossa; Urban II.

RELATED ARTICLES in *Great Events from History: The Middle Ages, 477-1453*: 1054: Beginning of the Rome-Constantinople Schism; November 27, 1095: Pope Urban II Calls the First Crusade.

Gregory IX

Italian pope (1227-1241)

With perseverance, courage, and conviction, under difficult circumstances, Gregory IX defended the Church from every perceived threat, encouraging spiritual life and learning within its structure, particularly in canon law.

Born: c. 1170; Anagni (now in Italy)
Died: August 22, 1241; Rome (now in Italy)
Also known as: Ugo of Segni (given name); Ugolino of Segni (variant of given name); Ugo or Ugolino di Segni (Italian version)
Areas of achievement: Religion and theology, church reform

Early Life

Little is known of the early life of Gregory IX. He was born Ugo or Ugolino, son of the count of Segni, and was descended from equally distinguished noblemen on his mother's side of the family. Ugo was a relative of Innocent III, arguably the most powerful pope of the Middle Ages. Research indicates that he was probably Innocent's grandnephew.

Contemporary biographers describe Ugo as a man of pleasing form, handsome features, and aristocratic bearing. He was also described as possessing a remarkable memory and an active mind. He was an eloquent speaker, and a biblical scholar of distinction who enjoyed discussion of scriptural texts. Said to have been a model of virtue, kind to others, and compassionate to those less fortunate than he, Ugo seems to have been genuinely interested in the spiritual life. Intellectually gifted, he studied at the University of Paris, and probably at Bologna, before being named chaplain to Innocent III. He was elevated to the position of cardinal-deacon of the Church of Saint Eustachius in 1198, and became cardinal-bishop of Ostia in 1206.

Throughout his pontificate, Ugo was close to Innocent III, accepting many embassies in his name, and traveling widely to represent papal interests. He was legate to the Germanies when rival claimants to the imperial crown brought on a war. German problems occupied Ugo until 1206. He also represented the pope in northern Italy, in both Tuscany and Lombardy. Innocent's successor, Honorius III, also used Ugo's negotiating skills in those territories to create peaceful cooperation between cities and to facilitate the preaching of a crusade. Wherever assigned, Ugo sought always to preserve ecclesiastical rights against secular encroachment and to foster clerical reform.

During Bishop Ugo's mission to northern Italy, he met Saint Francis of Assisi and was deeply impressed by his piety, simplicity, and zeal. Francis found in the bishop a man to be admired and trusted. Their lasting friendship played a great part in the future of the Franciscan order.

In 1220, Ugo was in Rome for the coronation of Holy Roman Emperor Frederick II and to encourage the new ruler to lead a crusade against the Turks as he had earlier sworn to do. Ugo returned to Lombardy for a period in 1221; from 1222 until Honorius III's death in 1227, he appears to have been in attendance at the papal court as a principal adviser. On March 19, 1227, after the burial ceremonies for Honorius III, the cardinals met and elected Ugo to the Papacy as Gregory IX. His coronation took place on Easter Sunday, April 11, 1227.

Life's Work

Gregory IX's fourteen-year pontificate was profoundly influenced by the long struggle with Frederick II, which seems to have been its dominant theme. Although this problem is central to any consideration of his papacy, Gregory did accomplish other goals worthy of attention. Gregory had the misfortune of inheriting old problems of church-state relations, as well as a powerful adversary in Frederick, called by his contemporaries "the wonder of the world."

Frederick II inherited from his father, Henry VI, claims to German lands and the imperial title. From his mother, Constance, he held Norman lands in southern Italy and Sicily. Ecclesiastical authorities in Rome perceived these combined realms, which surrounded the Papal States, as constituting a threat to church interests. Frederick's personality and ambition caused further concern. The twelfth and thirteenth centuries saw noteworthy growth in the power of medieval kingship. The Papacy, too, had developed as a medieval monarchy as well as a religious fount. This was to be an era of much dispute on the relative powers of the two jurisdictions. Clashes and challenges were inevitable.

From the moment of Gregory's accession, he urged the emperor and the faithful of Europe to undertake the promised crusade. Reluctantly, Frederick sailed in September of 1227, after keeping the crusading armies waiting for three months. Because disease and disaffection daily diminished the ranks of the fighting men, public opinion became critical of pope and emperor alike. Two days after the embarkation, Frederick returned, pleading ill health. Crusaders who finally arrived in the Holy Land found themselves leaderless and returned—or died in skirmishes resulting from this failed endeavor.

Gregory IX promptly excommunicated the emperor, who ignored the pope's action. Despite his public stance, Gregory privately sought a reconciliation by letter and by sending legates to the emperor. Frederick refused all overtures, and began his long struggle to become the absolute ruler of the territories he claimed, further antagonizing the Papacy by his treatment of clerics within his realm.

In June, 1228, Frederick left Italy for the Holy Land without notifying the pope of his intentions or asking that the excommunication be lifted. He took with him only a small army, since he intended not to fight but to negotiate a treaty with the Saracen authorities. The action brought on a second excommunication. Frederick concluded a treaty with the sultan that returned Jerusalem to Christian hands but failed to provide any defense against the Saracen power. Fearing papal intervention among his vassals, Frederick returned to Italy to assert his independence and regain control of his ancestral lands. From 1228 to 1229, negotiators tried to lessen the tensions between the two parties. In July of 1230, the Treaty of San Germano ushered in an uneasy truce that lasted until 1236. Hostilities were resumed when Frederick invaded Lombardy, arousing on the part of the pope support for the Lombard League against him. The struggle continued through the remaining years of the pontificate, ultimately contributing to the death of Gregory in 1241.

Despite the distraction of this struggle, Gregory was able to accomplish many of his goals. His devotion to learning resulted in a statement of privileges to the masters and students of Paris in 1231 that is regarded as the true charter of the university. The document deals with the government of the school and guarantees its intellectual freedom. In 1210, the Aristotelian texts on natural philosophy had been proscribed by a council and were no longer taught. Gregory wanted the works reconsidered because he found much that was useful in them, in spite of some portions that were regarded as detrimental. He commissioned a distinguished group of masters to examine the books and remove any erroneous or scandalous material so that Aristotle might again be studied.

One of the most significant achievements of Gregory's pontificate was his contribution to the development of canon law. Gregory was himself a shrewd and able lawyer. His experience at the papal court and as a legate had taught him the need of systematizing and unifying the great mass of ecclesiastical law. In the twelfth century, the monk Gratian had collected earlier law, attempting to reconcile its differences and present his own conclusions and synthesis in a volume known as the *Decretum* (c. 1140). Much more still needed to be done, however, as nearly a century of scholarly activity had swelled the collection of materials.

To this end, Gregory appointed the Dominican friar Raymond of Peñafort to compile material including his own decretals (responses of the popes to questions put to them by their bishops on various points of law; scholars known as decretalists researched them and attempted to clarify and organize these responses). The result was a useful compendium that became the basic text at the law school at Bologna. Raymond compiled the materials in five books containing two thousand sections. The work was widely acclaimed and became the basis for the developing body of canon law as well as an influence on other European legal traditions.

Gregory's legal interests also led to the establishment of the Inquisition in 1233. Alarmed by the successful spread of old heresies into Spain and Italy, as well as by

Pope Gregory IX. (Library of Congress)

the popular mob actions against them, Gregory established a separate tribunal under the direction of the new Dominican order. The episcopal office, with its inherent inquisitorial powers, had too many other duties to meet the immediate need. The tribunal was firmly grounded in law, although it did not meet modern concepts of justice.

At the end of his pontificate as at the beginning, Frederick II was the pope's nemesis. The emperor had created dissension in Rome, captured a number of leading churchmen, hanged members of the pope's family in northern Italy, and written against him. Finally, he blockaded Rome, forcing the ill and grieving pope to endure the unhealthy summer months there. Gregory IX died on August 22, 1241.

Significance

At Gregory IX's death, he was praised as a good shepherd, a noble and dedicated man. An enlightened figure in many ways for the times, he was torn between his duty as pope and his own desire for peace. He was keenly aware that Innocent III had established precedents for him to follow, but he was uncomfortable with military and political solutions, quickly offering alternatives to his adversaries. It was his misfortune to be pitted against a man of Frederick's ability and ambition.

This pope was far more at ease structuring the rule for the Franciscan order, presiding over the canonization of Francis, or protecting and assisting orders for religious women. Gregory was the patron of Saint Clare, a friend and disciple of Saint Francis who founded the Order of Poor Clares. He also befriended Agnes, daughter of the king of Bohemia, who wished to enter religious life rather than marry. Placing her under his protection, the pope helped her enter the Poor Clares.

Gregory's concern for women under monasticism led to concern for all women, and in 1227 he approved the Order of Saint Mary Magdalene, founded as a refuge for repentant prostitutes. These women were permitted to take vows as nuns in the order or to return to the world and marry.

Gregory's interest in spreading the Gospel to Africa and the northern reaches of the Baltic was never realized. Too many problems (including the Mongol invasion of Russia) frustrated these ambitions. Also doomed was his desire for reconciliation with the Eastern church, although some negotiations were opened and some talks took place.

In many ways, Gregory IX was a victim of the clash of church-state rights. The office he inherited had become so embroiled in political affairs that the question of the role of the spiritual in the world had to be addressed. As a lawyer, Gregory believed that his responsibility as the spiritual leader extended to the social consequences of political action. He therefore felt the need to intervene in secular affairs. To that end, Gregory IX tirelessly directed his time and energy throughout his pontificate.

—Anne R. Vizzier

Further Reading

Abulafia, David. *Frederick II: A Medieval Emperor.* 1988. Reprint. London: Pimlico, 1992. A biography of Frederick II. Contains illustrations, maps, bibliography, and index.

O'Gorman, Bob, and Mary Faulkner. "Glad You Asked: Q&A on Church Teaching: What Was the Inquisition?" *U.S. Catholic* 66, no. 10 (October, 2001): 28. This brief article traces the development and progress of the Inquisition, including its establishment by Pope Gregory IX.

Powell, James M. *Anatomy of a Crusade, 1213-1221.* Philadelphia: University of Pennsylvania Press, 1986. An examination of the Fifth Crusade and Frederick II's role in it. Contains maps, illustrations, a bibliography, and an index.

Robson, Michael. *Saint Francis of Assisi: The Legend and the Life.* London: Geoffre Chapman, 1999. A biography of Saint Francis that describes both the legends and his life. Bibliography and index.

Sabatier, Paul. *The Road to Assisi: The Essential Biography of Saint Francis.* Brewster, Mass.: Paraclete Press, 2003. A new edition of a classic biography of Saint Francis of Assisi by a French Protestant.

Shannon, Albert Clement. *The Medieval Inquisition.* 2d ed. Collegeville, Minn.: Liturgical Press, 1991. An examination of the Inquisition, established by Gregory IX, in the Middle Ages. Bibliography and index.

See also: Saint Anthony of Padua; Giovanni da Pian del Carpini; Saint Clare of Assisi; Saint Elizabeth of Hungary; Saint Francis of Assisi; Frederick II; Innocent III; Louis IX; Raymond of Peñafort; William of Auvergne; William of Auxerre.

Related articles in *Great Events from History: The Middle Ages, 477-1453*: April 16, 1209: Founding of the Franciscans; 1227-1230: Frederick II Leads the Sixth Crusade; 1228-1231: Teutonic Knights Bring Baltic Region Under Catholic Control; 1233: Papal Inquisition; c. 1250-1300: Homosexuality Criminalized and Subject to Death Penalty; c. 1265-1273: Thomas Aquinas Compiles the *Summa Theologica*; 1305-1417: Avignon Papacy and the Great Schism.

Guido d'Arezzo

Italian musician

Guido is generally credited with reestablishing solmization and with perfecting staff notation. His Micrologus, *a treatise on musical practice, was one of the most widely copied and read books on music in the Middle Ages.*

Born: c. 991; possibly Arezzo, Tuscany (now in Italy)
Died: 1050; Avellana (now in Italy)
Also known as: Guido of Arezzo; Guy of Arezzo; Guido Aretinus
Area of achievement: Music

Early Life

Guido d'Arezzo (GWEE-doh duh-REHT-soh) was probably born in Arezzo, although at least one source assigns Paris as his birthplace. Nothing is known about his early life and parentage. Music historians have managed, however, to piece together an approximate outline of his career from allusions and references in two letters written by Guido—one to Bishop Theobald of Arezzo, Guido's patron and mentor, and the other to Brother Michael of Pomposa, possibly the co-author of one of Guido's early musical texts.

Guido was educated at the Benedictine abbey at Pomposa, close to Ferrara on the Adriatic coast. It was probably at this abbey that he began studying music theory and developing his ideas of staff notation; certainly, while he was there he gained acclaim for his ability to train singers to learn new chants in a short time and with a minimum of effort. With his fellow brother Michael, Guido drafted an antiphonary—a collection of liturgical chants—notated according to Guido's new system. Although the antiphonary is now lost, it attracted much favorable attention in monasteries throughout Italy as well as resentment and scorn from Guido's fellow monks at Pomposa, who were wary of any departures from tradition and therefore scorned Guido's innovation.

At some point during his early training, Guido may have spent some time at the monastery of Saint-Maur-des-Fossés near Paris—his familiarity with the music treatise of Odo of Saint-Maur-des-Fossés is evident in his ideas on staff notation, which may have been refined at the French monastery. In his letter to Brother Michael, Guido advocates close study of a work entitled *Enchiridion*, which he attributes to Odo and from which he claims to have learned many of the musical principles underlying his notation system.

Life's Work

Around 1025, Guido moved to Arezzo at the invitation of Bishop Theobald, who appointed him to a teaching post at the cathedral school. Bishop Theobald later commissioned the *Micrologus de disciplina artis musicae* (after 1026; best known as *Micrologus*), which was dedicated to him at its completion. Guido remained under the protection of Bishop Theobald until at least 1036. As a music teacher, he trained singers for the cathedral services, presumably by using the new notation described in the antiphonary.

The *Micrologus*—one of the most influential books of its time—was designed for singers, with the object of improving their skill in using the new notation and in sightsinging both familiar and unfamiliar chants. Although much of the work is highly theoretical in both language and content, two chapters are of interest to lay musicians. In one, Guido compares the elements of a melody to the elements in a stanza of poetry: Individual melodic sounds correspond to letters of the alphabet, groups of sounds correspond to syllables, and groups of syllables become analogous to poetic feet. The other chapter, on organum—an early form of polyphony, or music with two or more independent voices—marks an important development in the history of counterpoint. Although common practice decreed two voices moving in parallel fourths and fifths, Guido introduced the idea of independent voices that could occasionally move apart or even cross, although the intervals between voices were restricted to consonances (sounds that were restful rather than discordant). As a comprehensive document on music theory and practice, the *Micrologus* was used extensively in both monasteries and universities during the Middle Ages and survives today in about seventy manuscripts dating from the eleventh to the fifteenth century.

Sometime around 1028, Guido traveled to Rome in the company of Dom Peter of Arezzo and Abbot Grunwald, possibly of Badicroce, to the south of Arezzo. The journey was undertaken at the request of Pope John XIX, who may have seen or heard of Guido and Brother Michael's antiphonary and the new system of notation and who wished to have Guido explain his pedagogical system. Before he could accomplish that task, Guido had to leave Rome as a result of ill health, although he did promise to return and resume his explanation of the new notation to the clergy. On the trip home, Guido paused for a visit with the abbot at Pomposa, who, having heard of Guido's visit to Rome, counseled Guido to avoid cities and to settle in a monastery, preferably Pomposa. Guido declined that invitation and about a year later joined the Camaldolese monastery in Avellana, where he eventually became prior.

Not long after his visit to Rome, Guido wrote the *Epistola de ignoto cantu* (c. 1028), a letter to Brother Michael in which he gave a full description of his theory of solmization, or the method of singing any liturgical melody through the use of the Aretinian scale, involving the six syllables—ut, re, mi, fa, sol, la—which today correspond to the first six tones of the major scale. Although Guido is often credited with inventing solmization, that technique was in fact known to the ancient Greeks; his contribution to music was to establish the practical application of solmization in singing technique. Guido derived the six syllables from a hymn to Saint John—*Ut queant laxis*—in which the six different phrases of the melody begin on six different notes in the ascending order of today's major scale. As with so many of Guido's contributions to music theory, a bit of scholarly controversy surrounds the origin of the hymn. Early historians credited Guido with its authorship, although later scholars identified the text in a manuscript dated around 800. The melody may be Guido's; in fact, he may have composed it as a pedagogical device to use in teaching sightsinging, a valuable skill for clergy and laymen charged with singing during church services. In the letter, Guido informed Brother Michael that the new system had enabled his choirboys to learn new chants rapidly; weeks of training, he wrote, had given way to singing chants on sight.

Two other pieces of writing by Guido are mentioned in some detail in medieval manuscripts. Written after 1030, both were apparently intended as introductory pieces for the lost antiphonary. The *Aliae regulae* (c. 1020-1025), intended as a guide to using the antiphonary, laments the time spent by young singers in learning liturgical chants and committing them to memory and outlines the advantages of a system of line notation—involving four lines and three spaces—based on height of pitch. In this essay, Guido proposes that the lines and spaces composing the system be named after the letters of the pitches they represent. Although he does not specify the number of lines to be thus identified, he does point out that he uses a yellow line for C and a red line for F, with a black line above C and another between C and F. Some manuscripts show a green line for B-flat, with other lines drawn in when necessary, although music historians believe these features to be additions by others and not Guido. The neumes (modern-day musical notes) rest on the lines and in the spaces. Although a number of eleventh and twelfth century manuscripts display the new notation with Guido's colors, thirteenth century manuscripts show that the colored lines were eventually deemed unnecessary. The letter identifications survive today in the C, F, and G clefs. Guido did not invent alphabetical notation; the French were already using an alphabetical system involving the letters from A to P in the late 990's. As with solmization, Guido perfected an awkward system already in use. Guido's system of letter notation uses only the letters A to G in series of capital letters, small letters, and double small letters. The *Regulae rhythmicae in antiphonarii sui prologum prolate* (c. 1025-1027; *Guido D'Arezzo's "Regule rithmice," "Prologue in antiphonarium," and "Epistola ad michahelem,"* 1999), also a prologue and written in verse, contains short explanations of several musical concepts—such as intervals and modes and the gamut, or range, of notes available to the singer—described in the *Micrologus*. In addition, Guido expounds further his ideas of a system of notation using colored and lettered lines.

Sigibertus Gemblacensis, a twelfth century theorist, credits Guido with the invention of a pedagogical device called the Guidonian Hand, also known as a hexachord. This device involved labeling each of the nineteen phalanges of the open left hand with nineteen of the notes in the gamut, with the twentieth note in the air above the tip of the middle finger. The Guidonian Hand functioned as an aid in teaching solmization by providing the singer with a visible aid to memorizing intervals. Popular during the Middle Ages, the Guidonian Hand was widely used by singers in learning Gregorian chants. Modern music historians have discounted the notion that Guido invented the Guidonian Hand (although it was named for him); the basic idea of the hand appears in manuscripts dating before Guido's lifetime. More than likely, he popularized and refined an older technique that had been largely ignored by lay musicians and music teachers.

SIGNIFICANCE

Although Guido's enthusiastic admirers through the centuries have credited him with various musical inventions, it seems clear that he was a popularizer rather than an inventor. He himself acknowledged, in the letter to Brother Michael, that he was merely simplifying ideas already in circulation among innovative musicians. Nevertheless, Guido's significant contributions to music are many: He was a renowned teacher in an age when music pedagogy was just becoming a discipline; he saw the practical applications of theoretical concepts and devised ways to teach those applications to singers; and he disseminated his ideas to the world through his writing.

The extent of Guido's influence as a musicologist and teacher is evident in the number of commentaries on his work from the eleventh century to the Renaissance. Written by other music theorists—many of them anonymous—from Italy, England, and Belgium, these commentaries demonstrate the impact of Guido's innovations and reforms on the development of polyphonic liturgical music and on the pedagogical methods used in training singers in monasteries and the great cathedral schools of the Middle Ages. Guido's ideas were disseminated through these commentaries and through copies of his works, which were distributed widely. As late as the sixteenth century, an elaborately illustrated compilation consisting mainly of Guido's *Regulae rhythmicae in antiphonarii prologum prolate* and the *Epistola de ignoto cantu* was circulated as Guido's *Introductorium*.

—*E. D. Huntley*

FURTHER READING

Brockett, Clyde Waring, Jr. "A Comparison of the Five Monochords of Guido of Arezzo." *Current Musicology* 32 (1981): 29-42. A discussion of the five versions of the monochord (a single-string pitch finder and interval-measuring device) described in the musical treatises of Guido d'Arezzo. The author uses the descriptions as a point of departure for a comparison of the ideas elaborated in Guido's writings.

Burtius, Nicolaus. *Musices Opusculum*. Translated by Clement A. Miller. Neuhausen-Stuttgart: Hänssler-Verlag, 1983. A translation of a fifteenth century work on music theory that discusses Guido. Bibliography and index.

Crocker, Richard, and David Hiley, eds. *The Early Middle Ages to 1300*. 2d ed. New York: Oxford University Press, 1990. Part of the New Oxford History of Music series, this work presents a history and criticism of music in the early Middle Ages. Bibliography and index.

Flynn, William T. *Medieval Music as Medieval Exegesis*. Lanham, Md.: Scarecrow Press, 1999. This examination of liturgical music in the Middle Ages includes a discussion of the teaching of singing. Bibliography and index.

Pesce, Dolores. *Guido d'Arezzo's "Regule rithmice," "Prologus in antiphonarium," and "Epistola ad michahelem": A Critical Text and Translation with an Introduction, Annotations, Indices, and New Manuscript Inventories*. Ottawa, Canada: Institute of Mediaeval Music, 1999. A translation of some of the writings on music theory by Guido. Bibliography and indexes.

SEE ALSO: Adam de la Halle; John Dunstable; Hildegard von Bingen; Francesco Landini; Guillaume de Machaut; Johannes de Muris; Pérotin; Philippe de Vitry; Wang Wei.

RELATED ARTICLES in *Great Events from History: The Middle Ages, 477-1453*: 590-604: Reforms of Pope Gregory the Great; After 1000: Development of Miracle and Mystery Plays.

JOHANN GUTENBERG

German inventor

Gutenberg invented printing with movable metal type and initiated the printing of the forty-two-line Bible, setting in motion a cultural revolution.

BORN: 1394-1399; Mainz (now in Germany)
DIED: Probably February 3, 1468; Mainz
ALSO KNOWN AS: Johannes Gensfleisch zur Laden (given name)
AREAS OF ACHIEVEMENT: Science and technology, literature

EARLY LIFE

Johann Gutenberg (YOH-hahn GEW-tehn-buhrg) was born in Mainz, an important German city on the Rhine River that was the seat of an archbishop. In the absence of a documented record, his birth date is placed between 1394 and 1399. His family, known as Gensfleisch zur Laden, was of the patrician class, but they were generally called Gutenberg, after their place of residence. Most members of his father's family were skilled metal craftsmen for the archbishop's mint in Mainz. Although there is no firm evidence about Gutenberg's education, he presumably continued his family's association with metalworking by being trained in this craft.

During his youth, Mainz was experiencing political turmoil because of conflicts between patrician and working classes. This civil strife led Gutenberg's father, Friele zum Gutenberg, to go into exile from the city in 1411. After similar disruptions in 1428, during which the Mainz guilds revoked civic privileges from the patricians, Gutenberg, who was probably around thirty years old at that time, settled in Strasbourg, a German city on the Rhine.

LIFE'S WORK

Gutenberg's activities during his mature life are of primary interest because of the evidence they contribute to knowledge about the invention of printing with movable type in Western Europe. His life and work can be divided into two chronological periods. During the first period, between 1428 and 1448, when he was living in Strasbourg, he probably began developing the printing process. In the last twenty years of his life, from 1448 to 1468, he returned to Mainz, where he brought his invention of printing with movable metal type to fruition in a Bible (now known as the Gutenberg Bible, the first complete book printed with movable metal type in Europe) and other printed books.

Johann Gutenberg. (Library of Congress)

Information about Gutenberg's life in Strasbourg comes mainly from court records of lawsuits in which he was involved. Except for one case in 1436, when he was sued for breach of promise regarding marriage, these records are important because they show that he both practiced metalworking and was developing printing technology. One lawsuit in 1439 provides useful insights into Gutenberg's involvement with printing. The suit arose because, in 1438, Gutenberg had formed a partnership with several Strasbourg citizens to produce mirrors to be sold to pilgrims on a forthcoming pilgrimage to Aachen. On learning that the pilgrimage was to take place a year later than they had anticipated, the partners entered into a new contract with Gutenberg so that he would instruct them in other arts that he knew. One clause stipulated that if a partner died, his heirs would receive monetary compensation instead of being taken into the partnership. Soon after the contract was negotiated, one of the partners, Andreas Dritzehn, died, and his two brothers sued to become partners. The court determined that the contract was valid, and Gutenberg won the case.

Testimony of witnesses for this lawsuit has been interpreted as showing that Gutenberg was experimenting with printing using movable metal type. A goldsmith testified that Gutenberg paid him for "materials pertaining to printing." One witness mentioned purchases of metal, a press, and *Formen* (which became the German word for type). Another described how Gutenberg instructed him to dismantle and place on the press an object consisting of four pieces held together with screws that had been reconstructed as a typecasting mold. These combined references indicate that Gutenberg was working out the printing process, but no tangible evidence of his work with printing from this Strasbourg period has survived.

By 1448, Gutenberg had returned to Mainz. One document—a record of an oath made by Johann Fust on November 6, 1455, during a lawsuit that Fust, a Mainz businessman, had brought against Gutenberg—helps to reconstruct Gutenberg's work in Mainz from around 1448 to 1455. The document, known as the Helmasperger Instrument from the name of the notary who drew it up, also has been used to connect this activity with the production of the Gutenberg Bible.

Fust was suing to recover loans that he had made to Gutenberg. The first loan of eight hundred guilders at 6 percent interest was made in 1450 and the second, also for eight hundred guilders with interest, in 1452. The loans were intended to provide for expenses in making equipment, paying workers' wages, and purchasing paper, parchment, and ink. In the second loan, Fust and Gutenberg became partners for "the work of the books." Testimony also establishes that Gutenberg had several workers and assistants. Peter Schoeffer, who had earlier been a scribe, was a witness for Fust, and soon thereafter Fust and Schoeffer established a flourishing printing business in Mainz. Gutenberg's two witnesses, Berthold Ruppel and Heinrich Kefer, who were his servants or workmen, also later became independent printers. Fust won the suit, since the court decided that Gutenberg should repay the original loan with interest. This document indicates that Gutenberg, using capital loaned to him by Fust, was operating a workshop with assistants for the purpose of producing books, probably by printing.

Bibliographical study of the Gutenberg Bible adds evidence to support the theory that Gutenberg's primary "work of the books" was printing the Gutenberg Bible. Notation in a copy of this Bible at the Bibliothèque Nationale in Paris indicates that Heinrich Cremer, vicar of the Church of Saint Stephen at Mainz, completed its rubrication and binding in two volumes in August, 1456. Study of paper, ink, and typography of the Gutenberg Bible suggests that it was in production between 1452 and 1454. This analysis also demonstrates that several presses were printing this Bible simultaneously. Thus, evidence from examination of surviving copies of the Gutenberg Bible correlates with information from Fust's lawsuit to show that the Bible was at or near completion at the time of the 1455 suit. Also, the substantial amount of money loaned and the types of expenses for equipment, supplies, and wages for several workmen are consistent with the production scale using several presses. Scholars have thus concluded that soon after Gutenberg returned to Mainz, he was responsible for producing the first complete printed book in Western Europe, the Gutenberg Bible.

A major question about Gutenberg's later life concerns his continued production of printed books after Fust's lawsuit in 1455. Again, documented evidence about this period is meager. He seems to have received some patronage and support from Konrad Humery, a Mainz canonist, who, after Gutenberg's death in early February, 1468, attested that he owned Gutenberg's printing equipment and materials. In addition, in 1465, the archbishop of Mainz had accorded Gutenberg a civil pension whose privileges included an annual allowance for a suit of clothes, allotments of corn and wine, and exemption from taxes.

Determining Gutenberg's production of printed matter besides the Gutenberg Bible therefore depends on interpretation of these documents, including the financial ramifications of the 1455 lawsuit, and especially bibliographical analysis of early examples of printing. One group of these printed materials is called the B36 group. The name comes from a Gothic type similar to but somewhat larger and less refined than the type used for the forty-two-line Gutenberg Bible. Works associated with this group include some broadsides, traditional grammar texts by the Roman author Donatus, and a thirty-six-line Bible printed in Bamberg, dated 1458-1459. Another group comes from the press that printed the *Catholicon*, a Latin dictionary put together in a smaller Gothic type by Johannes Balbus in Mainz in 1460. At least two other books and broadsides are connected with this press.

According to some sources, Gutenberg had to give up his printing materials to satisfy repayment to Fust. This financial disaster, combined with the somewhat inferior quality of printing using variants of the thirty-six-line Bible type, suggests that few, if any, other surviving early printed works can be attributed to Gutenberg. Another interpretation holds that the settlement with Fust did not deplete Gutenberg's financial or material resources to which Humery's support added. The comparative irregularities in the B36 type show that it was being developed earlier than the perfected Gutenberg Bible font, and this evidence suggests that Gutenberg was printing other works concurrently with and subsequently to the Gutenberg Bible using this more experimental type. Technical innovations in the type and setting of the *Catholicon*, along with its colophon extolling the new printing process, make Gutenberg, the inventor of printing, the person most likely to have executed the printing from the *Catholicon* press. Thus, it makes sense that Gutenberg probably printed various items comprising the B36 and *Catholicon* press groups throughout his career based in Mainz.

SIGNIFICANCE

While further research in many areas will continue to add greater precision to identifying the corpus of Johann Gutenberg's printed works, his most significant achievement is the invention of printing with movable metal type. From the 1430's to the completion of the Gutenberg Bible around 1455, Gutenberg utilized his metalworking skills to develop a process of casting individual letters that could be arranged repeatedly into any alphabetic text. When combined with paper, his new oil-based typographic ink, and a printing press, Gutenberg's process succeeded in merging several distinct technologies, making possible the production of multiple identical copies of a text. Although the changes that printing brought developed gradually during the succeeding centuries, the use of printing has had major effects on almost every aspect of human endeavor—including communications and literacy, economic patterns of investment, production, and marketing, and a wide range of intellectual ideas.

The Gutenberg Bible is an outstanding symbol of his invention. The copies that are still extant (forty-eight out of an original printing of about 180) demonstrate the high level of technical and aesthetic perfection that this 1,282-page book attained. The regularity of the lines, the justification of the margins, the quality of the ink, and especially the beautiful design of the type show how Gutenberg raised the printing process beyond a technological invention to an art.

—*Karen K. Gould*

FURTHER READING

Davies, Martin. *The Gutenberg Bible.* London: British Library, 1996. Examines both how the Bible was printed and the spread and impact of printing across Europe. Bibliography.

Febvre, Lucien, and Henri-Jean Martin. Translated by David Gerard. 1976. Reprint. *The Coming of the Book: The Impact of Printing, 1450-1800.* London: Verso, 1997. Discusses Gutenberg's role in the invention of printing in the context of the transition from manuscripts to printed books. Also examines the impact of printing on varied aspects of book production and the book trade in early modern Europe. Maps, bibliography, index.

Fuhrmann, Otto W. *Gutenberg and the Strasbourg Documents of 1439: An Interpretation.* New York: Press of the Woolly Whale, 1940. Gives a transcription of the original German text of the lawsuit against Gutenberg in Strasbourg in 1439 that is important for reconstructing Gutenberg's early printing efforts. The book provides translations in modern English, German, and French, as well as a discussion of the meaning of the Strasbourg suit.

Goff, Frederick R. *The Permanence of Johann Gutenberg.* Austin: University of Texas at Austin, Humanities Research Center, 1969. Includes an essay on Gutenberg's invention and evidence for what he printed. Also discusses the significance of Gutenberg's invention.

Ing, Janet. "Searching for Gutenberg in the 1980's." *Fine Print* 12 (1986): 212-215. This article summarizes the technical bibliographical studies concerning Gutenberg's printing during the twentieth century. Its focus is on scientific methods of analysis of paper and ink and typographical studies done in the 1970's and 1980's. References are included.

Kapr, Albert. *Johann Gutenberg: The Man and His Invention.* Translated by Douglas Martin. Brookfield, Vt.: Scolar Press, 1996. Covers Gutenberg's origins, early life, apprenticeship, and travel; the technical problems of inventing the printing press; his business; the Mainz archbishops' war; and more. Illustrations, bibliography, index.

Lehmann-Haupt, Helmut. *Gutenberg and the Master of the Playing Cards.* New Haven, Conn.: Yale University Press, 1966. Suggests that Gutenberg may have been involved with developing techniques for printed reproduction of designs for book decoration and illustration necessary to produce, in printed form, the effect of finely illuminated manuscripts.

McMurtrie, Douglas C. *The Gutenberg Documents.* New York: Oxford University Press, 1941. Contains all the known documents associated with Gutenberg in English translation. Includes notes.

Man, John. *Gutenberg: How One Man Remade the World with Words.* New York: John Wiley & Sons, 2002. Explores the vast effects of Gutenberg's invention on science, literature, the understanding of the past, Christian (dis)unity, politics and the rise of nation-states, and more. Also examines Gutenberg as a determined and ambitious risk taker in the often repressive context of his times. Bibliography, index.

Needham, Paul. "Johann Gutenberg and the Catholicon Press." *Papers of the Bibliographical Society of America* 76 (1982): 395-456. Discusses bibliographical problems relating particularly to evidence from paper and typography in works from the *Catholicon* press. Needham's conclusions summarize arguments for Gutenberg's role in printing material in the *Catholicon* press group.

Painter, George D. "Gutenberg and the B36 Group: A Re-Consideration." In *Essays in Honor of Victor Scholderer,* edited by Dennis F. Rhodes. Mainz: Karl Pressler, 1970. This article discusses the examples of

printing in the B36 group and argues that Gutenberg printed these pieces.
Scholderer, Victor. *Johann Gutenberg: The Inventor of Printing*. 1963. Rev. ed. London: Trustees of the British Museum, 1970. The most complete biography of Gutenberg in English. It covers the various types of evidence for documenting Gutenberg's life and activity as the inventor of printing. Contains bibliographical references and good illustrations.

SEE ALSO: Jean Froissart; Poggio.

RELATED ARTICLES in *Great Events from History: The Middle Ages, 477-1453*: 7th-8th centuries: Papermaking Spreads to Korea, Japan, and Central Asia; 713-741: First Newspapers in China; 868: First Book Printed; c. 1045: Bi Sheng Develops Movable Earthenware Type; c. 1450: Gutenberg Pioneers the Printing Press.

GUY DE CHAULIAC

French writer and historian

Guy de Chauliac wrote the most important treatise on surgery during the later Middle Ages. For more than two centuries, he was considered the leading authority on such diverse medical topics as dissection, surgical procedure, professional ethics, leprosy, anatomical structure, pharmaceutical drugs, dental care, ophthalmology, and plague origins, symptoms, and preventions.

BORN: c. 1290; Chauliac, Auvergne, France
DIED: July 25, 1368; Avignon, France
ALSO KNOWN AS: Guigo (or Guido) de Chaulhaco (or Cauliaco, Caillat, or Chaulhac)
AREAS OF ACHIEVEMENT: Medicine, historiography

EARLY LIFE

Of agrarian, peasant stock, Guy de Chauliac (gee-duh-shohl-yahk) exhibited intellectual abilities early in his youth and was supported in his subsequent academic pursuits by the lords of Mercœur. He first studied medicine in Toulouse and completed his initial medical training in Montpellier under Raymond of Molières. Later, in Bologna, he mastered anatomy under Niccolò Bertruccio, renowned for his pioneering achievements in describing the construction and operation of the brain. Guy perfected his surgical techniques under Alberto of Bologna.

Bologna was vitally important to Guy's career because of its long and distinguished medical history. As early as the middle of the twelfth century, it had a medical faculty that taught Latin translations of Arabic texts, especially those of Avicenna. Of particular significance to Guy's development were the writings of William of Saliceto, a surgeon who produced a treatise in 1275 describing human dissection; Thaddeus of Florence, who encouraged scholar-physicians to make direct translations from the Greek masters; and Mondino dei Liucci, who publicly dissected corpses. Mondino's *Anatomia*, a practical manual of dissection completed in 1316, was the most popular textbook on anatomy before that of Vesalius in the sixteenth century. Finally, Henry of Mondeville, a fellow student of Mondino at Bologna, brought these techniques in the first decade of the fourteenth century to Montpellier. All of these brilliant masters played a major role in Guy's perspective, procedure, and philosophy of medicine.

After his university career, Guy practiced medicine in Paris from 1315 to 1320. Thereafter, he served for an extended period of time in Lyon, where he also was a canon and provost of Saint-Just; he acquired similar posts later at Reims and at Mende. For much of his later life he resided in Avignon, where he was the personal physician to Clement VI, Innocent VI, and Urban V. He also served these pontiffs as a personal auditor and judge.

It was during these Avignonese years that Guy witnessed some of the most catastrophic events in human history: the Black Death of the mid-1300's, which killed approximately one-third of Europe's population, and the initial bloody episodes of the Hundred Years' War (1337-1453) between England and France. In this tragic setting, Guy wrote the most important medical text of the later Middle Ages.

LIFE'S WORK

In 1363, Guy finished his masterpiece—the *Chirurgia magna* (*The Cyrurgie of Guy de Chauliac*, 1971)—and dedicated it to his former colleagues and masters at Montpellier, Bologna, Paris, and Avignon. Systematic and comprehensive, this work contains a synthesis of the best medical ideas of his age, an intensive analysis of earlier literature, especially the treatises of Galen, Aristotle,

Rhazes, Albucasis, Avicenna, and Averroës, and a litany of hundreds of his own personal observations.

The Cyrurgie of Guy de Chauliac consists of seven major sections (*tractates*), but it is preceded by an introduction (*capitulum singulare*) that provides personal information on Guy's life and advises physicians to acquire a liberal education, maintain a proper diet, keep excellent care of their instruments, and conduct correct surgical procedures. He warned them not to shun patients out of fear as was commonplace during the outbreaks of the Black Death and lambasted the fables perpetrated by some of his predecessors. He cautioned against relying on the occult even though he himself occasionally slipped and recommended occult remedies. Guy was concerned with the total education of physicians, their health and physical appearance, their office procedures and equipment, and their ethics and personal deportment. Not since Hippocrates had this facet of the profession been given such intensive emphasis.

In the first section of *The Cyrurgie of Guy de Chauliac*, Guy presents a brief exegesis on anatomy based largely on Galen and Bertruccio. More detailed than the anatomical treatise of Mondino, it stresses the need for all surgeons to be knowledgeable in all facets of this discipline. Some of the format was based on Guy's experience of assisting at dissections and postmortems.

The next section is one of the most popular, durable, and influential in the book. Dealing generally with carbuncles, abscesses, and tumors, Guy recommended operating on cancer in its earliest stages. He described in detail the plague that had recently ravaged Avignon. Based on personal observation and a brief bout with the disease, he described its origins in Asia, its causes (unfortunately ascribing them to a number of popular superstitions), its contagious nature, and its prevention. Concerning plague symptoms, Guy lists fever, pains in the side or chest, coughing, shortness of breath, rapid pulse, vomiting of blood, and the appearance of buboes in the groin, under the armpit, or behind the ears. Distinguishing between the bubonic and pneumonic types, he recommended such divergent preventive measures as the avoidance of damp places, the burning of aromatic wood, the abstention from violent exercise and hot baths, and the use of antidotes and drugs.

Section 3 deals with various kinds of wounds, diets for wounded persons, diseases contracted after being wounded, and treatments. Once again, it was unfortunate that he recommended the Galenic method of applying salves and ointments. His contemporary Mondeville had

Engraving of Guy de Chauliac by Ambroise Tardieu. (Library of Congress)

pioneered in the antiseptic treatment of wounds that included cleaning them with wine, stitching their edges, keeping them dry and clean, and permitting nature to heal them. These techniques became standard by the later stages of the Hundred Years' War. Nevertheless, Guy did provide valuable insights in his discussions of the escape of the cerebrospinal fluid, the effect of pressure on respiration, the closing of chest wounds, and the extreme caution needed in treating abdominal wounds.

After describing the numerous types of ulcers in section 4, Guy devoted the entire next section to fractures and dislocations. Although he contributed little original to existing literature, he provided a detailed procedure for treating fractures with splints, pulleys, and weights. His treatments for dislocations of the hands and feet endured for centuries.

In section 6, Guy covered such diverse topics as sciatica, leprosy, localized illnesses, bladder stones, proper eye and dental care, and medical and dental equipment. His work in leprosy was of great importance. He drew attention to the excessive greasiness of a leper's skin and recommended segregation and proper medical treatment. So successful were these methods that by the sixteenth century there was a dramatic reduction in the number of new cases and some of the methods were applied to other diseases. He may have been the first to recommend the use of the catheter to diagnose stones in the bladder. He prescribed a powder made from cuttlebones and other substances for cleaning teeth, the use of ox bone for the replacement of lost teeth, and the fastening of gold wire around loose teeth for strengthening. He even prescribed spectacles as a remedy for poor sight after salves and lotions had failed. The last section catalogs an extremely comprehensive antidotary in which Guy lists about 750 medical substances. In the process, he was one of the first physicians to warn patients about the dangers of excessive or sustained drug use.

SIGNIFICANCE

Guy was the most famous and successful surgical writer of the Middle Ages. His *Chirurgia magna* was translated into French, Provençal, Catalan, Italian, English, Dutch, Hebrew, and Irish. Although criticized by some modern writers for his lack of originality, his primary intention was to summarize the knowledge of the most significant medical writers of his own and of preceding ages. Even the longer title of his work—*Inventorium sive collectorium in parte chirurgiciali medicine* (the inventory or collectory of surgery)—testifies to this overall goal. Consequently, he became a founder of didactic surgery—a teacher of surgery as well as a practicing physician-scientist.

Although never a professor of surgery in a prestigious university, Guy had the title of master of medicine conferred on him by the administrative authorities of the University of Montpellier shortly before his death. His surgical work was unparalleled until Ambroise Paré amended it toward the end of the sixteenth century, while his anatomical observations served as the scientific model until 1534 when Vesalius published his great treatise. In the fields of surgery, medicine, and anatomy, Guy served as a standardizer, transmitter, and synthesizer. He was a harbinger of the many significant breakthroughs in these fields that occurred in the scientific revolution.

—*Ronald Edward Zupko*

FURTHER READING

Campbell, Anna M. *The Black Death and Men of Learning*. New York: Columbia University Press, 1931. A classic study, with excellent coverage of the medical opinions of fourteenth century physicians on one of the greatest medical catastrophes in recorded history.

Crombie, A. C. *Augustine to Galileo: The History of Science, A.D. 400-1650*. London: Falcon Press, 1952. Extols Guy's position as the leading medical writer in Western Europe prior to the sixteenth century.

Hall, A. R. *The Scientific Revolution: 1500-1800*. 2d ed. Boston: Beacon Press, 1966. This work includes a discussion of the great debt that Ambroise Paré, the most famous sixteenth century French surgeon, owed to *The Cyrurgie of Guy de Chauliac*.

Kibre, Pearl. *Studies in Medieval Science: Alchemy, Astrology, Mathematics, and Medicine*. London: Hambledon Press, 1984. Discusses treatises by Guy and other contemporary medical writers found in the medieval libraries of Western Europe.

Mellick, S. A. "The Montpellier School and Guy de Chauliac." *Australian and New Zealand Journal of Surgery* 69, no. 4 (April, 1999): 297-301. Profiles Guy and his work, especially *The Cyrurgie of Guy de Chauliac*, and places the surgeon within the history of the ancient French university at Montpellier.

O'Boyle, Cornelius. *The Art of Medicine: Medical Teaching at the University of Paris, 1250-1400*. Boston: Brill, 1998. Discusses the history of the study and practice of medicine as art at the time of Guy. Includes an extensive bibliography and index.

Sarton, George. *Introduction to the History of Science: Science and Learning in the Fourteenth Century*. Vol. 3. Baltimore: Williams and Wilkins, 1947-1948. Comprehensively covers Guy's contributions to medieval anatomy and surgery. A landmark study in the history of science.

Sedgwick, W. T., and H. W. Tyler. *A Short History of Science*. Reprint. New York: Macmillan, 1939. This study describes Guy's debt to his Bolognese medical masters and to Henry of Mondeville, who brought the Italian methods to Montpellier.

Singer, Charles. *A Short History of Anatomy from the Greeks to Harvey*. Reprint. Mineola, N.Y.: Dover, 1957. Highlights Guy's position as a standardizer of medieval surgical practices.

Thorndike, Lynn. *A History of Magic and Experimental Science: The Fourteenth and Fifteenth Centuries*. Vols. 3 and 4. New York: Columbia University Press, 1934. Chapter 30 is devoted to Guy and his contemporary physicians, with a special emphasis on the impact of the Black Death on their work and their respective societies.

Wallner, Bjorn, ed. *The Middle English Translation of Guy de Chauliac's Anatomy, with Guy's Essay on the History of Medicine*. Lund, Sweden: CWK Gleerup,

1964. A valuable late fourteenth or early fifteenth century rendering of a portion of *The Cyrurgie of Guy de Chauliac*.

SEE ALSO: Pietro d'Abano; Arnold of Villanova; Averroës; Avicenna; Jacqueline Félicie; Saint Fulbert of Chartres; Hildegard von Bingen; Saint Isidore of Seville; Moses Maimonides; Paul of Aegina; al-Rāzī; Trotula.

RELATED ARTICLES in *Great Events from History: The Middle Ages, 477-1453*: 809: First Islamic Public Hospital; c. 1010-1015: Avicenna Writes His *Canon of Medicine*; 1100-1300: European Universities Emerge; c. 1150: Moors Transmit Classical Philosophy and Medicine to Europe; 1337-1453: Hundred Years' War; 1347-1352: Invasion of the Black Death in Europe.

GWENLLIAN VERCH GRUFFYDD

Welsh hereditary royalty

Gwenllian verch Gruffydd fought against Norman expansion and domination of medieval Wales. She is a legendary figure in Welsh history and is argued by some to be the compiler of the Mabinogion, *a group of medieval Welsh tales relating four loosely related adventures.*

BORN: c. 1085; Aberffraw Castle, Anglesey, Wales
DIED: 1136; Cydweli (now Kidwelly), Carmarthenshire, Wales
AREAS OF ACHIEVEMENT: Military, literature

EARLY LIFE

Gwenllian verch Gruffydd (ga-wen-lil-yun vurk GRIHF-ihth) was one of fourteen children born to Gruffydd ap Cynan, king of Gwynedd and lord of North Wales. She was sister to the great Owain Gwynedd, prince of North Wales (1137 to 1170). At eighteen Gwenllian eloped and married the prince of South Wales, Gruffydd ap Rhys ap Tewdwr, later king of Deheubarth in Dyfed, and son of her father's close ally and covictor of the Battle of Mynydd Carn in 1081. Gwenllian and Gruffydd had ten children.

LIFE'S WORK

Few details of Gwenllian's life are known, other than that she fought in the Battle of Maes in 1136 in an attempt to stave off a Norman incursion into South Wales. The background to this battle provides some insight into her life.

In 1095, when Gwenllian was about ten years old, the Anglo-Normans began a campaign to regain control of Wales. A core of Welsh resistance lay in the resurgent kingdom of Gwynedd, and the Normans directed their efforts in that area. The Welsh responded to Norman invasion by using guerrilla warfare, which had frustrated efforts of previous Norman expeditionary forces since the initial Norman invasion of Britain in 1066.

The Norman military machine was made up predominantly of professional, specialized, full-time mounted soldiers. This type of military was a rapid-response force adapted to fighting in open flat lands and was employed to seize and hold large tracts of land and bases of power. The military organization of the Welsh was very different. Welsh society consisted of tribes and clans that prized their autonomy and lived in mostly forested and mountainous terrain. The Welsh military was a loosely organized, part-time, volunteer infantry force designed to pursue feuds and conduct raiding and looting expeditions. The capture of loot and booty, especially cattle and agricultural goods, was a major focus of Welsh society. The Welsh were not an agrarian people; raiding and looting were means of survival and social advancement. The long series of Welsh revolts against Anglo-Norman rule was motivated less by feelings of nationalism and cultural pride and more by the loss of rich hereditary lands as sources of goods.

Previously, the Normans had attempted conquest of Wales through devastation and destruction of Welsh forces. This was ineffective, because Welsh clans had little property to destroy and their armies were not organized into a mass field force that could be defeated in outright combat. The Normans, on the other hand, were not able to fight the irregular warfare necessary to meet the Welsh on their own fighting terms. To assert their power, the Normans began a strategy of building castles in Wales. By using this construction gambit, they altered the way warfare was conducted in Wales, shifting military objectives from open combat to positional warfare. A strategically positioned castle could control vast areas of land. It could protect and hold conquered fertile lands to its rear and guard exits and entrances to safe havens of the Welsh uplands. Welsh raiders did not wish to risk slaughter by quick hitting Norman cavalry, so they began to stay in isolated Welsh-held territories.

However, the Normans became militarily complacent as a result of castle building. The Norman culture was based on mounted knights and massive landed estates. Mountainous and wooded hills were environments in which the horse brought no military power and the estates no profits. Unwilling to change their cultural strategy, the Normans did not produce a new military capable of waging successful mountain warfare. By not meeting this challenge, the Normans allowed the isolated forested and mountainous regions of Wales to become bastions for Welsh clans and traditional society. In these areas, Welsh clans and tribes began to expand their culture in the face of Anglo-Norman rule. Eventually, calls for rebellion were raised against the invaders who controlled the rich grazing lands and fertile lowlands and coasts.

After the death of Henry I in 1135 precipitated civil war in England, the Welsh once more revolted against outside Anglo-Norman rule. A Welsh army was raised in West Brycheiniog (Breconshire) and attacked Anglo-Norman settlements in Glower. A battle fought between Loughor and Swansea resulted in a victory for the Welsh and the loss of more than five hundred Norman knights.

Gruffydd ap Rhys, Gwenllian's husband, was inspired by this Welsh victory with the prospect of expelling all foreigners from his hereditary lands in South Wales. Determined to reestablish the integrity of his hereditary kingdom and end Anglo-Norman advances into southern and western Wales, Gruffydd ap Rhys and Gwenllian began fighting a guerrilla-style campaign from their base in the forest of Ystrad Tywi. In 1136, Gruffydd ap Rhys traveled north with one of his sons, seeking reinforcements from his father-in-law, to stop a rumored invasion of his home in Cardigan. In his absence, a fresh advance of Norman forces around Cydweli led Gwenllian to try to protect her husband's kingdom.

Gwenllian became aware of a combined force of Norman and allied troops landing on the Galmorgan coast in an effort to reinforce Baron Maurice de Londre's forces at Kidwelly Castle. Kidwelly Castle dominates a prominent ridge overlooking the junction of two rivers, Gwendraeth Fawr and Gwendraeth Fach, and the flat sea marshes of Carmarthen Bay. It was one of several twelfth century Norman castles built during the reign of Henry I to reinforce Norman power along the southern coast of Wales and command passage of rivers across which the road to the west passed. The first defensive structure at the site was a semicircular earthwork built in 1106 by Roger de Caen, bishop of Salisbury. That earthwork was expanded with masonry work by William de Londres, a companion of Fitz Hamon and his conquering Norman knights and the father of Maurice de Londres.

Gruffydd had left no contingency plans for military action in his absence, but Gwenllian, sensing an imminent threat, gathered her available forces and marched to intercept the Normans and their allies. She brought with her two of her young sons, Maelgwn and Morgan. Gwenllian marched from Ystrad Tywi to Cydweli and set an ambush at Mynydd y Garreg (Mount of Rocks), about one mile north of Kidwelly Castle. Her scouts reported the recently landed combined Norman force marching toward her position, so she ordered a large detachment to intercept them while the rest of her force remained in reserve. The Norman reinforcements, led by a Welsh traitor, Gruffudd ap Llewelyn, evaded the Welsh interception force and approached Mynydd y Garreg under cover of surrounding forest. There the Normans waited to attack. Two days after taking up position near Mynydd y Garreg, the full complement of Norman troops charged over the top of the hill in a surprise attack. Maurice de Londres and Geoffrey, constable of the bishop, simultaneously led mounted Norman knights from Kidwelly Castle, trapping Gwenllian's force in the field below Mynydd y Garreg. The field is still known as Maes Gwenllian, or Gwenllian's Field.

Gwenllian personally rallied and led her Welsh forces against the two-pronged, overwhelming Norman onslaught. Her force was overrun and quickly slaughtered around her. Her son, Maelgwn, died fighting at her side. Only a small number of prisoners were taken, including Gwenllian and her young son, Morgan. Though Gwenllian was wounded, Maurice de Londres, already carrying with him a reputation for brutality, showed no mercy and ordered Gwenllian's immediate battlefield execution. While the victorious Normans cheered, Gwenllian was beheaded in front of her son Morgan. Morgan was taken prisoner and died nine years later in prison.

Significance

Folk legend depicts Gwenllian in a heroic light: a beautiful, Boudicca-like British warrior, hair flowing from beneath a gleaming helmet, bloody sword in hand, exhorting her fighters on by her own gallant example. To whatever extent this image of Gwenllian is true, the reality is that she remains a footnote to history, about whom very little of substance is known. Nevertheless, her heroism and the very fact that legends grew around her is some indication of the esteem in which she is held for her role in the Battle of Maes, the history of Wales in general, and for influencing the Celtic attitudes toward the Norman invaders.

A legend persists that Gwenllian's headless ghost wandered Maes Gwenllian for centuries until someone finally searched the ancient battlefield, found her skull, and reunited it with her grave. A carved circular stone memorial to Gwenllian bearing an inscription and a Celtic knot presently rests outside the main entrance to Kidwelly Castle, Wales.

Another legend concerning Gwenllian verch Gruffydd suggests that she is the possible author or compiler of the *Mabinogion*, a group of medieval Welsh tales relating four loosely related adventures. The *Mabinogion* is in four parts, or branches, and draws on myths and the history of Celtic Britain with settings largely within Wales and the otherworld. While some researchers—notably Andrew Breeze—have suggested, based on textual evidence, that Gwenllian may have been instrumental in the construction of this medieval work, most scholars argue that the work evolved over centuries and passed from storyteller to storyteller, until being collected and compiled sometime during the late twelfth century.

—*Randall L. Milstein*

FURTHER READING

Breeze, Andrew. *Subverting Patriarchy: Princess Gwenllian and "The Mabinogi."* Proceedings of the Eleventh International Congress of Celtic Studies, Cork, Ireland, 1999. A scholarly argument suggesting Gwenllian's part in the composition or constructing of the *Mabinogion*.

Davies, John. *A History of Wales*. New York: Penguin Books, 1994. A comprehensive history of Wales and the Welsh peoples.

Ford, Patrick K. *The Mabinogi and Other Medieval Welsh Tales*. Berkeley: University of California Press, 1977. A modern translation of the *Mabinogion* with accompanying references and interpretations.

Jones, Thomas. *Brut y Tywysogyon: Or, The Chronicle of the Princes*. 2d ed. Cardiff: University of Wales Press, 1973. The translated text of the *Brut y Tywysogyon*, which chronicles the lives of the hereditary Welsh rulers.

Morris, Jan. *The Matter of Wales: Epic Views of a Small Country*. New York: Oxford University Press, 1984. A good general history of Wales with many photographs and maps.

Nelson, L. H. *The Normans in South Wales, 1070-1171*. Austin: University of Texas, 1966. An exploration of the Norman conquest of England and Southern Wales with a good accounting of the cultural differences between the native Welsh and invading continental Europeans.

Walker, David. *The Normans in Britain*. Oxford, England: Blackwell, 1995. An overview of the Anglo-Norman period in Wales, England, Scotland, and Ireland.

SEE ALSO: Henry I; Nest verch Rhys ap Tewdwr.

RELATED ARTICLE in *Great Events from History: The Middle Ages, 477-1453*: October 14, 1066: Battle of Hastings.

HAFIZ

Persian poet

The premier lyric poet in more than a millennium of literary expression in the Persian language, Hafiz represents the culmination of lyrical styles and modes that began some five centuries before him and remains a model for Iranian poets today.

BORN: c. 1320; Shīrāz, Persia (now in Iran)
DIED: 1389 or 1390; Shīrāz
ALSO KNOWN AS: Shams al-Dīn Muḥammed (given name); Ḥāfez
AREA OF ACHIEVEMENT: Literature

EARLY LIFE

Hafiz (KAH-fehz) was born sometime around 1320. His merchant father, who had emigrated from Eşfahān (Isfahan) sometime earlier, apparently died when Hafiz was young. Hafiz received a traditional education in Arabic, Qurʾānic studies, science, and literature. His poetry reveals an intimate familiarity with the five centuries of Persian literature that preceded him, as well as his knowledge of Islamic sciences and his special competence in Arabic. His pen name testifies to this last skill, because the word "Hafiz" denotes a person who has memorized the Qurʾān.

Little specific information is available on the private life of the most acclaimed Persian lyric poet in history. Citations in biographical dictionaries, references in chronicles and other historical sources, and possible autobiographical details in his poems are mostly unverifiable. Information is available, however, about the tumultuous political history of Hafiz's native province of Fārs and its capital, Shīrāz, during his lifetime.

At the time of Hafiz's birth, Maḥmūd Shāh Inju ruled Fārs in the name of the Il-Khanid ruler Abū Saʿīd. The latter's successor executed Maḥmūd in 1335. Anarchy ensued, as Maḥmūd's four sons strove to gain control over their father's kingdom. One of them, Abū Isḥāq, took over Shīrāz seven years later and ruled, albeit with opposition, until 1352. During this period, Hafiz composed poems in praise of Abū Isḥāq and one of his viziers; these poems show that he was a seriously regarded court poet by the time he was thirty years of age.

In 1353 came the capture of Shīrāz by the Mozaffarid leader called Mubāriz al-Dīn Muḥammad, who had Abū Isḥāq summarily beheaded in front of the Achaemenid ruins at Persepolis. Mubāriz al-Dīn, whose family was to control Shīrāz until 1393, imposed strict, puritanical Sunni religious observation on the city during his five-year reign, a situation Hafiz bewailed in several poems. In addition, Hafiz's signature on a manuscript dated 1355 implies that he had to seek work as a scribe at that time, either because he was not yet economically established as a poet or because he was out of favor with the Mozaffarid court. In 1358, Mubāriz al-Dīn was deposed, blinded, and succeeded by his son Jalāl al-Dīn Shāh Shujāʿ. Hafiz, whose lot improved when Shāh Shujāʿ ascended the throne, eulogized this royal patron in a number of poems.

LIFE'S WORK

It was during the long reign of Shah Shujāʿ, between 1358 and 1384, that Hafiz's fame began to spread throughout the Persian-speaking world, westward to the Arab world and Ottoman Empire, and eastward to Mughal India (Mogul Empire). Altogether, he composed some five hundred *ghazal* poems and a handful of poems in other traditional Persian verse forms. The fourteenth century was the culminating age of the Persian *ghazal*, and Hafiz was its apogee.

The *ghazal* is a conventional composition of usually between five and thirteen couplets, the first closed and the others open, resulting in a monorhyme pattern such as *aabaca*. Each constituent verse exhibits the same quantitative metrical pattern. The poet's nom de plume generally appears in a *ghazal*'s final couplet.

The basic subject of these poems was idealized love, treated with conventional, stylized imagery in an equally conventional diction. The Hafizian *ghazal*, while displaying amatory, mystical, and panegyrical modes typical of the verse form up to his day, is distinctive in its merging of modes, in Hafiz's creation of an ambivalent lyric world of love in which readers can sense both love of God and passion for a romanticized, this-worldly beloved. An example is the very famous *ghazal* with which Hafiz's *Dīvān* (c. 1368; *The Divan*, 1891) usually begins.

> O cupbearer, pass around a cup and hand it to me;
> for love appeared at first easy, but difficulties arose.
> In hope of the musk pod the zephyr eventually opens
> from those tresses, what blood spilt in hearts because
> of musky curls.
> Color the prayer-carpet with wine should the Magian
> elder so advise;
> for the wayfarer knows the way, and the stages.
> At beloved's abodes what security of pleasure can exist?

Every second the caravan bells cry out: tie up the loads.
Dark night, the fear of the waves, and such a terrifying
whirlpool—how can the lightburdened and shore-
bound fathom my state?
Everything has dragged me from self-interest to infamy;
how can that secret which inspires gatherings remain
secret?
If you desire the beloved's presence, Hafiz, don't be
absent;
when you meet whom you desire, let the world go, give
it up.

A reader's first impression of this poem is of polysemy and multiplicity of patterns of imagery, which is another typical feature of the Hafizian *ghazal*. Once the two levels of the speaker's emotional state as a lover are discerned, however, one begins to sense the poem's integrity. A quasi-temporal and physical setting is implied in the address in the opening couplet of the cupbearer. The speaker may be in a tavern, seeking consolation in wine for the pains of love. Those who have not given themselves wholeheartedly to love and who have not done the apparently blasphemous bidding of the Zoroastrian priest who is presumed privy to secrets of the heart cannot understand the lover's state. The true lover may lose his reputation. Nevertheless, as the speaker advises at the poem's close, a true lover has to be ready to give up everything.

As for the nature of this love, the seriousness of tone and the religious commitment voiced imply that the speaker is enamored of a romantic beloved but that at the same time he senses the presence of the Creator in the beloved or the potential proximity to God that might be achieved by heeding no calls but love. The translation communicates nothing of the aural force of tight patterns of rhyme, meter, and alliteration of the original Persian or its rhetorical richness in echoing earlier poets and employing conventional figures with touches of novelty. The original is quintessential Hafiz in its thematic ambivalence, powerful imagery, and rich decorativeness.

In 1365, Shah Shujāʿ's brother Maḥmūd laid siege to Shīrāz along with the Jalāyrid Shaykh Uways. Hafiz may have lived for a year or two in the 1370's in Eṣfahān or Yazd, but he spent most of his life in Shīrāz. In 1384, Zayn al-ʿĀbidīn succeeded Shah Shujāʿ, and internecine feuds continued within the Mozaffarid family. In 1387, Tamerlane, who had massacred seventy thousand people in Eṣfahān, reached Shīrāz and brought the Mozaffarid Dynasty under his control. He named Yaḥyā his local ruler. Soon, however, Yaḥyā's nephew Manṣūr overthrew his uncle, which brought Tamerlane's wrath down on Manṣūr and the whole Mozaffarid family, all of whom Tamerlane proceeded to execute. Hafiz, who had briefly enjoyed the patronage of Yaḥyā and Manṣūr, died two or three years before Tamerlane's second invasion of Shīrāz in 1393.

By the end of his life, Hafiz had become the most respected Middle Eastern lyric poet, a reputation that he retains to the present day. Curiously, however, he never authorized or supervised a collection of his poems. Consequently, the first manuscripts containing all of his *ghazals* were not compiled until a generation after his death, which led to textual problems persisting today with respect to the authenticity of some *ghazals*, of some of their constituent couplets, of the order of couplets within *ghazals*, and of verbal variants. Editorial efforts in Iran since the beginning of World War II have brought the text as close to reliability as is possible.

A further difficulty in the critical appreciation of Hafiz's *ghazals* is that only in the 1960's did serious literary criticism and analysis begin to be applied to Hafiz. Still, Hafiz's popularity has never diminished from his death to the present time.

SIGNIFICANCE

It would be difficult to exaggerate the admiration and respect that poetry lovers in the Persian-speaking world feel for Hafiz. Iranians from all walks of life still use verses from Hafiz's *The Divan* for prognostication; the Qurʾān is the only other book so used. Hafiz's tomb is Shīrāz's most popular monument. Modernist Iranian poets routinely declare their devotion to him and his relevance as inspiration for them. The recitation of Hafizian *ghazals* is a common activity at social gatherings.

Dating back to Sir William Jones's "A Persian Song" (1771), a rendition of the most famous among Hafiz's *ghazals* in the West, more attempts at translating his verses into English have been made than with respect to any other Persian poet. These translations, however, have generally failed to capture Hafiz's spirit and subtlety. Such literary giants as Johann Wolfgang von Goethe and Ralph Waldo Emerson have sensed and rightly lauded Hafiz's poetic genius, but English-speaking readers have only recently experienced convincing evidence in the form of appealing translations.

Part of the explanation for the unfortunate fact that a poet so revered and influential in his own culture should remain almost unknown in the English-speaking world six centuries after his death is that Hafiz's voice has had no Edward FitzGerald, as Omar Khayyám's epigrammatic quatrains did, nor a Matthew Arnold, as did Firdusi's epic *Shahnamah* (c. 1010; the book of kings) episode about Sohrab (Suhrāb) and his father Rostam (Rustam). In addition, lyric poetry, especially when very culture-specific in form and imagery, seems resistant to translation more than other literary species. The foregoing description of the *ghazal* verse form highlights two almost insurmountable translation problems: transmission of pervasive aural elements and effects from traditional Persian verse to English, and the communication in English of the textual richness and resonances of conventional images, themes, and vocabulary.

As for the nature of Hafiz's special appeal, one Iranian view sees him as a combination of the questioning spirit of Omar Khayyám (1048?-1123?), the lyricism and skill at versification of Saʿdi (1200-1291), and the intensity of feeling and spirit exhibited in the poetry of Jalāl al-Dīn Rūmī (1207-1273). From another perspective, Hafiz's special talent is seen as the ability to create a texture of ambivalence in his poetic world, continually forcing the reader to sense both material and spiritual planes of experience. In addition, above and beyond Khayyamic echoes in carpe diem invitations and assertions to the effect that scientific inquiry will not fathom the point to life, Hafiz's *ghazals* have a further appeal to Iranian readers in their frequent images of libertines, scandalous models of behavior who answer only to themselves and who disregard what others think or what those in power bid one to do. As this sort of libertine, Hafiz remains inspirational to readers whose own lives do not often allow for such defiant free-spiritedness. Finally, Hafiz's persistent joie de vivre and concomitant refusal to be depressed by the difficult times in which he lived have given hope to later readers who have found many reasons to despair.

—*Michael Craig Hillmann*

FURTHER READING

Browne, Edward G. "Hafiz of Shīrāz." In *A Literary History of Persia*. 1926. 4 vols. Reprint. Vol. 3. Cambridge, England: Cambridge University Press, 1969. A review by an eminent Western Persianist of the biographical lore on Hafiz, as well as a commentary on Hafiz translations and attendant problems. Bibliography.

Hafiz. *The Divan of Hafez: A Bilingual Text, Persian-English*. Translated by Reza Saberi. Lanham, Md.: University Press of America, 2002. Presents a translation of Hafiz's *Divan*, with facing Persian-English pages. Hafiz's life and work are discussed in the introduction. Includes a glossary.

_______. *Hafez: Dance of Life*. Translated by Michael Boylan. Washington, D.C.: Mage, 1988. Twelve plates by a leading Iranian painter giving a Sufi interpretation to twelve poems, which are translated freely by an American poet who emphasizes their earthbound and romantic elements, followed by an afterword that treats reasons for Hafiz's special appeal to Iranians. Brief bibliography.

_______. *Poems from the "Divan" of Hafiz*. 1897. New ed. Translated by Gertrude Lowthian Bell. London: William Heinemann, 1928. Still the most highly regarded English versions of Hafiz, containing forty-three *ghazals* in translation following a lengthy (and sometimes inaccurate) introduction presenting the historical background, the standard biographical lore, and a recapitulation of the extent of Sufi influence on Hafiz.

Hillmann, Michael C. "Classicism, Ornament, Ambivalence, and the Persian Muse." In *Iranian Culture: A Persianist View*. Lanham, Md.: University Press of America, 1988. An attempt to discern enduring Iranian cultural attitudes in an examination of aesthetic aspects and criteria discernible in Hafiz's *ghazals*, among them appreciation of tradition, formality, and ceremony, a penchant for embellishment and the ornamental, and a capacity for ambivalence in attitudes, ideas, beliefs, and standards. Bibliography.

_______. *Unity in the Ghazals of Hafez*. Minneapolis, Minn.: Bibliotheca Islamica, 1976. A formalist analysis of sixteen Hafizian *ghazals* in a response to long-standing charges by Iranian scholars and scholars of Asia that Hafiz's poems lack unity. Includes an extensive list in notes and bibliography of writings on Hafiz in European languages. Bibliography, index.

Meisami, Julie Scott. *Medieval Persian Court Poetry*. Princeton, N.J.: Princeton University Press, 1987. A medievalist's attempt to rescue traditional Persian court poetry from the disfavor into which it has fallen, through a demonstration of its similarities with medieval literature in the West. A chapter entitled "*Ghazal:* The Ideals of Love," deals with Sanāʾī (1050-1131) and Hafiz, who stand at the beginning and end of the period in which *ghazal* writing was at its peak. Bibliography, index.

Pourafzal, Haleh, and Roger Montgomery. *The Spiritual Wisdom of Haféz: Teachings of the Philosopher of Love*. Rochester, Vt.: Inner Traditions, 1998. A good introduction to Hafiz's poetry. Explores how his work speaks to current scholarship in philosophy, psychology, social theory, and education. Bibliographical references, index.

Yarshater, Ehsan, comp. and ed. *Persian Literature*. Albany, N.Y.: Bibliotheca Persica, 1988. The first comprehensive overview of Persian literature since shortly after World War II, with an article on medieval lyric poetry and another on Hafiz. Bibliography, index.

SEE ALSO: Firdusi; al-Jāḥiẓ; Omar Khayyám; Jalāl al-Dīn Rūmī; Saʿdi; Tamerlane.

RELATED ARTICLES in *Great Events from History: The Middle Ages, 477-1453*: 637-657: Islam Expands Throughout the Middle East; 1010: Firdusi Composes the *Shahnamah*; 1273: Sufi Order of Mawlawīyah Is Established.

AL-ḤALLĀJ

Persian mystic

Al-Ḥallāj's martyrdom for his unorthodox religious beliefs, including his experiences of mystical communion with Allāh, can be seen as both his intense personal faith and determined resistance to what he considered political wrongdoing and corruption at the highest levels of Islamic government in the tenth century.

BORN: c. 858; Ṭūr (now in Iran)
DIED: March 26, 922; Baghdad (now in Iraq)
ALSO KNOWN AS: Abū al-Mughīth al-Ḥusayn ibn Manṣūr al-Ḥallāj (full name)
AREAS OF ACHIEVEMENT: Religion and theology, philosophy

EARLY LIFE

Al-Ḥallāj (ahl-kahl-AHJ), whose surname ibn Manṣūr al-Ḥallāj means "son of Manṣūr the wool carder," was born in southern Iran. As a youth, he helped his father in the wool trade in various textile centers both in Iran and Iraq. While living in the ʿAbbāsid caliphal city of Wasit, half way between Baghdad and Basra, he gained his earliest education in Qurʾānic studies following the strict and literalist Sunni orthodox Hanbalite school of law.

After the family returned to Tustar in Iran, his exposure to Sunnism continued under the tutelage of the famous scholar Sahl. Sahl's influence, however, contained elements of esoteric interpretations of religious sources, some of which reflected patterns associated with Islam's earliest and perhaps most famous Sufi mystic, al-Ḥasan al-Baṣrī (642-728). Indeed al-Ḥallāj was soon attracted to Basra, known to be the center of Sufism, at that date dominated by the figure of al-Junayd (d. 910) and his contemporary ʿAmr al-Makki. Both of these mystics emphasized the importance of inner religious experience and withdrawal from society and matters of this world. In 877, al-Ḥallāj married the daughter of one of al-Junayd's secretaries and Sufi associate of ʿAmr al-Makki, Abū Yaʿqūb al-Aqta. One of the male children of this union, Hamd, would eventually compile the only firsthand account of his father's life and the controversy surrounding his teachings.

Already in this early stage of his life, al-Ḥallāj was opposed to signs of conflict between Muslim sectarian movements, and he sought a path that would emphasize unity and justice for all believers. However, he was exposed to tensions that had already led to violence between Sunnis (orthodox Muslims) and Shīʿites (a major sectarian offshoot). In particular, he witnessed firsthand strife at the time of the Shīʿite-supported black slave (Zanj) revolt in southern Iraq. This may have impelled him toward eclectic combinations from both mainstreams of Islam, as well as elements from other monotheistic traditions. This tendency soon led to Sunni accusations that he had abandoned his orthodox origins.

Al-Ḥallāj was so moved by his first experience of the minor pilgrimage to Mecca sometime in the mid-880's that he remained in the Holy City for an entire year. This sojourn among pilgrims from so many different areas seems to have strengthened his view that Sufi quietism and detachment was an imperfect path to the realization of true Islam.

LIFE'S WORK

Al-Ḥallāj's form of mysticism clearly combined individual religious inspiration with concern for the actual state of human existence on earth. It was his denunciation of the ruling elite's acceptance of, and participation in, the atmosphere of greed and corruption pervading Baghdad society that eventually led to his condemnation and execution in 922. Tradition has attributed to al-Ḥallāj's contemporary (and would-be protector), the official grand chamberlain Nasr, a revealing testimony: "Those who want him dead are the ministerial scribes."

It was al-Ḥallāj's rejection of ascetic quietism in Sufi

mysticism—the path originally attributed to al-Baṣrī—that brought him into a number of conflicts with critics in several different camps, including supporters of the "finality" of formal religious law, or Shariᶜa (referred to here as canonists, meaning guided by the text of religious law).

Perhaps it was the mixed influence of various Arabicized Iranian elements in his Tustar and Ahwaz homeland area between Iraq and Iran that impelled al-Ḥajjāj to integrate eclectic components into his teachings. Certainly one can find elements of Nestorian Christian (a mid-fifth century offshoot from Orthodox Christianity concentrated in Iraq and Iran), Jewish, pre-Islamic Zoroastrian, and unorthodox Muslim Mutazilite beliefs crisscrossing in his philosophy of religion. One of the most controversial components of this eclecticism would be al-Ḥallāj's views that Jesus was the true Mahdī (guide) who would return to right the spiritual errors of humankind and establish the "true" canonical path of Islamic laws.

However, there also was a political side to his teaching that displeased the ᶜAbbāsid caliph's elite bureaucracy. Reactions against him as a supposed agent of the Qarmathians (an extreme form of Shia opposition) may have served as an excuse to arrest him temporarily in 887 in the region between Sus in Iran and the official ᶜAbbāsid city of Wasit in Iraq and to subject him to public flogging. This public humiliation compelled him to quit the ᶜAbbāsid coreland altogether for the next five years. During this time he traveled through the Eastern Iranian province of Khorāsān and into the largely Turkish-speaking area near and beyond the Oxus River. By 893, however, he not only returned to his family in western Iran, but seems to have turned his methods of preaching to even more extreme subjects. His detractors gathered hearsay evidence that, for example, he was being welcomed in towns and villages in Fārs as a miracle worker.

Although such claims were clearly exaggerated, there is no doubt that mystical currents reflected in al-Ḥallāj's poetic corpus (destroyed after his martyrdom, but passed on in secondary manuscripts kept by his disciples) began to support two strains that made his fame, but also led to his demise as a presumed heretic. One of these strains was his claim that he had experienced direct communion with Allāh. Expressing this personal religious experience bordered on heresy, for Islam insists on the total unity of Allāh's existence, which is thought to surpass any comparison with human conceptions of existence. One of the most famous statements attributed to al-Ḥallāj, and certainly one that would have outraged orthodox scholars of *tawhid* (divine singularity), occurred when he proclaimed publicly, "I am the absolute truth" ("*Ana al-Haqq*"), a qualification reserved exclusively to describe Allāh. The other strain in al-Ḥallāj's teaching that fomented considerable controversy was his sense of, and apparent willing acceptance of, his impending martyrdom. Martyrdom seemed to be a condition for the final realization of his religious experience; he would finally embrace Allāh and disappear into (that is, become one with) the supreme deity.

After a second pilgrimage to Mecca in 894 (an event marked by the gathering of hundreds of his disciples dressed in rags to symbolize the rejection of worldly possessions), al-Ḥallāj's resumption of itinerant teaching carried him as far as India and into the Uighur Turkish regions of Central Asia. Islam had not penetrated fully in this region, and elements of Manichaeism (based on the dualism of good and evil) were still prevalent. Al-Ḥallāj preached against dualistic beliefs, predicting the coming of self-sacrificing (thus martyred) saints whose devotion to the love of Allāh (*mahaba*) would turn the balance of religion against the temptations of evil.

From this point al-Ḥallāj was almost certain to meet with denunciation for heresy if he returned (as he did in 902) to the conservative religious and political capital of Baghdad. Although supporters of strict interpretations of Islamic canon law, led by Muḥammad ibn Dāwūd, denounced al-Ḥallāj to Caliph al-Mutadid himself, the mystic escaped formal judgment once again. Nonetheless, after a third (two-year) extended pilgrimage to Mecca, he returned to restate openly the nonconformist tenets that finally led to his condemnation by a vizierial (ministerial) court.

Once again resident in Baghdad, al-Ḥallāj shocked conservative observers by building a replica of the Holy Shrine of Mecca (the Kaaba) in the courtyard of his house and carrying out the rituals of pilgrimage—an act that was considered a direct violation of Islamic law. When this was combined with his supposed involvement in a plot to remove the infant caliph al-Muqtadir and substitute a rival under his own spiritual guidance, there was no alternative but to flee again. This time, however, he was pursued, arrested, and held for nine years as a prisoner of the palace. Although he received personal patronage and protection from the grand chamberlain Nasr, intrigues that were political and financial as much as religious multiplied the denunciations against him, and the vizierial court condemned him to death.

After his public execution in 922, the martyred mystic's head was displayed in Baghdad and throughout the provinces (as far as Khorāsān), most likely to discourage would-be disciples from furthering reformist zeal. By reformist zeal, al-Ḥallāj's judges meant either the preaching of nonconformist religious tenets or opposing vizierial speculation and questionable financial dealings affecting the state and its responsibilities to the Islamic community.

SIGNIFICANCE

Al-Ḥallāj's life and martyrdom were certainly not typical, even considering the tolerable limits of marginality presented by Islamic mystics either before or after the zenith of Islamic society and culture around 1000 to 1100. Al-Ḥallāj's intense belief in the cause he espoused and the way he actively preached his beliefs set him apart from the other mystics of his time.

The accusations he leveled at ordinary Islamic belief patterns were one thing; his denunciation of high-level figures in the caliph's court was quite a different matter, making him a dangerous public figure. Reports that al-Ḥallāj drew fairly large numbers of disciples suggest he may even have been considered a potential candidate for the political leadership of a quasi-revolutionary movement against the status quo of the ʿAbbāsid caliphate. He used religious fervor as a rallying force to attract those who were disillusioned with the arrogant attitudes and corrupt practices of the ruling elite. Perhaps this explains why al-Ḥallāj and his work are still remembered. Indeed, his cause has been reborn and carried, although not always successfully, by religious zealots opposed to unjust government in a number of time periods and places across the Islamic world.

—*Byron D. Cannon*

FURTHER READING

Ernst, Carl W., trans., and comp. *Teachings of Sufism.* Boston: Shambhala, 1999. Presents a study of the doctrines of Sufism, including the work of al-Ḥallāj. Also discusses the mystical understanding of the Qurʾān. Includes an index of relevant passages from the Qurʾān and prophetic sayings, a bibliography, and general index.

Kahn, Masood Ali, and S. Ram, eds. *Encyclopaedia of Sufism.* 12 vols. New Delhi: Anmol, 2003. A collection introducing Sufism and its basics in Islam, and Sufism's tenets, doctrines, literature, saints, and philosophy. Bibliography, index.

Lings, Martin. *What Is Sufism?* 1975. Reprint. Cambridge, England: Islamic Texts Society, 1999. A useful general survey of the principles of mysticism and the various representatives of nonconformist religious practice and thinking in Islam. Bibliography, index.

Mason, Herbert. *Al-Ḥallāj.* Richmond, Surrey, England: Curzon Press, 1995. This is probably the most readable account of al-Ḥallāj's life and work, based on the author's earlier, more specialized studies. Discusses the theme of "disappearance," universalism, uniqueness, and al-Ḥallāj's place in Sufism. Bibliography, index.

Massignon, Louis. *The Passion of Al-Ḥallāj: Mystic and Martyr of Islam.* Translated by Herbert Mason. Princeton, N.J.: Princeton University Press, 1994. A translation of Vol. 4 of the original work in French, this is an extensive, analytical, and sympathetic study of al-Ḥallāj. Evaluates sources and examines al-Ḥallāj's influence on later philosophers and theologians.

Sells, Michael A., ed. and trans. *Early Islamic Mysticism: Sufi, Qurʾān, Mirʿaj, Poetic, and Theological Writings.* New York: Paulist Press, 1996. Explores the sources of Islamic mysticism, with a chapter on al-Ḥallāj and a chronology of major figures in the development of Sufism. Bibliography, index.

SEE ALSO: Blessed Angela of Foligno; al-Ashʿarī; Beatrice of Nazareth; al-Ghazzālī; al-Ḥasan al-Baṣrī; Joan of Arc; Jalāl al-Dīn Rūmī.

RELATED ARTICLES in *Great Events from History: The Middle Ages, 477-1453*: 637-657: Islam Expands Throughout the Middle East; 869-883: Zanj Revolt of African Slaves; 1273: Sufi Order of Mawlawīyah Is Established.

HAROLD II
King of England (r. 1066)

Harold Godwinson was elected English king in 1066 and defeated a Norse invasion at Stamford Bridge, but he was defeated at Hastings by William the Conqueror and the Normans, marking the start of the Norman Conquest of England.

BORN: c. 1022; East Anglia, England
DIED: October 14, 1066; near Hastings, England
ALSO KNOWN AS: Harold Godwinson (given name)
AREAS OF ACHIEVEMENT: Government and politics, military

EARLY LIFE

Harold Godwinson (Harold II) lived during, and was part of, the domination of Saxon England by Viking invaders. Although sometimes called "the last Saxon king," Harold II was not of royal birth and was half Danish. His father, Godwin, was an English warrior during the confused attempts of King Ethelred II, the Unready (r. 978-1013 and 1014-1016) to resist Scandinavian invaders. After Ethelred's death, Godwin supported the Danish monarch Canute the Great as English king (r. 1017-1035), became earl of Wessex, and fathered a family of eight by marriage to a Danish noblewoman. Godwin's support of Canute's heirs may have involved him in the treacherous murder of Ethelred's son Prince Alfred in 1036. However, when Canute's last son died in 1042 "as he stood at his drink," Godwin supported Ethelred's remaining son, Edward, recently returned from exile in Normandy. King Edward the Confessor (r. 1043-1066) married Godwin's daughter Edith in 1045 but abstained from sexual relations in symbolic gratitude for church protection during his Norman exile. A future succession problem was thus inevitable. Meanwhile, though, the Godwins prospered, and in 1045 Godwin's second son, Harold, was made earl of East Anglia.

Young Harold Godwinson's administration of his extensive earldom was apparently at least satisfactory. He was reasonable, congenial, and persuasive in counsel, although sometimes impatient in military situations. Physically, Harold was moderately tall, strong, and athletic, with the blond hair and flowing mustache of a "Viking type." Early on he began family life with a mistress, Edith Swan-neck, who became the mother of five (or six) of his children. Harold gained more prominence in the conflicts caused by his older brother, Sweyn, who was exiled once for violating an abbess and again for the murder of a cousin. With Sweyn's death in 1052, Harold became heir-presumptive to the heritage of Godwin.

Early in 1051, King Edward put Earl Godwin on the defensive by ordering him to punish the citizens of Dover for a brawl with the traveling party of Eustace of Boulogne. The aging earl and his sons defied the royal order, but in an armed confrontation with Edward's forces, Godwin's allies backed down. The Godwins were outlawed for treason and exiled late in 1051; Harold found refuge in Ireland.

King Edward used the absence of the Godwins to appoint several Norman administrators to English positions in church and state. The Norman rulers, although themselves a Franco-Norse mixture, were his mother's people, and a youth spent in Normandy made Edward feel more comfortable with them than with the Anglo-Danish Godwins. According to some accounts, in late 1051 or early 1052, King Edward's cousin, the illegitimate but powerful twenty-four-year-old duke William of Normandy (William the Conqueror), himself visited England and received Edward's promise of succession to the English throne. Why Edward did not make this promise a matter of widespread public record in England is unclear. By the spring of 1052, however, anti-Norman sentiment in England allowed the Godwins to return in force and obtain pardon and restoration. Earl Godwin died in April of 1053, and Harold succeeded him as earl of Wessex.

LIFE'S WORK

From 1053 to 1066, Harold not only increased the lands and power of his family but also became the chief shaper and manager of national policy under Edward. He led armies in two hard-fought and successful wars against the Welsh, and he negotiated with the Scots and with rival earldoms in Mercia and Northumbria. Another ongoing problem was the status of Stigand, who had been appointed archbishop of Canterbury in 1052 but who did not prove acceptable to Vatican authorities. If Harold did make a visit to Rome about 1057, as sometimes alleged, he did not solve this problem, for when Alexander II became pope in 1062, the Vatican reformers made replacing Stigand part of their agenda. Also, the English succession problem deepened in 1057, when King Edward the Confessor invited the return of Ethelred's grandson, Edward the Exile, who landed in England, fell ill, and died. This left no adult English prince at hand as an alternative to the possible succession of William of Normandy.

Norman accounts describe a voyage by Harold, probably in 1064, to Ponthieu, where the ruler turned him over to William of Normandy. The duke treated his "guest" well, "invited" him to share in a campaign against Brittany, and "rewarded" him with a ceremony equivalent to knighthood in exchange for Harold's oath of loyalty, support for William's succession as English king, and also a promise to marry one of William's daughters. In some versions, concealed holy relics reinforced the loyalty oaths. Harold later argued that he made promises under duress so as to be free to leave. Why Harold undertook the trip at all is not clear.

Harold returned from Normandy in 1065 to find trouble in Northumbria. Harold's brother Tostig governed this earldom harshly, provoking a rebellion. Harold agreed to outlaw and exile Tostig, replacing him with Morcar, a brother to Earl Edwin of Mercia. He subsequently agreed to marry Aldgyth, a sister to Edwin and Morcar, a union that, when it took place in 1065 or early 1066, constituted an apparent breach of his alleged promises to Duke William.

Edward's final choice of a successor, according to the Saxon accounts, was his deathbed selection of Harold Godwinson on January 5, 1066. A council of the Witan elected Harold king on the following day, apparently to forestall other claimants to the throne. William of Normandy quickly publicized his own case and gained papal support, while Harold "Hardrada"("hard ruler") of Norway claimed England as the promised reward for his victory in a war against Denmark. The exiled earl Tostig and his freebooters were ready to help either of these challengers. In addition, the Welsh and Scots were traditionally hostile, and Edwin and Morcar, the "northern earls," were doubtfully loyal.

Harold II gives his oath to William of Normandy. (Library of Congress)

By April of 1066, when Halley's Comet was seen as a portent of fateful events to come, Norman and Norwegian shipbuilding operations were well underway. Earl Tostig's forces on the Isle of Wight began to raid England's south coast, while Harold mobilized the English fleet and fyrd (militia) in June. However, Harold's advantage of a large militia at hand soon posed a significant supply problem. The potential invaders spent the summer of 1066 waiting for Harold's militia to disband for want of food. As Tostig changed his base to Scotland and Hardrada's fleet advanced to the Orkneys, King Harold's soldiers began to desert for their own harvests. On September 8, Harold demobilized the militia and moved his fleet to London for supplies and refitting. At the same time, William shifted his base to Saint-Valery-sur-Somme, but he was held in port by unfavorable winds.

In the second week of September, Hardrada's fleet arrived off Northumbria and was joined by Tostig. Their combined force, carried in perhaps three hundred ships, traveled up the Humber and Ouse Rivers to a landing in Yorkshire on September 18. While Harold assembled troops, his allies Edwin and Morcar were defeated in a major battle at Gate Fulford on September 20. Hardrada and Tostig, welcomed in York, scattered their forces in search of plunder. Harold's ready forces, gathering militia en route, covered two hundred miles from London to Tadcaster in from four to five days, surprising the dispersed

DANISH KINGS OF ENGLAND, 1016-1066

Reign	*Monarch*
1016-1035	CANUTE THE GREAT
1035-1040	Harold I Harefoot
1040-1042	Harthacnut
1043-1066	EDWARD THE CONFESSOR
1066	HAROLD II

Note: Both Edward and Harold II were of mixed Danish and Saxon ancestry.

invaders. On September 25, Harold won a hard-fought and decisive battle at Stamford Bridge, Hardrada and Tostig were killed, and Harold allowed the Norwegian survivors an unmolested departure to avoid further losses of his own before facing the next invader.

William's landing near Hastings on September 28 compelled the English to make another forced march south, arriving at London on October 6. Harold summoned militia, but Edwin and Morcar held back, while Harold's own earldoms of Wessex and Kent were immediately threatened by the invaders. The prospects of national resistance over the winter were uncertain, and Harold decided to do battle with the force he had at hand. Most of his army arrived after nightfall on October 13 on the South Downs ridge at Senlac, an area now occupied by the town of Battle, more or less ready for action on the following day, Saturday, October 14.

Harold aligned perhaps eight thousand infantry—some Danish soldiers, but mostly Saxon militia—along the summit crest at Senlac, with each flank reasonably well anchored; the uphill road to London was squarely blocked. His deployment was well defended by the thrusting spears and battle axes of his warriors. However, in a long day of sporadic combat, the superior equipment, training, and mobility of the invaders—about five thousand infantry and two thousand cavalry—became apparent. Norman horsemen cut up any Saxon attempts at attack, confining Harold to a static defense. William was able to direct probing assaults and battle maneuvers, while stories of Harold's combat valor say nothing of any actions to support his gradually weakening right wing. As dusk approached, superior Norman archery proved decisive. An arrow struck Harold in the right eye and killed him; with his death, the English center broke. As night fell, the Saxons managed a ragged retreat, but thereafter the English cause had no active and accepted leader.

Harold's scattered remains were collected, by William's order, for burial "by the shore he defended so well" rather than in hallowed ground. Tradition holds that a subsequent reburial was made in Waltham Abbey. A new church, Battle Abbey, was built by William on the spot where Harold was killed. However, the estates of Harold and his followers at Senlac were confiscated as being the property of rebels in arms against William their lawful king. Norman references to "King Harold of England" soon changed to "Harold Godwinson" and then to "Harold the usurper."

SIGNIFICANCE

Saxon chroniclers mourned Harold's defeat as a national calamity, describing William the Conqueror as a stern ruler and his Normans as greedy oppressors. Puritan nationalism in the seventeenth century and Romantic nationalism in the nineteenth century glorified Harold as a fallen hero in the cause of Anglo-Saxon freedom. Twentieth century historians argued that most eleventh century Saxons were not free and that their victory at Senlac would have perpetuated Anglo-Danish barbarism, while the Norman Conquest restored closer commercial, linguistic, and religious contacts with the Latin civilization of Southern Europe. Such interpretations, based on later ideas of national destiny, may somewhat distort the issues of 1066, but certainly Harold II represents a significant "might have been" in the field of "history if."

—K. Fred Gillum

FURTHER READING

Barlow, Frank. *Edward the Confessor.* Berkeley: University of California Press, 1970. A scholarly study that includes many references to Harold.

Butler, Denis. *1066: The Story of a Year.* New York: Putnam, 1966. A readable narrative but compiled using some unreliable chronicles and expanded by fictitious details.

Freeman, Edward A. *The Norman Conquest of England: Its Causes and Results.* 6 vols. New York: AMS Press, 1977. Especially useful and comprehensive work, which glorifies Harold and the Saxons.

Hodgkin, Thomas. *The History of England from the Earliest Times to the Norman Conquest.* London: Longmans, Green, 1931. A scholarly and well-balanced use of source material, though with few notations. Appendix on sources and historians.

Stenton, F. M. *Anglo-Saxon England.* 3d ed. New York: Oxford University Press, 1989. A classic history that is critical of eleventh century English leadership and heavily dependent on pro-Norman sources. Still a good source for the period.

Walker, David. *The Normans in Britain*. Cambridge, Mass.: Blackwell, 1995. Offers an overview of the Anglo-Norman period in England, Scotland, Ireland, and Wales, beginning with the Battle of Hastings.

Walker, Ian W. *Harold, the Last Anglo-Saxon King*. Gloucestershire, England: Sutton, 1997. Discusses Harold's family background, his exile and return, and his and William the Conqueror's roles in the Norman Conquest.

Whitelock, Dorothy, David C. Douglas, and Susie I. Tucker, eds. *The Anglo-Saxon Chronicle*. 2d ed. New Brunswick, N.J.: Rutgers University Press, 1989. A basic contemporary source with later chronicles by Florence of Worcester, William of Malmesbury, and William of Jumieges.

Wright, Peter Poyntz. *The Battle of Hastings*. Salisbury, England: Michael Russell, 1986. A short book filled with illustrations and maps and devoted entirely to the Battle of Hastings. Traces the events leading to the battle, its tactics and strategies, and the immediate aftermath.

SEE ALSO: Canute the Great; Edward the Confessor; Ethelred II, the Unready; William the Conqueror.

RELATED ARTICLE in *Great Events from History: The Middle Ages, 477-1453*: October 14, 1066: Battle of Hastings.

HARṢA

Indian raja (r. 606-c. 647)

One of the last great rulers of the classical age of Hindu India, Harṣa defended Buddhism in its homeland, established relations with the Chinese empire, and distinguished himself in classical Sanskrit theater.

BORN: c. 590; probably Thānesar, India
DIED: c. 647; possibly Kanauj, India
ALSO KNOWN AS: Harsha; Harṣavardhana; Shilāditya
AREAS OF ACHIEVEMENT: Government and politics, warfare and conquest, religion and theology, theater

EARLY LIFE

Much of the information recorded about the youth of Harṣa (HUHR-shuh) comes from the account of Bāṇa, a contemporary Sanskrit poet. Harṣa was the second son of Prabhākaravardhana, the raja of Thānesar (probably a small, independent state in the Punjab). The death of his father ultimately led Harṣa, however reluctantly, to rule for more than forty years over a great north Indian empire. Yet the path to the throne was neither easy nor obvious.

After their mother, Yasomati, committed suttee—self-sacrifice on her husband's funeral pyre—both Harṣa and his elder brother, Rājyavardhana, declined the succession. This situation persisted until their sister, Rājyasrī, who had married Grahavarman, the Maukhari king of Kanauj, was imprisoned after the death of her husband by Devagupta, king of Malwa (Malava; in west-central India). Rājyavardhana, abandoning his ascetic life, defeated Devagupta; unfortunately, the young king was assassinated by Devagupta's ally, Ṣaṣāṇka, king of Gauḍa (modern Bengal). On learning of her brother's death, Rājyasrī—who had been freed by a sympathetic noble—wandered into the Vindhya Mountains, while Rājyavardhana's army fell into disarray. Harṣa, who had been left in charge of the government by his brother, rallied the royal forces; formed an alliance with another of Ṣaṣāṇka's enemies, Bhaskaravarman, king of Kāmarūpa; and found his sister, who was about to mount a funeral pyre in the mountains.

Vowing vengeance against Ṣaṣāṇka, his brother's murderer, the sixteen-year-old Harṣa began a war of universal conquest. Although his objective would not be achieved, he nevertheless managed to transform a desperate situation. According to tradition, his initial hesitance about ascending the throne was overcome by encouragement from the statue of Avalokiteṣvara Bodhisattva (the merciful, earthly manifestation of the eternal Buddha). Although apocryphal, this story of the statue certainly indicates the spiritual dimension of Harṣa's personality.

LIFE'S WORK

The rich details provided by Bāṇa in *Sri Harṣcarita* (seventh century; *The Harshacharita of Banabhatta*, 1892) break off abruptly with Harṣa's reunion with his sister. Aside from royal seals and inscriptions, the account of a contemporary Buddhist pilgrim, Xuanzang (Hsüan-tsang; c. 602-664), is the only record of the remainder of

Harṣa's lengthy reign. Unfortunately, Xuangzang met the king only around 643 and left India in 644, three years before Harṣa's death. Therefore, much about Harṣa's reign remains unknown.

Harṣa, who was always on the move, amassed a huge standing army; his forces easily exceeded those of Chandragupta Maurya in the fourth century B.C.E., even if figures of 60,000 elephants, 100,000 cavalry, and perhaps 1 million infantry are discounted as hyperbole. Although he apparently campaigned vigorously even in the early years of his reign, by about 620, he was deeply involved in warfare, battling the forces of King Pulakeśin II of the Cālukya Dynasty of the northern Deccan and, after 636, annexing much of Bengal, Bihar, and Orissa. These facts somewhat modify contemporary claims of thirty years of peace under his rule.

Historical opinion is divided as to the extent of his conquests and the range of his empire. He suffered defeat at the hands of the Cālukya, which may or may not have established the sacred Narmada River as his southern boundary. He never apparently defeated his avowed enemy Ṣaṣāṇka (who cut down the Bodhi tree at Bodh Gayā), only making his eastern acquisitions sometime after the latter's death in about 637. Apparently, Harṣa also had little success against the states of western India. Lāṭa, Malwa, and Gurjara were buffer states protected by Pulakeśin II, and powerful Sindh fought him off, although Dharasena IV of Valabhī became his son-in-law.

Harṣa's political power, based in Kanauj (now a minor village with few traces left of his era), embraced the populous, traditional heartland of the Gangetic plain. His prestige and influence extended throughout northern India but was counterbalanced by the Cālukya of the Deccan plateau region. His empire was not a centralized one under his direct control as has sometimes been asserted.

The state was highly organized, yet few details about it are known. In a traditional society based on bureaucratic villages, tours of inspection through the provinces and districts were the means of control. Taxes were light, and 50 percent of the budget went to religion and the arts. (At quinquennial assemblies, the treasury surpluses of the past five years were distributed to religious sects and the solitary poor.) An infrastructure to protect travelers, the poor, and the sick—including rest houses, stupas, and monasteries—was in place. The judicial system (inherited from the Gupta, a north Indian dynasty that ruled from the early fourth to the mid-sixth century) was based on social morality and filial duty; its deterrents included imprisonments, mutilations, banishments, and fines. The economy, based on textiles and metals, was prosperous, as was shown by the fact that the assembly's distributed wealth was always replenished in the following ten days.

Although a Hindu (probably a Shaivite), Harṣa seems to have been committed early to Buddhism, most likely its Māhayāna form, although it was not uncommon for rulers to follow a tolerant and eclectic religious policy. His brother Rājyavardhana had been a Buddhist and his sister Rājyasrī became a Buddhist nun. In 643, Harṣa demanded the presence of the illustrious Chinese Buddhist Xuanzang (Hsüan-tsang; c. 602-664), who had studied at Nalanda University in his realm, bringing him from the court of his ally, Bhaskaravarman of Kāmarūpa, by threat of force.

In the last years of his reign, Harṣa sought to model himself after Aśoka the Great as the chief patron of his religion—at a time when Buddhism was losing its position to Hinduism. At the sixth quinquennial assembly at Prayaqa in 643, he favored Buddhism in his distribution of the wealth. He also convoked a grand religious assembly at Kanauj—attended by twenty kings—marked by twenty-one days of festival centered on a 100-foot (30-meter) tower holding a life-size statue of the Buddha. During this festival, Harṣa arranged a theological disputation, with Xuanzang as the Buddhist champion. The tensions arising from this advocacy led to two frustrated murder conspiracies: Hīnayānist Buddhists conspired against Xuanzang, and on the last day of the festival, they used a diversionary fire to attack Harṣa with a knife.

Harṣa opened diplomatic relations with the Chinese empire in 641. This action led to a series of Chinese embassies in 641, 643, and, stimulated by Xuanzang's return to China, in 647, under Wang Huienze. The last embassy arrived after Harṣa's death and apparently was attacked by Harṣa's usurping minister, Arjuna. Wang's embassy, with Nepalese, Tibetan, and Kāmarūpa help, captured Arjuna and brought him to China. Wang returned to India in 657 and 664, and the Chinese connection lasted until 787. Xuanzang, who had received gold and an elephant from Harṣa, returned to China with 520 cases of Indian religious documents and founded the Buddhist Consciousness Only School, which later strongly influenced Japanese Buddhism.

In addition to these achievements, Harṣa was a leading Sanskrit playwright in the mold of Kālidāsa, writing *Ratnāvāli* (seventh century; *Retnavali: Or, The Necklace*, 1827) and *Priyadarśikā* (seventh century; English translation, 1923), which contains the new device of a play-within-a-play. His last work, the *Nágánanda* (seventh century; *Nágánanda: Or, The Joy of the Snake-World*,

1872), contains Buddhist themes of the bodhisattva and self-sacrifice in a Hindu framework (perhaps Harṣa played Garuda, the redeemed mythical bird). Although his authorship of the plays has been disputed, Harṣa clearly was a patron of learning and the arts in a period marked by the breakdown of the classical Gupta achievement.

Significance

Though the uniqueness of Harṣa's role in Indian history has been seriously challenged, including the true extent of his empire, his military record, and his depiction as the last great Buddhist-Hindu ruler before Islam, the fact remains that Harṣa constructed a dominant, celebrated political entity out of a petty state amid the disintegration of the Gupta world, holding it together for more than forty years, although it fragmented on his death. Indeed, one of the chronological eras of Indian history is fixed on his reign. Harṣa's advocacy of Buddhism in a Hindu frame was a factor in encouraging Xuanzang to carry its message to the Far East, even as that religion was about to lose force in its homeland. Harṣa was essentially a philosopher-king inspired by *dharma* in his character and in his rule of an enlightened welfare state. He was a lion of activity, who ignored food and sleep and found the day too short. The power of his personality is shown by the grim humor of his reply to Bhaskaravarman, who had offered to send his head in place of Xuanzang to Harṣa's court, "Send head per bearer," and by his defense of Xuanzang's life at Kanauj, when he threatened to cut out the tongues of the pilgrim's enemies.

—*Ralph Smiley*

Further Reading

Bāṇa. *The Harsa-carita*. Translated by E. B. Cowell and F. W. Thomas. London: Royal Asiatic Society, 1897. Bāṇa, a Brahman and Harṣa's court poet, covers Harṣa's life until he gained the throne in 612. Written in a masterly, highly ornate style, his work is the first Sanskrit biography.

Devahuti, Deva. *Harsha: A Political Study*. Rev. ed. New York: Oxford University Press, 1998. An updated assessment, written from the Indian perspective, of Harṣa's role in Indian history. Includes genealogical tables and twelve plates.

_______. *The Unknown Hsüan-tsang*. New York: Oxford University Press, 2001. A collection of translations of Xuanzang's translations into Chinese, with a biographical account of the monk by an Indian scholar.

Mookerji, R. K. *Harsha*. Oxford, England: H. Milford, 1926. Part of the Rulers of India series, Mookerji's seminal study was one of the first to promote Harṣa's importance in classical India. This biography gathers together all the then-known information about this myth-shrouded figure. Includes indexes and notes.

Panikkar, K. M. *Sri Harsha of Kanauj: A Monograph on the History of India in the First Half of the Seventh Century A.D.* Bombay: D. B. Taraporevaja Sons, 1922. One of the pioneer studies in Indian history, this work builds up Harṣa as a king of enormous influence and power, setting him against the background of his era. Includes indexes and notes.

Thapar, Romila. *Early India: From the Origins to A.D. 1300*. Berkeley: University of California Press, 2002. A general overview of the early history of India, covering its states and cities.

Wriggins, Sally Hovey. *Xuanzang: A Buddhist Pilgrim on the Silk Road*. Boulder, Colo.: Westview Press, 1996. A readable and accessible biography of Xuanzang.

Xuanzang. *Si-yu-ki: Buddhist Records of the Western World*. Translated by Samuel Beal. 2 vols. 1884. Reprint. London: Routledge, 2000. The Chinese Buddhist pilgrim Xuanzang covers Harṣa's reign historically, although with a pronounced religious bias. This panegyric was written after Xuanzang's return to China in 645.

See also: Xuanzang.

Related articles in *Great Events from History: The Middle Ages, 477-1453*: 606-647: Reign of Harṣa of Kanauj; c. 611-642: Reign of Pulakeśin II; 618: Founding of the Tang Dynasty; 629-645: Pilgrimage of Xuanzang.

HARTMANN VON AUE

German poet

Through its language, style, and literary form, Hartmann's work provided a model for the composition of courtly epic verse and stands at the beginning of the Hohenstaufen renaissance in German literature.

BORN: c. 1160-1165; Swabia (now in Germany)
DIED: c. 1210-1220; Swabia
ALSO KNOWN AS: Hartmann von Ouwe
AREA OF ACHIEVEMENT: Literature

EARLY LIFE

As is often the case with medieval literary figures, what is known about the life of Hartmann von Aue (HAHRT-mahn fuhn OW) is mainly conjecture. What knowledge there is does not come from official documents of the time but rather from personal comments that he makes in his own works and an analysis of his language. There are also several brief references to him in the work of his contemporaries and a coat of arms found in manuscript illustrations. Thus, even his place of birth is questioned by some scholars. Because of the peculiarities of his language, which point to the Alammanic dialect area in southwestern Germany, it is generally believed that Hartmann was born in Swabia.

Hartmann was probably a ministerial or landless nobleman in service to a patron. A miniature dating from the fourteenth century shows him on horseback with the armor and dress of a knight. His work includes a lament of the loss of his liege lord and a vow to go on a crusade, either in 1189 under Frederick I Barbarossa or in 1197 under Henry VI. Hartmann was an educated man, possibly receiving his formal education at the monastery school at Reichenau, a conclusion drawn from his introductory words to *Der arme Heinrich* (c. 1195; English translation, 1931), where he describes himself as an educated knight (*Ritter*) and a vassal in service at Aue.

The exact order in which Hartmann's work was written is open to debate by scholars, although there seems to be more general agreement as to the order of the works than as to their dates of composition. Among his early works is a long, didactic poem on love, sometimes referred to as *Das Büchlein* (little book) but more often called *Die Klage* (c. 1180; *The Lament*, 2001). His other major early work is an adaptation of a work by Chrétien de Troyes, *Erek* (c. 1190; *Erec*, 1982). Both *The Lament* and *Erec*—as well as some of Hartmann's earlier lyric poetry (*Lieder*), or courtly love songs—were written in the period between 1180 and 1190.

The Lament shows Hartmann's ability to manipulate the forms of the tradition of courtly love. His poem (1,914 verses long) presents an argument between the heart and the body in which the ideals of service to the beloved and self-denial are extolled. The basis for these ideas comes from twelfth century songs of the Provençal troubadours, although Hartmann's own clear style and didactic tone reveal two characteristics appearing in his mature works as well.

His Arthurian romance *Erec* demonstrates his talent in the genre where he is considered strongest and where he is certainly best known, the courtly epic. His source was the earliest Arthurian romance of the same name by Chrétien, and, although the basic plot is not changed, the purpose behind the story is altered to stress the concept of moderation, or *mâze*, in a knight's life. Erec realizes through his experiences that neither complete devotion to his lady nor total dedication to brave deeds can produce an ideal knight. Instead, he must attain a proper balance between the two.

Both *The Lament* and *Erec* lay the groundwork for Hartmann von Aue's later compositions, showing a gradual mastery of literary form and establishing themes that form the basis of subsequent works. In fact, Hartmann returned to the Arthurian romance for *Iwein* (c. 1190-1205; *Iwein: The Knight with the Lion*, 1979), his last courtly epic.

LIFE'S WORK

With *Erec*, Hartmann composed the first German Arthurian romance and set the focus of his later epics, the question of moral conduct and ideal character. This work also stands at the beginning of several generations of German poets who drew on the same Arthurian legends and the ideals of chivalry. In Hartmann's work there are two parallel threads: the profane literature of his love lyrics and Arthurian romances and the religious themes of his crusade poetry, *Gregorius* (c. 1190-1197; English translation, 1955, 1966) and *Der arme Heinrich*. These two strands reflect opposing currents of his times but are by no means totally separate within his own work.

Hartmann's love lyrics, or *Minne*, which follow the medieval courtly tradition, are most often classified among his earliest compositions. In general, they have been regarded with less esteem than his later crusading poems, which have often been singled out for special attention. In addition, some of the themes and elements in-

MAJOR WORKS BY HARTMANN VON AUE

Date	Work
c. 1180	*Die Klage* (*The Lament*)
c. 1190	*Erek*
c. 1190-1197	*Gregorius*
c. 1190-1205	*Iwein*
c. 1195	*Der arme Heinrich*

troduced in the lyric poetry have parallels in his narrative works. From traditional devotional songs to a noble lady, he progressed to the praise of love for women of a humbler station, for example; then in *Der arme Heinrich*, the unselfish girl who saves her noble lord is the daughter of a peasant, and her immense value is in her willingness to sacrifice herself for him. The themes of estrangement, or alienation from a loved one, reappear in the romances *Erec* and *Iwein*.

One event frequently mentioned in discussing Hartmann's life is the death of his master, which seems to have moved him deeply and to which he refers in a poem showing great devotion. After this event, he may have gone on a crusade (1197), although this is by no means certain, and the crusade may have been an earlier one. Some critics have also suggested that this death marked a turning away from profane love songs to his crusading poems showing a new way of life in the service of Christ (*Gottesminne*). The unhappiness of the lover who admires a lady who withholds her notice is now transformed into the happiness of a more dangerous but also more rewarding love. The religious sanction of the Crusades transforms the enterprise into a loving service of God. The conclusion that such a change was brought about by the shock of his master's death has been disputed by other critics, who remind the reader that medieval poetry was often an expression of societal ideals and feelings and cannot be so directly related to an individual's personal experience as modern verse is. Hartmann's poetry, including courtly love songs, songs renouncing this love, and crusade songs, places him in the tradition of Reinmar von Hagenau and Walther von der Vogelweide and can be considered to accompany the full span of his narrative work.

In his Arthurian romances, Hartmann was concerned with questions of moral conduct, even though the story was essentially profane or secular. Following *Erec*, however, he wrote two narratives specifically concerned with humility before the power of God, *Gregorius* and *Der arme Heinrich*. Hartmann's source for *Gregorius* was an older version of a French poem, appearing in two versions in the twelfth century. Yet he added his own style and language as well as a strong religious-didactic element. The legend tells of a noble sinner who repents of his sin of unknowing incest and inflicts a penance on himself so strict that he is purified. As a sign of his purification, he is chosen as pope, and both he and his mother are forgiven. The clear lesson is that sinful man can obtain salvation, no matter how grievous his sin, through repentance and atonement.

His following narrative, *Der arme Heinrich*, tells of a nobleman suffering from leprosy who learns humility through the unselfish example of a peasant's daughter. Although this premise offered Hartmann the opportunity to describe the horrible ravages of the disease in gruesome detail, he chose to concentrate instead on its tragic effect on Heinrich's life as he is abandoned to his fate and, most intently, on the young girl who demonstrates the pure spirit of self-sacrifice when she agrees to offer her blood to cleanse him. When Heinrich finds the humility to refuse her sacrifice, he is miraculously cured. In this work, Hartmann blends a religious legend with realistic and historic elements of medieval life. Instead of using a noble to illustrate the highest virtues, he presents a peasant as his ideal figure.

Hartmann's most popular work in his own time was his second Arthurian romance, *Iwein*, which is referred to in other medieval works and of which some twenty-eight manuscripts exist. The main theme, as with *Erec*, deals with the chivalric code of the knights, complete with the elements of love, generosity, refinement, and *mâze*. The poet uses the external symbols of the Church in all of his courtly epics, but the role of God is not confined to his two versions of religious legends. His introduction to *Iwein* clearly states that true kindness (or goodness) receives God's favor and men's honor (or esteem). Thus, the currents of religious and secular rewards are combined for individuals with this important quality. Just as surely, pride or haughtiness (*superbia*) without regard for compassion is punished. Heinrich's sin in *Der arme Heinrich* was not so very different, nor was Gregorius's first error, as he abandoned the religious life for which he was destined to pursue adventure as a knight. Hartmann's work shows clearly how important moral and social commitments were for him; both religious and secular currents shaped his work.

SIGNIFICANCE

The appearance of four particularly gifted poets paved the way for the development of a body of high-quality literature in the German language rather than in Latin as had been the norm before the period of the High Middle Ages. This new literature reached a level of refinement above previous attempts in the vernacular. Among the best-known poets of the period are Walther von der Vogelweide in the area of lyric poetry and Gottfried von Strassburg and Wolfram von Eschenbach along with Hartmann von Aue in the area of the courtly epic. Hartmann's lasting fame rests mainly on his Arthurian romances. His polished verses found favor at the courts and stand as a model for future developments in narrative literature in German. Furthermore, in the amount and versatility of his work, he is exceptional for his times.

Hartmann's very strong sense of moral rectitude and his concern for the correct knightly behavior of the code of chivalry permeate his work and are in harmony with the medieval period. His great individual contribution is a clarity of style, reflecting, according to some critics, the practice of the *ornatus facilis* of medieval rhetoric, which is characterized by figures of repetition while avoiding forced imagery and artificiality. Gottfried von Strassburg praised Hartmann's refined language, eloquence, and clearness by using the image of crystalline words to emphasize what he considered to be his contemporary's greatest literary quality. Contrasting with that of earlier German narratives, Hartmann's polished language and style exerted strong influence on the medieval poets Wolfram von Eschenbach, Walther von der Vogelweide, and Reinmar von Hagenau. Later medieval poets were also familiar with Hartmann's work, which continued to influence courtly novels and heroic narrative well beyond his lifetime. For his contributions, Hartmann is certainly to be counted among the master poets of medieval German literature.

—*Susan L. Piepke*

FURTHER READING

Bell, Clair Hayden. *Peasant Life in Old German Epics: Meier Helmbrecht and "Der arme Heinrich."* New York: Columbia University Press, 1931. Contains an English translation of *Der arme Heinrich*, with explanatory endnotes as well as a bibliography. The introduction discusses points of comparison between *Gregorius* and an epic poem by Wernher der Gärtner, *Meier Helmbrecht* (c. 1250; partially translated as *Meier Helmbrecht, a German Farmer of the Thirteenth Century*, 1894). Includes general information about Hartmann and his work and discussion of the role of the peasant in medieval times.

Hartmann von Aue. *Hartmann von Aue: "Gregorius, the Good Sinner."* Translated by Sheema Zeben Buehne. New York: Frederick Ungar, 1966. This volume includes short introductory remarks about the work and the translation but is most valuable for the complete text of *Gregorius*, with original language on one side and English translation on the other, and helpful explanatory notes.

Hasty, Will. *Adventures in Interpretation: The Works of Hartmann von Aue and Their Critical Reception*. Columbia, S.C.: Camden House, 1996. A survey of criticism of Hartmann von Aue's work from the Enlightenment to postmodernism, which concludes that the interpretations by modern readers have been shaped mainly by critical trends.

Jackson, W. H. *Chivalry in Twelfth-Century Germany: The Works of Hartmann von Aue*. Rochester, N.Y.: D. S. Brewer, 1994. A study of Hartmann von Aue's poetic representation of knighthood and chivalric values with consideration of historical, literary, and linguistic influences.

Jackson, W. H., and S. A. Ranawake, eds. *The Arthur of the Germans: The Arthurian Legend in Medieval German and Dutch Literature*. Cardiff: University of Wales Press, 2000. A group of essays includes chapters on the emergence of the German Arthurian romance.

Jackson, W. T. H. *The Literature of the Middle Ages*. New York: Columbia University Press, 1960. A major study of the literature of the Middle Ages, including information on the development of the literature and its various forms. In the discussion of the romance, Hartmann is considered in the context of his times. He is compared with his contemporaries, and *Erec* and *Iwein* are analyzed specifically. Includes a chronology of the important works of the period and an extensive bibliography arranged by topic.

Loomis, Roger Shermann. *Arthurian Literature in the Middle Ages: A Collaborative History*. Oxford: Clarendon Press, 1959. An important survey of literature dealing with the Arthurian legend, with articles by specialists in each field. An individual chapter, "Hartmann von Aue and His Successors," focuses on the development of the German Arthurian romance. Related chapters discuss Chrétien de Troyes, the source for Hartmann's romances, and Hartmann's contemporaries Wolfram von Eschenbach and Gottfried von Strassburg. Footnotes supply bibliographical information for each topic.

Resler, Michael. Introduction to *Hartmann von Aue: "Erec."* Philadelphia: University of Pennsylvania

Press, 1987. An extensive introduction including general historical and cultural background, specific information on the life of Hartmann, a discussion of Arthurian romance, and a full consideration of the sources, structure, and thematic issues of this work. This volume also contains a translation of *Erec* plus explanatory endnotes. Includes helpful selected bibliography, although the majority of the references are to sources in German.

Richey, M. F. *Essays on Mediaeval German Poetry.* New York: Barnes and Noble Books, 1969. With an explanation of *Minne*, individual chapters on various medieval German poets (including the study of a poem by Hartmann), and a short selection of German sources, this volume provides a good orientation to the literary form but no extensive information on Hartmann. The article by Leslie Seiffert is especially helpful.

Sayce, Olive. *The Poets of the Minnesang*. Oxford: Clarendon Press, 1967. A representative survey of lyric poetry written in Germany, Austria, and Switzerland from 1150 to 1400. Good material on the origins and conventions of the *Minne*. With specific reference to Hartmann, including a representative sample of his poems in their original form without English translation.

Seiffert, Leslie. "Hartmann von Aue and His Lyric Poetry." *Oxford German Studies* 3 (1968): 1-29. Very informative article supplementing the more general references by Richey and Sayce. Considers the place of Hartmann in medieval lyric poetry and shows the role such poetry played in his life and literary production. Discusses briefly the research and current opinion on his lyric poetry and examines themes, motifs, and a pattern of moods within the work. Detailed interpretations of poems are included.

Sullivan, Robert G. *Justice and the Social Context of Early Middle High German Literature.* New York: Routledge, 2001. A history of the Holy Roman Empire hinging on an examination of High German literature and its authors' focus on social, political, and spiritual issues during a time of transformation. Bibliographical references, index.

Thomas, J. W. Introduction to *Hartmann von Aue: "Erec."* Lincoln: University of Nebraska Press, 1982. Includes information on Hartmann's life and works, as well as the theme, plot structure, motifs, and style of the translated work. Explanatory notes at the end provide bibliographical information on each of these topics. A readable translation of the text follows.

_______. Introduction to *Hartmann von Aue: "Iwein."* Lincoln: University of Nebraska Press, 1979. An informative introduction with an overview of Hartmann's works and discussions of the theme of *Iwein*, structure and motifs, and the narrative style. Notes include important bibliographical references as well as helpful information. The translation included in this volume is very readable.

Tobin, Frank J. *"Gregorius" and "Der arme Heinrich": Hartmann's Dualistic and Gradualistic Views of Reality.* Bern, Switzerland: Verlag Herbert Lang, 1973. A scholarly treatment of the two works, with important insights into the view of the world implicit in these texts. Includes extensive discussion of the content and themes of the two works, as well as an orientation to the terms "dualism" and "gradualism" as applied to the analysis. The bibliography includes both German and English references.

Wapnewski, Peter. *Hartmann von Aue*. Stuttgart, Germany: Metzler, 1979. Critical analysis of Hartmann von Aue's work, with bibliographic references. Published in German.

Zeydel, Edwin H., and B. Q. Morgan, eds. *"Gregorius": A Medieval Oedipus Legend by Hartmann von Aue.* Chapel Hill: University of North Carolina Press, 1955. Introduction and explanatory endnotes accompany this translation of *Gregorius* into rhyming couplets. Contains commentary on the verse form and the Gregorius legend, along with related legends in literature, particularly the Oedipus legend. Also includes information about the life of Hartmann and the surviving manuscripts of this work.

SEE ALSO: Chrétien de Troyes; Gottfried von Strassburg; Walther von der Vogelweide; Wolfram von Eschenbach.

RELATED ARTICLES in *Great Events from History: The Middle Ages, 477-1453*: After 1000: Development of Miracle and Mystery Plays; c. 1025: Scholars at Chartres Revive Interest in the Classics; c. 1100: Rise of Courtly Love; 1100-1300: European Universities Emerge; 1136: Hildegard von Bingen Becomes Abbess; c. 1180: Chrétien de Troyes Writes *Perceval*; 1189-1192: Third Crusade; c. 1306-1320: Dante Writes *The Divine Comedy*; c. 1350-1400: Petrarch and Boccaccio Recover Classical Texts.

HĀRŪN AL-RASHĪD
Persian caliph (r. 786-809)

Hārūn al-Rashīd counts among the most famous holders of the office of caliph in the ʿAbbāsid Dynasty in Baghdad (eighth to thirteenth century). His most notable accomplishments were quelling revolts, establishing peace, and promoting intellectual activity, industry, and trade.

BORN: February, 766; Rayy, Persia (now in Iran)
DIED: March 24, 809; probably Khorāsān (now in Iran)
ALSO KNOWN AS: Hārūn al-Rashīd ibn Muḥammad al-Mahdī ibn al-Manṣūr al-ʿAbbāsī (full name)
AREAS OF ACHIEVEMENT: Government and politics, warfare and conquest, military

EARLY LIFE

Hārūn al-Rashīd (hah-RUH-nahl-rahsh-EED), who was to become the fifth Islamic caliph in the line of the ʿAbbāsid family, was born in 766 in north-central Iran. He was the third son of Caliph al-Mahdī and the second child of al-Mahdī's wife al-Khayzurān, a former slave of the fourth ʿAbbāsid caliph. Had it not been for the influence of al-Khayzurān and others close to the seat of power in Baghdad, Hārūn might never have ascended the throne. His older brother al-Hādī, who was the initial successor to al-Mahdī, reigned only a year (785-786) following the death of their father. Al-Hādī's death was said to have been the result of a court conspiracy, and Hārūn's claim to succession at the very young age of twenty required the concentrated action of supporters who could intervene on his behalf. His chief supporter was Yaḥyā the Barmakid (d. 805), who had been the prince's secretarial aide and instructor during his early youth. Yaḥyā's loyalty to the claimant probably stemmed from the circumstances of Hārūn's earliest appointments to key positions appropriate to an ʿAbbāsid prince. During a period of renewed warfare between the Arab caliphate and the Byzantine Greek Empire (779-780 and 781-782), Hārūn had been named commander of two expeditions, one of which penetrated as far as the shores of the Bosporus opposite the Byzantine capital at Constantinople. Despite the fact that the real commanders of these military campaigns were accomplished soldiers and officials, the prince received several honorific governorships for his service in the field. These included posts in Ifriqiyah (now Tunisia), Egypt, Syria, Armenia, and Azerbaijan Province in Iran. On each occasion, the real man in control seems to have been Yaḥyā, Hārūn's adviser.

The fruit of Hārūn's close dependence on his former tutor was to be seen in Yaḥyā's intervention, with the assistance of the prince's mother, al-Khayzurān, to secure Hārūn's selection as second heir to the throne. This became very critical when intrigues broke out over al-Mahdī's apparent last-minute decision to bypass al-Hādī in favor of Yaḥyā's protégé. As soon as Hārūn succeeded to the throne following al-Hādī's murder, he recognized Yaḥyā and his two sons as his official viziers, or primary ministers. This ascendancy of a small group of caliphal advisers lasted until the Barmakids themselves fell victim to court intrigues nearly two decades later (in 803).

This pattern in Hārūn al-Rashīd's early life might seem to suggest that, as caliph, it would be his nature to bend to the will of others. His accomplishments as ruler of the ʿAbbāsid Empire until 809, however, left a very different legacy.

LIFE'S WORK

Apparently, Hārūn al-Rashīd's early experiences as prince-commander of the caliphal armies sent against the Byzantine emperor left a strong mark. Throughout his reign, he placed great emphasis on defending the Islamic-Christian border. He would even create a special military province, called Al-Awasim, in the zone separating the two empires. Particular care went into the strengthening of the fortifications of Tarsus, which would serve as a military deployment zone. The state of the caliph's military preparedness was tested at the very outset of his reign, when Constantine VI, son of the Byzantine empress Irene, came of age and denounced his mother's generally peaceful relations with the caliph of Baghdad. Border fighting surged between 795 and 797. In the latter year, the empress overthrew her young successor, blinded him, and restored general terms of peace with caliph Hārūn.

Conditions deteriorated dramatically later in Hārūn's reign when Irene was overthrown by Nicephorus, a rebellious Byzantine aristocrat, in 802. Nicephorus broke relations with Baghdad and attacked in 804, only to be vigorously repulsed by an army led by Caliph Hārūn. This force advanced well into Asia Minor and menaced the city of Constantinople itself. Hārūn laid down new terms of peace in 806, including a humiliating clause requiring the Byzantine emperor to pay annual tribute to Baghdad. A few years earlier, Arab naval forces temporarily recaptured the island of Cyprus, which had re-

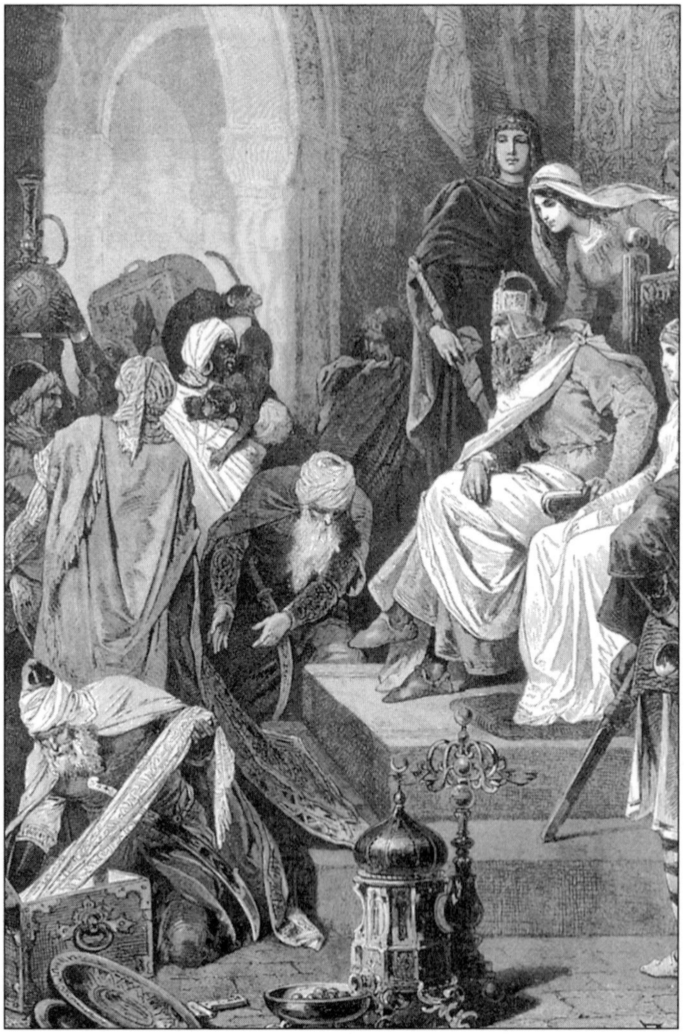

Charlemagne receives the embassy of Hārūn al-Rashīd. (F. R. Niglutsch)

turned to Christian hands shortly after the earliest years of Arab Muslim campaigns against Constantinople in the mid-seventh century.

Perhaps the reason that Hārūn's victories against the Christian Byzantines were not carried further at this time is to be found in the many signs of internal division that had appeared within the Islamic Empire. These divisions had both a geographic and a religio-cultural schismatic side to them. On the one hand, there is no doubt that, by the time of Hārūn's reign, the central caliphate showed signs of being unable to control its most distant provinces. Both along the southern coasts of the Mediterranean (the Maghrib, or western provinces of what is now Morocco, Algeria, and Tunisia) and in the east (primarily the province of Khorāsān, in eastern Iran, but also in the core provinces of Arabia and Iraq), revolts and independence movements troubled Hārūn's reign on many occasions. These weakened his capacity to impose not only political but also important economic bonds of caliphal control.

In addition, one must take into consideration the fact that Islamic schismatic movements—most under the banner of the ʿAlīds, Shia followers of the imamate descending from the Prophet's son-in-law ʿAlī—had weakened the cultural and religious authority of the Baghdad caliphate. Hārūn's methods of dealing with ʿAlīd threats were sometimes preemptive, bordering on outright persecution. Members of families descending from ʿAlī were warned against establishing themselves in distant retreats and teaching ʿAlīd doctrines that might be turned against the caliph. Some, including Yaḥyā ibn Abdullah, brother of the defeated ʿAlīd pretender Muḥammad al-Nafs al-Zakiyya, were brought to Baghdad under a promise of security, only to be imprisoned for life. Such treacherous policies undoubtedly alienated many others whose loyalty to the Islamic realm, irrespective of questions of religious doctrines, was wearing thin by the time of Hārūn's death in 809.

The circumstances surrounding Hārūn's succession bear witness to growing divisions that were weakening the political ascendancy of the ʿAbbāsid caliphate. Several years before his death, at a time when his ruling strength seemed to be at its zenith, Hārūn revealed what came to be known as the Covenant of the Kaaba. This document designated his firstborn son, Muḥammad al-Amīn, as Hārūn's successor to the caliphate. Al-Amīn's younger brothers, al-Maʾmūn (Hārūn's son by a Persian slave) and al-Muʿtaṣim, were assigned full powers as governors of the eastern (Iranian) provinces and Mesopotamia (Iraq), respectively. Hārūn's intention was that, while al-Amīn would assume the office and functions of caliph, his other heirs would have a nearly equal share in the responsibilities of imperial rule. Al-Amīn's almost immediate redefinition of the extent of al-Muʿtaṣim's authority in Iraq and his attempts to exclude al-Maʾmūn from his assumed eventual right to succeed to the caliphate, however, deteriorated into a situation of civil war by 810. Although al-Maʾmūn succeeded in overcoming the forces of Hārūn's first-chosen successor, he managed this only with the aid of Iranian forces under the command of Tāhir ibn al-Ḥusayn, victor in an important battle at Rayy. Later, Tahir proceeded to Baghdad, where, in 813, his forces killed Caliph al-Amīn and proclaimed the succession of Hārūn's second son, al-Maʾmūn (r. 813-833). The fact that the new caliph remained behind for some time in the capital of the province of Khorāsān before assuming the responsibilities of his office in Baghdad itself is significant. It underlined the determination of his Iranian "protectors" to make certain that no caliph after Hārūn al-Rashīd would assume that the eastern provinces could be ruled from Baghdad. Thus, Hārūn's mistake in trying to arrange his own succession cost the institution of the caliphate a high price. This price involved the emergence, in a few years' time, of the first autonomous dynasty of non-Arab governors over Iran. Its founder was Tāhir ibn al-Ḥusayn himself. Its main cities, especially Nishapur and Samarqand, would soon attract as many eminent representatives of medieval Islamic civilization and culture as had Hārūn al-Rashīd's capital city of Baghdad.

SIGNIFICANCE

Too frequently the name Hārūn al-Rashīd has been associated with a romantic, if not even mythological, vision of the Islamic world in the time of the Baghdad caliphs. This tendency to glorify and romanticize has not been limited to accounts of his reign in the Western world. The themes of the famous undated and anonymously written collection of legends of *Alf layla wa-layla* (fifteenth century; *The Arabian Nights' Entertainments*, 1706-1708; also known as *The Thousand and One Nights*) are products of the literary and cultural imagination of the Islamic world in which he lived; inevitably, therefore, they contributed to subsequent romantic images in European accounts.

On a political level, the temptation has been strong to compare Hārūn al-Rashīd to his equally famous Catholic contemporary, the emperor Charlemagne. Traditional but undocumented accounts tell of diplomatic contacts between the two and even of exchanges to support mutual recognition of respective imperial spheres—at the expense of their shared rival on the throne of the Byzantine Empire at Constantinople. Probably more important than such comparisons, however, is the challenge to study indices of economic exchanges, which, at the height of the caliphs' ascendancy over all Islamic provinces east and west, had come to represent an interregional network that was capable of deciding the future material fate of the Byzantine Empire. Hence, Hārūn's dealings with the Byzantines and, even more, his dealings with distant eastern zones (the Red Sea, the Persian Gulf, and the eastern provinces of Iran bordering on Turkistan) that tied the Islamic Empire to sources of trade in the Far East had to do with much more than mere political ascendancy. These contacts would determine which of the two empires, Islamic or Greek Byzantine, would hold sway over world trade.

In such a geopolitical framework, the relatively recent phenomenon of a restored "Roman" Empire in the West must have been considered of very peripheral importance. An objective approach to Hārūn al-Rashīd's reign,

THE ʿABBĀSID CALIPHS, 750-1256

Reign	*Caliph*
750-754	Abū al-ʿAbbās al-Saffāḥ
754-775	al-Manṣūr
775-785	al-Mahdī
785-786	al-Hādī
786-809	HĀRŪN AL-RASHĪD
809-813	al-Amīn
813-833	al-Maʾmūn (Maʾmūn the Great)
833-842	al-Muʿtaṣim
842-847	al-Wathīq
847-861	al-Mutawakkil
861-862	al-Muntaṣir
862-866	al-Mustaʿin
866-869	al-Muʿtazz
869-870	al-Muqtadī
870-892	al-Muʿtamid
892-902	al-Muʿtaḍid
902-908	al-Muktafī
908-932	al-Muqtadir
932-934	al-Qāhir
934-940	al-Rāḍī
940-944	al-Mustaqfī
946-974	al-Mutī
974-991	al-Tāʾiʿ
991-1031	al-Qadir
1031-1075	al-Qāʾim
1075-1094	al-Muqtadī
1094-1118	al-Mustazhir
1118-1135	al-Mustarshid
1135-1136	al-Rashīd
1136-1160	al-Muqtafī
1160-1170	al-Mustanjid
1170-1180	al-Mustadī
1180-1225	al-Nāṣir
1225-1226	al-Zāhir
1226-1242	al-Mustanṣir
1242-1256	al-Mustaʿṣim

therefore, would study interlinking political, economic, social, and cultural factors that either helped the caliphs of his era to retain the greatness of Baghdad as a world capital or presaged its decline. The caliphs' religious policy, as well as attitudes toward provincial autonomy from Baghdad's direct control, were factors that had, by the time of Hārūn's reign, become issues reflecting future dilemmas, and the eventual decline, of the ʿAbbāsid caliphate.

—*Byron D. Cannon*

FURTHER READING

Bishai, Wilson B. *Islamic History of the Middle East: Backgrounds, Development, and Fall of the Arab Empire*. Boston: Allyn and Bacon, 1968. This survey of Islamic history is less detailed than Brockelmann's 1939 synthesis of Middle Eastern developments from the rise of Muḥammad into the twentieth century (see below). It tends, however, to be somewhat freer in interpretative analysis than are more traditional histories; this makes the work more readable, if less precisely documented. A full section is devoted to the career of Hārūn, based mainly on al-Ṭabarī's *History*. Maps, bibliography.

Brockelmann, Carl. *History of the Islamic Peoples*. Translated by Joel Carmichael and Moshe Perlmann. New York: Routledge, 2000. This volume is still the classic work on Islamic history and civilization and its main dynasties, including the ʿAbbāsid period. The synopsis on Hārūn is among the most developed and useful case studies in the book. Maps, bibliography, index.

Gabrieli, Francesco. *The Arabs: A Compact History*. New York: Hawthorn Books, 1963. This book is less detailed than Bishai's and Brockelmann's works, but the coverage of the reign of Hārūn nevertheless covers several subjects that merit more attention than many more complete political histories offer. These include tax policies and attitudes of the caliph toward "loyal" critics among Sunni jurisprudents responsible for the elaboration of Islamic law.

Glubb, John Bagot. *Haroon al Rasheed and the Great ʿAbbāsids*. London: Hodder and Stoughton, 1976. This monograph was written by "Glubb Pasha," British commanding officer of the Arab Legion in Jordan until his retirement in 1956. A very readable book, especially for its picturesque accounts of the social and cultural milieu of Baghdad during the reign of Hārūn. Bibliography, index.

Hibri, Tayeb el-. *Reinterpreting Islamic Historiography: Hārūn al-Rashīd and the Narrative of the ʿAbbāsid Caliphate*. New York: Cambridge University Press, 1999. Argues that past historical accounts of the eighth and ninth century caliphate were not written as portraits of the time, but instead as a means to convey the religious, political, and social issues that were then prominent. Bibliography, index.

Sourdel, Dominique. "The ʿAbbāsid Caliphate." In *The Cambridge History of Islam*, edited by Peter M. Holt, Ann K. Lambton, and Bernard Lewis. Vol. 1. Cambridge, England: Cambridge University Press, 1977. A brief but scholarly account of the Baghdad caliphate. Covers the main aspects of military and religious history, including the key question of civil war following Hārūn's death. Extensive bibliography, glossary.

SEE ALSO: Charlemagne; Saint Irene; al-Ṭabarī.

RELATED ARTICLES in *Great Events from History: The Middle Ages, 477-1453*: 780: Beginning of the Harem System; 786-809: Reign of Hārūn al-Rashīd; 809: First Islamic Public Hospital.

al-Ḥasan al-Baṣrī
Islamic leader

Al-Ḥasan was the most famous of Muslim teachers and preachers of the generation that followed the age of the Prophet Muḥammad and his companions. His views on religion and politics in the early stages of the Islamic Empire, as well as his code of conduct, made him the model of the pious Muslim in the formative age of Islam.

Born: 642; Medina, Arabia (now in Saudi Arabia)
Died: 728; Basra (now in Iraq)
Also known as: Abū Saʿīd ibn Abī al-Ḥasan Yasār al-Baṣrī (full name)
Area of achievement: Religion and theology

Early Life

Al-Ḥasan al-Baṣrī (ahl-KEH-sahn ahl-BAHS-ree) was born in Medina, ten years after the death of the Prophet Muḥammad. His father, Yasar, of non-Arab origin, had been taken prisoner when the Muslims conquered Maysan in Iraq. He was brought to Medina, where he was manumitted by his owner, and married Ḥasan's mother, Khayrah, also a slave. Some medieval Arab historians assert that al-Ḥasan's parents were manumitted only after his birth.

Al-Ḥasan's childhood is surrounded by the mist of legend. The tradition that was formed around him after his death placed his childhood in the sacred circle of the Prophet Muḥammad himself. It is said that as an infant he was at times suckled by one of the wives of the Prophet, Umm Salama, who owned his mother. One source has it that by drinking from a pitcher that had been used by the Prophet, the boy imbibed divine wisdom.

He grew up in Wadi al-Qura, near Medina, where he was exposed to the pure Arabic tongue of the Bedouins, who were Arab desert nomads. The child accompanied his mother while she served in the house of Umm Salama. Thus he was exposed, at a very early age, to the circle of the Prophet's house and to some of the companions (*sahaba*) of the Prophet who were still living. At fourteen, al-Ḥasan had already memorized the Qurʾān and was adept in writing and arithmetic.

Al-Ḥasan grew up to be tall and handsome, with a fair complexion and blue eyes. His appearance was slightly marred by a small deformation of his nose, the result of a riding accident. His family moved to Basra, Iraq, in 657. At age twenty-two, al-Ḥasan participated in the campaigns of Arab conquests in the East. He saw action in northeastern Persia and in Afghanistan, assisting at the storming of Kabul. At age thirty, he became a secretary to the governor of Khorāsān Province.

Life's Work

Al-Ḥasan returned from the East at age thirty-two to reside in Basra until the end of his life. Basra was a bustling city situated between Arabia and the newly conquered territories to the east. The Arabs who were flocking to Basra shared the city with an increasing number of *mawali* (non-Arab Muslims who were clients of Arabian tribes), whose influence in the economic, political, and religious life of the Islamic Empire was increasing steadily.

Being one of the *mawali* did not hinder al-Ḥasan from becoming the most celebrated teacher of his age. Most of the religious scholars of that age, in fact, were of this class. He was one of many learned men who established a circle of followers and students. He met with his disciples at the mosque, or occasionally at his residence, lecturing on and discussing theological and ethical subjects. At this early stage of Islamic history, these circles were the closest thing to a collegiate institution of learning.

Al-Ḥasan's fame spread to other areas of the expanding Islamic Empire. He was well known and respected by the governors of the province of Iraq as well as at the seat of the caliphate in Damascus. He was a contemporary of ten caliphs, some of whom sought his advice on matters of policy, dogma, and ethics. A letter by al-Ḥasan to the Umayyad caliph ʿAbd al-Malik (r. 685-705) has been preserved; it responds to an inquiry by the caliph as to al-Ḥasan's opinions on the subject of free will.

To draw a fully accurate picture of al-Ḥasan's lifework may prove an impossible task, despite the fact that most Arabic medieval chroniclers, historians, and theologians make reference to him. He emerges from these writings as a man for all seasons, a teacher of universal appeal. Almost all Islamic sects and schools of thought that came after his time regarded him as a champion or patron. It is impossible to separate totally the legend from the historical man.

The rebellion that led to the assassination of the third caliph, ʿUthmān ibn ʿAffān (r. 644-656)—which al-Ḥasan witnessed in Medina as a boy of fourteen—along with the wars of conquest in Asia, was instrumental in forming al-Ḥasan's lifelong philosophy of peaceful living and religious piety. He spoke eloquently against both insurrection and the divisive political and religious argumentation that was rampant at that time. It was this attitude that kept him from arousing the ire of the governors and caliphs of his time, although he did occasionally criticize their incessant pursuit of wealth and power; indeed, he pointed out their misdeeds with clarity and audacity.

Al-Ḥasan's teaching career was not the only reason for his legendary status among his contemporaries and later generations. His powerful Arabic prose style and rhetoric, resplendent with vivid images and striking antitheses, were praised and imitated by later writers and preachers. There is a wealth of pronouncements and clever sayings in flawless Arabic attributed to him by medieval Arab authors.

Al-Ḥasan's lifestyle was another important factor in the making of the legend. Islamic mystics (Sufis) honor him as their first master. He preached the renunciation of this world and its goods in order to seek the rewards of the afterlife, a principle that he applied to his own conduct. His fear of God and constant awareness of the coming Day of Judgment made him a sober man who rarely smiled. Al-Ḥasan ruled himself and his household by the principle of *zuhd*, voluntary poverty. For example, he refused a grant of uncultivated state land; when he received a gift or donation, he would distribute most of it to the poor, keeping only enough to meet his immediate needs. He refused to give his daughter in marriage to a rich man, for he judged that such a wealthy individual either must have amassed his money by dishonest means or must be selfish and miserly.

Al-Ḥasan flourished during that critical period of Islamic history that followed the murder of the caliph ʿUthmān. It was a time of divisiveness in the political and religious life of the Islamic realm. The party of ʿAlī (Shia) was emerging as a strong movement of opposition to the newly established Umayyad Dynasty in Damascus; it was also presenting a challenge to the doctrinal unity of Islam. Disputes over succession and the governance of the new empire were causing political and religious schisms. A variety of schools of Qurʾānic interpretation emerged in support of various political parties. Numerous Arab tribal conflicts, inherited from pre-Islamic time, were also re-emerging. The generation of *sahaba*, or companions of the Prophet, who were regarded as authorities on the interpretation of the Qurʾān, was dying out. The Prophet's followers (called *tabiʿun*) were taking over the task of interpretation and judgment. Al-Ḥasan was the earliest and most prominent member of this group.

In this atmosphere of heterodoxy, dissension, and revolutions in Islam, religious scholars often championed and promoted one party or the other. Al-Ḥasan managed to steer a course above narrow partisanship. He did not refrain from criticizing those in power, yet he managed to avoid undermining their authority. There were times when he went into hiding after speaking openly and forcefully against the governor of Iraq, al-Ḥajjāj, who was known for his strictness and cruelty. Nevertheless, the two men occasionally exchanged visits and counsel.

Al-Ḥasan was able to survive and flourish in this age of conflict because of his categorical opposition to revolt against established authority. He taught that people should try to reform their own lives before taking on themselves the reformation of the state. Thus the Umayyads, who had their hands full with revolts in Iraq and farther east and who sometimes used excessive force in putting down these revolts, tolerated and even appreciated al-Ḥasan, despite his criticisms of them.

The Umayyad caliph ʿUmar II (r. 717-720), who was a devout and pious man, had a good rapport with al-Ḥasan. They exchanged many letters, and the caliph sought al-Ḥasan's advice on matters of policy. ʿUmar's reforms reflected some of al-Ḥasan's teachings, and the caliph's simple lifestyle reflected the model of piety set by al-Ḥasan.

It was during this period of time that al-Ḥasan was appointed a judge. He resigned after a short tenure, possibly because of his old age. Shortly after the death of ʿUmar II, and at the height of the Islamic Empire's territorial expansion, al-Ḥasan died. The Muslims' trend toward power and wealth—and toward political and religious dissension—would continue unabated.

Al-Ḥasan did not leave any written legacy. Tradition has it that on his deathbed he ordered his books and all of his writings burned so that, as he put it, there would be nothing in them that might incriminate him on Judgment Day.

Significance

Most of the Islamic schools of thought and mystic orders that flourished in the following centuries claimed al-Ḥasan as a founder or a member. The Sufi mystics, for example, claimed him as their first master. Opposing parties of later generations often quoted him in support of their causes. As a result, the figure of al-Ḥasan al-Baṣrī came to assume mythic proportions. During his long and distinguished career, he was obsessed mostly with two things: his personal salvation and pious conduct, and the unity and propagation of Islam. Without his writings, and in the absence of any impartial contemporary accounts of his life, al-Ḥasan must remain a figure of legend as much as of history.

—Hassan S. Haddad

FURTHER READING

Brockelmann, Carl. *History of the Islamic Peoples.* Translated by Joel Carmichael and Moshe Perlmann. New York: Routledge, 2000. This volume, first published in 1948, is still the classic work on Islamic history and civilization. Places al-Ḥasan within the political, cultural, and religious context of his time. Maps, bibliography, index.

Obermann, Julian. "Political Theory in Early Islam." *Journal of the American Oriental Society* 55 (1935): 138-162. Addresses the question of the authenticity of the letter to Caliph ʿAbd al-Malik, attributed to al-Ḥasan. The author rules that it was al-Ḥasan's own work.

Ritter, H. "Ḥasan al-Baṣrī." In *The Encyclopaedia of Islam.* Leiden, the Netherlands: E. J. Brill, 1971. This is a concise and useful sketch of his life and work. It contains a bibliography of the most prominent sources on al-Ḥasan in medieval Arabic writings. It also includes a short list of works in French and German in which al-Ḥasan is mentioned.

Schimmel, Annemarie. *Mystical Dimensions of Islam.* Chapel Hill: University of North Carolina Press, 1975. One of the best treatments of its subject. The discussion is aimed primarily at scholars, yet the book is eminently readable. Bibliography.

Smith, Margaret. *The Way of the Mystics: The Early Christian Mystics and the Rise of the Sufis.* 1931. Reprint. New York: Oxford University Press, 1976. Discusses al-Ḥasan within the context of the mystical tradition, drawing parallels between early Christianity and Sufism. A scholarly work, yet accessible to the general reader. Bibliography.

Ṭabarī, al-. *Biographies of the Prophet's Companions and Their Successors.* Translated by Ella Landau-Tasseron. Albany: State University of New York Press, 1998. A translation of the Arab historian al-Ṭabarī's *History*, an authoritative late ninth century work on the era of Prophet Muḥammad, with some discussion of al-Ḥasan and other companions of the Prophet. Bibliography, index.

SEE ALSO: ʿAbd al-Malik; Aḥmad ibn Ḥanbal; Khadīja; Muḥammad; Rābiʿah al-ʿAdawiyah; ʿUmar I.

RELATED ARTICLES in *Great Events from History: The Middle Ages, 477-1453*: c. 610-632: Muḥammad Receives Revelations; 637-657: Islam Expands Throughout the Middle East; October 10, 680: Martyrdom of Prophet's Grandson Ḥusayn; 872-973: Publication of the *History of al-Ṭabarī*; 1273: Sufi Order of Mawlawīyah Is Established.

HENRY THE LION

Duke of Saxony (1142-1180) and Bavaria (1156-1180)

Henry was the most important of the twelfth century German nobles who resisted the authority of the Holy Roman Emperor. He was also a leader in the movement to extend German colonization into Slavic territory.

BORN: 1129; place unknown
DIED: August 6, 1195; Brunswick, Saxony (now in Germany)
ALSO KNOWN AS: Heinrich der Löwe; Henry III; Henry XII (duke of Bavaria)
AREA OF ACHIEVEMENT: Government and politics

EARLY LIFE

Even kings considered themselves clients of Henry the Lion, duke of Saxony and Bavaria. He was a very capable and determined person, but these traits alone would not have made him one of the most important people of the age. The timing of his birth and the political conditions in Germany allowed him to attain a degree of power and influence seldom reached in the twelfth century by anyone without royal status. Between 1076, when Pope Gregory VII attempted to depose Emperor Henry IV, and Henry the Lion's birth in 1129, the German nobility gained so much independence from the throne that the result was nearly anarchy. This situation had arisen because the emperors were distracted by the conflict with the Papacy and because they had lost their struggle to make succession to the imperial throne hereditary. The conflict with the various popes required concentration on Italy rather than Germany, and the principle of election to the throne meant that feuds, granting of favors in return for electoral support, and uncertainty about the future created political instability. Enjoying freedom from imperial control, aggressive knights carved out domains for themselves and began to give themselves territorial designations based on the names of their castles: thus Lothair of Supplinburg, grandfather of Henry the Lion.

Engraved depiction of Henry the Lion, standing center, receiving a plea for assistance from a kneeling Frederick Barbarossa. (R. S. Peale and J. A. Hill)

Lothair was one of the new men, so new that his family is unknown except for the name of his father. Yet he was able to become duke of Saxony and, finally, Holy Roman Emperor Lothair III. He had no sons, but he married his daughter, Gertrude, to Henry the Proud, a member of the Bavarian Welf family. Despite all of his efforts to have Henry the Proud recognized as his successor, when Lothair died in 1137, Henry was not elected. Throughout Lothair's reign, a feud had continued between the Welf and Hohenstaufen families. The Hohenstaufen party not only prevented Henry the Proud's election but also deprived him of his title as duke of Saxony. The Saxons, however, remained loyal to him and war broke out between his forces and those of Albert the Bear, the newly appointed duke of Saxony. Henry the Proud appeared to be winning when he suddenly died in 1139, leaving his ten-year-old son, Henry the Lion, to carry on the struggle.

Contrary to expectation, the Welf cause did not collapse with the death of Henry the Proud. The Saxon nobles and the Welf family continued the fight until a negotiated settlement in 1142 recognized Henry the Lion as duke of Saxony. As part of the settlement, Gertrude, Henry the Lion's mother, married the newly named duke of Bavaria. She died in childbirth the next year, leaving Henry alone at the age of fourteen. Albert the Bear lost his title but remained a problem for the Welfs. He was given a small territory on the Saxon border and remained Henry's archenemy for the rest of his life.

LIFE'S WORK

In addition to his struggle to maintain and increase his influence and holdings at the expense of his fellow nobles and the emperor, Henry expanded his domain, and consequently that of German culture, into previously Slavic regions. These activities made him second in power only to the emperor within Germany and a prominent figure in international affairs. He displayed the ruthless methods he would use throughout his life from the very beginning of his tenure as duke of Saxony at the age of thirteen. One of his first acts was to claim the lands of one of his vassals who died childless. In the course of the ensuing dispute, he imprisoned the archbishop of Bremen, who was the deceased's brother, and other church officials. He released them only after the emperor intervened. These high-handed methods were to be the primary cause of the revolt by his vassals that led to his deposition in 1180.

Henry's campaign against the Slavs was similarly characterized by ruthless determination. As early as 1147, Henry had been involved in the crusade against the heathen Slavs that had been authorized by the pope in lieu of warring in the Holy Land. The Crusade of 1147 had few results because of the quarreling among the Crusaders, but Albert the Bear and Henry the Lion—as well as other Saxon nobles—continued the attempt to establish colonies beyond their eastern borders. Albert cooperated with the Church, although he would not allow Church officials to impose heavier tithes on the converted Slavs than on the German colonists. He also prevented the Crusade of 1157 from being conducted in his territory. Henry, on the other hand, was less interested in Christianizing the Slavs than in obtaining tribute from them. He crossed the Elbe River in 1160 and subdued the area around Mecklenburg, which he managed to hold for seven years. Even after he was forced to return most of it to a Slav prince, the acquisition and exploitation of Slavic lands remained a constant feature of his policy. By the time of his deposition in 1180, the area between the Elbe and the Baltic Sea to the Danish border had been colonized by Germans and was under Saxon control.

Henry was also interested in extending his power by encouraging trade and commerce. One of his most successful enterprises was the development and promotion of the city of Lübeck into an important commercial center on the Baltic coast. The city was founded in 1143, and Henry had gained control of it with his usual ruthless tactics by 1160. Thereafter, he favored it in every way he could and in return received considerable revenue from its markets. In a similar way, he raised the city of Munich to commercial importance by building a bridge for the transport of salt from Salzburg. Bishop Otto of Freising complained that Henry had, in effect, stolen the tolls from the salt trade by diverting traffic to Munich from the bishop's territory, but the complaint produced no results.

These high-handed methods and efforts to increase his power finally brought Henry to grief. He took every opportunity to weaken the Saxon nobility, who bitterly resented him. The practice that aroused the most fury was the seizure of the lands of vassals who died without adult male heirs. He added insult to injury by attempting to make the counts into his direct administrative subordinates. By the standards of a later age, this movement toward centralization and the attempt to gain control of independent, frequently feuding, and continually troublesome nobles may seem laudable, but in the twelfth century, the view was that nobles should be free to govern their lands as they pleased as long as they met their feudal obligations. That was the position of Henry's vassals, who protested vigorously to his overlord, Emperor Frederick I Barbarossa.

Henry probably could not have withstood the conspiracies against him by the Saxon nobles as long as he did without the support of the emperor. Frederick, who had been elected emperor in 1152, was a staunch friend to Henry as well as being his first cousin. Frederick's mother, Judith, was Henry the Proud's sister. This kinship did not, however, make Frederick a Welf partisan, for he had equal ties of kinship to the Hohenstaufen family. It seems that the two men were genuinely fond of each other. At any rate, they supported each other. Frederick allowed Henry to do as he pleased in Saxony, and Henry participated in Frederick's military campaigns in Italy. It was after the Italian campaign of 1155, in which Henry had performed particularly valuable service, that Frederick made him duke of Bavaria as well as Saxony and thus returned the old Welf territories to the family that had traditionally possessed them. By the time his arch rival, Albert the Bear, died in 1170, Henry had been able to quell the rebellions against him so successfully and had become so powerful that a period of relative peace ensued. He felt secure enough to leave his lands in the care of his wife and go on a crusade to Jerusalem in 1172, but he returned after only a short stay.

Relations between Henry and Frederick became less cordial after 1174. Henry apparently refused to take part in the Italian campaign of that year even though his troops were desperately needed. The two men are reported to have met for the last time in 1176, when Frederick is supposed to have gone so far as to beg for Henry's help in Italy. Henry is said to have demanded the important castle and fief of Goslar in return for military aid. Frederick refused, and the two parted on bad terms. The negotiations at this meeting, if it actually occurred, are matters of speculation. No contemporary record of it exists.

Whatever the immediate circumstances of the quarrel between Henry and Frederick, it was the result of the policies both men had pursued. Frederick was attempting to assert his authority in Germany and Italy just as Henry was trying to consolidate his in Saxony. While Henry wanted to subordinate his own vassals, he also wanted to maintain his freedom from imperial control. The demand for Goslar, regardless of whether it occurred, is symbolic of this struggle for power.

Part of the struggle involved Henry's dealings with foreign princes. A civil war in Denmark enabled him to make the king of Denmark practically a vassal in return for his support. The king paid tribute to Henry and remained under his control from 1157 until 1171, when he tried to break away. The attempt failed, and Denmark remained a Saxon client until Henry's fall. Frederick was less concerned with Henry's Danish venture than with his friendship toward foreign enemies of imperial policy. He was particularly disturbed by Henry's relations with some of the Italian nobles Frederick was trying to subdue. Henry also visited the Byzantine emperor, who was unfriendly to Frederick. Another of Frederick's enemies, Henry II of England, was a potential problem, as Henry the Lion had married his daughter, Matilda, in 1168.

The final break with the emperor came in 1178. A bishop who had been dispossessed of some of his lands by Henry appealed to Frederick for justice. Naturally, the Saxon nobility supported the bishop. Frederick, who had dismissed many such complaints against Henry on previous occasions, took this opportunity to call his overly powerful vassal to account. Henry ignored three different summonses to appear at the imperial court during 1179 and was outlawed in January, 1180. Bernard of Anhalt, a son of Albert the Bear, became duke of Saxony, and Saxony became a much smaller territory as many of its fiefs went back to the Church or to other magnates. Frederick was careful not to create such a powerful threat to imperial authority as Henry had.

Henry attempted to fight back but without success. His former vassals proved undependable, and his appeals to foreign courts for aid went unheeded. Finally, in 1182, he went into exile at the court of his father-in-law, Henry II of England. He and his family were well treated in England. His son, Otto, became a favorite of Richard I, who became king of England in 1189. Richard and Otto were first cousins and similar in appearance as well as tastes. Richard made him earl of York in 1190, when he was only eight years old, tried to obtain the Scottish throne for him, and was his primary supporter when he was elected Holy Roman Emperor Otto IV.

The differences between Frederick and Henry were reconciled. Frederick died in 1190, and Henry returned to Germany in 1194. He established a court at Brunswick, where he patronized the troubadours who were to make him the hero of many ballads. He also saw to the building of the church where he and his wife are buried. His interest in history led him to collect a number of chronicles and to oversee the writing of an informational book that he titled *Lucidarius*. Despite the Latin title, it is written in the vernacular German of the period. He had only one year to enjoy these activities, as he died in 1195.

Significance

Henry the Lion was in many ways a product of his time, but his personal attributes qualified him for his time very well. He was probably the most powerful and archetypal of the nobles who prevented the Holy Roman Emperor from establishing a unified government in Germany. There were many other reasons for the failure of Germany to develop a central government after the French or English model, but the ability of the great nobles to maintain their own authority at the expense of central government was one of the key factors.

He was also one of the most important figures in the expansion of Germany to the east. The territory he wrested from the Slavs may have fallen from his personal control, but those areas settled by German colonists were to remain permanently Germanized.

It is interesting to speculate about the results if Henry had succeeded in establishing a centralized, independent Saxony. Bavaria and Saxony, as they then existed, constituted about one third of modern Germany. Such a state in Central Europe would have had profound consequences. He failed, however, and remains interesting only as a prime example of the powerful subjects whose defeat was such an important feature of nation building by medieval European kings. The difference in this case is that there was no building of a German state.

—*Philip Dwight Jones*

Further Reading

Barraclough, Geoffrey. *The Origins of Modern Germany*. Reprint. New York: W. W. Norton, 1984. Although published originally in 1947, this book remains the standard work in English on medieval Germany. Barraclough takes the position that Henry resented giving up Goslar to Frederick in 1168 and was determined to regain it but that Henry lost all chance of success when Frederick made peace with the Church in 1177. The author also believes that Frederick pursued a policy of keeping the nobles weak after Henry's fall.

_______, ed. *Medieval Germany, 911-1250: Essays by German Historians*. 2 vols. Oxford: Basil Blackwell, 1961. The issue of most interest to modern historians is the interpretation of the constitutional struggle between Frederick and Henry, and some of the articles in this work deal with this topic.

Ehlers, Joachim. *Heinrich der Löwe: Europäisches Fürstentum im Hochmittelalter.* Göttingen, Germany: Muster-Schmidt, 1997. One of the few biographies of Henry, in German. Illustrations, bibliography.

Eyck, Frank. *Religion and Politics in German History: From the Beginnings to the French Revolution*. New York: St. Martin's Press, 1998. An analysis of how Germanic peoples preserved links with classical civilization through their ability to assimilate other cultures and peoples, from their alliances with eighth century popes through the Reformation and Counter-Reformation. The initial bond between the Germanic rulers and popes turned to conflict as the Papacy gained power. Tables, maps, bibliography, index.

Hampe, Karl. *Germany Under the Salian and Hohen-*

staufen Emperors. London: Rowman and Littlefield, 1973. A classic work, with an introduction by Ralph Bennet that comments on the latest German and English works in this field and gives the latest interpretations of the constitutional struggle between Frederick and Henry.

Jeep, John M., et al., eds. *Medieval Germany: An Encyclopedia*. New York: Garland, 2001. An A-Z encyclopedia that addresses all aspects of the German- and Dutch-speaking medieval world from 500 to 1500. Entries include individuals, events, and broad topics such as feudalism and pregnancy. Bibliographical references, index.

Jordan, Karl. *Henry the Lion: A Biography*. Translated by P. S. Falla. New York: Oxford University Press, 1986. A rare English-language biography of Henry. Illustrations, maps, bibliography, index.

Moore, Robert Ian. *The First European Revolution, c. 970-1215*. Malden, Mass.: Blackwell, 2000. According to the publisher, "a radical reassessment of Europe from the late tenth to the early thirteenth centuries [arguing that] the period witnessed the first true 'revolution' in European society," supported by transformation of the economy, family life, political power structures, and the rise of the non-Mediterranean cities. Bibliography, index.

Munz, Peter. *Frederick Barbarossa: A Study in Medieval Politics*. Ithaca, N.Y.: Cornell University Press, 1969. Munz believes that assigning motives of modern state building to twelfth century figures is anachronistic and that Frederick did not want to centralize his authority. He argues that Frederick's real aim was to keep the German nobles embroiled with one another so he would be free to go on crusades.

Otto of Freising. *The Deeds of Frederick Barbarossa*. 1953. Rev. ed. New York: W. W. Norton, 1966. There is little about Henry in this work, but it is worth looking at because Otto was a contemporary of Henry and was involved in a quarrel with him. It is also worthwhile in that it deals extensively with Frederick, who is of obvious importance to Henry's story.

Thompson, James Westfall. *Feudal Germany*. Chicago: University of Chicago Press, 1928. Dated, but probably one of the more readily available works. Thompson champions Henry as a forward-looking ruler who was trying to build a modern, centralized state and who was patriotically trying to prevent abortive, wasteful military campaigns in Italy. He further argues that one of Frederick's greatest wrongs was the destruction of Saxony.

SEE ALSO: Frederick I Barbarossa; Gregory VII; Henry the Lion; Henry IV (of Germany); Richard I.

RELATED ARTICLES in *Great Events from History: The Middle Ages, 477-1453*: c. 1150-1200: Rise of the Hansa Merchant Union; 1152: Frederick Barbarossa Is Elected King of Germany; September 17, 1156: Austria Emerges as a National Entity.

PRINCE HENRY THE NAVIGATOR

Portuguese military leader and explorer

Although Prince Henry considered crusading against the North African Muslims to be his primary task, it was his African explorations that later put Portugal at the forefront of the European age of discovery.

BORN: March 4, 1394; Porto, Portugal
DIED: November 13, 1460; Sagres, Portugal
AREAS OF ACHIEVEMENT: Exploration, warfare and conquest, religion and theology

EARLY LIFE

On February 14, 1387, King John I of Portugal married Philippa (of Portugal), the eldest daughter of Prince John of Gaunt of England. The union proved quite fertile, and the queen gave birth to a succession of children: Duarte in 1391, Pedro in 1392, and her best-known child, Henry (or Enrique) on March 4, Ash Wednesday, 1394. These children were followed by a daughter, Isabel, and two more sons, John and Fernando. Little is known about Prince Henry's youth, although it appears that he grew up in close association with his two elder brothers. They received the usual upbringing of noble youths, learning horsemanship, hunting, and the skills and values associated with late medieval chivalry.

Chivalric values were new to late fourteenth century Portugal, with its isolated location on Western Europe's periphery. It appears that these values arrived with the chaste Queen Philippa from England, and King John I quite readily adopted chivalric ideals for his court and family. Chivalry imposed restraint and sophistication on the rough-and-ready crusading spirit that had long been indigenous to the Iberian Peninsula. These twin value systems of chivalry and crusade against infidels would be the predominant influences on Prince Henry's actions through his entire life.

In 1411, King John I made peace with Castile and declared that he would celebrate the occasion with a joust during which his three oldest sons would be knighted. His sons objected, however, and asked that they be given a chance to earn their knighthood in actual combat according to the best chivalric practices. Because Portugal had just reached a peace treaty with neighboring Castile, the warlike energies of John I's sons needed to be directed farther afield. The Moorish city of Ceuta, located strategically opposite Gibraltar, became their objective. It would be the first major Portuguese move against Islamic territory since about 1250. The expedition was quite large, consisting of 240 ships, thirty thousand sailors, and twenty thousand soldiers, and took two years to prepare. Sailing from the Tagus River on July 23, 1415, the expedition landed at Ceuta on August 21 and immediately assaulted the city. An easy and overwhelming victory resulted for the Crusaders. John's three sons all fought bravely and earned their knighthoods. Furthermore, Pedro obtained the additional reward of the dukedom of Coimbra, while Henry received the dukedom of Viseu. Returning to Portugal, the young Prince Henry took up frontier guard duty at Viseu for the next several years.

Prince Henry the Navigator. (Hulton|Archive at Getty Images)

LIFE'S WORK

The capture of Ceuta proved quickly to be an expensive disappointment for the Portuguese. Its thriving caravan trade was soon diverted to other coastal cities, while the surrounding Muslim states maintained an attitude of implacable hostility. One party of Portuguese had opposed the expedition to Ceuta from the beginning, and after the conquest, its members advocated immediate evacuation. Another party, which included Prince Henry, called for the retention of Ceuta and further expansion against the Muslim powers. Their ultimate goal was the winning of North Africa for Christendom. To achieve their objective, Prince Henry advanced a policy of attacking the Muslims head-on in the region of Ceuta, while at the same time trying to approach them from behind by a flanking movement down the west coast of Africa.

In 1416, King John I appointed Prince Henry as governor of Ceuta, although the young man continued to reside at Viseu. A Muslim threat against Ceuta in 1418 prompted Portugal to organize a relief expedition under Henry's command. By this time, the character of the young prince was formed, and he was at the height of his physical powers. According to his chronicler, Gomes Eannes de Zurara, Prince Henry was tall and dark, with a large build and thick, shaggy black hair. His face wore a grave expression that aroused a sense of fear in those around him. Unlike many profligate noblemen of the late Middle Ages, he ascetically shunned both wine and women. In fact, he never married and was reputed to have died a virgin. Instead, Prince Henry directed his energies into crusading and exploring.

Crusading and exploration were expensive enterprises, and throughout his life, Prince Henry, who enjoyed living in a princely style, was chronically short of money. He drew revenues from his dukedom of Viseu, to which were added the governorship of Algarve in 1419 and the headship of the Military Order of Christ in 1420. Still, these were not enough, and Henry continually had to seek further sources of revenue. It was this constant quest for money that explains his role in the settlement of Madeira and the Azores Islands and in the Castilian-Portuguese rivalry over the Canary Islands.

It is possible that Europeans discovered the Madeiras as early as 1339, but it is definite that they knew about the islands by 1417, when a strong Castilian expedition visited Porto Santo. Portugal reacted by quickly occupying the islands during 1419 and 1420 with settlers from Prince Henry's province of Algarve. In 1433, King Duarte granted the islands to Henry as a fief, and he drew income from their production of dye-stuffs and grain. The same situation applied to the Azores, which the Portuguese Diogo de Senill discovered in 1427. Domestic animals were dropped off on the islands during the early 1430's in preparation for human settlement. It was not until 1439 that the regent Dom Pedro gave his brother Prince Henry a charter to settle the islands; colonization was begun in the early 1440's. Once again, the production of dye-stuffs and grain provided the profits that helped to fuel Prince Henry's explorations and crusades.

Meanwhile, the exploration of the African coast was delayed by the navigational and psychological barrier of Cape Bojador. This barren promontory extended twenty-five miles out into the Atlantic, where great waves crashed and adverse winds and currents made sailing treacherous. Beyond lay the "Green Sea of Darkness" from which no one ever returned. Between 1424 and 1434, Prince Henry sent out fifteen expeditions with orders to round it. Finally, in 1434 or 1435, a squire of Prince Henry's household, Gil Eanes, sailed past the dreaded cape on his second attempt. His success removed a formidable psychological barrier to exploration, although the cape still remained a serious navigational menace. The conquest of Cape Bojador was probably Prince Henry's most important contribution to European exploration.

After the passage of Cape Bojador, exploration of the African coast made greater progress. In 1436, the explorer Afonso Gonçalves Baldia reached the bay that he mistakenly called the Rio de Ouro. After that, however, exploration stopped temporarily while Prince Henry concentrated on his true love, a crusade against the Muslims in what became the disastrous Tangier expedition of 1437. From 1438 to 1441, the tumultuous early years of the minority of Afonso V intervened to occupy Portuguese energies, until Henry's brother Pedro defeated the queen-mother Lenora for the regency.

A return of stability brought a resumption of exploration. In 1441, Antao Gonçalves brought back the first black slaves from Africa, beginning a profitable but inhumane trade, while Nuno Tristão discovered Cape Blanco. The next year, 1442, saw the first African gold brought back to Portugal, an achievement that allowed them to bypass the Muslim caravan trade. At that point, Prince Henry obtained a royal monopoly of all trading south of Cape Bojador and proceeded for a fee to issue trading licenses to eager merchants.

By 1446, trading expeditions far outnumbered voyages of further discovery. Still, exploration also progressed rapidly with the encouragement of both Prince Henry and his brother Dom Pedro, whose role in early Portuguese exploration has been unfairly ignored. With their encouragement, Dinís Dias discovered Cape Verde in 1444, while Alvaro Fernandes reached the Gambia River the following year. After Pedro fell into disgrace in 1448, however, and was killed at the Battle of Alfarrobeira on May 20, 1449, much of the drive for new discoveries appears to have ended. It revived somewhat during 1454, when the Venetian merchant Alvise Cadamosto joined the service of Prince Henry. He reached Portuguese Guinea in 1455 and proceeded even farther south the following year, accidentally discovering the Cape Verde Islands and the Bissagos Islands. Cadamosto's primary interest was trading, and it was between 1455 and 1461 that Prince Henry established the fortress-trading post on Arguim Island, near Cape Blanco.

Meanwhile, back in Portugal, the siren call of a crusade against the Muslims tempted the aging Prince Henry once again. During 1456 and 1457, Portugal prepared for a papal crusade against the Ottoman Turks in response to their capture of Constantinople in 1453. When the general crusade failed to materialize, the Portuguese simply redirected their efforts against the Muslims of North Africa. Their fleet, including King Afonso and Prince Henry, sailed on October 17, 1458, and arrived off the Muslim city of Alcacer-Seguer on October 22, capturing it two days later. It was to be Prince Henry's last crusade.

Exploration of the African coast also slowed during Henry's last years, although a brisk trade continued. Pedro de Sintra may have reached Sierra Leone in 1460, but as the farthest point of Portuguese discovery achieved in Prince Henry's lifetime, it was not a particularly impressive addition to the achievements of Cadamosto in 1456. Back in Portugal, the old Prince Henry fell ill at his residence of Sagres and died on November 13, 1460.

SIGNIFICANCE

Prince Henry the Navigator is one of the romantic historical figures of whom stories are told to schoolchildren in the Western world. Modern society finds this Henry attractive, since he was supposedly a lone giant pushing back the darkness of geographic ignorance. It is claimed that he was a navigational innovator, the founder of a school and an observatory for geographic studies at Sagres, and a systematic promoter of exploration, with a view to reaching India by sea. In fact, he was none of these things. Recent scholarship finds no evidence for any technical innovations, any school, or any systematic plan of exploration, especially anything including India as its ultimate goal. Present-day Portuguese do not even recognize him as "the Navigator"; that title was bestowed on him by his English biographer Richard Henry Major in 1868.

The fact is that Prince Henry was a man of the late Middle Ages; chivalric and crusading values motivated him to attack the Muslims and to explore Africa. In addition, as his chronicler Zurara pointed out, his actions befitted the stars under which he was born. Prince Henry's horoscope showed that he "should toil at high and mighty conquests, especially in seeking out things that were hidden from other men and secret." People in medieval times took these predictions seriously, and it was as a medieval Crusader that Prince Henry uncovered places that were hidden and secret and inadvertently helped to open up the great age of discovery in the late fifteenth and sixteenth centuries.

—*Ronald H. Fritze*

FURTHER READING

Aczel, Amir D. *The Riddle of the Compass: The Invention That Changed the World.* New York: Harcourt, 2001. A brief but detailed and thorough account of the invention of the compass. Also discusses the history of navigation to the fifteenth century.

Beazley, Charles Raymond. *Prince Henry the Navigator: The Hero of Portugal and of Modern Discovery, 1394-1460 A.D.* 1894. Reprint. New York: Burt Franklin, 1968. The author follows Major's work in viewing Prince Henry as a man of science living before his true time and as a great precursor of the age of exploration. Almost half the book deals with geographical, scientific, and political developments leading up to the time of Prince Henry.

Diffie, Bailey W., and George D. Winius. *Foundations of the Portuguese Empire, 1415-1580.* Minneapolis: University of Minnesota Press, 1977. Although part of a general history of the Portuguese Empire, the first quarter of the volume provides information and interpretation of Prince Henry's career. It is a well-written study and is solidly based on primary and secondary sources. Prince Henry clearly appears as a medieval Crusader.

Major, Richard Henry. *The Life of Prince Henry of Portugal, Surnamed the Navigator, and Its Results.* 1868. Reprint. London: Frank Cass, 1967. The author is responsible for Prince Henry being popularly known throughout the English-speaking world as "the Navigator." This biography remains useful, even though it is quite dated in its attribution to Henry of a scientific spirit and of the sole motivating force behind Portuguese exploration.

Russell, Peter. *Prince Henry "the Navigator": A Life.* New Haven, Conn.: Yale University Press, 2000. A history of Prince Henry and his expeditions. Provides many illustrations, a map of discoveries, and a translated letter of Henry's, written to his father. Includes an extensive bibliography and index.

Sanceau, Elaine. *Henry the Navigator: The Story of a Great Prince and His Times.* New Haven. Conn.: Archon Books, 1969. Written by an author of several biographies of great figures from the age of Portuguese expansion. Artfully blends documentary evidence into an exciting narrative. This biography should be preferred to the one by Ure.

Ure, John. *Prince Henry the Navigator.* London: Constable, 1977. Written by an English diplomat who served in Portugal, this full-scale biography does a good job of emphasizing Henry's medieval crusading mentality. It unfortunately also continues to view him as possessing a modern spirit of inquiry and so is largely a mild updating of the earlier romantic interpretations of Prince Henry as the indispensable man of the age of discovery.

Winius, George D., ed. *Portugal, the Pathfinder: Journeys from the Medieval Toward the Modern World, 1300-Circa 1600.* Madison, Wis.: Hispanic Seminary of Medieval Studies, 1995. Chapters look at figures such as Prince Henry, Vasco de Gama, and their successors; the "discovery" of the Atlantic as an autonomous geographical space; the evidence of medieval maps; and Portuguese expansion in West Africa. Includes a bibliography and index.

Zurara, Gomes Eannes de. *The Chronicle of the Discovery and Conquest of Guinea.* 2 vols. Edited and translated by Charles Raymond Beazley and Edgar Prestage. 1896-1899. Reprint. New York: B. Franklin, 1963. These contemporary chronicles are extensive sources for an account of the early Portuguese discoveries and are the only source for some incidents. The values of chivalry and crusading likely influenced the author, who was a member of the Order of Christ and the official historian of Prince Henry's career.

See also: Petrus Peregrinus de Maricourt.

Related articles in *Great Events from History: The Middle Ages, 477-1453*: c. 1145: Prester John Myth Sweeps Across Europe; c. 1250: Improvements in Shipbuilding and Navigation; 1415-1460: Prince Henry the Navigator Promotes Portuguese Exploration; May 29, 1453: Fall of Constantinople.

Henry I

King of England (r. 1100-1135)

Henry I did much to organize and regularize the laws and government of England, reforming judicial and fiscal matters. By his marriage to Matilda of Scotland, a descendant of Edward the Confessor, Henry I won the support of many of his English subjects, although the marriage was less pleasing to Normans.

Born: c. September, 1068; Selby, Yorkshire, England
Died: December 1, 1135; Lyons-la-Forêt, Normandy (now in France)
Also known as: Henry Beauclerc
Areas of achievement: Government and politics, law, military

Early Life

Henry I was the only English-born son of William the Conqueror and the only one of his sons to have been born after their father had become king of England; his brothers had been born while William was duke of Normandy. It is reputed that Henry I learned to read and write Latin and studied the English language and law, but scholars have found little to support his supposed intellectual habits, although they do concede that he had some knowledge of Latin and spoke some English. On the death of William the Conqueror, in 1087, Normandy was willed to his eldest son, Robert, while England was awarded to his second son, William Rufus. Henry received lands in both Normandy and England. As he thus became a vassal of both of his brothers, he was inevitably brought into the quarrels between them.

Henry was a member of the royal hunting party, in the New Forest, when William Rufus was fatally injured by an arrow, whether by accident or murder (this question has never been answered). There have been hints that Henry may have had at least a guilty knowledge of the events that led to the death of William Rufus, if, indeed, there was a plot. At the time of the death of William Rufus, Robert was returning to Europe from a crusade. Henry knew of an agreement between Robert and William Rufus with regard to the succession; each was to be his brother's heir. Henry moved to consolidate his position. He rode from the New Forest to Winchester and took possession of the royal treasury. He was chosen king the next day by those councillors in Winchester at the time. At the time of his coronation, he issued a charter of liberties, designed to win support of the people and the Church. He promised to put an end to the evil customs of William Rufus and to assure that the laws of Edward the Confessor would be upheld, subject to the amendments made by William the Conqueror. He invited the exiled Saint Anselm, archbishop of Canterbury (1093-1109), to return to England and to resume his office. On Anselm's

Henry I. (Library of Congress)

return, Henry raised the question of the investiture of church appointees by the king, lay investiture. Anselm refused to accept this concept of investiture. The issue was settled by a compromise, in which it was agreed that the king was to be informed of election of churchmen but would allow their investment by the Church. In reality, the king had surrendered a hollow ceremony and retained a real power.

In the spring of 1101, Robert of Normandy returned to Western Europe and made plans to invade England in support of his claim to the English throne. The landing of Robert at Portsmouth was followed by a meeting of the two brothers. An agreement was reached. By the terms of their agreement, Henry gave up all of his Norman holdings except Domfront, restored the lands in England of Robert's supporters, and paid the duke an annual pension. For his part, Robert gave up his claim to the English throne and paid homage to Henry for his English lands.

The rule of Robert over Normandy caused some of his vassals to appeal to Henry for aid. A decisive battle between the two brothers was fought at Tinchebray, and as a result of this engagement, Robert fell prisoner to Henry. Robert would be retained as his brother's prisoner until Robert's death in 1134. With the fall of Robert, England and Normandy were reunited.

Although Henry had many illegitimate children, he had only two legitimate heirs, Matilda and William. Until 1120, the succession appeared secure. In that year, returning to England from Normandy following his betrothal and marriage, William was to drown at sea.

Suddenly, the succession question was no longer settled. All of Henry's plans were now in a state of total confusion. He sent for his widowed daughter, Matilda, who had been married to Holy Roman Emperor Henry V. At a December, 1126, meeting of his council, Henry forced his barons and prelates to swear to support Matilda should Henry die without a male heir. Although many prelates and barons favored his nephew, Stephen of Blois (who became King Stephen, r. 1135-1154), they were afraid to oppose Henry's wishes. In the spring of 1127, he secured for Matilda a new husband, Geoffrey of Anjou. In 1133, a child, the future Henry II, was born to this marriage.

Life's Work

It was to be in the field of government that Henry I would make his major contribution to English history. Henry made a wise choice in naming as his principal adviser and justiciar Roger of Salisbury. During his reign, Henry began to meet less with his Great Council of tenants-in-chief and to meet more frequently with a small working council of a few barons and his major officials. This smaller group traveled with the king at all times. While the Great Council remained essentially a feudal body and met only on formal occasions, the smaller body was mainly an administrative council, a legislative body, a financial agency, and a court of law. Although the Great Council could disavow decisions of the smaller council, it seldom did so.

Norman Kings of England, 1066-1189

Reign	*Monarch*
1066-1087	WILLIAM I THE CONQUEROR
1087-1100	William II Rufus
1100-1135	HENRY I BEAUCLERC
1135-1154	Stephen
1154-1189	HENRY II (Plantagenet line begins)

Under the direction of Roger of Salisbury, the financial and judicial functions of the council became more specialized. When the small council met for financial reasons, it came to be spoken of as the Exchequer. For the accomplishment of its financial duties, it was divided into the Lower Exchequer, which received moneys due the Crown, and the Upper Exchequer, which settled accounts and financially oriented judicial disputes. During Henry's reign judicial reforms also took place. Henry commenced a practice of sending out royal justices on circuits to provide the king's justice in the local areas. This use of such officials, known as itinerant justices, was only begun under Henry's rule; it was expanded during the reign of his grandson, Henry II.

Because much of the reform work of Henry I was lost during the period of civil war that followed his death, later scholars have tended to forget the work of Henry I and his minister, Roger of Salisbury, and attribute this work to Henry II. In truth, Henry II's work was at least in part restoration.

Significance

Henry I has not received due recognition. In addition to his work in government, Henry should also be credited with the reunification of England and Normandy under the Norman rulers of England. This reunification may have been a mixed blessing, as it kept England's king abroad for great periods of time and caused substantial amounts of England's resources to be expended on its troubled French territories.

—*Van Mitchell Smith*

Further Reading

Chrimes, S. B. *An Introduction to the Administrative History of Mediaeval England*. 3d ed. New York: Barnes and Noble Books, 1966. Written primarily for scholars, but also valuable for general readers.

Hollister, C. Warren. *Henry I*. New Haven, Conn.: Yale University Press, 2001. Part of the Yale English Monarchs series, an extensive biography of Henry. Includes a bibliography and index.

Kealey, Edward J. *Roger of Salisbury, Viceroy of England*. Berkeley: University of California Press, 1972. Although this work deals primarily with the life and career of Roger of Salisbury, it is one of the more extensive sources of the reign of Henry I.

Poole, Austin L. *From Domesday Book to Magna Carta, 1087-1216*. New York: Oxford University Press, 1993. This volume, from the Oxford History of England series, includes discussion of the reign of Henry I.

Robertson, A. J., ed. and trans. *The Laws of the Kings of England from Edmund to Henry I*. Felinfach, Wales: Llanerch, 2000. A survey of the legal history of English kings.

Taswell-Langmead, Thomas Pitt. *English Constitutional History, from the Teutonic Conquest to the Present Time*. 11th ed. Boston: Houghton Mifflin, 1960. Still one of the standard sources of English constitutional history. Covers the time of Henry I.

Williamson, David. *Debrett's Kings and Queens of Europe*. Topsfield, Mass.: Salem House, 1988. A brief entry of Henry I and Queen Matilda. Includes genealogical tables.

See also: Saint Anselm; David I; Gwenllian verch Gruffydd; Henry II; Nest verch Rhys ap Tewdwr; King Stephen; William the Conqueror.

Related articles in *Great Events from History: The Middle Ages, 477-1453*: 1154-1204: Angevin Empire Is Established; c. 1200: Common-Law Tradition Emerges in England.

Henry II

French-born king of England (r. 1154-1189)

Beginning his reign after a time of civil war, Henry II reestablished order. Henry sought to build on the reforms of his grandfather Henry I, fostered the study of the laws of England, and advocated constitutional law.

Born: March 5, 1133; Le Mans, Maine (now in France)
Died: July 6, 1189; near Tours (now in France)
Also known as: Henry of Anjou; Henry Plantagenet; Henry Fitzempress; Henry Curtmantle
Areas of achievement: Law, government and politics

Early Life

Henry II was the eldest child of Matilda, daughter of Henry I, by her second husband, Geoffrey, count of Anjou. After the death of William, the only legitimate son of Henry I, in 1120, Henry I was obliged to rebuild his shattered succession plan around Matilda. He forced his major barons and prelates to swear their allegiance to her. Although many had serious misgivings about having a female ruler, their fear of the king caused them to accede to his wishes. On the death of Henry I, however, Stephen of Blois, his nephew, moved quickly to secure the throne (as King Stephen) and to acquire the support of the barons and prelates. Although he had acquired the throne with surprising ease, Stephen found it much more difficult to hold it. As neither Matilda nor Stephen proved to be an effective leader, the struggle did not reach a decisive point until Henry, Matilda's son, appeared as a major figure.

The dynastic fight would be settled with the Treaty of Winchester in 1153, by the terms of which Stephen would retain the throne for his life and would be succeeded by young Henry. Stephen died in 1154, and Henry came to the throne as Henry II.

Henry II was of medium height, stocky, and strong. His face was said to resemble that of a lion, especially when he was angry. Although his temperament was generally cold and calculating, he was subject to sudden and violent mood shifts. Being an outdoorsman, he wore his hair close-cropped and was judged to be handsome; although he dressed simply, his bearing was regal and commanded respect and admiration.

Life's Work

By inheritance and marriage, Henry found himself the ruler of a vast realm. From his mother, he inherited Normandy and Maine; from his father, he inherited the lands of Anjou; and through his marriage to Eleanor of Aquitaine, he secured the duchy of Aquitaine. During his reign, he would establish overlordships in Wales and portions of Ireland, and he would reestablish a vague overlordship over Scotland. Like many monarchs before him, he found that such an empire was easier to gain than to rule. His territories comprised an array of feudal states ruled by independent-minded, often rebellious vassals. His position in France was complicated by the fact that he held such lands as a vassal of his rival the king of France. The later years of Henry's reign would be complicated by the intrigues of Eleanor with the French king, involving Henry's sons in rebellions against their father. During the summer of 1189, the final intrigue would play itself out against an aging and ailing Henry. Henry died on the sixth of July, that summer. Thus, after times of greatness and an assured place in the development of the English constitution, Henry would die a vanquished man, defeated by the house he could not rule—his own.

Henry's reign would also be marked, as were those of many of his Norman predecessors, by stormy relations with the Church. His main purpose was to regain the powers held by his grandfather, powers that had been lost during the civil war period. In the reign of Stephen, the Church, taking advantage of the weakness of the monarchy, had expanded the areas of church judicial jurisdiction. On the death of the archbishop of Canterbury, Henry saw an opportunity to control the Church from within its ranks, by proposing the appointment of his friend and chancellor, Thomas Becket (later Saint Thomas Becket). Although Becket was opposed to the plan, Henry was adamant. As adviser and chancellor, Becket had been fanatically loyal to the king. When he became the archbishop and leader of the English church, he defended the interests of his new master with the same zeal. It is possible that Becket may have overreacted in his effort to prove to the Church and the nation that he was not the king's man in his new post.

Henry II. (Library of Congress)

Meeting the church leaders at Clarendon in 1164, Henry sought to lessen the jurisdiction of the church courts. By the terms of the *Constitutions of Clarendon* (1164), Henry asked that the clergy, under Becket, give their oaths to support the customs of the realm as they had existed in the reign of Henry I. The prelates agreed with great reluctance. Taking advantage of the fact that these customs were unwritten, Henry had his court create a written presentation of the customs as they had existed during the reign of Henry I. He now asked the prelates to place their signatures on the list of written customs, and although the other bishops agreed to sign, Becket refused.

The events that followed Clarendon brought Becket and Henry into a series of confrontations. Thereupon, Henry failed to secure the pope's approval of his written statement of customs. Henry sought to bring Becket to submission by placing charges against him for misappropriation of funds while he was chancellor. Becket appealed to the pope, and Henry charged that the archbishop had violated the statement of written customs. Just as the bishops declined to accept charges of treason against Becket, the lay barons hesitated to move the secular charges against him.

Becket fled to the Continent, and an attempt to arrange a reconciliation between Henry and Becket failed. At length a settlement was reached between Henry and Becket. On his return to England, Becket took action against the bishops who had cooperated with the king in his absence. Tradition holds that Henry, on hearing this news, made a most intemperate remark concerning Becket. Four of Henry's knights left the king and went to Canterbury, where they murdered the archbishop. To cleanse himself of blame for murder, Henry came to terms with the Church authorities and surrendered all of his earlier gains in which he had decreased the jurisdiction of the church courts in England.

It is in the realm of government, the English constitution, and the study of English constitutional history that the reign of Henry II earned for him a leading place in English history and earned for Henry the designation as a great king.

During the time of Henry II, a beginning was made in the study of constitutional history. Richard Fitz Neal wrote a volume entitled *The Dialogue* (c. 1198) that surveyed the work and the workers connected with the Exchequer. In the field of law, Ranulf de Glanville wrote the first study on the subject, *Tractatus de legibus et consuetudinibus regni Angliae* (c. 1188; *Treatise on the Laws and Customs of the Kingdom of England*, 1900). The volume traced the development of the royal courts and the justice they administered. It demonstrated the interest of Henry and some of his advisers in the past laws of England and the manner of their application. A third major study was *Polycraticus* (c. 1159; selected English translation, 1938), the "stateman's handbook," an account of political philosophy as conceived in the Middle Ages, written by the distinguished theologian and scholar John of Salisbury.

PLANTAGENET KINGS OF ENGLAND, 1154-1399

Reign	*Monarch*
1154-1189	HENRY II (with ELEANOR OF AQUITAINE, r. 1154-1189)
1189-1199	RICHARD I THE LION-HEARTED
1199-1216	JOHN I LACKLAND
1216-1272	HENRY III
1272-1307	EDWARD I LONGSHANKS
1307-1327	EDWARD II (with ISABELLA OF FRANCE, r. 1308-1330)
1327-1377	EDWARD III (with PHILIPPA OF HAINAUT, r. 1327-1369)
1377-1399	RICHARD II

Henry's reign was also marked by more accurate and extensive record-keeping and an increase in nongovernment writings. Henry II sought to improve the quality of government and to extend the reforms of his grandfather. He wanted to strengthen royal control and to decrease the king's dependency on the feudal system, while lessening the role of the feudal barons in both civil government and military service.

He began to decrease the role of the Great Council, dominated by his great barons, and to depend more on a small working body that came to be known as the Small Council. This body was dominated by officials of his court, together with a few of the barons. It traveled with the king on trips to the various regions of his kingdom. The Great Council came to meet only three times a year, and its meetings became more ceremonial than practical. This lessened the burden of the barons for attendance on the king. In addition, he instituted a tax, scutage, which allowed these vassals to substitute a money payment in place of military service. Although the barons were at first pleased by the lessening of their attendance at court and the lessening of their military service, they were soon to discover that both reforms lessened their role in government and their power and influence at court.

Henry's reign also saw a considerable change in the judicial work of the Small Council; in 1178, he created a permanent subcommittee of the council to devote itself exclusively to judicial matters. In time, from this arrangement, the three great common-law courts would develop. Henry also re-established the use of the itinerant justices created under Henry I. He expanded and systematized the use of the justices by establishing regular circuits for the itinerant justices. He also used the justices as royal officials to check on local officials, namely the sheriffs. The use of the grand or accusing jury was definitely established by the Assize of Clarendon in 1166. The writ, as a means of bringing a case before the royal justice, was also developed at this time.

Also during Henry's reign a permanent subcommittee for financial matters was formed. Its work fell under two main classifications—the collection of taxes due from the sheriffs of the various counties and cases arising from financial concerns. In time, it also controlled the storage of the king's resources. By the end of his reign, Henry had created a more organized central administration, an arrangement that decreased the role of feudalism and the role of the individual barons in government.

SIGNIFICANCE

Henry II is generally regarded as one of England's greatest kings, the father of English constitutional law, the founder of a modern structure for the government of England, and a stern foe of the power of the feudal barons and of feudalism in government. Although his numerous wars and skirmishes to defend and expand the Continental holdings of the Angevins were colorful, they were not to be a lasting success and would be lost under his son John.

—*Van Mitchell Smith*

FURTHER READING

Appleby, John T. *Henry II: The Vanquished King*. New York: Macmillan, 1962. A very competent work on all aspects of the reign of Henry II.

Barber, Richard. *The Devil's Crown: A History of Henry II and His Sons*. London: British Broadcasting Corporation, 1978. This volume is based on the BBC television series. It is a popularly styled version of the period and extremely well done.

Gillingham, John. *The Angevin Empire*. New York: Holmes and Meier, 1984. A brief study of all aspects of the Angevin Empire. Particularly good in explaining Angevin government.

Harvey, John Hooper. *The Plantagenets*. Rev. ed. New York: B. T. Batsford, 1959. A useful work that deals with the Plantagenet family. It has a short but well-considered section about Henry II and his court and Queen Eleanor.

Kelly, Amy. *Eleanor of Aquitaine and the Four Kings*. Cambridge, Mass.: Harvard University Press, 1950. A fine presentation of the role played by Eleanor of Aquitaine in the life of her two husbands and in the lives of her sons by Henry II.

Maitland, Frederic William. *The Collected Papers of Frederic William Maitland*. 3 vols. Edited by H. A. L. Fisher. 1911. Reprint. Holmes Beach, Fla.: Gaunt, 1999. Presents the papers of the influential scholar of British constitutional history.

May, Thomas. *The Reigne of King Henry the Second, Written in Seauen Books*. Edited by Götz Schmitz. Tempe, Ariz.: Arizona Center for Medieval and Renaissance Studies and the Renaissance English Text Society, 1999. Presents the 1633 work of the Renaissance scholar Thomas May, who wrote seven manuscripts on Henry II. This text analyzes the manuscripts in detail and includes genealogical tables; appendixes featuring information on Henry II's coronation, his character, his death, and more; and provides sources for further study.

Warren, W. L. *Henry II*. Berkeley: University of California Press, 1977. A well-written study of the reign of Henry II.

SEE ALSO: Alexander III; Saint Thomas Becket; Henry de Bracton; Christina of Markyate; Eleanor of Aquitaine; Henry I; King John; Marie de France; Philip II; Richard I; King Stephen.

RELATED ARTICLES in *Great Events from History: The Middle Ages, 477-1453*: c. 1100: Rise of Courtly Love; 1136: Hildegard von Bingen Becomes Abbess; 1147-1149: Second Crusade; 1154-1204: Angevin Empire Is Established; 1169-1172: Normans Invade Ireland; December 29, 1170: Murder of Thomas Becket; c. 1200: Common-Law Tradition Emerges in England; 1453: English Are Driven from France.

HENRY II THE SAINT

King of Germany (r. 1002-1024) and Holy Roman Emperor (r. 1014-1024)

Using patience, common sense, and a realistic approach to the intrigues and problems of eleventh century Germany and Italy, Henry restored the monarchy north of the Alps and supported and encouraged church reforms.

BORN: May 6, 973; Abbach, Bavaria (now in Germany)

DIED: July 13, 1024; near Göttingen, Saxony (now in Germany)

ALSO KNOWN AS: Heinrich der Heilige

AREAS OF ACHIEVEMENT: Government and politics, church reform

EARLY LIFE

The son of Duke Henry II of Bavaria and Gisela (daughter of Conrad, king of Burgundy), Henry could claim direct descent through his father's line from Henry the Fowler. In addition, his grandfather was the younger brother of the emperor Otto the Great. When Duke Henry I was imprisoned by Otto III for leading a rebellion against the emperor, young Henry was placed in the care of Abraham, bishop of Freising, and then sent to Hildesheim, where he was reared and educated. Because it was believed that he would enter the Church, his education was that of a cleric and scholar, not of a soldier and king.

When his father was freed and restored to his duchy, however, the boy returned to Bavaria, where his education and training were put into the hands of Wolfgang of Ratisbon. The death of his father in 995 made him duke of Bavaria at the age of twenty-two. Shortly thereafter, he married Kunigunde, the daughter of Siegfried, count of Luxemburg. As duke of Bavaria, Henry remained loyal to Otto III, accompanying him on two Italian campaigns, until the emperor's death in 1002.

Otto died without an heir, thus ending the direct male line of Otto the Great and opening the way for a struggle to determine the new king of Germany and Holy Roman Emperor. The former was decided by heredity or by election; the latter required the cooperation of the pope. Several of the great German dukes wished to succeed Otto as king of Germany, notably the duke of Carinthia, grandson of Otto the Great. Others who sought the kingship were Henry of Bavaria, who was descended from the direct, male, imperial line, and Eckhard, Margrave of Meissen, who was the choice of the Saxon princes. When Eckhard was killed in April, 1002, and Otto pledged his support to Henry, however, the matter was settled. Henry was elected king of Germany and crowned on June 7, 1002, at Mayence (Mainz).

The new German king was a well-educated, pious, and sensitive young man. Although not brilliant, he possessed the admirable qualities of common sense and good judgment, which served him well throughout his life. His physical appearance seems to have been quite ordinary, as there is little written on the subject. Allegations that he was lame are legends, not facts. His health was generally poor, however, and should be considered when assessing the limited success of his reign.

LIFE'S WORK

Henry's coronation at Mayence was not universally recognized by the German nobility. He had little more than the support of the Bavarians and Franconians. Following his coronation, Dietrich, duke of Upper Lorraine, pledged his support, but Lower Lorraine, Saxony, and Swabia refused to accept Henry. He first secured recognition from the Saxon nobility by agreeing to respect their local laws and customs. Then he turned his attention to Lower Lorraine and through diplomacy won over its support. Only Swabia remained; when the local duke found himself isolated, he negotiated and finally submitted. Germany was at last, if only temporarily, united, but Henry's troubles had only begun. As the emperor's heir apparent, he also aspired to the vacant imperial throne. Otto III, however, had left a weakened and disunited empire: Poland, Bohemia, and Lombardy were all in varying stages of rebellion.

Detail of Henry II, the Saint. (Hulton|Archive at Getty Images)

The most serious challenge came from the east. Bolesław Chrobry, the son of Mieszko, had been installed as duke of Poland in 992 on the death of his father. He united the various tribes of the Oder and Vistula and won major concessions from Otto III. With the death of the emperor in 1002, Bolesław sought total independence from German vassalage. At the head of a strong army, he conquered the lands west of the Elbe and when Henry refused to recognize his conquests, took advantage of the turbulent conditions in Bohemia to add that duchy to his expanded holdings. Henry was unable to deal with this eastern threat, because internal problems required his full attention. He first put an end to disloyalty in Lorraine and then turned to face a more serious rebellion, supported by the duke of Poland, that included his own brother, Bruno. The fighting, bitter at times, lasted into 1004, but the king prevailed; once again peace and order were restored within the kingdom.

Henry was now ready to address the problems of the empire. While the Polish/Bohemian situation may have been the most serious, it would also be the most difficult to resolve. A favorable solution in Italy, on the other hand, seemed more attainable. Thus Henry gathered his army and crossed the Alps. The campaign itself was successful, but it did not solve the German monarch's fundamental problem of lasting control. Marching by way of Trent and Verona, picking up support along the way, he reached Pavia in May, 1004. There he was elected king of the Lombards on May 14 and crowned the following day in the Basilica of Saint Michael. His rival, Ardoin, marquess of Ivrea, who had himself been crowned king of the Lombards two years earlier in the same church, fled to the west as his support faded. Henry's triumph seemed complete, although it was marred when fighting broke out between the Germans and Italians in Pavia. The city was partially destroyed, with substantial loss of life. Unfortunately, Henry was not able to remain in Italy to consolidate his newly won position. Bohemia and Bolesław required his immediate attention. In June, Henry marched back across the Alps leaving behind a dubiously loyal Lombardy.

On his return to Germany, Henry reorganized his army and prepared for a Bohemian campaign. Crossing the Erzgebirge without opposition, he was joined by Jaromir, the deposed duke of Bohemia. The Bohemians, who had no love for the duke of Poland, posed no obstacle. Bolesław, fully aware of the approaching danger and without local support, withdrew to the north. Henry entered Prague amid rejoicing and restored Jaromir. The duke of Bohemia, realizing that his position depended on German assistance, remained faithful to Henry and supported him in his Polish wars. Bolesław's setback, however, in no way eliminated Henry's eastern problems: Although a temporary peace was made while Bolesław turned his attention to Kiev, Henry was forced to make repeated campaigns in order to secure his eastern frontier. Finally, a more lasting peace was signed at Bautzen in 1018, although it represented no German victory, merely recognizing the status quo. Bolesław kept the lands east of the Elbe and was virtually independent of any German control, even proclaiming himself king of Poland before Henry's death. Bohemia, however, remained loyal, and at last Henry had true peace on his eastern border.

SAXON KINGS OF GERMANY, 919-1024

Reign	*King*
919	Henry I the Fowler (Saxon, not crowned)
936-973	OTTO I
973-983	Otto II
983-1002	Otto III
1002-1024	HENRY II THE SAINT
1024	Franconian/Salian line begins (Conrad II)

In the west, Henry also had problems. The great nobles of Lorraine defied him at every opportunity, and he was forced to make several campaigns across the Rhine in order to maintain even nominal control. Burgundy was also defiant. King Rudolf III was a weak monarch who struggled constantly (and usually unsuccessfully) with his nobles. In 1016, he sought Henry's support. The German king, who claimed to be the rightful heir to the throne of Burgundy when his uncle should die, was very willing to intervene. Rudolf acknowledged Henry's right of succession, and in 1018, having secured his eastern border, Henry undertook an expedition into Burgundy. The affair was not a success. The Burgundian nobility remained lawless, and Henry's claim remained doubtful; it became a moot issue when he died before Rudolf.

Italy provided yet another source of frustration. In the ten years that passed following his first expedition south of the Alps, Henry's authority and influence had waned, and civil war was the normal state of affairs. The pro-German faction, primarily the bishops and abbots, rallied about Bishop Leo of Vercelli. Ardoin, the deposed Lombard king, led the defiant faction, which was largely secular. Henry not only needed to restore his rule in Lombardy but also wished to be crowned Holy Roman Emperor. This additional title would add strength to his position in both Germany and Italy. Therefore, he marched south accompanied by Queen Kunigunde in late fall of 1013. By Christmas, he was in Pavia, and in January, 1014, he moved on to Ravenna. At a synod he convened in Ravenna, Henry put the affairs of northern Italy in order; Ardoin's support melted away. He reached Rome on February 14 and was crowned that same day by Pope Benedict VIII. Unfortunately, within a week of the coronation fighting broke out between his German entourage and the Romans. Withdrawing from the city, Henry returned to Lombardy and in June recrossed the Alps. Henry's second Italian expedition was at least a partial success: New life was given to the empire and relations were established between the pope and the new emperor. Yet northern Italy remained unsettled. With the emperor's departure, civil war again broke out, and even after the abdication and later death of Ardoin, the Lombards resisted Henry's authority.

He made one last expedition to Italy in 1021-1022. The principal purpose of the journey was a campaign against the Byzantine province in the south, where some Lombard princes had allied themselves with the Byzantine forces. At Verona in early December, Henry's formidable German army was joined by his Italian supporters; in January, 1022, they marched south. Sickness became rampant in his army, however, and he turned back, having made only a minor impact on southern Italy. Back in Lombardy, he turned his attention to church reform and was more successful than he had been with political affairs. In the autumn, he returned to Germany, where he died on July 13, 1024, and was buried in Bamberg.

SIGNIFICANCE

Henry II's life was a continual struggle to revive the political institutions of the German kingdom and Holy Roman Empire following their decline. He was able to achieve a considerable degree of success in Germany but was less successful in Italy. His greatest triumphs were the improvement of church-state relations and religious reform. Henry strengthened the position of the Church in both Germany and Italy, following an aggressive policy of granting lands and titles to the bishops and abbots as a means of reducing the power and influence of the secular nobility, over whom he had less influence and control. Having the right to nominate, Henry installed loyal bishops on whom he could depend to remain faithful in his unceasing wars with his vassals. He also strongly supported reform within the Church, particularly the Cluniac movement. At the synod of Pavia, August, 1022, with the support of Pope Benedict, he was able to secure the denunciation of clerical marriage in both Germany and Italy.

—*John G. Gallaher*

FURTHER READING

Bryce, James. *The Holy Roman Empire*. Rev. ed. New York: Macmillan, 1922. This work provides a good general introduction to the medieval German Empire, although it does not deal with Henry in detail.

Eyck, Frank. *Religion and Politics in German History: From the Beginnings to the French Revolution*. New York: St. Martin's Press, 1998. An analysis of how Germanic peoples preserved links with classical civilization through their ability to assimilate other cultures and peoples, from their alliances with eighth century popes through the Reformation and Counter-Reformation. The initial bond between the Germanic rulers and popes turned to conflict as the Papacy gained power. Tables, maps, bibliography, index.

Fisher, Herbert. *The Medieval Empire*. 2 vols. Reprint. New York: AMS Press, 1969. Although Fisher wrote these two volumes at the turn of the century, they continue to hold up well under modern scrutiny. His approach is topical rather than chronological, thus the reign of Henry is found in several chapters in both volumes.

Gwatkin, H. M., J. P. Whitney, J. R. Tanner, and C. W. Previté-Orton, eds. *The Cambridge Medieval History*. Vol. 3, *Germany and the Western Empire*. New York: Cambridge University Press, 1957. Chapter 10 of this volume, entitled "The Emperor Henry II," provides one of the most comprehensive accounts of the life and times of Henry II. It is primarily a political history of his reign, although other chapters cover related individuals and events that are not central to his life. There is an extensive bibliography and index.

Henderson, Ernest F. *A History of Germany in the Middle Ages*. Reprint. New York: Haskell House, 1968. Chapter 11 of Henderson's straightforward political narrative is devoted to the reigns of Henry II and Conrad II. A good starting point for a study of the last male descendant of Otto the Great.

Jeep, John M., et al., eds. *Medieval Germany: An Encyclopedia*. New York: Garland, 2001. An A-Z encyclopedia that addresses all aspects of the German- and Dutch-speaking medieval world from 500 to 1500. Entries include individuals, events, and broad topics such as feudalism and pregnancy. Bibliographical references, index.

Mann, Horace K. *The Lives of the Popes in the Early Middle Ages*. Vols. 4-5, *The Popes in the Days of Anarchy: Formosa to Damascus II, 891-1048*. London: Kegan Paul, Trench, Trübner, 1925. This work provides a good account of the reign of Henry II from the point of view of the Papacy, as well as portraying the Church in both Germany and Italy. Although concentrating on Pope Benedict VIII and his relationship with the emperor, because of the involvement of the clergy in secular affairs, the study also considers political intrigues and warfare.

Moore, Robert Ian. *The First European Revolution, c. 970-1215*. Malden, Mass.: Blackwell, 2000. According to the publisher, "a radical reassessment of Europe from the late tenth to the early thirteenth centuries [arguing that] the period witnessed the first true 'revolution' in European society," supported by transformation of the economy, family life, political power structures, and the rise of the non-Mediterranean cities. Bibliography, index.

Thompson, James Westfall. *Feudal Germany*. Chicago: University of Chicago Press, 1928. 2d ed. New York: Frederick Ungar, 1962. Thompson treats medieval German history primarily in terms of the relationship between church and state and tends to emphasize the conflict between Henry II and Benedict VIII.

SEE ALSO: Gershom ben Judah.

RELATED ARTICLES in *Great Events from History: The Middle Ages, 477-1453*: August 10, 955: Otto I Defeats the Magyars; 976-1025: Reign of Basil II.

HENRY III

King of England (r. 1216-1272)

Henry's reign witnessed the growing role of the community of the realm in the rule of England. By the end of Henry's reign, the rule of England could no longer be exercised by the king alone.

BORN: October 1, 1207; Winchester, Hampshire, England

DIED: November 16, 1272; London, England

ALSO KNOWN AS: Henry III Plantagenet; Henry of Winchester

AREA OF ACHIEVEMENT: Government and politics

EARLY LIFE

Henry III was the eldest son of the luckless King John (who died in 1216) and his queen, Isabella of Angoulême. Little is known of Henry's childhood before he became king, but he was crowned at Gloucester in October of 1216, at nine years of age. He inherited a turbulent kingdom. The last years of his father's reign had been roiled by baronial rebellion and by war with France over the possessions on the Continent claimed by the king of England. At Henry's coronation, England was subject to sporadic civil war, caused in large part by the ephemeral ambitions of Prince Louis of France to seize the throne of England. Henry, however, had the support of the principal magnates of England, and, unlike King John, had no enemies. The king's supporters, led by his regent William Marshal, earl of Pembroke, combined military victory (in 1217) with twice reissuing the Magna Carta (in 1216 and 1217) to ensure the crown and the kingdom to the boy king. The period of the marshal's regency, which terminated with his death in 1219, is chiefly notable for enlarging the share of the nobility in the governance of the realm.

Henry's minority continued until 1227, a period characterized, after the death of the regent, by conflict between royalist ministers and loyalist barons for control of the young king and of the kingdom. The most important constitutional act of the mid-1220's was the royal reissue of the Magna Carta in 1225; the first clear instance of a grant of taxation in return for a royal boon, this version of the Great Charter was that which was confirmed by future kings in times of apparent constitutional crisis.

Henry had the appearance and manner of a monarch. He was of medium height and athletic in build. The young king was generous, intelligent, a man interested in scholarship, and a patron of architecture—a chiefly royal form of secular patronage in the Middle Ages because of its expense. He was very religious, although the traditional view that he was under the control of the Papacy needs minor qualification. Henry had negative qualities as well: He was profligate with money, he could be bullheaded, was often deficient as a judge of character, and, in the earlier years of his reign, was too subservient to the ambitions and to the policies of Poitevin advisers, such as Peter des Roches and Peter des Rivaux.

LIFE'S WORK

From the end of Henry's minority in 1227 until the great rebellion of 1258, Henry struggled to rule as well as to reign. His program was characterized by a growing disillusionment with papal authority as expressed in England and by firm, if at times thwarted, attempts to defend his prerogative powers against encroachment by lords both great and small in political status. The 1230's were testing years. Henry's political problems were exacerbated, and their principles often obscured, because of the opposition between his natural counselors, the baronage of England, and the influence of Provençal and Savoyard nobles who had flocked to the English court in the wake of his queen, Eleanor of Provençe, who became his wife in 1236. The traditional counselors of the king bitterly resented the intrusion of men unfamiliar with English ways into the intimate circle of the king's advisers. Yet the magnates were unable to produce a program that would exclude the Frenchmen from positions of political influence over the king until the Paper Constitution of 1244, a document that, although it came to nothing in practical terms, asserted the right of the community of the realm to participate in all policies of the government that affected the kingdom as well as the king.

Henry's problems were complicated by foreign affairs. The confusion of Henry's failed policy in Wales, and the worsening of Anglo-Scottish relations, eventuated in a victory for Wales, under Henry's son Edward I, and in a bleeding sore in the case of Scotland (a problem that lasted until the early eighteenth century). Moreover, Henry's attempts to recover lands in France north of the Loire, which had been lost under King John, were unsuccessful. Although the English made several concerted attempts to regain the territories, attempts that were to continue through the ultimately unsuccessful Hundred Years' War (1337-1453), the lands had been irrevocably lost under King John's rule. The period of conflict in the reign of Henry III ended with the Treaty of Paris in 1259, through which Henry recognized the loss of the Angevin lands north of the Loire, while Louis IX acknowledged Henry's dominion over Gascony and some of Aquitaine. Furthermore, Henry's feckless attempts to make his brother Richard of Cornwall the ruler of Sicily, in response to papal invitation, did not enhance his reputation with his barons.

Foreign failures, then, aggravated internal relations between the king and his barons. The seminal problem of contention in internal politics from the mid-1240's to the end of the reign was this: Could the barons control the power of the king? This effort failing, how could they assume the powers of kingship themselves? By what means could the barons force the king to take their counsel, because the king must be free to choose his own counselors? Not for the first time in English history, the fundamental issues had been raised: What is the role of the king and what that of his chosen counselors in the rule of England? What is the role of the community of the realm? How were these roles to be defined, and by whom, and how were the defined relationships to be enforced? Before 1258, the problem was explored primarily in a political context; in and after 1258, relatively peaceful means of addressing the problem of governance having failed, England was plunged into civil war. The feudal regime was becoming archaic; hence, its modes of operation were no longer relevant to the changing conditions of the mid-thirteenth century. Yet, no one in a position of power really understood this fact, nor did the polity have a clearly grasped idea of discovering new institutions and new political tools to replace old ways that no longer reflected reality. Thus, in 1258, England fell into civil war.

The Provisions of Oxford of that year, proposed by the baronial opposition to the king, attempted in essence to place kingship in a conjoint form of rule with the community of the realm. This movement in government included, for the first time, a stratum ranking in social status below the great landed lords, the class that in the Tudor period would be known as the gentry, those substantial people whose rise to political influence reflected their economic importance. The five years preceding the baronial rebellion, which was to be led by Simon de Montfort, earl of Leicester, were characterized by great

Henry III. (Library of Congress)

uncertainty both in the baronial and in the royal advocates' positions. Neither side had been able to formulate a definite position in the question of who ruled England, and how. Yet the weight of precedent fortified the royal view of monarchial powers. On the other hand, emerging political realities dictated the participation of the wider community in the governance of England. Political compromise failed; the result was therefore a civil war over the right to rule in and over England. The civil war continued until its putative end by the Mise of Amiens in 1264, an arbitration that was delivered by Louis IX of France. Louis judged Henry III in the right in the dispute. Not surprisingly, the rebel barons under Montfort's leadership refused the arbitration's result, and civil war again broke out, seemingly ending with the victory of the Montfort party at the Battle of Lewes (1264). Yet the immediately following Mise of Lewes, which again included gentry in a program to reform the realm, failed to provide a solution to the seemingly intractable political problems of the reign. War again erupted, and Montfort was killed at the Battle of Evesham in 1265. With the death of its leader, the reform movement collapsed.

The last seven years of Henry III's reign, in which the actual ruler of England was his son, the Lord Edward (to succeed as King Edward I in 1272), were characterized by political compromise. The Dictum of Kenilworth (1266) encompassed the reissue of the Magna Carta, the redress of some specific grievances of the opposition, and a strong statement of the monarch's right to exercise royal authority "without impediment or contradiction." The cause of Henry's death is unknown.

PLANTAGENET KINGS OF ENGLAND, 1154-1399

Reign	*Monarch*
1154-1189	HENRY II (with ELEANOR OF AQUITAINE, r. 1154-1189)
1189-1199	RICHARD I THE LION-HEARTED
1199-1216	JOHN I LACKLAND
1216-1272	HENRY III
1272-1307	EDWARD I LONGSHANKS
1307-1327	EDWARD II (with ISABELLA OF FRANCE, r. 1308-1330)
1327-1377	EDWARD III (with PHILIPPA OF HAINAUT, r. 1327-1369)
1377-1399	RICHARD II

SIGNIFICANCE

When Henry III died, he could have regarded his reign with some satisfaction. Despite the internal and external problems of his reign, he had brought his stewardship of the realm to a conclusion that would have appeared unlikely when he acceded to the throne in 1216: The monarchy's powers were undiminished, although now exercised in cooperation with the magnates and with the middling knights, by now expressed in Parliament. The developments of this reign saw the king of England well on the way to being a constitutional monarch, a ruler whose willfulness was restrained by institutionalized opposition. "Loyal opposition" in any other nation of the thirteenth century would have appeared to be an oxymoron. In addition, Henry was the first English king to be a significant patron of architecture; Westminster Abbey is his greatest monument.

—*James W. Alexander*

FURTHER READING

Carpenter, D. A. "King Henry's 'Statute' Against Aliens: July 1263." *English Historical Review* 107, no. 425 (1992). Presents the text of the provisions, which includes a declaration for the exclusion from England of foreign-born persons and for the future governing of England by native-born men only.

Clanchy, Michael T. *England and Its Rulers, 1066-1272: Foreign Lordship and National Identity.* Totowa, N.J.: Barnes and Noble Books, 1983. Covers the non-English rule of England.

Denholm-Young, Noël. *Richard of Cornwall.* New York: William Salloch, 1947. Argues that Henry III's younger brother "influenced, and at times of crisis dominated, his brother's policy."

Powicke, F. M. *The Battle of Lewes, 1264: Its Place in English History.* Lewes, England: Friends of Lewes Society, 1964. Assesses the importance of this battle in broad historical context—political, constitutional, and military—and stresses the role of Montfort.

_______. *King Henry III and the Lord Edward.* 2 vols. Oxford, England: Clarendon Press, 1947. A standard narrative study of the reign and of the importance of Lord Edward's influence in its closing years.

Powicke, Maurice. *The Thirteenth Century, 1216-1307.* 2d ed. Oxford, England: Clarendon Press, 1962. An excellent study of British history during the reign of Henry III.

Treharne, Reginald F. *The Baronial Plan of Reform, 1258-1263.* 1932. Reprint. Manchester, England: Manchester University Press, 1971. Traces in depth the history of the Barons' War, emphasizing its political and constitutional aspects.

_______. *Simon de Montfort and Baronial Reform: Thirteenth-Century Essays*. Edited by E. B. Fryde. London: Hambleton Press, 1968. The principal concentration of these essays is on the period 1258-1264, the reign's crisis years.

Treharne, Reginald F., and I. J. Sanders. *Documents of the Baronial Movement of Reform and Rebellion, 1258-1267*. Oxford, England: Clarendon Press, 1973. Reprints documents in Latin and Anglo-Norman French, with English translations and commentaries.

Valente, Claire. *The Theory and Practice of Revolt in Medieval England*. Burlington, Vt.: Ashgate, 2003. Addresses in its opening chapter the study of revolts and also discusses theories of resistance, the Magna Carta, and the concept of the community of the realm.

Weiler, Björn K. U., ed. *England and Europe in the Reign of Henry III (1216-1272)*. Burlington, Vt.: Ashgate, 2002. Looks at Henry's reign as it affected England and the Continent.

See also: Hubert de Burgh; Edward I; Henry IV (of England); King John; Louis IX; Simon de Montfort.

Related articles in *Great Events from History: The Middle Ages, 477-1453*: c. 1200: Common-Law Tradition Emerges in England; June 15, 1215: Signing of the Magna Carta; 1258: Provisions of Oxford Are Established; 1285: Statute of Winchester.

Henry IV (of England)

King of England (r. 1399-1413)

The circumstances of Henry's reign invested the English Parliament with new authority regarding royal power: Kings would rule by parliamentary title.

Born: April 3, 1367; Bolingbroke Castle, near Spilsby, Lincolnshire, England

Died: March 20, 1413; London, England

Also known as: Henry of Lancaster; Henry Bolingbroke

Area of achievement: Government and politics

Early Life

Henry of Lancaster—or Henry Bolingbroke, as he came to be known—was the only surviving son of John of Gaunt and his first wife, Blanche of Lancaster. Henry's parentage in large part determined his destiny as England's future king, for John of Gaunt, duke of Lancaster, was the third of five surviving sons of King Edward III, while Henry's mother was descended from King Henry III. John was in possession of several earldoms, including Derby; from about the age of ten, his son Henry was known as the earl of Derby, as well as being the nominal head of the Lancastrian estates. (John would secure other assurances for his son's future as well, including a marriage, in 1380 or 1381, to the second wealthiest heiress in England, Mary of Bohun, when she was still a child.)

On the death of King Edward's son, Edward the Black Prince, in 1376, and the death of the king himself a year later, the son of the Black Prince, Richard II, ascended the throne. Henry's cousin was only ten or eleven years old—about the same age as Henry—and it fell on John of Gaunt, the young king's uncle, to lead the kingdom in function if not in title. John's government was not a popular one; he was blamed for trying to secure the succession for himself and for unpopular policies such as poll taxes, and consequently, in 1381, while he was away in the north, the Peasants' Revolt erupted in London. Henry and Richard took refuge in the Tower.

It was in this setting that Henry was reared and in which he received the training that would lead him to stake his claim to the throne against Richard twenty years later. As a young nobleman, he led the itinerant life typical of those in his position—overseeing his lands and tenants, as well as his own, growing, household: Between 1387 and 1394, four sons and two daughters were born to him and Mary; Mary died, however, giving birth to their last child. Henry also accompanied his father on expeditions abroad: to Flanders in 1383-1384 and to Scotland in 1385. In contrast to the physically weaker, if more imaginative and creative, Richard, Henry continued the Lancastrian tradition of physical prowess in knightly sport, gaining for himself a reputation as a Crusader as well as a warrior. In 1390, he attended a great tournament held near Calais and, with an English contingent of three hundred knights, accompanied the duke of Bourbon on the expedition that captured Tunis. Henry twice joined the Teutonic Knights on their military expeditions eastward along the Baltic coast. In 1392-1393, he visited the Holy Land, but he returned disappointed in his inability to visit the Holy Sepulchre. In September of 1396, he would command English knights against the Turks at the disastrous battle of Nicopolis along the lower Danube.

Henry's entrance into politics came in 1386, when, along with his close associate Thomas Mowbray, earl of Nottingham, he joined with three other lords who opposed the king: the dukes of Gloucester, Arundel, and Warwick. Together, the five men, who came to be known as the five lords appellants, joined their forces and took London in late 1387 (the year of the future Henry V's birth). Richard was effectively deposed, but he was allowed to keep the throne on relenting to the five lords' demand that Simon Burley, his tutor and confidant, be executed. Nevertheless, the lords dominated rule of the kingdom until 1389, when Richard, now a young man, rebelled against the officials who had been placed in power by the five lords and insisted on his right as king to rule. Henry's aristocratic combine floundered, and over the next few years, troubles in the north that required the attention of the duke of Gloucester and John of Gaunt, as well as internal jealousies and suspicions, effectively defused the opposition as Richard took more personal control over his kingdom. His hold on the throne would remain a weak one, however, ensured primarily by the iron hand of John of Gaunt; in 1394, Richard's last friend, his wife, Queen Anne, died. John of Gaunt was often out of the country conducting foreign negotiations, and Richard himself went to Ireland to quell unrest there. Henry remained in London, attending Parliament and sitting on the council that ruled the country.

Henry IV of England. (Library of Congress)

In 1397, the duke of Gloucester initiated a scheme to seize the throne and the power behind it: the dukes of Lancaster (John of Gaunt) and York. Henry, it is believed, was invited to join the conspiracy, but it came to nothing: Richard discovered the plan. The outcome was the deaths of Gloucester and Arundel, and the banishment of Warwick. Henry's part in the affair remains uncertain, as the plot would have involved his going against his own father. It appears, however, that he was reconciled with Richard, for, in a sweep of housecleaning, the king replaced his old enemies with a host of new dukes, among them Henry, as duke of Hereford.

LIFE'S WORK

The events that led to Henry's conspiracy against Richard II began in 1398. Henry brought an accusation against a royal favorite, his old colleague Thomas Mowbray, now the duke of Norfolk. The aristocratic quarrel ended when the king banished both dukes. Henry chose Paris for his exile. John of Gaunt, the power behind Richard's throne, died in the following year. Richard, in the face of both law and a special promise to his cousin, declared the vast Lancastrian estates forfeit. The seizure of his lands gave Henry an excuse to return to England. When he landed in Yorkshire in June of 1399, he protested that his return was occasioned only by his wish to restore his family holdings. However sincere Henry may have been, his return marked the beginning of a rebellion. England was rife with the discontent that had plagued Richard's entire reign: The nation had been overtaxed, the aristocracy was afraid of the Richardian absolutism, complaints had arisen about the king's counselors, and the king had been out of the country for several weeks.

Once in England, Henry's strength grew; most of the great nobles rallied to his side: They feared a king who could attack the estates of the most powerful family of the realm. By the time the king returned from Ireland, royal support had almost completely evaporated and Henry's rallying forces had become a flood tide. Richard surrendered and placed himself at his cousin's mercy. From his prison in the Tower of London, the king was perhaps hopeful that time would, as it had in 1388, provide an opening for him to regain power. Richard approved an abdication statement on September 29, 1399. That "pure and free resignation" was presented to Parliament the next day, and Parliament acted effectively to depose the king.

The following events were to prove extremely consequential for England. Having determined to seize the throne, Henry had to struggle with plausible arguments for his right to do so. The only attempt to prove his legitimate rights was tortured, fantastical, and unacceptable. His thought of claiming the throne by conquest, which was how he had achieved his control, was disturbing. A conqueror could erase existing laws and reshape the kingdom to his desires, but Henry's supporters did not want to destroy the legal traditions that benefited them. In the end, Henry simply claimed the vacant throne before the parliamentary session that had deposed the king. He held his coronation on October 13, 1399. The former King Richard was kept alive until a rebellion in his name proved too much of a threat to the new king, and he was murdered in his prison at the Lancastrian castle of Pontefract, in Yorkshire.

The circumstances of Henry IV's usurpation offered excuses for rebellion against him and caused him to be cautious and conciliatory toward both his opponents and his parliaments. His throne was insecure and Parliament—as well as his political enemies, among whom at times would be his eldest son, Henry—would take advantage of the inherent difficulties of his claim to the crown.

The Crown's inability to finance its governmental needs placed Henry IV at the mercy of the House of Commons. Forced to rely on monies raised through taxation, Henry had to make concessions that allowed the Commons to demand that he curtail governmental expenses, to appoint councils designed to supervise his administration, and to criticize his military policies. If Parliament could create a king, it was better able to control his reign: Parliament eagerly took advantage of a weakened royalty.

Henry was faced with constant warfare and rebellion. The Scots had taken advantage of the northern English earls' involvement in internal politics to wreak havoc on the border areas. The Scottish invasion was finally stopped by the Percy family, the leading aristocratic family of the north. The king, however, was unable to reward the great northern family adequately, either for their aid in his rebellion or for their defending of the border. The elder Percy, the duke of Northumberland, angrily renounced his oath of allegiance to Henry. The family revolted and launched an armed uprising against the king. Almost simultaneously, Owen Glendower, a northern Welsh landowner, became the leader of Welsh discontent. The Welsh felt exploited by the government of the English marcher lords. Glendower sparked a revolt throughout Wales. The rebellion fused with anti-Henrician English factions. It was joined by Sir Edmund Mortimer, who had been captured by Glendower but was not ransomed by the king, and then by the Percys as the duke of Northumberland's son Henry Percy (the "Hotspur" of William Shakespeare's plays), Mortimer's brother-in-law, sided with the rebels. The king defeated the Percys: Henry Percy was killed in battle in 1403, and the duke of Northumberland was finally captured and executed in 1408. It was not until 1410, however, that the Glendower rebellion was effectively ended.

Adding to Henry IV's military complications were England's relations with France. Following the death of Richard II, the French had demanded the return of his widow, Isabella, the daughter of the French king, and her dowry. Denied his chance to continue peaceful relations with France by marrying his son to Isabella, and denied her use in negotiations once she and her dowry were returned to her homeland, Henry discovered his relations with France worsening. The French began to send military assistance to the Glendower rebellion, raided the southern coast of England, and troubled English merchants in the Channel. Popular English hostility toward France increased. The merchants wanted reprisals, and the magnates longed for a renewal of the plundering expeditions into France. Henry, however, had no plans to become involved in a war against France. His policy of siding with first one and then another French faction unfortunately appeared to be a policy of vacillation and pleased no English faction.

Kings of England: House of Lancaster

Reign	*Monarch*
1327-1377	Edward III
1377-1399	Richard II
1399-1413	Henry IV
1413-1422	Henry V
1422-1461	Henry VI
1470-1471	Henry VI, Lancaster

KINGS OF ENGLAND: HOUSE OF YORK

Reign	*Monarch*
1461-1470	Edward IV
1471-1483	Edward IV, restored
1483	Edward V
1483-1485	Richard III Hunchback
1485	Tudor ascendancy: Henry VII

Difficulties within the royal family also hampered Henry's effectiveness toward the end of his reign. His ambitious, dashing, pushy, and impatient son Henry of Monmouth, prince of Wales (the famous Prince Hal of Shakespeare's *Henry V*), for a time in 1411 became king in all but name. Before that, the prince had quarreled with his father over governmental policy, supported his father's political opponents in France and led an unauthorized invasion of France, resisted an attempt to inquire into the Lollard heresy, and opposed the king's ministers. The prince twice moved troops to London as if he intended to overthrow the government. There were also indications that the Beaufort branch of the royal family, the king's half brothers descended from the marriage of John of Gaunt and Katherine Swynford, were allied with Prince Hal.

Henry IV spent his last years in dismal disillusionment. His health, never good, was now broken, as was his spirit. Feeble, trembling, itchy with a skin disease rumored to be leprosy, and hardly able to walk, he may well have wondered what had gone wrong with his life. In his youth, he had been accustomed to riches and magnificence; as king, he had scarcely enough money to provide for his government. As a young aristocrat, he was known for his martial skills and his earned military glory; as king, he was eventually able to achieve domestic military success but it apparently resolved little and bestowed no fame. His refusal to engage in military expeditions against France cost him valuable public opinion. He began his reign as a successful usurper of a throne; he ended it troubled by those who wished that his son would usurp the father. He had been well liked as Henry Bolingbroke; as Henry IV, he was unpopular. Shakespeare wrote the line "Uneasy lies the head that wears a crown" for Henry IV—Shakespeare's interpretation was insightful.

Henry's last thoughts were of plans that might have been successfully conceived and carried out in his aristocratic youth. A bewildered old man—old before his time, even in the fifteenth century—the king spoke of invading France, of leading a new crusade to recapture the Holy Land, of making a pilgrimage to Jerusalem. Instead, he suffered a seizure in 1413 while praying in Westminster Abbey. He was carried into the Jerusalem Chamber, where he died. His trip to Jerusalem was appropriately ironic: Not much of his life was as he thought it would be.

SIGNIFICANCE

Henry IV had usurped the throne of Richard II and placed his family, the Lancastrians, in power, initiating the dynastic struggle between the great aristocratic families of Lancaster and York known as the Wars of the Roses (1455-1485). The manner in which Parliament was allowed to depose Richard and accept Henry as the royal successor provided the opportunity for Parliament to gain more power than it had ever held before: The Lancastrian kings would rule by parliamentary title, and in the fifteenth century political theories would place great stress on the legal limitations of royal power.

—*Dale E. Landon*

FURTHER READING

Brown, A. L. "The Commons and the Council in the Reign of Henry IV." *English Historical Review* 79 (January, 1964): 1-30. Attributes the actions of the Commons in the reign of Henry to a desire for good and economical government. Argues against any constitutional program established by the first of the Lancastrian kings.

Dodd, Gwilyn, and Douglas Biggs, eds. *Henry IV: The Establishment of the Regime, 1399-1406*. Rochester, N.Y.: Boydell Press, 2003. A biography of Henry, with discussion of his seizure of power.

Jacob, E. F. *The Fifteenth Century, 1399-1485*. Oxford, England: Clarendon Press, 1961. Chapters 1-3 present chronological accounts of Henry IV's reign dominated by political history. A good introduction to the political problems of the reign.

Kirby, J. L. *Henry IV of England*. London: Archon Books, 1971. A scholarly political biography that adequately covers Henry and his problems—a rather conventional account.

Pollard, A. J. *The Wars of the Roses*. 2d ed. New York: Palgrave, 2001. A brief introduction to the wars. Includes genealogical tables and maps.

Wilkinson, Bertie. "The Deposition of Richard II and the Accession of Henry IV." *English Historical Review* 54 (April, 1939): 215-239. Sets forth an argument that Parliament did not grant Henry Bolingbroke a parliamentary title. His failure to obtain such a title revealed one of his major political weaknesses.

Wylie, James H. *History of England Under Henry the Fourth*. 4 vols. 1884-1898. Reprint. New York: AMS Press, 1968. Still of value for its coverage of the politics of Henry's reign and, more important, for the sources it contains.

See also: Edward III; Henry III; Henry V; Richard II.
Related articles in *Great Events from History: The Middle Ages, 477-1453*: 12th-14th centuries: Social and Political Impact of Leprosy; c. 1145: Prester John Myth Sweeps Across Europe.

Henry IV (of Germany)

King of Germany (r. 1056-1106) and Holy Roman Emperor (r. 1084-1106)

Henry's struggles with the German nobility and the Papacy had a decisive impact on the future constitutional and political development of Germany. Although his tenacious defense of the rights and prerogatives of the monarchy was largely unsuccessful, it still marked him as one of the greatest of the German kings.

Born: November 11, 1050; Goslar, Saxony (now in Germany)
Died: August 7, 1106; Liège, Lorraine (now in Belgium)
Also known as: Henry VIII (duke of Bavaria); Heinrich IV
Area of achievement: Government and politics

Early Life

Henry IV was born on November 11, 1050, the son and heir of Henry III and his wife, Agnes of Poitou. Henry was well educated for the period: He could read and write, knew Latin, and had an interest in music and architecture. His childhood was very tumultuous and would have an inordinate influence on his personality and his later decisions.

In 1056, his father died. The German nobles accepted the five-year-old Henry as king only because his father had earlier forced them three times to swear allegiance to him. Control of the monarchy quickly fell to Henry's mother, a weak, retiring woman thoroughly unsuited to the rough world of German politics. She did her best, but under her regency the interests of the monarchy were not advanced, royal lands were alienated to various princes, and the political situation in Germany began to unravel.

These problems became very clear when in April, 1062, Archbishop Anno of Cologne enticed the twelve-year-old Henry onto a gaily decorated boat on the Rhine River at Kaiserwerth and kidnapped him. Henry tried to escape by jumping over the side and was rescued only with great difficulty. The conspirators' motivation was simply to satisfy their own selfish desires while allowing Henry only a semblance of power. Probably relieved to be done with the responsibility of being regent, Agnes made no objection, nor did any other significant group in Germany, to the kidnapping; instead she fulfilled her long-held desire to enter a convent.

By 1066, when he was able to assume power for himself at the age of sixteen, Henry was a tall, attractive man, who despite frequent illnesses had an imposing physical presence. Lacking the piety of his father, Henry reacted against the restraints of his childhood by living a dissolute life. His experiences with the German princes during the regency not only had taught him trickery, deceit, and cunning, but also had filled him with an intense pride in the dignity of the monarchy and a burning desire to preserve and defend its rights. The protection of the monarchy would remain the constant goal of his reign; in 1066, Henry was ready to begin the arduous task of restoring the power and prestige of the crown.

Life's Work

Because of the erosion of royal authority during the regency, Henry's first priority was to create a firm economic foundation for the monarchy, enabling it to act independently of the desires of the German nobility. That required the reinstitution of royal properties in Saxony, making it the center of royal power. Such a program was certain to be opposed by the Saxon nobles, who would see it as a threat to the gains they had made during the regency, and by the free Saxon peasants, who correctly perceived any increase in the monarchy's power as leading to servitude. Led by Otto von Nordheim and Magnus Billung, these groups rebelled in 1070. Although the Saxons had some success against Henry, the issue was never in serious doubt and on June 9, 1075, the imperial army decisively defeated a Saxon army of nobles and peasants at Langensalza on the river Unstrutt. Broken and crushed, Saxony appeared completely subjugated and Henry was poised to govern it directly through royal officials, *ministeriales*, with Goslar as his capital. Had this success proved lasting, there is little doubt that Henry would have completed the political program of the Ottonian and Salian kings: the creation of a German "state" like that of Norman England. At the very moment of his greatest victory, however, Henry was suddenly faced with an even more perilous enemy in the person of Pope Gregory VII.

Gregory, formerly the Cluniac monk Hildebrand, was elected pope in 1073 while Henry was preoccupied with Saxony. At first, relations between the two were quite friendly. Gregory followed ancient custom by informing the German king of his election and requesting Henry's confirmation, which was granted. Had Henry understood the true aims and beliefs of Gregory, however, this approval would not have been forthcoming.

Henry IV of Germany. (Library of Congress)

Within this short, pale, and plebeian fifty-year-old pope burned a revolutionary vision of the Church and its place in society. Essentially, Gregory saw himself called by God to free the Church from the chains of secular authority. He envisioned a Church, under the absolute control of the Papacy, having ultimate primacy over all society. All authority, secular and clerical, would serve the will of the pope. Indeed, Gregory attacked the German king and the German church precisely because it was the most organized and disciplined in Europe. It had been reformed by Henry II and Henry III and therefore was attached to the Crown and not to the Papacy. Thus, if absolute papal control of the Church and society were to become a reality in Europe, first the secular control of the German church had to be destroyed. His contemporaries were very aware that Gregory's program was revolutionary, breaking with ancient custom and tradition.

Gregory carefully planned his move against Henry, choosing to strike just as the Saxon revolt was coming to its climax. At the Lenten Synod of 1075, Gregory, as part of a sweeping reform program against simoniac German clergy, forbade Henry to perform any lay investitures or else suffer severe penalties—a mortal challenge to the monarchy's ability to rule. The German kings had long used prelates as the chief officials of the kingdom and to deny them the power to appoint and to invest the bishops and the abbots of the imperial abbeys was to shred the crown's capacity to govern.

Henry ignored the pope's decree, and once the Saxons were reduced, he turned his attention to Milan, where he appointed an archbishop in direct opposition to Gregory, who had supported another candidate. The pope retaliated with his famous letter of December 8, 1075, in which he called Henry to penance and threatened him with the loss of his throne. He also ordered his messengers to berate Henry personally for his moral faults, making it clear that if the king did not submit, excommunication and deposition would follow.

Gregory had miscalculated. By taking such an extreme position, one that imperiled civil order in Germany, he drove the German bishops and Henry together; on January 24, 1076, they met at Worms. There Henry and his bishops approved a letter castigating the pope. It began "Hildebrand, no longer pope but false monk" and concluded by stating "We Henry, king by the grace of God, with all our bishops say to you: come down, come down!" This letter reached Gregory in February, 1076, but now it was Henry who had overreached. The pope immediately excommunicated and deposed the king and absolved all of his subjects of their fealty to him.

Within months Henry found himself isolated, deserted by his former allies, and facing an increasingly more powerful opposition. In October, the German nobility met at Tribur to decide how to treat the excommunicated monarch. Henry had to agree to remove the excommunication within a year or the nobles would no longer consider him king. They apparently believed that Henry would be unable to fulfill this requirement, for they also invited Gregory to meet with them as a mediator at Augsburg on February 2, 1077. Henry realized that if the Augsburg meeting took place the monarchy was doomed.

At this juncture Henry performed a brilliant political maneuver. Secretly crossing the Alps, for all the major passes were blocked by nobles hostile to the monarchy, he appeared before Gregory at Canossa on January 25, 1077; for three days Henry stood in the cold and snow wearing only sackcloth as penance. Gregory was reluctant to grant absolution, but he was a priest and a priest could not refuse forgiveness to a sincere penitent, as Henry well knew. As a result of this dramatic action Henry was absolved and restored to his throne.

The German princes were furious with Gregory. The meeting at Augsburg had only been a week away, but now with the excommunication removed, they had no legitimate reason for rebellion. Nevertheless, they elected Rudolf of Swabia as antiking and Germany was plunged into three years of civil war. Henry knew that Rudolf was not a serious threat as long as Gregory did not recognize Rudolf as the rightful king. Gregory remained neutral for three years and then, possibly fearful that Henry was reconsolidating his power, excommunicated him again at the Lenten Synod of 1080 and declared Rudolf the legitimate king. Rudolf, however, was killed in battle the following October; this time, the German clergy and nobility stood by Henry, for they realized that Gregory posed as much a threat to their privileges as to the king's. With this support, Henry held a council at Mainz that deposed Gregory and established an antipope. It was now Gregory who was isolated, and in 1081, Henry invaded Italy. Gregory took refuge in the Castle Sant'Angelo in Rome, and though faced with certain defeat, he refused to compromise. He was finally rescued by his Norman allies, with whom he retreated to southern Italy. Broken by this extraordinary conflict, Gregory died at Salerno on May 25, 1085.

It appeared that Henry had achieved his goals. Gregory had been driven into exile and Henry's position in Germany never seemed stronger. In 1087, his eldest son, Conrad, was crowned the next king, and in 1089, after his wife Bertha's death, Henry married Adelheid, the daughter of a Russian prince. Yet within a few years, Henry's world began to collapse around him. In 1088, Bishop Otto of Ostia was elected Pope Urban II. Because of his political genius, Urban was a much more potent adversary than was his predecessor; he successfully exploited conditions in Germany to advance the papal program. Urban was aided by Henry's family problems.

FRANCONIAN (SALIAN) KINGS OF GERMANY, 1024-1125

Reign	*King*
1024-1039	Conrad II
1039-1056	Henry III
1056-1106	HENRY IV
1106-1125	Henry V
1125	Franconian/Salian line ends

In 1093, the papal party persuaded the impressionable Conrad to desert his father and be crowned king of the Lombards. Simultaneously, Henry's young wife, Adelheid, after being imprisoned for adultery, escaped and spread incredible tales about Henry's moral corruption. The forces that Henry had opposed since 1066 once again arrayed themselves against him; from 1090 to 1096 he was trapped in a castle near Verona. In 1096, however, Henry was able to return to Germany and at Mainz he held a diet that deposed Conrad (who died in 1101) and crowned his brother, Henry, heir. Henry also tried to make peace with Urban, but the pope refused these overtures and renewed Henry's excommunication. At this moment young Henry betrayed his father. Henry IV, who by now was understandably suspicious of his family, was nevertheless tricked by his son into leaving his armed escort and accompanying him to the castle at Böckelheim. There Henry became his son's prisoner and was forced to confess his sins and to renounce his rights to the throne. Henry V had staged a successful coup; before he could mount a counterstroke, Henry IV died at Liège on August 7, 1106.

SIGNIFICANCE

Henry IV's reign was a turning point in German history. His political goal had been to continue the policy initiated by Conrad II of consolidating royal power at the expense of the German nobility and clergy. Henry's vision was for a feudal monarchy whose every aspect would be inspired and controlled by the king. He was well aware of the strong opposition he would face in attempting to achieve this ambitious plan, but Henry was never dismayed by adversity and he did have some success. A royal capital was created, royal lands were extended, and for a period of time the nobility was held in check. Henry's development of a bureaucratic government employing civil servants called *ministeriales* anticipated similar reforms accomplished under the Capetians in France and the Plantagenets in England.

The Investiture Controversy halted the evolution toward a strong, centralized monarchy, however, and started a steady dissolution of the crown's authority. With the monarchy preoccupied with its fight with the Papacy, developing noble families, such as the Zahringer of Swabia, were able to consolidate their own position. By the time of Henry's death in 1106, the German nobility was already in the ascendancy and Germany had started down the long, tortuous path of feudalism just as the other monarchies in France and England were beginning to create new types of royal government and to extend their authority into broader areas of society.

It is not difficult to see the heroic character of Henry IV. He struggled mightily and with extraordinary courage to preserve and to expand royal power. In his mind's eye, Henry had grasped the vague outline of the future course of government better than had any of his contemporaries. If it is true, as James Westfall Thompson states, that "a man is to be judged not by what he achieves, but by what he labors to accomplish," then Henry IV was the greatest German monarch of the Middle Ages.

—*Ronald F. Smith*

FURTHER READING

Barraclough, G. *The Origins of Modern Germany.* 4th ed. Oxford: Basil, Blackwell and Mott, 1962. This is a very impressive survey of Germany from 800 to 1939. Constitutional issues and the development of a central government are stressed. The period of 1025-1075 is seen as a time of royal consolidation, while the era from 1075, when the Investiture Controversy breaks out, to 1152 is perceived as a period of decline for the German monarchy.

Eyck, Frank. *Religion and Politics in German History: From the Beginnings to the French Revolution.* New York: St. Martin's Press, 1998. An analysis of how Germanic peoples preserved links with classical civilization through their ability to assimilate other cultures and peoples, from their alliances with eighth century popes through the Reformation and Counter-Reformation. The initial bond between the Germanic rulers and popes turned to conflict as the Papacy gained power. Tables, maps, bibliography, index.

Fuhrmann, Horst. *Germany in the High Middle Ages, 1050-1200.* New York: Cambridge University Press, 1986. This work provides an outstanding summary of Henry IV's reign and places it within the context of the history of medieval Germany. The discussion of the Investiture Controversy and the Saxon rebellion is concise yet detailed. The bibliography is the best of any of the works cited here and details only those studies done in English.

Hampe, Karl. *Germany Under the Salian and Hohenstaufen Emperors.* Translated by Ralph Bennett. Totowa, N.J.: Rowman and Littlefield, 1973. Originally published in 1909, this book is still regarded as one of the most readable and reliable accounts of eleventh and twelfth century Germany. Hampe sees Henry IV's policies as reactionary with their object of restoring ancient rights of the monarchy. There are some excellent insights regarding Henry's motives and character. Highly recommended.

Jeep, John M., et al., eds. *Medieval Germany: An Encyclopedia.* New York: Garland, 2001. An A-Z encyclopedia that addresses all aspects of the German- and Dutch-speaking medieval world from 500 to 1500. Entries include individuals, events, and broad topics such as feudalism and pregnancy. Bibliographical references, index.

Joachimsen, Paul. "The Investiture Contest and the German Constitution." In *Studies in Medieval History: Medieval Germany, 911-1250.* Vol. 2, *Essays by German Historians*, edited by G. Barraclough. 4th ed. London: Basil, Blackwell and Mott, 1967. Considered by some to be a classic in the field, this article succinctly discusses the constitutional issues of the Investiture Controversy and maintains that the historical significance of Henry IV's reign is the fact that he took issue with the Papacy's view that the German monarchy was solely an electoral monarchy with no regard given to the rights of blood or heredity.

Moore, Robert Ian. *The First European Revolution, c. 970-1215.* Malden, Mass.: Blackwell, 2000. According to the publisher, "a radical reassessment of Europe from the late tenth to the early thirteenth centuries [arguing that] the period witnessed the first true 'revolution' in European society," supported by transformation of the economy, family life, political power structures, and the rise of the non-Mediterranean cities. Bibliography, index.

Robinson, Ian Stuart. *Henry IV of Germany, 1056-1106.*

New York: Cambridge University Press, 1999. The first English-language work on Henry IV and the seminal events occurring during his reign over kingdoms of Germany, Italy, and Burgundy, including the beginning of the church-state confrontation. Maps, bibliography, index.

Thompson, James Westfall. *Feudal Germany.* Chicago: University of Chicago Press, 1928. This book was criticized when first published for not including the latest scholarship. It maintains that the root of Henry's struggle with the Papacy was economic. Rome wanted to gain complete control of the Church in Germany and Henry IV could not allow this to happen. There is a very detailed description of the Saxon rebellion and some fine descriptions of Henry.

SEE ALSO: Frederick I Barbarossa; Gregory VII; Henry the Lion; Saint László I; Leo IX; Matilda of Canossa; Urban II.

RELATED ARTICLES in *Great Events from History: The Middle Ages, 477-1453*: August 10, 955: Otto I Defeats the Magyars; 976-1025: Reign of Basil II; 1054: Beginning of the Rome-Constantinople Schism; November 27, 1095: Pope Urban II Calls the First Crusade.

HENRY V

King of England (r. 1413-1422)

Henry gave England justice and stability at home, while his military and political genius enabled him to proceed in the conquest of France and his claim to its crown. He left England a strong power in European affairs.

BORN: September 16?, 1387; Monmouth Castle, Monmouthshire, England

DIED: August 31, 1422; Bois de Vincennes, France

ALSO KNOWN AS: Henry of Monmouth (given name)

AREAS OF ACHIEVEMENT: Government and politics, military

EARLY LIFE

The man who would become Henry V, king of England and regent of France, is familiar to modern readers and audiences as the Prince Hal of William Shakespeare's plays, but his contemporaries knew him in his youth as Henry of Monmouth. His father, Henry, duke of Lancaster, was similarly known from his birthplace as Henry Bolingbroke (Henry IV) and was the cousin of the reigning monarch, Richard II.

Henry was well educated; the records for the duchy of Lancaster show early payments for his books, a harp, and a sword. Unverified tradition says that he was educated at Oxford. Whatever his background, during his reign he showed considerable ability in a variety of fields, from the military (he was an outstanding general) to the musical (he composed several pieces of church music).

In 1389, Richard II exiled Henry Bolingbroke, whose sons were taken into the court, partly as kinsmen, partly as hostages. Richard displayed real affection for the younger Henry, taking him in May, 1399, on an expedition to Ireland, where the king himself knighted the youth. In August of that year, however, Bolingbroke returned to England in revolt; Richard rebuked his young relative, but Henry seems to have had no forewarning of his father's actions.

Bolingbroke was quickly able to depose Richard, largely because the king's erratic and willful actions had seriously undermined his support among the nobility. In October, Bolingbroke was crowned Henry IV in London; his son participated in the ceremony and two days later was made earl of Chester, duke of Cornwall, and prince of Wales. He was soon after given the title of duke of Aquitaine, the English possession on the Continent, and duke of Lancaster, his father's former title.

From 1400 until 1408, Henry was occupied in subduing rebellion in his princedom of Wales. First, as figurehead of a council of nobles, and later on his own, he planned and led raids and skirmishes against the Welsh. In 1403, this struggle was interrupted by the conspiracy of the powerful Percy family of northern England. Henry IV and his son combined their forces to defeat the Percys at the Battle of Berwick (July 21, 1403), during which the prince was wounded in the face but continued in the fight.

By 1408, the Welsh had been hammered into submission, and Henry was more active in London and in the king's council. In 1409, he was made warden of the Cinque Ports and constable of Dover, both important military posts. He also took a larger part in the government, partly because of Henry IV's steadily weakening condition, caused by an unknown but disfiguring disease. By 1410, the prince probably was ruling in his father's name, aided by his relative Thomas Beaufort, the new chancellor. The Beauforts were to be valuable servants during Henry V's reign. In 1410, Henry was also given the vital post of captain of Calais, England's stronghold in France.

An attempt to have the king abdicate in favor of his son led to the removal of Beaufort as chancellor and the temporary withdrawal of Henry from the court and council, but on March 20, 1413, Henry IV died, and his son, at age twenty-six, became king of England.

There are several contemporary descriptions and portraits of Henry V, and they generally agree that he struck an appropriately kingly figure. He was above medium height, with a slender, athletic body, and was known as an exceptionally swift runner. His hair was smooth, brown, and thick; he had a cleft chin and small ears. The feature most noted by Henry's subjects was his eyes, which were said to be those of a dove in peace but a lion's when he was angered.

LIFE'S WORK

Henry V was crowned on April 9, 1413 (Passion Sunday), in an unusual spring snowstorm. Equally unusual, and commented on by his contemporaries, was the marked change in his character, which immediately became more somber and regal. The total reversal is heightened, however, in Shakespeare's *Henry V* (1598-1599) for dramatic emphasis; Henry's youth had been spent largely in camp and council, rather than in taverns and the streets.

One of the complaints voiced in Henry's first parliament, in 1413, was the weakness of royal power during his father's last years. The son moved decisively to counter this and appointed such skilled and experienced officers as his kinsman and new chancellor, Henry Beaufort. Throughout his reign, Henry was well served by his officers and officials.

In December, 1413, Henry had the remains of Richard II, the monarch deposed and perhaps ordered killed by his father, reburied with royal pomp at Westminster. This action was an indication both of Henry's affections for the man and of his allegiance to the ideal of kingship as a station partially sacramental in nature.

Henry was noted for his orthodoxy and concern for the unity of the Church, and he was greatly concerned with the growing Lollard movement in England, which threatened both ecclesiastical and social stability. The Lollards, a form of early protestants, were led by Sir John Oldcastle, who was arrested in September, 1413, and interrogated by numerous officials, including the king himself. Oldcastle escaped and early the next year devised a plot to seize the king and his brothers. Acting with his customary decisiveness, Henry surprised the rebels as they gathered at St. Giles' Field outside London, and crushed the revolt. Sir John escaped again but was later captured and executed in 1418 while Henry was campaigning in France.

Henry V. (G. T. Devereux)

France was the dominant theme of Henry's reign. English kings had held territory in France, and Henry was determined to reconquer that which had been lost; he also sought the Crown of France itself. In the Parliament of 1414, Henry's claims were asserted, and support was given for a military expedition.

The English asserted title to the provinces of Normandy, Touraine, Anjou, Maine, and Ponthieu, as well as border territories ceded to them by previous treaties. Henry also desired a marriage with Catherine, daughter of the French king Charles VI, and a large dowry for the bride. The demands were considerable, but they were made at an appropriate moment.

Charles VI was a weak monarch, frequently insane, and control of France was split between the dauphin and his supporters, the Armagnacs, and John, duke of Burgundy. Although powerful, France was largely incapable of using that power. By contrast, Henry V brought to the struggle both unshakable personal conviction and national unity.

The first of Henry's three expeditions to France began on August 11, 1415, when he sailed with twenty-five hundred men-at-arms and eight thousand archers from Portsmouth. After a two-month siege, the port of Harfleur capitulated. Rather than return by sea to England, Henry marched overland toward Calais in a striking demonstration of claim to the disputed territory. The march also put his small army in great danger.

On October 25, 1415, near the castle of Agincourt, and only two days' march from the safety of Calais, Henry and his now seven thousand men found their way blocked by at least fifty thousand French troops. The English line drew up between two forests, with their front protected by pointed stakes driven into the ground. When the heavily armored French knights attacked across a muddy field, the English longbowmen devastated their ranks. Continued French assaults only increased the disaster, and an English counterattack finished the French. Henry arrived in England with more than two thousand prisoners from the French nobility, and the battle won on St. Crispan's Day became the centerpiece of Shakespeare's *Henry V* and an enduring part of England's national mythology.

The new importance of Henry and England was signaled in 1416 by the visit of Sigismund, the Holy Roman Emperor. The emperor and Henry concluded a treaty that ended the schism in the Church between rival popes by the election of a new pontiff, Martin V, and promised a joint crusade in the future. Henry's long-range goal was to lead a united Europe in reconquest of the Holy Land.

As part of that plan he pressed his claim to the French crown. In the fall of 1416, he carefully prepared for his second expedition, and his extensive shipbuilding efforts can justly qualify him as the founder of the Royal Navy.

In July, 1417, Henry sailed with fifty thousand troops. He landed in Normandy, cut off the province's communications with the rest of France, and secured a base of operations. This was done through a series of sieges conducted by Henry and his lieutenants. By the end of July, Henry had invested the strategic town of Rouen, which held out until January of 1419 but which was forced to surrender because of famine and lack of support. Significantly, the French, split between Armagnac and Burgundian factions, were unable to relieve the town.

Henry skillfully exploited this internecine feud in his negotiations, which brought success in May, 1420, with the Treaty of Troyes. This agreement between Henry, Philip the Good (his father, John, having been killed), and Charles VI excluded the dauphin from succession, recognized Henry as the heir to the Crown after Charles's death, and made him regent during the king's life. It also confirmed Philip the Good in alliance against the dauphin and granted Catherine to Henry in marriage. The marriage was celebrated on June 2, 1420 (Trinity Sunday); a son, Henry, was born on December 6, 1421.

After the treaty, Henry entered Paris and established his officers there. By the end of the year, the royal couple had sailed to England, where Catherine was crowned at Westminster on February 24, 1421. A triumphal royal progress through England was cut short in April with the news of the defeat and death of Henry's brother, the duke of Clarence, in France. On June 10, Henry left England on his third, and final, expedition.

Once in France, Henry quickly reversed the military situation in favor of the English. On October 6, he invested the town of Meaux; the siege lasted until May, 1422, and during the long winter months, in the crowded, unsanitary conditions of the camp, Henry contracted the dysentery that would kill him.

During the spring and summer, Henry grew steadily weaker, and in August, he was carried to Vincennes, his health rapidly failing. Realizing his state, he made arrangements for the education of his son, for the government of England and France, and for the continuation of his policies. He died early in the morning of August 31, 1422, at the age of thirty-five. There was an elaborate funeral procession that culminated on November 11 with his burial at the Chapel of Edward the Confessor at Westminster Abbey. On his splendid tomb, his effigy lay, carved in oak with a cover of silver gilt and a head of solid silver. The head was stolen in 1545 but replaced by a bronze one in 1972. After many centuries, Henry V remains one of England's most favored kings.

Significance

Henry V was judged by his contemporaries to be an outstanding, even exemplary, monarch. According to the standards of the time, he indeed was, since he brought his realm peace and justice at home and legitimate martial glory abroad.

Within England, Henry V's reign was marked by tranquillity and order. Failure to ensure such order was probably the worst fault attributable to a late medieval monarch. Such failure had led to the fall of Richard II and had darkened the last years of Henry's father. Largely because of his personal example and wise selection of deputies, Henry V provided his kingdom with the peace it desired.

Henry was noted for his sense of justice, which at times seemed to border on the inflexible. In this, however, as in his steadfast devotion to the Catholic Church, Henry was motivated by the ideal standards he believed should guide a monarch. In any event, his consistent adherence to these standards helped ensure a quiet realm in England, even though he was on campaign for almost half of his nine-year reign.

Henry's campaigns in France form the keystone to Henry V's fame during his life and his enduring memory after his death. His wars were supported by his countrymen for many reasons, but chief among them were Henry's careful presentation of his efforts as a legitimate response to French provocations and his continued victories. Judged as a military monarch, Henry was outstanding, not only for the famous victory at Agincourt but particularly for his careful and thorough planning of his expeditions and his acute sense of possibilities and appropriate, effective strategy. He shared the hardships of campaigns with his troops, and his combination of talent and leadership made him the outstanding warrior of his day.

That day was short, but while he lived, Henry accomplished two of his goals. He had gained, although not consolidated, his claims to French territory and was assured the French crown at the death of Charles VI. By an irony of history, the victorious, younger king died before the insane, older one, and Henry V never had the opportunity to rule both England and France, or to lead Europe on a new crusade. Still, while what might have been remains unknown, it is clear that the young King Henry V left England a stronger nation for his reign, and a name that yet lives.

—*Michael Witkoski*

FURTHER READING

Curry, Anne, ed. *Agincourt, 1415: Henry V, Sir Thomas Erpingham, and the Triumph of the English Archers*. Charleston, S.C.: Arcadia, 2000. Looks at Henry's role in the Battle at Agincourt and, especially, the use of longbows by the victors.

Hutchinson, Harold. *Henry V: A Biography*. New York: John Day, 1967. A biography of Henry V and his time, with admirable treatment of the background and milieu of the early fifteenth century. A good introduction for readers unfamiliar with the characters or characteristics of the late Middle Ages.

Jacob, E. F. *Henry V and the Invasion of France*. 1947. Rev. ed. New York: Collier Books, 1966. A thorough study of Henry's campaigns. Since his conquest of France is considered the most important aspect of his kingship, this comprehensive overview is extremely valuable for understanding Henry's accomplishments.

Keegan, John. *The Face of Battle*. New York: Viking Press, 1976. This is a remarkable book that explores and explains the nature of warfare from the participant's point of view. The section on Agincourt is a stunning re-creation of medieval combat and gives the reader a real understanding of what must have happened and why.

Larbarge, Margaret Wade. *Henry V: The Cautious Conqueror*. New York: Stein and Day, 1975. An account of the life and actions of the king. Best for readers with some familiarity with the time period.

McFarlane, Kenneth B. *Lancastrian Kings and Lollard Knights*. Oxford, England: Clarendon Press, 1972. Divided into two sections, the first primarily about Henry IV, the second about the Lollard movement in fourteenth century England. There is, however, a good general essay titled "Henry V: A Personal Portrait," which is an excellent starting place for the beginning student.

Seward, Desmond. *Henry V as Warlord*. New York: Penguin Books, 2001. A biography of Henry, focusing on his military leadership.

Wylie, James H. *The Reign of Henry the Fifth*. 3 vols. Cambridge, England: Cambridge University Press, 1914-1929. Still a definitive study of Henry V's kingship, this work goes into great detail on every aspect of the reign.

SEE ALSO: Henry IV (of England); Philip the Good; Richard II.

RELATED ARTICLES in *Great Events from History: The Middle Ages, 477-1453*: c. 700: Bow and Arrow Spread into North America; 1154-1204: Angevin Empire Is Established; August 26, 1346: Battle of Crécy; 1414-1418: Council of Constance; May 4-8, 1429: Joan of Arc's Relief of Orléans; 1453: English Are Driven from France.

Heraclius

Byzantine emperor (r. 610-641)

Seizing the East Roman (Byzantine) imperial throne amid seemingly fatal crises, Heraclius turned back the onslaughts of the Persians and Avars, only to see his work largely undone by the Arab conquests. Nevertheless, he and his successors initiated institutional reorganization that would revitalize the empire.

Born: c. 575; Cappadocia, Byzantine Empire (now in Turkey)

Died: February 11, 641; Constantinople, Byzantine Empire (now Istanbul, Turkey)

Areas of achievement: Government and politics, warfare and conquest

Early Life

Heraclius (heh-rak-LEE-uhs) came from a wealthy and distinguished Cappadocian family in central Asia Minor, possibly (though not incontrovertibly) of Armenian descent. His father, an able general of the same name, was rewarded for his services by his old friend the emperor Maurice (c. 539-602) with the office of exarch, or viceroy, of North Africa. When his father took up residence in its capital, Carthage, about 600, the younger Heraclius was about twenty-five years old. No information survives about the son's life until then.

In 602, the emperor Maurice was dethroned and cruelly murdered by a crude, half-barbarian usurper named Phocas. His regime became a reign of terror against the nobility in the capital, Constantinople, while the previously strong military efforts against the empire's enemies were totally neglected. The elder Heraclius was apparently planning some action of his own against the murderer of his old friend and benefactor when he was invited in 608 by exasperated leaders in Constantinople to assist them in removing the tyrant. Too old to lead the action in person, the exarch organized a long-range strategy of rebellion to be led by his kinsmen. Under his nephew, Nicetas, son of the exarch's brother, and his chief-of-staff, Gregory, a force was able to win control of the strategic province of Egypt by late 609 or early 610.

The second phase of the project was a naval expedition led by the exarch's son, the younger Heraclius, then about thirty-four or thirty-five years old. He reached Constantinople by the end of September, 610, and his arrival prompted a rising there that brought down Phocas. With the usurper roughly dispatched, there was apparently some uncertainty about the choice of his successor, and his dissident son-in-law, the general Priscus, may have hoped to claim it. However, the senate and the populace declared Heraclius their rescuer. Thus, on October 5, 610, Heraclius was crowned emperor and, at the same time, was married to his first wife, Eudoxia.

Life's Work

Heraclius assumed rule of a state that soon seemed headed for destruction from paired foreign threats. In the Balkans, the Turkic Avars and their Slavic subject peoples were breaking through the borders and mounting a drive toward Constantinople itself. Meanwhile, Khosrow II (590-628), the Persian king, had invaded the imperial territory supposedly to avenge his former ally Maurice, but his aggression soon became a campaign to restore the great empire of Achaemenid days. Imperial forces were unable to hold back a series of Persian attacks that captured Antioch, Damascus, and Jerusalem, the latter with terrible slaughter and calculated violation of the supreme Christian shrines. Egypt was invaded and overrun by 620, and attacks were launched at Asia Minor, with talk of the new Xerxes crossing soon to Europe.

Against these threats, Heraclius seems to have done little in his first ten years of reign. Although physically strong, brave, and intelligent, Heraclius displayed fluctuations between boldness and indecisiveness; patterns of emotional imbalance in his family suggest that he may have been bipolar (manic-depressive). He also faced acute problems, both personal and political, in his early years in power. Following the death of his father, the old exarch, came the death in 612 of his epileptic wife, Eudoxia, after she had given birth to two children. In his grief, he was persuaded by his mother to marry, about eighteen months later, his own niece, Martina, twenty-three years his junior. This intelligent and devoted, if ambitious, woman made him a good wife, but the marriage provoked Church indignation and popular hostility, while the fact that most of their eventual ten children were born disabled in some way was taken as proof of divine retribution for their incest.

Heraclius also had to assert his right to lead. Priscus, resentful perhaps because he missed his chance at the throne, was openly rude and unreliable; only by a carefully planned ruse was Heraclius able, in late 612, to strip him of command and imprison him. Beyond this, Heraclius had to deal with the veritable collapse of the empire's once-fine military system and the rapid dwindling of resources and revenue. Heraclius was by no means inactive, but he may well have had his moments of despair. According to one source, around 619 he considered leaving Constantinople to make Carthage his base for a military counter effort. According to this report, panic in the capital prompted the patriarch Sergius I to exact an oath from Heraclius that he would never abandon Constantinople. The story reflects the fact that Sergius made an understanding with the emperor by which vast quantities of the Church's wealth were made available as its contribution to the vindication of both empire and Christian faith. With these resources, Heraclius seems to have begun building a new military force, one emphasizing cavalry. He is said to have retired to study strategy and military lore intensively, and it is possible that the *Strategikon* (sixth century; *Maurice's Strategikon: Handbook of Byzantine Military Strategy*, 1984), traditionally attributed to the emperor Maurice, might have been written, or at least rewritten, by Heraclius during this period of military buildup.

Engraving of Heraclius patterned after a sculpture. (Library of Congress)

Heraclius also broke a tradition of more than two centuries, that the emperor left military campaigning to his generals, by insisting that he would lead his troops in person. After a solemn departure ceremony on April 4, 622, Heraclius crossed to Asia Minor, outmaneuvered the Persian forces for some months, and then won a handsome victory in February, 623, temporarily relieving the threat to that area. Back in Constantinople, he was obliged to negotiate anew with the restless Avars, from whom he had already purchased a truce at the cost of heavy tribute; at one point, he barely escaped capture by them in a treacherous ambush. With no response to his overtures for peace with the Persians, Heraclius renewed his offensive in early 624, determined to carry the war into the Persians' land. Invading by way of Armenia and causing the Persian king to flee, Heraclius stormed and desecrated the Zoroastrian shrine city, in retaliation for the profanation of Jerusalem. Heraclius spent the following year cultivating allies among the peoples of the Caucasia and trying to take control of Armenian territories.

In 626, as his operations returned to Asia Minor, Heraclius faced a new crisis. The Persians had menaced Constantinople only passingly before, but now they entered into an agreement with the Avars, encouraging and supporting them in a direct attack on the capital. The Avars seemed genuinely determined to take the city, while the Persians hoped that the attack would force Heraclius to come to its rescue, thereby abandoning his campaign against them. The emperor, however, gambled that the city could hold out without him, relying on its magnificent fortifications, its able commanders, and the leadership of Sergius. His risk proved worth taking: After a ferocious siege, from late June to early August, the Avars admitted failure and withdrew, their power in the Balkans crumbling. Heraclius, who had continued his operations meanwhile in Asia Minor, was able now to redouble his efforts with enhanced prestige.

Much of 627 was spent in further building of his

forces and arranging an alliance with the powerful Khazars of the Caucasia. At the end of the year, he resumed his invasion of Persian territory, and on December 12, 627, he confronted the Persian army before the ruins of ancient Nineveh. The outcome was a crushing defeat for the Persians, whose army was broken, but the emperor failed to follow up on his victory immediately, resuming his pursuit of the fleeing Persian king only after some weeks. Taking one royal capital, Dastagird, the vacillating Heraclius decided not to attack another. Yet obstinate to the end, Khosrow was dethroned by a rebellion and murdered in late February, 628, his place taken by his son. The new king sued for peace, and Heraclius gladly negotiated a reestablishment of original boundaries and restoration of holy relics. Making a triumphal procession to Constantinople, Heraclius entered it amid wild rejoicing in September, 628. During the next two years, Heraclius supervised the recovery of the liberated territories and at some point ceremonially restored the Holy Cross to Jerusalem as a symbol of Christian victory.

Aging and worn out, Heraclius devoted the ensuing years to securing the reestablishment of imperial government in the recovered territories, to pursuing religious pacification, and to arranging provisions of succession among members of his growing family. Yet he was not allowed to rest on his laurels: Barely was his heroic war of recovery ended when he was faced with the unexpected onslaught of the Arab conquests. Newly unified under the banner of the Prophet Muḥammad and taking advantage of the mutual exhaustion of Persia and the empire, the Arabs launched initial raids that soon turned into programs of conquest. Imperial forces resisting them were twice defeated in 634 and again the following year, when the Arabs were able to take Damascus. Heraclius attempted to coordinate a defensive program in person and gathered a final, large army. Yet its ambush and destruction on the banks of the Yarmūk River in August, 636, removed all hope of successful resistance. Heraclius abandoned Syria in despair while the cities of the region fell in rapid succession to the conquerors: Jerusalem capitulating in 638, and the imperial capital of Caesarea in 640. By that time, with Syria-Palestine overrun, the Arabs had begun their invasion of Egypt.

Meanwhile, broken and ailing, Heraclius halted his progress to Constantinople at the Bosporos Thracius, refusing for many months to cross into his capital. A congenital hydrophobia, reinforced by a prophecy of his death by water, held him back until, in early 638, under threats of conspiracies and succession problems, a crossing was arranged: A vast pontoon bridge was built across the channel, with trees and shrubbery planted on either side to hide the water from view as he moved across. Back in his capital, Heraclius attempted to resolve the long-standing religious disputes, hoping to mollify the dissident Monophysites, whose unrest in Syria-Palestine and Egypt is thought to have undermined the defense of those areas. Later in 638, he issued his doctrinal decree on this matter, the *Ekthesis*, and thereafter attempted to negotiate its acceptance among various branches of the Church. Heraclius's health continued to decline, and he died on February 11, 641.

Byzantine Emperors: Heraclian Line, 610-717

Reign	*Emperor*
610-641	Heraclius
620's	Avar and Visigothic incursions
636	Palestine lost to ʿUmar I
641	Constantine III and Heracleonas
641	Egypt, Genoa lost
641-668	Constans II Pogonatus
668-685	Constantine IV
674-677	Muʾāwiyah lays siege to Constantinople
685-695	Justinian II Rhinotmetus
693	Armenia lost
695-698	Leontius (non-Heraclian)
698	Carthage falls
698-705	Tiberius III
705-711	Justinian II (restored)
711-713	Philippicus Bardanes
713-715	Anastasius II
716-717	Theodosius III

Significance

Heraclius's sometimes inconsistent character, together with the disasters of his last years, has compromised the brilliance of his real achievements. It is true that, after saving the empire heroically from one nearly fatal crisis, he died unable to protect it from another. Yet he was fighting external forces beyond his control. Also foredoomed was his effort to resolve the Monophysite dissent: By introducing the compromise doctrine of Monothelitism in his *Ekthesis*, he only complicated further an already unsolvable situation. Nevertheless, if he left a set of grim legacies behind him, he also left the dynasty he founded, including several emperors of dedication and talent, who were to cope with these legacies through the rest of the sixth century.

He also left at least the beginnings of a governmental transformation that would help make possible the successful struggle of his heirs. Much controversy has surrounded the development of the so-called Theme System, which is dated generally to the sixth century. Under this system, Asia Minor was divided into a set of military districts, garrisoned by native troops supported by the revenues of small agricultural freeholds. This military pattern soon took over the local civil functions and was eventually applied to other parts of the empire's territories, becoming in time the basis for the surviving empire's military, administrative, agrarian, and fiscal organization. It has been traditional to credit Heraclius with initiating these organizational reforms—whether as a part of his preparations for war with the Persians or after his victory over them (and even in imitation of their institutions)—but historians are by no means agreed on how clear or complete such credit should be. To Heraclius's age is attributed also the final abandonment of older Roman administrative forms and Latin titles and their replacement with a more fully Hellenized chancery.

While controversy about him and his achievements will remain, there is no doubt of Heraclius's genuine role as a savior of his state and of his age as a turning point in the transformation of the late Roman into the Byzantine Empire. In the later medieval West, he would be remembered as a prototype of the "Crusader" sovereign, triumphant over unbelievers in the cause of the Christian faith.

—*John W. Barker*

FURTHER READING

Bury, J. B. *A History of the Later Roman Empire: From Arcadius to Irene (395 A.D. to 800 A.D.)*. 2 vols. New York: Macmillan, 1889. An older set with still useful chapters on the life and age of Heraclius.

Kaegi, Walter E. *Heraclius: Emperor of Byzantium*. New York: Cambridge University Press, 2003. A thorough overview of Heraclius's life and times. Includes an extensive bibliography and an index.

Maurice. *Maurice's Strategikon: Handbook of Byzantine Military Strategy*. Translated by George T. Dennis. Philadelphia: University of Pennsylvania Press, 1984. This important military manual is still ascribed to Heraclius's most significant predecessor, but its contents reflect the kind of organization with which Heraclius achieved his victories. Has a useful introduction.

Ostrogorsky, George. *History of the Byzantine State*. Translated by Joan Hussey. Rev. ed. New Brunswick, N.J.: Rutgers University Press, 1969. A comprehensive one-volume study of the history and institutions of the empire from the early fourth through the mid-fifteenth century. Arguments on the Theme System are no longer fully acceptable, but the treatment of the age of Heraclius and his successors still puts the system in excellent perspective.

Reinink, Gerrit J., and Bernard H. Stolte, eds. *The Reign of Heraclius (610-641): Crisis and Confrontation*. Dudley, Mass.: Peeters, 2002. A collection of conference papers exploring Heraclius's reign and influence. Includes an extensive bibliography and index.

Stratos, Andreas N. *Byzantium in the Seventh Century*. 2 vols. Translated by Marc Ogilvie-Grant and Harry T. Hionides. Amsterdam: Adolf M. Hakkert, 1968, 1972. The opening volumes (of six in the original Greek version, five in the English translation) of a massive work on the entire seventh century. Volumes 1 and 2 discuss in detail the confused and fragmentary sources from this epoch. A comprehensive and exhaustive study.

Theophanes. *The Chronicle of Theophanes Confessor: Byzantine and Near Eastern History, A.D. 284-813*. Translated by Cyril Mango and Roger Scott. New York: Oxford University Press, 1997. Provides an excellent introduction and notes clarifying some of the problems involved with using Theophanes's work as a source. The *Chronicle* is still one of the most important surviving texts on the Heraclian age.

SEE ALSO: Justinian I; Saint Sergius I; Theodora.

RELATED ARTICLES in *Great Events from History: The Middle Ages, 477-1453*: 630-711: Islam Expands Throughout North Africa; August 15-20, 636: Battle of Yarmūk; 637-657: Islam Expands Throughout the Middle East; 726-843: Iconoclastic Controversy.

Saint Hilda of Whitby

English abbess

One of the most important women of her day, Hilda founded and headed monasteries, advised leaders of church and state, mediated ecclesiastical disputes, and promoted learning and literary production.

Born: 614; Northumbria (now in England)
Died: November 17, 689; Whitby, Yorkshire, England
Also known as: Hild (variant of given name)
Areas of achievement: Religion and theology, literature, monasticism, patronage of the arts

Early Life

Hilda (HIHL-duh) was born a member of the royal household of Deira, one of the two kingdoms in Northumbria, in northern England. Her father, Hereric, was an Anglo-Saxon, and her mother, Breguswith, a Celt; thus even at her birth Hilda represented the union of two peoples whose cultures were often at war with each other.

Hilda's early life was marked by turmoil. When Deira was seized by the ruler of Bernicia, the other Northumbrian kingdom, her family had to flee. They took refuge at Elmete, in Yorkshire, but shortly thereafter, her father, Hereric, was poisoned by the petty king Cerdic. It was reported, however, that her mother, Breguswith, was consoled by a dream in which she was desperately searching for her missing husband. Though she never reached him, she did find under her clothing a necklace holding a jewel so bright that it illuminated all of Britain. She knew that the jewel signified her young daughter Hilda.

In 616, Hereric's uncle, Edwin, defeated the Bernicians and united both their county and Deira into a single kingdom, Northumbria, and the two-year-old Hilda went to live at his court. There she was taught to worship the pagan gods. However, when his first wife died in 625, King Edwin married Æthelburgh, the daughter of the king of Kent, where Saint Augustine was based. As part of the marriage agreement, she was permitted to continue worshiping as a Christian. She brought with her to Northumbria the monk Paulinus, who had been sent from Rome to Kent so that he could assist Augustine in his mission of converting the pagans. At first Edwin resisted Christianity, but after surviving an assassination attempt, he agreed to change his faith. On April 12, 627, Paulinus baptized the king and most of his court, including his great-niece Hilda, in the river at York.

When Hilda was eighteen, her great-uncle was killed in battle, and the queen, her daughter Eanfled, and most of the court fled to Kent. Paulinus, who had been the archbishop of York, was among the refugees. Thus, northern England was left under the control of the Celtic Christians rather than of those who followed the dictates of Rome.

It is not known what happened to Hilda between 632 and 647. It is very possible that she married and then, after being widowed, resolved to end her days in a convent. The lives of many noblewomen followed this pattern. Hilda's sister Hereswith, the widow of the king of East Anglia, was now in a French convent at Chelles near Paris. At any rate, whether or not Hilda had once been married, at thirty-three she was considered well past middle age. It would have seemed logical that she retire from the world and become a nun like her sister.

As it turned out, Hilda did not join Hereswith as she had planned. Although she would take holy orders, she would not retire from the world.

Life's Work

In 647, Hilda went to East Anglia, where her nephew was now the king, for a final year at court. However, shortly before she was to leave for France, she was summoned to Northumbria by Bishop Aidan, a Celtic monk who had founded the monastery at Lindisfarne. At his request, Hilda helped to form a small religious house on the bank of the River Wear. In 649, Aidan appointed her abbess of the large "double" monastery at Hartlepool, so termed because the community included both men and women.

With her close connections to the court, it was inevitable that Hilda's progress in her vocation would often be influenced by political developments. For example, in 655, Oswiu, the king of Bernicia, who had married Edwin's daughter Eanfled, promised that if God would give him victory in battle, thus making him king of a united Northumbria, he would dedicate his one-year-old daughter Elfleda to the church and also would provide enough land for twelve new monasteries. After Oswiu triumphed, he fulfilled his vow. Princess Elfleda was sent to Hartlepool and put in the care of her kinswoman, and Hilda was given some twelve hundred acres at Streonashalh (or Whitby, as it was renamed by the Danes), where she was to establish another double monastery and become its first abbess. Princess Elfleda, whom she took with her, eventually became a nun and later, abbess of Whitby.

In 657, Hilda founded what would be the most important religious house in northeast England. Because of her reputation for godliness as well as worldly wisdom, Hilda was consulted by kings and princes, as well as by Church leaders, who met at Whitby to discuss important issues and to seek Hilda's counsel. Thus, she become one of the most influential figures in the Church of her time. However, Hilda, who came to be known as "mother," was just as accessible to the poor and destitute as to those of high social rank.

At Whitby, as at Wear and at Hartlepool, Hilda established a rule of life that included the usual monastic virtues of poverty, chastity, and devotion but, above all, stressed charity and peace. From the beginning, the abbess herself had been known as a peacemaker. This quality was to serve her well in one of the great crises of the medieval church, the conflict between the practices of the Celtic churchmen, who had been converting pagans in the northern regions of Britain before 300, and those of the missionaries sent from Rome in the fifth and sixth centuries, whose influence prevailed in the south and east.

Even though Hilda had been baptized by the Roman monk Paulinus and may have spent some time in Kent—a center of Roman influence—with Queen Æthelburgh—who was strongly committed to Rome—in later life Hilda turned to the Celtic traditions that prevailed in the north, where all of the religious houses with which she was associated were located. Among her closest friends were the great Celtic leader Aidan; Finan, who succeeded him as bishop of Lindisfarne; and Colman, who was Finan's successor and who, like the other two, had come to Northumbria from Ireland, which still observed Celtic traditions. As a native of the island of Iona, which lies off the west coast of Scotland, King Oswiu also held to Celtic ways. However, like her mother Æthelburgh, Oswiu's wife Eanfled was convinced that Rome was right.

It should be stressed that the Celtic Christians and the Romans did not disagree on doctrine; their two major differences were the following: Which calendar should be used to calculate the date of Easter and how should the tonsures of monks be shaped. The Easter question was especially troublesome; as dissension escalated, in some places Easter was observed twice. However, there was an underlying issue that would influence the course of history: whether or not the English Church should submit to Roman governance.

Eventually the leaders of the Roman faction, which included Queen Eanfled, her son Prince Alhfrith, and her protegé Wilfred, who had been made bishop of York, succeeded in putting enough pressure on Oswiu so that in 664 he called a meeting of Church leaders in order to get their differences settled. Because this historic gathering was held at Hilda's monastery, it came to be known as the Synod of Whitby. Although Hilda strongly supported the Celtic position, the Synod voted to abide by Roman practices. Bishop Colman was so furious that he resigned his see. However, Hilda accepted the decision and even tried to make peace between the two parties, though she would be an outspoken opponent of Wilfred her entire life.

Under Hilda's direction, Whitby became known as a great center of learning, offering students access to a fine library and instruction in Latin language and literature. Because those in her charge were so well-versed in the Holy Scriptures and so well-trained in godly behavior, the men were in great demand as priests. According to Saint Bede the Venerable, Whitby produced no less than five bishops.

Hilda was also responsible for encouraging an illiterate cowherd named Cædmon, who was employed at Whitby, to become England's first great poet. Tradition says that Cædmon had always left the room at times when it was his turn to sing. However, one night he dreamed that when someone ordered him to sing about the glory of God, he obeyed. On awakening, not only did he recall the verses he had sung, but he even found himself adding to them. He reported these strange events to the reeve, or steward, of Whitby, who promptly informed Hilda. After examining him, Hilda became convinced that Cædmon had been touched by the grace of God and ordered him to take monastic vows. Then she saw to it that he was taught sacred history, which Cædmon then turned into magnificent verse. Because his poetry was written in the Anglo-Saxon vernacular, it became popular with the common people, who did not know Latin. Cædmon's verses were said to be responsible for converting many from paganism.

Hilda remained at Whitby until her death in 680. Even though she was ill during the last seven years of her life, Bede tells us that up to the end, she kept on instructing her flock and exhorting them to live in godliness and peace. According to Bede, on the night that Hilda died, a nun in a monastery thirty miles away had a vision in which she saw the abbess being welcomed into Heaven. Saint Hilda is commemorated in the Roman calendar on November 17.

SIGNIFICANCE

Hilda was a pivotal figure in the development of Christianity in seventh century England. It can hardly be overestimated how much her promotion of learning, her patronage of poetry, and the wise counsel she offered so freely to commoners, bishops, princes, and kings changed her world for the better. Thirteen centuries after her death, she is still admired as a woman who was fully involved in her world and her church but never forgot that her primary allegiance was to her Maker.

—*Rosemary M. Canfield Reisman*

Further Reading

Bede. *The Ecclesiastical History of the English People; The Greater Chronicle; Bede's Letter to Egbert.* Edited by Judith McClure and Roger Collins. New York: Oxford University Press, 1994. Bede's history, completed in 731, is the primary source for information about the medieval English church. Two chapters are devoted to Hilda and her protegé Cædmon.

Macdonald, Iain, ed. *Saints of Northumbria: Cuthbert, Aidan, Oswald, Hilda.* Edinburgh: Floris Books, 1997. A collection of seventh and eighth century texts, which not only relate supernatural events associated with the saints but also discuss their involvement in political and ecclesiastical disputes.

Pullen, Bruce Reed. *Discovering Celtic Christianity: Its Roots, Relationships, and Relevance.* Mystic, Conn.: Twenty-Third/Bayard, 1999. An informative account of the author's pilgrimage to Celtic religious sites in Great Britain and Ireland. Includes historical charts, illustrations, and bibliography, as well as travel suggestions.

Sellner, Edward C. *Wisdom of the Celtic Saints.* Notre Dame, Ind.: Ave Maria Press, 1993. The lives of twenty Celtic saints of the sixth to the ninth centuries. The stories collected by this prominent Catholic scholar reveal the importance of women such as Hilda in the Celtic church. A thought-provoking study. Illustrated.

Smith, Lesley, and Jane H. M. Taylor, eds. *Women, the Book, and the Godly: Selected Proceedings of the St. Hilda's Conference, 1993.* Rochester, N.Y.: D. S. Brewer, 1995. Explores women's roles in the medieval church in England, including as readers, biblical scholars, writers, and religious authorities.

Szarmach, Paul E., ed. *Holy Men and Holy Women: Old English Prose Saints' Lives and Their Contexts*, edited by Paul E. Szarmach. Vol. 3. Albany: State University of New York Press, 1996. Excellent background essays. Hilda is discussed at length in an essay entitled "Saints and Companions to Saints: Anglo-Saxon Royal Women Monastics in Context." Good indexes.

Walsh, James Joseph, comp. *These Splendid Sisters.* 1927. Reprint. Freeport, N.Y.: Books for Libraries Press, 1970. Despite its dated style, this brief essay would be a good starting point for general readers. Includes a chapter on Hilda.

See also: Saint Bede the Venerable; Saint Brigit; Cædmon; Christina of Markyate; Gwenllian verch Gruffydd; Hildegard von Bingen; Joan of Arc.

Related articles in *Great Events from History: The Middle Ages, 477-1453*: 635-800: Founding of Lindisfarne and Creation of the *Book of Kells*; 731: Bede Writes *Ecclesiastical History of the English People*; 1136: Hildegard von Bingen Becomes Abbess.

HILDEGARD VON BINGEN

German mystic and writer

The first major German mystic, Hildegard, in her prolific writings and extensive preaching, exerted a widespread influence on religious and political figures in twelfth century Europe.

BORN: 1098; Bermersheim bei Alzey, Rheinhessen (now in Germany)

DIED: September 17, 1179; Rupertsberg bei Bingen, Rheinhessen

ALSO KNOWN AS: Saint Hildegard; Hildegard of Bingen; Sybil of the Rhine

AREAS OF ACHIEVEMENT: Religion and theology, literature, music, social reform

EARLY LIFE

Born in 1098 in Bermersheim bei Alzey, Hildegard von Bingen (HIHL-deh-gahrd fuhn BIHN-gehn) was the tenth and last child of Hildebert von Bermersheim, a knight in the service of Meginhard, Count of Spanheim, and his wife, Mechthild. At her birth, her parents consecrated Hildegard to God as a tithe. As early as the age of three, Hildegard had her first vision, of a dazzling white light, which she was later to call the *umbra viventis lucis* (shadow of the living Light), which appeared to her as reflected in a *fons vitae* (shining pool). Other visions followed, along with accurate premonitions of the future. When she was eight years old, her parents entrusted her to the care of the learned Jutta of Spanheim, a holy anchoress attached to the Benedictine abbey of Mount Saint Disibode.

Hildegard's visions continued during her adolescence, but, embarrassed when she began to realize that she was alone in seeing them, she began to keep them to herself, confiding only in Jutta. In spite of her ill health, Hildegard began her studies under Jutta, learning to read and sing Latin. Her further education was entrusted to the monk Volmar of Saint Disibode, who, over time, became her lifelong friend, confidant, and secretary. At age fourteen, she took vows and received the veil from Bishop Otto von Bamberg, the hermitage of Jutta having by this time attracted enough followers to become a community under the Rule of Saint Benedict.

The next two decades were formative years for Hildegard: She acquired an extensive knowledge of the Scriptures, the church fathers and later church writers, the monastic liturgy, science, medicine, and philosophy. From her later writings it is possible to trace specific writers she studied during this period: Saint Augustine, Boethius, Saint Isidore of Seville, Bernard Silvestris, Aristotle, Galen, Messahalah, Constantine the African, Hugh of Saint Victor, and Alberic the Younger. Meanwhile, she continued to experience the charisma of her mystical visions. When Jutta died in 1136, Hildegard, at thirty-eight, was unanimously elected abbess by the nuns of her community.

LIFE'S WORK

The turning point in Hildegard's life came in 1141, when she received a commandment from God: "Write, what you see and hear! Tell people how to enter the kingdom of salvation!" She initially went through a period of self-doubt: How could she, *ego paupercula feminea forma* (a poor little figure of a woman), be chosen as a mouthpiece for God? She questioned whether others would give credence to her visions. She finally confided fully in her confessor, the monk Godfrey, who referred the matter to his abbot, Kuno. Kuno ordered Hildegard to write down some of her visions, which he then submitted to the archbishop of Mainz. The archbishop determined that Hildegard's visions were indeed divinely inspired, and Hildegard ultimately came to accept a view of herself as a woman chosen to fulfill God's work.

A ten-year collaboration between Hildegard and her secretary Volmar began, as she dictated to him her principal work, *Scivias* (1141-1151; English translation, 1986), an abbreviation for *nosce vias (Domini)*, or "know the ways of the Lord," consisting of twenty-six visions dealing with the relationships and interdependence between the triune God and humans through the Creation, Redemption, and Church. The visions also contained apocalyptic prophecies and warnings, which would motivate Hildegard to begin an extensive correspondence of more than one hundred letters to popes, emperors, kings, archbishops, abbots, and abbesses; she also began to journey throughout Germany and France preaching against the abuses and corruption of the Church. As her visions led her to an active role in church and social reform, she came to accept her link with the tradition of the female prophets (Deborah, Olda, Hannah, and Elizabeth).

In 1147, when Pope Eugenius III held a synod in Trier, he appointed a commission to examine Hildegard's writing. Bernard of Clairvaux, with whom Hildegard had corresponded, spoke affirmatively of her. Subsequently, in a letter to Hildegard, the pope approved her visions as authentic manifestations of the Holy Spirit and, warning her against pride, gave her apostolic license to continue writing and publishing. Hildegard, in return, wrote the pope a long letter urging him to work for reform in the Church and the monasteries. The woman who initially had felt timid serving as a mouthpiece for the Word of God was beginning to speak with the uncompromising sense of justice that was to characterize her prophetic and apostolic mission for the rest of her life.

With the pope's endorsement of her visions, Hildegard's renown and the number of postulants at her convent grew, and she determined to separate from the monastery of Saint Disibode and to found a new community at Rupertsberg, near Bingen, a site that had been revealed to her in a vision. Despite the objections of the monks of Saint Disibode and their abbot, Kuno, who would lose prestige and revenue with her departure, Hildegard used family connections with the archbishop of Mainz to secure the property and personally oversaw the construction of a convent large enough to house fifty nuns. In 1150, she moved to Rupertsberg with eighteen other nuns. As abbess, Hildegard managed to obtain exclusive rights to the Rupertsberg property from Abbot Kuno in 1155, and several years later it was arranged that she would respond directly to the archbishop of Mainz as her superior rather than to the abbot of Saint Disibode.

Under Hildegard's leadership, the new community flourished, as did her own work and creative production. In 1151, she completed *Scivias*, concluding the work with a liturgical drama set to music, *Ordo virtutum*, the earliest known morality play and a dramatic work of considerable originality and merit. Between 1151 and 1158, seventy-seven individual hymns and canticles that she had written for her nuns were collected in a lyrical cycle entitled *Symphonia harmonia caelestium revelationum* (the harmonious symphony of heavenly revelations), which, according to Peter Dronke, contains "some of the most unusual, subtle, and exciting poetry of the twelfth century." Her music, ranging in mood from tranquil lyricism to declamatory intensity, includes some of the finest songs written in the Middle Ages.

Hildegard, who in addition to her responsibilities as abbess served in the convent infirmary, commenced work on two books on natural history and medicine. Characterized by careful scientific observation, Hildegard's medical and scientific studies contain the prototypes of some modern methods of diagnosis and anticipate certain later discoveries such as circulation of the blood and psychosomatic illness.

She also wrote a commentary on the Gospels, an explication of the Rule of Saint Benedict and one of the Athanasian Creed, and the lives of Saint Rupert and Saint Disibode.

It was primarily for her mystical trilogy that Hildegard was known in her day: that is, *Scivias*, a treatise on ethics entitled *Liber vitae meritorum* (1158-1163; book of life's merits), and *De operatione Dei* (1163-1173; *Book of Divine Works*, 1987), a vast cosmology and theodicy. It is these works, together with her letters, that primarily account for the late twentieth century renaissance in Hildegard scholarship. The illuminated manuscript of *Scivias* that was prepared at her scriptorium in 1165 is of interest not only to modern theologians and art historians but also to the layperson desiring access to her prolific and sometimes abstruse work.

Known by her twelfth century contemporaries as the *prophetissa Teutonica*, or Sibyl of the Rhine, Hildegard continued, into her seventies and eighties, to travel

Seventeenth century engraving of Hildegard von Bingen. (Hulton|Archive at Getty Images)

widely in Germany and France, providing spiritual direction and preaching. Pilgrims flocked to her convent; her advice was sought by popes and archbishops, emperors and kings, religious and laypeople of all classes. Her influence in twelfth century Europe was considerable. Through the years, she corresponded with four popes—Eugene III, Anastasius IV, Adrian IV, and Alexander III—and with two German emperors, Conrad III and his son and successor Frederick I Barbarossa, whom she rebuked for supporting an antipope. She also sent letters to Henry II of England and his queen Eleanor, the divorced wife of Louis VII. She corresponded with Bernard of Clairvaux and preached his crusade in her travels. She corresponded continuously with the archbishop of Mainz and with bishops and clergy throughout Germany, the Low Countries, and Central Europe. Moreover, she maintained a personal correspondence with twenty-five abbesses of various convents. Constant and uncompromising themes in her letters were condemnation of the abuses and corruption within both church and secular government and the need for social justice, compassion, and wisdom.

The year before her death, when she was in her eighties, Hildegard faced a difficult ethical trial. Her community was placed under interdict for having buried in the convent cemetery a revolutionary youth who had been excommunicated. Hildegard refused to have the body exhumed and removed as ordered; instead, she blessed the grave with her abbatial staff and removed all traces of it. In her view, although the young man had been excommunicated, because he had been absolved and reconciled with the Church before dying, he merited a sacred burial. The interdict forbade the community to hear Mass, receive the Eucharist, or sing the Divine Office. As painful as the interdict was to Hildegard, her sense of justice and her fidelity to her "living Light," no matter what the cost to her, led her to withstand the pressure to give in; she would not let the letter of the law stand before the spirit of the law. Hildegard wrote numerous letters of protest to the appropriate authorities, until finally her argument prevailed and the interdict was removed. Six months later, in 1179, she died.

SIGNIFICANCE

The first major German mystic, Hildegard von Bingen has never been formally canonized (three proceedings were initiated in the thirteenth and fourteenth centuries, but none was ever completed), yet she is included in the martyrologies and in the Acta Sanctorum under the title "saint," and in 1979 Pope John Paul II, on the 800th anniversary of Hildegard's death, referred to her as "an outstanding saint." Through her preaching, writings, and correspondence, she actively influenced the decisions and policies of religious and political leaders of her day. The founder of the Rhineland mystic movement, she influenced later medieval mystics, including Mechthild of Magdeburg and Meister Eckhart. Further, the themes of ecology, social responsibility, the co-creativity of human beings, feminine aspects of the divine, and the interconnectivity of the cosmos in her visionary writings have been noted by Creation-centered theologians in the twentieth century.

Although philosophically Abbess Hildegard accepted the Catholic medieval view of woman's subordination to man, based on the doctrine of the Fall, her visions encouraged her to become highly independent in her thinking, actions, and creations. She made significant contributions in her medical writings. Her poetry, music, and liturgical drama *Ordo virtutum* are original in form and ideas. Her visionary works, while they also provide a compendium of contemporary thought, are a unique phenomenon in twelfth century letters, as are the manuscript illuminations that accompany them. Considering the originality of her visionary cosmology, it is not surprising that Hildegard von Bingen has been compared to both Dante and William Blake.

—*Jean T. Strandness*

FURTHER READING

Bobko, Jane, comp. and ed. *Vision: The Life and Music of Hildegard von Bingen*. New York: Penguin Studio, 1995. Focuses on Hildegard's music. Bibliographical references.

Craine, Renate. *Hildegard: Prophet of the Cosmic Christ*. New York: Crossroad, 1997. Covers the life and works of Hildegard with emphasis on her multiple roles as visionary, mystic, author, artist, musician and composer, holistic healer, theologian, and Benedictine abbess. Hildegard did not accept her gift until the age of forty-two but still left behind a vast legacy that is discussed in this revealing biography.

Dronke, Peter. *Poetic Individuality in the Middle Ages: New Departures in Poetry, 1000-1150*. Oxford: Oxford University Press, 1970. An excellent study of the poetic imagery of Hildegard's lyrics, with numerous textual examples in the Latin original and in translation. Analyzes the *Ordo virtutum* as a fusion between a morality play and the expression of mystical experience. Contains the complete Latin text of the *Ordo virtutum* and the musical transcriptions of two of Hildegard's melismatic sequences from the *Symphonia harmoniae caelestium revelationum.*

_______. *Women Writers of the Middle Ages.* New York: Cambridge University Press, 1984. A substantial study of the nature of Hildegard's visionary experiences and their influence on the development of her cosmological thought. Focuses on Hildegard's autobiographical writings, her letters, and her medical treatises, including excerpts from selected texts and letters in the Latin original and in translation.

Hildegard of Bingen. *Book of Divine Works, with Letters and Songs.* Translated and edited by Matthew Fox. Santa Fe, N.Mex.: Bear, 1987. Contains translations of important primary source material: Hildegard's third major visionary opus, forty-two selected letters; and twelve songs. Also contains a good summary introduction to Hildegard's life and works.

_______. *Illuminations of Hildegard of Bingen.* Edited by Matthew Fox. Santa Fe, N.Mex.: Bear, 1985. Color reproductions of the illuminations of Hildegard's visionary manuscripts, accompanied by extensive commentary on the themes of her cosmology.

_______. *Scivias.* Translated by Bruce Hozeski. Santa Fe, N.Mex.: Bear, 1986. The translated text of Hildegard's major visionary cycle, accompanied by black-and-white illustrations of the text's illuminations. Introductory essays include a biographical sketch, a review of her work, and an analysis of the structure and contents of *Scivias.*

Kraft, Kent. "The German Visionary: Hildegard of Bingen." In *Medieval Women Writers*, edited by Katharina Wilson. Athens: University of Georgia Press, 1984. An interpretive study of significant events in Hildegard's life and their influence on her works. Provides a summary review and analysis of her important creative work, followed by selected excerpts from her works.

Lagorio, Valerie M. "The Medieval Continental Women Mystics: An Introduction." In *An Introduction to the Medieval Mystics of Europe*, edited by Paul E. Szarmach. Albany: State University of New York Press, 1984. An insightful survey of important European women mystics from Hildegard of Bingen in the twelfth century to Saint Catherine of Siena in the fourteenth century.

Maddocks, Fiona. *Hildegard von Bingen: The Woman of Her Age.* New York: Doubleday, 2001. A careful and balanced biography of Hildegard. Maddocks is a music critic, well aware of arguments against Hildegard's authorship of certain works, but her treatment of her subject allows for a full appreciation of the philosopher's many talents. Draws on previously unavailable materials.

Newman, Barbara. *Sister of Wisdom: St. Hildegard's Theology of the Feminine.* Berkeley: University of California Press, 1987. A comprehensive scholarly study that examines Hildegard's contributions within the context of twelfth century thought and also as part of the sapiential tradition.

_______, ed. *Voice of the Living Light: Hildegard of Bingen and Her World.* Berkeley: University of California Press, 1998. Compiled in conjunction with the 900th anniversary of Hildegard's birth, the nine essays in this book offer an intriguing look at the life and work of this remarkable woman. She was the first woman given permission by the pope to write theological books, and she also preached openly to both the clergy and the common people.

Pernoud, Regine. *Hildegard of Bingen: Inspired Conscience of the Twelfth Century.* Translated by Paul Duggan. New York: Marlowe, 1998. In addition to discussing the writings and visions of this influential twelfth century abbess, Pernoud provides information about Hildegard's life. He offers insight into the turbulent political times she lived in and the effect she had on princes, the populace, and popes through her correspondence.

Schipperges, Heinrich. H. *The World of Hildegard von Bingen: Her Life, Times, and Visions.* Translated by John Cumming. Collegeville, Minn.: Liturgical Press, 1998. A complete biography issued by a Christian publisher that has published several titles with Hildegard as the focus. Chapters address her early life, her musical, artistic, and medical works, and her philosophy of life. Bibliographical references, index.

Throop, Priscilla, trans. *Hildegard von Bingen's "Physica": The Complete English Translation of Her Classic Work on Health and Healing.* Rochester, Vt.: Healing Arts Press, 1998. The first complete translation of her natural healing system.

See also: Saint Benedict of Nursia; Saint Bernard of Clairvaux; Boethius; Saint Brigit; Saint Catherine of Siena; Christina of Markyate; Saint Clare of Assisi; Dhuoda; Saint Hilda of Whitby; Saint Isidore of Seville; Julian of Norwich; Margery Kempe; Mechthild von Magdeburg; Marguerite Porete.

Related article in *Great Events from History: The Middle Ages, 477-1453*: 1136: Hildegard von Bingen Becomes Abbess.

HROSVITHA

German-Saxon poet, playwright, and historian

A learned Benedictine canoness whose writings were in Latin, Hrosvitha was the first Saxon poet, the first known dramatist of Christianity, and the earliest known historian of Germany.

BORN: c. 930-935; probably Gandersheim, Lower Saxony (now in Germany)
DIED: c. 1002; probably the Benedictine convent of Gandersheim
ALSO KNOWN AS: Hrosuind; Hroswitha; Hrotsvit; Hrotsvitha; Hrotswitha; Roswitha; Clamor Validus (Latin interpretation of the Saxon root of her name meaning "strong voice")
AREAS OF ACHIEVEMENT: Literature, historiography, monasticism, religion and theology

EARLY LIFE

Hrosvitha (rohz-VEE-tah) was a tenth century canoness who lived in the Benedictine convent of Gandersheim in Lower Saxony. Little is known about her life apart from what can be construed from the times in which she lived and from her writings, including a chronicle in verse on the history of the convent of Gandersheim, from its founding in 856 to the year 919, called *Primordia coenobii Gandershemensis* (c. 973; founding of the Gandersheim monastery, translated into English by Sister Mary Bernardine Bergman in *Hrosvithae Liber terius: A Text with Translation*, 1943). Duke Liudolf and his Frankish wife Oda, whose mother Æda had seen a vision of Saint John the Baptist telling her that her noble son-in-law would establish a monastery for saintly women, founded the convent.

Hrosvitha writes in her history of Gandersheim that Liudolf was in the service of King Louis I, grandson of Charlemagne (742-814). The Carolingian Empire that Charlemagne initiated in the ninth century led to a renaissance of enlightened learning in Germany during the "Dark Ages," including the founding of twenty monasteries in Saxony, including eleven for women. The first three abbesses of Gandersheim were daughters of Liudolf and Oda.

Otto I (Otto the Great, 912-973), a descendant of Liudolf, ruled Germany during Hrosvitha's time. After he conquered northern Italy and was crowned king of the Lombards, Otto I was given the Imperial crown by Pope John XII in 951 and thus became the first Holy Roman Emperor. Hrosvitha's writings formed part of the literary activity by which the age of Otto the Great sought to emulate that of Charles the Great. She wrote an epic chronicle of his reign called *Gesta Ottonis* (973; the deeds of Otto, partial translation in *Hrosvithae Liber terius: A Text with Translation*, 1943).

The niece of Otto I, Princess Gerberga II, was consecrated as abbess of Gandersheim in 959. She became a teacher and friend of Hrosvitha, who is believed by some to have entered the convent in 955, the year in which Otto II was born. He later ruled with his father as coemperor of the Holy Roman Empire and was a friend of Hrosvitha. She once wrote that her abbess, Princess Gerberga, was younger than she, leading to the suggestion that because Gerberga was born in 940, Hrosvitha was born sometime between 930 and 935. The literary efforts of Hrosvitha were encouraged by the abbess and by a teacher and nun named Richarda.

Because only novices from noble families were chosen to enter the monasteries of her time, Hrosvitha was probably of noble birth. She may have entered the abbey at a very young age, because her skill in Latin indicates that she had many years of training in the language and it is known that some young women made the decision to pursue the religious life as early as twelve years of age. She also may have learned Greek because she often used Greek sources in her stories and Abbess Gerberga and her sister had studied Greek.

The monasteries of Saxony were considered "free" abbeys, meaning that even in the convents the abbesses were responsible to the king rather than to the church. However, in 947, Otto I freed the Gandersheim Abbey from royal rule, giving the abbess complete authority. Contrary to later restrictions on women, she had her own court of law, coined her own money, had a seat in the Imperial Diet, and even sent soldiers to battle. She was directly responsible for the nuns and canonesses in the abbey.

The office of canoness first appeared in the eighth century and included vows of chastity and obedience, but not the vow of poverty as taken by the nuns. Although they followed the Rule of Saint Benedict, including communal living and daily recitation of the Divine Office, they had more freedom than the nuns. They could receive guests, own books and property, have servants, and enter and leave the monastery with permission.

Hrosvitha's writings indicate a wide knowledge of both classical and religious literature, suggesting that Gandersheim had a generous collection of manuscripts and a first-rate library. By her own admission, she obtained all her information from the convent's library, except for some personal accounts of contemporary events from guests and friends. Her writings indicate a familiarity with Scholastic philosophy, mathematics, astronomy, music, and the works of such writers as Vergil, Terence, Ovid, and Boethius.

Life's Work

Hrosvitha's works reflect a deep devotion and dedication to God and an attitude of humility and openness to truth from any source. It is clear from the prefaces to her writings that the sole desire behind her intellectual and literary efforts was to glorify God and the saints through literary forms borrowed from pagan sources. She admits that some of her work is based on questionable material but that even such material can reveal truth.

Hrosvitha produced a series of writings in three different genres, all in Latin, which in the tenth century was the only language used for literary composition. In addition to her two chronicles on the *Gesta Ottonis* and *Primordia coenobii Gandershemensis*, she wrote eight epic poems and six dramas based on Bible stories and legends of saints and martyrs. The themes of her works are conversion, chastity, and faithfulness to Christ, even unto martyrdom. Most of her writings are themselves a conversion of pagan forms and vices into Christian literature extolling virtues. She often demonstrated how feminine faithfulness could defeat male might.

Her least important writings were her eight narrative poems, all around 959-962. Two are biblical poems, one on the life of Mary and one on the ascension of Christ, the former based on the Bible and the apocryphal Gospel of Saint James. Six are legends of saints and martyrs: of Saint Gangolf, a Burgundian prince; on the youthful Saint Pelagius, based on firsthand reports she heard of the recent martyrdom of a young Christian captive who resists the homosexual advances of the caliph of Córdoba; on the fall and conversion of Theophilus, the earliest poem based on the medieval legend of Faust; on Basilius, a similar story about an unhappy young man saved from a pact with the devil; on the martyrdom of Saint Dionysius; and on the martyrdom of Saint Agnes, based on a biography by Saint Ambrose.

Hrosvitha, seated second from right, reads from a book. (Hulton|Archive at Getty Images)

Hrosvitha's literary reputation rests on her six dramatic works, all written after 963, which mark the beginning of nonliturgical Christian theater in Europe. She used the Roman dramatist Terence (c. 190-159 B.C.E.) as her model, but she replaced his depiction of the victory of vice with the triumph of purity in saintly virgins. She confesses to embarrassment in her portrayal of unholy love. This especially applies to several dramas based on the theme of sensual love in which the stronger is the temptation, the greater is the triumph of virtue.

Three of the plays, *Gallicanus*, *Dulcitius*, and *Sapientia* (all translated into English in 1923), describe the struggle between infant Christianity and paganism, including martyrdoms under Hadrian, Diocletian, and Julian the Apostate. In *Gallicanus*, this pagan general of Emperor Constantine seeks to marry his daughter, Constantia, who has taken a vow of chastity, but the suitor is converted and dies as a martyr. *Dulcitius*, a prefect of Diocletian, imprisons three Christian maidens in a kitchen and tries to seduce them in the night, but he suffers a delusion in which he embraces the sooty pots and pans before the maidens are martyred. *Sapientia* describes the legend of three holy virgins, Faith, Hope, and Charity, who were tortured by the emperor Hadrian and martyred in the presence of their mother, Wisdom.

The three plays *Callimachus* (English translation, 1923), *Abraham* (English translation, 1923), and *Paphnutius* (English translation, 1914) describe the conflict between the flesh and the spirit and the penance required by those who allow the flesh to triumph. In *Callimachus*, the title character's guilty passion for Drusiana follows her to the grave; but after he is bitten by a serpent, both he and Drusiana are raised from the dead by the prayers of Saint John the Apostle. In *Abraham*, a holy hermit in the disguise of a lover rescues his niece Mary from harlotry and leads her to conversion followed by twenty years of penance. In *Paphnutius*, another hermit disguised as a lover exhorts Thais to renounce her evil life, leading to her conversion and three years of penance in a narrow cell.

Hrosvitha often gives insights into her mastery of medieval knowledge. In *Sapientia* she confounds Hadrian by answering his question about the ages of her daughters with a discussion of number theory as given by Boethius. She defines a perfect number as one that equals the sum of its factors (28 = 1 + 2 + 4 + 7 + 14) and gives four that were known to the Greeks (6, 28, 496, 8,128). In *Paphnutius* she describes the mathematical relationship between music and astronomy, noting the ratios between concordant tones in the seven intervals of the octave corresponding to those in the seven planets, and concludes that "God has set all things in number and measure and weight."

SIGNIFICANCE

Through her prefaces, it is clear that Hrosvitha was commissioned by her abbess Gerberga, Otto II, and other "learned and virtuous men," sharing her manuscripts with them. However, her works seemed to have had little influence beyond Gandersheim, where they were probably read aloud by the nuns and may have been performed at the convent or even at the court of Otto II. They probably also served in educating the nuns.

After five centuries of neglect, they were discovered in 1493 by the German humanist Conrad Celtes in the Benedictine monastery at Saint Emmeram at Regensburg. After editing by Celtes, they were published in 1501 at Nuremberg, with eight woodcuts, thought to be by Albrecht Dürer, illustrating incidents in the plays. The frontispiece shows Hrosvitha presenting her works to Otto II and Abbess Gerberga. Subsequent editions were published in 1707 at Wittenberg, a French translation in 1845 at Paris, a German translation at Lübeck in 1857, and many more translations since. Modern performances of her plays began with marionette performances in 1888 at Paris and continued to the professional stages of London and New York.

In addition to being the first known dramatist of Christianity, Hrosvitha was also the earliest known historian of Germany, and her chronicles have been of considerable value to modern historians. Her works reveal the breadth of knowledge in early medieval monasteries, including musical theory, astronomical knowledge, number theory, and classical history and philosophy.

—*Joseph L. Spradley*

FURTHER READING

Dronke, Peter. *Women Writers of the Middle Ages: A Critical Study of Texts from Perpetua to Marguerite Potete*. New York: Cambridge University Press, 1984. This study has a good twenty-nine-page chapter on Hrosvitha and her writings.

Haight, Anne Lyon, ed. *Hroswitha of Gandersheim: Her Life, Her Times, Her Works*. New York: Hroswitha Club, 1965. The most complete book about Hrosvitha and her works in English, including sections by Marjorie Dana Barlow listing performances of her plays since 1888 and printed editions of her works.

Penrose, Mary E. *Roots Deep and Strong: Great Men and Women of the Church*. New York: Paulist Press, 1995. A popular account of early church men and women with a chapter, "Hroswitha: Playwright and Poet," describing her life and times.

St. John, Christopher, trans. *The Plays of Roswitha*. New York: Cooper Square, 1966. This English translation of the plays includes the prefaces to all her works and has two good introductions to her life and her plays.

Thiebaux, Marcelle. *The Writings of Medieval Women*. 2d ed. New York: Garland, 1994. A chapter on Hrosvitha, "Hagiographer, Playwright, Epic Historian," has a good introduction to her legend *Pelagius* and her play *Dulcitius*.

SEE ALSO: Saint Benedict of Nursia; Otto I.

RELATED ARTICLES in *Great Events from History: The Middle Ages, 477-1453*: 590-604: Reforms of Pope Gregory the Great; August 10, 955: Otto I Defeats the Magyars; March 21, 1098: Foundation of the Cistercian Order.

JÁNOS HUNYADI

Hungarian military leader

By organizing, financing, and leading Hungarian and Central European military forces, Hunyadi halted the Ottoman Empire's advance at the Balkan Mountains, postponing for some seventy years the Turkish conquest of central Hungary.

BORN: c. 1407; place unknown
DIED: August 11, 1456; Zimony, Hungary (now Zemun, Serbia)
ALSO KNOWN AS: John Hunyadi; John Huniades
AREAS OF ACHIEVEMENT: Warfare and conquest, government and politics

EARLY LIFE

Popularly believed to be the son of Sigismund, king of Hungary and Holy Roman Emperor, János Hunyadi (JAHN-ohs HOON-yood-ee) was in fact the eldest child of Vojk, a noble of Walachian origin who had moved to Hungary around 1395 and then had married into a Hungarian noble family. Besides János, the marriage produced two sons, as well as at least one daughter. János's father became a royal soldier and counselor, and in 1409 he received for his services an estate in Transylvania—called Vajdahunyad—from which the family took its name.

Little is known of Hunyadi's youth, since few extant records of the period mention him. Nevertheless, since he was for the most part a resident at the court of Sigismund, he presumably received early military training. This is all the more likely since soldierly prowess was generously rewarded with sizable grants of land, which in turn meant wealth and power.

Said to have been a born soldier, Hunyadi cut an impressive figure. He was of medium height and had a thick neck, long chestnut-brown hair, a well-proportioned body, and large, penetrating eyes. He began his military career in the 1420's under Pipo of Ozora. Around 1428 he married Erzsébet Szilágyi, herself a daughter of a noble family. Their marriage produced two sons, László and Mátyás, the latter destined to become perhaps Hungary's most illustrious king as Matthias Corvinus (r. 1458-1490).

In 1430, Hunyadi entered the service of the king, accompanying Sigismund to Italy. There the young soldier served Fillippo Maria Visconti, duke of Milan (1412-1447), for a time. In 1433, Hunyadi was reunited with Sigismund and accompanied him on many trips, including one to Bohemia in 1437. By then expertly trained in mercenary warfare, well acquainted with the most up-to-date Italian and Hussite military tactics and procedures, and experienced in the methods of the Turkish armies, Hunyadi dedicated himself to the struggle against the Ottomans.

LIFE'S WORK

In the fifteenth century, the Ottoman Empire was still dedicated to expansion and military conquest. This awesome momentum, created by economic need and religious fervor, had by Sigismund's time already carried the Turks deep into the Balkan Peninsula. The Ottoman wave would soon sweep over Hungary, whose own southern frontier reached into the Balkans.

Unfortunately, the Hungarian distribution of land and wealth, favoring the aristocrats at the expense of the crown, did not seem a likely source for the centralized, unified effort that would be required to hold the great Turkish empire in check. Nevertheless, the single most powerful aristocrat in the country was a man both eminently qualified and highly motivated to stem the Ottoman advance: János Hunyadi.

According to the chronicler Thuróczy, Hunyadi's military virtues were great; the account cites his strength and courage as a soldier as well as his strategical and tactical acumen. Though an accurate portrayal of him, Thuróczy's account fails nevertheless to consider certain other necessary aspects of Hunyadi's character. He was also a crafty politician who, though disliked by his fellow aristocrats, managed to create important if short-lived alliances with his peers. Moreover, able to count on neither the king, whose own landholdings had seriously dwindled, nor the barons, who were reluctant to dip into their vast resources, Hunyadi organized and financed his armies himself, drawing on the revenue of his approximately six million acres of property.

Under Albert II of Habsburg (r. 1438-1439), Sigismund's son-in-law and successor, Hunyadi and his brother served as joint military governors of Szörény (Severin). Hunyadi continued as bán of Severin until 1446, protecting that area from the Ottoman menace. It was, from all accounts, these experiences that hastened his assimilation. To Hunyadi, himself an immigrant without a Magyar pedigree, the *patria* encompassed not merely the nobility but the people as a whole.

In 1440, a few months after Albert's death, the Polish king Władysław III was elected king of Hungary by the diet. Władysław, who saw Hunyadi as the real leader against the Turks, put him in charge of the key fortress in Belgrade and of the southern border region as a whole. In 1441, he appointed Hunyadi both *voivode* of Transylvania and *ispán* of Temesvár (Timişoara), offices he would hold until 1446. Hunyadi organized and equipped an army composed mainly of Bohemian Hussite mercenaries, but he rounded it out with his own adherents, relatives, noble vassals, and even peasants. He enjoyed his first victory over the Ottomans in 1442, driving the invading army out of Transylvania. This was the first such defeat ever suffered by the Ottomans in Europe, and news of it quickly spread, reviving hopes that the Balkans would indeed be liberated from the Turkish yoke.

Doubting that a passive defense would be adequate to deal with the Turkish menace, Hunyadi decided to take the offensive. Pressing toward the heart of the Ottoman Empire, he led his forces to one victory after another, occupying as he went the towns of Nish and Sofia. Though his long march was stalled not long after, his victories persuaded Ottoman Sultan Murad II (r. 1421-1451) to negotiate for peace. Unfortunately, the treaty had no sooner been signed with the sultan's emissaries in Szeged than, at the behest of the papal legate, Władysław broke his word and launched a new attack. The foreign support that had been promised failed to materialize, and Hunyadi's forces were routed at Varna in 1444. The king fell in battle, while Hunyadi managed a narrow escape.

János Hunyadi leads an assault on Belgrade. (F. R. Niglutsch)

Although the diet of 1445 recognized the succession of Albert's son László, Emperor Frederick III (r. 1440-1493), who had custody of the young Habsburg, refused to surrender him. The problem of the succession was given a temporary but happy solution the following year: Hunyadi was acclaimed the Hungarian regent, a result largely of the vigorous campaign of János Vitéz, bishop of Várad (Oradea).

It was not until 1448 that Hunyadi built up sufficient strength for a new offensive. Leading his army deep into the Balkans, he engaged the Turkish army at Kosovo. Betrayed, however, by the Serbian despot George Brankovich, Hunyadi was not only defeated but taken captive temporarily as well. In 1450, Hunyadi concluded an agreement with Frederick III that recognized the legitimacy of László. In 1453, the once-vacant throne now occupied, Hunyadi dutifully resigned as regent but was appointed by László his commander in chief and royal treasurer.

Unfortunately, the king fell under the influence of Austrian noble Ulrich II von Cilli, a longtime rival of Hunyadi. Cilli now became allied with several aristocrats against Hunyadi. In addition, Hunyadi's old friend and ally János Vitéz, always a staunch foe of baronial power, put forward a plan for centralization that would have seriously weakened Hunyadi's position. When the Hungarians learned that Constantinople had fallen (in 1453) and

KINGS OF HUNGARY, 1290-1490

Reign	*Ruler*
1290-1301	Andrew III (end of the Árpád line)
1301-1304	Wenceslaus (Václav) II
1304-1308	Otto I of Bavaria
1305-1306	Wenceslaus (Václav) III
1306	End of the Přemlysid line
1306-1310	Instability
1310-1342	Károly (Charles Robert) I
1342-1382	Lajos (Louis) I
1382-1395	Maria
1387-1437	Sigismund
1438-1439	Albert II of Habsburg
1440-1444	Ulaslo I (Władysław III, Poland)
1444-1457	László V
1458-1490	Matthias (Matyas) Corvinus

that Ottoman Sultan Mehmed II (r. 1451-1481) was gathering his forces to attack Hungary, Vitéz's plan was prudently withdrawn from consideration.

In 1456, the Ottomans besieged Belgrade, sending forth an army 100,000 strong. Neither the king, who fled the country, nor the barons came to the aid of Hunyadi's hopelessly outnumbered army. Eventually, however, help came. Franciscan friar John of Capistrano (1386-1456), sent by the pope to organize a Crusade, managed to recruit into Hunyadi's army some twenty thousand soldiers. On July 21, the city's walls already penetrated, the Turks launched an all-out attack but were defeated and withdrew en masse.

Not for another seventy years would a major battle be fought between Hungarian and Ottoman forces. Hunyadi, who had saved Hungary from Turkish conquest, died of the plague not long thereafter.

SIGNIFICANCE

Hungary in the fifteenth century was poised between the Middle Ages and the Renaissance. It was also the meeting place of Western and Eastern Europe. Themselves the scourge of the West some five centuries earlier, the Hungarians, now Christian and in possession of one of the most powerful states in Europe, hoped to bar the way of the new terror of Europe, the Ottoman Turks. It was mainly through Hunyadi's efforts that Hungary survived and Western Europe was spared the Turkish scourge. Yet—and this cast a dark shadow over Hungary—virtually all the border fortresses had fallen to the Turks.

When Hunyadi died, his first son, László, was killed by anti-Hunyadi conspirators, while his other son, Mátyás, was imprisoned. On King László's unexpected death in 1457, however, the diet elected Mátyás king. Exploiting the peace created by his father, Mátyás, called Matthias Corvinus, inaugurated a glorious era for Hungary. Not only did it grow stronger both militarily and economically, but it became the center of Renaissance culture in East Central Europe as well. That this era would not last, indeed would pass into a century-and-a-half-long nightmare beginning with the Battle of Mohács in 1526, was the result at least in part of Mátyás's almost total neglect of the slumbering, but by no means extinct, Ottoman threat.

—*Gregory Nehler*

FURTHER READING

Bideleux, Robert, and Ian Jeffries. *A History of Eastern Europe: Crisis and Change*. New York: Routledge, 1998. Although no chapter deals solely with Hunyadi, this comprehensive work explores, among other topics, the history between the Ottomans and the Hungarians before, during, and after Hunyadi's time. Maps, bibliography, index.

Held, Joseph. *Hunyadi: Legend and Reality*. Boulder, Colo.: East European Monographs, 1985. A detailed work on Hunyadi's life and leadership. Includes a bibliography, an index, a list of place names, maps, illustrations, and a brief note on primary sources.

Macartney, C. A. *Hungary: A Short History*. 1962. Reprint. Chicago: Aldine, 1968. An excellent overview of Hungarian history by an eminent British historian. Though it gives only a brief account of Hunyadi, it is stylishly written and includes an index, maps, photographs, tables, a comparative chronology, biographies, and a bibliography.

Muresanu, Camil. *John Hunyadi: Defender of Christendom*. Translated by Laura Treptow. Iaşi, Romania: Center for Romanian Studies, 2001. Considers Hunyadi as soldier and statesman. Although this work might be difficult to locate and obtain, it is one of only a few sources in English on Hunyadi. Bibliography, index.

Sinor, Denis. *History of Hungary*. 1959. Reprint. Westport, Conn.: Greenwood Press, 1976. A crossover effort, this entertaining treatment of Hungarian history was written by an Inner-Asian specialist and it includes an account of Hunyadi. Chronology of events, index.

Vámbéry, Armin. *Hungary in Ancient, Medieval, and Modern Times*. 1886. Reprint. Freeport, N.Y.: Books for Libraries Press, 1972. In this still-useful survey, a full chapter is devoted to the career of Hunyadi. Illustrations, index.

Zarek, Otto. *History of Hungary*. Translated by Peter P. Wolkowsky. London: Selwyn and Blount, 1939. The sixth chapter of this work is mainly devoted to Hunyadi. Features an index, a map, and an aid to pronunciation.

SEE ALSO: Árpád; Saint László I; Mehmed II; Stephen I.

RELATED ARTICLES in *Great Events from History: The Middle Ages, 477-1453*: August 10, 955: Otto I Defeats the Magyars; June 28, 1389: Turkish Conquest of Serbia; 1442-1456: János Hunyadi Defends Hungary Against the Ottomans; 1444-1446: Albanian Chieftains Unite Under Prince Skanderbeg.

JAN HUS

Czech religious leader

Through preaching and writing against the abuses of the medieval church attendant on the divided Papacy, the greedy and indolent clergy, and the rigid anti-layperson doctrines, Hus laid the foundation for the Protestant Reformation one hundred years later. His martyrdom at the Council of Constance made him a national hero to the Czech people.

BORN: 1372 or 1373; Husinec, southern Bohemia (now in Czech Republic)

DIED: July 6, 1415; Constance (now in Germany)

AREAS OF ACHIEVEMENT: Religion and theology, church reform

EARLY LIFE

Jan Hus (yahn hews) derived his name from the small hamlet in which he was born, Husinec, which literally means "Goosetown." No agreement exists about his exact date of birth or the nature of his early schooling, but it is known that his family was poor and his mother vowed that her son would enter the priesthood. In 1390, Hus entered the University of Prague, and by 1398, he had garnered both the bachelor of arts and master's degree to join the arts faculty as a full member. During the winter semester of 1401/1402 he served for a term as dean of the arts faculty before enrolling in the faculty of theology to pursue the highest degree available in a medieval university, the doctor's degree in theology. After earning the bachelor of divinity degree in 1404, as a first step he began to lecture on the Bible and then, in 1407, on Peter Lombard's *Sententiarum libri IV* (1148-1151; *The Books of Opinions of Peter Lombard*, 1970; better known as *Sentences*). He was within a year or two of his goal when his life was engulfed in controversy. From humble origins, Hus had climbed to the top rung of the academic ladder in his native land.

What was going on in his mind and heart during these years? Not much is known about these personal matters. All students and faculty were members of the clergy at that time, which did not mean that they were ordained as priests or monks but which did preclude marriage and secular occupations. Hus does not tell how he survived his prolonged apprenticeship in the lower ranks of the university, and unlike his celebrated successors in the Reformation (especially Martin Luther, 1483-1546), he does not divulge his religious thinking. He was ordained as a priest in June of 1400 and appointed preacher at the Bethlehem Chapel on March 14, 1402. This privately endowed religious institution in Prague had only been established in 1391, but it had already become a center for the Czech reform movement. Hus was to become its most famous advocate.

Amid the disarray caused by the papal problems in the fourteenth century—the Babylonian Captivity in Avignon, France, from 1305 to 1378, which was sharpened by the Great Schism from 1378 to 1417—there were calls for church reform throughout Europe. Add to this the chronic political unrest caused by the Hundred Years' War (1337-1453) and the ghastly Black Death outbreaks beginning in 1347-1348, all of which spawned the peasant revolts of 1356 in France and 1381 in England, and the calls for reform became cries for revolution. It was out of this context that John Wyclif emerged to become the leading religious reformer and the spiritual mentor of Hus.

LIFE'S WORK

Hus's philosophy was formed by the Czech reform movement and the theology of Wyclif. The Czech reform movement had been started in 1363, when the Holy Roman Emperor Charles IV and the Archbishop Ernest of Pardubice called to Prague an Augustinian preacher from Vienna named Conrad Waldhauser. This preacher castigated the German clerics and merchants with electrifying zeal, and in the process he converted John Milíč of

Kroměříž, who took up the call to exhort his own people to repent and reform. Following Milíč came Matthew of Janov, who in his short life translated the Bible into Czech and compiled five volumes of theology called *Regulae veteris et novi testamenti* (1388-1392). This full-fledged religious movement prepared Hus to receive and respond to the powerful message from across the English Channel.

Wyclif cast his heavy shadow over the life and career of Hus. Although the Czechs in general and Hus in particular were strongly attracted to Wyclif's views on church reform and Christian doctrine, they did not agree completely with him. Hus differed from Wyclif on most of the views certified as heretical, but he was labeled as a follower of Wyclif and burned at the stake as a heretic because of his sympathy for Wyclif.

As a moralist, Wyclif questioned the legitimacy of the pope, the sacramental authority of the clergy, and even secular lords and kings, when corrupt. Although many of his followers in England, called Lollards, were persecuted and suppressed, Wyclif himself managed to stay out of trouble and died just as his doctrinal pronouncements were beginning to disturb the peace of Christendom. The Czech religious leaders were learning about Wyclif when Hus was becoming a preacher.

As a theologian, Wyclif denied the doctrine of transubstantiation in the sacrament of Holy Communion. The Fourth Lateran Council in 1215 had pronounced that the bread and wine were "transubstantiated" into the body and blood of Christ. Wyclif, rejecting this dogma, argued that it was impossible for the "real" elements, that is, the bread and the wine, to be annihilated by their transformation into the body and blood of Christ. This denial of transubstantiation led him to question the legitimacy of priests who administered the sacrament, to challenge the pope, who was the chief priest of the church, and even to attack the tithes collected to support the Church. Moreover, Wyclif proposed that Communion be offered to the laity "in both kinds," which meant giving wine as well as bread to the laity. Finally, he based his criticism of transubstantiation and other doctrines on the Bible, as well as on philosophical arguments. Emphasizing the need for scrip-

Scene depicting the execution of Jan Hus. (Library of Congress)

tural grounding of doctrine, he became a stout supporter of the translation of the Bible into vernacular languages.

Hus began as an orthodox teacher and preacher. From 1402 to 1408, he exhorted his parishioners at the Bethlehem Chapel to stop sinning and to improve their lives. Yet he did not confine his criticism to the meek and lowly of his parish and community. He recognized that many of the problems that led his parishioners to suffer and sin were caused by clerical abuses and the corruption of the clergy. Being a proud Czech in a world dominated politically and ecclesiastically by Germans, Hus did not hesitate to lambaste the German leaders, clerical and lay, for the evils of the world and the confusion in doctrine. In so doing, Hus became a leader of discontented poor people who wanted to revolt against tyranny and a spokesman for discontented Czechs of all classes who wanted to overthrow the German Holy Roman Emperor. Even though Hus himself entertained no such exalted revolutionary ambition, he was accused of being subversive.

Hus was actually a theologian rather than a political ideologue. He assumed that human wretchedness was a consequence of the Fall in the Garden of Eden. He believed that the sacraments of the Church could restore the spiritual virtues that were not entirely destroyed by Original Sin. Baptism and Communion were essential for salvation. While Hus did not deny the importance of the other five sacraments, he and his peers focused attention on these two. Baptism was not yet the issue it would become in the next century. The controversy that was going to convulse the Christian world for the next two centuries revolved around Communion.

Hus did not subscribe to Wyclif's rejection of transubstantiation, but he welcomed his anticlericalism and his reliance on the Bible. Because of his sympathy for Wyclif's reform sentiments, Hus defended Wyclif against the charge of heresy. That made Hus vulnerable to the ever-increasing assault from the theologians and ecclesiastical politicians who would ignore his fine distinctions. The assault began in 1402 in Prague and ended only at Constance in 1415.

When the new archbishop of Prague, Zbyněk Zajíc of Hasenburk, attacked Wyclif's theology in 1402, he provoked Hus to argue that the transubstantiated bread remained in the sacrament after its consecration. While Hus did not accept Wyclif's position theologically, for Hus did accept the doctrine that Christ's real body and blood were present physically, he did agree with Wyclif's position philosophically. That is, Hus did believe that it was "real" bread that contained Christ's physical remains. The theologians who were dominant in Bohemia and who prevailed at the Council of Constance were scandalized by the notion that there was anything "real" like bread in the sacrament. They held further that Christ's body and blood could be perceived only by faith.

Hus's opponents also insisted that even a wicked priest could confer a valid Communion sacrament, which was orthodox doctrine from Saint Augustine's pronouncements a thousand years earlier. Beginning in 1407, however, they provoked Hus to reply that a layperson who knowingly receives the sacrament from a wicked priest is guilty of a grave sin. While Wyclif's original argument had verged on a heretical denial of ordination, Hus remained orthodox by affirming the validity of ordination while denying the corrupt priest any possibility of salvation. Since Hus persisted in defending the Wyclifite excoriation of bad priests and sinfully obedient laypeople, he opened himself up to be condemned as a Wyclifite.

The ecclesiastical politicians launched their successful assault in 1411 when they provoked Hus to oppose the papal crusade against the king of Naples, who supported Gregory XII. Not only did Hus protest against the secular use of papal power, but he also railed against the sale of indulgences that supported the enterprise. On October 18, 1412, the antipope John XXIII excommunicated Hus for nonobedience (not for heresy) and placed Prague under interdict until Hus left. Hus went into exile in southern Bohemia, where he lived with many nobles in several different castles. During his exile, he wrote his principal work, *De ecclesia* (*The Church*, 1915), and several polemical articles against his critics. Again, he vainly struggled to disentangle his respect for Wyclif the reformer from his nonadherence to Wyclif's heretical ideas.

On October 31, 1413, Emperor Sigismund compelled John XXIII to call a new council to convene in Constance (1414-1418) exactly one year later. The emperor then invited Hus to leave his safe retreats and attend the council. He promised him safe conduct to the conference, and he gave the impression that he promised him safe conduct to return home. It made little difference though, because once Hus had been lured to the conference, he was doomed. On November 3, 1414, Hus arrived at Constance, six weeks ahead of the emperor's entourage. The council was formally opened on November 16, and Hus was arrested on November 28 and imprisoned in a monastery dungeon from December 6 to March 24 of the next year. After many postponements, Hus was granted two public hearings in June, but there was no debate allowed. On July 6, 1415, Hus was formally condemned for Wyclifite heresy, and when he refused to recant, he was burned at the stake.

Significance

Jan Hus was a Czech leader in a political system dominated by Germans. He was a Wyclifite reformer in an ecclesiastical setting run by opponents of Wyclif, whose books were burned on February 10, 1413, in front of the basilica of Saint Peter in Rome. As a conscientious human being, Hus was unlucky to live at a time when religious reform was necessary to fight for but not possible to achieve. Yet Hus was not a failure in the ultimate sense. By the standards of his own age and religion, he was vindicated by his martyrdom.

As a child of his age, Hus shared the theologically shaped view of the world and differed from his peers mostly by placing greater emphasis on scriptural authority and patristic teachings of the first five centuries of the Christian era. In this respect, he stood on the threshold of the Reformation, which preferred the Bible to the pope. As the subsequent intellectual revolutions in science and democracy have repudiated the medieval worldview and superseded the authority of the Christian clergy, Hus the embattled Wyclifite theologian (who tried not to follow Wyclif into heresy) has faded away. All that remains is Hus the martyr. In his moral stature, his unyielding devotion to truth as he knew it, the purity and integrity of his character, and his unswerving loyalty to Christianity as he believed it, Hus has become an inspirational figure to many generations. In the last analysis, Hus was not the victim of the Council of Constance; he stands as its judge.

—*David R. Stevenson*

Further Reading

Fudge, Thomas A. *The Magnificent Ride: The First Reformation in Hussite Bohemia*. Brookfield, Vt.: Ashgate, 1998. Presents a cultural and social history of the reform movement in Bohemia. Maps, bibliography, index.

Loomis, Louise R. *The Council of Constance: The Unification of the Church*. New York: Columbia University Press, 1961. A primary source on the proceedings of the Council of Constance and the condemnation of Hus.

Lützow, Franz. *The Life and Times of Master John Hus*. New York: E. P. Dutton, 1921. An older but highly readable biography.

Odložilík, Otakar. *Wyclif and Bohemia*. Prague: Nákladem Královské ceské spolecnosti nauk, 1936. A Czech view of Wyclif's impact on Christian reform sentiment in Bohemia.

Schaff, David S. *John Hus: His Life, Teachings, and Death After Five Hundred Years*. New York: Charles Scribner's Sons, 1915. This is the best older biography. It is very sympathetic to Hus and his cause.

Spinka, Matthew. *John Hus and the Czech Reform*. Chicago: University of Chicago Press, 1941. Spinka is the outstanding Hus scholar writing in English. This biography places Hus in his Czech setting, which Spinka believes is essential to understand Hus. Spinka writes in the shadow of the Munich Conference in 1938, and this event colors his interpretation of Hus's betrayal by the German emperor at the Council of Constance.

_______. *John Hus at the Council of Constance*. New York: Columbia University Press, 1965. Contains the proceedings of the Council of Constance and Hus's correspondence.

_______. *John Hus' Concept of the Church*. Princeton, N.J.: Princeton University Press, 1966. Spinka's presentation of Hus's theology attempts to establish Hus as a major medieval theologian who admired Wyclif but did not follow him into heresy. He points out that many of Wyclif's other Czech followers were more heretical, even though they opposed Hus and supported Hus's condemnation.

Stacey, John. *John Wyclif and Reform*. Philadelphia: Westminster Press, 1964. Wyclif is seen as a religious reformer in theology who remained prudent in politics.

Ullman, W. *The Origins of the Great Schism*. London: Burns, Oates, and Washbourne, 1948. Gives the background for the religious corruption and moral confusion that set the stage for Hus's career. It deals with the rise of two popes, two Colleges of Cardinals, and two papal genealogies in the century preceding Hus.

Wylie, James Hamilton. *The Council of Constance to the Death of John Hus*. London: Longmans, Green, 1900. A comprehensive source in English for this subject.

See also: Charles IV; Thomas à Kempis; Wenceslaus; John Wyclif; Jan Žižka.

Related articles in *Great Events from History: The Middle Ages, 477-1453*: c. 1175: Waldensian Excommunications Usher in Protestant Movement; November 11-30, 1215: Fourth Lateran Council; 1305-1417: Avignon Papacy and the Great Schism; 1337-1453: Hundred Years' War; 1377-1378: Condemnation of John Wyclif; 1414-1418: Council of Constance; July 6, 1415: Martyrdom of Jan Hus.

IBN AL-ʿARABĪ
Islamic scholar and philosopher

Ibn al-ʿArabī formulated and made explicit the inner doctrines of Sufism and was the link between the Eastern and Western schools of that philosophy.

BORN: July 28, 1165; Murcia, Valencia (now in Spain)
DIED: November 16, 1240; Damascus, Ayyūbid Empire (now in Syria)
ALSO KNOWN AS: Abū Bakr Muḥammad ibn al-ʿArabī al-Ḥātimī al-Ṭaʾī; Muḥyī al-Dī Abū ʿAbd Allāh Muḥammad ibn ʿAlī ibn Muḥammad ibn al-ʿArabī al-Ḥātimī al-Ṭāʾī ibn al-ʿArabī
AREAS OF ACHIEVEMENT: Religion and theology, philosophy, monasticism

EARLY LIFE

Abū Bakr Muḥammad ibn al-ʿArabī al-Ḥātimī al-Ṭaʾī, commonly known as Ibn al-ʿArabī (ihb-nool-ar-a-BEE) was born in Islamic Spain to a well-to-do and respected family. He spent his early years in Murcia, moving first to Lisbon and later to the more cosmopolitan Seville, where his family settled. There he received his formal education and was given the leisure to pursue a developing interest in mystical approaches to religion and the teachings of Sufism. In search of spiritual enlightenment, he sought out individuals known for their wisdom and spiritual insights who would be willing to take him on as a pupil and guide him in his quest. One such figure, Fatimah of Córdoba, an elderly yet vigorous woman at ninety-five, became Ibn al-ʿArabī's spiritual adviser for several years.

Students of Islamic philosophy customarily pursued a formal program of study in such subjects as cosmology, the metaphysical doctrines of Islam, analysis of the Qurʾān for hidden meaning, and the science of letters and numbers. In addition, the student gained skills in the practice of private activities such as meditation, vigil, fasting, and prayer. On fulfilling these requirements, the successful aspirant was prepared to experience, understand, and control supersensory communications of several types. He was empowered with such gifts as visions, precognition, communing with the spirits of the dead, and healing. Ibn al-ʿArabī is reported to have been a proficient student who enjoyed numerous mystical experiences; he frequently visited cemeteries, where he spoke with the dead. It was during this intellectually fertile period of his life that he married the first of three wives, a woman named Maryam—the daughter of a man of influence and wealth—who was eager to partake of her husband's spiritual experiences and quest.

At age twenty, and already initiated into the Sufi way, Ibn al-ʿArabī began to travel throughout Andalusia in search of greater enlightenment. During one of his stays in the city of Córdoba, he was invited to the home of Averroës, the most celebrated Islamic disciple of Aristotelian philosophy of the age and a friend of his father. The well-established scholar and the young visionary represented opposite approaches to the question of knowledge: Averroës proposed that reason was the foundation of wisdom, while to Ibn al-ʿArabī, true knowledge resulted from spiritual vision. Nevertheless, Averroës fully understood Ibn al-ʿArabī's goals and recognized that his visitor had attained a level of understanding superior to most. Ibn al-ʿArabī describes Averroës' reaction to the visit thus:

> He had thanked God, I have been told, to have lived at a time when he could have seen someone who had entered into spiritual retreat ignorant and had left it as I had done. He said: "It was a case whose possibility I had affirmed myself without however as yet encountering someone who had experienced it. Glory be to God that I have been able to live at a time when there exists a master of this experience, one of those who open the locks of His doors. Glory be to God to have made me the personal favor of seeing one of them with my own eyes."

Ibn al-ʿArabī continued his peripatetic existence in Andalusia and North Africa, visiting sages, holding debates, and writing. He was also subject to frequent visions. In one such vision, received in 1198, he was ordered to depart for Asia. Heeding the command, he arrived in Mecca in 1201 and remained there for four years, devoting himself to study, public discussion of his views, and writing. During his stay in the holy city of Islam, he married his second wife, wrote several works—including a famous collection of love poems—and began composition of his most famous book, *al-Futūhāt al-Makkīyah* (thirteenth century; the Meccan revelations), a lengthy compendium of esoteric knowledge.

LIFE'S WORK

Sufism represents an Islamic tradition, as old as the religion itself, of a small group of devout believers—exemplified by the earliest followers of Muḥammad the Prophet—who renounce the rewards and temptations of this world in order to lead a life of contemplation and prayer. The emphasis of the group is on the direct experience of God; its fundamental tenet is that "there is no reality but the Reality (God), and that all other realities are purely relative and dependent upon His reality." The cumulative experiences and insights of those who followed the early Sufis constitute a complex doctrine; as a tradition, it was wrapped in heavy symbolism and obscure references, accessible only to those who could receive the dogma orally from an enlightened master. Ibn al-ʿArabī succeeded in changing the pattern of transmission by recording much of this wisdom in books, making it possible for the tradition, full of veiled allusion, to be communicated to wider audiences in clearer and more accessible form. He is known among the Sufis as "the greatest Shaikh" for his role as the first to set in writing the vast amount of doctrine contained in the Sufi oral tradition.

Ibn al-ʿArabī was a prolific writer, believed to have authored 250 separate titles. Aside from his writings on Sufism, he composed short treatises, letters, poetry, and abstract philosophical works. His most impressive work, however, is *al-Futūḥāt al-Makkīyah*. The motivation for writing the book, as the title implies, came from a compelling outside source—divine revelation—and the author is spoken of as simply the vehicle through which the message was recorded. The lengthy treatise, considered the main sourcebook of the sacred sciences of Islam, is made up of 560 chapters; it records the sayings of the earlier Sufis, explains the principles of metaphysics and various sacred sciences, and describes Ibn al-ʿArabī's own spiritual development. A second important work, *Fuṣūs al-ḥikam* (1229; *The Bezels of Wisdom*, 1980), is Ibn al-ʿArabī's spiritual testament. This twenty-seven-chapter book, which contains the basic doctrines of Islamic esotericism, was inspired by a vision of the Prophet holding a book and ordering the writer to transmit the word to future generations.

Because Ibn al-ʿArabī's metaphysical doctrines came from inspiration rather than meditation, his works generally lack coherence and frustrate those who read them hoping to gather from them a systematic and comprehensive view of the universe. Students of Ibn al-ʿArabī suggest that his aim was not to give a rationally satisfying explanation of reality. In fact, some would argue that he was not a philosopher at all, since he was not interested in constructing a complete and consistent system of thought. What he attempted to do, rather, was to present a vision of reality, the attainment of which depended on the practice of certain methods of realization.

At the core of Ibn al-ʿArabī's thought, as for all Sufism, is the concept of the transcendent unity of Being: Though God is separate from the universe, he encompasses all of it. While God manifests himself in the creation, he transcends it. While God is above all qualities, he is not devoid of them. The qualities, or Names, are infinite, yet they are summarized in the Qurʾān to make them understandable. Knowledge of these Names, then, leads to knowledge of God, and to spiritual realization. One who has attained this level, the "Universal Man," is one who has understood the Names, has mastered all the stages of enlightenment, and has been able to combine the fullness of being and of knowledge. The Prophet Muḥammad was such a Universal Man, as were the great saints of Islam who, over the generations, transcended material reality and understood all the spiritual possibilities of the universe.

The goal of all Sufis is union with the Divine, achieved in the gradual ascent through several levels of spiritual attainment culminating in a state of complete contemplation of God. The desired union with the Divine Being only comes after the arduous ascent, as if climbing a mountain, toward spiritual purification. Prayer is the essential element of this climb and also its ultimate goal; humans begin by praying to God and end their search by purifying their soul and allowing God to pray within them. Humans thus become the mirrors of God and finally understand all of God's Names.

Each step in this spiritual quest requires passage from the outward reality to the inner one, to the true essence of things: from the external, or exoteric, to the hidden, or esoteric. The nonmaterial nature of the quest makes the use of ordinary words insufficient. For this reason, the Sufis often rely on a language full of symbols, the only adequate tool to describe the hidden meaning of nature, the true significance of the religious experience, and the inner workings of a person's soul.

Ibn al-ʿArabī's articulation of the ideals of Sufism brought him fame, notoriety, and even some enemies. He spent the last part of his life living and lecturing in different areas of the Middle East and Asia Minor, coming into contact with numerous influential writers and thinkers. One of his disciples, Sadr al-Dīn al-Qunawi, is considered the essential bridge between Western Sufism and the equally vigorous school developing in Iran during the thirteenth century. Ibn al-ʿArabī eventually settled in Damascus in 1223, where he remained for most of the rest of his life. There he devoted himself to teaching and writing and, as a respected sage, was able to influence future generations of Sufis, both Eastern and Western. He was survived by two sons and a daughter. One of the sons became an accomplished poet; of the daughter it is said that she was able to respond to difficult theological questions at an early age.

SIGNIFICANCE

It is evident that Sufism, like similar schools of thought whose goal is spiritual communion with an Absolute, defies a simple and precise definition. Moreover, the experiences its adherents seek cannot be understood easily or even appreciated by the uninitiated; nor can they be described, with any clarity, using ordinary everyday language. Ibn al-ʿArabī's most notable contribution was to record his own understanding of how this communion with a Supreme Being was attained, recounting, in the process, centuries-old insights hitherto transmitted only orally by enlightened individuals. He thus gave later generations a language with which to describe their experiences and a definitive doctrine from which to continue to develop the theoretical foundations of Sufism.

Through the centuries, Ibn al-ʿArabī's influence has been enormous; he has been read and studied as seriously by his detractors as by his disciples. Clear links have been traced from Ibn al-ʿArabī to all subsequent Sufi schools of thought and religious orders throughout the Islamic world. In modern times, his works continue to be read as far east as India and Pakistan; his odes are recited in Sufi monasteries in Egypt and North Africa. Some scholars have suggested that Ibn al-ʿArabī strongly, if indirectly, influenced Dante, whose works reveal parallels with the spiritual quest of the Sufi.

—*Clara Estow*

FURTHER READING

Addas, Claude. *Ibn ʿArabī: The Voyage of No Return.* Translated by David Streight. Cambridge, England: Islamic Texts Society, 2000. Part of the Muslim Personalities series, this book examines Ibn al-ʿArabī and Sufism. Includes a bibliography.

Affifi, Abul E. *The Mystical Philosophy of Muhyid Din-Ibnul ʿArabī.* 1939. Reprint. New York: AMS Books, 1974. The first serious and comprehensive examination of Ibn al-ʿArabī's philosophy, this work attempts to make the Muslim sage understandable to Western readers. Refers to Ibn al-ʿArabī as a pantheist and a typical mystic philosopher, labels that other scholars find difficult to justify. Useful bibliography and an informative appendix.

Asín Palacios, Miguel. *Islam and the Divine Comedy.* Translated by Harold Sunderland. London. 1926. Rev. ed. Lahore, Pakistan: Qausain, 1977. The seminal work by the distinguished Spanish Arabist and translator of Ibn al-ʿArabī. The author was the first scholar to suggest the link between Dante and Islamic mysticism. A fascinating study of the transmission of philosophical and literary motifs.

Coates, Peter. *Ibn ʿArabī and Modern Thought: The History of Taking Metaphysics Seriously.* Oxford, England: Anqa, 2002. Explores the metaphysics of Ibn al-ʿArabī in the context of modern philosophy.

Corbin, Henry. *Alone with the Alone: Creative Imagination in the Sufism of Ibn ʿArabī.* Translated by Ralph Manheim. Princeton, N.J.: Princeton University Press, 1998. Explores in great detail Ibn al-ʿArabī's notion of the creative imagination, which, according to the author, is the goal of the mystical experience. A serious and erudite work displaying great familiarity with Eastern and Western schools of mystical philosophy. The author attempts to understand Ibn al-ʿArabī's thought in relation to these traditions.

Ibn al-ʿArabī. *Sufis of Andalusia: The "Ruh al-quds" and "al-Durrat al-Fakhirah" of Ibn ʿArabī.* Translated with an introduction and notes by R. W. J. Austin. London: Allen and Unwin, 1971. A translation of one of Ibn al-ʿArabī's most accessible works, his account of Hispano-Muslim sages who influenced and guided him in his search for enlightenment. Of particular interest is Ibn al-ʿArabī's mention of numerous female role models, described as having reached high levels of spirituality within a tradition that generally excludes women from such pursuits. The volume contains a fairly informative biographical portrait.

Knysh, Alexander. *Ibn ʿArabī in the Later Islamic Tradition: The Making of a Polemical Image in Medieval Islam.* Albany: State University of New York Press, 1999. Examines the controversy surrounding Ibn al-ʿArabī's philosophy in the tradition of Islam, a tradition suspicious of his mysticism. Looks at the intellectual strategies used by his detractors over time.

Nasr, Seyyed Hossein. *Three Muslim Sages.* 1969. Reprint. Delmar, N.Y.: Caravan Books, 1976. A third of the book is devoted to Ibn al-ʿArabī, emphasizing the importance of the medieval thinker in the development of Sufism in particular and Islam in general. Dismisses much of the criticism against Ibn al-ʿArabī by asserting that his thought is highly original and resulted from divine inspiration.

Shah, Idries. *The Sufis.* 1964. Reprint. London: Octagon Press, 1984. A serious and readable account of the theories, development, and principal figures of Sufism. The author uses numerous examples of ways in which Sufi motifs and practices found their way into European letters and institutions. Suggests that Sufism was disseminated mainly by its poets and quotes Ibn al-ʿArabī's poetry as a possible model for the development of the cult of the Virgin Mary.

See also: Aḥmad ibn Ḥanbal; Averroës; Dante; al-Ḥallāj; al-Ḥasan al-Baṣrī; Jalāl al-Dīn Rūmī.

Related articles in *Great Events from History: The Middle Ages, 477-1453*: c. 610-632: Muḥammad Receives Revelations; Early 10th century: Qarakhanids Convert to Islam; 1273: Sufi Order of Mawlawīyah Is Established.

Ibn Baṭṭūṭah

Arab traveler

Driven by an exceptional wanderlust, Ibn Baṭṭūṭah became the greatest Muslim traveler. His peregrinations through India, Russia, China, the East Indies, North Africa, and the Middle East were recorded in the most famous of all Islamic travelogs, the Riḥlah.

Born: February 24, 1304; Tangier, Morocco
Died: c. 1377; Morocco
Also known as: Abū ʿAbd Allāh Muḥammad ibn-ʿAbd Allāh al-Lawātī al-Ṭanji ibn Baṭṭūṭah (full name)
Area of achievement: Exploration

Early Life

Abū ʿAbd Allāh Muḥammad ibn-ʿAbd Allāh al-Lawātī al-Tanji ibn Baṭṭūṭah, who came to be known as Ibn Baṭṭūṭah (IHB-uhn bat-TEW-tah), was born in Tangier, Morocco. His family had a long tradition of serving as religious judges, and his educational training prepared him for such a career. Well before he undertook the first of his many journeys at the age of twenty-one, Ibn Baṭṭūṭah had studied Islamic theology and law in Tangier. His first journey, which commenced in June of 1325, took the form of a pilgrimage to Mecca, but it had much broader ramifications. In a fashion reminiscent of the grand tours which Europeans would undertake in later centuries to finish their education, his trip to Mecca supplied Ibn Baṭṭūṭah with diverse opportunities.

Ever the astute observer and inquisitive intellectual, Ibn Baṭṭūṭah talked and studied with scholars he encountered as he made an unhurried progress eastward. Evidently his family was an affluent one, with extensive connections throughout the Islamic world. Their belief—a view seemingly shared by Ibn Baṭṭūṭah—was that his experiences would be ideally suited to the duties of a magistrate, which he was expected to assume on his return. His purse, personality, and contacts with powerful officials readily opened many doors for the young man, and his winning ways, together with a considerable degree of curiosity he aroused as an individual from the outer geographic reaches of Islam, stood him in good stead. He was greeted with hospitality wherever he went.

Ibn Baṭṭūṭah's initial journey was a momentous one in a number of ways. He traveled to Cairo, probably the greatest city of the time, making stops, en route from Tangier, in most of the major ports of the southern Mediterranean. He reveled in the time he spent in that renowned intellectual center of ancient times, Alexandria. His experiences in Egypt aroused in him an insatiable wanderlust. He reached Damascus in August, 1326, and it was there that he took his first wife. After a brief courtship and honeymoon, he joined a caravan of pilgrims wending their way to Mecca.

The pilgrims' travels were arduous in the extreme. After passing through what is now Jordan and Syria, the faithful rested for several days at Al-Karak, for the ordeal of a desert crossing lay before them. They managed the crossing of the Wadi al-Ukhaydir—Ibn Baṭṭūṭah characterized it as the valley of hell—by moving at night until they reached the Al-ʿUla oasis. Thence they moved onward to the holy city of Medina and then progressed to Mecca. As was the case with all of his peregrinations, Ibn Baṭṭūṭah produced vivid accounts of his experiences in and impressions of Mecca. He departed from Mecca sometime in November of 1326, now a *hajji* (one who has made the pilgrimage to Mecca) as well as a man determined to see much more of the world.

Life's Work

The essence of Ibn Baṭṭūṭah's achievement lies in his wide-ranging travels. Yet there was much more to his repeated journeys than merely visiting strange and faraway places. The reader of *Tuḥfat al-nuẓẓār fi gharaʿib al-amsar wa-ʿajaʿib al-asfar* (1357-1358; *Travels of Ibn Battuta*, 1958-2000, best known as the *Riḥlah*) becomes immediately aware of Ibn Baṭṭūṭah's keen eye for detail; clearly, he was a man of rare curiosity and intellect. Anything and everything interested him. From unusual religious beliefs to the economies of the regions through which he trekked, from methods of dress to the basics of diet, he noted the varied aspects of the lifestyles he encountered. Indeed, what Ibn Baṭṭūṭah saw and reported is at least as important as where he went.

Returning with his two wives to Tangier, Ibn Baṭṭūṭah tarried only a short time before succumbing again to his desire to travel. His next major undertaking was a second *hajj*, and this time he gave himself ample time to sense and savor all Mecca had to offer. His visit lasted for some three years. This must have been quite expensive, but evidently the family fortunes were ample to support such extended periods of travel.

Next, Ibn Baṭṭūṭah decided to sail down the Red Sea to the renowned trading center of Aden. He provides a singular description of the strategically located seaport and the way in which it depended on great cisterns for its water supply. After some time in Aden, he continued southward along the African coast and visited the important trade centers of Kilwa and Mombasa. On his return journey, he stopped in the major cities of Oman and Hormuz. In fact, in a fashion which was to become characteristic of all his endeavors, he attempted to visit every reachable site of major significance.

After touring the Gulf of Aden and its environs, he traversed the considerable breadth of Arabia while making the *hajj* for a third time. A trip across the Red Sea followed, with a risky, demanding journey to Syene (modern Aswān) and thence via the Nile to Cairo. By this juncture, Arabia, Africa's Mediterranean coast, and the lower reaches of the Nile had become familiar territory, and, not surprisingly for a man of his inclinations, Ibn Baṭṭūṭah began to look farther afield.

He passed through the various Turkish states in Asia Minor, crossed the Black Sea to reach Kaffa (modern Feodosiya, the first Christian city he had seen), and moved northeastward into Kipchak. This Russian region was then under the control of Khan Muḥammad Özbeg, and Ibn Baṭṭūṭah joined his peripatetic camp. In this way he was able to visit the outer reaches of Mongolia, where he marveled at the brevity of summer nights.

On leaving the khan's camp, Ibn Baṭṭūṭah linked his travel fortunes to a Byzantine princess, whom he accompanied to Constantinople. There, in what he considered one of the most important moments of his career, he enjoyed an interview with Emperor Andronicus III Palaeologus. From the emperor's court he journeyed eastward, crossing the steppes of southern Asia en route to Kabul and thence over the Hindu Kush. In September of 1333, he reached the Indus River. He had, in eight years of traveling, made three pilgrimages to Mecca, seen most of the southern and eastern Mediterranean, floated on the Nile, braved the desert sands of Arabia, and penetrated deep into Russia. It is at this juncture that he ends his first narrative, and by any standard of measurement his achievements had been considerable. Still, though he was probably the most traveled man of his time, the clarion call to adventure drew him as strongly as ever.

He wandered throughout the Sind and eventually moved on to Delhi at the invitation of the ruler, Muḥammad ibn Tughluq. This capricious, bloodthirsty monarch was a bit too much even for Ibn Baṭṭūṭah's eclectic tastes: "No day did his palace gate fail to witness the elevation of some abject to affluence and the torture and murder of some living soul." Yet somehow he managed to get along with this extraordinary ruler, and he became *qāḍī* (judge) of Delhi at a very high salary. He served in this capacity for the next eight years. Yet, far from prospering, he fell into considerable debt. Scholars have ascribed this to his extravagance, and his living beyond his means may have figured prominently in his eventual decline into disfavor.

Resilient soul that he was, however, Ibn Baṭṭūṭah turned potential ruin into what to him must have been a glorious assignment. He was chosen to head a delegation which was paying a visit to the last Mongol emperor of China. Leaving in 1342, the group made its way to Calcutta en route to China. Here fate intervened, however, in the form of a shipwreck that completely destroyed the junk on which he and the other envoys were to travel. This was a disaster of the first magnitude, for Ibn Baṭṭūṭah lost not only his personal possessions but also the lavish gifts he had been delegated to carry to China.

Accordingly, Ibn Baṭṭūṭah remained in the region, visiting various cities on India's western coast and also the Maldive Islands, where he rose to prominence as a judge and added four wives to his harem. Yet he did not tarry overlong, for August, 1344, found him leaving the Maldives for Sri Lanka. Further adventures followed, and eventually he reached Java after having stopped briefly in Burma (now Myanmar). From Java he finally made his way to China, where he visited Amoy (Xiamen), Canton (Guangzhou), and Beijing, among other major sites. Returning westward, he revisited Sumatra, Malabar, Oman,

Persia, and a host of other locations. On reaching Damascus, he learned of his father's death some fifteen years earlier. It was the first news of home he had had in that many years.

It was also during this period that Ibn Baṭṭūṭah witnessed, at first hand, the ravages of the bubonic plague (sometimes called the Black Death). His graphic reports on what he saw in Damascus, where more than two thousand unfortunate souls died in a single day, is one of the finest surviving accounts of the plague. Perhaps thereby reminded of his mortality, he then revisited Jerusalem and Cairo in the process of making a fourth *hajj*. Finally, having been away from home almost constantly for more than twenty-four years, he returned to Morocco on November 8, 1349.

Even then, his travels were not over. After spending a relatively short time in Tangier, he made his way to Spain and toured Andalusia. His final major journey was into central Africa. Journeying from oasis to oasis across the Sahara, he reached the fabled desert entrepôt of Timbuktu, where the mighty Niger River (which he wrongly called the Nile) begins its great westward sweep to the ocean. At this point, his king called him home, thereby bringing an end to nearly thirty years of travel encompassing an estimated 75,000 miles (120,000 kilometers). His final years were more settled; he was in his early seventies when he died in his native Morocco.

SIGNIFICANCE

With the possible exception of the voyages of Marco Polo, there is nothing prior to the European Renaissance to compare with the nature and extent of Ibn Baṭṭūṭah's travels. He single-handedly made the world a smaller place, and thanks to his remarkable accounts modern knowledge of much of Asia during the fourteenth century is considerably richer than otherwise would have been the case. As the chronicler Ibn Juzayy, who recounted Ibn Baṭṭūṭah's travels by royal decree, stated:

> This Shaykh is the traveller of our age; and he who should call him the traveller of the whole body of Islam would not exceed the truth.

—*James A. Casada*

FURTHER READING

Arno, Joan, and Helen Grady. *Ibn Battuta, a View of the Fourteenth-Century World: A Unit of Study for Grades 7-10*. Los Angeles: National Center for History in the Schools, University of California, Los Angeles, 1998. A seventy-three-page teacher's manual for teaching both Ibn Baṭṭūṭah and fourteenth century North Africa. Illustrations, maps, bibliographical references.

Cooley, William D. *The Negroland of the Arabs Examined and Explained*. London: J. Arrowsmith, 1841. Although there are some problems with Cooley's transcriptions from the Arabic, this is a useful early English account of that portion of Ibn Baṭṭūṭah's travels devoted to the Sahara and Niger regions.

Dunn, Ross E. *The Adventures of Ibn Battuta: A Muslim Traveller of the Fourteenth Century*. Berkeley: University of California Press, 1989. More than a dozen chapters outline Baṭṭūṭah's travel's, including a dozen detailed maps. Glossary, bibliography, index.

Hamdun, Said, and Noël King, trans. and eds. *Ibn Battuta in Black Africa*. Foreword by Ross Dunn. Princeton, N.J.: M. Wiener, 1994. Illustrations, maps, bibliographical references, index. A selection of Ibn Baṭṭūṭah's writings during his two sub-Saharan trips—his second, to Mali, being his last recorded adventure.

Hamilton, Paul. "Seas of Sand." In *Exploring Africa and Asia*, by Nathalie Ettinger, Elspeth J. Huxley, and Paul Hamilton. Garden City, N.Y.: Doubleday, 1973. The section titled "The Traveler of Islam" constitutes a useful, accessible account of Ibn Baṭṭūṭah's first journey to Mecca. Illustrated.

Ibn Baṭṭūṭah. *Travels of Ibn Battuta*. Translated and edited by H. A. R. Gibb. 4 vols. Cambridge, England: Cambridge University Press, 1958-2000. This careful, amply annotated translation is by far the most important English-language source of information on the man and his milieu. Gibb's introduction and notes offer useful historical background.

Mackintosh-Smith, Tim. *Travels with a Tangerine: A Journey in the Footnotes of Ibn Baṭṭūṭah*. New York: Welcome Rain, 2002. Includes illustrations, maps, bibliographical references, index.

Rumford, James. *Traveling Man: The Journey of Ibn Battuta, 1325-1354*. Boston: Houghton Mifflin, 2001. Color illustrations, maps. Designed for young readers, a semi-fictional biography.

Tucker, William. "Ibn-Battuta, Abu Abd-Allah Muhammad." In *The Discoverers: An Encyclopedia of Exploration*, edited by Helen Delpar. New York: McGraw-Hill, 1980. A succinct, useful summation of the high points of Ibn Baṭṭūṭah's career. This volume includes short biographies of many other explorers as well. Bibliographies and an index.

SEE ALSO: Mansa Mūsā; Raziya; William of Rubrouck; Zheng He.

RELATED ARTICLES in *Great Events from History: The Middle Ages, 477-1453*: 1062-1147: Almoravids Conquer Morocco and Establish the Almoravid Empire; 1271-1295: Travels of Marco Polo; 1324-1325: Mansa Mūsā's Pilgrimage to Mecca Sparks Interest in Mali Empire; 1325-1355: Travels of Ibn Baṭṭūṭah; 1340: Al-ʿUmarī Writes a History of Africa; 1377: Ibn Khaldūn Completes His *Muqaddimah*.

IBN GABIROL

Jewish poet and philosopher

Ibn Gabirol created a form of poetry written in biblical Hebrew. His version of Neoplatonic philosophy came to be integrated within Christian Augustinian thought.

BORN: c. 1020; probably Málaga, Caliphate of Córdoba (now in Spain)

DIED: c. 1057; probably Valencia, Kingdom of Valencia (now in Spain)

ALSO KNOWN AS: Ibn Gabirol, Solomon ben Yehuda (full name); Avicebron (Latin name)

AREAS OF ACHIEVEMENT: Literature, philosophy, religion and theology

EARLY LIFE

Solomon ben Yehuda ibn Gabirol (IHB-uhn gah-BEE-rawl) was probably born in Málaga. The sources for his biographical data are allusions in his poems, references in the works of the Jewish commentator Moses ibn Ezra (c. 1060-c. 1139) and the Arabic historian Ibn Saʿid (c. 1029-1070), and Hebrew legends, many of which were published in the sixteenth century in Italy and the Ottoman Empire.

Western scholars index his name in a variety of ways: Most list him as Ibn Gabirol, others as Gabirol, and a few as Solomon ibn Gabirol. His name in Arabic was Abū Ayyūb Sulaymān ibn Yaḥya ibn Gabirūt; in Latin, he was known as Avicebron, Avicenebrol, Albenzubron, and variations thereof. There is no agreement as to the meaning of the name Gabirol. Some have suggested that it is a diminutive of the Arabic word *yabir* (power), while others see it as affixing the Hebrew word *El* (God), to *yabir.* The uncertainty in dates is caused, in part, by the sources' use of different calendars. Ibn Ezra wrote of poets and poetics in the eighth century of the fourth millennium (4800 of the Hebrew year), which approximates 1040, while Ibn Saʿid used the Muslim calendar.

In 4800 (of the Hebrew year), according to Ibn Ezra, "lived Abū Ayyūb Selomo son of Yehuda ibn Gabirol, the Cordoban." From this, it has been concluded that Ibn Gabirol's parents had lived in Córdoba, capital of Muslim Iberia, whence they fled, probably in 1013 during the fundamentalist revolution that shattered the unity of the Umayyad caliphate. The family went to Málaga, where Solomon was born—an inference from his custom of appending "Malki," meaning "of Málaga," to his name in his writings. His poems suggest that his father had been prominent in Cordoban society before the turmoil and that his parents suffered from something akin to tuberculosis.

According to his self-description, Ibn Gabirol was small, homely, and weak; he suffered from a skin disease. He was educated in Hebrew, Arabic, and Greek literature as well as philosophy, science, and theology; indeed, Ibn Gabirol was wont to complain that he was treated as a Greek. Various sources describe him as vain, argumentative, and hot-tempered.

LIFE'S WORK

By his own report, Ibn Gabirol's first five poems were written when he was sixteen or younger. The most significant of these is *Azharot*, a nonmetrical versification of the 613 Commandments. Shortly after this time, the family moved to Saragossa, where Mundir I (r. 1029-1038) had established an independent kingdom that attempted to maintain the sophisticated lifestyle of the Umayyads. Mundir and his immediate heirs welcomed all poets and philosophers. One of the leading figures at court was the Jewish Yekutiel ibn Hasan, who befriended the young poet. During this period, Ibn Gabirol wrote several works, including elegies on the death of Hai ben Sherira Gaon (939-1038), leader of the Hebrew Academy at Pumbedita, and *Anaq* (necklace), a four-hundred-line didactic poem on the importance of Hebrew grammar, of which only eighty-eight lines have survived.

Around 1039, Ibn Gabirol lost his father and his patron: His father apparently succumbed to tuberculosis, and Yekutiel was assassinated by rivals at the palace. In 1040, Ibn Gabirol wrote two elegies in honor of his former patron. Around the same time, he wrote a poem that he dedicated and sent to Samuel ha-Nagid (Ibn Nagrella; 993-1056), vizier to Badis, king of Granada, whose forces had just defeated the rival king of Seville. Samuel, one of the most influential Jews of the period, sent financial assistance to the poet, who remained in Saragossa completing, in Arabic, his major study of ethics, *Kitāb iṣlāḥ al-akhlāq* (1045; *The Improvement of Moral Qualities*, 1901). About that time, Ibn Gabirol's mother died. Alone in the world and dependent on a patron for support, he went to Granada. Apparently, Samuel had known Ibn Gabirol's parents in Málaga. He took the orphan under his protection, and Ibn Gabirol came to call him "my father."

After arriving in Granada, Ibn Gabirol wrote a long, mournful poem expressing his feeling of despair on leaving Saragossa. In 1048, Nissim ben Jacob ben Nissim ibn Shahim, leader of the Kairwan (Tunisia) Jewish community, arrived in Granada to arrange a marriage between his daughter and Samuel's son. Nissim (c. 990-1062) was a noted theologian, and Ibn Gabirol spent a year listening to his public disputations and commentaries. It has been surmised that Samuel had abandoned Ibn Gabirol because of some uncomplimentary comments the poet had made about Samuel's poetic style, and that Ibn Gabirol became dependent on Nissim. This interpretation, however, seems doubtful, since Nissim himself was dependent on Samuel's largesse and Ibn Gabirol was not the type to sit at anyone's feet.

Ibn Gabirol was the first of the significant Hispano-Hebrew poets and philosophers who wrote in both biblical Hebrew and Arabic. At this time, all Jews could read Ibn Gabirol's Hebrew poetry, but Jews and Christians who lived outside the Arabic world could not read works written in Arabic. During the period 1167-1186, Judah ben Saul ibn Tibbon translated *The Improvement of Moral Qualities* into Hebrew. Meanwhile, Christians had become interested in Ibn Gabirol's philosophical work. In the mid-twelfth century, his major philosophical study, of which no Arabic copy has surfaced, was translated from Arabic into Latin as *Fons vitae* (fountain of life; English translation, 1963). A century later, Shem Tov ben Joseph Falaquera translated portions of the Arabic manuscript into Hebrew, but the Hebrew reading public found it of little interest.

As time went by, most of the Arabic manuscripts were either lost or destroyed by Muslim fundamentalists. Jews preserved the Hebraic poetic and ethical works and Christians the Latin philosophical works. The result was that Jews knew nothing of Ibn Gabirol's philosophical opera; certain fifteenth and sixteenth century Portuguese Jewish philosophers, for example, considered "Albenzubron" a Muslim. Christians, on the other hand, knowing nothing of his Hebrew poetry, considered "Avicebron" a Muslim or an Arab convert to Christianity. In the mid-nineteenth century, Solomon Munk realized that Falaquera's Hebrew translation and the Latin *Fons vitae* were based on the same lost Arabic source. Munk published an extensive work demonstrating that Ibn Gabirol and Avicebron were one and the same.

Ibn Gabirol worked simultaneously on religious and philosophical poetry and prose. Except where internal evidence is available, there is little indication as to the order of composition of his works.

Hebrew was not the daily language of Iberian Jews; most spoke Arabic. Biblical Hebrew and the Hebrew of the commentaries, however, were known to all Jews. Secular poetry, if it had existed in biblical times, did not survive. There developed in Palestine under Byzantine influence, however, a form of poetry (*payytanim*) that was used in religious services and for special occasions. This form, based on stress rather than meter, and with various patterns of rhyme, was brought to Iberia and flourished there. During the height of the Umayyad caliphate, Jewish courtiers employed this poetic form for secular purposes. Around the same time, Jewish scholars embarked on an intensive study of biblical Hebrew; the result was an expansion of the biblical vocabulary. Ibn Gabirol was a proponent of biblical Hebrew, and his earliest poems followed the model of the *payytanim*. Gradually, his poems took on the characteristics of the most sophisticated Arabic stylists, but the language was the expanded biblical Hebrew. His secular poems became models, and copies quickly spread throughout the Mediterranean.

It was in Ibn Gabirol's religious poetry, however, that he reached the summit of his creativity. Using biblical Hebrew but infusing the poems with imagery and meters derived from Arabic poetry, he created works of such lasting beauty that they are still used in Hebrew prayer books. There is a pessimistic quality to these poems. While this dark mood is consistent with the stylistic temper of Arabic poets during the last decades of Umayyad Iberia, it also reflects Ibn Gabirol's own experience of being forced into exile after the death of Yekutiel and his family's memories of the flight from Córdoba. There is a yearning for redemption in his poetry; the poems are mystical and personal. Unlike his secular poems, which are marked by bravado and arrogance, Ibn Gabirol's religious works are filled with longing and humility.

The poem *Keter Malkhut* (*The Kingly Crown*, 1911) is, in part, a restatement of Ibn Gabirol's philosophy and a confession of sins. In his system, the incorporeal God, derived from a Platonic or Neoplatonic conceptualization, is all-powerful: "Thou art Lord, and all creatures are Thy servants and adorers." Following Plato, Ibn Gabirol visualized the soul as temporarily inhabiting the body, but he did not fall into the Platonic concept of reincarnation. The work demonstrates Ibn Gabirol's knowledge of Islamic science, particularly astronomy. The last portion of the poem, the confession of sins, is used in some Sephardic prayer books at Yom Kippur (the Day of Atonement).

Ibn Gabirol was a Neoplatonist at a time when Jewish intellectual life was focused on Aristotelian ideas. Scholars such as Judah ibn Tibbon or Moses Maimonides (1135-1204) either did not know or thought unimportant Ibn Gabirol's philosophical writings, while Falaquera thought him a follower of Empedocles. In reality, one can trace Ibn Gabirol's philosophy to ideas in Aristotle, Galen, Plotinus, Proclus, and various Hebrew and Muslim philosophers and theologians. The form of *Fons vitae* is the Platonic dialogue, and Plato is the only philosopher mentioned.

Rejected by Jewish and Christian Aristotelians, Ibn Gabirol was quickly accepted by Christian Augustinians. Because he had developed a philosophical and theological system without reference to Hebrew tradition, Christians considered his work a valid instrument for bolstering Augustinian teaching. Starting with the translator/commentator Dominicus Gundissalinus, Ibn Gabirol's cosmology and methodology influenced thirteenth century Christian theologians such as William of Auvergne, Robert Grosseteste, Saint Albertus Magnus, Roger Bacon, Saint Bonaventure, and Raymond Lull. The Christians took Ibn Gabirol's concepts of light and of the plurality of forms and incorporated them into Augustinian Scholasticism.

The Improvement of Moral Qualities, an ethical work that has survived in both the Arabic original and Ibn Tibbon's translation, became popular among Jews. Because of the numerous biblical citations, it was clearly marked as Jewish and seemed to hold little interest for Christians. The work is original in that the author lists twenty personal traits, each of which he links to one of the five senses. In the Arabic original, there is a diagram later used by Kabbalists in developing their theories.

If Ibn Gabirol wrote any biblical commentaries or Kabbalist tracts, none has survived. Abraham ibn Ezra of Tudela (1089-1164), a noted theologian, cited Ibn Gabirol seven times in his comments on the Bible. There is extant a comment by Ibn Gabirol on the Garden of Eden passage in Genesis in which that passage is treated allegorically: Eden is dealt with not as a specific place but as a generalized preexisting atmosphere, while the garden represents the real world. There is also extant a satirical poem in which, like the Kabbalist writers, Ibn Gabirol makes use of the fact that each Hebrew letter has a numerical value. The values of the letters in the word for water, for example, total ninety, while those in the word for wine total seventy, proving that water is superior to wine.

Through the years, scholars have been discovering bits and pieces of Ibn Gabirol's canon; a *diwan* (collection of poems), for example, was found in Cairo. References to many undiscovered poems exist. Ibn Gabirol boasted that he had written twenty books, but only two have been found. Two others attributed to him, a Latin translation titled *De anima* and a Hebrew translation titled *Mivhar ha-Peninim* (maxims; 1546), are questioned by most authorities.

Ibn Gabirol never married; he averred that his only loves were poetry and philosophy, avenues to truth. According to Ibn Ezra, Ibn Gabirol was thirty years old when he died in Valencia. That would be around 1050 or 1051. Hebrew tradition places his death in the year 4830, or 1069/1070, when he was fifty. Ibn Saʿid states that "Sulaiman ibn Yakhaya, known by the name of ibn Gabirūl of Sarakotha . . . died . . . in the year 450," that is, between February, 1057, and February, 1058. Scholars accept the latter date because it is the most exact; moreover, whatever is reported regarding Ibn Gabirol after 1057/1058 seems to involve magic and fantasy: that he created a female golem out of wood, or that he was murdered in Valencia by a rival Arabic poet who hid Ibn Gabirol's body under a fig grove, and the deed was discovered when a tree began to produce miraculous fruit.

SIGNIFICANCE

Ibn Gabirol was the product of a sophisticated Arabic civilization that permitted intellectual and religious freedom. During its zenith, that society accepted Greek science and philosophy. The Iberian Jews not only adapted aspects of Arabic culture and learning but also began a renaissance of biblical studies. Ibn Gabirol was an extraordinary stylist in both Arabic and Hebrew. He helped fashion the philosophical vocabulary of Arabic and the sensual vocabulary of Hebrew. As the author of at least 175 religious and 146 secular poems in biblical Hebrew, he was known as the Nightingale; his philosophical works crossed sectarian lines. That the Muslim fundamentalists burned his manuscripts while the Jews rejected his philosophy and the Christians paid no attention to his poetry reflects the limitations of Muslim, Jewish, and Christian civilizations and not the genius of Ibn Gabirol.

—*J. Lee Shneidman*

FURTHER READING

Gilson, Étienne. *History of Christian Philosophy in the Middle Ages*. New York: Random House, 1955. A significant work, written by a leading Thomist who pays special attention to the Aristotelian aspects of Hebrew and Arabic philosophy but also includes a brief summary of Ibn Gabirol's Platonism and its impact on Christian thinkers.

Goldberg, Isaac, ed. and comp. *Solomon Ibn Gabirol: A Bibliography of His Poems in Translation*. Washington, D.C.: Word Works, 1998. A collection listing translations of Ibn Gabirol's poetry into more than a dozen languages, including English.

Husik, Isaac. *A History of Mediaeval Jewish Philosophy*. 1916. Reprint. New York: Atheneum, 1969. One of the earliest studies of the subject. Includes an excellent chapter on the development of Ibn Gabirol's philosophy and ethics. The section on ethics is perhaps one of the best available.

Ibn Gabirol. *Selected Poems of Solomon Ibn Gabirol*. Translated by Peter Cole. Princeton, N.J.: Princeton University Press, 2001. Part of the Lockert Library of Poetry in Translation series, this collection provides a selection of Ibn Gabirol's poems. Includes a bibliography and index.

Myer, Isaac. *Qabbalah*. 1888. Reprint. New York: Ktav Publishing House, 1970. Links Ibn Gabirol with the Kabbalists. The work is interesting, though quite speculative. Author's explanation of the drawings in Ibn Gabirol is significant.

Sarna, Nahum M. "Hebrew and Bible Studies in Medieval Spain." In *The Sephardi Heritage: Essays on the History and Cultural Contribution of the Jews of Spain and Portugal*, edited by R. D. Barnett. New York: Ktav Publishing House, 1971. An excellent study of the Hebrew renaissance in Muslim Iberia, placing Ibn Gabirol's work in the context of both that Hebrew renaissance and the dominant Arabic civilization.

Sirat, Colette. *A History of Jewish Philosophy in the Middle Ages*. New York: Cambridge University Press, 1985. The author examines the intellectual sources of Hebrew philosophy—the Bible, tradition, Aristotelianism, and Platonism—demonstrating how each of these helped shape emerging philosophical positions. One section details Ibn Gabirol's fusion of Hebrew religious thought with Neoplatonism.

Tanenbaum, Adena. *The Contemplative Soul: Hebrew Poetry and Philosophical Theory in Medieval Spain*. Boston: Brill, 2002. Presents a critical history of writing about the soul in Hebrew poetry and Jewish philosophy in Andalusian Spain, including the work of Ibn Gabirol. Provides an extensive bibliography and index.

SEE ALSO: Abū Ḥanīfah; Saint Albertus Magnus; Alhazen; Averroës; Roger Bacon; Saint Bonaventure; Fakhr al-Dīn al-Rāzī; al-Ḥallāj; Raymond Lull; Moses Maimonides; Moses de León; Naḥmanides; William of Auvergne.

RELATED ARTICLES in *Great Events from History: The Middle Ages, 477-1453*: April or May, 711: Ṭārik Crosses into Spain; 1031: Caliphate of Córdoba Falls; c. 1150: Moors Transmit Classical Philosophy and Medicine to Europe; 1190: Moses Maimonides Writes *The Guide of the Perplexed*; c. 1275: The *Zohar* Is Transcribed.

IBN KHALDŪN

Arab historian

Ibn Khaldūn formulated highly original and widely acclaimed theories on the rise and fall of empires and established himself as one of the most distinguished intellectual figures of Western Islam in the late Middle Ages.

BORN: May 27, 1332; Tunis (now in Tunisia)
DIED: March 17, 1406; Cairo, Egypt
ALSO KNOWN AS: Abū Zayd ʿAbd al-Raḥmān ibn Khaldūn (full name)
AREA OF ACHIEVEMENT: Historiography

EARLY LIFE

Abū Zayd ʿAbd al-Raḥmān Ibn Khaldūn (ihbn kahl-DOON) was born in North Africa to a respected family of Muslim public servants and intellectuals. The Khaldūn clan, believed to have resided in Andalusia, Spain, since the eighth century, had left the Iberian Peninsula and settled in Tunis shortly before the last stage of the Christian Reconquest of much of Muslim Andalusia in the mid-thirteenth century.

The successful advance of the Spanish Christian armies that displaced the Khaldūn family was one of many factors leading to political instability in the western Mediterranean, a situation that continued to characterize the area throughout Ibn Khaldūn's life. Centralized political power in the once extensive and glorious Islamic empire had disintegrated, leaving a collection of small, often poor kingdoms of indeterminate frontiers, constantly threatened from without and suffering from endemic political strife. Palace plots, court intrigues, political assassinations, armed revolts, and usurpations were commonplace.

The tumultuous career of Ibn Khaldūn must be understood in the political context of the period. Much of what is known about his career comes from his own autobiographical recollections, wherein the author candidly shares his failures as well as his triumphs. Expected to follow family tradition and pursue a career in learning and public service, Ibn Khaldūn received a classical education that included instruction in both religious and secular subjects. This dual orientation, and the conflict inherent in it, would be a permanent feature of Ibn Khaldūn's career and thought. He was schooled in the Qurʾān, Islamic law, and Arabic grammar, as well as in philology, poetry, logic, and philosophy. He received his first official appointment in 1352 at age twenty, when he was named sealbearer by the Ḥafṣid ruler of Tunis. His duty was to sign and seal the sultan's chancery documents. Ibn Khaldūn, however, soon became embroiled in the political maelstrom of the region, falling prey to his own restlessness and political ambitions.

After the defeat of the ruler of Tunis by the emir of Constantine, Ibn Khaldūn moved to Tilimsan, where he accepted the patronage of Sultan Abū ʿInān, who appointed him to a post similar to the one he had held in Tunis. In 1357, however, Ibn Khaldūn was discovered conspiring against his master and was kept in prison for nearly two years, gaining release after the sultan's death. When the Marīnid Abū Salim became ruler of Morocco—a development Ibn Khaldūn had supported—the ruler appointed the young scholar secretary of state and judge. Ibn Khaldūn occupied these positions until 1362, when palace intrigues led him to seek protection in the Nasrid kingdom of Granada, across the Strait of Gibraltar. His stay in Iberia was marred, however, by a growing rivalry with the Granadine prime minister Ibn al-Khaṭīb, leading Ibn Khaldūn to accept the opportunity to become prime minister in the court of the newly successful Ḥafṣid conqueror of Bejaia. Back in North Africa in 1365, Ibn Khaldūn combined his ministerial duties with writing and teaching jurisprudence. It was a prolific and relatively stable period of his life.

After his benefactor was defeated and killed—at the hands of a royal cousin—Ibn Khaldūn, who had initially welcomed the usurper and remained in his government, fell out of favor and left Bejaia to pursue a policy hostile to the ruler. After changing political sides several times, Ibn Khaldūn decided in 1375 to retire from public life, at least temporarily, in order to devote himself to writing. He settled among nomadic tribes, where he composed the first drafts of his most important historical works. Growing tired of isolation after four years, he sought to return to a more active life in his home city of Tunis.

LIFE'S WORK

When, at age forty-four, Ibn Khaldūn abandoned his political career to live among the nomads to reflect and write, he was motivated by a desire to understand and reconcile the conflict he had experienced between spiritual demands and political realities. He also wished to understand the social milieu of various periods in the past, an interest that led him to the study of history. His approach to the past, his emphasis on the role of social causation in particular, sets him apart from traditional historians. Ibn Khaldūn perceived the writing of history as requiring two separate, and innovative, steps. The first was to ascertain the truth of a particular event; this step would be accomplished through the verification of all facts related to the event. The second was to understand the event as the logical outcome of the interplay of forces within the society in which it occurred. Pursuing this dual approach, Ibn Khaldūn attempted to discover the value system of a particular society, to extract its first principles, believing that these were responsible for historical change. He was interested first and foremost in the Islamic world, the world with which he was most familiar. He examined the growth and development of Islam through the centuries in order to formulate a theory that would explain the rise and decline not only of the powerful Islamic state but also that of all great empires through the ages. His observations were recorded in *Muqaddimah* (1375-1379; *The Muqaddimah*, 1958), a work that outlines the principles of what Ibn Khaldūn called the "science of human association," a discipline he believed to be totally new.

The low ebb of Islam during Ibn Khaldūn's lifetime, the fourteenth century, attributed by traditionalists to society's abandonment of the original Islamic ideals, was perceived rather differently by Ibn Khaldūn. He viewed all historical events as a natural—and entirely nonspiritual—process resulting from history's own dynamics. While Ibn Khaldūn believed that Allāh, omniscient and omnipresent, was behind all change, he dismissed as hypocritical those traditionalists who embraced an idealistic thought-style, insisting on the primacy of the spiritual in the material world. Truly pious men, Ibn Khaldūn argued, would retire from this world to devote themselves to worship; they would not meddle in the affairs of society, because the spiritual and the secular have different spheres. Even the Prophet Muḥammad himself, according to Ibn Khaldūn, operated within a particular social system, achieving his sacred mission within the limits set by the system's rules.

Rather than appealing to spiritual causation, Ibn Khaldūn believed that societies are controlled by forces generated from inside the sociopolitical group. Man, he stated, is a social being who seeks naturally to associate with others and form a community. What follows is the emergence of a leader who gives cohesiveness to the group, nurturing the growth of an essential quality known as *ʿaṣabīyah*, or group spirit. It is the degree of *ʿaṣabīyah* present in a society at a particular point in its history that determines its success. Change comes about when local chieftains, backed by their group's high level of *ʿaṣabīyah*, attack neighboring tribes, grow, and eventually establish a dynasty. Larger populations in turn lead to the founding of cities, greater prosperity, division of labor, capital accumulation, and the flourishing of arts and crafts. Larger populations also make possible the creation of empires.

Furthermore, while civilization (here contrasted to the primitive existence of nomadic tribes, described as illiterate and violent) can only exist under the auspices of an empire, it also contains the seeds of its own destruction. *ʿAṣabīyah* weakens with the passage of time, and the vigor and energy that made for successful conquest give way to vice and moral laxity. Dynasties also founder; by their fourth generation, qualities of leadership among the rulers have usually dissipated and have been replaced by a desire to dominate others. Empires thus weakened become the target of fierce and ambitious new groups and are eventually defeated by them, and a new historical cycle is ready to begin.

History, then, argues Ibn Khaldūn, is the rise and fall of empires resulting from the inevitable clash between civilization and nomadism. This process, although essentially cyclical in structure, is not repetitive in its outcome; it builds on itself. Each new empire does not reject the accomplishments of the one it replaces; instead, it absorbs and integrates many of those qualities and uses them to refine its own institutions and values. Something new and different is thus created. Furthermore, a new empire, at least during its formative years, promotes novel forms of cultural and artistic expression and represents an unequaled opportunity for religious and moral renewal.

Perhaps in search of his own moral renewal, Ibn Khaldūn left Tunis in 1382 to make a pilgrimage to Mecca. En route, however, he stopped in Cairo and was prevailed on to stay there. His family, traveling from Tunis to join him, died in a shipwreck in 1384. During his time in Cairo, Ibn Khaldūn devoted himself to preaching, teaching, writing, and carrying out the duties of a Malikite judge. Although he believed that during this stage of his career he had comported himself with the utmost honesty, he was unable to escape censure. He died in 1406, shortly after being named judge for the sixth time, and was buried in a Cairo cemetery.

SIGNIFICANCE

Ibn Khaldūn's views of the historical process emphasize the temporal over the spiritual and employ a relativist, nonabsolutist interpretation of Islamic principles. A case in point is the interpretation of the traditional dictum, traced to the Prophet Muḥammad himself, that a caliph must be from the tribe of Quraysh. Since there were no survivors of this group by Ibn Khaldūn's time, a fact ignored by traditionalists, Ibn Khaldūn argued that the reason that the Prophet had chosen the Quraysh was that this tribe was the strongest in Arabia during his lifetime. As conditions had changed markedly in the intervening seven hundred years, argued Ibn Khaldūn, the caliph should come from a tribe whose present qualities of strength most resembled the Prophet's original choice. In this instance, as in countless others, Ibn Khaldūn proposed a temporal and revisionist interpretation of the tradition and sayings of the Prophet.

The ambitious and universal qualities of Ibn Khaldūn's quest for the causes of historical change have contributed to making *The Muqaddimah* a document of importance for several disciplines; the text has been adopted by sociologists, economists, and historians as a meaningful statement and antecedent of their own methodology. Through the centuries, the work has been used to support a wide array of ideologies, ranging from orthodox Marxism to supply-side economics.

—*Clara Estow*

FURTHER READING

Ahmad, Zaid. *The Epistemology of Ibn Khaldūn*. New York: Routledge, 2003. Analytical approach to Khaldūn's epistemology, with a close examination of chapter 6 of the *Muqaddimah*, in which Khaldūn sketches his thoughts on the relationship and usefulness of science to human civilization.

Azmeh, Aziz al-. *Ibn Khaldūn: An Essay in Reinterpretation*. 1981. Reprint. New York: Central European University Press, 2003. One of the foremost authorities on Ibn Khaldūn reexamines the *Muqaddimah*. Aims both to inform the reader concerning the most distinguished and innovative elements of Ibn Khaldūn's work and to reclaim (and rescue) Ibn Khaldūn from thinkers in numerous disciplines who over the centuries have misappropriated his thoughts and misapplied his ideas. Includes a detailed bibliography of works on Ibn Khaldūn in various languages.

Brett, Michael. *Ibn Khaldūn and the Medieval Maghrib*. Brookfield, Vt.: Ashgate/Variorum, 1999. Brett, who sees his work as revising French colonial scholarship, approaches Islamization, Arabization, and urbanization through the prism of Ibn Khaldūn, seeing Islamization as a process of colonization through trade and conversion, not conquest. Index, map.

Enan, M. A. *Ibn Khaldūn: His Life and Work*. Lahore, India: Sh. Muhammad Ashraf, 1941. The first biography in English of the great historian and philosopher of Islam. Compares Khaldūn's thought with that of later scholars and philosophers using accessible language. Based on original sources.

Fischel, J. Walter. *Ibn Khaldūn in Egypt*. Berkeley: University of California Press, 1967. Fischel, a well-known student of Islamic culture, appraises Ibn Khaldūn's contribution to the field of historiography, exploring the historian's years in Egypt and the Egyptian influence in Ibn Khaldūn's works.

Lacoste, Yves. *Ibn Khaldūn: The Birth of History and the Past of the Third World*. Translated by David Macey. London: Verso Editions, 1984. An eminent geographer explores ways to apply Ibn Khaldūn's analysis of the complex forces operating in fourteenth century North Africa to modern problems of underdevelopment in the Third World. Lacoste considers the *Muqaddimah* as the outcome of Ibn Khaldūn's struggle to reconcile rationalism and mystical tendencies both in his own thought and in the society in which he lived.

Lawrence, Bruce B., ed. *Ibn Khaldūn and Islamic Ideology*. Leiden, the Netherlands: E. J. Brill, 1984. A collection of articles from a symposium at Duke University to commemorate the 650th anniversary of Ibn Khaldūn's birth. In "Ibn Khaldūn and His Time," Franz Rosenthal argues against efforts to view Ibn Khaldūn as a forerunner of subsequent ideologies. What is of interest, Rosenthal asserts, is the man Ibn Khaldūn in relation to his times. Other noteworthy articles in this volume explore such topics as the literary merits of *The Muqaddimah*, Ibn Khaldūn's attitude toward Jewish history, and the impact of his ideas on Islamic society.

Mahdi, Muhsin. *Ibn Khaldūn's Philosophy of History*. Chicago: University of Chicago Press, 1964. Examines the philosophical principles on which Ibn Khaldūn's new science of culture is based to demonstrate that he ultimately relied on philosophical principles to explain history. Rejects the efforts of commentators who attempt to show that Ibn Khaldūn should be considered the father of the modern social sciences.

Rosenthal, Franz. Introduction to *The Muqaddimah: An Introduction to History*, by Ibn Khaldūn. Rev. ed. 3 vols. Princeton, N.J.: Princeton University Press, 1967. A complete English translation. Rosenthal introduces the first volume with a long and informative section on the life and work of Ibn Khaldūn and

the many factors that might have influenced his views.
Simon, Róbert. *Ibn Khaldūn: History as Science and the Patrimonial Empire*. Translated by Klara Pogatsa. Budapest: Akadémiai Kiadó, 2002. Examines Khaldūn's epistemology as it informs his concept of human social organization.

SEE ALSO: ʿAbd al-Muʾmin; Hārūn al-Rashīd; al-Masʿūdī; Mansa Mūsā; Tamerlane.

RELATED ARTICLES in *Great Events from History: The Middle Ages, 477-1453*: 1325-1355: Travels of Ibn Baṭṭūṭah; 1340: Al-ʿUmarī Writes a History of Africa; 1377: Ibn Khaldūn Completes His *Muqaddimah.*

AL-IDRĪSĪ

Arab geographer and cartographer

A world traveler, al-Idrīsī eventually collaborated with the Norman king of Sicily, Roger II, to produce a major geography and several significant maps of the medieval world. For more than five hundred years, these works served as models for productions in the field.

BORN: 1100; Sebta, Morocco (now Ceuta, Spain)
DIED: Between 1164 and 1166; near Sebta, Morocco
ALSO KNOWN AS: Edrisi; Abū ʿAbd Allāh Muḥammad ibn Muḥammad ʿAbd Allāh ibn Idrīs al-Ḥammūdī al-Ḥasanī al-Idrīsī (full name)
AREAS OF ACHIEVEMENT: Geography, cartography

EARLY LIFE

Al-Idrīsī (al ih-DREE-sih) was born in 1100 in Sebta, now the Spanish enclave Ceuta, in Morocco. He was a Shīʿite Muslim, descended from the Prophet Muḥammad, of the noble house of Alavi Idrīsīs, claimants to the caliphate. His family had migrated from Málaga and Algeciras in Spain to Sabtah and Tangier in the eleventh century, and al-Idrīsī studied in Córdoba, the capital of Islamic Spain.

Al-Idrīsī was a student of medicine, a poet, a world traveler, and a merchant-adventurer. His wanderings, which began at age sixteen, eventually took him on the routes of many of the historic Muslim conquests. He traveled far and wide across much of the known world—west to Madeira and the Canary Islands, north to France and England, and east to Asia Minor and Central Asia—and meticulously gathered information along the way about what he saw and what lay beyond.

A natural curiosity about the world, along with the wealth and freedom to satisfy it, was probably the principal motivation behind these journeys. Al-Idrīsī's identity as a great noble and a descendant of Muḥammad periodically put his life in danger from assassins hired by rival Islamic noble houses or religious factions. This ever-present danger probably kept him on the move. Whatever the cause of his wanderings, they gradually gained for him the reputation of a worldly wise and learned man. Under the pretext of offering him protection from his enemies, but probably because of his growing fame as a scholar and traveler, in 1140 the Norman Christian king of Sicily, Roger II, invited al-Idrīsī to join his court. Al-Idrīsī's acceptance of the offer led to a twenty-year stay at the Sicilian court and initiated a fifteen-year geographic and cartographic collaboration with Roger.

LIFE'S WORK

Sicily had been granted to Roger II and the Normans under the Treaty of Saint-Germain in 1139, and he promptly made Palermo his capital. Before the coming of the Normans, Palermo also had been the capital of Islamic Sicily. During the Middle Ages, under both the Muslims and the Normans, Palermo was a major crossroads of the Mediterranean world. It was a traditional meeting place for sailors, merchants, pilgrims, Crusaders, scholars, adventurers, and other travelers.

During Roger's reign, Palermo also became an intellectual center of medieval Europe. He was interested in fostering learning of any kind, and he was generous with his patronage. Perhaps for pragmatic reasons of expansionism and trade, Roger was devoted to geography. Undoubtedly, he believed that al-Idrīsī's princely status might help him further his own political aims. In any case, he seems to have been dissatisfied with the existing Arabic and Greek works on geography and cartography—one of the major reasons for the summons to al-Idrīsī.

At Roger's court, al-Idrīsī was honored as a noble, scholar, and traveler, and it was there that his real fame as a geographer and cartographer came. During the fifteen years of their collaboration, al-Idrīsī produced a celestial globe, a disk-shaped 1.5-by-3.5-meter (5-by-11.5-foot) tablet map of the known world, and many other maps. The globe and the world map were made of solid silver, weighing 450 Roman pounds. The globe and map in turn were based on al-Idrīsī's encyclopedic geography, *Kitāb nuzhat al-mushtāq fī ikhtirāq al-āfāq* (1154; the pleasure excursion of one who is eager to traverse the regions of the world; also known as *Kitāb ar-Rujārī*, literally "book of Roger"), which was completed under Roger's patronage. The world map and presumably also the globe fell into the hands of a mob in 1160 and were smashed, but many of the seventy manuscript maps made by al-Idrīsī from the world map shortly before Roger's death in 1154 luckily survived. Sadly, no complete version of *Kitāb ar-Rujārī* survives in any language. It first appeared in the West in Rome in an abridged version in 1592 and was translated into Latin in Paris in 1619, but no full translation into English ever has been made.

After the death of Roger, al-Idrīsī continued to work for his son and successor, King William I (William the Bad), and wrote another geographic treatise. No complete version of this second book survives either, but a shortened version, a seventy-three-map atlas, remains. In about 1160, al-Idrīsī left Sicily for his native Morocco to live out his life, where sometime between 1164 and 1166 he died, probably near Sabtah.

Al-Idrīsī's great world map was a monument to medieval Islamic geography and cartography, but today it exists only in several reconstructions created by scholars from the surviving fragments of his works. It was divided into seven horizontal climatic zones (probably derived from the classical Greco-Roman worldview and the works of Ptolemy), each divided vertically into eleven sections to create a primitive grid, a system of longitude and latitude for more accurate place location. The map also contained a wealth of information, an abundance of detail, and a degree of clarity rarely achieved previously. It was most accurate for the Mediterranean region; perhaps understandably, Sicily is shown as an exceptionally large island. Its accuracy and detail also extended elsewhere. For example, al-Idrīsī showed the source of the Nile River as an unnamed lake in Central Africa. Yet, while his maps were drawn very correctly for the time, they were not drawn mathematically.

On al-Idrīsī's world map, the Islamic and Norman worlds were joined. In preparation for the creation of al-Idrīsī's maps and geographies, Roger had sent out reliable agents and draftsmen to collect data from many lands. Al-Idrīsī relied heavily on classic Muslim sources, such as the works of al-Khwarizmi and al-Masʿūdī, and classic Greek, Roman, and Hellenistic sources, such as the works of Ptolemy, the father of modern geography and cartography. Al-Idrīsī's grid system (but not his projections) probably was based on those of Ptolemy and a copy of Ptolemy's altered version of the world map of Marinus of Tyre. As his great world map demonstrates, however, al-Idrīsī was often much more than a mere modifier of Ptolemy. Al-Idrīsī also utilized Indian astronomical studies. Yet, perhaps most important, he relied heavily on his recollections of his own journeys and those of other travelers for reliable information.

Significance

Al-Idrīsī's work was far more influential than Ptolemy's in the East, but less so in Europe. Still, his maps opened European eyes to some of what the Muslims knew about Africa and Asia in the Middle Ages. Perhaps because he spent much of his adult life in the service of the Christian kings of Sicily, for centuries—even into the twentieth century—al-Idrīsī and his achievements were ignored by Muslim scholars. In so doing, they deprived their Western counterparts of a fuller understanding of him as well. Only recently has al-Idrīsī's full impact begun to be realized, especially within the context of the study of the history of science and the history of cartography.

In short, al-Idrīsī represents by far the best example of Islamic-Christian scientific collaboration in the Middle Ages in geography. *Kitāb ar-Rujārī* was the most important geographic work of the period, and in its various forms it served as a major European and Muslim textbook for several centuries. Maps clearly based on those of al-Idrīsī were produced well into the seventeenth century. He applied scientific methodology and precision to the heretofore largely imaginative arts of geography and cartography. Al-Idrīsī truly deserved the epithet "Strabo of the Arabs," which was applied to him in his own lifetime.

—*Dennis Reinhartz*

Further Reading

Badeau, John S., et al., eds. *The Genius of Arab Civilization: Source of Renaissance*. New York: New York University Press, 1975. 2d ed. Cambridge, Mass.: MIT Press, 1983. Contains a relatively brief but significant factual account of al-Idrīsī and his work by Florence Amzallag Tatistcheff, putting them into perspective with the broader medieval Arab achievement. Plate of one map.

Bagrow, Leo, and R. A. Skelton. *History of Cartography*. Cambridge, Mass.: Harvard University Press, 1964. 2d ed. Chicago: Precedent, 1985. Contains a brief section on al-Idrīsī and his work which only begins to put him into perspective in the history of cartography. Plates of four maps.

Curtis, Edmund. *Roger of Sicily and the Normans in Lower Italy, 1016-1154*. New York: G. P. Putnam's Sons, 1912. A very good biography of the much-neglected King Roger II, containing a significant section on his collaboration with al-Idrīsī. Includes extensive excerpts from al-Idrīsī's works.

Lock, C. B. Muriel. *Geography and Cartography: A Reference Handbook*. Hamden, Conn.: Linnet Books, 1976. Contains an entry on al-Idrīsī. Especially helpful with regard to some of the various abridgments and other editions of his now-classic works.

SEE ALSO: ʿAbd al-Muʾmin; Benjamin of Tudela; Ibn Baṭṭūṭah; Marco Polo; William of Rubrouck; Zheng He.

RELATED ARTICLES in *Great Events from History: The Middle Ages, 477-1453*: 1271-1295: Travels of Marco Polo; 1325-1355: Travels of Ibn Baṭṭūṭah; 1377: Ibn Khaldūn Completes His *Muqaddimah*; 1405-1433: Zheng He's Naval Expeditions; 1415-1460: Prince Henry the Navigator Promotes Portuguese Exploration.

INNOCENT III

Italian pope (1198-1216)

At a period of crisis in the Catholic church, Pope Innocent III succeeded in affirming the power of his office against challenges from powerful lay rulers and from the Albigensian heresy, and in so doing became the most powerful pope of the Middle Ages. Through sweeping ecclesiastical reform, he also attempted to mute the arguments of the critics of an increasingly venal, poorly educated, and self-indulgent clergy.

BORN: 1160 or 1161; Anagni, the Roman Campagna, Papal States (now in Italy)

DIED: July 16, 1216; Perugia (now in Italy)

ALSO KNOWN AS: Lothario of Segni (given name); Lotario di Segni; Lotario de Conti; Giovanni Lotario, comte de Segni

AREAS OF ACHIEVEMENT: Religion and theology, government and politics

EARLY LIFE

The future Pope Innocent III was born Lothario of Segni at Anagni, in the Roman Campagna, the son of Trasmondo of Segni and Claricia, née Scotti, both members of prominent Roman aristocratic families. Occasionally one encounters the surname of Conti for Lothario. This name, Italian for "count," was assumed by the family after Innocent III's pontificate. It was one of the most powerful Roman families and furnished several popes to the Church in the thirteenth century. The surviving fragment of a mosaic and a painting of Innocent III confirm that he was short of stature, with a round face, high-arched eyebrows, a straight nose, and a small mouth. Contemporaries also noted his ability to express himself verbally in an incisive fashion and a well-modulated voice that commanded the attention of his audience.

The young Lothario, who was vowed to the clergy, was able to indulge an appetite for learning that he exhibited at an early age. He first studied at Rome under Peter Ismael, whom, in recognition, he later named bishop of Sutri. His happiest years, according to his later testimony, were spent at the University of Paris, where he studied theology under Peter of Corbeil, whom he later rewarded with two high ecclesiastical appointments. Innocent always retained a great affection for France and its people. After his time in Paris, he studied civil and canon law, two subjects in which he excelled, at the University of Bologna, mainly under the great canonist Huguccio of Pisa. Lothario did not forget his teacher and companions at Bologna when he became pope. Huguccio became bishop of Ferrara, and Lothario's fellow students and companions were awarded other important posts in the Church. Lothario's studies in theology and the civil and canon law were to prepare him well for his later pontificate.

On completion of his studies at Bologna, Lothario returned to Rome, where his education, family contacts, and relationship with several cardinals assured his rapid advance as a cleric. In 1187, Pope Gregory VIII ordained him subdeacon. In 1189 or 1190, Pope Clement III made him cardinal deacon of the Church of Saint Sergius and Saint Bacchus in the Roman forum, where he served during the pontificate of Celestine III. His years there were devoted to the reconstruction and embellishing of his church building and, most important, to writing. While wisely maintaining a distance from the machinations and intrigues of the Papal Curia (the administrative office of the Church), Lothario composed several theological treatises, including *De contemptu mundi* (*The Mirror of Mans Lyfe*, 1580; also as *De miseria conditionis huma-*

Pope Innocent III. (Library of Congress)

nae; *On the Misery of the Human Condition*, 1978) and *De sacro alteris mysterio* (the sacred mystery of the altar). These works contributed to his growing prestige as a theologian, moralist, and writer and undoubtedly had something to do with his election as pope at the very young age of thirty-seven.

On the death of the nonagenarian Celestine III on January 8, 1198, several candidates were nominated to succeed him. The new pope was elected on the same day on the second ballot. Although Lothario received the greatest number of votes on the first ballot, concern over his youth necessitated a second. His learning, unquestionable morality, and vigor, however, overcame initial concerns about his age. Lothario of Segni was elected by a unanimous vote and ascended the papal throne as Innocent III.

Life's Work

Innocent became pope at a crucial time in European history. The institutions of manorialism and feudalism were succumbing to the economic and political forces of the growth of towns and a new merchant class and of monarchs bent on creating centralized territorial states. The secular authority of the pope was being challenged by ambitious rulers, and the Church itself, and especially the clergy, increasingly came under attack from critics attracted to various heresies. In addition, the Muslims retained control over Jerusalem and the Holy Places. From the first day of his reign, Innocent recognized the necessity for strong papal leadership and immediately laid claim to broad powers in the exercise of his authority over ecclesiastical government and, as vicar of Christ, over temporal affairs having a bearing on the Church's well-being.

Innocent has been accused by some historians of selfish and excessive ambition because of his attempt to exercise power over European lay rulers. Indeed, the pope did devote considerable time to diplomatic and political matters, and he did not hesitate to use the powers of his office to force obedience. His actions were motivated, however, by his sincere conviction that spiritual issues were at stake and that Christian unity and tranquillity necessitated recognition of the pope's supremacy as ruler and judge throughout the Christian world. Although Innocent intervened in the affairs of numerous European kingdoms, including Portugal, Aragon, Castile, Hungary, and Poland, his interventions in the Holy Roman Empire, England, and France most clearly illustrate his motives.

Innocent intervened first in the Holy Roman Empire over the election of the emperor, and he was to remain involved there during almost all of his pontificate because of a series of complex events. The emperor, Henry VI, who had extended his control over a large part of the Papal States and over Sicily, died a few months before Innocent's election. The electors split over two claimants to the imperial title, while ignoring Henry's young son, Frederick II of Sicily. Frederick, who as king of Sicily was a vassal of the pope, became Innocent's ward. Innocent intervened in the disputed election for two reasons. First, he wanted to separate Sicily from the imperial holdings and to reassert control over the Papal States. Second, he claimed special rights within the empire dating to the papal coronation of Charlemagne in 800. Innocent interpreted this event as a transfer of power from the Eastern Roman Empire (Byzantine Empire) to the West by papal authority. He asserted, therefore, that, although the princes of the Holy Roman Empire had the right to elect, their choice was subject to papal confirmation and that he should be the sole arbiter in a disputed election. Following a lengthy civil war, Innocent finally secured the election of his choice, Otto IV, whom he crowned in 1209. Otto, however, failed to keep his promise to restore the papal lands to the Church and even laid plans to invade Sicily. Innocent promptly excommunicated him and declared him deprived of the imperial title. Innocent then threw his support to Frederick II in return for his promise to separate the administration of Sicily from his German holdings and to undertake a crusade to the Holy Land. Frederick was crowned in 1220. Innocent had effectively asserted papal power against disobedient lay rulers and had, at least temporarily, restored tranquillity to a war-torn Europe. In addition, papal lands that had been lost earlier were restored.

Although Innocent found himself at odds on several occasions with his most troublesome lay adversary, King John of England, the bitterest and longest dispute was over the election of the primate of the English church, the archbishop of Canterbury, following the death, in 1205, of Archbishop Hubert Walter. Ultimately, two archbishops were elected: the choice of a group of monks of the cathedral chapter and the king's choice, a subservient courtier and civil servant, John de Grey, archbishop of Norwich. Innocent rejected both claimants. He offered his own candidate, the English scholar and ecclesiastical statesman Stephen Langton. Despite John's opposition, Innocent consecrated Langton as archbishop of Canterbury and gave him the *pallium*, the symbol of his office, in June, 1207. John's rejection of Langton led to a long and complicated struggle between king and pope. In March, 1208, Innocent placed England under an interdict—a territorial excommunication that denied some of the sacraments to John's subjects. John responded by seizing all Church properties in England and collecting the revenues they provided. In November, 1209, the pope excommunicated the king. The conflict was not resolved, however, until 1213, when, under the threat of an invasion of England by Philip Augustus (Philip II of France), John gave in. He agreed to accept Langton, to return church properties, and to repay the revenues he had collected from them since the imposition of the interdict (this last promise, however, he failed to keep). John further agreed to recognize the pope as his feudal lord and to receive his kingdom back as a fief from the Papacy. Thus, Innocent had used the powers of his office to force lay obedience and to secure recognition of the best candidate for England's highest ecclesiastical office.

Innocent also intervened in France, in the domestic problems of Philip II. In 1193, Philip had married a Danish princess, Ingeborg, for money and political expediency. Tiring of his queen, Philip forced a group of French prelates to annul the marriage on the totally insupportable grounds of consanguinity. Ingeborg and her Danish relatives appealed to the pope, and Celestine III voided the annulment. Philip, however, ignored the pope and, in 1196, married Agnes, the daughter of a Bavarian nobleman. On his accession, Innocent quickly intervened. He sent a legate to persuade the king, under threat of an interdict, to accept Celestine's prohibition and recognize Ingeborg. Philip refused to yield, and the interdict was imposed in January, 1200. Six months later, however, Agnes died, the king submitted, and the interdict was removed. Philip, however, expressed his intention of reopening the case and did not formally restore Ingeborg as queen until 1213. Nevertheless, Innocent had won on an issue directly related to the spiritual authority of the pope and the Church: the sacrament of marriage.

Innocent was also committed to asserting the power of the Church against the twin threats of heresy and Islam. The Catharists (Albigensians), a heretical sect that had its origins in one of Christianity's early competitors in the Roman Empire, Manichaeanism, enjoyed great popularity in areas of southern France. Rejecting the organization of the Catholic Church and its sacramental system, the Cathari posed a significant, though localized, threat to the pope's authority. Accordingly, in 1208, Innocent called knights of northern France to embark on a crusade against the Cathari. The pope, whose intention had been to convert the heretics, was soon grieved to find his religious crusade degenerating into a bloody war of territorial conquest; he did not foresee the brutality of the Inquisition, established by his successor, which resulted in the total extirpation of the heresy.

Earlier, in 1202, Innocent had preached a crusade (the Fourth Crusade) to capture Jerusalem and the Holy Places from the Muslims. This undertaking, to the pope's disappointment, was diverted from its goal by the selfish interests of the Crusaders, especially the Venetians, who instead took Constantinople. Innocent was preparing to launch a new crusade against the Muslims at the time of his death.

Innocent's greatest and most enduring achievement, and the one in which he took greatest interest and pride, was in the sphere of ecclesiastical reform. Aware of the inroads of heresy that had gained impetus from the Church's failure to define its doctrines and discipline its clergy, Innocent convoked the Fourth Lateran Council of the Church in 1215. In attendance were more than four hundred bishops, eight hundred abbots, and representatives of all major European rulers. The council enacted extensive reform legislation. The main tenets of Catholicism were restated, and the seven sacraments were defined. The doctrine of transubstantiation, which enhanced the role of the clergy as joint participants in the miracle of transforming the bread and wine into the body and blood of Christ, was affirmed. In addition, Catholics were required to confess their sins annually to a priest. Clerical participation in judicial ordeals was prohibited, thus requiring secular courts to devise more rational methods of determining guilt. Vacant bishoprics were to be filled within three months, and in every church province an episcopal council was to meet yearly to discipline its wayward members. Steps were taken to improve clerical morality. Celibacy and sobriety were encouraged, and gambling, hunting, engaging in trade, frequenting taverns, and the wearing of flashy, ornate clothing were forbidden. In addition, clergymen were not to hold more than one benefice in which they were required to exercise pastoral responsibilities.

The work of the council, which owed its inspiration directly to Innocent, went far, at least temporarily, in muting criticisms of the Church. An unfortunate decree of the council, however, was that Jews should be distinguished as outcasts by being required to wear a yellow label. This was an affirmation of Innocent's earlier advocacy of the ghettoization of the Jews. The Fourth Lateran Council marks the culmination of the papacy of Innocent III. He died suddenly in Perugia, on July 16, 1216, probably from malaria.

Significance

Innocent III is perhaps the most controversial figure in the history of the Papacy. His exercise of the authority of his office, which he, as vicar of Christ, regarded as all-encompassing, often involved him in temporal matters. Some historians have argued, therefore, that he was more concerned with enhancing the temporal authority of the Papacy than in fulfilling the spiritual and pastoral duties of his office. Others, however, have argued that Innocent regarded his intervention in temporal affairs as an extension of his spiritual duties. His interventions were motivated by moral concerns—his desire to punish sin or to prevent its commission.

Indisputably, Innocent became pope at a period of crisis in the Church and succeeded in effectively asserting the powers of his office and transforming the Church into the most powerful and respected institution in Europe. His program of ecclesiastical reform, reflected in the work of the Fourth Lateran Council, had it been implemented more thoroughly, might have helped the Church to avoid the divisions and corruption of the succeeding centuries that led ultimately to the Protestant Reformation and the division of Western Christendom, the unity of which Innocent had labored to ensure.

—*J. Stewart Alverson*

Further Reading

Bolton, Brenda. *Studies on Papal Authority and Pastoral Care*. Brookfield, Vt.: Variorum, 1995. Bolton aims to restore to Pope Innocent III some of the respect of which later generations have deprived him because of contradictory political evidence. By means of a very comprehensive analysis of the Pope's sermons and documents about his personal lifestyle, she argues that Innocent III possessed exceptional spirituality and excelled in the performance of his duties as bishop of Rome and head of the Church.

Moore, John C. *Pope Innocent III: To Root Up and to Plant*. Boston: Brill, 2003. A biography of Pope Innocent III by a noted scholar. Bibliography and index.

Moore, John C., Brenda Bolton, et al., eds. *Pope Innocent and His World*. Brookfield, Vt.: Ashgate, 1999. A collection of papers presented at a conference on Pope Innocent III at Hofstra University. Bibliography and index.

Powell, James M., ed. *Innocent III: Vicar of Christ or Lord of the World?* 2d ed. Washington, D.C.: Catholic University of America Press, 1994. The book is a compilation of works, representing two conflicting views on Innocent and the Papacy: the spiritual perspective and the political perspective. The essays add insight to the controversial question of the extension of Innocent's papal authority into secular matters and whether it brought about the decline of power following the rule of Innocent IV. The book also discusses certain issues of monastic reform.

Sayers, Jane. *Innocent III: Leader of Europe, 1198-1216*. New York: Longman, 1994. Sayers analyzes the way Innocent III's authority operated, as well as how his subjects reacted to his rule. She discusses at length the intellectual and psychological formation that gave Innocent his interest in pastoral work and law. Emphasizing the role of tradition, Sayers illustrates that because of the spiritual and legal characteristics of his office, the Pope was not a free agent.

See also: Saint Albertus Magnus; Saint Dominic; Saint Francis of Assisi; Frederick II; Gregory VII; Gregory IX; Innocent IV; James I the Conqueror; King John; Philip II; Valdemar II; William of Moerbeke.

RELATED ARTICLES in *Great Events from History: The Middle Ages, 477-1453*: 963: Foundation of the Mount Athos Monasteries; 1048: Zīrids Break from Fāṭimid Dynasty and Revive Sunni Islam; 1100-1300: European Universities Emerge; c. 1175: Waldensian Excommunications Usher in Protestant Movement; April 16, 1209: Founding of the Franciscans; 1209-1229: Albigensian Crusade; 1212: Children's Crusade; July 27, 1214: Battle of Bouvines; June 15, 1215: Signing of the Magna Carta; November 11-30, 1215: Fourth Lateran Council; 1217-1221: Fifth Crusade; 1227-1230: Frederick II Leads the Sixth Crusade; 1233: Papal Inquisition.

INNOCENT IV

Italian pope (1243-1254)

Throughout his pontificate, Innocent IV defended the temporal and spiritual authority of the Papacy and upheld its supremacy over secular rulers.

BORN: c. 1180; Genoa (now in Italy)
DIED: December 7, 1254; Naples (now in Italy)
ALSO KNOWN AS: Sinibaldo Fieschi (given name)
AREAS OF ACHIEVEMENT: Religion and theology, government and politics

EARLY LIFE

Sinibaldo Fieschi, who would later take the name Innocent IV, was the sixth son of ten children of Hugo, count of Lavagna, in northern Italy. The family was well connected in political and ecclesiastical circles, especially in Genoa, where Sinibaldo was born. During the bitter and recurring struggles between the Holy Roman Emperors and the pope, the Fieschi were generally regarded as being proimperial—an ironic situation in the light of Sinibaldo's later actions as pope.

Fieschi was an exceptionally intelligent and gifted young man who showed particular aptitude for the law, especially church or canon law. He studied at Parma under his uncle, a bishop, and then at Bologna, where he became a master of canon law. He served as the canon at the cathedral in Genoa and then at Parma before being named bishop of Albenga in 1225.

During the papacy of Honorius III (1216-1227), Fieschi was summoned to Rome to serve the pope. The next pontiff, Gregory IX (1227-1241), appointed Fieschi as his vice chancellor and elevated him to the position of cardinal priest of Saint Lawrence in Lucina.

Fieschi's activities as jurist and diplomat were recognized by Gregory, himself a strong and able administrator. From 1235 through 1240, Fieschi was governor of the March of Ancona, part of the secular territory under the rule of the Papacy. There he demonstrated his tough, realistic approach to government and politics, a foreshadowing of his later actions as pope.

During this time, Gregory IX and the Holy Roman Emperor, Frederick II of Sicily (r. 1220-1250), were engaged in a deadly contest for supreme power, Frederick pointing to the precedent of the ancient empire, the pope claiming supreme authority through apostolic succession. On the death of Gregory in 1241, Frederick seized a number of cardinals, hoping to force them into electing a pope favorable to him. Their choice, Celestine IV, ruled for only seventeen days in 1241, and there followed an interregnum of almost two years. Finally, enough cardinals escaped from Frederick's control to hold a new election; their choice was Sinibaldo Fieschi, who was elected on June 25, 1243.

The new pope took the name Innocent IV, which was a telling choice because the last pope to use that name, Innocent III, had brought the power of the Papacy to its greatest height, both spiritually and temporally. His successor was determined to do the same; this meant inevitable conflict with Frederick II.

The surviving portraits of Innocent IV show a clean-shaven, rather full-faced man with dark, intelligent eyes and a determined set to his mouth. Among his contemporaries, he was noted for his intelligence, learning, and tenacity. He was attuned to the practical and administrative, rather than the spiritual or mystical, but was still a friend and protector of Saint Francis of Assisi. His overriding concern was to maintain the supreme position of the Church.

LIFE'S WORK

Frederick and Gregory had long been engaged in open hostilities, and the emperor hoped that Innocent would be more favorably disposed to his cause. Very soon after Innocent came to the papal throne, however, he made it clear that he would continue Gregory's policies of maintaining the supremacy of the Church.

The relationship between Innocent and Frederick quickly deteriorated, and within months of the election, they were virtually at war. Repeated attempts at negotiation broke down, and in 1244, Frederick advanced on Rome hoping to take the pope hostage. Innocent slipped out of the city on June 28, 1244, and fled to Genoa with a number of his cardinals. In December, they moved to Lyon, technically a part of the empire, but actually ruled by its archbishop and protected by the French, who were officially neutral but favored the cause of the pope. Innocent thus became the first pope to receive official asylum outside Italy. He would not return to Italy until after the death of Frederick; for ten years, he remained in Lyon, making it the center of the Church's administration and the headquarters for his battle against the emperor.

Innocent summoned a general council of the Church. The First Council of Lyon met from June 26 through July 12, 1245, and had a number of items on its official agenda: conversion of the Mongols, reunification of the Latin and Greek churches, and a new crusade to the Holy Land. These paled beside the dominant issue: the

Pope Innocent IV. (Library of Congress)

Church's struggle with Frederick. The emperor was accused of perjury, breach of the peace, sacrilege, and heresy. Although ably defended by the noted jurist Thaddeus of Suessa, Frederick was found guilty on all charges, excommunicated from the Church, and deposed from his throne. Innocent proclaimed a crusade against Frederick, and began raising money and support throughout Europe.

The rest of Innocent's pontificate was one long war with Frederick. The reaction from the emperor to his excommunication was muted (he had faced this action on several occasions before), but his deposition caused an all-out assault on the position of the Church: Within his domains, he plundered churches and monasteries, dispersed monks, and abolished the clergy's exemptions from taxes and their authority over the laity. He sent messages to other rulers, urging them to join him in making a complete break between church and state, and so securing supreme power for the secular monarchs.

Frederick II was a remarkable man. Known to his contemporaries as Stupor Mundi (the wonder of the world), his kingdom in Sicily was one of the most advanced of its time, with a court that delighted in arts and learning. In addition to wearing the imperial crown, he was king of Jerusalem, having secured peace through negotiations with the sultan of Egypt. His burning ambition was to establish the empire and its ruler as the supreme power in Europe, unbeholden in any way to the pope.

Supporters of the imperial cause were known as Ghibellines, a name taken from the territory of Waiblingen in Franconia, which had long been territory of Frederick's family, the Hohenstaufens. Their opponents, who favored the pope, were known as Guelphs. It was at this time that these two names first became widely used, especially in Italy, where the two factions tore the countryside apart in internecine struggles.

Frederick's position of separation of church and state is often regarded as the more modern or advanced theory, one that looked forward to the Renaissance and modern times. Innocent's quest for papal authority, on the other hand, is considered by many to be a throwback to the ideas of the Middle Ages. Actually, these views are possible only in hindsight. At the time, both Frederick and Innocent made compelling cases for their views.

After the Council of Lyon had deposed Frederick, Innocent maneuvered for the election of a new emperor. First, Henry Raspe, landgrave of Thuringia, was selected, and following his death in 1247, William of Holland was chosen. This election helped weaken Frederick's power in the north, especially in conjunction with the tacit support of Louis IX of France, later canonized as Saint Louis.

The main struggle was conducted in the south, in Italy, with Frederick campaigning on the peninsula and Innocent directing events from Lyon. In 1248, Frederick suffered a serious defeat when the city of Parma revolted from his rule and was seized by the Guelphs. That undermined Frederick's position in northern Italy and forced him to spend the next two years repairing his fortunes. Innocent continued to favor rival kings and pretenders and even encouraged disloyal nobles in an attempt to poison the emperor. Just as Frederick had begun to regain his position, he suddenly died on December 13, 1250. Innocent returned to Italy.

His victory, however, was not yet complete. Conrad IV, Frederick's son, assumed the crown of Sicily and aspired to the imperial throne. Sicily had once been a fief of the Papacy, and Innocent wished to restore that situation. He offered the crown to a number of people, including Charles of Anjou in France, England's Richard of Cornwall, and the English king Henry III. Henry accepted for his young son, Edmund, but on the death of Conrad in 1254, Frederick's illegitimate son Manfred took the crown and promised to recognize the pope as his overlord.

The peace was short-lived, for Manfred soon renounced his allegiance. Innocent wearily but determinedly began to prepare for yet another phase in this incessant struggle. He became ill, however, and he died on December 7, 1254, in Naples. He was buried in the cathedral in that city; on his tomb were carved the words, "He destroyed the serpent Frederick, Christ's enemy."

Significance

Many of the contemporaries of Innocent IV, as well as later historians, have seen him only as a pope intent on securing and enlarging the secular power of the Papacy. Engaged in a ten-year struggle with Frederick, Innocent may have lowered the prestige and moral authority of the Church through his political manipulations, his demands for funds, and his unyielding tactics. In this view, Innocent IV was less a spiritual leader than a political one, and his concerns were with secular power and its preservation.

On the other hand, it must be noted that Innocent's actions were based on motives that were primarily theological and canonical. In his view, and as articulated by the Council of Lyon, the pope wielded an authority transcending that of secular monarchs, precisely because the pope's authority was spiritual: The vicar of Christ took precedence over the vicar of Caesar. As a practical matter, Innocent preferred that the pope rule as a sovereign in his own right, but he always insisted that the pope held ultimate authority over all secular monarchs.

Thus, the pope had the authority to depose kings and emperors. When Frederick was found guilty of exceptionally serious offenses, Innocent "translated" or removed the empire from him. Frederick, a firm believer in the divine right of kings, naturally rejected this and the pope's claims. There could never be the possibility of peace between the two great contenders.

Because of the preoccupation with political and military struggles during his pontificate, Innocent's other achievements have sometimes been ignored. Actually, he proved to be quite notable in several areas, and is regarded by church historians as important for a number of reasons other than his lengthy confrontation with Frederick.

Innocent made several serious efforts to reunify the Church, and some writers believe that had he not died at a critical moment in the talks, a breakthrough could well have been accomplished. Regardless of whether this is true, at least he made the most determined attempt at reunion during this entire period. More audacious and less successful were his efforts to have missionaries convert Kublai Khan and his Mongols to Christianity. Although this aim may seem a fantasy today, it should be remembered that much of the eastern part of Europe had only recently been opened to Christianity, and there was reason to believe that the process of conversion might well continue.

It was in education and within the administration of the Church that Innocent made his most lasting impact. He was a learned man himself, and encouraged learning in others. During his exile in Lyon, he established schools for theology, canon law, and civil law. He founded a university at Piacenza, approved the establishment of another in Valencia, and granted to it and to the university at Toulouse the same rights as those enjoyed by the long-established University of Paris.

Innocent appointed outstanding and able men to the Papal Curia and provided strong and capable government for the Church. One of his first but longest-lasting actions as pope took place in 1245, when he gave the cardinals the distinctive red hats that they wear today.

Finally, Innocent IV is remembered as an outstanding canon lawyer and scholar. He published three collections of his own judicial works as pope, and his most famous production is a commentary on the decretals (letters that contain a papal ruling, usually on a matter of canonical law) of his predecessor, Gregory IX.

An intelligent, practical man, Innocent defended the rights and authority of the Papacy through ten years of desperate struggle, and left the Church strong and vigorous on his death.

—*Michael Witkoski*

FURTHER READING

Abulafia, David. *Frederick II: A Medieval Emperor.* 1988. Reprint. London: Pimlico, 1992. A biography of Frederick II. Contains illustrations, maps, bibliography, and index.

Figueira, Robert C. "Innocent IV." In *The Great Popes Through History: An Encyclopedia*, edited by Frank J. Coppa. Westport, Conn.: Greenwood Press, 2002. An examination of the role of Pope Innocent IV in history. Bibiography and index.

Maxwell-Stuart, P. G. *Chronicle of the Popes: The Reign-by-Reign Record of the Papacy from Saint Peter to the Present.* New York: Thames and Hudson, 1997. A look at the Papacy, one pope at a time. Covers Innocent IV. Contains illustrations, maps, and index.

Morris, Colin. *The Papal Monarchy: The Western Church from 1050 to 1250.* New York: Oxford University Press, 1989. A history of the Church in the Middle Ages, including during Innocent IV's papacy.

Robinson, I. S. *The Papacy, 1073-1198: Continuity and Innovation.* New York: Cambridge University Press, 1990. An examination of the Papacy during the Middle Ages, including the relations between church and state. Index.

Ullmann, Walter. *A Short History of the Papacy in the Middle Ages.* 1972. Reprint. New York: Routledge, 2003. This history of the popes focuses on the Middle Ages, including Innocent IV. Bibliography and index.

SEE ALSO: Giovanni da Pian del Carpini; Saint Clare of Assisi; Saint Francis of Assisi; Frederick II; Gregory IX; Innocent III; Kublai Khan; Louis IX; Sorghagtani Beki; Jean de Venette; William of Auvergne; William of Saint-Amour.

RELATED ARTICLES in *Great Events from History: The Middle Ages, 477-1453*: 1204: Genghis Khan Founds Mongol Empire; 1227-1230: Frederick II Leads the Sixth Crusade; 1233: Papal Inquisition; 1248-1254: Failure of the Seventh Crusade; 1258: Provisions of Oxford Are Established.

SAINT IRENE

Byzantine empress (r. 797-802)

Irene was the first woman to rule the Christian Roman Empire as sole authority, and she was instrumental in temporarily halting iconoclasm. Her reign saw the emergence of two distinctive European cultures, one centered on Rome and the Atlantic states in the west and the other centered on Constantinople and the east.

BORN: c. 752; Athens, Byzantine Empire (now in Greece)

DIED: August 9, 803; island of Lesbos, Byzantine Empire (now in Greece)

AREAS OF ACHIEVEMENT: Government and politics, religion and theology

EARLY LIFE

Historians know little about Irene's life before her marriage to Leo, crown prince of the Byzantine Empire. Her hometown, Athens, boasted a glorious past, and Irene was well connected with a local family of aristocrats. In Byzantine times, however, Athens had become a rather ordinary port town, and the empire swarmed with notable families eager to marry into the ruling family. A stranger to the capital, Constantinople, Irene was in her mid-twenties and orphaned by her parents and had few clear allies at the court. Whatever qualities brought Irene to wed Leo, she emerged dramatically after his death as a decisive, inspiring, versatile, and occasionally ruthless leader.

LIFE'S WORK

At the time Irene arrived in Constantinople, Emperor Constantine V Copronymus (r. 741-775), found himself preoccupied with three interlocking crises that had bedeviled the realm for decades. First came the strategic threats endangering Byzantium. From the Middle East and North Africa, the armies of the ʿAbbāsid caliphs, holding the banners of Islam, regularly invaded Anatolia and the Mediterranean. To the north, Slavs and Bulgarians menaced the European side. The danger of fighting two enemies on two distant fronts threatened Constantinople with constant encirclement. Second, treacheries within Byzantine forces themselves required unceasing vigilance. Ambitious generals, ethnic and regional animosities, and other conflicts within the ranks required

Constantine to keep his troops busy at war or circulating among garrisons. Third, a monumental religious controversy kept the Byzantine state, church, and society in constant turmoil. That struggle was the Iconoclastic Controversy.

Icons are paintings depicting Christ, Christian saints, and Biblical scenes. Illustrated by monks, Eastern Orthodox Christians display icons in churches, homes, monasteries, and public places to remind themselves of God's presence. They are used in worship, in private devotions, and for educational purposes. Although the use of icons in worship reflected a long-standing practice in Byzantine Christianity, some in the empire viewed them as idolatrous and wanted all icons removed and destroyed. These "icon-breakers" were called iconoclasts; icon defenders were called iconophiles or iconodules. In 726, Emperor Leo III (r. 717-741) ordered the destruction of every icon in the realm. Despite resistance from bishops, monks, and commoners, and even the condemnation of the pope, Leo made iconoclasm official state policy. His son, Constantine V, went even further. At the Council of Heiria (754), he forced Church leaders to declare icons heretical and started a vicious persecution to impose iconoclasm by force. Bishops, priests, monks, and nuns went to jail and into exile; some were blinded, mutilated, or executed. Constantine not only purged the Church of iconophiles but the state and officer corps as well, using iconoclastic reform as a justification to restructure the military. Ironically, however, whether from ignorance or indifference, he missed one significant iconophile within his own household: Irene, his daughter-in-law and wife of his heir. At his death, Constantine left Byzantine secure from outside threats but seething within from his brutality.

Young and insecure, Constantine's son, Leo IV (r. 775-780), tempered his iconoclasm with caution. Besides the angry factionalism generated by his father, Leo inherited ambitious brothers and uncles ready to challenge him at any misstep. Thus, in 776, with vivid displays of committed support from the generals and hierarchy, he crowned the six-year-old Constantine VI as his heir. Military victories raised his prestige and allowed Leo to make some gestures of reconciliation toward iconophiles throughout the Church and society. Persecution of monks, one of Constantine V's most controversial policies, ceased. How Irene's affection for icons and monastics played in Leo's moderation went unrecorded. In 780, Leo and Irene broke over the volatile issue of iconoclasm, a break both public and nasty. The emperor discovered that several courtiers had smuggled icons into the palace for Irene's private devotions. Always alert for potential conspiracies (as any emperor had to be), the queen's subterfuge enraged him. He had the courtiers whipped in the streets, jailed several iconodule clergy, rebuked Irene, and banished her from his personal quarters. Then, that September, Leo contracted a sudden fever and died. Irene was now empress.

Instead of stepping quietly aside as most Byzantine queens had done, Irene declared herself regent for the child Constantine VI and pointedly reminded courtiers, nobles, clergy, and soldiers of their recent oaths. Because Constantine was only ten, Irene could also entitle herself coemperor. Even before the end of 780, conspirators concocted a scheme to depose Irene and Constantine in favor of Leo's brother, Nicephorus. The empress responded with speed and theatrics. She arrested all five of Leo's brothers and compelled them to become priests, thereby barring them for life from the throne. Energetic and decisive, her enemies completely off balance, Irene began salting her supporters throughout state service and within the officer corps. Resounding victories in the Balkans and a truce with Muslims in Anatolia strengthened her domestic hand as well. All these successes steeled her resolve to launch a political, religious, and cultural revolution greater than any war—the destruction of iconoclasm.

The official restoration of icon veneration in the Orthodox Church required careful but deliberate action. Irene sensed that devotion to the spirituality that icons embodied remained broad and deep throughout the Byzantine Empire, despite the violent intimidation of the clergy, the bureaucracy, and the public by three consecutive iconoclast emperors. The iconodules were cowed but not converted. Letters to Pope Adrian I, a militant opponent of iconoclasm, indicated that Rome and the Latin churches would happily join in a council to endorse a return of the icons. Still, more than fifty years of imperial religious policy could not be repudiated overnight. Therefore, the empress waited several years, steadily replacing high-level iconoclasts with loyal iconophiles and phasing out enforcement of anti-icon regulations.

In 786, Irene and Constantine inaugurated the Council of Constantinople with the intention of reversing the 754 Council of Heiria. The Council of Constantinople declared iconoclasm a heresy and made icon imagery standard again in the eastern churches. However, mobs of soldiers and others opposed to Irene broke into the conference, set off street protests, and forced her to cancel the council. Undaunted, Irene rotated loyal troops and officers into the more manageable city of Nicaea while eliminating intractable iconoclasts and disgruntled sol-

BYZANTINE EMPERORS: SYRIAN (ISAURIAN) LINE, 717-802

Reign	*Emperor*
717-718	Sulaimān and ʿUmar II lay siege to Constantinople
717-741	Leo III the Isaurian (the Syrian)
726-843	Iconoclastic Controversy
741-775	Constantine V Copronymus
754	Ravenna lost to Lombards
775-780	Leo IV the Khazar
780-797	Constantine VI
786-809	Reign of Hārūn al-Rashīd
787	Council at Nicaea sanctions icons
797-802	SAINT IRENE (regent, 780-790)
800	Pope Leo III crowns Charlemagne as emperor

diers. The next year, in the autumn of 787, the seventh ecumenical council at Nicaea gave Irene what she wanted. More than 350 bishops as well as attending priests, monks, and civil servants declared iconoclasm a heresy and made icon veneration again a legitimate expression of Christian worship. The only real dissent at the council came from a minority of iconophiles who wanted the defeated iconoclast clergy treated as criminals and punished severely. These irreconcilables resented Irene's merciful declaration that, after due submission and repentance, former iconoclasts would remain in holy orders and even keep their posts.

Despite their cooperation at Nicaea, Irene's and Constantine's position soured rapidly. Constantine reached his maturity in the same year of the holding of the second Nicene council. However, a proposed marriage between Constantine and Rotrude, daughter of Frankish and Lombardian king (and later Holy Roman Emperor) Charlemagne, fell through despite Irene's efforts, and he married instead a local nobleman's granddaughter. On top of that embarrassment, military reverses in Anatolia, Bulgaria, and Italy eroded Byzantine prestige. Finally, Irene clearly had no intention of respecting the tradition to step aside so the adolescent Constantine might become sole emperor. In 790, a dispute between Irene and Constantine over a courtier escalated into a showdown between the two, and Byzantine generals forced a solution. They made Constantine VI sole emperor but allowed his deposed mother rooms at the palace instead of exile, prison, or worse. Totally inept and incompetent, Constantine brought his mother back as coruler two years later.

However, mistrust and paranoia between Constantine and Irene continued to polarize both state and military, with Constantine increasingly coming off the loser. His wars in Bulgaria were unsuccessful. When dissident soldiers tried a second time to raise his priest-uncle Nicephorus to the throne in 793, Constantine had Nicephorus blinded and his other uncles mutilated. Troops throughout Anatolia mutinied and the revolt went on another year. What role Irene played in these affairs is unclear, but blame fell entirely on her son. In 795, Constantine abandoned his first wife to marry his mistress, an act that made the emperor—the head of Byzantine Christendom—an adulterer under Orthodox canon law. Compounding frictions with the Church, the emperor increasingly displayed pro-iconoclast sympathies, attitudes guaranteed to horrify his mother. In June, 797, perhaps appalled over Constantine's reckless incompetence or just unable to contain her ambition, Irene and her supporters staged a coup. They captured her son, imprisoning him in the palace. On August 15, in the same room in which he was born, the plotters blinded Constantine. Traumatized, abandoned, and shut away, Constantine died shortly thereafter. Irene was now sole ruler of Byzantium and surrounded by dangers. New conspiracies arose from the male partisans of Leo's family. Defeats in the Balkans and Anatolia sharpened the dangers created by mutinies. The support of the Church and the public vacillated. Iconoclasm was not dead, female rule had no legal precedent, and horror at a mother complicit in the murder of her own son unleashed waves of revulsion despite disgust at Constantine's character.

Ever determined, Irene moved briskly. She insisted on the title emperor, not empress. She cut taxes and tariffs, raised salaries, and stimulated trade. Irene became a lavish patron of the churches and monasteries, founding schools for training clergy and civil servants. Protection money to buy off Bulgarian chieftains and Muslim invaders kept the peace. Conspiracies were crushed ruthlessly, but executions kept to a minimum. Irene's prestige nonetheless eroded. Financial burdens resulting from her personal largesse and tax concessions merged with the humiliating weight of tributes paid to foreign enemies, creating a profound economic and military crisis. At some time in 799, she contracted an unknown illness that debilitated her legendary stamina. Her weariness provoked another plot that she barely managed to contain. An unexpected challenge from abroad came in 800—Charlemagne's coronation as Roman emperor.

Charlemagne and Irene had bumped heads before, when Charlemagne blocked the marriage of his daughter to Constantine VI in 787. Then, involving himself in religious issues, he denounced both the Council of Heiria and the second Nicene council, often in language that alarmed Pope Adrian and flirted with iconoclasm. Charlemagne belittled the Byzantine emperors as "mere kings" and declared that no woman (in this case, Irene) could lawfully rule a state or preside over religious councils. In 794, despite Pope Adrian's strenuous efforts to talk him out of it, Charlemagne staged his Council of Frankfurt and had more harsh words for the Byzantines. Thus, when Pope Leo III crowned him emperor on Christmas Day, 800, the implications for the Byzantine Empire and for Irene were chilling—Charlemagne now seemed to claim the leadership of Christian Europe.

Instead of confrontation, however, emissaries between Charlemagne and Irene raised the idea of reconciliation through marriage. Their union would unite political Christendom, strengthen both rulers against domestic enemies, and settle a vast range of frictions between Rome and Constantinople. Irene, whether from inspiration, desperation, or romantic motives, apparently favored the proposal; her courtiers, clergy, and officers did not. In October, 802, as Charlemagne's representatives prepared to discuss marriage details with Irene's people, the plotters occupied the palace and arrested the empress. Poised in defeat, Irene accepted her overthrow without resistance. The new emperor, Nicephorus I (r. 802-811) exiled her to a convent on the island of Lesbos, where, in 803, she died.

Significance

Assessing Irene is controversial. In general, she has received usually positive acclaim for her joint reign with Constantine VI, especially for her handling of religious conflicts and military affairs. Nonetheless, iconoclasm enjoyed a resurgence for several decades until eliminated decisively in 843 by another iconophile empress, Theodora. Her reign also marked the accelerated separation of western Europe from eastern Europe, most notably in the creation of a distinctive and independent imperial state by Charlemagne.

—*Weston F. Cook, Jr.*

Further Reading

Garland, Lynda. *Byzantine Empresses: Women and Power in Byzantium, A.D. 527-1204*. New York: Routledge, 1999. Explores the history of the empresses of the Byzantine Empire. Includes a chapter on Irene. Map, extensive bibliography, index.

Herrin, Judith. *Women in Purple: Rulers of Medieval Byzantium*. Princeton, N.J.: Princeton University Press, 2001. Studies women in Byzantine politics. Includes a chapter on Irene. Maps, extensive bibliography, and index.

James, Liz. *Empresses and Power in Early Byzantium*. New York: Leicester University Press, 2001. Surveys the governmental and political history of the reigns of empresses of early Byzantium, setting the stage for Irene's time.

Norwich, John Julius. *Byzantium: The Early Centuries*. New York: Alfred Knopf, 1994. First of a three-volume history of Byzantium. Pages 366-382 focus on Irene, but the author's depiction is harsh and unflattering.

Ostrogorsky, George. *History of the Byzantine State*. Translated by Joan Hussey. Rev. ed. New Brunswick, N.J.: Rutgers University Press, 1969. A classic English-language Byzantine history. Comprehensive study of the empire from the early fourth to the mid-fifteenth century.

Treadgold, Warren. *A History of the Byzantine State and Society*. Stanford, Calif.: Stanford University Press, 1997. A lucid depiction of political, military, cultural, and religious contexts for Irene's life and work.

Whittow, Mark. *The Making of Byzantium, 600-1025*. Berkeley: University of California Press, 1996. A history of the Byzantine Empire and the Orthodox Church. Maps, bibliography, and index.

See also: Alcuin; Charlemagne; Hārūn al-Rashīd; John of Damascus; Theophanes the Confessor.

Related articles in *Great Events from History: The Middle Ages, 477-1453*: 726-843: Iconoclastic Controversy; 781: Alcuin Becomes Adviser to Charlemagne; 786-809: Reign of Hārūn al-Rashīd.

ISABELLA OF FRANCE

French-born queen of England (r. 1308-1327 and 1327-1330)

For many years, Isabella was queen of the English king Edward II, whose incompetence, eccentricities, and male lovers eventually forced her to oppose him. She played a leading role in his eventual deposition, imprisonment, and execution.

BORN: c. 1292; place unknown
DIED: August 23, 1358; Hertford, England
ALSO KNOWN AS: Isabelle of France; Isabella the She-Wolf; Isabella the Fair; She-Wolf of France
AREA OF ACHIEVEMENT: Government and politics

EARLY LIFE

Isabella (ihz-uh-BEHL-uh) was the daughter of Philip IV the Fair, king of France, and of his wife, Joan of Champagne and Navarre. Although it is impossible to be precise, there can be no doubt that Isabella was very young in 1298, when as a part of the peace treaty between her father and Edward I of England, she was betrothed to the prince of Wales. The marriage was carried out in January of 1308, followed by the coronation in Westminster a month later. Thus began the public portion of her career. From that point until the time of her political downfall in 1330, Isabella would play a pivotal role in the politics of the age.

LIFE'S WORK

For much of Edward II's reign, Isabella was a dutiful queen and a faithful wife. She struggled to adapt to a new country and had to cope with Edward's political ineptitude, his eccentric behavior, and a predilection for what the chroniclers of the age called "evil counselors." The most offensive member of the king's troupe was Piers Gaveston, an imperious Gascon knight who had earlier been exiled by Edward I. Gaveston was the king's intimate companion and adviser, the recipient of many gifts, grants, and titles that might otherwise have been bestowed on Isabella and his English nobles. The relationship most assuredly alienated many powerful people, including the king's cousin, Thomas, earl of Lancaster. As a result, few people, including Isabella, grieved when Gaveston was seized in 1312 and executed by his political enemies.

Gaveston's death and the imposition of reforms by Thomas and the nobility weakened the position of the king. Over the next five years, the king was beset by many problems, not the least among which was yet another Scottish uprising, which resulted in one of the worst defeats in English military history (Battle of Bannockburn, 1314) and a Great Famine that ravaged the land for three years. Interestingly enough, these events seem to have worked to the advantage of the troubled marriage and, at the same time, thrust the queen into a prominent political position. Between 1312 and 1321, Isabella worked hard to effect peace between her husband and the disaffected nobles while serving as a mediator with the king of France. Along the way, she bore the king four children, including an heir, the future Edward III.

In the performance of her duties as queen, Isabella was oftentimes put in harm's way. In 1319, while the king besieged Berwick, Isabella was very nearly abducted by the Scots near York. The plot was foiled when a captured spy revealed the plan and Isabella was able to safely make her escape to Nottingham. On another occasion, Isabella avoided capture by the Scots at Byland Abbey (now North Yorkshire) only by fleeing to the coast, where she was forced to make her escape through a perilous voyage by sea. She was sometimes roughed up by her own English subjects. In 1321, while traveling to Canterbury, she and her party became embroiled in a struggle with Lady Badlesmere, wife of one of the king's political enemies, over her refusal to admit Isabella and her entourage for lodging at Leeds Castle near Maidstone. The matter was only resolved after the king entered the dispute and laid siege to the castle.

Whatever hope there might have been for a normal relationship between the king and queen, however, was shattered by the emergence of the prominent and influential Despenser (Spencer) family as a major factor in politics after 1318. Hugh le Despenser the Younger, in a manner reminiscent of Gaveston, quickly won a place in the king's heart and probably also his bed. Unscrupulous and greedy, the Despensers proved to be even more objectionable than the king's earlier favorites. Their enemies were imprisoned, executed, or driven from the land and their money, lands, and titles confiscated. In retribution, Thomas and other dissidents gathered enough support in a parliament held in London to banish the greedy pair from the country for a short period of time. However, in 1322 Edward regained the upper hand, gathered an army, and routed Thomas's forces in the decisive Battle of Boroughbridge. The Despensers, now back in the country, were free to "pillage, plunder, and persecute their enemies" during the next five years.

Under the rule of Edward and the Despensers, Isabella was made to suffer many indignities. Her property was confiscated and her every move was watched, in large part because of her connections with a number of dissidents, including some of the most influential ecclesiastical lords of the kingdom and her fairly obvious ties with the French monarchy. Even so, in a move that defies explanation, Edward did allow the queen to journey to Paris in March of 1325 as a representative of the English government on the occasion of her youngest brother's coronation as king. The decision would prove to be a fatal mistake, one that was exacerbated when Prince Edward was permitted to join his mother on the Continent in the fall of that year, ostensibly to render homage to the new French king. Edward fully expected mother and son to discharge their political duties and return to England in a timely manner. Now free of a husband she loathed and free of his evil minions, Isabella, the king's protestations notwithstanding, adamantly refused to return to England. Her defiant stance endeared her to many, including those English exiles and criminals who had taken refuge in France. Foremost among them was the Welsh lord Roger Mortimer, whose family had suffered grievously at the hands of the Despensers. Isabella soon formed a close attachment to Mortimer that, in the words of one source, "soon ripened into criminal intimacy."

With her motley crew in tow, Isabella and Mortimer crossed the Channel and landed in Essex on September 24, 1326, where they were enthusiastically embraced by all who had grievances. The king, finding that he had little support, fled westward with the queen in pursuit. The Despensers were soon apprehended and executed. The king was captured not long thereafter in Wales and brought before Parliament in London on January 7, where he was forced to abdicate in favor of his son and heir, Edward III. Edward II was then imprisoned at Berkeley Castle, where he was starved, tortured, and eventually murdered. Isabella's complicity in the crime has earned for her a not-so-special niche in the history of the English monarchy. A seventeenth century writer would dub Isabella the She-Wolf, an epithet that has colored the judgment of historians for generations.

From 1327 to 1330, Isabella and Mortimer governed England on behalf of the youthful Edward III. The two proved to be no less rapacious than the Despensers. Their arrogance and extravagance, coupled with a political policy of appeasement for both Scotland and France, alienated the young king and many of his adherents. On October 18, 1330, a coup was carried out that swept the queen mother and her paramour from power. Mortimer, despite Isabella's pitiful pleas for mercy, was executed. Isabella was spared, though she would spend the last twenty-eight years of her life in honorable confinement. Although Isabella was excluded by her son from the affairs of government, she seems to have led a comfortable existence—though subject to bouts of melancholia—at Castle Rising and other places, amid her books, jewelry, religious relics, and gifts of food and wine. Her last days were spent in the religious habit of the sisters of Santa Clara. She died on August 23, 1358, and was buried in November in the Franciscan church at Newgate in London.

SIGNIFICANCE

Isabella has had few apologists. On the contrary, most scholars and novelists have portrayed her as an adulterer and a murderer. Her involvement in Edward's deposition, imprisonment, and murder cannot be denied, nor can her image be totally rehabilitated. However, it might be argued that the sins of her youth were the inevitable results of a life spent with an incompetent king who was domi-

Isabella of France. (Hulton|Archive at Getty Images)

nated by his male favorites. To stress these sins is to overlook the fact that for most of her public career, Isabella was dutiful. On numerous occasions, Isabella interceded with the nobility to bring peace and stability to the kingdom. It was only after the king spurned his wife for the Despensers that Isabella became the leader of the opposition movement. Had it not been for the tragic events of 1325-1327, Isabella might well have taken her place among the greatest queens of the age.

—*Larry W. Usilton*

FURTHER READING

Davies, James Conway. *The Baronial Opposition to Edward II, Its Character and Policy: A Study in Administrative History.* 1918. Reprint. New York: Barnes and Noble Books, 1967. Still considered one of the best studies of Edward II's reign. Isabella appears throughout, but not always in a favorable light.

Doherty, Paul. *Isabella and the Strange Death of Edward II.* New York: Carroll and Graf, 2003. An engaging look at Isabella's role in the controversy and intrigue surrounding Edward's deposition and death.

Hutchison, Harold. *Edward II, 1284-1327.* 1971. Reprint. New York: Barnes and Noble Books, 1996. A sympathetic biography that attempts to exonerate the king of the charges of incompetence and cowardice, while citing mitigating circumstances for his vices. The author is, however, less charitable to Isabella.

Johnstone, Hilda. "Isabella, the She-Wolf of France." *History* 21 (1936): 208-218. The author attempts to paint a more favorable picture of Isabella by citing some of the concerns—especially the king's relationship with Gaveston—that forced her into opposition. Much of the article focuses on the queen's years of honorable confinement.

McKisack, May. *The Fourteenth Century, 1307-1399.* 1959. Reprint. Oxford, England: Clarendon Press, 1971. A volume in the Oxford History of England series long regarded as one of the most comprehensive studies of the fourteenth century.

Menache, Sophia. "Isabelle of France, Queen of England—A Reconsideration." *Journal of Medieval History* 10 (1984): 107-124. An excellent short study of the queen's life, and a sympathetic look at a queen considered here to be powerful, very influential, and one who was oftentimes used as a peacemaker between the king and his enemies.

Mortimer, Ian. *The Greatest Traitor: The Life of Sir Roger Mortimer, First Earl of March, Ruler of England, 1327-1330.* London: Jonathan Cape, 2003. A historical analysis of Mortimer for the general reader, one that presents an unfavorable, critical perspective.

Strickland, Agnes. *Lives of the Queens of England: From the Norman Conquest.* New York: Harper and Bros., 1886. An oft-cited study of the many queens of England. The author's relatively short sketch of Isabella tells a familiar story from Isabella's betrothal to her last years at Castle Rising.

SEE ALSO: Edward I; Edward II; Edward III; Philip IV the Fair; Philippa of Hainaut.

RELATED ARTICLE in *Great Events from History: The Middle Ages, 477-1453*: June 23-24, 1314: Battle of Bannockburn.

SAINT ISIDORE OF SEVILLE
Spanish scholar

Through his defense of education, Isidore of Seville not only preserved the classical traditions of his people but also helped forge a national identity.

BORN: c. 560; Cartagena or Seville (now in Spain)
DIED: April 4, 636; Seville
ALSO KNOWN AS: Isidorus Hispalensis
AREAS OF ACHIEVEMENT: Education, literature, religion and theology, government and politics

EARLY LIFE

Isidore, the second son of prominent Hispano-Roman parents, possibly was born in the city of Seville, where his parents had fled after the sacking of their native Cartagena by the Arian Visigoths. All the children in Isidore's strongly orthodox family committed themselves to service in the Church: The only daughter, Florentina, entered a convent, and the three sons, Leander, Isidore, and Fulgentius, became priests. After the early death of their parents, Severian and Theodora, Leander, already a priest, assumed complete responsibility for the education of his sister and brothers and enrolled them in convent and monastery schools. Fulgentius, the youngest, became bishop of Écija, while both Leander and Isidore became archbishops of the see of Seville and, later, bishops (primates) of all Spain. Both also were canonized.

Although Isidore's entire life was dedicated to the Church, the world around him was definitely not a Catholic one, nor even predominantly Christian. The Roman Empire in the West had been divided into many Germanic kingdoms. In the old Roman territory of Hispania, it was the Visigoths, perhaps the most Romanized of the Germanic peoples, who finally became the dominant power. By the time of Isidore's birth, they had managed to subdue most of the peninsula except for a small enclave of the Suevi in Galicia, the Byzantines in the south and east, and the Basques, who remained independent in their mountain strongholds. This military success was only a beginning. The Visigoths faced formidable religious and cultural differences in achieving their goal of a united Hispanic state. They were the ruling class, but their Hispano-Roman subjects, who greatly outnumbered them, considered them to be little more than heretics and barbarians.

After much internecine warfare, including a civil war among members of the royal family itself, the religious question was at least superficially settled by the conversion of Recared to orthodox Catholicism in 587. This act, which did much to mitigate Hispano-Roman tensions, was brought about largely through the efforts of Leander, Isidore's brother and bishop of Seville. Although completely disparate in outlook and heritage, Leander and Recared did share one ideal: a unified Spain. It was a concept that Leander was to pass on to Isidore, who was not only his brother but also his fervent disciple. Therefore, after his brother's death, it was only natural for Isidore to succeed to the see of Seville and take his place as the spokesperson of the orthodox Christian tradition. Although little is known of Isidore's early life, his ascension to the most influential religious post in Hispania brought Isidore to the forefront of his country's history. His desire was not only to record that history but also to alter its direction.

LIFE'S WORK

Isidore's main achievements were his defense of education and his preservation of knowledge that he gleaned from the writings of ancient pagan authors and of the Church fathers. His concepts were seldom abstract or esoteric. He used his learning, influence, and great writing skill to further specific practical ends. He was perhaps the preeminent scholar of his time.

Little is known of Isidore's personality. By the testimony of his own words, it is evident that he could be ruthless and cynical. He exercised almost absolute control over the Spanish church and at times was unforgiving of religious nonconformity. In cultural and scientific fields, however, Isidore exhibited a rare tolerance and openness that merits praise.

Isidore's first major achievement after his ordination as a bishop was the reorganization of the educational system, which the Church controlled. At the Fourth Council of Toledo in 633, he ordered that schools specializing in the liberal arts be set up in the cities of all dioceses of Hispania and that the course of study for priests be formalized and strengthened. Because the Catholic clergy represented or influenced almost all literate people, this decree brought about a rise in the standard of literacy for the entire peninsula. Isidore himself wrote many treatises outlining specifically the duties and obligations of the clergy as well as several commentaries on the Old and New Testaments. Isidore's also was the guiding hand in the much-needed revision and standardization of the old Spanish liturgy.

Saint Isidore of Seville. (Library of Congress)

The bishop then turned from the education of the common man to the education of princes. After Leander's death, Isidore became the adviser, both spiritual and political, to the Visigothic monarchs. Notwithstanding his Hispano-Roman descent, Isidore considered himself to be a Spaniard. He admired the Visigoths for their courage and driving energy in unifying his beloved country. At the beginning of his historical chronicle of the Goths, there are the famous words of his "De laude Hispaniae" (in praise of Spain): "Of all the lands that extend from the west to India, thou are the fairest, oh sacred Hispania, ever-fecund mother of princes and peoples, rightful queen of all the provinces, from whom west and east draw their light."

A great nation needed a just and wise king, and to Isidore fell the task of shaping the Visigothic concept of kingship and of civilizing its barbaric nature. He wrote that a king must not only defend his people against outside attack but also serve as an example by his ethical Christian conduct. Isidore even went so far as to insist that a king who ruled unjustly had surrendered all rights of kingship, and therefore his people had the moral obligation to overthrow him. The bishop also advocated hereditary monarchy in order to ensure political stability. Many of his concepts were far ahead of his time. Any attempt by the Visigoths to abandon their old elective system of leadership generally ended in bloodshed. It is interesting to note, however, that it is not to the Visigothic reality but to Isidore's idealized rendering of that reality that later generations would turn in the quest for unity against the Moors.

In legal matters, Isidore was more immediately successful. One of the stumbling blocks to the true unification of the Hispano-Roman and Gothic peoples of the peninsula had been the lack of a uniform code of law. Finally, about 654, Recceswinth promulgated the first binding body of laws for the entire state, a code influenced significantly by Isidore's writings. The Liber Judiciorum, better known as the Fuero Juzgo, was to serve as the law of the land until modern times. So important had Isidore's contribution been that later generations adopted the custom of taking oaths in both criminal and civil cases on the saint's shrine in León. It was believed that any perjury would cause the death of the miscreant within the year.

Isidore also served as the Visigothic historian, producing an informative chronicle entitled *Historia de regibus Gothorum, Vandalorum, et Suevorum* (624; *History of the Kings of the Goths, Vandals, and Suevi*, 1966). He wrote many religious, scientific, and historical studies, but it was his last and most comprehensive work, *Etymologiae* (late sixth or early seventh century; partial translation in *An Encyclopedist of the Dark Ages*, 1912), which earned for him lasting fame and the title of Egregious Doctor. Edited and divided into twenty books after his death by his friend and former student, Braulio, bishop of Saragossa, *Etymologiae* is a summarization of all the knowledge available to Isidore in the seventh century. The first of the medieval encyclopedias, it attempted to synthesize classical Greco-Roman traditions with Christian morals and doctrine. The subjects range from cosmology, language study, anthropology, the liberal arts, psychology, medicine, and shipbuilding to the planning of country gardens. *Etymologiae* was the standard reference work of its time; one thousand medieval manuscripts still survive, and the actual number was exceeded only by copies of the Vulgate Bible. Much of the information recorded in the encyclopedia is now only of intellectual curiosity. Nevertheless, it served as a beacon of classical learning throughout many centuries of scholarly twilight and, in its painstaking attention to detail and observation, provided a base on which various disciplines could be built. For example, Isidore's discussion regarding medicines is remarkably free from magical or religious influences; thus, he continued the tradition of medicine as a scientific discipline and transmitted and expanded a universal medical terminology that could be understood by all of its practitioners.

Isidore died on April 4, 636. The Visigothic kingdom he described and defended was to vanish soon after with the coming of the Moors in 711. His fame and influence, however, continued to grow. He was canonized by the Church, and because of his ardent support of Spanish nationalism, he became a symbol of the Reconquest. During the Middle Ages, the liberation of his remains from Muslim territory became a cause célèbre. Finally, in 1063, his tomb became a shrine on the pilgrim road to Santiago de Compostela. Word of his miracles spread all through Europe. Visions of Saint Isidore before a battle were said to ensure victory for the Christian forces. A Leonese legend tells how before the important Battle of Las Navas de Tolosa (1212), El Cid himself knocked on the door of the shrine to summon Saint Isidore to the fight.

Isidore's fame as a scholar also increased with Luke, bishop of Tuy's biography, compiled centuries after the saint's death. Dante numbered him among the great theologians, and, in 1722, Isidore was declared a doctor of the Church by Pope Innocent XIII. His feast day is April 4, but in Spain it has traditionally been celebrated on July 25 or December 30.

SIGNIFICANCE

There are, in reality, two Isidores: the pragmatic scholar and educator and the legendary warrior-saint. Both personae converge in his influential role as a developer of Spanish culture and identity. His countrymen were to draw on his vision of a unified Spain as a rallying point in later battles for national identity. He was ahead of his time in understanding the value of education as a tool for forging cultural union; it was this awareness that motivated him to compile and make accessible the information necessary for a literate society.

A strong believer in tradition, Isidore wished to preserve the great classical heritage of learning he had received from his Hispano-Roman forebears. Although not original in content, his encyclopedic writings achieved this purpose and became part of the foundation for the new intellectual awakening of the Renaissance.

Isidore's true originality lay in his concept of welding the contemporary to the classical. His history of the Visigoths offers valuable insight into his times, an era he himself did so much to shape. He was the principal adviser to several kings and tried to use his prestige and scholarship to elevate Visigothic culture. Drawing on tales of the great leaders of Rome, he created the ideal of the perfect Christian prince. Though the Visigothic kings proved intractable, Isidore's ideas served as the basis for numerous future philosophical writings on the essence of kingship and power.

Isidore's influence on daily affairs was enormous. He revised the educational system of his jurisdiction, instituted clerical reform, and insisted on the standardization of religious texts. This influence was not limited to his own time and place. With the adoption of the Fuero Juzgo, the official law of all Christian Spain, Isidore's precepts on law and justice held sway until the twentieth century.

—*Charlene E. Suscavage*

FURTHER READING

Evans, G. R. *Fifty Key Medieval Thinkers*. New York: Routledge, 2002. Succinct biographies of important thinkers—mainly theologians and philosophers—of the Middle Ages, including Isidore. Also provides a bibliography and index.

Isidore of Seville. *History of the Kings of the Goths, Vandals, and Suevi*. Translated by Guido Donini and Gordon B. Ford, Jr. 2d rev. ed. Leiden, The Netherlands: E. J. Brill, 1970. A helpful translation of Isidore's chronicle of the Visigothic monarchy.

_______. *The Medical Writings*. Translated and edited by William D. Sharpe. *Transactions of the American Philosophical Society* 54, no. 2 (1964): 3-75. The editor, a physician, has compiled and translated portions of the *Etymologiae* having to do with medicine. He presents useful background information on Isidore's sources.

Ladner, Gerhart B. *God, Cosmos, and Humankind: The World of Early Christian Symbolism*. Translated by Thomas Dunlap. Berkeley: University of California Press, 1995. Includes the chapter "The Symbolism of the Word and the Name: The Etymologies of Isidore of Seville," which discusses Isidore's use of symbolic language in his *Etymologiae*.

Lear, F. S. "The Public Law of the Visigothic Code." *Speculum* 26 (1951): 1-23. Analysis of the law code Isidore influenced so greatly.

O'Callaghan, Joseph F. *A History of Medieval Spain*. Ithaca, N.Y.: Cornell University Press, 1975. Contains a chapter on the Visigothic era with special emphasis on the drive for unity.

O'Donovan, Oliver, and Joan Lockwood O'Donovan, eds.

From Irenaeus to Grotius: A Sourcebook in Christian Political Thought, 100-1625. Grand Rapids, Mich.: William B. Eerdmans, 1999. An extensive collection. Part 2 includes a section on the Christian-based political ideas of Isidore.

Starkie, Walter. *The Road to Santiago: Pilgrims of St. James*. Reprint. Berkeley: University of California Press, 1965. An impressionistic description of Saint Isidore's shrine and its associated legends.

Thompson, E. A. *The Goths in Spain*. Oxford, England: Clarendon Press, 1969. A good general history of the rise and collapse of the Visigoth empire.

SEE ALSO: Saint Albertus Magnus; Averroës; Roger Bacon; Henry de Bracton; El Cid; John Duns Scotus; Louis IX; Raymond Lull; Paul of Aegina; Rabanus Maurus; al-Rāzī; Thomas Aquinas.

RELATED ARTICLES in *Great Events from History: The Middle Ages, 477-1453*: April or May, 711: Ṭārik Crosses into Spain; October 11, 732: Battle of Tours.

ITZCÓATL

King of the Aztecs (r. 1427?-1440)

As the founder of the Mexican state, Itzcóatl was largely responsible both for the strengths that enabled it to survive until the Spanish conquest of 1519 and for the weaknesses that contributed to its destruction.

BORN: c. 1382; place unknown

DIED: 1440; probably Tenochtitlán (now Mexico City, Mexico)

AREAS OF ACHIEVEMENT: Government and politics, military

EARLY LIFE

Itzcóatl (EETZ-coh-waht-uhl)—meaning "obsidian serpent"—was the illegitimate son of Acamapichtli, the first king of the Mexica, the Aztec tribe that founded Tenochtitlán and came in time to dominate central Mexico. His mother was a seller of herbs or vegetables and apparently a slave, but Itzcóatl distinguished himself as a military commander and statesman before he himself became king of the Mexica about 1427. Except for the remarkable fact of his parentage, nothing is known of his personal life, and his public life can be understood only in relation to the political development of Mexico in his lifetime.

The early struggle of the Mexica to establish themselves in the Valley of Mexico and to achieve hegemony over its various tribes must not be understood as a war among nations but as a conflict of city-states that fought each other in loose alliances. The arena of this struggle was a relatively small area in the vicinity of what is now called Mexico City, the heart of which is the site of Tenochtitlán.

The various chronicles of early Mexican history, all written from memory after the Spanish conquest, do not agree as to dates. The Mexica entered the Valley of Mexico from the north in the latter half of the thirteenth century, the last Náhuatl-speaking tribe to make this migration. They were in their beginnings a poor tribe of nomads, without the complex social and political structure or the elaborate system of religious ritual that they developed later. When they arrived, the valley was dominated by Azcapotzalco, the premier Tepenecan city on the west shore of Lake Texcoco; Tlacopán, on the mainland due west of Tenochtitlán; Coyoacán, on the southwest shore; Xochimilco and Chalco, in the south; and Texcoco, the intellectual center of the valley and the dominant power east of the lake. The Mexica, possessing no lands, indeed no resources but the prowess of their warriors, enlisted as mercenaries in the employ of other cities. In the early fourteenth century, one faction of the Mexica, defeated by the enemies of their employers, fled to a swampy area in the lake and began the slow process of building up the land on which they established the town of Tlatilulco. Later—in 1369, according to one account—another faction, also forced to flee from their mainland enemies, established a second town nearby: Tenochtitlán.

In their wanderings and their early years in central Mexico, the basic organs of civil and military management of the Mexica were the clans, each of which was governed by its own council of elders, a headman, and a "speaker" who represented it in the council of the Mexica. After the founding of Tenochtitlán, however, a steady process of centralization began, and by 1375, when Acamapichtli was chosen the first king of Tenochtitlán, this process was virtually complete, so that a great gulf had opened between the council and the commoners, with real power concentrated in the hands of an oligarchy composed of a few great families who dominated the council and monopolized all administrative and religious power.

Acamapichtli's successor was his son, Huitzilhuitl, who became king in 1404, married the daughter of Tezozómoc, the king of Azcapotzalco, and was succeeded in 1416 by his ten-year-old son Chimalpopoca, during whose reign the inevitable conflict with Azcapotzalco came to a head.

Life's Work

Itzcóatl may have been speaker under Huitzilhuitl, and he certainly filled this post during the reign of Chimalpopoca. In that role, he astutely and cautiously extended the trade and influence of the Mexica to the shore towns while avoiding an open clash with Azcapotzalco. In 1426, Tezozómoc of Azcapotzalco died and was succeeded by his son Maxtla, who was determined to end the rivalry of the upstart Mexica and, according to one account, arranged the murder of Chimalpopoca in 1427.

Another account, however, suggests that Chimalpopoca was murdered by the war faction in the Mexican council. According to this story, the Mexica demanded materials from Tezozómoc for building a causeway to bring water from Chapultepec, on the west shore of the lake. The allies of Azcapotzalco, realizing that such a causeway would strengthen Tenochtitlán, resisted this demand and determined to destroy the Mexica. They cut off all trade and other contact with Tenochtitlán, and when Tezozómoc died, Chimalpopoca, no longer able to count on his grandfather's protection, was murdered. In any case, the council of the Mexica elected Itzcóatl as his successor.

Itzcóatl was recognized for both his bravery and his prudence; in fact, one source gives credit to him as a military leader and an important administrator as early as 1407. Another says that he had commanded armies for three decades. These achievements probably account for his election in spite of his illegitimacy. He was at that time about forty-five years old.

Itzcóatl's situation when he became king was precarious because of the forces arrayed against the Mexica, but he had strong allies in Tlacopán and in the king of Texcoco, his nephew Nezahualcóyotl, who was putting together an alliance of all the cities east of the lake. It was also at this time that Itzcóatl succeeded, perhaps by marriage to a princess of the other Mexican city in the lake, Tlatilulco, in achieving an alliance that led eventually to the merger of the two cities. Itzcóatl's further achievement of a triple alliance of Tenochtitlán-Tlatilulco with Texcoco and Tlacopán was perhaps his greatest political achievement, and it survived, with Tenochtitlán the dominant force in the alliance, until the Spanish conquest.

In 1428, Itzcóatl gathered the council in Tenochtitlán and demanded war against Azcapotzalco and its west-shore allies. Strong arguments were made in the council for peace, but the military party had everything to gain from a war. The power of the state, in the hands of the oligarchy, had been partially thwarted by certain elements in Tenochtitlán society that would be rendered powerless by a major victory against the city's enemies. In fact, the accounts that blame the Tepanecs for the death of Chimalpopoca may have been written to justify the war with them. In any case, Itzcóatl, encouraged by his nephew Tlacaelel, who shared his sense of the destiny of the Mexica to rule all the Valley of Mexico, prevailed in the council. A peace proposal was sent to Azcapotzalco, combined with a threat of war if it were not accepted. Its rejection was followed by a Tepanecan attack across the causeway from the mainland. Nezahualcóyotl had brought his Texcoco warriors to Tenochtitlán, and the Mexica of Tenochtitlán and Tlatilulco were united. As a result, the Tepanecs, completely routed, fled to Azcapotzalco, which fell to the allies after a siege of four months. It was completely destroyed, and the few of its population who did not escape were exterminated or enslaved.

In 1429-1430, the Mexica repaid Nezahualcóyotl for his support by helping him recover control of those cities east of the lake that had rebelled with the encouragement of Azcapotzalco. In 1430, Tenochtitlán asked—or demanded—that Xochimilco provide stone and logs for the expansion of the temple of Huitzilopochtli. When these materials were denied, Xochimilco was blockaded and eventually conquered. Its lands were distributed among Itzcóatl's closest supporters, and Xochimilco agreed to provide the materials and the slave labor to build a great causeway to join Tenochtitlán to the mainland from the south. A year later, Coyoacán broke off trading relations with Tenochtitlán, in effect declaring war, and was subsequently conquered. In all, according to one account (the Codex Mendoza), Itzcóatl is credited with the conquest of twenty-four towns.

In 1431, Nezahualcóyotl was crowned emperor of the three-city league, but events had already set in motion the process by which Tenochtitlán and its kings would be the dominant power in Mexico. For a period of five or six years after the war, the slave laborers and the tribute won in the war were used to erect palaces, expand

Tenochtitlán-Tlatilulco, build canals within the city, and erect greater shrines to the gods. In the center of Tenochtitlán was built the monumental shrine to the god of war, Huitzilopochtli.

The primary result of the war was the total reorganization of Mexican society. Itzcóatl created twenty-one titles for the greatest families and established a system of succession that endured until the Spanish conquest: When a king was chosen, four brothers or other close relatives were elevated to special titles, and one of them was named to be his successor. The conquered agricultural lands were distributed to a relatively small number of Mexican leaders, thus magnifying the power of the oligarchy; political power was concentrated in the hands of the king, the speaker, and the council; and the power of the military class was considerably enhanced. Above all, the cult of Huitzilopochtli, the god of war whose demands for sacrificial victims, as interpreted by the priests, were virtually insatiable, was greatly augmented. The result, in other words, was profoundly ideological—the dictatorship of the oligarchy supported by the warrior elite was justified by a constant state of war, and warfare was required by the constant need for sacrificial victims. Political, military, and religious concerns were supportive of one another.

Several accounts maintain that before the attack on Azcapotzalco the commoners were fearful of the consequences of a possible defeat. According to one account, Itzcóatl is supposed to have offered a wager to them: If the warriors failed, the king and his council would permit themselves to be killed and eaten. The commoners, in turn, agreed that if the warriors were victorious, they would accept a state of virtual slavery. This strange wager would seem, however, to be pure propaganda written after the event. In fact, most accounts agree that after the Mexica had won the Tepanec War, Itzcóatl ordered the destruction of existing accounts of the Mexican past and their rewriting to emphasize the grandeur and the justice of Tenochtitlán's rise to power. Apparently, the reforms also included a manipulation of education and of art and literature in the service of the state: Itzcóatl was the first king of Tenochtitlán to have his likeness carved in stone. Clearly, the most appalling aspect of the ideological reforms of Itzcóatl's reign was the sharp increase in the magnitude of human sacrifice.

Most accounts agree that Itzcóatl died in 1440 and was succeeded by Moctezuma I (also known as Montezuma I; r. 1440-1469), who expanded the Aztec Empire by using the methods and the ideology that his predecessor had developed.

SIGNIFICANCE

Itzcóatl must be credited with the foundation of the Mexican monarchy, which became the dominant power in central Mexico under the rule of his successors, and he established the political and military institutions, including the political alliance with Texcoco and Tlacopán, that made possible the Aztec Empire, which endured until the arrival of the Spanish in 1519. The human cost of this achievement, however, was by modern standards outrageously high.

The state that Itzcóatl was primarily responsible for creating existed for its own glorification. Even European monarchies of the time were less powerful in their control of their people—if only because they were subject to the disapproval of the Church—than was the oligarchy to which Itzcóatl gave power. Indeed, Itzcóatl, with the aid of like-minded individuals, created the kind of absolute totalitarian state that Europe did not suffer until the twentieth century. The oligarchy controlled the education of young nobles, who were taught to serve the state, and literary and artistic culture was dedicated to the glorification of the state. Furthermore, the destruction of historical chronicles and rewriting of history to make the state and its keepers the absolute political reality was something unknown in Europe until modern times.

Itzcóatl's use of the cult of Huitzilopochtli for political ends, considering that it was a cult that demanded human sacrifice, is the most extraordinary aspect of the totalitarian system he created. Admittedly, the numbers of sacrificial victims were inflated by Spanish chroniclers, but even when those numbers are reduced, the hard kernel of historical fact still horrifies. This religion of blood was put to the service of the state, and the state engaged in warfare to serve the religion. This inevitably vicious circle produced slaughter too appalling to condone, whatever the numbers. Certainly, Itzcóatl, though he had the encouragement of his colleagues, must receive the largest share of the blame. After the conquest of Azcapotzalco, he issued an edict proclaiming Huitzilopochtli the supreme god of the Mexica, and after the conquest of Coyoacán, he issued another that defined the divine mission of the Mexica as bringing all the nations of the world to the worship of that god by force of arms. The "flower wars" that provided victims for the priest-executioners of Tenochtitlán during the eighty years after Itzcóatl's death were the terrible legacy of his reign, and they contributed more than anything else to the destruction of the state he created, for the Spanish were welcomed by the enemies those wars produced.

Considering all this, it is an error to condemn Hernán Cortés and the Spanish conquest without taking account of the fact that, in spite of the excesses of that conquest, it did not introduce to the Mexican people any violence, exploitation, or infringement of liberty that was new to them. If the priests who accompanied Cortés burned Aztec libraries, Itzcóatl had done the same before them; if they enslaved the Aztecs, the enemies of the Aztecs also had been enslaved; if they enforced conversion to Christianity, the Aztecs had sought the same ends on behalf of Huitzilopochtli, whose demands on the common people of Mexico were infinitely bloodier.

—Robert L. Berner

FURTHER READING

Brundage, Burr Cartwright. *A Rain of Darts: The Mexica Aztecs*. Austin: University of Texas Press, 1972. A thorough one-volume history of the Aztecs, from their obscure origins to the destruction of Tenochtitlán in 1521. Carefully weighs all the evidence of the codices and provides the most likely dates for the events of Aztec history. Maps, bibliography.

Carrasco, Pedro. *The Tenochca Empire of Ancient Mexico: The Triple Alliance of Tenochtitlán, Tetzcoco, and Tlacopan*. Norman: University of Oklahoma Press, 1999. Presents a history of the politics and government of the tripartite Aztec alliance. Maps, bibliography, and index.

Conrad, Geoffrey W., and Arthur A. Demarest. *Religion and Empire: The Dynamics of Aztec and Inca Expansionism*. New York: Cambridge University Press, 1984. A comparative study that thoroughly examines the political and social factors that led to Aztec expansion and evaluates the theories modern scholars have proposed to account for it. Illustrations and extensive bibliography.

Durán, Diego. *The Aztecs: The History of the Indies of New Spain*. Translated by Doris Heyden and Fernando Horcasitas. New York: Orion, 1964. The author was a contemporary Dominican friar who was in Mexico only twenty years after the Spanish conquest and based his account on the codices and the memory of informants. The text was written to help Christian missionaries understand Aztec paganism, but it reveals considerable sympathy for the Indians.

Gillmor, Frances. *The King Danced in the Marketplace*. 1964. Reprint. Salt Lake City: University of Utah Press, 1977. The king of the title is Moctezuma I, but this book deals also with the events of Itzcóatl's reign. Based on solid research and thoroughly documented, but written in a novelistic style. Map, genealogical table, bibliography, and index.

Kimmel, Eric A. *Montezuma and the Fall of the Aztecs*. New York: Holiday House, 2000. Briefly traces the life and reign of Moctezuma II and the fall of the Aztec Empire after the Spanish conquest. Written for young readers. Colored map, bibliography.

Meyer, Michael C., William L. Sherman, and Susan M. Deeds. *The Course of Mexican History*. 6th ed. New York: Oxford University Press, 1999. A 732-page history of Mexico prior to, during, and after the reign of Itzcóatl and the time of the Aztecs. Maps, bibliography, and index.

Padden, R. C. *The Hummingbird and the Hawk: Conquest and Sovereignty in the Valley of Mexico, 1503-1541*. Columbus: Ohio State University Press, 1967. A thoroughly researched study of the conflict of Aztec and Spanish religious beliefs during the reign of Moctezuma II, the conquest, and its aftermath, this account offers many insights into the rise of the Mexica during the reign of Itzcóatl. Maps, bibliography.

Radin, Paul. "The Sources and Authenticity of the History of the Ancient Mexicans." *University of California Publications in American Archaeology and Ethnology* 17 (1920-1926): 1-150. Provides translations of various Aztec codices, including the lengthy Codex Ramírez, which deals more fully than most of the primary documents with the events of the reigns of Itzcóatl and his predecessors.

RELATED ARTICLES in *Great Events from History: The Middle Ages, 477-1453*: c. 7th-8th centuries: Maya Build Astronomical Observatory at Palenque; 600-950: El Tajín Is Built; c. 700-1000: Building of Chichén Itzá; c. 950-1150: Toltecs Build Tula; 1325-1519: Aztecs Build Tenochtitlán.

ABŪ MŪSĀ JĀBIR IBN ḤAYYĀN
Arabian chemist and alchemist

The greatest alchemist of Islam, Jābir is regarded as the father of Arabian chemistry. His many works influenced later Arabian and European chemists considerably, and his alchemical ideas and recipes helped advance chemical theory and experimentation.

BORN: 721; Tūs (now in Iran)
DIED: 815; Al-Kūfa (now in Iraq)
AREA OF ACHIEVEMENT: Science and technology, chemistry

EARLY LIFE

It must be said at the outset that many scholars, some from as long ago as the tenth century, have believed that Jābir ibn Ḥayyān (JAHB-IHR ihb-ehn hi-YAHN) did not exist at all, but belief in his existence has always had its defenders. Those accepting his authenticity think that his family came from the southern Arabian Azd tribe that had settled, during the rise of Islam, in Al-Kūfa, then a rapidly growing city on the Euphrates River just south of the ruins of Babylon. Abū Mūsā Jābir ibn Ḥayyān, Jābir's father (with whom he shares his name), was a Shīʿite apothecary in Khorāsān in eastern Persia, and he supported the powerful ʿAbbāsid family, who hoped to overthrow the Umayyad caliph. (The Umayyad Dynasty had ruled the Muslim Empire since 661.) The ʿAbbāsids sent Abū Mūsā throughout Persia to prepare the way for a revolution. In the course of this political mission he visited Ṭūs, near what is now Mashhad in northeast Iran, and there, around 721, his son was born and named for him. While the younger Jābir was still a child, his father was captured by the caliph's agents and beheaded.

Jābir was sent to southern Arabia, where he studied all branches of Eastern learning, including alchemy and medicine. Some scholars say that he was taught by Jaʿfar ibn Muḥammad (699/700 or 702/703-765), the sixth Shīʿite imam, who was a descendant of ʿAlī, the cousin and son-in-law of Muḥammad. In his later writings, Jābir often stated that he was nothing but a spokesperson for Jaʿfar's doctrines. Besides being a Shīʿite, Jābir was also a Sufi, a mystic Muslim, and illustrators have depicted him with high forehead and curly hair and beard, and dressed in woolen Sufic robes. The Sufis taught Jābir a doctrine ascribing hidden meanings to numbers and letters, which had a great influence on his alchemical theories.

Because the Umayyads remained in power until Jābir was in his late twenties, he lived a life of concealment, roaming through various countries without settling in one place because he feared that the caliph would have him executed. Around 750, when the ʿAbbāsids succeeded in their revolution, he became associated with the viziers of the ʿAbbāsids, the powerful Barmakids. He had earned the grand-vizier's gratitude by curing one of his mortally ill harem girls. The Barmakid family became patrons of Jābir and obtained a position for him at the court of Hārūn al-Rashīd, the famous caliph of the legendary collection of tales about Central Asia, *Alf layla wa-layla* (fifteenth century; *The Arabian Nights' Entertainments*, 1706-1708; also known as *The Thousand and One Nights*), which is of uncertain authorship and date. Jābir, for his part, deemed it an honor to compose works for this caliph.

LIFE'S WORK

In some lists, the writings that bear Jābir's name number more than three thousand. According to many scholars, these works are sufficiently different in style, vocabulary, approach, and content to establish separate authorship for many of them. For example, in some of the works certain terms from late ninth century Greek translations are used, indicating that they were written long after Jābir's death. Many historians of science now regard as probable the thesis that, though some of these works may have been written by Jābir, most were composed by members of the Ismāʿīlīs, a Shīʿite sect that believed that Muḥammad ibn Ismāʿil was the seventh imam and which was particularly interested in mysticism, numerology, alchemy, and astrology. Although some recent scholars are more willing than their earlier colleagues to grant historical reality to Jābir and his works, all agree that many of the surviving writings contain later Ismāʿīlī modifications and additions.

To complicate matters further, several alchemical texts that appeared in the thirteenth and fourteenth centuries with Jābir's name have no Arabic equivalents, and their style and content reveal that they were written by a Western, most likely Spanish, alchemist who lived in the later Middle Ages. This anonymous Spanish alchemist adopted Jābir's name to add authority to his work. Scholars therefore completely disregard the Latin texts by Jābir and exclusively consider the Arabic texts when discussing Jābir ibn Ḥayyān.

The majority of the Arabic Jabirian texts are alchemical, but others concern medicine, cosmology, astrology, mathematics, magic, music, and philosophy. The most important books include the *Kitāb al-sabʿīn* (c. late ninth century; the seventy books) and the *Kitāb al-mawāzīn* (early tenth century; the book of balances). Unfortunately, the bulk of the Jabirian writings remain unstudied, even though they constitute the most significant body of alchemical works in Arabic and a principal source of Latin alchemy.

To appreciate Jābir's achievements, one must understand his relationship to Greek philosophy and early alchemy. In his theory of matter, he derived many of his basic ideas from Aristotle, but not without modification. For example, Aristotle regarded the four principles, heat, cold, moisture, and dryness, as accidental qualities, whereas Jābir saw them as material natures that could be separated and combined in definite proportions to form new substances. Other Jabirian ideas can be traced to the Greek alchemists of Alexandria. These early alchemical writings, however, are often confusing and superstitious, so when Jābir used these ideas, he justified them both rationally and empirically.

In Jābir's scheme of things, science was divided into two interdependent halves, the religious and the secular. He then divided secular knowledge into alchemy and techniques. The task of the alchemist was to use various techniques to isolate pure natures, determine the proportion in which they entered into substances, and then combine them in proper amounts to give desired products. Ideally, the practice of alchemy should raise the alchemist to a higher level of knowledge where both his soul and the world will be transformed. Practically, alchemy centered on the transmutation of metals, notably the changing of base metals such as lead and iron into the valuable metals such as silver and gold.

Jābir's system of alchemy was logical and precise. For example, his classification of substances shows great clarity of thought. He divided minerals into three groups, each having certain specific qualities based on the predominance of one of the pure natures: first, spirits, or substances that completely evaporate in fire (for example, sulfur, mercury, and camphor); second, metals, or meltable and malleable substances that shine and ring when hammered (such as lead, copper, and gold); and third, pulverizable substances that, meltable or not, are not malleable and that shatter into powder when hammered (malachite, turquoise, mica, and the like).

Jābir was a firm believer in the possibility of transmutation, since this was a logical conclusion from his sulfur-mercury theory of metals. This theory suggested that all metals were composed of different proportions of idealized sulfur and idealized mercury. These idealized, or pristine, substances bore some resemblance to common sulfur and mercury, but the idealized substances were much purer than anything that could be produced alchemically. Jābir's theory probably derived from Aristotle's *Meteorologica* (335-323 B.C.E.; English translation, 1812), where the process of exhalations from the earth forming minerals and metals is discussed. For Aristotle, earthy smoke consisted of earth in the process of changing into fire, and watery vapor was water undergoing conversion into air. Difficult-to-melt minerals consisted mainly of the earthy smoke, while easy-to-melt metals were formed from the watery vapor. In Jābir's view, sulfur and mercury were formed under planetary influence in the interior of the earth as intermediates between the exhalations and the minerals and metals.

To explain the existence of different kinds of metals, Jābir assumed that the sulfurous and mercurial principles were not always pure and that they did not always unite in the same proportions. If they were perfectly pure and combined in the most perfect manner, then the product was the perfect metal, gold. Defects in proportion or purity resulted in the formation of other metals. Because all metals were composed of the same constituents as gold, the transmutation of less valuable metals into gold could be effected by means of an elixir.

For the alchemists, the elixir, also called the philosopher's stone, was a substance that brought about the rapid transmutation of base metals into gold. The term was initially used for a substance that cured human illnesses (the Arabic *al-iksir* was derived from a Greek word for medicinal powder). In an analogous fashion, an elixir might "perfect," or cure, imperfect metals. A peculiarity of Jābir's system was its emphasis on the use of vegetable and animal substances in the preparation of the elixir (earlier alchemists used inorganic materials). In his search for materials from which the elixir could be extracted, Jābir investigated bone marrow, lion's hair, jasmine, onions, ginger, pepper, mustard, anemones, and many other materials from the plant and animal kingdoms.

An essential part of Jābir's sulfur-mercury theory was his numerological system, used to calculate the balance of the metals necessary to achieve transmutation. Balance, or *mizan*, was the central concept used by Jābir to catalog and number the basic qualities of all substances. Therefore all alchemical work involved establishing the correct proportion of the natures—hot, cold, moist, and dry—and then expressing this proportion in numbers.

In applying this idea of balance to metals, Jābir noted that each metal had two exterior and two interior qualities. For example, gold was inwardly cold and dry, outwardly hot and moist. He determined the nature of each metal by a complex number system whose key numbers, 17 and 28, were derived from a magic square. Its top row contained the numbers 4, 9, and 2; the middle row, 3, 5, and 7; and the bottom row, 8, 1, and 6. Adding the numbers of the top row to the bottom two numbers of the last vertical column yields 28. The numbers of the remaining, smaller square add up to 17. It is likely that 28, a number to which the Sufis attached great value, was astrological in origin, since it is the product of the number of known planets (7) and the number of Aristotelian elements (4). Twenty-eight is also a perfect number in that it is equal to the sum of its divisors (1, 2, 4, 7, and 14). In evaluating the nature of metals, Jābir used the numbers in the smaller square, 1, 3, 5, and 8. Thus, in his system, the contrary natures, hot and cold, or moist and dry, could fuse only in the proportions 1 to 3 or 5 to 8. The sum of these numbers is 17, and 17 is the number of powers that Jābir attributed to the metals. Each quality, moreover, had 4 degrees and 7 subdivisions, or 28 parts altogether. He assigned each of these 28 parts to one of the letters of the Arabic alphabet. He then composed tables interrelating the values of the Arabic letters (which depended on the Arabic name for each metal) and the amounts of the 4 natures.

Beyond its purely alchemical meaning, the term *mizan*, or balance, was a basic principle of Jābir's worldview. Balance also meant the harmony of the various tendencies of the Neoplatonic world soul, the organizer of the basic qualities. Balance was therefore related to Jābir's monism, which opposed the dualistic worldview of Manichaeanism (the struggle against this religion was a chief concern of Islam at the time). This religious side of Jābir's thought was based on the appearance of the word *mizan* in the Qurʾān, where it is used in the sense of a balance that weighs one's good and bad deeds at the Last Judgment.

Astrology also played an important part in Jābir's system. The stars were not only constituents of the world but they also influenced earthly events. All natural substances had specific properties that linked them to the upper world, and this link allowed talismans to be used effectively. The talisman bore the power of the stars and, when used properly, could provide domination over events. Thus, for Jābir, the same causality determined astrology and alchemy. Both sciences imitated the Creator, since Creator and alchemist worked with the same materials and were governed by the same laws.

Despite his great fame as court astrologer and alchemist, Jābir fell out of favor in 803 because of his association with the Barmakids. When these powerful ministers had been discovered plotting against the caliph, some were executed; others were expelled. Jābir shared the banishment of the Barmakids, and he withdrew to Al-Kūfa in eastern Persia. One account states that he returned to court under the new caliph, al-Maʾmūn (r. 813-833); another states that he spent the rest of his life in obscurity. The date of his death is uncertain, though it is usually given as 815. Two centuries after his death, during building operations in a quarter of Al-Kūfa known as the Damascus Gate, Jābir's cellar laboratory was discovered along with a golden mortar weighing two hundred pounds.

SIGNIFICANCE

Jābir ibn Ḥayyān is important for both the history of alchemy and the development of Islamic culture. Although from the vantage point of later centuries his scientific thought seems strange and superstitious, he did help to advance chemical theory and experiment. In searching for the secret of transmutation, he mastered many basic chemical techniques, such as sublimation and distillation, and became familiar with the preparation and properties of many basic chemicals. For example, he was fascinated with sal ammoniac (now called ammonium chloride), a substance unknown to the Greeks. The volatility of this salt greatly impressed the Arabs. Jābir was a skilled and ingenious experimenter, and he described for the first time how to prepare nitric acid. More clearly than any other early chemist, he stated and recognized the importance of the experimental process. In his work he also described and suggested improvements in such chemical technological processes as dyeing and glassmaking.

His work also belongs to the legacy of Islam. The Shīʿites state that he is one of their great spiritual guides. Scarcely a single later Arabic alchemical text exists in which he is not quoted. When, in the twelfth and thirteenth centuries, Islamic science was transmitted to Latin Christianity, the fame of Jābir went with it. His sulfur-mercury theory persisted and was at last modified into the phlogiston theory of Johann Becher and George Stahl in the seventeenth and eighteenth centuries. In the guise of Jābir's works, Arabic alchemy exerted considerable influence on the development of modern chemistry.

—*Robert J. Paradowski*

FURTHER READING

Federmann, Reinhard. *The Royal Art of Alchemy.* Translated by Richard H. Weber. Philadelphia: Chilton,

1969. This book, originally published in 1964, is a popular account of the history of alchemy. It also includes a chapter specifically devoted to Jābir's life and work. Bibliography.

Haq, Syed Nomanul. *Names, Natures and Things: The Alchemist Jābir ibn Ḥayyān and His Kitāb al-Ahjar (Book of Stones)*. Boston: Kluwer Academic, 1994. Explores Jābir's alchemical work, especially its focus on taxonomy (the naming of things) and materialism. Part of the Studies in the Philosophy of Science series. Extensive bibliography and an index.

Holmyard, E. J. *Alchemy*. 1957. Reprint. New York: Dover, 1990. The author, who has published extensively on Jābir's writings, presents a good general survey of alchemy. He accepts Jābir's existence and presents a detailed reconstruction of his life. Bibliography, index.

Leicester, Henry M. *The Historical Background of Chemistry*. 1956. Reprint. New York: Dover, 1971. The author follows the evolution of chemistry through the ideas of chemists rather than their lives. His chapter on Arabic alchemy contains an insightful account of the body of writings associated with Jābir. Bibliography.

Nasr, Seyyed Hossein. *Islamic Science: An Illustrated Study*. Westerham, England: World of Islam Festival, 1976. The first illustrated account of Islamic science ever undertaken. Using traditional Islamic concepts, the author discusses various branches of science, including alchemy, and places Jābir's work in its Islamic setting.

_______. *Science and Civilization in Islam*. New York: New American Library, 1968. This book is the first one-volume work in English to deal with Islamic science from the Muslim rather than the Western point of view. Its approach is encyclopedic rather than analytic, but it does contain a discussion of Jābir's life and work in its Muslim context.

Rashed, Roshdi, ed. *Encyclopedia of the History of Arabic Science*. 3 vols. New York: Routledge, 1996. Vol. 1 surveys the history of technology, alchemy, and the life sciences in Arabic science. Bibliography, index.

Read, John. *Prelude to Chemistry: An Outline of Alchemy, Its Literature and Relationships*. Cambridge, Mass.: MIT Press, 1966. First published in 1936, this book offers a bird's-eye view of alchemy from its origins in Egypt and India to the era of the phlogiston theory. Its emphasis is on the relationship of alchemy to literature. Bibliography, notes.

Schacht, Joseph, and C. E. Bosworth, eds. *The Legacy of Islam*. 2d ed. New York: Oxford University Press, 1974. This version of a work edited in 1931 by Thomas Arnold and Alfred Guillaume analyzes the contributions of Islamic civilization to the world. The chapter "The Natural Sciences and Medicine" contains brief remarks on Jābir. Bibliography, index.

Taylor, F. Sherwood. *The Alchemists*. 1949. Reprint. New York: Arno Press, 1974. Still the best of the general works on alchemy. It clearly and sympathetically surveys the field from ancient to modern times. Bibliography.

Turner, Howard R. *Science in Medieval Islam: An Illustrated Introduction*. Austin: University of Texas Press, 1997. Explores the world of science, including alchemy, in medieval Islam. Good for those interested in an introduction to the topic. Maps, bibliography, and index.

SEE ALSO: al-Ḥallāj; Hārūn al-Rashīd; Rābiʿah al-ʿAdawiyah; al-Rāzī; Jalāl al-Dīn Rūmī.

RELATED ARTICLES in *Great Events from History: The Middle Ages, 477-1453*: 786-809: Reign of Hārūn al-Rashīd; Mid-9th century: Invention of Gunpowder and Guns; c. 1150: Moors Transmit Classical Philosophy and Medicine to Europe.

Jacopo della Quercia

Italian sculptor

Heir to the late Gothic sculptural style of fourteenth century Italy and influenced by the spatial massing of form found in ancient classical art, Jacopo forged an independent, monumental style of great expressive power. Along with Lorenzo Ghiberti, Donatello, and Nanni di Banco, he is considered one of the most significant sculptors working in the early decades of the Italian Renaissance.

Born: c. 1374; probably Siena, Republic of Siena (now in Italy)
Died: October 20, 1438; Siena, Republic of Siena
Area of achievement: Art

Early Life

Although the sculptural commissions executed during the mature career of Jacopo della Quercia (YAWK-oh-poh dayl-lah KWEHR-chah) are amply documented, very little is known about his early life. His father, Piero di Angelo, was a Sienese goldsmith and wood-carver who was married in 1370. Giorgio Vasari, a sixteenth century art historian, has left two versions of Jacopo's life. In the first version, written in 1550, he attributes to Jacopo an equestrian statue of the condotierre (mercenary military leader) Giovanni d'Arco that was executed in 1391 but is now lost. To receive such a commission, Jacopo would have to have been at least nineteen years of age, placing his birth date around 1371. Vasari's second version, written in 1568, claims that Jacopo was sixty-four years of age when he died in 1438, which calculates to a slightly later birthdate. What is known for certain is that by 1401, when Jacopo entered the famous competition for the Florentine baptistery doors commission, he must have been a master sculptor of some renown.

The meaning and origins of the name "della Quercia" is a mystery. He was identified by this name as early as the mid-fifteenth century, but early documents refer to him as "Jacopo di Maestro Piero," after his father, and even later he is occasionally called "Jacopo delle Fonte" in reference to his work on the Fonte Gaia in Siena. It is possible he either inherited the "della Quercia" from his grandfather, or that it refers to a district of Siena in which he was born or lived. It is extremely doubtful that it indicates a birthplace outside Siena.

Jacopo's early career is the subject of scholarly conjecture. It is safe to assume that, in the tradition of the time, he received his initial training from his father, who worked as a wood-carver. Piero di Angelo did not carve in stone, however, nor was there much activity in that medium in Siena during the last years of the fourteenth century. It is generally accepted that during the 1490's Jacopo probably traveled to one of the Italian cities where major stone or marble sculptural programs were in progress. The possibilities include Bologna, Milan, or Venice, but theories concerning his activities in any of these cities are purely tentative.

The first firmly documented event in his life is his participation in the competition for the commission to create a set of bronze doors for the baptistery of the cathedral in Florence. Lorenzo Ghiberti won the competition, and Jacopo's bronze relief competition panel has not survived.

In 1403, Jacopo was in Ferrara, where he began an altar for the Silvestri family, completion of which occurred in 1408. A marble Madonna and Child created for this altar is the earliest extant work universally accepted by scholars as being an example of his style. (Earlier works have been attributed to him, but the attributions are controversial.) During these same years, he also traveled to Lucca to execute the sepulchral monument to Ilaria del Carretto-Guinigi, who died in 1405.

These two youthful works demonstrate a flexibility of expression that would mark his entire career. The *Silvestri Madonna* is boldly carved, forthright, and monumental. The Ilaria sepulcher, with its graceful effigy and sarcophagus base, presents a quieter, more romantic expression fitting to its subject. In both works, one finds a classical, spatial massing of form coexisting with a rhythmic, elegant line derived from Gothic antecedents.

Life's Work

In 1408, Jacopo received a commission that would occupy him, on and off, until 1419. That was for the Fonte Gaia in Siena, a large fountain in the center of town, which would serve as a civic focal piece. Contemporary documents indicate that physical work on the fountain did not begin until 1414. The plan of the fountain ultimately included numerous figural and decorative reliefs and statues. The overall scheme, as well as the handling of the human figures and decorative motifs, was heavily influenced by antique classicism. In particular, the high reliefs depicting scenes from Genesis display, despite their badly weathered condition, an unusually well-developed sense of classically inspired physicality and of the potential for form to create emotional expression.

Concurrent with the Sienese project, Jacopo was executing commissions in Lucca. In 1412, Lorenzo Trenta, a wealthy Lucchese merchant, began building a family burial chapel in the Church of San Frediano. Jacopo was put in charge of the project, which was not totally finished until 1422. The archaic gothicisms that flavor the chapel's tomb markers and altar, especially surprising in the light of the contemporary Fonte Gaia, reflect Jacopo's willingness and ability to alter his style in the interests of harmonizing his work to the taste and style of its surroundings.

The documentary sources reveal that Jacopo was an ambitious sculptor who rarely refused an important commission. The result was delay and procrastination, as he attempted to juggle his various commitments. For example, while under contract for both the Fonte Gaia and the Trenta chapel, he accepted yet another assignment. In 1417, he was commissioned to make two bronze reliefs for the Siena baptistery font. By 1425, he still had not delivered the reliefs and the Opera del Duomo (cathedral works committee), which had already reassigned one panel to the Florentine sculptor Donatello, sued Jacopo for return of the money advanced. Not until 1430 would Jacopo be paid for completing his relief depicting the Annunciation to Zacchariah. Despite his procrastination, in 1427 he was placed in charge of the entire baptistery font program, perhaps in a bid to secure his attention.

In 1425, Jacopo began work on his most famous sculptural program, the main portal (porta magna) of the Church of San Petronio in Bologna. From then until his death in 1438, he would maintain two workshops, one in Bologna and one in Siena. The Sienese would try to keep him at home with commissions (the Vari-Bentivoglio monument and the Casini altar), fines, and finally, in 1435, an appointment as architect-in-chief of the cathedral works. Despite these demands, Jacopo would make one of his greatest artistic statements in the San Petronio sculpture, where the low relief Old Testament scenes display simplified, monumental compositions and classically rendered human nudes. The *Madonna and Child* for the project is admired for its handling of spatial massing, and all the sculpture is marked by a rippling, mobile line.

A fairly complete picture of Jacopo the sculptor emerges from the historical and physical evidence of his professional career. He personally traveled to marble quarries to choose the raw material for his projects but had little compunction about leaving major programs in the hands of assistants when other commitments required his absence. The work secured to his hand displays an ability to infuse classical forms with a high level of emotion. His compositions are marked by rhythms of line and form that imbue them with an unmistakable sense of movement. Rarely in sculpture does one find works in which line and mass coexist on such equal footing.

Jacopo is considered an independent artist, partly because his career took place outside of Florence, the major Italian center for sculpture in the early fifteenth century. He was well aware of the achievements of the Florentine artists but forged a different, almost idiosyncratic, style connected to theirs but, at the same time, separate. The Florentine achievements in pictorial space, for example, never really concerned Jacopo. His emphasis was always on the heroically scaled foreground figures. Backgrounds and details were reduced to a minimum. His insistent, rippling line, at times poetic and at other times nervous and expressive, defined outlines and contours and had no equivalent among his major contemporaries.

The picture of Jacopo the man is less complete. Little is known about his private life. An impending marriage is recorded in 1424, but there is no evidence that it took place and neither a wife nor children were mentioned in his will. In 1413, he was involved in an affair with the wife of a wealthy Lucchese merchant, and that year, he and one of his assistants were accused of theft, rape, and sodomy. The assistant spent several years in prison, but Jacopo escaped Lucca, only returning on receipt of safe conduct in 1416. This event did not seem to affect either his professional or social position. In 1418 and 1435, he was elected to the Sienese City Council, and in 1420, he was chosen to serve as the prior of his district in Siena. His inimitable style seems to have secured for him a fair degree of wealth, position, and protection. It certainly secured for him a prominent place in the history of art.

SIGNIFICANCE

Although Jacopo exerted some stylistic influence during his career and immediately after his death, full appreciation of his legacy did not develop until one hundred years later. In the late fifteenth century, another sculptor, also an independent and also fascinated by the expressive possibilities of form and heroic physicality, would be greatly impressed by exposure to Jacopo's work. That sculptor was Michelangelo. That Michelangelo studied Jacopo's sculpture is proved not only by historical documentation but also by the frequent quotations of Jacopo's San Petronio reliefs in Michelangelo's Sistine Chapel paintings. In Jacopo, Michelangelo found a stylistic ancestor. In Michelangelo, Jacopo's experiments in heroic form found their fulfillment.

A study of Jacopo's sculpture forces the viewer to confront the complexities of artistic style at the dawn of the Italian Renaissance. The Gothic style had not disappeared overnight. The forms and techniques of ancient classical art were not revived indiscriminately. The two traditions had been influencing Italian sculptors since the mid-thirteenth century, and they continued to coexist in Jacopo's work. Jacopo's responses to these traditions, however, were personal and independent. Gothic line and classical form were reinterpreted to ends that were expressive without being expressionistic and were classical without being revivalistic.

—*Madeline Cirillo Archer*

Further Reading

Beck, James. *Jacopo della Quercia*. New York: Columbia University Press, 1991. 2 vols. A biography of thenoted sculptor. Illustrated, with bibliography and index.

Beck, James, and Auerlio Amendola. *Ilaria del Carretto di Jacopo Della Quercia*. Milano, Italy: Silvana Editoriale, 1988. A look at Jacopo's work on the Ilaria del Carretto tomb. In English and Italian.

Hanson, Anne Coffin. *Jacopo della Quercia's Fonte Gaia*. Oxford, England: Clarendon Press, 1965. A monograph on one of Jacopo's most important commissions, giving special emphasis to the fountain's iconographic program and its joint civic and religious function.

Pope-Hennessy, John. *Italian Gothic Sculpture*. 4th ed. London: Phaidon Press, 1996. The chapter on Jacopo places him at the end of the development of late Gothic Italian sculpture. Comparative photographs support the often-neglected stylistic ties of Jacopo to this older tradition. Includes critical analysis, biographical and bibliographical summaries, an index, and photographs of major works with accompanying catalog entries.

Seymour, Charles. *Jacopo della Quercia: Sculptor*. New Haven, Conn.: Yale University Press, 1973. Discusses the documentary evidence of the major works and includes insightful critical commentary. Ample photographic reproductions including many details. Includes a chronological compendium of the documents, as well as the actual text of major contracts (not translated). Includes an index and a selected bibliography.

Vasari, Giorgio. *Lives of the Most Eminent Painters, Sculptors, and Architects*. Reprint. New York: Alfred A. Knopf, 1996. A translation of the 1568 edition of Vasari's biographies. An expanded biography of Jacopo, based most likely on oral tradition.

See also: Filippo Brunelleschi; Donatello; Lorenzo Ghiberti; Giotto; Andrea Orcagna; Andrea Pisano; Nicola Pisano and Giovanni Pisano.

Related article in *Great Events from History: The Middle Ages, 477-1453*: c. 1410-1440: Florentine School of Art Emerges.

AL-JĀḤIẒ
Arabic writer

As the first important Arabic prose writer, al-Jāḥiẓ employed his vast erudition and innovative stylistic technique to free the Arabic language from its theological and philological restraints, making it a tool for the long-term cultural cohesion of the diverse cultures of Islam.

Born: c. 776; Basra (now in Iraq)
Died: 868; Basra
Also known as: Abū ʿUthmān ʿAmr ibn Baḥ ibn Maḥbūb al-Jāḥiẓ (full name)
Areas of achievement: Literature, religion and theology

Early Life

Al-Jāḥiẓ (ehl-JAHK-ihz) might have been the child of East African slaves, who were numerous in southern Iraq in the eighth and ninth centuries. His ancestry is uncertain, however. The sobriquet al-Jāḥiẓ (goggle-eyed) refers to a remarkable physical condition that observers may have attributed to African origins. People of his time described al-Jāḥiẓ as an exceptionally ugly individual.

Al-Jāḥiẓ studied in his hometown of Basra, then went off to Baghdad for advanced education. He appears to have been employed early as a clerical official or copyist for the government. His unusual stylistic flair came to the attention of high officials, and the ʿAbbāsid caliph al-Maʾmūn (r. 813-833) commissioned him to write a series of essays justifying the ʿAbbāsid seizure of power from the previous Ummayad Dynasty in Damascus around 750. According to some sources, the caliph once considered employing al-Jāḥiẓ as a personal tutor for his sons, but was so unnerved by his physical appearance that he decided against him. (In fairness to the caliph, it should be noted that al-Jāḥiẓ also had a reputation for a bitter and irascible temperament.)

Al-Jāḥiẓ was an active and productive individual, involved, like many Muslim intellectuals of this time, in a variety of arenas. He followed the rationalist Mutazilite school of Islamic thought, which reveled in logical analysis and lively debate; the Mutazilite sect that he founded appears to have espoused some radical theological views. Al-Jāḥiẓ was fond of defending unpopular positions in public debate even when he did not personally agree with them. He also dabbled in the natural sciences; his zoological treatise, *Kitāb alhayawan* (ninth century; book of animals), constituted one of the earliest attempts in Islam to formulate orders of living things. Of the more than 120 works attributed to al-Jāḥiẓ by thirteenth century geographer and biographer Yaqut (1179-1229), however, only a few are extant.

Al-Jāḥiẓ, who was fluent in Greek as well as Arabic, borrowed heavily from the Hellenistic tradition, frequently quoting or citing Aristotle and other Greek intellectual figures. Among Arabic scholars of his time, he was one of the most inclined to acknowledge his debt to Greek learning.

LIFE'S WORK

The literary career of al-Jāḥiẓ owes much to the development in Islam of the concept of *adab*, or high culture. *Adab* demanded of its practitioners not only an eclectic knowledge base but also certain mannerisms and styles of expression considered appropriate to a cultivated intellectual elite. The content of *adab* might vary according to the personality of the individual; theology and Islamic canon law (Shariʿa) were considered appropriate subject matter. The keystone of *adab*, however, was literary and rhetorical expression. Eloquence was considered one of the essential virtues; indeed, in rigorously pious circles the spoken word was one of the few forms of emotional expression to which one might manifest visible reaction. Conventions of verbal elegance soon came to be applied in literary practice as well, so that good writing was elevated alongside rhetoric as a quality of the cultivated.

The evolution of *adab* raised difficulties concerning the heretofore restricted and unimaginative use of Arabic in written form. Written Arabic often adhered slavishly to Qurʾānic expression, and in al-Jāḥiẓ's age prose style was rigid and inflexible. Writers were essentially clerks and secretaries who compiled rather than created. There was a heavy emphasis on such traditional topics as the life of Muḥammad and early Islam, as well as a consuming regard for philology at the expense of experiment. Matters of everyday life and those not directly related to the Qurʾān or canon law were addressed only in poetry.

Al-Jāḥiẓ sensed that Arabic literary expression was at a dead end—that if current trends continued, Arabic would soon be relegated to use in religious observances only. To overcome this problem, he struck out in new directions with a prose style intended, as he described it, to be both educational and entertaining and to reach a broader segment of the literate public. Al-Jāḥiẓ combined a witty and satirical style with his breadth of learning to produce a large corpus of works on all aspects of contemporary life. He made extensive use of anecdotes to make his writing accessible by varying its structure and pace. Al-Jāḥiẓ's frequent use of a rhymed, cadenced prose style called *sajʾ* deeply influenced *adab* culture even in media such as personal correspondence. He was also one of the first Arabic writers to employ irony as a literary device.

Among the surviving works of al-Jāḥiẓ, one that well illustrates his style is *Kitāb al-bukhalāʾ* (book of misers), in which he rebukes members of the Persian urban middle class, contrasting their behavior with the generosity of the Arabs. It is not the dubious ethnic stereotypes that make the work interesting, however, but the manner of presentation. Marked by witty, vibrant prose, the work is filled with anecdotes about well-known past and contemporary figures who serve as negative examples of the virtue of generosity. Some have suggested that the format and style of the work continues in Arabic a tradition going back to the *Charactēres ethikōi* (c. 319 B.C.E.; *The Moral Characters of Theophrastus*, 1702, best known as *Characters*) of Theophrastus (c. 372-c. 287 B.C.E.), in that al-Jāḥiẓ replicates the Greek philosopher's brief and vigorous descriptions of moral character types.

Never one to dodge controversy, al-Jāḥiẓ wrote on a wide variety of issues of the time. In his *Kitāb al-Bayan wa-al-Tabyin* (book of eloquence and exposition), he attacked the populist Shuubi movement, which proclaimed the superiority of non-Arabs over Arabs in religious and cultural achievement. Not surprisingly, many Shuubis were Persians, who, in the view of al-Jāḥiẓ, were most responsible for the clerical and bureaucratic pedantry to which Arabic literature had been reduced. Besides an essay that extolled the virtues of the Turks, al-Jāḥiẓ wrote one on black Africans and several on corruption and venality in government.

If al-Jāḥiẓ was something of a muckraker, he was also

a devout Muslim. Deeply concerned by what he saw as a growing cynicism and infidelity among the literate classes, he never lost an opportunity to weave theology into his commentaries on everyday life and his descriptions of exemplary behavior.

Significance

As a scholar and man of letters, al-Jāḥiẓ had a lasting effect on Islamic culture. His zoological treatise, which, though wide-ranging and imaginative, treats zoology almost as a branch of philology and literature, found many emulators. Among them were the cosmographer al-Qazwīnī and the thirteenth century Egyptian scientist al-Damīrī, generally regarded as the greatest Muslim figure in early zoology.

Al-Jāḥiẓ changed for all time the nature and function of Arabic prose; without him, the development of Arabic secular writing would have been almost unthinkable. No longer would Arabic be restricted merely to government reports, theology, and the recounting of the life of Muḥammad and the Arab conquests; no longer would Arabic literacy be limited to a privileged few. Al-Jāḥiẓ showed that Arabic is a subtle and supple literary language, able to express the entire spectrum of human activity and desire, a vehicle in which literary devices could be exploited to their fullest effect.

Al-Jāḥiẓ was to become something of a cultural hero in Muslim Spain, setting of one of the greatest cultural flowerings in the medieval world. Spanish Muslims who traveled to Syria and Iraq to study heard al-Jāḥiẓ lecture and eagerly sought copies of his manuscripts to take home, where they became models of literary style for several centuries to come.

—*Ronald W. Davis*

Further Reading

De Somogyi, J. "Al-Jāḥiẓ and Ad-Damīrī." *Annual of the Leeds University Oriental Society* 1 (1958-1959): 55-60. A brief examination of the influence of al-Jāḥiẓ on this Muslim scientist who, several centuries later, used his work as a model.

Dodge, Bayard, ed. and trans. *The Fihrist of al-Nadīm: A Tenth-Century Survey of Muslim Culture*. Vol. 1. New York: Columbia University Press, 1970. This volume contains a brief biography of al-Jāḥiẓ in traditional Muslim form, also listing some of the scholars associated with him, by a tenth century chronicler. A good example of biographical treatment at the time, it provides a sense of the intellectual environment in which al-Jāḥiẓ lived and worked.

Hirschfeld, H. "A Volume of Essays by al-Jāḥiẓ." In *A Volume of Oriental Essays Presented to Edward G. Brown*, edited by T. W. Arnold and R. A. Nicolson. Cambridge, England: Clarendon Press, 1922. Offers commentary on a previously untranslated group of essays and notes.

Hodgson, Marshall G. S. *The Venture of Islam: Conscience and History in a World Civilization*. 3 vols. Chicago: University of Chicago Press, 1974. Vol. 1 includes a discussion of the characteristics and development of *adab* culture and the role al-Jāḥiẓ played in articulating its literary aspects. Shows the great breadth of intellectual and literary activity embraced by *adab* and the diversity of knowledge required of its practitioners.

Jāḥiẓ, al-. *Sobriety and Mirth: A Selection of the Shorter Writings of al-Jāḥiẓ*. Translated by Jim Colville. New York: Kegan Paul, 2002. Writings on social and moral issues, including "This Life and the Life to Come," "The Superiority of Blacks to Whites," "Anthropomorphism Refuted," "Drink and Drinkers," and "On Women."

Marshall, D. R. "An Arab Humorist: Al-Jāḥiẓ and 'The Book of Misers.'" *Journal of the Faculty of Arts of the University of Malta* 4 (1970): 77-97. Emphasizes secular as opposed to theological overtones of al-Jāḥiẓ's work and discusses the various literary devices and idioms that gave his writing wide appeal.

Menocal, Maria Rosa, Raymond P. Scheindlin, and Michael Sells, eds. *The Literature of Al-Andalus*. New York: Cambridge University Press, 2000. Surveys the literature of Muslim Spain. Includes illustrations, a bibliography, and index.

Ouyang, Wen-chin. *Literary Criticism in Medieval Arabic-Islamic Culture: The Making of a Tradition*. Edinburgh: Edinburgh University Press, 1997. Chapter 3 explores the early tradition of medieval Arabic-Islamic literary criticism and discusses literary value and al-Jāḥiẓ's work. Bibliography, index.

Pellat, Charles. Introduction to *The Life and Works of Jāḥiẓ: Translations of Selected Texts*. Translated by D. M. Hawke. Berkeley: University of California Press, 1969. The essays in this volume cover topics such as politics, theology, rhetoric, science, manners, love, and society. The short introduction is a useful discussion of the career and significance of al-Jāḥiẓ.

Zahniser, Mathias. "Source Criticism in the Uthmaniyya of al-Jāḥiẓ." *Muslim World* 70 (1980): 134-141. Argues that al-Jāḥiẓ belonged to a sect called Uthmaniyya, which opposed the claims of the Shiis regarding the right of succession in Islam. Al-Jāḥiẓ may have written tracts for the ʿAbbāsid caliphate supporting the rightful claim of Abū Bakr, the first caliph, to leadership.

See also: Pietro d'Abano; Firdusi; Hafiz; Omar Khayyám; Jalāl al-Dīn Rūmī; Saʿdi; Yaqut.

Related articles in *Great Events from History: The Middle Ages, 477-1453*: April or May, 711: Ṭārik Crosses into Spain; 786-809: Reign of Hārūn al-Rashīd; 869-883: Zanj Revolt of African Slaves; c. 950: Court of Córdoba Flourishes in Spain; 1010: Firdusi Composes the *Shahnamah*; 1031: Caliphate of Córdoba Falls.

James I the Conqueror

French-born king of Spain (r. 1217-1276)

James conquered three Islamic principalities in Spain and reorganized his many realms in Mediterranean Spain and Occitania (now southern France) into a great and prosperous state, rivaling Genoa for control of western Mediterranean naval power and trade. An autobiographer, he also founded a university and promulgated the first Romanized law code of general application in Europe.

Born: February 2, 1208; Montpellier, County of Toulouse (now in France)
Died: July 27, 1276; Valencia (now in Spain)
Also known as: James I; James the Conqueror
Areas of achievement: Government and politics, warfare and conquest, literature, education

Early Life

James I the Conqueror was born in the port city of Montpellier, whose sovereign lordship was held by his mother, Marie of Montpellier. His father was Peter II the Catholic, victor at Las Navas de Tolosa (1212) over the Islamic Almohad empire when James was a child. Because of his incompetence in war, Peter lost the Battle of Muret (1213) to the French Crusaders against the Albigensians—and, with it, his life and his dynasty's control over much of what is now southern France.

The crusade's leader, Simon de Montfort, kidnapped the child James, planning eventually to marry him to his own daughter. James's mother, Marie, went to Rome, persuaded Pope Innocent III to rescue her son and protect his kingdom during the child's minority, and then died (1213). Thus James was an orphan, sometimes poor and hungry, at the castle of Monzón, headquarters of the Knights Templars, who coruled his rebellious kingdom for him under papal orders.

In 1217, James began his personal rule. Although he was to call himself "king from the Rhone River to Valencia," his main realms were the inland kingdom of Aragon and the coastal county of Catalonia. Aragon was a feudal, stock-raising land; Catalonia was a far wealthier and more powerful urban region. Each had its own language, law, government, economy, and culture. James himself spoke mainly Catalan, and doubtless some Aragonese and the Occitan of his trans-Pyrenean holdings. Still a teenager, James was knighted and, to help stabilize his restless realms, married in 1221 to an older woman, Princess Leonor of Castile. The unhappy union was annulled in 1229, after the birth of a son, Alfonso.

In his prime, James was an imposing figure, taller than his contemporaries, of athletic build, with blond hair and handsome countenance. His portrait at about age fifty was to show an alert majestic personage, with a small beard and the longish hair of his generation. His character was bold, impulsive, generous, and courteously chivalric. He was also cruel on occasion, as when he had the tongue of the bishop of Gerona cut out in 1246.

James was also notorious in Christendom as a womanizer. He dearly loved his second wife, Princess Yolande of Hungary (1235), who gave him two daughters and two sons. At her death, he married and soon repudiated his third wife, Teresa Gil de Vidaure (1255), after having two more sons. James also had at least five illegitimate children.

Life's Work

James spent much of his life conquering the Islamic regions to his south, already weakened by the breakup of the Almohad empire after his father's victory at Las Navas de Tolosa. In 1229, James gathered a large fleet and army for an amphibious assault on the emirates of the Balearic Islands. Majorca Island fell in 1229, Minorca became a tributary in 1232, and Ibiza fell in 1235. Long after young James's abortive invasion of the Islamic province, or principality, of Valencia in 1225, his raiding knights in 1232 began the long war of conquest there. James kept it going until 1245, in constant maneuvering and bypassing, with few pitched battles but with major sieges of Burriana (1233), the city of Valencia (1238), and Biar (1245). The Siege of Játiva was rather a series of feints and interim arrangements from 1239 to 1252.

Meanwhile, the Franks of Francia, in the wake of the Albigensian crusade, were absorbing ever more of Occitania; James counteracted the French moves ineffectively. In 1245, he patched up a final truce in southern Valencia with the local leader, declared his Valencian crusade finished, and plunged into Occitan affairs. He also projected in 1246 an ambitious crusade to support Latin Byzantium against Greek reconquest. As a result of all these programs abroad, the Valencian Muslims were able to revolt successfully from 1247 into 1258, to James's anger and frustration.

James I the Conqueror prepares to embark with his troops for the Balearic Islands. (F. R. Niglutsch)

In 1258, James gave up all but a coastal stretch of Occitania to Louis IX of France by the Treaty of Corbeil. He continued to organize his Majorcan and Valencian conquests, each as a "kingdom" with a multiethnic population of Muslims, Christians, and Jews as parallel, semiautonomous communities. In 1261, he called the first *corts* (parliament) of Valencia, which promulgated the final version of his pioneering Roman law code, the *furs* (laws). When a countercrusade drove his Castilian neighbors out of the kingdom of Murcia to the south of Valencia, James reconquered that region for the Castilians. In 1269, he mounted a crusade to the Holy Land, although contrary winds and domestic worries aborted his personal role in that adventure. James had been in contact with the Mongols in 1267, exchanging diplomatic-military missions with an eye to allying with this new menace so as to reconquer Jerusalem.

During all this time, and fitted in between his crusading conquests in Spain, James led an energetic life on many other fronts. Besides his constant concern with Occitania, which involved him in the intrigues and battles of the English (from their bases in English Aquitaine) and of principalities such as Toulouse and Marseilles, he was also involved intimately with Castile, at times lending support against the Muslims there and at times angrily on the very edge of war with its people. As the French grew stronger in Occitania, James turned to their rivals the Hohenstaufens of Sicily and Germany, marrying his son Peter to the Hohenstaufen heiress and surely already envisioning the Catalan seizure of Sicily by Peter in 1282. In between conquests and international projects, James also had to fight sporadic baronial rebellions, as well as two serious revolts by his sons.

James's greatest international triumph occurred in 1274, when he briefly became the adviser on crusade matters at the Second Council of Lyon in France. He devotes twenty chapters of his autobiography to that culminating point in his career. James died as he had lived, a conquering warrior. In the last year of his long life, the Muslims of Valencia again revolted, supported by invading armies from Granada and North Africa. James fought desperately to stem their reconquest of Valencia; when death claimed him in the process (1276), his son Peter had to bury him temporarily in Valencia and continue to subdue the Muslims. Later, James was interred in a splendid tomb at Poblet Monastery, near Tarragona.

KINGS OF ARAGON

Reign	*Ruler*
1035-1063	Ramiro I
1063-1094	Sancho Ramirez
1094-1104	Pedro I
1104-1134	Alfonso I (co-ruled León and Castile, 1109-1126)
1134-1137	Ramiro II
1137	Union with County of Barcelona
1137-1162	Petronilla
1162-1196	Alfonso II
1196-1213	Pedro II
1213-1276	JAMES I THE CONQUEROR (under regency to 1217)
1276-1285	Pedro III
1285-1291	Alfonso III
1291-1327	James II
1327-1336	Alfonso IV
1336-1387	Peter IV
1387-1395	John I
1395-1410	Martin I
1412-1416	Ferdinand I
1416-1458	Alfonso V
1458-1479	John II
1479-1516	Ferdinand II

More than a warrior and statesman, James conspicuously advanced the laws, institutions, and commerce of his realms. The *corts* of his several principalities matured under him, both in their regional and general forms. By exploiting the cheap paper available to him after his conquest of that Islamic industry at Játiva in Valencia, he built the first extensive archives of any European secular state. He multiplied a hierarchy of functionaries in a sophisticated administrative bureaucracy and tirelessly traveled his realms every year in person. James was a leader in the renaissance of Roman law in his century; besides the Valencian *Furs* (1261), he promulgated the Aragonese *Fueros* (1247), the *Costums* of Lérida (1228), and the *Costums de la Mar* (1258) that evolved into the famed *Consulate of the Sea*. His reorganization of communal government, especially at Barcelona and in the towns of Valencia and Majorca, lent stability to his municipalities.

Commerce and naval power expanded marvelously under James's direction; they may have been a major purpose of his conquests. He took over the "circle trade" between North Africa, Valencia, Majorca, and parts of southern France. His merchants became the major European presence in Tunis (effectively a client state of James) and in Alexandria, Egypt.

As part of this affluence, James encouraged Jewish immigration; despite some aggressive proselytism, as in the disputation of Barcelona (1263), his reign is remembered as a political golden age and cultural renaissance for his Jewish communities in Spain and southern France. James presided over and contributed personally to the flowering of the Catalan language and literature. The work of historians Ramón Muntaner and Bernat Desclot, the prolific philosopher-mystic Raymond Lull, the troubadour Cerverí de Girona—and especially the king's autobiography, *Libre dels feyts* (thirteenth century; *The Chronicle of James I, King of Aragon, Surnamed the Conqueror*, 1883)—exemplify this major moment in the Romance languages. Also, James did not neglect higher education; he founded a university at Valencia in the wake of his conquest, and he intruded so forcefully with statutes and reorganization at the University of Montpellier that he is remembered as a kind of second founder there. In addition, his reign saw a renewed enthusiasm for building sweep over the land, from Lérida to Valencia.

SIGNIFICANCE

James I the Conqueror is universally recognized as the founder of the greatness of the realms of Aragon and as one of the handful of main leaders of the Spanish Reconquest. He and his older contemporary Ferdinand III of Castile virtually brought that movement to its dramatic close. Because James's realms joined with Castile some two hundred years later to start the beginning of the country now called Spain, he is therefore a great figure for Spain as well. The Catalans particularly honor him as their own greatest ruler, administrator, and military figure, and as the main promoter of their rise to commercial, imperial, and cultural greatness.

His life—from helpless child-hostage and ward of the Knights Templars in a poor and unstable kingdom to eventual eminence as the most successful Crusader of Christendom and head of a major world power—makes a colorful and stirring tale. Despite his solid achievements in administration, law, commerce, culture, and international affairs, James preferred to see himself in the role of chivalric knight and warrior-conqueror. His autobiography leaves out almost every other aspect of his career, concentrating, as its title says, on his deeds of war. His book's structure owes much to the Islamic ruler-(auto)biography genre, and its tone echoes the troubadour poems it often incorporates in prose form. Yet, with its naïve self-reflection and vigorous spirit, it reveals much of the private James as well, providing a rare, personal view of a remarkable medieval king.

—*Robert I. Burns*

FURTHER READING

Bisson, Thomas N. *The Medieval Crown of Aragon: A Short History.* New York: Oxford University Press, 1986. Chapter 3 provides a compendious summation of James's reign, and a fine general history of the region is covered in other chapters. Especially good on the reign's constitutional and fiscal aspects, with a long section on the king's early years and another on conquests and foreign relations.

Burns, Robert I. *The Crusader Kingdom of Valencia: Reconstruction on a Thirteenth-Century Frontier.* 2 vols. Cambridge, Mass.: Harvard University Press, 1967. Covers the conquest and, particularly, James's use of Church institutions as his main resource for consolidating his hold and restructuring the conquered kingdom's elements. With chapters on James's school system, hospitals, appointed bishops, military orders, economic foundations, and more. Includes a bibliography.

_______. *Islam Under the Crusaders: Colonial Survival in the Thirteenth-Century Kingdom of Valencia.* Princeton, N.J.: Princeton University Press, 1973. Describes the collapse of the Almohads and Islamic Valencia, James's crusade and its extension in the form of Muslim revolts, and especially the role and transformation of Valencia's postcrusade Muslims. Covers James's surrender concessions and treaties thoroughly, his incorporation of the military elites into his feudal system, and the subject communities' law, worship, economic life, local dynasties, and organization. Includes illustrations, maps, and a bibliography.

_______. *Medieval Colonialism: Postcrusade Exploitation of Islamic Valencia.* Princeton, N.J.: Princeton University Press, 1975. Studies James's handling of Valencia's conquered Muslims, drawing social history especially from the taxes he imposed. Covers public monopolies, agrarian and commercial taxes, irrigation and similar fees, the shops and taverns, military obligations, and the means of harvesting these taxes. Includes a bibliography, maps, and illustrations.

_______. *Moors and Crusaders in Mediterranean Spain: Collected Studies.* London: Variorum, 1978. Sixteen selected articles on James. Chapter 1 is a psychohistorical analysis of his personality and behavior. Other chapters discuss the Muslims taken into his feudal ranks, proselytism and converts, the anti-Moor riots of 1276, James's importation of more Muslims for economic reasons, his modes of inviting surrender and making peace, and more.

_______. *Muslims, Christians, and Jews in the Crusader Kingdom of Valencia.* Cambridge, England: Cambridge University Press, 1984. Discusses prominent themes in James's realms: the language barrier, redrawing the maps of the conquered kingdom, the role of his corsairs and of pirates, the king's Jews, the surrender constitutions, the proselytizing movement, the revolt of al-Azraq, and James's continuing role in southern France, especially his personal raid to kidnap the heiress of Provence in Marseilles. Includes a bibliography and maps.

_______. *Society and Documentation in Crusader Valencia.* Princeton, N.J.: Princeton University Press, 1985. Examines in detail the archival registers of James in thirty-eight specialized chapters. Describes his traveling court and household and his chancery. Six chapters cover the Paper Revolution, by which cheap paper from conquered Játiva transformed and bureaucratized James's administration. Other chapters discuss Valencia's many languages, the notarial profession, the archives, and the themes most prominent in James's records.

_______, ed. *The Worlds of Alfonso the Learned and James the Conqueror: Intellect and Force in the Middle Ages.* Princeton, N.J.: Princeton University Press, 1985. From a symposium comparing and contrasting the neighboring kings. Reviews James's accomplishments, with a five-page dateline for both Spain and Europe in synchrony with the lives of James and Alfonso. Analyzes kingship and constitution under James, Catalan literature in his day, his town militia, and his policy in southern France.

Burns, Robert I., and Paul E. Chevedden. "A Unique Bilingual Surrender Treaty from Muslim-Crusader Spain." *Historian: A Journal of History* 62, no. 3 (Spring, 2000). Discusses the vast number of truces, pacts, and alliances that helped define Muslim-Christian relationships at the time of the Crusades. This article looks at an often-ignored bilingual treaty specifically.

Hillgarth, Jocelyn N. *The Spanish Kingdoms, 1250-1516.* 2 vols. Oxford, England: Clarendon Press, 1976-1978. Includes an excellent assessment of James and his achievements and failures. By a specialist, this work is especially good on the chronicle sources and on the economy. The volume offers generous background for all elements of Castilian and Aragonese history from about 1250.

James I the Conqueror. *The Chronicle of James I, King of Aragon, Surnamed the Conqueror.* Translated by John Forster. 1883. Reprint. Farnborough, England: Gregg International, 1968. The king's own *Llibre dels feyts*, or book of deeds, the main source for his personality and military achievements. Literary battles have established its authenticity and primary authorship, have clarified the inclusion of prosified poems, and have suggested plausible stages and circumstances of its redaction.

Van Landingham, Marta. *Transforming the State: King, Court, and Political Culture in the Realms of Aragon, 1213-1387.* Boston: Brill, 2002. A study of the political, legal, and regnal culture of medieval Aragon in the time of James. Includes a bibliography and index.

SEE ALSO: Innocent III; Louis IX; Raymond Lull; Simon de Montfort.

RELATED ARTICLE in *Great Events from History: The Middle Ages, 477-1453*: 1209-1229: Albigensian Crusade.

JOACHIM OF FIORE

Italian historian and religious leader

Joachim developed a persuasive system of historical understanding that evolved through three successive stages, culminating in what he termed as an age of the Holy Spirit filled with bliss and understanding.

BORN: c. 1135; Celico, Kingdom of Naples (now in Italy)

DIED: 1202; Fiore (now in Italy)

ALSO KNOWN AS: Gioacchino da Fiore

AREAS OF ACHIEVEMENT: Religion and theology, historiography

EARLY LIFE

Joachim of Fiore (yoh-AH-keem uhv FYOH-ray) was born to Maurus, a notary, and Gemma in Celico. Although later writers would claim that the family members were converted Jews, there is no convincing evidence to support this statement. Joachim, who was trained to be a court bureaucrat and notary, entered the service of King William II of Sicily at Palermo as a young man. About 1167, after an illness, he left William's service to go on a pilgrimage to the Holy Land, where he decided to follow a religious life. While meditating on Mount Tabor, he experienced his first revelation; as a result, he believed that God had given to him a special insight into scriptural understanding.

Joachim returned to Sicily and lived as a hermit on Mount Etna for a few weeks, then he traveled back to the vicinity of Cosenza, where he began to live the life of a hermit-preacher. In 1170, he entered the novitiate at a monastery at Corazzo and rose to the position of prior shortly after taking his vows. Seven years later, he was elected abbot of the monastery. Either shortly before his election or shortly thereafter, Corazzo chose to join the Cistercian community.

As the new abbot, Joachim's first task was to seek association for the Corazzo monastery with a Cistercian motherhouse. Thus, he began to travel almost immediately in search of a monastery that would assume that obligation, going both to Sambucina and to Casamari. He was unsuccessful in convincing the Cistercians in either place to accept Corazzo. Finding a motherhouse for his monastery was doubly important to Joachim as he was anxious to begin writing about his scheme of history and theology. The Cistercian General Council would not authorize his scholarly activities until Corazzo was officially within the Cistercian community. Frustrated with the Cistercians and anxious to begin his writing, he appealed to Pope Lucius III in 1184. Permission was granted to him to begin his studies, and the pope also allowed him a leave of absence from his duties as abbot.

LIFE'S WORK

Joachim returned to Casamari and began to write *Liber de concordia Novi ac Veteris Testamenti* (1519; book of concords between the Old and New Testaments) and *Expositio in Apocalypsim* (1527; exposition on the Apocalypse) simultaneously. As he wrote, he realized that he still did not have a clear understanding of the relationship between the Trinity and biblical concords; thus, on Pentecost, 1183 or 1184, he received his second revelation. This revelation was so graphic that he put aside the two manuscripts on which he was working and wrote the first book of his third major treatise, *Psalterium decem chordarum* (1527; ten-stringed psaltery). Utilizing the imagery of the strings on the musical instrument, Joachim presented a full explanation of the mystery of the Trinity.

Returning to Corazzo the following year, he continued his writing; after failing to understand the meanings of the apocalyptic writings in the Bible, he received his third revelation. While he was again in deep meditation, it seemed as if curtains were lifted within his mind causing "a certain clearness of understanding before the eyes of my mind which exposed to me the fullness of this book of the Apocalypse and the entire concord of the Old and New Testaments."

In 1186, Joachim visited the new pope, Urban III, and received renewed permission and encouragement to continue his writing. In 1187, however, Urban died; Joachim traveled again to Rome in 1188 to visit Urban's successor, Clement III. Clement, too, endorsed his writings. By 1189, Joachim was feeling the pressures of growing fame and recognition as an exegete of prophecy, and he was becoming more and more disenchanted with the Cistercian order, which he believed to be too lax in its religious life. In late winter of that year, he went deep into the Sila Mountains to seek a place of peace and quiet. In May, he settled at San Giovanni in Fiore. As a result, the leadership of the Cistercian order considered him a renegade. He finally broke with the order when Henry VI, the Holy Roman Emperor, issued a charter to Joachim on October 21, 1194, authorizing a new monastery at San Giovanni in Fiore with Joachim as its abbot. With the charter in hand, Joachim approached Pope Celestine III seeking approval of a constitution for a new religious order; the pope did so by a papal bull on August 25, 1196. Thus the Order of Fiore was born with its motherhouse located in San Giovanni in Fiore in Calabria.

Despite periodic revelations, Joachim never claimed to be a prophet. Instead, he insisted that God had given him the gift of a clearer exegetical understanding of Scripture that enabled him to display a new system of theology and historiography. Joachim's apocalyptic attitudes and theology of history were a significant departure from the Augustinian tradition in that he viewed history as dynamic rather than static. The Calabrian abbot perceived three progressive *status* (ages), or a threefold pattern of history, in which each member of the Trinity played guiding roles. The first *status*, in which God the Father directed the course of human events, began with Adam and ended with Christ's Incarnation. The second *status*, characterized by the leadership of Jesus Christ, overlapped back into the first *status* and lasted until the thirteenth century. The third *status* was more complicated. Its origins were in both the first and second *status*—a double origin and progression from the Old and New Testaments and the Father and Son; it would be guided by the Holy Spirit.

Saint Bernard of Clairvaux was the precursor to the third age. His rule had laid the groundwork for a future monastic community that eventually would encompass all Christians: monks, clerics, and laymen. Two new orders would appear and usher in the age followed by the first appearance of the Antichrist. The Antichrist would cause terrible trials and tribulations, but he would be defeated by Christians. After the Antichrist was defeated, the Holy Spirit would guide life until the second appearance of the Antichrist and Doomsday. It was with the concept of the third *status* that Joachim broke from the Augustinian tradition by placing eschatological events into human history. As a dreamer of the future, he did not look backward in time to some golden age, such as the apostolic age, in which people would emulate Christ and his disciples; rather, he concluded that the future time would be a true *renovatio*, unlike anything in the past, led by the Holy Spirit. Such ideas became fertile ground for scores of future movements of reform.

In Joachim's schema, each age was progressive toward the next; collectively, they moved toward an ideal human existence. The first age, for example, had been lived under Law, the second had been lived under grace, and the third would be lived in full freedom and understanding. Each of Joachim's three *status* was divided into seven *estates* (times) with five concordant types or species and seven *typicus intellectus*. For example, the twelve patriarchs of the Old Testament were precursors to the twelve Apostles, and one would expect a similar concordant type in the third age. Thus, history is given continuity.

Joachim has frequently been described as a "picture thinker." Toward the end of his life, he began to make elaborate and colorful drawings that graphically explained his main ideas. These drawings were compiled around 1227-1239 as *Liber figurarum* by his disciples and provide visual explanations of the intricacies of his thought.

The peace and understanding of the third age, an age that would accomplish true monastic contemplation, would be phased in exactly as the second had emerged from the first. Two new monastic orders, contemplative in the pattern of Moses and evangelical in the pattern of Elijah, would usher in the age, guiding human history from the second *status* to the third. All human history would reach fruition when "the new order of the people of God," as Joachim called it, was established. This future state of the church and society would be a physical commune based on the monastic utopian model that he drew in *Liber figurarum* and entitled *Dispositio novi ordinis pertinens ad tercium statum*. The community, which in the drawing is heavily annotated with explanatory details, would feature a contemplative society of monks, clerics, and laity living harmoniously together under the direction of a spiritual father and his councillors.

By 1200, Joachim had finished his major works, and many minor ones too, presenting them with a testamentary letter to Pope Innocent III. Joachim died just before Easter, 1202.

Significance

Joachim was the most important apocalyptic writer and exegete of prophecy in the Middle Ages. He introduced an optimistic pattern of history that challenged future generations to view human events in terms of progress instead of deterioration.

Joachim's influence has been significant but difficult to measure because many thinkers whose ideas reflect his tripartite scheme of history cannot be shown to have had direct access to his texts. It is certain that he influenced millenarian sects of the thirteenth century whose teachings, unlike his own, were thoroughly heretical, and references to his ideas can be tracked through subsequent centuries. The nineteenth century brought an upsurge of interest in Joachim; in particular, Joachimite thought entered the current of esoteric lore that profoundly influenced nineteenth century European literature. As a consequence, modern writers as diverse as William Butler Yeats and D. H. Lawrence were familiar with Joachim's ideas and appropriated them in fashioning their own apocalyptic visions of history.

—*Delno West*

Further Reading

Gould, Warwick, and Marjorie Reeves. *Joachim of Fiore and the Myth of the Eternal Evangel in the Nineteenth Century*. Rev. ed. New York: Oxford University Press, 2001. A revised and enlarged edition of the 1987 study. The book analyzes the influence of Joachim, including major literary figures of the eighteenth and nineteenth centuries who utilized the ideas of Joachim in their own works.

Joachim of Fiore. *Liber de concordia Novi ac Veteris Testamenti*. Edited by E. Randolph Daniel. Philadelphia: American Philosophical Society, 1983. A modern edition of one of Joachim's major works. Introductory chapters answer perplexing questions about the abbot's extant manuscripts and technical aspects of his schema.

McGinn, Bernard. *The Calabrian Abbot: Joachim of Fiore in the History of Western Thought*. New York: Macmillan, 1985. Through both new essays and reprints of past articles by the author, this book firmly places Joachim in the history of Western thought. A good introduction to Joachim and his thought.

Reeves, Marjorie. *The Influence of Prophecy in the Later Middle Ages: A Study in Joachimism*. 1969. Reprint. Notre Dame, Ind.: University of Notre Dame, 1993. This remains the classic study of Joachim, his life, his works, his teachings, and his influence up to the sixteenth century. An appendix contains lists of Joachim's authentic and spurious works, and a preface has been added to the new edition.

_______. *Joachim of Fiore and the Prophetic Future: A Medieval Study in Historical Thinking*. Rev. ed. Stroud: Sutton, 1999. A revision of the 1976 edition, this work examines Joachim's vision of history and its progression. Illustrated, with bibliography and index.

Reeves, Marjorie, and Beatrice Hirsch-Reich. *The Figurae of Joachim of Fiore*. Oxford, England: Clarendon Press, 1972. The most definitive study of Joachim's drawing and symbols. Chapters address major themes in Joachim's scheme through his own visual portrayal of those themes.

Wessley, Stephen E. *Joachim of Fiore and Monastic Reform*. New York: Peter Lang, 1990. A study of the religious thoughts of Joachim, particularly his views of monasticism.

West, Delno, ed. *Joachim of Fiore in Christian Thought*. 2 vols. New York: Burt Franklin, 1975. A sequence of journal articles in several languages that are generally unavailable in American libraries. Essays relate to Joachim and Joachimite themes studied over the twentieth century.

West, Delno, and Sandra Zimdars-Swartz. *Joachim of Fiore: A Study in Spiritual Perception and History*. Bloomington: Indiana University Press, 1983. Meant as an introduction for the general reader, this book is focused on Joachim's life and teachings as a major contribution to Western intellectual history.

See also: Innocent III; William of Ockham; Marguerite Porete; Salimbene.

Related articles in *Great Events from History: The Middle Ages, 477-1453*: March 21, 1098: Foundation of the Cistercian Order; November 11-30, 1215: Fourth Lateran Council.

JOAN OF ARC

French warrior and martyr

Joan's military victories initiated the withdrawal of English troops from France to end the Hundred Years' War, and she made possible the coronation of Charles VII at Reims. As a martyr to her vision and mission, she had as much influence after her death as in her lifetime.

BORN: c. 1412; Domrémy, France
DIED: May 30, 1431; Rouen, France
ALSO KNOWN AS: Joan the Maid; Jehanne la Pucelle; Jeanne la Pucelle; Jeanne d'Arc
AREAS OF ACHIEVEMENT: Military, religion and theology, government and politics

EARLY LIFE

Usually identified with the province of Lorraine, Joan of Arc grew up a daughter of France in Domrémy, a village divided between the king's territory and that of the dukes of Bar and Lorraine. Bells from the church next to her home sounded the events of her youth. Her father, Jacques, was a peasant farmer and respected citizen. Joan learned piety from her mother, Isabelle Romée, as part of a large family. She took special pride in spinning and sewing; she never learned to read or write. By custom, she would have assumed her mother's surname, but in her public career she was called the Maid of Orléans, or Joan the Maid (with the double sense of virgin and servant).

Joan was born into the violence of the Hundred Years' War (1337-1453). Henry V, king of England, had gained control of most of northern France and, with the aid of the French duke of Burgundy, claimed the crown from the insane Charles VI. The heir to the throne, Charles VII—or the dauphin, as he was called—was young and apparently believed that his cause was hopeless. Five years after his father's death, he was still uncrowned, and Reims, the traditional coronation site, was deep in English territory. Domrémy, on the frontier, was exposed to all the depredations of the war and was pillaged on at least one occasion during Joan's childhood.

Joan began to hear voices and believed she received visits by the patron saints of France, Saint Michael, Saint Catherine, and Saint Margaret, when she was thirteen or fourteen years old. She claimed that she heard and saw the saints, who became her companions and directed her every step. Initially, she took the voices as calling her to a holy life, and she pledged her virginity and piety. Later she came to believe that it was her mission to deliver France from the English.

Paintings and medals were made of Joan, but no genuine portrait has been identified; a contemporary sketch survives by a man who never saw her. Three carved limestone heads in helmets (now in Boston, Loudun, and Orléans) may represent near-contemporary portraits. They show a generous nose and mouth and heavy-lidded eyes. She had a ruddy complexion; black hair in a documentary seal (now lost) indicated her coloring. Sturdy enough to wear armor and live a soldier's life, she had a gentle voice. She wore a red frieze dress when she left Domrémy; when she approached the dauphin at Chinon, she wore men's clothing: black woolen doublet and laced leggings, cap, cape, and boots. She wore her hair short like a man's, or a nun's, cut above the ears in the "pudding basin" style that facilitated wearing a helmet and discouraged lustful thoughts. Later, the dauphin provided her with armor and money for fashionable clothing. The gold-embroidered red costume in which she was finally captured may have been made from cloth sent to her by the captive duke of Orléans.

LIFE'S WORK

In 1428, Joan attempted to gain support from Robert de Baudricourt, the royal governor of Vaucouleurs. (The pregnancy of a kinswoman living two miles from Vaucouleurs provided Joan with a pretext to leave home.) Baudricourt, after rejecting her twice—as the voice had predicted—became caught up in Joan's mission. The English had besieged Orléans, as she had told him they would, and he, similarly besieged, had to agree to surrender his castle unless the dauphin came to his aid by a specified date. Before sending Joan to the dauphin, he had her examined and exorcised.

Charles agreed to the interview with Joan in desperation. Orléans, besieged since October of 1428, had great strategic importance; its fall would shake the loyalty of his remaining supporters and the readiness of his cities to provide money. Joan's appearance at court on February 25, 1429, after traveling through enemy territory for eleven days, brought fresh hope. She identified the dauphin at once in the crowded room, and she gave him some sign, "the king's secret," which confirmed her mission but whose nature is still debated. A second exhaustive investigation of Joan occurred at Poitiers, where her piety and simplicity impressed everyone. Charles established a household for her. She had a standard made and adopted an ancient sword, which was discovered, through her directions, buried in the church of Sainte-Catherine-de-Fierbois.

On April 29, 1429, Joan and an expedition, believing they were on a supply mission, arrived upstream of Orléans. Joan addressed the English commander, calling on him to retreat. She turned rough French soldiers into Crusaders, conducting daily assemblies for prayer and insisting that they rid themselves of camp followers and go to confession. When a party bringing supplies to the city on the opposite bank found the wind blowing against them, she predicted the sudden change of wind that permitted the boats to cross. Nonplussed Englishmen allowed another shipment led by priests to pass without firing on it; they explained their lack of action as the result of bewitchment. Within the city, Joan's inspired leadership encouraged the troops to follow her famous standard and her ringing cry, "In God's name, charge boldly!" On May 7, though seriously wounded as she had predicted, she rallied the troops to victory at the Tourelles fortification, after the French captains had given up hope. The next day, the English withdrew from Orléans.

In little more than a week, with much plunder and killing of prisoners, the French drove their enemies from the remaining Loire strongholds of Jargeau, Meung, and Beaugency. Though Joan took part in these actions, her principal influence remained her extraordinary attraction and rallying of forces; she later said that she had killed no one. The troops of Arthur de Richemont, brother of the duke of Brittany, who now joined the dauphin, counted decisively in another victory at Patay on June 17.

Charles's coronation on July 17 at Reims, deep in enemy territory, clearly shows Joan's influence. Counselors and captains advised Charles to take advantage of his victories and move against Normandy. Joan persuaded him instead to travel to Reims, and city after city yielded to siege or simply opened its gates to the dauphin: Auxerre, Troyes, Châlons, and Reims itself. The stunned English regent, the duke of Bedford, offered no resistance.

After the coronation, Joan's single-minded drive to take Paris and gain the release of the duke of Orléans conflicted with a royal policy of caution and diplomacy based on the expectation that Burgundy, too, would rally peacefully to Charles. Charles ennobled Joan and her family and provided her with attendants and money, but she was too popular to permit her return to Domrémy. Her voices warned that she had little time. By September 8, when the assault on Paris finally began, the English had regained their aplomb. Joan, again wounded, unsuccessfully urged an evening attack. Charles's orders the next day forbade an attack, though the baron of Montmorency and his men came out of the city to join the royal army, and on September 13, Charles withdrew his troops.

Joan now joined in a holding action to prevent the English forces from using the extended truce to retake their lost positions. Her men took Saint-Pierre-le-Moûtier, but lack of supplies forced her to abandon La Charité. In the spring of 1430, she led volunteers to stiffen the resistance of Compiègne against the Burgundians, contrary to the royal policy of pacification. That helps to explain Charles's failure to negotiate her release after her capture at Compiègne on May 23—an event also predicted by her voices. The Burgundians sold her to the English authorities.

Nineteenth century engraving of Joan of Arc. (Library of Congress)

Joan's trial, which ran from January 9 through May 30, 1431, tested her faith and gave her a final opportunity to uphold the French cause. Her death was a foregone conclusion; the English reserved their right to retry her if the Church exonerated her. Bishop Pierre Cauchon of Beauvais took the lead, realizing that a church trial, by proving her a witch, would turn her victories to Anglo-Burgundian advantage. Indeed, her captors may have believed her a camp trollop and sorceress until a physical examination by the duchess of Bedford, the sister of Philip of Burgundy, proved Joan's virginity. That made it clear that she had not had carnal relations with Satan, a sure sign of sorcery.

After twice attempting to escape (for which her voices blamed her), she stood trial in Rouen. The two earlier investigations and Joan's impeccable behavior obliged Cauchon to falsify evidence and maneuver her into self-incrimination. She showed great perspicacity—her voices told her to answer boldly. Cauchon finally reduced the seventy-two points on which she had been examined to twelve edited points, on which her judges and the faculty of the University of Paris condemned her.

Seriously ill and threatened by her examiners, Joan apparently signed a recantation that temporarily spared her life. Cauchon claimed that she had renounced her voices; some historians claim forgery, admission to lesser charges, or some code by which she indicated denial. In any case, she returned to woman's clothing as ordered and to her cell. She was later found wearing men's clothing (perhaps partly to protect herself from her guards). When questioned, Joan replied that her voices had rebuked her for her change of heart. On May 29, the judges agreed unanimously to give Joan over to the English authorities. She received Communion on the morning of May 30 and was burned as a heretic.

SIGNIFICANCE

Mystics with political messages abounded in Joan's world, but none had Joan's impact on politics. Widespread celebration in 1436 of Claude des Armoises, claiming to be Joan escaped from the flames, demonstrated her continuing popularity. Orléans preserved Joan's cult, and Domrémy became a national shrine. A surge of interest beginning in the nineteenth century with Napoleon has made Joan one of the most written-about persons in history, but efforts to analyze her in secular terms reaffirm the continuing mystery of her inspiration.

Many people in the huge crowd that witnessed Joan's death believed in her martyrdom and reported miracles. English insistence on complete destruction of her body, with her ashes thrown into the Seine River, underscored the point. When he took Rouen and the trial records in 1450, Charles VII ordered her case reopened, but only briefly. Too many influential living persons were implicated in Joan's condemnation, and a reversal of the verdict would also support papal claims to jurisdiction in France. A papal legate, Guillaume d'Estouteville, later encouraged Joan's aged mother to appeal to the pope, which brought about rehabilitation proceedings and the declaration of her innocence in 1456. Even then, the revised verdict merely revoked the earlier decision on procedural grounds without endorsing Joan's mission or condemning her judges. Joan was canonized by Pope Benedict XV on May 16, 1920, and France honors her with a festival day on the second Sunday of May.

—*Paul Stewart*

FURTHER READING

Elliott, Dyan. "Seeing Double: John Gerson, the Discernment of Spirits, and Joan of Arc." *American Historical Review* 107, no. 1 (February, 2002). Argues that the work of the French theologian Jean de Gerson (1363-1429) attempted to use clerical control to "contain" female spirituality, including the spirituality of Joan.

Fabre, Lucien. *Joan of Arc*. Translated by Gerard Hopkins. New York: McGraw-Hill, 1954. An account that reflects the French and Catholic positions on Joan's life. The author bases conclusions about the various puzzles on documents and provides a guide to the vast literature.

Guillemin, Henri. *The True History of Joan "of Arc."* Translated by William Oxferry. London: Allen and Unwin, 1972. An example of the tradition believing that Joan did not die in 1431. One of the many variations in this tradition makes her the sister of Charles VII.

Hanawalt, Barbara A., and Susan Noakes. "Trial Transcript, Romance, Propaganda: Joan of Arc and the French Body Politic." *Modern Language Quarterly* 57, no. 4 (December, 1996). An examination of the political narrative and metaphor surrounding Joan's "restoring" the "wholeness" both of the dauphin's body and the body politic of France.

Lucie-Smith, Edward. *Joan of Arc*. London: Allen Lane, 1976. The necessary counterbalance to Fabre's biography. An objective and scholarly accounting, but it treats Joan's voices as hallucinations.

Pernoud, Régine. *Joan of Arc by Herself and Her Witnesses*. Translated by Edward Hyams. 1966. Reprint.

Lanham, Md.: Scarborough House, 1994. A work of great integrity and judgment by the former director of the Centre Jeanne d'Arc in Orléans, who culled documents of Joan's own times for this extremely useful book.

_______. *The Retrial of Joan of Arc: The Evidence of the Trial for Her Rehabilitation, 1450-1456*. Translated by J. M. Cohen. New York: Harcourt, Brace, 1955. Though incomplete, this text includes the essential 1455-1456 testimony by 144 persons who knew Joan at various stages of her life, making her life one of the best-documented of her century. Intended to counteract the earlier trial, it proves something of a whitewash, but it also gives a valid picture of what Joan meant to the French people.

Sackville-West, Vita. *Saint Joan of Arc*. New York: Grove Press, 2001. A biographical account of Joan, first published in 1936, including discussion of the history of France during the reign of Charles VII.

Warner, Marina. *Joan of Arc: The Image of Female Heroism*. Berkeley: University of California Press, 2000. The author ranges through the centuries and provides a hard look at how little is known about Joan's appearance and image as a hero.

Wheeler, Bonnie, and Charles T. Wood, eds. *Fresh Verdicts on Joan of Arc*. New York: Garland, 1999. A collection of essays ranging from topics such as Joan's military leadership of men, her gender expression, her interrogation at trial, errors in histories of Joan, comparisons with Christine de Pizan, and more.

SEE ALSO: Charles d'Orléans; Alain Chartier; Christina of Markyate; Christine de Pizan; Fredegunde; Henry V; Damia al-Kāhina; Margery Kempe; Lady Alice Kyteler; Philip the Good.

RELATED ARTICLES in *Great Events from History: The Middle Ages, 477-1453*: 1233: Papal Inquisition; 1250-1300: Homosexuality Criminalized and Subject to Death Penalty; July 2, 1324: Lady Alice Kyteler Is Found Guilty of Witchcraft; 1337-1453: Hundred Years' War; May 4-8, 1429: Joan of Arc's Relief of Orléans; 1453: English Are Driven from France.

JŌCHŌ

Japanese sculptor

Jōchō established an indigenous Japanese style of wood sculpture using a joined-wood technique.

BORN: Date unknown; probably Kyoto, Japan
DIED: 1057; probably Kyoto, Japan
ALSO KNOWN AS: Kōshō
AREA OF ACHIEVEMENT: Art

EARLY LIFE

Very little is known about the first twenty years of the life of Jōchō (joh-choh). At the age of twenty, he became a disciple of Kōjō, according to a book called *Chūgaishō* (compiled in the twelfth century). Kōjō was a prestigious court sculptor in Kyoto, and he and Jōchō collaborated on many projects. Their works were enshrined at the Hōjōji Muryōjuin (Amida hall) in Kyoto, which was built for the former prime minister Fujiwara Michinaga (regent, 996-1017). That was the first time Jōchō met Michinaga, who was the most powerful politician in the late Heian period. To be invited to make a sculpture for Michinaga was considered a great honor.

According to an entry for the year 1020 in the *Chūgaishō*, Jōchō deeply impressed Michinaga with his sculptures. This source also maintains that, with Michinaga's help, Jōchō became one of the top artists of the late Heian period. (Jōchō's age at this time is disputed among scholars.)

Aside from the *Chūgaishō*, there is no source that describes Jōchō's early life. It is assumed that Jōchō spent his days of apprenticeship under Kōjō. Kōjō, who may have been Jōchō's father, had the greatest influence on him. It is fair to say that Kōjō created the foundation, in both style and method, for Jōchō's achievement in art.

Kōjō was active from the end of the tenth century until his death around 1022. His style was calm and elegant, with soft modeling, refined details, and naturalistic proportions, as seen in the Fudō Myōō (bright king) image at Dōshuin, Kyoto. His work was a great change from the solid-wood sculptures of the previous period, with their massive, powerful forms but rather stiff style.

Kōjō was well connected with the upper class of society, including the court, aristocracy, and dominant monasteries. His lifetime relationship with Michinaga and his association with a monk of the Tendai Buddhist sect, Genshin, were particularly influential. According to Genshin's Pure Land (Jōdo) teaching, the aristocracy should strive to be reborn in paradise after leaving this world.

Hōjōji was Michinaga's project to visualize paradise in this world. The nine Amida Buddhas and two bodhisattvas at the Muryōjuin were icons for the salvation of Michinaga on his deathbed. In fact, Michinaga died holding the colorful strings extending from the hands of the nine Buddhas. The late Heian sculpture style (also called the Fujiwara style) was the art of Pure Land Buddhism. Kōjō made a great step toward this style, and after his death, Jōchō carried on the attempt to create an ideal form of the Buddha for the aristocracy.

Life's Work

Jōchō's active period was roughly from 1020 to 1057. His accomplishments cover three distinct phases: the image making for the Hōjōji, the engagement in the Kōfukuji reconstruction, and the creation of the Amida for the Byōdōin Hōōdō (Phoenix Hall). Two years after his debut at the Muryōjuin, Jōchō made thirteen images for the halls of Kondō (golden hall) and Godaidō (hall of five deities) at Hōjōji. After Kōjō's death, Michinaga assigned Jōchō to complete the Hōjōji project. Some of the statues that Jōchō made for the two halls are the Buddha figures of Dainichi, Shaka, and Yakushi, bodhisattva figures of Monju and Miroku, and various great kings and other deities. For this incomparable contribution, Jōchō was awarded the Buddhist rank of *hokkyō* (bridge of law) in 1022; he was the first sculptor to be so honored. The award enhanced the social status of sculptors; during later periods, other sculptors became eligible for this honor.

In the following year, Jōchō made the images for the Yakushidō Hall in the Hōjōji. There were twenty-five statues in all. In 1026, he made twenty-seven life-size images within two months for one of Michinaga's daughters, Empress Takeko. Not only the quantity but also the size of the work was characteristic of Jōchō's sculptures. In the case of the Hōjōji, the images vary from about 6-30 feet (2-10 meters) in height for standing figures and 3-15 feet (1-5 meters) for seated figures. During this period, the *jōroku* (seated Buddha) was a popular figure, measuring approximately 9 feet (3 meters) in height.

One of Jōchō's accomplishments was the establishment of a studio system. Responding to the popularity of icon making among the aristocracy, his studio increased its scale so that it could mass produce huge sculptures. About one hundred sculptors worked under Jōchō to make the Hōjōji imagery. By using a multiple-block technique of assembling wood, many images could be produced in a short time. A division of labor was established: There were *daibusshi* (major Buddhist sculptors) and *shōbusshi* (minor Buddhist sculptors). Several *shōbusshi* worked under each *daibusshi*, and Jōchō supervised all *daibusshi*. This system proved to be effective and was adopted by sculptors in later periods.

The technique popular during the early Heian period, which involved solid wood, was replaced by Jōchō's *Kiyosehō*, or joined-wood method, which was more economical with wood, produced relatively lightweight sculptures, helped prevent cracking, and allowed for mass production. The thinner wood used in this process forced changes in the style and type of carving. Instead of deep and sharp grooves, which produced the *honpa-shiki* (rolling wave style) seen during previous periods, the figures now featured shallow carving, with the result that the surface had a soft, gentle quality. This change of style suited the taste of the aristocracy.

In 1048, Jōchō acquired the even higher Buddhist rank of *hōgen* (eyes of law) for his efforts in reconstructing the images of the Kōfukuji. The Kōfukuji, a temple of the Fujiwara family in Nara, burned down in 1046. The next year, Fujiwara Yorimichi (regent, 1017-1068), Michinaga's son, began to reconstruct the temple. Jōchō's participation in this project provided a good opportunity for him to learn the Nara style of sculpture. He also made the Buddha Shaka for one of the halls of the Yakushiji, Tōin Hakkaku Endō, in Nara. For this image, he is said to have copied the Shaka of Daianji, which is one of the excellent works from the Nara period (710-794). Jōchō's study of the classic style of Nara later appeared in the perfect form of the Amida in the Phoenix Hall of the Byōdōin in Uji, Kyoto. Jōchō surpassed Kōjō by adopting the Nara style in his sculpture.

Of Jōchō's masterpieces, the Amida image in the Phoenix Hall is his only work that is known to exist in modern times. A diary of Taira Sadaie, who was Yorimichi's secretary, states that on the nineteenth day of the second month of 1053, the Amida was enshrined in the Amida hall of Byōdōin. It mentions that Jōchō received gifts for the making of the statue on the day the image was enshrined. This entry proves that the Amida that is now at Phoenix Hall was made by Jōchō.

The Byōdōin was first the villa of Michinaga, and after his death, it became Yorimichi's villa. In 1052, at the age of sixty-one, Yorimichi converted this villa into a temple. In the next year, the dedication of the Phoenix Hall was held, and the Amida image was brought from Kyoto and placed inside. The Phoenix Hall is a building with wings on each side and a tail extending to the rear, and it is completely surrounded by ponds. Two phoenix birds are set on each side of the roof of the hall. The Amida is seated on a lotus pedestal in the altar placed in the center of the hall. It is backed by a boat-shaped mandorla decorated with clouds and angels. Above the mandorla is an elaborate canopy. The fifty-two cloud-riding bodhisattvas are suspended from the walls, and the Pure Land paintings are depicted below on the door panels and walls. The ceiling, pillars, brackets, and other woodwork are decorated with bird and flower motifs. The entire hall is decorated splendidly to express a world of paradise. Phoenix Hall is an excellent representative of Fujiwara aristocratic art, which blended landscape, architecture, sculpture, painting, and craft.

Jōchō and his studio were probably engaged in the making of all the sculptural works for the hall. The Amida, however, was the supreme work. The seated Buddha is perfectly balanced and softly modeled. Every line is fluid and curvilinear; there is no distortion or imperfection. The face of the image has been described as being as round as a full moon. The facial expression is calm, tender, and full of affection. The thin robe is softly fitted to the body, and the folds of the simple drapery flow naturally. The folds are shallowly carved; Jōchō no longer used the early Heian style of carving that Kōjō used. The Buddha sits comfortably, hands folded in the posture of meditation.

The naturalness of this image reflects Jōchō's mastery of proportion. In 1134, the sculptors Inkaku and Inchō measured more than sixty sections of another Amida image made by Jōchō. The precise proportions of Jōchō's images are possible because of the innovative joined-wood method he used. Inspired by the aristocratic taste of the time, Jōchō's work reflects a sense of elegance. It is believed that Jōchō died on the first day of the eighth month of 1057.

SIGNIFICANCE

Jōchō's Amida became a standard model for the seated Amida Buddha. During the twelfth century, the Jōchō style dominated Japanese sculpture. With the popularity of Pure Land Buddhism, images similar to the Phoenix Hall Amida were made throughout Japan. Some of the examples include the Chūsonji and the Hakusui Amidadō, both in northern Japan. Most of these images remained faithful to Jōchō's style, reflecting little of the later sculptors' personalities. In fact, sculptors who attempted to emulate Jōchō's work tended to create stylized and lifeless figures. The limitations of Jōchō's style were those of the elite society of the period. His patrons were aristocrats and other members of the ruling class who were successful politically and economically. Thus, the style he pioneered lost its vitality following the decline of the aristocracy and was eventually replaced by the Kamakura style.

Jōchō's contribution to the development of Japanese art was enormous. With Jōchō, Japanese Buddhist sculpture first achieved its own indigenous style. For centuries after the introduction of Buddhism to Japan in the early sixth century, Buddhist sculpture in Japan was imitative of Chinese and Korean art. Jōchō, following Kōjō's principle, was able to express the distinctively Japanese sense of beauty, serenity, and elegance in his images.

—*Yoshiko Kainuma*

FURTHER READING

Fukuyama, Toshio. *Heian Temples: Byōdō-in and Chūson-ji*. Translated by Ronald K. Jones. New York: Weatherhill, 1976. A finely illustrated book dealing with the art of Pure Land Buddhism of the late Heian period. It contains the Hōjōji and Byōdōin Phoenix Hall of the eleventh century and the Chūsonji and others of the twelfth century.

Horomitsu, Washizuka, et al. *Enlightenment Embodied: The Art of the Japanese Buddhist Sculptor, Seventh to Fourteenth Centuries*. Translated and edited by Reiko Tomii and Kathleen M. Fraiello. New York: Agency for Cultural Affairs, Government of Japan, and Japan Society, 1997. This catalog of an exhibition at the Japan Society Gallery in 1997 features Buddhist art, much of it contemporary with Jōchō's work.

Kuno, Takeshi, ed. *A Guide to Japanese Sculpture*. Tokyo: Maruyama, 1963. Useful for a survey of the major trends of the history of Japanese sculpture. Contains helpful glossary and charts.

Morse, Anne Nishimura, and Nobuo Tsuji, eds. *Japanese Art in the Museum of Fine Arts, Boston*. 2 vols. Boston: The Museum, 1998. This catalog of Buddhist art in the Museum of Fine Arts, Boston, presents a wide array of art, including painting, sculpture, Nō masks, robes, and paintings from the Kano and Rimpa schools.

Nishikawa, Kyōtarō, and Emily J. Sano. *The Great Age of Japanese Buddhist Sculpture, A.D. 600-1300*. Fort Worth, Tex.: Kimbell Art Museum, 1982. The catalog of an exhibition of Japanese Buddhist sculpture at the Kimbell Art Museum. A good source for the sculpture of Byōdōin Phoenix Hall.

Okazaki, Jōji. *Pure Land Buddhist Painting*. Translated by Elizabeth ten Grotenhuis. Tokyo: Kodansha Inter-

national and Shibundō, 1977. A useful source for understanding Pure Land Buddhism and its art, which flourished among the Fujiwara aristocracy.
Stanley-Baker, Joan. *Japanese Art*. Rev. ed. New York: Thames and Hudson, 2000. A general work on Japanese art. Chapter 4 focuses on the Heian period, covering the period in which Jōchō worked.

SEE ALSO: Fujiwara Michinaga; Kōken; Unkei.
RELATED ARTICLES in *Great Events from History: The Middle Ages, 477-1453*: 538-552: Buddhism Arrives in Japan; 593-604: Regency of Shōtoku Taishi; 794-1185: Heian Period; 858: Rise of the Fujiwara Family; 1175: Hōnen Shōnin Founds Pure Land Buddhism.

KING JOHN

King of England (r. 1199-1216)

John's poor statesmanship was primarily responsible for the downfall of the Angevin Empire and the decreased power of the English monarch, as reflected in the Magna Carta.

BORN: December 24, 1166; Beaumont Palace, Oxford, Oxfordshire, England
DIED: October 18, 1216; Newark Castle, Nottinghamshire, England
ALSO KNOWN AS: John Lackland
AREA OF ACHIEVEMENT: Government and politics

EARLY LIFE

John was the youngest son of King Henry II and his queen, Eleanor of Aquitaine, younger by eleven years than Prince Henry, by nine than Richard the Lion-Hearted (Richard I), by eight than Geoffrey. At 5 feet, 5 inches (165 centimeters) tall, he never measured up to his tall elder brothers. The effigy on his tomb at Worcester Cathedral, carved fifteen years after his death, shows a resemblance to those of Henry II and Richard, but with better defined, bonier features. Unlike their father, John and Richard wore mustaches and trimmed beards; John's hair covered his ears in the thirteenth century style. No physical description survives from John's lifetime, but fuller archives than for any previous reign preserve many details of his lifestyle. Even as a child, he had a reputation for luxury rather than knightly valor; as king, he used sugar and spices, wore a dressing gown (a novelty), collected jewels, and read books.

Prejudice against his enemies and the Angevin technique of ruling through fear do not suffice to explain John's reputation for malignancy. He may not have murdered his nephew Arthur of Brittany in a drunken rage, but it would have been in character. In 1170, partly because of Henry II's infidelities, Queen Eleanor withdrew to Aquitaine, her own property, to plot against him with Richard, Geoffrey, and her first husband, King Louis VII of France. Richard, already designated heir of Aquitaine, and Geoffrey, married to the heiress of Brittany, were to gain from Prince Henry's Continental inheritance. Though involved in these conspiracies, John remained with his father and so gained a reputation for deceit.

Henry II called his youngest son "Lackland," in reference to his small expectations as the youngest heir, and in 1185 he knighted John and sent him to take control of Ireland. John, however, showed himself a paltry statesman and warrior and alienated both Irish and English chieftains. He cut an even more despicable figure early in Richard's reign (1189-1199). Their brothers' deaths and Richard's childlessness left the succession in dispute between John and Geoffrey's son Arthur. Before departing on the Third Crusade, Richard granted extensive properties to John, but he recognized Arthur as heir. John challenged Richard's regent, William Longchamp, bishop of Ely, and plotted with Philip II (Augustus), king of France, to establish his own control. He bowed to the strong will of dowager Queen Eleanor, however, and even paid to ransom Richard, who had been imprisoned in Germany on his way home from the Crusade. During the last half of Richard's reign, John fought well and loyally for his brother, and on his deathbed the king recognized John as heir instead of Arthur.

LIFE'S WORK

John's underlying problem remained the difficulty of controlling by feudal government the Angevin Empire, stretching from Scotland to Spain. His sovereignty over his French territories depended on the whims of innumerable barons, each of whom could decide not to accept John as his feudal lord. Duchess Constance, mother of twelve-year-old Arthur, gained the support of Philip for her son's cause. Dowager Queen Eleanor, however, strengthened John's position by making him duke of Aquitaine; Richard had served merely as her coregent.

English and Norman barons preferred John to a Breton. William des Roches, the most powerful baron of Anjou and commander of Breton forces, went over to John's side. The Treaty of Le Goulet on May 22, 1200, settled the succession. Philip and Arthur recognized John's rights, and John accepted Philip as his overlord in France.

The unstable provinces of Maine, Anjou, and Tourraine, connecting Normandy on the north with Aquitaine, proved the weakest link in John's empire. To the west lay Arthur's Brittany; to the east, Philip's home territory. A strong line of fortresses protected the northern frontier, but the lands of Aquitaine continued the fragmented middle zone. To bolster his strength here, in 1201, John married the young Isabelle of Angoulême, who had been betrothed to Hugh of Lusignan. (The pope annulled his first marriage, to Isabelle of Gloucester.) The political advantage of the match could only have enhanced John's passion for the young girl. John soon turned his advantage into liability. Rather than compensate Hugh for his loss, as was the custom, he challenged him (with professional duelists) for plotting against Richard. The Lusignan family responded by leading the barons of the middle zone into revolt. John demonstrated remarkable heroism, rescuing his mother, besieged at Mirebeau, and, assisted by William des Roches, capturing a party of rebel leaders including his cousin Arthur of Brittany.

A defiant King John accepts his excommunication from the papal embassy of Innocent III. (F. R. Niglutsch)

Again, however, John's domineering personality spoiled his triumph. William had demanded a voice in Arthur's fate, and when he was denied, he turned against John. Arthur's mysterious disappearance branded his uncle a villain; afterward, Philip would rally French barons by the demand that John free Arthur.

John lost Normandy for various reasons, but it proved the watershed of John's reign. Himself a conspirator, he now feared hostile conspiracy everywhere. He became cautious in warfare and relied on younger knights, which offended Norman magnates, and on mercenary troops, who plundered Norman populations. The admirable frontier defenses proved vulnerable; the surrender of Château Gaillard in April, 1204, brought the collapse of John's control over Normandy.

A conflict with Pope Innocent III compounded John's problems. In 1205, the Canterbury monks asserted their independence by electing their prior as archbishop. Then, under royal pressure, they elected the king's secretary as archbishop. Thus, two delegations in Rome sought papal confirmation. When a runoff election produced a tie vote, Innocent appointed Cardinal Stephen Langton, an Englishman who was serving in the papal chancery. John rejected the appointment. An eight-year contest of wills followed. At first, Innocent had little success; neither interdict nor excommunication seemed to change John's position. Only in 1213, with the pope about to depose him and sponsor Philip's crusade against him, did John give in. He surrendered dramatically, accepting Langton and turning England and Ireland over to the pope as fiefs. This tribute gained for him Innocent's firm support.

From the first, John had showed more interest than any predecessor in traveling throughout England, participating in local courts. Barons resented this interference, and John, because of his firsthand acquaintance with local government and because of the desertions he had suffered in Normandy, distrusted the barons. Yet during his quarrel with the pope, the king strengthened his position in England. He not only definitively established royal supremacy in Ireland, brought King William the Lion of Scotland to heel, and pacified Wales, but also developed a naval defense system. In 1212, at Damme, an English fleet crippled a French invasion fleet of seventeen hundred ships. In 1214, with British frontiers secured, at peace with Rome, John sought revenge for his defeat a decade earlier. He and his nephew, the Holy Roman Emperor Otto IV of Brunswick, planned a combined war operation. Though John had success at Poitou, Otto's decisive defeat by Philip II at Bouvines in 1214 frustrated their strategy, and John returned to England with nothing gained.

A triumph in 1214 might have brightened John's tarnished reputation. English barons had paid heavily for his wars: eleven scutages in sixteen years, compared to three in Richard's ten-year reign, and many barons had lost estates in Normandy. Reconciliation with the Church brought home troublesome exiles, and Langton proved a capable spokesperson for the barons. Faced with unified baronial opposition, John signed the Great Charter, or Magna Carta, and, at least temporarily, agreed that even the king was subordinate to the "law of the land."

In 1215, England's barons divided: London, the north, and some of the west in revolt; the Midlands and south still supporting the king. Though many baronial leaders, such as Robert Fitzwalter, were merely self-seeking, the men who framed the charter, Langton and William Marshal, both recently at odds with John, now were committed royalists. The charter emerged, therefore, a compromise document, aiming for efficient functioning of the king's courts, not for destruction of his power. It limited the king by law, but only according to specific grievances and not in principle. The irrelevance of any compromise to the forces contending in 1215-1216 soon became clear. After signing the charter at Runnymede on June 15, 1215, John appealed to the pope to annul it. Innocent complied: He decreed excommunicate anyone who revolted against John and suspended Langton from office. On the other side, Fitzwalter's Army of God never disbanded. Yet, although two-thirds of the barons now accepted Prince Louis (Louis IX), son of Philip, as king of England, one-third still remained irrevocably loyal. John established himself in the north, but misfortune ended his reign. A storm hurt his new fleet, enabling the French to land, and he died of dysentery while campaigning against them.

SIGNIFICANCE

King John's reign marks a turning point in English historiography. Richard I's reputation lives on, glorified by legend and chronicle. John's rule was documented by an unprecedented supply of government documents and the writings of his clerical enemies, such as Roger of Wendover. If the loss of Normandy hurt John's reputation, it forced his vassals to choose to be English or Norman-French and thus began the great expansion of the French national monarchy, which ended only with the Hundred Years' War (1337-1453). John's legend belongs to the seventeenth century when historians such as Edward Coke misread the Great Charter as a monument to traditional English freedom against Continental despotism. In fact, only in its last clause did the charter reject monarchical control, establishing a council of barons to guarantee the king's adherence. Periodically, in various transmutations, this conciliar ideal kept England in disorder for two hundred years and helped bring about its final defeat by France. The rallying of barons behind nine-year-old Henry III stands as a fitting epitaph for his father's preservation of the monarchical center of English government.

—*Paul Stewart*

FURTHER READING

Alexander, Michael V. C. *Three Crises in Early English History: Personalities and Politics During the Norman Conquest, the Reign of King John, and the Wars of the Roses*. Lanham, Md.: University Press of America, 1998. A thorough look at John's personal and political role in the signing of the Magna Carta.

Church, S. D., ed. *King John: New Interpretations*. Rochester, N.Y.: Boydell Press, 1999. Discusses topics and persons such as John and the English economy, the Church in Rome, Eleanor of Aquitaine, Philip II, and relations with Scotland, Wales, and Ireland.

Holt, James Clarke. *Magna Carta*. New York: Cambridge University Press, 1965. Concentrates on the political context of 1215 but follows through to the charter's influence in later centuries.

_______. *The Northerners: A Study in the Reign of King John*. Oxford, England: Oxford University Press, 1961. A detailed look at politics from 1212 to 1216 and at the formation of something like a political party based on geography and opposition to royal policies.

Kelly, Amy. *Eleanor of Aquitaine and the Four Kings*. Cambridge, Mass.: Harvard University Press, 1950. Interpretive biography of King John's mother, a strong influence on his reign until her death. The kings discussed are Louis VII of France, Henry II, Richard I, and John.

Painter, Sidney. *The Reign of King John*. Baltimore: Johns Hopkins University Press, 1949. An excellent history of the whole reign. Analyzes the baronial group through family connections, property claims, and personalities.

_______. *William Marshal, Knight-Errant, Baron and Regent of England*. Baltimore: Johns Hopkins University Press, 1933. Describes the British perspective, as opposed to Eleanor's and Langton's Continental view. Marshal served before and after John's reign.

Powicke, Frederick Maurice. *The Loss of Normandy, 1189-1204*. Manchester, England: Manchester University Press, 1913. Offers background on Richard's reign and points up John's problems and weaknesses.

_______. *Stephen Langton*. Oxford, England: Oxford University Press, 1928. At the heart of the controversies of the reign, Langton had his own viewpoint on church-state relations.

Turner, Ralph Vernon. *The King and His Courts: The Role of John and Henry III in Administration and Justice, 1199-1240*. Ithaca, N.Y.: Cornell University Press, 1968. A constitutional history showing John's best facet.

Warren, Wilfred Lewis. *King John*. London: Eyre and Spottiswoode, 1961. A good biography, offering balanced judgment not only on John but also on various scholarly puzzles of his reign.

SEE ALSO: Hubert de Burgh; Eleanor of Aquitaine; Frederick II; Henry II; Henry III; Louis IX; Philip II; Richard I.

RELATED ARTICLES in *Great Events from History: The Middle Ages, 477-1453*: c. 1150-1200: Rise of the Hansa Merchant Union; 1154-1204: Angevin Empire Is Established; 1189-1192: Third Crusade; July 27, 1214: Battle of Bouvines; June 15, 1215: Signing of the Magna Carta; November 11-30, 1215: Fourth Lateran Council.

JOHN OF DAMASCUS

Syrian-born writer, monk, and religious scholar

During the Iconoclastic Controversy of the eighth century, John wrote a series of theological tracts defending the use of images in Christian worship, thus establishing the theological position of Eastern Orthodoxy.

BORN: c. 675; Damascus (now in Syria)
DIED: December 4, 749; near Jerusalem (now in Israel)
ALSO KNOWN AS: John Damascene
AREAS OF ACHIEVEMENT: Religion and theology, literature

EARLY LIFE

John of Damascus (deh-MAS-kehs) was born in the city with which he is identified at a time when Syria was under the rule of the caliphs. His family name was Manṣūr, meaning "victory." John's father was Sergius Manṣūr, a wealthy Christian who served at the court of the Umayyad caliph ʿAbd al-Malik. Because of the practice of toleration by the Umayyad Dynasty, it was not unusual for Christians to serve the caliphs. When Sergius was elevated to the rank of prime minister, he was troubled at the thought that his son John would adopt Arab ways. He placed him under the instruction of the Sicilian monk Cosmas, who had been brought to Damascus as a slave.

It was customary for the Arabs to go on plundering excursions along the Mediterranean coasts and to return with a number of prisoners, whom they made slaves. Among a group of prisoners brought back from the coast of Sicily was the monk Cosmas. Cosmas was an ordained priest and a teacher. He knew grammar and logic and as much arithmetic as Pythagoras and as much geometry as Euclid. He had also studied music, poetry, and astronomy.

The usual practice was to sell such prisoners to farmers, who would work them in the fields until they dropped dead. There existed laws against introducing slaves into the houses of official families. John's father managed, however, to buy Cosmas for a great price from Malik and took him into his home; from that point onward the learned monk became John's tutor and master. Thus John acquired a formidable knowledge of theology, rhetoric, natural history, music, and astronomy. He learned from Cosmas much about the world and about spiritual theory.

John became deeply religious and, like his father, was given to good works. On his father's death, however, Caliph ʿAbd al-Malik appointed John to the high position of chief secretary. In an Eastern court, only the position of councillor of state was higher. In time, John enjoyed the powers once possessed by his father. While serving in the Eastern court, John continued to practice the Christian virtues of charity and humility. He was obsessed by the thought of offering up all of his wealth to the poor and then following his teacher and master, Cosmas, into a monastery. It is clear that the humble Cosmas exerted more influence over John than did the mighty caliph. Cosmas had retired to the monastery of St. Sabas in Palestine when he had completed John's education. John remained at his position in the caliph's court until approximately 730, when he, too, entered the monastery of St. Sabas. Yet already before he left the secular world, John had begun the great work of his life, the refutation of iconoclasm (the opposition to religious imagery).

LIFE'S WORK

Iconoclasm was the latest in a series of challenges—beginning with Arianism—that the Eastern church had had to face. The Iconoclastic Controversy began with Byzantine emperor Leo III and continued through the reign of his successor, Constantine V. It was a conflict over images and the particular significance attached to them. In the Eastern (or Greek) church, the practice of venerating icons was widespread by the seventh century. The opponents of this practice maintained that Christianity, as a purely spiritual religion, must proscribe the cult of icons. This opposition was strong in the Byzantine Empire, so long the cradle of religious ferment. There were considerable remnants of Monophysitism, and the Paulicians, a sect hostile to any ecclesiastical cult, were gaining ground.

Defenders of the practice of venerating icons attributed Leo's hostility to images to Jewish and Muslim influences. Mosaic teaching requires strict repudiation of image worship, but it was contact with the Muslim world that had intensified the distrust of icons. Muslims have an abhorrence of any pictorial representation of the human countenance. They teach that "images are an abomination of the works of Satan."

In 726, the Greek islands of Thera and Therasia were shaken by a marine volcanic eruption. At the request of iconoclastic bishops of Asia Minor, Leo III responded to this natural disaster by issuing a decree declaring that the eruption was the result of God's wrath on the idolatry of the Greeks; therefore, all paintings, mosaics, and statues representing Christ and his saints had to be destroyed. Another decree ordered the destruction of the great statue of Christ over the bronze gate of the palace in Constantinople. A riot ensued when imperial officers tore down this statue. The emperor then ordered the execution of those who had tried to protect the statue; the victims were the first martyrs of the Iconoclastic Controversy.

In order to strengthen his position, Leo attempted to win over the pope and the patriarch of Constantinople. His proposals were decisively rejected by the aged patriarch Germanus I (715-730), and his correspondence with Pope Gregory II (715-731) only produced negative results. After these two authorities, the emperor's principal opponent was John of Damascus.

As images, paintings, and statues were being destroyed, John wrote to the emperor. He argued that figures of the cherubim and seraphim adorned the ark of the covenant. Further, citing the Scriptures, John wrote that

John of Damascus. (Library of Congress)

Solomon was ordered to adorn the walls of the temple with living figures, flowers, and fruit. He concluded that it was fitting that Christians should adorn their churches. John's letter was reasoned and scholarly, replete with quotations from the Bible.

Leo was determined that the images be removed. He believed that Christianity needed purifying and that this could only come about with the destruction of the images. Leo was determined that Christianity survive the increasing power of Islam. Failing to get any support from Germanus, who had joined the side of the image-worshiping Christians, Leo replaced him with Anastasius.

Still in the caliph's court in 730, John issued a formidable attack, quoting the evidence of the Church fathers who favored the worship of images. He quoted from Saint Basil, Dionysius the Areopagite, Gregory of Nyssa, and Saint John Chrysostom as evidence that they openly supported the use of images. The image worshipers, he wrote, were not circumscribing God but were venerating God, which was right and proper. John closed his letter by deliberately misquoting Galatians 1:8 and accusing Leo of preaching a gospel contrary to the Bible. This letter ushered in hostility between the emperor and John.

Unable to overwhelm John by force of argument, the emperor determined to destroy him by stratagem. He forged letters addressed to himself, signing John's name to them. The letters informed the Byzantine emperor that the guards surrounding Damascus were weak and negligent and could easily be subdued. The letters urged the emperor to send an army immediately against Damascus, stating that Leo would have the cooperation of John.

These forged letters were sent by messenger to the caliph. John was summoned and asked how he could explain them. When he could offer no explanation, the caliph ordered John's right hand severed. All that night, holding his severed hand to his wrist, John prostrated himself before an icon of the Virgin Mary. According to Adrian Fortescue's text *The Greek Fathers* (1908), John said the following prayer:

> Lady and purest mother, who didst give birth to my God, because of the holy icons my right hand is cut off. Thou knowest well the cause, that Leo the emperor rages; so help me at once and heal my hand by the power of the Most High, who became man from thee, who works many wonders by thy prayers. May he now heal this hand through thy intercession, and it shall in future always write poetry in thy honour, O Theotokos, and in honour of thy Son made man in thee and for the true faith. Be my advocate, for thou canst do anything, being mother of God.

In the morning, there was only the mark of a suture to show where the knife had passed. Soon afterward, John begged the caliph to relieve him of office. Reluctantly, for he valued his service, the caliph let him go. In the year 730, after he sold all of his worldly possessions and gave the proceeds to the poor, John set out for the monastery of St. Sabas in Palestine.

At the monastery, John did not take an active part in the Iconoclastic Controversy as it continued to rage throughout the East. The statues and paintings were destroyed, but he had nothing more to say about them. As a monk, John took the vow of complete silence; he was charged to renounce all secular learning and ordered not to write. About 735, he was ordained for the priesthood, and then the restrictions were removed.

Living in a small cell, John wrote voluminously: homilies, commentaries, ascetic tracts, liturgical canons, and hymns. One of his works, to which no definite date can be attached, was the comprehensive *Echdosis tēs orthodoxon pisteōs* (*Exposition of the Orthodox Faith*, 1899). In it, he wrote briefly about images. At first God had no form, John wrote, but God became human out of pity for humans and to save humans. As human, God lived on Earth among humankind, worked miracles, suffered, was crucified, rose again, and ascended to Heaven. All these things, he wrote, actually happened and were written down for those who were not alive at the time. When humans look on the image of God, then, they remember God's saving passion, and they fall and worship what is represented there.

It was during his time at the monastery of St. Sabas that John formulated a fuller defense of holy images, which was his only original contribution to theology. Because of this contribution, he is recognized as the last of the Greek fathers. This defense is in the form of three treatises, collectively known as *Logoi treis apologētikoi pros toms diabollontas tas agaias eikonas* (c. 730; *On Holy Images*, 1898). The crucial argument of the treatises is the continual insistence that in the Incarnation a decisive and abiding change took place in the relationship between God and material creation. John wrote that before the Incarnation, God, being without form or body, could not be represented. Since the Incarnation, however, God has emerged in the flesh and lived among humans, and representations can be made of Him. Humans do not worship matter, wrote John, but worship the creator of matter.

He accused the iconoclasts, who insisted that the Old Testament's prohibition of idolatry applied to images, of quoting Scripture out of context. He proceeded to cite passages showing how God, having forbidden the making of idols, yet commanded the use of material objects and images in divine worship, instructing that his temple be adorned with the likenesses of plants and animals—images that were not to be worshiped as idols.

On the basis of Scripture, John made a distinction between absolute worship, or adoration, and relative worship, or veneration. The Bible records many occasions when the patriarchs and prophets worshiped, venerated, and bowed before places or things to whom such honor was due, yet never with the attitude of adoration that is to be reserved for God alone. John argued that it is wrong to identify every image with its prototype. Only Jesus the Son, as the pure image of God the Father, can be said to mirror his prototype with absolute faithfulness. All other images, John wrote, whether natural, symbolic, or allegorical, are essentially different from their prototypes.

Only God, he wrote, is worthy of absolute worship, or adoration. Relative worship, or veneration, is given to the Mother of God, the saints, or sacred objects. Thus, veneration given by a Christian to an image of Christ is ontologically the same as the reverence he or she ought to give his or her fellow Christians, who are also images of Christ, but it is ontologically different from the adoration that is due God alone.

Significance

The Council of Nicaea in 787 under the Byzantine empress Irene (r. 797-802) restored the use of images in Christian worship. Whereas the Iconoclast Synod of Constantinople in 754 cursed John of Damascus, the church council in 787 looked on him as a great hero. With the end of the Iconoclastic Controversy, the honor of John's name was spread throughout Christendom. An early ninth century chronicler, Theophanes the Confessor, writes that John was rightly surnamed Chrysorroas, after the chief river of his city. This name was chosen because through his life and teachings, John gleamed like gold. This name, however, did not become the common one associated with John; he has been known and honored through the centuries as John of Damascus. In the Eastern Christian church, John's feast day is December 4. Pope Leo III of the Western Christian church declared John a doctor of the Church and appointed March 27 as his feast day. Throughout Christendom, John is known for his virtue, piety, and learning—and for defending the worship of holy images.

—*Bill Manikas*

Further Reading

Anderson, David. *St. John of Damascus: On the Divine Images*. Crestwood, N.Y.: St. Vladimir's Seminary Press, 1980. Contains an analysis of John's three treatises on images.

Cavarnos, Constantine. *Guide to Byzantine Iconography: Detailed Explanation of the Distinctive Characteristics of Byzantine Iconography, With a Concise Systematic Exposition of Saint John Damascene's Defense of Holy Icons*. Boston: Holy Transfiguration Monastery, 1993. Explores John's work defending icons in the Church. An excellent resource on the icons of the orthodox church, explaining the theology of icons. Bibliography, index.

Fortescue, Adrian. *The Greek Fathers*. London: Catholic Truth Society, 1908. Written by an expert in the field, this classic volume contains a chapter on John of Damascus, together with translations of some of his works. Generously documented.

Louth, Andrew. *St. John Damascene: Tradition and Originality in Byzantine Theology*. New York: Oxford University Press, 2002. Explores John's work on faith, with three sections covering his life, his logic, and iconoclasm. Bibliography, index.

Ostrogorsky, George. *History of the Byzantine State*. Translated by Joan Hussey. Rev. ed. New Brunswick, N.J.: Rutgers University Press, 1969. An excellent and thorough history of the period. Contains a section on the iconoclastic controversy. Illustrations, colored maps, bibliography.

Parry, Kenneth. *Depicting the Word: Byzantine Iconophile Thought of the Eighth and Ninth Centuries*. New York: E. J. Brill, 1996. Surveys John's intellectual contributions defending the veneration of icons, controversial literature on iconoclasm, and more. Bibliography, index.

Payne, Robert. *The Holy Fire: The Story of the Fathers of the Eastern Church*. Crestwood, N.Y: St. Vladimir's Seminary Press, 1980. Contains a chapter on John of Damascus, together with a discussion of some of his writings.

Runciman, Steven. *Byzantine Civilization*. London: E. Arnold, 1966. Contains a chapter on Byzantine literature and makes frequent references to the works of John of Damascus. Includes bibliographic notes.

Schönborn, Christoph. *God's Human Face: The Christ-icon*. Translated by Lothar Krauth. San Francisco: Ignatius Press, 1994. An exploration of the nature and history of iconoclasm and the iconoclastic controversy, the theology of images, the representation of the body, and much more. Chapters also cover "The Icon as Grace-Filled Matter: John Damascene" and the second Council of Nicea. Bibliography, index.

Valantasis, Richard, ed. *Religions of Late Antiquity in Practice*. Princeton, N.J.: Princeton University Press, 2000. A study that includes the chapter "Texts on Iconoclasm: John of Damascus and the Council of Hiereia." Bibliography, index.

See also: ʿAbd al-Malik; Charlemagne; Saint Irene; Theoleptus of Philadelphia; Theophanes the Confessor.

Related articles in *Great Events from History: The Middle Ages, 477-1453*: 726-843: Iconoclastic Controversy; 1054: Beginning of the Rome-Constantinople Schism.

Judah ha-Levi

Hebrew poet and philosopher

Judah ha-Levi, one of the greatest Hebrew poets, was also an important medieval religious philosopher of the Arabic-Aristotelian tradition.

Born: c. 1075; Tudela, Kingdom of Pamplona (now in Spain)
Died: July, 1141; Egypt
Also known as: Yehuda ben Shemuel ha-Levi (Hebrew name); Abū al-Ḥasan (Arabic name)
Areas of achievement: Literature, philosophy, religion and theology

Early Life

The son of Samuel ha-Levi, Judah ha-Levi (JEW-duh hah-LEE-vi) was born in Muslim Spain. As a member of an affluent, well-educated Jewish family, ha-Levi began the study of Hebrew and religion when he was quite young, but his schooling was not limited to those subjects. Growing up during a golden age of Jewish life in Spain, he was exposed to a wide range of learning—Arabic, mathematics, astronomy, philosophy. Because of the fluidity of religious demarcations in Spain during this period, he also learned Castilian, and the languages of all three Spanish religions (Hebrew, Arabic, and Castilian) are employed in his poetry.

When Judah ha-Levi was about fifteen, he may have gone to Lucena to study under the noted Talmudist Isaac Alfasi. According to some sources, after this teacher's death in 1103 ha-Levi remained at Lucena for some time, serving as secretary to Alfasi's successor, Joseph ibn Megash. The death of Alfasi and the succession and marriage of Ibn Megash occasioned some of ha-Levi's earliest verses. Sometime in his youth, he also became friendly with a celebrated older Jewish poet, Moses ibn Ezra of Granada. Ha-Levi had participated in a poetry contest at Córdoba, the object being to write an imitation of a complex poem by Ibn Ezra. Ha-Levi's entry won, and it so impressed the senior poet that he invited ha-Levi to visit him. After meeting the handsome, dark-haired youth, Moses ibn Ezra wrote,

> How can a boy so young in years
> Bear such a weight of wisdom sage,
> Nor 'mongst the greybeards find his peers
> While still in the very bloom of age?

The two remained lifelong friends. Ha-Levi for a time lived in Ibn Ezra's house, and the older man's death in 1139 elicited a moving elegy from ha-Levi.

Ha-Levi was making other important friendships as well. From Baruch Albalia he may have derived his interest in Arabic-Aristotelian philosophy, while Levi al-Taban of Saragossa, Judah ben Gajath of Granada, and Abraham ibn Ezra shared and encouraged his poetic interest. Abraham ibn Ezra became an especially close friend. The two enjoyed discussing biblical exegesis, and Ibn Ezra's important commentaries occasionally show evidence of ha-Levi's influence. Tradition maintains that Ibn Ezra's son married ha-Levi's daughter.

Life's Work

Throughout his life, ha-Levi was a poet first, a physician and philosopher only secondarily. Of his literary work, some eight hundred poems survive. Though most are religious, a substantial number are secular; of these, about eighty are love poems in the manner of Arabic and Christian verses of the day. In these poems, the lady typically is cruel to her lover; the lover yearns for her and fills buckets with his tears; the lady shines even in the darkest night; her eyes slay the lover. Despite their highly stylized formula, the poems reveal technical virtuosity in the use of internal rhyme and musicality, and the imagery can be strikingly original, as when he likens a face surrounded by long red hair to the setting sun turning the sky crimson. Humor, too, surfaces in these poems.

> Awake, my dear, from your slumber arise,
> The sight of you will ease my pain;
> If you dream of one who is kissing your eyes,
> Awake, and soon the dream I'll explain.

Throughout his life, ha-Levi would admire and celebrate female beauty.

Ha-Levi was also sensitive to the beauty and grandeur of nature. Celebrating the return of spring, he wrote,

> And now the spring is here with yearning eyes
> Midst shimmering golden flower beds,
> On meadows a tapestry of bloom over all;
> And myriad-eyed young plants upspring,
> White, green, or red like lips that to the mouth
> Of the beloved one sweetly cling.

On another occasion, a storm at sea prompted him to proclaim the power of nature and to recognize a person's weakness in the face of elemental rage. Commenting on these nature poems, Heinrich Graetz has observed,

> One can see in his lines the flowers bud and glisten; one inhales their fragrance; one sees the branches bending beneath the weight of golden fruits, and hears the songsters of the air warble their love songs. . . . When he describes the fury of a storm-tossed sea, he imparts to his readers all the sublimity and terror which he himself felt.

Another, larger group of ha-Levi's secular poems are occasional pieces, such as those composed for the death of his teacher and the marriage of Ibn Megash. Most of the extant poems in this category are eulogies or laments, which often combine personal grief with a sense of cosmic desolation, for in the death of a friend or fellow Jew he read the fate of the Jewish nation.

> There is no sanctuary and no rest,
> in the West or in the East.
> Should Edom [Christianity] or Ishmael [Islam] be victor,
> the Jew is always the vanquished.

This concern for the Jewish condition also informs ha-Levi's religious poetry. About half the surviving poems, some 350, are prayers for festivals (*piyyutim*), many of which continue to be recited. His models here were not only the biblical lamentations of Job and Jeremiah but also contemporary Hebrew and Arabic verses. Most focus on national tragedies, though he sometimes describes personal experiences and expresses a desire for salvation. The Psalms provided examples for other, more personal religious poetry in which he recorded his fears and struggles, failures and joys.

Only about thirty-five known poems deal directly with Zion, yet on these more than any others rest his fame and reputation as a poet, for into these works he poured his deepest, most powerful feelings. "My heart is in the East, and I am in the uttermost West—/ How can I find savor in food? How shall it be sweet to me?" For him, the vision of Israel was not an abstraction but a reality that he saw before him daily. Recognizing the plight of the Jews in the Diaspora, subject to the whims of mobs and petty tyrants, he asks rhetorically,

> Have we either in the east or in the west
> A place of hope wherein we may trust,
> Except the land that is full of gates,
> Toward which the gates of Heaven are open—
> Like Mount Sinai and Carmel and Bethel,
> And the houses of the prophets, the envoys,
> And the thrones of the priests of the Lord's throne,
> And the thrones of the kings, the anointed?

Of these poems, none is more moving than the "Zionide" (Ode to Zion), still recited in synagogues around the world each Ninth of Ab, the fast commemorating the destruction of the first and second Temples in Jerusalem and, fittingly, the 1492 exile of the Jews from Spain, a disaster ha-Levi had feared and foreseen. In four stanzas with but a single rhyme throughout, ha-Levi expresses the Jewish longing for Jerusalem, the joy and grief for its past glories, the sense of hope unfulfilled, and the anticipation of joyful redemption when "the chosen are returned to thee/ And thy first youth in glory is renewed." The Hebrew poet Israel Efros has declared, "If the hearts of the Jews of all time could be formed into one great throbbing heart and made to turn toward the East, the song that it would sing would be" ha-Levi's "Ode to Zion."

Ha-Levi's poetry circulated widely in manuscript, and from the beginning of printing his works were incorporated into prayer books. They have been translated into many languages, including German (1845), English (1851), Italian (1871), Hungarian (1910), Dutch (1929), and Spanish (1932).

Poetry could not, however, earn for ha-Levi a living, so he was forced to turn to medicine. His attitude toward the profession is conveyed in a letter to a friend.

> I occupy myself in the hours which belong neither to the day nor to the night with the vanity of the medical sci-

> ence, although I am unable to heal. . . . I cry to God that He quickly send deliverance to me and give me freedom to enjoy rest, that I may repair to some place of living knowledge, to the fountain of wisdom.

His disclaimer of skill notwithstanding, he apparently served as court physician to Alfonso VI of Toledo, which had fallen to the Christians in 1085. The murder of his patron, Solomon ibn Ferrizuel, in 1108 shocked ha-Levi; together with the sufferings caused by fundamentalist Muslims and the Christian Crusaders, this event reemphasized the precariousness of the Jewish position in exile.

The death of Ibn Ferrizuel seems to have driven ha-Levi from Toledo. During the following years, he traveled throughout Spain, visiting Granada, Málaga, Córdoba, and Seville. In this last city, he became friendly with the court physicians Abū Ayūb Solomon ibn al-Muᶜallim and Abū al-Ḥasan ben Meir ibn Kamniel, and here he married in 1120. Further travel took him back to Toledo (1130) and Córdoba (c. 1134). Increasingly, he felt alienated from his native land; after the deaths of his wife and his close friend Moses ibn Ezra, he resolved to follow his heart to Israel. Shortly before leaving Spain, he codified a treatise he had been developing for almost twenty years, his *Kītab al-Ḥujjah waal dalīl fi nasr al-dīn al dhalīl* (1139; *Judah Halevi's Kitab al Khazari*, 1905; best known as *Book of the Kuzari*).

The work is based on the conversion to Judaism of Bulan, king of the Khazars, a Tartar tribe in Russia, in 740. Hasdai ibn Shaprut (c. 910-970) had corresponded with Joseph, another Khazar king, who had sent an account of the religious debates among Christians, Muslims, and Jews that had led to Bulan's decision to convert; ha-Levi was familiar with these letters and may have conversed with Khazar descendants living in Spain. The *Book of the Kuzari*, however, transcends a mere attempt at historical re-creation. Ha-Levi was concerned with the Karaite movement in Judaism that sought to reject all Talmudic tradition in favor of a literal reading of the Torah, the five books of Moses, and he was equally concerned with the inroads of Arabic-Aristotelian philosophy. He had apparently studied Avicenna and al-Fārābi, as well as their opponent, the mystical al-Ghazzālī, and had sided with the latter. These concerns combined with ha-Levi's personal convictions to create a brilliant explication and defense of Judaism.

As the *Book of the Kuzari* opens, Bulan is troubled by a dream in which an angel has told him that while the king's intentions please God, his actions do not. Bulan therefore summons a philosopher to help him. The philosopher replies that purity of heart is more important than action, but Bulan's dream has already demonstrated the error of such a view. The king then calls in a Muslim and a Christian theologian; because the Jews are persecuted and universally despised, he does not invite a representative of that faith. As the Christian and the Muslim speak, though, Bulan realizes that both draw heavily from Judaism, and at the end of the first section he brings in a Jewish spokesman, the Haver (friend).

In the succeeding four sections, the king and the Haver, who serves as ha-Levi's spokesperson, discuss the nature of Judaism. Bulan first wants to know how the Jews understand God. The Haver replies that actual experience is more important than theoretical speculation. He then links the Jewish people, Israel, and the Hebrew language, a fusion that ha-Levi increasingly believed to be essential: The Jew could survive only with a homeland in which he spoke his own language. In the third section, the Haver explains Bulan's dream by saying that to worship God one must fulfill his commandments. Section four finally addresses the question Bulan had asked about the nature of God. As Elohim, the Haver replies, God is remote, but as Adonai he has revealed himself through history and prophecy. Only the Jews have enjoyed this intimate revelation from and relationship with God, so all other religions must approach God through the Jews.

Thus far, the Haver has focused on distinguishing Judaism from the other major religions. In the final section, he returns to the philosopher. Acknowledging Aristotle's authority in matters of logic and mathematics, he maintains that in spiritual matters speculation is handicapped because the philosopher knows God only indirectly. The Prophet, on the other hand, has experienced God directly. Herein lies the strength of Judaism; 600,000 people saw the parting of the Red Sea and heard God's voice at Sinai. No other religion can claim such an immediate encounter with the divine, an encounter cherished through an unbroken chain of tradition. Ha-Levi thus indicates the weakness of the Karaite view: The rejection of the Talmudic heritage would leave Judaism with no stronger claim to validity than that of Christianity or Islam, since without the historical link to Sinai Judaism would lose its unique experience of revelation.

At the end of the *Book of the Kuzari*, the Haver tells Bulan of his intention to go to Israel. Why, the king replies, should the Haver undertake a dangerous journey to a perilous land? Since the destruction of the Temple, God no longer physically resides in Israel, so one can find God anywhere if one seeks with a pure heart. Speaking for ha-Levi, the Haver responds that heart and soul are perfectly pure only in the place selected by God. Though God has removed his physical presence from Israel, God's spirit remains, and therefore the Haver must go.

Still, ha-Levi's own decision to leave was not reached easily. In the *Book of the Kuzari*, Bulan anachronistically warns the Haver of the anti-Jewish sentiments of the Crusaders then controlling the Holy Land. Ha-Levi's letters express doubts about the journey, as does the following introspective poem:

> Yet he feared and trembled with falling tears
> To cast Spain from him and seek shores beyond;
> To ride upon ships, to tread through wastes,
> Dens of lions, mountains of leopards.

In 1140, though, he finally set off for Israel, arriving in Alexandria on September 8. Like his Spanish compatriots, the Jews of Egypt sought to dissuade him from further travel. Why leave the comforts and safety of civilization for a desolate, war-torn land? Still, ha-Levi pressed onward toward his goal, passing through Cairo, Tyre, and Damascus.

Did he ever reach Israel? Was he able to "pass to Hebron, where the ancient graves/ Still wait for me, and wander in the dusk/ Of the forest of Carmel"? Did he "stand upon the summit of the mountains/ Where once the unforgotten brothers stood/ And the light of them was seen throughout the world"? Did he "fall to the earth and press my lips into the dust and weep thy desolation/ Till I am blind, and, blind, still comfort thee"? Were these words of his "Ode to Zion" prophecy or dream? No one knows; his final resting place, like that of Moses, remains undiscovered. Yet legend maintains that he did indeed reach the Wailing Wall, and that there, as he prostrated himself to kiss the sacred ground, an Arab horseman trampled or stabbed him to death even as ha-Levi was uttering the words of his "Ode to Zion."

Significance

Shortly after ha-Levi's death, Judah ibn Tibbon translated the *Book of the Kuzari* into Hebrew (c. 1150); ha-Levi had chosen to write in Arabic to make the work accessible to a wider audience. In later years, it was translated into many other languages and enjoyed popularity not only in Jewish but also in Christian and Muslim circles for its championship of faith above reason. The *Book of the Kuzari* impressed Johann Gottlieb von Herder, for example, who claimed that in writing his dialogues he used ha-Levi rather than Plato as his model.

Yet it was as a poet that ha-Levi saw himself, and it is as a poet that his reputation has chiefly survived. More than six centuries after his death, Herder's countryman Heinrich Heine called ha-Levi's poetry "pure and true and blemish-free," and in 1882 Emma Lazarus published translations of a number of ha-Levi's poems in *Songs of a Semite*. Brilliant in technique, striking in imagery, adept in musicality, they reveal a talent of the first order. His contemporaries and successors repeatedly sang his praises. To Moses ibn Ezra, he was "the pearl diver and lord of most rare jewels." The thirteenth century poet Judah ben Solomon Harizi declared that ha-Levi's poetry

> shines like a crown over the congregation of Israel, adorns its neck like the most precious strand of pearls. . . . All are his followers and attempt to sing in his manner, but they do not reach even the dust of his chariot, and humbly they kiss his feet.

Later, Abraham Bedersi referred to his verses as "the Urrim and Tummim of Jewish song."

Such praise is merited; his poems are living jewels, sighing for the tragedies of the Jews and panting for salvation. He expressed the dreams of an exiled, homeless people and offered hope that despite the present darkness they might yet "behold in wonderment/ the beauteous splendor" of their land. The rhythms of ha-Levi's lines are the heartbeats of his nation. Judah ha-Levi is the enduring poet laureate of Zion.

—*Joseph Rosenblum*

Further Reading

Cohen, Richard A., ed. *Ninety-two Poems and Hymns of Yehuda Halevi*. Translated by Thomas Kovach, Eva Jospe, and Gilya Gerda Schmidt. Albany: State University of New York Press, 2000. Provides translations of ha-Levi's hymns and poems, including "Ode to Zion." Also includes an introductory essay.

Druck, David. *Yehuda Halevy: His Life and Works*. Translated by M. Z. R. Frank. New York: Bloch, 1941. Good introduction to ha-Levi's life and writings, and the discussions of the *Book of the Kuzari* and the poetry remain useful.

Efros, Israel. "Some Aspects of Yehudah Halevi's Mysticism." *Proceedings of the American Academy of Jewish Research* 11 (1941): 27-41. An erudite discussion of the *Book of the Kuzari*'s treatment of mysticism and rationalism. Notes ha-Levi's sources and explores the meanings of certain obscure terms in the work.

Feldman, Leon A. "Yehudah Halevi: An Answer to a

Historical Challenge." *Jewish Social Studies* 3 (1941): 243-272. Based on an address given at the octocentennial observance of ha-Levi's death. Calls ha-Levi "the greatest Hebrew poet after the conclusion of the Bible." Solid historical and philosophical background on medieval Spain and the relationship of that milieu to ha-Levi's ideas. Concludes with a discussion of ha-Levi's enduring significance.

Kayser, Rudolf. *The Life and Time of Jehudah Halevi*. Translated by Frank Gaynor. New York: Philosophical Library, 1949. Places ha-Levi within the context of the Jewish golden age in Spain and also within the context of the conflict between Western rationalism and Eastern mysticism. In the *Book of the Kuzari* and in his emigration, ha-Levi reveals his sympathy with the latter.

Menocal, Maria Rosa, Raymond P. Scheindlin, and Michael Sells, eds. *The Literature of Al-Andalus*. New York: Cambridge University Press, 2000. Part of the Cambridge History of Arabic Literature series, provides a biographical look at the literature of ha-Levi in Arabic Andalusia.

Minkin, Jacob S. "Judah Halevi." In *Great Jewish Personalities in Ancient and Medieval Times*, edited by Simon Noveck. Washington, D.C.: B'nai B'rith Department of Adult Jewish Education, 1959. A chronological presentation of the life and works. Draws on the poetry and the *Book of the Kuzari* to gain insights into ha-Levi's experiences and thoughts.

Silman, Yochanan. *Philosopher and Prophet: Judah Halevi, the Kuzari, and the Evolution of His Thought*. Translated by Lenn J. Schramm. Albany: State University of New York Press, 1995. Explores the whole range of ha-Levi's philosophical and religious thought, from Aristotelianism, to form and matter, divinity, theology, anthropology, god and world, and more.

Zinberg, Israel. "Jehudah Halevi the Poet." In *A History of Jewish Literature*, translated and edited by Bernard Martin, vol. 1. Cleveland, Ohio: Press of Case Western Reserve University, 1972. Analyzes the evolution of ha-Levi's poetry as the writer matured. Includes generous excerpts from ha-Levi's verses.

SEE ALSO: Averroës; Avicenna; El Cid; al-Ghazzālī; Moses Maimonides.

RELATED ARTICLES in *Great Events from History: The Middle Ages, 477-1453*: c. 950: Court of Córdoba Flourishes in Spain; 1031: Caliphate of Córdoba Falls; November 1, 1092-June 15, 1094: El Cid Conquers Valencia; November 27, 1095: Pope Urban II Calls the First Crusade; c. 1150: Moors Transmit Classical Philosophy and Medicine to Europe; 1190: Moses Maimonides Writes *The Guide of the Perplexed*.

JULIAN OF NORWICH

English mystic

Julian was a significant English medieval mystic, whose book, The Showings of Julian of Norwich, *made her the first-recognized English female author.*

BORN: 1342; probably Norwich, Norfolk, England
DIED: After 1416; Norwich
ALSO KNOWN AS: Juliana of Norwich
AREAS OF ACHIEVEMENT: Religion and theology, literature, philosophy

EARLY LIFE

A contemporary of the great English authors Geoffrey Chaucer and William Langland and of the theologian John Wyclif, little is known of Julian of Norwich's (NOHR-ihch) life. Even the name Julian by which she is best known might not have been her given name but instead arisen from the name of the church that contained her anchorhold. The scant, verifiable, biographical details available come from a few autobiographical references in her book, *The Showings of Julian of Norwich* (written c. 1373-1393; published c. 1650-c. 1670, 1901; also known as the *Revelations of Divine Love*), a brief description of a meeting with fellow East Anglian mystic Margery Kempe, described in Kempe's autobiography, *The Book of Margery Kempe* (1940), and from several contemporary wills that record bequests to Julian and her servant.

Julian lived during the turmoil in fourteenth century Europe and England, including the Babylonian Captivity of the Church (1309-1377), the Great Schism of the Papacy (1378-1417), the Hundred Years' War (1337-1453), the Black Death throughout Europe (1347-1352) and recurrent plague, bad harvests, outbreaks of cattle disease, and the Peasants' Revolt in England (1381). These events might help explain the great number of English mystics such as Walter Hilton, Richard Rolle, Margery Kempe, and the unknown author of the mystical prose work *The Cloud of Unknowing* (fourteenth century), who were devout seekers of not only refuge but also answers through solitude, meditation, and prayer.

Because Julian vividly described colors and cloth in her book and possibly because she had familiarity with paintings of the crucifixion extant in Norwich, it is thought that she came from a wealthy family engaged in the Norwich textile trade. Apparently familiar with the contemplative life, it is possible that she may have been a Benedictine nun prior to becoming an anchoress, a holy recluse, who lived in a cell (or anchorhold), at the Church of Saints Julian and Edward in Norwich, East Anglia, England. To become an anchoress, she would have had to face an interview by the local bishop to ascertain whether she had a genuine "calling" to a life of devotion. Such a vocation would have been unusual for Julian, as most women, especially the wealthy, were expected to marry, have children, and keep house or assist in the management of the family estate. Julian's church, located on the main road in England's second largest city, would have been in close proximity to the bell in the Cathedral of Norwich, which would have helped regulate her devotion or prayer. The cathedral dated to Norman times and about thirty churches existed in the city at the time, making it an important center of religion and religious artifacts in England.

LIFE'S WORK

At the age of just over thirty years (according to Julian's account), Julian was stricken with a serious ailment of seven nights' and six days' duration. She believed she was taken ill as a result of previous prayers for three gifts from God, a better knowledge of Christ's suffering, a severe illness and the wounds of contrition, and compassion and longing like those of the martyred Saint Cecilia. She was given the last rites on the fourth day, and on the seventh day, she went numb from the waist down and again received the last rites. At one point Julian's mother closed Julian's eyes thinking her daughter had died. On either May 8 or May 13, 1373 (the manuscript sources differ), she recovered and received sixteen visions, revelations, or "showings," as she called them, which she believed to be of divine origin as she meditated on the crucifix a local curate had brought to her. The crucifix appeared to come to life in a re-enactment of Christ's crucifixion. Scholarly, medical explanations for her illness range from diagnoses of self-induced psychosomatic episode to botulism, cardiac arrest, ergotism, or a reaction to herbs.

The sixteen visions she reportedly experienced were the following:

1. The crowning of Christ with thorns
2. The signs of Christ's passion
3. The almighty, all-knowing, all-loving God has made everything
4. The beatings of Christ's body and the shedding of his blood
5. The devil is defeated by Christ's passion and sufferings
6. The heavenly reward for God's faithful
7. The experiences of God's grace bringing joy and the experience of temptation bringing sadness
8. Christ's suffering and death
9. The joy that the Trinity experienced because of the sufferings and death of Christ
10. Christ shows his heart divided in half
11. The revelation of Christ's mother, Mary
12. The Lord is the essence of all there is
13. That believers should appreciate the creation of nature, the creation of human beings, and Christ's atonement
14. That Christ is the basis of believers' prayers
15. Believers will enter their reward in heaven leaving their pain behind
16. The Trinity lives eternally in the souls of the believers, and through his love the believers will not be overtaken by the devil

Feeling compelled to share these "showings" with others, even though she was a woman, Julian prepared in the first-person vernacular a short description (usually referred to by scholars as the Short Text) soon after the visions, although some scholars argue the work was composed as late as 1388. Julian pondered these visions for about twenty years, and around 1393, she wrote an expanded version (called the Long Text) roughly six times the length of the Short Text, which is highly regarded for its poetic, spiritual, devotional, and theological elements and makes her the first recognized English female author.

Julian's contemporary reputation as a holy woman attracted the attention of Margery Kempe, who sought out Julian in 1413 for advice about the uncontrollable weeping Kempe experienced. According to Kempe, their visit lasted "many days," and Julian assured Kempe that the tears were a gift from God and not the devil. A bequest by a local man in 1416 to Julian and her servant indicated that she was alive at that date and still an anchoress.

SIGNIFICANCE

Julian's description of the revelations, which she maintained were rooted in God's expression of love for humanity and intended to benefit others and not just herself, has attracted considerable scholarly attention. Commentators have focused on a number of passages in her book, the depiction of the universe as a "hazel nut" in God's hand, the parable of the Lord and the servant, the discussion of sin and the problem of evil, the attack of the devil, the motherhood of God, and the Trinity, specifically the second member of the Trinity, Jesus.

Other areas of interest lie in examinations of the differences between the Short and Long Texts. For example, Julian noted that the Short Text was aimed primarily to a readership in the contemplative life. However, this is not mentioned in the Long Text. So it appears that she reached out to a wider, lay readership in the Long Text. There is much greater detail of the physical aspects of the crucifixion in the Long Text. In the Long Text she provides cross references to the revelations as a type of index for the benefit of the reader, and the revelations are numbered.

Believers may accept the visions as of divine origin; skeptics, while rejecting that explanation, focus on interpreting the visions in the manner in which Julian understood them given her religious background and her understanding of biblical and theological works within her own cultural context. This has led to speculation about Julian's educational background because she referred to herself as "unlettered." It may have been that she was just being humble because she obviously had a broad understanding of the Bible and theological works, or it may have referred to the fact that she had no formal training in Greek and Latin and was largely self taught. The complex content and sophisticated treatment of her material as well as the intricate reasoning and rhetoric indicate a superior intellect whatever the status of her education.

Her book has drawn greater attention to the position of women in late Medieval England. Her description of Jesus as a mother, unusual and original although not unique to Christian writings, has led many scholars, especially feminists, to explore gender-related theological issues and may be one of the factors that has led to the usage of female pronouns and terms to describe the God mentioned in the Bible.

Among the deep theological issues with which Julian grappled is the concept of origin of sin. Her answer explained that Adam (the servant) wandered away from God (the Lord)—an act that was unintentional and involved no wickedness—and God in love sought out Adam. She did not ascribe wrath to God as had many earlier theologians. God is said to allow sin and tolerate evil because it will result in the positive, beneficial goals of Christ's crucifixion: the atonement of sin and the providing of salvation so that "all shall be well." Although she remained orthodox, Julian came close to Universalism (the belief that all will be saved) when she maintained that God will perform "on the last day" a special deed for the benefit of sinners who had been destined for eternal damnation. In such a fashion, she was able to focus on the purpose of the revelations—manifestation of God's love to humanity.

—*Mark C. Herman*

FURTHER READING

Abbott, Christopher. *Julian of Norwich: Autobiography and Theology.* Rochester, N.Y.: D. S. Brewer, 1999. Part of the Cambridge Studies in Medieval Mysticism series, this text explores the meanings of autobiography, such as that composed by Julian in her *Revelations*, in the context of women and mysticism.

Baker, Denise Nowakowski. *Julian of Norwich's "Showings": From Vision to Book.* Princeton, N.J.: Princeton University Press, 1994. Focuses on Julian's development and significance as a thinker and theologian within her religious background.

Beer, Frances. *Women and Mystical Experience in the Middle Ages.* Woodbridge, England: Boydell Press, 1992. A comparative study useful for placing Julian within the context of medieval women mystics.

Colledge, Edmund, and James Walsh, eds. *A Book of Showings to the Anchoress Julian of Norwich.* 2 vols. Toronto: Pontifical Institute of Mediaeval Studies, 1978. A scholarly edition with an excellent introduction.

Jantzen, Grace M. *Julian of Norwich: Mystic and Theologian.* Mahwah, N.J.: Paulist Press, 2000. A full consideration of Julian's life, spirituality, and theology.

Jones, Catherine. "The English Mystic: Julian of Norwich." In *Medieval Women Writers*, edited by Katharina M. Wilson. Athens: University of Georgia Press, 1984. A brief consideration of Julian that focuses on her message of optimism. Contains selections from her work.

Julian of Norwich. *Revelations of Divine Love.* Translated by Clifton Wolters. Baltimore: Penguin Books, 1973. A very accessible translation for the general reader.

Kempe, Margery. *The Book of Margery Kempe: A New Translation, Contexts, Criticism.* Translated and edited by Lynn Staley. New York: Norton, 2001. This critical edition of Kempe's autobiographical work contains an excerpt of her "Shewings of Julian of Norwich," and places Kempe in historical context.

McEntire, Sandra J., ed. *Julian of Norwich: A Book of Essays.* New York: Garland, 1998. Provides an excellent overview of scholarship from the late 1990's. Comprehensive bibliography will greatly assist students and other researchers.

Stone, Robert Karl. *Middle English Prose Style: Margery Kempe and Julian of Norwich.* The Hague, the Netherlands: Mouton, 1970. A detailed, critical literary analysis of two great late-medieval prose devotional works, *The Book of Margery Kempe* and Julian's *Revelations*.

Yuen, Wai Man. *Religious Experience and Interpretation: Memory as the Path to the Knowledge of God in Julian of Norwich's Showings.* New York: Peter Lang, 2003. Part of the Feminist Critical Studies in Religion and Culture series, this text looks closely at Julian's *Revelations* and the experience of memory in intellectual life.

SEE ALSO: Geoffrey Chaucer; Christina of Markyate; Hildegard von Bingen; Margery Kempe; Mechthild von Magdeburg; John Wyclif.

RELATED ARTICLES in *Great Events from History: The Middle Ages, 477-1453*: 1136: Hildegard von Bingen Becomes Abbess; 1305-1417: Avignon Papacy and the Great Schism; 1347-1352: Invasion of the Black Death in Europe; 1377-1378: Condemnation of John Wyclif; c. 1380: Compilation of the Wise Sayings of Lal Ded; May-June, 1381: Peasants' Revolt in England; 1387-1400: Chaucer Writes *The Canterbury Tales*.

JUSTINIAN I

Byzantine emperor (r. 527-565)

A conscientious man of somber judgment and religious zeal, Justinian was the pivotal emperor in the transition from the later Roman Empire to the Byzantine Empire. He left a legacy of great buildings, a legal compilation that became the foundation of European law, and an enhanced autocratic tradition that helped the Byzantine Empire guard against the encroachment of Islam.

BORN: Probably May 11, 483; Tauresium, Dardania, Illyricum (now in Serbia)

DIED: November 14, 565; Constantinople, Byzantine Empire (now Istanbul, Turkey)

ALSO KNOWN AS: Justinian the Great; Justinianus, Flavius Petrus Sabbatius (full Latin name)

AREAS OF ACHIEVEMENT: Government and politics, religion and theology, architecture

EARLY LIFE

Justinian I (Juh-STIN-ee-uhn) was born in Illyricum, but nothing else is known of his youth. His parents were from peasant families originally from Macedonia and had given their son the name Flavius Petrus Sabbatius. When Justinian was about twenty he was brought to Constantinople by his uncle, Justin I, who had risen through the ranks of the military and had become an important officer in the royal guard. Justin was married but had no children and had brought several of his nephews to the empire's capital, where they were given a good education and trained for the military. When Justinian proved the most adept and promising, he was adopted by his uncle and added the name Justinianus. In time, Justinian received a commission in the elite *candidati*, the emperor's personal bodyguard.

On July 8, 518, Emperor Anastasius I died with neither an heir nor any provision for the succession. Justin, who by this time commanded the royal guard, took advantage of the situation and arranged to have himself proclaimed emperor. He was not, however, experienced in administration or well educated (he may even have been illiterate); thus, his reign did not begin with much promise. Justinian, who had such capabilities in abundance, soon demonstrated his worth to his uncle and rose rapidly to become virtual emperor before succeeding his uncle on the throne when the latter died in 527. Justinian first commanded the military troops in Constantinople and kept order in the difficult early days of his uncle's reign. Justin had only one major rival for the throne, and Justinian arranged to have him assassinated by 520, with Justin's cooperation. Justinian then assumed the office of consul in 521 and of caesar in 525. Justinian was careful in these years to cultivate a popular following, which may have played a part in influencing his uncle to keep promoting him. When Justin became seriously ill in early 527, at the

Depiction of Justinian I kneeling before Christ, who is flanked by Mary, left, and the archangel Michael on the right. (Library of Congress)

age of seventy-seven, he officially crowned Justinian coemperor, with the title of augustus, on Easter Sunday, April 4, 527. The old emperor died on August 1, 527, and Justinian, who had been the virtual ruler since almost 518, was now proclaimed emperor in name as well.

Shortly after Justin's accession to the emperor's throne, Justinian had met and fallen passionately in love with Theodora, one of the most remarkable women of history. She was of humble origins but a great beauty, highly intelligent and talented. There was some trouble with Justin's wife over the affair because of Theodora's questionable past as an actress, and marriage had to wait until after her death, shortly before Justin's. Although Theodora could be cruel, was often deceitful, and loved power, she had uncanny political judgment and an iron will. She was able to exercise more influence over Justinian than anyone else at court.

LIFE'S WORK

As emperor, Justinian surrounded himself with able, if somewhat flawed, advisers and assistants. Next to Theodora, John of Cappadocia, Justinian's chief financial officer, was the most important. John was infamous for his cruelty, ruthlessness, depraved personal life, and incredible greed, but Justinian ignored all that because John was also shrewd and endlessly resourceful in raising money. Justinian had inherited a full treasury, but the nearly constant warfare that faced him and the cost of his various grand projects soon depleted it. In John, Justinian found someone who could find new sources of revenue and administer the system more efficiently. John created misery and a crushing tax burden for the empire's subjects, which caused Theodora to believe that he was a threat to the public interest of the realm. For this reason, and probably because he was her rival for influence over Justinian, Theodora waged a ruthless campaign against him until she entrapped him in a bogus conspiracy against Justinian; John was banished in 541.

Another important person Justinian recruited into his service was Tribonian (d. 545), a lawyer reputed to have the finest legal mind in the empire. Although Tribonian was a pagan, Justinian made him chief of the imperial judicial system. Tribonian was very nearly as avaricious as John of Cappadocia and has been accused by scholars of

BYZANTINE EMPERORS: JUSTINIAN LINE, 518-610

Reign	*Emperor*
518-527	Justin I
527-548	THEODORA (empress)
527-565	JUSTINIAN I THE GREAT
540	Khosrow I sacks Antioch
565-578	Justin II
578-582	Tiberius II Constantinus
582-602	Maurice
602-610	Phocas (non-Justinian)

corrupting the whole legal system. Nevertheless, he contributed significantly to the success of Justinian's reign by directing the remarkable legal reforms that took place. Belisarius (c. 505-565), the outstanding general of the age in tactics and administration—and who excelled as a field commander—also served Justinian well. An honest and honorable man with no ambitions beyond serving his emperor, he was trusted by everyone but the ever-suspicious Justinian.

Nearly all the major figures in Justinian's administration were of humble origins, as was the emperor himself. He was always on the lookout for talent and kept the offices of the empire filled with the best he could find. Justinian did not, however, delegate all the work to others. He was a serious and diligent monarch who paid careful attention to detail, supervised his chief officers closely, and worked such long hours that he became known popularly as "the emperor who never sleeps."

The great crisis of Justinian's reign was the Nika Riots of 532. The Blues and Greens were organizations that supported rival chariot racing teams at the Hippodrome but represented different political positions as well. When rioting broke out between the two, they forgot their differences and joined forces against Justinian when he intervened to end the violence. It looked for a time as though Justinian would be forced to flee, and several chief ministers recommended that he leave. Theodora, however, never vacillated and convinced Justinian to stand firm and await the proper moment to crush the rioters. As many as thirty thousand people may have died before Belisarius brought Constantinople under control again, and much of the city was in ruins. Two important results came from the Nika Riots. Neither the aristocratic nor the popular faction ever fully recovered, and Justinian was able to rule as an absolute monarch thereafter. Furthermore, the destruction of so much of the city provided Justinian with the opportunity for an epic building program.

Justinian was at war defending the empire's borders for most of his reign. His most celebrated military project, however, was the recovery of the territories of the Western Roman Empire that had been overrun by barbarians. In June of 533, Justinian sent Belisarius with a small force of sixteen thousand to Carthage, where he gained an easy victory over the unprepared and incompetently led Vandals. In 535, Justinian decided to attempt the next and major step by overthrowing the Ostrogothic kingdom of Italy and reestablishing imperial rule. Belisarius again had an easy victory in Sicily and in southern Italy, reaching Rome late in 536. From that point onward, however, Justinian's refusal to entrust Belisarius with adequate troops and supplies prolonged the war and brought terrible hardships to the Italian people. Believing the situation hopeless, Belisarius arranged to have himself recalled to Constantinople in 548 and went into retirement. In 550, Justinian sent Narses to Italy. Although Narses was not the military genius Belisarius was, he was given more adequate supplies, and in 552, he was able to defeat decisively the Ostrogoth forces at Taginae and had pacified Italy by 554. By this time, much of Italy had been destroyed or ravaged.

There was constant trouble from the various peoples living on the northern and eastern borders, which kept the empire almost constantly at war. In Spain, the Visigoths maintained constant pressure on the shrinking area in the south that remained under imperial rule. The Franks and others constantly harassed Italy. In the Balkans, the Slavs and Avars were a constant threat. The Persians to the east and Arabs to the southeast were at war with the empire on and off throughout Justinian's reign. The revenues required to sustain this military effort were actually beyond the empire's capabilities. Justinian had to use diplomacy and tribute to supplement the military effort, particularly in the Balkans and with Persia.

The role of caesaropapist emperor, one who exercises supreme authority over ecclesiastical matters, was well suited to Justinian's personality and temperament. His education had included theological training, an interest he maintained all of his life, especially after Theodora's death. Christianity was beset with schismatics, and in this age of intolerance and willingness of so many to fight and die for their particular interpretation, these divisions threatened to disrupt the empire. The chief problem was the conflict between the Monophysites, who denied that Jesus Christ had human attributes, and the orthodox Chalcedonians, who claimed that Christ was both human and divine. Justinian tried, through a variety of means, to find a compromise but never succeeded for long. In the process, however, he acquired considerable authority over the Church and its councils, including even the pope on occasion. In the end, he probably did as much as anyone to ensure the eventual split between the Roman Catholic and the Orthodox churches.

The legal system developed by the Roman Empire has been called its grandest contribution to history. By Justinian's time, the practical application of Roman law had come to be based on various collections of imperial edicts and *constitutiones*. This development made it difficult to research points of law, and much of it was obsolete or inadequate to the changed circumstances of the empire. On February 13, 528, some six months after becoming emperor in his own name, Justinian called together a commission of legal scholars led by Tribonian. Their first assignment was to prepare a new edition of the laws. The new code was to be updated, with repetitions and contradictions removed, and organized in a clear and rational manner. The first edition of *Codex Iustinianus* (529, 534; English translation, 1915; better known as *Justinian's Codification*) was published in 529, but revision became necessary after later parts of the whole work were completed. The second part was a compilation of all the interpretations of the laws written by renowned Roman jurists over the centuries. These opinions, explaining the law, were important guides for the lawyers and others who applied the laws.

In 533, Tribonian and his assistants had finished the work of collating, abridging, and modernizing the old texts, and the *Digesta* (533 C.E., also known as *Pandectae*; *The Digest of Justinian*, 1920) was published. At the same time, Tribonian finished revising and updating Gaius's older commentaries on Roman law. This third part, known as the *Institutiones* (second century C.E.; *Institutes of Gaius*, 1946-1953, also known as *Institutes*), was to serve as a textbook or handbook for law students. At this point *Justinian's Codification* had to be revised to bring it in line with *The Digest of Justinian* and the *Institutes*. Together, *Justinian's Codification*, *The Digest of Justinian*, and the *Institutes* made up the *Corpus juris civilis* (body of civil law), which was intended to serve all the legal needs of the empire. It was in this form that Roman law was passed on to succeeding generations and Western civilization. *Justinian's Codification* contained the actual laws, *The Digest of Justinian* the definitive literature of jurisprudence, and the *Institutes* the official manual for law students. In time, 160 Novels, or new laws adopted by Justinian, were added. The historical impact of the *Corpus juris civilis* on the development of Western law has been enormous and stands as Justinian's greatest achievement.

Although Justinian was a conservative who perceived his duty to include preserving the empire intact in form as well as in territory, he was actually something of an innovator. In the same manner as he combined control of the political and religious life into a powerful caesaropapist concept of the emperor's office, he also streamlined and consolidated the authority of imperial administration. He dropped the now-meaningless office of consul, discarded the principle of strict separation between civil and military authority, and, in general, established precedents for future emperors to tighten imperial authority to make it more autocratic. He insisted that all subordinates be loyal and efficient servants of the state and rewarded and promoted anyone with talent. He also sought to reduce the abuses by officials of their offices but found the goal of honest government elusive, not to mention compromised by his own toleration of corrupt but efficient revenue officers. The problem with the tax system, however, was not unusual. Emperors had been trying for two centuries before Justinian to bring reform with no greater success.

Following the example of many of his predecessors, Justinian was determined to leave his mark on the empire by a building program that included practical as well as ornamental structures. Among the practical buildings, military forts on the frontiers, and sometimes in the interior of the empire as well, made up the largest category. Justinian also built many bridges, aqueducts, and roads, and various buildings for general public use, such as law courts, baths, great cisterns, storehouses, and asylums. Ornamental buildings included additions to the imperial palace and numerous monasteries and churches, many of which still stand. The great fortress-monastery of Saint Catherine of Mount Sinai is among those that have survived, and its original parts remain an invaluable repository of early Christian and Byzantine art.

Besides Constantinople, the primary focus of Justinian's church building was in and around Jerusalem and Ravenna, Italy. It is in the unusually richly decorated octagonal Church of San Vitale in Ravenna that the best portraits of Justinian and Theodora were discovered. They are full-length portraits in mosaic panels. These are not particularly detailed portraits and no detailed descriptions of the two monarchs have survived. From what is known, he was of moderate height and medium build, with a pleasant, round face that seems to have been without any particularly remarkable features.

The destruction that accompanied the Nika Riots created the need for the most important category of Justinian's building projects and provided him with the opportunity to begin the process of turning the city into the most splendid of medieval Christendom. He built several giant colonnaded cisterns, two of which still survive, all manner of public buildings, and the great Augustan forum. He also substantially enlarged the Grand Palace of the Emperors and, in general, beautified the area around the city. His greatest passion seems to have been building or rebuilding churches and monasteries. The monumental Church of the Holy Apostles, which no longer exists, was the regular site for the emperors' tombs and is reputed to have looked like the Church of San Marco in Venice.

Two other churches of particular note, both of which have survived, were also reconstructions of buildings originally erected by Constantine the Great. Hagia Eirene (Holy Peace) has suffered over the years, but Hagia Sophia (Holy Wisdom) still demonstrates the glory of Byzantine art and architecture. The Turks made it into a mosque in 1453, when they took Constantinople, covering its magnificent mosaics with whitewash. The Turkish statesman and president Kemal Atatürk (1881-1938) converted it into a museum in 1935, and some of its former beauty has been painstakingly restored in the years since. It was a complex building of a then radically new design featuring a great central dome resting on a square base through the use of pendentives, semidomes on each side of the nave to add spaciousness, colonnades, and galleries. It was the greatest church of Christendom in its day and remains one of the world's great architectural masterpieces.

Theodora died of cancer on June 28, 548. The loss of her stabilizing influence and support seems to have signaled the end of the positive and creative part of Justinian's reign. Although he was to have some temporary successes in resolving the theological disputes that so plagued the empire, a permanent solution eluded him, and the problem was nearly out of control by the time he died. The crushing effects of his fiscal policies on the populace were becoming more noticeable, and the brilliance of his earlier days was giving way to exhaustion in the empire. Justinian was increasingly unable to defend the empire's borders and had to resort to diplomacy and bribes. The problem became critical in the Balkans, where the Avars and Slavs had begun pushing into the empire's territory during Justin's reign. The defensive capabilities of the empire had degenerated so far that Justinian was forced to call Belisarius out of retirement in 559 to defend the capital, while the remainder of the Balkan people were left to fend off the invaders as best they could. The Italian reconquest was brought to a successful conclusion, but at the cost of an impoverished Italy. Even the Blues and Greens circus factions reappeared to disturb Justinian's last years.

On November 14, 565, when Justinian died at the age of eighty-two, the news was greeted with relief by his subjects. He and Theodora had had no children, and Justinian made his nephew Justin his heir. Amid popular rejoicing that the old tyrant was dead and a new era was dawning, Justinian was buried in the Church of the Holy Apostles. In truth, a great age had ended, and a terrible one was to follow.

SIGNIFICANCE

Justinian I misunderstood the changing nature of his time. Reconquering the Western Roman Empire was a doomed effort to re-create a Christian version of the classical Roman state that left the surviving eastern part of the empire exhausted and dangerously exposed. His lavish building program made the economic situation worse while he failed to protect adequately the empire's borders. By becoming personally involved in the theological disputes of his time, he did expand the role of emperor to a caesaropapist autocracy—but at the expense of contributing significantly to the permanent split in the Christian community between the Roman Catholic and the Orthodox churches. His misplaced religious zeal extended even to requiring adherence to Orthodox Christianity as a prerequisite to teaching in the empire and to closing the schools of higher learning in Athens in 529. Not only were those subjects with a classical education deprived of a living, but they were also driven from the empire, destroying the tradition of Plato's Academy and thus breaking an important link with antiquity. Yet he is not entirely to blame for these mistakes. Justinian was acting within the Roman tradition of what was expected of an emperor. It was only toward the end of his reign, when the consequences of these policies began to pile up, that his subjects began to complain so bitterly, not during the early years of glory and achievement.

Whatever blame may be assigned for Justinian's mistakes, it is clear that he left a remarkable legacy for the future of Western civilization, one any monarch would envy. He set a standard of dedication to duty, personal honor, and integrity rarely matched by an emperor. He sought little for himself and everything for the empire's welfare as he understood it. The *Corpus juris civilis* strengthened the empire by improving the administration of justice, establishing legal standards by which most other law in Western civilization would come to be measured, and ultimately becoming the foundation of most modern European legal systems. His building projects helped make Constantinople one of the great cities of the medieval world and an inspiration that helped sustain Byzantine civilization for centuries. These achievements, and the improvements in imperial administration, contributed to the longevity of the empire and its historic role as the bastion of Christendom in the East, guarding Europe from conquest by Islam.

—*Richard L. Hillard*

FURTHER READING

Baker, G. P. *Justinian: The Last Roman Emperor.* 1931. Reprint. New York: Cooper Square Press, 2002. A biographical account of Justianian's reign and the history of the Roman and Byzantine Empires during his time. Maps, bibliography, index.

Barker, John W. *Justinian and the Later Roman Empire.* Madison: University of Wisconsin Press, 1966. An excellent, balanced biography of Justinian and his reign. Begins with an illuminating background chapter on the Roman world before Justinian and ends with a discussion of the long-term results of his reign.

Calkins, Robert G. *Medieval Architecture in Western Europe: From A.D. 300 to 1500.* New York: Oxford University Press, 1998. Explores the history of Western European architecture of the Middle Ages, including the buildings of Justinian. Illustrations, extensive bibliography, index.

Downey, Glanville. *Constantinople in the Age of Justinian.* Norman: University of Oklahoma Press, 1960. An excellent description of Justinian's empire and its base in Constantinople. A useful introduction especially to the history of the city. Part of the Centers of Civilization series.

Evans, James Allan. *The Age of Justinian: The Circumstances of Imperial Power.* New York: Routledge, 1996. Surveys the imperial tactics of Justinian's empire, with discussion of the early years of power; the empire's people; the Nika Revolt; the wars in Africa, Persia, and Italy; and the empire's administration. Maps, extensive bibliography, and index.

_______. *The Empress Theodora: Partner of Justinian.* Austin: University of Texas Press, 2002. A brief look at the life of Theodora and her role as empress. Maps, bibliography, index.

Grant, Michael. *From Rome to Byzantium: The Fifth Century A.D.* New York: Routledge, 1998. Contextualizes the history of the Byzantine Empire in the era immediately preceding Justinian's reign, from the fall of the Roman Empire to the rise of Byzantium. Maps, bibliography, and index.

Jones, A. H. M. *The Later Roman Empire, 284-602: A Social, Economic, and Administrative Survey.* 2 vols. 1964. Reprint. Oxford, England: Basil Blackwell, 1986. Analytical survey from Diocletian and the conversion of the empire to Asian despotism and the final collapse and loss of the western half of the empire. Includes the reign of Justinian.

Procopius. *The Anecdota: Or, Secret History.* Vol. 6 in *Procopius.* Translated by H. B. Dewing. Cambridge, Mass.: Harvard University Press, 1960-1962. The original source for much of the historical knowledge about Theodora, written by a contemporaneous historian. Perhaps the most important eyewitness account of Justinian's reign.

Runciman, Steven. *Byzantine Civilization.* 1933. Reprint. London: E. Arnold, 1966. A brief essay by an accomplished scholar that provides an excellent introduction to the sweep of Byzantine history.

Ure, P. N. *Justinian and His Age.* 1951. Reprint. Westport, Conn.: Greenwood Press, 1979. A balanced and detailed evaluation of accounts by Procopius and other eyewitnesses of Justinian's reign but not a chronological narrative history. Recommended for those engaged in an in-depth study of Justinian.

Veyne, Paul, ed. *From Pagan Rome to Byzantium.* Vol. 1 in *A History of Private Life,* edited by Philippe Ariès and Georges Duby. Cambridge, Mass.: Harvard University Press, 1987. A rewarding historical survey of the hidden and intimate daily life of people rich and poor. Especially interesting is the startling contrast of the triumph of Christianity with the undisciplined private lives of so many in Byzantium.

SEE ALSO: Amalasuntha; Basil the Macedonian; Khosrow I; Theodora.

RELATED ARTICLES in *Great Events from History: The Middle Ages, 477-1453*: February 2, 506: Alaric II Drafts the *Breviarum Alarici*; 529-534: Justinian's Code Is Compiled; 532-537: Building of Hagia Sophia; 563: Silk Worms Are Smuggled to the Byzantine Empire; 568-571: Lombard Conquest of Italy; 1054: Beginning of the Rome-Constantinople Schism; 1295: Model Parliament.

DAMIA AL-KĀHINA

Berber queen (r. c. 667-c. 702)

Damia al-Kāhina was queen of a Berber tribe and led the resistance to Arab expansion into North Africa in the seventh century.

BORN: c. 650; Aures Mountains (now in Algeria)
DIED: c. 702; North Africa (now Algeria)
ALSO KNOWN AS: el-Cahena; Damya; Dehya; Dihya; Kahena, Diah or Dahia; el-Kahena
AREAS OF ACHIEVEMENT: Government and politics, warfare and conquest

EARLY LIFE

Damia al-Kāhina (DAY-mee-uh uhl-kah-HEE-nah), the Jewish queen of the Berbers, was born into the Jarawa tribe of Berbers, who were located in the Aures Mountains of Algeria. She has been called the Deborah of the Berbers (after the biblical Deborah) because of her military leadership of the tribe, and French writers have referred to her as the Joan of Arc of Africa. The name of al-Kāhina's father was Tabita or Tatit, and some sources say that he was the chief of the group.

On her father's death, al-Kāhina replaced him, although apparently after considerable infighting. Some reports say that she had two sons, one with a man of Byzantine (and thus Christian) origin and another who was Berber and perhaps Jewish, which indicates the cultural mixing that was occurring at the time. The Berbers in the region were known by the name Amazigh, which means "free" or "noble" and refers to their sense of independence. They were spread out over a vast region, including those occupying Libya, Tunisia, Algeria, and Morocco. Although the Berbers were organized into various tribes under different rulers, they had common links of language and culture.

By the seventh century, when al-Kāhina was born, the various Berber tribes adhered to a mosaic of religious practices, especially Jewish and Christian. The Christian Berbers were allied with the Byzantine rulers, who, in turn, were known for persecuting the Jews. Before the confrontation between Christianity and Islam, it was not uncommon for entire tribes to convert to Judaism if their leaders did, and several tribes in the eastern world did convert to Judaism, including Yemenites, Khazars, and Berbers such as the Jerawa. In addition to the Berber Jews, who were mostly rural, Middle Eastern Jews resided in the urban centers along the coast and Spanish Jews fled the Visigothic repression in Spain. Although Jews in both North Africa and Spain were oppressed by their respective Christian kingdoms, they reacted differently to the Muslim invasion. The Spanish Jews welcomed it, while the Berber Jews resisted it, probably because their tradition of local autonomy was threatened by the Arab invasion. North Africa produced the unusual circumstance of Jews uniting with Christians, who had persecuted them, in order to oppose the Muslim advance.

The origin of the name Kāhina seems to have its roots in the Arabic word *kahin*, which means diviner, sorcerer, or priest; *Kāhinah* is the feminine form of the word. The comparable word in Hebrew is *kohen*, which has led to speculation that Kāhina might have been from a priestly Jewish family. For a thousand years after she died, her life was discussed almost exclusively in Arabic, and as a result the Arabic name became the established one. In pre-Islamic Arabia, the *kahins* were the guardians of holy places, and powers of sorcery or magic were also attributed to them. In the civil unrest in Arabia following the death of the Prophet Muḥammad, the local *kahins* frequently led the revolts. By calling this woman leader a *Kāhinah*, the early Arab narrators were identifying her as a non-Muslim and a diviner, or sorcerer. At that moment historically, the name probably also carried the implication of being a troublemaker or revolt leader.

The first reference to Damia al-Kāhina was made by the Muslim writer al-Wāqidī (747-823). Other writers from the same time period who mentioned her leadership in resisting the Arabs were Khalīfa ibn Khayyāt and al-Balādhurī. In later centuries, ʿAbd al-Hakam (ninth century), ʿAbd Bakrī (eleventh), and Ibn al-Athīr (thirteenth) also described the events surrounding her life. The account of Ibn Khaldūn, the respected Muslim cultural historian of the fourteenth century, synthesized the information from the earlier writers to make the most complete story of her life.

LIFE'S WORK

Initially, Damia al-Kāhina's power was limited to her tribe, but as the Arabs encroached from Egypt, she was able to rally the disparate Berber tribes to fight the invaders. Although she may have been the ruler of her tribe for as many as thirty-five years, it was her leadership of the broader Berber coalition against the Arabs that projected her into history. Eventually, she had wide influence over Ifriqiya, the Berber term for the area west of Egypt and the term that eventually gave its name to the entire continent. The Byzantine Christians had a strong presence in

North Africa in the 600's, with their power concentrated in cities such as Carthage. The first Arabs arrived to Tunisia in 647, and by the 670's, there were Muslim converts and a Muslim military presence. The dominant Berber leader at the onset of the Arab advance was Kusayla, who initially sought to ally with them rather than fight, but he was later killed by one of the Arab leaders.

The assassination of Kusayla was seen as a traitorous act by the Berbers, and it seems to have led al-Kāhina to lose trust in the Arabs as well as to propel her into action against them. As al-Kāhina's power grew, she suspended the practice of Muslim law and reportedly oppressed Muslim residents. Arab writers described a situation of civil unrest in the region that led Caliph Muʾāwiyah I of the Umayyad Dynasty to intervene. He was religiously moderate, and he saw the Jews as allies against the Christian kingdoms and even established settlements of Jews in Tripoli, but he could not ignore what seemed to be a challenge to Islam. The war against al-Kāhina became a *jihād* in which the Arabs were committed to defend their co-religionists in the area and to spread the rule of Islam. She was accused of being a sorceress and cruel to her people, and this seems to have been part of the justification for invading and establishing Arab rule.

The caliph sent General Ḥassān ben al-Nuʿmān to quell the disturbances between Berbers and Muslims. The solution to the conflict was peaceful, and the general accepted a peace treaty with the Berbers, who agreed to pay an annual tribute. He remained in the region until the death of Caliph Muʾāwiyah in 680. Eleven years later, there was renewed resistance from the Berbers, and he was again sent to the Maghreb by Caliph ʿAbd al-Malik. In 692, General Hassān marched with a large army to Carthage, which was the seat of the Byzantine rulers who had allied with al-Kāhina. The Byzantines abandoned the city in the face of the Arab advance, which marked the end of their influence in the region. After taking Carthage, Hassān turned toward the Aures Mountains, which were the stronghold of the Berber forces under al-Kāhina. Part of her strategy was a scorched-earth policy in which her forces withdrew from certain areas, leaving nothing behind for the advancing Arab army. She even destroyed her own fortified capital to keep it from being converted into an Arab stronghold. Hassān finally attacked the Berber forces led by al-Kāhina near the River of Tribulation (*nahr al-balā*). After a fierce battle, the Berbers defeated the Arabs and inflicted severe losses on them.

Among the Muslim prisoners taken by the Berbers was one named Khālid, whom al-Kāhina liked and adopted as her son. She released the others. The defeat was so disastrous for the Arab forces that Hassān withdrew and established the remainder of his army in a safe area on the coast near Barca in present-day Libya. Some writers suggest that al-Kāhina made attempts to establish peace with the Arabs at this point, but to no avail. Hassān did not attack again for another seven years, during which time he accumulated reinforcements, and he contacted Khālid to spy on the Berber forces. Khālid apparently complied, because there are stories of his hidden messages to Hassān being found inside a loaf of bread on one occasion and in the horn of a saddle on another.

In 697 or 698, General Hassān marched once again against the Berbers, some of whom defected to the Arab side, either because they saw the struggle to be futile or because of opposition to policies of al-Kāhina. Knowing about the divisions within her own people and the size of the approaching Arab army, al-Kāhina warned her sons that they might lose. She asked Khālid to use his contacts with the Arabs to protect her two sons as his own brothers in the case of her defeat. Even though she knew about his perfidy, he was her bridge to the Muslim world and her best means of protecting the lives of her sons.

The final battle came in 701 or 702, and the Berber forces were routed by the Arab army. Damia al-Kāhina was captured and killed, and oral tradition said that she died near a well that bore her name for centuries afterward. Her defeat and death did not end the confrontation, and the Berbers continued to resist the Arabs. Although most Berbers eventually converted to Islam, they still rejected Arabization. Jewish communities survived and did well under the Arabs, but the Arab-Berber conflict diminished only when the latter eventually regained power in the new Muslim North Africa.

After the Berber defeat, the two sons of al-Kāhina joined the Arab forces, and they were named the military leaders of the Jarawa and Aures regions under the new Muslim administration, the former being their mother's tribe and the latter being her home region. The references by Arab writers to Berber defections and the naming of the two sons to important military positions in the Arab army emphasize the collaboration by Berbers with Arabs after their defeat.

SIGNIFICANCE

Damia al-Kāhina was important as an extraordinary leader who not only ruled her people for many years but also was a strategic military commander. She united the Berbers in a way that perhaps no other leader has been able to do. Every cultural group in North Africa developed its own stories about her, and al-Kāhina became an even more complex persona in folklore.

The Arab groups against which she fought for so long portray her as an impediment to the eventual spread of Islam into North Africa. French writers have emphasized the Jewishness of al-Kāhina, claiming her as the representation of Western values staving off the advance of Muslim orthodoxy. They emphasize the Roman and Byzantine (that is, European and Christian) influences in the area, and they also refer to the presence of Byzantine forces in helping the resistance against the Arabs. Contemporary North African scholars celebrate her as a heroine and leader of the Berber people and as an example of their strength and resolution. More recently, Jewish writers also have described and evaluated the complex traditions surrounding al-Kāhina's life. Some claim her as an example of leadership, willing to give her own life for her people, while others question her Jewishness. Feminist thinkers refer to her as an example of a strong woman who was successful in the traditionally male world of military leadership.

Damia al-Kāhina has a distinct significance to each group of people affected by her, and each group emphasizes different aspects of her life. She is beyond history, and she has become a legend with all of the elaborations on her life story expected of a legend.

—*Ronald Joseph Duncan*

FURTHER READING

Corcos, David. "Kāhina." In *Encyclopedia Judaica*. Vol. 10. New York: Macmillian, 1972. The Kāhina was the queen of the Jerawa tribe of Berber converts to Judaism. She defeated the armies of Islam but was later betrayed and defeated. Her origins are controversial.

Hannoum, Abdelmajid. *Colonial Histories, Post-colonial Memories: The Legend of the Kāhina, a North African Heroine*. Portsmouth, N.H.: Heinemann, 2001. Hannoum provides the most complete scholarly coverage in English of the folklore surrounding Damia al-Kāhina. He presents the various accounts of her life and traces the changes in them from the earliest Arab narrators to the present, including French colonialists, contemporary North Africans, feminists, and Jewish authors.

Roth, Norman. "The Kāhina: Legendary Materials in the Accounts of the 'Jewish Berber Queen.'" *The Maghreb Review* 7, nos. 5/6 (1982): 122-125. A review of important sources that discuss the history and folklore surrounding the Kāhina tradition, including Arab, French, and Jewish sources. Roth evaluates the potential validity of the various aspects of the story, including al-Kāhina's name, her sons, her Jewishness, and strategic details.

Talbi, Mohamed. "Al-Kāhina." In *Encyclopedia of Islam*. Vol. 4. Leiden: E. J. Brill, 1986. A concise description of al-Kāhina's life and works.

SEE ALSO: Ibn Khaldūn; Ṭāriq ibn-Ziyād.

RELATED ARTICLES in *Great Events from History: The Middle Ages, 477-1453*: c. 610-632: Muḥammad Receives Revelations; 630-711: Islam Expands Throughout North Africa; 685-691: Building of the Dome of the Rock; April or May, 711: Ṭārik Crosses into Spain; October 11, 732: Battle of Tours; 1048: Zīrids Break from Fāṭimid Dynasty and Revive Sunni Islam; 1062-1147: Almoravids Conquer Morocco and Establish the Almoravid Empire.

MARGERY KEMPE

English mystic

Margery Kempe was one of the earliest creators of travel literature and memoir in England, and her religious visions place her among the early English mystics.

BORN: c. 1373; Bishop's Lynn (now King's Lynn), Norfolk, England
DIED: c. 1440; place unknown
ALSO KNOWN AS: Margery Brunham (given name)
AREAS OF ACHIEVEMENT: Literature, religion and theology

EARLY LIFE

Margery Kempe was born into a prosperous merchant family in Bishop's Lynn in the English county of Norfolk. Lynn was then among England's leading seaports and, in terms of size and density of population, was second only to London. German merchants of the Hanseatic League, despite occasional conflicts with English merchants, landed goods directly in Lynn; from there, the wares could be transported to village and town fairs and to London. In this environment, merchants formed a kind of middle-class aristocracy, and, through guilds, took responsibility for civic government.

Kempe's father was probably John Brunham. Although Brunham's occupation is unknown, he became an important force in governing the town, serving as mayor in 1370, 1377, 1378, 1385, and 1391. He was probably the John Brunham who served as alderman of the important Holy Trinity Guild from 1394 to 1401. If this identification is correct, Margery Kempe would have been raised in some luxury. Kempe herself records little detail of her early life, but the suggestion of prosperity is reinforced by her distaste for the filth and vermin she encountered on her travels and by her admission to the Guild of the Trinity in 1437-1438. She was, however, apparently illiterate; possibly, she was literate enough for daily affairs but not skilled enough to read or write her own account of her visions, sufferings, and travels. Instead, religious writings were instead read to her and she had scribes write for her.

John and Margery Kempe were married when she was about twenty; she then bore fourteen children. Only one is mentioned in her memoirs, but in an age of high infant mortality and in a seaport ravaged by frequent epidemics, only one may have survived to adulthood. After the first difficult childbirth, Kempe lapsed into insanity. Apparently feeling herself guilty of some unnamed sin she could not confess, she became self-destructive, vividly envisioning hell and envisioning herself swallowed up by demons. She had to be restrained with chains from harming herself, and scars on her hands remained with her through her life. In the midst of this torment, Christ appeared to her, offering her consolation. She was immediately healed, but, according to her memoirs, she lapsed back into worldliness and vanity. Dissatisfied with her life, she became a brewer, a trade often practiced by women. For several years, she was among the most important brewers in Lynn, but the brewings failed. Still determined to become wealthy, she bought a mill, two horses, and a servant and went into business grinding customers' corn until her horses refused to work and her servants quit. At this point, she finally renounced her worldliness.

LIFE'S WORK

After experiencing a vision of heaven while lying in bed, Kempe committed herself to frequent churchgoing and lengthy fasts and urged her husband to live with her chastely. Because of his refusal, she continued to bear his children. (He apparently did not notice the hair shirt she wore beneath her clothing as part of her penitence.) Her church attendance was marked by loud crying and wailing. This would increase with time, especially after her pilgrimage to Jerusalem, but, from the beginning, neighbors thought her visions and emotional outpourings marked the return of her insanity. Although her emotionalism was in the tradition of personal religion in her time, she began to arouse considerable hostility and needed the approval of Roman Catholic churchmen and churchwomen.

She began with a series of pilgrimages to shrines and to individuals within England. In the period between 1413 and 1415, she visited Norwich, Great Yarmouth, Canterbury, London, York, and Bristol, among other places. Traveling mainly on foot, she visited individuals such as the mystic Julian of Norwich and religious houses such as that maintained by the Order of Minoresses in Cambridgeshire. Together, John and Margery Kempe visited Bishop Philip Repingdon of Lincoln, who granted their wish to take public vows of chastity. Kempe's voices, however, also had commanded her to wear white clothes, and this proved controversial throughout these years. Repingdon deferred the matter. White was symbolic of purity, especially sexual purity, and Kempe had born fourteen children. From Bishop Thomas

Arundel of Norwich she received permission to select her own confessor and to take weekly communion; during this time period in history, Roman Catholics were required to attend mass weekly but to take communion only once a year.

Margery Kempe ventured abroad without John Kempe, primarily to Rome, the Holy Land, and the Spanish shrine of Saint James Compostela, the three principal overseas pilgrimages in her time. To reach the Holy Land, Kempe embarked at Yarmouth, landed in the Netherlands, and, with a party of pilgrims, set out from Venice. From there, after a lengthy stay, they sailed to Jerusalem. Kempe spent about three weeks in the Holy Land before returning to Venice. From there, she set out for Rome. The trip to Spain was a later, separate, venture.

Both types of journeys, local and international, exposed Kempe to extreme peril. In England, she risked being burned as a heretic. As early as 1401, new laws permitted royal officers to arrest suspected heretics and the government to burn relapsed heretics; these laws allowed the burning of Kempe's great French contemporary, Joan of Arc, by the English. The first person to be executed under these laws was William Sawtre, a parish priest in Lynn. Kempe must have been aware of the risk she was running when, as frequently happened, she was accused of being a Lollard. Lollards shared no common creed but generally were followers of John Wyclif of Oxford, who had condemned the corruption and wealth of the Church and questioned the reality of transubstantiation in the mass and the need for priests to intervene between Christians and God. Lollards were "accused" of allowing women to speak in church. Kempe's insistence of the validity of her visions and voices, her outspoken criticism of some clerics, and her habit of calling attention to herself placed her in grave danger. When she was tried, she escaped punishment, probably because she made a point of deferring to the wisdom of Catholic churchmen.

Her problems on her international trips were more mundane. Just as she aroused criticism among her neighbors, she irritated her fellow pilgrims who refused to put up with her behavior. Kempe apparently monopolized mealtime conversation with her account of her meditations, life, and visions; she refused to tolerate worldly conversation and pleasures, and she frequently succumbed to violent sobbing. Other travelers ousted her from their companies. In Rome, for example, she was forced to find a German confessor when deserted by the English. The German assigned Kempe, no longer a young woman, to be servant to a destitute woman; Kempe slept on the floor amid vermin and was forced to beg.

She returned safely to England. John and Margery Kempe had lived separately for many years, but, at about the age of sixty, John fell, badly injuring his head. At the insistence of the community, his wife took him in, caring for him as his body and mind failed and he became incontinent. He died in 1431, shortly before the death of their son, the only child mentioned in the memoirs, who had come from the Continent with his wife on a visit. Kempe's last journey was to accompany the younger woman back to Danzig (now Gdansk), although Kempe's confessor had forbidden her the journey. This trip, too, was fraught with problems and ended as a pilgrimage to the Precious Blood at Wilsnak. Some time before 1436, Kempe, determined to record her memoirs, dictated to at least two scribes. She was known to be alive as late as 1440. The circumstances and date of her death are not known.

Her memoirs, in their existing form, consist of two parts, the first of eighty-nine chapters, the second, ten. The copy that survives, presently in the British Library, was made by a scribe known only as Salthows and was held in the library of Mount Grace Priory in Yorkshire. English printer Wynkyn de Worde published seven pages of devotional extracts in 1500-1501 under the title *Here begynneth a shorte treatyse of contemplacyon taught by our lorde Jhesu cryste, or taken out of the boke of Margerie Kempe of Lynn*. These passages were reprinted by Henry Pepwell in 1521. The body of the text remained unknown until discovered in the Butler-Bowdon family library in Lancashire. The first scholarly, annotated edition was published in 1940 as *The Book of Margery Kempe*. Other translations have followed.

Significance

Kempe's emotionalism and self-righteousness, which pervade her book, often disturb later readers and scholars as badly as they disturbed the neighbors and traveling companions of her time, but, through this material, Kempe emerges as a figure who, like Joan of Arc, was standing on the bridge between the medieval world and the modern. She earnestly attempted to submit herself to the Roman Catholic Church; that her strong personality kept her from entirely doing so is transparently clear. This conflicted personality is why Kempe's work remains readable to ordinary readers as well as those interested in religious mysticism. In the literature of her time, her memoirs are unique in depicting a woman wrestling with the problems of religion, marriage, childbearing, and a sense of personal destiny.

—*Betty Richardson*

FURTHER READING

Ashley, Kathleen. "Historicizing Margery: The Book of Margery Kempe as Social Text." *Journal of Medieval and Early Modern Studies* 28 (Spring, 1998): 371-388. Analyzes Kempe's memoir as a reflection on the social life of the times.

Atkinson, Clarissa W. *Mystic and Pilgrim: The Book and the World of Margery Kempe*. Ithaca, N.Y.: Cornell University Press, 1983. Offers a clear description of Kempe and her time, especially the ways in which she violated social convention and religious conformity.

Collis, Louise. *Memoirs of a Medieval Woman: The Life and Times of Margery Kempe*. New York: Harper, 1983. This reprint of a 1964 publication offers an unparalleled and lively glimpse of life on religious pilgrimage in Kempe's time. The author, generally more sympathetic to Kempe's fellow travelers than to Kempe herself, uses contemporary writings to fill in the detail of everyday life that Kempe herself omits.

Gallyon, Margaret. *Margery Kempe of Lynn and Medieval England*. Norwich, England: Canterbury Press, 1995. A readable, serious study of Kempe as mystic, with a clear explanation of the rites and customs of the Roman Catholic Church in Kempe's age.

Goodman, Anthony. *Margery Kempe and Her World*. London: Longman, 2002. A detailed, readable account, especially of Kempe's surroundings and the urban gender roles of her time.

Lerner, Gerda. *The Creation of Feminist Consciousness from the Middle Ages to Eighteen-Seventy*. New York: Oxford University Press, 1993. Places Kempe within a tradition of feminine mysticism that redefined women's roles in the process of finding salvation.

McEntire, Sandra J. *Margery Kempe: A Book of Essays*. New York: Garland, 1992. This collection includes essays for the general reader among those directed to scholars. Among those for the general reader are "Margery Kempe and Her Calling" and "Margery Kempe and King's Lynn."

Rawcliffe, Carole. *Medicine and Society in Later Medieval England*. Phoenix Mill, England: Alan Sutton, 1995. While Kempe is only briefly mentioned, this volume examines how her contemporaries would have viewed her mental breakdown after childbirth and similar problems.

Staley, Lynn, trans. and ed. *The Book of Margery Kempe: A New Translation, Contexts, Criticism*. New York: Norton, 2001. Provides critical essays designed for advanced students and readers and also contains excerpts from the mystics, such as Julian of Norwich and Saint Brigit of Sweden, who most influenced Kempe's life and thought, and an excerpt from *The Constitutions of Thomas Arundel* (1409), which laid the groundwork for eradicating the heresy for which Kempe was accused.

SEE ALSO: Blessed Angela of Foligno; Saint Brigit; Saint Catherine of Siena; Christina of Markyate; Dante; Hildegard von Bingen; Joan of Arc; Julian of Norwich; Mechthild von Magdeburg; John Wyclif.

RELATED ARTICLES in *Great Events from History: The Middle Ages, 477-1453*: 1136: Hildegard von Bingen Becomes Abbess; c. 1150-1200: Rise of the Hansa Merchant Union; 1377-1378: Condemnation of John Wyclif; c. 1380: Compilation of the Wise Sayings of Lal Ded.

KHADĪJA

Arab merchant and religious leader

Khadīja was the first convert to Islam. Her support of her husband, the prophet Muḥmmad, and his revelations, and her conversion, helped lead the way to the promotion of Islam. She used her wealth to support his mission and to promote the spread of Islam in the Arabian Peninsula.

BORN: c. 554; Mecca, Arabia (now in Saudi Arabia)
DIED: 619; Mecca
ALSO KNOWN AS: Khadījah; Khadījah bint Khuwaylid; Khadījah al-Kubra; Khadeejah bint Khuwaylid
AREA OF ACHIEVEMENT: Religion and theology

EARLY LIFE

Khadīja (Khah-DEE-jah) was born in Mecca, in the western part of the Arabian Peninsula, to Khuwaylid ibn Asad and Fāṭimah bint Zaidah. Her father was a successful merchant and businessman, and his wealth and the family's position as a member of the powerful Quraysh tribe combined to make the family prominent in the city of Mecca. Khadīja's mother died around 575, and when Khadīja's father died about ten years later, Khadīja and her siblings inherited his businesses and wealth, and Khadīja inherited her father's business skills.

Already wealthy from her inheritance, Khadīja soon demonstrated her intellectual abilities and own commercial savvy. She sent trade caravans to various locations in the region, making substantial profits on these trips; some sources refer to her as the richest trader in the city of Mecca. Her ability to expand her wealth and her consistent success in business earned her the nicknames princess of the Quraysh and princess of Mecca.

Nevertheless, Khadīja was not known only for her wealth; her nobility of character and her good morals also earned her the nickname "al-tahira" (the pure one). Khadīja was known to use her prominence in Meccan society and her wealth for the good of others, undertaking charitable activities such as providing assistance to orphans and funds for poor people to marry and set up households.

Before her father's death, Khadīja married and was widowed. Some sources mention only one husband, others mention two husbands; a very small minority assert that Khadīja was never married before her marriage to Muḥammad. Most sources agree that Khadīja had at least two sons with her first husband, and that both of these sons later died in battle.

LIFE'S WORK

Khadīja's wealth did not allow her to travel with her trade caravans; doing so would deviate from what was expected of "respectable" widows. Instead, she hired agents to act on her behalf. In 595, on the recommendation of several of her relatives, she hired the twenty-five-year-old Muḥammad ibn ʿAba Allāh, a distant cousin, to accompany her trade caravan to Syria and conduct her commercial affairs there. Although Muḥammad did not have much experience in this field, having only observed trading negotiations previously, he had already earned a reputation in Mecca as an honest, reliable man; he was known throughout Mecca as al-Amin (the trustworthy).

When Muḥammad returned from Syria, he brought with him enormous profits—some sources estimate the profits were at least twice what Khadīja expected to earn from the trade. One of Khadīja's servants, Maysarah, who had accompanied the caravan, provided Khadīja with glowing accounts of Muḥammad's conduct and business skills; Khadīja's relatives were also impressed with this young man. Khadīja employed Muḥammad again, this time for an equally profitable trip into the southern region of the Arabian Peninsula (now Yemen). Khadīja decided that despite her decision not to marry again, Muḥammad was a remarkable man with an outstanding character who would be an ideal husband. Muḥammad was also impressed with Khadīja's character, but as she had rejected offers of marriage from some of the wealthiest and most elite men of Mecca, he did not anticipate any possibility of marriage. Khadīja therefore initiated the union, first through sending one of her friends to discuss the matter with Muḥammad and then through discussions with her relatives. Shortly thereafter, with the consent of their families, the two were wed.

Khadīja was twice widowed before her marriage to Muḥammad; both husbands died during the frequent tribal warfare in the Arabian Peninsula during this era. She and her first husband, Abū Hālah Hind ibn Zarah, had three sons (Hind, Hālah, and al-Ṭāhir). Although most scholars believe that Khadīja's four daughters were by Muḥammad, a small minority argue that her first three daughters were by her second husband, Ateeq ibn ʿAaith, and some assert that the first three were in fact Khadīja's nieces who grew up in her household. Khadīja and Muḥammad also had at least two sons, both of whom died as infants. The four daughters who survived into adulthood were Zaynab, Ruqayyah, Umm Kulthūm, and Fāṭimah (c. 605-633).

Khadīja and Muḥammad lived happily together, devoting themselves to their family and to each other, for approximately fifteen years. Both continued to feel compassion for those less fortunate and to offer their assistance to widows, to orphans, and to the poor. During this time, Muḥammad began exploring questions of religion and faith and listening to the discussions of others. He often retreated to the hills near Mecca to consider and meditate on these issues. During one of these retreats in 610, Muḥammad received the first of his revelations from God. Delivered through the angel Gabriel, this revelation marks the beginning of Muḥammad's prophethood; the revelations received were later recorded and compiled into the Qur'ān, the holy book of the new religion of Islam.

Her husband's revelation changed the course of Khadīja's life. Muḥammad himself, though impressed with the truth and beauty of the first revelation, was rather troubled by the experience. Returning home in a feverish state, he told Khadīja what had happened. She was convinced that the revelation was indeed from God and that Muḥammad was God's messenger, and she expressed these views to him. Her immediate and unquestioning acceptance of the revelation and her husband's role as Prophet not only made Khadīja the first Muslim, or believer in Islam; it also made Khadīja an important, moving figure in the acceptance of Muḥammad and his revelations as worthy and prophetic. Khadīja's conversion influenced other women to convert as well; as an older, respectable, wealthy woman, she was an influential figure within the Quraysh tribe.

Muḥammad's status as Prophet was also confirmed by Waraqah ibn Nawfal, one of Khadīja's cousins who was a Christian. Waraqah compared Muḥammad's revelation with Christian scriptures, declaring Muḥammad's experience to be similar to what had happened to Moses. For the first three years after the revelations began, Muḥammad shared them with family and friends, many of whom also began to believe in the revelations. Although some were skeptical, including his uncle, Abū Ṭālib (fl. sixth century), who had raised Muḥammad after the deaths of Muḥammad's parents, trouble did not begin until Muḥammad began preaching publicly in Mecca in 613. In his public preaching, Muḥammad condemned the worship of the old gods of Mecca, thus angering the city's elite. Although none dared act directly against the Prophet because of his family's and his wife's status in the community, other converts to the emerging religion were not so fortunate. New Muslims of the poorer classes and without powerful families to protect them were harassed, attacked, and seized. This persecution led to the emigration of a group of converts to Abyssinia (now Ethiopia), where they were protected and allowed to worship freely.

Despite these troubling developments, Khadīja's faith in her husband never wavered. She reassured him when he expressed doubts and frustration. She continued to support him emotionally, intellectually, and religiously, and she continued to use her financial resources to support his mission. The continued financial support of Khadīja had earlier allowed Muḥammad to pursue his spiritual activities, free from the necessity of constantly working to earn a living; now her financial support and her confidence in him enabled him to fully embrace his role as messenger of God. When Khadīja died, neither her husband nor her daughters inherited from her, perhaps an indication that her considerable wealth had either been spent by the time she died or that she had somehow lost her wealth as a consequence of the persecution of the Muslims of Mecca.

In spite of the attacks on the small Muslim community, Muḥammad continued to deliver his message publicly, calling on Meccans to renounce polytheism and worship the one, true God. His activities resulted in a lengthy boycott of the Hashim clan, the clan of the Quraysh tribe to which Muḥammad belonged, by the other clans of the tribe. This boycott was designed to pressure Muḥammad into ceasing his public denunciations and preaching. As leader of the clan, Abū Ṭālib continued to protect Muḥammad, Khadīja, and their family, even though he himself never converted to Islam. When he died, however, the Muslim community lost one of its most influential allies, and Muḥammad began looking for a new base for himself and his followers. Before the Muslim community relocated to the new site (Yathrib, or Medina, in 622), Khadīja died from a fever in Mecca at the approximate age of sixty-five. Although the Prophet remarried several times after her death, Khadīja remained the wife whom he held up to others as an example of piety and faithfulness.

Significance

Khadīja's significance lies in her belief that Muḥammad's revelations were authentic and her belief in the consequent religion of Islam. Her support of Muḥmmad and her conversion helped lead the way to the promotion of Islam.

Khadīja is considered to have been an exemplary

wife, an exemplary mother, and an exemplary Muslim. Moreover, she is considered by Muslims to be one of the four perfect women in history, in company with Fāṭimah, one of the Prophet's daughters; Mary, mother of Jesus; and Asiya, wife of the pharaoh, who rescued Moses from the Nile, according to Muslim belief. Because of her devotion to her husband, to her children, and to God and Islam, Khadīja remains a role model for Muslims.

—*Amy J. Johnson*

FURTHER READING

Ahmed, Leila. *Women and Gender in Islam*. New Haven, Conn.: Yale University Press, 1992. This book discusses the changing roles and norms ascribed to Muslim women throughout history. Although the author's discussion of Khadīja and the early years of Islam is relatively brief, the work is valuable in tracing the development of gender roles in Islamic history.

Denny, Frederick Mathewson. *An Introduction to Islam*. New York: Macmillan, 1994. This book discusses the religion of Islam and its history, including its foundation and Khadīja's significance in that history.

Esposito, John, ed. *The Oxford History of Islam*. New York: Oxford University Press, 1999. Good general history of the religion and its role in political expansion. Chapters 1 and 2 are most valuable to those interested in Khadīja, as they discuss the foundation of Islam.

Haykal, Muḥammad Husayn. *The Life of Muḥammad*. Translated by Ismail Ragi A. al-Faruqi. Indianapolis, Ind.: North American Trust, 1976. A translation from a well-known Arabic biography of the Prophet that provides a full and detailed account of Muḥammad's work. It blends historical information with references to religious texts and Hadith reports. Bibliography, index.

Roded, Ruth, ed. *Women in Islam and the Middle East: A Reader*. New York: I. B. Tauris, 1999. Provides a collection of original sources on women in Islam in the Middle East, from the Middle Ages through the twentieth century. Looks at the legal, cultural, political, religious, and domestic contexts of women's experience in a discussion of the Qurʾān, the foundations of Islam, selective quotation of the Prophet's words, and the death of Khadīja and Muḥammad's daughter Fāṭimah. Bibliography, index.

Rubin, Uri. *The Eye of the Beholder: The Life of Muḥammad as Viewed by the Early Muslims*. Princeton, N.J.: Darwin Press, 1995. An exploration of Muḥammad's life from the perspective of his contemporaries, including a chapter on the viewpoints of Khadīja and her cousin Waraqah. Bibliography, index.

Ṭabarī, Abu Jafar Muhammad ibn Jarir al-. *Taʾrīkh al-rusul wa al-mulūk*. Translated and annotated by Ella Landau-Tasseron. Albany: State University of New York Press, 1998. Al-Ṭabarī chronicles the early history of Islam and is a valuable source for information on Khadīja and Muḥammad and his companions.

Wadud, Amina. *Qurʾān and Woman: Rereading the Sacred Text from a Woman's Perspective*. 2d ed. New York: Oxford University Press, 1999. The author's unique reading of the Qurʾān sheds light on the role of women and relations between women and men presented in the book of Islam. Chapters explore the biases of earlier interpretations and its effects on tradition and Islamic culture and society, equality between men and women, and more. Includes a list of women mentioned in the Qurʾān, a bibliography, and an index.

SEE ALSO: Anna, Princess of the Byzantine Empire; Saint Clotilda; Muḥammad; Rābiʿah al-ʿAdawiyah; al-Ṭabarī.

RELATED ARTICLES in *Great Events from History: The Middle Ages, 477-1453*: c. 610-632: Muḥammad Receives Revelations; 630-711: Islam Expands Throughout North Africa; 637-657: Islam Expands Throughout the Middle East.

KHOSROW I

King of Persia (r. 531-579)

Through courage and shrewd practical intelligence, Khosrow I restored and revitalized the threatened Sāsānian monarchy, bringing Persian civilization to a peak of wealth, prestige, and security. He also introduced administrative, civil, and military innovations that radically transformed government, earning him the title Anushirvan (of the Immortal Spirit).

BORN: c. 510; probably Ctesiphon, Mesopotamia (now in Iraq)
DIED: 579; probably Ctesiphon
ALSO KNOWN AS: Khosrow Anūshirvan (Khosrow the Just)
AREAS OF ACHIEVEMENT: Government and politics, warfare and conquest, military, patronage of the arts, architecture

EARLY LIFE

Khosrow I (kaws-RAHW) was born at a time when the ancient culture of Mesopotamia was disrupted by internal convulsions and threatened by several external forces—migrations of tribes displaced by the Huns and Avars, defensive maneuvers by factions of the deteriorating Roman Empire, and uprisings among the Arabs. His father, Kavadh I (r. 488-496, 499-531), struggled against these forces, establishing strategies that Khosrow I would perfect. Kavadh himself had seized the throne in a rebellion of nobles fomented by the Hephthalite Huns, with whom he had lived as a prisoner or hostage. For this reason, his control was precarious. During the first part of his reign, he alienated some of his aristocratic supporters by engineering the assassination of his prime minister, Zarmiha (Sokhra), who had helped put him on the throne. His major problem, however, was with the Mazdakites, followers of the heretical Zoroastrian priest Mazdak (fl. late fifth century).

Kavadh promoted the Mazdakite causes—mostly based on a revival of prescribed Manichaean principles, modified by pacifism and principles of community property—apparently because he needed the support of a cohesive group to oppose the power of the aristocracy. The strategy backfired. When rebellion broke out among the subject Armenians and Arabs, and the Byzantine emperor withheld support, the nobles conspired to depose Kavadh and replace him with his brother Jamasp. Kavadh managed, however, to escape from prison, make his way to the Hephthalite frontier, and persuade his former allies to send an army to restore him to power. Thus, in 498, Kavadh secured his power by an unusual policy of conciliation.

During the next few years, Kavadh engaged in intermittent and indecisive war with the Byzantines, which ended in a treaty in 506. Thereafter, Kavadh concerned himself with internal affairs. Mazdakite agitation persisted, and Kavadh began to moderate his earlier tolerance. He became preoccupied with the question of succession. Singling out his youngest and ablest son, Khosrow, as most likely to secure and extend his achievements, he tried for a while to persuade the Byzantine emperor, Justinian I (r. 527-565), to adopt Khosrow, thereby to gain support from that quarter. This plan fell through, and war broke out again. Khosrow began influencing policy even before his accession, taking the lead in the persecution of the Mazdakites, even bringing about the execution of Mazdak. Kavadh was able to make alliances both north and south of Persia, partly through the diplomatic efforts of Khosrow, who—young, vigorous, a splendid horseman with a commanding presence—was able to inspire immediate confidence.

LIFE'S WORK

In spite of Kavadh's preparations, Khosrow's ascent to the throne of the Sāsānian Empire was not uncontested. His brothers Kaus and Zham launched a revolt of dissident nobles, which Khosrow suppressed with little difficulty; he then had his brothers executed. He decided that internal reforms had to take precedence over imperial ambitions, especially because the Mazdakite disruptions had damaged both economy and administration. This initial attention to the details of management set the pattern for his major achievement, a radical reform of methods of government.

Kavadh had recognized that inconsistencies in the registration of property and possessions as well as in the census itself had hampered the collection of taxes and fees. To amend this, he had begun a program of surveying and measuring the land. Khosrow completed and extended this undertaking to tabulating sources of revenue, such as date palms and olive trees, systematizing the registration of land titles, and regularizing the census. In conjunction, Khosrow replaced the old system of assessing taxes on the produce of land with a new fixed tax based on averages. At the same time, he imposed a fixed head tax on the common people. Both were to be paid in money, not kind, and payments were to be made three times a year. The effect of these reforms was remarkable: The central administration could now calculate in advance the exact revenue to be collected at any time, and that made accurate national budgeting possible.

Khosrow's army reforms were almost equally important. Previously, armies had been levied from the personal troops of the landed nobles, who served without pay, supporting their retainers by shares in plunder. Khosrow instead enrolled all nobles in the army, paying them a fixed salary and providing their equipment. This system secured the principal allegiance of the military class for the king and his army and reduced the power of the great magnates. In effect, Khosrow had created a knightly class loyal to him. During his lifetime, these nobles came to form the central class of the Persian social system: the knights who owned villages. Khosrow planted several such villages on the borders, with the explicit mission of taking up arms whenever the frontier was threatened.

Khosrow followed these reforms with further administrative changes. Dividing the empire into quarters, he appointed generals to head each part. Thus, the empire's frontiers were secured; improved military roads and communications systems made it possible to reinforce quickly any threatened sector. Khosrow was now free to carry out military operations without having to be concerned with defending his borders. He began his military expeditions almost immediately, perhaps sensing an opportunity in Justinian I's preoccupation with the western part of his empire.

Woodcut of Khosrow I, on left. (Library of Congress)

In 540, Khosrow invaded Syria, conquering Antioch. Because of his western involvement, Justinian could not employ his full military force against the Persians. Khosrow withdrew slowly, extorting ransom from Byzantine cities as he did as the price of their safety. When he actually besieged one of them to increase this forced tribute, Justinian denounced the truce and sent Belisarius, his best general, to push back the Persians.

Returning to Persia, Khosrow built a new city on the model of Antioch near Ctesiphon. He called it Veh az Antiok Khosrow, meaning "Khosrow's better than Antioch," and populated it with prisoners; it became known as Rumagan, the town of the Greeks, and formed part of the opulent capital complex. When the campaign resumed, Khosrow won some initial success in the north, but eventually the war settled into a three-year stalemate. In 544, after Belisarius had returned to the west, Khosrow besieged the principal city of Edessa, intending to gain control over all Byzantine trans-Euphrates possessions. Edessa resisted the siege heroically, forcing Khosrow to retreat. Justinian was able to forge a five-year truce.

Four years later, the Byzantines broke the truce to recover the Black Sea holdings. They succeeded in retaking Petra in

551 after routing two Persian armies. This resulted in a partial truce, made permanent after the Byzantines had regained Lazica in 556. Final settlement was reached in 561 in the form of a fifty-year treaty. Khosrow agreed to this primarily to free his armies for operations in the east, where opportunities for expansion had suddenly improved. He formed an alliance with the Turks in 557 to destroy the Hephthalites and divide their territory. In this way, Khosrow dramatically extended Persian control across the Oxus River, possibly pushing all the way to India.

Khosrow also proved able to extend Persian power into southern Arabia. The Byzantines were interested in controlling this region for two reasons: to protect the various Christian interests there and to break down Persian control of the spice and silk trade routes with India. Khosrow was prevented from sending aid for a while, but in 572, he dispatched an army with a small fleet under Vahriz. After taking time to work out alliances with Arab groups, Vahriz mounted a successful campaign that made southern Arabia a Sāsānian dependency in 577.

Meanwhile, Justinian was succeeded in 565 by Justin II (r. 565-578), who was eager to recover Byzantine territory in the east. Taking advantage of an Armenian uprising in 571, he invited the rebels into the empire and sent an army to back them the following year. The Persians, however, profited from dissension among officers of the invading army, driving them back and occupying new Byzantine possessions. Justin sued for peace, but because no agreement had been reached regarding Armenia, Khosrow invaded again in 575. For the next four years, the rival empires traded successes, until the Byzantine emperor Maurice (r. 582-602) gained the upper hand at the same moment that the Armenian rebels returned to the Sāsānian fold. Negotiations for peace were taking place when Khosrow died in 579.

SĀSĀNIAN KINGS, 309-821

Reign	*Ruler*
309-379	Shāpūr II
379-383	Ardashīr II
383-388	Shāpūr III
388-399	Barham (Varahran) IV
399-421	Yazdgard I
421-439	Barham (Varahran) V
439-457	Yazdgard II
457-459	Hormizd III
459-484	Peroz
484-488	Valash
488-496	Kavadh I
496-498	Jamasp
499-531	Kavadh I (restored)
531-579	KHOSROW (Khusro or Chosroes) I
579-590	Hormizd IV
590-628	Khosrow II
628	Kavadh II
628-629	Ardashīr III
629-630	Boran
630-632	Hormizd V and Khosrow III
633-651	Yazdgard III
651	Islamic conquest
651-656	ʿUthmān ibn ʿAffān
656-661	Alī ibn Abī Ṭālib
661-750	Umayyad caliphs
750-821	ʿAbbāsid caliphs

SIGNIFICANCE

Khosrow I brought the Sāsānian Empire to the pinnacle of its glory. Had that empire endured longer, it is quite possible that his name would be as well known in Western societies as those of David and Solomon, who achieved considerably less. His wisdom and accomplishments remain proverbial even today among the common people of the Near East, and Kisra, an Arabic corruption of his name, became the Arabs' designation for all Sāsānian rulers. Peasants in Iraq still routinely point to any ruin as the work of Kisrá Ānūshirvān, and in many cases they are right. Khosrow directed more new construction—of caravanserais, roads, bridges, official buildings, even whole towns—than had any previous Persian ruler. This network not only interconnected the parts of the empire in unprecedented ways but also promoted a remarkable economic expansion that financed Khosrow's colonial and military enterprises. He also constructed defensive walls and supporting forts on all four frontiers, designed for the protection of his four commanding generals.

The wealth supporting these activities came basically from agriculture, which expanded significantly during this period. Much of the expansion came from bringing new land under cultivation, promoted by Khosrow's painstaking survey and registration programs. He also systematically encouraged the practice of irrigation, bringing tunnel and canal systems into use throughout the empire. Irrigation had been a common practice in this region for centuries, but it was Khosrow who developed it as a state policy. Iraq owes to him the great Nahsawan canal system, which brought about a geometrical increase in that country's agricultural production.

Unlike most monarchs of his time, Khosrow permitted little religious persecution; his attacks on the Mazdakites stemmed from social and political motives. Furthermore, he advanced the cause of learning, even providing a refuge for some of the scholars and philosophers exiled by Justinian when he closed the academy at Athens. Khosrow maintained a circle of scholars at his court; a medical school established during his reign flourished into Islamic times. Numerous translations of important works date from his period.

One measure of his significance is the appellation of "the Just" attached to his name from early times. Several collections of *andarz* or "advice books"—somewhat like how-to manuals for noblemen, especially rulers—are attributed to him, much as the Book of Psalms is to David or Proverbs to Solomon. Like these and other semilegendary figures, Khosrow's eminence was such that many tales arose concerning his special powers. That in itself, however, testifies only to his hold on the popular imagination. More concrete witnesses appear in the wealth of artifacts and architectural remnants dating from his reign, including many silver plates and engraved stones preserved in museum collections. What remains standing of the palatial Taq Kisra in Ctesiphon (believed to have been built during Khosrow I's time), with its particularly magnificent central arch, speaks across the ages of the stature of Khosrow I.

—*James L. Livingston*

FURTHER READING

Curtis, John, ed. *Mesopotamia and Iran in the Parthian and Sāsānian Periods: Rejection and Revival c. 238 B.C.-A.D. 642*. London: British Museum Press, 2000. Collected papers from a conference on Sāsānian and early Iranian civilization. Includes discussion of the art of the period. Bibliography.

Firdusi. *The Epic of the Kings: Shāh-nāma, the National Epic of Persia, by Ferdowsi*. Translated by Reuben Levy. Chicago: University of Chicago Press, 1967. A translation of the poet-historian Firdusi's *Shahnamah* (c. 1010), a monumental epic poem on the history of Persia from its eponymous beginnings through the conquest by the Muslims. Contains much information on Khosrow, both historical and legendary, presented from the perspective of Persian historiography. Part of UNESCO's Persian Heritage series. (An abridged 1996 translation with a new introduction is also available from Mazda Publishers, Costa Mesa, Calif.)

Frye, Richard N. *The Heritage of Persia*. Cleveland, Ohio: World, 1963. Similar to the fuller account in *The Cambridge History of Iran*, though more tentative. A good discussion of Khosrow's influence on pre-Islamic Persia. Illustrations.

_______. "The Political History of Iran Under the Sāsānians." In *The Cambridge History of Iran*, edited by Ehsan Yarskater. Vol. 3. Cambridge, England: Cambridge University Press, 1983. The most thorough account in English of the achievements of Khosrow and their background, with complete bibliography and photographs of relevant artifacts. Other chapters on different aspects of Iranian history are also relevant to Khosrow, showing, for example, his image in Persian literature.

Ghirshman, Roman. *Iran: Parthians and Sāssānians*. Translated by Stuart Gilbert and James Emmons. London: Thames and Hudson, 1962. A solid and incisive presentation, focusing on Khosrow's social, military, and civil accomplishments. Part of the Arts of Mankind series. Maps, bibliography.

Sicker, Martin. *The Pre-Islamic Middle East*. Westport, Conn.: Praeger, 2000. A concise yet comprehensive survey of the Middle Eastern world from early antiquity to the end of the Sāsānid Empire. Bibliography, index.

Sykes, Percy. *A History of Persia*. 2 vols. 1915. Reprint. New York: Barnes and Noble Books, 1969. A dated account, but it provides a substantial overview of Khosrow, his achievements, and his role in the development of Persian culture. Maps, bibliography.

Wiesehofer, Josef. *Ancient Persia: From 550 B.D. to 650 A.D.* Translated by Azizeh Azodi. New York: I. B. Tauris, 1996. A comprehensive study of the Persian Empire under the Achaeminids, the Parthians, and the Sāsānians. Focuses primarily on Persian written and archaeological sources rather than often inaccurate Greek or Roman accounts. Includes black-and-white plates, bibliographical essays, a chronological table, and a list of dynasties and kings.

SEE ALSO: Alp Arslan; Firdusi; Hārūn al-Rashīd; Heraclius; Justinian I.

RELATED ARTICLES in *Great Events from History: The Middle Ages, 477-1453*: 563: Silk Worms Are Smuggled to the Byzantine Empire; 567-568: Sāsānians and Turks Defeat the White Huns; 786-809: Reign of Hārūn al-Rashīd; 1010: Firdusi Composes the *Shahnamah*; 1040-1055: Expansion of the Seljuk Turks.

AL-KHWĀRIZMĪ

Arabic mathematician and astronomer

Al-Khwārizmī is the author of several important mathematical works. The Latin translations of his writings introduced the concepts of algebra and Hindu-Arabic numerals into the mathematics of medieval Europe. He also compiled a set of astronomical tables used widely in the Islamic Near East.

BORN: c. 780; place unknown
DIED: c. 850; possibly Baghdad (now in Iraq)
ALSO KNOWN AS: Muḥ ibn Mūsā al-Khwārizmī (full name)
AREAS OF ACHIEVEMENT: Mathematics, astronomy, geography, science and technology

EARLY LIFE

Very little is known of the life of al-Khwārizmī (ahl-KWAHR-ihz-mee). The name al-Khwārizmī means literally "the man from Khwārizm"; the epithet may also, however, be interpreted to indicate the origin of one's "stock." The historian al-Ṭabarī asserts that al-Khwārizmī actually came from Qutrubull, a district not far from Baghdad, between the Tigris and Euphrates Rivers. Some sources even give his place of birth as Baghdad. Historians do agree that he lived at Baghdad in the early ninth century under the caliphates of al-Maʾmūn (r. 813-833) and al-Muʿtaṣim (r. 833-842).

In *Kitāb al-Fihrist* (c. 987; book of chronicles), Ibn al-Nadīm's entry on al-Khwārizmī reads,

> al-Khwārizmī. His name was Muhammad ibn Mūsā and his family origin was from Khwārazm. He was temporarily associated with the Treasury of the "House of Wisdom" of al-Maʾmūn. He was one of the leading scholars in astronomy. People both before and after the observations [conducted under al-Maʾmūn] used to rely on his first and second *zījes* [astronomical tables] which were both known by the name *Sindhind*. His books are (as follows): (1) the *Zīj*, in two [editions], the first and the second; (2) the book on sundials; (3) the book on the use of the astrolabe; (4) the book on the construction of the astrolabe; and (5) the [chronicle].

Al-Nadim's list is, however, incomplete. He mentions only the astronomical studies and omits an algebra, an arithmetic, a study of the quadrivium, and an adaptation of Ptolemy's geography. Al-Khwārizmī was apparently well known in Baghdad for his scholarly works on astronomy and mathematics. His inheritance tables on the distribution of money were widely used.

LIFE'S WORK

Al-Khwārizmī is credited by early Arab scholars Ibn Khaldūn (1332-1406) and Kâtib Çelebî (1609-1657) with being the first mathematician to write about algebra. The word "algebra" comes from the second word of the title, *Kitāb al-jabr wa al-muqābalah* (c. 820). It is his best-known work. Literally, the title means "the book of integration and equation." It contained rules for arithmetical solutions of linear and quadratic equations, for elementary geometry, and for inheritance problems concerning the distribution of wealth according to proportions. The algebra was based on a long tradition originating in Babylonian mathematics of the early second millennium B.C.E. When it was first translated into Latin in the twelfth century, the rules for the distribution of wealth, which had been so popular in the Near East, were omitted. Translated into English from a Latin version in 1915 by Louis Charles Karpinski, the book opens with a pious exhortation that reveals al-Khwārizmī's belief in an ordered universe.

> *The Book of Algebra and Almucabola, concerning arithmetical and Geometrical problems.*
> In the name of God, tender and compassionate, begins the book of Restoration and Opposition of number put forth by Mohammed Al-Khowarizmi, the son of Moses. Mohammed said, Praise God the creator who has bestowed on man the power to discover the significance of numbers. Indeed, reflecting that all things which men need require computation, I discovered that all things involve number and I discovered that number is nothing other than that which is composed of units. Unity therefore is implied in every number. Moreover I discovered all numbers to be so arranged that they proceed from unity up to ten.

In the same introduction, al-Khwārizmī describes three kinds of numbers, "roots, squares, and numbers." He sums up the relationships among them in the following way:

> Squares equal to roots,
> Squares equal to numbers, and
> Roots equal to numbers.

Karpinski explains that these three types, designated as "simple" by Omar Khayyám and other Arab mathematicians, "correspond in modern algebraic notation to the following: $ax^2 = bx$, $ax^2 = n$, and $bx = n$.

The first six chapters of al-Khwārizmī's algebra deal with the following mathematical relationships, those relationships concerning "squares equal to roots," "squares equal to numbers," "roots equal to numbers," "squares and roots equal to numbers," "squares and numbers equal to roots," and "roots and numbers equal to a square." These chapters are followed by illustrative geometrical demonstrations and then many problems with their solutions.

Some of his problems are purely formal, whereas others appear in practical contexts. One of his formal problems states,

> If from a square I subtract four of its roots and then take one-third of the remainder, finding this equal to four of the roots, the square will be 256.

His explanation is simple:

> Since one-third of the remainder is equal to four roots, one knows that the remainder itself will equal 12 roots. Therefore, add this to the four, giving 16 roots. This (16) is the root of the square.

This relationship can also be stated $\frac{1}{3}(x^2 - 4x) = 4x$.

An interesting chapter on mercantile transactions asserts that "mercantile transactions and all things pertaining thereto involve two ideas and four numbers." Karpinski explains,

> The two ideas appear to be the notions of quantity and cost; the four numbers represent unit of measure and price per unit, quantity desired and cost of the same.

Al-Khwārizmī's last mercantile problem is,

> A man is hired to work in a vineyard 30 days for 10 pence. He works six days. How much of the agreed price should he receive?
> *Explanation.* It is evident that six days are one-fifth of the whole time; and it is also evident that the man should receive pay having the same relation to the agreed price that the time he works bears to the whole time, 30 days. What we have proposed, is explained as follows. The month, i.e., 30 days, represents the measure, and ten represents the price. Six days represents the quantity, and in asking what part of the agreed price is due to the worker you ask the cost. Therefore multiply the price 10 by the quantity 6, which is inversely proportional to it. Divide the product 60 by the measure 30, giving 2 pence. This will be the cost, and will represent the amount due to the worker.

For Muslims, al-Khwārizmī's astronomical works are perhaps even more important than his algebra. His astronomical tables were used for accurate timekeeping. In Islam, the times of the five daily prayers are determined by the apparent position of the sun in the sky and vary naturally throughout the year. In al-Khwārizmī's work on the construction and use of the astrolabe, the times of midday and afternoon prayers are determined by measuring shadow lengths. These timekeeping techniques were widely used for centuries.

Al-Khwārizmī also created tables to compute the local direction of Mecca. This is fundamental to Muslims because it is the direction they face when they pray, bury their dead, and perform various ritual acts. It is no wonder that in Islamic texts, al-Khwārizmī is referred to as "the astronomer."

Al-Khwārizmī's book on arithmetic has been preserved in only one version. Translated into Latin and published in Rome in 1857 by Prince Baldassare Boncompagni, al-Khwārizmī's *Algoritmi de numero indorum* appears as part 1 of a volume entitled *Tratti d'aritmetica*. The title means "al-Khwārizmī concerning the Hindu art of reckoning." This is the derivation of the word "algorithm." The arithmetic introduced Arabic numerals and the art of calculating by decimal notation. The only copy of this work is in the Cambridge University library.

His study of the *quadrivium*—the medieval curriculum of arithmetic, music, astronomy, and geometry—is entitled *Liber ysagogarum Alchorismi in artem astronomicam a magistro A. compositus* (1126). It was the first of al-Khwārizmī's writings to appear in Europe. The identity of the writer "A" is not certain, but he is assumed to be the English mathematician and scholar Adelard of Bath (c. 1075-after 1142-1146), who is known as the translator of al-Khwārizmī's tables. These trigonometric tables were among the first of the Arabic studies in mathematics to appear in Europe.

Al-Khwārizmī enjoyed an excellent reputation among his fellow Arab scholars. Some of his numerical examples were repeated for centuries, becoming so standardized that many subsequent mathematicians did not consider it necessary to acknowledge al-Khwārizmī as the source. Karpinski observes that "the equation $x^2 + 10x = 39$ runs like a thread of gold through the algebras for several centuries."

The geography *Kitāb surat al-ard* (book of the form of the earth) differs in several respects from Ptolemy's geography. Like Ptolemy's, it is a description of a world map and contains a list of the coordinates of the principal places on it, but al-Khwārizmī's arrangement is radically different, and it is clear that the map to which it refers is not the same as the map Ptolemy described. It is supposed that al-Khwārizmī's world map was the one constructed by al-Maʾmūn. This map was an improvement over Ptolemy's, correcting distortions in the supposed length of the Mediterranean. It was far more accurate, too, in its description of the areas under Islamic rule. Because it contained errors of its own, however, the geography written by al-Khwārizmī failed to replace the Ptolemaic geography used in Europe.

Significance

Al-Khwārizmī's importance in the history of mathematics is inarguable. Two notable arithmetic books, Alexander de Villa Dei's *Carmen de Algorismo* (twelfth century) and Johannes de Sacrobosco's *Algorismus vulgaris* (thirteenth century), owe much to al-Khwārizmī's arithmetic and were widely used for several hundred years. In the ninth century, Abū Kāmil drew on al-Khwārizmī's works for his own writings on algebra. In turn, mathematician and scholar Leonardo of Pisa (c. 1170-c. 1240) was influenced by Abū Kamīl. Numerous commentaries on Abū Kamīl's work kept al-Khwārizmī's influence alive in the Middle Ages and during the Renaissance.

Karpinski states concisely what appears to be the consensus of opinion among historians.

> Mathematical science was more vitally influenced by Moḥhammed ibn Mūsā than by any other writer from the time of the Greeks to Regiomontanus (1436-1476).

—*Catherine Gilbert*

Further Reading

Bell, Eric T. *The Development of Mathematics*. New York: McGraw-Hill, 1945. Begins with a historical review of the field of mathematics from the first-known texts through successive stages of discoveries, ending at midpoint in the twentieth century. The chapter of most interest to students of Islamic science is entitled "Detour Through India, Arabia, and Spain, 400-1300."

Cajori, Florian. *A History of Mathematics*. 1931. 5th ed. Providence, R.I.: AMS Chelsea, 2000. This classic work has several important characteristics that still merit mention. It covers standard non-Western mathematical traditions (Hindu and Islamic). The author manages to give detailed information on individual mathematicians' original findings while keeping information accessible to the general reader.

Hogendijk, Jan P., and Abdelhamid I. Sabra, eds. *The Enterprise of Science in Islam: New Perspectives*. Cambridge, Mass.: MIT Press, 2003. A collection surveying the history of Islamic science, including mathematics and astronomy. Illustrations, bibliography, index.

Karpinski, Louis Charles. *Robert of Chester's Latin Translation of the Algebra of Al-Khowarizmi*. New York: Macmillan, 1915. Dated, but an admirable work of scholarship, with useful commentary. Contains Latin and English translations on facing pages and pages from selected works by al-Khwārizmī in the original Islamic text.

Kennedy, E. S., ed. *Studies in the Islamic Exact Sciences*. Edited by David A. King and Mary Helen Kennedy. Beirut: American University of Beirut Press, 1983. Provides a rather technical treatment of several scientific disciplines that flourished in early Islamic times, including the development, through trigonometry, of accurate astronomical calculations. Written especially for those with a substantial background in mathematics.

King, D. A. *Al-Khwārizmī and New Trends in Mathematical Astronomy in the Ninth Century*. New York: Hagop Kevorkian Center for Near Eastern Studies, New York University, 1983. Discusses some newly discovered works of al-Khwārizmī. While it presupposes a background in mathematics, this work contains interesting charts and graphs that offer a taste of al-Khwārizmī's methods.

Nasr, Seyyed Hossein. *Islamic Science: An Illustrated Study*. London: World of Islam Festival, 1976. A carefully researched photographic record of the tools of Islamic science. Textual treatment of historical figures is more limited than in the author's book below. Illustrations from Islamic astronomy.

_______. *Science and Civilization in Islam*. Cambridge, Mass.: Harvard University Press, 1968. Contains a broad historical setting against which to view al-Khwārizmī.

Usmanov, Z. D., and I. Hodjiev. "The Legacy of al-Khwārizmī." *Quantum* 8, no. 6 (July-August, 1998). A brief overview of al-Khwārizmī's foundational work in algebra. Presents several algebraic figures as examples.

See also: Abul Wefa; Saint Albertus Magnus; Alhazen; Roger Bacon; al-Battānī; al-Bīrūnī; Brahmagupta; Jean Buridan; Saint Fulbert of Chartres; Leonardo of Pisa; Levi ben Gershom; Omar Khayyám; Petrus Peregrinus de Maricourt.

Related articles in *Great Events from History: The Middle Ages, 477-1453*: 595-665: Invention of Decimals and Negative Numbers; 7th-8th centuries: Maya Build Astronomical Observatory at Palenque; c. 950: Court of Córdoba Flourishes in Spain; c. 1100: Arabic Numerals Are Introduced into Europe; 1328-1350: Flowering of Late Medieval Physics.

Kōbō Daishi

Japanese monk

Kōbō Daishi founded the Shingon sect of Buddhism. One of the most important intellectuals in Japanese Buddhist history, he introduced esoteric Buddhism and the study of Sanskrit to Japan, wrote pioneering treatises on Chinese poetics, and was a revered calligrapher.

Born: July 27, 774; Byōbugaura (now Zentsūji), Sanuki Province (now Kagawa Prefecture), Japan
Died: April 22, 835; Mount Kōya, Japan
Also known as: Kūkai
Areas of achievement: Religion and theology, literature, art

Early Life

Kūkai, who was given the name Kōbō Daishi (koh-boh di-shee) posthumously in 931, was born to lady Atō Tamayori and Saeki Tagimi, aristocrats whose family was in political decline. A prodigy, at age fifteen, he began studying Chinese classics with a renowned Confucian scholar Atō Ōtari and, at age eighteen, entered the National University, typically a path to an elite bureaucratic career. However, Kūkai eventually dropped out, becoming a wandering Buddhist ascetic without official status.

Kūkai spent years alternately studying scriptures in Nara and meditating in remote regions, where he associated with mountain ascetics of the Natural Wisdom school (*Jinenchi shu*). In 797, he wrote *Sangō shiiki* ("Indications of the Goals of the Three Teachings," 1972), a fictional dialogue comparing Buddhism, Confucianism, and Daoism. It was the first pro-Buddhist polemic in Japan, broad in scholarship and bold in placing even Daoism, then a proscribed religion, above government-promoted Confucianism. It was also a personal justification of a career choice that deeply disappointed Kūkai's family. He continued to be a *shidosō* (irregular unordained monk) for six more years.

In 804, a life-changing opportunity arrived: participation, as a Buddhist student (he was officially ordained only on the eve of departure), in an embassy to Chang'an, the capital of the Tang Dynasty (T'ang; 618-907). Apparently his goal was to understand the *Mahāvairocana Sūtra*, challenging because it was a product of unfamiliar esoteric (tantric) Buddhism and written partly in Sanskrit. Fluent in Chinese, he served as secretary to the ambassador before being placed in Ximing Monastery, a great center of Buddhist scholarship. He studied Sanskrit and south Indian Brahmanical philosophy with Prajñā (734-810?), translator and a master of the *Tipiṭaka* (compiled c. 250 B.C.E.; English translation in *Buddhist Scriptures*, 1913).

Esoteric Buddhism, then scarcely ninety years old in China, was in vogue in court and had its first native Chinese patriarch, Huiguo (Hui-kuo; 746-805), of the Chonglong (Green Dragon) Monastery. Remarkably, Huiguo quickly accepted Kūkai as a favored student, imparted to him in three months the most secret truths of the esoteric tradition (which depended on personal secret transmission from master to disciple, versus the public, written transmission of exoteric Buddhism), and ordained him a master. Before dying soon after, Huiguo designated Kūkai and Yiming (I-ming), the imperial chaplain, as the two chief transmitters of his teaching, which he enjoined Kūkai to quickly establish in Japan. Kūkai was already depleting his resources by making copies of scriptures, paintings, and ritual implements. Thus, though he apparently had planned to study in China for twenty years, he returned to Japan after an absence of thirty months.

Given the Japanese elite's proclivity to emulate the high culture of China, Kūkai's new status as an esoteric Buddhism master seemed to assure a triumphal homecoming. A twist of fate dictated otherwise. Kūkai's great clerical contemporary, Tendai sect founder Saichō (767-822), who had also gone on the 804 embassy to China, was waiting for a ship back to Japan after spending six months in China, when he encountered an esoteric master who quickly initiated him into esoteric Buddhism. On his return, Emperor Kammu (r. 781-806) recognized Saichō as an esoteric master and had him perform an initiation rite for leading clerics, the first esoteric service in Japan. Thus, Kūkai returned to find a court hesitant to accept his claim to be an authentic master of esoteric Buddhism.

In late 806, in Kyushu, Kūkai sent the emperor *Shōrai mokuroru* ("A Memorial Presenting a List of Newly Imported Sutras and Other Items," 1972), describing his accomplishments in China and listing the 142 sutras, 42 Sanskrit texts, 32 commentaries, and 10 paintings he had brought from China. He had to remain outside the capital for three years, awaiting the court's reply. In 809, he was finally ordered to Takaosanji (now Jingoji), a mountain temple on the northwestern outskirts of Kyoto, where he resided as abbot until 823.

LIFE'S WORK

Although discouraged for many years by the slow progress of his efforts to disseminate the teachings of Huiguo, Kūkai gradually established himself as a religious and cultural leader in early Heian (794-1185) society, partly through his relationship with the new emperor, Saga (r. 809-823), who, like Kūkai, had extraordinary talent in poetry and calligraphy—they are remembered as two of the *sampitsu* (three brushes), Japan's greatest calligraphers. Saga valued Kūkai's talent, knowledge of Chinese poetics, and the poetry books he had brought from China, and he often invited the monk to poetry sessions at the palace. In addition, Saga supported his efforts to further esoteric Buddhism.

In 810, Kūkai was allowed to form a group of disciples and perform the initiation ritual (*abhiseka*). Two years later, Saichō and more than 190 others, including leading Nara priests and members of the court, received the *abhiseka* from Kūkai, now accepted as an esoteric master. He trained many of Saichō's disciples and loaned Saichō many scriptures he had brought from China, though insisting they could not be truly understood without personal instruction—an issue that eventually divided the two.

Needing a larger esoteric meditation site for his own growing school, in 816, Kūkai obtained from the emperor Saga Mount Kōya, which he had seen as a wandering ascetic. Mount Kōya, along with Tendai's Mount Hiei, became one of Japan's two great mountain monasteries. In 823, Saga presented Kūkai with Tōji, one of two state temples flanking Kyoto's southern entrance, as a training center for his new school, the Shingon (mantra or true words).

Kūkai's brilliance, energy, organizational skills and versatility made him enormously productive. Still active in court poetry, he wrote studies of Chinese poetics: *Bumkyō bifu ron* (819; "The Secret Treasure-house of the Mirrors of Poetry," 1972), condensed the following year as *Bumpitsu ganshin shō* (820; "The Essentials of Poetry and Prose," 1972). These works influenced later poets such as Fujiwara no Teika, editor of the *Shinkokinshū* (1216; new collection of ancient and modern poems), and seventeenth century haiku master Matsuo Bashō.

Donning a civil engineer's cap, in 821, Kūkai returned to his naive Sanuki Province to build a reservoir (which survives, bearing his name). He also took over construction of still-unfinished Tōji, building the *kōdō* (lecture hall) and designing its sculptural program to express central Shingon concepts. It is one of the greatest surviving ensembles of early Heian sculpture. In 826, as an adjunct to Tōji, he established the first school in Japan open to children of any class. This noble enterprise, sadly, survived his death a scant decade. The dictionary he created for its students is the oldest extant in Japan.

Although Saichō and his Tendai sect withdrew from older Buddhist institutions, dispensing with Hīnayāna monastic rules (*vinaya*), seeking to escape the authority of the *sōgō* (the state board governing Buddhism), and securing separate Tendai ordination on Mount Hiei, Kūkai became part of the establishment, maintaining ties with the Great Nara temples by giving lectures and conducting services there, and initiating large numbers of Nara priests into esotericism. In 822, he constructed an *abhiseka* hall in front of the Great Buddha Hall of Tōdaiji, the greatest state temple in Japan. He became a leading official in the *sōgō* in 823 and administrative head of Daianji, the great Nara temple, in 829. In this manner, he made esotericism part of mainstream Japanese Buddhism, a fluid relationship persisting for centuries. Thus, contrary to the conventional view, the Shingon that Kūkai established was not an exclusive sect sharply separated from older Nara Buddhist institutions.

Nevertheless, Shingon espoused many radical notions. Although older traditions (Hīnayāna, Mahāyāna) had emphasized subduing one's passions or emulating compassionate bodhisattvas, esotericism promised enlightenment (Buddhahood) in this present existence through magical rituals. Its chief scriptures, the *Mahāvairocana* and *Vajrasekhara Sūtras*, were declared not to be revelations from Śākyamuni, the historical Buddha (the traditional view of all sutras), but from Mahāvairocana (Dainichi in Japanese), the cosmic Buddha, whom Kūkai conceived in pantheistic terms—the source of and thus identical with all Buddhas, bodhisattvas, and sentient beings. Although previous Buddhist concepts of such an ultimate cosmic divinity emphasized formlessness and incomprehensibility, Kūkai personalized Mahāvairocana as wise and compassionate.

Mahāvairocana is revealed through the three mysteries of body, speech, and mind, which are manifested in esoteric ritual in mudras (poses and hand gestures), mantras (the "sound seed" counterparts of other reality), and mandalas (pictorial diagrams conveying profound, ineffable truths). Kūkai asserted that proper performance of esoteric meditation and rituals with mudras, mantras, and mandalas has far greater efficacy than older practices such as simply reciting sutras (as ineffectual, he declared, as reading a medical book to the sick). Kūkai's belief in the possibility of enlightenment "in this very body" rested on his rigorous nondualism. Mind and body are one, for the Six Great Elements, the "body of Dainichi"—earth, water, fire, wind, space, and consciousness, Kūkai's variant of the Chinese five element theory—are all identical with one another.

Because Mahāvairocana is one with everything in the universe, his wisdom is in every person, though for most it is still unrealized. Esoteric ritual meditation, whose form follows detailed prescriptions regarding mudras, mantras, and visualization of mandalas, is the method of realizing Mahāvairocana's all-embracing wisdom here and now, which is simply, as the *Mahāvairocana Sūtra* states, to know one's own mind as it really is.

Kūkai propounded the superiority of esoteric over exoteric Buddhism in *Benkenmitsu nikyō ron* (c. 814; "The Difference Between Exoteric and Esoteric Buddhism," 1972); *Jūjūshin ron* (830; "The Ten Stages of the Development of Mind," 1972), his most famous work, a broad synthesis of Buddhism and other beliefs that places Shingon at the apex; its abridgement, *Hizō hōyaku* (830; "The Precious Key to the Secret Treasury," 1972); and *Hannya shingyō hiken* (c. 834; "The Secret Key to the Heart Sutra," 1972). He explicated Shingon's core assertion that one can achieve enlightenment in this life in *Sokushin jōbutsu gi* (817; "Attaining Enlightenment in This Very Existence," 1972), the most systematic exposition of his thought; *Shōji jissō gi* (c. 817; "The Meanings of Sound, Word, and Reality," 1972); and *Unji gi* (c. 817; "The Meanings of the Word Hūm," 1972). Kūkai's more practical works treat methods of meditation, revealing a preoccupation with ritual procedures that confirms the magical cast of Shingon.

Kūkai's profound interest in Sanskrit reflected his desire to understand esoteric rituals and preserve the sounds of their mantras (which Chinese transliterations altered) to guarantee their efficacy. Notably, 20 percent of the texts his novices studied were in Sanskrit. He regarded the phonetic signs of Sanskrit to be truer than Chinese characters because the latter were grounded in illusory objects, according to Buddhism. This view of language dignified the emerging syllabary, *kana* (which tradition inaccurately says he invented) as a legitimate, even superior, method of writing Japanese. *Kana*, which caused a cultural revolution in Heian Japan, was clearly shaped by the Sanskrit studies of Kūkai and later esoteric priests.

Significance

Kūkai created an enduring intellectual and institutional structure for Japanese esoteric Buddhism. As a poet, interpreter of Chinese poetry, sponsor of art, instigator of gorgeous religious rituals that captivated the aristocracy, and contributor to the development of *kana*, Kūkai was a major shaper of Heian court culture, whose influence has endured. The anti-intellectual, magical character of Shingon and its identification of ultimate reality with ordinary phenomena, like popular legends about Kūkai's miracles and immortality, helped perpetuate the nonrationalistic, nonphilosophical quality of Japanese culture.

Because Shingon asserted that all other divinities derived from Dainichi and shared with Shintō magical use of words (mantra, *kotodama*), sanctified ritual space, and chief divinities identified with the sun (Dainichi, Amaterasu), it was inevitable that the two faiths would meld together, adding to the blending of Shintō and Buddhism that characterized pre-modern Japan. Finally, the personal master-disciple transmission of Shingon, later replicated in Zen, set a pattern for the teaching of all Japan's traditional arts.

—*R. Craig Philips*

Further Reading

Abé, Ryūichi. *The Weaving of Mantra: Kūkai and the Construction of Esoteric Buddhist Discourse*. New York: Columbia University Press, 1999. A brilliant study of great interest to all students of Japanese Buddhism, it persuasively challenges conventional characterizations of Heian Buddhism.

Hadeda, Yoshito S. *Kūkai, Major Works: Translated with an Account of His Life and a Study of His Thought*. New York: Columbia University Press, 1972. The standard English source on his life and writings.

Kitagawa, Joseph Mituo. *On Understanding Japanese Religion*. Princeton, N.J.: Princeton University Press, 1987. Contains an interesting chapter on the posthumous worship of Kūkai.

Saunders, E. Dale. *Buddhism in Japan, with an Outline of its Origins in India*. Tuttle: Tokyo, 1976. A useful survey.

See also: Kōken; Nichiren.

Related articles in *Great Events from History: The Middle Ages, 477-1453*: 538-552: Buddhism Arrives in Japan; 593-604: Regency of Shōtoku Taishi; 607-839: Japan Sends Embassies to China; 794-1185: Heian Period; c. 800: *Kana* Syllabary Is Developed; 1175: Hōnen Shōnin Founds Pure Land Buddhism.